The Writer's Presence
A Pool of Readings

The Writer's Presence
A Pool of Readings

EIGHTH EDITION

EDITED BY

DONALD MCQUADE
University of California, Berkeley

ROBERT ATWAN
Series Editor, The Best American Essays

Bedford/St. Martin's   Boston ♦ New York

For Bedford/St. Martin's

Vice President, Editorial, Macmillan Higher Education Humanities: Edwin Hill
Editorial Director for English: Karen S. Henry
Publisher for Composition, Business and Technical Writing,
*   and Developmental Writing:* Leasa Burton
Executive Editor: John Sullivan
Senior Developmental Editor: Adam Whitehurst
Publishing Services Manager: Andrea Cava
Senior Production Supervisor: Lisa McDowell
Marketing Manager: Jane Helms
Editorial Assistant: Kathleen Wisneski
Project Management: Books By Design, Inc.
Director of Rights and Permissions: Hilary Newman
Senior Art Director: Anna Palchik
Text Design: Tom Carling; Books By Design, Inc.
Cover Design: William Boardman
Cover Photo: Graffiti Artist © Getty Images
Composition: Books By Design, Inc.
Printing and Binding: RR Donnelley and Sons

1   0   9   8   7   6
f   e   d   c   b   a

For information, write: Bedford/St. Martin's, 75 Arlington Street, Boston, MA 02116
   (617-399-4000)

ISBN 978-1-319-09008-1

Acknowledgments

Text acknowledgments and copyrights appear at the back of the book on pages 878–83, which constitute an extension of the copyright page. Art acknowledgments and copyrights appear on the same page as the art selections they cover. It is a violation of the law to reproduce these selections by any means whatsoever without the written permission of the copyright holder.

Preface for Instructors

At the center of our work on this new edition of *The Writer's Presence* is our commitment to creating an effective tool for teaching critical reading and writing. We have designed *The Writer's Presence* to achieve three fundamental instructional objectives: to introduce students to a wide range of prose genres emphasizing a strong authorial presence and voice; to provide writing instructors maximum flexibility in assigning reading materials and writing models; and to support composition teachers and students as effectively as possible with helpful, though unobtrusive, editorial and pedagogical features. We remain confident that the readings we have selected, the ways we have chosen to arrange that material, and the instructional resources we have provided both in the book and in the comprehensive instructor's manual as well as online will make this a uniquely useful collection that will satisfy the requirements of most first-year writing programs.

The Writer's Presence combines eminently readable—and teachable—writing with a simple organization and minimal editorial apparatus. Each selection showcases a writer's unique voice and provides students with accessible models they can use to develop their own voices in the writing they produce. Engaging readings arranged alphabetically by author and by four types of writing—personal, expository, and argumentative essays, as well as short fiction—offer instructors the freedom to explore a wide range of pedagogical options, readily adaptable to the specific abilities and needs of particular students.

ESTABLISHED FEATURES OF *THE WRITER'S PRESENCE*

We continue to work diligently to ensure that the book's enduring features are as useful to instructors and as helpful to students as possible. (For information on features new to this edition, see page viii.)

Diverse Selections with a Strong Writer's Presence

Each selection in *The Writer's Presence* displays the distinctive signature that characterizes memorable prose: the presence of a lively individual imagination attempting to explore the self, shape information into meaning, or contend with issues. There are 94 essays, including 2 graphic selections and 6 short stories, plus 31 writer's commentaries offering an array of voices, genres, and styles from different times and cultures. We include a strong representation of women writers and writers of color. Ranging widely across subjects, methods of development, and stylistic patterns, the selections also illustrate both the expectations and the uncertainties that surface when a writer attempts to create a memorable presence in prose.

We have built this book—like previous editions—out of first-rate reading and teaching material proven to work in the writing classroom. We continue to feature a large number of authors whose works instructors have repeatedly enjoyed teaching over the years. These classroom favorites include such acclaimed writers as Maya Angelou, James Baldwin, Joan Didion, Annie Dillard, Malcolm Gladwell, Edward Hoagland, Langston Hughes, Jamaica Kincaid, George Orwell, Jonathan Swift, Alice Walker, E. B. White, and Virginia Woolf. In fact, as this list of writers clearly indicates, *The Writer's Presence* could also serve as an introduction to the essay as a literary genre and to literary nonfiction in general. For instructors with even more literary ambitions, we have included paired selections to highlight how such writers as Jhumpa Lahiri, Sherman Alexie, and Jamaica Kincaid work in two different genres.

Flexible Organization

The organization of *The Writer's Presence* displays a broad range of private, personal, expository, argumentative, and creative writing without imposing an order or specifying an instructional context in which to work with individual selections. In that sense, the contents of *The Writer's Presence* can truly be called "a pool of readings." We have divided the nonfiction selections that constitute the first three parts into the three most commonly taught types of nonfiction—personal essays, exposition, and argumentation. That is the extent of the book's overarching structure. Within each part, we present the writers in alphabetical order to make the selections easy to retrieve, assign, analyze, and interpret, regardless of instructional emphasis. To make it even easier to explore different pedagogical approaches, *The Writer's Presence* includes alternate tables of contents that enable the book to be used as a thematic reader, a short prose reader, or a rhetorical modes reader with an emphasis on contemporary argument, with each selection chosen to play multiple roles.

Helpful and Unobtrusive Apparatus

As in previous editions, we continue to keep instructional apparatus to a minimum, striving for a middle ground between too much and too little. The headnotes in *The Writer's Presence* provide important biographical information and publication lists, along with engaging and useful quotations from the author, and, whenever possible, they indicate the selection's original source. Many selections provide provocative glimpses of lives and places, and readers naturally want to know when a selection was written and how and where it originally appeared. We don't want readers to infer mistakenly that an excerpt is actually an essay, as this would distort their approach to the selection and could also be unfair to the author. For example, we want readers to know at the outset that Maya Angelou's "What's Your Name, Girl?" is taken from her award-winning autobiography, *I Know Why the Caged Bird Sings*, and was not originally intended to stand alone as an essay.

Our classroom experience suggests that many students will benefit in analyzing or rereading a selection from having access to carefully constructed follow-up questions. In this edition, we have retained "The Reader's Presence," the small collection of questions after each selection. These questions can be used by student readers and writers to enhance their understanding of the selection, or the questions can stimulate productive analysis and group discussion in the classroom.

We have designed "The Reader's Presence" to cover some of the dominant features of the selection and to refer to matters of content, style, and structure. As the title indicates, the questions will often draw attention to the specific ways in which readers are present in a piece of writing—either as an implied reader (the reader imagined by the writer) or as an actual reader. We discuss the concept of presence—both the writer's and the reader's—more fully in the "Introduction for Students."

"Writer at Work" Selections

These thirty-one supplemental readings include excerpts from interviews and essays in which authors discuss their writing processes and their identities as writers or in which a writer's work or composing process is analyzed. We chose each to demonstrate to students that effective writing is thoughtful work done by a wide range of writers.

Uniquely Extensive Instructor's Manual

Although the amount of instructional apparatus in *The Writer's Presence* is carefully managed, a wealth of specific instructional activities appears in *Resources for Teaching The Writer's Presence*, the most comprehensive instructor's manual available for any composition reader.

The resources in this guide to *The Writer's Presence* include the following four parts in each entry:

- "Approaching the Essay" provides a thorough overview of pedagogically effective ways to work with the essay in the classroom.

- "Additional Activities" offers imaginative classroom material and exercises, connections to other essays in the book, and collaborative projects.

- "Generating Writing" includes a range of writing exercises—from suggestions for informal writing to essay assignments and ideas for research papers.

- "The Reader's Presence" addresses the questions following each selection in the text, pointing to illuminating passages in the selection and anticipating possible responses from students.

This comprehensive teaching tool is available in print or as a PDF, which is downloadable at the book's catalog page: **macmillanhighered.com/catalog/writerspresence**.

FEATURES NEW TO THIS EDITION

For the eighth edition of *The Writer's Presence*, we have strengthened one of the book's key features, its emphasis on authorial presence, and focused additional attention on rhetorical strategies. We have also introduced new features that we believe will enhance the book's appeal to teachers and students in and beyond the classroom.

Twenty-Seven New Selections

The compelling new essays include works by such well-known contemporary authors as Dorothy Allison, Joan Didion, Annie Dillard, Andre Dubus III, Ian Frazier, Jhumpa Lahiri, Bill McKibben, Steven Pinker, Michael Pollan, Annie Proulx, Mary Roach, Patti Smith, Cheryl Strayed, and John Edgar Wideman.

Introductions to Rhetorical Strategies for Common Essay Types

In response to instructor feedback, each section of the book now begins with an introduction familiarizing students with the conventions of personal, expository, and argumentative essays, as well as fiction. Designed to provide quick access to strategies for reading and writing, these introductions are packed with examples from the text that illustrate rhetorical moves common to each type of writing in the book.

Four New Sample Student Papers

The Writer's Presence features additional highly teachable examples of successful student writing by including six source-driven sample essays, each paired as a direct or an indirect response to the professional essays. Students can follow other undergraduates as they engage in meaningful terms with the thinking and writing of professional writers, all with an eye on improving their own compositional efforts. To highlight the specifics of how students can effectively respond to published writing, we now annotate each student essay.

More Teachable Images and Visual Texts

The Writer's Presence introduces "Visual Presence" questions for essays that include images. These questions are designed to help students connect images with their reading in order to extend their critical reading and analysis practice to visual texts. Rather than treating images as decorative, The Writer's Presence features visuals with pedagogical purpose.

More "Writer at Work" Selections

For the eighth edition, we have expanded the acclaimed "Writer at Work" commentaries in which authors discuss their writing habits and identities as writers. This edition features, for example, an interview with Brian Doyle on his process for creating very short but highly impactful essays.

GET THE MOST OUT OF YOUR COURSE WITH THE WRITER'S PRESENCE

Bedford/St. Martin's offers resources and format choices that help you and your students get even more out of your book and course. To learn more about or to order any of the following products, contact your Bedford/St. Martin's sales representative, e-mail sales support (**sales_support@bfwpub.com**), or visit the Web site at **macmillanhighered .com/catalog/writerspresence**.

LaunchPad Solo for The Writer's Presence: Where Students Learn

LaunchPad Solo provides engaging content and new ways to get the most out of your course. Get **unique, book-specific materials** in a fully customizable course space; then assign and mix our resources with yours. Visit **macmillanhighered.com /writerspresence8e**.

- **Curated Content**—including readings, videos, tutorials, and more—is **easy to adapt and assign** by adding your own materials and mixing them with our high-quality multimedia content and ready-made assessment options, such as **LearningCurve** adaptive quizzing.

- LaunchPad Solo also offers access to a **gradebook** that provides a clear window on the performance of your whole class, individual students, and even individual assignments.

- A **streamlined interface** helps students focus on what's due, and social commenting tools let them **engage**, make connections, and learn from each other.

To get the most out of your course, order LaunchPad Solo for *The Writer's Presence* packaged with the print book **at no additional charge**. (LaunchPad Solo for *The Writer's Presence* can also be purchased on its own.) An activation code is required. To order LaunchPad Solo for *The Writer's Presence* with the print book, use **ISBN 978-1-319-10062-9**.

Package with Another Bedford/St. Martin's Title and Save

Get the most value for your students by packaging *The Writer's Presence* with a Bedford/St. Martin's handbook or any other Bedford/St. Martin's title for a significant discount. To order, please request a package ISBN from your sales representative or e-mail sales support (**sales_support@bfwpub.com**).

Select Value Packages

Add value to your text by packaging one of the following resources with *The Writer's Presence*. To learn more about package options for any of the following products, contact your Bedford/St. Martin's sales representative or visit **macmillanhighered.com /catalog/writerspresence**.

LearningCurve for Readers and Writers, Bedford/St. Martin's adaptive quizzing program, quickly learns what students already know and helps them practice what they don't yet understand. Game-like quizzing motivates students to engage with their course, and reporting tools help teachers discern their students' needs. *LearningCurve for Readers and Writers* can be packaged with *The Writer's Presence* at a significant discount. An activation code is required. To order *LearningCurve* packaged with the print book, contact your sales representative for a package ISBN. For details, visit **learningcurveworks.com**.

Portfolio Keeping, **Third Edition, by Nedra Reynolds and Elizabeth Davis**, provides all the information students need to use the portfolio method successfully in a writing course. *Portfolio Teaching*, a companion guide for instructors, provides the practical information instructors and writing program administrators need to use the portfolio method successfully in a writing course. To order *Portfolio Keeping* packaged with the print book, contact your sales representative for a package ISBN.

Instructor Resources

macmillanhighered.com/catalog/writerspresence

You have a lot to do in your course. Bedford/St. Martin's wants to make it easy for you to find the support you need—and to get it quickly.

Resources for Teaching The Writer's Presence is available as a PDF that can be downloaded from the Bedford/St. Martin's online catalog at the URL above. In addition to chapter overviews and teaching tips, the instructor's manual includes sample syllabi and suggestions for classroom activities.

TeachingCentral offers the entire list of Bedford/St. Martin's print and online professional resources in one place. You'll find landmark reference works, sourcebooks on pedagogical issues, award-winning collections, and practical advice for the classroom—all free for instructors. Visit **macmillanhighered.com/teachingcentral**.

Bits collects creative ideas for teaching a range of composition topics in an easily searchable blog format. A community of teachers—leading scholars, authors, and editors—discuss revision, research, grammar and style, technology, peer review, and much more. Take, use, adapt, and pass the ideas around. Then, come back to the site to comment or share your own suggestions. Visit **bedfordbits.com**.

ACKNOWLEDGMENTS

Each revision of *The Writer's Presence* has been developed through frequent correspondence and conversations—on the phone, in person, in letters, and on the Internet—with the many teachers and an appreciable number of students who have worked with *The Writer's Presence* in their writing classes. We continue to learn a great deal from these discussions, and we are grateful to the colleagues and friends who graciously have allowed us into their already crowded lives to seek advice and encouragement. Since its inception, *The Writer's Presence* has been and continues to be a truly collaborative enterprise.

In the same way we originally developed *The Writer's Presence*, this revision has emerged from spirited discussions with instructors. We are grateful to these colleagues across the country who took the time to tell us about what did—and did not—work well when they used the seventh edition: Lisa Breunig, Fairfield University; David Calonne, Eastern Michigan University; Lisa del Rosso, New York University; Shelley Girdner, University of New Hampshire; Rachel Golland, St. Thomas Aquinas College; Geri Harmon, Georgia Gwinnett College; Leslie Jewkes, College of Western Idaho; Vali Karr, Houston Community College System; Linda Legters, Norwalk Community College; Ailish Hopper Meisner, Goucher College; Chuck Sweetman, Washington University; Marsha Temlock, Norwalk Community College; Erika Watkins, Christel House Academy (DORS).

We would especially like to acknowledge our colleagues from the Expository Writing Program at New York University who talked with us and shared their ideas as we planned the first edition of this book—Lisa Altomari, Karen Boiko, Darlene Forrest, Alfred Guy, Mary Helen Kolisnyk, Jim Marcall, Denice Martone, and Will McCormack.

We also extend our thanks to the professional staff at Bedford/St. Martin's for their innumerable contributions to this revision. We are enormously grateful for the unfailing support and many useful suggestions we received from our editor, Adam Whitehurst. We are also most grateful to Deja Earley Ruddick, instructor at Auburn University, who has managed every aspect of this eighth edition with great insight, excellent judgment, and unfailing dedication. We want to thank as well Kathleen Wisneski for her superb work and resourcefulness bringing together the inevitable and the innumerable loose ends throughout the project's development. Many thanks to Herb Nolan of Books By Design, Inc., for his outstanding work moving this large manuscript through production with such good cheer and exemplary professionalism. Special thanks to Andrea Cava for managing the entire process with impeccable and quiet attentiveness and intelligence. We extend our thanks as well to Margaret Gorenstein and Linda Winters, who managed the challenging process of securing reprint permissions with great skill and attentiveness, and to Julie Tesser, who made the work of art research and permissions gathering seem effortless.

As ever, Joan Feinberg offered us spirited encouragement and first-rate and rigorous advice, as well as engaging suggestions for improving the project. When our conversations veered occasionally toward uncertainty, we relied on her steady editorial presence — and that of Editor in Chief Karen Henry — to help us convert pedagogical principle into sound instructional practice.

Sam Ruddick, Ph.D., along with Deja Earley Ruddick, researched and wrote the headnotes for this edition, in addition to preparing the comprehensive instructor's manual that accompanies this collection, *Resources for Teaching The Writer's Presence*. Dr. Ruddick is a lecturer in English and composition at Auburn University. We are very grateful to Sam and Deja for the intelligence, imagination, energy, and wealth of teaching experience they bring to the project. Their work remains an invaluable pedagogical tool to help instructors teach their students to read and write more effectively.

We continue to be grateful to Cassandra Cleghorn of Williams College; Alfred Guy of Yale University; Joanna Imm of the University of Arizona; the late Jon Roberts of St. Thomas Aquinas College; Shelley Salamensky of the University of Louisville, Los Angeles; Alix Schwartz of the University of California, Berkeley; Kate Silverstein; Darryl Stephens; and MaryJo Thomas; their helpful suggestions are still amply evident in the instructor's manual. Christine McQuade, Michael Hsu, Julian Miller, Alaska Quilici, and Ela Provost offered invaluable assistance in strengthening the research and pedagogy that informs this project. As always, continued thanks are due to Gregory Atwan for his unfailing support.

Donald McQuade
Robert Atwan
September 2014

Contents

1. PERSONAL WRITING
Exploring Our Own Lives   23

absent from entire professions, such as academia, the media, and filmmaking. It's appalling that people should be content to cut themselves off from everyone unlike themselves."

laboratory tables and shelves. . . . The long chemical names on the little white labels were as mystifying to me as medieval Latin. These odd-sounding things would be mixed and poured and turned into new substances, like magic potions."

"Can one experience nostalgia for a time and place one did not know? I believe so. You could put me in solitary with Abbott's photograph of 'Blossom Restaurant' and I wouldn't notice the months pass away as I studied the menu chalked on the blackboard at its entrance."

"In the U.S., millennials are the children of baby boomers, who are also known as the Me Generation, who then produced the Me Me Me Generation, whose selfishness technology has only exacerbated."

"It was as if someone had taken a tiny bead of pure life and decking it as lightly as possible with down and feathers, had set it dancing and zigzagging to show us the true nature of life."

"I got out this diary and read, as one always does read one's own writing, with a kind of guilty intensity. I confess that the rough and random style of it, often so ungrammatical, and crying for a word altered, afflicted me somewhat."

3. ARGUMENTATIVE WRITING
Contending with Issues 579

"Immersing myself in a book or a lengthy article used to be easy. My mind would get caught up in the narrative or the turns of the argument, and I'd spend hours strolling through long stretches of prose. That's rarely the case anymore. Now my concentration often starts to drift after two or three pages. I get fidgety, lose the thread, begin looking for something else to do."

 e-Readings > Linda Stone, *On Continuous Partial Attention* [video]

macmillanhighered.com/writerspresence8e

that Hollywood isn't going to make movies like the ones I imagined. Hollywood isn't going to make movies that are class-conscious, or antiwar, or conscious of the need for racial equality or gender equality."

4. THE SHORT STORY
Six Modern Classics   793

"Victor didn't have any money. Who does have money on a reservation, except the cigarette and fireworks salespeople? His father had a savings account waiting to be claimed, but Victor needed to find a way to get to Phoenix. Victor's mother was just as poor as he was, and the rest of his family didn't have any use at all for him."

"Wash the white clothes on Monday and put them on the stone heap; wash the color clothes on Tuesday and put them on the clothesline to dry; don't walk barehead in the hot sun."

"This mother in 'Girl' was really just giving the girl an idea about the things she would need to be a self-possessed woman in the world."

e-Readings > Jamaica Kincaid, *Girl* [audio]

"They were on their way to see the Sun Temple at Konarak. It was a dry, bright Saturday, the mid-July heat tempered by a steady ocean breeze, ideal weather for sightseeing."

"She went into the kitchen and approached the door slowly, then hung out the screen door, her bare toes curling down off the step. There were two boys in the car and now she recognized the driver: he had shaggy, shabby black hair that looked crazy as a wig and he was grinning at her."

"Some years ago in the American Southwest there surfaced a tabloid psychopath known as 'The Pied Piper of Tucson.' I have forgotten his name, but his specialty was the seduction and occasional murder of teenage girls."

"The grandmother had the peculiar feeling that the bespectacled man was someone she knew. His face was as familiar to her as if she had known him all her life but she could not recall who he was."

"I often ask myself what makes a story work, and what makes it hold up as a story, and I have decided that it is probably some action, some gesture of a character that is unlike any other in the story, one which indicates where the real heart of the story lies."

"[I]n the guise of a Deep South horror story, O'Connor gave American letters something else altogether: a religiously audacious work of literature, a spiritual puzzle — a small miracle."

"'Sammy, you don't want to do this to your Mom and Dad,' he tells me. It's true, I don't. But it seems to me that once you begin a gesture it's fatal not to go through with it."

Alternate Tables of Contents

Selections Arranged by Theme

EDUCATION

ETHICS AND MORALITY

GENDER ROLES

HISTORY AND BIOGRAPHY

LANGUAGE AND LITERATURE

LAW, POLITICS, AND SOCIETY

THE NATURAL ENVIRONMENT

PHILOSOPHY, SPIRITUALITY, AND RELIGION

POPULAR CULTURE AND MASS MEDIA

PSYCHOLOGY AND HUMAN BEHAVIOR

RACIAL AND ETHNIC IDENTITY

SCIENCE AND TECHNOLOGY

A SENSE OF PLACE

Selections Arranged by Common Rhetorical Modes and Patterns of Development

CONSTRUCTING NARRATIVES

Narratives That Recount Other Lives

WRITING DESCRIPTION: PERSONS, PLACES, THINGS

USING COMPARISONS

DEFINING WORDS AND CONCEPTS

SUPPLYING INSTANCES AND EXAMPLES

CLASSIFYING IDEAS

FORMING ANALOGIES

FASHIONING ARGUMENTS: EIGHT METHODS

Arguing from Personal Experience

Arguing from Factual Evidence

Short Essay Contents
A Complete Short Essay Reader (6 pages or fewer)

Introduction for Students:
The Writer's Presence

PRESENCE IS A WORD—like *charisma*—that we reserve for people who create powerful and memorable impressions. Many public figures and political leaders are said to "have presence"—Martin Luther King Jr., Eleanor Roosevelt, and John F. Kennedy and his wife Jacqueline Kennedy Onassis are a few superb historical examples—as well as many athletes, dancers, and musicians. In fact, the quality of presence is found abundantly in the performing arts, where top entertainers and actors self-consciously fashion—through style, costume, and gesture—an instantly recognizable public presence. Clearly, people with presence are able to command our attention. How do they do it?

Presence is far easier to identify than it is to define. We recognize it when we see it, but how do we capture it in words? Virtually everyone would agree, for example, that when LeBron James steps onto a basketball court, he displays an exceptional degree of presence; we acknowledge this regardless of whether we are basketball fans. But what is it about such individuals that commands our attention? How can we begin to understand this elusive characteristic known as presence?

On one level, *presence* simply means "being present." But the word is more complex than that; it suggests much more than the mere fact of being physically present. Most dictionaries define *presence* as an ability to project a sense of self-assurance, poise, ease, or dignity. We thus speak of someone's "stage presence" or "presence of mind." But the word is also used today to suggest an impressive personality, an individual who can make his or her presence felt. As every college student knows, to be present in a classroom is not the same thing as *having a presence* there. We may be present in body but not in spirit. In that sense, presence is also a matter of individual energy and exertion, of putting something of ourselves into whatever we do.

Presence is especially important in writing, which is what this book is about. Just as we notice individual presence in sports or music or conversation, so too we discover it in good writing. If what we read seems dreary, dull, or dead, it's usually because the writer forgot to include an important ingredient: *personal presence*. That doesn't mean that your essays should be written *in* the first-person singular (this book contains many exceptional essays that aren't) but that your essays should be written *by* the first-person singular. Interesting essays are produced by a real and distinct person, not an automaton following a set of mechanical rules and abstract principles.

PRESENCE IN WRITING

How can someone be present in writing? How can you project yourself into an essay so that it seems that you're personally there, even though all your reader sees are words on a piece of paper?

The Writer's Presence shows you how this is done. It shows how a wide variety of talented writers establish a distinct presence in many different kinds of writing and for many different purposes and audiences. Although the book offers numerous examples of methods for establishing presence, several are worth pointing out at the start. Let's examine four of the chief ways an experienced writer can be present in an essay.

1. Through Personal Experience. One of the most straightforward ways for the writer to make his or her presence felt in an essay is to include appropriate personal experiences. Of course, some assignments call for a personal essay and, in those cases, you will naturally be putting episodes from your own life at the center of your writing. But writers also find ways to build their personal experiences into essays that are informative or argumentative, essays on topics other than themselves. They do this to show their close connection with a subject, to offer testimony, or to establish their personal authority on a subject. Many essays in this collection offer clear illustrations of how writers incorporate personal experience into an essay on a specific topic or issue.

Look, for example, at the essay by Amy Cunningham, "Why Women Smile" (page 369). This essay is primarily an explanation of a cultural phenomenon — the way women are socially conditioned to maintain a smiling attitude. However, Cunningham begins the essay not with a general observation but with a personal anecdote: "After smiling brilliantly for nearly four decades, I now find myself trying to quit." Although her essay is not "personal," her opening sentence, besides establishing her own connection with the topic, provides readers with a personal motive for her writing.

2. Through Voice. Another way a writer makes his or her presence felt is through creating a distinctive and an identifiable *voice*. Good writers want their words to be heard. They want their sentences to have rhythm, cadence, and balance. Experienced authors revise a great deal of their writing just to make sure the sentences *sound* right. They're writing for the reader's ear as well as the reader's mind. Therefore, whenever we read a piece of writing, we ought to think of it as an experience similar to listening to someone speak aloud. Doing so adds drama to writing and reading. Here is what the poet Robert Frost has to say on the subject:

> Everything written is as good as it is dramatic. . . . A dramatic necessity goes deep into the nature of the sentence. Sentences are not different enough to hold the attention unless they are dramatic. No ingenuity of varying structure will do. All that can save

them is the speaking tone of voice somehow entangled in the words and fastened to the page for the ear of the imagination. That is all that can save poetry from singing, all that can save prose from itself. (Preface to *A Way Out*, in *Selected Prose of Robert Frost*)

Frost spent a good portion of his celebrated public life encouraging people to cultivate what he called "the hearing imagination." For more on voice and tone of voice, see the introduction to Part 1, page 25.

3. Through Point of View. Another sure way for writers to establish presence is through the point of view they adopt toward a subject. Often, especially in personal essays, the writer will make clearly known his or her specific location. A good example of this can be found in Langston Hughes's recollection of a tense childhood moment during a revivalist meeting in his church, where he locates his physical presence explicitly (see "Salvation," page 157).

Point of view is not always a matter of a specific location or position. Writers are not always present in their essays as dramatic characters. In many reflective, informative, or argumentative essays, the point of view is determined more by a writer's intellectual attitude or opinions—an angle of vision—than by a precise physical perspective. As an example of how a writer establishes a personal perspective without a dominant first-person narrator, consider the following passage from John Taylor Gatto's "Against School" (page 607), an argumentative essay against America's traditional school system. Although Gatto from time to time introduces his own personal background, he makes his point of view—opposition to modern education—clear to the reader without ever referring directly to himself. Note his comparison between how schools train children and how concerned parents might better handle the job:

> Now for the good news. Once you understand the logic behind modern schooling, its tricks and traps are fairly easy to avoid. School trains children to be employees and consumers; teach your own to be leaders and adventurers. School trains children to obey reflexively; teach your own to think critically and independently. Well-schooled kids have a low threshold for boredom; help your own to develop an inner life so that they'll never be bored. Urge them to take on the serious material, the *grown-up* material, in history, literature, philosophy, music, art, economics, theology—all the stuff schoolteachers know well enough to avoid. Challenge your kids with plenty of solitude so that they can learn to enjoy their own company, to conduct inner dialogues.

There is no first-person singular here, nor a dramatically rendered self. Yet this passage conveys a distinct point of view.

4. Through Style. Writers also establish a presence in their writing through what is usually termed *style*. By a *writing style*, critics usually mean an aggregate of verbal techniques that add up to a distinctive way of saying something. Many creative writers develop a characteristic manner of speaking that depends often on word selection, sentence structure, tone of voice, imagery, and many other elements that contribute to a distinctive and personal identity on the page. Developing a distinctive style demands more than following grammatical rules and established usage. Throughout this book, discussion questions will often target particular instances of a writer's style. For a fuller treatment of prose style, see the introduction to Part 1, "Personal Writing," on page 25.

THE SELECTIONS IN THIS BOOK

Many selections in this book feature the first-person point of view directly. These selections appear mostly in Part 1, "Personal Writing: Exploring Our Own Lives." In most of these selections, the writer appears as both narrator and main character, and the writer's presence is quite observable.

But private and personal writing provide only a fraction of the different types of nonfiction that appear regularly in books, newspapers, and magazines. Many essays are written on specific topics and deal with specific issues. Most of the essays appearing in America's major periodicals, for example, are intended to be either informative or persuasive; the author wants to convey information about a particular subject (a Civil War battle, for example) or wants to express an opinion about a particular issue (such as how to deal with terrorism). Parts 2 and 3, "Expository Writing: Shaping Information" and "Argumentative Writing: Contending with Issues," contain a large number of selections that illustrate writing intended to inform, argue, and persuade.

You'll notice, however, a strong writer's presence in many of the informative and persuasive essays. This is deliberate. To write informatively or persuasively about subjects other than yourself doesn't mean that you have to disappear as a writer. Sometimes you will want to insert your own experiences and testimony into an argumentative essay; at other times, you will want to assume a distinct viewpoint concerning a piece of information; and at still other times—though you may not introduce the first-person singular—you will make your presence strongly felt in your tone of voice or simply in the way you arrange your facts and juxtapose details (see the Gatto passage on page 607). As we'll discuss further in the introduction to Part 2, at the heart of the word *information* is *form*. Writers don't passively receive facts and information in a totally finished format; they need to shape their information, to give it form. This shaping or patterning is something the writer *contributes*. A large part of the instructional purpose of this collection is to encourage you to pay more attention to the different ways writers are present in their work.

THE READER'S PRESENCE

Because almost all writing (and *all* published writing) is intended to be read, we can't dismiss the importance of the reader. Just as we find different levels of a writer's presence in a given piece of writing, so too can we detect different ways in which a reader can be present.

An author writes a short essay offering an opinion about gun control. The author herself has been the victim of a shooting, and her piece, though it includes her personal experiences, is largely made up of a concrete plan to eliminate all guns—even hunting rifles—from American life. She would like lawmakers to adopt her plan. Yet, in writing her essay, she imagines that there will be a great deal of resistance to her argument. In other words, she imagines a reader who will most likely disagree with her and who needs to be won over. Let's imagine she has her opinion essay published in a national magazine.

Now imagine three people in a dentist's office who within the same afternoon pick up this issue of the magazine and read the essay. One of them has also been victimized by guns (her son was accidentally wounded by a hunter), and she reads the essay with great sympathy and conviction. She understands perfectly what this woman has gone through and believes in her plan completely. The next reader, a man who has never once in his life committed a crime and has no tolerance for criminals, is outraged by the essay. He was practically brought up in the woods and loves to hunt. He could never adopt a gun control plan that would in effect criminalize hunting. He's ready to fire off a letter attacking this woman's plan. The third reader also enjoys hunting and has always felt that hunting rifles should be exempt from any government regulation of firearms. But he finds the writer's plan convincing and feasible. He spends the rest of the day trying to think of counterarguments.

Obviously, these are only three of many possibilities. But you can see from this example the differences between the reader imagined by the writer and some actual readers. The one person who completely agreed with the writer was not the kind of reader the author had originally imagined or was trying to persuade; she was already persuaded. And though the other two readers were part of her intended audience, one of them could never be persuaded to her point of view, whereas the other one might.

The differences briefly outlined here are distinctions between what can be called *implied readers* and *actual readers*. The implied reader is the reader imagined by the writer for a particular piece of writing. In constructing arguments, for example, it is usually effective to imagine readers we are *trying* to win over to our views. Otherwise, we are simply asking people who already agree with us to agree with us—what's commonly known as "preaching to the converted" or "preaching to the choir."

In informative or critical essays, a writer also needs to be careful about the implied reader. For example, it's always important to ask how much your intended audience may already know about your subject. Here's a practical illustration. If you were asked to write a review of a recent film for your college newspaper, you would assume your readers had not yet seen the film (or else you might annoy them by giving away some surprises, or "spoilers"). However, if you were asked to write a critical essay about the same movie for a film course, you could assume your readers had seen the film. It's the same movie, and you have the same opinions about it, but your two essays have two different purposes, and in the process of writing them you imagine readers with two different levels of knowledge about the film.

Actual readers, of course, differ from implied readers in that they are real people who read the writing—not readers intended or imagined by the writer. As you read the essays in this collection, you should be aware of at least two readers—(1) the reader you think the writer imagines for the essay and (2) the reader you are in actuality. Sometimes you will seem very close to the kind of reader the writer is imagining. In those cases, you might say that you "identify" with a particular writer, essay, or point of view. At other times, however, you will notice a great distance between the reader the author imagines and you as an actual reader. For example, you may feel excluded by the author on the basis of race, gender, class, or expected knowledge and educational level. Or you may feel you know more than the author does about a particular topic.

To help you get accustomed to your role as a reader, each selection in the book is followed by a set of questions, "The Reader's Presence." These questions are designed to orient you to the various levels of reading suggested by the selection. Some questions will ask you to identify the kind of reader you think the author imagines; other questions will prompt you to think about specific ways you may differ from the author's intended reader; still others will help you to make connections between and among the selections and authors. In general, the questions are intended to make you more deeply aware of your *presence* as a reader.

In this brief introduction, we covered only two types of readers (imagined and actual), but some literary essays, such as Jonathan Swift's "A Modest Proposal" (page 752) and David Foster Wallace's "Consider the Lobster" (page 760), demand more complex consideration. Whenever we think more than these two types of readers need to be identified in an essay, we will introduce this information in the questions.

We hope you will find *The Writer's Presence* a stimulating book to read and think about. To make our presence felt as writers is as much a matter of self-empowerment as it is of faith. It requires the confidence that we can affect others, determine a course of action, or even surprise ourselves by coming up with new ideas or by acquiring new powers of articulation.

Part of the enduring pleasure of writing is precisely that element of surprise, of originality—that lifelong pleasure of discovering new resources of language, finding new means of knowing ourselves, and inventing new ways to be present in the world.

ON WRITING:
Practical Advice from

ONE OF THE MOST reassuring discoveries any student of writing can make is that there is no single way to write, no fail-proof formula to produce successful essays. Anyone seriously interested in learning to write can benefit from reading what other writers have to say about the challenges and pleasures of the writing process. The pages that follow provide an opportunity for you to study the writing process from the points of view of experienced writers—from how they search for an idea and then develop it in a first draft to how they revise and then prepare that idea for presentation in a final draft.

Like all writers, published authors invariably speak of the problems and the pleasures of struggling to convey a clear sense of their ideas. They frequently touch on their respect for and anxiety about mastering the skills required to write effective prose. They also describe the distinctive ways in which they compose: how they go about generating ideas for an essay, how they deal with the frustrations of procrastination and the dead ends that disrupt their progress, how they revise, and how they determine when their essays are finished and ready to be read by an audience.

The perspectives these writers present on the composing process are as varied as their backgrounds and interests. Yet the methods they follow when writing can be grouped into three general phases: **getting started, drafting, and revising**. Experienced writers usually start by searching for and then deciding on a subject to write about, developing their ideas about the subject, clarifying their purpose in writing, organizing their thoughts, and considering the audience they want to address. In the drafting phase, they usually carry out their detailed plan in a first draft. In the revising phase, they study what they have written and determine how they can re-envision and improve it. These designations are not a lock-step series of discrete stages that writers work through in exactly the same manner each

GETTING STARTED

IN THE FIRST of the three phases of the writing process, a writer chooses a subject to write about if one has not been assigned, discovers a purpose for writing about the subject, generates a thesis or a controlling idea (also called a *governing idea*), and then develops that idea in various preliminary writing exercises (often involving brainstorming and freewriting) or in an outline or some other form that will serve as the basis for producing a first draft of an essay. This is the most difficult phase of writing for most people. Because they usually face so many challenges and obstacles at this point in the writing process, most writers have more to say about this phase than any other.

Successful Writers

time. They are simply patterns of activities that describe what happens when writers write.

As every writer knows, at least intuitively, writing is not a linear but a recursive process. Writing rarely proceeds neatly from one phase to the next. Rather, the phases frequently overlap, making the process often appear messy. Yet, in tracing the movements of a writer's mind at work on an idea, we can discover and describe patterns, but the specific circumstances and the particular moves writers make are never exactly the same every time.

Integral to each phase of the composing process is **reading**. Reading and writing function much like breathing in and breathing out. Writers read what others have written with a sense of purpose: to gather information, to understand concepts and the details that support them, to evaluate ideas, to engage in critical thinking, to assess explanations and the assumptions that inform arguments, to be entertained, to visit or envision other places and people, to challenge or inspire others, to persuade others to act, or to expand the limits of what is imagined as possible.

Reading what other writers have to say about writing should assure you that all writers—whether they are professionals, classmates, or you—grapple with many of the same basic issues as well as the same frustrations and pleasures of writing. You may also be pleasantly surprised and pleased to learn that in many instances the observations and solutions of the professional writers quoted in the pages that follow are similar to those you may have developed in your own writing. In addition, you may find that these writers will offer new suggestions that can help you improve your writing. Recognizing what is unique and shared about the writing experience will enable you to place yourself in the company of other writers while developing your own voice and distinguishing it from theirs.

▓ MARK TWAIN

"The secret of getting ahead is getting started. The secret of getting started is breaking your complex overwhelming tasks into small manageable tasks, and then starting on the first one."

(Samuel Langhorne Clemens, 1835–1910, American author and humorist)

▓ JACK LONDON

"You can't wait for inspiration. You have to go after it with a club."

(1876–1916, American author and journalist)

▓ MAYA ANGELOU

"When I start a project, the first thing I do is write down, in longhand, everything I know about the subject, every thought I've ever had on it."

(1928–2014, American poet and autobiographer. See also page 55.)

■ JOHN STEINBECK

"Write freely and as rapidly as possible and throw the whole thing on paper. Never correct or rewrite until the whole thing is down. Rewriting in process is usually found to be an excuse for not going on."

(1902–1968, American novelist)

■ AKHIL SHARMA

"Writing . . . is very hard and the fact that you will find it very hard does not mean that you are stupid."

(b. 1971, Indian American author)

DEALING WITH PROCRASTINATION

The tendency to procrastinate remains one of the most common obstacles many writers face when they set out to put pen to paper or fingers on the keyboard. There is no one easy aspect of writing, other than postponing it. Many writers—whether they are professionals or students—share this trait.

■ MARGARET ATWOOD

"If I waited for perfection, I would never write a word."

(b. 1939, Canadian author and literary critic)

■ PAUL RUDNICK

"Writing is 90 percent procrastination: reading magazines, eating cereal out of the box, watching infomercials. It's a matter of doing everything you can to avoid writing, until it is about four in the morning and you reach the point where you have to write."

(b. 1957, American playwright and novelist)

■ BRIAN DOYLE

"Make a note instantly when an idea or a line or a caught remark or a memory or an epiphany hits you suddenly in the kidney. INSTANTLY. Use dollar bills and children's necks if necessary. (I once started an essay on my son Liam's neck at the beach.) Then hustle to a keyboard as fast as you can and take the note out for a stroll and see what happens. Don't think. Just start typing and see what happens. Don't control it. Don't even think 'this will be an essay.' Just start. I find that often the piece soon enough tells you what shape it wishes to take."

(b. 1956, American essayist and novelist. See also page 387.)

■ TAYARI JONES

"[To deal with writer's block] I just keep at it. I think it's a lot like using a pen that isn't working. You can make the scribbling motion and nothing happens, until suddenly it does. Who knows why. But it does. Thank the lord."

(b. 1970, African American novelist)

■ DOUGLAS ADAMS

"I love deadlines. I like the whooshing sound they make as they fly by."

(1952–2001, English author and playwright)

ELIZABETH HARDWICK

"I'm not sure I understand the process of writing. There is, I'm sure, something strange about imaginative concentration. The brain slowly begins to function in a different way, to make mysterious connections. Say, it is Monday, and you write a very bad draft, but if you keep trying, on Friday, words, phrases, appear almost unexpectedly. I don't know why you can't do it on Monday, or why I can't. I'm the same person, no smarter, I have nothing more at hand. . . . It's one of the things writing students don't understand. They write a first draft and are quite disappointed, or often should be disappointed. They don't understand that they have merely begun, and that they may be merely beginning even in the second or third draft."

(1916–2007, American author and literary critic)

MARTIN AMIS

"A lot of the time seems to be spent making coffee or trolling around, or throwing darts, or playing pinball, or picking your nose, trimming your fingernails, or staring at the ceiling. . . . Writing is waiting, for me certainly. It wouldn't bother me a bit if I didn't write one word in the morning. I'd just think, you know, not yet."

(b. 1949, English novelist)

MAYA ANGELOU

"One of the problems we have as writers is we don't take ourselves seriously while writing; being serious is setting aside a time and saying if it comes, good; if it doesn't come, good, I'll just sit here."

(1928–2014, American poet and autobiographer. See also page 55.)

ANNA QUINDLEN

"People have writer's block not because they can't write, but because they despair of writing eloquently."

(b. 1953, American author and columnist)

WILLIAM JAMES

"Nothing is so fatiguing as the eternal hanging on of an uncompleted task."

(1842–1910, American psychologist and philosopher)

ERNEST HEMINGWAY

"There is no rule on how to write. Sometimes it comes easily and perfectly: sometimes it's like drilling rock and then blasting it out with charges."

(1899–1961, American author and journalist)

RICHARD FORD

"Writing can be complicated, exhausting, isolating, abstracting, boring, dulling, briefly exhilarating; it can be made to be grueling and demoralizing. And occasionally it can produce rewards. But it's never as hard as, say, piloting an L-1011 into O'Hare on a snowy night in January, or doing brain surgery when you have to stand up for ten hours straight, and once you start you can't just stop. If you're a writer, you can stop anywhere, any time, and no one will care or ever know. Plus, the results might be better if you do."

(b. 1944, American author)

GENERATING IDEAS

Writers rely on a seemingly limitless supply of strategies and tactics to generate a subject for an essay and to start exploring their ideas about these subjects—from deliberate reading and research to discussions with friends as well as random mental associations. For many writers, as Henry Miller (1891–1980, American novelist and painter) observes, "writing, like life itself, is a voyage of discovery."

In order to develop practiced confidence in their ability to choose an engaging subject to focus on in an essay, many writers identify subjects in the issues and concerns in the world around them. To help keep track of their ideas about a subject, writers often rely on a journal, a daily written record of one's experiences and thoughts on particular subjects. Journal entries are usually more focused and interrelated than those in a diary, which poses no restrictions on subject or focus.

Many writers find that they can discover ideas about a subject by writing down everything they know about it. Often called *freewriting* or *nonstop writing*, this strategy involves pouring out words, thoughts, or feelings, without concern for grammar or punctuation or coherence. Other writers prefer to develop ideas through *brainstorming*. Unlike freewriting, which produces ideas by linking or associating one thought with another, brainstorming records thoughts as they occur, with no regard for their relation to one another. When writers brainstorm, they often leap from one thought to another without stopping to explore the seeming connections between what may be two completely unrelated ideas.

Exercises such as freewriting and brainstorming are excellent confidence builders, especially for relatively inexperienced writers. They can help writers generate a great deal of prose in a short time. These exercises also enable writers to see quickly what they have to say about a subject—while resisting the urge to edit their work prematurely. Whether you write in a journal or on the back of a napkin, thinking in writing is the best way to discover the potential of a subject to engage an audience. After all, a practiced writer is usually an effective writer.

■ E. L. DOCTOROW

"Writing is an exploration. You start from nothing and learn as you go. . . . Writing is like driving at night in the fog. You can only see as far as your headlights, but you can make the whole trip that way. . . . "

(b. 1931, American novelist)

■ JOAN DIDION

"I write entirely to find out what I'm thinking, what I'm looking at, what I see and what it means. What I want and what I fear."

(b. 1934, American essayist and novelist. See also page 376.)

■ CHERYL STRAYED

"I find the most important thing for aspiring writers is for them to give themselves permission to be brave on the page, to write in the presence of fear, to go to those places that you think you can't write—really that's exactly what you need to write."

(b. 1968, American memoirist, essayist, and novelist. See also page 266.)

ENVISIONING AN AUDIENCE

Imagining an audience looms large in the mind of every writer. The writer's view of the reader helps determine the extent of an essay's success. The writer asks: "Who is my reader? What do I need to do to help that person to understand and appreciate what I want to say about my particular subject?" The first question addresses the knowledge, background, and predispositions of the reader toward the subject. The second points to the kinds of information or appeals to which the reader is most likely to respond.

Not all writers concern themselves with the question of audience from the outset of their work. Some writers regard audience as a matter for revision—as an important consideration only after they have articulated their idea and established control of their

■ FRANÇOIS MAURIAC

"Each of us is like a desert, and a literary work is like a cry from the desert, or like a pigeon let loose with a message in its claws, or like a bottle thrown into the sea. The point is: to be heard—even if by one single person."

(1885–1970, French author and Nobel Laureate)

■ F. SCOTT FITZGERALD

"All good writing is swimming under water and holding your breath."

(1896–1940, American novelist)

■ ALAN LIGHTMAN

"I spend a lot of time with the first paragraph and even the first sentence because this is really the beginning of the creation of the world that I want my reader to inhabit, and I think that the first paragraph really sets the tone, the voice of the writer, and the scene, and invites the reader into the imaginary world."

(b. 1948, American professor of physics at MIT and essayist. See also page 469.)

■ JHUMPA LAHIRI

"All writing, all art is just a wild leap off a cliff because there's nothing to support you. You're creating something out of nothing."

(b. 1967, Indian American novelist and essayist. See also pages 181, 816.)

■ ERNEST HEMINGWAY

"Work every day. No matter what has happened the day or night before, get up and bite on the nail."

(1899–1961, American novelist and Nobel Laureate)

■ WILLIAM FAULKNER

"Get it down. Take chances. It may be bad, but it's the only way you can do anything really good."

(1897–1962, American novelist and Nobel Laureate)

■ ANDRE DUBUS III

"I think if I've learned anything over the years about writing, I've learned to follow where the writing wants to go. More times than not, I don't want to go where it wants to go at all. . . . I try to approach the act of writing in a humble state, as in I'm humbling myself to the writing and I'm opening myself up. That's why I never outline; that's more of a willful approach. I trust the writing to take me someplace that I can't foresee when I begin writing."

(b. 1959, American novelist and essayist. See also page 112.)

■ JOHN EDGAR WIDEMAN

"That sense of beginning anew, and that sense of having a direction, or at least the urge to find a direction every day means that I have set aside a kind of place in my life for words and for language to live, and that place is—reciprocates, it gives me a place to live."

(b. 1941, American novelist and essayist and professor of English at Brown University. See also page 778.)

■ JOYCE CAROL OATES

Read, observe, listen intensely!—as if your life depended upon it."

(b. 1938, American novelist and essayist. See also page 834.)

----

thinking in writing. Given that student writers prepare papers to satisfy course requirements, they are also of course mindful of their instructor's presence in their audience. Some students are intimidated by this recognition, others imagine themselves writing for a teacher with whom they feel comfortable, still others write with peers and an instructor in mind. But whether they are writing for a teacher, peers, or an audience beyond the classroom, the fact that someone will read their writing imposes a good deal of discipline on most student writers. Thinking about readers helps writers make decisions about appropriate subjects, the kinds of examples to use, the kind and level of diction to use, and the overall organization of the essay—each of which enables them to be clear and compelling in their prose.

■ DON DeLILLO

"I don't have a sense of a so-called ideal reader and certainly not of a readership, that terrific entity. I write for the page."

(b. 1936, American novelist and essayist)

■ MARIANNE MOORE

"Any writer overwhelmingly honest about pleasing himself is almost sure to please others."

(1887–1972, American poet)

■ BARBARA KINGSOLVER

"Close the door. Write with no one looking over your shoulder. Don't try to figure out what other people want to hear from you; figure out what you have to say. It's the one and only thing you have to offer."

(b. 1955, American novelist and essayist)

■ ANNIE DILLARD

"Write as if you were dying. At the same time, assume you write for an audience consisting solely of terminal patients. That is, after all, the case. What would you begin writing if you knew you would die soon? What could you say to a dying person that would not enrage by its triviality?"

(b. 1945, American essayist. See also page 382.)

■ PICO IYER

"Writing is, in the end, that oddest of anomalies: an intimate letter to a stranger."

(b. 1957, British-born essayist and novelist of Indian origin. See also page 439.)

DRAFTING

WRITERS WORK in a strikingly wide range of different ways to produce a complete first draft. Some write to discover what they want to say. In one sense, these writers need to see what their ideas look like on paper in order to explore, develop, and revise a first draft. Other writers proceed at a much slower pace: they think carefully about what they want to say before they commit themselves to writing. These writers usually regard thinking and writing as separate, sequential intellectual activities. Still other writers create their own distinctive blend of these write/rewrite and think/write styles of drafting.

■ IAIN BANKS

"Writing is like everything else: the more you do it the better you get. Don't try to perfect as you go along, just get to the end of the damn thing. Accept imperfections. Get it finished and then you can go back. . . ."

(1954–2013, Scottish author)

■ JACQUES BARZUN

"Convince yourself that you are working in clay, not marble, on paper, not eternal bronze: Let that first sentence be as stupid as it wishes."

(1907–2012, French-born American historian of ideas and culture)

■ TOBIAS WOLFF

"For a young writer, the best thing to do is get it out. I certainly have to. I have to write at length before I can write in brief. I have to see what the terrain is before I single out that telling moment, that telling detail and cut away the others. But I have to write the others to get to that one. So you don't want to start off in a stingy way when you write. You want to be extravagant. You know you're going to rewrite anyway, so what the hell? Pump it out, see what comes. And be free in your composition. You can be an editor later. But you don't want to be an editor and a writer at the same time, when you're doing that first draft. I think that's a mistake."

(b. 1945, American memoirist, essayist, and short story writer)

 macmillanhighered.com/writerspresence8e
LearningCurve > Topic sentences and supporting details; Topics and main ideas

DOROTHY ALLISON

"Sometimes, after reading the work of young authors in a work-shop, I find myself asking them 'Who do you write for? Who do you write to?' Some answer me immediately—my daddy, my mama, my first lover, the preacher who scared me so badly when I was thirteen. But some just stare at me, not knowing how important the question actually is. Of course, we write for ourselves. Of course. But even making notes in a journal or commenting anonymously on some blog, we have an observer in the back of our heads—a reader, a witness. It is that witness that shapes the work—focuses it or, now and then, pushes us past what we are first willing to share. Tell me the truth, that reader/witness demands. Say what you fear. Say what you love. Tell me something no one else has ever told me. Out of that demand comes the best work—the richest most revealing nar-ratives, what we never imagined we could share but discover in the writing."

(b. 1949, American novelist and essayist. See also page 37.)

GABRIEL GARCÍA MÁRQUEZ

"When I'm writing I'm always aware that this friend is going to like this, or that another friend is going to like that paragraph or chapter, always thinking of specific people. In the end all books are written for your friends."

(1928–2014, Colombian novelist and journalist)

ELMORE LEONARD

"My most important piece of advice to all you would-be writers: when you write, try to leave out all the parts readers skip."

(1925–2013, American novelist and screenwriter)

ANNIE DILLARD

"When you write, you lay out a line of words. The line of words is a miner's pick, a woodcarver's gouge, a surgeon's probe. You wield it, and it digs a path you follow. Soon you find yourself deep in new territory. Is it a dead end or have you located the real subject? You will know tomorrow, or this time next year."

(b. 1945, American essayist. See also page 382.)

MICHAEL POLLAN

"As I'm editing, I'm hearing it in my head, or sometimes I whisper it aloud to myself as I write. My ear is a very im-portant part of how I write."

(b. 1955, American journalist, essayist, and professor of journalism at the University of California, Berkeley. See also page 527.)

YAEL HEDAYA

"This is what I always tell my students. Writing is not about leaping forward like an antelope, or some other graceful creature. Writing is about moving like a crab. Sideways."

(b. 1964, Israeli novelist)

WALTER MOSLEY

"Your first sentence will start you out, but don't let it trip you up. The beginning is only a draft. Drafts are imperfect by definition. Your first draft is like a rich uncultivated field for the farmer: it is waiting for you to bring it into full bloom."

(b. 1952, American novelist and essayist. See also page 682.)

MALCOLM GLADWELL

"Good writing does not succeed or fail on the strength of its ability to persuade. It succeeds or fails on the strength of its ability to engage you, to make you think, to give you a glimpse into someone else's head."

(b. 1963, Canadian author. See also page 422.)

■ ZADIE SMITH

"Try to read your own work as a stranger would read it, or even better, as an enemy would."

(b. l975, British novelist, essayist, and short story writer)

■ LILLIAN HELLMAN

"Nothing you write, if you hope to be any good, will ever come out as you first hoped."

(1905–1984, American playwright)

■ JHUMPA LAHIRI

"The key is to try to understand what are the elements that are failing and why, and then you move onto the next draft with a little more clarity."

(b. 1967, Indian American novelist and essayist. See also pages 181, 816.)

REVISING

WHEN WRITERS REVISE, they reexamine what they have written with an eye on strengthening their control over their ideas. In some instances, as they revise, they expand or delete, substitute or reorder. In other instances, they revise to clarify or to emphasize—to reinforce or tone down particular points. More generally, they often revise either to simplify what they have written or to add a nuance. Revising provides writers with the opportunity to rethink their drafts, to help them accomplish their intentions more clearly or more fully. Revising also involves such larger concerns as determining whether the draft is logically consistent, whether its thesis or main idea is supported adequately, whether it is organized clearly enough, and whether it satisfies its audience's reasonable expectations or needs—in engaging and accessible terms. Revising enables writers to make sure their essays are as clear, precise, and effective as possible. Revising is crucial to successful writing.

■ ELIE WIESEL

"Writing is not like painting where you add. It is not what you put on the canvas that the reader sees. Writing is more like a sculpture where you remove, you eliminate in order to make the work visible. Even those pages you remove somehow remain."

(b. 1928, Jewish-American author and Nobel Laureate. See also page 300.)

■ DINAW MENGESTU

"A good writing day is one in which I don't end up flinging myself against a wall or curled up on a couch in a state of nearly blinding frustration. On a good writing day the sentences come out easily, and I know when I'm finished that they are the right ones, whether there are hundreds of them or two."

(b. 1978, African novelist. See also page 202.)

■ ROBERT CORMIER

"The beautiful part of writing is that you don't have to get it right the first time, unlike, say, a brain surgeon. You can always do it better, find the exact word, the apt phrase, the leaping simile."

(1925–2000, American author and columnist)

■ MICHAEL CHABON

"I love cutting. It hurts for a second but it immediately feels great afterward. You feel lighter, relieved of bad dreams and heavy burdens. I can watch two or three hundred pages go down the tubes with the equanimity of a lab assistant gassing a rat."

(b. 1963, American novelist and essayist)

 macmillanhighered.com/writerspresence8e
LearningCurve > Commas; Fragments; Run-ons and comma splices; Active and passive voice; Appropriate language; Subject-verb agreement; Working with sources (MLA); Working with sources (APA)

GEORGE ORWELL

"A scrupulous writer, in every sentence that he writes, will ask himself at least four questions, thus: (1) What am I trying to say? (2) What words will express it? (3) What image or idiom will make it clearer? (4) Is this image fresh enough to have an effect?"

(1903–1950, English novelist and essayist. See also pages 216, 515.)

E. M. FORSTER

"How do I know what I think until I see what I say?"

(1879–1970, English novelist and essayist)

NAOMI SHIHAB NYE

"If a teacher told me to revise, I thought that meant my writing was a broken-down car that needed to go to the repair shop. I felt insulted. I didn't realize the teacher was saying, 'Make it shine. It's worth it.' Now I see revision as a beautiful word of hope. It's a new vision of something. It means you don't have to be perfect the first time. What a relief!"

(b. 1952, Palestinian poet and novelist)

SUSAN SONTAG

"I don't write easily or rapidly. My first draft usually has only a few elements worth keeping. I have to find what those are and build from them and throw out what doesn't work, or what simply is not alive."

(1933–2004, American essayist)

ISAAC BASHEVIS SINGER

"The waste basket is the writer's best friend."

(1902–1991, American author and Nobel Laureate)

VLADIMIR NABOKOV

"I have rewritten—often several times—every word I have ever published. My pencils outlast their erasers."

(1899–1977, Russian novelist)

ELLEN GOODMAN

"I rewrite a great deal. I'm always fiddling, always changing something. I'll write a few words—then I'll change them. I add. I subtract. I work and fiddle and keep working and fiddling, and I only stop at the deadline."

(b. 1941, American columnist)

E. B. WHITE

"The main thing I try to do is write as clearly as I can. Because I have the greatest respect for the reader, and if he's going to the trouble of reading what I've written—I'm a slow reader myself and I guess most people are—why, the least I can do is make it as easy as possible for him to find out what I'm trying to say, trying to get at. I rewrite a good deal to make it clear."

(1899–1985, American essayist. See also page 293.)

CHRIS ABANI

"I cut the parts I love the most."

(b. 1966, Nigerian author and poet)

JOHN MCPHEE

"[T]he aural part of writing is a big, big thing to me. I can't stand a sentence until it sounds right, and I'll go over it again and again. . . . I always read the second draft aloud, as a way of moving forward. . . . I read aloud so I can hear if it's fitting together or not. It's just as much a part of the composition as going out and buying a ream of paper."

(b. 1931, American author of narrative nonfiction)

WORKING WITH WORDS

One of the most important principles to learn about writing well is that ideas don't generate writing as much as thinking in writing produces ideas. To write effectively doesn't mean that writers are required to come up with as many new ideas—or words—as possible about a subject but rather that they focus on generating the greatest impact from the ideas that they have already committed to paper. As soon as words appear on a page, it's possible to see whether they express adequately the idea the writer is trying to convey, whether the word choices bring the subject to life or smother it with too many syllables or adjectives. Successful writers realize that there is power and elegance in simple prose and in carefully chosen diction and punctuation. Arranging and rearranging words, deciding whether an exclamation point or a semicolon best supports the writer's purpose—these basic decisions are the means by which the craft of writing is elevated to art.

PICO IYER

"Punctuation marks are the road signs placed along the highways of our communication—to control speeds, provide directions, and prevent head-on collisions."

(b. 1957, British-born essayist and novelist. See also page 439.)

STEPHEN KING

"Any word you have to hunt for in a thesaurus is the wrong word. There are no exceptions to this rule."

(b. 1947, American novelist. See also page 447.)

WENDELL BERRY

"A sentence is both the opportunity and the limit of thought—what we have to think with, and what we have to think in."

(b. 1934, American novelist and essayist)

ROBERT FROST

"All the fun is in how you say a thing."

(1874–1963, American poet)

LEWIS THOMAS

"Exclamation points are the most irritating of all. Look! they say, look at what I just said! How amazing is my thought! It is like being forced to watch someone else's small child jumping up and down crazily in the center of the living room shouting to attract attention. If a sentence really has something of importance to say, something quite remarkable, it doesn't need a mark to point it out. And if it is really, after all, a banal sentence needing more zing, the exclamation point simply emphasizes its banality!"

(1913–1993, American physician and essayist)

■ SCOTT ADAMS

"Creativity is allowing yourself to make mistakes. Art is knowing which ones to keep."

(b. 1957, American creator of the *Dilbert* comic strip and the author of several nonfiction works)

■ ANNIE DILLARD

"On plenty of days the writer can write three or four pages, and on plenty of other days he concludes he must throw them away."

(b. 1945, American essayist. See also page 382.)

■ ELMORE LEONARD

"If it sounds like writing, I rewrite it."

(1925–2013, American novelist and screenwriter)

■ BARBARA TUCHMAN

"Nothing is more satisfying than to write a good sentence. It is no fun to write lumpishly, dully, in prose the reader must plod through like wet sand. But it is a pleasure to achieve, if one can, a clear running prose that is simple yet full of surprises. This does not just happen. It requires skill, hard work, a good ear, and continued practice."

(1912–1989, American historian)

■ MARK TWAIN

"I notice that you use plain, simple language, short words and brief sentences. That is the way to write English — it is the modern way and the best way. Stick to it; don't let fluff and flowers and verbosity creep in. When you catch an adjective, kill it. No, I don't mean utterly, but kill most of them — then the rest will be valuable. They weaken when they are close together. They give strength when they are wide apart. An adjective habit, or a wordy, diffuse, flowery habit, once fastened upon a person, is as hard to get rid of as any other vice. . . . Substitute 'damn' every time you're inclined to write 'very'; your editor will delete it and the writing will be just as it should be."

(Samuel Langhorne Clemens, 1835–1910, American author and humorist)

■ DINAW MENGESTU

"Like most writers, I take apart my sentences over and over. A bad or unpolished sentence or phrase can ruin an entire paragraph for me so I try as much as possible to work over each sentence without destroying any of its initial integrity."

(b. 1978, African novelist. See also page 202.)

■ JONATHAN SWIFT

"Proper words in proper places, make the true definition of style."

(1667–1745, Anglo-Irish satirist and essayist. See also page 752.)

■ DONALD HALL

"The paragraph [is] a mini-essay; it is also a maxi-sentence."

(b. 1928, American poet and essayist)

■ B. J. CHUTE

"Grammar is to a writer what anatomy is to a sculptor, or the scales to a musician. You may loathe it, it may bore you, but nothing will replace it, and once mastered it will support you like a rock."

(1913–1987, American novelist)

READING

ONE OF THE MOST productive exercises for any writer to practice is to read with a writer's eye. Successful writers read with focused and sustained attention to the choices writers make and to the consequences of those choices—much like how a director views a well-made film, how a musician hears a beautiful piece of music, or how a pastry chef envisions someone savoring a delicious croissant. They take pleasure and satisfaction in practicing their craft, but they also seek to learn from what they create. They notice what works and what doesn't, and they continuously ask themselves why. The same principle applies to writers: successful writers know that careful reading can produce clear and engaging prose.

◼ EUDORA WELTY

"There's still a strange moment with every book when I move from the position of writer to the position of reader and I suddenly see my words with the eyes of the cold public. It gives me a terrible sense of exposure, as if I'd gotten sunburned."

(1909–2001, American novelist)

◼ TONY HILLERMAN

"When I was teaching writing—and I still say it—I taught that the best way to learn to write is by reading. Reading critically, noticing paragraphs that get the job done, how your favorite writers use verbs, all the useful techniques. A scene catches you? Go back and study it. Find out how it works."

(1925–2008, American author of detective novels)

◼ TESS GALLAGHER

"When you start reading in a certain way, that's already the beginning of your writing. You're learning what you admire and you're learning to love other writers. The love of other writers is an important first step. To be a voracious, loving reader."

(b. 1943, American poet and essayist)

◼ JOYCE CAROL OATES

"Read widely, and without apology. Read what you want to read, not what someone tells you you should read. . . . Young or beginning writers must be urged to read widely, ceaselessly, both classics and contemporaries, for without an immersion in the history of the craft, one is doomed to remain an amateur: an individual for whom enthusiasm is ninety-nine percent of the creative effort."

(b. 1938, American novelist and essayist. See also page 834.)

◼ GEORGE BERNARD SHAW

"As soon as I open [a book], I occupy the book, I stomp around in it. I underline passages, scribble in the margins, leave my mark. . . . I like to be able to hear myself responding to a book, answering it, agreeing and disagreeing in a manner I recognize as peculiarly my own."

(1856–1950, Irish playwright)

◼ ANNIE PROULX

"I'm basically a reader, which is the best way to learn to write. . . . You should write because you love the shape of stories and sentences and the creation of different worlds on a page. Writing comes from reading, and reading is the finest teacher of how to write. I read omnivorously—technical manuals, history, all sorts of things."

(b. 1935, American journalist and novelist. See also page 222.)

macmillanhighered.com/writerspresence8e
LearningCurve > Critical reading
Tutorials > Critical Reading > Active reading strategies; Reading visuals: Purpose; Reading visuals: Audience

BRIAN DOYLE

"No reading, no writing. You have got to hear lots of voices on the page to learn how to get voices onto pages. The best education for a young writer is wild wide reading. Read everything of all sorts. Get a sense of how stories can be shaped and shared. Then get your butt in the chair every day, 'lower your standards,' as the great Oregon poet William Stafford said, and type like a maniac."

(b. 1956, American essayist and novelist. See also page 387.)

CYNTHIA OZICK

"I read in order to write. I read out of obsession with writing. . . . I read in order to find out what I need to know."

(b. 1928, American novelist and essayist)

WILLIAM FAULKNER

"Read, read, read. Read everything—trash, classics, good and bad, and see how they do it. Just like a carpenter who works as an apprentice and studies the master. Read! You'll absorb it. Then write. If it is good, you'll find out. If it's not, throw it out the window."

(1897–1962, American novelist and Nobel Laureate)

STEPHEN KING

"The real importance of reading is that it creates an ease and intimacy with the process of writing; one comes to the country of the writer with one's papers and identification pretty much in order. Constant reading will pull you into a place (a mindset, if you like the phrase) where you can write eagerly and without self-consciousness. It also offers you a constantly growing knowledge of what has been done and what hasn't, what is trite and what is fresh, what works and what just lies there dying (or dead) on the page. The more you read, the less apt you are to make a fool of yourself with your pen or word processor. . . . '[R]ead a lot, write a lot' is the great commandment."

(b. 1947, American novelist. See also page 447.)

JHUMPA LAHIRI

"I love that line of Saul Bellow's: 'A writer is nothing but a reader moved to emulation.' I really do believe that."

(b. 1967, Indian American novelist and essayist. See also pages 181, 816.)

MASON COOLEY

"Reading gives us someplace to go when we have to stay where we are."

(1927–2002, American aphorist)

EDMUND BURKE

"To read without reflecting is like eating without digesting."

(1729–1797, Anglo-Irish statesman, author, orator, political theorist, and philosopher)

NATHANIEL HAWTHORNE

"Easy reading is damned hard writing."

(1804–1864, American novelist. See also page 432.)

WALTER SAVAGE LANDOR

"What is reading but silent conversation?"

(1775–1864, English writer and poet)

WRITING IS A SKILL that develops over time and with frequent practice. Writing flourishes when someone has something important to say—and responds to the writer's interest in wanting to have an idea understood by others. Developing the ability to surprise oneself—to be able to express something that one did not previously think one knew or could express —can be an enormously satisfying experience. In this sense, writing offers the opportunity to transform the world already formed by the words of others into a world of possibility—a world that writers create with the words they craft on a blank page.

PART 1

PERSONAL WRITING

Exploring Our Own Lives

WHAT IS PERSONAL WRITING?

Thanks to the Internet and the rapid rise of social media, more personal writing occurs now than ever before in history. At any moment, millions of people around the globe are telling others where they happen to be, what they are doing, who they are with, and what they are seeing and hearing. This is often accomplished quickly, in various shorthand codes, without full attention to the conventional rules of writing—grammar, spelling, and punctuation.

Whatever form or media it uses, **personal writing** is essentially writing in which someone recounts his or her own experiences. It has traditionally taken the form of diaries, journals, and—as is the focus of this part—personal essays. Such writing often (though not always) is written in the first-person singular, depends much on memory, relies heavily on narration and description, and often blends these with personal observations and reflection. In fact, of all the kinds of essays that appear in this book, the personal essay comes closest to literature. Many personal essays—such as E. B. White's "Once More to the Lake" (page 293) and George Orwell's "Shooting an Elephant" (page 216) are considered literary in the same way as are poetry, fiction, and drama. In these essays, writers pay particular attention to establishing a personal presence, turning their story into a compelling narrative, and writing literary (or artful) prose.

Though this type of writing seems commonplace now, personal essays are a relatively new form of literature. Various types of essays existed in ancient times, but critics usually consider a French writer, Michel de Montaigne (1533–1592) as the first essayist. An important part of the reason for this is that Montaigne coined the term "essay" (*essai,* in French). The word means *attempt* or *try out* and has connotations of informality and inconclusiveness. In his confessional and digressive essays, Montaigne hoped to share with readers his inner life with all its embarrassing moments, conflicting emotions, differing attitudes, and shifts of opinion. As a writer, you may decide the personal essay format best fits your writing situation if your personal story is essential to the topic at hand, if you're interested in working out something you don't quite understand about your thoughts or your experiences, or if it makes a topic that readers are unfamiliar with more immediately relatable.

STRATEGIES FOR ESTABLISHING YOUR
PERSONAL PRESENCE

In writing about themselves, writers normally rely on the **first-person singular**, that ubiquitous one-letter capital "I." It may look like a simple word, but it isn't. First, though the "I" may purport to be you—the person recounting the experiences—the word can't refer to your entire character and personality, only a small portion of which may be conveyed in an essay. You don't necessarily express yourself simply by saying "I." The sentence "I went to the mall to look for a pair of jeans" does not tell us anything about you, except that you wanted to find jeans at the mall. Usually, writers need to add more personal information to make the "I" more individualized: "I went to the mall thinking that a new pair of jeans would improve my mood." Now we have more than an empty "I" that is merely an agent; we have an "I" that is becoming a character in our essay. As the essayist Scott Russell Sanders reminds us, there is a big difference between the first-person singular and the "singular first person."

As you begin writing a personal essay, don't simply assume that when you use the word "I" a reader will automatically see a one-to-one connection between that word and you. Unless you are a celebrity, the reader will only know about you from what you tell. You will need to inhabit the "I," make your presence and personality felt in the writing itself. You are not present in flesh and blood but only as the speaker of the essay. That is why your tone of voice (which we'll discuss shortly) plays such a significant role in establishing your presence as an individual.

But be warned: to avoid appearing overly self-absorbed, writers often moderate their use of "I." When every sentence begins with that pronoun—or if it appears in every sentence—then the writer will seem narcissistic and the writing monotonous. As you begin reading the essays in this section, notice how writers use (and avoid) the word "I" to give you a sense of themselves as the compelling subject of the essay.

As you begin to think of the "I" in your essay as a character, it's also useful to consider **point of view**, the physical location from where you tell the story. For writers, the point of view is often a literal reality, an actual place or situation in which writers physically locate themselves. This occurs most frequently in autobiographical essays in which the writer is present both as the narrator and as a character. For example, in "A Clack of Tiny Sparks: Remembrances of a Gay Boyhood" (page 98), Bernard Cooper is meticulous about telling us his actual location at any given moment in his writing. The essay begins, "Theresa Sanchez sat behind me in ninth-grade algebra."

Or consider the tremendous importance of point of view—this time in terms of perspective—to another essayist, Brent Staples. This is how Staples opens his essay:

> My first victim was a woman—white, well dressed, probably in her early twenties. I came upon her late one evening on a deserted street in Hyde Park, a relatively affluent neighborhood in an otherwise mean, impoverished section of Chicago. As I swung onto the avenue behind her, there seemed to be a discreet, uninflammatory distance between us. Not so. She cast back a worried glance. To her, the youngish black man—a broad six feet two inches with a beard and billowing hair, both hands shoved into the pockets of a bulky military jacket—seemed menacingly close. After a few more quick glimpses, she picked up her pace and was soon running in earnest. Within seconds she disappeared into a cross street. **Brent Staples**, "Just Walk on By: A Black Man Ponders His Power to Alter Public Space" (page 260)

To see why he frightens people, Staples needs to see himself in the stereotypical ways that others see him. Thus, by the middle of this opening paragraph (in the sentence beginning "To her"), he switches the point of view from his own perspective to that of the young and terrified white woman, describing his appearance as she would perceive it.

Point of view is not always a matter of a specific location or position. Writers are not always present in their essays as dramatic characters. In many reflective, informative, or argumentative essays, the point of view is determined more by a writer's intellectual attitude or opinions—an angle of vision—than by a precise physical perspective. Examples of these will be covered in the introductions to Parts 2 and 3.

Another way to give your personal essay presence is to think about the words you write as sounds, and your writing as something that has a **voice**. All words are composed of sounds, and language itself is something nearly all of us originally learned through *hearing*. Any piece of writing can be read aloud, though many readers have developed such ingrained habits of silent reading that they no longer *hear* the writing. Good writers, however, want their words to be heard. They want their sentences to have rhythm, cadence, and balance. Experienced authors revise a great deal of their writing just to make sure the sentences *sound* right. They're writing for the reader's ear as well as for the reader's mind.

In many respects, voice is the writer's "signature," what finally distinguishes the work of one writer from another. Consider how quickly we recognize voice. We've *heard* only the opening lines of a comedy routine on television, yet we instantly recognize the speaker. So, too, whenever we read a piece of writing, we ought to think of it as an experience similar to listening to someone speak aloud.

A more-specific dimension of voice is **tone**, which refers to the manner the writer adopts in addressing the reader and to the implied relationship of the writer to the reader. Tone suggests not the writer's attitude itself but the way that attitude is revealed. Our tone in writing is what we use to convey to readers a sense of our personality—do we sound formal, breezy, irreverent, satirical, matter-of-fact, flippant, bitter, nostalgic? It also demonstrates our attitude toward our subject and audience—do we seem in awe of another person, hostile about an issue, open to various points of view, surprised by another's opinion, contemptuous of our readers?

In practical terms, tone is usually a matter of diction and individual word choice. Observe how Henry Louis Gates Jr. chooses his words carefully in order to convey tone—in this case, how he felt about Sammy Davis Jr.'s versus Nat King Cole's hair.

> Sammy Davis's process I detested. It didn't look good on him. Worse still, he liked to have a fried strand dangling down the middle of his forehead, shaking it out from the crown when he sang. But Nat King Cole's hair was a thing unto itself, a beautifully sculpted work of art that he and he alone should have had the right to wear.
> **Henry Louis Gates Jr.**, "In the Kitchen" (page 126)

Note how you come to know as a reader what Gates feels about "Sammy Davis's process": he chooses to use the stronger verb "detested" instead of the more common "hated," and when speaking of Nat King Cole's hair, he sounds almost reverential, using phrases like "work of art." In addition to simply telling us what he thinks, Gates's overall tone of voice in the essay—which he establishes by means of very particular word choices (note the negative impact of "fried strand dangling")—helps us understand how he *feels* about his subject.

STRATEGIES FOR TURNING YOUR STORY INTO A COMPELLING NARRATIVE

Put simply, we **narrate** when we tell a story that recounts a sequence of events: "x happened, then y happened, and then z happened." We narrate such stories all the time in our daily conversations: "After class, I walked to the parking lot and ran into a friend I hadn't seen since high school. We decided to go to the cafeteria for coffee."

Narration also plays a large role in writing personal essays. But in writing we need to be far more selective. We all know people who go on and on in conversation—I did this, then I went there, then I saw that, and so on. If such rambling is dull to hear in real life, it is much worse in writing, where a reader expects that a point will be reached or a story will be clear and coherent. When we write, we need not only to consider a sequence of events but also to show how events are interconnected, how one event causes or motivates another, how one thing leads to another. Suppose we revise our brief example:

> After class, I walked to the parking lot and ran into a friend I hadn't seen since high school. A lot had happened to him since then, so we decided to go to the cafeteria for coffee and to catch up.

Notice that now there's a closer connection among the sequence of events and our narrative can continue to say what exactly has happened to our friend and what we went on to talk about. But we can still do better; we can make it more interesting by including description.

In the personal narrative essay, narration and **description** usually go hand in hand. As we tell our story, we often need to describe objects, people, and places. We need to both show and tell. A personal narrative with no physical details would provide no information for readers to visualize the events you are relating. Let's further revise our example:

> After biology class, I walked through the heavy snowfall to the commuter's parking lot and literally bumped into a friend I hadn't seen since high school. Gary now sported a perfectly trimmed goatee, wore fashionable glasses, and looked like he had lost about fifty pounds. We stood in the snow and talked for a few awkward minutes. It was clear a lot had happened to him since we last saw each other, so we decided to trudge over to the cafeteria for steaming hot coffee and to catch up on our lives. I was eager to hear about his.

Note how filling in just a few details—of weather, people, movement, place—helps create a scene and allows us to picture a particular incident.

Good description demands that we observe the world around us attentively and then try to put our observations into words that will best help our readers visualize what we see. In writing, adjectives will do part of this work for us, but writers need to remember that many common adjectives are so abstract that they tell us very little. To say that something is "beautiful" or that a food is "delicious" does not get us far; these overused words merely convey the writer's impressions. Effective description is usually concrete: what exactly makes something "beautiful" or "delicious"?

When describing objects, it helps to know precise terms. There are many varieties of lettuce: were you looking at romaine or iceberg? Was the bird a cardinal or a bluejay? Is the tree you refer to a maple or an oak—and, remember, there are different kinds of maple and oak trees. Specificity can be important to descriptive writing, especially when the writer strives for precision and accuracy. Writing descriptively offers us a good opportunity to expand our vocabularies and know the world around us more intimately.

In the following example, note all of the specific details Judith Ortiz Cofer includes to describe life in her apartment building.

> The walls were thin, and voices speaking and arguing in Spanish could be heard all day. *Salsas* blasted out of radios, turned on early in the morning and left on for company. Women seemed to cook rice and beans perpetually—the strong aroma of boiling red kidney beans permeated the hallways. **Judith Ortiz Cofer**, "Silent Dancing" (page 88)

What is the significance of Cofer describing the odor in the hallways as "the strong aroma of boiling red kidney beans" rather than simply "the smell of beans"? What other details in the passage are enhanced by their specificity?

One topic people talk about most is talk, whether it's friendly gossip, what a celebrity said, or what was reported on the news. Because personal essays usually include other people—often friends, parents, and siblings—we will occasionally need to not only describe them but also refer to things they've said. The personal essay often differs from expository or argumentative writing in that quotation usually entails what someone has *said*, not something we're quoting from our reading. To report **dialogue** in writing, we use essentially two methods of quotation: direct and indirect.

A direct quotation normally appears in quotation marks and tries to capture the exact words and tone of the person speaking. Richard Rodriguez provides a good example of this:

> The nun said, in a friendly but oddly impersonal voice: "Boys and girls, this is Richard Rodriguez." (I heard her sound it out: *Rich-heard Road-ree-guess*.) **Richard Rodriguez**, "Aria: A Memoir of a Bilingual Childhood" (page 227)

An indirect quotation doesn't require quotation marks and is usually a nonverbatim report of what someone said. It does not claim to repeat someone's words exactly. Here is an example from Jamaica Kincaid. She is referring to a phone conversation with her mother:

> During a conversation over the telephone, she had once again let me know that my accomplishments—becoming a responsible and independent woman—did not amount to very much, that the life I lived was nothing more than a silly show, that she truly wished me dead. **Jamaica Kincaid**, "The Estrangement" (page 169)

Most essayists will blend direct and indirect quotation in their writing. Of course, we are seldom making an audio recording of our conversations and it is difficult to recall exact language—especially during emotional situations—from what could be many years ago. Personal essayists depend heavily on memory and try to reconstruct conversations as best they can. These are usually compressed—we don't need every line of the conversation, just the most interesting or representative parts. Here's how adding direct and indirect dialogue can contribute to our previous example.

> After biology class, I walked through the heavy snowfall to the commuter's parking lot and literally bumped into a friend I hadn't seen since high school. "Dude?" Gary seemed surprised. "What are you doing here?" He looked at me curiously, uncertain. He now sported a perfectly trimmed goatee, wore fashionable glasses, and looked like he had lost about fifty pounds. We stood in the snow and talked for a few awkward minutes. He mentioned that he had just driven to campus to visit a girl he met at a big party last weekend. It was clear a lot had happened to him since we last saw each other, so we decided to trudge over to the cafeteria for steaming hot coffee and to catch up on our lives. I was eager to hear about his.

Look back at our original telling of this encounter with a friend on page 28. What impact does it have to be deliberate about our narrative, and to add description and dialogue? Note that as various elements were added to the first simply stated version, a personal story began to take shape, with a specific setting, a dramatic incident, a forward movement, and characters we might want to learn more about.

STRATEGIES FOR WRITING LITERARY PROSE

As mentioned earlier, the personal essay is the most literary type of essay. Unlike most other essay types, its main purpose is not explanatory, informative, or persuasive. It uses many characteristics we associate with fiction, such as narration, description, character, dialogue, and setting. It can also resemble poetry in its language and style. Although we won't cover all the literary elements here, it's worth mentioning how metaphors and similes can contribute to an effective essay, and how thinking about style and noticing verbal patterns can help your writing, too.

One challenge with personal writing is translating your personal experience into something that readers who don't know you will understand and engage with. Although common to nearly all essay forms, the use of **metaphor** allows personal essayists to communicate personal details in ways that show universal significance. Writers use metaphor when they find resemblances between different kinds of things or ideas. Similar to metaphor, a **simile** explicitly states the resemblance by adding "like" or "as." To say, "She's a rock," is to use a metaphor; to say, "She's like a rock," is to use a simile.

As you come across metaphors and similes throughout this book, you'll find they are not merely decorative but often play a significant role in the writer's expression and the essay's overall structure and design. Good writers enjoy making up original similes and metaphors and try to avoid the usual clichéd or stale ones that come to mind easily, such as calling someone's abs a "six pack," a drink "smooth as silk," a friend "smart as a whip," or an idea "crystal clear." Note the original simile the renowned American essayist Edward Hoagland uses to open his essay "On Stuttering" (page 152): "Stuttering is like trying to run with loops of rope around your feet."

As Hoagland's simile demonstrates, writers use metaphor and simile to make their writing more vivid and to offer readers a chance to visualize something in a way they may never have considered. Note that Hoagland's simile invites us to *see* the vocal act of stuttering.

Literary essayists will also embed metaphors and similes into their writing to reinforce an essay's dominant imagery. Many well-crafted essays depend on a network of words and images that relate to and echo each other. The writer expects the reader to connect the dots, to see and appreciate how one image at one point in the essay interacts with another. To see how this works in a piece of writing, look at Anne Fadiman's "Under Water" (page 120). At one point in this essay about a disastrous whitewater canoeing trip, the author notices a fellow student in her wilderness program "standing at a strange angle at the middle of the river." She imagines that an instructor will soon appear and "pluck him out, like a twig from a snag." An inattentive reader may easily overlook that simile, but an attentive reader will remember that her essay begins with a reference to streams in her childhood and how she liked to drop twigs into the water and watch them float downstream, and how "if they hit a snag, I freed them." The simile is an integral part of a pattern of imagery that recurs throughout the essay.

In your own writing, look for ways to use the metaphors and similes that come to you as you write. The figurative language you include can not only make an image or idea clear but also echo your larger point.

As observed in Fadiman's deliberate use of imagery, the literary essayist is always consciously crafting and shaping his or her work. This artistic presence is not always obvious. Yet when we begin to detect in our reading certain kinds of repeated elements—a metaphor or an image, a twist on an earlier episode, a conclusion that echoes the opening—we become aware that someone is deliberately shaping experience or ideas in a special manner. We often find this type of presence in imaginative literature—especially in novels and poems—as well as in essays that possess a distinct literary flavor.

To see an example of creating a style and presence through verbal patterns, look at the opening paragraph of E. B. White's now-classic essay, "Once More to the Lake."

> One summer, along about 1904, my father rented a camp on a lake in Maine and took us all there for the month of August. We all got ringworm from some kittens and had to rub Pond's Extract on our arms and legs night and morning, and my father

rolled over in a canoe with all his clothes on; but outside of that the vacation was a success and from then on none of us ever thought there was any place in the world like that lake in Maine. We returned summer after summer—always on August 1st for one month. I have since become a salt-water man, but sometimes in summer there are days when the restlessness of the tides and the fearful cold of the sea water and the incessant wind that blows across the afternoon and into the evening make me wish for the placidity of a lake in the woods. A few weeks ago this feeling got so strong I bought myself a couple of bass hooks and a spinner and returned to the lake where we used to go, for a week's fishing and to revisit old haunts. **E. B. White**, "Once More to the Lake" (page 293)

If, in rereading this opening, you circle every use of the word *and*, you will clearly see a pattern of repetition. *And*, of course, is a very unobtrusive word, and you may not notice right away how White keeps it present throughout the passage. This repetition alone may strike you at first as of no special importance, but as you read through the essay and see how much of White's central theme depends on the idea of return and repetition (reinforced by the title's "Once More"), you will get a better sense of why the little word *and*—a word that subtly reinforces the idea of repetition itself—is so significant. Nearly all the literary essays in Part 1 will demand such attentive reading.

READING PERSONAL ESSAYS: A Checklist

To benefit the most from the readings in this part, we recommend that you read each selection, paying close attention to a number of different elements. As noted in this introduction, the personal essay requires careful reading, with special attention to both the essay's content and the writer's craft. The following checklist will serve as a convenient guide as you approach the selections in Part 1.

- Consider carefully the essay's title. In what ways does it or doesn't it reflect the author's topic? In one sentence, summarize the relationship of the title to the topic.

- Describe your immediate response to the way the essay opens, either the first sentence or the entire first paragraph. Explain what, if anything, drew you into the essay or pushed you away. To what extent did you react to content or tone of voice?

- Describe the speaker's tone of voice. What words would you use to characterize the way the person sounds to you?

- Consider how the tone of the essay reflects the writer's attitude or stance toward his or her topic. To what extent do you identify with or disagree with the writer's attitude?

- Identify the "I" of the essay. Do you get the impression that the "I" speaking is the same person as the writer? Or do you think the "I" is made up for the purposes of the essay?

- How is the essay narrated? Is the time frame in strict chronological order, or is the story told in other ways? To what extent is the time frame compressed?

- Identify the dominant tense of the essay. Is most of the telling in the past or present tense? Note changes of tense and evaluate the reasons for them.

- Try to assess how much time has elapsed between the essay's main action and its actual composition. How much of the essay depends on memory?

- Consider the writer's use of dialogue. Is the report of conversation most often direct or indirect? Do you find the dialogue realistic or artificial?

- Do you find the characters, settings, and objects described in the essay easy or difficult to visualize? Assess the writer's descriptive abilities.

- Summarize the central point of the essay. Is that point explicitly stated or was it hidden or buried?

- Describe the speaker's point of view. Is the point of view connected to the speaker's physical presence in the essay? Do we see people, places, and objects from a single point of view? To what extent does the "I" of the essay appear as a main character?

- Annotate the essay's verbal patterns. Underline repeated words or phrases. Note the use of similar images that repeatedly occur. Note any other repetitions you find.

Sherman Alexie

THE JOY OF READING AND WRITING: SUPERMAN AND ME

SHERMAN ALEXIE (b. 1966) is a Spokane/Coeur d'Alene Indian who grew up on the Spokane Indian Reservation in Wellpinit, Washington. He was born hydrocephalic and underwent a brain operation at the age of six months, which he was not expected to survive. As a youth, Alexie left the reservation for a public high school where he excelled in academics and became a star player on the basketball team. He attended Gonzaga University in Spokane on a scholarship and then transferred to Washington State University, where his experience in a poetry workshop encouraged him to become a writer. Soon after graduation he received the Washington State Arts Commission Poetry Fellowship and a National Endowment for the Arts Poetry Fellowship. His first collection of short stories, *The Lone Ranger and Tonto Fistfight in Heaven* (1993), received a PEN/Hemingway Award for Best First Book of Fiction. He was subsequently named one of Granta's Best of Young American Novelists and published a novel titled *Reservation Blues* (1995), followed the next year by *Indian Killer* (1996). Alexie's screenplay for the movie *Smoke Signals*, based on his short story "This Is What It Means to Say Phoenix, Arizona" (page 803), received the Christopher Award in 1999. He has published some twenty books of fiction and poetry, including *Ten Little Indians* (2003), short stories; *Dangerous Astronomy* (2005), poetry; *Flight* (2007), a novel; *The Absolutely True Diary of a Part-Time Indian* (2007), his first book aimed at young adults, which won the 2007 National Book Award for Young People's Literature; *War Dances* (2010), which won the PEN/Faulkner Award for Fiction; and, most recently, *Blasphemy* (2012), a book of new and collected short stories.

> "I'm a good writer who may be a great writer one day. I'm harder on myself than anybody."

Alexie has commented on his own work, "I'm a good writer who may be a great writer one day. I'm harder on myself than anybody."

I LEARNED TO READ with a Superman comic book. Simple enough, I suppose. I cannot recall which particular Superman comic book I read, nor can I remember which villain he fought in that issue. I cannot remember the plot, nor the means by which I obtained the comic book. What I can remember is this: I was 3 years old, a Spokane Indian boy living with his family on the Spokane Indian Reservation in eastern Washington state. We were poor by most standards, but one of my parents usually managed to find some minimum-wage job or another, which made us middle-class by reservation standards. I had a brother and three sisters. We lived on a combination of irregular paychecks, hope, fear, and government surplus food.

My father, who is one of the few Indians who went to Catholic school on purpose, was an avid reader of westerns, spy thrillers, murder mysteries, gangster epics, basketball player biographies, and anything else he could find. He bought his books by the pound at Dutch's Pawn Shop, Goodwill, Salvation Army, and Value Village. When he had extra money, he bought new novels at supermarkets, convenience stores, and hospital gift shops. Our house was filled with books. They were stacked in crazy piles in the bathroom, bedrooms, and living room. In a fit of unemployment-inspired creative energy, my father built a set of bookshelves and soon filled them with a random assortment of books about the Kennedy assassination, Watergate, the Vietnam War, and the entire 23-book series of the Apache westerns. My father loved books, and since I loved my father with an aching devotion, I decided to love books as well.

I can remember picking up my father's books before I could read. The words themselves were mostly foreign, but I still remember the exact moment when I first understood, with a sudden clarity, the purpose of a paragraph. I didn't have the vocabulary to say "paragraph," but I realized that a paragraph was a fence that held words. The words inside a paragraph worked together for a common purpose. They had some specific reason for being inside the same fence. This knowledge delighted me. I began to think of everything in terms of paragraphs. Our reservation was a small paragraph within the United States. My family's house was a paragraph, distinct from the other paragraphs of the LeBrets to the north, the Fords to our south, and the Tribal School to the west. Inside our house, each family member existed as a separate paragraph but still had genetics and common experiences to link us. Now, using this logic, I can see my changed family as an essay of seven paragraphs: mother, father, older brother, the deceased sister, my younger twin sisters, and our adopted little brother.

At the same time I was seeing the world in paragraphs, I also picked up that Superman comic book. Each panel, complete with picture, dialogue, and narrative was a three-dimensional paragraph. In one panel, Superman breaks through a door. His suit is red, blue, and yellow. The brown door shatters into many pieces. I look at the narrative above the picture. I cannot read the words, but I assume it tells me that "Superman is breaking down the door." Aloud, I pretend to read the words and say, "Superman is breaking down the door." Words, dialogue, also float out of Superman's mouth. Because he is breaking down the door, I assume he says, "I am breaking down the door." Once again, I pretend to read the words and say aloud, "I am breaking down the door." In this way, I learned to read.

This might be an interesting story all by itself. A little Indian boy teaches himself to read at an early age and advances quickly. He reads "Grapes of

Wrath" in kindergarten when other children are struggling through "Dick and Jane." If he'd been anything but an Indian boy living on the reservation, he might have been called a prodigy. But he is an Indian boy living on the reservation and is simply an oddity. He grows into a man who often speaks of his childhood in the third person, as if it will somehow dull the pain and make him sound more modest about his talents.

A smart Indian is a dangerous person, widely feared and ridiculed by Indians and non-Indians alike. I fought with my classmates on a daily basis. They wanted me to stay quiet when the non-Indian teacher asked for answers, for volunteers, for help. We were Indian children who were expected to be stupid. Most lived up to those expectations inside the classroom but subverted them on the outside. They struggled with basic reading in school but could remember how to sing a few dozen powwow songs. They were monosyllabic in front of their non-Indian teachers but could tell complicated stories and jokes at the dinner table. They submissively ducked their heads when confronted by a non-Indian adult but would slug it out with the Indian bully who was 10 years older. As Indian children, we were expected to fail in the non-Indian world. Those who failed were ceremonially accepted by other Indians and appropriately pitied by non-Indians.

I refused to fail. I was smart. I was arrogant. I was lucky. I read books late into the night, until I could barely keep my eyes open. I read books at recess, then during lunch, and in the few minutes left after I had finished my classroom assignments. I read books in the car when my family traveled to powwows or basketball games. In shopping malls, I ran to the bookstores and read bits and pieces of as many books as I could. I read the books my father brought home from the pawnshops and secondhand. I read the books I borrowed from the library. I read the backs of cereal boxes. I read the newspaper. I read the bulletins posted on the walls of the school, the clinic, the tribal offices, the post office. I read junk mail. I read auto-repair manuals. I read magazines. I read anything that had words and paragraphs. I read with equal parts joy and desperation. I loved those books, but I also knew that love had only one purpose. I was trying to save my life.

Despite all the books I read, I am still surprised I became a writer. I was going to be a pediatrician. These days, I write novels, short stories, and poems. I visit schools and teach creative writing to Indian kids. In all my years in the reservation school system, I was never taught how to write poetry, short stories, or novels. I was certainly never taught that Indians wrote poetry, short stories, and novels. Writing was something beyond Indians. I cannot recall a single time that a guest teacher visited the reservation. There must have been visiting teachers. Who were they? Where are they now? Do they exist? I visit the schools as often as possible. The Indian kids crowd the classroom. Many are writing their own poems, short stories, and novels. They have read my books. They have read many other books. They look at me with bright eyes and arrogant wonder. They are trying to save their lives. Then there are the sullen and already defeated Indian kids who sit in the back rows and ignore me with theatrical precision. The pages of their notebooks are empty. They carry neither pencil nor pen. They stare out the window. They refuse and resist. "Books," I say to them. "Books," I say. I throw my weight against their locked doors. The door holds. I am smart. I am arrogant. I am lucky. I am trying to save our lives.

The Reader's Presence

1. What does literacy mean to Alexie? What are his associations with reading? with writing? How does he use his reading and his writing to establish his ties to the community? What aspects of his identity are bound up with reading and writing?

2. How did the young Alexie use popular culture to educate himself? What did comic books teach him? How does Alexie use the figure of Superman, and aspects of action-hero stories more generally, to give structure and coherence to his essay?

3. **CONNECTIONS:** Alexie uses the metaphor of "breaking down the door" to describe the act of learning to read. What are the connotations of this metaphor? How does it compare with Frederick Douglass's account of his acquisition of literacy in "Learning to Read and Write" (page 106) in which he says that he sometimes felt as though "learning to read had been a curse rather than a blessing" (paragraph 6)? As he encountered arguments for and against slavery in the books he read, Douglass felt that reading deepened his already vivid experience of slavery: "It had given me a view of my wretched condition, without the remedy" (paragraph 6). Is literacy a means to freedom for Alexie as it was, ultimately, for Douglass? If so, freedom from what or freedom to do what?

Dorothy Allison

A QUESTION OF CLASS

DOROTHY ALLISON (b. 1949) is an American writer and feminist. Born to a fifteen-year-old, unwed mother in Greenville, South Carolina, Allison grew up with a keen awareness of class. She was the first member of her family to graduate high school, and she attended Florida Presbyterian College (now Eckerd College) on a National Merit Scholarship. She eventually moved to New York City, pursuing a graduate degree in anthropology at the New School for Social Research. She published a chapbook of poetry, *The Women Who Hate Me*, with Long Haul Press in 1983, followed by a collection of short stories, *Trash*, with Firebrand

Books, in 1988. But it was not until the publication of *Bastard Out of Carolina* (1992) that she achieved mainstream recognition. A best-selling novel and the basis for an award-winning film, *Bastard Out of Carolina* was a finalist for the National Book Award and the winner of the Ferro Grumley Prize, an American Library Association (ALA) Award for Gay and Lesbian Writing. Her second novel, *Cavedweller* (1998), was also a best-seller.

> Dorothy Allison said that when she first encountered the feminist movement, "It was like opening [her] eyes under water."

Allison credits militant feminists for encouraging her to write. Of the tremendous influence, personally and professionally, that the early feminist movement had on her, she has said, "It was like opening your eyes under water. It hurt, but suddenly everything that had been dark and mysterious became visible and open to change." Accordingly, her writing often reflects a concern with social-justice issues, especially those related to class, sex, and sexual orientation. She won the Robert Penn Warren Award for Fiction in 2007.

THE FIRST TIME I HEARD, "They're different than us, don't value human life the way we do," I was in high school in Central Florida. The man speaking was an army recruiter talking to a bunch of boys, telling them what the army was really like, what they could expect overseas. A cold angry feeling swept over me. I had heard the word *they* pronounced in that same callous tone before. *They*, those people over there, those people who are not us, they die so easily, kill each other so casually. They are different. *We*, I thought. *Me*.

When I was six or eight back in Greenville, South Carolina, I had heard that same matter-of-fact tone of dismissal applied to me. "Don't you play with her. I don't want you talking to them." Me and my family, we had always been *they*. Who am I? I wondered, listening to that recruiter. Who are my people? We die so easily, disappear so completely — we/they, the poor and the queer. I pressed my bony white trash fists to my stubborn lesbian mouth. The rage was a good feeling, stronger and purer than the shame that followed it, the fear and the sudden urge to run and hide, to deny, to pretend I did not know who I was and what the world would do to me.

My people were not remarkable. We were ordinary, but even so we were mythical. We were the *they* everyone talks about — the ungrateful poor. I grew up trying to run away from the fate that destroyed so many of the people I loved, and having learned the habit of hiding, I found I had also learned to hide from myself. I did not know who I was, only that I did not want to be *they*, the ones who are destroyed or dismissed to make the "real" people, the important people, feel safer. By the time I understood that I was queer, that habit of hiding was deeply set in me, so deeply that it was not a choice but an instinct. Hide, hide to survive, I thought, knowing that if I told the truth about my life, my family, my sexual desire, my history, I would move over into that unknown territory, the land of they, would never have the chance to name my own life, to understand it or claim it.

Why are you so afraid? my lovers and friends have asked me the many times I have suddenly seemed a stranger, someone who would not speak to them, would not do the things they believed I should do, simple things like applying for a job, or a grant, or some award they were sure I could acquire easily. Entitlement, I have told them, is a matter of feeling like we rather than they. You think you have a right to things, a place in the world, and it is so intrinsically a part of you that you cannot imagine people like me, people who seem to live in your world, who don't have it. I have explained what I know over and over, in every way I can, but I have never been able to make clear the degree of my fear, the extent to which I feel myself denied: not only that I am queer in a world that hates queers, but that I was born poor into a world that despises the poor. The need to make my world believable to people who have never experienced it is part of why I write fiction. I know that some things must be felt to be understood, that despair, for example, can never be adequately analyzed; it must be lived. But if I can write a story that so draws the reader in that she imagines herself like my characters, feels their sense of fear and uncertainty, their hopes and terrors, then I have come closer to knowing myself as real, important as the very people I have always watched with awe.

I have known I was a lesbian since I was a teenager, and I have spent   5
a good twenty years making peace with the effects of incest and physical abuse. But what may be the central fact of my life is that I was born in 1949 in Greenville, South Carolina, the bastard daughter of a white woman from a desperately poor family, a girl who had left the seventh grade the year before, worked as a waitress, and was just a month past fifteen when she had me. That fact, the inescapable impact of being born in a condition of poverty that this society finds shameful, contemptible, and somehow deserved, has had dominion over me to such an extent that I have spent my life trying to overcome or deny it. I have learned with great difficulty that the vast majority of people believe that poverty is a voluntary condition.

I have loved my family so stubbornly that every impulse to hold them in contempt has sparked in me a countersurge of pride—complicated and undercut by an urge to fit us into the acceptable myths and theories of both mainstream society and a lesbian-feminist reinterpretation. The choice becomes Steven Spielberg movies or Erskine Caldwell novels, the one valorizing and the other caricaturing, or the patriarchy as villain, trivializing the choices the men and women of my family have made. I have had to fight broad generalizations from every theoretical viewpoint.

Traditional feminist theory has had a limited understanding of class differences and of how sexuality and self are shaped by both desire and denial. The ideology implies that we are all sisters who should only turn our anger and suspicion on the world outside the lesbian community. It is easy to say that the patriarchy did it, that poverty and social contempt are products of the world of the fathers, and often I felt a need to collapse my sexual history into what I was willing to share of my class background, to pretend that my life both as a lesbian and as a working-class escapee was constructed by the patriarchy. Or conversely, to ignore how much my life was shaped by growing up poor and talk only about what incest did to my identity as a woman and as a lesbian. The difficulty is that I can't ascribe everything that has been problematic about my life simply and easily to the patriarchy, or to incest, or even to the invisible and much-denied class structure of our society.

In my lesbian-feminist collective we had long conversations about the mind/body split, the way we compartmentalize our lives to survive. For years I thought that that concept referred to the way I had separated my activist life from the passionate secret life in which I acted on my sexual desires. I was convinced that the fracture was fairly simple, that it would be healed when there was time and clarity to do so—at about the same point when I might begin to understand sex. I never imagined that it was not a split but a splintering, and I passed whole portions of my life—days, months, years—in pure directed progress, getting up every morning and setting to work, working so hard and so continually that I avoided examining in any way what I knew about my life. Busywork became a trance state. I ignored who I really was and how I became that person, continued in that daily progress, became an automaton who was what she did.

I tried to become one with the lesbian-feminist community so as to feel real and valuable. I did not know that I was hiding, blending in for safety just as I had done in high school, in college. I did not recognize the impulse to forget. I believed that all those things I did not talk about, or even let myself think too much about, were not important, that none of them defined me. I had constructed a life, an identity in which I took pride, an alternative lesbian family in which I felt safe, and I did not realize that the fundamental me had almost disappeared.

It is surprising how easy it was to live that life. Everyone and everything   10 cooperated with the process. Everything in our culture—books, television, movies, school, fashion—is presented as if it is being seen by one pair of eyes, shaped by one set of hands, heard by one pair of ears. Even if you know you are not part of that imaginary creature—if you like country music not symphonies, read books cynically, listen to the news unbelievingly, are lesbian not heterosexual, and surround yourself with your own small deviant community—you are still shaped by that hegemony, or your resistance to it. The only way I found to resist that homogenized view of the world was to make myself part of something larger than myself. As a feminist and a radical lesbian organizer, and later as a sex radical (which eventually became the term, along with pro-sex feminist, for those who were not anti-pornography but anti-censorship, those of us arguing for sexual diversity), the need to belong, to feel safe, was just as important for me as for any heterosexual, nonpolitical citizen, and sometimes even more important because the rest of my life was so embattled.

Photo by Jill Posener

Dorothy Allison, 1992.

The first time I read the Jewish lesbian Irena Klepfisz's poems,[1] I experienced a frisson of recognition. It was not that my people had been "burned off the map" or murdered as hers had. No, we had been encouraged to destroy ourselves, made invisible because we did not fit the myths of the noble poor generated by the middle class. Even now, past forty and stubbornly proud of my family, I feel the draw of that mythology, that romanticized, edited version of the poor. I find myself looking back and wondering what was real, what was true. Within my family, so much was lied about, joked about, denied, or told with deliberate indirection, an undercurrent of humiliation or a brief pursed grimace that belied everything that had been said. What was real? The poverty depicted in books and movies was romantic, a backdrop for the story of how it was escaped.

The poverty portrayed by left-wing intellectuals was just as romantic, a platform for assailing the upper and middle classes, and from their perspective, the working-class hero was invariably male, righteously indignant, and inhumanly noble. The reality of self-hatred and violence was either absent or caricatured. The poverty I knew was dreary, deadening, shameful, the women powerful in ways not generally seen as heroic by the world outside the family.

My family's lives were not on television, not in books, not even comic books. There was a myth of the poor in this country, but it did not include us,

[1] *A Few Words in the Mother Tongue: Poems, Selected and New* (Eighth Mountain Press: Portland, Oregon, 1990). — ALLISON'S NOTE.

no matter how hard I tried to squeeze us in. There was an idea of the good poor—hard-working, ragged but clean, and intrinsically honorable. I understood that we were the bad poor: men who drank and couldn't keep a job; women, invariably pregnant before marriage, who quickly became worn, fat, and old from working too many hours and bearing too many children; and children with runny noses, watery eyes, and the wrong attitudes. My cousins quit school, stole cars, used drugs, and took dead-end jobs pumping gas or waiting tables. We were not noble, not grateful, not even hopeful. We knew ourselves despised. My family was ashamed of being poor, of feeling hopeless. What was there to work for, to save money for, to fight for or struggle against? We had generations before us to teach us that nothing ever changed, and that those who did try to escape failed.

My mama had eleven brothers and sisters, of whom I can name only six. No one is left alive to tell me the names of the others. It was my grandmother who told me about my real daddy, a shiftless pretty man who was supposed to have married, had six children, and sold cut-rate life insurance to poor Black people. My mama married when I was a year old, but her husband died just after my little sister was born a year later.

When I was five, Mama married the man she lived with until she died.   15
Within the first year of their marriage Mama miscarried, and while we waited out in the hospital parking lot, my stepfather molested me for the first time, something he continued to do until I was past thirteen. When I was eight or so, Mama took us away to a motel after my stepfather beat me so badly it caused a family scandal, but we returned after two weeks. Mama told me that she really had no choice: she could not support us alone. When I was eleven I told one of my cousins that my stepfather was molesting me. Mama packed up my sisters and me and took us away for a few days, but again, my stepfather swore he would stop, and again we went back after a few weeks. I stopped talking for a while, and I have only vague memories of the next two years.

My stepfather worked as a route salesman, my mama as a waitress, laundry worker, cook, or fruit packer. I could never understand, since they both worked so hard and such long hours, how we never had enough money, but it was also true of my mama's brothers and sisters who worked hard in the mills or the furnace industry. In fact, my parents did better than anyone else in the family. But eventually my stepfather was fired and we hit bottom—nightmarish months of marshals at the door, repossessed furniture, and rubber checks. My parents worked out a scheme so that it appeared my stepfather had abandoned us, but instead he went down to Florida, got a new job, and rented us a house. He returned with a U-Haul trailer in the dead of night, packed us up, and moved us south.

The night we left South Carolina for Florida, my mama leaned over the backseat of her old Pontiac and promised us girls, "It'll be better there." I don't know if we believed her, but I remember crossing Georgia in the early morning, watching the red clay hills and swaying grey blankets of moss recede through the back window. I kept looking at the trailer behind us, ridiculously small to contain everything we owned. Mama had packed nothing that wasn't fully paid off, which meant she had only two things of worth: her washing and sewing machines, both of them tied securely to the trailer walls. Throughout the trip I fantasized an accident that would burst that trailer, scattering old clothes and cracked dishes on the tarmac.

I was only thirteen. I wanted us to start over completely, to begin again as new people with nothing of the past left over. I wanted to run away from who we had been seen to be, who we had been. That desire is one I have seen in other members of my family. It is the first thing I think of when trouble comes—the geographic solution. Change your name, leave town, disappear, make yourself over. What hides behind that impulse is the conviction that the life you have lived, the person you are, is valueless, better off abandoned, that running away is easier than trying to change things, that change itself is not possible. Sometimes I think it is this conviction—more seductive than alcohol or violence, more subtle than sexual hatred or gender injustice—that has dominated my life and made real change so painful and difficult.

Moving to Central Florida did not fix our lives. It did not stop my stepfather's violence, heal my shame, or make my mother happy. Once there, our lives became controlled by my mother's illness and medical bills. She had a hysterectomy when I was about eight and endured a series of hospitalizations for ulcers and a chronic back problem. Through most of my adolescence she superstitiously refused to allow anyone to mention the word *cancer*. When she was not sick, Mama and my stepfather went on working, struggling to pay off what seemed an insurmountable load of debts.

By the time I was fourteen, my sisters and I had found ways to discourage most of our stepfather's sexual advances. We were not close, but we united against him. Our efforts were helped along when he was referred to a psychotherapist after he lost his temper at work, and was prescribed drugs that made him sullen but less violent. We were growing up quickly, my sisters moving toward dropping out of school while I got good grades and took every scholarship exam I could find. I was the first person in my family to graduate from high school, and the fact that I went on to college was nothing short of astonishing. 20

We all imagine our lives are normal, and I did not know my life was not everyone's. It was in Central Florida that I began to realize just how different we were. The people we met there had not been shaped by the rigid class structure that dominated the South Carolina Piedmont. The first time I looked around my junior high classroom and realized I did not know who those people were—not only as individuals but as categories, who their people were and how they saw themselves—I also realized that they did not know me. In Greenville, everyone knew my family, knew we were trash, and that meant we were supposed to be poor, supposed to have grim low-paid jobs, have babies in our teens, and never finish school. But Central Florida in the 1960s was full of runaways and immigrants, and our mostly white working-class suburban school sorted us out not by income and family background but by intelligence and aptitude tests. Suddenly I was boosted into the college-bound track, and while there was plenty of contempt for my inept social skills, pitiful wardrobe, and slow drawling accent, there was also something I had never experienced before: a protective anonymity, and a kind of grudging respect and curiosity about who I might become. Because they did not see poverty and hopelessness as a foregone conclusion for my life, I could begin to imagine other futures for myself.

In that new country, we were unknown. The myth of the poor settled over us and glamorized us. I saw it in the eyes of my teachers, the Lion's Club representative who paid for my new glasses, and the lady from the Junior League who told me about the scholarship I had won. Better, far better, to be one of the mythical poor than to be part of the *they* I had known before. I also experienced a new level of fear, a fear of losing what had never before been imaginable. Don't let me lose this chance, I prayed, and lived in terror that I might suddenly be seen again as what I knew myself to be.

As an adolescent I thought that my family's escape from South Carolina played like a bad movie. We fled the way runaway serfs might have done, with the sheriff who would have arrested my stepfather the imagined border guard. I am certain that if we had remained in South Carolina, I would have been trapped by my family's heritage of poverty, jail, and illegitimate children — that even being smart, stubborn, and a lesbian would have made no difference.

My grandmother died when I was twenty, and after Mama went home for the funeral, I had a series of dreams in which we still lived up in Greenville, just down the road from where Granny died. In the dreams I had two children and only one eye, lived in a trailer, and worked at the textile mill. Most of my time was taken up with deciding when I would finally kill my children and myself. The dreams were so vivid, I became convinced they were about the life I was meant to have had, and I began to work even harder to put as much distance as I could between my family and me. I copied the dress, mannerisms, attitudes, and ambitions of the girls I met in college, changing or hiding my own tastes, interests, and desires. I kept my lesbianism a secret, forming a relationship with an effeminate male friend that served to shelter and disguise us both. I explained to friends that I went home so rarely because my stepfather and I fought too much for me to be comfortable in his house. But that was only part of the reason I avoided home, the easiest reason. The truth was that I feared the person I might become in my mama's house, the woman of my dreams — hateful, violent, and hopeless.

It is hard to explain how deliberately and thoroughly I ran away from   25
my own life. I did not forget where I came from, but I gritted my teeth and hid it. When I could not get enough scholarship money to pay for graduate school, I spent a year of rage working as a salad girl, substitute teacher, and maid. I finally managed to find a job by agreeing to take any city assignment

where the Social Security Administration needed a clerk. Once I had a job and my own place far away from anyone in my family, I became sexually and politically active, joining the Women's Center support staff and falling in love with a series of middle-class women who thought my accent and stories thoroughly charming. The stories I told about my family, about South Carolina, about being poor itself, were all lies, carefully edited to seem droll or funny. I knew damn well that no one would want to hear the truth about poverty, the hopelessness and fear, the feeling that nothing I did would ever make any difference and the raging resentment that burned beneath my jokes. Even when my lovers and I formed an alternative lesbian family, sharing what we could of our resources, I kept the truth about my background and who I knew myself to be a carefully obscured mystery. I worked as hard as I could to make myself a new person, an emotionally healthy radical lesbian activist, and I believed completely that by remaking myself I was helping to remake the world.

For a decade, I did not go home for more than a few days at a time.

When in the 1980s I ran into the concept of feminist sexuality, I genuinely did not know what it meant. Though I was, and am, a feminist, and committed to claiming the right to act on my sexual desires without tailoring my lust to a sex-fearing society, demands that I explain or justify my sexual fantasies have left me at a loss. How does anyone explain sexual need?

The Sex Wars are over, I've been told, and it always makes me want to ask who won. But my sense of humor may be a little obscure to women who have never felt threatened by the way most lesbians use and mean the words *pervert* and *queer*. I use the word queer to mean more than lesbian. Since I first used it in 1980 I have always meant it to imply that I am not only a lesbian but a transgressive lesbian—femme, masochistic, as sexually aggressive as the women I seek out, and as pornographic in my imagination and sexual activities as the heterosexual hegemony has ever believed.

My aunt Dot used to joke, "There are two or three things I know for sure, but never the same things and I'm never as sure as I'd like." What I know for sure is that class, gender, sexual preference, and prejudice—racial, ethnic, and religious—form an intricate lattice that restricts and shapes our lives, and that resistance to hatred is not a simple act. Claiming your identity in the cauldron of hatred and resistance to hatred is infinitely complicated, and worse, almost unexplainable.

I know that I have been hated as a lesbian both by "society" and by the   30 intimate world of my extended family, but I have also been hated or held in contempt (which is in some ways more debilitating and slippery than hatred) by lesbians for behavior and sexual practices shaped in large part by class. My sexual identity is intimately constructed by my class and regional background, and much of the hatred directed at my sexual preferences is class hatred—however much people, feminists in particular, like to pretend this is not a factor. The kind of woman I am attracted to is invariably the kind of woman who embarrasses respectably middle-class, politically aware lesbian feminists. My sexual ideal is butch, exhibitionistic, physically aggressive, smarter than she wants you to know, and proud of being called a pervert. Most often she is working class, with an aura of danger and an ironic sense of humor. There is a lot of contemporary lip service paid to sexual tolerance, but the fact that my sexuality is constructed within, and by, a butch/femme and leather fetishism is widely viewed with distaste or outright hatred.

For most of my life I have been presumed to be misguided, damaged by incest and childhood physical abuse, or deliberately indulging in hateful and retrograde sexual practices out of a selfish concentration on my own sexual satisfaction. I have been expected to abandon my desires, to become the normalized woman who flirts with fetishization, who plays with gender roles and treats the historical categories of deviant desire with humor or gentle contempt but never takes any of it so seriously as to claim a sexual identity based on these categories. It was hard enough for me to shake off demands when they were made by straight society. It was appalling when I found the same demands made by other lesbians.

One of the strengths I derive from my class background is that I am accustomed to contempt. I know that I have no chance of becoming what my detractors expect of me, and I believe that even the attempt to please them will only further engage their contempt, and my own self-contempt as well. Nonetheless, the relationship between the life I have lived and the way that life is seen by strangers has constantly invited a kind of self-mythologizing fantasy. It has always been tempting for me to play off of the stereotypes and misconceptions of mainstream culture, rather than describe a difficult and sometimes painful reality.

I am trying to understand how we internalize the myths of our society even as we resist them. I have felt a powerful temptation to write about my family as a kind of morality tale, with us as the heroes and middle and upper classes as the villains. It would be within the romantic myth, for example, to pretend that we were the kind of noble Southern whites portrayed in the movies, mill workers for generations until driven out by alcoholism and a family propensity for rebellion and union talk. But that would be a lie. The truth is that no one in my family ever joined a union.

Taken to its limits, the myth of the poor would make my family over into union organizers or people broken by the failure of the unions. As far as my family was concerned union organizers, like preachers, were of a different class, suspect and hated however much they might be admired for what they were supposed to be trying to achieve. Nominally Southern Baptist, no one in my family actually paid much attention to preachers, and only little children went to Sunday school. Serious belief in anything—any political ideology, any religious system, or any theory of life's meaning and purpose—was seen as unrealistic. It was an attitude that bothered me a lot when I started reading the socially conscious novels I found in the paperback racks when I was eleven or so. I particularly loved Sinclair Lewis's novels and wanted to imagine my own family as part of the working man's struggle.

"We were not joiners," my aunt Dot told me with a grin when I asked   35
her about the union. My cousin Butch laughed at that, told me the union
charged dues, and said, "Hell, we can't even be persuaded to toss money
in the collection plate. An't gonna give it to no union man." It shamed me
that the only thing my family whole-heartedly believed in was luck and the
waywardness of fate. They held the dogged conviction that the admirable
and wise thing to do was keep a sense of humor, never whine or cower, and
trust that luck might someday turn as good as it had been bad—and with
just as much reason. Becoming a political activist with an almost religious
fervor was the thing I did that most outraged my family and the Southern
working-class community they were part of.

Similarly, it was not my sexuality, my lesbianism, that my family saw as
most rebellious; for most of my life, no one but my mama took my sexual
preference very seriously. It was the way I thought about work, ambition,
and self-respect. They were waitresses, laundry workers, counter girls. I was
the one who went to work as a maid, something I never told any of them.
They would have been angry if they had known. Work was just work for
them, necessary. You did what you had to do to survive. They did not so
much believe in taking pride in doing your job as in stubbornly enduring
hard work and hard times. At the same time, they held that there were some
forms of work, including maid's work, that were only for Black people, not
white, and while I did not share that belief, I knew how intrinsic it was to
the way my family saw the world. Sometimes I felt as if I straddled cultures
and belonged on neither side. I would grind my teeth at what I knew was
my family's unquestioning racism while continuing to respect their pragmatic endurance. But more and more as I grew older, what I felt was a deep
estrangement from their view of the world, and gradually a sense of shame
that would have been completely incomprehensible to them.

"Long as there's lunch counters, you can always find work," I was told
by my mother and my aunts. Then they'd add, "I can get me a little extra
with a smile." It was obvious there was supposed to be nothing shameful
about it, that needy smile across a lunch counter, that rueful grin when you
didn't have rent, or the half-provocative, half-pleading way my mama could
cajole the man at the store to give her a little credit. But I hated it, hated the
need for it and the shame that would follow every time I did it myself. It was
begging, as far as I was concerned, a quasi-prostitution that I despised even
while I continued to rely on it. After all, I needed the money.

"Just use that smile," my girl cousins used to joke, and I hated what I
knew they meant. After college, when I began to support myself and study
feminist theory, I became more contemptuous rather than more understanding of the women in my family. I told myself that prostitution is a skilled
profession and my cousins were never more than amateurs. There was a
certain truth in this, though like all cruel judgments rendered from the outside, it ignored the conditions that made it true. The women in my family,
my mother included, had sugar daddies, not johns, men who slipped them

money because they needed it so badly. From their point of view they were nice to those men because the men were nice to them, and it was never so direct or crass an arrangement that they would set a price on their favors. Nor would they have described what they did as prostitution. Nothing made them angrier than the suggestion that the men who helped them out did it just for their favors. They worked for a living, they swore, but this was different.

I always wondered if my mother hated her sugar daddy, or if not him then her need for what he offered her, but it did not seem to me in memory that she had. He was an old man, half-crippled, hesitant and needy, and he treated my mama with enormous consideration and, yes, respect. The relationship between them was painful, and since she and my stepfather could not earn enough to support the family, Mama could not refuse her sugar daddy's money. At the same time the man made no assumptions about that money buying anything Mama was not already offering. The truth was, I think, that she genuinely liked him, and only partly because he treated her so well.

Even now, I am not sure whether there was a sexual exchange between them. Mama was a pretty woman, and she was kind to him, a kindness he obviously did not get from anyone else in his life. Moreover, he took extreme care not to cause her any problems with my stepfather. As a teenager, with a teenager's contempt for moral failings and sexual complexity of any kind, I had been convinced that Mama's relationship with that old man was contemptible. Also, that I would never do such a thing. But the first time a lover of mine gave me money and I took it, everything in my head shifted. The amount was not much to her, but it was a lot to me and I needed it. While I could not refuse it, I hated myself for taking it and I hated her for giving it. Worse, she had much less grace about my need than my mama's sugar daddy had displayed toward her. All that bitter contempt I felt for my needy cousins and aunts raged through me and burned out the love. I ended the relationship quickly, unable to forgive myself for selling what I believed should only be offered freely—not sex but love itself.

When the women in my family talked about how hard they worked, the men would spit to the side and shake their heads. Men took real jobs—harsh, dangerous, physically daunting work. They went to jail, not just the cold-eyed, careless boys who scared me with their brutal hands, but their gentler, softer brothers. It was another family thing, what people expected of my mama's people, mine. "His daddy's that one was sent off to jail in Georgia, and his uncle's another. Like as not, he's just the same," you'd hear people say of boys so young they still had their milk teeth. We were always driving down to the county farm to see somebody, some uncle, cousin, or nameless male relation. Shaven-headed, sullen, and stunned, they wept on Mama's shoulder or begged my aunts to help. "I didn't do nothing, Mama," they'd say, and it might have been true, but if even we didn't believe them, who would? No one told the truth, not even about how their lives were destroyed.

One of my favorite cousins went to jail when I was eight years old, for breaking into pay phones with another boy. The other boy was returned to the custody of his parents. My cousin was sent to the boys' facility at the county farm. After three months, my mama took us down there to visit, carrying a big basket of fried chicken, cold cornbread, and potato salad. Along with a hundred others we sat out on the lawn with my cousin and watched him eat like he hadn't had a full meal in the whole three months. I stared at his near-bald head and his ears marked with fine blue scars from the carelessly handled razor. People were laughing, music was playing, and a tall, lazy, uniformed man walked past us chewing on toothpicks and watching us all closely. My cousin kept his head down, his face hard with hatred, only looking back at the guard when he turned away.

"Sons-a-bitches," he whispered, and my mama shushed him. We all sat still when the guard turned back to us. There was a long moment of quiet, and then that man let his face relax into a big wide grin.

"Uh-huh," he said. That was all he said. Then he turned and walked away. None of us spoke. None of us ate. He went back inside soon after, and we left. When we got back to the car, my mama sat there for a while crying quietly. The next week my cousin was reported for fighting and had his stay extended by six months.

My cousin was fifteen. He never went back to school, and after jail he couldn't join the army. When he finally did come home we never talked, never had to. I knew without asking that the guard had had his little revenge, knew too that my cousin would break into another phone booth as soon as he could, but do it sober and not get caught. I knew without asking the source of his rage, the way he felt about clean, well-dressed, contemptuous people who looked at him like his life wasn't as important as a dog's. I knew because I felt it too. That guard had looked at me and Mama with the same expression he used on my cousin. We were trash. We were the ones they built the county farm to house and break. The boy who was sent home was the son of a deacon in the church, the man who managed the hardware store.

As much as I hated that man, and his boy, there was a way in which I also hated my cousin. He should have known better, I told myself, should have known the risk he ran. He should have been more careful. As I grew older and started living on my own, it was a litany I used against myself even more angrily than I used it against my cousin. I knew who I was, knew that the most important thing I had to do was protect myself and hide my despised identity, blend into the myth of both the good poor and the reasonable lesbian. When I became a feminist activist, that litany went on reverberating in my head, but by then it had become a groundnote, something so deep and omnipresent I no longer heard it, even when everything I did was set to its cadence.

By 1975 I was earning a meager living as a photographer's assistant in Tallahassee, Florida. But the real work of my life was my lesbian-feminist activism, the work I did with the local women's center and the committee

45

to found a women's studies program at Florida State University. Part of my role, as I saw it, was to be a kind of evangelical lesbian feminist, and to help develop a political analysis of this woman-hating society. I did not talk about class, except to give lip service to how we all needed to think about it, the same way I thought we all needed to think about racism. I was a determined person, living in a lesbian collective—all of us young and white and serious—studying each new book that purported to address feminist issues, driven by what I saw as a need to revolutionize the world.

Years later it's difficult to convey just how reasonable my life seemed to me at that time. I was not flippant, not consciously condescending, not casual about how tough a struggle remaking social relations would be, but like so many women of my generation, I believed absolutely that I could make a difference with my life, and I was willing to give my life for the chance to make that difference. I expected hard times, long slow periods of self-sacrifice and grinding work, expected to be hated and attacked in public, to have to set aside personal desire, lovers, and family in order to be part of something greater and more important than my individual concerns. At the same time, I was working ferociously to take my desires, my sexuality, my needs as a woman and a lesbian more seriously. I believed I was making the personal political revolution with my life every moment, whether I was scrubbing the floor of the childcare center, setting up a new budget for the women's lecture series at the university, editing the local feminist magazine, or starting a women's bookstore. That I was constantly exhausted and had no health insurance, did hours of dreary unpaid work and still sneaked out of the collective to date butch women my housemates thought retrograde and sexist never interfered with my sense of total commitment to the feminist revolution. I was not living in a closet: I had compartmentalized my own mind to such an extent that I never questioned why I did what I did. And I never admitted what lay behind all my feminist convictions—a class-constructed distrust of change, a secret fear that someday I would be found out for who I really was, found out and thrown out. If I had not been raised to give my life away, would I have made such an effective, self-sacrificing revolutionary?

The narrowly focused concentration of a revolutionary shifted only when I began to write again. The idea of writing stories seemed frivolous when there was so much work to be done, but everything changed when I found myself confronting emotions and ideas that could not be explained away or postponed until after the revolution. The way it happened was simple and unexpected. One week I was asked to speak to two completely different groups: an Episcopalian Sunday school class and a juvenile detention center. The Episcopalians were all white, well-dressed, highly articulate, nominally polite, and obsessed with getting me to tell them (without their having to ask directly) just what it was that two women did together in bed. The delinquents were all women, 80 percent Black and Hispanic, wearing green uniform dresses or blue jeans and workshirts, profane, rude, fearless, witty, and just as determined to get me to talk about what it was that two women did together in bed.

I tried to have fun with the Episcopalians, teasing them about their fears   50
and insecurities, and being as bluntly honest as I could about my sexual
practices. The Sunday school teacher, a man who had assured me of his liberal inclinations, kept blushing and stammering as the questions about my
growing up and coming out became more detailed. I stepped out into the
sunshine when the meeting was over, angry at the contemptuous attitude
implied by all their questioning, and though I did not know why, so deeply
depressed I couldn't even cry.

The delinquents were another story. Shameless, they had me blushing
within the first few minutes, yelling out questions that were part curiosity
and partly a way of boasting about what they already knew. "You butch or
femme?" "You ever fuck boys?" "You ever want to?" "You want to have children?" "What's your girlfriend like?" I finally broke up when one very tall,
confident girl leaned way over and called out, "Hey, girlfriend! I'm getting
out of here next weekend. What you doing that night?" I laughed so hard I
almost choked. I laughed until we were all howling and giggling together.
Even getting frisked as I left didn't ruin my mood. I was still grinning when
I climbed into the waterbed with my lover that night, grinning right up to
the moment when she wrapped her arms around me and I burst into tears.

That night I understood, suddenly, everything that had happened to my
cousins and me, understood it from a wholly new and agonizing perspective,
one that made clear how brutal I had been to both my family and myself. I
grasped all over again how we had been robbed and dismissed, and why I
had worked so hard not to think about it. I had learned as a child that what
could not be changed had to go unspoken, and worse, that those who cannot
change their own lives have every reason to be ashamed of that fact and to
hide it. I had accepted that shame and believed in it, but why? What had I or
my cousins done to deserve the contempt directed at us? Why had I always
believed us contemptible by nature? I wanted to talk to someone about all
the things I was thinking that night, but I could not. Among the women I
knew there was no one who would have understood what I was thinking, no
other working-class woman in the women's collective where I was living. I
began to suspect that we shared no common language to speak those bitter
truths.

In the days that followed I found myself remembering that afternoon
long ago at the county farm, that feeling of being the animal in the zoo, the
thing looked at and laughed at and used by the real people who watched us.
For all his liberal convictions, that Sunday school teacher had looked at me
with the eyes of my cousin's long-ago guard. I felt thrown back into my childhood, into all the fears I had tried to escape. Once again I felt myself at the
mercy of the important people who knew how to dress and talk, and would
always be given the benefit of the doubt, while my family and I would not.

I experienced an outrage so old I could not have traced all the ways it
shaped my life. I realized again that some are given no quarter, no chance,
that all their courage, humor, and love for each other is just a joke to the ones

who make the rules, and I hated the rule-makers. Finally, I recognized that part of my grief came from the fact that I no longer knew who I was or where I belonged. I had run away from my family, refused to go home to visit, and tried in every way to make myself a new person. How could I be working class with a college degree? As a lesbian activist? I thought about the guards at the detention center. They had not stared at me with the same picture-window emptiness they turned on the girls who came to hear me, girls who were closer to the life I had been meant to live than I could hear to examine. The contempt in their eyes was contempt for me as a lesbian, different and the same, but still contempt.

While I raged, my girlfriend held me and comforted me and tried to get   55
me to explain what was hurting me so bad, but I could not. She had told me so often about her awkward relationship with her own family, the father who ran his own business and still sent her checks every other month. She knew almost nothing about my family, only the jokes and careful stories I had given her. I felt so alone and at risk lying in her arms that I could not have explained anything at all. I thought about those girls in the detention center and the stories they told in brutal shorthand about their sisters, brothers, cousins, and lovers. I thought about their one-note references to those they had lost, never mentioning the loss of their own hopes, their own futures, the bent and painful shape of their lives when they would finally get free. Cried-out and dry-eyed, I lay watching my sleeping girlfriend and thinking about what I had not been able to say to her. After a few hours I got up and made some notes for a poem I wanted to write, a bare, painful litany of loss shaped as a conversation between two women, one who cannot understand the other, and one who cannot tell all she knows.

It took me a long time to take that poem from a raw lyric of outrage and grief to a piece of fiction that explained to me something I had never let myself see up close before—the whole process of running away, of closing up inside yourself, of hiding. It has taken me most of my life to understand that, to see how and why those of us who are born poor and different are so driven to give ourselves away or lose ourselves, but most of all, simply to disappear as the people we really are. By the time that poem became the story "River of Names,"[2] I had made the decision to reverse that process: to claim my family, my true history, and to tell the truth not only about who I was but about the temptation to lie.

By the time I taught myself the basics of storytelling on the page, I knew there was only one story that would haunt me until I understood how to tell it—the complicated, painful story of how my mama had, and had not, saved me as a girl. Writing *Bastard Out of Carolina*[3] became, ultimately, the way to claim my family's pride and tragedy, and the embattled sexuality I had fashioned on a base of violence and abuse.

---

2 *Trash* (Firebrand Books: Ithaca, New York, 1988).—ALLISON'S NOTE.
3 Dutton: New York, 1992.—ALLISON'S NOTE.

The compartmentalized life I had created burst open in the late 1970s after I began to write what I really thought about my family. I lost patience with my fear of what the women I worked with, mostly lesbians, thought of who I slept with and what we did together. When schisms developed within my community; when I was no longer able to hide within the regular dyke network; when I could not continue to justify my life by constant political activism or distract myself by sleeping around; when my sexual promiscuity, butch/femme orientation, and exploration of sadomasochistic sex became part of what was driving me out of my community of choice—I went home again. I went home to my mother and my sisters, to visit, talk, argue, and begin to understand.

Once home I saw that as far as my family was concerned, lesbians were lesbians whether they wore suitcoats or leather jackets. Moreover, in all that time when I had not made peace with myself, my family had managed to make a kind of peace with me. My girlfriends were treated like slightly odd versions of my sisters' husbands, while I was simply the daughter who had always been difficult but was still a part of their lives. The result was that I started trying to confront what had made me unable really to talk to my sisters for so many years. I discovered that they no longer knew who I was either, and it took time and lots of listening to each other to rediscover my sense of family, and my love for them.

It is only as the child of my class and my unique family background that   60 I have been able to put together what is for me a meaningful politics, to regain a sense of why I believe in activism, why self-revelation is so important for lesbians. There is no all-purpose feminist analysis that explains the complicated ways our sexuality and core identity are shaped, the way we see ourselves as parts of both our birth families and the extended family of friends and lovers we invariably create within the lesbian community. For me, the bottom line has simply become the need to resist that omnipresent fear, that urge to hide and disappear, to disguise my life, my desires, and the truth about how little any of us understand—even as we try to make the world a more just and human place. Most of all, I have tried to understand the politics of *they*, why human beings fear and stigmatize the different while secretly dreading that they might be one of the different themselves. Class, race, sexuality, gender—and all the other categories by which we categorize and dismiss each other—need to be excavated from the inside.

The horror of class stratification, racism, and prejudice is that some people begin to believe that the security of their families and communities depends on the oppression of others, that for some to have good lives there must be others whose lives are truncated and brutal. It is a belief that dominates this culture. It is what makes the poor whites of the South so determinedly racist and the middle class so contemptuous of the poor. It is a myth that allows some to imagine that they build their lives on the ruin of others, a secret core of shame for the middle class, a goad and a spur to the marginal working class, and cause enough for the homeless and poor to feel no constraints on hatred or violence. The power of the myth is made even more apparent when we examine how, within the lesbian and feminist communities where we have addressed considerable attention to the politics of marginalization, there is still so much exclusion and fear, so many of us who do not feel safe.

I grew up poor, hated, the victim of physical, emotional, and sexual violence, and I know that suffering does not ennoble. It destroys. To resist destruction, self-hatred, or lifelong hopelessness, we have to throw off the conditioning of being despised, the fear of becoming the *they* that is talked about so dismissively, to refuse lying myths and easy moralities, to see ourselves as human, flawed, and extraordinary. All of us — extraordinary. ●

The Reader's Presence

1. Allison's essay underscores the ways in which she views herself as different from mainstream American women. Consider her use of pronouns and how they relate to these issues of difference and identity as well as to the narrative as a whole. What effect does the speaker's use of "they" have in terms of the story and her sense of personal identity? Compare and contrast the opening and final sentences of the essay. What does Allison's use of "us" in the final sentence reveal? What role do contradictions play in the essay? How do they shape what the narrator calls "the fundamental me" (paragraph 9)? How does this sense of inner conflict affect the narrator?

2. Allison discusses the myths of our society and the importance of representation as it relates to one's identity. "My family's lives were not on television, not in books, not even comic books" (paragraph 13). To what extent do external forces shape the narrator's identity? How does the end of the essay reconcile this realization? How convincingly does Allison demonstrate that matters of class exist within lesbian and activist communities?

3. **VISUAL PRESENCE:**   Examine the photograph of Dorothy Allison on a motorcycle (page 41). How does Allison establish her presence in the portrait? In what specific ways does this image illustrate the points she makes about class and identity in her essay? Support your answer with details from the image.

4. **CONNECTIONS:**   Compare and contrast Allison's essay to Walter Mosley's "Get Happy" (page 682). To what extent does Mosley seem to describe Allison's experiences when he writes, "many of us suffer under a corporatized bureaucracy where homelessness, illiteracy, poverty, malnourishment (both physical and spiritual) and an unrelenting malaise are not only possible but likely" (paragraph 9)? In what specific way(s) does Allison's essay connect with Mosley's call "to expand the possibilities for happiness" (paragraph 12)? To what extent do you view Allison's concluding sentence ("All of us — extraordinary") as embracing happiness in the face of "class stratification, racism, and prejudice" (paragraph 61)?

Maya Angelou

"WHAT'S YOUR NAME, GIRL?"

MAYA ANGELOU (1928–2014) grew up in St. Louis, Missouri, and in Stamps, Arkansas, a victim of poverty, discrimination, and abuse. Angelou confronts the pain and injustice of her childhood in *I Know Why the Caged Bird Sings* (1969), from which the selection "'What's Your Name, Girl?'" is taken. James Baldwin, who suggested she write about her childhood, praised this book as the mark of the "beginning of a new era in the minds and hearts of all black men and women." Angelou, who received more than thirty honorary degrees, was the Reynolds Professor of American Studies at Wake Forest University. In addition to the several volumes of her autobiography, Angelou was the author of articles, short stories, and poetry. Some of her publications include *Hallelujah! The Welcome Table* (2004), a collection of essays, and several books of poetry, including *Amazing Peace: A Christmas Poem* (2005), *Mother: A Cradle to Hold Me* (2006), and *Poetry for Young People: Maya Angelou* (2007). At the request of President Bill Clinton, Angelou composed "On the Pulse of the Morning," a poem she read at his inauguration in 1993. She later served on two presidential committees and was awarded the Presidential Medal of Arts in 2000 and the Presidential Medal of Freedom in 2011. She also received three Grammy Awards, including a Grammy in 2002 for her recording of *A Song Flung Up to Heaven*, the sixth book in her autobiographical series. Her most recent book was *Mom & Me & Mom* (2013), a nonfiction book delving into Angelou's relationship with her mother.

> **"When I'm writing, everything shuts down."**

Angelou described a typical day in her life as a writer in this way: "When I'm writing, everything shuts down. I get up about five. . . . I get in my car and drive off to a hotel room: I can't write in my house, I take a hotel room and ask them to take everything off the walls so there's me, the Bible, *Roget's Thesaurus*, and some good, dry sherry and I'm at work by 6:30. I write on the bed lying down—one elbow is darker than the other, really black from leaning on it—and I write in longhand on yellow pads. Once into it, all disbelief is suspended, it's beautiful. I hate to go, but I've set for myself 12:30 as the time to leave, because after that it's an indulgence, it becomes stuff I am going to edit out anyway. . . . After dinner I re-read what I have written . . . if April is the cruellest month, then 8:00 at night is the cruellest hour because that's when I start to edit and all that pretty stuff I've written gets axed out. So if I've written ten or twelve pages in six hours, it'll end up as three or four if I'm lucky."

RECENTLY A WHITE WOMAN from Texas, who would quickly describe herself as a liberal, asked me about my hometown. When I told her that in Stamps[1] my grandmother had owned the only Negro general merchandise store since the turn of the century, she exclaimed, "Why, you were a debutante." Ridiculous and even ludicrous. But Negro girls in small Southern towns, whether poverty-stricken or just munching along on a few of life's necessities, were given as extensive and irrelevant preparations for adulthood as rich white girls shown in magazines. Admittedly the training was not the same. While white girls learned to waltz and sit gracefully with a teacup balanced on their knees, we were lagging behind, learning the mid-Victorian values with very little money to indulge them. (Come and see Edna Lomax spending the money she made picking cotton on five balls of ecru tatting thread. Her fingers are bound to snag the work and she'll have to repeat the stitches time and time again. But she knows that when she buys the thread.)

We were required to embroider and I had trunkfuls of colorful dishtowels, pillowcases, runners, and handkerchiefs to my credit. I mastered the art of crocheting and tatting, and there was a lifetime's supply of dainty doilies that would never be used in sacheted dresser drawers. It went without saying that all girls could iron and wash, but the finer touches around the home, like setting a table with real silver, baking roasts, and cooking vegetables without meat, had to be learned elsewhere. Usually at the source of those habits. During my tenth year, a white woman's kitchen became my finishing school.

Mrs. Viola Cullinan was a plump woman who lived in a three-bedroom house somewhere behind the post office. She was singularly unattractive until she smiled, and then the lines around her eyes and mouth which made her look perpetually dirty disappeared, and her face looked like the mask of an impish elf. She usually rested her smile until late afternoon when her women friends dropped in and Miss Glory, the cook, served them cold drinks on the closed-in porch.

The exactness of her house was inhuman. This glass went here and only here. That cup had its place and it was an act of impudent rebellion to place it anywhere else. At twelve o'clock the table was set. At 12:15 Mrs. Cullinan sat down to dinner (whether her husband had arrived or not). At 12:16 Miss Glory brought out the food.

It took me a week to learn the difference between a salad plate, a bread plate, and a dessert plate.   5

Mrs. Cullinan kept up the tradition of her wealthy parents. She was from Virginia. Miss Glory, who was a descendant of slaves that had worked for the Cullinans, told me her history. She had married beneath her (according to Miss Glory). Her husband's family hadn't had their money very long and what they had "didn't 'mount to much."

---

[1] **Stamps:** A town in southwestern Arkansas. —EDS.

As ugly as she was, I thought privately, she was lucky to get a husband above or beneath her station. But Miss Glory wouldn't let me say a thing against her mistress. She was very patient with me, however, over the housework. She explained the dishware, silverware, and servants' bells.

The large round bowl in which soup was served wasn't a soup bowl, it was a tureen. There were goblets, sherbet glasses, ice-cream glasses, wine glasses, green glass coffee cups with matching saucers, and water glasses. I had a glass to drink from, and it sat with Miss Glory's on a separate shelf from the others. Soup spoons, gravy boat, butter knives, salad forks, and carving platter were additions to my vocabulary and in fact almost represented a new language. I was fascinated with the novelty, with the fluttering Mrs. Cullinan and her Alice-in-Wonderland house.

Her husband remains, in my memory, undefined. I lumped him with all the other white men that I had ever seen and tried not to see.

On our way home one evening, Miss Glory told me that Mrs. Cullinan   10 couldn't have children. She said that she was too delicate-boned. It was hard to imagine bones at all under those layers of fat. Miss Glory went on to say that the doctor had taken out all her lady organs. I reasoned that a pig's organs included the lungs, heart, and liver, so if Mrs. Cullinan was walking around without these essentials, it explained why she drank alcohol out of unmarked bottles. She was keeping herself embalmed.

When I spoke to Bailey[2] about it, he agreed that I was right, but he also informed me that Mr. Cullinan had two daughters by a colored lady and that I knew them very well. He added that the girls were the spitting image of their father. I was unable to remember what he looked like, although I had just left him a few hours before, but I thought of the Coleman girls. They were very light-skinned and certainly didn't look very much like their mother (no one ever mentioned Mr. Coleman).

My pity for Mrs. Cullinan preceded me the next morning like the Cheshire cat's smile. Those girls, who could have been her daughters, were beautiful. They didn't have to straighten their hair. Even when they were caught in the rain, their braids still hung down straight like tamed snakes. Their mouths were pouty little cupid's bows. Mrs. Cullinan didn't know what she missed. Or maybe she did. Poor Mrs. Cullinan.

For weeks after, I arrived early, left late, and tried very hard to make up for her barrenness. If she had had her own children, she wouldn't have had to ask me to run a thousand errands from her back door to the back door of her friends. Poor old Mrs. Cullinan.

Then one evening Miss Glory told me to serve the ladies on the porch. After I set the tray down and turned toward the kitchen, one of the women asked, "What's your name, girl?" It was the speckled-face one. Mrs. Cullinan said, "She doesn't talk much. Her name's Margaret."

"Is she dumb?"   15

---

[2] ***Bailey:*** Angelou's brother. —EDS.

"No. As I understand it, she can talk when she wants to but she's usually quiet as a little mouse. Aren't you, Margaret?"

I smiled at her. Poor thing. No organs and couldn't even pronounce my name correctly.[3]

"She's a sweet little thing, though."

"Well, that may be, but the name's too long. I'd never bother myself. I'd call her Mary if I was you."

I fumed into the kitchen. That horrible woman would never have the 20 chance to call me Mary because if I was starving I'd never work for her. I decided I wouldn't pee on her if her heart was on fire. Giggles drifted in off the porch and into Miss Glory's pots. I wondered what they could be laughing about.

Whitefolks were so strange. Could they be talking about me? Everybody knew that they stuck together better than the Negroes did. It was possible that Mrs. Cullinan had friends in St. Louis who heard about a girl from Stamps being in court and wrote to tell her. Maybe she knew about Mr. Freeman.[4]

My lunch was in my mouth a second time and I went outside and relieved myself on the bed of four-o'clocks. Miss Glory thought I might be coming down with something and told me to go on home, that Momma would give me some herb tea, and she'd explain to her mistress.

I realized how foolish I was being before I reached the pond. Of course Mrs. Cullinan didn't know. Otherwise she wouldn't have given me the two nice dresses that Momma cut down, and she certainly wouldn't have called me a "sweet little thing." My stomach felt fine, and I didn't mention anything to Momma.

That evening I decided to write a poem on being white, fat, old, and without children. It was going to be a tragic ballad. I would have to watch her carefully to capture the essence of her loneliness and pain.

The very next day, she called me by the wrong name. Miss Glory and I 25 were washing up the lunch dishes when Mrs. Cullinan came to the doorway. "Mary?"

Miss Glory asked, "Who?"

Mrs. Cullinan, sagging a little, knew and I knew. "I want Mary to go down to Mrs. Randall's and take her some soup. She's not been feeling well for a few days."

Miss Glory's face was a wonder to see. "You mean Margaret, ma'am. Her name's Margaret."

"That's too long. She's Mary from now on. Heat that soup from last night and put it in the china tureen and, Mary, I want you to carry it carefully."

---

[3] ***couldn't even pronounce my name correctly:*** Angelou's first name is actually Marguerite. —EDS.

[4] ***Mr. Freeman:*** A friend of Angelou's mother; he was convicted of raping Angelou when she was a child. —EDS.

Every person I knew had a hellish horror of being "called out of his   30
name." It was a dangerous practice to call a Negro anything that could be
loosely construed as insulting because of the centuries of their having been
called niggers, jigs, dinges, blackbirds, crows, boots, and spooks.

Miss Glory had a fleeting second of feeling sorry for me. Then as she
handed me the hot tureen she said, "Don't mind, don't pay that no mind.
Sticks and stones may break your bones, but words . . . You know, I been
working for her for twenty years."

She held the back door open for me. "Twenty years; I wasn't much older
than you. My name used to be Hallelujah. That's what Ma named me, but
my mistress give me 'Glory,' and it stuck. I likes it better too."

I was in the little path that ran behind the houses when Miss Glory
shouted, "It's shorter too."

For a few seconds it was a toss-up over whether I would laugh (imagine
being named Hallelujah) or cry (imagine letting some white woman rename
you for her convenience). My anger saved me from either outburst. I had to
quit the job, but the problem was going to be how to do it. Momma wouldn't
allow me to quit for just any reason.

"She's a peach. That woman is a real peach." Mrs. Randall's maid was   35
talking as she took the soup from me, and I wondered what her name used
to be and what she answered to now.

For a week I looked into Mrs. Cullinan's face as she called me Mary. She
ignored my coming late and leaving early. Miss Glory was a little annoyed
because I had begun to leave egg yolk on the dishes and wasn't putting
much heart in polishing the silver. I hoped that she would complain to our
boss, but she didn't.

Then Bailey solved my dilemma. He had me describe the contents of
the cupboard and the particular plates she liked best. Her favorite piece
was a casserole shaped like a fish and the green glass coffee cups. I kept
his instructions in mind, so on the next day when Miss Glory was hanging
out clothes and I had again been told to serve the old biddies on the porch,
I dropped the empty serving tray. When I heard Mrs. Cullinan scream,
"Mary!" I picked up the casserole and two of the green glass cups in readi-
ness. As she rounded the kitchen door I let them fall on the tiled floor.

I could never absolutely describe to Bailey what happened next, because
each time I got to the part where she fell on the floor and screwed up her
ugly face to cry, we burst out laughing. She actually wobbled around on the
floor and picked up shards of the cups and cried, "Oh, Momma. Oh, dear
Gawd. It's Momma's china from Virginia. Oh, Momma, I sorry."

Miss Glory came running in from the yard and the women from the
porch crowded around. Miss Glory was almost as broken up as her mistress.
"You mean to say she broke our Virginia dishes? What we gone do?"

Mrs. Cullinan cried louder. "That clumsy nigger. Clumsy little black   40
nigger."

Old speckled-face leaned down and asked, "Who did it, Viola? Was it
Mary? Who did it?"

Everything was happening so fast I can't remember whether her action preceded her words, but I know that Mrs. Cullinan said, "Her name's Margaret, goddamn it, her name's Margaret!" And she threw a wedge of the broken plate at me. It could have been the hysteria which put her aim off, but the flying crockery caught Miss Glory right over her ear and she started screaming.

I left the front door wide open so all the neighbors could hear.

Mrs. Cullinan was right about one thing. My name wasn't Mary.

The Reader's Presence

1. At the center of this autobiographical episode is the importance of people's names in African American culture. Where does Angelou make this point clear? If she hadn't explained the problem of names directly, how might your interpretation of the episode be different? To what extent do the names of things also play an important role in the essay? What does it mean to be "called out of [one's] name" (paragraph 30)?

2. Consider Marguerite's final act carefully. What turns her sympathetic feelings for Mrs. Cullinan to anger? Why does she respond by deliberately destroying Mrs. Cullinan's china? What else could she have done? Why was that act especially appropriate? What does the china represent? How does Angelou establish our sympathy, or lack thereof, for Marguerite in the final paragraphs?

3. **CONNECTIONS:**   Many coming-of-age stories involve an account not only of the child's acquisition of language but also, and perhaps more important, of the importance of social context to communication. Miss Glory's training of Marguerite as a maid involves "additions to [her] vocabulary and in fact almost represented a new language" (paragraph 8). How does Angelou's education compare to that of Richard Rodriguez in "Aria: A Memoir of a Bilingual Childhood" (page 227)? What is the relation between language and power in each essay?

James Baldwin
NOTES OF A NATIVE SON

JAMES BALDWIN (1924–1987) grew up in New York City but moved to France in 1948 because he felt personally and artistically stifled as a gay African American man in the United States. His first novels, *Go Tell It on the Mountain* (1953) and *Giovanni's Room* (1956), and his first collection of essays, *Notes of a Native Son* (1955), were published during Baldwin's first stay abroad, where he was able to write critically about race, sexual identity, and social injustice in America. "Once I found myself on the other side of the ocean," he told an interviewer, "I could see where I came from very clearly, and I could see that I carried myself, which is my home, with me. You can never escape that. I am the grandson of a slave, and I am a writer. I must deal with both."

After nearly a decade in France, he returned to New York and became a national figure in the civil rights movement. After Baldwin's death, Henry Louis Gates Jr. eulogized him as the conscience of the nation, for he

> "I am the grandson of a slave, and I am a writer. I must deal with both."

"educated an entire generation of Americans about the civil-rights struggle and the sensibility of Afro-Americans as we faced and conquered the final barriers in our long quest for civil rights." Baldwin continued to educate through his essays, collected in *The Price of the Ticket: Collected Nonfiction* (1985).

When asked if he approached the writing of fiction and nonfiction in different ways, Baldwin responded, "Every form is different, no one is easier than another. . . . An essay is not simpler, though it may seem so. An essay is clearly an argument. The writer's point of view in an essay is always absolutely clear. The writer is trying to make the readers see something, trying to convince them of something. In a novel or a play you're trying to show them something. The risks, in any case, are exactly the same."

The title essay of the book *Notes of a Native Son* first appeared in *Harper's* magazine in 1955. In it, Baldwin recounts the death of his father, whose funeral took place on Baldwin's nineteenth birthday—the same day a bloody race riot broke out in Harlem.

ONE

On the twenty-ninth of July, in 1943, my father died. On the same day, a few hours later, his last child was born. Over a month before this, while all our energies were concentrated in waiting for these events, there had been, in Detroit, one of the bloodiest race riots of the century. A few hours after my father's funeral, while he lay in state in the undertaker's chapel, a race riot broke out in Harlem. On the morning of the third of August, we drove my father to the graveyard through a wilderness of smashed plate glass.

The day of my father's funeral had also been my nineteenth birthday. As we drove him to the graveyard, the spoils of injustice, anarchy, discontent, and hatred were all around us. It seemed to me that God himself had devised, to mark my father's end, the most sustained and brutally dissonant of codas. And it seemed to me, too, that the violence which rose all about us as my father left the world had been devised as a corrective for the pride of his eldest son. I had declined to believe in that apocalypse which had been central to my father's vision; very well, life seemed to be saying, here is something that will certainly pass for an apocalypse until the real thing comes along. I had inclined to be contemptuous of my father for the conditions of his life, for the conditions of our lives. When his life had ended I began to wonder about that life and also, in a new way, to be apprehensive about my own.

I had not known my father very well. We had got on badly, partly because we shared, in our different fashions, the vice of stubborn pride. When he was dead I realized that I had hardly ever spoken to him. When he had been dead a long time I began to wish I had. It seems to be typical of life in America, where opportunities, real and fancied, are thicker than anywhere else on the globe, that the second generation has no time to talk to the first. No one, including my father, seems to have known exactly how old he was, but his mother had been born during slavery. He was of the first generation of free men. He, along with thousands of other Negroes, came North after 1919 and I was part of that generation which had never seen the landscape of what Negroes sometimes call the Old Country.

He had been born in New Orleans and had been quite a young man there during the time that Louis Armstrong, a boy, was running errands for the dives and honky-tonks of what was always presented to me as one of the most wicked of cities—to this day, whenever I think of New Orleans, I also helplessly think of Sodom and Gomorrah. My father never mentioned Louis Armstrong, except to forbid us to play his records; but there was a picture of him on our wall for a long time. One of my father's strong-willed female relatives had placed it there and forbade my father to take it down. He never did, but he eventually maneuvered her out of the house and when, some years later, she was in trouble and near death, he refused to do anything to help her.

He was, I think, very handsome. I gather this from photographs and from my own memories of him, dressed in his Sunday best and on his way to preach a sermon somewhere, when I was little. Handsome, proud, and

5

ingrown, "like a toenail," somebody said. But he looked to me, as I grew older, like pictures I had seen of African tribal chieftains: he really should have been naked, with warpaint on and barbaric mementos, standing among spears. He could be chilling in the pulpit and indescribably cruel in his personal life and he was certainly the most bitter man I have ever met; yet it must be said that there was something else in him, buried in him, which lent him his tremendous power and, even, a rather crushing charm. It had something to do with his blackness, I think—he was very black—with his blackness and his beauty, and with the fact that he knew that he was black but did not know that he was beautiful. He claimed to be proud of his blackness but it had also been the cause of much humiliation and it had fixed bleak boundaries to his life. He was not a young man when we were growing up and he had already suffered many kinds of ruin; in his outrageously demanding and protective way he loved his children, who were black like him and menaced, like him; and all these things sometimes showed in his face when he tried, never to my knowledge with any success, to establish contact with any of us. When he took one of his children on his knee to play, the child always became fretful and began to cry; when he tried to help one of us with our homework the absolutely unabating tension which emanated from him caused our minds and our tongues to become paralyzed, so that he, scarcely knowing why, flew into a rage and the child, not knowing why, was punished. If it ever entered his head to bring a surprise home for his children, it was, almost unfailingly, the wrong surprise and even the big watermelons he often brought home on his back in the summertime led to the most appalling scenes. I do not remember, in all those years, that one of his children was ever glad to see him come home. From what I was able to gather of his early life, it seemed that this inability to establish contact with other people had always marked him and had been one of the things which had driven him out of New Orleans. There was something in him, therefore, groping and tentative, which was never expressed and which was buried with him. One saw it most clearly when he was facing new people and hoping to impress them. But he never did, not for long. We went from church to smaller and more improbable church, he found himself in less and less demand as a minister, and by the time he died none of his friends had come to see him for a long time. He had lived and died in an intolerable bitterness of spirit and it frightened me, as we drove him to the graveyard through those unquiet, ruined streets, to see how powerful and overflowing this bitterness could be and to realize that this bitterness now was mine.

When he died I had been away from home for a little over a year. In that year I had had time to become aware of the meaning of all my father's bitter warnings, had discovered the secret of his proudly pursed lips and rigid carriage: I had discovered the weight of white people in the world. I saw that this had been for my ancestors and now would be for me an awful thing to live with and that the bitterness which had helped to kill my father could also kill me.

He had been ill a long time—in the mind, as we now realized, reliving instances of his fantastic intransigence in the new light of his affliction and endeavoring to feel a sorrow for him which never, quite, came true. We had not known that he was being eaten up by paranoia, and the discovery that his cruelty, to our bodies and our minds, had been one of the symptoms of his illness was not, then, enough to enable us to forgive him. The younger children felt, quite simply, relief that he would not be coming home anymore. My mother's observation that it was he, after all, who had kept them alive all these years meant nothing because the problems of keeping children alive are not real for children. The older children felt, with my father gone, that they could invite their friends to the house without fear that their friends would be insulted or, as had sometimes happened with me, being told that their friends were in league with the devil and intended to rob our family of everything we owned. (I didn't fail to wonder, and it made me hate him, what on earth we owned that anybody else would want.)

His illness was beyond all hope of healing before anyone realized that he was ill. He had always been so strange and had lived, like a prophet, in such unimaginably close communion with the Lord that his long silences which were punctuated by moans and hallelujahs and snatches of old songs while he sat at the living-room window never seemed odd to us. It was not until he refused to eat because, he said, his family was trying to poison him that my mother was forced to accept as a fact what had, until then, been only an unwilling suspicion. When he was committed, it was discovered that he had tuberculosis and, as it turned out, the disease of his mind allowed the disease of his body to destroy him. For the doctors could not force him to eat, either, and, though he was fed intravenously, it was clear from the beginning that there was no hope for him.

In my mind's eye I could see him, sitting at the window, locked up in his terrors; hating and fearing every living soul including his children who had betrayed him, too, by reaching toward the world which had despised him. There were nine of us. I began to wonder what it could have felt like for such a man to have had nine children whom he could barely feed. He used to make little jokes about our poverty, which never, of course, seemed very funny to us; they could not have seemed very funny to him, either, or else our all too feeble response to them would never have caused such rages. He spent great energy and achieved, to our chagrin, no small amount of success in keeping us away from the people who surrounded us, people who had all-night rent parties[1] to which we listened when we should have been sleeping, people who cursed and drank and flashed razor blades on Lenox Avenue. He could not understand why, if they had so much energy to spare, they could not use it to make their lives better. He treated almost everybody on our block with a most uncharitable asperity and neither they, nor, of course, their children were slow to reciprocate.

---

[1] **rent parties:** Part of a Harlem tradition; musicians were often hired and contributions taken to help pay the rent for needy tenants.—EDS.

The only white people who came to our house were welfare workers   10
and bill collectors. It was almost always my mother who dealt with them,
for my father's temper, which was at the mercy of his pride, was never to be
trusted. It was clear that he felt their very presence in his home to be a violation: this was conveyed by his carriage, almost ludicrously stiff, and by his
voice, harsh and vindictively polite. When I was around nine or ten I wrote
a play which was directed by a young, white schoolteacher, a woman, who
then took an interest in me, and gave me books to read and, in order to corroborate my theatrical bent, decided to take me to see what she somewhat
tactlessly referred to as "real" plays. Theater-going was forbidden in our
house, but, with the really cruel intuitiveness of a child, I suspected that the
color of this woman's skin would carry the day for me. When, at school, she
suggested taking me to the theater, I did not, as I might have done if she had
been a Negro, find a way of discouraging her, but agreed that she should
pick me up at my house one evening. I then, very cleverly, left all the rest to
my mother, who suggested to my father, as I knew she would, that it would
not be very nice to let such a kind woman make the trip for nothing. Also,
since it was a schoolteacher, I imagine that my mother countered the idea of
sin with the idea of "education," which word, even with my father, carried
a kind of bitter weight.

Before the teacher came my father took me aside to ask *why* she was
coming, what *interest* she could possibly have in our house, in a boy like
me. I said I didn't know but I, too, suggested that it had something to do
with education. And I understood that my father was waiting for me to say
something—I didn't quite know what; perhaps that I wanted his protection
against this teacher and her "education." I said none of these things and
the teacher came and we went out. It was clear, during the brief interview
in our living room, that my father was agreeing very much against his will
and that he would have refused permission if he had dared. The fact that
he did not dare caused me to despise him: I had no way of knowing that
he was facing in that living room a wholly unprecedented and frightening
situation.

Later, when my father had been laid off from his job, this woman became
very important to us. She was really a very sweet and generous woman and
went to a great deal of trouble to be of help to us, particularly during one
awful winter. My mother called her by the highest name she knew: she said
she was a "Christian." My father could scarcely disagree but during the
four or five years of our relatively close association he never trusted her and
was always trying to surprise in her open, Midwestern face the genuine,
cunningly hidden, and hideous motivation. In later years, particularly when
it began to be clear that this "education" of mine was going to lead me to
perdition, he became more explicit and warned me that my white friends
in high school were not really my friends and that I would see, when I was
older, how white people would do anything to keep a Negro down. Some of
them could be nice, he admitted, but none of them were to be trusted and
most of them were not even nice. The best thing was to have as little to do

with them as possible. I did not feel this way and I was certain, in my innocence, that I never would.

But the year which preceded my father's death had made a great change in my life. I had been living in New Jersey, working in defense plants, working and living among southerners, white and black. I knew about the south, of course, and about how southerners treated Negroes and how they expected them to behave, but it had never entered my mind that anyone would look at me and expect *me* to behave that way. I learned in New Jersey that to be a Negro meant, precisely, that one was never looked at but was simply at the mercy of the reflexes the color of one's skin caused in other people. I acted in New Jersey as I had always acted, that is as though I thought a great deal of myself—I had to *act* that way—with results that were, simply, unbelievable. I had scarcely arrived before I had earned the enmity, which was extraordinarily ingenious, of all my superiors and nearly all my co-workers. In the beginning, to make matters worse, I simply did not know what was happening. I did not know what I had done, and I shortly began to wonder what *anyone* could possibly do, to bring about such unanimous, active, and unbearably vocal hostility. I knew about Jim Crow but I had never experienced it. I went to the same self-service restaurant three times and stood with all the Princeton boys before the counter, waiting for a hamburger and coffee; it was always an extraordinarily long time before anything was set before me; but it was not until the fourth visit that I learned that, in fact, nothing had ever been set before me: I had simply picked something up. Negroes were not served there, I was told, and they had been waiting for me to realize that I was always the only Negro present. Once I was told this, I determined to go there all the time. But now they were ready for me and, though some dreadful scenes were subsequently enacted in that restaurant, I never ate there again.

It was the same story all over New Jersey, in bars, bowling alleys, diners, places to live. I was always being forced to leave, silently, or with mutual imprecations. I very shortly became notorious and children giggled behind me when I passed and their elders whispered or shouted—they really believed that I was mad. And it did begin to work on my mind, of course; I began to be afraid to go anywhere and to compensate for this I went places to which I really should not have gone and where, God knows, I had no desire to be. My reputation in town naturally enhanced my reputation at work and my working day became one long series of acrobatics designed to keep me out of trouble. I cannot say that these acrobatics succeeded. It began to seem that the machinery of the organization I worked for was turning over, day and night, with but one aim: to eject me. I was fired once, and contrived, with the aid of a friend from New York, to get back on the payroll; was fired again, and bounced back again. It took a while to fire me for the third time, but the third time took. There were no loopholes anywhere. There was not even any way of getting back inside the gates.

That year in New Jersey lives in my mind as though it were the year   15
during which, having an unsuspected predilection for it, I first contracted
some dread, chronic disease, the unfailing symptom of which is a kind of
blind fever, a pounding in the skull and fire in the bowels. Once this disease
is contracted, one can never be really carefree again, for the fever, without
an instant's warning, can recur at any moment. It can wreck more important
things than race relations. There is not a Negro alive who does not have this
rage in his blood—one has the choice, merely, of living with it consciously
or surrendering to it. As for me, this fever has recurred in me, and does, and
will until the day I die.

My last night in New Jersey, a white friend from New York took me to
the nearest big town, Trenton, to go to the movies and have a few drinks. As
it turned out, he also saved me from, at the very least, a violent whipping.
Almost every detail of that night stands out very clearly in my memory. I
even remember the name of the movie we saw because its title impressed
me as being so patly ironical. It was a movie about the German occupation
of France, starring Maureen O'Hara and Charles Laughton and called *This
Land Is Mine*. I remember the name of the diner we walked into when the
movie ended: it was the "American Diner." When we walked in the count-
erman asked what we wanted and I remember answering with the casual
sharpness which had become my habit: "We want a hamburger and a cup of
coffee, what do you think we want?" I do not know why, after a year of such
rebuffs, I so completely failed to anticipate his answer, which was, of course,
"We don't serve Negroes here." This reply failed to discompose me, at least
for the moment. I made some sardonic comment about the name of the diner
and we walked out into the streets.

This was the time of what was called the "brownout," when the lights
in all American cities were very dim. When we reentered the streets something happened to me which had the force of an optical illusion, or a nightmare. The streets were very crowded and I was facing north. People were
moving in every direction but it seemed to me, in that instant, that all of
the people I could see, and many more than that, were moving toward
me, against me, and that everyone was white. I remember how their faces
gleamed. And I felt, like a physical sensation, a *click* at the nape of my neck
as though some interior string connecting my head to my body had been
cut. I began to walk. I heard my friend call after me, but I ignored him.
Heaven only knows what was going on in his mind, but he had the good
sense not to touch me—I don't know what would have happened if he
had—and to keep me in sight. I don't know what was going on in my mind,
either; I certainly had no conscious plan. I wanted to do something to crush
these white faces, which were crushing me. I walked for perhaps a block or
two until I came to an enormous, glittering, and fashionable restaurant in
which I knew not even the intercession of the Virgin would cause me to be
served. I pushed through the doors and took the first vacant seat I saw, at a
table for two, and waited.

I do not know how long I waited and I rather wonder, until today, what I could possibly have looked like. Whatever I looked like, I frightened the waitress who shortly appeared, and the moment she appeared all of my fury flowed toward her. I hated her for her white face, and for her great, astounded, frightened eyes. I felt that if she found a black man so frightening I would make her fright worthwhile.

She did not ask me what I wanted, but repeated, as though she had learned it somewhere, "We don't serve Negroes here." She did not say it with the blunt, derisive hostility to which I had grown so accustomed, but, rather, with a note of apology in her voice, and fear. This made me colder and more murderous than ever. I felt I had to do something with my hands. I wanted her to come close enough for me to get her neck between my hands.

So I pretended not to have understood her, hoping to draw her closer. 20 And she did step a very short step closer, with her pencil poised incongruously over her pad, and repeated the formula: ". . . don't serve Negroes here."

Somehow, with the repetition of that phrase, which was already ringing in my head like a thousand bells of a nightmare, I realized that she would never come any closer and that I would have to strike from a distance. There was nothing on the table but an ordinary watermug half full of water, and I picked this up and hurled it with all my strength at her. She ducked and it missed her and shattered against the mirror behind the bar. And, with that sound, my frozen blood abruptly thawed, I returned from wherever I had been, I *saw*, for the first time, the restaurant, the people with their mouths open, already, as it seemed to me, rising as one man, and I realized what I had done, and where I was, and I was frightened. I rose and began running for the door. A round, potbellied man grabbed me by the nape of the neck just as I reached the doors and began to beat me about the face. I kicked him and got loose and ran into the streets. My friend whispered, "*Run!*" and I ran.

My friend stayed outside the restaurant long enough to misdirect my pursuers and the police, who arrived, he told me, at once. I do not know what I said to him when he came to my room that night. I could not have said much. I felt, in the oddest, most awful way, that I had somehow betrayed him. I lived it over and over and over again, the way one relives an automobile accident after it has happened and one finds oneself alone and safe. I could not get over two facts, both equally difficult for the imagination to grasp, and one was that I could have been murdered. But the other was that I had been ready to commit murder. I saw nothing very clearly but I did see this: that my life, my *real* life, was in danger, and not from anything other people might do but from the hatred I carried in my own heart.

TWO

I had returned home around the second week in June—in great haste because it seemed that my father's death and my mother's confinement were both but a matter of hours. In the case of my mother, it soon became clear that she had simply made a miscalculation. This had always been her tendency and I don't believe that a single one of us arrived in the world, or has since arrived anywhere else, on time. But none of us dawdled so intolerably about the business of being born as did my baby sister. We sometimes amused ourselves, during those endless, stifling weeks, by picturing the baby sitting within in the safe, warm dark, bitterly regretting the necessity of becoming a part of our chaos and stubbornly putting it off as long as possible. I understood her perfectly and congratulated her on showing such good sense so soon. Death, however, sat as purposefully at my father's bedside as life stirred within my mother's womb and it was harder to understand why he so lingered in that long shadow. It seemed that he had bent, and for a long time, too, all of his energies toward dying. Now death was ready for him but my father held back.

All of Harlem, indeed, seemed to be infected by waiting. I had never before known it to be so violently still. Racial tensions throughout this country were exacerbated during the early years of the war, partly because the labor market brought together hundreds of thousands of ill-prepared people and partly because Negro soldiers, regardless of where they were born, received their military training in the south. What happened in defense plants and army camps had repercussions, naturally, in every Negro ghetto. The situation in Harlem had grown bad enough for clergymen, policemen, educators, politicians, and social workers to assert in one breath that there was no "crime wave" and to offer, in the very next breath, suggestions as to how to combat it. These suggestions always seemed to involve playgrounds, despite the fact that racial skirmishes were occurring in the playgrounds, too. Playground or not, crime wave or not, the Harlem police force had been augmented in March, and the unrest grew—perhaps, in fact, partly as a result of the ghetto's instinctive hatred of policemen. Perhaps the most revealing news item, out of the steady parade of reports of muggings, stabbings, shootings, assaults, gang wars, and accusations of police brutality, is the item concerning six Negro girls who set upon a white girl in the subway because, as they all too accurately put it, she was stepping on their toes. Indeed she was, all over the nation.

I had never before been so aware of policemen, on foot, on horseback, 25
on corners, everywhere, always two by two. Nor had I ever been so aware of small knots of people. They were on stoops and on corners and in doorways, and what was striking about them, I think, was that they did not seem to be talking. Never, when I passed these groups, did the usual sound of a curse or a laugh ring out and neither did there seem to be any hum of gossip. There was certainly, on the other hand, occurring between them communication extraordinarily intense. Another thing that was striking was the unexpected diversity of the people who made up these groups. Usually, for example, one would see a group of sharpies standing on the street corner, jiving the passing chicks; or a group of older men, usually, for some reason, in the

vicinity of a barber shop, discussing baseball scores, or the numbers, or making rather chilling observations about women they had known. Women, in a general way, tended to be seen less often together—unless they were church women, or very young girls, or prostitutes met together for an unprofessional instant. But that summer I saw the strangest combinations: large, respectable, churchly matrons standing on the stoops or the corners with their hair tied up, together with a girl in sleazy satin whose face bore the marks of gin and the razor, or heavy-set, abrupt, no-nonsense older men, in company with the most disreputable and fanatical "race" men,[2] or these same "race" men with the sharpies, or these sharpies with the churchly women. Seventh Day Adventists and Methodists and Spiritualists seemed to be hobnobbing with Holyrollers and they were all, alike, entangled with the most flagrant disbelievers; something heavy in their stance seemed to indicate that they had all, incredibly, seen a common vision, and on each face there seemed to be the same strange, bitter shadow.

The churchly women and the matter-of-fact, no-nonsense men had children in the Army. The sleazy girls they talked to had lovers there, the sharpies and the "race" men had friends and brothers there. It would have demanded an unquestioning patriotism, happily as uncommon in this country as it is undesirable, for these people not to have been disturbed by the bitter letters they received, by the newspaper stories they read, not to have been enraged by the posters, then to be found all over New York, which described the Japanese as "yellow-bellied Japs." It was only the "race" men, to be sure, who spoke ceaselessly of being revenged—how this vengeance was to be exacted was not clear—for the indignities and dangers suffered by Negro boys in uniform; but everybody felt a directionless, hopeless bitterness, as well as that panic which can scarcely be suppressed when one knows that a human being one loves is beyond one's reach, and in danger. This helplessness and this gnawing uneasiness does something, at length, to even the toughest mind. Perhaps the best way to sum all this up is to say that the people I knew felt, mainly, a peculiar kind of relief when they knew that their boys were being shipped out of the south, to do battle overseas. It was, perhaps, like feeling that the most dangerous part of a dangerous journey had been passed and that now, even if death should come, it would come with honor and without the complicity of their countrymen. Such a death would be, in short, a fact with which one could hope to live.

It was on the twenty-eighth of July, which I believe was a Wednesday, that I visited my father for the first time during his illness and for the last time in his life. The moment I saw him I knew why I had put off this visit so long. I had told my mother that I did not want to see him because I hated him. But this was not true. It was only that I *had* hated him and I wanted to hold on to this hatred. I did not want to look on him as a ruin: it was not a ruin I had

2 *"race" men:* Baldwin seems to be thinking of self-appointed spokesmen for racial consciousness and not serious black leaders.—EDS.

hated. I imagine that one of the reasons people cling to their hates so stubbornly is because they sense, once hate is gone, that they will be forced to deal with pain.

We traveled out to him, his older sister and myself, to what seemed to be the very end of a very Long Island. It was hot and dusty and we wrangled, my aunt and I, all the way out, over the fact that I had recently begun to smoke and, as she said, to give myself airs. But I knew that she wrangled with me because she could not bear to face the fact of her brother's dying. Neither could I endure the reality of her despair, her unstated bafflement as to what had happened to her brother's life, and her own. So we wrangled and I smoked and from time to time she fell into a heavy reverie. Covertly, I watched her face, which was the face of an old woman; it had fallen in, the eyes were sunken and lightless; soon she would be dying, too.

In my childhood—it had not been so long ago—I had thought her beautiful. She had been quick-witted and quick-moving and very generous with all the children and each of her visits had been an event. At one time one of my brothers and myself had thought of running away to live with her. Now she could no longer produce out of her handbag some unexpected and yet familiar delight. She made me feel pity and revulsion and fear. It was awful to realize that she no longer caused me to feel affection. The closer we came to the hospital the more querulous she became and at the same time, naturally, grew more dependent on me. Between pity and guilt and fear I began to feel that there was another me trapped in my skull like a jack-in-the-box who might escape my control at any moment and fill the air with screaming.

She began to cry the moment we entered the room and she saw him 30 lying there, all shriveled and still, like a little black monkey. The great, gleaming apparatus which fed him and would have compelled him to be still even if he had been able to move brought to mind, not beneficence, but torture; the tubes entering his arm made me think of pictures I had seen when a child, of Gulliver, tied down by the pygmies on that island. My aunt wept and wept, there was a whistling sound in my father's throat; nothing was said; he could not speak. I wanted to take his hand, to say something. But I do not know what I could have said, even if he could have heard me. He was not really in that room with us, he had at last really embarked on his journey; and though my aunt told me that he said he was going to meet Jesus, I did not hear anything except that whistling in his throat. The doctor came back and we left, into that unbearable train again, and home. In the morning came the telegram saying that he was dead. Then the house was suddenly full of relatives, friends, hysteria, and confusion and I quickly left my mother and the children to the care of those impressive women, who, in Negro communities at least, automatically appear at times of bereavement armed with lotions, proverbs, and patience, and an ability to cook. I went downtown. By the time I returned, later the same day, my mother had been carried to the hospital and the baby had been born.

THREE

For my father's funeral I had nothing black to wear and this posed a nagging problem all day long. It was one of those problems, simple, or impossible of solution, to which the mind insanely clings in order to avoid the mind's real trouble. I spent most of that day at the downtown apartment of a girl I knew, celebrating my birthday with whisky and wondering what to wear that night. When planning a birthday celebration one naturally does not expect that it will be up against competition from a funeral and this girl had antici-pated taking me out that night, for a big dinner and a night club afterwards. Sometime during the course of that long day we decided that we would go out anyway, when my father's funeral service was over. I imagine I decided it, since, as the funeral hour approached, it became clearer and clearer to me that I would not know what to do with myself when it was over. The girl, stifling her very lively concern as to the possible effects of the whisky on one of my father's chief mourners, concentrated on being conciliatory and practi-cally helpful. She found a black shirt for me somewhere and ironed it and, dressed in the darkest pants and jacket I owned, and slightly drunk, I made my way to my father's funeral.

The chapel was full, but not packed, and very quiet. There were, mainly, my father's relatives, and his children, and here and there I saw faces I had not seen since childhood, the faces of my father's one-time friends. They were very dark and solemn now, seeming somehow to suggest that they had known all along that something like this would happen. Chief among the mourners was my aunt, who had quarreled with my father all his life; by which I do not mean to suggest that her mourning was insincere or that she had not loved him. I suppose that she was one of the few people in the world who had, and their incessant quarreling proved precisely the strength of the tie that bound them. The only other person in the world, as far as I knew, whose relationship to my father rivaled my aunt's in depth was my mother, who was not there.

It seemed to me, of course, that it was a very long funeral. But it was, if anything, a rather shorter funeral than most, nor, since there were no over-whelming, uncontrollable expressions of grief, could it be called—if I dare to use the word—successful. The minister who preached my father's funeral sermon was one of the few my father had still been seeing as he neared his end. He presented to us in his sermon a man whom none of us had ever seen—a man thoughtful, patient, and forbearing, a Christian inspiration to all who knew him, and a model for his children. And no doubt the children, in their disturbed and guilty state, were almost ready to believe this; he had been remote enough to be anything and, anyway, the shock of the incontro-vertible, that it was really our father lying up there in that casket, prepared the mind for anything. His sister moaned and this grief-stricken moaning was taken as corroboration. The other faces held a dark, noncommittal thoughtful-ness. This was not the man they had known, but they had scarcely expected to be confronted with *him*; this was, in a sense deeper than questions of fact,

the man they had not known, and the man they had not known may have
been the real one. The real man, whoever he had been, had suffered and now
he was dead: this was all that was sure and all that mattered now. Every man
in the chapel hoped that when his hour came he, too, would be eulogized,
which is to say forgiven, and that all of his lapses, greeds, errors, and stray-
ings from the truth would be invested with coherence and looked upon with
charity. This was perhaps the last thing human beings could give each other
and it was what they demanded, after all, of the Lord. Only the Lord saw the
midnight tears, only He was present when one of His children, moaning and
wringing hands, paced up and down the room. When one slapped one's child
in anger the recoil in the heart reverberated through heaven and became
part of the pain of the universe. And when the children were hungry and sullen and distrustful and one watched them, daily, growing wilder, and further
away, and running headlong into danger, it was the Lord who knew what
the charged heart endured as the strap was laid to the backside; the Lord
alone who knew what one *would* have said if one had had, like the Lord, the
gift of the living word. It was the Lord who knew of the impossibility every
parent in that room faced: how to prepare the child for the day when the
child would be despised and how to *create* in the child—by what means?—a
stronger antidote to this poison than one had found for oneself. The avenues,
side streets, bars, billiard halls, hospitals, police stations, and even the playgrounds of Harlem—not to mention the houses of correction, the jails, and
the morgue—testified to the potency of the poison while remaining silent
as to the efficacy of whatever antidote, irresistibly raising the question of
whether or not such an antidote existed; raising, which was worse, the question of whether or not an antidote was desirable; perhaps poison should be
fought with poison. With these several schisms in the mind and with more
terrors in the heart than could be named, it was better not to judge the man
who had gone down under an impossible burden. It was better to remember:
Thou knowest this man's fall; but thou knowest not his wrassling.

While the preacher talked and I watched the children—years of changing their diapers, scrubbing them, slapping them, taking them to school,
and scolding them had had the perhaps inevitable result of making me love
them, though I am not sure I knew this then—my mind was busily breaking
out with a rash of disconnected impressions. Snatches of popular songs, inde-
cent jokes, bits of books I had read, movie sequences, faces, voices, political
issues—I thought I was going mad; all these impressions suspended, as it
were, in the solution of the faint nausea produced in me by the heat and
liquor. For a moment I had the impression that my alcoholic breath, ineffi-
ciently disguised with chewing gum, filled the entire chapel. Then someone
began singing one of my father's favorite songs and, abruptly, I was with
him, sitting on his knee, in the hot, enormous, crowded church which was
the first church we attended. It was the Abyssinian Baptist Church on 138th
Street. We had not gone there long. With this image, a host of others came. I
had forgotten, in the rage of my growing up, how proud my father had been
of me when I was little. Apparently, I had had a voice and my father had

liked to show me off before the members of the church. I had forgotten what he had looked like when he was pleased but now I remembered that he had always been grinning with pleasure when my solos ended. I even remembered certain expressions on his face when he teased my mother—had he loved her? I would never know. And when had it all begun to change? For now it seemed that he had not always been cruel. I remembered being taken for a haircut and scraping my knee on the footrest of the barber's chair and I remembered my father's face as he soothed my crying and applied the stinging iodine. Then I remembered our fights, fights which had been of the worst possible kind because my technique had been silence.

I remembered the one time in all our life together when we had really   35
spoken to each other.

It was on a Sunday and it must have been shortly before I left home. We were walking, just the two of us, in our usual silence, to or from church. I was in high school and had been doing a lot of writing and I was, at about this time, the editor of the high school magazine. But I had also been a Young Minister and had been preaching from the pulpit. Lately, I had been taking fewer engagements and preached as rarely as possible. It was said in the church, quite truthfully, that I was "cooling off."

My father asked me abruptly, "You'd rather write than preach, wouldn't you?"

I was astonished at his question—because it was a real question. I answered, "Yes."

That was all we said. It was awful to remember that that was all we had *ever* said.

The casket now was opened and the mourners were being led up the   40
aisle to look for the last time on the deceased. The assumption was that the family was too overcome with grief to be allowed to make this journey alone and I watched while my aunt was led to the casket and, muffled in black, and shaking, led back to her seat. I disapproved of forcing the children to look on their dead father, considering that the shock of his death, or, more truthfully, the shock of death as a reality, was already a little more than a child could bear, but my judgment in this matter had been overruled and there they were, bewildered and frightened and very small, being led, one by one, to the casket. But there is also something very gallant about children at such moments. It has something to do with their silence and gravity and with the fact that one cannot help them. Their legs, somehow, seem *exposed*, so that it is at once incredible and terribly clear that their legs are all they have to hold them up.

I had not wanted to go to the casket myself and I certainly had not wished to be led there, but there was no way of avoiding either of these forms. One of the deacons led me up and I looked on my father's face. I cannot say that it looked like him at all. His blackness had been equivocated by powder and there was no suggestion in that casket of what his power had or could have been. He was simply an old man dead, and it was hard to believe that he had ever given anyone either joy or pain. Yet, his life filled that room. Further up the avenue his wife was holding his newborn child. Life and death so close together, and love and hatred, and right and wrong, said something to me which I did not want to hear concerning man, concerning the life of man.

After the funeral, while I was downtown desperately celebrating my birthday, a Negro soldier, in the lobby of the Hotel Braddock, got into a fight with a white policeman over a Negro girl. Negro girls, white policemen, in or out of uniform, and Negro males—in or out of uniform—were part of the furniture of the lobby of the Hotel Braddock and this was certainly not the first time such an incident had occurred. It was destined, however, to receive an unprecedented publicity, for the fight between the policeman and the soldier ended with the shooting of the soldier. Rumor, flowing immediately to the streets outside, stated that the soldier had been shot in the back, an instantaneous and revealing invention, and that the soldier had died protecting a Negro woman. The facts were somewhat different—for example, the soldier had not been shot in the back, and was not dead, and the girl seems to have been as dubious a symbol of womanhood as her white counterpart in Georgia usually is, but no one was interested in the facts. They preferred the invention because this invention expressed and corroborated their hates and fears so perfectly. It is just as well to remember that people are always doing this. Perhaps many of those legends, including Christianity, to which the world clings began their conquest of the world with just some such concerted surrender to distortion. The effect, in Harlem, of this particular legend was like the effect of a lit match in a tin of gasoline. The mob gathered before the doors of the Hotel Braddock simply began to swell and to spread in every direction, and Harlem exploded.

The mob did not cross the ghetto lines. It would have been easy, for example, to have gone over Morningside Park on the west side or to have crossed the Grand Central railroad tracks at 125th Street on the east side, to wreak havoc in white neighborhoods. The mob seems to have been mainly interested in something more potent and real than the white face, that is, in white power, and the principal damage done during the riot of the summer of 1943 was to white business establishments in Harlem. It might have been a far bloodier story, of course, if, at the hour the riot began, these establishments had still been open. From the Hotel Braddock the mob fanned out, east and west along 125th Street, and for the entire length of Lenox, Seventh, and Eighth avenues. Along each of these avenues, and along each major side street—116th, 125th, 135th, and so on—bars, stores, pawnshops, restaurants, even little luncheonettes had been smashed open and entered and looted—looted, it might be added, with more haste than efficiency. The shelves really looked as though a bomb had struck them. Cans of beans and soup and dog food, along with toilet paper, corn flakes, sardines and milk tumbled every which way, and abandoned cash registers and cases of beer leaned crazily out of the splintered windows and were strewn along the avenues. Sheets, blankets, and clothing of every description formed a kind of path, as though people had dropped them while running. I truly had not realized that Harlem *had* so many stores until I saw them all smashed open; the first time the word *wealth* ever entered my mind in relation to Harlem was when I saw it scattered in the streets. But one's first, incongruous impression of plenty was countered immediately by an impression of waste. None of this was doing anybody any good. It would have been better to have left the plate glass as it had been and the goods lying in the stores.

It would have been better, but it would also have been intolerable, for Harlem had needed something to smash. To smash something is the ghetto's chronic need. Most of the time it is the members of the ghetto who smash each other, and themselves. But as long as the ghetto walls are standing there will always come a moment when these outlets do not work. That summer, for example, it was not enough to get into a fight on Lenox Avenue, or curse out one's cronies in the barber shops. If ever, indeed, the violence which fills Harlem's churches, pool halls, and bars erupts outward in a more direct fashion, Harlem and its citizens are likely to vanish in an apocalyptic flood. That this is not likely to happen is due to a great many reasons, most hidden and powerful among them the Negro's real relation to the white American. This relation prohibits, simply, anything as uncomplicated and satisfactory as pure hatred. In order really to hate white people, one has to blot so much out of the mind—and the heart—that this hatred itself becomes an exhausting and self-destructive pose. But this does not mean, on the other hand, that love comes easily: the white world is too powerful, too complacent, too ready with gratuitous humiliation, and, above all, too ignorant and too innocent for that. One is absolutely forced to make perpetual qualifications and one's own reactions are always canceling each other out. It is this, really, which has driven so many people mad, both white and black. One is always in the position of having to decide between amputation and gangrene. Amputation is swift but time may prove that the amputation was not necessary—or one may delay the amputation too long. Gangrene is slow, but it is impossible to be sure that one is reading one's symptoms right. The idea of going through life as a cripple is more than one can bear, and equally unbearable is the risk of swelling up slowly, in agony, with poison. And the trouble, finally, is that the risks are real even if the choices do not exist.

"But as for me and my house," my father had said, "we will serve the   45
Lord." I wondered, as we drove him to his resting place, what this line had meant for him. I had heard him preach it many times. I had preached it once myself, proudly giving it an interpretation different from my father's. Now the whole thing came back to me, as though my father and I were on our way to Sunday school and I were memorizing the golden text: *And if it seem evil unto you to serve the Lord, choose you this day whom you will serve; whether the gods which your fathers served that were on the other side of the flood, or the gods of the Amorites, in whose land ye dwell: but as for me and my house, we will serve the Lord.* I suspected in these familiar lines a meaning which had never been there for me before. All of my father's texts and songs, which I had decided were meaningless, were arranged before me at his death like empty bottles, waiting to hold the meaning which life would give them for me. This was his legacy: nothing is ever escaped. That bleakly

memorable morning I hated the unbelievable streets and the Negroes and whites who had, equally, made them that way. But I knew that it was folly, as my father would have said, this bitterness was folly. It was necessary to hold on to the things that mattered. The dead man mattered, the new life mattered; blackness and whiteness did not matter; to believe that they did was to acquiesce in one's own destruction. Hatred, which could destroy so much, never failed to destroy the man who hated and this was an immutable law.

It began to seem that one would have to hold in the mind forever two ideas which seemed to be in opposition. The first idea was acceptance, the acceptance, totally without rancor, of life as it is, and men as they are: in the light of this idea, it goes without saying that injustice is a commonplace. But this did not mean that one could be complacent, for the second idea was of equal power: that one must never, in one's own life, accept these injustices as commonplace but must fight them with all one's strength. This fight begins, however, in the heart and it now had been laid to my charge to keep my own heart free of hatred and despair. This intimation made my heart heavy and, now that my father was irrecoverable, I wished that he had been beside me so that I could have searched his face for the answers which only the future would give me now. ●

The Reader's Presence

1. Why does Baldwin open with three events: his father's death, his youngest sibling's birth, and the race riots in Detroit and Harlem? How did the death of his father serve to change Baldwin's thinking about how he would deal with racism in his life? How does Baldwin make peace with his father's memory?

2. At the end of the essay, Baldwin remembers a biblical passage his father used to quote (paragraph 45). How does Baldwin reinterpret the passage after his father's death? What does it mean in the context of being his father's son? How does it help him make sense of the race riots in Harlem?

3. **VISUAL PRESENCE:**   Look carefully at the portrait of James Baldwin (page 78). In what ways is Baldwin's posture consistent with the tone of his piece? How would you characterize his body language? Use specific details from the image in developing your response.

4. **CONNECTIONS:**   Examine Baldwin's description of the Harlem race riots in the third section of his essay. How does Baldwin approach the riots as a native of Harlem and as an African American? What explanations does he give for the violence? How does he use the riots to explain the relations between white and black America? Compare Baldwin's discussion of the Harlem race riots to Martin Luther King Jr.'s consideration of nonviolence in "Letter from Birmingham Jail" (page 643) written eight years later. Which author takes a more personal view of race relations at the time? In your opinion, would King concur with Baldwin's assessment of the riots? Do you think after reading Baldwin's essay that Baldwin would agree with King's philosophy? These are long essays and among the most important documents of African American literary history. Compare and contrast the racial attitudes of both Baldwin and King as reflected in these two outstanding works.

The Writer at Work

JAMES BALDWIN on Black English

Everett Collection/Superstock

In the following piece, Baldwin takes up a subject that is periodically scrutinized by the American mass media: Is black English a language and, if so, what kind of language is it? Whatever its current status in the eyes of the dominant society, black English is an indisputable fact of everyday life for many Americans. When Baldwin writes that blacks have "endured and transcended" American racism by means of language, he echoes William Faulkner's belief that our compulsion to talk is what will save the human race.

Since Baldwin wrote this piece in 1979, the language he so ardently defends as necessary to African American strength in the face of "brutal necessity" (that is, in defense against racism) has entered the mainstream through the spread of hip-hop culture. What might Baldwin say about white speakers of black English? Are they simply another example of the appropriation of subcultural forms by the dominant culture, a means of containing or defusing resistance? The "rules of the language are dictated by what the language must convey," Baldwin writes. Who is using black English today? For what purposes?

❝The argument concerning the use, or the status, or the reality, of black English is rooted in American history and has absolutely nothing to do with the question the argument supposes itself to be posing. The argument has nothing to do with language itself but with the *role* of language. Language, incontestably, reveals the speaker. Language, also, far more dubiously, is meant to define the other—and, in this case, the other is refusing to be defined by a language that has never been able to recognize him.

People evolve a language in order to describe and thus control their circumstances, or in order not to be submerged by a reality that they cannot articulate. (And, if they cannot articulate it, they are submerged.) A Frenchman living in Paris speaks a subtly and crucially different language from that of the man living in Marseilles; neither sounds very much like a man living in Quebec; and they would all have great difficulty in apprehending what the man from Guadeloupe, or Martinique, is saying, to say nothing of the man from Senegal—although the "common" language of all these areas is French. But each has paid, and is paying, a different price for this "common" language, in which, as it turns out, they are not saying, and cannot be saying, the

same things: They each have very different realities to articulate, or control.

What joins all languages, and all
men, is the necessity to confront life, in
order, not inconceivably, to outwit death:
The price for this is the acceptance, and
achievement, of one's temporal identity.
So that, for example, though it is not
taught in the schools (and this has the
potential of becoming a political issue)
the south of France still clings to its ancient and musical Provençal, which resists
being described as a "dialect." And much
of the tension in the Basque countries,
and in Wales, is due to the Basque and
Welsh determination not to allow their
languages to be destroyed. This determination also feeds the flames in Ireland,
for among the many indignities the Irish
have been forced to undergo at English
hands is the English contempt for their
language.

It goes without saying, then, that
language is also a political instrument,
means, and proof of power. It is the
most vivid and crucial key to identity: It
reveals the private identity, and connects
one with, or divorces one from, the larger,
public, or communal identity. There have
been, and are, times, and places, when
to speak a certain language could be
dangerous, even fatal. Or, one may
speak the same language, but in such a
way that one's antecedents are revealed,
or (one hopes) hidden. This is true in
France, and is absolutely true in England:
The range (and reign) of accents on
that damp little island make England
coherent for the English and totally
incomprehensible for everyone else. To
open your mouth in England is (if I may
use black English) to "put your business
in the street": You have confessed your
parents, your youth, your school, your
salary, your self-esteem, and, alas, your
future.

Now, I do not know what white
Americans would sound like if there
had never been any black people in the
United States, but they would not sound
the way they sound. *Jazz,* for example,
is a very specific sexual term, as in *jazz
me, baby,* but white people purified it
into the Jazz Age. *Sock it to me,* which
means, roughly, the same thing, has been
adopted by Nathaniel Hawthorne's descendants with no qualms or hesitations
at all, along with *let it all hang out* and
right on! Beat to his socks, which was
once the black's most total and despairing
image of poverty, was transformed into a
thing called the Beat Generation, which
phenomenon was, largely, composed
of *uptight,* middle-class white people,
imitating poverty, trying to *get down,* to
get *with it,* doing their *thing,* doing their
despairing best to be *funky,* which we,
the blacks, never dreamed of doing—we
were funky, baby, like *funky* was going
out of style.

Now, no one can eat his cake and
have it, too, and it is late in the day to attempt to penalize black people for having
created a language that permits the nation its only glimpse of reality, a language
without which the nation would be even
more *whipped* than it is.

I say that the present skirmish is
rooted in American history, and it is.
Black English is the creation of the black
diaspora. Blacks came to the United
States chained to each other, but from
different tribes: Neither could speak the
other's language. If two black people,
at that bitter hour of the world's history,
had been able to speak to each other,
the institution of chattel slavery could
never have lasted as long as it did. Subsequently, the slave was given, under the
eye, and the gun, of his master, Congo
Square, and the Bible—or in other words,
and under these conditions, the slave

began the formation of the black church, and it is within this unprecedented tabernacle that black English began to be formed. This was not, merely, as in the European example, the adoption of a foreign tongue, but an alchemy that transformed ancient elements into a new language: *A language comes into existence by means of brutal necessity, and the rules of the language are dictated by what the language must convey.*

There was a moment, in time, and in this place, when my brother, or my mother, or my father, or my sister, had to convey to me, for example, the danger in which I was standing from the white man standing just behind me, and to convey this with a speed, and in a language, that the white man could not possibly understand, and that, indeed, he cannot understand, until today. He cannot afford to understand it. This understanding would reveal to him too much about himself, and smash that mirror before which he has been frozen for so long.

Now, if this passion, this skill, this (to quote Toni Morrison) "sheer intelligence," this incredible music, the mighty achievement of having brought a people utterly unknown to, or despised by "history" — to have brought this people to their present, troubled, troubling, and unassailable and unanswerable place — if this absolutely unprecedented journey does not indicate that black English is a language, I am curious to know what definition of language is to be trusted.

A people at the center of the Western world, and in the midst of so hostile a population, has not endured and transcended by means of what is patronizingly called a "dialect." We, the blacks, are in trouble, certainly, but we are not doomed, and we are not inarticulate because we are not compelled to defend a morality that we know to be a lie.

The brutal truth is that the bulk of white people in America never had any interest in educating black people, except as this could serve white purposes. It is not the black child's language that is in question, it is not his language that is despised: It is his experience. A child cannot be taught by anyone who despises him, and a child cannot afford to be fooled. A child cannot be taught by anyone whose demand, essentially, is that the child repudiate his experience, and all that gives him sustenance, and enter a limbo in which he will no longer be black, and in which he knows that he can never become white. Black people have lost too many black children that way.

And, after all, finally, in a country with standards so untrustworthy, a country that makes heroes of so many criminal mediocrities, a country unable to face why so many of the nonwhite are in prison, or on the needle, or standing, futureless, in the streets — it may very well be that both the child, and his elder, have concluded that they have nothing whatever to learn from the people of a country that has managed to learn so little. **"**

Raymond Carver

MY FATHER'S LIFE

Son of a laborer and a homemaker in Clatskanie, Oregon, **RAYMOND CARVER** (1938–1988) resembled the characters in the short stories for which he is widely acclaimed. Once a manual laborer, a gas station attendant, and a janitor himself, Carver acquired his vision of the working class and the desperate lives of ordinary folk through direct experience. The Pacific Northwest of Carver's writing is peopled with types such as "the waitress, the bus driver, the mechanic, the hotel keeper" — people Carver feels are "good people." First published in *Esquire* in 1984, "My Father's Life," Carver's account of his father's hardships during the Great Depression, puts a biographical spin on these "good people." Carver's short story collections, *Will You Please Be Quiet, Please?* (1976), *Cathedral* (1984), and *Where I'm Calling From* (1988), were all nominated for the National Book Critics Circle Award. Both *Cathedral* and *Where I'm Calling From* were also nominated for the Pulitzer Prize for fiction in 1985 and 1989, respectively. Carver's poetry is collected in *Where Water Comes Together with Other Water* (1985), recipient of the 1986 Los Angeles Times Book Prize; *Ultramarine* (1986); and *A New Path to the Waterfall* (1989).

> **"Writers don't need tricks or gimmicks."**

In his essay "On Writing," Carver states, "Writers don't need tricks or gimmicks or even necessarily to be the smartest fellows on the block. At the risk of appearing foolish, a writer sometimes needs to be able to just stand and gape at this or that thing—a sunset or an old shoe—in absolute and simple amazement."

MY DAD'S NAME was Clevie Raymond Carver. His family called him Raymond and friends called him C. R. I was named Raymond Clevie Carver, Jr. I hated the "Junior" part. When I was little my dad called me Frog, which was okay. But later, like everybody else in the family, he began calling me Junior. He went on calling me this until I was thirteen or fourteen and announced that I wouldn't answer to that name any longer. So he began calling me Doc. From then until his death, on June 17, 1967, he called me Doc, or else Son.

When he died, my mother telephoned my wife with the news. I was away from my family at the time, between lives, trying to enroll in the School of Library Science at the University of Iowa. When my wife answered the phone, my mother blurted out, "Raymond's dead!" For a moment, my wife thought my mother was telling her that I was dead. Then my mother made it clear *which* Raymond she was talking about and my wife said, "Thank God. I thought you meant *my* Raymond."

My dad walked, hitched rides, and rode in empty boxcars when he went from Arkansas to Washington State in 1934, looking for work. I don't know whether he was pursuing a dream when he went out to Washington. I doubt it. I don't think he dreamed much. I believe he was simply looking for steady work at decent pay. Steady work was meaningful work. He picked apples for a time and then landed a construction laborer's job on the Grand Coulee Dam. After he'd put aside a little money, he bought a car and drove back to Arkansas to help his folks, my grandparents, pack up for the move west. He said later that they were about to starve down there, and this wasn't meant as a figure of speech. It was during that short while in Arkansas, in a town called Leola, that my mother met my dad on the sidewalk as he came out of a tavern.

"He was drunk," she said. "I don't know why I let him talk to me. His eyes were glittery. I wish I'd had a crystal ball." They'd met once, a year or so before, at a dance. He'd had girlfriends before her, my mother told me. "Your dad always had a girlfriend, even after we married. He was my first and last. I never had another man. But I didn't miss anything."

They were married by a justice of the peace on the day they left for Washington, this big, tall country girl and a farmhand-turned-construction worker. My mother spent her wedding night with my dad and his folks, all of them camped beside the road in Arkansas.   5

In Omak, Washington, my dad and mother lived in a little place not much bigger than a cabin. My grandparents lived next door. My dad was still working on the dam, and later, with the huge turbines producing electricity and the water backed up for a hundred miles into Canada, he stood in the crowd and heard Franklin D. Roosevelt when he spoke at the construction site. "He never mentioned those guys who died building that dam," my dad said. Some of his friends had died there, men from Arkansas, Oklahoma, and Missouri.

He then took a job in a sawmill in Clatskanie, Oregon, a little town alongside the Columbia River. I was born there, and my mother has a picture of my dad standing in front of the gate to the mill, proudly holding me up to face the camera. My bonnet is on crooked and about to come untied. His hat is pushed back on his forehead, and he's wearing a big grin. Was he going in to work or just finishing his shift? It doesn't matter. In either case, he had a job and a family. These were his salad days.

In 1941 we moved to Yakima, Washington, where my dad went to work as a saw filer, a skilled trade he'd learned in Clatskanie. When war broke out, he was given a deferment because his work was considered necessary to the war effort. Finished lumber was in demand by the armed services, and he kept his saws so sharp they could shave the hair off your arm.

After my dad had moved us to Yakima, he moved his folks into the same neighborhood. By the mid-1940s the rest of my dad's family—his brother, his sister, and her husband, as well as uncles, cousins, nephews, and most of their extended family and friends—had come out from Arkansas. All because my dad came out first. The men went to work at Boise Cascade, where my dad worked, and the women packed apples in the canneries. And in just a little while, it seemed—according to my mother—everybody was better off than my dad. "Your dad couldn't keep money," my mother said. "Money burned a hole in his pocket. He was always doing for others."

The first house I clearly remember living in, at 1515 South Fifteenth   10 Street, in Yakima, had an outdoor toilet. On Halloween night, or just any night, for the hell of it, neighbor kids, kids in their early teens, would carry our toilet away and leave it next to the road. My dad would have to get somebody to help him bring it home. Or these kids would take the toilet and stand it in somebody else's backyard. Once they actually set it on fire. But ours wasn't the only house that had an outdoor toilet. When I was old enough to know what I was doing, I threw rocks at the other toilets when I'd see someone go inside. This was called bombing the toilets. After a while, though, everyone went to indoor plumbing until, suddenly, our toilet was the last outdoor one in the neighborhood. I remember the shame I felt when my third-grade teacher, Mr. Wise, drove me home from school one day. I asked him to stop at the house just before ours, claiming I lived there.

I can recall what happened one night when my dad came home late to find that my mother had locked all the doors on him from the inside. He was drunk, and we could feel the house shudder as he rattled the door. When he'd managed to force open a window, she hit him between the eyes with a colander and knocked him out. We could see him down there on the grass. For years afterward, I used to pick up this colander—it was as heavy as a rolling pin—and imagine what it would feel like to be hit in the head with something like that.

It was during this period that I remember my dad taking me into the bedroom, sitting me down on the bed, and telling me that I might have to go live with my Aunt LaVon for a while. I couldn't understand what I'd done that meant I'd have to go away from home to live. But this, too—whatever prompted it—must have blown over, more or less, anyway, because we stayed together, and I didn't have to go live with her or anyone else.

I remember my mother pouring his whiskey down the sink. Sometimes she'd pour it all out and sometimes, if she was afraid of getting caught, she'd only pour half of it out and then add water to the rest. I tasted some of his whiskey once myself. It was terrible stuff, and I don't see how anybody could drink it.

After a long time without one, we finally got a car, in 1949 or 1950, a 1938 Ford. But it threw a rod the first week we had it, and my dad had to have the motor rebuilt.

"We drove the oldest car in town," my mother said. "We could have   15 had a Cadillac for all he spent on car repairs." One time she found someone else's tube of lipstick on the floorboard, along with a lacy handkerchief. "See this?" she said to me. "Some floozy left this in the car."

Once I saw her take a pan of warm water into the bedroom where my dad was sleeping. She took his hand from under the covers and held it in the water. I stood in the doorway and watched. I wanted to know what was going on. This would make him talk in his sleep, she told me. There were things she needed to know, things she was sure he was keeping from her.

Every year or so, when I was little, we would take the North Coast Limited across the Cascade Range from Yakima to Seattle and stay in the Vance Hotel and eat, I remember, at a place called the Dinner Bell Cafe. Once we went to Ivar's Acres of Clams and drank glasses of warm clam broth.

In 1956, the year I was to graduate from high school, my dad quit his job at the mill in Yakima and took a job in Chester, a little sawmill town in northern California. The reasons given at the time for his taking the job had to do with a higher hourly wage and the vague promise that he might, in a few years' time, succeed to the job of head filer in this new mill. But I think, in the main, that my dad had grown restless and simply wanted to try his luck elsewhere. Things had gotten a little too predictable for him in Yakima. Also, the year before, there had been the deaths, within six months of each other, of both his parents.

But just a few days after graduation, when my mother and I were packed to move to Chester, my dad penciled a letter to say he'd been sick for a while. He didn't want us to worry, he said, but he'd cut himself on a saw. Maybe he'd got a tiny sliver of steel in his blood. Anyway, something had happened and he'd had to miss work, he said. In the same mail was an unsigned postcard from somebody down there telling my mother that my dad was about to die and that he was drinking "raw whiskey."

When we arrived in Chester, my dad was living in a trailer that belonged   20
to the company. I didn't recognize him immediately. I guess for a moment I didn't want to recognize him. He was skinny and pale and looked bewildered. His pants wouldn't stay up. He didn't look like my dad. My mother began to cry. My dad put his arm around her and patted her shoulder vaguely, like he didn't know what this was all about, either. The three of us took up life together in the trailer, and we looked after him as best we could. But my dad was sick, and he couldn't get any better. I worked with him in the mill that summer and part of the fall. We'd get up in the mornings and eat eggs and toast while we listened to the radio, and then go out the door with our lunch pails. We'd pass through the gate together at eight in the morning, and I wouldn't see him again until quitting time. In November I went back to Yakima to be closer to my girlfriend, the girl I'd made up my mind I was going to marry.

He worked at the mill in Chester until the following February, when he collapsed on the job and was taken to the hospital. My mother asked if I would come down there and help. I caught a bus from Yakima to Chester, intending to drive them back to Yakima. But now, in addition to being physically sick, my dad was in the midst of a nervous breakdown, though none of us knew to call it that at the time. During the entire trip back to Yakima, he didn't speak, not even when asked a direct question. ("How do you feel, Raymond?" "You okay, Dad?") He'd communicate, if he communicated at all, by moving his head or by turning his palms up as if to say he didn't know or care. The only time he said anything on the trip, and for nearly a month afterward, was when I was speeding down a gravel road in Oregon and the car muffler came loose. "You were going too fast," he said.

Back in Yakima a doctor saw to it that my dad went to a psychiatrist. My mother and dad had to go on relief, as it was called, and the county paid for the psychiatrist. The psychiatrist asked my dad, "Who is the President?" He'd had a question put to him that he could answer. "Ike," my dad said. Nevertheless, they put him on the fifth floor of Valley Memorial Hospital and began giving him electroshock treatment. I was married by then and about to start my own family. My dad was still locked up when my wife went into this same hospital, just one floor down, to have our first baby. After she had delivered, I went upstairs to give my dad the news. They let me in through a steel door and showed me where I could find him. He was sitting on a couch with a blanket over his lap. *Hey*, I thought. *What in hell is happening to my dad?* I sat down next to him and told him he was a grandfather. He waited a minute and then he said, "I feel like a grandfather." That's all he said. He didn't smile or move. He was in a big room with a lot of other people. Then I hugged him, and he began to cry.

Somehow he got out of there. But now came the years when he couldn't work and just sat around the house trying to figure what next and what he'd done wrong in his life that he'd wound up like this. My mother went from job to crummy job. Much later she referred to that time he was in the hospital, and those years just afterward, as "when Raymond was sick." The word *sick* was never the same for me again.

In 1964, through the help of a friend, he was lucky enough to be hired on at a mill in Klamath, California. He moved down there by himself to see if he could hack it. He lived not far from the mill, in a one-room cabin not much different from the place he and my mother had started out living in when they went west. He scrawled letters to my mother, and if I called she'd read them aloud to me over the phone. In the letters, he said it was touch and go. Every day that he went to work, he felt like it was the most important day of his life. But every day, he told her, made the next day that much easier. He said for her to tell me he said hello. If he couldn't sleep at night, he said, he thought about me and the good times we used to have. Finally, after a couple of months, he regained some of his confidence. He could do the work and didn't think he had to worry that he'd let anybody down ever again. When he was sure, he sent for my mother.

He'd been off from work for six years and had lost everything in that 25 time—home, car, furniture, and appliances, including the big freezer that had been my mother's pride and joy. He'd lost his good name too—Raymond Carver was someone who couldn't pay his bills—and his self-respect was gone. He'd even lost his virility. My mother told my wife, "All during that time Raymond was sick we slept together in the same bed, but we didn't have relations. He wanted to a few times, but nothing happened. I didn't miss it, but I think he wanted to, you know."

During those years I was trying to raise my own family and earn a living. But, from one thing and another, we found ourselves having to move a lot. I couldn't keep track of what was going down in my dad's life. But I did have a chance one Christmas to tell him I wanted to be a writer. I might as well have told him I wanted to become a plastic surgeon. "What are you going to write about?" he wanted to know. Then, as if to help me out, he said, "Write about stuff you know about. Write about some of those fishing trips we took." I said I would, but I knew I wouldn't. "Send me what you write," he said. I said I'd do that, but then I didn't. I wasn't writing anything about fishing, and I didn't think he'd particularly care about, or even necessarily understand, what I was writing in those days. Besides, he wasn't a reader. Not the sort, anyway, I imagined I was writing for.

Then he died. I was a long way off, in Iowa City, with things still to say to him. I didn't have the chance to tell him goodbye, or that I thought he was doing great at his new job. That I was proud of him for making a comeback.

My mother said he came in from work that night and ate a big supper. Then he sat at the table by himself and finished what was left of a bottle of whiskey, a bottle she found hidden in the bottom of the garbage under some coffee grounds a day or so later. Then he got up and went to bed, where my mother joined him a little later. But in the night she had to get up and make a bed for herself on the couch. "He was snoring so loud I couldn't sleep," she said. The next morning when she looked in on him, he was on his back with his mouth open, his cheeks caved in. *Graylooking*, she said. She knew he was dead—she didn't need a doctor to tell her that. But she called one anyway, and then she called my wife.

Among the pictures my mother kept of my dad and herself during those early days in Washington was a photograph of him standing in front of a car, holding a beer and a stringer of fish. In the photograph he is wearing his hat back on his forehead and has this awkward grin on his face. I asked her for it and she gave it to me, along with some others. I put it up on my wall, and each time we moved, I took the picture along and put it up on another wall. I looked at it carefully from time to time, trying to figure out some things about my dad, and maybe myself in the process. But I couldn't. My dad just kept moving further and further away from me and back into time. Finally, in the course of another move, I lost the photograph. It was then that I tried to recall it, and at the same time make an attempt to say something about my dad, and how I thought that in some important ways we might be alike. I wrote the poem when I was living in an apartment house in an urban area south of San Francisco, at a time when I found myself, like my dad, having trouble with alcohol. The poem was a way of trying to connect up with him.

PHOTOGRAPH OF MY FATHER IN HIS TWENTY-SECOND YEAR

October. Here in this dank, unfamiliar kitchen
I study my father's embarrassed young man's face.
Sheepish grin, he holds in one hand a string
of spiny yellow perch, in the other
a bottle of Carlsberg beer.

In jeans and flannel shirt, he leans
against the front fender of a 1934 Ford.
He would like to pose brave and hearty for his posterity,
wear his old hat cocked over his ear.
All his life my father wanted to be bold.

But the eyes give him away, and the hands
that limply offer the string of dead perch
and the bottle of beer. Father, I love you,
yet how can I say thank you, I who can't hold my liquor either
and don't even know the places to fish.

The poem is true in its particulars, except that my dad died in June and 30
not October, as the first word of the poem says. I wanted a word with more
than one syllable to it to make it linger a little. But more than that, I wanted
a month appropriate to what I felt at the time I wrote the poem — a month
of short days and failing light, smoke in the air, things perishing. June was
summer nights and days, graduations, my wedding anniversary, the birthday of one of my children. June wasn't a month your father died in.

After the service at the funeral home, after we had moved outside, a
woman I didn't know came over to me and said, "He's happier where he
is now." I stared at this woman until she moved away. I still remember the
little knob of a hat she was wearing. Then one of my dad's cousins — I didn't
know the man's name — reached out and took my hand. "We all miss him,"
he said, and I knew he wasn't saying it just to be polite.

I began to weep for the first time since receiving the news. I hadn't been
able to before. I hadn't had the time, for one thing. Now, suddenly, I couldn't
stop. I held my wife and wept while she said and did what she could do to
comfort me there in the middle of that summer afternoon.

I listened to people say consoling things to my mother, and I was glad
that my dad's family had turned up, had come to where he was. I thought I'd
remember everything that was said and done that day and maybe find a way
to tell it sometime. But I didn't. I forgot it all, or nearly. What I do remember
is that I heard our name used a lot that afternoon, my dad's name and mine.
But I knew they were talking about my dad. *Raymond*, these people kept
saying in their beautiful voices out of my childhood. *Raymond.* ●

The Reader's Presence

1. You may have noticed that Carver begins and ends his essay with a reference to his
   and his father's name. Of what importance is this information at the opening? What
   do we learn about his relationship with his father through their names? How do
   names matter in the final paragraph?

2. Reread the essay with particular attention to the conversations between father and
   son. How many reported conversations can you find? What do the conversations
   sound like? Can you find any pattern to them? If so, describe that pattern. To what
   extent do these conversations help you understand Carver's relationship with his
   father?

3. **CONNECTIONS:**   Carver includes one of his own poems in his essay (paragraph 29), as does Alice Walker in "Beauty: When the Other Dancer Is the Self" (page 275). How do these writers explore the margins between poetry and prose? What do you think a poem communicates that a passage of prose may not?

Judith Ortiz Cofer

SILENT DANCING

Born in Puerto Rico in 1952, **JUDITH ORTIZ COFER** moved to New Jersey in 1955. Her poetry has appeared in numerous literary magazines, and several collections of her poems have been published. Her first novel, *The Line of the Sun* (1989), was nominated for the Pulitzer Prize. "Silent Dancing" is from Cofer's 1990 essay collection, *Silent Dancing: A Partial Remembrance of a Puerto Rican Childhood*, which won a PEN/Martha Albrand special citation for nonfiction. Among her notable books are *The Latin Deli: Prose and Poetry* (1993), *An Island Like You: Stories of the Barrio* (1995), *Woman in Front of the Sun* (2000), *The Meaning of Consuelo* (2003), and *Call Me Maria* (2004). In 2012 she published a children's picture book titled *The Poet Upstairs*.

> **"The 'infinite variety' and power of language interest me."**

Reflecting on her life as a writer, Cofer has said, "The 'infinite variety' and power of language interest me. I never cease to experiment with it. As a native Puerto Rican, my first language was Spanish. It was a challenge, not only to learn English, but to master it enough to teach it and—the ultimate goal—to write poetry in it." Cofer is professor of English and creative writing at the University of Georgia.

WE HAVE A HOME MOVIE of this party. Several times my mother and I have watched it together, and I have asked questions about the silent revelers coming in and out of focus. It is grainy and of short duration, but it's a great visual aid to my memory of life at that time. And it is in color—the only complete scene in color I can recall from those years.

We lived in Puerto Rico until my brother was born in 1954. Soon after, because of economic pressures on our growing family, my father joined the United States Navy. He was assigned to duty on a ship in Brooklyn Yard—a place of cement and steel that was to be his home base in the States until his retirement more than twenty years later. He left the Island first, alone, going to New York City and tracking down his uncle who lived with his family across the Hudson River in Paterson, New Jersey. There my father found a tiny apartment in a huge tenement that had once housed Jewish families but was just being taken over and transformed by Puerto Ricans, overflowing from New York City. In 1955 he sent for us. My mother was only twenty years old, I was not quite three, and my brother was a toddler when we arrived at *El Building*, as the place had been christened by its newest residents.

My memories of life in Paterson during those first few years are all in shades of gray. Maybe I was too young to absorb vivid colors and details, or to discriminate between the slate blue of the winter sky and the darker hues of the snow-bearing clouds, but that single color washes over the whole period. The building we lived in was gray, as were the streets, filled with slush the first few months of my life there. The coat my father had bought for me was similar in color and too big; it sat heavily on my thin frame.

I do remember the way the heater pipes banged and rattled, startling all of us out of sleep until we got so used to the sound that we automatically shut it out or raised our voices above the racket. The hiss from the valve punctuated my sleep (which has always been fitful) like a nonhuman presence in the room—a dragon sleeping at the entrance of my childhood. But the pipes were also a connection to all the other lives being lived around us. Having come from a house designed for a single family back in Puerto Rico—my mother's extended-family home—it was curious to know that strangers lived under our floor and above our heads, and that the heater pipe went through everyone's apartments. (My first spanking in Paterson came as a result of playing tunes on the pipes in my room to see if there would be an answer.) My mother was as new to this concept of beehive life as I was, but she had been given strict orders by my father to keep the doors locked, the noise down, ourselves to ourselves.

It seems that Father had learned some painful lessons about prejudice   5
while searching for an apartment in Paterson. Not until years later did I hear how much resistance he had encountered with landlords who were panicking at the influx of Latinos into a neighborhood that had been Jewish for a couple of generations. It made no difference that it was the American phenomenon of ethnic turnover which was changing the urban core of Paterson, and that the human flood could not be held back with an accusing finger.

"You Cuban?" one man had asked my father, pointing at his name tag on the Navy uniform—even though my father had the fair skin and light-brown hair of his northern Spanish background, and the name Ortiz is as common in Puerto Rico as Johnson is in the United States.

"No," my father had answered, looking past the finger into his adversary's angry eyes. "I'm Puerto Rican."

"Same shit." And the door closed.

My father could have passed as European, but we couldn't. My brother and I both have our mother's black hair and olive skin, and so we lived in El Building and visited our great-uncle and his fair children on the next block. It was their private joke that they were the German branch of the family. Not many years later that area too would be mainly Puerto Rican. It was as if the heart of the city map were being gradually colored brown—*café con leche*[1] brown. Our color.

The movie opens with a sweep of the living room. It is "typical" immi-   10
grant Puerto Rican decor for the time: The sofa and chairs are square and hard-looking, upholstered in bright colors (blue and yellow in this instance), and covered with the transparent plastic that furniture salesmen then were so adept at convincing women to buy. The linoleum on the floor is light blue; if it had been subjected to spike heels (as it was in most places), there were dime-sized indentations all over it that cannot be seen in this movie. The room is full of people dressed up: dark suits for the men, red dresses for the women. When I have asked my mother why most of the women are in red that night, she has shrugged, "I don't remember. Just a coincidence." She doesn't have my obsession for assigning symbolism to everything.

The three women in red sitting on the couch are my mother, my eighteen-year-old cousin, and her brother's girlfriend. The novia is just up from the Island, which is apparent in her body language. She sits up formally, her dress pulled over her knees. She is a pretty girl, but her posture makes her look insecure, lost in her full-skirted dress, which she has carefully tucked around her to make room for my gorgeous cousin, her future sister-in-law. My cousin has grown up in Paterson and is in her last year of high school. She doesn't have a trace of what Puerto Ricans call la mancha (literally, the stain: the mark of the new immigrant—something about the posture, the voice, or the humble demeanor that makes it obvious to everyone the person has just arrived on the mainland). My cousin is wearing a tight, sequined, cocktail dress. Her brown hair has been lightened with peroxide around the bangs, and she is holding a cigarette expertly between her fingers, bringing it up to her mouth in a sensuous arc of her arm as she talks animatedly. My mother, who has come up to sit between the two women, both only a few years younger than herself, is somewhere between the poles they represent in our culture.

It became my father's obsession to get out of the barrio, and thus we were never permitted to form bonds with the place or with the people who lived there. Yet El Building was a comfort to my mother, who never got over yearning for *la isla*. She felt surrounded by her language: The walls were thin, and voices speaking and arguing in Spanish could be heard all day.

---

[1] *café con leche:* Coffee with cream. In Puerto Rico it is sometimes prepared with boiled milk. —COFER'S NOTE.

Salsas blasted out of radios, turned on early in the morning and left on for company. Women seemed to cook rice and beans perpetually—the strong aroma of boiling red kidney beans permeated the hallways.

Though Father preferred that we do our grocery shopping at the supermarket when he came home on weekend leaves, my mother insisted that she could cook only with products whose labels she could read. Consequently, during the week I accompanied her and my little brother to *La Bodega*—a hole-in-the-wall grocery store across the street from El Building. There we squeezed down three narrow aisles jammed with various products. Goya's and Libby's—those were the trademarks that were trusted by her *mamá*, so my mother bought many cans of Goya beans, soups, and condiments, as well as little cans of Libby's fruit juices for us. And she also bought Colgate toothpaste and Palmolive soap. (The final *e* is pronounced in both these products in Spanish, so for many years I believed that they were manufactured on the Island. I remember my surprise at first hearing a commercial on television in which Colgate rhymed with "ate.") We always lingered at La Bodega, for it was there that Mother breathed best, taking in the familiar aromas of the foods she knew from Mamá's kitchen. It was also there that she got to speak to the other women of El Building without violating outright Father's dictates against fraternizing with our neighbors.

Yet Father did his best to make our "assimilation" painless. I can still see him carrying a real Christmas tree up several flights of stairs to our apartment, leaving a trail of aromatic pine. He carried it formally, as if it were a flag in a parade. We were the only ones in El Building that I knew of who got presents on both Christmas day and *dia de Reyes*, the day when the Three Kings brought gifts to Christ and to Hispanic children.

Our supreme luxury in El Building was having our own television set. It   15 must have been a result of Father's guilty feelings over the isolation he had imposed on us, but we were among the first in the barrio to have one. My brother quickly became an avid watcher of Captain Kangaroo and Jungle Jim, while I loved all the series showing families. By the time I started first grade, I could have drawn a map of Middle America as exemplified by the lives of characters in *Father Knows Best*, *The Donna Reed Show*, *Leave It to Beaver*, *My Three Sons*, and (my favorite) *Bachelor Father*, where John Forsythe treated his adopted teenage daughter like a princess because he was rich and had a Chinese houseboy to do everything for him. In truth, compared to our neighbors in El Building, *we* were rich. My father's Navy check provided us with financial security and a standard of life that the factory workers envied. The only thing his money could not buy us was a place to live away from the barrio—his greatest wish, Mother's greatest fear.

In the home movie the men are shown next, sitting around a card table set up in one corner of the living room, playing dominoes. The clack of the ivory pieces was a familiar sound. I heard it in many houses on the Island and in many apartments in Paterson. In Leave It to Beaver, *the Cleavers played bridge in every other episode; in my childhood, the men started every social occasion with a hotly debated round of dominoes. The women would sit around and watch, but they never participated in the games.*

Here and there you can see a small child. Children were always brought to parties and, whenever they got sleepy, were put to bed in the host's bedroom. Babysitting was a concept unrecognized by the Puerto Rican women I knew: A responsible mother did not leave her children with any stranger. And in a culture where children are not considered intrusive, there was no need to leave the children at home. We went where our mother went.

Of my preschool years I have only impressions: the sharp bite of the wind in December as we walked with our parents toward the brightly lit stores downtown; how I felt like a stuffed doll in my heavy coat, boots, and mittens; how good it was to walk into the five-and-dime and sit at the counter drinking hot chocolate. On Saturdays our whole family would walk downtown to shop at the big department stores on Broadway. Mother bought all our clothes at Penney's and Sears, and she liked to buy her dresses at the women's specialty shops like Lerner's and Diana's. At some point we'd go into Woolworth's and sit at the soda fountain to eat.

We never ran into other Latinos at these stores or when eating out, and it became clear to me only years later that the women from El Building shopped mainly in other places—stores owned by other Puerto Ricans or by Jewish merchants who had philosophically accepted our presence in the city and decided to make us their good customers, if not real neighbors and friends. These establishments were located not downtown but in the blocks around our street, and they were referred to generically as *La Tienda, El Bazar, La Bodega, La Botánica.* Everyone knew what was meant. These were the stores where your face did not turn a clerk to stone, where your money was as green as anyone else's.

One New Year's Eve we were dressed up like child models in the Sears   20
catalogue: my brother in a miniature man's suit and bow tie, and I in black patent-leather shoes and a frilly dress with several layers of crinoline underneath. My mother wore a bright red dress that night, I remember, and spike heels; her long black hair hung to her waist. Father, who usually wore his Navy uniform during his short visits home, had put on a dark civilian suit for the occasion: We had been invited to his uncle's house for a big celebration. Everyone was excited because my mother's brother Hernan—a bachelor who could indulge himself with luxuries—had bought a home movie camera, which he would be trying out that night.

Even the home movie cannot fill in the sensory details such a gathering left imprinted in a child's brain. The thick sweetness of women's perfumes mixing with the ever-present smells of food cooking in the kitchen: meat and plantain *pasteles*, as well as the ubiquitous rice dish made special with pigeon peas—*gandules*—and seasoned with precious *sofrito*[2] sent up from

2 **sofrito:** A cooked condiment. A sauce composed of a mixture of fatback, ham, tomatoes, and many island spices and herbs. It is added to many Puerto Rican dishes for a distinctive flavor.—COFER'S NOTE.

the Island by somebody's mother or smuggled in by a recent traveler. *Sofrito* was one of the items that women hoarded, since it was hardly ever in stock at La Bodega. It was the flavor of Puerto Rico.

The men drank Palo Viejo rum, and some of the younger ones got weepy. The first time I saw a grown man cry was at a New Year's Eve party: He had been reminded of his mother by the smells in the kitchen. But what I remember most were the boiled *pasteles*—plantain or yucca rectangles stuffed with corned beef or other meats, olives, and many other savory ingredients, all wrapped in banana leaves. Everybody had to fish one out with a fork. There was always a "trick" pastel—one without stuffing—and whoever got that one was the "New Year's Fool."

There was also the music. Long-playing albums were treated like precious china in these homes. Mexican recordings were popular, but the songs that brought tears to my mother's eyes were sung by the melancholy Daniel Santos, whose life as a drug addict was the stuff of legend. Felipe Rodríguez was a particular favorite of couples, since he sang about faithless women and brokenhearted men. There is a snatch of one lyric that has stuck in my mind like a needle on a worn groove: *De piedra ha de ser mi cama, de piedra la cabezera . . . la mujer que a mi me quiera . . . ha de quererme de veras. Ay, Ay, Ay, corazón, porque no amas.*[3] . . . I must have heard it a thousand times since the idea of a bed made of stone, and its connection to love, first troubled me with its disturbing images.

The five-minute home movie ends with people dancing in a circle—the creative filmmaker must have set it up so that all of them could file past him. It is both comical and sad to watch silent dancing. Since there is no justification for the absurd movements that music provides for some of us, people appear frantic, their faces embarrassingly intense. It's as if you were watching sex. Yet for years I've had dreams in the form of this home movie. In a recurring scene, familiar faces push themselves forward into my mind's eyes, plastering their features into distorted close-ups. And I'm asking them: "Who is *she*? Who is the old woman I don't recognize? Is she an aunt? Somebody's wife? Tell me who she is."

> "See the beauty mark on her cheek as big as a hill on the lunar landscape of her face—well, that runs in the family. The women on your father's side of the family wrinkle early; it's the price they pay for that fair skin. The young girl with the green stain on her wedding dress is *La Novia*—just up from the Island. See, she lowers her eyes when she approaches the camera, as she's supposed to. Decent girls never look at you directly in the face. *Humilde*, humble, a girl should express humility in all her actions. She will make a good wife for your cousin. He should consider himself lucky to have met her only weeks after she arrived here. If he marries her quickly, she will make him a good Puerto Rican–style wife; but if he waits too long, she will be corrupted by the city—just like your cousin there."

---

[3] ***De piedra ha de ser . . . amas:*** Lyrics from a popular romantic ballad (called a *bolero* in Puerto Rico). Freely translated: "My bed will be made of stone, of stone also my headrest (or pillow), the woman who (dares to) love me, will have to love me for real. Ay, Ay, Ay, my heart, why can't you (let me) love. . . ." —COFER'S NOTE.

"She means me. I do what I want. This is not some primitive island I live on. Do they expect me to wear a black mantilla on my head and go to mass every day? Not me. I'm an American woman, and I will do as I please. I can type faster than anyone in my senior class at Central High, and I'm going to be a secretary to a lawyer when I graduate. I can pass for an American girl anywhere—I've tried it. At least for Italian, anyway—I never speak Spanish in public. I hate these parties, but I wanted the dress. I look better than any of these *humildes* here. My life is going to be different. I have an American boyfriend. He is older and has a car. My parents don't know it, but I sneak out of the house late at night sometimes to be with him. If I marry him, even my name will be American. I hate rice and beans—that's what makes these women fat."

"Your *prima*[4] is pregnant by that man she's been sneaking around with. Would I lie to you? I'm your *Tía Política*,[5] your great-uncle's common-law wife—the one he abandoned on the Island to go marry your cousin's mother. *I* was not invited to this party, of course, but I came anyway. I came to tell you that story about your cousin that you've always wanted to hear. Do you remember the comment your mother made to a neighbor that has always haunted you? The only thing you heard was your cousin's name, and then you saw your mother pick up your doll from the couch and say: 'It was as big as this doll when they flushed it down the toilet.' This image has bothered you for years, hasn't it? You had nightmares about babies being flushed down the toilet, and you wondered why anyone would do such a horrible thing. You didn't dare ask your mother about it. She would only tell you that you had not heard her right, and yell at you for listening to adult conversations. But later, when you were old enough to know about abortions, you suspected.

"I am here to tell you that you were right. Your cousin was growing an *Americanito* in her belly when this movie was made. Soon after she put something long and pointy into her pretty self, thinking maybe she could get rid of the problem before breakfast and still make it to her first class at the high school. Well, *Niña*,[6] her screams could be heard downtown. Your aunt, her mamá, who had been a midwife on the Island, managed to pull the little thing out. Yes, they probably flushed it down the toilet. What else could they do with it—give it a Christian burial in a little white casket with blue bows and ribbons? Nobody wanted that baby—least of all the father, a teacher at her school with a house in West Paterson that he was filling with real children, and a wife who was a natural blonde.

"Girl, the scandal sent your uncle back to the bottle. And guess where your cousin ended up? Irony of ironies. She was sent to a village in Puerto Rico to live with a relative on her mother's side: a place so far away from civilization that you have to ride a mule to reach it. A real change in scenery. She found a man there—women like that cannot live without male company—but believe me, the men in Puerto Rico know how to put a saddle on a woman like her. *La Gringa*,[7] they call her. Ha, ha, ha. *La Gringa* is what she always wanted to be. . . ."

The old woman's mouth becomes a cavernous black hole I fall into. And as I fall, I can feel the reverberations of her laughter. I hear the echoes of her last

---

4 ***prima:*** Female cousin. — COFER'S NOTE.
5 ***Tía Política:*** Aunt by marriage. — COFER'S NOTE.
6 ***Niña:*** Girl. — COFER'S NOTE.
7 ***La Gringa:*** Derogatory epithet used here to ridicule a Puerto Rican girl who wants to look like a blonde North American. — COFER'S NOTE.

mocking words: *La Gringa, La Gringa!* And the conga line keeps moving silently past me. There is no music in my dream for the dancers.

When Odysseus visits Hades to see the spirit of his mother, he makes an   25 offering of sacrificial blood, but since all the souls crave an audience with the living, he has to listen to many of them before he can ask questions. I, too, have to hear the dead and the forgotten speak in my dream. Those who are still part of my life remain silent, going around and around in their dance. The others keep pressing their faces forward to say things about the past.

My father's uncle is last in line. He is dying of alcoholism, shrunken and shriveled like a monkey, his face a mass of wrinkles and broken arteries. As he comes closer I realize that in his features I can see my whole family. If you were to stretch that rubbery flesh, you could find my father's face, and deep within *that* face—my own. I don't want to look into those eyes ringed in purple. In a few years he will retreat into silence, and take a long, long time to die. *Move back, Tío*, I tell him. *I don't want to hear what you have to say. Give the dancers room to move. Soon it will be midnight. Who is the New Year's Fool this time?* ▣

The Reader's Presence

1. In "Silent Dancing," Cofer explores the personal, familial, and communal transformations that resulted from moving in the 1950s to Paterson, New Jersey—to "a huge tenement that had once housed Jewish families" (paragraph 2) and to a new community that emerged from the sprawling barrio that Puerto Ricans "overflowing from New York City" (paragraph 2) called home. Reread the essay carefully, and summarize the transformations that occurred in the life of the narrator, her family, and their larger Puerto Rican community.

2. Cofer uses an account of a home movie to create a structure for her essay. What are the specific advantages and disadvantages of this strategy? How, for example, does the home movie serve as "a great visual aid" (paragraph 1) to recounting life in the barrio of Paterson, New Jersey? What effect does the fact that the home movie is in color have on what Cofer notices? on how she writes?

3. Because Cofer's essay is built around the occasion of watching a home movie, the narrator assumes the position of an observer of the scenes and people Cofer describes. What specific strategies as a writer does Cofer use to establish a presence for herself in this narrative and descriptive account of growing up?

4. **VISUAL PRESENCE:** Cofer selected a photograph of herself when she was two years old for the cover of *Silent Dancing*. (See page 96.) Why do you think Cofer chose this image for the cover? What message about the author does this picture convey? Cite specific details from the image in your response.

5. **CONNECTIONS:** In his attempt to aid the family's "assimilation" into American culture, Cofer's father forbids his wife and children from making friends in "El Building." Cofer and her mother were expected "to keep the doors locked, the noise down, ourselves to ourselves" (paragraph 4). As a result, Cofer at times feels alienated from her own relatives. How does her situation compare to that of the narrator of Maxine Hong Kingston's "No Name Woman" (page 453)?

The Writer at Work

JUDITH ORTIZ COFER on Memory and Personal Essays

SILENT DANCING:
A Partial Remembrance of a Puerto Rican Childhood

JUDITH ORTIZ COFER

In setting out to write essays recounting her family history, Judith Ortiz Cofer found in Virginia Woolf a brilliant mentor and guide who taught her how to release the creative power of memory. In the following preface to *Silent Dancing: A Partial Remembrance of a Puerto Rican Childhood*, Cofer pays tribute to Woolf, who "understood that the very act of reclaiming her memories could provide a writer with confidence in the power of art to discover meaning and truth in ordinary events." How do Cofer's remarks in the preface (which she called "Journey to a Summer's Afternoon"), along with Woolf's "The Death of the Moth" (page 574), help illuminate the artistry of Cofer's own essay, "Silent Dancing"?

The author at the age of two, from the cover of *Silent Dancing: A Partial Remembrance of a Puerto Rican Childhood*, by Judith Ortiz Cofer. Published in 1990 by Arte Publico Press (Houston, Texas).

❝As one gets older, childhood years are often conveniently consolidated into one perfect summer's afternoon. The events can be projected on a light blue screen; the hurtful parts can be edited out, and the moments of joy brought in sharp focus to the foreground. It is our show. But with all that on the cutting room floor, what remains to tell?

Virginia Woolf, whose vision guided my efforts as I tried to recall the faces and words of the people who are a part of my "summer's afternoon," wrote of the problem of writing truth from memory. In "A Sketch of the Past" she says, "But if I turn to my mother, how difficult it is to single her out as she really was; to imagine what she was thinking, to put a single sentence into her mouth." She accepts the fact that in writing about one's life, one often has to rely on that combination of memory, imagination, and strong emotion that may result in "poetic truth." In preparing to write her memoirs Woolf said, "I dream, I make up pictures of a summer's afternoon."

In one of her essays from her memoir *Moments of Being*, Woolf recalls the figure of her beautiful and beloved mother who died while the author was still a child, leaving her a few precious "moments of being" from which the mature woman must piece together a childhood. And she does so not to showcase her life, extraordinary as it was, but rather out of a need most of us feel at some point to study ourselves and our lives in retrospect; to understand what people and events formed us (and, yes, what and who hurt us, too).

From "A Sketch of the Past": "Many bright colors; many distinct sounds; some human beings, caricatures; several violent moments of being, always including a circle of the scene they cut out: and all surrounded by a vast space—that is a rough visual description of childhood. This is how I shape it; and how I see myself as a child. . . ."

This passage illustrates the approach that I was seeking in writing about my family. I wanted the essays to be, not just family history, but also creative explorations of known territory. I wanted to trace back through scenes based on my "moments of being" the origins of my creative imagination. As a writer, I am, like most artists, interested in the genesis of ideas: How does a poem begin? Can the process be triggered at will? What compels some of us to examine and re-examine our lives in poems, stories, novels, memoirs?

Much of my writing begins as a meditation on past events. But memory for me is the "jumping off" point; I am not, in my poetry and my fiction writing, a slave to memory. I like to believe that the poem or story contains the "truth" of art rather than the factual, historical truth that the journalist, sociologist, scientist—most of the rest of the world—must adhere to. Art gives me that freedom. But in writing these "essays" (the Spanish word for essay, *ensayo*, suits my meaning here better—it can mean "a rehearsal," an exercise or practice), I faced the possibility that the past is mainly a creation of the imagination also, although there are facts one can research and confirm. The biographer's time-honored task can be employed on one's own life too. There are birth, marriage, and death certificates on file, there are letters and family photographs in someone's desk or attic; and there are the relatives who have assigned themselves the role of genealogist or family bard, recounting at the least instigation the entire history of your clan. One can go to these sources and come up with a *Life* in several volumes that will make your mother proud and give you the satisfaction of having "preserved" something. I am not interested in merely "canning" memories, however, and Woolf gave me the focus that I needed to justify this work. Its intention is not to chronicle my life—which in my case is still very much "in-progress," nor are there any extraordinary accomplishments to showcase; neither is it meant to be a record of public events and personal histories (in fact, since most of the characters in these essays are based on actual, living persons and real places, whenever I felt that it was necessary to protect their identities, I changed names, locations, etc.). Then, what is the purpose of calling this collection nonfiction or a memoir? Why not just call it fiction? Once again I must turn to my literary mentor for this project, Virginia Woolf, for an answer: like her, I wanted to try to connect myself to the threads of lives that have touched mine and at some point converged into the tapestry that is my memory of childhood. Virginia Woolf understood that the very act of reclaiming her memories could provide a writer with confidence in the power of art to discover meaning and truth in ordinary events. She was a time-traveler who saw the past as a real place one could return to by following the tracks left by strong emotions: "I feel that strong emotion must leave its trace; and it is only a question of discovering how we can get ourselves attached to it, so that we shall be able to live our lives through from the start."[1]

It was this winding path of memory, marked by strong emotions, that I followed in my *ensayos* of a life.**"**

[1]All quotes by Virginia Woolf are from *Moments of Being* (Harcourt Brace Jovanovich, Inc.).— Cofer's Note.

Bernard Cooper

A CLACK OF TINY SPARKS:
REMEMBRANCES OF A GAY BOYHOOD

Born and raised in Los Angeles, **BERNARD COOPER** (b. 1951) received his BFA and MFA from the California Institute of the Arts. His two collections of personal essays, *Maps to Anywhere* (1990) and *Truth Serum* (1996), cover a wide range of topics from the aging of his father, to his gay awakening, to the future of American life and culture. A collection of short stories, *Guess Again*, was published in 2000 and his latest memoir, *The Bill from My Father*, in 2006.

> **"The world only seems real and vivid and meaningful to me in the smaller details."**

Cooper was an art critic for *Los Angeles Magazine* for many years. He is currently a faculty member in the MFA program at Bennington College, and he teaches at the University of Southern California in the Master of Professional Writing program. He's won a PEN/Ernest Hemingway Award, an O. Henry Prize, a Guggenheim Fellowship, and a National Endowment for the Arts fellowship. Cooper contributes to various periodicals, including *Harper's*, where "A Clack of Tiny Sparks: Remembrances of a Gay Boyhood" first appeared in January 1991.

Commenting on his 1993 novel, *A Year of Rhymes*, Cooper notes, "One of the reasons why there is so much detail in my work is that I'm a person that essentially shies away from abstractions, from Large Issues and Big Ideas. The world only seems real and vivid and meaningful to me in the smaller details, what's heard and felt and smelled and tasted."

THERESA SANCHEZ sat behind me in ninth-grade algebra. When Mr. Hubbley faced the blackboard, I'd turn around to see what she was reading; each week a new book was wedged inside her copy of *Today's Equations*. The deception worked; from Mr. Hubbley's point of view, Theresa was engrossed in the value of X, but I knew otherwise. One week she perused *The Wisdom of the Orient*, and I could tell from Theresa's contemplative expression that the book contained exotic thoughts, guidelines handed down from high. Another week it was a paperback novel whose

macmillanhighered.com/writerspresence8e
How does kid logic about the nature of love change as we get older?
e-Readings > Howie Chackowicz, "The Game Ain't Over 'til the Fatso Man Sings" (audio essay)

title, *Let Me Live My Life*, appeared in bold print atop every page, and whose cover, a gauzy photograph of a woman biting a strand of pearls, head thrown back in an attitude of ecstasy, confirmed my suspicion that Theresa Sanchez was mature beyond her years. She was the tallest girl in school. Her bouffant hairdo, streaked with blond, was higher than the flaccid bouffants of other girls. Her smooth skin, plucked eyebrows, and painted fingernails suggested hours of pampering, a worldly and sensual vanity that placed her within the domain of adults. Smiling dimly, steeped in daydreams, Theresa moved through the crowded halls with a languid, self-satisfied indifference to those around her. "You are merely children," her posture seemed to say. "I can't be bothered." The week Theresa hid *101 Ways to Cook Hamburger* behind her algebra book, I could stand it no longer and, after the bell rang, ventured a question.

"Because I'm having a dinner party," said Theresa. "Just a couple of intimate friends."

No fourteen-year-old I knew had ever given a dinner party, let alone used the word "intimate" in conversation. "Don't you have a mother?" I asked.

Theresa sighed a weary sigh, suffered my strange inquiry. "Don't be so naïve," she said. "Everyone has a mother." She waved her hand to indicate the brick school buildings outside the window. "A higher education should have taught you that." Theresa draped an angora sweater over her shoulders, scooped her books from the graffiti-covered desk, and just as she was about to walk away, she turned and asked me, "Are you a fag?"

There wasn't the slightest hint of rancor or condescension in her voice.   5
The tone was direct, casual. Still I was stunned, giving a sidelong glance to make sure no one had heard. "No," I said. Blurted really, with too much defensiveness, too much transparent fear in my response. Octaves lower than usual, I tried a "Why?"

Theresa shrugged. "Oh, I don't know. I have lots of friends who are fags. You remind me of them." Seeing me bristle, Theresa added, "It was just a guess." I watched her erect, angora back as she sauntered out the classroom door.

She had made an incisive and timely guess. Only days before, I'd invited Grady Rogers to my house after school to go swimming. The instant Grady shot from the pool, shaking water from his orange hair, freckled shoulders shining, my attraction to members of my own sex became a matter I could no longer suppress or rationalize. Sturdy and boisterous and gap-toothed, Grady was an inveterate backslapper, a formidable arm wrestler, a wizard at basketball. Grady was a boy at home in his body.

My body was a marvel I hadn't gotten used to; my arms and legs would sometimes act of their own accord, knocking over a glass at dinner or flinching at an oncoming pitch. I was never singled out as a sissy, but I could have been just as easily as Bobby Keagan, a gentle, intelligent, and introverted boy reviled by my classmates. And although I had always been aware of a tacit rapport with Bobby, a suspicion that I might find with him a rich friendship, I stayed away. Instead, I emulated Grady in the belief that being seen with him, being like him, would somehow vanquish my self-doubt, would make me normal by association.

Apart from his athletic prowess, Grady had been gifted with all the trappings of what I imagined to be a charmed life: a fastidious, aproned mother who radiated calm, maternal concern; a ruddy, stoic father with a knack for home repairs. Even the Rogerses' small suburban house in Hollywood, with its spindly Colonial furniture and chintz curtains, was a testament to normalcy.

Grady and his family bore little resemblance to my clan of Eastern Euro-   10
pean Jews, a dark and vociferous people who ate with abandon—matzo and halvah and gefilte fish; foods the goyim couldn't pronounce—who cajoled one another during endless games of canasta, making the simplest remark about the weather into a lengthy philosophical discourse on the sun and the seasons and the passage of time. My mother was a chain-smoker, a dervish in a frowsy housedress. She showed her love in the most peculiar and obsessive ways, like spending hours extracting every seed from a watermelon before she served it in perfectly bite-sized, geometric pieces. Preoccupied and perpetually frantic, my mother succumbed to bouts of absentmindedness so profound she'd forget what she was saying midsentence, smile and blush and walk away. A divorce attorney, my father wore roomy, iridescent suits, and the intricacies, the deceits inherent in his profession, had the effect of making him forever tense and vigilant. He was "all wound up," as my mother put it. But when he relaxed, his laughter was explosive, his disposition prankish: "Walk this way," a waitress would say, leading us to our table, and my father would mimic the way she walked, arms akimbo, hips liquid, while my mother and I were wracked with laughter. Buoyant or brooding, my parents' moods were unpredictable, and in a household fraught with extravagant emotion it was odd and awful to keep my longing secret.

One day I made the mistake of asking my mother what a "fag" was. I knew exactly what Theresa had meant but hoped against hope it was not what I thought; maybe "fag" was some French word, a harmless term like "naïve." My mother turned from the stove, flew at me, and grabbed me by the shoulders. "Did someone call you that?" she cried.

"Not me," I said. "Bobby Keagan."

"Oh," she said, loosening her grip. She was visibly relieved. And didn't answer. The answer was unthinkable.

For weeks after, I shook with the reverberations from that afternoon in the kitchen with my mother, pained by the memory of her shocked expression and, most of all, her silence. My longing was wrong in the eyes of my mother, whose hazel eyes were the eyes of the world, and if that longing continued unchecked, the unwieldy shape of my fate would be cast, and I'd be subjected to a lifetime of scorn.

During the remainder of the semester, I became the scientist of my own   15
desire, plotting ways to change my yearning for boys into a yearning for girls. I had enough evidence to believe that any habit, regardless of how compulsive, how deeply ingrained, could be broken once and for all: The plastic

cigarette my mother purchased at the Thrifty pharmacy — one end was red to approximate an ember, the other tan like a filtered tip — was designed to wean her from the real thing. To change a behavior required self-analysis, cold resolve, and the substitution of one thing for another: plastic, say, for tobacco. Could I also find a substitute for Grady? What I needed to do, I figured, was kiss a girl and learn to like it.

This conclusion was affirmed one Sunday morning when my father, seeing me wrinkle my nose at the pink slabs of lox he layered on a bagel, tried to convince me of its salty appeal. "You should try some," he said. "You don't know what you're missing."

"It's loaded with protein," added my mother, slapping a platter of sliced onions onto the dinette table. She hovered above us, cinching her housedress, eyes wet from onion fumes, the mock cigarette dangling from her lips.

My father sat there chomping with gusto, emitting a couple of hearty grunts to dramatize his satisfaction. And still I was not convinced. After a loud and labored swallow, he told me I may not be fond of lox today, but sooner or later I'd learn to like it. One's tastes, he assured me, are destined to change.

"Live," shouted my mother over the rumble of the Mixmaster. "Expand your horizons. Try new things." And the room grew fragrant with the batter of a spice cake.

The opportunity to put their advice into practice, and try out my plan to 　20 adapt to girls, came the following week when Debbie Coburn, a member of Mr. Hubbley's algebra class, invited me to a party. She cornered me in the hall, furtive as a spy, telling me her parents would be gone for the evening and slipping into my palm a wrinkled sheet of notebook paper. On it were her address and telephone number, the lavender ink in a tidy cursive. "Wear cologne," she advised, wary eyes darting back and forth. "It's a make-out party. Anything can happen."

The Santa Ana wind blew relentlessly the night of Debbie's party, careening down the slopes of the Hollywood hills, shaking the road signs and stoplights in its path. As I walked down Beachwood Avenue, trees thrashed, surrendered their leaves, and carob pods bombarded the pavement. The sky was a deep but luminous blue, the air hot, abrasive, electric. I had to squint in order to check the number of the Coburns' apartment, a three-story building with glitter embedded in its stucco walls. Above the honeycombed balconies was a sign that read BEACHWOOD TERRACE in lavender script resembling Debbie's.

From down the hall, I could hear the plaintive strains of Little Anthony's "I Think I'm Going Out of My Head." Debbie answered the door bedecked in an Empire dress, the bodice blue and orange polka dots, the rest a sheath of black and white stripes. "Op art," proclaimed Debbie. She turned in a circle, then proudly announced that she'd rolled her hair in orange juice cans. She patted the huge unmoving curls and dragged me inside. Reflections from the swimming pool in the courtyard, its surface ruffled by wind, shuddered over the ceiling and walls. A dozen of my classmates were seated

on the sofa or huddled together in corners, their whispers full of excited immi-
nence, their bodies barely discernible in the dim light. Drapes flanking the
sliding glass doors bowed out with every gust of wind, and it seemed that the
room might lurch from its foundations and sail with its cargo of silhouettes
into the hot October night.

Grady was the last to arrive. He tossed a six-pack of beer into Debbie's
arms, barreled toward me, and slapped my back. His hair was slicked back
with Vitalis, lacquered furrows left by the comb. The wind hadn't shifted a
single hair. "Ya ready?" he asked, flashing the gap between his front teeth
and leering into the darkened room. "You bet," I lied.

Once the beers had been passed around, Debbie provoked everyone's
attention by flicking on the overhead light. "Okay," she called. "Find a
partner." This was the blunt command of a hostess determined to have her
guests aroused in an orderly fashion. Everyone blinked, shuffled about, and
grabbed a member of the opposite sex. Sheila Garabedian landed beside
me — entirely at random, though I wanted to believe she was driven by
passion — her timid smile giving way to plain fear as the light went out.
Nothing for a moment but the heave of the wind and the distant banter of
dogs. I caught a whiff of Sheila's perfume, tangy and sweet as Hawaiian
Punch. I probed her face with my own, grazing the small scallop of an ear,
a velvety temple, and though Sheila's trembling made me want to stop, I
persisted with my mission until I found her lips, tightly sealed as a private
letter. I held my mouth over hers and gathered her shoulders closer, resigned
to the possibility that, no matter how long we stood there, Sheila would be
too scared to kiss me back. Still, she exhaled through her nose, and I listened to the squeak of every breath as though it were a sigh of inordinate
pleasure. Diving within myself, I monitored my heartbeat and respiration,
trying to will stimulation into being, and all the while an image intruded, an
image of Grady erupting from our pool, rivulets of water sliding down his
chest. "Change," shouted Debbie, switching on the light. Sheila thanked
me, pulled away, and continued her routine of gracious terror with every boy
throughout the evening. It didn't matter whom I held — Margaret Sims, Betty
Vernon, Elizabeth Lee — my experiment was a failure; I continued to picture
Grady's wet chest, and Debbie would bellow "change" with such fervor, it
could have been my own voice, my own incessant reprimand.

Our hostess commandeered the light switch for nearly half an hour.   25
Whenever the light came on, I watched Grady pivot his head toward the
newest prospect, his eyebrows arched in expectation, his neck blooming
with hickeys, his hair, at last, in disarray. All that shuffling across the carpet
charged everyone's arms and lips with static, and eventually, between low
moans and soft osculations, I could hear the clack of tiny sparks and see
them flare here and there in the dark like meager, short-lived stars.

I saw Theresa, sultry and aloof as ever, read three more books — *North
American Reptiles, Bonjour Tristesse,* and *MGM: A Pictorial History* — before
she vanished early in December. Rumors of her fate abounded. Debbie

Coburn swore that Theresa had been "knocked up" by an older man, a traffic cop, she thought, or a grocer. Nearly quivering with relish, Debbie told me and Grady about the home for unwed mothers in the San Fernando Valley, a compound teeming with pregnant girls who had nothing to do but touch their stomachs and contemplate their mistake. Even Bobby Keagan, who took Theresa's place behind me in algebra, had a theory regarding her disappearance colored by his own wish for escape; he imagined that Theresa, disillusioned with society, booked passage to a tropical island, there to live out the rest of her days without restrictions or ridicule. "No wonder she flunked out of school," I overheard Mr. Hubbley tell a fellow teacher one afternoon. "Her head was always in a book."

Along with Theresa went my secret, or at least the dread that she might divulge it, and I felt, for a while, exempt from suspicion. I was, however, to run across Theresa one last time. It happened during a period of torrential rain that, according to reports on the six o'clock news, washed houses from the hillsides and flooded the downtown streets. The halls of Joseph Le Conte Junior High were festooned with Christmas decorations: crepe-paper garlands, wreaths studded with plastic berries, and one requisite Star of David twirling above the attendance desk. In Arts and Crafts, our teacher, Gerald (he was the only teacher who allowed us—*required* us—to call him by his first name), handed out blocks of balsa wood and instructed us to carve them into bugs. We would paint eyes and antennae with tempera and hang them on a Christmas tree he'd made the previous night. "Voilà," he crooned, unveiling his creation from a burlap sack. Before us sat a tortured scrub, a wardrobe-worth of wire hangers that were bent like branches and soldered together. Gerald credited his inspiration to a Charles Addams cartoon he's seen in which Morticia, grimly preparing for the holidays, hangs vampire bats on a withered pine. "All that red and green," said Gerald. "So predictable. *So boring.*"

As I chiseled a beetle and listened to rain pummel the earth, Gerald handed me an envelope and asked me to take it to Mr. Kendrick, the drama teacher. I would have thought nothing of his request if I hadn't seen Theresa on my way down the hall. She was cleaning out her locker, blithely dropping the sum of its contents—pens and textbooks and mimeographs—into a trash can. "Have a nice life," she sang as I passed. I mustered the courage to ask her what had happened. We stood alone in the silent hall, the reflections of wreaths and garlands submerged in brown linoleum.

"I transferred to another school. They don't have grades or bells, and you get to study whatever you want." Theresa was quick to sense my incredulity. "Honest," she said. "The school is progressive." She gazed into a glass cabinet that held the trophies of track meets and intramural spelling bees. "God," she sighed, "this place is so . . . barbaric." I was still trying to decide whether or not to believe her story when she asked me where I was headed. "Dear," she said, her exclamation pooling in the silence, "that's no ordinary note, if you catch my drift." The envelope was blank and white; I looked up at Theresa, baffled. "Don't be so naïve," she muttered, tossing an empty bottle of nail polish into the trash can. It struck bottom with a resolute thud. "Well," she said, closing her locker and breathing deeply, "bon voyage." Theresa swept through the double doors and in seconds her figure was obscured by rain.

As I walked toward Mr. Kendrick's room, I could feel Theresa's insinu-   30
ation burrow in. I stood for a moment and watched Mr. Kendrick through the pane in the door. He paced intently in front of the class, handsome in his shirt and tie, reading from a thick book. Chalked on the blackboard behind him was THE ODYSSEY BY HOMER. I have no recollection of how Mr. Kendrick reacted to the note, whether he accepted it with pleasure or embarrassment, slipped it into his desk drawer or the pocket of his shirt. I have scavenged that day in retrospect, trying to see Mr. Kendrick's expression, wondering if he acknowledged me in any way as his liaison. All I recall is the sight of his mime through a pane of glass, a lone man mouthing an epic, his gestures ardent in empty air.

Had I delivered a declaration of love? I was haunted by the need to know. In fantasy, a kettle shot steam, the glue released its grip, and I read the letter with impunity. But how would such a letter begin? Did the common endearments apply? This was a message between two men, a message for which I had no precedent, and when I tried to envision the contents, apart from a hasty, impassioned scrawl, my imagination faltered.

Once or twice I witnessed Gerald and Mr. Kendrick walk together into the faculty lounge or say hello at the water fountain, but there was nothing especially clandestine or flirtatious in their manner. Besides, no matter how acute my scrutiny, I wasn't sure, short of a kiss, exactly what to look for—what semaphore of gesture, what encoded word. I suspected there were signs, covert signs that would give them away, just as I'd unwittingly given myself away to Theresa.

In the school library, a *Webster's* unabridged dictionary lay on a wooden podium, and I padded toward it with apprehension; along with clues to the bond between my teachers, I risked discovering information that might incriminate me as well. I had decided to consult the dictionary during lunch period, when most of the students would be on the playground. I clutched my notebook, moving in such a way as to appear both studious and nonchalant, actually believing that, unless I took precautions, someone would see me and guess what I was up to. The closer I came to the podium, the more obvious, I thought, was my endeavor; I felt like the model of The Visible Man in our science class, my heart's undulations, my overwrought nerves legible through transparent skin. A couple of kids riffled through the card catalogue. The librarian, a skinny woman whose perpetual whisper and rubber-soled shoes caused her to drift through the room like a phantom, didn't seem to register my presence. Though I'd looked up dozens of words before, the pages felt strange beneath my fingers. *Homer* was the first word I saw. *Hominid. Homogenize.* I feigned interest and skirted other words before I found the word I was after. Under the heading HO·MO·SEX·U·AL was the terse definition: *adj. Pertaining to, characteristic of, or exhibiting homosexuality.—n. A homosexual person.* I read the definition again and again, hoping the words would yield more than they could. I shut the dictionary, swallowed hard, and, none the wiser, hurried away.

As for Gerald and Mr. Kendrick, I never discovered evidence to prove or dispute Theresa's claim. By the following summer, however, I had overheard from my peers a confounding amount about homosexuals: They wore green on Thursday, couldn't whistle, hypnotized boys with a piercing glance. To this lore, Grady added a surefire test to ferret them out.

"A test?" I said.

"You ask a guy to look at his fingernails, and if he looks at them like this"—Grady closed his fingers into a fist and examined his nails with manly detachment—"then he's okay. But if he does this"—he held out his hands at arm's length, splayed his fingers, and coyly cocked his head—"you'd better watch out." Once he'd completed his demonstration, Grady peeled off his shirt and plunged into our pool. I dove in after. It was early June, the sky immense, glassy, placid. My father was cooking spareribs on the barbecue, an artist with a basting brush. His apron bore the caricature of a frazzled French chef. Mother curled on a chaise lounge, plumes of smoke wafting from her nostrils. In a stupor of contentment she took another drag, closed her eyes, and arched her face toward the sun.

Grady dog-paddled through the deep end, spouting a fountain of chlorinated water. Despite shame and confusion, my longing for him hadn't diminished; it continued to thrive without air and light, like a luminous fish in the dregs of the sea. In the name of play, I swam up behind him, encircled his shoulders, astonished by his taut flesh. The two of us flailed, pretended to drown. Beneath the heavy press of water, Grady's orange hair wavered, a flame that couldn't be doused.

I've lived with a man for seven years. Some nights, when I'm half-asleep and the room is suffused with blue light, I reach out to touch the expanse of his back, and it seems as if my fingers sink into his skin, and I feel the pleasure a diver feels the instant he enters a body of water.

I have few regrets. But one is that I hadn't said to Theresa, "Of course I'm a fag." Maybe I'd have met her friends. Or become friends with her. Imagine the meals we might have concocted: hamburger Stroganoff, Swedish meatballs in a sweet translucent sauce, steaming slabs of Salisbury steak.

The Reader's Presence

1. Cooper's first stirrings of attraction for his friend Grady occur in a swimming pool. What importance does swimming play in Cooper's essay? How does it provide him with a cluster of images for sexual experience?

2. Why does Cooper attend the "make-out party" (paragraph 20)? What does he hope will happen? Why do you think he ends his description of the party with the observation of the "clack of tiny sparks" (paragraph 25)? Why do you think he used that image for his title?

3. **CONNECTIONS:**   In paragraph 15, Cooper writes that he became "the scientist of [his] own desire," as he tried to understand—and to resist—his "yearning for boys." In what ways does Cooper's process of self-discovery resemble that of Dorothy Allison in "A Question of Class" (page 37)? What differences do you find in the authors' processes of self-discovery? Children often turn to dictionaries to solve mysteries they are too shy to ask people about. How does Cooper's discovery of the definition of "homosexual" compare to Frederick Douglass's attempt to discover the meaning of "abolition" in the following essay, "Learning to Read and Write"?

Frederick Douglass

LEARNING TO READ AND WRITE

Born into slavery, **FREDERICK DOUGLASS** (1817?–1895) was taken from his mother as an infant and denied any knowledge of his father's identity. He escaped to the north at the age of twenty-one and created a new identity for himself as a free man. He educated himself and went on to become one of the most eloquent orators and persuasive writers of the nineteenth century. He was a national leader in the abolition movement and, among other activities, founded and edited the *North Star* and *Douglass' Monthly*. His public service included appointments as U.S. marshal and consul general to the Republic of Haiti. His most lasting literary accomplishment was his memoirs, which he revised several times before they were published as *The Life and Times of Frederick Douglass* (1881 and 1892). "Learning to Read and Write" is taken from these memoirs.

> **Born into slavery, Frederick Douglass was taken from his mother as an infant and denied any knowledge of his father's identity.**

Douglass overcame his initial reluctance to write his memoirs because, as he put it, "not only is slavery on trial, but unfortunately, the enslaved people are also on trial. It is alleged that they are, naturally, inferior; that they are so low in the scale of humanity, and so utterly stupid, that they are unconscious of their wrongs, and do not apprehend their rights." Therefore, wishing to put his talents to work "to the benefit of my afflicted people," Douglass agreed to write the story of his life.

I LIVED IN MASTER HUGH'S FAMILY about seven years. During this time, I succeeded in learning to read and write. In accomplishing this, I was compelled to resort to various stratagems. I had no regular teacher. My mistress, who had kindly commenced to instruct me, had, in compliance with the advice and direction of her husband, not only ceased to instruct, but had set her face against my being instructed by anyone else. It is due, however, to my mistress to say of her, that she did not adopt this course of treatment immediately. She at first lacked the depravity indispensable to shutting me up in mental darkness. It was at least necessary for her to have some training in the exercise of irresponsible power, to make her equal to the task of treating me as though I were a brute.

My mistress was, as I have said, a kind and tender-hearted woman; and in the simplicity of her soul she commenced, when I first went to live with her, to treat me as she supposed one human being ought to treat another. In entering upon the duties of a slaveholder, she did not seem to perceive that I sustained to her the relation of a mere chattel, and that for her to treat me as a human being was not only wrong, but dangerously so. Slavery proved as injurious to her as it did to me. When I went there, she was a pious, warm, and tender-hearted woman. There was no sorrow or suffering for which she had not a tear. She had bread for the hungry, clothes for the naked, and comfort for every mourner that came within her reach. Slavery soon proved its ability to divest her of these heavenly qualities. Under its influence, the tender heart became stone, and the lamb-like disposition gave way to one of tiger-like fierceness. The first step in her downward course was in her ceasing to instruct me. She now commenced to practice her husband's precepts. She finally became even more violent in her opposition than her husband himself. She was not satisfied with simply doing as well as he had commanded; she seemed anxious to do better. Nothing seemed to make her more angry than to see me with a newspaper. She seemed to think that here lay the danger. I have had her rush at me with a face made all up of fury, and snatch from me a newspaper, in a manner that fully revealed her apprehension. She was an apt woman; and a little experience soon demonstrated, to her satisfaction, that education and slavery were incompatible with each other.

From this time I was most narrowly watched. If I was in a separate room any considerable length of time, I was sure to be suspected of having a book, and was at once called to give an account of myself. All this, however, was too late. The first step had been taken. Mistress, in teaching me the alphabet, had given me the *inch*, and no precaution could prevent me from taking the *ell*.

The plan which I adopted, and the one by which I was most successful, was that of making friends of all the little white boys whom I met in the street. As many of these as I could, I converted into teachers. With their kindly aid, obtained at different times and in different places, I finally succeeded in learning to read. When I was sent to errands, I always took my book with me, and by doing one part of my errand quickly, I found time to get a lesson before my return. I used also to carry bread with me, enough of which was always in the house, and to which I was always welcome; for I was much better off in this regard than many of the poor white children in our neighborhood. This bread I used to bestow upon the hungry little urchins, who, in return, would give me that more valuable bread of knowledge. I am strongly tempted to give the names of two or three of those little boys, as a testimonial of the gratitude and affection I bear them; but prudence forbids — not that it would injure me, but it might embarrass them; for it is almost an unpardonable offense to teach slaves to read in this Christian country. It is enough to say of the dear little fellows, that they lived on Philpot Street, very near Durgin and Bailey's ship-yard. I used to talk this matter of slavery over with them. I would sometimes say to them, I wished I could be as free as they would be when they got to be men. "You will be free as soon as you are twenty-one, *but I am a slave for life!* Have not I as good a right to be free as you have?" These words used to trouble them; they would express for me the liveliest sympathy, and console me with the hope that something would occur by which I might be free.

I was now about twelve years old, and the thought of being *a slave for*   5
life began to bear heavily upon my heart. Just about this time, I got hold of a book entitled *The Columbian Orator.* Every opportunity I got, I used to read this book. Among much of other interesting matter, I found in it a dialogue between a master and his slave. The slave was represented as having run away from his master three times. The dialogue represented the conversation which took place between them, when the slave was retaken the third time. In this dialogue, the whole argument in behalf of slavery was brought forward by the master, all of which was disposed of by the slave. The slave was made to say some very smart as well as impressive things in reply to his master — things which had the desired though unexpected effect; for the conversation resulted in the voluntary emancipation of the slave on the part of the master.

In the same book, I met with one of Sheridan's[1] mighty speeches on and in behalf of Catholic emancipation. These were choice documents to me. I read them over and over again with unabated interest. They gave tongue to interesting thoughts of my own soul, which had frequently flashed through my mind, and died away for want of utterance. The moral which I gained from the dialogue was the power of truth over the conscience of even a slaveholder. What I got from Sheridan was a bold denunciation of slavery, and a powerful vindication of human rights. The reading of these documents enabled me to utter my thoughts, and to meet the arguments brought forward to sustain slavery; but while they relieved me of one difficulty, they brought on another even more painful than the one of which I was relieved. The more I read, the more I was led to abhor and detest my enslavers. I could regard them in no other light than a band of successful robbers, who had left their homes, and gone to Africa, and stolen us from our homes, and

---

1 *Sheridan's:* Richard Brinsley Butler Sheridan (1751–1816), Irish dramatist and orator. — EDS.

1855 advertisement to capture a runaway slave.

in a strange land reduced us to slavery. I loathed them as being the meanest as well as the most wicked of men. As I read and contemplated the subject, behold! that very discontentment which Master Hugh had predicted would follow my learning to read had already come, to torment and sting my soul to unutterable anguish. As I writhed under it, I would at times feel that learning to read had been a curse rather than a blessing. It had given me a view of my wretched condition, without the remedy. It opened my eyes to the horrible pit, but to no ladder upon which to get out. In moments of agony, I envied my fellow-slaves for their stupidity. I have often wished myself a beast. I preferred the condition of the meanest reptile to my own. Anything, no matter what, to get rid of thinking! It was this everlasting thinking of my condition that tormented me. There was no getting rid of it. It was pressed upon me by every object within sight or hearing, animate or inanimate. The silver trump of freedom had roused my soul to eternal wakefulness. Freedom now appeared, to disappear no more forever. It was heard in every sound, and seen in every thing. It was ever present to torment me with a sense of my wretched condition. I saw nothing without seeing it, I heard nothing without hearing it, and felt nothing without feeling it. It looked from every star, it smiled in every calm, breathed in every wind, and moved in every storm.

I often found myself regretting my own existence, and wishing myself dead; and but for the hope of being free, I have no doubt but that I should have killed myself, or done something for which I should have been killed. While in this state of mind, I was eager to hear anyone speak of slavery. I was a ready listener. Every little while, I could hear something about the abolitionists. It was some time before I found what the word meant. It was always used in such connections as to make it an interesting word to me. If a slave ran away and succeeded in getting clear, or if a slave killed his master, set fire to a barn, or did anything very wrong in the mind of a slaveholder, it was spoken of as the fruit of *abolition*. Hearing the word in this connection very often, I set about learning what it meant. The dictionary afforded me little or no help. I found it was "the act of abolishing"; but then I did not know what was to be abolished. Here I was perplexed. I did not dare to ask anyone about its meaning, for I was satisfied that it was something they wanted me to know very little about. After a patient waiting, I got one of our city papers, containing an account of the number of petitions from the North, praying for the abolition of slavery in the District of Columbia, and of the slave trade between the States. From this time I understood the words *abolition* and *abolitionist*, and always drew near when that word was spoken, expecting to hear something of importance to myself and fellow-slaves. The light broke in upon me by degrees. I went one day down on the wharf of Mr. Waters; and seeing two Irishmen unloading a scow of stone, I went, unasked, and helped them. When we had finished, one of them came to me and asked me if I were a slave. I told him I was. He asked, "Are ye a slave for life?" I told him that I was. The good Irishman seemed to be deeply affected by the statement. He said to the other that it was a pity so fine a little fellow as myself should be a slave for life. He said it was a shame to hold me. They both advised me to run away to the North; that I should find friends there, and that I should be free. I pretended not to be interested in what they said, and treated them as if I did not understand them; for I feared they might be treacherous. White men have been known to encourage slaves to escape, and then, to get the reward, catch them and return them to their masters. I was afraid that these seemingly good men might use me so; but I nevertheless remembered their advice, and from that time I resolved to run away. I looked forward to a time at which it would be safe for me to escape. I was too young to think of doing so immediately; besides, I wished to learn how to write, as I might have occasion to write my own pass. I consoled myself with the hope that I should one day find a good chance. Meanwhile, I would learn to write.

The idea as to how I might learn to write was suggested to me by being in Durgin and Bailey's shipyard, and frequently seeing the ship carpenters, after hewing, and getting a piece of timber ready for use, write on the timber the name of that part of the ship for which it was intended. When a piece of timber was intended for the larboard side, it would be marked thus — "L."

When a piece was for the starboard side, it would be marked thus — "S." A piece for the larboard side forward, would be marked thus — "L.F." When a piece was for starboard side forward, it would be marked thus — "S.F." For larboard aft, it would be marked thus — "L.A." For starboard aft, it would be marked thus — "S.A." I soon learned the names of these letters, and for what they were intended when placed upon a piece of timber in the shipyard. I immediately commenced copying them, and in a short time was able to make the four letters named. After that, when I met with any boy who I knew could write, I would tell him I could write as well as he. The next word would be, "I don't believe you. Let me see you try it." I would then make the letters which I had been so fortunate as to learn, and ask him to beat that. In this way I got a good many lessons in writing, which it is quite possible I should never have gotten in any other way. During this time, my copy-book was the board fence, brick wall, and pavement; my pen and ink was a lump of chalk. With these, I learned mainly how to write. I then commenced and continued copying the Italics in *Webster's Spelling Book*, until I could make them all without looking in the book. By this time, my little Master Thomas had gone to school, and learned how to write, and had written over a number of copy-books. These had been brought home, and shown to some of our near neighbors, and then laid aside. My mistress used to go to class meeting at the Wilk Street meeting-house every Monday afternoon, and leave me to take care of the house. When left thus, I used to spend the time in writing in the spaces left in Master Thomas's copy-book, copying what he had written. I continued to do this until I could write a hand very similar to that of Master Thomas. Thus, after a long, tedious effort for years, I finally succeeded in learning how to write.

The Reader's Presence

1. What sort of audience does Douglass anticipate for his reminiscence? How much does he assume his readers know about the conditions of slavery?

2. What books seem to matter most to Douglass? Why? What are his motives for wanting to read and write? For Douglass, what is the relationship between literacy and freedom? How does he move from curiosity to anguish to "eternal wakefulness" in paragraph 6? What is the relationship between learning to read and learning to write?

3. **VISUAL PRESENCE:** Examine the nineteenth-century advertisement designed to capture a runaway slave (page 109). In what specific ways does the language of this advertisement reflect the slave owner's attitude toward the slave? How does this language correspond to Douglass's description of his life as a slave? Support your answer with specific examples.

4. **CONNECTIONS:** Read Azar Nafisi's excerpt from "Reading Lolita in Tehran" (page 499) and consider Nafisi's students' challenges in obtaining an education. What obstacles do the girls overcome to join Nafisi's class? How do the difficulties Douglass faced in getting an education compare with those of Nafisi's students?

Andre Dubus III

THE LAND OF NO: LOVE IN A CLASS-RIVEN AMERICA

ANDRE DUBUS III (b. 1959) is the author of several novels, most famously *House of Sand and Fog* (1999), which became the basis for a critically acclaimed film of the same name. In addition to his novels, Dubus has written a collection of short stories, *The Cage Keeper: And Other Stories* (1989) and a memoir, *Townie* (2011), describing his youth and early adulthood, as well as his relationship with his father, Andre Dubus, who was a highly regarded writer. Andre Dubus III grew up, for the most part, in rough, economically depressed mill towns in the Merrimack Valley of Massachusetts. As a youth, he was a street fighter; later, a boxer. He eventually renounced violence and began writing fiction at age twenty-two, shortly after graduating from the University of Texas at Austin, where he had earned a bachelor's degree in sociology. He has worked as a carpenter, a bartender, an office cleaner, a halfway-house counselor, and even, for six months, an assistant to a private investigator and bounty hunter. He has taught writing at Harvard University, Tufts University, Emerson College, and the University of Massachusetts Lowell, where he is currently a full-time faculty member. He also has been awarded a Guggenheim Fellowship, the National Magazine Award for fiction, and the Pushcart Prize, and he was a finalist for the Rome Prize Fellowship from the Academy of Arts and Letters.

> "Most of the time I feel stupid, insensitive, mediocre, talentless and vulnerable . . . and wrong. I've found that when that happens, it usually means I'm writing pretty well."

The range of Dubus's experiences—his journey from a difficult childhood through a variety of professions, leading eventually to a successful career as a writer, teacher, and speaker—may be responsible for giving him a unique insight into many different walks of life, insight that not only fuels his fiction but also allows for the sort of understanding that made "The Land of No: Love in Class-riven America," originally published in the *New Republic*, possible. Demonstrating a remarkable awareness of class distinctions in America, Dubus observes the chasm between rich and poor without passing judgment on the people who stand on either side. His writing process is informed by a similar humility. He has said that "[m]ost of the time I feel stupid, insensitive, mediocre, talentless and vulnerable . . . and wrong. I've found that when that happens, it usually means I'm writing pretty well." His latest book, *Dirty Love*, is a series of interconnected novellas, published in 2013.

EMILY WAS 23 YEARS OLD and had a $2 million trust fund. She also had a warm smile, spoke kindly to everyone she met, and was tall and blonde and beautiful with the erect posture of the skier and gymnast she'd once been. We lived together in Manhattan in a tiny first-floor apartment. Six shifts a week, I tended bar at a chophouse down in the garment district.

Emily (not her real name) didn't have to work, but, while she was looking for an internship at a TV studio, she found a job in a bookstore. She said she was grateful for her inherited wealth but did not earn it so would not use it. Sometimes, though, she'd dip into it to buy me things she thought I needed: a new leather jacket, hand-stitched cowboy boots, a wool sweater from Ireland. I was grateful for these things but felt undeserving. I'd never been around anyone with money before—someone who could just buy whatever she wanted whenever she wanted it.

This was in the 1980s, a decade when there were 5,000 homeless families in New York City, and what seemed like a millionaire on every block. The homeless would be huddled in the concrete corner of a subway station, or curled up under dirty blankets on a grate outside a hotel or apartment building, the smaller children tucked between a mother or father and the granite wall. I found myself giving a lot of my tips to them, more than I could afford, though in some shadowed sliver of my psyche I knew I had Emily and what was given to her: a soft, deep place to fall, something my family had never known.

It was the summer of 1970, I was eleven years old, and in our small, rented house there was no escape. They got under your clothes, under your shirt and pants and underwear, an itch you could never quite reach—between your shoulder blades, up your neck, behind your knees, and in your hair. If you took a shower and stood wet and naked in front of a window fan it helped, but only until you were dry again. Then they seemed to rise up out of your own skin: fleas, gnats, bedbugs, lice—whatever they were exactly we didn't know, only that we were besieged by them, and no matter how many times our mother called the landlord, he never sent anyone to fix the problem.

We were living in northern Massachusetts then, in an old ship-building   5 town on the Merrimack River three miles from the Atlantic. Its downtown was an abandoned cluster of mill buildings with no glass in their windows; the sidewalks buckled and were littered with trash. Dry weeds sprouted in cracks down the center of the asphalt streets, and the only working businesses were a diner, a newsstand, and a barroom, its dim interior filled with the shadows of men and women drinking.

But it was a place of cheap rents, and it was the first town to which our young mother moved her four kids after the divorce from our father. Twenty-eight years old, she got jobs as a nurse's aide and a waitress, then earned her way through school till she was out and working in social services, helping poor families like us.

We moved often, one year three times, always for a cheaper rent. We kids spent too much time watching television, roaming the streets, getting high on stoops waiting for the school bus. Children got pregnant at 14, boys went off to reform school and later prison, my best friend to an early grave, his own knife stuck into his liver by the girlfriend he'd tormented far too long.

As predictably as leaves dropping from their branches in the fall, the landlord would be at our door asking for the rent check our mother just did not have, and we'd be moving again, loading up a U-Haul truck with what little we owned, our clothes tossed into plastic trash bags, my mother's boyfriend driving the truck while the rest of us piled into whatever Mom drove at the time — usually Japanese cars that still lived after 200,000 miles and once a '67 Cadillac that ran on only three of its eight cylinders. Our mother called it "the pig."

Some summers, we escaped all this by heading 2,000 miles south to Louisiana, where our maternal grandparents lived. We never owned a car that could make that trip so the five of us would take a bus into Boston, to a squat concrete building behind chain-link and barbed wire, its oil-spotted yard crowded with new-looking cars. Our mother would sign some papers, then we'd be climbing into a VW van, or a four-door Buick, or once a black Trans-Am with leather seats, air-conditioning, and an 8-track player with quadraphonic sound. These were repo cars, and our mother would be paid to drive them to New Orleans. It gave her enough money for gas and two rooms at a motel with a pool, then five Greyhound tickets from New Orleans to Fishville, Louisiana.

Swimming in a Holiday Inn pool somewhere south of Knoxville, I could   10
see the last of the sun glinting off our black Trans Am in the parking lot, and I knew that after we'd all cooled off there'd be enough money for burgers and Cokes, and later we'd all be lying on our hotel beds watching a color television in air-conditioned rooms. *This is what it's like to be rich*, I remember thinking. *This must be it.*

One night, crossing Third Avenue for the bar on the corner, Emily and I were talking about an old friend of mine, a woman who'd gotten pregnant in high school, dropped out, then had two more kids with the same man — someone who beat her up regularly, who had knocked out some of her teeth and put her in the hospital. After years of this, she left him, went back to school, and became a registered nurse. Emily had met her once. She liked and admired her. As we crossed Third Avenue she said, "You know the first thing I'd do if I were her?"

"What?"

"I'd get my teeth fixed."

Weeks before this, she and I had spent the night at her family's home. It was one of five they owned; her parents were away that weekend at their ranch in the Southwest. I'd never been in a house like this. It had rooms off of rooms, and in each of them were deep sofas and chairs, woven carpet over polished hard-wood floors, tasteful paintings on the walls. She asked if I was hungry, and she opened the fridge and it was stuffed with food—cold cuts and cheeses, fresh vegetables and fruit and imported condiments, milk and orange juice and European beer. Emily was the youngest of five, all of them grown and out of the house. How was it possible for a refrigerator to hold so much? Especially in a home of only two?

She was surprised at my surprise. I tried to tell her how little my mother 15 had been able to give us, how one night a friend came over with a case of beer and I just opened the fridge, and he put it on one of three empty shelves beside a jar of mustard. She looked at me as if I were exaggerating. How could I tell her how differently we'd been raised? In the circular driveway in front of her house were five Porsches her father had shipped over from England to sell here for a profit, something she told me was called the "gray market." In my family, the market was where we went for food, if there was enough money to buy some.

I did not feel sorry for myself; I felt the superior pain of the inferior, the pride of the sufferer, the shame of the poor. I could also see that my dark mood was pulling her down and that she was beginning to feel guilty for something that had little to do with her. I kept quiet and felt far away from this kind young woman who seemed to love me just the way I was, this woman I judged when she was doing no such thing to me.

But now, stepping onto the sidewalk on the other side of Third Avenue, I heard myself yelling: "You don't think she'd like to have new *teeth*? Of course she would, Emily, but she doesn't have that kind of *money*, and, if she did, it would mean no oil in the burner that month, no food in the fridge. It would mean being late with the fucking rent. But you can't even think those things because you're from the Land of Yes when the rest of us are from the Land of No. We don't even *think* we can have these things you take for granted, like new fucking *teeth*."

It wasn't the first time I'd done this to her, and it wouldn't be the last. She stood there staring at me. In her eyes was hurt and a resigned sadness, then the hard light of resentment as she turned and walked down Third Avenue, lengthening her stride, getting as far away from me as fast as she could.

Two weeks later, business at the chophouse having been slow for months, I got laid off. I spent the next month walking from one restaurant to another looking for work, but there was none. Rent was past due, and I had no money in the bank.

Maybe because of our fights over her privileged life, Emily told me she 20 would not even consider dipping into her trust fund, though she did not make enough at the bookstore to support us both. I could see she was beginning to worry.

In the fourth week, I stopped looking for bartending work and got a job cleaning apartments and offices, but I earned half what I'd made serving drinks. Any day now, the landlord would stand at our door the way he'd always stood at my mother's, his hand out for the check that would not be coming. Emily and I would have to move, but where? I saw us huddled together on a grate, or curled under blankets beneath hedges in Central Park, and I remembered one night when those bugs had gotten so bad my mother and I had slept in the pig parked out in the street. It was a humid July night, my sisters and brother miraculously asleep inside. My mother took the front, and I lay in the back. The bars had closed hours ago so we weren't worried about the drunks; we opened our windows all the way. For a long while, I stared at the ripped fabric of the ceiling. I could hear the fan in my sister's window, then the even breaths of my sleeping mother. She worked so hard and always fell asleep so fast.

Now it was dusk in Manhattan, and I was walking uptown from my new cleaning job, preparing myself to tell Emily it was time for us to start packing. But, when I walked into our tiny place, she was pulling roasted chicken from the oven, her hair pulled up and back, and she kissed me and handed me a cold European beer.

"I paid our rent."

"How?"

"How do you think?" She smiled recklessly, like she was flirting with a   25
stranger and knew she probably shouldn't but would anyway. She seemed a little drunk.

"I thought you weren't going to do that."

"We're paid up for six months." She grabbed her glass of wine and moved past me and sat on the couch. She snatched up the remote and flicked on our color television.

I couldn't deny the relief I felt. Like standing naked and wet in front of that window fan, all the itching gone. And it was clear she did not want to discuss it. I sat next to her on the couch. I sipped the beer she'd paid for. I watched whatever it was she was watching. Her hand rested in her lap, and I wanted to reach over and hold it. It was only inches away, but it may as well have been in another country, another land, one we both knew we would never be living in together. ▒

The Reader's Presence

1. Dubus opens by describing Emily's affluent background and then proceeds to write about the homeless in New York. What compositional purpose and significance do you assign to beginning his essay with this dichotomy? To what extent does this beginning foreshadow the remainder of his essay?

2. Consider the interlude Dubus presents (paragraphs 4 through 10), where he recounts growing up in northern Massachusetts. What strategic purpose does this recounting of his childhood serve? Why does the narrator yell at Emily? What has she done to provoke his anger? Why does Dubus write, "I heard myself yelling" (paragraph 17)? Consider the amount of detail in the story: "a new leather jacket, hand-stitched cowboy boots, a wool sweater from Ireland" (paragraph 2). What does Dubus's invoking such detail tell us about the narrator and his identification with "the Land of No" (paragraph 17)?

3. **CONNECTIONS:** After describing his upbringing, Dubus writes, "I felt the superior pain of the inferior, the pride of the sufferer, the shame of the poor" (paragraph 16). Compare the narrator's conflicted feelings about his upbringing to those of Dorothy Allison in "A Question of Class" (page 37). To what extent—and why—are both authors susceptible to feelings of rage?

The Writer at Work

ANDRE DUBUS III on the Risks of Memoir Writing

Lawrence Lucier/FilmMagic/Getty Images

Memoir writing can be a risky business. When writers publish a memoir they often find that they have offended people from their past who may feel misrepresented, insulted, injured, and perhaps angry enough to initiate legal action. Well-known as a novelist, Andre Dubus III ventured into the dangerous territory of memoir writing when he published *Townie* in 2011. The following year, he wrote an essay about the experience, appropriately called "Writing & Publishing a Memoir: What in the Hell Have I Done?" published in *River Teeth*, Volume 14 (2013). Following is a small portion of the essay (which includes how his hometown of Haverhill, Massachusetts, responded to "The Book").

❝In my hometown of Haverhill, Massachusetts, the mill town where I grew up and the setting for *Townie*, I'm told it's referred to as "The Book." . . .

Just weeks after it was published, I was to give a reading at the Haverhill Public Library. Over five hundred people showed up. The librarian introduced me, and there was enthusiastic applause, a few raucous whoops and shouts from the rear of the room. I looked out over the crowd and took them in. Many were my age, in their late forties or early fifties. Behind aging skin and hair and a few extra pounds, I recognized a face here, the eyes of another there, people I hadn't seen in over thirty years, when we'd all attended the same high school with its undercover narcs and drug dealing, its high-achieving jock kids from across the river, the leather-wearing, pony-tailed losers like me on the mill side, the kids or grandkids of immigrants from Ireland and Italy, Greece and Puerto Rico and the Dominican Republic. And there were older men and women there, too, the parents of those of us who grew up in the shadow of the Vietnam War and Watergate and Nixon flying away from the presidency in his helicopter, an echo image of what so many of our own fathers had done, though they'd driven away in Chevys or hopped a bus or just hit the road with a thumb out.

I thanked everyone for coming, then I read a few brief passages and took some questions. Mostly, though, the audience offered comments, and mostly these were words of thanks for telling our story. "Our story." I liked hearing this and was grateful for their gratitude, but I was also confused by it. I knew what they meant, that I'd written about that in-between generation we were members of; ten years younger than the Vietnam baby boomers but ten years older than Generation X, we were kids who grew up listening to early Aerosmith on eight-tracks in Z28s, drinking Haffenreffer tall boys and smoking angel dust. We grew our hair to our waists and carried pints of Southern Comfort in our Dingo boots like Janis Joplin, but the party had moved on years ago and so we were left wearing costumes, having sex too young, drinking too much, fighting in barrooms and in the street, our broke single mothers too overwhelmed to do much about it. I knew what they were thanking me for, but still, wasn't *Townie* essentially *my* story?

Years ago I read an interview with the writer Janet Burroway, in which she says that when readers go to the novel, what we're really saying to it is this: "Give me *me*." Most of us know this to be true. If the writer goes deeply enough into her characters and their stories, then they'll go deeply enough into us too, their own natures resonating with ours, like an easterly breeze moving wind chimes on a porch we'd never even known about. But with creative nonfiction/memoir, the breeze seems to be even more direct, the wind chimes closer to the front door of the house in which we live.

"Hey, don't tell me, but I know who the Murphy brothers really are. The Pecker Street gang."

The man who said that wore a dark sweater and Dickie work pants, broken capillaries blooming across his upper cheeks. He was my age, and looked pleased with himself, and I liked him right away.

"You got it," I said.

"Andre." A woman was raising her hand from the crowded center of the room. She had short gray hair and a plump, warm-looking face, her eyes lit with a street-savvy light I wouldn't want to mess with: "Now when I want people to know about my life, I just have them read your book. But what do you think of what the mayor's saying about it?"

Just days before, the Mayor of Haverhill had written on his Facebook page that I was "embellishing details" and that Haverhill had never been the tough mill town I wrote about in *Townie*. If this were a novel, his words wouldn't have bothered me at all, but this was a memoir, and when that word is printed beneath the title of a book, the contract between its writer and the reader is this:

Dear Reader,
    Everything you read in this book happened, at least to the best of my memory, which like everyone's is seen through a deeply subjective emotional lens. Still, I have tried to be loyal to the facts as I remember them, which isn't always the truth, but it is my truth.

I was on tour when I heard about the mayor's postings. I called him and told him I was concerned, that a charge like that against a memoir could very well undermine the authority of that book. And I had not "embellished." He apologized and told me he'd only begun to read my book that morning, that he'd been reacting to published reviews and interviews which referred to 1970s Haverhill as a "depressed crime-ridden mill town."

"But Mr. Mayor, it *was*."

"Not in my neighborhood."

"Where'd you live?"

"Riverside."

"Well, I lived across from the Avenues. A much different neighborhood."

We talked a while longer. The mayor said he'd read the first hundred pages of my book, and he could see I wasn't writing so much about the town as I was about my boyhood and my family. In fact, he said, it was clear to him that I hadn't called Haverhill any of those things the newspapers were calling it, and he had to admit, there were parts of our city then, especially the bars along the river of an almost entirely boarded-up downtown, that were pretty rough.

"In fact, when I was a young lawyer, my first clients were drug dealers from near where you lived."

"Thank you."

"And my wife did remind me that I took boxing lessons to defend myself then."

"That's all I'm saying."

But the mayor, who has worked diligently to make downtown Haverhill a much more vibrant place than it was forty years ago, had every right to worry about how it was being described by the national press now. I told him I would make sure to mention things are different today. He promised to stop posting charges of embellishments on his website.

I told the woman in that library crowd that I respected the mayor, and now that he'd begun to actually read my book, he was taking back what he wrote about it.

A man standing near a window raised his hand. He looked over six feet tall and well over two hundred pounds, and he wore a black beret and a black sweater and black pants. He was my age or younger, but he was leaning on a cane. His goatee was wispy and just beginning to gray.

I called on him.

"You know your friend Cleary? Your best friend when you were kids?"

His voice was reedy and restrained, like he was trying to hold back an emotion that wasn't all good.

"Yeah? What about Cleary?"

"He was my brother."

Cleary, always clowning and stealing and drinking and getting high, the son of a hopelessly alcoholic mother and distant father, my best friend when I was thirteen, fourteen, and fifteen, stabbed to death at age twenty-five by the common-law wife he used to beat.

"Mark? Is that you?"

He nodded, and I left the podium and walked down the side aisle to Cleary's younger brother I hadn't seen in years. I hugged him and he hugged me back, and then the crowd began to clap, and I walked back to the microphone and told them just who he was.

Later, at the book-signing table, he asked me to inscribe a copy to their father. Mark told me how happy his old man was to hear that his oldest son, dead far too soon, had made it into the pages of a real book, that his son would live on now, that he wouldn't be forgotten. On the title page of the book, I wrote how much I loved and missed his son, and I wrote his son's real name and wished the father well, and signed my own.

But a week or two later, I received an email from Mark's girlfriend telling me Mark's father had read the book and that he was very, very upset. And why wouldn't he be? How could I not have thought of this earlier? I described his son as having been a wife-beater in his last days; I described how deeply alcoholic his mother had been, this woman who died of her disease not long after her oldest child had been stabbed to death; I wrote how absent he, the father, had seemed to me during those years. My God, what had I *done*?

I'd written as truly of that time as I could, that's what I'd done, but my intention never was to hurt anyone. Ever. These things rarely happen when what you write and publish is fiction.**"**

Anne Fadiman

UNDER WATER

ANNE FADIMAN (b. 1953) is an American author and teacher. Her first book, *The Spirit Catches You and You Fall Down*, an account of an epileptic Hmong child and her family living in Merced, California, won the National Book Critics' Circle Award in 1997. She was the editor of the prestigious American literary quarterly, *The American Scholar*, for seven years, and her essays have appeared in *Harper's*, the *New Yorker*, and the *New York Times*, among many other publications. She has won national magazine awards for both reporting and essays, and in 2012 she was appointed as the inaugural Francis Writer in Residence at Yale University, where she teaches in the English Department and mentors students who wish to become writers and editors. Her other books include *Ex Libris: Confessions of a Common Reader* (1998) and *At Large and At Small: Familiar Essays* (2007), an essay collection from which this selection is taken.

> **"Books wrote our life story."**

In *Ex Libris*, Anne Fadiman reflected on the role of books in her life by saying that "books wrote our life story, and as they accumulated on our shelves (and on our windowsills, and underneath our sofa, and on top of our refrigerator), they became chapters in it themselves."

I WAS AN IMPATIENT CHILD who disliked obstructions: traffic jams, clogged bathtub drains, catsup bottles you had to bang. I liked to drop twigs into the stream that ran through our backyard and watch them float downstream, coaxed around rocks and branches by the distant pull of the ocean. If they hit a snag, I freed them.

When I was eighteen, rushing through life as fast as I could, I was a student on a month-long wilderness program in western Wyoming. On the third day of the course we went canoeing on the Green River, a tributary of the Colorado that begins in the glaciers of the Wind River range and flows south across the sagebrush plains. Swollen by warm-weather runoff from an unusually deep snowpack, the Green was higher and swifter that month—June of 1972—than it had been in forty years. A river at flood stage can have strange currents. There is not enough room in the channel for the water to move downstream in an orderly fashion, so it collides with itself and forms whirlpools and boils and souseholes.[1] Our instructors decided to stick to their

---

[1] **boils and souseholes:** Terms from whitewater canoeing or rafting. Boils are small spots of agitated or swirling water; souseholes are formed by water flowing over submerged objects, usually rocks. —EDS.

itinerary nevertheless, but they put in at a relatively easy section of the Green, one that the flood had merely upgraded, in the international system of white-water classification, from Class I to Class II. There are six levels of difficulty, and Class II was not an unreasonable challenge for novice paddlers.

The Green River did not seem dangerous to me. It seemed magnificently unobstructed. Impediments to progress—the rocks and stranded trees that under normal conditions would protrude above the surface—were mostly submerged. The river carried our aluminum canoe high and lightly, like a child on a pair of broad shoulders. We could rest our paddles on the gunwales and let the water do our work. The sun was bright and hot. Every few minutes I dipped my bandanna in the river, draped it over my head, and let an ounce or two of melted glacier run down my neck.

I was in the bow of the third canoe. We rounded a bend and saw, fifty feet ahead, a standing wave in the wake of a large black boulder. The students in the lead canoe were attempting to avoid the boulder by backferrying, slipping crabwise across the current by angling their boat diagonally and stroking backward. Done right, backferrying allows paddlers to hover midstream and carefully plan their course instead of surrendering to the water's impetuous pace. But if they lean upstream—a natural inclination, as few people choose to lean toward the difficulties that lie ahead—the current can overflow the lowered gunwale and flip the boat. And that is what happened to the lead canoe.

I wasn't worried when I saw it go over. Knowing that we might capsize   5
in the fast water, our instructors had arranged to have our gear trucked to our next campsite. The packs were safe. The water was little more than waist-deep, and the paddlers were both wearing life jackets. They would be fine. One was already scrambling onto the right-hand bank.

But where was the second paddler? Gary, a local boy from Rawlins a year or two younger than I, seemed to be hung up on something. He was standing at a strange angle in the middle of the river, just downstream from the boulder. Gary was the only student on the course who had not brought sneakers, and one of his mountaineering boots had become wedged between two rocks. The instructors would come around the bend in a moment and pluck him out, like a twig from a snag.

But they didn't come. The second canoe pulled over to the bank and ours followed. Thirty seconds passed, maybe a minute. Then we saw the standing wave bend Gary's body forward at the waist, push his face underwater, stretch his arms in front of him, and slip his orange life jacket off his shoulders. The life jacket lingered for a moment at his wrists before it floated downstream, its long white straps twisting in the current. His shirtless torso was pale and undulating, and it changed shape as hills and valleys of water flowed over him, altering the curve of the liquid lens through which we watched him. I thought: *He looks like the flayed skin of St. Bartholomew in the Sistine Chapel.*[2] As soon as I had the thought, I knew that

---

[2] **Sistine Chapel:** The famed ceiling of the Sistine Chapel in Rome, one of the artistic wonders of the world, was painted by Michelangelo between 1508 and 1512. The figure of St. Bartholomew appears in one of the ceiling's many panels. —Eds.

Scala/Art Resource, NY

Detail from Michelangelo's famed "Sistine Chapel" showing the figure of St. Bartholomew.

it was dishonorable. To think about anything outside the moment, outside Gary, was a crime of inattention. I swallowed a small, sour piece of self-knowledge: I was the sort of person who, instead of weeping or shouting or praying during a crisis, thought about something from a textbook (H. W. Janson's *History of Art*, page 360).

Once the flayed man had come, I could not stop the stream of images: Gary looked like a piece of seaweed. Gary looked like a waving handkerchief, Gary looked like a hula dancer. Each simile was a way to avoid thinking about what Gary *was*, a drowning boy. To remember these things is dishonorable, too, for I have long since forgotten Gary's last name and the color of his hair and the sound of his voice.

I do not remember a single word that anyone said. Somehow we got into one of the canoes, all five of us, and tried to ferry the twenty feet or so to the middle of the river. The current was so strong, and we were so incompetent, that we never even got close. Then we tried it on foot, linking arms to form a chain. The water was so cold that it stung. And it was noisy, not the roar and crash of whitewater but a groan, a terrible bass grumble, from the stones that were rolling and leaping down the riverbed. When we got close to Gary, we couldn't see him. All we could see was the reflection of the sky. A couple of times, groping blindly, one of us touched him, but he was as slippery as soap. Then our knees buckled and our elbows unlocked, and we rolled downstream, like the stones. The river's rocky load, moving invisibly beneath its smooth surface, pounded and scraped us. Eventually the current heaved us, blue-lipped and panting, onto the bank. In that other world above the water, the only sounds were the buzzing of bees and flies. Our wet sneakers kicked up red dust. The air smelled of sage and rabbitbrush and sunbaked earth.

We tried again and again, back and forth between the worlds. Wet, dry, 10 cold, hot, turbulent, still.

At first I assumed that we would save him. He would lie on the bank and the sun would warm him while we administered mouth-to-mouth resuscitation. If we couldn't get him out, we would hold him upright in the river; maybe he could still breathe. But the Green River was flowing at nearly three thousand cubic feet—about ninety tons—per second. At that rate, water can wrap a canoe around a boulder like tinfoil. Water can uproot a tree. Water can squeeze the air out of a boy's lungs, undo knots, drag off a life jacket, lever a boot so tightly into the riverbed that even if we had had ropes—the ropes that were in the packs that were in the trucks—we never could have budged him.

We kept going in, not because we had any hope of saving Gary after the first ten minutes but because we needed to save face. It would have been humiliating if the instructors had come around the bend and found us sitting in the sagebrush, a docile row of five with no hypothermia and no skinned knees. Eventually, they did come. The boats had been delayed because one of them had nearly capsized, and the instructors had made the students stop and practice backferrying until they learned not to lean upstream. Even though Gary had already drowned, the instructors did all the same things we had done, more competently but no more effectively, because they, too, would have been humiliated if they hadn't skinned their knees. Men in wetsuits, belayed with ropes, pried the body out the next morning.

Twenty-seven years have passed. My life seems too fast now, so obstructions bother me less than they once did. I am no longer in a hurry to see what is around the next bend. I find myself wanting to backferry, to hover midstream, suspended. If I could do that, I might avoid many things: harsh words, foolish decisions, moments of inattention, regrets that wash over me, like water. ■

The Reader's Presence

1. Read Anne Fadiman's opening paragraph very carefully. What is its relevance to the rest of her short personal essay? What images in the paragraph will be repeated later? What would you consider the key word of the paragraph? In what ways does that word inform the entire essay?

2. At the moment of crisis, the author says she pictured a figure that appears in Michelangelo's famous ceiling painting in the Sistine Chapel in Rome (paragraph 7). Why does Fadiman consider her thought "dishonorable"? What do you think she means by a "crime of inattention"? How do these self-criticisms reappear in the essay's final paragraph?

3. **CONNECTIONS:**   Compare and contrast Anne Fadiman's "Under Water" to George Orwell's classic essay, "Shooting an Elephant" (page 216). Both essays depend on an unfolding narrative; in what way does each writer rely on similar methods of storytelling? How do spectators play a role in the story? When she writes "we needed to save face" (paragraph 12), do you see any connections to Orwell's essay? What other similarities can you find?

The Writer at Work

ANNE FADIMAN on the Art of Editing

Chester Higgins Jr./The New York Times/Redux

Anne Fadiman has not only written numerous personal and reflective essays but also served for years as the chief editor of one of the country's finest literary quarterlies, *The American Scholar*. She recalls that experience in the introductory essay she contributed to her 2003 edition of *The Best American Essays*. As readers, we see only the final published efforts of writers (whether novelists, poets, or essayists) and it's important for student readers to understand that everything they encounter in a book like this has not only been edited professionally but re-edited and then probably edited again. In this passage from her introductory essay, Fadiman pays tribute to the importance of fastidious editing.

❝A few years ago, the author of an autobiographical essay I was planning to publish in *The American Scholar*—a very fine writer—died suddenly. The writer had no immediate relatives, so I asked his longtime editor at *The New Yorker* if he would read the edited piece, hoping he might be able to guess which of my minor changes the writer would have been likely to accept and which he would have disliked. Certainly, said the editor. Two days later, he sent the piece back to me with comments on my edits and some additional editing of his own. "My suggestions are all small sentence tweaks," he wrote. "I could hear ———'s voice in my head as I did them and I'm pretty sure they would have met with his approval—most of them, anyway." Some examples: "A man who looked unmusical" became "a man so seemingly unmusical." "They made a swift escape to their different homes" became "They scattered swiftly to their various homes." "I felt that that solidity had been fostered by his profession" became "That solidity, I felt, had been fostered by his profession." These were, indeed, only small tweaks, but their precision filled me with awe. Of *course* you couldn't look unmusical. Of *course* it was awkward to use "escape" (singular) with "homes" (plural). Of *course* I should have caught "that that." I faxed the piece to my entire staff because editors rarely get a chance to see the work of other editors; we see only its results. This was like having a front-row seat at the Editing Olympics.

Five days later, the editor sent the piece back to us, covered with a second round of marginalia. "No doubt this is more than you bargained for," he wrote. "It's just that when the more noticeable imperfections have been taken care of, smaller ones come into view . . . I've even edited some of my own edits—e.g., on page 25, where I've changed 'dour,' which I inserted in the last go-round, to 'glowering.' This is because 'dour' is too much like 'pinched,' which I'm also suggesting."

If you're not a writer; this sort of compulsiveness may seem well nigh pathological. You may even be thinking, "What's the difference?" But if you *are* a writer, you'll realize what a gift the editor gave his old friend. Had not a word been changed, the essay still would have been excellent. Each of these "tweaks"—there were perhaps a hundred, none more earthshaking than the ones I've quoted—made it a little better, and their aggregate effect was to transform an excellent essay into a superb one.**❞**

Henry Louis Gates Jr.

IN THE KITCHEN

The critic, educator, writer, and activist **HENRY LOUIS GATES JR.** (b. 1950) is one of the more recent in a long line of African American intellectuals who are also public figures. In 1979 he became the first African American to earn a PhD from Cambridge University in its eight-hundred-year history. He has been the recipient of countless honors, including a Carnegie Foundation Fellowship, a Mellon Fellowship, a MacArthur "genius" grant for his work in literary theory, and the 1998 National Medal for the Humanities. Gates is the Alphonse Fletcher University Professor and the director of the W. E. B. Du Bois Institute for African and African American Research at Harvard University. He has been at the forefront of the movement to expand the literary canon that is studied in American schools to include the works of non-European authors. He is also known for his work as a "literary archaeologist," uncovering thousands of previously unknown stories, poems, and reviews written by African American authors between 1829 and 1940 and making those texts available to modern readers. Gates has written and produced a number of documentaries aired on public television, including *African American Lives* in 2006 and *Finding Your Roots with Henry Louis Gates, Jr.* in 2012, which further examined the genealogical and genetic heritage of African Americans.

> **"I'm trying to recollect a lost era . . . a whole world that simply no longer exists."**

Gates's more recent books include *Black in Latin America* (2011), *Life Upon These Shores: Looking at African American History, 1513–2008* (2011), and *Encyclopedia of Africa* (2010), which he edited with Kwame Anthony Appiah.

"In the Kitchen" is taken from Gates's 1995 book *Colored People*, a memoir of his early life as part of the middle-class "colored" community of Piedmont, West Virginia. About *Colored People*, Gates says, "I'm trying to recollect a lost era, what I can call a *sepia time*, a whole world that simply no longer exists."

WE ALWAYS HAD A GAS STOVE in the kitchen, though electric cooking became fashionable in Piedmont, like using Crest toothpaste rather than Colgate, or watching Huntley and Brinkley rather than Walter Cronkite. But for us it was gas, Colgate, and good ole Walter Cronkite, come what may. We used gas partly out of loyalty to Big Mom, Mama's mama, because she was mostly blind and still loved to cook, and she could feel her way better with gas than with electric.

But the most important thing about our gas-equipped kitchen was that Mama used to do hair there. She had a "hot comb"—a fine-tooth iron instrument with a long wooden handle—and a pair of iron curlers that opened and closed like scissors: Mama would put them into the gas fire until they glowed. You could smell those prongs heating up.

I liked what that smell meant for the shape of my day. There was an intimate warmth in the women's tones as they talked with my mama while she did their hair. I knew what the women had been through to get their hair ready to be "done," because I would watch Mama do it herself. How that scorched kink could be transformed through grease and fire into a magnificent head of wavy hair was a miracle to me. Still is.

Mama would wash her hair over the sink, a towel wrapped round her shoulders, wearing just her half-slip and her white bra. (We had no shower until we moved down Rat Tail Road into Doc Wolverton's house, in 1954.) After she had dried it, she would grease her scalp thoroughly with blue Bergamot hair grease, which came in a short, fat jar with a picture of a beautiful colored lady on it. It's important to grease your scalp real good, my mama would explain, to keep from burning yourself.

Of course, her hair would return to its natural kink almost as soon as   5
the hot water and shampoo hit it. To me, it was another miracle how hair so "straight" would so quickly become kinky again once it even approached some water.

My mama had only a "few" clients whose heads she "did"—and did, I think, because she enjoyed it, rather than for the few dollars it brought in. They would sit on one of our red plastic kitchen chairs, the kind with the shiny metal legs, and brace themselves for the process. Mama would stroke that red-hot iron, which by this time had been in the gas fire for a half hour or more, slowly but firmly through their hair, from scalp to strand's end. It made a scorching, crinkly sound, the hot iron did, as it burned its way through the damp kink, leaving in its wake the straightest of hair strands, each of them standing up long and tall but drooping at the end, like the top of a heavy willow tree. Slowly, steadily, with deftness and grace, Mama's hands would transform a round mound of Odetta kink[1] into a darkened swamp of everglades. The Bergamot made the hair shiny; the heat of the hot iron gave it a brownish-red cast. Once all the hair was as straight as God allows kink to get, Mama would take the well-heated curling iron and twirl the straightened strands into more or less loosely wrapped curls. She claimed that she owed her strength and skill as a hairdresser to her wrists, and her little finger would poke out the way it did when she sipped tea. Mama was a southpaw, who wrote upside down and backwards to produce the cleanest, roundest letters you've ever seen.

The "kitchen" she would all but remove from sight with a pair of shears bought for this purpose. Now, the *kitchen* was the room in which we were

---

[1] **Odetta kink:** A reference to Odetta Holmes Felious Gordon, a popular African American folk singer of the 1960s who helped popularize the hairstyle known as the "afro." —EDS.

Odetta Holmes Felious Gordon.

sitting, the room where Mama did hair and washed clothes, and where each of us bathed in a galvanized tub. But the word has another meaning, and the "kitchen" I'm speaking of now is the very kinky bit of hair at the back of the head, where our neck meets the shirt collar. If there ever was one part of our African past that resisted assimilation, it was the kitchen. No matter how hot the iron, no matter how powerful the chemical, no matter how stringent the mashed-potatoes-and-lye formula of a man's "process," neither God nor woman nor Sammy Davis, Jr., could straighten the kitchen. The kitchen was permanent, irredeemable, invincible kink. Unassimilably African. No matter what you did, no matter how hard you tried, nothing could dekink a person's kitchen. So you trimmed it off as best you could.

When hair had begun to "turn," as they'd say, or return to its natural kinky glory, it was the kitchen that turned first. When the kitchen started creeping up the back of the neck, it was time to get your hair done again. The kitchen around the back, and nappy edges at the temples.

Sometimes, after dark, Mr. Charlie Carroll would come to have his hair done. Mr. Charlie Carroll was very light-complected and had a ruddy nose, the kind of nose that made me think of Edmund Gwenn playing Kris Kringle in *Miracle on 34th Street*. At the beginning, they did it after Rocky and I had gone to sleep. It was only later that we found out he had come to our house so Mama could iron his hair—not with a comb and curling iron but with our very own Proctor-Silex steam iron. For some reason, Mr. Charlie would conceal his Frederick Douglass mane[2] under a big white Stetson hat, which

---

[2] ***Frederick Douglass mane:*** Frederick Douglass (1817?–1895), an escaped slave who became a prominent African American writer, abolitionist, and orator (see page 106).—EDS.

Library of Congress

Frederick Douglass.

I never saw him take off. Except when he came to our house, late at night, to have his hair pressed.

(Later, Daddy would tell us about Mr. Charlie's most prized piece of knowledge, which the man would confide only after his hair had been pressed, as a token of intimacy. "Not many people know this," he'd say in a tone of circumspection, "but George Washington was Abraham Lincoln's daddy." Nodding solemnly, he'd add the clincher: "A white man told me." Though he was in dead earnest, this became a humorous refrain around the house—"a white man told me"—used to punctuate especially preposterous assertions.)

My mother furtively examined my daughters' kitchens whenever we went home for a visit in the early eighties. It became a game between us. I had told her not to do it, because I didn't like the politics it suggested of "good" and "bad" hair. "Good" hair was straight. "Bad" hair was kinky. Even in the late sixties, at the height of Black Power, most people could not bring themselves to say "bad" for "good" and "good" for "bad." They still said that hair like white hair was "good," even if they encapsulated it in a disclaimer like "what we used to call 'good.'"

Maggie would be seated in her high chair, throwing food this way and that, and Mama would be cooing about how cute it all was, remembering how I used to do the same thing, and wondering whether Maggie's flinging her food with her left hand meant that she was going to be a southpaw too. When my daughter was just about covered with Franco-American SpaghettiOs, Mama would seize the opportunity and wipe her clean, dipping her head, tilted to one side, down under the back of Maggie's neck. Sometimes, if she could get away with it, she'd even rub a curl between her fingers, just to make sure that her bifocals had not deceived her. Then she'd sigh with satisfaction and relief, thankful that her prayers had been answered. No kink . . . yet. "Mama!" I'd shout, pretending to be angry. (Every once in a while, if no one was looking, I'd peek too.)

I say "yet" because most black babies are born with soft, silken hair. Then, sooner or later, it begins to "turn," as inevitably as do the seasons or the leaves turn on a tree. And if it's meant to turn, it *turns*, no matter how hard you try to stop it. People once thought baby oil would stop it. They were wrong.

Everybody I knew as a child wanted to have good hair. You could be as ugly as homemade sin dipped in misery and still be thought attractive if you had good hair. Jesus Moss was what the girls at Camp Lee, Virginia, had called Daddy's hair during World War II. I know he played that thick head of hair for all it was worth, too. Still would, if he could.

My own hair was "not a bad grade," as barbers would tell me when they 15 cut my head for the first time. It's like a doctor reporting the overall results of the first full physical that he had given you. "You're in good shape" or "Blood pressure's kind of high; better cut down on salt."

I spent much of my childhood and adolescence messing with my hair. I definitely wanted straight hair. Like Pop's.

When I was about three, I tried to stick a wad of Bazooka bubble gum to that straight hair of his. I suppose what fixed that memory for me is the spanking I got for doing so: he turned me upside down, holding me by the feet, the better to paddle my behind. Little *nigger*, he shouted, walloping away. I started to laugh about it two days later, when my behind stopped hurting.

When black people say "straight," of course, they don't usually mean "straight" literally, like, say, the hair of Peggy Lipton (the white girl on *The Mod Squad*) or Mary of Peter, Paul and Mary fame; black people call that "stringy" hair. No, "straight" just means not kinky, no matter what contours the curl might take. Because Daddy had straight hair, I would have done *anything* to have straight hair—and I used to try everything to make it straight, short of getting a process, which only riffraff were dumb enough to do.

Of the wide variety of techniques and methods I came to master in the great and challenging follicle prestidigitation, almost all had two things in common: a heavy, oil-based grease and evenly applied pressure. It's no accident that many of the biggest black companies in the fifties and sixties made hair products. Indeed, we do have a vast array of hair grease. And I have tried it all, in search of that certain silky touch, one that leaves neither the hand nor the pillow sullied by grease.

I always wondered what Frederick Douglass put on *his* hair, or Phillis   20
Wheatley.[3] Or why Wheatley has that rag on her head in the little engraving in the frontispiece of her book. One thing is for sure: you can bet that when Wheatley went to England to see the Countess of Huntington, she did not stop by the Queen's Coiffeur on the way. So many black people still get their hair straightened that it's a wonder we don't have a national holiday for Madame C. J. Walker, who invented the process for straightening kinky hair, rather than for Dr. King. Jheri-curled or "relaxed" — it's still fried hair.

I used all the greases, from sea-blue Bergamot, to creamy vanilla Duke (in its orange-and-white jar), to the godfather of grease, the formidable Murray's. Now, Murray's was some *serious* grease. Whereas Bergamot was like oily Jell-O and Duke was viscous and sickly sweet, Murray's was light brown and *hard*. Hard as lard and twice as greasy, Daddy used to say whenever the subject of Murray's came up. Murray's came in an orange can with a screw-on top. It was so hard that some people would put a match to the can, just to soften it and make it more manageable. In the late sixties, when Afros came into style, I'd use Afro-Sheen. From Murray's to Duke to Afro-Sheen: that was my progression in black consciousness.

We started putting hot towels or washrags over our greased-down Murray's-coated heads, in order to melt the wax into the scalp and follicles. Unfortunately, the wax had a curious habit of running down your neck, ears, and forehead. Not to mention your pillowcase.

Another problem was that if you put two palmfuls of Murray's on your head, your hair turned white. Duke did the same thing. It was a challenge: if you got rid of the white stuff, you had a magnificent head of wavy hair. Murray's turned kink into waves. Lots of waves. Frozen waves. A hurricane couldn't have blown those waves around.

That was the beauty of it. Murray's was so hard that it froze your hair into the wavy style you brushed it into. It looked really good if you wore a part. A lot of guys had parts *cut* into their hair by a barber, with clippers or a straight-edge razor. Especially if you had kinky hair — in which case you'd generally wear a short razor cut, or what we called a Quo Vadis.

Being obsessed with our hair, we tried to be as innovative as possible.   25
Everyone knew about using a stocking cap, because your father or your uncle or the older guys wore them whenever something really big was about to happen, secular or sacred, a funeral or a dance, a wedding or a trip in which you confronted official white people, or when you were trying to look really sharp. When it was time to be clean, you wore a stocking cap. If the event was really a big one, you made a new cap for the occasion.

A stocking cap was made by asking your mother for one of her hose, cutting it with a pair of scissors about six inches or so from the open end, where

---

[3] ***Phillis Wheatley*** (1753?–1784): An African-born slave who became America's first major black poet. — EDS.

the elastic goes to the top of the thigh. Then you'd knot the cut end, and behold—a conical-shaped hat or cap, with an elastic band that you pulled down low on your forehead and down around your neck in the back. A good stocking cap, to work well, had to fit tight and snug, like a press. And it had to fit that tightly because it *was* a press: it pressed your hair with the force of the hose's elastic. If you greased your hair down real good and left the stocking cap on long enough—*voilà*: you got a head of pressed-against-the-scalp waves. If you used Murray's, and if you wore a stocking cap to sleep, you got a *whole lot* of waves. (You also got a ring around your forehead when you woke up, but eventually that disappeared.)

And then you could enjoy your concrete 'do. Swore we were bad, too, with all that grease and those flat heads. My brother and I would brush it out a bit in the morning so it would look—ahem—"natural."

Grown men still wear stocking caps, especially older men, who generally keep their caps in their top drawer, along with their cuff links and their see-through silk socks, their Maverick tie, their silk handkerchief, and whatever else they prize most.

A Murrayed-down stocking cap was the respectable version of the process, which, by contrast, was most definitely not a cool thing to have, at least if you weren't an entertainer by trade.

Zeke and Keith and Poochie and a few other stars of the basketball team all used to get a process once or twice a year. It was expensive, and to get one you had to go to Pittsburgh or D.C. or Uniontown, someplace where there were enough colored people to support a business. They'd disappear, then reappear a day or two later, strutting like peacocks, their hair burned slightly red from the chemical lye base. They'd also wear "rags" or cloths or handkerchiefs around it when they slept or played basketball. Do-rags, they were called. But the result was *straight* hair with a hint of wave. No curl. Do-it-yourselfers took their chances at home with a concoction of mashed potatoes and lye.

The most famous process, outside of what Malcolm X describes in his *Autobiography* and maybe that of Sammy Davis, Jr., was Nat King Cole's. Nat King Cole had patent-leather hair.

"That man's got the finest process money can buy." That's what Daddy said the night Cole's TV show aired on NBC, November 5, 1956. I remember the date because everyone came to our house to watch it and to celebrate one of Daddy's buddies' birthdays. Yeah, Uncle Joe chimed in, they can do shit to his hair that the average Negro can't even *think* about—secret shit.

Nat King Cole was *clean*. I've had an ongoing argument with a Nigerian friend about Nat King Cole for twenty years now. Not whether or not he could sing; any fool knows that he could sing. But whether or not he was a handkerchief-head for wearing that patent-leather process.

Sammy Davis's process I detested. It didn't look good on him. Worse still, he liked to have a fried strand dangling down the middle of his forehead, shaking it out from the crown when he sang. But Nat King Cole's hair was

Gems/Redferns/Getty Images

Nat King Cole.

a thing unto itself, a beautifully sculpted work of art that he and he alone should have had the right to wear.

The only difference between a process and a stocking cap, really, was   35 taste; yet Nat King Cole—unlike, say, Michael Jackson—looked *good* in his process. His head looked like Rudolph Valentino's in the twenties, and some say it was Valentino that the process imitated. But Nat King Cole wore a process because it suited his face, his demeanor, his name, his style. He was as clean as he wanted to be.

I had forgotten all about Nat King Cole and that patent-leather look until the day in 1971 when I was sitting in an Arab restaurant on the island of Zanzibar, surrounded by men in fezzes and white caftans, trying to learn how to eat curried goat and rice with the fingers of my right hand, feeling two million miles from home, when all of a sudden the old transistor radio sitting on top of a china cupboard stopped blaring out its Swahili music to play "Fly Me to the Moon" by Nat King Cole. The restaurant's din was not affected at all, not even by half a decibel. But in my mind's eye, I saw it: the King's sleek black magnificent tiara. I managed, barely, to blink back the tears. ■

The Reader's Presence

1. At what point in the essay do you, as a reader, begin to become aware of the social or political significance of the hair-straightening process? At what point in his own development does Gates begin to ascribe a political significance to hair? How would you describe his attitude toward the "kitchen"? toward the "process"? toward the prominent black Americans whom he names in the essay?

2. How would you characterize the author's voice in this essay? Which words and phrases hark back to the language of his home and family? How does Gates integrate these words and phrases into the text? What difference, if any, does it make to you as a reader when he puts certain words, such as *kitchen* or *good*, in quotation marks, as opposed to the passages in which phrases (such as "ugly as homemade sin dipped in misery" [paragraph 14]) are not set off in the text in this way?

3. **VISUAL PRESENCE:** Compare and contrast the portraits of Odetta Holmes Felious Gordon (page 128), Frederick Douglass (page 129), and Nat King Cole (page 133). What words and phrases would you choose to describe each person's appearance? After reading Gates's essay, how does each person's hairstyle affect how you perceive him or her? Support your answer with specific evidence from the text.

4. **CONNECTIONS:** Compare and contrast Gates's essay with James Baldwin's "Notes of a Native Son" (page 61). How does each writer come to terms with a sense of his racial identity? To what specific extent are Gates's ideas about black resistance to assimilation, published in 1995, similar to and different from those of Baldwin, published in 1955? Which essay did you find more compelling to read? Explain why.

The Writer at Work

HENRY LOUIS GATES JR. on the Writer's Voice

AP Photo/Gretchen Ertl

Skilled at critical and academic writing, Henry Louis Gates Jr. hoped to find ways to tell stories about his growing up in a small West Virginia community. In writing his memoir, *Colored People*, Gates found the voice he wanted. The following comments appeared in a 1995 collection, *Swing Low: Black Men Writing*, edited by Rebecca Carroll.

❝ My father told stories all the time when I was growing up. My mother used to call them "lies." I didn't know that "lies" was the name for stories in the black vernacular, I just thought it was her own word that she had made up. I was inspired by those "lies," though, and knew that I wanted to tell some too one day.

When I was ten or twelve, I had a baseball column in the local newspaper. I was the scorekeeper for the minor-league games in my town—I would compile all of the facts, and then the editor and I would put together a narrative. I did that every week during the summer. The best part was seeing my name in print. After that, I was hooked—hooked to seeing my name in black and white on paper.

At fourteen or fifteen, I read James Baldwin's work and became fascinated with the idea of writing. When I started reading about black people through the writings of black people, suddenly I was seized by the desire to write. I was in awe of how writers were able to take words and create an illusion of the world that people could step into—a world where people opened doors and shut doors, fell in love and out of love, where people lived and died. I wanted to be able to create those worlds too. I knew I had a voice even before I knew what a "writer's voice" meant. I didn't know what it was, but I could hear it, and I knew when my rhythm was on—it was almost as if I could hear myself write. I thought I had a unique take on the world and trusted my sensibility. It struck me that perhaps it would be a good thing to share it with other people. . . .

I don't think that the prime reason for writing is to save the world, or to save black people. I do it because it makes me feel good. I want to record my vision and to entertain people. When I was writing reviews, although it was an intriguing way to discuss literature, I would have a lot of black people say to me, "I'm having a hard time understanding you, brother." I've always had two conflicting voices within me, one that wants to be outrageous and on the edge, always breaking new ground, and another that wants to be loved by the community for that outrageousness. It is very difficult to expect that people will let you have it both ways like that. Those who really care about a community are the ones who push the boundaries and create new definitions, but generally they get killed for doing that, which is what I mean when I refer to myself as a griot in the black community—the one who makes the wake-up call, who loves his people enough to truly examine the status quo.

The wonderful thing about *Colored People* is that everybody gets it and can appreciate it because it is a universal story. It is my segue from nonfiction to fiction. I wrote it to preserve a world that has passed away, and to reveal some secrets—not for the shock value, but because I want to re-create a voice that black people use when there are no white people around. Oftentimes in black literature, black authors get all lockjawed in their writing because they are doing it for a white audience, and not for themselves. You don't hear the voice of black people when it's just us in the kitchen, talking out the door and down the road, and that is the voice that I am trying to capture in *Colored People*. Integration may have cost us that voice. We cannot take it for granted and must preserve it whenever possible. I don't know what kind of positive language and linguistic rituals are being passed down in the fragmented, dispossessed black underclass. I think it's very different from when and where I was raised, when there was a stronger sense of community, and that language was everywhere I turned. ❞

Michihiko Hachiya

FROM *HIROSHIMA DIARY*

On August 6, 1945, the United States dropped an atomic bomb on the Japanese city of Hiroshima and introduced a new, devastating weapon into modern war. Two days later, the U.S. military dropped another bomb, on Nagasaki, forcing the Japanese government into an unconditional surrender. For years, the Japanese survivors of the blasts suffered from unhealing burns, radiation poisoning, cancers, and a score of other illnesses. At first, the Japanese had no idea what had hit them, though rumors of a new secret weapon circulated rapidly.

Most Americans today know of the bombing mainly through repeated images of the mushroom cloud itself; rarely do they see photographs or footage of the destruction and casualties. One of the most vivid accounts of the bombing and its immediate aftermath can be found in a diary kept by a Hiroshima physician, **MICHIHIKO HACHIYA** (1903–1980), who, though severely injured himself, miraculously found the time to record both his professional observations of a medical nightmare and his human impressions of an utterly destroyed community. Published on the tenth anniversary of the bombing of Hiroshima, *Hiroshima Diary* (1955) gained widespread attention. The diary runs only for some two months, from the moment of the blast on the sunny morning of August 6 to the end of September, when the American occupation was well under way.

> At first, the Japanese had no idea what had hit them, though rumors of a new secret weapon circulated rapidly.

 WHAT HAD HAPPENED?

August 6, 1945

Badly injured from the blast, Dr. Hachiya managed to make his way to the hospital where he served as director and which, fortunately, was quite near his house. He spent several days in bed and did not begin writing his diary until August 8. As we can see from the following passage, however, the events were still fresh in his mind.

THE HOUR WAS EARLY; the morning still, warm, and beautiful. Shimmering leaves, reflecting sunlight from a cloudless sky, made a pleasant contrast with shadows in my garden as I gazed absently through wide-flung doors opening to the south.

Clad in drawers and undershirt, I was sprawled on the living room floor exhausted because I had just spent a sleepless night on duty as an air warden in my hospital.

Suddenly, a strong flash of light startled me—and then another. So well does one recall little things that I remember vividly how a stone lantern in the garden became brilliantly lit and I debated whether this light was caused by a magnesium flare or sparks from a passing trolley.

Garden shadows disappeared. The view where a moment before all had been so bright and sunny was now dark and hazy. Through swirling dust I could barely discern a wooden column that had supported one corner of my house. It was leaning crazily and the roof sagged dangerously.

Moving instinctively, I tried to escape, but rubble and fallen timbers 5 barred the way. By picking my way cautiously I managed to reach the *rōka*[1] and stepped down into my garden. A profound weakness overcame me, so I stopped to regain my strength. To my surprise I discovered that I was completely naked. How odd! Where were my drawers and undershirt?

What had happened?

All over the right side of my body I was cut and bleeding. A large splinter was protruding from a mangled wound in my thigh, and something warm trickled into my mouth. My cheek was torn, I discovered as I felt it gingerly, with the lower lip laid wide open. Embedded in my neck was a sizable fragment of glass which I matter-of-factly dislodged, and with the detachment of one stunned and shocked I studied it and my blood-stained hand.

Where was my wife?

Suddenly thoroughly alarmed, I began to yell for her: "Yaeko-san! Yaeko-san! Where are you?"

Blood began to spurt. Had my carotid artery been cut? Would I bleed to 10 death? Frightened and irrational, I called out again: "It's a five-hundred-ton bomb! Yaeko-san, where are you? A five-hundred-ton bomb has fallen!"

Yaeko-san, pale and frightened, her clothes torn and blood-stained, emerged from the ruins of our house holding her elbow. Seeing her, I was reassured. My own panic assuaged, I tried to reassure her.

"We'll be all right," I exclaimed. "Only let's get out of here as fast as we can."

She nodded, and I motioned for her to follow me.

The shortest path to the street lay through the house next door so through the house we went—running, stumbling, falling, and then running again until in headlong flight we tripped over something and fell sprawling into the street. Getting to my feet, I discovered that I had tripped over a man's head.

"Excuse me! Excuse me, please!" I cried hysterically. 15

There was no answer. The man was dead. The head had belonged to a young officer whose body was crushed beneath a massive gate.

We stood in the street, uncertain and afraid, until a house across from us began to sway and then with a rending motion fell almost at our feet. Our

---

[1] *rōka:* A narrow outside hall.—EDS.

own house began to sway, and in a minute it, too, collapsed in a cloud of dust. Other buildings caved in or toppled. Fires sprang up and whipped by a vicious wind began to spread.

It finally dawned on us that we could not stay there in the street, so we turned our steps towards the hospital. Our home was gone; we were wounded and needed treatment; and after all, it was my duty to be with my staff. This latter was an irrational thought—what good could I be to anyone, hurt as I was.

We started out, but after twenty or thirty steps I had to stop. My breath became short, my heart pounded, and my legs gave way under me. An overpowering thirst seized me and I begged Yaeko-san to find me some water. But there was no water to be found. After a little my strength somewhat returned and we were able to go on.

I was still naked, and although I did not feel the least bit of shame, I was   20
disturbed to realize that modesty had deserted me. On rounding a corner we came upon a soldier standing idly in the street. He had a towel draped across his shoulder, and I asked if he would give it to me to cover my nakedness. The soldier surrendered the towel quite willingly but said not a word. A little later I lost the towel, and Yaeko-san took off her apron and tied it around my loins.

Our progress towards the hospital was interminably slow, until finally, my legs, stiff from drying blood, refused to carry me farther. The strength, even the will, to go on deserted me, so I told my wife, who was almost as badly hurt as I, to go on alone. This she objected to, but there was no choice. She had to go ahead and try to find someone to come back for me.

Yaeko-san looked into my face for a moment, and then, without saying a word, turned away and began running towards the hospital. Once, she looked back and waved and in a moment she was swallowed up in the gloom. It was quite dark now, and with my wife gone, a feeling of dreadful loneliness overcame me.

I must have gone out of my head lying there in the road because the next thing I recall was discovering that the clot on my thigh had been dislodged and blood was again spurting from the wound. I pressed my hand to the bleeding area and after a while the bleeding stopped and I felt better.

Could I go on?

I tried. It was all a nightmare—my wounds, the darkness, the road   25
ahead. My movements were ever so slow; only my mind was running at top speed.

In time I came to an open space where the houses had been removed to make a fire lane. Through the dim light I could make out ahead of me the hazy outlines of the Communications Bureau's big concrete building, and beyond it the hospital. My spirits rose because I knew that now someone would find me; and if I should die, at least my body would be found.

I paused to rest. Gradually things around me came into focus. There were the shadowy forms of people, some of whom looked like walking ghosts. Others moved as though in pain, like scarecrows, their arms held out from their bodies with forearms and hands dangling. These people puzzled me until I suddenly realized that they had been burned and were holding their arms out to prevent the painful friction of raw surfaces rubbing together. A naked woman carrying a naked baby came into view. I averted my gaze. Perhaps they had been in the bath. But then I saw a naked man, and it occurred to me that, like myself, some strange thing had deprived them of their clothes. An old woman lay near me with an expression of suffering on her face; but she made no sound. Indeed, one thing was common to everyone I saw — complete silence. . . .

PIKADON

August 9, 1945

As the wounded poured into Dr. Hachiya's hospital, the physicians tried to make sense of the symptoms and injuries, which did not resemble those of ordinary bombings. Because many of the patients with horrible symptoms showed no obvious signs of injuries, Dr. Hachiya could only speculate about what might have occurred. He had no idea as yet what type of weapon had been used against them.

Today, Dr. Hanaoka's[2] report on the patients was more detailed. One observation particularly impressed me. Regardless of the type of injury, nearly everybody had the same symptoms. All had a poor appetite, the majority had nausea and gaseous indigestion, and over half had vomiting.

Not a few had shown improvement since yesterday. Diarrhea, though, continued to be a problem and actually appeared to be increasing. Distinctly alarming was the appearance of blood in the stools of patients who earlier had only diarrhea. The isolation of these people was becoming increasingly difficult.

One seriously ill man complained of a sore mouth yesterday, and today, 30 numerous small hemorrhages began to appear in his mouth and under his skin. His case was the more puzzling because he came to the hospital complaining of weakness and nausea and did not appear to have been injured at all.

This morning, other patients were beginning to show small subcutaneous hemorrhages, and not a few were coughing and vomiting blood in addition to passing it in their stools. One poor woman was bleeding from her privates. Among these patients there was not one with symptoms typical of anything we knew, unless you could excuse those who developed signs of severe brain disease before they died.

---

2 **Dr. Hanaoka:** Head of internal medicine. — EDS.

Dr. Hanaoka believed the patients could be divided into three groups:

1. Those with nausea, vomiting, and diarrhea who were improving.

2. Those with nausea, vomiting, and diarrhea who were remaining stationary.

3. Those with nausea, vomiting, and diarrhea who were developing hemorrhage under the skin or elsewhere.

Had these patients been burned or otherwise injured, we might have tried to stretch the logic of cause and effect and assume that their bizarre symptoms were related to injury, but so many patients appeared to have received no injury whatsoever that we were obliged to postulate an insult heretofore unknown.

The only other possible cause for the weird symptoms observed was a sudden change in atmospheric pressure. I had read somewhere about bleeding that follows ascent to high altitudes and about bleeding in deep

People walking through the ruins of Hiroshima in the weeks following the atomic bomb blast. Photo by Bernard Hoffman.

sea divers who ascend too rapidly from the depths. Having never seen such injury I could not give much credence to my thoughts.

Still, it was impossible to dismiss the thought that atmospheric pressure   35
had had something to do with the symptoms of our patients. During my student days at Okayama University, I had seen experiments conducted in a pressure chamber. Sudden, temporary deafness was one symptom everyone complained of if pressure in the chamber was abruptly altered.

Now, I could state positively that I heard nothing like an explosion when we were bombed the other morning, nor did I remember any sound during my walk to the hospital as houses collapsed around me. It was as though I walked through a gloomy, silent motion picture. Others whom I questioned had had the same experience.

Those who experienced the bombing from the outskirts of the city characterized it by the word: *pikadon*.[3]

How then could one account for my failure and the failure of others to hear an explosion except on the premise that a sudden change in atmospheric pressure had rendered those nearby temporarily deaf: Could the bleeding we were beginning to observe be explained on the same basis?

Since all books and journals had been destroyed, there was no way to corroborate my theories except by further appeal to the patients. To that end Dr. Katsube[4] was asked to discover what else he could when he made ward rounds.

It was pleasing to note my scientific curiosity was reviving, and I lost no   40
opportunity to question everyone who visited me about the bombing of Hiroshima. Their answers were vague and ambiguous, and on one point only were they in agreement: a new weapon had been used. *What* the new weapon was became a burning question. Not only had our books been destroyed, but our newspapers, telephones, and radios as well. . . .

The Reader's Presence

1. In many ways, it is fortunate that one of the diaries kept immediately after the atomic blast was written by a medical doctor. Why? How does it contribute to the diary's historical value? Could this be a disadvantage? Would you have preferred to read a patient's diary instead? Why or why not?

2. Hachiya's first entry, on August 6, was written a few days after the events it depicts. What indications do you receive from the writing that the entry was predated? Can you detect any differences from the second entry (August 9), which was apparently composed on the stated day?

---

[3]**pikadon:** *Pika* means a glitter, sparkle, or bright flash of light, like a flash of lightning. *Don* means a boom! or loud sound. Together, the words came to mean to the people of Hiroshima an explosion characterized by a flash and a boom. Hence: "flash-boom!" Those who remember the flash only speak of the "*pika*"; those who were far enough from the hypocenter to experience both speak of the "*pikadon*." —EDS.

[4] *Dr. Katsube:* Chief of surgery. —EDS.

3. **VISUAL PRESENCE:**   Examine carefully the photograph of Hiroshima after the atomic bomb blast (page 140). What were your initial reactions to the photograph? How does the image compare with Hachiya's description of the events immediately following the attack? Support your response with specific details from the photograph and Hachiya's essay.

4. **CONNECTIONS:**   Hachiya's confusion reveals itself in his writing in many ways: short paragraphs, multiple questions, and unconfirmed guesses. Throughout, his matter-of-fact language belies his panic. In what specific ways does Hachiya's characterization of the bombing of Hiroshima compare with Christopher Hitchens's account of being waterboarded ("Believe Me, It's Torture," page 616)?

Silas Hansen

BLANK SLATE

SILAS HANSEN (b. 1987), an American essayist, grew up in western New York. In 2010, he graduated from the State University of New York at Brockport in English, Women and Gender Studies, and Political Science, and in 2013 he received his MFA in creative writing from Ohio State University. His essays have appeared in such publications as *Slate*, *The Normal School*, *Hayden's Ferry Review*, *Redactions*, and *Puerto del Sol*, among others, and in 2013 he won an AWP Intro Journals award in nonfiction and was nominated for a Pushcart Prize.

> **"I'm okay with [reading] things that are sad, but I want them to try to transcend that sadness."**

He has said, of his reading habits, "For the most part I'll read anything. . . . I'm okay with [reading] things that are sad, but I want them to try to transcend that sadness."

"Blank Slate" is a poignant account of Hansen deciding on a new first name after a transgender transformation. It originally appeared in the *Colorado Review* in 2013, and was subsequently reprinted at Slate.com in the same year.

FOUR YEARS BEFORE I CHANGED MY NAME to Silas, when I was twenty, I briefly dated a girl who was deaf. When we were together, I still identified as a lesbian—a butch lesbian. I was a feminist, a women's studies major, a frequent attendee at Ani DiFranco concerts. I was also firmly in denial about my gender identity. I was still pretending I was comfortable living as a woman, still proclaiming my pride in my body, in my female identity.

We went out for only a few weeks, and we were never serious, but she grew tired of fingerspelling my name pretty quickly—I did, too—so she gave me a name sign to streamline the process. A hearing person can't pick her own name—someone who is deaf has to give her one. The person who names you usually picks up on some characteristic about you and bases your name sign on it. Laughing a lot might result in your name sign containing the sign for "giggle"; being an artist might mean it will be somehow related to the sign for "paintbrush."

We were sitting next to each other on the couch in her dorm room, watching a movie with the subtitles on, when she made the letter L with her right hand, for Lindsay, and brought it to her face, running her thumb down the side, from her temple to her chin—the sign for "girl."

And even then, when I smiled and brought my fingertips to my lips and then moved my hand out, toward her—"thank you"—it felt wrong, like in the summer when my brown hair lightens in the sun and people tell me I'm blond, or the time I went to the doctor and she told me I was a full inch-and-a-half shorter than I've always believed. I don't care that there is evidence to the contrary: my hair color when I look in the mirror, the numbers on the measuring stick, the F on my driver's license, my birth certificate. I know, deep down, who I am: I have brown hair. I am five feet, ten inches tall. I am not a girl.

Once, during my first year of graduate school, when I was twenty-three, I was having lunch with my friend Nicole. I don't remember the initial topic of conversation, but somehow it shifted to names, and, more specifically, to what our parents almost named us. I told her about my dad's plan to name me Erin Karen—or Scott Timothy if I'd been born a boy. Nicole said that her parents had considered Madeline. "Can you imagine how cool it would be if I'd been a Maddy?" she said.

I knew what she meant. I have always disliked my birth name—Lindsay Rebecca. I disliked it even in preschool, long before I understood why it didn't feel like it fit. In elementary school I would wish my name were something different, something more interesting. I imagine a lot of kids feel that way, especially those of us with too-common names. There were too many Lindsays in the eighties and nineties, just as there were too many Jessicas and Sarahs. But by the time Nicole and I talked, the feeling had only gotten worse for me: over the past two years, I had started to question my gender identity, and though I hadn't yet admitted what I feared—that I might be

5

transgender—I still hated telling people my name. I wished it were something more androgynous, like Alex, so it wouldn't give me away so easily, so it didn't sound quite so feminine. I wished it were something that felt like it belonged to me.

But Nicole and I had been friends for only a couple of months, were still getting to know each other, and I felt weird steering the conversation in a direction she hadn't intended, so I didn't say this. Instead, I made a joke: "Well, when I write my memoir someday and you're a character in it, I'll call you Maddy to protect your identity. Deal?"

She sighed. She looked dejected. "I didn't live the life of a Maddy, though. I've lived the life of a Nicole."

I brought this conversation up about a year later, not long after I'd started calling myself Silas, but she didn't remember it. But why would she? For Nicole, the subject is one she can afford to have a casual interest in—the wish that her name had been something other than what it is, but no drive to actually change it. But months, almost a year later, I was still thinking about what it means to live the life of a certain name. How would my life be different if my mom hadn't vetoed Erin Karen because of the near rhyme? Who would Erin Karen have been? What would her childhood have been like? What if there hadn't been some prenatal mistake, some sort of cosmic event—I don't know what caused the incongruence between mind and body—and I had been born a boy and called Scott? Would I still be here, the person I am now, or would my male body, and the name I carried, have taken me in a completely different direction?

And then I wonder: Have I lived the life of a Lindsay? Or did I live the   10
life of a Silas for twenty-four years without even knowing?

The September after I turned twenty-four, four months after I asked my friends to start calling me Silas, I told my family that I am transgender. It was a shock to them, though my mom insists it wasn't that much of a shock—I had been embracing my masculine side for years already. They simply thought I was a lesbian, even though I had never confirmed nor denied my family's assumptions. At first, when I was twenty and just admitting to myself that I liked girls, and that I might be different, I was afraid to tell them. Still, as my hair got shorter, eventually finding its way into a fauxhawk, as my fashion choices slowly became more masculine, as more and more of my social life revolved around friends who were gay and organizations like my school's gay/straight alliance, my parents realized something was going on. By the time they started to ask questions, I had started to realize that being a butch lesbian wasn't the life I was meant to live, and I didn't know how to tell them that, although I did date women, I wasn't gay.

Although my family's reaction was positive—my parents told me they loved me no matter what, and my grandmother said, "I don't care. Why would I care?" and changed the subject to tell me about the ongoing saga of her kitchen remodel—things weren't easy for them, or for me. Part of me thought that, in telling them, a weight would be lifted—and it was, but then it was replaced with the burden of relearning our family dynamics, how we're supposed to interact with each other. For months after I told them, I had to remind myself when I talked to them that the boundaries were different, that I could let my guard down a little and let them see the real me. Although none of them have told me this, I'm sure they sometimes felt—perhaps still feel—the same way.

My mom and my grandmother started calling me Silas just before I went to visit for the holidays a couple of months later, but my dad and my brother took longer to get used to the change. Because I hadn't started hormones yet, and because I'd had short hair and worn men's clothing for a few years already, the name change was, for them, the biggest difference. It was the only one they could see. And they hated it.

It was jarring when they used my old name. I startled every time they said it—and they did frequently that Thanksgiving and Christmas, and a little less often in the months that followed. I don't think they even meant to, necessarily—it was just a habit they hadn't broken yet, but also probably a habit they weren't all that interested in fighting.

I was a little angry with them for not calling me Silas, for insisting on calling me Lindsay—a name I rarely heard anymore in my everyday life. I had already told my friends and had been living full-time as Silas for four months by the time I told my family. Everyone I saw on a daily basis had already made the transition, and it was difficult, when I was visiting, to be patient.

I would have been more likely to understand if Lindsay meant something special, but it doesn't. It's not a family name, and it means "from the lake settlement island"—which I'm not. It's not even as if my parents picked it because it would connote hope, or courage, or brilliance. Lindsay just happened to be popular the year I was born. It was, in fact, the forty-ninth most popular girls' name, which means that 6,530 American girls born in 1987 were named Lindsay. Two were in my class from kindergarten to twelfth grade. My parents simply heard it somewhere—they don't remember where exactly—and decided they liked it, and that it sounded good alongside my brother's name, Michael. And yet, they picked it. They gave it to me. They thought long and hard about what would sound good with our last name, about what name they could picture themselves yelling across a crowded playground. The very fact that they called their only daughter that for twenty-four years makes it mean something, to them at least. And I gave it up. I threw it away.

I get it. I understand why it's so hard, because—for a while—it was hard for me, too.

The first person to call me Silas out loud, after I e-mailed my friends asking them to do so, was my friend Meg. I almost cried, but not from happiness. We were sitting at my friend Heather's dining room table, and my

15

friends were all painting their nails and I was sitting there, drinking a margarita and trying to concentrate on the conversation and not think about the e-mail. They had all sent me texts or e-mails in response, telling me I had their support, but it had been only twelve hours and no one had said anything in person yet. Everyone was acting like everything was normal.

"Silas," Meg said, "can you pass me the Kleenex?"

I don't know if the others heard her or, if they did hear, if it was weird for them, too, but I suddenly couldn't breathe. It felt so weird, so not normal, to be called Silas instead of Lindsay. I immediately regretted my decision. What if this meant I was wrong about being transgender and I never should have asked people to call me something else? What if I was right, but had chosen the wrong name? Was it too late to send another e-mail, begging everyone to call me Andrew, or Charlie, or Sam? I hadn't expected it to be so hard—not for me at least, since I had wanted a new name—a male name—for so long, and since Silas felt so perfect in theory.

That was the beginning of June, at the end of my first year of graduate school, but by the time I went to visit my family for the Fourth of July, I had gotten used to hearing it, and it felt different—better—than being called Lindsay ever had, even before I started to wonder about my gender identity. Suddenly I had a hard time remembering to answer when my parents (whom I still didn't know how to tell) called me Lindsay.

Although I didn't feel connected to my birth name, I was attached to my nicknames: Linds, which my closest friends used to call me, their voices full of kindness and sometimes—when I was stressing out over something insignificant—loving exasperation. Lin, which my brother used to say in a short burst of familiarity when he was in a good mood, like it's five syllables long when we were arguing. A.Y., which always differentiated me from E.Y., Lindsey, my best friend in college.

I was even attached to Binz—the nickname my parents called me since they brought me home from the hospital. I used to hate it, begged my parents not to call me that in public; not to say it in front of my friends because they'd all laugh and call me that for days until they got bored; not to call me that anymore, at all, ever again. And yet, in the months between when my friends started calling me Silas and before my family knew Silas even existed, I used to call home sometimes just to hear my mom say it, just to bask in that familiarity, in that sense of normal. As hard as it was to hear her call me Lindsay all the time, over and over in the course of a single conversation, sometimes it felt good to hear her say it in her voice, to hold onto that and remember my past.

I've always been interested in names. A few years ago, my grandma wanted help finding some of our family history using the Internet. I was fascinated by what I found and ended up spending the entire summer researching our family tree. But nothing I found—not Ralph Waldo Emerson's place on one of the branches, not ancestors who came over on the Mayflower—was as interesting to me as the names of my great-grandmother and the other four Emerson sisters: Hazel Ruth, Grace Pearl, Gladys Rose, Maude Daisy, and—my personal favorite—Myrtle Fern.

After my grandmother's questions were answered, I continued to   25 research my ancestors because I wanted to know more about my dad's family, which I have never understood, and in which I have never felt like I really belonged. Since my paternal grandmother died when I was eight, we've seen that side of the family only once a year, at most, even though all of them still live in the same small town. I have only one cousin's number stored in my phone, and I haven't so much as sent Tiffany a "Merry Christmas" text message in at least two years. Still, my only living male relatives are on my dad's side, and that was the summer when I finally started asking myself the right questions about gender. I felt like I needed to know these men, to find out where I fit, and where I came from. My grandfather Otto, who came to the United States from Denmark, died in 1964, when my dad was three, and I can't navigate any of the Danish records, leaving me with nothing but questions. All I have are a handful of names: Otto, Erik, Knute—names that repeat in my father's family, though not for my brother and me.

I remember when I was little, when I'd hear my aunt call my cousin by his full name—Otto Knute Hansen, after our grandfather and great-grandfather—and how jealous I was of how exotic yet familial it sounded. I wanted a name like his, one that signified who I was, where I had come from. One that tied me, I have come to realize, to those men.

Researching names became a hobby of mine in college. I like to find out the meanings of names and when they were popular. I like to find new names—ones I've never heard before. Sometimes I'll go on baby-name websites and start judging people on what they name their kids, or offer suggestions on what middle names sound good with the first name they've picked, or what spelling they should choose—Lukas or Lucas, Zachary or Zackary. When friends tell me they're pregnant, I'm the first person to suggest names. When they have their kids and announce what they've picked, I secretly grade them: A for Eliza, B+ for Daniel, F for Pheonix spelled e-o instead of o-e.

I've been told that I have very traditional taste in names—too traditional is what's implied. I once got into an argument with someone on one of those baby-name websites because I said I hated it when people name their daughters traditionally male names, like James or Elliot or Eli. Gender-neutral names are different, I said, maybe even preferable in some cases (like in mine), but why make a child's life more difficult than it has to be? She argued that gendering names is pointless, that they always change over time anyway—that Lindsay, Stacy, Meredith, used to be male names, that a girl with a boy's name might be discriminated against less because people will assume she's male when they simply see the name in writing. "Besides," she said, "the names sound strong." The implication, of course, is that masculinity means strength, and femininity does not.

To say that a name has to sound male to sound strong is sexist, I argued. Wrong. Misogynistic. Who's to say that a Victoria can't be just as strong as an Elliot? Maybe even stronger? What's wrong with finding strength in femininity?

But the moment I asked this question, and looked back at the list of 30 male names I'd been making in Microsoft Word, ones I was considering for myself, my reason for being in this name forum in the first place, I felt like a hypocrite.

When I first started talking to my friends about being transgender, I told them I was thinking about a name for myself—a new name, a boy's name—and people told me, "But Lindsay is a boy's name. Or it can be, anyway." They suggested I keep it, or at least change it to something similar. Or something with the same nicknames. Or keep it as a middle name.

But the connotation of the name, for me, growing up in the nineties, is female. It makes me feel female when people call me that. It makes me feel as if I should have been someone completely different, someone I can never be. I see Lindsay as a cheerleader. I always picture girls with names that end in y (or worse, in *i*) as cheerleaders, as bottle blondes. Lindsay, Courtney, Stacy, Nikki. They're too cutesy. Lindsay is a teenager who goes to football games on Friday nights with her friends, watches romantic comedies, has an athletic boyfriend with a one-syllable name like Joe or Rob or Steve.

When I look in the mirror, I don't see a Lindsay. I never have, even when I still called myself that, still told other people to call me that. I always felt like a fraud, like the name didn't belong to me—it belonged to someone else—and I needed to give it back. I needed to get rid of it.

I thought for a while that I might pick the name Andrew. For a long time, I thought that was who I was. I'd look in the mirror and think, that could be me. I hate the name Andy because of my brother's weird friend from high school, and I don't like Drew, either—it just doesn't sound like a real name to me. But Andrew is undoubtedly masculine, without question, and yet there's a softness to it in that last syllable. It's a name I felt I could live up to.

A few months before I chose my name, though, I moved to Ohio for 35 graduate school and met two more Andrews. Two guys whose company, it turns out, I enjoy immensely, but who are just two more additions to a long list of Andrews who are nothing like me. Now, when I hear the name Andrew, I picture specific people—my friend Andrew the PhD student and my friend Andrew the fiction writer. I couldn't see myself as an Andrew anymore; I would have to change too much of myself to become one. Just like with Lindsay, it felt like a name I was borrowing, one I had to give back.

So I started looking again.

I made a list of popular names from 1987, thinking that maybe I could pick a name that would sound right, that would sound like I was really named that, like that had always been what people called me. None of those names felt right, though: Michael, Christopher, Matthew, Joshua, David, Daniel, James, Justin, Robert. I kept going further and further down the list—Brandon, Anthony, Nicholas, Zachary, Aaron, Mark, Paul, Gregory, Jose—and none of those felt right, either. I kept looking, thinking I'd find something eventually, but I started to lose hope. I started to think I'd never find the name that felt like mine. Then I thought maybe the reason I couldn't find a name was that I was wrong about being transgender—maybe it wasn't the answer to all the questions I'd had for years. And so I stopped looking for a while.

Eventually, someone suggested picking a family name. I gave it some thought—maybe Charlie, after my great-grandfather, but I'd grown up hearing stories about him from my grandmother, his daughter, and the name seemed like too much to live up to, like naming myself after a legend. I kept wishing I could pick something from my dad's side—something Danish—but the ones I knew were all taken by my uncles and their sons, and it felt weird to name myself after a living relative I hardly knew.

Then, on a list of popular names in Denmark, I found it: Silas, #21. It's not Danish, actually—it's from the Bible. But it's more popular in Denmark now than in any other country. If you search for my first and last name on Facebook, most of the men who show up live in Copenhagen, Odense, Frederiksberg. It means "man of the forest," and though I'm not a survivalist, I was a Girl Scout for fifteen years, and most of my best childhood memories take place in the woods behind my parents' house.

That night, I looked in the mirror and said it out loud a few times. Silas   40
Hansen. Silas. Si. I didn't cringe the way I did with some of the others, didn't shake my head in disgust, didn't feel like a fraud using someone else's name. Finally, it felt right, like it had been my name all along.

My cousin Holly has known other transgender people and didn't ask me anything about that. Her only question, via e-mail, was why I chose the name Silas. I didn't know how to answer the question—it was too hard to explain it all, so I told her I didn't know, it just sounded right, felt right. "I just like it," I said. It wasn't a lie, but it wasn't the whole truth, either. She didn't press for more.

She responded a few hours later and said she expected a long story about why I had chosen it, some sort of significance. "For the record," she said, "I think it's the right choice."

She explained that Silas is the contracted form of Silvanus, and that Silvanus is an important character in the New Testament, a friend of the apostles Paul and Timothy. "Isn't that cool?" she said. Our family isn't all that religious, so it surprised me that she knew this, even more that she found significance in it. And yet, there it is: my father is Tim, my brother is Michael Paul. "Silas, Paul, Tim," Holly said. "All in one family."

I haven't read the Bible in years, not since I stopped going to church after I started college, and I don't remember ever reading about Silvanus. Maybe I just skipped over those parts, or maybe I've forgotten. I'm agnostic now, not sure if I believe in a higher power at all, let alone the Christian concept of God. But I like the idea of Silvanus, a writer, a teacher—like me. I like the image of the three names alongside each other—Silas, Paul, Timothy—like my name belongs there, like it was meant to be this way.

My eighty-eight-year-old grandmother has never been good with names. It's a trait that's carried on the second X-chromosome in my family, along with bad knees and asthma and anxiety. Grandma says it started with her mother and her four sisters. They'd all be in the same room and one of them would leave, and they'd end up calling each other by the wrong names. "Maude," Hazel would say to Myrtle, when Maude had just left, "can you hand me that glass?" And Myrtle would respond, without even thinking.

To my grandmother, I have never been Lindsay—always Kim, my mother's name, or Andrea, my cousin's. My mom is always Terry, her older sister. Aunt Terry is also always Kim. She calls my cousins Holly and Andrea by each other's names. Now that Holly has two daughters, Kelsey and Katelyn, she calls them each other's names, or their mother's, or mine. My brother, Mike, is Tim, after our dad, or Floyd or Don, my grandmother's brothers, who have both been dead almost a decade.

"I'm not senile," she says. "I've done this for years."

A few weeks after I told my family I was trans, when I was home visiting for Thanksgiving, my grandmother started using my new name, except she couldn't say it. She kept saying "Cyrus" instead. My mom kept making jokes out of it, like calling me "Billy Ray." A few weeks later, the night I got into town for Christmas break, she asked me to pass the salt at dinner, but called me Mike, then Tim. "Sorry," she said. "I mean Cyrus."

My friend Dyan told me after I picked the name Silas that she liked it because all the letters in Silas are in the name Lindsay. Although I didn't think about it before I picked it, I like the idea of it. It's like I'm taking parts of my old self along with me as I move forward—not the whole, but the parts that fit.

Kathy, one of my coworkers from my job in college, is a grandmother of five: Noah, Emma, Devin, Colby, and Cora. "None of them look like their names, though," she tells people. She shows pictures, tells them that Noah should be Miles, Devin should be Eli.

On a trip back to western New York the summer after I told my friends but before I told my parents, I told Kathy about my name change. She had known for a few months that it was something I was considering and had always been supportive, but she shook her head. "Jack," she said. "You look like a Jack."

I started biweekly testosterone injections the February after I told my parents I was transgender, and—after paying a $140 fee and swearing in front of a judge that I wasn't changing my name to avoid debt or for other fraudulent purposes—legally changed my name that June. Even now that my voice has dropped, and my facial hair is slowly filling in, and my driver's license has the right name and gender, I still wonder sometimes if Kathy is right. What if, five years from now, after the hormones have truly made their mark, I stop thinking Silas is the right name for me? I honestly don't know what it means to look like a name, but I'm also guilty of name-stereotyping. There was a guy I knew in college, an older student with long gray hair and a beard down to his chest; he dressed like a biker. And he went by James. I always thought he should have been Jim, at least, if not something more nontraditional: Spike, maybe.

But the thing I love most about the name Silas is that I don't know anyone else with that name. I've never met another Silas and so I don't have a picture in my head of what one looks like, sounds like, acts like. Silas is a blank slate. If I were a Matt or a Jack or an Andrew, I'd feel as if I had to live up to that name, as if I had to do it justice. If I were a Charlie, I'd feel as if I were carrying around my great-grandfather's name, his legacy. But Silas is mine.

I can change the way I look and grow into an entirely different personality. I can learn to act like a stereotypical guy—which I don't, most of the time—and still be Silas, or I can stay the way I am now and the name still works. Sometimes, since strangers do not always read me as male right away, people assume that I am a girl named Silas—it doesn't sound all that masculine, at least not the way a name like John or Joseph does. Part of me hates it when this happens, but at the same time, I'm a little bit grateful that the name straddles the border between masculine and feminine, the way I do. I see Silas as someone who can cross over into one or the other anytime he wants, anytime he needs to. My friends joke that I'm the type of person who can calm a crying baby and change the oil in a car, probably at the same time. Although I actually know nothing about changing the oil in a car, I like the way this sounds, and I think the sentiment behind it is what's important. I'm the guy they call when they need someone to help move their couch, or when they need something off the top shelf but can't reach it. I'm also the guy they call when they can't remember how to cast on stitches for the scarf they're knitting, or when they need a good chocolate chip cookie recipe. That's why Silas works for me. I can carry that name with me as I learn how to be a man, learn to navigate this land of men's bathrooms and facial hair and talking to girls as a straight man without losing sight of who I am, who I used to be. And, in the end, what more could I want from a name?

The Reader's Presence

1. Reread carefully the beginning of the essay. What strategic effect does Hansen elicit from readers by beginning with various categories—such as "feminist," "women's studies major," "frequent attendee at Ani DiFranco concerts"—to define himself? How did these categories illustrate Hansen's identity? How do they relate to the importance of one's name? In what specific ways do "boundaries" mark the narrator's life before, during, and after the transition in his life?

2. When Hansen and his friend Nicole discuss ideal names, Nicole imagines what it would have been like to be named Maddy instead. What does Nicole mean when she says, "I didn't live the life of a Maddy, though. I've lived the life of a Nicole" (paragraph 8)? To what extent has the narrator lived the life of a "Lindsay"? What sort of things does the narrator associate with the name Lindsay? How important is it for the narrator to feel connected to his name? Why is it important for Hansen to choose a name that is "a blank slate" (paragraph 53)? To what extent does Hansen succeed?

3. **CONNECTIONS:**   The American philosopher William James observed, "Life is in the transitions as much as in the terms connected." Reflect on Hansen's essay and on the transitions that Silas Hansen has experienced. What specific moments in the essay can you point to that support—or contradict—whether Hansen would endorse or refute James's assertion?

Edward Hoagland

On Stuttering

EDWARD HOAGLAND (b. 1932) is an essayist, a nature writer, and a novelist. In 1951, Hoagland joined the Ringling Bros. and Barnum & Bailey Circus and wrote a novel about his experience: *Cat Man* (1956) was accepted for publication before he graduated from Harvard and the book won the Houghton Mifflin Literary Fellowship Award. He has received several other honors, including two Guggenheim

> **"Most of us live like stand-up comedians on a vaudeville stage."**

Fellowships, an O. Henry Award, an award from the American Academy of Arts and Letters, and a Lannan Foundation Award. Having taught at Bennington College in Vermont for almost twenty years, Hoagland retired in 2005.

Hoagland's essays cover a wide range of topics, such as personal experiences, wild animals, travels to other countries, and ecological crises. Among his many highly regarded books are *Walking the Dead Diamond River* (1973), *African Calliope* (1979), *Balancing Acts* (1992), *Tigers & Ice* (1999), and *Hoagland on Nature* (2003). His latest book, *Children Are Diamonds: An African Apocalypse*, was published in 2013.

In his memoir, *Compass Points* (2001), Hoagland writes: "Most of us live like stand-up comedians on a vaudeville stage—the way an essayist does—by our humble wits, messing up, swallowing an aspirin, knowing Hollywood won't call, thinking no one we love will die today, just another day of sunshine and rain."

STUTTERING is like trying to run with loops of rope around your feet. And yet you feel that you do want to run because you may get more words out that way before you trip: an impulse you resist so other people won't tell you to "calm down" and "relax." Because they themselves may stammer a little bit when jittery or embarrassed, it's hard for a real stutterer like me to convince a new acquaintance that we aren't perpetually in such a nervous state and that it's quite normal for us to be at the mercy of strangers. Strangers are usually civilized, once the rough and sometimes inadvertently hurtful process of recognizing what is wrong with us is over (that we're not laughing, hiccuping, coughing, or whatever) and in a way we plumb them for traces of schadenfreude. A stutterer knows who the good guys are in any crowded room, as well as the location of each mocking gleam, and even the St. Francis type, who will wait until he thinks nobody is looking to wipe a fleck of spittle off his face.

I've stuttered for more than sixty years, and the mysteries of the encumbrance still catch me up: being reminded every morning that it's engrained in my fiber, although I had forgotten in my dreams. Life can become a matter of measuring the importance of anything you have to say. Is it better to remain a pleasant cipher who ventures nothing in particular but chuckles immoderately at everyone else's conversation, or instead to subject your several companions to the ordeal of watching you struggle to expel opinions that are either blurred and vitiated, or made to sound too emphatic, by all the huffing and puffing, the facial contortions, tongue biting, blushing, and suffering? "Write it down," people often said to me in school; indeed I sold my first novel before I left college.

Self-confidence can reduce a stutter's dimensions (in that sense you do "outgrow" it), as will affection (received or felt), anger, sexual arousal, and various other hormonal or pheromonal states you may dip into in the shorter term. Yet it still lurks underfoot, like a trapdoor. I was determined not to be impeded and managed to serve a regular stint in the Army by telling the draft-board psychiatrist that I wanted to and was only stammering from "nervousness" with him. Later I also contrived to become a college professor, thanks to the patience of my early students. Nevertheless, through childhood and adolescence, when I was almost mute in public, I could talk without much difficulty to one or two close friends, and then to the particular girl I was necking with. In that case, an overlapping trust was then the lubricant, but if it began to evaporate as our hopes for permanence didn't pan out, I'd start regretfully, apologetically but willy-nilly, to stutter with her again. Adrenaline, when I got mad, operated in a similar fashion, though only momentarily. That is, if somebody made fun of me or treated me cavalierly and a certain threshold was crossed, a spurt of chemistry would suddenly free my mouth and — like Popeye grabbing a can of spinach — I could answer him. Poor Billy Budd[1] didn't learn this technique (and his example frightened me because of its larger implications). Yet many stutterers develop a snappish temperament, and from not just sheer frustration but the fact that being more than ready to "lose one's temper" (as Billy wasn't) actually helps. As in jujitsu, you can trap an opponent by employing his strength and cruelty against him; and bad guys aren't generally smart enough to know that if they wait me out, I'll bog down helplessly all over again.

Overall, however, stuttering is not so predictable. Whether rested or exhausted, fibbing or speaking the Simon-pure truth, and when in the company of chums or people whom I don't respect, I can be fluent or tied in knots. I learned young to be an attentive listener, both because my empathy for others' worries was honed by my handicap and because it was in my best interest that they talk a lot. And yet a core in you will hemorrhage if you become a mere assenter. How many opinions can you keep to yourself before you choke on them (and turn into a stick of furniture for everybody else)? So, instead, you measure what's worth specifying. If you agree with two-thirds of what's being suggested, is it worth the labor of breathlessly elaborating upon the one-third where you differ? There were plenty of times when a subject might come up that I knew more about than the rest of the group, and it used to gall me if I had held my peace till maybe closeted afterward with a close friend. A stymieing bashfulness can also slide a stutterer into slack language because accurate words are so much harder to say than bland ones. You're tempted to be content with an approximation of what you mean in order to escape the scourge of being exact. A sort of football game is going on in your head — the tacklers live there too — and the very effort of pausing to figure out the right way to describe something will alert them to how to pull you down. Being glib and sloppy generates less blockage.

But it's important not to err in the opposite direction, on the side of tendentiousness, and insist on equal time only because you are a pain in the neck with a problem. You can stutter till your tongue bleeds and your chest is sore from heaving, but so what, if you haven't anything to say that's worth the humiliation? Better to function as a kind of tuning fork, vibrating to other people's anguish or apprehensiveness, as well as your own. A handicap can be cleansing. My scariest moments as a stutterer have been (1) when my daughter was learning to talk and briefly got the impression that she was supposed to do the same; (2) once when I was in the woods and a man shot in my direction and I had to make myself heard loud and fast; and (3) when anticipating weddings where I would need either to propose a toast or say "I

5

---

[1] ***Poor Billy Budd:*** A reference to the main character in Herman Melville's novella, *Billy Budd* (published 1924). Billy Budd's speech impediment plays a pivotal role in the plot, leading to his hanging. — EDS.

do." Otherwise my impediment ceased to be a serious blight about the time I lost my virginity: just a sort of cleft to step around—a squint and gasp of hesitation that indicated to people I might want to be friends with or interview that I wasn't perfect either and perhaps they could trust me.

At worst, during my teens, when I was stuttering on vowels as well as consonants and spitting a few words out could seem interminable, I tried some therapies. But "Slow Speech" was as slow as the trouble itself; and repeatedly writing the first letter of the word that I was stuttering on with my finger in my pocket looked peculiar enough to attract almost as much attention. It did gradually lighten with my maturity and fatherhood, professional recognition, and the other milestones that traditionally help. Nothing "slew" it, though, until at nearly 60 I went semiblind for a couple of years, and this emergency eclipsed—completely trumped—the lesser difficulty. I felt I simply had to talk or die, and so I talked. Couldn't do it gratuitously or lots, but I talked enough to survive. The stutter somehow didn't hold water and ebbed away, until surgery restored my vision and then it returned, like other normalcies.

Such variations can make a stutter seem like a sort of ancillary eccentricity, or a personal Godzilla. But the ball carrier in your head is going to have his good days too—when he can swivel past the tacklers, improvising a broken-field dash so that they are out of position—or even capture their attention with an idea so intriguing that they stop and listen. Not for long, however: The message underlying a stutter is rather like mortality, after all. Real reprieves and fluency are not for you and me. We blunder along, stammering—then not so much—through minor scrapes and scares, but not unscathed. We're not Demosthenes, of course. And poor Demosthenes, if you look him up, ended about as sadly as Billy Budd. People tend to. ◼

The Reader's Presence

1. Why does Hoagland compare his stutter to a football game (paragraph 4)? Explore the metaphor fully. For example, what position does Hoagland play? Who are the tacklers who are trying to pull him down? How many touchdowns does he score in his life, according to his essay? What strategies does he develop to avoid anticipated blockers? Would you say he's winning or losing? Why?

2. In what specific ways do Hoagland's sentences and paragraphs begin and end as you might have anticipated? Can you detect written signs of his stutter? What kinds of verbal hesitations and restatements happen when someone stutters? Where—and with what effects—are there similar hesitations and restatements in Hoagland's essay? Imagine Hoagland speaking this essay. At which points do you think that he would hesitate? Rewrite a paragraph to include the imagined stuttering and compare it to the original paragraph. What changes in meaning occur in the rewritten version?

3. **CONNECTIONS:**   Read David Sedaris's "Me Talk Pretty One Day" (page 252) and compare his and Hoagland's approaches to handling difficulties with speech. What strategies do they use to deal with being less than fluent? To what extent do their limitations affect their feelings about themselves? about the world around them? Who deals more effectively with not being able to communicate easily? Why?

The Writer at Work

EDWARD HOAGLAND on What an Essay Is

© Oscar White/Corbis

Known as one of America's finest essayists, Edward Hoagland began his career writing fiction. In this passage from his Introduction to *The Best American Essays 1999*, Hoagland describes how he thinks essays work and the idiosyncratic ways essayists—like himself—approach the act of writing them. Essays, he reminds us, are different from articles and documents: They don't necessarily offer objective information and they don't require their writers to be authorities about anything other than their own experiences. All good essays, he suggests, encapsulate their writer's presence. In these literary beliefs he is a direct descendant of Montaigne (1533–1592), whom many consider the inventor of the modern essay. Montaigne, too, was skeptical of authority and wrote essays that appear to follow the drifts of an interior dialogue carried on with himself. After reading Hoagland's brief but thoughtful passage, consider how it comments on his essay on stuttering.

“ Essays are how we speak to one another in print—caroming thoughts not merely in order to convey a certain packet of information, but with a special edge or bounce of personal character in a kind of public letter. You multiply yourself as a writer, gaining height as though jumping on a trampoline, if you can catch the gist of what other people have also been feeling and clarify it for them. Classic essay subjects, like the flux of friendship, "On Greed," "On Religion," "On Vanity," or solitude, lying, self-sacrifice, can be major-league yet not require Bertrand Russell to handle them. A layman who has diligently looked into something, walking in the mosses of regret after the death of a parent, for instance, may acquire an intangible authority, even without being memorably angry or funny or possessing a beguiling equanimity. *He* cares; therefore, if he has tinkered enough with his words, we do too.

An essay is not a scientific document. It can be serendipitous or domestic, satire or testimony, tongue-in-cheek or a wail of grief. Mulched perhaps in its own contradictions, it promises no sure objectivity, just the condiment of opinion on a base of observation, and sometimes such leaps of illogic or superlogic that they may work a bit like magic realism in a novel: namely, to simulate the mind's own processes in a murky and incongruous world. More than being instructive, as a magazine article is, an essay has a slant, a seasoned personality behind it that ought to weather well. Even if we think the author is telling us the earth is flat, we might want to listen to him elaborate upon the fringes of his premise because the bristle of his narrative and what he's seen intrigues us. He has a cutting edge, yet balance too. A given body of information is going to be eclipsed, but what lives in art is spirit, not factuality, and we respond to Montaigne's human touch despite four centuries of technological and social change. **”**

Langston Hughes
SALVATION

One of the leading figures of the Harlem Renaissance, **LANGSTON HUGHES** (1902–1967) was a prolific writer. He started his career as a poet, but he also wrote fiction, autobiography, biography, history, and plays, and he worked at various times as a journalist. One of his most famous poems, "The Negro Speaks of Rivers," was written while he was in high school. Although Hughes traveled widely, most of his writings are concerned with the lives of urban working-class African Americans.

> "I only knew the people I had grown up with, and they weren't the people whose shoes were always shined, who had been to Harvard, or who had heard of Bach. But they seemed to me good people too."

Hughes used the rhythms of blues and jazz to bring to his writing a distinctive expression of black culture and experience. His work continues to be popular today, especially collections of short stories such as *The Ways of White Folks* (1934), volumes of poetry such as *Montage of a Dream Deferred* (1951), and his series of vignettes on the character Jesse B. Simple, collected and published from 1950 to 1965. Hughes published two volumes of autobiography; "Salvation" is taken from the first of these, *The Big Sea* (1940).

Throughout his work, Hughes refused to idealize his subject. "Certainly," he said, "I personally knew very few people anywhere who were wholly beautiful and wholly good. Besides I felt that the masses of our people had as much in their lives to put into books as did those more fortunate ones who had been born with some means and the ability to work up to a master's degree at a Northern college." Expressing the writer's truism on writing about what one knows best, he continued, "Anyway, I didn't know the upper-class Negroes well enough to write much about them. I only knew the people I had grown up with, and they weren't the people whose shoes were always shined, who had been to Harvard, or who had heard of Bach. But they seemed to me good people too."

I WAS SAVED FROM SIN when I was going on thirteen. But not really saved. It happened like this. There was a big revival at my Auntie Reed's church. Every night for weeks there had been much preaching, singing, praying, and shouting, and some very hardened sinners had been brought to Christ, and the membership of the church had grown by leaps and bounds. Then just before the revival ended, they held a special meeting for children, "to bring the young lambs to the fold." My aunt spoke of it for days ahead. That night I was escorted to the front row and placed on the mourners' bench with all the other young sinners, who had not yet been brought to Jesus.

My aunt told me that when you were saved you saw a light, and something happened to you inside! And Jesus came into your life! And God was with you from then on! She said you could see and hear and feel Jesus in your soul. I believed her. I had heard a great many old people say the same thing and it seemed to me they ought to know. So I sat there calmly in the hot, crowded church, waiting for Jesus to come to me.

The preacher preached a wonderful rhythmical sermon, all moans and shouts and lonely cries and dire pictures of hell, and then he sang a song about the ninety and nine safe in the fold, but one little lamb was left out in the cold. Then he said: "Won't you come? Won't you come to Jesus? Young lambs, won't you come?" And he held out his arms to all us young sinners there on the mourners' bench. And the little girls cried. And some of them jumped up and went to Jesus right away. But most of us just sat there.

A great many old people came and knelt around us and prayed, old women with jet-black faces and braided hair, old men with work-gnarled hands. And the church sang a song about the lower lights are burning, some poor sinners to be saved. And the whole building rocked with prayer and song.

Still I kept waiting to *see* Jesus.   5

Finally all the young people had gone to the altar and were saved, but one boy and me. He was a rounder's son named Westley. Westley and I were surrounded by sisters and deacons praying. It was very hot in the church, and getting late now. Finally Westley said to me in a whisper: "God damn! I'm tired o' sitting here. Let's get up and be saved." So he got up and was saved.

Then I was left all alone on the mourners' bench. My aunt came and knelt at my knees and cried, while prayers and song swirled all around me in the little church. The whole congregation prayed for me alone, in a mighty wail of moans and voices. And I kept waiting serenely for Jesus, waiting, waiting—but he didn't come. I wanted to see him, but nothing happened to me. Nothing! I wanted something to happen to me, but nothing happened.

I heard the songs and the minister saying: "Why don't you come? My dear child, why don't you come to Jesus? Jesus is waiting for you. He wants you. Why don't you come? Sister Reed, what is this child's name?"

"Langston," my aunt sobbed.

"Langston, why don't you come? Why don't you come and be saved? Oh,   10 Lamb of God! Why don't you come?"

Now it was really getting late. I began to be ashamed of myself, holding everything up so long. I began to wonder what God thought about Westley, who certainly hadn't seen Jesus either, but who was now sitting proudly on the platform, swinging his knickerbockered legs and grinning down at me, surrounded by deacons and old women on their knees praying. God had not struck Westley dead for taking his name in vain or for lying in the temple. So I decided that maybe to save further trouble, I'd better lie, too, and say that Jesus had come, and get up and be saved.

So I got up.

Suddenly the whole room broke into a sea of shouting, as they saw me rise. Waves of rejoicing swept the place. Women leaped in the air. My aunt threw her arms around me. The minister took me by the hand and led me to the platform.

When things quieted down, in a hushed silence, punctuated by a few ecstatic "Amens," all the new young lambs were blessed in the name of God. Then joyous singing filled the room.

That night, for the first time in my life but one—for I was a big boy   15 twelve years old—I cried. I cried, in bed alone, and couldn't stop. I buried my head under the quilts, but my aunt heard me. She woke up and told my uncle I was crying because the Holy Ghost had come into my life, and because I had seen Jesus. But I was really crying because I couldn't bear to tell her that I had lied, that I had deceived everybody in the church, that I hadn't seen Jesus, and that now I didn't believe there was a Jesus anymore, since he didn't come to help me. ●

The Reader's Presence

1. Pay close attention to Hughes's two opening sentences. How would you describe their tone? How do they suggest the underlying pattern of the essay? How do they introduce the idea of deception right from the start? Who is being deceived in the essay? Is it the congregation? God? Hughes's aunt? the reader?

2. Hughes's essay is full of hyperbole, much of it expressing the heightened emotion of religious conversion. What is the purpose of the exclamation points Hughes uses in paragraph 2? Who is speaking these sentences? Where are other examples of over-statement? How does Hughes incorporate lyrics from songs into his prose (see especially paragraph 3)? Why not simply quote from the songs directly? How do these stylistic decisions affect your sense of the scene? Do you feel aligned with Hughes? Why or why not?

3. **CONNECTIONS:**   How does Hughes use the character of Westley? To what extent is Westley essential in the narrative? Explain why. How does Westley's role compare to secondary characters such as, for example, Theresa in Bernard Cooper's "A Clack of Tiny Sparks: Remembrances of a Gay Boyhood" (page 98) or Yafei in Ha Jin's "Arrival" (page 161)?

The Writer at Work

LANGSTON HUGHES on *How to Be a Bad Writer (in Ten Easy Lessons)*

Established authors are frequently asked for tips on writing. Here Langston Hughes reverses the practice and offers young writers some memorable advice on how to write poorly. "How to Be a Bad Writer" first appeared in the *Harlem Quarterly* (Spring 1950). Some of Hughes's suggestions no longer seem applicable today, thanks in part to his own literary efforts. But which lessons do you think are still worth paying attention to?

❝1. Use all the clichés possible, such as "He had a gleam in his eye," or "Her teeth were white as pearls."

2. If you are a Negro, try very hard to write with an eye dead on the white market—use modern stereotypes of older stereotypes—big burly Negroes, criminals, low-lifers, and prostitutes.

3. Put in a lot of profanity and as many pages as possible of near-pornography and you will be so modern you pre-date Pompei in your lonely crusade toward the best-seller lists. By all means be misunderstood, unappreciated, and ahead of your time in print and out, then you can be felt-sorry-for by your own self, if not the public.

4. Never characterize characters. Just name them and then let them go for themselves. Let all of them talk the same way. If the reader hasn't imagination enough to make something out of cardboard cut-outs, shame on him!

5. Write about China, Greece, Tibet, or the Argentine pampas—anyplace you've never seen and know nothing about. Never write about anything you know, your home town, or your home folks, or yourself.

6. Have nothing to say, but use a great many words, particularly high-sounding words, to say it.

7. If a playwright, put into your script a lot of hand-waving and spirituals, preferably the ones everybody has heard a thousand times from Marion Anderson to the Golden Gates.

8. If a poet, rhyme June with moon as often and in as many ways as possible. Also use *thee*'s and *thou*'s and *'tis* and *o'er*, and invert your sentences all the time. Never say, "The sun rose, bright and shining." But, rather, "Bright and shining rose the sun."

9. Pay no attention to spelling or grammar or the neatness of the

manuscript. And in writing letters, never sign your name so anyone can read it. A rapid scrawl will better indicate how important and how busy you are.

10. Drink as much liquor as possible and always write under the influence of alcohol. When you can't afford alcohol yourself, or even if you can, drink on your friends, fans, and the general public.

If you are white, there are many more things I can advise in order to be a bad writer, but since this piece is for colored writers, there are some things I know a Negro just will not do, not even for writing's sake, so there is no use mentioning them. **"**

Ha Jin

ARRIVAL

HA JIN (b. 1956) is an award-winning Chinese American author. Born Jin Xuefei, in the Liaoning province of northern China, he grew up in rural China and joined the People's Liberation Army of China at age fourteen, serving for several years along what was then the Sino-Soviet border. He left the army at nineteen and began his studies at Heilongjiang University in Harbin, China, when he was twenty-one. He received a bachelor's degree in English from Heilongjiang in 1981 and a master's degree in American literature at Shandong University in 1984. In 1985, he left China to work toward a PhD in English at Brandeis University in

> Ha Jin grew up in rural China and joined the People's Liberation Army of China at age fourteen.

Massachusetts. Although his original intention had been to return to China to teach and write, he decided to remain in the United States after the Tiananmen Square massacre in 1989. He took the pen name "Ha Jin" when he decided to write exclusively in English, and has published more than a dozen books under that name since 1990, including critically acclaimed novels as well as collections of poetry and short stories. He had only been writing in English for a dozen years when his novel *Waiting* won the National Book Award in 1999. He has also received two PEN/Faulkner Awards, the Flannery O'Connor Award for short fiction, the PEN/Hemingway Award, and the Asian American Literary Award. His most recent books include *Nanjing Requiem: A Novel* (2011); *A Good Fall* (2009), a short story collection; and *The Writer as Migrant* (2008), a book of nonfiction on writing in the migrant tradition. He teaches writing at Boston University.

Explaining how the Tiananmen Square massacre changed him, Ha Jin said, "I served in the Chinese army, and the army was called the People's Army, so we were from the people and supposed to serve the people and protect the people. I was shocked that the field armies would go into the city and really suppress civilians. Then my son arrived. That was a turning point. It was clear that he would be an American."

IN COLLEGE, English meant humiliation to me. When I was assigned to major in the language in 1977 at Heilongjiang University,[1] I knew only dozens of English words and was put in the lowest class, where I stayed four years. We were the first group of undergraduates admitted through the entrance exams after the Cultural Revolution,[2] after colleges had been closed for a decade. There was no hope for a late starter like me to catch up with the students in the faster English classes, so I kind of gave up and avoided working hard on my English. But in 1980, writers such as Hemingway, Faulkner, Bellow and Malamud suddenly became immensely popular in China after American literature had mostly been banned for three decades. I was fascinated by their fiction: Their literary subject matter was not confined to politics and social movements, as it was in China, and the techniques they used — such as stream of consciousness and multiple narrative points of view — were unheard of to me. I made up my mind to study American literature after college. For that, I would have to pass an advanced English test, so I began applying myself.

In 1982, I got into the graduate program in American literature at Shandong University,[3] but I was not a good student — at least, my professor didn't like me, probably because I married in my first year there when I was supposed to concentrate on my studies. There were only three graduate students in my year, and we had American professors teaching us most of the time. Back then, no doctoral degree in our field was offered in China, so the only way to continue my graduate work was to go abroad. Beatrice Spade, my American literature professor, encouraged me to apply to some U.S. universities, and in the winter of 1984, I started sending out applications.

---

[1] **Heilongjiang University:** Located in Harbin, China, the university today numbers 34,000 students. — EDS.

[2] **Cultural Revolution:** A massive political reform movement launched by Mao Zedong in 1965 mainly to suppress counterrevolutionary activities. — EDS.

[3] **Shandong University:** With some 54,000 students on a sprawling campus in Jinan, the university is one of the largest and most prestigious in China. — EDS.

The next spring, Brandeis University,[4] which I knew nothing about and which had been recommended to me by Professor Spade, notified me of my admission and offered me a scholarship, but I wasn't very excited. I was 28, and unable to imagine living outside of China.

Since childhood, I had lived a peripatetic life, most of the time separated from my parents, so I was quite independent. But the United States was so far away and so enigmatic that ever since I had started the application, I had been possessed by a relentless emotion, as if I was about to fall ill. The previous October, Professor Spade had introduced me to a group of top American scholars in a delegation that visited our university. They were staying at a hotel in Jinan City, and I spoke with Professor Alan Trachtenberg, the head of American studies at Yale, for a preliminary interview. I was a bundle of nerves, and when he asked if I had questions for him, I blurted out, "I don't know if I can survive in America." The question, more existential than literal, must have been tormenting me for months and just gushed out. Professor Trachtenberg's eyes flashed behind his glasses—he was surprised, but there was no way for me to clarify, to say that physically I could survive for sure, but that I was more concerned about my quest for a meaningful existence, which I had no idea how to accomplish in the United States.

So, I blew my opportunity with Yale. I had my scholarship from Brandeis, though, and now I had to get permission from my university to go abroad. That meant I would have a J-1 visa that required its holder to return after graduation. To me, this was no problem, as I viewed my studies in America as no more than a sojourn. Besides, the authorities, to prevent me from defecting, would not allow my wife and child to go with me, so I would have to return anyway, the sooner, the better. 5

A schoolmate, Yafei, and I were allowed to leave together. He was going to MIT to study linguistics. After mid-August, we went to Beijing to go through a few days of "the training," which was more like a formality consisting of speeches given by officials and brief introductions to the United States.

One of the officials, a squat, smiling man, told us to be careful about sexual contact with foreigners and not to catch VD, but he also said, "It's understandable if you have a fling with someone when you are there, because we are not puritans."

Everything went smoothly in Beijing, except that three days before our scheduled departure, we were informed that the plane tickets were no longer available, though our school had paid for them long before. Apparently, our tickets had been given to "more important people." Desperate, Yafei contacted a distant relative who had some pull with the airport. To get the tickets, we would have to give the man some brand-name cigarettes. His

---

[4] ***Brandeis University:*** A noted university in Waltham, Massachusetts, just outside Boston.— EDS.

wife was fond of 555's, and we decided to offer him two cartons. I didn't smoke and had no idea where to buy foreign cigarettes, which regular stores didn't carry. Yafei, always resourceful, got them without difficulty, and we split the cost, each paying 30 yuan,[5] almost half our monthly salary. We took a bus to the man's home to hand him the bribe. He met us in the doorway of his apartment and gave us the plane tickets after taking the cigarettes. Though he didn't let us in, through a narrow pane of glass on a door I caught a glimpse of his wife lying in bed smoking. On our way back to our dorm, Yafei said that the woman's father was a high-ranking official. Years later, whenever I thought of going back to China, the image of the young woman with a haggard face and bedraggled hair smoking expensive cigarettes would come to mind and make me wince.

Yafei and I boarded a plane without anyone seeing us off. I had never flown before, so the shifting and tilting cityscape of Beijing viewed from the air was exhilarating. However, the Boeing had a peculiar smell that nauseated us. It was a typical American odor, sharp and artificial, like a combination of chemicals and perfumes. Even lunch, Parmesan chicken and salad, tasted strange and gave off the same awful smell. I would find it everywhere in America, even on vegetables and fruits in supermarkets, but in a week or so I would get used to it, unable to detect it anymore.

Professor Peter Swiggart, a middle-aged man with chestnut hair and a   10 roundish, good-natured face, was assigned by the international program at Brandeis to be my host, so he agreed to pick me up at Logan International Airport.

The moment I sat in the passenger seat of his car, he told me to "buckle up." I had no clue what he was talking about. He pulled his seat belt; still, I didn't know how to use mine, never having seen one in a car before. I thought to myself, *This is like a ride on a plane.* That was the only connection I could make with the seat belt. Professor Swiggart helped me push the buckle into the slot.

My graduate dormitory at Brandeis was a three-story building by the Charles River. I had two roommates. Benny was from Israel, and Hosan from South Korea. Hosan, a broad-framed man with a square face, was a second-year graduate student in the chemistry department, which had a number of Chinese students, so he spread the word among them about my arrival, probably because I was an oddity studying literature instead of science.

The next afternoon, I strolled along the Charles. The sky was clear and high, much higher than the sky in China, thanks to the absence of smog. A pudgy angler was fishing with a tallboy of beer in his hand. Behind us, Canada geese strutted and mallards waddled. A young mother and her toddler boy were tossing potato chips at the waterfowl. Soon the man caught a bass, about a foot and a half long, wriggling like crazy. He unhooked the

---

[5] **yuan:** Basis of Chinese currency; in 2011, a yuan was worth approximately 16 cents. —EDS.

fish, observed it for a few seconds. "Dammit, it's you again," he said, and, to my amazement, dropped it back into the water.

"You don't keep your fish?" I asked him.

"Nope."   15

"You can't eat it?" I was still baffled.

"I'm fishin' jus' for fun."

It occurred to me that people here had a different view of nature. That night, I wrote in my first letter to my best friend: "By comparison, our old land must be overused and exhausted. Nature is extraordinarily generous to America."

My roommate Benny was a first-year graduate student in Judaic studies. He was a skinny man and had a German girlfriend, Bettina, who had just arrived as a special student, doing graduate work at Brandeis for one year. At first, I thought that they both spoke English fluently, but I soon discovered that their vocabulary wasn't that rich and that they might not know more English than I did. Yet compared with theirs, my spoken English was quite shabby, partly because I had learned it mainly from books. For example, several times I introduced myself as "a freshman," assuming that the word referred to a first-year grad student as well. I couldn't understand the news on TV at all, and it took me two months to be able to follow TV shows. Some Chinese students in our dorm loved watching American wrestling, believing that the stunts, the moves, the pain were all real.

Below us, on the first floor, lived a young Indian couple, both graduate   20 students. The wife, Aparna, was tall and vivacious, specializing in social policy and management. One evening, as we were having tea in their living room, she asked me, "Why didn't you bring your wife and child with you?"

"They were not allowed to come with me," I said.

"Who didn't allow them?"

"The government."

"Why not sue your government?"

Stumped, I didn't know how to answer. But the question has stayed with   25 me since. It shook me, as I realized that democracy fundamentally meant the equality between the individual and the country. Such a thought was something few Chinese would dare to entertain.

When I left home, it was understood between my wife, Lisha, and me that I would live abroad for four years without coming back to visit her, because I was unlikely to be able to afford the airfare. Our 2-year-old son had been staying with her parents, and, right before my departure, Lisha and I went to see him; he was too young to worry about my imminent absence from his life. Even when I said goodbye, he hardly paid me any mind. After my arrival in Boston, I noticed that some Chinese graduate students had their spouses with them, so I began to figure out how to bring Lisha over. I spoke to a woman at the graduate school admissions at Brandeis, saying: "I want my wife to join me here. I miss her terribly." She didn't respond, her face wooden and her eyes dropped, as if I had asked for something beyond reason. The prolonged silence made clear that no assistance would come from her office.

Gradually, I found out that everyone who came here was entitled to have a visa for his or her spouse, but there was another difficulty, namely money. The U.S. Embassy in Beijing would demand that my wife show that I had at least $4,000 in my bank account. To earn that amount, I began working on and off campus. I started in the periodical section of the main library and learned to operate the copiers and the microfilm and microfiche machines. My fellow graduate student Dan Morris used to be a custodian at Waltham Hospital, but now he was too busy with his studies to keep all the hours, so he split the job with me. We each worked 20 hours a week in the medical building, vacuuming floors, cleaning toilets, washing glass doors, picking up trash from the offices and keeping the parking lot clean. We wore beepers at work so that the doctors and nurses could page us if they needed help. The job was undemanding, but I often got confused. For instance, a patient once told me to keep an eye on his "burgundy station wagon" because its lock was broken. I had no idea what kind of car a station wagon was and had to ask several people about that. A physician who spoke English with a Greek accent often wiggled his forefinger to summon me over when he wanted me to change a light bulb or clean away a patch of vomit on his office floor. I hated that gesture, which at first seemed to mean that he could pull me around with just one finger. But gradually I became accustomed to it as I saw that many others used it without any condescension. Despite some twinge of discomfort, I liked the job, mainly because I could rest my mind while I worked. I had to be very careful about my time and energy. At the outset of the semester, the director of graduate studies had told me that the English department had admitted Asian PhD candidates before, but none of them had survived the intensity of the graduate work, so I had to prove that I could manage it.

For new arrivals in America, there was always the sinister attraction of money. Suddenly one could make $4 or $5 an hour, which was equal to a whole week's wages back home. If you were not careful, you could fall into the money-grubbing trap. Some Chinese students didn't continue with their graduate work because they couldn't stop making money. One fellow from Shanghai started working part time in a museum on campus but soon stopped showing up in his lab in the physics department, dropped out of graduate school within a semester, and began taking courses to learn how to sell real estate. Another in American studies, who loved teaching as a profession, could no longer write his dissertation after taking a clerical job in a bank—sometimes he put in more than 60 hours a week, the overtime even harder to resist.

One evening, as I was cleaning the front entrance of the medical building, a slender Hispanic woman carrying a baby stopped to watch me work. She was under 30, with honey-colored hair, and might have been a single mother. A moment later, she stepped closer and handed her pacifier-sucking baby to me, saying, "You like kids?" Her round eyes were glowing while a hesitant smile cracked her face.

I was perplexed but managed to say, "Sorry, I am busy now." I kept spray- 30
ing Windex on the glass door. After scraping the glass clean, I observed my face in the mirror inside the men's room. I looked a bit melancholy and frazzled. But how on earth, I wondered, had that woman sensed my yearning for family?

My coursework and two part-time jobs kept me so busy that I rarely ate dinner. I would cook twice a week—a potful of rice or spaghetti mixed with vegetables and chicken generally lasted me a few days. Back home, I wouldn't eat chicken or beef, because, unlike pork, they had tasted strange to me. But now I just ate whatever I could get. Fortunately, in America, food was very affordable. But my eating habit soon gave me a stomachache. I went to the infirmary, and the doctor said I had developed a digestive disorder and must eat regularly, three meals a day. That was out of the question, thanks to my hectic schedule. But my stomach problem made Lisha eager to join me here.

Despite my effort to earn money for her visa, she was not sure if she would be able to come. With the help of a doctor's letter about my illness, she had obtained a three-month leave from the school where she taught, but the Chinese authorities wouldn't let her bring our child. She was having difficulty getting a passport even for herself. For two months, she went to various offices every day to ask for permission to visit me. Sometimes she swept floors and wiped desks in those places just to earn the officials' mercy so they might issue her the papers.

During my absence, she had been raising our child alone on her teacher's salary. I missed him and often looked at the photos she mailed me. I could not afford to call home, since it cost more than $3 a minute. Worse, very few families in China had a phone back then, and if I was going to call, Lisha would have to go to an office to wait for the call. When she spoke, there would be people around, listening. Once in a while, she would send me the imprints of our child's hands and feet to give me a better sense of how much he had grown. In the Boston area, I had encountered young couples from China who had their children with them, and I could see that eventually I might be able to bring my son over, too, but the first step was to get his mother out.

However, even after Lisha got her passport, she began having second thoughts about leaving our son behind and coming alone. In her letters, she even bragged teasingly about how orderly her life had become without me around and said that, as we had planned, she could manage without seeing me for four years. I assured her that our family would be reunited in time, but she should come over first. She was worried about her lack of English, as well, and I told her that she could easily learn it once she was here. I also wrote her about American amenities: She could take a hot shower at home every day; she could do laundry in a washer and dryer,

no need to hand-launder anything; and she needn't burn honeycomb bri-
quettes to cook, as electric and gas stoves were commonplace in America.
What's more, the air here was so fresh and clean that your collar didn't get
black even after you wore a white shirt for days, and that you needn't wipe
your shoes.

After a few more exchanges of letters, she finally decided to come once   35
I had earned the $4,000.

At the end of the semester, I completed my four courses with decent
grades, which convinced the department of my ability. Then, one evening,
my friend Jia-yang, a first-year graduate student in the biology department,
came by to ask if he could borrow $1,000 from me, saying that his wife was
going to apply for a visa, and he needed enough money in his bank account.
I was stupefied, as it had never crossed my mind that I could have borrowed
cash from friends, perhaps because it was such a big sum. I lent Jia-yang the
money, and he promised to lend me some when Lisha began her application.
And, two months later, he did. Now Lisha and I wouldn't have to wait for
long to be together again, for me to show her my new American life.

The Reader's Presence

1. Before coming to the United States to study, Jin worried whether he could survive in
   America. "Arrival" is an account of his survival. What did Jin worry about mostly? For
   example, what do you think he means when he writes "that physically I could survive
   for sure, but . . . I was more concerned about my quest for a meaningful existence,
   which I had no idea how to accomplish in the United States" (paragraph 4)? Based
   on Jin's essay, do you think Jin achieves "a meaningful existence" in America? Why
   or why not?

2. At one point in his essay, Jin suggests that he never forgot an image associated with
   the bribe he was forced to make to obtain his plane ticket: "Years later, whenever I
   thought of going back to China, the image of the young woman with a haggard face
   and bedraggled hair smoking expensive cigarettes would come to mind and make
   me wince" (paragraph 8). Why do you think that image affected Jin so powerfully?
   How is it associated with his native country?

3. **CONNECTIONS:**   Compare Jin's "Arrival" with Dinaw Mengestu's "Home at Last"
   (page 202). What immigrant experiences do you find similar in each selection? Of
   what importance, for example, is the role of family for each writer?

Jamaica Kincaid

THE ESTRANGEMENT

Born in Antigua in 1949, **JAMAICA KINCAID** moved to the United States at seventeen to work as an au pair in New York. Although she is known primarily for her fiction, Kincaid is by no means a stranger to nonfiction: she began her writing career as a journalist, penning articles for the *Village Voice* and *Ingenue* magazines. In 1976, she became a staff writer for the *New Yorker*, a position she kept for nine years. Her first book of fiction, a collection of unified short stories centering on the coming of age of a Caribbean girl and titled *At the Bottom of the River* (1983), won the Morton Darwen Zabel Award of the American Academy of Arts and Letters and was nominated for the

> **Born in Antigua in 1949, Jamaica Kincaid moved to the United States at seventeen to work as an au pair in New York.**

PEN/Faulkner Award. Her first novel, *Annie John* (1983), was a finalist for the 1985 international Ritz Paris Hemingway Award. Her 1996 book, *The Autobiography of My Mother*, was a finalist for the PEN/Faulkner Award. Her most recent book, *See Now Then: A Novel*, was published in 2013. She teaches literature and creative writing at Claremont McKenna College, in Claremont, California.

THREE YEARS before my mother died, I decided not to speak to her again. And why? During a conversation over the telephone, she had once again let me know that my accomplishments—becoming a responsible and independent woman—did not amount to very much, that the life I lived was nothing more than a silly show, that she truly wished me dead. I didn't disagree. I didn't tell her that it would be just about the best thing in the world not to hear this from her.

And so, after that conversation, I never spoke to her, said a word to her of any kind, and then she died and her death was a shock to me, not because I would miss her presence and long for it, but because I could not believe that such a presence could ever be stilled.

For many years and many a time, her children, of which I was the only female, wondered what would happen to her, as we wondered what would happen to us; because she seemed to us not a mother at all but a God, not a Goddess but a God.

How to explain in this brief space what I mean? When we were children and in need of a mother's love and care, there was no better mother to provide such an ideal entity. When we were adolescents, and embracing with adolescent certainty our various incarnations, she could see through the thinness of our efforts, she could see through the emptiness of our aspirations; when we fell apart, there she was, bringing us dinner in jail or in a hospital ward, cold compresses for our temples, or just standing above us as we lay flat on our backs in bed. That sort of mother is God.

Her death was a shock, not because I would miss her, but because I could not believe such a presence could be stilled. 5

I am the oldest, by 9, 11, and 13 years, of four children. My three brothers and I share only our mother; they have the same father, I have a different one. I knew their father very well, better than they did, but I did not know my own. (When I was seven months in her womb, my mother quarreled with the man with whom she had conceived me and then ran away with the money he had been saving up to establish a little business for himself. He never forgave her.) I didn't mind not knowing my real father, because in the place I am from, Antigua, when people love you, your blood relationship to them is not necessarily the most important component. My mother's husband, the father of my brothers, loved me, and his love took on the shape of a father's love: he told me about himself when he was a boy and the things he loved to do and the ways in which his life changed for better and worse, giving me some idea about how he came to be himself, my father, the father of my brothers, the person married to my mother.

She was a very nice person, apparently; that is what everybody said about her at her funeral. There were descriptions of her good and selfless deeds, kindnesses, generosity, testaments of her love expressed in humor. We, her children, looked at one another in wonder then, for such a person as described was not at all known to us. The person we knew, our Mother, said horrible things to us more often than not.

The youngest of my three brothers died of AIDS when he was 33 years of age. In the years he spent actively dying, our mother tended to him with the greatest tenderness that was absent all the time before he was dying. Before he got sick, before he became afflicted with that disease, his mother, my mother too, quarreled with him and disparaged him. This was enabled by the fact that he did not know how to go off somewhere and make a home of any kind for himself. Yes, he had been unable to move out into the world, away from this woman, his mother, and become the sole possessor of his own destiny, with all the loss and gain that this implies.

The two remaining brothers and I buried her right next to him, and we were not sure we should have done that: for we didn't know even now, if he wanted to spend eternity lying beside her, since we were sure we would rather be dead than spend eternity lying next to her.

Is this clear? It is to me right now as I write it: I would rather be dead than spend eternity with our mother! And do I really mean that when I say it? Yes, I really mean just that: after being my mother's daughter, I would rather be dead than spend eternity with her. 10

By the time my mother died, I was not only one of her four children, I had become the mother of two children: a girl and then a boy. This was bliss, my two children in love with me, and I with them. Nothing has gone wrong, as far as I can see, but tears have been shed over my not being completely enthusiastic about going to a final basketball game in a snowstorm, or saying something I should have kept in my mind's mouth. A particularly unforgivable act in my children's eyes is a book's dedication I made to them; it read: "With blind, instinctive, and confused love to Annie and Harold, who from time to time are furiously certain that the only thing standing between them and a perfect union with their mother is the garden, and from time to time, they are correct."[1]

I wrote this with a feeling of overbrimming love for them, my children. I was not thinking of my own mother directly, not thinking of her at all consciously at that exact time, but then again, I am always thinking of my mother; I believe every action of a certain kind that I make is completely influenced by her, completely infused with her realness, her existence in my life.

I am now middle-aged (59 years of age); I not only hope to live for a very long time after this, I will be angry in eternity if this turns out not to be the case. And so in eternity will my children want to be with me? And in eternity will I, their mother, want to be with them?

In regard to my children, eternity is right now, and I always want to be with them. In regard to my mother, my progenitor, eternity is beyond now, and is that not forever? I will not speak to her again in person, of that I am certain, but I am not sure that I will never speak to her again. For in eternity is she in me, and are even my children speaking to her? I do not know, I do not know.

The Reader's Presence

1. Note how frequently Kincaid uses repetition in her brief essay—for example, the repetition of the word "eternity" toward the end of the selection. How does her use of repetition throughout the essay affect your response? Select a paragraph to read aloud. How would you describe Kincaid's tone of voice? For example, how would you interpret her tone of voice in her final sentence, which is also deliberately repetitive?

2. When Kincaid writes that she "would rather be dead than spend eternity with our mother" (paragraph 10), what do you think she means? In what way is that remark puzzling? How do you interpret it?

3. **CONNECTIONS:**   Kincaid wrote this essay for a magazine in 2009; compare it with her miniature, one-paragraph short story "Girl" (page 813), published in 1978. Based on this essay, do you think the story is autobiographical? In what ways does the story inform the essay?

[1] Kincaid is a dedicated gardener and has written several books on gardening. —EDS.

Geeta Kothari

IF YOU ARE WHAT YOU EAT, THEN WHAT AM I?

Writer and educator **GEETA KOTHARI** (b. 1962) was born in New York City of Indian parents who emigrated from New Delhi, India. Kothari is the fiction editor of the literary journal the *Kenyon Review* and teaches at the University of Pittsburgh. She is a two-time recipient of the fellowship in literature from the Pennsylvania Council on the Arts and the editor of an anthology, *Did My Mama Like to Dance? and Other Stories about Mothers and Daughters* (1994). Her fiction and nonfiction work has appeared in a number of journals, including the *Massachusetts Review* and *Fourth Genre*.

> **Geeta Kothari is a two-time recipient of the fellowship in literature from the Pennsylvania Council on the Arts.**

Her essay "If You Are What You Eat, Then What Am I?" was first published in the *Kenyon Review* in 1999 and was selected for the *Best American Essays 2000*.

Kothari clearly understands the relationship among culture, family, and food and "the tacit codes of the people you live with," as the Michael Ignatieff quotation that opens the essay underscores.

To belong is to understand the tacit codes of the people you live with.
—*MICHAEL IGNATIEFF, Blood and Belonging*

I

THE FIRST TIME my mother and I open a can of tuna, I am nine years old. We stand in the doorway of the kitchen, in semi-darkness, the can tilted toward daylight. I want to eat what the kids at school eat: bologna, hot dogs, salami—foods my parents find repugnant because they contain pork and meat by-products, crushed bone and hair glued together by chemicals and fat. Although she has never been able to tolerate the smell of fish, my mother buys the tuna, hoping to satisfy my longing for American food.

Indians, of course, do not eat such things.

The tuna smells fishy, which surprises me because I can't remember anyone's tuna sandwich actually smelling like fish. And the tuna in those sandwiches doesn't look like this, pink and shiny, like an internal organ. In fact, this looks similar to the bad foods my mother doesn't want me to eat.

She is silent, holding her face away from the can while peering into it like a half-blind bird.

"What's wrong with it?" I ask.

She has no idea. My mother does not know that the tuna everyone else's   5
mothers made for them was tuna *salad*.

"Do you think it's botulism?"

I have never seen botulism, but I have read about it, just as I have read about but never eaten steak and kidney pie.

There is so much my parents don't know. They are not like other parents, and they disappoint me and my sister. They are supposed to help us negotiate the world outside, teach us the signs, the clues to proper behavior: what to eat and how to eat it.

We have expectations, and my parents fail to meet them, especially my mother, who works full time. I don't understand what it means, to have a mother who works outside and inside the home; I notice only the ways in which she disappoints me. She doesn't show up for school plays. She doesn't make chocolate-frosted cupcakes for my class. At night, if I want her attention, I have to sit in the kitchen and talk to her while she cooks the evening meal, attentive to every third or fourth word I say.

We throw the tuna away. This time my mother is disappointed. I go to   10
school with tuna eaters. I see their sandwiches, yet cannot explain the discrepancy between them and the stinking, oily fish in my mother's hand. We do not understand so many things, my mother and I.

II

On weekends, we eat fried chicken from Woolworth's on the back steps of my father's first-floor office in Murray Hill. The back steps face a small patch of garden—hedges, a couple of skinny trees, and gravel instead of grass. We can see the back windows of the apartment my parents and I lived in until my sister was born. There, the doorman watched my mother, several months pregnant and wearing a sari, slip on the ice in front of the building.

My sister and I pretend we are in the country, where our American friends all have houses. We eat glazed doughnuts, also from Woolworth's, and french fries with catsup.

III

My mother takes a catering class and learns that Miracle Whip and mustard are healthier than mayonnaise. She learns to make egg salad with chopped celery, deviled eggs with paprika, a cream cheese spread with bits of fresh ginger and watercress, chicken liver pâté, and little brown and white checkerboard sandwiches that we have only once. She makes chicken *à la king* in puff pastry shells and eggplant parmesan. She acquires smooth wooden paddles, whose purpose is never clear, two different egg slicers, several wooden spoons, icing tubes, cookie cutters, and an electric mixer.

IV

I learn to make tuna salad by watching a friend. My sister never acquires a taste for it. Instead, she craves:

> bologna
> hot dogs
> bacon
> sausages

and a range of unidentifiable meat products forbidden by my parents. Their restrictions are not about sacred cows, as everyone around us assumes; in a pinch, we are allowed hamburgers, though lamb burgers are preferable. A "pinch" means choosing not to draw attention to ourselves as outsiders, impolite visitors who won't eat what the host serves. But bologna is still taboo.

V

Things my sister refuses to eat: butter, veal, anything with *jeera*.[1] The baby-   15
sitter tries to feed her butter sandwiches, threatens her with them, makes her cry in fear and disgust. My mother does not disappoint her; she does not believe in forcing us to eat, in using food as a weapon. In addition to pbj, my sister likes pasta and marinara sauce, bologna and Wonder bread (when she can get it), and fried egg sandwiches with turkey, cheese, and horseradish. Her tastes, once established, are predictable.

VI

When we visit our relatives in India, food prepared outside the house is carefully monitored. In the hot, sticky monsoons in New Delhi and Bombay, we cannot eat ice cream, salad, cold food, or any fruit that can't be peeled. Definitely no meat. People die from amoebic dysentery, unexplained fevers, strange boils on their bodies. We drink boiled water only, no ice. No sweets except for jalebi, thin fried twists of dough in dripping hot sugar syrup. If we're caught outside with nothing to drink, Fanta, Limca, Thums Up (after Coca-Cola is thrown out by Mr. Gandhi) will do. Hot tea sweetened with sugar, served with thick creamy buffalo milk, is preferable. It should be boiled, to kill the germs on the cup.

---

[1] **jeera:** Cumin. —EDS.

My mother talks about "back home" as a safe place, a silk cocoon frozen in time where we are sheltered by family and friends. Back home, my sister and I do not argue about food with my parents. Home is where they know all the rules. We trust them to guide us safely through the maze of city streets for which they have no map, and we trust them to feed and take care of us, the way parents should.

Finally, though, one of us will get sick, hungry for the food we see our cousins and friends eating, too thirsty to ask for a straw, too polite to insist on properly boiled water.

At my uncle's diner in New Delhi, someone hands me a plate of aloo tikki, fried potato patties filled with mashed channa dal[2] and served with a sweet and sour chutney. The channa, mixed with hot chilies and spices, burned my tongue and throat. I reach for my Fanta, discard the paper straw, and gulp the sweet orange soda down, huge draughts that sting rather than soothe.

When I throw up later that day (or is it the next morning, when a stom-   20
achache wakes me up from deep sleep?), I cry over the frustration of being singled out, not from the pain my mother assumes I'm feeling as she holds my hair back from my face. The taste of orange lingers in my mouth, and I remember my lips touching the cold glass of the Fanta bottle.

At that moment, more than anything, I want to be like my cousins.

VII

In New York, at the first Indian restaurant in our neighborhood, my father orders with confidence, and my sister and I play with the silverware until the steaming plates of lamb biryani[3] arrive.

What is Indian food? my friends ask, their noses crinkling up.

Later, this restaurant is run out of business by the new Indo-Pak-Bangladeshi combinations up and down the street, which serve similar food. They use plastic cutlery and Styrofoam cups. They do not distinguish between North and South Indian cooking, or between Indian, Pakistani, and Bangladeshi cooking, and their customers do not care. The food is fast, cheap, and tasty. Dosa, a rice flour crepe stuffed with masala[4] potato, appears on the same trays as chicken makhani.[5]

Now my friends want to know, Do you eat curry at home?   25

One time, my mother makes lamb vindaloo[6] for guests. Like dosa, this is a South Indian dish, one that my Punjabi mother has to learn from a cook-book. For us, she cooks everyday food—yellow dal, rice, chapati, bhaji. Len-tils, rice, bread, and vegetables. She has never referred to anything on our

---

2 **channa dal:** A dish made of the split kernel of beans in the chickpea family.—EDS.

3 **lamb biryani:** A dish made of lamb, spices, basmati rice, and yogurt.—EDS.

4 **masala:** A blend of spices common to Indian food, often includes cinnamon, cardamom, cum-in, caraway, and many others.—EDS.

5 **chicken makhani:** A dish combining chicken with a butter-based tomato sauce.—EDS.

6 **lamb vindaloo:** A spicy marinated lamb dish.—EDS.

table as "curry" or "curried," but I know she has made chicken curry for guests. Vindaloo, she explains, is a curry too. I understand, then, that curry is a dish created for guests, outsiders, a food for people who eat in restaurants.

VIII

I have inherited brown eyes, black hair, a long nose with a crooked bridge, and soft teeth with thin enamel. I am in my twenties, moving to a city far from my parents, before it occurs to me that jeera, the spice my sister avoids, must have an English name. I have to learn that haldi = turmeric, methi = fenugreek. What to make with fenugreek, I do not know. My grandmother used to make methi roti[7] for our breakfast, corn bread with fresh fenugreek leaves served with a lump of homemade butter. No one makes it now that she's gone, though once in a while my mother will get a craving for it and produce a facsimile ("The corn meal here is wrong") that only highlights what she's really missing: the smells and tastes of her mother's house.

I will never make my grandmother's methi roti or even my mother's unsatisfactory imitation of it. I attempt chapati:[8] it takes six hours, three phone calls home, and leaves me with an aching back. I have to write translations down: jeera = cumin. My memory is unreliable. But I have always known garam = hot.

IX

My mother learns how to make brownies and apple pie. My father makes only Indian food, except for loaves of heavy, sweet, brown bread that I eat with thin slices of American cheese and lettuce. The recipe is a secret, passed on to him by a woman at work. Years later, when he finally gives it to me, when I ask for it, I end up with three bricks of gluten that even the birds and my husband won't eat.

X

My parents send me to boarding school, outside of London. They imagine   30
that I will overcome my shyness and find a place for myself in this all-girls' school. They have never lived in England, but as former subjects of the British Empire, they find London familiar, comfortable in a way New York—my mother's home for over twenty years by now—is not. Americans still don't know what to call us; their Indians live on reservations, not in Manhattan.

---

[7] **roti:** A round puffy flatbread.—EDS.
[8] **chapati:** A type of roti, or flatbread.—EDS.

Because they understand the English, my parents believe the English understand us.

I poke at my first school lunch—thin, overworked pastry in a puddle of lumpy gravy. The lumps are chewy mushrooms, maybe, or overcooked shrimp.

"What is this?" I don't want to ask, but I can't go on eating without knowing.

"Steak and kidney pie."

The girl next to me, red-haired, freckled, watches me take a bite from my plate. She has been put in charge of me, the new girl, and I follow her around all day, a foreigner at the mercy of a reluctant and angry tour guide. She is not used to explaining what is perfectly and utterly natural.

"What, you've never had steak and kidney pie? Bloody hell."   35

My classmates scoff, then marvel, then laugh at my ignorance. After a year, I understand what is on my plate: sausage rolls, blood pudding, Spam, roast beef in a thin, greasy gravy, all the bacon and sausage I could possibly want. My parents do not expect me to starve.

The girls at school expect conformity; it has been bred into them, through years of uniforms and strict rules about proper behavior. I am thirteen and contrary, even as I yearn for acceptance. I declare myself a vegetarian and doom myself to a diet of cauliflower cheese and baked beans on toast. The administration does not question my decision; they assume it's for vague, undefined religious reasons, although my father, the doctor, tells them it's for my health. My reasons, from this distance of many years, remain murky to me.

Perhaps I am my parents' daughter after all.

XI

When she is three, sitting on my cousin's lap in Bombay, my sister reaches for his plate and puts a chili in her mouth. She wants to be like the grown-ups who dip green chilies in coarse salt and eat them like any other vegetable. She howls inconsolable animal pain for what must be hours. She doesn't have the vocabulary for the oily heat that stings her mouth and tongue, burns a trail through her small tender body. Only hot, sticky tears on my father's shoulder.

As an adult, she eats red chili paste, mango pickle, kimchee,[9] foods that   40
make my eyes water and my stomach gurgle. My tastes are milder. I order raita[10] at Indian restaurants and ask for food that won't sear the roof of my mouth and scar the insides of my cheeks. The waiters nod, and their eyes shift—a slight once-over that indicates they don't believe me. I am Indian,

---

[9] ***kimchee:*** A spicy Korean dish made of fermented cabbage and other vegetables. —EDS.
[10] ***raita:*** A yogurt-based condiment, often including cilantro, mint, and cucumber. —EDS.

aren't I? My father seems to agree with them. He tells me I'm asking for the impossible, as if he believes the recipes are immutable, written in stone during the passage from India to America.

XII

I look around my boyfriend's freezer one day and find meat: pork chops, ground beef, chicken pieces, Italian sausage. Ham in the refrigerator, next to the homemade Bolognese sauce. Tupperware filled with chili made from ground beef and pork.

He smells different from me. Foreign. Strange.

I marry him anyway.

He has inherited blue eyes that turn gray in bad weather, light brown hair, a sharp pointy nose, and excellent teeth. He learns to make chili with ground turkey and tofu, tomato sauce with red wine and portobello mushrooms, roast chicken with rosemary and slivers of garlic under the skin.

He eats steak when we are in separate cities, roast beef at his mother's   45
house, hamburgers at work. Sometimes I smell them on his skin. I hope he doesn't notice me turning my face, a cheek instead of my lips, my nose wrinkled at the unfamiliar, musky smell.

XIII

And then I realize I don't want to be a person who can find Indian food only in restaurants. One day, my parents will be gone, and I will long for the foods of my childhood, the way they long for theirs. I prepare for this day the way people on TV prepare for the end of the world. They gather canned goods they will never eat while I stockpile recipes I cannot replicate. I am frantic, disorganized, grabbing what I can, filing scribbled notes haphazardly. I regret the tastes I've forgotten, the meals I have inhaled without a thought. I worry that I've come to this realization too late.

XIV

Who told my mother about Brie? One day we were eating Velveeta, the next day Brie, Gouda, Camembert, Port Salut, Havarti with caraway, Danish fontina, string cheese made with sheep's milk. Who opened the door to these foreigners that sit on the refrigerator shelf next to last night's dal?

Back home, there is one cheese only, which comes in a tin, looks like Bakelite, and tastes best when melted.

And how do we go from Chef Boyardee to fresh pasta and homemade sauce, made with Redpack tomatoes, crushed garlic, and dried oregano? Macaroni and cheese, made with fresh cheddar and whole milk, sprinkled with bread crumbs and paprika. Fresh eggplant and ricotta ravioli, packed with marinara sauce and fresh mozzarella.

My mother will never cook beef or pork in her kitchen, and the foods   50
she knew in her childhood are unavailable. Because the only alternative to the supermarket, with its TV dinners and canned foods, is the gourmet Italian deli across the street, by default our meals become socially acceptable.

XV

If I really want to make myself sick, I worry that my husband will one day leave me for a meat-eater, for someone familiar who doesn't sniff him suspiciously for signs of alimentary infidelity.

XVI

Indians eat lentils. I understand this as absolute, a decree from an unidentifiable authority that watches and judges me.

So what does it mean that I cannot replicate my mother's dal? She and my father show me repeatedly, in their kitchen, in my kitchen. They coach me over the phone, buy me the best cookbooks, and finally write down their secrets. Things I'm supposed to know but don't. Recipes that should be, by now, engraved on my heart.

Living far from the comfort of people who require no explanation for what I do and who I am, I crave the foods we have shared. My mother convinces me that moong is the easiest dal to prepare, and yet it fails me every time: bland, watery, a sickly greenish-yellow mush. These imperfect imitations remind me only of what I'm missing.

But I have never been fond of moong dal.[11] At my mother's table it is   55
the last thing I reach for. Now I worry that this antipathy toward dal signals something deeper, that somehow I am not my parents' daughter, not Indian, and because I cannot bear the touch and smell of raw meat, though I can eat it cooked (charred, dry, and overdone), I am not American either.

I worry about a lifetime purgatory in Indian restaurants where I will complain that all the food looks and tastes the same because they've used the same masala.

XVII

About the tuna and her attempts to feed us, my mother laughs. She says, "You were never fussy. You ate everything I made and never complained."

---

11 *moong dal:* A dish made of split green lentils. —EDS.

My mother is at the stove, wearing only her blouse and petticoat, her sari carefully folded and hung in the closet. She does not believe a girl's place is in the kitchen, but she expects me to know that too much hing can ruin a meal, to know without being told, without having to ask or write it down. Hing = asafoetida.

She remembers the catering class. "Oh, that class. You know, I had to give it up when we got to lobster. I just couldn't stand the way it looked."

She says this apologetically, as if she has deprived us, as if she suspects   60
that having a mother who could feed us lobster would have changed the course of our lives.

Intellectually, she understands that only certain people regularly eat lobster, people with money or those who live in Maine, or both. In her catering class there were people without jobs for whom preparing lobster was a part of their professional training as caterers. Like us, they wouldn't be eating lobster at home. For my mother, however, lobster was just another American food, like tuna—different, strange, not natural yet somehow essential to belonging.

I learned how to prepare and eat lobster from the same girl who taught me tuna salad. I ate bacon at her house, too. And one day this girl, with her houses in the country and Martha's Vineyard, asked me how my uncle was going to pick me up from the airport in Bombay. In 1973, she was surprised to hear that he used a car, not an elephant. At home, my parents and I laughed, and though I never knew for sure if she was making fun of me, I still wanted her friendship.

My parents were afraid my sister and I would learn to despise the foods they loved, replace them with bologna and bacon and lose our taste for masala. For my mother, giving up her disgust of lobster, with its hard exterior and foreign smell, would mean renouncing some essential difference. It would mean becoming, decidedly, definitely, American—unafraid of meat in all its forms, able to consume large quantities of protein at any given meal. My willingness to toss a living being into boiling water and then get past its ugly appearance to the rich meat inside must mean to my mother that I am, somehow, someone she is not.

But I haven't eaten lobster in years. In my kitchen cupboards, there is a thirteen-pound bag of basmati rice, jars of lime pickle, mango pickle, and ghee,[12] cans of tuna and anchovies, canned soups, coconut milk, and tomatoes, rice noodles, several kinds of pasta, dried mushrooms, and unlabeled bottles of spices: haldi, jeera, hing. When my husband tries to help me cook, he cannot identify all the spices. He gets confused when I forget their English names and remarks that my expectations of him are unreasonable.

I am my parents' daughter. Like them, I expect knowledge to pass from   65
me to my husband without one word of explanation or translation. I want him to know what I know, see what I see, without having to tell him exactly what it is. I want to believe the recipes never change. ▧

---

12 ***ghee:*** Clarified butter. —EDS.

The Reader's Presence

1. Kothari worries in the essay whether she is "[her] parents' daughter" (paragraph 38). Why is this of concern? How is that concern related to the title of her essay? At the end of the essay, she says definitively: "I am my parents' daughter" (paragraph 65). How has she reached that conclusion in the process of writing the essay?

2. Consider the ways food relates to cultural identity. How does Kothari characterize American foods? In what ways does she enjoy them? In what ways does she find them distasteful? For example, how is her husband—who is never named—described in terms of his favorite foods? In what ways do husband and wife differ from each other? How does Kothari suggest that their culinary differences could affect their relationship?

3. **CONNECTIONS:** Read Kothari's essay in conjunction with Judith Ortiz Cofer's "Silent Dancing" (page 88). Although one writes about food and the other about ethnic values, discuss how each writer deals with conflict between a family's values and assimilation into a different culture. You might also consider Kothari's attention to ethnic cuisine in contrast to Eric Schlosser's description in "Why McDonald's Fries Taste So Good" (page 547) of American fast food. To what extent to you think fast-food chains help undermine cultural heritage as it is expressed in various ethnic cuisines, such as Kothari's Indian recipes? Support your points with specific references to each text.

Jhumpa Lahiri

MY TWO LIVES

JHUMPA LAHIRI (b. 1967) is perhaps best known for her debut collection of short stories, *Interpreter of Maladies* (1999), which won the Pulitzer Prize for Fiction in 2000 and has sold more than 15 million copies worldwide. Born in London, she is the daughter of Indian immigrants. Her family left the United Kingdom for the United States when she was two years old, and she has said that she considers herself American. She has received a number of prestigious literary awards, including the Pulitzer Prize (2000), the PEN/O. Henry Prize (1999), a Guggenheim Fellowship (2002), and the Asian-American Literary Award (2009) for her 2008 collection of short stories, *Unaccustomed Earth*. She is also the author of two novels: *The Lowland* (2013) and *The Namesake* (2003), which was the basis for a film of the same title in 2006. Her fiction is largely autobiographi-

cal, exploring the complicated identity issues faced by first- and second-generation Indian immigrants as they attempt to make sense of their lives in America within the context of Indian cultural values. Of growing up the child of Indian immigrants, she has said, "It

> Of growing up the child of Indian immigrants, Lahiri has said, "It was always a question of allegiance, of choice."

was always a question of allegiance, of choice. I wanted to please my parents and meet their expectations. I also wanted to meet the expectations of my American peers, and the expectations I put on myself to fit into American society."

I HAVE LIVED IN THE UNITED STATES for almost 37 years and anticipate growing old in this country. Therefore, with the exception of my first two years in London, "Indian-American" has been a constant way to describe me. Less constant is my relationship to the term. When I was growing up in Rhode Island in the 1970s I felt neither Indian nor American. Like many immigrant offspring I felt intense pressure to be two things, loyal to the old world and fluent in the new, approved of on either side of the hyphen. Looking back, I see that this was generally the case. But my perception as a young girl was that I fell short at both ends, shuttling between two dimensions that had nothing to do with one another.

At home I followed the customs of my parents, speaking Bengali and eating rice and dal with my fingers. These ordinary facts seemed part of a secret, utterly alien way of life, and I took pains to hide them from my American friends. For my parents, home was not our house in Rhode Island but Calcutta, where they were raised. I was aware that the things they lived for—the Nazrul songs they listened to on the reel-to-reel, the family they missed, the clothes my mother wore that were not available in any store in any mall—were at once as precious and as worthless as an outmoded currency.

I also entered a world my parents had little knowledge or control of: school, books, music, television, things that seeped in and became a fundamental aspect of who I am. I spoke English without an accent, comprehending the language in a way my parents still do not. And yet there was evidence that I was not entirely American. In addition to my distinguishing name and looks, I did not attend Sunday school, did not know how to ice-skate, and disappeared to India for months at a time. Many of these friends proudly called themselves Irish-American or Italian-American. But they were several generations removed from the frequently humiliating process of immigration, so that the ethnic roots they claimed had descended underground whereas mine were still tangled and green. According to my parents I was not American, nor would I ever be no matter how hard I tried. I felt doomed by their pronouncement, misunderstood and gradually defiant. In spite of the first lessons of arithmetic, one plus one did not equal two but zero, my conflicting selves always canceling each other out.

When I first started writing I was not conscious that my subject was the Indian-American experience. What drew me to my craft was the desire to force the two worlds I occupied to mingle on the page as I was not brave enough, or mature enough, to allow in life. My first book was published in 1999, and around then, on the cusp of a new century, the term "Indian-American" has become part of this country's vocabulary. I've heard it so often that these days, if asked about my background, I use the term myself, pleasantly surprised that I do not have to explain further. What a difference from my early life, when there was no such way to describe me, when the most I could do was to clumsily and ineffectually explain.

As I approach middle age, one plus one equals two, both in my work and   5 in my daily existence. The traditions on either side of the hyphen dwell in me like siblings, still occasionally sparring, one outshining the other depending on the day. But like siblings they are intimately familiar with one another, forgiving and intertwined. When my husband and I were married five years ago in Calcutta we invited friends who had never been to India, and they came full of enthusiasm for a place I avoided talking about in my childhood, fearful of what people might say. Around non-Indian friends, I no longer feel compelled to hide the fact that I speak another language. I speak Bengali to my children, even though I lack the proficiency to teach them to read or write the language. As a child I sought perfection and so denied myself the claim to any identity. As an adult I accept that a bicultural upbringing is a rich but imperfect thing.

While I am American by virtue of the fact that I was raised in this country, I am Indian thanks to the efforts of two individuals. I feel Indian not because of the time I've spent in India or because of my genetic composition but rather because of my parents' steadfast presence in my life. They live three hours from my home; I speak to them daily and see them about once a month. Everything will change once they die. They will take certain things with them—conversations in another tongue, and perceptions about the difficulties of being foreign. Without them, the back-and-forth life my family leads, both literally and figuratively, will at last approach stillness. An anchor will drop, and a line of connection will be severed.

I have always believed that I lack the authority my parents bring to being Indian. But as long as they live they protect me from feeling like an impostor. Their passing will mark not only the loss of the people who created me but the loss of a singular way of life, a singular struggle. The immigrant's journey, no matter how ultimately rewarding, is founded on departure and deprivation, but it secures for the subsequent generation a sense of arrival and advantage. I can see a day coming when my American side, lacking the counterpoint India has until now maintained, begins to gain ascendancy and weight. It is in fiction that I will continue to interpret the term "Indian-American," calculating that shifting equation, whatever answers it may yield. ▪

The Reader's Presence

1. Lahiri begins by asserting, "I have lived in the United States for almost 37 years and anticipate growing old in this country. Therefore, with the exception of my first two years in London, 'Indian-American' has been a constant way to describe me." Consider the significance of the syntax of her second sentence, in which "Indian-American" is placed before the personal pronoun "me." What does this suggest about how Lahiri views her divided cultural identity?

2. What role does writing play in Lahiri's sense of cultural identity? In what ways does writing allow her to attempt to come to terms with her "conflicted selves"? Through writing, Lahiri desires to "force the two worlds I occupied to mingle on the page" (paragraph 4), and yet she describes herself in plural terms ("my conflicting selves," paragraph 3). How does she rectify this conflict?

3. **CONNECTIONS:** Lahiri mentions "the traditions on either side of the hyphen" (paragraph 5) in reference to the hyphen separating her cultural descriptor, Indian-American. In what specific ways is the hyphen a metaphor for her experience with her "bicultural upbringing" (paragraph 5)? In what ways are Lahiri's experiences similar to those of Judith Ortiz Cofer, described in her essay "Silent Dancing" (page 88)?

Nancy Mairs
ON BEING A CRIPPLE

NANCY MAIRS (b. 1943) has contributed poetry, short stories, articles, and essays to numerous journals. "On Being a Cripple" comes from *Plaintext*, a collection of essays published in 1986. Her books include *Remembering the Bone House: An Erotics of Place and Space* (1989); *Carnal Acts* (1990); *Ordinary Time: Cycles in Marriage, Faith, and Renewal* (1993); *Waist-High in the World: A Life Among the Nondisabled* (1997); *A Troubled Guest: Life and Death Stories* (2001); and her

> "I want a prose that is allusive and translucent."

most recent, *A Dynamic God: Living an Unconventional Catholic Faith* (2007). From 1983 to 1985 Mairs served as assistant director of the Southwest Institute for Research on Women, and she has also taught at the University of Arizona and at UCLA.

In *Voice Lessons: On Becoming a (Woman) Writer* (1994), she writes, "I want a prose that is allusive and translucent, that eases you into me and embraces you, not one that baffles you or bounces you around so that you can't even tell where I am. And so I have chosen to work, very, very carefully, with the language we share, faults and all, choosing each word for its capacity, its ambiguity, the space it provides for me to live my life within it, relating rather than opposing each word to the next, each sentence to the next, 'starting on all sides at once . . . twenty times, thirty times, over': the stuttering adventure of the essay."

> *To escape is nothing. Not to escape is nothing.*
> — *Louise Bogan*

THE OTHER DAY I was thinking of writing an essay on being a cripple. I was thinking hard in one of the stalls of the women's room in my office building, as I was shoving my shirt into my jeans and tugging up my zipper. Preoccupied, I flushed, picked up my book bag, took my cane down from the hook, and unlatched the door. So many movements unbalanced me, and as I pulled the door open I fell over backward, landing fully clothed on the toilet seat with my legs splayed in front of me: the old beetle-on-its-back routine. Saturday afternoon, the building deserted, I was free to laugh aloud as I wriggled back to my feet, my voice bouncing off the yellowish tiles from all directions. Had anyone been there with me, I'd have been still and faint and hot with chagrin. I decided that it was high time to write the essay.

First, the matter of semantics. I am a cripple. I choose this word to name me. I choose from among several possibilities, the most common of which are "handicapped" and "disabled." I made the choice a number of years ago, without thinking, unaware of my motives for doing so. Even now, I'm not sure what those motives are, but I recognize that they are complex and not entirely flattering. People—crippled or not—wince at the word "cripple," as they do not at "handicapped" or "disabled." Perhaps I want them to wince. I want them to see me as a tough customer, one to whom the fates/gods/viruses have not been kind, but who can face the brutal truth of her existence squarely. As a cripple, I swagger.

But, to be fair to myself, a certain amount of honesty underlies my choice. "Cripple" seems to me a clean word, straightforward and precise. It has an honorable history, having made its first appearance in the Lindisfarne Gospel in the tenth century. As a lover of words, I like the accuracy with which it describes my condition: I have lost the full use of my limbs. "Disabled," by contrast, suggests any incapacity, physical or mental. And I certainly don't like "handicapped," which implies that I have deliberately been put at a disadvantage, by whom I can't imagine (my God is not a Handicapper

macmillanhighered.com/writerspresence8e
How do these photos of disabled athletes create an opportunity to discuss how society portrays people with disabilities?
e-Readings > Disabled Sports USA (screenshots)

General), in order to equalize chances in the great race of life. These words seem to me to be moving away from my condition, to be widening the gap between word and reality. Most remote is the recently coined euphemism "differently abled," which partakes of the same semantic hopefulness that transformed countries from "undeveloped" to "underdeveloped," then to "less developed," and finally to "developing" nations. People have continued to starve in those countries during the shift. Some realities do not obey the dictates of language.

Mine is one of them. Whatever you call me, I remain crippled. But I don't care what you call me, so long as it isn't "differently abled," which strikes me as pure verbal garbage designed, by its ability to describe anyone, to describe no one. I subscribe to George Orwell's thesis that "the slovenliness of our language makes it easier for us to have foolish thoughts."[1] And I refuse to participate in the degeneration of the language to the extent that I deny that I have lost anything in the course of this calamitous disease; I refuse to pretend that the only differences between you and me are the various ordinary ones that distinguish any one person from another. But call me "disabled" or "handicapped" if you like. I have long since grown accustomed to them; and if they are vague, at least they hint at the truth. Moreover, I use them myself. Society is no readier to accept crippledness than to accept death, war, sex, sweat, or wrinkles. I would never refer to another person as a cripple. It is the word I use to name only myself.

I haven't always been crippled, a fact for which I am soundly grateful.   5
To be whole of limb is, I know from experience, infinitely more pleasant and useful than to be crippled: and if that knowledge leaves me open to bitterness at my loss, the physical soundness I once enjoyed (though I did not enjoy it half enough) is well worth the occasional stab of regret. Though never any good at sports, I was a normally active child and young adult. I climbed trees, played hopscotch, jumped rope, skated, swam, rode my bicycle, sailed. I despised team sports, spending some of the wretchedest afternoons of my life, sweaty and humiliated, behind a field-hockey stick and under a basketball hoop. I tramped alone for miles along the bridle paths that webbed the woods behind the house I grew up in. I swayed through countless dim hours in the arms of one man or another under the scattered shot of light from mirrored balls, and gyrated through countless more as Tab Hunter and Johnny Mathis gave way to the Rolling Stones, Creedence Clearwater Revival, Cream. I walked down the aisle. I pushed baby carriages, changed tires in the rain, marched for peace.

When I was twenty-eight I started to trip and drop things. What at first seemed my natural clumsiness soon became too pronounced to shrug off. I consulted a neurologist, who told me that I had a brain tumor. A battery of tests, increasingly disagreeable, revealed no tumor. About a year and a half later I developed a blurred spot in one eye. I had, at last, the episodes "disseminated in space and time" requisite for a diagnosis: multiple sclerosis.

---

[1] **Orwell:** From his essay "Politics and the English Language" (page 515). —EDS.

I have never been sorry for the doctor's initial misdiagnosis, however. For almost a week, until the negative results of the tests were in, I thought that I was going to die right away. Every day for the past nearly ten years, then, has been a kind of gift. I accept all gifts.

Multiple sclerosis is a chronic degenerative disease of the central nervous system, in which the myelin that sheathes the nerves is somehow eaten away and scar tissue forms in its place, interrupting the nerves' signals. During its course, which is unpredictable and uncontrollable, one may lose vision, hearing, speech, the ability to walk, control of bladder and/or bowels, strength in any or all extremities, sensitivity to touch, vibration, and/or pain, potency, coordination of movements—the list of possibilities is lengthy and, yes, horrifying. One may also lose one's sense of humor. That's the easiest to lose and the hardest to survive without.

In the past ten years, I have sustained some of these losses. Characteristic of MS are sudden attacks, called exacerbations, followed by remissions, and these I have not had. Instead, my disease has been slowly progressive. My left leg is now so weak that I walk with the aid of a brace and a cane; and for distances I use an Amigo, a variation on the electric wheelchair that looks rather like an electrified kiddie car. I no longer have much use of my left hand. Now my right side is weakening as well. I still have the blurred spot in my right eye. Overall, though, I've been lucky so far. My world has, of necessity, been circumscribed by my losses, but the terrain left me has been ample enough for me to continue many of the activities that absorb me: writing, teaching, raising children and cats and plants and snakes, reading, speaking publicly about MS and depression, even playing bridge with people patient and honorable enough to let me scatter cards every which way without sneaking a peek.

Lest I begin to sound like Pollyanna, however, let me say that I don't like having MS. I hate it. My life holds realities—harsh ones, some of them—that no right-minded human being ought to accept without grumbling. One of them is fatigue. I know of no one with MS who does not complain of bone-weariness; in a disease that presents an astonishing variety of symptoms, fatigue seems to be a common factor. I wake up in the morning feeling the way most people do at the end of a bad day, and I take it from there. As a result, I spend a lot of time *in extremis* and, impatient with limitation, I tend to ignore my fatigue until my body breaks down in some way and forces rest. Then I miss picnics, dinner parties, poetry readings, the brief visits of old friends from out of town. The offspring of a puritanical tradition of exceptional venerability, I cannot view these lapses without shame. My life often seems a series of small failures to do as I ought.

I lead, on the whole, an ordinary life, probably rather like the one I would   10
have led had I not had MS. I am lucky that my predilections were already solitary, sedentary, and bookish—unlike the world-famous French cellist I have read about, or the young woman I talked with one long afternoon who wanted only to be a jockey. I had just begun graduate school when I found out something was wrong with me, and I have remained, interminably, a

graduate student. Perhaps I would not have if I'd thought I had the stamina to return to a full-time job as a technical editor; but I've enjoyed my studies.

In addition to studying, I teach writing courses. I also teach medical students how to give neurological examinations. I pick up freelance editing jobs here and there. I have raised a foster son and sent him into the world, where he has made me two grandbabies, and I am still escorting my daughter and son through adolescence. I go to Mass every Saturday. I am a superb, if messy, cook. I am also an enthusiastic laundress, capable of sorting a hamper full of clothes into five subtly differentiated piles, but a terrible housekeeper. I can do italic writing and, in an emergency, bathe an oil-soaked cat. I play a fiendish game of Scrabble. When I have the time and the money, I'd like to sit on my front steps with my husband, drinking Amaretto and smoking a cigar, as we imagine our counterparts in Leningrad and make sure that the sun gets down once more behind the sharp childish scrawl of the Tucson Mountains.

This lively plenty has its bleak complement, of course, in all the things I can no longer do. I will never run again, except in dreams, and one day I may have to write that I will never walk again. I like to go camping, but I can't follow George and the children along the trails that wander out of a campsite through the desert or into the mountains. In fact, even on the level I've learned never to check the weather or try to hold a coherent conversation: I need all my attention for my wayward feet. Of late, I have begun to catch myself wondering how people can propel themselves without canes. With only one usable hand, I have to select my clothing with care not so much for style as for ease of ingress and egress, and even so, dressing can be laborious. I can no longer do fine stitchery, pick up babies, play the piano, braid my hair. I am immobilized by acute attacks of depression, which may or may not be physiologically related to MS but are certainly its logical concomitant.

These two elements, the plenty and the privation, are never pure, nor are the delight and wretchedness that accompany them. Almost every pickle that I get into as a result of my weakness and clumsiness—and I get into plenty—is funny as well as maddening and sometimes painful. I recall one May afternoon when a friend and I were going out for a drink after finishing up at school. As we were climbing into opposite sides of my car, chatting, I tripped and fell, flat and hard, onto the asphalt parking lot, my abrupt departure interrupting him in mid-sentence. "Where'd you go?" he called as he came around the back of the car to find me hauling myself up by the door frame. "Are you all right?" Yes, I told him, I was fine, just a bit rattly, and we drove off to find a shady patio and some beer. When I got home an hour or so later, my daughter greeted me with "What have you done to yourself?" I looked down. One elbow of my white turtleneck with the green froggies, one knee of my white trousers, one white kneesock were blood-soaked. We peeled off the clothes and inspected the damage, which was nasty enough but not alarming. That part wasn't funny: The abrasions took a long time to heal, and one got a little infected. Even so, when I think of my friend talking earnestly, suddenly, to the hot thin air while I dropped from his view as though through a trap door, I find the image as silly as something from a Marx Brothers movie.

I may find it easier than other cripples to amuse myself because I live propped by the acceptance and the assistance and, sometimes, the amusement of those around me. Grocery clerks tear my checks out of my checkbook for me, and sales clerks find chairs to put into dressing rooms when I want to try on clothes. The people I work with make sure I teach at times when I am least likely to be fatigued, in places I can get to, with the materials I need. My students, with one anonymous exception (in an end-of-the-semester evaluation), have been unperturbed by my disability. Some even like it. One was immensely cheered by the information that I paint my own fingernails; she decided, she told me, that if I could go to such trouble over fine details, she could keep on writing essays. I suppose I became some sort of bright-fingered muse. She wrote good essays, too.

The most important struts in the framework of my existence, of course,   15
are my husband and children. Dismayingly few marriages survive the MS test, and why should they? Most twenty-two- and nineteen-year-olds, like George and me, can vow in clear conscience, after a childhood of chicken pox and summer colds, to keep one another in sickness and in health so long as they both shall live. Not many are equipped for catastrophe: the dismay, the depression, the extra work, the boredom that a degenerative disease can insinuate into a relationship. And our society, with its emphasis on fun and its association of fun with physical performance, offers little encouragement for a whole spouse to stay with a crippled partner. Children experience similar stresses when faced with a crippled parent, and they are more helpless, since parents and children can't usually get divorced. They hate, of course, to be different from their peers, and the child whose mother is tacking down the aisle of a school auditorium packed with proud parents like a Cape Cod dinghy in a stiff breeze jolly well stands out in a crowd. Deprived of legal divorce, the child can at least deny the mother's disability, even her existence, forgetting to tell her about recitals and PTA meetings, refusing to accompany her to stores or church or the movies, never inviting friends to the house. Many do.

But I've been limping along for ten years now, and so far George and the children are still at my left elbow, holding tight. Anne and Matthew vacuum floors and dust furniture and haul trash and rake up dog droppings and button my cuffs and bake lasagna and Toll House cookies with just enough grumbling so I know that they don't have brain fever. And far from hiding me, they're forever dragging me by racks of fancy clothes or through teeming school corridors, or welcoming gaggles of friends while I'm wandering through the house in Anne's filmy pink babydoll pajamas. George generally calls before he brings someone home, but he does just as many dumb thankless chores as the children. And they all yell at me, laugh at some of my jokes, write me funny letters when we're apart—in short, treat me as an ordinary human being for whom they have some use. I think they like me. Unless they're faking. . . .

Faking. There's the rub. Tugging at the fringes of my consciousness always is the terror that people are kind to me only because I'm a cripple. My mother almost shattered me once, with that instinct mothers have—blind, I think, in this case, but unerring nonetheless—for striking blows along the fault-lines of their children's hearts, by telling me, in an attack on my self-ishness, "We all have to make allowances for you, of course, because of the way you are." From the distance of a couple of years, I have to admit that I haven't any idea just what she meant, and I'm not sure that she knew either. She was awfully angry. But at the time, as the words thudded home, I felt my worst fear, suddenly realized. I could bear being called selfish: I am. But I couldn't bear the corroboration that those around me were doing in fact what I'd always suspected them of doing, professing fondness while silently putting up with me because of the way I am. A cripple. I've been a little cracked ever since.

Along with this fear that people are secretly accepting shoddy goods comes a relentless pressure to please—to prove myself worth the burdens I impose, I guess, or to build a substantial account of good will against which I may write drafts in times of need. Part of the pressure arises from social expectations. In our society, anyone who deviates from the norm had better find some way to compensate. Like fat people, who are expected to be jolly, cripples must bear their lot meekly and cheerfully. A grumpy cripple isn't playing by the rules. And much of the pressure is self-generated. Early on I vowed that, if I had to have MS, by God I was going to do it well. This is a class act, ladies and gentlemen. No tears, no recriminations, no faint-heartedness.

One way and another, then, I wind up feeling like Tiny Tim,[2] peering over the edge of the table at the Christmas goose, waving my crutch, piping down God's blessing on us all. Only sometimes I don't want to play Tiny Tim; I'd rather be Caliban,[3] a most scurvy monster. Fortunately, at home no one much cares whether I'm a good cripple or a bad cripple as long as I make vichyssoise with fair regularity. One evening several years ago, Anne was reading at the dining-room table while I cooked dinner. As I opened a can of tomatoes, the can slipped in my left hand and juice spattered me and the counter with bloody spots. Fatigued and infuriated, I bellowed, "I'm so sick of being crippled!" Anne glanced at me over the top of her book. "There now," she said, "do you feel better?" "Yes," I said, "yes, I do." She went back to her reading. I felt better. That's about all the attention my scurviness ever gets.

Because I hate being crippled, I sometimes hate myself for being a crip-   20
ple. Over the years I have come to expect—even accept—attacks of violent self-loathing. Luckily, in general our society no longer connects deformity and disease directly with evil (though a charismatic once told me that I have MS because a devil is in me) and so I'm allowed to move largely at will, even among small children. But I'm not sure that this revision of attitude has

---

2 **Tiny Tim:** Crippled boy in Charles Dickens's *A Christmas Carol.*—EDS.
3 **Caliban:** A character in William Shakespeare's play *The Tempest.*—EDS.

been particularly helpful. Physical imperfection, even freed of moral disapprobation, still defies and violates the ideal, especially for women, whose confinement in their bodies as objects of desire is far from over. Each age, of course, has its ideal, and I doubt that ours is any better or worse than any other. Today's ideal woman, who lives on the glossy pages of dozens of magazines, seems to be between the ages of eighteen and twenty-five; her hair has body, her teeth flash white, her breath smells minty, her underarms are dry; she has a career but is still a fabulous cook, especially of meals that take less than twenty minutes to prepare; she does not ordinarily appear to have a husband or children; she is trim and deeply tanned; she jogs, swims, plays tennis, rides a bicycle, sails, but does not bowl; she travels widely, even to out-of-the-way places like Finland and Samoa, always in the company of the ideal man, who possesses a nearly identical set of characteristics. There are a few exceptions. Though usually white and often blonde, she may be black, Hispanic, Asian, or Native American, so long as she is unusually sleek. She may be old, provided she is selling a laxative or is Lauren Bacall. If she is selling a detergent, she may be married and have a flock of strikingly messy children. But she is never a cripple.

Like many women I know, I have always had an uneasy relationship with my body. I was not a popular child, largely, I think now, because I was peculiar: intelligent, intense, moody, shy, given to unexpected actions and inexplicable notions and emotions. But as I entered adolescence, I believed myself unpopular because I was homely; my breasts too flat, my mouth too wide, my hips too narrow, my clothing never quite right in fit or style. I was not, in fact, particularly ugly, old photographs inform me, though I was well off the ideal; but I carried this sense of self-alienation with me into adulthood, where it regenerated in response to the depredations of MS. Even with my brace I walk with a limp so pronounced that, seeing myself on the videotape of a television program on the disabled, I couldn't believe that anything but an inchworm could make progress humping along like that. My shoulders droop and my pelvis thrusts forward as I try to balance myself upright, throwing my frame into a bony S. As a result of contractures, one shoulder is higher than the other and I carry one arm bent in front of me, the fingers curled into a claw. My left arm and leg have wasted into pipe-stems, and I try always to keep them covered. When I think about how my body must look to others, especially to men, to whom I have been trained to display myself, I feel ludicrous, even loathsome.

At my age, however, I don't spend much time thinking about my appearance. The burning egocentricity of adolescence, which assures one that all the world is looking all the time, has passed, thank God, and I'm generally too caught up in what I'm doing to step back, as I used to, and watch myself as though upon a stage. I'm also too old to believe in the accuracy of self-image. I know that I'm not a hideous crone, that in fact, when I'm rested, well dressed, and well made up, I look fine. The self-loathing I feel is neither physically nor intellectually substantial. What I hate is not me but a disease.

I am not a disease.

And a disease is not—at least not singlehandedly—going to determine who I am, though at first it seemed to be going to. Adjusting to a chronic incurable illness, I have moved through a process similar to that outlined by Elisabeth Kübler-Ross in *On Death and Dying*. The major difference—and it is far more significant than most people recognize—is that I can't be sure of the outcome, as the terminally ill cancer patient can. Research studies indicate that, with proper medical care, I may achieve a "normal" life span. And in our society, with its vision of death as the ultimate evil, worse even than decrepitude, the response to such news is, "Oh well, at least you're not going to *die*." Are there worse things than dying? I think that there may be.

I think of two women I know, both with MS, both enough older than I   25 to have served me as models. One took to her bed several years ago and has been there ever since. Although she can sit in a high-backed wheelchair, because she is incontinent she refuses to go out at all, even though incontinence pants, which are readily available at any pharmacy, could protect her from embarrassment. Instead, she stays at home and insists that her husband, a small quiet man, a retired civil servant, stay there with her except for a quick weekly foray to the supermarket. The other woman, whose illness was diagnosed when she was eighteen, a nursing student engaged to a young doctor, finished her training, married her doctor, accompanied him to Germany when he was in the service, bore three sons and a daughter, now grown and gone. When she can, she travels with her husband; she plays bridge, embroiders, swims regularly; she works, like me, as a symptomatic-patient instructor of medical students in neurology. Guess which woman I hope to be.

At the beginning, I thought about having MS almost incessantly. And because of the unpredictable course of the disease, my thoughts were always terrified. Each night I'd get into bed wondering whether I'd get out again the next morning, whether I'd be able to see, to speak, to hold a pen between my fingers. Knowing that the day might come when I'd be physically incapable of killing myself, I thought perhaps I ought to do so right away, while I still had the strength. Gradually I came to understand that the Nancy who might one day lie inert under a bedsheet, arms and legs paralyzed, unable to feed or bathe herself, unable to reach out for a gun, a bottle of pills, was not the Nancy I was at present, and that I could not presume to make decisions for that future Nancy, who might well not want in the least to die. Now the only provision I've made for the future Nancy is that when the time comes—and it is likely to come in the form of pneumonia, friend to the weak and the old—I am not to be treated with machines and medications. If she is unable to communicate by then, I hope she will be satisfied with these terms.

Thinking all the time about having MS grew tiresome and intrusive, especially in the large and tragic mode in which I was accustomed to considering my plight. Months and even years went by without catastrophe (at least without one related to MS), and really I was awfully busy, what with George and children and snakes and students and poems, and I hadn't the time, let alone the inclination, to devote myself to being a disease. Too, the richer my life became, the funnier it seemed, as though there were some connection between largesse and laughter, and so my tragic stance began to waver until, even with the aid of a brace and a cane, I couldn't hold it for very long at a time.

After several years I was satisfied with my adjustment. I had suffered my grief and fury and terror, I thought, but now I was at ease with my lot. Then one summer day I set out with George and the children across the desert for a vacation in California. Part way to Yuma I became aware that my right leg felt funny. "I think I've had an exacerbation," I told George. "What shall we do?" he asked. "I think we'd better get the hell to California," I said, "because I don't know whether I'll ever make it again." So we went on to San Diego and then to Orange, up the Pacific Coast Highway to Santa Cruz, across to Yosemite, down to Sequoia and Joshua Tree, and so back over the desert to home. It was a fine two-week trip, filled with friends and fair weather, and I wouldn't have missed it for the world, though I did in fact make it back to California two years later. Nor would there have been any point in missing it, since in MS, once the symptoms have appeared, the neurological damage has been done, and there's no way to predict or prevent that damage.

The incident spoiled my self-satisfaction, however. It renewed my grief and fury and terror, and I learned that one never finishes adjusting to MS. I don't know now why I thought one would. One does not, after all, finish adjusting to life, and MS is simply a fact of my life—not my favorite fact, of course—but as ordinary as my nose and my tropical fish and my yellow Mazda station wagon. It may at any time get worse, but no amount of worry or anticipation can prepare me for a new loss. My life is a lesson in losses. I learn one at a time.

And I had best be patient in the learning, since I'll have to do it like it 30 or not. As any rock fan knows, you can't always get what you want. Particularly when you have MS. You can't, for example, get cured. In recent years researchers and the organizations that fund research have started to pay MS some attention even though it isn't fatal; perhaps they have begun to see that life is something other than a quantitative phenomenon, that one may be very much alive for a very long time in a life that isn't worth living. The researchers have made some progress toward understanding the mechanism of the disease: It may well be an autoimmune reaction triggered by a slow-acting virus. But they are nowhere near its prevention, control, or cure. And most of us want to be cured. Some, unable to accept incurability, grasp at one treatment after another, no matter how bizarre: megavitamin therapy, gluten-free diet, injections of cobra venom, hypothermal suits, lymphocytopharesis, hyperbaric chambers. Many treatments are probably harmless enough, but none are curative.

The absence of a cure often makes MS patients bitter toward their doctors. Doctors are, after all, the priests of modern society, the new shamans, whose business is to heal, and many an MS patient roves from one to another, searching for the "good" doctor who will make him well. Doctors too think of themselves as healers, and for this reason many have trouble dealing with MS patients, whose disease in its intransigence defeats their aims and mocks their skills. Too few doctors, it is true, treat their patients as whole human beings, but the reverse is also true. I have always tried to be gentle with my doctors, who often have more at stake in terms of ego than I do. I may be frustrated, maddened, depressed by the incurability of my disease, but I am not diminished by it, and they are. When I push myself up from my seat in the waiting room and stumble toward them, I incarnate the limitation of their powers. The least I can do is refuse to press on their tenderest spots.

This gentleness is part of the reason that I'm not sorry to be a cripple. I didn't have it before. Perhaps I'd have developed it anyway—how could I know such a thing?—and I wish I had more of it, but I'm glad of what I have. It has opened and enriched my life enormously, this sense that my frailty and need must be mirrored in others, that in searching for and shaping a stable core in a life wrenched by change and loss, change and loss, I must recognize the same process, under individual conditions, in the lives around me. I do not deprecate such knowledge, however I've come by it.

All the same, if a cure were found, would I take it? In a minute. I may be a cripple, but I'm only occasionally a loony and never a saint. Anyway, in my brand of theology God doesn't give bonus points for a limp. I'd take a cure; I just don't need one. A friend who also has MS startled me once by asking, "Do you ever say to yourself, 'Why me, Lord?'" "No, Michael, I don't," I told him, "because whenever I try, the only response I can think of is 'Why not?'" If I could make a cosmic deal, who would I put in my place? What in my life would I give up in exchange for sound limbs and a thrilling rush of energy? No one. Nothing. I might as well do the job myself. Now that I'm getting the hang of it.

The Reader's Presence

1. Mairs's approach to her multiple sclerosis may come across as ironic, jaunty, or tough. Near the beginning of the essay she assumes that her reader is fundamentally alienated from her: "I refuse to pretend that the only differences between you and me are the various ordinary ones that distinguish any one person from another" (paragraph 4). What are those differences? How does the essay attempt to move the reader away from awkwardness or suspicion or hostility? Does it succeed? Why or why not?

2. What does the epigraph from Louise Bogan mean to you? What might it signify in relation to Mairs's essay? What is "escape," in Mairs's context? What meanings might the word *nothing* have?

3. **CONNECTIONS:** "Lest I begin to sound like Pollyanna, however, let me say that I don't like having MS. I hate it" (paragraph 9). Discuss Mairs's admission of hatred for the disease—and for herself (paragraph 20)—in relation to Alice Walker's "abuse" of her injured eye (paragraph 30) in "Beauty: When the Other Dancer Is the Self" (page 275). What is the role of self-loathing in personal growth?

The Writer at Work

NANCY MAIRS on Finding a Voice

fotosmith

In writing workshops and lectures, the essayist Nancy Mairs is often asked what appears to be a simple question: How did you find your voice as a writer? Yet is the question truly a simple one? In the following passage from her book "on becoming a (woman) writer," *Voice Lessons*, Mairs closely examines the question and suggests a way it might be answered. You might want to compare her concern about finding a voice to that of Henry Louis Gates Jr. in "The Writer at Work" on page 134.

❝ The question I am most often asked when I speak to students and others interested in writing is, How did you find your voice? I have some trouble with this locution because "find" always suggests to me the discovery, generally fortuitous, of some lack or loss. I have found an occasional four-leaf clover. I have found a mate. I have, more than once, found my way home. But is a voice susceptible of the same sort of revelation or retrieval? Hasn't mine simply always been there, from my earliest lallation to the "I love you" I called after my husband on his way to school several hours ago?

But of course, I remind myself, the question doesn't concern *my* voice at all but the voice of another woman (also named Nancy Mairs, confusingly enough) whose "utterances" are, except for the occasional public reading, literally inaudible: not, strictly speaking, a voice at all, but a fabrication, a device. And when I look again at the dictionary, I see that "find" can indeed also mean "devise." The voice in question, like the woman called into being to explain its existence, is an invention.

But of whom? For simplicity's sake, we assume that the voice in a work is that of the writer (in the case of nonfiction) or one invented by her (in the case of fiction). This assumption describes the relationship between writer (the woman in front of a luminous screen) and persona (whoever you hear speaking to you right now) adequately for most readers. And maybe for most writers, too. Until that earnest student in the second row waves a gnawed pencil over her head and asks, timidly as a rule because hers is the first question, "How did you find your voice?"

As though "you" were a coherent entity already existing at some original point, who had only to open her mouth and agitate her vocal chords—or, to be precise, pick up her fingers and diddle the keys—to call the world she had in mind into being. Not just a writer, an Author. But I've examined this process over and over in myself, and the direction of this authorial plot simply doesn't ring true. In the beginning, remember, was the *Word*. Not me. And the question, properly phrased, should probably be asked of my voice: How did you find (devise, invent, contrive) your Nancy? ❞

David Mamet

THE RAKE: A FEW SCENES FROM MY CHILDHOOD

DAVID MAMET (b. 1947) is a playwright, screenwriter, and director whose work is appreciated for the attention he pays to language as it is spoken by ordinary people in the contemporary world. His 1984 Pulitzer Prize–winning play, *Glengarry Glen Ross*, explores the psychology of ambition, competition, failure, and despair among a group of Chicago real estate agents who are driven to sell worthless property to unsuspecting customers.

Mamet has said that "playwriting is simply showing how words influence actions and vice versa. All my plays attempt to bring out the poetry in the plain, everyday language people use. That's the only way to put art back in the theater." Mamet's sensitivity to working-class language and experience is due in part to his own work experience in factories; at a real estate agency; and as a window washer, office cleaner, and taxi driver. Mamet has taught theater at several leading universities and published a number of books about theater and film, including *True and False: Heresy and Common Sense for the Actor* (1997), *Three Uses of the Knife: On the Nature and Purpose of Drama* (1998), and *Bambi vs. Godzilla: On the Nature, Purpose, and Practice of the Movie Business* (2007). Mamet's plays include the often-revived *American Buffalo* (1977), *Ricky Jay: On the Stem* (2002), *Romance* (2005), and *November*, his take on politics that opened in New York City in 2008. He has written and directed several films, including Oscar-nominated movies, *The Verdict* (1982) and *Wag the Dog* (1997), *State and Main* (2000), and *Heist* (2001). He was also the producer and writer of the television series *The Unit* (2006–2007). His latest book, *The Secret Knowledge: On the Dismantling of American Culture*, was published in 2011. "The Rake: A Few Scenes from My Childhood" appeared in *Harper's* in 1992.

> "Playwriting is simply showing how words influence actions and vice versa."

THERE WAS THE INCIDENT of the rake and there was the incident of the school play, and it seems to me that they both took place at the round kitchen table.

The table was not in the kitchen proper but in an area called "the nook," which held its claim to that small measure of charm by dint of a waist-high wall separating it from an adjacent area known as the living room.

All family meals were eaten in the nook. There was a dining room to the right, but, as in most rooms of that name at the time and in those surroundings, it was never used.

The round table was of wrought iron and topped with glass; it was noteworthy for that glass, for it was more than once and rather more than several times, I am inclined to think, that my stepfather would grow so angry as to bring some object down on the glass top, shattering it, thus giving us to know how we had forced him out of control.

And it seems that most times when he would shatter the table, as often   5
as that might have been, he would cut some portion of himself on the glass, or that he or his wife, our mother, would cut their hands on picking up the glass afterward, and that we children were to understand, and did understand, that these wounds were our fault.

So the table was associated in our minds with the notion of blood.

The house was in a brand-new housing development in the southern suburbs. The new community was built upon, and now bordered, the remains of what had once been a cornfield. When our new family moved in, there were but a few homes in the development completed, and a few more under construction. Most streets were mud, and boasted a house here or there, and many empty lots marked out by white stakes.

The house we lived in was the development's Model Home. The first time we had seen it, it had signs plastered on the front and throughout the interior telling of the various conveniences it contained. And it had a lawn, and was one of the only homes in the new community that did.

My stepfather was fond of the lawn, and he detailed me and my sister to care for it, and one fall afternoon we found ourselves assigned to rake the leaves.

Why this chore should have been so hated I cannot say, except that we   10
children, and I especially, felt ourselves less than full members of this new, cobbled-together family, and disliked being assigned to the beautification of a home that we found unbeautiful in all respects, and for which we had neither natural affection nor a sense of proprietary interest.

We went to the new high school. We walked the mile down the open two-lane road on one side of which was the just-begun suburban community and on the other side of which was the cornfield.

The school was as new as the community, and still under construction for the first three years of its occupancy. One of its innovations was the notion that honesty would be engendered by the absence of security, and so the lockers were designed and built both without locks and without the possibility of attaching locks. And there was the corresponding rash of thievery and many lectures about the same from the school administration, but it was difficult to point with pride to any scholastic or community tradition supporting the suggestion that we, the students, pull together in this new, utopian way. We were, in school, in an uncompleted building in the midst of a mud field in the midst of a cornfield. Our various sports teams were called The Spartans;

and I played on those teams, which were of a wretchedness consistent with their novelty.

Meanwhile my sister interested herself in the drama society. The year after I had left the school she obtained the lead in the school play. It called for acting and singing, both of which she had talent for, and it looked to be a signal triumph for her in her otherwise unremarkable and unenjoyed school career.

On the night of the play's opening, she sat down to dinner with our mother and our stepfather. It may be that they ate a trifle early to allow her to get to the school to enjoy the excitement of opening night. But however it was, my sister had no appetite, and she nibbled a bit at her food, and then she got up from the table to carry her plate back to scrape it in the sink, when my mother suggested that she sit down, as she had not finished her food. My sister said she really had no appetite, but my mother insisted that, as the meal had been prepared, it would be good form to sit and eat it.

My sister sat down with the plate and pecked at her food and she tried   15
to eat a bit, and told my mother that, no, really, she possessed no appetite whatever, and that was due, no doubt, not to the food, but to her nervousness and excitement at the prospect of opening night.

My mother, again, said that, as the food had been cooked, it had to be eaten, and my sister tried and said that she could not; at which my mother nodded. She then got up from the table and went to the telephone and looked the number up and called the school and got the drama teacher and identified herself and told him that her daughter wouldn't be coming to school that night, that, no, she was not ill, but that she would not be coming in. Yes, yes, she said, she knew her daughter had the lead in the play, and, yes, she was aware that many children and teachers had worked hard for it, et cetera, and so my sister did not play the lead in her school play. But I was long gone, out of the house by that time, and well out of it. I heard that story, and others like it, at the distance of twenty-five years.

In the model house our rooms were separated from their room, the master bedroom, by a bathroom and a study. On some weekends I would go alone to visit my father in the city and my sister would stay and sometimes grow frightened or lonely in her part of the house. And once, in the period when my grandfather, then in his sixties, was living with us, she became alarmed at a noise she had heard in the night; or perhaps she just became lonely, and she went out of her room and down the hall, calling for my mother, or my stepfather, or my grandfather, but the house was dark, and no one answered.

And, as she went farther down the hall, toward the living room, she heard voices, and she turned the corner, and saw a light coming from under the closed door in the master bedroom, and heard my stepfather crying, and the sound of my mother weeping. So my sister went up to the door, and she heard my stepfather talking to my grandfather and saying, "Jack.

Say the words. Just say the words . . ." And my grandfather in his Eastern European accent, saying with obvious pain and difficulty, "No. No. I can't. Why are you making me do this? Why?" And the sound of my mother crying convulsively.

My sister opened the door, and she saw my grandfather sitting on the bed, and my stepfather standing by the closet and gesturing. On the floor of the closet she saw my mother, curled in a fetal position, moaning and crying and hugging herself. My stepfather was saying, "Say the words. Just say the words." And my grandfather was breathing fast and repeating, "I can't. She knows how I feel about her. I can't." And my stepfather said, "Say the words, Jack. Please. Just say you love her." At which my mother would moan louder. And my grandfather said, "I can't."

My sister pushed the door open farther and said—I don't know what she   20
said, but she asked, I'm sure, for some reassurance, or some explanation, and my stepfather turned around and saw her and picked up a hairbrush from a dresser that he passed as he walked toward her, and he hit her in the face and slammed the door on her. And she continued to hear "Jack, say the words."

She told me that on weekends when I was gone my stepfather ended every Sunday evening by hitting or beating her for some reason or other. He would come home from depositing his own kids back at their mother's house after their weekend visitation, and would settle down tired and angry, and, as a regular matter on those evenings, would find out some intolerable behavior on my sister's part and slap or hit or beat her.

Years later, at my mother's funeral, my sister spoke to our aunt, my mother's sister, who gave a footnote to this behavior. She said when they were young, my mother and my aunt, they and their parents lived in a small flat on the West Side. My grandfather was a salesman on the road from dawn on Monday until Friday night. Their family had a fiction, and that fiction, that article of faith, was that my mother was a naughty child. And each Friday, when he came home, his first question as he climbed the stairs was, "What has she done this week . . . ?" At which my grandmother would tell him the terrible things that my mother had done, after which she, my mother, was beaten.

This was general knowledge in my family. The footnote concerned my grandfather's behavior later in the night. My aunt had a room of her own, and it adjoined her parents' room. And she related that each Friday, when the house had gone to bed, she, through the thin wall, heard my grandfather pleading for sex. "Cookie, please." And my grandmother responding, "No, Jack." "Cookie, please." "No, Jack." "Cookie, please."

And once, my grandfather came home and asked, "What has she done this week?" and I do not know, but I imagine that the response was not completed, and perhaps hardly begun; in any case, he reached and grabbed my mother by the back of the neck and hurled her down the stairs.

And once, in our house in the suburbs there had been an outburst by   25
my stepfather directed at my sister. And she had, somehow, prevailed. It

was, I think, that he had the facts of the case wrong, and had accused her of the commission of something for which she had demonstrably had no opportunity, and she pointed this out to him with what I can imagine, given the circumstances, was an understandable, and, given my prejudice, a commendable degree of freedom. Thinking the incident closed she went back to her room to study, and, a few moments later, saw him throw open her door, bat the book out of her hands, and pick her up and throw her against the far wall, where she struck the back of her neck on the shelf.

She was told, the next morning, that her pain, real or pretended, held no weight, and that she would have to go to school. She protested that she could not walk, or, if at all, only with the greatest of difficulty and in great pain; but she was dressed and did walk to school, where she fainted, and was brought home. For years she suffered various headaches; an X-ray taken twenty years later for an unrelated problem revealed that when he threw her against the shelf he had cracked her vertebrae.

When we left the house we left in good spirits. When we went out to dinner, it was an adventure, which was strange to me, looking back, because many of these dinners ended with my sister or myself being banished, sullen or in tears, from the restaurant, and told to wait in the car, as we were in disgrace.

These were the excursions that had ended, due to her or my intolerable arrogance, as it was explained to us.

The happy trips were celebrated and capped with a joke. Here is the joke: My stepfather, my mother, my sister, and I would exit the restaurant, my stepfather and mother would walk to the car, telling us that they would pick us up. We children would stand by the restaurant entrance. They would drive up in the car, open the passenger door, and wait until my sister and I had started to get in. They would then drive away.

They would drive ten or fifteen feet, and open the door again, and we 30 would walk up again, and they would drive away again. They sometimes would drive around the block. But they would always come back, and by that time the four of us would be laughing in camaraderie and appreciation of what, I believe, was our only family joke.

We were raking the lawn, my sister and I. I was raking, and she was stuffing the leaves into a bag. I loathed the job, and my muscles and my mind rebelled, and I was viciously angry, and my sister said something, and I turned and threw the rake at her and hit her in the face.

The rake was split bamboo and metal, and a piece of metal caught her lip and cut her badly.

We were both terrified, and I was sick with guilt, and we ran into the house, my sister holding her hand to her mouth, and her mouth and her hand and the front of her dress covered in blood.

We ran into the kitchen where my mother was cooking dinner, and my mother asked what happened.

Neither of us, myself out of guilt, of course, and my sister out of a desire   35
to avert the terrible punishment she knew I would receive, neither of us
would say what occurred.

My mother pressed us, and neither of us would answer. She said that
until one or the other answered, we would not go to the hospital; and so the
family sat down to dinner where my sister clutched a napkin to her face and
the blood soaked the napkin and ran down onto her food, which she had to
eat; and I also ate my food and we cleared the table and went to the hospital.

I remember the walks home from school in the frigid winter, along the
cornfield that was, for all its proximity to the city, part of the prairie. The
winters were viciously cold. From the remove of years, I can see how the
area might and may have been beautiful. One could have walked in the
stubble of the cornfields, or hunted birds, or enjoyed any of a number of
pleasures naturally occurring. ●

The Reader's Presence

1. Interwoven throughout Mamet's essay are descriptions of suburban developments
   and model homes; he even uses the word *utopian* (paragraph 12). What is Mamet's
   attitude toward these ideals? What is his tone in discussing them? Mamet says that
   he and his sister hated doing yard work, in part because they "had neither natural
   affection nor a sense of proprietary interest" (paragraph 10) toward their house.
   What does this mean?

2. Near the end of the essay, Mamet recalls a "joke" that his family shared. How does
   he present the joke to the reader? Do you think Mamet wants the reader to think the
   joke is funny? Why or why not? Would the joke seem different if Mamet had told it
   at the beginning of the essay? How does he connect this joke back to the story about
   the rake?

3. **CONNECTIONS:**   Mamet says that "the table was associated in our minds with the
   notion of blood" (paragraph 6). Do you think the rake also has symbolic value? If
   so, what does it represent? How does Mamet's use of symbolic objects compare to
   George Orwell's treatment of the gun and the elephant in "Shooting an Elephant"
   (page 216)? How does Mamet's account of his relationship with his sister compare
   to Alice Walker's account of her brothers' role in the "accident" in which she lost the
   sight in her eye in "Beauty: When the Other Dancer Is the Self" (page 275)?

Dinaw Mengestu

Home at Last

Ethiopian-born author **DINAW MENGESTU** (b. 1978) immigrated to the United States with his parents when he was just two years old. He received a BA in English from Georgetown University and an MFA in fiction writing from Columbia University. His debut novel, *The Beautiful Things That Heaven Bears* (2007), was a New York Times Notable Book and was named one of the ten best novels of 2007 by Amazon.com. He has also written extensively for magazines, such as *Harper's* and *Rolling Stone*, on global issues, including the situation in Darfur. He teaches at Georgetown University, where he's the Lannan Chair of Poetics, and he was selected as a MacArthur Fellow in 2012. His second novel, *How to Read the Air*,

> Dinaw Mengestu's novel is about "what it's like when you are not particularly attached to either of [the] two communities" you belong to.

was published in 2010. Mengestu has said that the novel, the story of an Ethiopian American, is "less about trying to figure out how you occupy these two cultural or racial boundaries and more about what it's like when you are not particularly attached to either of [the] two communities." A similar sentiment marks the following essay, "Home at Last," originally published in the Winter 2008 issue of *Open City*.

AT TWENTY-ONE I moved to Brooklyn hoping that it would be the last move I would ever make—that it would, with the gradual accumulation of time, memory, and possessions, become that place I instinctively reverted back to when asked, "So, where are you from?" I was born in Ethiopia like my parents and their parents before them, but it would be a lie to say I was *from* Ethiopia, having left the country when I was only two years old following a military coup and civil war, losing in the process the language and any direct memory of the family and culture I had been born into. I simply am Ethiopian, without the necessary "from" that serves as the final assurance of our identity and origin.

Since leaving Addis Ababa in 1980, I've lived in Peoria, Illinois; in a suburb of Chicago; and then finally, before moving to Brooklyn, in Washington, D.C., the de facto[1] capital of the Ethiopian immigrant. Others, I know, have

---

[1] *de facto:* A Latin term often used in the law; it means "in practice" or "for all intents and purposes." —EDS.

moved much more often and across much greater distances. I've only known a few people, however, that have grown up with the oddly permanent feeling of having lost and abandoned a home that you never, in fact, really knew, a feeling that has nothing to do with apartments, houses, or miles, but rather the sense that no matter how far you travel, or how long you stay still, there is no place that you can always return to, no place where you fully belong. My parents, for all that they had given up by leaving Ethiopia, at least had the certainty that they had come from some place. They knew the country's language and culture, had met outside of coffee shops along Addis's main boulevard in the early days of their relationship, and as a result, regardless of how mangled by violence Ethiopia later became, it was irrevocably and ultimately theirs. Growing up, one of my father's favorite sayings was, "Remember, you are Ethiopian," even though, of course, there was nothing for me to remember apart from the bits of nostalgia and culture my parents had imparted. What remained had less to do with the idea that I was from Ethiopia and more to do with the fact that I was not from America.

I can't say when exactly I first became aware of that feeling—that I was always going to and never from—but surely I must have felt it during those first years in Peoria, with my parents, sister, and me always sitting on the edge of whatever context we were now supposed to be a part of, whether it was the all-white Southern Baptist Church we went to every weekend, or the nearly all-white Catholic schools my sister and I attended first in Peoria and then again in Chicago at my parents' insistence. By that point my father, haunted by the death of his brother during the revolution and the ensuing loss of the country he had always assumed he would live and die in, had taken to long evening walks that he eventually let me accompany him on. Back then he had a habit of sometimes whispering his brother's name as he walked ("Shibrew," he would mutter) or whistling the tunes of Amharic[2] songs that I had never known. He always walked with both hands firmly clasped behind his back, as if his grief, transformed into something real and physical, could be grasped and secured in the palms of his hands. That was where I first learned what it meant to lose and be alone. The lesson would be reinforced over the years whenever I caught sight of my mother sitting by herself on a Sunday afternoon, staring silently out of our living room's picture window, recalling, perhaps, her father who had died after she left, or her mother, four sisters, and one brother in Ethiopia—or else recalling nothing at all because there was no one to visit her, no one to call or see. We had been stripped bare here in America, our lives confined to small towns and urban suburbs. We had sacrificed precisely those things that can never be compensated for or repaid—parents, siblings, culture, a memory to a place that dates back more than half a generation. It's easy to see now how even as a family we were isolated from one another—my parents tied and lost to their past; my sister and I irrevocably assimilated. For years we were strangers even among ourselves.

---

[2] ***Amharic:*** Language spoken in North Central Ethiopia. —EDS.

By the time I arrived in Brooklyn I had little interest in where I actually landed. I had just graduated college and had had enough of the fights and arguments about not being "black" enough, as well as the earlier fights in high school hallways and street corners that were fought for simply being black. Now it was enough, I wanted to believe, to simply be, to say I was in Brooklyn and Brooklyn was home. It wasn't until after I had signed the lease on my apartment that I even learned the name of the neighborhood I had moved into: Kensington, a distinctly regal name at a price that I could afford; it was perfect, in other words, for an eager and poor writer with inflated ambitions and no sense of where he belonged.

After less than a month of living in Kensington I had covered almost   5 all of the neighborhood's streets, deliberately committing their layouts and routines to memory in a first attempt at assimilation. There was an obvious and deliberate echo to my walks, a self-conscious reenactment of my father's routine that I adopted to stave off some of my own emptiness. It wasn't just that I didn't have any deep personal relationships here, it was that I had chosen this city as the place to redefine, to ground, to secure my place in the world. If I could bind myself to Kensington physically, if I could memorize and mentally reproduce in accurate detail the various shades of the houses on a particular block, then I could stake my own claim to it, and in doing so, no one could tell me who I was or that I didn't belong.

On my early-morning walks to the F train I passed in succession a Latin American restaurant and grocery store, a Chinese fish market, a Halal butcher shop, followed by a series of Pakistani and Bangladeshi takeout restaurants. This cluster of restaurants on the corner of Church and McDonald, I later learned, sold five-dollar plates of lamb and chicken biryani in portions large enough to hold me over for a day, and in more financially desperate times, two days. Similarly, I learned that the butcher and fish shop delivery trucks arrived on most days just as I was making my way to the train. If I had time, I found it hard not to stand and stare at the refrigerated trucks with their calf and sheep carcasses dangling from hooks, or at the tanks of newly arrived bass and catfish flapping around in a shallow pool of water just deep enough to keep them alive.

It didn't take long for me to develop a fierce loyalty to Kensington, to think of the neighborhood and my place in it as emblematic of a grander immigrant narrative. In response to that loyalty, I promised to host a "Kensington night" for the handful of new friends that I eventually made in the city, an evening that would have been comprised of five-dollar lamb biryani followed by two-dollar Budweisers at Denny's, the neighborhood's only full-fledged bar—a defunct Irish pub complete with terribly dim lighting and wooden booths. I never hosted a Kensington night, however, no doubt in part because I had established my own private relationship to the neighborhood, one that could never be shared with others in a single evening of cheap South Asian food and beer. I knew the hours of the call of the muezzin that rang from the mosque a block away from my apartment. I heard it in my

Ethnic diversity in Brooklyn's Kensington neighborhood.

bedroom every morning, afternoon, and evening, and if I was writing when it called out, I learned that it was better to simply stop and admire it. My landlord's father, an old gray-haired Chinese immigrant who spoke no English, gradually smiled at me as I came and went, just as I learned to say hello, as politely as possible, in Mandarin every time I saw him. The men behind the counters of the Bangladeshi takeout places now knew me by sight. A few, on occasion, slipped an extra dollop of vegetables or rice into my to-go container, perhaps because they worried that I wasn't eating enough. One in particular, who was roughly my age, spoke little English, and smiled wholeheartedly whenever I came in, gave me presweetened tea and free bread, a gesture that I took to be an acknowledgment that, at least for him, I had earned my own, albeit marginal, place here.

And so instead of sitting with friends in a brightly lit fluorescent restaurant with cafeteria-style service, I found myself night after night quietly walking around the neighborhood in between sporadic fits of writing. Kensington was no more beautiful by night than by day, and perhaps this very absence of grandeur allowed me to feel more at ease wandering its streets at night. The haphazard gathering of immigrants in Kensington had turned it into a place that even someone like me, haunted and conscious of race and identity at every turn, could slip and blend into.

Inevitably on my way home I returned to the corner of Church and McDonald with its glut of identical restaurants. On warm nights, I had found it was the perfect spot to stand and admire not only what Kensington had become with the most recent wave of migration, but what any close-knit community—whether its people came here one hundred years ago from Europe or a decade ago from Africa, Asia, or the Caribbean—has provided throughout Brooklyn's history: a second home. There, on that corner, made up of five competing South Asian restaurants of roughly equal quality, dozens of Pakistani and Bangladeshi men gathered one night after another to drink chai out of paper cups. The men stood there talking for hours, huddled in factions built in part, I imagine, around restaurant loyalties. Some nights I sat in one of the restaurants and watched from a corner table with a book in hand as an artificial prop. A few of the men always stared, curious no doubt as to what I was doing there. Even though I lived in Kensington, when it came to evening gatherings like this, I was the foreigner and tourist. On other nights I ordered my own cup of tea and stood a few feet away on the edge of the sidewalk, near the subway entrance or at the bus stop, and silently stared. I had seen communal scenes like this before, especially while living in Washington, D.C., where there always seemed to be a cluster of Ethiopians, my age or older, gathered together outside coffee shops and bars all over the city, talking in Amharic with an ease and fluency that I admired and envied. They told jokes that didn't require explanation and debated arguments that were decades in the making. All of this was coupled with the familiarity and comfort of speaking in our native tongue. At any given moment, they could have told you without hesitancy where they were from. And so I had watched, hardly understanding a word, hoping somehow that the simple act of association and observation was enough to draw me into the fold.

Here, then, was a similar scene, this one played out on a Brooklyn corner with a culture and history different from the one I had been born into, but familiar to me nonetheless. The men on that corner in Kensington, just like the people I had known throughout my life, were immigrants in the most complete sense of the word—their loyalties still firmly attached to the countries they had left one, five, or twenty years earlier. If there was one thing I admired most about them, it was that they had succeeded, at least partly, in re-creating in Brooklyn some of what they had lost when they left their countries of origin. Unlike the solitary and private walks my father and I took, each of us buried deep in thoughts that had nowhere to go, this nightly gathering of Pakistani and Bangladeshi men was a makeshift reenactment of home. Farther down the road from where they stood were the few

10

remaining remnants of the neighborhood's older Jewish community—one synagogue, a kosher deli—proof, if one was ever needed, that Brooklyn is always reinventing itself, that there is room here for us all.

While the men stood outside on the corner, their numbers gradually increasing until they spilled out into the street as they talked loudly among themselves, I once again played my own familiar role of quiet, jealous observer and secret admirer. I have no idea what those men talked about, if they discussed politics, sex, or petty complaints about work. It never mattered anyway. The substance of the conversations belonged to them, and I couldn't have cared less. What I had wanted and found in them, what I admired and adored about Kensington, was the assertion that we can rebuild and remake ourselves and our communities over and over again, in no small part because there have always been corners in Brooklyn to do so on. I stood on that corner night after night for the most obvious of reasons—to be reminded of a way of life that persists regardless of context; to feel, however foolishly, that I too was attached to something. ●

The Reader's Presence

1. Why does Mengestu consciously try to make the Kensington section of Brooklyn home? What had been previously missing in his life? Why can't he acknowledge that he is *from* Ethiopia? Do you think he succeeds in making Kensington home? How do you interpret his final paragraph?

2. What is Mengestu's reason for not hosting the "Kensington night" he had planned (paragraph 7)? Why do you think—though he says he made new friends in the city—that no friends appear in the essay? Note how often through the course of the essay he is either alone or at the edge of a group of people whose language he doesn't understand. How do you interpret this?

3. **VISUAL PRESENCE:**   Review the photograph of a storefront in Brooklyn's Kensington neighborhood (page 205.) What specific details in the image suggest the ethnic diversity of Mengestu's neighborhood? In what specific way(s) does your neighborhood reflect a similar diversity?

4. **CONNECTIONS:**   Compare Mengestu's essay to Geeta Kothari's "If You Are What You Eat, Then What Am I?" (page 172). How does each essay illuminate ethnic identity in America? What differences and similarities can you find between each author's presentation of separation and assimilation?

Manuel Muñoz

LEAVE YOUR NAME AT THE BORDER

MANUEL MUÑOZ (b. 1972) is a California native who received a BA from Harvard University and an MFA in creative writing from Cornell University. He has published two award-winning collections of short fiction, *Zigzagger* (2003) and *The Faith Healer of Olive Avenue* (2007), and his work has been published widely in mainstream publications, such as the *New York Times*, as well as in some of the most prestigious literary magazines in the country, including *Glimmer Train* and *Boston Review*. He received a Whiting Award and a PEN/O. Henry Award in 2009. His first

> **Manuel Muñoz has said that California's Central Valley and his hometown, Dinuba, "remain the foundation of [his] fiction."**

novel, *What You See in the Dark*, was published in 2011. Although he currently teaches in the Creative Writing Program at the University of Arizona, Tucson, he has said that California's Central Valley and his hometown, Dinuba, "remain the foundation of [his] fiction."

AT THE FRESNO AIRPORT, as I made my way to the gate, I heard a name over the intercom. The way the name was pronounced by the gate agent made me want to see what she looked like. That is, I wanted to see whether she was Mexican. Around Fresno, identity politics rarely deepen into exacting terms, so to say "Mexican" means, essentially, "not white." The slivered self-identifications Chicano, Hispanic, Mexican-American and Latino are not part of everyday life in the Valley. You're either Mexican or you're not. If someone wants to know if you were born in Mexico, they'll ask. Then you're From Over There — *de allá*. And leave it at that.

The gate agent, it turned out, was Mexican. Well-coiffed, in her 30s, she wore foundation that was several shades lighter than the rest of her skin. It was the kind of makeup job I've learned to silently identify at the mall when I'm with my mother, who will say nothing about it until we're back in the car. Then she'll stretch her neck like an ostrich and point to the darkness of her own skin, wondering aloud why women try to camouflage who they are.

I watched the Mexican gate agent busy herself at the counter, professional and studied. Once again, she picked up the microphone and, with authority, announced the name of the missing customer: "Eugenio Reyes, please come to the front desk."

You can probably guess how she said it. Her Anglicized pronunciation wouldn't be unusual in a place like California's Central Valley. I didn't have a Mexican name there either: I was an instruction guide.

When people ask me where I'm from, I say Fresno because I don't expect them to know little Dinuba. Fresno is a booming city of nearly 500,000 these days, with a diversity—white, Mexican, African-American, Armenian, Hmong and Middle Eastern people are all well represented—that shouldn't surprise anyone. It's in the small towns like Dinuba that surround Fresno that the awareness of cultural difference is stripped down to the interactions between the only two groups that tend to live there: whites and Mexicans. When you hear a Mexican name spoken in these towns, regardless of the speaker's background, it's no wonder that there's an "English way of pronouncing it."

I was born in 1972, part of a generation that learned both English and Spanish. Many of my cousins and siblings are bilingual, serving as translators for those in the family whose English is barely functional. Others have no way of following the Spanish banter at family gatherings. You can tell who falls into which group: Estella, Eric, Delia, Dubina, Melanie.

It's intriguing to watch "American" names begin to dominate among my nieces and nephews and second cousins, as well as with the children of my hometown friends. I am not surprised to meet 5-year-old Brandon or Kaitlyn. Hardly anyone questions the incongruity of matching these names with last names like Trujillo or Zepeda. The English-only way of life partly explains the quiet erasure of cultural difference that assimilation has attempted to accomplish. A name like Kaitlyn Zepeda doesn't completely obscure her ethnicity, but the half-step of her name, as a gesture, is almost understandable.

Spanish was and still is viewed with suspicion: always the language of the vilified illegal immigrant, it segregated schoolchildren into English-only and bilingual programs; it defined you, above all else, as part of a lower class. Learning English, though, brought its own complications with identity. It was simultaneously the language of the white population and a path toward the richer, expansive identity of "American." But it took getting out of the Valley for me to understand that "white" and "American" were two very different things.

Something as simple as saying our names "in English" was our unwittingly complicit gesture of trying to blend in. Pronouncing Mexican names correctly was never encouraged. Names like Daniel, Olivia and Marco slipped right into the mutability of the English language.

I remember a school ceremony at which the mathematics teacher, a white man, announced the names of Mexican students correctly and caused some confusion, if not embarrassment. Years later we recognized that he spoke in deference to our Spanish-speaking parents in the audience, caring teacher that he was.

These were difficult names for a non-Spanish speaker: Araceli, Nadira, Luis (a beautiful name when you glide the *u* and the *i* as you're supposed to). We had been accustomed to having our birth names altered for convenience.

Concepción was Connie. Ramón was Raymond. My cousin Esperanza was Hope—but her name was pronounced "Hopie" because any Spanish speaker would automatically pronounce the *e* at the end.

Ours, then, were names that stood as barriers to a complete embrace of an American identity, simply because their pronunciations required a slip into Spanish, the otherness that assimilation was supposed to erase. What to do with names like Amado, Lucio or Élida? There are no English "equivalents," no answer when white teachers asked, "What does your name mean?" when what they really wanted to know was "What's the English one?" So what you heard was a name butchered beyond recognition, a pronunciation that pointed the finger at the Spanish language as the source of clunky sound and ugly rhythm.

My stepfather, from Ojos de Agua, Mexico, jokes when I ask him about the names of Mexicans born here. He deliberately stumbles over pronunciations, imitating our elders who have difficulty with Bradley and Madelyn. "Ashley Sánchez. ¿Tú crees?"[1] He wonders aloud what has happened to the "nombres del rancho"—traditional Mexican names that are hardly given anymore to children born in the States: Heraclio, Madaleno, Otilia, Dominga.

My stepfather's experience with the Anglicization of his name—Antonio to Tony—ties into something bigger than learning English. For him, the erasure of his name was about deference and subservience. Becoming Tony gave him a measure of access as he struggled to learn English and get more fieldwork.

This isn't to say that my stepfather welcomed the change, only that he could not put up much resistance. Not changing put him at risk of being passed over for work. English was a world of power and decisions, of smooth, uninterrupted negotiation. There was no time to search for the right word while a shop clerk waited for him to come up with the English name of the correct part needed out in the field. Clear communication meant you could go unsupervised, or that you were even able to read instructions directly off a piece of paper. Every gesture made toward convincing an employer that English was on its way to being mastered had the potential to make a season of fieldwork profitable.

It's curious that many of us growing up in Dinuba adhered to the same rules. Although as children of farm workers we worked in the fields at an early age, we'd also had the opportunity to stay in one town long enough to finish school. Most of us had learned English early and splintered off into a dual existence of English at school, Spanish at home. But instead of recognizing the need for fluency in both languages, we turned it into a peculiar kind of battle. English was for public display. Spanish was for privacy—and privacy quickly turned to shame.

The corrosive effect of assimilation is the displacement of one culture over another, the inability to sustain more than one way of being. It isn't a code word for racial and ethnic acculturation only. It applies to needing and

15

---

[1] *¿Tú crees?:* Can you believe it? —EDS.

wanting to belong, of seeing from the outside and wondering how to get in and then, once inside, realizing there are always those still on the fringe.

When I went to college on the East Coast, I was confronted for the first time by people who said my name correctly without prompting; if they stumbled, there was a quick apology and an honest plea to help with the pronunciation. But introducing myself was painful: already shy, I avoided meeting people because I didn't want to say my name, felt burdened by my own history. I knew that my small-town upbringing and its limitations on Spanish would not have been tolerated by any of the students of color who had grown up in large cities, in places where the sheer force of their native languages made them dominant in their neighborhoods.

It didn't take long for me to assert the power of code-switching in public, the transferring of words from one language to another, regardless of who might be listening. I was learning that the English language composed new meanings when its constrictions were ignored, crossed over or crossed out. Language is all about manipulation, or not listening to the rules.

When I come back to Dinuba, I have a hard time hearing my name   20 said incorrectly, but I have an even harder time beginning a conversation with others about why the pronunciation of our names matters. Leaving a small town requires an embrace of a larger point of view, but a town like Dinuba remains forever embedded in an either/or way of life. My step-father still answers to Tony and, as the United States-born children grow older, their Anglicized names begin to signify who does and who does not "belong"—who was born here and who is *de allá*.

My name is Manuel. To this day, most people cannot say it correctly, the way it was intended to be said. But I can live with that because I love the alliteration of my full name. It wasn't the name my mother, Esmeralda, was going to give me. At the last minute, my father named me after an uncle I would never meet. My name was to have been Ricardo. Growing up in Dinuba, I'm certain I would have become Ricky or even Richard, and the journey toward the discovery of the English language's extraordinary power in even the most ordinary of circumstances would probably have gone unlearned.

I count on a collective sense of cultural loss to once again swing the names back to our native language. The Mexican gate agent announced Eugenio Reyes, but I never got a chance to see who appeared. I pictured an older man, cowboy hat in hand, but I made the assumption on his name alone, the clash of privileges I imagined between someone *de allá* and a Mexican woman with a good job in the United States. Would she speak to him in Spanish? Or would she raise her voice to him as if he were hard of hearing?

But who was I to imagine this man being from anywhere, based on his name alone? At a place of arrivals and departures, it sank into me that the currency of our names is a stroke of luck: because mine was not an easy name, it forced me to consider how language would rule me if I allowed it. Yet I discovered that only by leaving. My stepfather must live in the Valley, a place that does not allow that choice, every day. And Eugenio Reyes—I do not know if he was coming or going. ●

The Reader's Presence

1. Consider the way Muñoz structures his essay. What is his purpose in starting with a name heard over the intercom at the Fresno Airport? What does that incident trigger? In what ways does ending his essay with further reflections on that same moment reinforce his perspective about identity? In what ways does his final paragraph complicate that perspective?

2. As a reader, would you know how to pronounce the author's name correctly? Any of the other Mexican names he mentions? Why do you think Muñoz offers no guide to pronunciation that would help English-speaking readers say the names as the author thinks they should be said? What does he feel is lost when the Mexican names are Anglicized?

3. **CONNECTIONS:** Compare "Leave Your Name at the Border" to Dinaw Mengestu's "Home at Last" (page 202). What identity issues do both writers contend with? You might also compare Muñoz's essay with Richard Rodriguez's longer essay on the Spanish language, "Aria: A Memoir of a Bilingual Childhood" (page 227). What differences in attitude do you find between Muñoz and Rodriguez?

Student Essay

MILOS KOSIC
It's Not the Name That Matters

Courtesy of Milos Kosic

When he wrote "It's Not the Name That Matters," the Serbian-born Milos Kosic was a journalism student at Northwest College, a two-year college in Powell, Wyoming. Kosic received his BA in English from the City College of New York and is currently doing graduate work in Berlin, Germany.

Kosic's essay was originally written as a response to the following assignment (which we've adapted for this edition of *The Writer's Presence*):

In almost every culture, people's names are significant. What about your name? What is its significance to you, your family, and your community? In an essay of 750 to 1,000 words, consider the issues, both personal and cultural, surrounding naming. Be sure to take into consideration the essay by Manuel Muñoz, "Leave Your Name at the Border," which addresses cultural questions like what happens to non-English names in an English-centered society. Your essay should refer to Muñoz's essay while relating a personal experience and maintaining a personal point of view.

"Over 70,000 died," says Cody as we look at the black walls of Vietnam Veterans Memorial. It's raining so hard in Washington that even though we are under an open umbrella, our clothes are soaking wet. Our bodies shake from the cold, and our shoes squish with every step. But we are not concerned about whether we will get sick or not. Thinking about comfort here would be inappropriate.

"Did you get our shadows in it?" asks Cody, referring to our reflections in the wall.

"Yeah, I'm recording them," I answer.

"That's way cool, dude."

© Aurelie and Morgan David De Lossy/cultura/Corbis

Whenever he can, Cody avoids calling me Milos. Sometimes I feel sorry for him, because no matter how hard he tries, he always mispronounces it. Either he says "s" at the end instead of "sh" or makes the "o" sound too long. I believe that every time he tries to say "Milos" (pronounced Mee'-lösh) and a different word comes out of his mouth, he curses both my name and the people who gave it to me.

There's nobody to blame. My parents are innocent. They wanted to call me Marko, naming me after the most popular hero of Serbian traditional songs. But in the hospital wing where I came into the world, it happened that all of the baby boys in the nursery had been named Marko. Confronted with the sad discovery that their name choice was not so original, my father and mother, who believed that their child had to be unique, decided to look for a backup. Milos was the ad hoc second choice.

Luckily, Serbia has many heroes and historic figures. There was bound to be a famous Serbian Milos. I was determined to discover one and looked into the history books. I found out that the guy who killed a Turkish king a long time ago was also named Milos (Miloš Obilić, to be exact). Naming someone after a great person is a tradition in Serbia. Now instead of having to tell others that I am not the namesake of anyone special, my parents can proudly say, "He is like the famous warrior."

As I grew up, I didn't show any signs of becoming a hero. One thing that was remarkable about me, though, was my inability to pronounce the sounds "sh" and "ch," which meant that pronouncing my own name was a serious problem. Thanks to my lovely cousin Lidija, my speech disability did not pass unnoticed. Every time we had a big family gathering, Lidija would dedicate herself to drawing attention to what my "talent" was.

"Come on, tell us your name. Tell us what your parents called you!" she would insist.

Gullible kid as I was, I would answer, "My name is Miloff," and all around I would hear plenty of laughter.

At some point during my teenage years, as my voice changed, I overcame my speech disability. But if in my childhood I was the only one who couldn't pronounce Milos correctly, since I've come to the U.S., I'm now the only one who can.

When I came to the U.S. to attend college, I left my name at the border. Unlike Manuel Muñoz (author of "Leave Your Name at the Border"), however, I never thought that doing so was especially significant. It was something that made sense to me. Americans cannot say Serbian words and names correctly, and I sometimes mangle English with my strong Slavonic accent. If pronunciation really matters, then for the sake of saving their language, Americans should immediately escort me back to the border. I would have no right to complain. Luckily this hasn't happened. Now it's time for me to show, as Muñoz says, the ability "to sustain more than one way of being" (210).

Extends and deepens the theme of mispronunciation.

Meets the assignment's requirement by referring to the Muñoz essay. This reference allows Kosic to express his ideas in relation to others.

You can call me Milo. You can call me Miles or Meat-loaf, I'm fine. But I wonder what kind of person you see behind that name. Do you see a stranger? A good friend? Do you mispronounce my name because you simply cannot say it right, or you don't even want to try because for you, I'm unimportant, someone who doesn't deserve your respect?

In their essay "Trading Up: Where Do Baby Names Come From?" Steven D. Levitt and Stephen J. Dubner explain that parents choose their child's name believing that the right one can predict personal success (120). But when you meet someone named Donald, do think of someone like Donald Trump or Donald Rumsfeld — or Donald Duck?

At the Vietnam Veterans Memorial, among the 59,256 names, none of them seems better than another. As Maya Lin says in "Between Art and Architecture," "a sense of quiet, a reverence always surrounds those names" (126). The carved black stone memorial wall tells us one true thing about each of the people on it. Those Benjamins and Justins, Ricardos and Samuels fought and died in the same war. Even if I can't say some of those names correctly, every single one of them is equally honorable and worthy.

"Milos!"

Cody mispronounces my name again when he calls to point out an old guy wearing a soldier's uniform, standing in front of the memorial.

"Is he security or something?" I ask.

"No," answers Cody. "He must be looking for his old pal somewhere on the wall."

We are ready to go. The old guy remains there. In the heavy rain, he will continue searching, no matter what his pal was called. It's not the name that matters. It's the person who stands behind it.

Conclusion effectively returns to the opening and summarizes the essay's main point.

WORKS CITED

Provides a bibliography of sources the writer has drawn upon.

Lin, Maya. "Making the Memorial." *The New York Review of Books*, 2 Nov. 2000, www.nybooks.com/articles/2000/11/02/making-the-memorial/.

Manuel, Muñoz. "Leave Your Name at the Border." *The Writer's Presence,* edited by Donald McQuade and Robert Atwan, 8th ed., Bedford/St. Martin's, 2014, pp. 208–11.

Levitt, Steven D., and Stephen J. Dubner. "Trading Up: Where Do Baby Names Come From?" *Slate.com*, 12 Apr. 2005, www.slate.com/articles/business/the_dismal_science/2005/04/trading_up.html.

George Orwell

SHOOTING AN ELEPHANT

GEORGE ORWELL (1903–1950) was born Eric Arthur Blair in Bengal, India, the son of a colonial administrator. He was sent to England for his education and attended Eton on a scholarship, but rather than go on to university in 1922 he returned to the East and served with the Indian Imperial Police in Burma. Orwell hated his work and the colonial system; published posthumously, the essay "Shooting an Elephant" was based on his experience in Burma and is found in *Shooting an Elephant and Other Essays* (1950). In 1927, Orwell returned to England and began a career as a professional writer. He served briefly in the Spanish Civil War until he was wounded and then settled in Hertfordshire. Best remembered for his novels *Animal Farm* (1945) and *Nineteen Eighty-Four* (1949), Orwell also wrote articles, essays, and reviews, usually with a political point in mind.

> **"Good prose is like a windowpane."**

In 1969, Irving Howe honored Orwell as "the best English essayist since Hazlitt, perhaps since Dr. Johnson. He was the greatest moral force in English letters during the last several decades: craggy, fiercely polemical, sometimes mistaken, but an utterly free man."

In his 1946 essay "Why I Write," Orwell said that from a very early age "I knew that when I grew up I should be a writer." At first he saw writing as a remedy for loneliness, but as he grew up his reasons for writing expanded: "Looking back through my work, I see it is invariably when I lacked a *political* purpose that I wrote lifeless books." In his mature work, he relied on simple, clear prose to express his political and social convictions: "Good prose," he once wrote, "is like a windowpane."

IN MOULMEIN, in Lower Burma, I was hated by large numbers of people — the only time in my life that I have been important enough for this to happen to me. I was subdivisional police officer of the town, and in an aimless, petty kind of way anti-European feeling was very bitter. No one had the guts to raise a riot, but if a European woman went through the bazaars alone somebody would probably spit betel juice over her dress. As a police officer I was an obvious target and was baited whenever it seemed safe to do so. When a nimble Burman tripped me up on the football field and the referee (another Burman) looked the other way, the crowd yelled with hideous laughter. This happened more than once. In the end the sneering yellow faces of young men that met me everywhere, the insults hooted after me when I was at a safe distance, got badly on my nerves. The young Buddhist priests were the worst of all. There were several thousands of them in the town and none of them seemed to have anything to do except stand on street corners and jeer at Europeans.

All this was perplexing and upsetting. For at that time I had already made up my mind that imperialism was an evil thing and the sooner I chucked up my job and got out of it the better. Theoretically—and secretly, of course—I was all for the Burmese and all against the oppressors, the British. As for the job I was doing, I hated it more bitterly than I can perhaps make clear. In a job like that you see the dirty work of Empire at close quarters. The wretched prisoners huddling in the stinking cages of the lockups, the grey, cowed faces of the long-term convicts, the scarred buttocks of the men who had been flogged with bamboos—all these oppressed me with an intolerable sense of guilt. But I could get nothing into perspective. I was young and ill-educated and I had had to think out my problems in the utter silence that is imposed on every Englishman in the East. I did not even know that the British Empire is dying, still less did I know that it is a great deal better than the younger empires that are going to supplant it. All I knew was that I was stuck between my hatred of the empire I served and my rage against the evil-spirited little beasts who tried to make my job impossible. With one part of my mind I thought of the British Raj[1] as an unbreakable tyranny, as something clamped down, *in saecula saeculorum,*[2] upon the will of prostrate peoples; with another part I thought that the greatest joy in the world would be to drive a bayonet into a Buddhist priest's guts. Feelings like these are the normal by-products of imperialism; ask any Anglo-Indian official, if you can catch him off duty.

One day something happened which in a roundabout way was enlightening. It was a tiny incident in itself, but it gave me a better glimpse than I had had before of the real nature of imperialism—the real motives for which despotic governments act. Early one morning the subinspector at a police station the other end of town rang me up on the phone and said that an elephant was ravaging the bazaar. Would I please come and do something about it? I did not know what I could do, but I wanted to see what was happening and I got on to a pony and started out. I took my rifle, an old .44 Winchester and much too small to kill an elephant, but I thought the noise might be useful *in terrorem.*[3] Various Burmans stopped me on the way and told me about the elephant's doings. It was not, of course, a wild elephant, but a tame one which had gone "must."[4] It had been chained up, as tame elephants always are when their attack of "must" is due, but on the previous night it had broken its chain and escaped. Its mahout,[5] the only person who could manage it when it was in that state, had set out in pursuit, but had taken the wrong direction and was now twelve hours' journey away, and in the morning the elephant had suddenly reappeared in the town. The Burmese population had no weapons and were

[1] ***Raj:*** The British administration.—EDS.
[2] **in saecula saeculorum:** Forever and ever (Latin).—EDS.
[3] **in terrorem:** As a warning (Latin).—EDS.
[4] ***"must":*** Sexual arousal.—EDS.
[5] ***mahout:*** Keeper (Hindi).—EDS.

quite helpless against it. It had already destroyed somebody's bamboo hut, killed a cow, and raided some fruit stalls and devoured the stock; also it had met the municipal rubbish van and, when the driver jumped out and took to his heels, had turned the van over and inflicted violence upon it.

The Burmese subinspector and some Indian constables were waiting for me in the quarter where the elephant had been seen. It was a very poor quarter, a labyrinth of squalid bamboo huts, thatched with palmleaf, winding all over a steep hillside. I remember that it was a cloudy, stuffy morning at the beginning of the rains. We began questioning the people as to where the elephant had gone and, as usual, failed to get any definite information. That is invariably the case in the East; a story always sounds clear enough at a distance, but the nearer you get to the scene of events the vaguer it becomes. Some of the people said that the elephant had gone in one direction, some said that he had gone in another, some professed not even to have heard of any elephant. I had almost made up my mind that the whole story was a pack of lies, when we heard yells a little distance away. There was a loud, scandalized cry of "Go away, child! Go away this instant!" and an old woman with a switch in her hand came round the corner of a hut, violently shooing away a crowd of naked children. Some more women followed, clicking their tongues and exclaiming; evidently there was something that the children ought not to have seen. I rounded the hut and saw a man's dead body sprawling in the mud. He was an Indian, a black Dravidian[6] coolie, almost naked, and he could not have been dead many minutes. The people said that the elephant had come suddenly upon him round the corner of the hut, caught him with its trunk, put its foot on his back, and ground him into the earth. This was the rainy season and the ground was soft, and his face had scored a trench a foot deep and a couple of yards long. He was lying on his belly with arms crucified and head sharply twisted to one side. His face was coated with mud, the eyes wide open, the teeth bared and grinning with an expression of unendurable agony. (Never tell me, by the way, that the dead look peaceful. Most of the corpses I have seen looked devilish.) The friction of the great beast's foot had stripped the skin from his back as neatly as one skins a rabbit. As soon as I saw the dead man I sent an orderly to a friend's house nearby to borrow an elephant rifle. I had already sent back the pony, not wanting it to go mad with fright and throw me if it smelled the elephant.

The orderly came back in a few minutes with a rifle and five cartridges, and meanwhile some Burmans had arrived and told us that the elephant was in the paddy fields below, only a few hundred yards away. As I started forward practically the whole population of the quarter flocked out of the houses and followed me. They had seen the rifle and were all shouting excitedly that I was going to shoot the elephant. They had not shown much interest in the elephant when he was merely ravaging their homes, but it was different now that he was going to be shot. It was a bit of fun to them, as it would be to an English crowd; besides, they wanted the meat. It made me

5

---

6 **Dravidian:** A populous Indian group. —EDS.

vaguely uneasy. I had no intention of shooting the elephant—I had merely sent for the rifle to defend myself if necessary—and it is always unnerving to have a crowd following you. I marched down the hill, looking and feeling a fool, with the rifle over my shoulder and an ever-growing army of people jostling at my heels. At the bottom, when you got away from the huts, there was a metalled road and beyond that a miry waste of paddy fields a thousand yards across, not yet ploughed but soggy from the first rains and dotted with coarse grass. The elephant was standing eight yards from the road, his left side towards us. He took not the slightest notice of the crowd's approach. He was tearing up bunches of grass, beating them against his knees to clean them and stuffing them into his mouth.

I had halted on the road. As soon as I saw the elephant I knew with perfect certainty that I ought not to shoot him. It is a serious matter to shoot a working elephant—it is comparable to destroying a huge and costly piece of machinery—and obviously one ought not to do it if it can possibly be avoided. And at that distance, peacefully eating, the elephant looked no more dangerous than a cow. I thought then and I think now that his attack of "must" was already passing off; in which case he would merely wander harmlessly about until the mahout came back and caught him. Moreover, I did not in the least want to shoot him. I decided that I would watch him for a little while to make sure that he did not turn savage again, and then go home.

But at that moment, I glanced round at the crowd that had followed me. It was an immense crowd, two thousand at the least and growing every minute. It blocked the road for a long distance on either side. I looked at the sea of yellow faces above the garish clothes—faces all happy and excited over this bit of fun, all certain that the elephant was going to be shot. They were watching me as they would watch a conjuror about to perform a trick. They did not like me, but with the magical rifle in my hands I was momentarily worth watching. And suddenly I realized that I should have to shoot the elephant after all: The people expected it of me and I had got to do it; I could feel their two thousand wills pressing me forward, irresistibly. And it was at this moment, as I stood there with the rifle in my hands, that I first grasped the hollowness, the futility of the white man's dominion in the East. Here was I, the white man with his gun, standing in front of the unarmed native crowd—seemingly the leading actor of the piece; but in reality I was only an absurd puppet pushed to and fro by the will of those yellow faces behind. I perceived in this moment that when the white man turns tyrant it is his own freedom that he destroys. He becomes a sort of hollow, posing dummy, the conventionalized figure of a sahib. For it is the condition of his rule that he shall spend his life in trying to impress the "natives," and so in every crisis he has got to do what the "natives" expect of him. He wears a mask, and his face grows to fit it. I had got to shoot the elephant. I had committed myself to doing it when I sent for the rifle. A sahib has got to act like a sahib; he has got to appear resolute, to know his own mind and do definite things. To come all that way, rifle in hand, with two thousand people marching at my heels, and then to trail feebly away, having done nothing—no, that was impossible. The crowd would laugh at me. And my whole life, every white man's life in the East, was one long struggle not to be laughed at.

But I did not want to shoot the elephant. I watched him beating his bunch of grass against his knees, with that preoccupied grandmotherly air that elephants have. It seemed to me that it would be murder to shoot him. At that age I was not squeamish about killing animals, but I had never shot an elephant and never wanted to. (Somehow it always seems worse to kill a *large* animal.) Besides, there was the beast's owner to be considered. Alive, the elephant was worth at least a hundred pounds; dead, he would only be worth the value of his tusks, five pounds, possibly. But I had got to act quickly. I turned to some experienced-looking Burmans who had been there when we arrived, and asked them how the elephant had been behaving. They all said the same thing: He took no notice of you if you left him alone, but he might charge if you went too close to him.

It was perfectly clear to me what I ought to do. I ought to walk up to within, say, twenty-five yards of the elephant and test his behavior. If he charged, I could shoot; if he took no notice of me, it would be safe to leave him until the mahout came back. But also I knew that I was going to do no such thing. I was a poor shot with a rifle and the ground was soft mud into which one would sink at every step. If the elephant charged and I missed him, I should have about as much chance as a toad under a steamroller. But even then I was not thinking particularly of my own skin, only of the watchful yellow faces behind. For at that moment, with the crowd watching me, I was not afraid in the ordinary sense, as I would have been if I had been alone. A white man mustn't be frightened in front of "natives"; and so, in general, he isn't frightened. The sole thought in my mind was that if anything went wrong those two thousand Burmans would see me pursued, caught, trampled on, and reduced to a grinning corpse like that Indian up the hill. And if that happened it was quite probable that some of them would laugh. That would never do. There was only one alternative. I shoved the cartridges into the magazine and lay down on the road to get a better aim.

The crowd grew very still, and a deep, low, happy sigh, as of people who   10
see the theatre curtain go up at last, breathed from innumerable throats. They were going to have their bit of fun after all. The rifle was a beautiful German thing with cross-hair sights. I did not then know that in shooting an elephant one would shoot to cut an imaginary bar running from ear-hole to ear-hole. I ought, therefore, as the elephant was sideways on, to have aimed straight at his ear-hole; actually I aimed several inches in front of this, thinking the brain would be further forward.

When I pulled the trigger I did not hear the bang or feel the kick—one never does when a shot goes home—but I heard the devilish roar of glee that went up from the crowd. In that instant, in too short a time, one would have thought, even for the bullet to get there, a mysterious, terrible change had come over the elephant. He neither stirred nor fell, but every line of his body had altered. He looked suddenly stricken, shrunken, immensely old, as though the frightful impact of the bullet had paralyzed him without knocking him down. At last, after what seemed a long time—it might have been five seconds, I dare say—he sagged flabbily to his knees. His mouth slobbered. An enormous senility seemed to have settled upon him. One could have imagined him thousands of years old. I fired again into the same spot. At the second shot he did not collapse but climbed with desperate slowness to his feet and stood weakly upright, with legs sagging and head drooping. I fired a third time. That was the shot that did it for him. You could see the agony of it jolt his whole body and knock the last remnant of strength from his legs. But in falling he seemed for a moment to rise, for as his hind legs collapsed beneath him he seemed to tower upward like a huge rock toppling, his trunk reaching skywards like a tree. He trumpeted, for the first and only time. And then down he came, his belly towards me, with a crash that seemed to shake the ground even where I lay.

I got up. The Burmans were already racing past me across the mud. It was obvious that the elephant would never rise again, but he was not dead. He was breathing very rhythmically with long rattling gasps, his great mound of a side painfully rising and falling. His mouth was wide open. I could see far down into caverns of pale pink throat. I waited a long time for him to die, but his breathing did not weaken. Finally, I fired my two remaining shots into the spot where I thought his heart must be. The thick blood welled out of him like red velvet, but still he did not die. His body did not even jerk when the shots hit him, the tortured breathing continued without a pause. He was dying, very slowly and in great agony, but in some world remote from me where not even a bullet could damage him further. I felt I had got to put an end to that dreadful noise. It seemed dreadful to see the great beast lying there, powerless to move and yet powerless to die, and not even to be able to finish him. I sent back for my small rifle and poured shot after shot into his heart, and down his throat. They seemed to make no impression. The tortured gasps continued as steadily as the ticking of a clock.

In the end I could not stand it any longer and went away. I heard later that it took him half an hour to die. Burmans were bringing dahs[7] and baskets even before I left, and I was told they had stripped his body almost to the bones by the afternoon.

Afterwards, of course, there were endless discussions about the shooting of the elephant. The owner was furious, but he was only an Indian and could do nothing. Besides, legally I had done the right thing, for a mad elephant has to be killed, like a mad dog, if its owner fails to control it. Among the Europeans opinion was divided. The older men said I was right, the younger men said it was a damn shame to shoot an elephant for killing a coolie, because the elephant was worth more than any damn Coringhee coolie. And afterwards I was very glad that the coolie had been killed; it put me legally in the right and it gave me sufficient pretext for shooting the elephant. I often wondered whether any of the others grasped that I had done it solely to avoid looking a fool. ●

[7] **dahs:** Large knives. —EDS.

The Reader's Presence

1. At the end of paragraph 2, Orwell gives the perfect expression of ambivalence, the simultaneous holding of two opposed feelings or opinions: "With one part of my mind . . . with another part . . ." How would you describe Orwell's dilemma? How would you react in such a situation? Is Orwell recommending that readers see his behavior as a model of what to do in such a conflict? To what extent is Orwell responsible for the situation in which he finds himself? What does he mean when he says that his conflicted feelings "are the normal by-products of imperialism"?

2. Some literary critics doubt that Orwell really did shoot an elephant in Burma. No external historical documentation has ever been found to corroborate Orwell's account. Yet what *internal* elements in the essay—what details or features—suggest that the episode is fact and not fiction? In other words, what makes this piece seem to be an essay and not a short story?

3. **CONNECTIONS:** Orwell's essay describes a state of extreme personal self-consciousness, even vigilance, in a situation in which one's behavior feels somehow "scripted" by society. Orwell writes, "In reality I was only an absurd puppet pushed to and fro by the will of those yellow faces behind" (paragraph 7). How does Orwell's essay compare with Brent Staples's essay "Just Walk on By: A Black Man Ponders His Power to Alter Public Space" (page 260)? Compare especially Orwell's use of the word *fool* in his last paragraph and Staples's use of the same word in the second paragraph of the alternate version of his essay. Do you believe both authors?

Annie Proulx

A YARD OF CLOTH

E. ANNIE PROULX (b. 1935) is an American writer of English and French-Canadian ancestry. She is probably best known as the author of the short story "Brokeback Mountain," which was originally published in the *New Yorker* in 1997 and went on to become the basis for the Academy Award–winning film of the same name, released in 2005. But Proulx was already a very successful writer by that time. Her first novel, *Postcards* (1992), received the PEN/Faulkner Award for fiction, and her second novel, *The Shipping News* (1993), won the Pulitzer Prize and the National Book Award. It was also made into a film. Born in Norwich,

Connecticut, Proulx studied at the University of Vermont, and did not come to fiction writing until (compared to many writers) relatively late in her career, which actually began with commissioned books on subjects ranging from cooking to gardening and country living. She did not publish her first collection of short fiction, *Heart Songs and Other Stories*, until she was more than fifty years old, in 1988. Since then, she has become one of the most critically acclaimed fiction writers in America. Some of her other books include the novels *Accordion Crimes* (1996) and *That Old Ace in the Hole* (2002), as well as several collections of short

> **"I find it satisfying and intellectually stimulating to work with the intensity, brevity, balance and word play of the short story."**

fiction set in Wyoming, notably *Close Range* (1999) and *Bad Dirt* (2004). She has expressed a particular preference for writing shorter work, saying, "I find it satisfying and intellectually stimulating to work with the intensity, brevity, balance and word play of the short story."

IN THE LATE 1980s on the day after Thanksgiving my younger sister Roberta and I went to visit our mother in her little apartment complex of housing for the elderly. At the time we both lived in Vermont, on the west side of the Connecticut River, and tried to make this trip across the river to Bristol, New Hampshire, once a month to see our mother. She had been ill for years with bronchiectasis, a chronic degenerative lung disease. The day was mild for late November, but heavy overcast, light rain and fog, one of those dark days that New England breeds in autumn. There were deer hunters on the road driving slowly at twenty miles per hour, craning their necks to see into the scraggy woods.

Roberta and I drove into the gathering gloom of Bristol. On the corner, a block from our mother's building, there had once been a wonderful rock shop full of minerals, geodes, bits of agate, amethyst crystals, mud puppies, slabs of malachite. But the sign was gone and in its place was a drooping banner in the window: DECORATOR FABRICS LOWER THAN WHOLESALE. Roberta and I both like beads, cloth, yarn, needles. We agreed to look in the shop on the way back if it was still open.

The dinner was pork loin, creamed onions that tasted exactly the same as they had when we were children, sweet potatoes, applesauce Roberta had made from a neighbor's apples, swapping him a chicken. Our mother was tired, but in fairly good health and spirits. She had exhausted herself for two days making the dinner. (Guilt! Guilt!)

Late in the afternoon we left her. The light was fading. A thin mist blurred the small branches of the trees. At the corner we remembered the fabric-sale sign. The place was still open. I parked the truck and we went into the shop.

There was no one in the shop. No one. Piles of folded fabric were stacked on long tables, bolts of shimmering brocade leaned against the wall. The   5 shop stank of old minerals, stale cigarette smoke, and the scent of wet leaves and rain we brought in with us. The bolts of fabric were as awkward as loose walking sticks and slid and fell against each other when we tried to pull any one out. It was difficult to see the patterns without knocking down a dozen of them. As we wrestled with the slippery bolts the door opened and a man came in. In some inexplicable way he was repellent. His face was creased and seamed, his black hair combed over a narrow skull. Slack stubbled cheeks, discolored teeth. The bolts of fabric seemed viciously animated. The man began to talk to us in an obsequious, intimate tone of voice. His comments were inane, stupid.

"I know ladies like to rummage around with cloth."

The damn bolts of designer fabrics, probably hijacked, I thought, refused to stay in place. The man asked us where we came from. We evaded, saying simply "Vermont" and "across the river."

"Where in Vermont? What town?" He would not give up.

"Oh, central Vermont, around Montpelier," I lied.

Now he insisted we take his business card. The cards were just across   10
the street in his antique shop. No, no, we didn't want him to bother. We refused. I was suddenly wild to get away from this man. He began to wind clocks, set the hands. I hated him. The fabrics were rich and fine, the prices very low, but it was impossible to make a rational selection with the man talking on and on in his oily way. Snatching up a bolt of fabric without looking at it, I said I would take a yard of cloth, try it at home and see if the colors were right. Anything to get away.

He produced a grimy yardstick from under the counter and a pair of scissors with a broken point. My sister leaned silently over an empty birdcage still encrusted with droppings. With a little flourish, and promising "I'll give you more than a yard," the man measured, cut briefly with the scissors, then tore the fabric and folded it into a small square. In the exchange of money his hand — very graceful and long-fingered — touched mine. Fever hot.

Yet we still could not get away. A barrage of advice to drive carefully, to take care, warnings that it was a bad night, there was fog, the road was slippery followed us down the steps. I thought his persistence extraordinary. Finally, alone on the sidewalk, we told each other that we had had a singular encounter.

We drove west through the mist and damp. The light was a somber, northern gray, the road blurred with light rain. Fog hung over the Pemigewasset. On the outskirts of town the road widened. We were alone on the highway. My sister was reading a letter. We came into the broad, sweeping curve that follows the river's course. In front of us, skewed across the empty road in the smoking-gray silence, were two smashed gray cars, pillars of steam rising from each, the road a fine carpet of glass. We stopped. Silence, stillness, all as static as a stage scene. There seemed no one in the terribly smashed cars, all the vehicles' glass on the road, the metal torn and compressed. A broad red runner of radiator fluid glistened on the wet road. We went to the cars. I could see a slumped figure.

Other vehicles began to come up behind us, most of them pulling around and continuing on their way. A pickup stopped. Two young men leaped out and began to pull at the farthest crashed car's door.

"Don't move them," I called.   15

Their hands withdrew from something, someone. My sister and I were at the nearest car. We saw the humped man, the blood, we saw he was young with thick, light hair, the brilliant red soaking into a blond mustache, something on the seat beside him like a brace, some plastic soda bottles. He moaned. My sister touched his shoulder. His face was gray, his eyes closed. His clothes sparkled with glass. He made a twisting hunch. His legs rattled. My sister's hand lay lightly on his shoulder.

Now cars were coming from both directions, swerving and cutting around or pulling over, the people getting out to stare. No police.

"I'll go for help," I called to the young men.

"The police station!" they yelled back. "Half a mile down the road."

"Don't move, we'll get help, help is coming," I said to the injured man.   20 I doubted he heard me. I ran to my truck, looked back. My sister was still with him, her hand on his shoulder. I called to her. She stepped toward me, turned back to the injured man, again stepped toward me, but reluctantly, still looking at him, her hand still outstretched even as she came away from him, as though she couldn't bear to leave him.

At the station the dispatcher called for police, ambulances, the Jaws of Life, fire trucks, someone to control traffic. In minutes flashing lights and sirens went by. We did not go back to the scene but headed home by another, longer road, many miles out of our way and clogged with traffic crawling through the thickening fog. I drove slowly and carefully.

A few days later we learned he had died from his injuries.

My sister and I both believed the man in the shop had saved our lives with his delaying talk, his cautions. A minute or two earlier and it could have been us wrecked on the curve of the river road. It was a singular and disturbing incident and we both felt its importance.

That night I telephoned my mother and told her about the accident and about the man in the shop who gave us the creeps but had perhaps saved us.

"Ah," she said. There was a note of contemptuous amusement in her   25 voice. "You know what his name is, don't you, the man in the shop?"

"No. He wanted to give us his card but I didn't take it."

"His name is Proulx," she said. In her tone—or did I misinterpret?—was her family's careful Yankee neutrality toward my father, which I had come to see as rejection.

This disclosure had the effect of an electric shock. The private questions welled. My sister and I spoke intensely to each other. The silence of our childhood, adulthood, suddenly broken. Who was this man with our name? Who were we? Who were our people? We knew so little.

The American experience—the focus on individual achievement, the acquisition of goods and money to prove one's social value—is built on this

III

sense of loss, this alienation from the warmth of the home culture, isolation from genetic bonds. This separation from one's tribe creates an inner
loneliness that increases as one ages. There is in many people, especially
immigrants, a burning need to complete the puzzle, to find the missing
pieces. And what did it do to us, growing up as outsiders, as part of no
place—we moved more than twenty times by the time I was fifteen—as part
of no people except our mother's pale-eyed Yankee clan, who subtly gave us
the sense that we were different and somehow tainted? Now we regret not
speaking with the man who shared our name.

I have moved countless times in my adult life, too. Part of this peripatetic   30
behavior is because Americans are a mobile people, but I also come from a
Franco-American background, rootless people who have no national identity, who really belong nowhere in the United States. The groups closest to
fitting in, I suppose, are the French in Maine, who have chipped out a place,
and the French from the Canadian Maritimes, who after the 1755 expulsion from Acadia went to France, where they were not welcomed, then to
Louisiana, where they became Cajuns (a corruption of the word *Acadians*).
The places and habitations where we live have histories, though we rarely
know them.

We slide into houses and apartments others have built and rarely have a
clue about what went on there, if the first owner grew an orchard of cherries
and pears, how came that bizarre stairway with risers of varied heights, if
that large piece of slate in the backyard was a wolf stone, if Indians knew the
place and what they did there. I wondered about those things as my family
moved and moved again around New England, leaving our hearts in Vermont, on to North Carolina, then again in Maine, but not belonging to any
of those places. Jack Kerouac nailed it when he wrote, in a letter to the critic
Yvonne Le Maître, of "that horrible homelessness of all French-Canadians
abroad in America."

There was one year in my life when I lived in Montreal, and several
when I commuted there from Vermont to graduate school, picked up a little
joual, became familiar with the flat riverine landscape and the shapes of
faces. Years later came a weekend in my life when I went to a gathering of
Franco-American writers on an island in Maine. As I walked into the room I
was slammed with the shock of recognition. Here were non-Anglo people,
people with familiar lineaments, with long fingers and slender bones, with
dark eyes and hair and certain ways of moving and gesturing. Tears came to
my eyes and for a little while I felt the curious but lovely sensation of being
with the home herd and fantasized moving to Quebec City or Montreal or
the Gaspé or Montmagny. But by then I had been too long in solitude, too
anglicized for the joy to last. ◼

The Reader's Presence

1. What are the strategic consequences that follow Proulx's decision to begin the essay by writing about visiting her mother? What role does her "Yankee" mother play in her sense of alienation from her cultural identity? When Proulx first sees the fabric store clerk, she observes: "In some inexplicable way he was repellent" (paragraph 5). How do you account for the fact that he elicits such a strong, negative response from the narrator? What is the significance of the "inexplicable" nature of her response? How does her impression change as she learns of their shared name?

2. One of the most striking features of Proulx's essay is the tone (the attitude) she expresses toward the scenes and the people she describes. Choose one paragraph from the essay and read it aloud. How would you characterize the sound of the speaker's voice? Proulx expresses strong reactions, both positive and negative, when she is around "the home herd" (paragraph 32). Although the fabric clerk gives her "the creeps" (paragraph 24), she is moved to tears when around other Franco-American writers. How do you account for these contradictory emotions?

3. **CONNECTIONS:** Compare and contrast Proulx's essay with Andre Dubus III's "The Land of No: Love in a Class-riven America" (page 112). How does Proulx's desire to be with "the home herd" relate to Dubus's inability to connect with his girlfriend Emily? Focus your attention initially on considering the reasons human nature prompts us to surround ourselves with people we consider to be similar. What differences can you identify in the ways Proulx and Dubus address this question?

Richard Rodriguez

ARIA: A MEMOIR OF A BILINGUAL CHILDHOOD

RICHARD RODRIGUEZ (b. 1944) has contributed articles to many magazines and newspapers, including *Harper's*, *American Scholar*, the *Los Angeles Times*, and the *New York Times*. He's best known for his intellectual autobiography, *Hunger of Memory: The Education of Richard Rodriguez* (1982). In it, Rodriguez outlines his positions on issues such as bilingualism, affirmative action, and assimi-

> **"I have come to think of myself as engaged in writing graffiti."**

lation, and he concludes that current policies in these areas are misguided and serve only to reinforce current social inequalities. His other books include *Days of Obligation:*

|||||||||||||||||||||||||||||||||||||||||||||||||||||||||||||||||||||||||||||||||||||||||||||||||||||||||||||||||||||||||||||||||||||||||||||||||||||||||||

An Argument with My Mexican Father (1992) and *Brown: The Last Discovery of America* (2002).

About the experience of writing his autobiography, Rodriguez comments, "By finding public words to describe one's feelings, one can describe oneself to oneself. . . . I have come to think of myself as engaged in writing graffiti."

The following essay originally appeared in the *American Scholar* (winter 1980/81) and later served as the opening chapter in Rodriguez's autobiography *Hunger of Memory*.

I REMEMBER, to start with, that day in Sacramento, in a California now nearly thirty years past, when I first entered a classroom—able to understand about fifty stray English words. The third of four children, I had been preceded by my older brother and sister to a neighborhood Roman Catholic school. But neither of them had revealed very much about their classroom experiences. They left each morning and returned each afternoon, always together, speaking Spanish as they climbed the five steps to the porch. And their mysterious books, wrapped in brown shopping-bag paper, remained on the table next to the door, closed firmly behind them.

An accident of geography sent me to a school where all my classmates were white and many were the children of doctors and lawyers and business executives. On that first day of school, my classmates must certainly have been uneasy to find themselves apart from their families, in the first institution of their lives. But I was astonished. I was fated to be the "problem student" in class.

The nun said, in a friendly but oddly impersonal voice: "Boys and girls, this is Richard Rodriguez." (I heard her sound it out: *Rich-heard Road-ree-guess.*) It was the first time I had heard anyone say my name in English. "Richard," the nun repeated more slowly, writing my name down in her book. Quickly I turned to see my mother's face dissolve in a watery blur behind the pebbled-glass door.

Now, many years later, I hear of something called "bilingual education"—a scheme proposed in the late 1960s by Hispanic-American social activists, later endorsed by a congressional vote. It is a program that seeks to permit non-English-speaking children (many from lower class homes) to use their "family language" as the language of school. Such, at least, is the aim its supporters announce. I hear them, and am forced to say no: It is not possible for a child, any child, ever to use his family's language in school. Not to understand this is to misunderstand the public uses of schooling and to trivialize the nature of intimate life.

Memory teaches me what I know of these matters. The boy reminds the adult. I was a bilingual child, but of a certain kind: "socially disadvantaged," the son of working-class parents, both Mexican immigrants. 5

In the early years of my boyhood, my parents coped very well in America. My father had steady work. My mother managed at home. They were nobody's victims. When we moved to a house many blocks from the

Mexican-American section of town, they were not intimidated by those two or three neighbors who initially tried to make us unwelcome. ("Keep your brats away from my sidewalk!") But despite all they achieved, or perhaps because they had so much to achieve, they lacked any deep feeling of ease, of belonging in public. They regarded the people at work or in crowds as being very distant from us. Those were the others, *los gringos*. That term was interchangeable in their speech with another, even more telling: *los americanos*.

I grew up in a house where the only regular guests were my relations. On a certain day, enormous families of relatives would visit us, and there would be so many people that the noise and the bodies would spill out to the backyard and onto the front porch. Then for weeks no one would come. (If the doorbell rang, it was usually a salesman.) Our house stood apart—gaudy yellow in a row of white bungalows. We were the people with the noisy dog, the people who raised chickens. We were the foreigners on the block. A few neighbors would smile and wave at us. We waved back. But until I was seven years old, I did not know the name of the old couple living next door or the names of the kids living across the street.

In public, my father and mother spoke a hesitant, accented, and not always grammatical English. And then they would have to strain, their bodies tense, to catch the sense of what was rapidly said by *los gringos*. At home, they returned to Spanish. The language of their Mexican past sounded in counterpoint to the English spoken in public. The words would come quickly, with ease. Conveyed through those sounds was the pleasing, soothing, consoling reminder that one was at home.

During those years when I was first learning to speak, my mother and father addressed me only in Spanish; in Spanish I learned to reply. By contrast, English (*inglés*) was the language I came to associate with gringos, rarely heard in the house. I learned my first words of English overhearing my parents speaking to strangers. At six years of age, I knew just enough words for my mother to trust me on errands to stores one block away—but no more.

I was then a listening child, careful to hear the very different sounds   10 of Spanish and English. Wide-eyed with hearing, I'd listen to sounds more than to words. First, there were English (gringo) sounds. So many words still were unknown to me that when the butcher or the lady at the drugstore said something, exotic polysyllabic sounds would bloom in the midst of their sentences. Often the speech of people in public seemed to me very loud, booming with confidence. The man behind the counter would literally ask, "What can I do for you?" But by being so firm and clear, the sound of his voice said that he was a gringo; he belonged in public society. There were also the high, nasal notes of middle-class American speech—which I rarely am conscious of hearing today because I hear them so often, but could not stop hearing when I was a boy. Crowds at Safeway or at bus stops were noisy with the birdlike sounds of *los gringos*. I'd move away from them all—all the chirping chatter above me.

My own sounds I was unable to hear, but I knew that I spoke English poorly. My words could not extend to form complete thoughts. And the words I did speak I didn't know well enough to make distinct sounds. (Listeners would usually lower their heads to hear better what I was trying to say.) But it was one thing for *me* to speak English with difficulty; it was more troubling to hear my parents speaking in public: their high-whining vowels and guttural consonants; their sentences that got stuck with "eh" and "ah" sounds; the confused syntax; the hesitant rhythm of sounds so different from the way gringos spoke. I'd notice, moreover, that my parents' voices were softer than those of gringos we would meet.

I am tempted to say now that none of this mattered. (In adulthood I am embarrassed by childhood fears.) And, in a way, it didn't matter very much that my parents could not speak English with ease. Their linguistic difficulties had no serious consequences. My mother and father made themselves understood at the county hospital clinic and at government offices. And yet, in another way, it mattered very much. It was unsettling to hear my parents struggle with English. Hearing them, I'd grow nervous, and my clutching trust in their protection and power would be weakened.

There were many times like the night at a brightly lit gasoline station (a blaring white memory) when I stood uneasily hearing my father talk to a teenage attendant. I do not recall what they were saying, but I cannot forget the sounds my father made as he spoke. At one point his words slid together to form one long word—sounds as confused as the threads of blue and green oil in the puddle next to my shoes. His voice rushed through what he had left to say. Toward the end, he reached falsetto notes, appealing to his listener's understanding. I looked away at the lights of passing automobiles. I tried not to hear any more. But I heard only too well the attendant's reply, his calm, easy tones. Shortly afterward, headed for home, I shivered when my father put his hand on my shoulder. The very first chance that I got, I evaded his grasp and ran on ahead into the dark, skipping with feigned boyish exuberance.

But then there was Spanish: *español*, the language rarely heard away from the house; *español*, the language which seemed to me therefore a private language, my family's language. To hear its sounds was to feel myself specially recognized as one of the family, apart from *los otros*. A simple remark, an inconsequential comment could convey that assurance. My parents would say something to me and I would feel embraced by the sounds of their words. Those sounds said: *I am speaking with ease in Spanish. I am addressing you in words I never use with los gringos. I recognize you as someone special, close, like no one outside. You belong with us. In the family. Ricardo.*

At the age of six, well past the time when most middle-class children 15 no longer notice the difference between sounds uttered at home and words spoken in public, I had a different experience. I lived in a world compounded of sounds. I was a child longer than most. I lived in a magical world, surrounded by sounds both pleasing and fearful. I shared with my family a language enchantingly private—different from that used in the city around us.

Just opening or closing the screen door behind me was an important experience. I'd rarely leave home all alone or without feeling reluctance. Walking down the sidewalk, under the canopy of tall trees, I'd warily notice the (suddenly) silent neighborhood kids who stood warily watching me. Nervously, I'd arrive at the grocery store to hear there the sounds of the gringo, reminding me that in this so-big world I was a foreigner. But if leaving home was never routine, neither was coming back. Walking toward our house, climbing the steps from the sidewalk, in summer when the front door was open, I'd hear voices beyond the screen door talking in Spanish. For a second or two I'd stay, linger there listening. Smiling, I'd hear my mother call out, saying in Spanish, "Is that you, Richard?" Those were her words, but all the while her sounds would assure me: *You are home now. Come closer inside. With us.* "*Sí,*" I'd reply.

Once more inside the house, I would resume my place in the family. The sounds would grow harder to hear. Once more at home, I would grow less conscious of them. It required, however, no more than the blurt of the doorbell to alert me all over again to listen to sounds. The house would turn instantly quiet while my mother went to the door. I'd hear her hard English sounds. I'd wait to hear her voice turn to soft-sounding Spanish, which assured me, as surely as did the clicking tongue of the lock on the door, that the stranger was gone.

Plainly it is not healthy to hear such sounds so often. It is not healthy to distinguish public from private sounds so easily. I remained cloistered by sounds, timid and shy in public, too dependent on the voices at home. And yet I was a very happy child when I was at home. I remember many nights when my father would come back from work, and I'd hear him call out to my mother in Spanish, sounding relieved. In Spanish, his voice would sound the light and free notes that he never could manage in English. Some nights I'd jump up just hearing his voice. My brother and I would come running into the room where he was with our mother. Our laughing (so deep was the pleasure!) became screaming. Like others who feel the pain of public alienation, we transformed the knowledge of our public separateness into a consoling reminder of our intimacy. Excited, our voices joined in a celebration of sounds. *We are speaking now the way we never speak out in public—we are together*, the sounds told me. Some nights no one seemed willing to loosen the hold that sounds had on us. At dinner we invented new words that sounded Spanish, but made sense only to us. We pieced together new words by taking, say, an English verb and giving it Spanish endings. My mother's instructions at bedtime would be lacquered with mock-urgent tones. Or a word like *sí*, sounded in several notes, would convey added measures of feeling. Tongues lingered around the edges of words, especially fat vowels. And we happily sounded that military drum roll, the twirling roar of the Spanish *r*. Family language, my family's sounds: the voices of my parents and sisters and brother. Their voices insisting: *You belong here. We*

are family members. Related. Special to one another. Listen! Voices singing and sighing, rising and straining, then surging, teeming with pleasure
which burst syllables into fragments of laughter. At times it seemed there
was steady quiet only when, from another room, the rustling whispers of my
parents faded and I edged closer to sleep.

Supporters of bilingual education imply today that students like me
miss a great deal by not being taught in their family's language. What they
seem not to recognize is that, as a socially disadvantaged child, I regarded
Spanish as a private language. It was a ghetto language that deepened and
strengthened my feeling of public separateness. What I needed to learn in
school was that I had the right, and the obligation, to speak the public language. The odd truth is that my first-grade classmates could have become
bilingual, in the conventional sense of the word, more easily than I. Had they
been taught early (as upper middle-class children often are taught) a "second language" like Spanish or French, they could have regarded it simply as
another public language. In my case, such bilingualism could not have been
so quickly achieved. What I did not believe was that I could speak a single
public language.

Without question, it would have pleased me to have heard my teach-   20
ers address me in Spanish when I entered the classroom. I would have felt
much less afraid. I would have imagined that my instructors were somehow
"related" to me; I would indeed have heard their Spanish as my family's
language. I would have trusted them and responded with ease. But I would
have delayed—postponed for how long?—having to learn the language
of public society. I would have evaded—and for how long?—learning the
great lesson of school: that I had a public identity.

Fortunately, my teachers were unsentimental about their responsibility.
What they understood was that I needed to speak public English. So their
voices would search me out, asking me questions. Each time I heard them
I'd look up in surprise to see a nun's face frowning at me. I'd mumble, not
really meaning to answer. The nun would persist. "Richard, stand up. Don't
look at the floor. Speak up. Speak to the entire class, not just to me!" But I
couldn't believe English could be my language to use. (In part, I did not want
to believe it.) I continued to mumble. I resisted the teacher's demands. (Did
I somehow suspect that once I learned this public language my family life
would be changed?) Silent, waiting for the bell to sound, I remained dazed,
diffident, afraid.

Because I wrongly imagined that English was intrinsically a public
language and Spanish was intrinsically private, I easily noted the difference between classroom language and the language of home. At school,
words were directed to a general audience of listeners. ("Boys and girls . . .")
Words were meaningfully ordered. And the point was not self-expression
alone, but to make oneself understood by many others. The teacher quizzed:
"Boys and girls, why do we use that word in this sentence? Could we think
of a better word to use there? Would the sentence change its meaning if the

words were differently arranged? Isn't there a better way of saying much the same thing?" (I couldn't say. I wouldn't try to say.)

Three months passed. Five. A half year. Unsmiling, ever watchful, my teachers noted my silence. They began to connect my behavior with the slow progress my brother and sisters were making. Until, one Saturday morning, three nuns arrived at the house to talk to our parents. Stiffly they sat on the blue living-room sofa. From the doorway of another room, spying on the visitors, I noted the incongruity, the clash of two worlds, the faces and voices of school intruding upon the familiar setting of home. I overheard one voice gently wondering, "Do your children speak only Spanish at home, Mrs. Rodriguez?" While another voice added, "That Richard especially seems so timid and shy."

That Rich-heard!

With great tact, the visitors continued, "Is it possible for you and your husband to encourage your children to practice their English when they are home?" Of course my parents complied. What would they not do for their children's well-being? And how could they question the Church's authority which those women represented? In an instant they agreed to give up the language (the sounds) which had revealed and accentuated our family's closeness. The moment after the visitors left, the change was observed. "*Ahora*, speak to us only *en inglés*," my father and mother told us. 25

At first, it seemed a kind of game. After dinner each night, the family gathered together to practice "our" English. It was still then *inglés*, a language foreign to us, so we felt drawn to it as strangers. Laughing, we would try to define words we could not pronounce. We played with strange English sounds, often over-anglicizing our pronunciations. And we filled the smiling gaps of our sentences with familiar Spanish sounds. But that was cheating, somebody shouted, and everyone laughed.

In school, meanwhile, like my brother and sisters, I was required to attend a daily tutoring session. I needed a full year of this special work. I also needed my teachers to keep my attention from straying in class by calling out, "*Rich-heard!*"—their English voices slowly loosening the ties to my other name, with its three notes, *Ri-car-do*. Most of all, I needed to hear my mother and father speak to me in a moment of seriousness in "broken"—suddenly heartbreaking—English. This scene was inevitable. One Saturday morning I entered the kitchen where my parents were talking, but I did not realize that they were talking in Spanish until, the moment they saw me, their voices changed and they began speaking English. The gringo sounds they uttered startled me. Pushed me away. In that moment of trivial misunderstanding and profound insight, I felt my throat twisted by unsounded grief. I simply turned and left the room. But I had no place to escape to where I could grieve in Spanish. My brother and sisters were speaking English in another part of the house.

Again and again in the days following, as I grew increasingly angry, I was obliged to hear my mother and father encouraging me: "Speak to us *en inglés*." Only then did I determine to learn classroom English. Thus, sometime afterward it happened: one day in school, I raised my hand to volunteer an answer to a question. I spoke out in a loud voice and I did not think it remarkable when the entire class understood. That day I moved very far from being the disadvantaged child I had been only days earlier. Taken hold at last was the belief, the calming assurance, that I *belonged* in public.

Shortly after, I stopped hearing the high, troubling sounds of *los gringos*. A more and more confident speaker of English, I didn't listen to how strangers sounded when they talked to me. With so many English-speaking people around me, I no longer heard American accents. Conversations quickened. Listening to persons whose voices sounded eccentrically pitched, I might note their sounds for a few seconds, but then I'd concentrate on what they were saying. Now when I heard someone's tone of voice—angry or questioning or sarcastic or happy or sad—I didn't distinguish it from the words it expressed. Sound and word were thus tightly wedded. At the end of each day I was often bemused, and always relieved, to realize how "soundless," though crowded with words, my day in public had been. An eight-year-old boy, I finally came to accept what had been technically true since my birth: I was an American citizen.

But diminished by then was the special feeling of closeness at home. Gone was the desperate, urgent, intense feeling of being at home among those with whom I felt intimate. Our family remained a loving family, but one greatly changed. We were no longer so close, no longer bound tightly together by the knowledge of our separateness from *los gringos*. Neither my older brother nor my sisters rushed home after school any more. Nor did I. When I arrived home, often there would be neighborhood kids in the house. Or the house would be empty of sounds.

Following the dramatic Americanization of their children, even my parents grew more publicly confident—especially my mother. First she learned the names of all the people on the block. Then she decided we needed to have a telephone in our house. My father, for his part, continued to use the word *gringo*, but it was no longer charged with bitterness or distrust. Stripped of any emotional content, the word simply became a name for those Americans not of Hispanic descent. Hearing him, sometimes, I wasn't sure if he was pronouncing the Spanish word *gringo*, or saying gringo in English.

There was a new silence at home. As we children learned more and more English, we shared fewer and fewer words with our parents. Sentences needed to be spoken slowly when one of us addressed our mother or father. Often the parent wouldn't understand. The child would need to repeat himself. Still the parent misunderstood. The young voice, frustrated, would end up saying, "Never mind"—the subject was closed. Dinners would be noisy with the clinking of knives and forks against dishes. My mother would smile softly between her remarks; my father, at the other end of the table, would chew and chew his food while he stared over the heads of his children.

My mother! My father! After English became my primary language, I no longer knew what words to use in addressing my parents. The old Spanish words (those tender accents of sound) I had earlier used—*mamá* and

30

papá—I couldn't use any more. They would have been all-too-painful reminders of how much had changed in my life. On the other hand, the words I heard neighborhood kids call their parents seemed equally unsatisfactory. "Mother" and "father," "ma," "papa," "pa," "dad," "pop" (how I hated the all-American sound of that last word)—all these I felt were unsuitable terms of address for *my* parents. As a result, I never used them at home. Whenever I'd speak to my parents, I would try to get their attention by looking at them. In public conversations, I'd refer to them as my "parents" or my "mother" and "father."

My mother and father, for their part, responded differently, as their children spoke to them less. My mother grew restless, seemed troubled and anxious at the scarceness of words exchanged in the house. She would question me about my day when I came home from school. She smiled at my small talk. She pried at the edges of my sentences to get me to say something more. ("What . . . ?") She'd join conversations she overheard, but her intrusions often stopped her children's talking. By contrast, my father seemed to grow reconciled to the new quiet. Though his English somewhat improved, he tended more and more to retire into silence. At dinner he spoke very little. One night his children and even his wife helplessly giggled at his garbled English pronunciation of the Catholic "Grace Before Meals." Thereafter he made his wife recite the prayer at the start of each meal, even on formal occasions when there were guests in the house.

Hers became the public voice of the family. On official business it was she, not my father, who would usually talk to strangers on the phone or in stores. We children grew so accustomed to his silence that years later we would routinely refer to his "shyness." (My mother often tried to explain: Both of his parents died when he was eight. He was raised by an uncle who treated him as little more than a menial servant. He was never encouraged to speak. He grew up alone—a man of few words.) But I realized my father was not shy whenever I'd watch him speaking Spanish with relatives. Using Spanish, he was quickly effusive. Especially when talking with other men, his voice would spark, flicker, flare alive with varied sounds. In Spanish he expressed ideas and feelings he rarely revealed when speaking English. With firm Spanish sounds he conveyed a confidence and authority that English would never allow him.

The silence at home, however, was not simply the result of fewer words passing between parents and children. More profound for me was the silence created by my inattention to sounds. At about the time I no longer bothered to listen with care to the sounds of English in public, I grew careless about listening to the sounds made by the family when they spoke. Most of the time I would hear someone speaking at home and didn't distinguish his sounds from the words people uttered in public. I didn't even pay much attention to my parents' accented and ungrammatical speech—at least not at home. Only when I was with them in public would I become alert to their accents. But even then their sounds caused me less and less concern. For I was growing increasingly confident of my own public identity.

35

I would have been happier about my public success had I not recalled, sometimes, what it had been like earlier, when my family conveyed its intimacy through a set of conveniently private sounds. Sometimes in public, hearing a stranger, I'd hark back to my lost past. A Mexican farm worker approached me one day downtown. He wanted directions to some place. "*Hijito . . . ,*" he said. And his voice stirred old longings. Another time I was standing beside my mother in the visiting room of a Carmelite convent, before the dense screen which rendered the nuns shadowy figures. I heard several of them speaking Spanish in their busy, singsong, overlapping voices, assuring my mother that, yes, yes, we were remembered, all our family was remembered, in their prayers. Those voices echoed faraway family sounds. Another day a dark-faced old woman touched my shoulder lightly to steady herself as she boarded a bus. She murmured something to me I couldn't quite comprehend. Her Spanish voice came near, like the face of a never-before-seen relative in the instant before I was kissed. That voice, like so many of the Spanish voices I'd hear in public, recalled the golden age of my childhood.

Bilingual educators say today that children lose a degree of "individuality" by becoming assimilated into public society. (Bilingual schooling is a program popularized in the seventies, that decade when middle-class "ethnics" began to resist the process of assimilation—the "American melting pot.") But the bilingualists oversimplify when they scorn the value and necessity of assimilation. They do not seem to realize that a person is individualized in two ways. So they do not realize that, while one suffers a diminished sense of *private* individuality by being assimilated into public society, such assimilation makes possible the achievement of *public* individuality.

Simplistically again, the bilingualists insist that a student should be reminded of his difference from others in mass society, of his "heritage." But they equate mere separateness with individuality. The fact is that only in private—with intimates—is separateness from the crowd a prerequisite for individuality; an intimate "tells" me that I am unique, unlike all others, apart from the crowd. In public, by contrast, full individuality is achieved, paradoxically, by those who are able to consider themselves members of the crowd. Thus it happened for me. Only when I was able to think of myself as an American, no longer an alien in gringo society, could I seek the rights and opportunities necessary for full public individuality. The social and political advantages I enjoy as a man began on the day I came to believe that my name is indeed *Rich-heard Road-ree-guess.* It is true that my public society today is often impersonal; in fact, my public society is usually mass society. But despite the anonymity of the crowd, and despite the fact that the individuality I achieve in public is often tenuous—because it depends on my being one in a crowd—I celebrate the day I acquired my new name. Those middle-class ethnics who scorn assimilation seem to me filled with decadent self-pity, obsessed by the burden of public life. Dangerously, they romanticize public separateness and trivialize the dilemma of those who are truly socially disadvantaged.

If I rehearse here the changes in my private life after my Americaniza- 40
tion, it is finally to emphasize a public gain. The loss implies the gain. The
house I returned to each afternoon was quiet. Intimate sounds no longer
greeted me at the door. Inside there were other noises. The telephone rang.
Neighborhood kids ran past the door of the bedroom where I was reading my
schoolbooks — covered with brown shopping-bag paper. Once I learned the
public language, it would never again be easy for me to hear intimate family
voices. More and more of my day was spent hearing words, not sounds. But
that may only be a way of saying that on the day I raised my hand in class
and spoke loudly to an entire roomful of faces, my childhood started to end.

I grew up the victim of a disconcerting confusion. As I became fluent
in English, I could no longer speak Spanish with confidence. I continued
to understand spoken Spanish, and in high school I learned how to read
and write Spanish. But for many years I could not pronounce it. A powerful
guilt blocked my spoken words; an essential glue was missing whenever I
would try to connect words to form sentences. I would be unable to break
a barrier of sound, to speak freely. I would speak, or try to speak, Spanish,
and I would manage to utter halting, hiccuping sounds which betrayed my
unease. (Even today I speak Spanish very slowly, at best.)

When relatives and Spanish-speaking friends of my parents came to the
house, my brother and sisters would usually manage to say a few words
before being excused. I never managed so gracefully. Each time I'd hear
myself addressed in Spanish, I couldn't respond with any success. I'd know
the words I wanted to say, but I couldn't say them. I would try to speak, but
everything I said seemed to me horribly anglicized. My mouth wouldn't form
the sounds right. My jaw would tremble. After a phrase or two, I'd stutter,
cough up a warm, silvery sound, and stop.

My listeners were surprised to hear me. They'd lower their heads to
grasp better what I was trying to say. They would repeat their questions
in gentle, affectionate voices. But then I would answer in English. No, no,
they would say, we want you to speak to us in Spanish (*"en español"*). But
I couldn't do it. Then they would call me *Pocho*. Sometimes playfully, teasing, using the tender diminutive — *mi pochito*. Sometimes not so playfully
but mockingly, *pocho*. (A Spanish dictionary defines that word as an adjective meaning "colorless" or "bland." But I heard it as a noun, naming the
Mexican-American who, in becoming an American, forgets his native society.) *"¡Pocho!"* my mother's best friend muttered, shaking her head. And my
mother laughed, somewhere behind me. She said that her children didn't
want to practice "our Spanish" after they started going to school. My mother's smiling voice made me suspect that the lady who faced me was not
really angry at me. But searching her face, I couldn't find the hint of a smile.

Embarrassed, my parents would often need to explain their children's
inability to speak fluent Spanish during those years. My mother encountered the wrath of her brother, her only brother, when he came up from Mexico one summer with his family and saw his nieces and nephews for the very
first time. After listening to me, he looked away and said what a disgrace it

was that my siblings and I couldn't speak Spanish, "*su propria idioma.*" He made that remark to my mother, but I noticed that he stared at my father.

One other visitor from those years I clearly remember: a long-time friend   45
of my father from San Francisco who came to stay with us for several days in late August. He took great interest in me after he realized that I couldn't answer his questions in Spanish. He would grab me, as I started to leave the kitchen. He would ask me something. Usually he wouldn't bother to wait for my mumbled response. Knowingly, he'd murmur, "*¿Ay pocho, pocho, donde vas?*" And he would press his thumbs into the upper part of my arms, making me squirm with pain. Dumbly I'd stand there, waiting for his wife to notice us and call him off with a benign smile. I'd giggle, hoping to deflate the tension between us, pretending that I hadn't seen the glittering scorn in his glance.

I recount such incidents only because they suggest the fierce power that Spanish had over many people I met at home, how strongly Spanish was associated with closeness. Most of those people who called me a *pocho* could have spoken English to me, but many wouldn't. They seemed to think that Spanish was the only language we could use among ourselves, that Spanish alone permitted our association. (Such persons are always vulnerable to the ghetto merchant and the politician who have learned the value of speaking their clients' "family language" so as to gain immediate trust.) For my part, I felt that by learning English I had somehow committed a sin of betrayal. But betrayal against whom? Not exactly against the visitors to the house. Rather, I felt I had betrayed my immediate family. I knew that my parents had encouraged me to learn English. I knew that I had turned to English with angry reluctance. But once I spoke English with ease, I came to feel guilty. I sensed that I had broken the spell of intimacy which had once held the family so close together. It was this original sin against my family that I recalled whenever anyone addressed me in Spanish and I responded, confounded.

Yet even during those years of guilt, I was coming to grasp certain consoling truths about language and intimacy — truths that I learned gradually. Once, I remember playing with a friend in the backyard when my grandmother appeared at the window. Her face was stern with suspicion when she saw the boy (the *gringo* boy) I was with. She called out to me in Spanish, sounding the whistle of her ancient breath. My companion looked up and watched her intently as she lowered the window and moved (still visible) behind the light curtain, watching us both. He wanted to know what she had said. I started to tell him, to translate her Spanish words into English. The problem was, however, that though I knew how to translate exactly what she had told me, I realized that any translation would distort the deepest meaning of her message: it had been directed only to me. This message of intimacy could never be translated because it did not lie in the actual words she had used but passed through them. So any translation would have seemed wrong; the words would have been stripped of an essential meaning. Finally I decided not to tell my friend anything — just that I didn't hear all she had said.

This insight was unfolded in time. As I made more and more friends outside my house, I began to recognize intimate messages spoken in English in a close friend's confidential tone or secretive whisper. Even more remarkable were those instances when, apparently for no special reason, I'd become conscious of the fact that my companion was speaking *only to me*. I'd marvel then, just hearing his voice. It was a stunning event to be able to break through the barrier of public silence, to be able to hear the voice of the other, to realize that it was directed just to me. After such moments of intimacy outside the house, I began to trust what I heard intimately conveyed through my family's English. Voices at home at last punctured sad confusion. I'd hear myself addressed as an intimate—in English. Such moments were never as raucous with sound as in past times, when we had used our "private" Spanish. (Our English-sounding house was never to be as noisy as our Spanish-sounding house had been.) Intimate moments were usually moments of soft sound. My mother would be ironing in the dining room while I did my homework nearby. She would look over at me, smile, and her voice sounded to tell me that I was her son. *Richard.*

Intimacy thus continued at home; intimacy was not stilled by English. Though there were fewer occasions for it—a change in my life that I would never forget—there were also times when I sensed the deep truth about language and intimacy: *Intimacy is not created by a particular language; it is created by intimates.* Thus the great change in my life was not linguistic but social. If, after becoming a successful student, I no longer heard intimate voices as often as I had earlier, it was not because I spoke English instead of Spanish. It was because I spoke public language for most of my day. I moved easily at last, a citizen in a crowded city of words.

As a man I spend most of my day in public, in a world largely devoid of   50
speech sounds. So I am quickly attracted by the glamorous quality of certain alien voices. I still am gripped with excitement when someone passes me on the street, speaking in Spanish. I have not moved beyond the range of the nostalgic pull of those sounds. And there is something very compelling about the sounds of lower-class blacks. Of all the accented versions of English that I hear in public, I hear theirs most intently. The Japanese tourist stops me downtown to ask me a question and I inch my way past his accent to concentrate on what he is saying. The eastern European immigrant in the neighborhood delicatessen speaks to me and, again, I do not pay much attention to his sounds, nor to the Texas accent of one of my neighbors or the Chicago accent of the woman who lives in the apartment below me. But when the ghetto black teenagers get on the city bus, I hear them. Their sounds in my society are the sounds of the outsider. Their voices annoy me for being so loud—so self-sufficient and unconcerned by my presence, but for the same reason they are glamorous: a romantic gesture against public acceptance. And as I listen to their shouted laughter, I realize my own quietness. I feel envious of them—envious of their brazen intimacy.

I warn myself away from such envy, however. Overhearing those teen-agers, I think of the black political activists who lately have argued in favor of using black English in public schools—an argument that varies only slightly from that of foreign-language bilingualists. I have heard "radi-cal" linguists make the point that black English is a complex and intricate version of English. And I do not doubt it. But neither do I think that black English should be a language of public instruction. What makes it inappro-priate in classrooms is not something in the language itself but, rather, what lower-class speakers make of it. Just as Spanish would have been a dan-gerous language for me to have used at the start of my education, so black English would be a dangerous language to use in the schooling of teenagers for whom it reinforces feelings of public separateness.

This seems to me an obvious point to make, and yet it must be said. In recent years there have been many attempts to make the language of the alien a public language. "Bilingual education, two ways to understand . . ." television and radio commercials glibly announce. Proponents of bilingual education are careful to say that above all they want every student to acquire a good education. Their argument goes something like this: Children per-mitted to use their family language will not be so alienated and will be better able to match the progress of English-speaking students in the crucial first months of schooling. Increasingly confident of their ability, such children will be more inclined to apply themselves to their studies in the future. But then the bilingualists also claim another very different goal. They say that children who use their family language in school will retain a sense of their ethnic heritage and their family ties. Thus the supporters of bilingual educa-tion want it both ways. They propose bilingual schooling as a way of help-ing students acquire the classroom skills crucial for public success. But they likewise insist that bilingual instruction will give students a sense of their identity apart from the English-speaking public.

Behind this scheme gleams a bright promise for the alien child: One can become a public person while still remaining a private person. Who would not want to believe such an appealing idea? Who can be surprised that the scheme has the support of so many middle-class ethnic Americans? If the barrio or ghetto child can retain his separateness even while being publicly educated, then it is almost possible to believe that no private cost need be paid for public success. This is the consolation offered by any of the number of current bilingual programs. Consider, for example, the bilingual voter's ballot. In some American cities one can cast a ballot printed in several lan-guages. Such a document implies that it is possible for one to exercise that most public of rights—the right to vote—while still keeping oneself apart, unassimilated in public life.

It is not enough to say that such schemes are foolish and certainly doomed. Middle-class supporters of public bilingualism toy with the confusion of those Americans who cannot speak standard English as well as they do. Moreover, bilingual enthusiasts sin against intimacy. A Hispanic-American tells me, "I will never give up my family language," and he clutches a group of words as though they were the source of his family ties. He credits to language what he should credit to family members. This is a convenient mistake, for as long as he holds on to certain familiar words, he can ignore how much else has actually changed in his life.

It has happened before. In earlier decades, persons ambitious for 55 social mobility, and newly successful, similarly seized upon certain "family words." Workingmen attempting to gain political power, for example, took to calling one another "brother." The word as they used it, however, could never resemble the word (the sound) "brother" exchanged by two people in intimate greeting. The context of its public delivery made it at best a metaphor; with repetition it was only a vague echo of the intimate sound. Context forced the change. Context could not be overruled. Context will always protect the realm of the intimate from public misuse. Today middle-class white Americans continue to prove the importance of context as they try to ignore it. They seize upon idioms of the black ghetto, but their attempt to appropriate such expressions invariably changes the meaning. As it becomes a public expression, the ghetto idiom loses its sound, its message of public separateness and strident intimacy. With public repetition it becomes a series of words, increasingly lifeless.

The mystery of intimate utterance remains. The communication of intimacy passes through the word and enlivens its sound, but it cannot be held by the word. It cannot be retained or ever quoted because it is too fluid. It depends not on words but on persons.

My grandmother! She stood among my other relations mocking me when I no longer spoke Spanish. *Pocho,* she said. But then it made no difference. She'd laugh, and our relationship continued because language was never its source. She was a woman in her eighties during the first decade of my life—a mysterious woman to me, my only living grandparent, a woman of Mexico in a long black dress that reached down to her shoes. She was the one relative of mine who spoke no word of English. She had no interest in gringo society and remained completely aloof from the public. She was protected by her daughters, protected even by me when we went to Safeway together and I needed to act as her translator. An eccentric woman. Hard. Soft.

When my family visited my aunt's house in San Francisco, my grandmother would search for me among my many cousins. When she found me, she'd chase them away. Pinching her granddaughters, she would warn them away from me. Then she'd take me to her room, where she had prepared for my coming. There would be a chair next to the bed, a dusty jellied candy nearby, and a copy of *Life en Español* for me to examine. "There," she'd say. And I'd sit content, a boy of eight. *Pocho,* her favorite. I'd sift through the pictures of earthquake-destroyed Latin-American cities and blonde-wigged Mexican movie stars. And all the while I'd listen to the sound of my grandmother's voice. She'd pace around the room, telling me stories of her life. Her past. They were stories so familiar that I couldn't remember when I'd heard them for the first time. I'd look up sometimes to listen. Other times she'd look over at me, but she never expected a response. Sometimes I'd smile or nod. (I understood exactly what she was saying.) But it never seemed to matter to her one way or the other. It was enough that I was there. The words she spoke were almost irrelevant to that fact. We were content. And the great mystery remained: intimate utterance.

I learn nothing about language and intimacy listening to those social activists who propose using one's family language in public life. I learn much more simply by listening to songs on a radio, or hearing a great voice at the opera, or overhearing the woman downstairs at an open window singing to herself. Singers celebrate the human voice. Their lyrics are words, but, animated by voice, those words are subsumed into sounds. (This suggests a central truth about language: All words are capable of becoming sounds as we fill them with the "music" of our life.) With excitement I hear the words yielding their enormous power to sound, even though their meaning is never totally obliterated. In most songs, the drama or tension results from the way that the singer moves between words (sense) and notes (song). At one moment the song simply "says" something; at another moment the voice stretches out the words and moves to the realm of pure sound. Most songs are about love: lost love, celebrations of loving, pleas. By simply being occasions when sounds soar through words, however, songs put me in mind of the most intimate moments of life.

Finally, among all types of music, I find songs created by lyric poets most compelling. On no other public occasion is sound so important for me. Written poems on a page seem at first glance a mere collection of words. And yet, without musical accompaniment, the poet leads me to hear the sounds of the words that I read. As song, a poem moves between the levels of sound and sense, never limited to one realm or the other. As a public artifact, the poem can never offer truly intimate sound, but it helps me to recall the intimate times of my life. As I read in my room, I grow deeply conscious of being alone, sounding my voice in search of another. The poem serves, then, as a memory device; it forces remembrance. And it refreshes; it reminds me of the possibility of escaping public words, the possibility that awaits me in intimate meetings.

The child reminds the adult: To seek intimate sounds is to seek the company of intimates. I do not expect to hear those sounds in public. I would dishonor those I have loved, and those I love now, to claim anything else. I would dishonor our intimacy by holding on to a particular language and calling it my family language. Intimacy cannot be trapped within words; it passes through words. It passes. Intimates leave the room. Doors close. Faces move away from the window. Time passes, and voices recede into the dark. Death finally quiets the voice. There is no way to deny it, no way to stand in the crowd claiming to utter one's family language.

The last time I saw my grandmother I was nine years old. I can tell you some of the things she said to me as I stood by her bed, but I cannot quote the message of intimacy she conveyed with her voice. She laughed, holding my hand. Her voice illumined disjointed memories as it passed them again. She remembered her husband—his green eyes, his magic name of Narcissio, his early death. She remembered the farm in Mexico, the eucalyptus trees nearby (their scent, she remembered, like incense). She remembered the family cow, the bell around its neck heard miles away. A dog. She remembered working as a seamstress, how she'd leave her daughters and son for long hours to go into Guadalajara to work. And how my mother would come running toward her in the sun—in her bright yellow dress—on her return. "MMMAAAAMMMMÁÁÁÁÁ," the old lady mimicked her daughter (my mother) to her daughter's son. She laughed. There was the snap of a cough. An aunt came into the room and told me it was time I should leave. "You can see her tomorrow," she promised. So I kissed my grandmother's cracked face. And the last thing I saw was her thin, oddly youthful thigh, as my aunt rearranged the sheet on the bed.

At the funeral parlor a few days after, I remember kneeling with my relatives during the rosary. Among their voices I traced, then lost, the sounds of individual aunts in the surge of the common prayer. And I heard at that moment what since I have heard very often—the sound the women in my family make when they are praying in sadness. When I went up to look at my grandmother, I saw her through the haze of a veil draped over the open lid of the casket. Her face looked calm—but distant and unyielding to love. It was not the face I remembered seeing most often. It was the face she made in public when the clerk at Safeway asked her some question and I would need to respond. It was her public face that the mortician had designed with his dubious art. ●

The Reader's Presence

1. The writer blames the intrusion of English into his family's private language, Spanish, for a breakdown of communication, and even of caring. How does the Spanish language appear in the essay? What associations does it have for the author? Why does Rodriguez end the essay with the scene of his dying grandmother followed by a glimpse of her corpse?

2. Rodriguez's rhetorical style alternates between persuasive argument and personal drama. Find examples of each. Do these divergent tactics undercut or reinforce each other? Why? What is the purpose of the exclamation points at the beginning of paragraph 33?

3. **CONNECTIONS:** Rodriguez opposes proposals to teach bilingual children in their native languages, wishing to keep native language "private" and fearing that teaching bilingual children in their native languages will further contribute to the marginalization of minorities. Read Walter Benn Michaels's essay, "The Trouble with Diversity" (page 673). Based on your analysis and understanding of Michaels's argument, how do you think Michaels would react to Rodriguez's proposition about bilingual education? Which writer do you find more persuasive, and why?

The Writer at Work

RICHARD RODRIGUEZ on a Writer's Identity

Christopher Felver/Corbis

How important is cultural or ethnic identity to a writer? Some writers clearly draw creative strength from their allegiances and affiliations, whereas others prefer to remain independent of groups, even those they are undeniably part of. In the following passage from a 1997 interview published in *The Sun* magazine, Scott London asks Richard Rodriguez some tough questions about Rodriguez's various "identities." Could you have anticipated Rodriguez's responses based on his essay, "Aria: A Memoir of a Bilingual Childhood"?

❝ *London:* Many people feel that the call for diversity and multiculturalism is one reason the American educational system is collapsing.

Rodriguez: It's no surprise that at the same time that American universities have engaged in a serious commitment to diversity, they have been thought-prisons. We are not talking about diversity in any real way. We are talking about brown, black, and white versions of the same political ideology. It is very curious that the United States and Canada both assume that diversity means only race and ethnicity. They never assume it might mean more Nazis, or more Southern Baptists. That's diversity, too, you know.

London: What do *you* mean by diversity?

Rodriguez: For me, diversity is not a value. Diversity is what you find in Northern Ireland. Diversity is Beirut. Diversity is brother killing brother. Where diversity is *shared*—where I share with you my difference—that can be valuable. But the simple fact that we are unlike each other is a terrifying notion. I have often found myself in foreign settings where I became suddenly aware that I was not like the people around me. That, to me, is not a pleasant discovery.

London: You've said that it's tough in America to lead an intellectual life outside the universities. Yet you made a very conscious decision to leave academia.

Rodriguez: My decision was sparked by affirmative action. There was a point in my life when affirmative action would have meant something to me—when my family was working-class, and we were struggling. But very early in life I became part of the majority culture and now don't think of myself as a minority. Yet the university said I was one. Anybody who has met a real minority—in the economic sense, not the numerical sense—would understand how ridiculous it is to describe a young man who is already at the university, already well into his studies in Italian and English Renaissance literature, as a minority. Affirmative action ignores our society's real minorities—members of the disadvantaged classes, no matter what their race. We have this ludicrous, bureaucratic sense that certain racial groups, regardless of class, are minorities. So what happens is those "minorities" at the very top of the ladder get chosen for everything.

London: Is that what happened to you?

Rodriguez: Well, when it came time for me to look for jobs, the jobs came looking for me. I had teaching offers from the best universities in the country. I was about to accept one from Yale when the whole thing collapsed on me.

London: What do you mean?

Rodriguez: I had all this anxiety about what it meant to be a minority. My professors—these same men who taught me the intricacies of language—just shied away from the issue. They didn't want to talk about it, other than to suggest I could be a "role model" to other Hispanics—when I went back to my barrio, I suppose. I came from a white, middle-class neighborhood. Was I expected to go back there and teach the woman next door about Renaissance sonnets? The embarrassing truth of the matter was that I was being chosen because Yale University had some peculiar idea about what my skin color or ethnicity signified. Who knows what Yale thought it was getting when it hired Richard Rodriguez? The people who offered me the job thought there was nothing wrong with that. I thought there was something very wrong. I still do. I think race-based affirmative action is crude and absolutely mistaken.

London: I noticed that some university students put up a poster outside the lecture hall where you spoke the other night. It said, "Richard Rodriguez is a disgrace to the Chicano community."

Rodriguez: I sort of like that. I don't think writers should be convenient examples. I don't think we should make people

feel settled. I don't try to be a gadfly, but I do think that real ideas are troublesome. There should be something about my work that leaves the reader unsettled. I intend that. The notion of the writer as a kind of sociological sample of a community is ludicrous. Even worse is the notion that writers should provide an example of how to live. Virginia Woolf ended her life by putting a rock in her sweater one day and walking into a lake. She is not a model for how I want to live my life. On the other hand, the bravery of her syntax, of her sentences, written during her deepest depression, is a kind of example for me. But I do not want to become Virginia Woolf. That is not why I read her.

London: What's wrong with being a role model?

Rodriguez: The popular idea of a role model implies that an adult's influence on a child is primarily occupational, that all a black child needs is to see a black doctor, and then this child will think, "Oh, I can become a doctor, too." I have a good black friend who is a doctor, but he didn't become a doctor because he saw other black men who were doctors. He became a doctor because his mother cleaned office buildings at night, and because she loved her children. She grew bowlegged from cleaning office buildings at night, and in the process she taught him something about courage and bravery and dedication to others. I became a writer not because my father was one—my father made false teeth for a living. I became a writer because the Irish nuns who educated me taught me something about bravery with their willingness to give so much to me.

London: There used to be a category for writers and thinkers and intellectuals—"the intelligentsia." But not anymore.

Rodriguez: No, I think the universities have co-opted the intellectual, by and large. But there is an emerging intellectual set coming out of Washington think tanks now. There are people who are leaving the universities and working for the government or in think tanks, simply looking for freedom. The university has become so stultified since the sixties. There is so much you can't do at the university. You can't say this, you can't do that, you can't think this, and so forth. In many ways, I'm free to range as widely as I do intellectually precisely because I'm not at a university. The tiresome Chicanos would be after me all the time. You know: "We saw your piece yesterday, and we didn't like what you said," or, "You didn't sound happy enough," or, "You didn't sound proud enough."

London: You've drawn similar responses from the gay community, I understand.

Rodriguez: Yes, I've recently gotten in trouble with certain gay activists because I'm not gay enough! I am a morose homosexual. I'm melancholy. *Gay* is the last adjective I would use to describe myself. The idea of being gay, like a little sparkler, never occurs to me. So if you ask me if I'm gay, I say no.

After the second chapter of *Days of Obligation*, which is about the death of a friend of mine from AIDS, was published in *Harper's*, I got this rather angry letter from a gay-and-lesbian group that was organizing a protest against the magazine. It was the same old problem: political groups have almost no sense of irony. For them, language has to say exactly what it means. "Why aren't you proud of being gay?" they wanted to know. "Why are you so dark? Why are you so morbid? Why are you so sad? Don't you realize, we're all OK? Let's celebrate that fact." But that is not what writers do. We don't celebrate being "OK." If you want to be OK, take an aspirin.

London: Do you consider yourself more Mexican, or more American?

Rodriguez: In some ways I consider myself more Chinese, because I live in San Francisco, which is becoming a predominantly Asian city. I avoid falling into the black-and-white dialectic in which most of America still seems trapped. I have always recognized that, as an American, I am in relationships with other parts of the world; that I have to measure myself against the Pacific, against Asia. Having to think of myself in relationship to that horizon has liberated me from the black-and-white checkerboard.**"**

Marjane Satrapi

MY SPEECH AT WEST POINT

Writer-illustrator and graphic novelist **MARJANE SATRAPI** (b. 1969) was born in Iran and, after a sojourn in Europe and a return to Tehran, now lives and works in France. Her graphic memoir, *Persepolis: The Story of a Childhood* (2003), recounts in comic-book form growing up in Iran from ages six to fourteen, years that saw the overthrow of the Shah, the triumph of the Islamic Revolution, and the devastating effects of war with Iraq. The book was an immediate hit in France, selling more than 150,000 copies, and has been translated into numerous languages. In the United States, *Persepolis* was named a *New York Times* Notable Book and one of *Time* magazine's "Best Comix of the Year." Satrapi co-directed the feature film, *Persepolis*, which won numerous awards including an Oscar nomination for Best Animated Feature Film of 2007. A live-action adaptation of *Chicken with Plums* came out in 2011. *Persepolis 2: The Story of a Return* (2004) picks up her story with Satrapi's departure for Austria when she was fourteen and continues through her college years back in Tehran. Satrapi's most-recent graphic memoirs are *Embroideries* (2005) and *Chicken with Plums* (2006). She has also written several children's books, and her commentary and comics appear in newspapers and magazines around the world, including the *New York Times* and the *New Yorker*.

> "I figured out a long time ago that, whatever I think I know, I don't know anything. Once I realized that, I really started learning."

Satrapi was invited to West Point to speak in 2005. After her visit, her book *Persepolis* was put on the required reading list at the academy. "My Speech at West Point" appeared on the Op-Ed page of the *New York Times* on May 29, 2005.

In an interview with *Believer* magazine, Satrapi talked about what she learned not only at West Point but also through traveling and listening to people from so many disparate cultures: "I figured out a long time ago that, whatever I think I know, I don't know anything. Once I realized that, I really started learning. That's a great strength: I know that I don't know. There are some people in Iran who are fundamentalist and others who are not. I have very good Israeli friends. And I have very good American friends. We come from different cultures but share points of view. It's humanism, which we're steadily losing. That's what the comics are about in a way, trying to stop that loss."

When I was invited to speak at West Point, this is how I thought it would be: I'll go to West Point...

The major will show me around without saying a word...

Then, he will shout at me...

YOU DON'T SMOKE HERE

Then, I'll eat with 4,000 cadets in the mess hall...

The meal won't be tasty... Pizza... half pepperoni

half cheese

After lunch, I will speak in front of 600 people...

I AM AGAINST THE WAR IN IRAQ.

They will all shout at me again...

I will have to continue my speech...

Democracy is not a present you give to people by bombing them.

Their general will order them to hang me...

I will DIE....

The Reader's Presence

1. How would you describe Satrapi's expectations of West Point as opposed to what she actually experienced on her visit? What do her expectations imply about her view of the military academy? Where may she have received these views? In what ways do they complicate her experience? What elements of Satrapi's narrative do you find humorous? Why?

2. Satrapi's personal narrative is not just told but drawn in black and white. How would you describe her artistic style? What sort of imagery does it resemble? Do you think that the way she depicts herself in the art reinforces the way she describes herself in words? Why or why not? Explain how you see the interrelation of words and images in this graphic essay.

3. **CONNECTIONS:**   Consider Satrapi's graphic essay in connection with other short personal narratives that dramatize a complicated personal experience, such as Jerald Walker's "Scattered Inconveniences" (page 282) or Brent Staples's "Just Walk on By: A Black Man Ponders His Power to Alter Public Space" (page 260). How do these narratives convey complicated moments and emotions and introduce competing perspectives? Of the three selections, choose the one you believe achieves the most satisfying resolution and explain the reasons for your choice.

The Graphic Memoirist at Work

MARJANE SATRAPI on the Language of Words and Images

Fred Hayes/Getty Images

In an interview with the literary journal *Fourth Genre*, Marjane Satrapi spoke about the unique interaction of words and images in her graphic memoirs and comics in general. The interview was conducted in November 2006 by the journal's interview editor, Robert Root, and it was published in Fall 2007.

❝ Root: I'm interested in the use of illustration in the service of autobiography or memoir or other kinds of nonfiction and how that affects the "nonfictionness" of it, the truth of it. People keep referring to your books and to Art Spiegelman's *Maus* and to Alison Bechdel's *Fun Home* as "graphic novels," but it seems to me that a more accurate term would be "graphic memoirs," since they are all autobiographical on some level.

Satrapi: Yes, they *are* autobiographical, but at the same time they search for truth. . . . If you're looking for truth you have to ask it from the Fox News and the *New York Times*. As soon as you write your story, it is a story; this is not a documentary. Of course you have to make fiction, you have to cheat, you have to make some angle around there, because the story has to turn, so that is the reconstruction of what we do. For instance, I don't know, when I write something about people and I'm mean to them, of course I would not use the real names and the real figures, even not the real story. I will create this new personage around myself. Of course, they will always be related to my experiences—what I have seen and what I have heard, or whatever—but any writer will do that, even in science fiction you do that. So the use of the drawing for me is that first of all, I am a very lousy writer. I have tried actually, you know, at one time to write. If I had to write this short article or something, here I am good. But for a novel, just forget about it. I lose all my sense of humor, I lose completely all my decency, and I become completely lousy and pathetic. If I say to myself, "Now you are a serious girl and now you are going to make some serious work," there's nothing worse than wanting to make a serious work for me. So drawing gives me the possibility of this sense of saying what I want to say.

Also, there are many things that you can say through images that you cannot say with the writing. The comics is the only media in the whole world that you can use the image plus the writing plus the imagination and plus be active while reading it. When you watch a picture, a movie, you are passive. Everything is coming to you. When you are reading comics, between one frame to the other what is happening, you have to imagine it yourself. So you are active; you have to take part actually when you read the story. It is the only medium that uses the images in this way. So, for me, comics has only convenience. . . .

Root: You've mentioned before the two languages that you work with, the language of words and the language of image, and how they come together. I wish you would elaborate a little more on that. You've said that you don't write the story and then find images to illustrate the text, that they go together and bounce off of one another. How does that work?

Satrapi: I have a small page on which I know more or less what I want to write in my story. When I start, I have these small little sketches with small drawings of people, and I have short, short dialogues going together, and once in a while I write the dialogue, and once in a while I go the other way. It's like a baby growing up. You don't have first the nose come up and then one eye and then one hand or one leg—all of it grows at the same time. Another thing also: when I work, you know, I am completely in a trance. I'm so concentrated on the work that I don't look at myself working. And I work alone on my books. So since I don't watch myself, it's very difficult for me to know what I'm doing, since I don't see what I'm doing. **"**

David Sedaris

ME TALK PRETTY ONE DAY

DAVID SEDARIS (b. 1956) was born in Johnson City, New York, and raised in Raleigh, North Carolina. He is a dramatist whose plays (one of which won an Obie Award), written in collaboration with his sister, Amy, have been produced at La Mama and Lincoln Center. Sedaris launched his career as a wry, neurotically self-disparaging humorist on National Public Radio's *Morning Edition*, when he read aloud from "The Santaland Diaries," an autobiographical piece about working as a Christmas elf at Macy's. He has since published a number of best-selling collections, including *Naked* (1997), *Holidays on Ice* (1997), *Me Talk Pretty One Day* (2000), *When You Are Engulfed in Flames* (2008), and his newest book, *Let's Explore Diabetes with Owls* (2013), which became an immediate best-seller. His collection of fables titled *Squirrel Seeks Chipmunk: A Modest Bestiary* (with illustrations by Ian Falconer) was published in 2010 and immediately hit the *New York Times* best-seller list for fiction. His essays appear regularly in the *New Yorker* and *Esquire*. In 2001, Sedaris was named Humorist of the Year by *Time* magazine and received the Thurber Prize for American Humor. *New York Magazine* had dubbed Sedaris "the most brilliantly witty New Yorker since Dorothy Parker." He currently lives in England.

> "It doesn't really matter what your life was like, you can write about anything."

Sedaris, who for two years taught writing at the Art Institute of Chicago, laments that the students in his writing classes "were ashamed of their middle-class background . . . they felt like unless they grew up in poverty, they had nothing to write about." Sedaris feels that "it doesn't really matter what your life was like, you can write about anything. It's just the writing of it that is the challenge."

AT THE AGE OF FORTY-ONE, I am returning to school and have to think of myself as what my French textbook calls "a true debutant." After paying my tuition, I was issued a student ID, which allows me a discounted entry fee at movie theaters, puppet shows, and Festyland, a far-flung amusement park that advertises with billboards picturing a cartoon stegosaurus sitting in a canoe and eating what appears to be a ham sandwich.

I've moved to Paris with hopes of learning the language. My school is an easy ten-minute walk from my apartment, and on the first day of class I arrived early, watching as the returning students greeted one another in the school lobby. Vacations were recounted, and questions were raised concerning mutual friends with names like Kang and Vlatnya. Regardless of their nationalities, everyone spoke in what sounded to me like excellent French. Some accents were better than others, but the students exhibited an ease and confidence I found intimidating. As an added discomfort, they were all young, attractive, and well dressed, causing me to feel not unlike Pa Kettle trapped backstage after a fashion show.

The first day of class was nerve-racking because I knew I'd be expected to perform. That's the way they do it here—it's everybody into the language pool, sink or swim. The teacher marched in, deeply tanned from a recent vacation, and proceeded to rattle off a series of administrative announcements. I've spent quite a few summers in Normandy, and I took a monthlong French class before leaving New York. I'm not completely in the dark, yet I understood only half of what this woman was saying.

"If you have not *meimslsxp* or *lgpdmurct* by this time, then you should not be in this room. Has everyone *apzkiubjxow*? Everyone? Good, we shall begin." She spread out her lesson plan and sighed, saying, "All right, then, who knows the alphabet?"

It was startling because (a) I hadn't been asked that question in a while 5 and (b) I realized, while laughing, that I myself did *not* know the alphabet. They're the same letters, but in France they're pronounced differently. I knew the shape of the alphabet but had no idea what it actually sounded like.

"Ahh." The teacher went to the board and sketched the letter *a*. "Do we have anyone in the room whose first name commences with an *ahh*?"

Two Polish Annas raised their hands, and the teacher instructed them to present themselves by stating their names, nationalities, occupations, and a brief list of things they liked and disliked in this world. The first Anna hailed from an industrial town outside of Warsaw and had front teeth the size of tombstones. She worked as a seamstress, enjoyed quiet times with friends, and hated the mosquito.

"Oh, really," the teacher said. "How very interesting. I thought that everyone loved the mosquito, but here, in front of all the world, you claim to detest him. How is it that we've been blessed with someone as unique and original as you? Tell us, please."

The seamstress did not understand what was being said but knew that this was an occasion for shame. Her rabbity mouth huffed for breath, and she stared down at her lap as though the appropriate comeback were stitched somewhere alongside the zipper of her slacks.

The second Anna learned from the first and claimed to love sunshine 10 and detest lies. It sounded like a translation of one of those Playmate of the Month data sheets, the answers always written in the same loopy handwriting: "Turn-ons: Mom's famous five-alarm chili! Turnoffs: insecurity and guys who come on too strong!!!!"

The two Polish Annas surely had clear notions of what they loved and hated, but like the rest of us, they were limited in terms of vocabulary, and this made them appear less than sophisticated. The teacher forged on, and we learned that Carlos, the Argentine bandonion player, loved wine, music, and, in his words, "making sex with the womens of the world." Next came a beautiful young Yugoslav who identified herself as an optimist, saying that she loved everything that life had to offer.

The teacher licked her lips, revealing a hint of the saucebox we would later come to know. She crouched low for her attack, placed her hands on the young woman's desk, and leaned close, saying, "Oh yeah? And do you love your little war?"

While the optimist struggled to defend herself, I scrambled to think of an answer to what had obviously become a trick question. How often is one asked what he loves in this world? More to the point, how often is one asked and then publicly ridiculed for his answer? I recalled my mother, flushed with wine, pounding the tabletop late one night, saying, "Love? I love a good steak cooked rare. I love my cat, and I love . . ." My sisters and I leaned forward, waiting to hear our names. "Tums," our mother said. "I love Tums."

The teacher killed some time accusing the Yugoslavian girl of masterminding a program of genocide, and I jotted frantic notes in the margins of my pad. While I can honestly say that I love leafing through medical textbooks devoted to severe dermatological conditions, the hobby is beyond the reach of my French vocabulary, and acting it out would only have invited controversy.

When called upon, I delivered an effortless list of things that I detest: blood sausage, intestinal pâtés, brain pudding. I'd learned these words the hard way. Having given it some thought, I then declared my love for IBM typewriters, the French word for *bruise*, and my electric floor waxer. It was a short list, but still I managed to mispronounce *IBM* and assign the wrong gender to both the floor waxer and the typewriter. The teacher's reaction led me to believe that these mistakes were capital crimes in the country of France.

"Were you always this *palicmkrexis?*" she asked. "Even a *fiuscrzsa ticiwelmun* knows that a typewriter is feminine."

I absorbed as much of her abuse as I could understand, thinking—but not saying—that I find it ridiculous to assign a gender to an inanimate object incapable of disrobing and making an occasional fool of itself. Why refer to Lady Crack Pipe or Good Sir Dishrag when these things could never live up to all that their sex implied?

The teacher proceeded to belittle everyone from German Eva, who hated laziness, to Japanese Yukari, who loved paintbrushes and soap. Italian, Thai, Dutch, Korean, and Chinese—we all left class foolishly believing that the worst was over. She'd shaken us up a little, but surely that was just an act designed to weed out the deadweight. We didn't know it then, but the coming months would teach us what it was like to spend time in the presence of a wild animal, something completely unpredictable. Her temperament was not based on a series of good and bad days but, rather, good and bad

15

moments. We soon learned to dodge chalk and protect our heads and stomachs whenever she approached us with a question. She hadn't yet punched
anyone, but it seemed wise to protect ourselves against the inevitable.

Though we were forbidden to speak anything but French, the teacher
would occasionally use us to practice any of her five fluent languages.

"I hate you," she said to me one afternoon. Her English was flawless. 20
"I really, really hate you." Call me sensitive, but I couldn't help but take it
personally.

After being singled out as a lazy *kfdtinvfm*, I took to spending four hours
a night on my homework, putting in even more time whenever we were
assigned an essay. I suppose I could have gotten by with less, but I was
determined to create some sort of identity for myself: David the hard worker,
David the cut-up. We'd have one of those "complete this sentence" exercises, and I'd fool with the thing for hours, invariably settling on something
like "A quick run around the lake? I'd love to! Just give me a moment while
I strap on my wooden leg." The teacher, through word and action, conveyed
the message that if this was my idea of an identity, she wanted nothing to
do with it.

My fear and discomfort crept beyond the borders of the classroom and
accompanied me out onto the wide boulevards. Stopping for a coffee, asking directions, depositing money in my bank account: these things were out
of the question, as they involved having to speak. Before beginning school,
there'd been no shutting me up, but now I was convinced that everything
I said was wrong. When the phone rang, I ignored it. If someone asked me
a question, I pretended to be deaf. I knew my fear was getting the best of
me when I started wondering why they don't sell cuts of meat in vending
machines.

My only comfort was the knowledge that I was not alone. Huddled in
the hallways and making the most of our pathetic French, my fellow students and I engaged in the sort of conversation commonly overheard in refugee camps.

"Sometime me cry alone at night."

"That be common for I, also, but be more strong, you. Much work and 25
someday you talk pretty. People start love you soon. Maybe tomorrow, okay."

Unlike the French class I had taken in New York, here there was no
sense of competition. When the teacher poked a shy Korean in the eyelid
with a freshly sharpened pencil, we took no comfort in the fact that, unlike
Hyeyoon Cho, we all knew the irregular past tense of the verb *to defeat*. In
all fairness, the teacher hadn't meant to stab the girl, but neither did she
spend much time apologizing, saying only, "Well, you should have been
vkkdyo more *kdeynfulh*."

Over time it became impossible to believe that any of us would ever
improve. Fall arrived and it rained every day, meaning we would now
be scolded for the water dripping from our coats and umbrellas. It was
mid-October when the teacher singled me out, saying, "Every day spent

with you is like having a cesarean section." And it struck me that, for the first time since arriving in France, I could understand every word that someone was saying.

Understanding doesn't mean that you can suddenly speak the language. Far from it. It's a small step, nothing more, yet its rewards are intoxicating and deceptive. The teacher continued her diatribe and I settled back, bathing in the subtle beauty of each new curse and insult.

"You exhaust me with your foolishness and reward my efforts with nothing but pain, do you understand me?"

The world opened up, and it was with great joy that I responded, "I 30 know the thing that you speak exact now. Talk me more, you, plus, please, plus."

The Reader's Presence

1. How did Sedaris take his experience—auditing a beginner's language class—and turn it into a humorous essay? What were the funniest parts of the essay? An interviewer once wrote that Sedaris's signature is "deadpan" humor. What is deadpan humor? Identify—and characterize the effectiveness of—examples of it in "Me Talk Pretty One Day."

2. Which English words would you substitute for the nonsense words that represent Sedaris's difficulties understanding his teacher's French? Have a classmate tell you what he or she thinks such words as *meimslsxp* (paragraph 4), *palicmkrexis* (paragraph 16), or *kdeynfulh* (paragraph 26) might mean. Did he or she pick the same or similar words to the ones you picked? Point to the clues Sedaris includes in the essay to hint at what such words mean. How would you rewrite the passage with different clues to indicate a different possible meaning for the nonsense words?

3. **CONNECTIONS:** How surprised were you by the last line in the essay? To what extent did you expect that Sedaris would speak fluently because he understood his teacher's French perfectly? Look at some other unexpected last lines in essays that you've read in this collection, such as Bernard Cooper's "A Clack of Tiny Sparks: Remembrances of a Gay Boyhood" (page 98) or Jamaica Kincaid's "The Estrangement" (page 169) or any two other last lines you found surprising, and identify how each author goes about setting up the surprise. When you look back, at what point in each essay might you have expected the unexpected? Be as specific as possible in your response.

Patti Smith

STICKY FINGERS

PATTI SMITH (b. 1946) is sometimes referred to as the "Godmother of Punk" and is widely recognized for her influence on the punk rock movement in 1970s New York. Although she is perhaps best known as a singer-songwriter, Smith is also a visual artist and an award-winning author. She was born in Chicago but raised in the New Jersey suburbs of Philadelphia, where she graduated from high school in 1964. Her mother was a Jehovah's Witness and the young Smith had a strict Bible education, but she ultimately rejected organized religion. After working in a factory and briefly attending Glassboro State College (now Rowan University), she moved to New York City in 1967, where she met her life-long friend, Robert Mapplethorpe, and began to experiment with various creative outlets, including painting, acting, writing, and music. By 1974, she was performing her own music in various New York City venues, and in 1975 she was signed by Arista Records. In December of that year, her debut album, *Horses*, was released to critical acclaim. Often cited as one of the greatest albums in rock history, it blends a punk rock sound with spoken word poetry.

> **"You just keep doing your work because you have to, because it's your calling."**

Smith went on to release ten more albums over nearly forty years, including *Radio Ethiopia* (1976), *Easter* (1978), *Dream of Life* (1988), *Peace and Noise* (1997), *Gung Ho* (2000), and *Twelve* (2007), among others. Her most recent studio recording is *Banga*, released in 2012 by Columbia Records. Smith has cited eighteenth-nineteenth-century British poet William Blake and nineteenth-century French poet Arthur Rimbaud as her influences, and she has given literary lectures on their work. In 2005, she was named a Commander of the Ordre des Arts et des Lettres by the French Ministry of Culture. In 2007, she was inducted into the Rock and Roll Hall of Fame and, in 2010, she won the National Book Award for her memoir, *Just Kids*, which documents her relationship with Robert Mapplethorpe, who went on from their experiments with art to become an acclaimed artist and photographer. Of working as a writer and an artist she has said, "[You] can't expect to be embraced by the people . . . you write poetry books that maybe, you know, fifty people read, and you just keep doing your work because you have to, because it's your calling." "Sticky Fingers" was published in the *New Yorker* in October 2011.

WHEN I WAS TEN YEARS OLD, I lived with my family in a small ranch house in rural South Jersey. I often accompanied my mother to the A. & P. to buy groceries. We did not have a car, so we walked, and I would help her carry the bags.

My mother had to shop very carefully, as my father was on strike. She was a waitress, and her paycheck and tips barely sustained us. One day, while she was weighing prices, a promotional display for the World Book Encyclopedia caught my eye. The volumes were cream-colored, with forest-green spines stamped in gold. Volume I was ninety-nine cents with a ten-dollar purchase.

All I could think of, as we combed the aisles for creamed corn, dry milk, cans of Spam, and shredded wheat, was the book, which I coveted with all my being. I stood at the register with my mother, holding my breath as the cashier rang up the items. It came to over eleven dollars. My mother produced a five, some singles, and a handful of change. As she was counting out the money, I somehow found the courage to ask for the encyclopedia. "Could we get one?" I said, showing her the display. "It's only ninety-nine cents."

I did not understand my mother's mounting anxiety; she did not have enough change and had to sacrifice a large can of Le Sueur peas to pay the amount. "Not now, Patricia," she said sternly. "Today is not a good day." I packed the groceries and followed her home, crestfallen.

The next Saturday, my mother gave me a dollar and sent me to the A. & P. alone. Two quarts of milk and a loaf of bread: that's what a dollar bought in 1957. I went straight to the World Book display. There was only one first volume left, which I placed in my cart. I didn't need a cart, but took one so I could read as I went up and down the aisles. A lot of time went by, but I had little concept of time, a fact that often got me in trouble. I knew I had to leave, but I couldn't bear to part with the book. Impulsively I put it inside my shirt and zipped up my plaid windbreaker. I was a tall, skinny kid, and I'm certain every contour of the book was conspicuous. 5

I strolled the aisles for several more minutes, then went through the checkout, paid my dollar, swiftly bagged the three items, and headed home with my heart pounding.

Suddenly I felt a heavy tap on my shoulder and turned to find the biggest man I had ever seen. He was the store detective, and he asked me to hand it over. I just stood in silence. "We know you stole something — you will have to be searched." Horrified, I slid the heavy book out from the bottom of my shirt.

He looked at it quizzically. "This is what you stole, an encyclopedia?"

"Yes," I whispered, trembling.

"Why didn't you ask your parents?" 10

"I did," I said, "but they didn't have the money."

"Do you know it's wrong?"

"Yes."

"Do you go to church?"

"Yes, twice a week." 15

"Well, you're going to have to tell your parents what you did."

"No, please."

"Then I will do it. What's the address?"

I was silent.

"Well, I'll have to walk you home." 20

"No, please, I will tell them."

"Do you swear?"

"Yes, yes, sir."

My mother was agitated when I arrived home. "Where were you? I needed the bread for your father's sandwiches. I told you to come right home."

And suddenly everything went green, like right before a tornado. My 25 ears were ringing, I felt dizzy, and I threw up.

My mother tended to me immediately, as she always did. She had me lie on the couch and got a cold towel for my head and sat by me with her anxious expression.

"What is it, Patricia?" she asked. "Did something bad happen?"

"Yes," I whispered. "I stole something." I told her about my lust for the book, my wrongdoing, the big detective. My mother was a good mother, but she could be explosive, and I tensed, waiting for the barrage of verbal punishment, the sentencing that always seemed to outweigh the crime. But she said nothing. She told me that she would call the store and tell the detective I had confessed, and that I should sleep.

When I awoke, sometime later, the house was silent. My mother had taken my siblings to the field to play. I sat up and noticed a brown-paper bag with my name on it. I opened it and inside was the World Book Encyclopedia, Volume I. ▪

The Reader's Presence

1. From the moment Smith lays eyes on the encyclopedia, she cannot bear to be without it: "All I could think of . . . was the book, which I coveted with all my being" (paragraph 3). Why is the encyclopedia so important to Smith? The encyclopedia is sold in the supermarket alongside such staples as milk and bread. What specific reasons can you offer in defense of the assertion that books are a necessary staple of one's life? Would you offer the same rationale in defense of the need for an encyclopedia? Why or why not? Would Smith?

2. Smith describes her desire for the encyclopedia with such words as "covet" and "lust," both of which carry religious connotations. What does Smith gain—and risk—by using language bearing such connotations? What specific language would you use to convey a clear sense of your attitude toward—and relationship with—books? with an encyclopedia?

3. **CONNECTIONS:** Compare and contrast Smith's essay with Jhumpa Lahiri's "My Two Lives" (page 181). In what specific ways is Smith's desire for the encyclopedia related to the importance of writing in Lahiri's life? Prepare a detailed account of the ways in which you believe writing and reading are connected.

Brent Staples

JUST WALK ON BY: A BLACK MAN PONDERS HIS POWER TO ALTER PUBLIC SPACE

As he describes in *Parallel Time: Growing Up in Black and White* (1994), **BRENT STAPLES** (b. 1951) escaped a childhood of urban poverty through success in school and his determination to be a writer. Although Staples earned a PhD in psychology from the University of Chicago in 1982, his love of journalism led him to leave the field of psychology and start a career that has taken him to the *New York Times*, where he has served on the editorial board since 1990. Staples contributes to several national magazines, including *Harper's*, the *New York Times Magazine*, and *Ms.*, in which "Just Walk on By" appeared in 1986.

Staples's 1994 memoir, *Parallel Time*, received the Anisfield Wolff Book Award, previously won by such writers as James Baldwin, Ralph Ellison, and Zora Neale Hurston. In it he remembers how in Chicago he prepared for

> "I traveled to distant neighborhoods, sat on their curbs, and sketched what I saw in words."

his writing career by keeping a journal. "I wrote on buses, on the Jackson Park el—though only at the stops to keep the writing legible. I traveled to distant neighborhoods, sat on their curbs, and sketched what I saw in words. Thursdays meant free admission at the Art Institute. All day I attributed motives to people in paintings, especially people in Rembrandts. At closing time I went to a nightclub in The Loop and spied on patrons, copied their conversations and speculated about their lives. The journal was more than 'a record of my inner transactions.' It was a collection of stolen souls from which I would one day construct a book."

MY FIRST VICTIM was a woman—white, well dressed, probably in her early twenties. I came upon her late one evening on a deserted street in Hyde Park, a relatively affluent neighborhood in an otherwise mean, impoverished section of Chicago. As I swung onto the avenue behind her, there seemed to be a discreet, uninflammatory distance between us. Not so. She cast back a worried glance. To her, the youngish black man—a broad six feet two inches with a beard and billowing hair, both hands shoved into the pockets of a bulky military jacket—seemed menacingly close. After a few more quick glimpses, she picked up her pace and was soon running in earnest. Within seconds she disappeared into a cross street.

That was more than a decade ago. I was twenty-two years old, a graduate student newly arrived at the University of Chicago. It was in the echo of that terrified woman's footfalls that I first began to know the unwieldy inheritance I'd come into—the ability to alter public space in ugly ways. It was clear that she thought herself the quarry of a mugger, a rapist, or worse. Suffering a bout of insomnia, however, I was stalking sleep, not defenseless wayfarers. As a softy who is scarcely able to take a knife to a raw chicken—let alone hold it to a person's throat—I was surprised, embarrassed, and dismayed all at once. Her flight made me feel like an accomplice in tyranny. It also made it clear that I was indistinguishable from the muggers who occasionally seeped into the area from the surrounding ghetto. That first encounter, and those that followed, signified that a vast, unnerving gulf lay between nighttime pedestrians—particularly women—and me. And I soon gathered that being perceived as dangerous is a hazard in itself. I only needed to turn a corner into a dicey situation, or crowd some frightened, armed person in a foyer somewhere, or make an errant move after being pulled over by a policeman. Where fear and weapons meet—and they often do in urban America—there is always the possibility of death.

In that first year, my first away from my hometown, I was to become thoroughly familiar with the language of fear. At dark, shadowy intersections in Chicago, I could cross in front of a car stopped at a traffic light and elicit the *thunk, thunk, thunk, thunk* of the driver—black, white, male, or female—hammering down the door locks. On less traveled streets after dark, I grew accustomed to but never comfortable with people who crossed to the other side of the street rather than pass me. Then there were the standard unpleasantries with police, doormen, bouncers, cabdrivers, and others whose business is to screen out troublesome individuals *before* there is any nastiness.

I moved to New York nearly two years ago and I have remained an avid night walker. In central Manhattan, the near-constant crowd cover minimizes tense one-on-one street encounters. Elsewhere—visiting friends in Soho,[1] where sidewalks are narrow and tightly spaced buildings shut out the sky—things can get very taut indeed.

Black men have a firm place in New York mugging literature. Norman Podhoretz[2] in his famed (or infamous) 1963 essay, "My Negro Problem—And Ours," recalls growing up in terror of black males; they "were tougher than we were, more ruthless," he writes—and as an adult on the Upper West Side of Manhattan, he continues, he cannot constrain his nervousness when he meets black men on certain streets. Similarly, a decade later, the essayist and novelist Edward Hoagland extols a New York where once "Negro bitterness bore down mainly on other Negroes." Where some see mere panhandlers, Hoagland sees "a mugger who is clearly screwing up his nerve to do more than just *ask* for money." But Hoagland has "the New

5

---

1 **Soho:** A district of lower Manhattan known for its art galleries. —EDS.
2 **Podhoretz:** A well-known literary critic and editor of *Commentary* magazine. —EDS.

Yorker's quick-hunch posture for broken-field maneuvering," and the bad guy swerves away.

I often witness that "hunch posture," from women after dark on the warrenlike streets of Brooklyn where I live. They seem to set their faces on neutral and, with their purse straps strung across their chests bandolier style, they forge ahead as though bracing themselves against being tackled. I understand, of course, that the danger they perceive is not a hallucination. Women are particularly vulnerable to street violence, and young black males are drastically overrepresented among the perpetrators of that violence. Yet these truths are no solace against the kind of alienation that comes of being ever the suspect, against being set apart, a fearsome entity with whom pedestrians avoid making eye contact.

It is not altogether clear to me how I reached the ripe old age of twenty-two without being conscious of the lethality nighttime pedestrians attributed to me. Perhaps it was because in Chester, Pennsylvania, the small, angry industrial town where I came of age in the 1960s, I was scarcely noticeable against a backdrop of gang warfare, street knifings, and murders. I grew up one of the good boys, had perhaps a half-dozen fistfights. In retrospect, my shyness of combat has clear sources.

Many things go into the making of a young thug. One of those things is the consummation of the male romance with the power to intimidate. An infant discovers that random flailings send the baby bottle flying out of the crib and crashing to the floor. Delighted, the joyful babe repeats those motions again and again, seeking to duplicate the feat. Just so, I recall the points at which some of my boyhood friends were finally seduced by the perception of themselves as tough guys. When a mark cowered and surrendered his money without resistance, myth and reality merged—and paid off. It is, after all, only manly to embrace the power to frighten and intimidate. We, as men, are not supposed to give an inch of our lane on the highway; we are to seize the fighter's edge in work and in play and even in love; we are to be valiant in the face of hostile forces.

Unfortunately, poor and powerless young men seem to take all this nonsense literally. As a boy, I saw countless tough guys locked away; I have since buried several, too. They were babies, really—a teenage cousin, a brother of twenty-two, a childhood friend in his midtwenties—all gone down in episodes of bravado played out in the streets. I came to doubt the virtues of intimidation early on. I chose, perhaps even unconsciously, to remain a shadow—timid, but a survivor.

The fearsomeness mistakenly attributed to me in public places often has   10
a perilous flavor. The most frightening of these confusions occurred in the late 1970s and early 1980s when I worked as a journalist in Chicago. One day, rushing into the office of a magazine I was writing for with a deadline story in hand, I was mistaken for a burglar. The office manager called security and, with an ad hoc posse, pursued me through the labyrinthine halls, nearly to my editor's door. I had no way of proving who I was. I could only move briskly toward the company of someone who knew me.

Another time I was on assignment for a local paper and killing time before an interview. I entered a jewelry store on the city's affluent Near North Side. The proprietor excused herself and returned with an enormous red Doberman pinscher straining at the end of a leash. She stood, the dog extended toward me, silent to my questions, her eyes bulging nearly out of her head. I took a cursory look around, nodded, and bade her good night. Relatively speaking, however, I never fared as badly as another black male journalist. He went to nearby Waukegan, Illinois, a couple of summers ago to work on a story about a murderer who was born there. Mistaking the reporter for the killer, police hauled him from his car at gunpoint and but for his press credentials would probably have tried to book him. Such episodes are not uncommon. Black men trade tales like this all the time.

In "My Negro Problem—And Ours," Podhoretz writes that the hatred he feels for blacks makes itself known to him through a variety of avenues—one being his discomfort with that "special brand of paranoid touchiness" to which he says blacks are prone. No doubt he is speaking here of black men. In time, I learned to smother the rage I felt at so often being taken for a criminal. Not to do so would surely have led to madness—via that special "paranoid touchiness" that so annoyed Podhoretz at the time he wrote the essay.

I began to take precautions to make myself less threatening. I move about with care, particularly late in the evening. I give a wide berth to nervous people on subway platforms during the wee hours, particularly when I have exchanged business clothes for jeans. If I happen to be entering a building behind some people who appear skittish, I may walk by, letting them clear the lobby before I return, so as not to seem to be following them. I have been calm and extremely congenial on those rare occasions when I've been pulled over by the police.

And on late-evening constitutionals along streets less traveled by, I employ what has proved to be an excellent tension-reducing measure: I whistle melodies from Beethoven and Vivaldi and the more popular classical composers. Even steely New Yorkers hunching toward nighttime destinations seem to relax, and occasionally they even join in the tune. Virtually everybody seems to sense that a mugger wouldn't be warbling bright, sunny selections from Vivaldi's *Four Seasons*. It is my equivalent of the cowbell that hikers wear when they know they are in bear country.

The Reader's Presence

1. Why does Staples use the word *victim* in his opening sentence? In what sense is the white woman a "victim"? How is Staples using the term? As readers, how might we interpret the opening sentence upon first reading? How does the meaning of the term change in rereading?

2. In rereading the essay, pay close attention to the way Staples handles points of view. When does he shift viewpoints or perspectives? What is his purpose in doing so? What are some of the connections Staples makes in this essay between the point of view one chooses and one's identity?

3. **CONNECTIONS:**   How does Staples behave on the street? How does he deal with the woman's anxiety? How has he "altered" his own public behavior? In what ways is his behavior on the street similar to his "behavior" as a writer? Compare this version of the essay to the alternate version that follows. What are the changes and how do those changes influence the essay's effect on the reader? How do you compare Staples's strategies — in both versions — to those of Manuel Muñoz in "Leave Your Name at the Border" (page 208)?

The Writer at Work

Another Version of *Just Walk on By*

Courtesy of Brent Staples

When he published his memoir, *Parallel Time*, in 1994, Brent Staples decided to incorporate his earlier essay into the book. He also decided to revise it substantially. As you compare the two versions, note the passages Staples retained and those he chose not to carry forward into book form. Do you agree with his changes? Why in general do you think he made them? If you had been his editor, what revision strategy would you have suggested?

❝At night, I walked to the lakefront whenever the weather permitted. I was headed home from the lake when I took my first victim. It was late fall, and the wind was cutting. I was wearing my navy pea jacket, the collar turned up, my hands snug in the pockets. Dead leaves scuttled in shoals along the streets. I turned out of Blackstone Avenue and headed west on 57th Street, and there she was, a few yards ahead of me, dressed in business clothes and carrying a briefcase. She looked back at me once, then again, and picked up her pace. She looked back again and started to run. I stopped where I was and looked up at the surrounding windows. What did this look like to people peeking out through their blinds? I was out walking. But what if someone

had thought they'd seen something they hadn't and called the police. I held back the urge to run. Instead, I walked south to The Midway, plunged into its darkness, and remained on The Midway until I reached the foot of my street.

I'd been a fool. I'd been walking the streets grinning good evening at people who were frightened to death of me. I did violence to them by just being. How had I missed this? I kept walking at night, but from then on I paid attention.

I became expert in the language of fear. Couples locked arms or reached for each other's hand when they saw me. Some crossed to the other side of the street. People who were carrying on conversations went mute and stared straight ahead, as though avoiding my eyes would save them. This reminded me of an old wives' tale: that rabid dogs didn't bite if you avoided their eyes. The determination to avoid my eyes made me invisible to classmates and professors whom I passed on the street.

It occurred to me for the first time that I was big. I was 6 feet 1½ inches tall, and my long hair made me look bigger. I weighed only 170 pounds. But the navy pea jacket that Brian had given me was broad at the shoulders, high at the collar, making me look bigger and more fearsome than I was.

I tried to be innocuous but didn't know how. The more I thought about how I moved, the less my body belonged to me; I became a false character riding along inside it. I began to avoid people. I turned out of my way into side streets to spare them the sense that they were being stalked. I let them clear the lobbies of buildings before I entered, so they wouldn't feel trapped. Out of nervousness I began to whistle and discovered I was good at it. My whistle was pure and sweet—and also in tune. On the street at night I whistled popular tunes from the Beatles and Vivaldi's *Four Seasons*. The tension drained from people's bodies when they heard me. A few even smiled as they passed me in the dark.

Then I changed. I don't know why, but I remember when. I was walking west on 57th Street, after dark, coming home from the lake. The man and the woman walking toward me were laughing and talking but clammed up when they saw me. The man touched the woman's elbow, guiding her toward the curb. Normally I'd have given way and begun to whistle, but not this time. This time I veered toward them and aimed myself so that they'd have to part to avoid walking into me. The man stiffened, threw back his head and assumed the stare: eyes dead ahead, mouth open. His face took on a bluish hue under the sodium vapor streetlamps. I suppressed the urge to scream into his face. Instead I glided between them, my shoulder nearly brushing his. A few steps beyond them I stopped and howled with laughter. I called this game Scatter the Pigeons.

Fifty-seventh Street was too well lit for the game to be much fun; people didn't feel quite vulnerable enough. Along The Midway were heart-stopping strips of dark sidewalk, but these were so frightening that few people traveled them. The stretch of Blackstone between 57th and 55th provided better hunting. The block was long and lined with young trees that blocked out the streetlight and obscured the heads of people coming toward you.

One night I stooped beneath the branches and came up on the other side, just as a couple was stepping from their car into their town house. The woman pulled her purse close with one hand and reached for her husband with the other. The two of them stood frozen as I bore down on them. I felt a surge of power: these people were mine; I could do with them as I wished. If I'd been younger, with less to lose, I'd have robbed them, and it would have been easy. All I'd have to do was stand silently before them until they surrendered their money. I thundered, "Good evening!" into their bleached-out faces and cruised away laughing.

I held a special contempt for people who cowered in their cars as they waited for the light to change at 57th and Woodlawn. The intersection was always deserted at night, except for a car or two stuck at the red. *Thunk! Thunk! Thunk!* they hammered down the door locks when I came into view. Once I had hustled across the street, head down, trying to seem harmless. Now I turned brazenly into the headlights and laughed. Once across, I paced the sidewalk, glaring until the light changed. They'd made me terrifying. Now I'd show them how terrifying I could be.**"**

Cheryl Strayed

INTO THE WOODS

CHERYL STRAYED (b. 1968) is the best-selling author of *Wild: From Lost to Found on the Pacific Crest Trail* (2012). The memoir details her 1,100-mile hike along the famous long-distance trail, a hike she chose to take after the death of her mother and her separation from her then husband. *Wild* was the first selection for Oprah's Book Club 2.0 and won a number of prestigious literary awards, including the Indie Choice Award. It is the basis for a film of the same name, scheduled for release in 2014.

Strayed has an MFA in creative writing from Syracuse University, where her focus was actually fiction writing. Her first published book was a novel, *Torch* (2006), which received favorable reviews, but it did not generate the commercial success she has since had with nonfiction. She has said that "[m]emoir is the art of subjective truth, and while I feel a strong obligation to the truth piece of that, I also firmly plant that truth within the context of my own subjectivity." Her essays

> **"Memoir is the art of subjective truth."**

have appeared in *The Best American Essays*, the *New York Times Magazine*, the *Washington Post Magazine*, *Vogue*, and *Salon*, among many other publications. She has been writing the advice column "Dear Sugar" for *The Rumpus* since 2010, and her book *Tiny Beautiful Things* (2012) is a collection of those columns published by Vintage Books in response to her growing popularity. Strayed was the guest editor of *The Best American Essays* in 2013, and her books have been translated into thirty languages.

Strayed spent most of her youth in rural Minnesota, where she had the unusual experience of growing up in a house without indoor plumbing. A long-time feminist, she currently resides in Portland, Oregon, with her husband and children. "Into the Woods" is excerpted from *Wild*, originally published in *Vogue* in February 2012, one month before the full memoir appeared in bookstores.

MY SOLO HIKE on the Pacific Crest Trail—three months, 1,100 miles—had many beginnings. There was the first, flip decision to do it, followed by the second, more serious decision to actually do it, and then the weeks of shopping and packing and preparing to do it. There was the quitting of my job as a waitress and finalizing my divorce from a man I still loved and selling almost everything I owned and visiting my mother's grave one

last time. There was the driving across the country from Minneapolis to Portland, Oregon, and, a few days later, catching a flight to Los Angeles and a
ride to the town of Mojave.

At which point, at long last, there was the actual doing it, quickly followed by the grim realization of what it meant to do it, followed by the decision to quit doing it because doing it was absurd and ridiculously difficult
and I was profoundly unprepared to do it.

And then there was the real live truly doing it.

Before I began my hike, I'd thought myself somewhat ready. I was someone who could be described as outdoorsy. My family vacations had always
involved some form of camping. As an adult, I'd slept in the back of my
truck in national forests more times than I could count. Plus, I'd spent my
teen years in the Minnesota northwoods in a house my mother and stepfather built that didn't have an indoor toilet, electricity, or running water. My
mother planted a garden and pickled vegetables, baked bread and carded
wool, and made half the clothes my siblings and I wore.

My mother and I were college seniors when we learned she had cancer. 5
She'd begun college when I did, pursuing a dream after years of setting it
aside. Her college was in Duluth, mine in Minneapolis. We'd always been
close—her love for me and my sister and my brother was all-encompassing
and full-throttle—but in my college years we became even closer, talking
almost every night on the phone. I was married by then, to a man named
Paul I'd wed in our woods, wearing a white satin-and-lace dress my mother
had sewn.

Until she was dying, it hadn't occurred to me that my mother would die.
She was monolithic and insurmountable, the keeper of my life. She would
grow old and more beautiful and still work in the garden. This image was
fixed in my mind. And yet the doctors all said the same thing: There was no
cure. She was 45.

I folded my life down. I told Paul not to count on me. I wanted to quit
school, but my mother insisted that I still get my degree. She herself needed
to complete only a couple more classes to graduate; she would get her B.A. if
it killed her, she said, and we laughed and then looked at each other darkly.

I cut my classes down to two days a week and afterward drove the three
hours north to be with my mother. On good days she sat in a chair and
talked to me. There was nothing much to say. She'd been so transparent
and effusive and I so inquisitive all my life that we'd already covered everything. I knew the names of the horses she had loved as a girl: Pal and Buddy
and Bacchus. I knew she'd lost her virginity at seventeen with a boy named
Mike. I knew how she met my father the next year and what he seemed
like to her on their first few dates. How, when she'd broken the news of her
unwed teen pregnancy to her parents, her father had dropped a spoon. All
growing up I'd asked and asked, making her describe those scenes, wanting to know who said what and how, what she'd felt inside while it was
going on. And she'd told me, laughing and asking why on earth I wanted to

know. I couldn't explain. But now that she was dying, I knew everything. My mother was in me already. Not just the parts of her that I knew, but the parts of her that had come before me, too.

I was wrong about it being impossible for my mother to die: She lived only 49 days after learning she had cancer.

Three and a half years later, I was at an outdoor store in Minneapolis. It was December 1994. On a shelf I saw a book called *The Pacific Crest Trail: Volume 1: California.* I picked it up. The PCT, I learned, was a continuous wilderness trail, 2,650 miles long, that traversed the entire length of California, Oregon, and Washington, passing through national parks and forests; through deserts and mountains; across rivers and highways. I turned the book over and gazed at its front cover—a boulder-strewn lake surrounded by rocky crags against a blue sky—then placed it back on the shelf and left.

But later I returned and bought the book. I couldn't explain it. Something bloomed inside me as I traced the jagged line of the trail with my finger.

I pulled into the town of Mojave, California, as the June sun dipped into the Tehachapi Mountains a dozen miles behind me to the west—mountains I'd be hiking the next day. "You can stop here," I said to the brother of a friend, who'd given me a ride from L.A., gesturing to an old-style neon sign that said WHITE'S MOTEL. By the worn look of the building, I guessed it was the cheapest place in town.

"You sure you're OK?" he said.

"Yes," I replied with false confidence and then watched him drive away. I'd spent the past six months imagining this moment, but now that it was here, I felt less exuberant than I had thought I would.

After checking in, I went to my room and sat on the soft bed. I was dressed in the clothes I'd been wearing since I'd left Portland the night before, every last thing brand-new. Wool socks, leather hiking boots, navy-blue shorts, underwear made of a special quick-dry fabric, and a white T-shirt over a sports bra. I felt like a fraud. I'd spent the previous months diligently preparing for my trip—addressing boxes of dehydrated food and camping supplies that a friend would mail to me throughout the summer to places along the PCT with evocative names like Echo Lake and Soda Springs. But now I didn't have any of the certainty I'd had when I'd sealed those boxes neatly shut with tape. It occurred to me just then that I'd never actually walked into the wilderness with a backpack on and spent the night. Not even once. *I've never gone backpacking!* I thought with rueful hilarity.

I walked over to my backpack, which was forest green and trimmed with black, and touched its top as if I were caressing a child's head. I opened one of its compartments and pulled out an orange whistle, whose packaging proclaimed it to be "the world's loudest." I ripped it open and held the whistle up by its yellow lanyard, then put it around my neck. Was I supposed to hike wearing it like this? Like so much else, I hadn't thought it all the way through.

The next morning, after the last shower I'd have for days, I piled all my belongings on the bed. I worked my way through the mountain of things—the thick fleece anorak, the camp chair, the snakebite kit, the tiny collapsible stove—wedging and cramming them into every available space of my pack. I wrapped bungee cords around all the things that didn't fit. When I was done, I sat on the floor, sweaty from my exertions, and then I remembered one last thing: water.

I guessed it would take me two days to reach the first water source—seventeen miles into my hike—and I would have to carry enough to get me through. I filled two 32-ounce bottles in the bathroom sink and put them in my pack's mesh side pockets. I dug out my Dromedary and filled up all 2.6 gallons of it. I don't know how much my pack weighed on that first day, but I do know the water alone was almost 26 pounds.

Finally, when everything I was going to carry was in place, a hush came over me. I was ready. I put on my watch, looped my sunglasses around my neck by their pink neoprene holder, donned my sun hat, and looked at my pack. It was at once enormous and compact, mildly adorable and intimidatingly self-contained. It had an animate quality; in its company, I didn't feel entirely alone. Standing, it came up to my waist. I gripped it and bent to lift it.

It wouldn't budge.   20

I squatted and grasped its frame more robustly and tried to lift it again. Again it did not move. It was exactly like attempting to lift a Volkswagen Beetle. It looked so cute, so ready to be lifted—and yet it was impossible to do.

I sat down beside it and pondered my situation. How could I carry a backpack more than 1,000 miles over rugged mountains and waterless deserts if I couldn't even budge it an inch in an air-conditioned motel room? It was true that the salespeople at REI had mentioned weight rather often in their soliloquies, but I hadn't paid much attention.

It was now or never. I sat down right in front of the pack, wove my arms through the shoulder straps, and clipped a strap across my chest. I took a deep breath and began rocking back and forth until I finally hurled myself forward onto my hands and knees. My backpack still seemed like a Volkswagen Beetle, only now it seemed like a Volkswagen Beetle that was parked on my back. The frame of the pack squeaked as I rose, it too straining from the tremendous weight.

I staggered and swayed around the room, my center of gravity pulled in any direction I so much as leaned. It felt pretty awful, and yet perhaps this was how it felt to be a backpacker. I didn't know.

I made my way to the nearby gas station. Unless I wanted to walk twelve   25
miles along the broiling shoulder of the highway to reach the trail, I needed a ride. Horrible things happened to hitchhikers, I knew, especially to women hitchhiking alone. But hitchhiking was simply what PCT hikers did on occasion. And I was a PCT hiker, right? *Right?*

I bought a can of Coke and drank it with a casual air that belied the fact that I could not stand up properly. A minivan pulled up and two men, clearly a father and son, got out. I asked for a ride. "Sure," the older one said finally, with obvious reluctance.

"Thank you," I trilled girlishly.

Fifteen minutes later, I was standing by the silent highway. Small clouds of dust blew in swirling gusts beneath the glaring noon sun. Surrounded in all directions by beige, barren-looking mountains, I was at the southern foot of the Sierra Nevada, which stretched north for more than 400 miles. On a fence post beyond the ditch I spied a palm-size metal blaze that said PACIFIC CREST TRAIL. I was here.

I cinched my pack and took the first steps down the trail to a brown metal box tacked to another fence post. Inside was the trail register. I wrote my name and the date and read the notes from previous hikers, most of them men traveling in pairs, not one of them a woman alone.

The trail headed east, paralleling the highway for a while, dipping down into rocky washes and back up again. *I'm hiking!* I thought. And then, *I am hiking on the Pacific Crest Trail!* What is hiking but walking, after all? I can walk! I'd argued when Paul had expressed his concern about my never actually having gone backpacking. But after about fifteen minutes, it was clear that I had never walked into desert mountains with a pack that weighed significantly more than half of what I did strapped onto my back. Which, it turns out, resembles walking less than it does hell. 30

I began panting and sweating immediately, dust caking my boots and calves as the trail turned north and began to climb. Each step was a toil as I ascended higher and higher still, interrupted only by the occasional short descent, which was a new kind of hell because I had to brace myself against each step, lest gravity's pull cause me to catapult forward. Soon the voice inside my head was screaming, *What have I gotten myself into?* I tried to ignore it, to hum as I hiked, though humming proved too difficult to do while also panting. The only possible distraction was my vigilant search for rattlesnakes. The landscape was made for them, it seemed. And also for mountain lions and wilderness-savvy serial killers.

Three hours in, I came to a rare level spot near a gathering of Joshua trees. To my monumental relief, there was a large boulder upon which I could sit and remove my pack. Amazed to be free of its weight, I strolled around and accidentally brushed up against one of the trees and was bayoneted by its sharp spikes. Blood instantly spurted out of three stab wounds on my arm. The wind blew so fiercely that when I removed my first-aid kit from my pack and opened it up, all of my Band-Aids blew away. I chased them uselessly across the flat plain and then they were gone, down the mountain and out of reach.

I'd never been so exhausted in all of my life. I retrieved my guidebook and held the fluttering pages against the wind, hoping that the familiar words and maps would dispel my growing unease. But paging through it for the first time while actually sitting on the trail was less reassuring than I'd hoped. There were things I'd overlooked, I saw now, such as a quote on page six by a fellow named Jim Podlesney that said, "How can a book describe the psychological factors a person must prepare for . . . the despair, the alienation, the anxiety and especially the pain, both physical and mental, which slices to the very heart of the hiker's volition, which are the real things that must be planned for? No words can transmit those factors. . . ."

I sat pie-eyed, with a lurching knowledge that indeed no words could transmit those factors. I wrapped my arms around my legs and pressed my face into the tops of my bare knees. When I opened my eyes several minutes later, I saw that I was sitting next to a plant I recognized. This sage was less verdant than the sage my mother had grown in our yard for years, but its shape and scent were the same. I reached over and picked a handful of the leaves and rubbed them between my palms, then put my face in them and inhaled deeply, the way my mother had taught me to do. It gives you a burst of energy, she'd always declared on those long days when we'd been working to build our house and our spirits had flagged.

Inhaling it now, I didn't so much smell the sharp, earthy scent of the 35 desert sage as I did the potent memory of my mother. I looked up at the blue sky, feeling my mother's presence, remembering why it was that I'd thought I could hike this trail. Of all the things I'd made myself believe so I could hike the PCT, the death of my mother was the thing that made me believe the most deeply in my safety: Nothing bad could happen to me, I thought. The worst thing already had.

I stood and let the wind blow the sage leaves from my hands. I could see the mountains that surrounded me for miles, sloping gently down into a wide desert valley. White, angular wind turbines lined the ridges in the distance. As I stood there, I knew I was done for the day. Too tired to light my stove and too exhausted to be hungry in any case, I pitched my tent, though it was only four in the afternoon. I pushed the pack in and crawled in behind it. I was relieved to be inside, even though inside meant only a cramped green nylon cave.

The next morning, as I began to walk, I felt experienced in a way I hadn't the day before, sore but stronger beneath my pack. That strength crumbled within fifteen minutes, as I ascended into the rocky mountains. My upper back and shoulders were soon bound in tense, hot knots. By noon I was up over 6,000 feet, and the air had cooled, the sun suddenly disappearing behind clouds. Yesterday it had been hot in the desert, but now I shivered as I ate my lunch of a protein bar and dried apricots. Afterward, I lay down on my tarp to rest for a few minutes and, without meaning to, fell asleep.

I woke to raindrops falling on my face and looked at my watch. I'd slept for nearly two hours. It was as if someone had come up behind me and knocked me unconscious with a rock. I saw that I was engulfed in a cloud, the mist so impenetrable I couldn't see beyond a few feet. I buckled my pack and continued hiking through the light rain. I wasn't thinking, *I'm hiking on the Pacific Crest Trail.* I wasn't even thinking, *What have I gotten myself into?* I was thinking only of moving myself forward.

After hours of this, I found a spot flat enough to pitch my tent. The tiny thermometer that dangled from my pack said it was 42 degrees. Too tired to make dinner, I peeled off my sweaty clothes and draped them over a bush to dry before I crawled into my tent. In the morning, I had to force them on. Rigid as boards, they'd frozen overnight.

A few hours into my third day on the trail, I reached Golden Oak   40
Springs. The sight of the square concrete pool lifted my spirits enormously, not only because it meant water, but also because humans had so clearly constructed it. I took out my purifier and began to pump the way I'd practiced in my kitchen sink in Minneapolis. It was harder to do than I remembered, but it had to be done. My next water source was a daunting nineteen miles away.

The sun warm on my body, I spent the day there with my compass in hand, reading a book about how to use a compass called *Staying Found*. I found north, south, east, and west. I walked jubilantly down a jeep road to see what I could see. It was spectacular to walk without my pack on. Later, I set up my stove and attempted to make myself my first hot meal, but I couldn't get it to sustain a flame. I pulled the little instruction book out and learned that I'd filled the stove's canister with the wrong kind of gas. I ate a handful of tuna-jerky flakes and fell asleep before sunset.

After leaving the springs the next morning, I realized I was having a kind of strange, abstract, retrospective fun. Despite my various agonies, I noticed the beauty that surrounded me: the color of a desert flower that brushed against me on the trail or the grand sweep of the sky as the sun faded over the mountains. I was in the midst of such a reverie when I skidded on pebbles and fell, landing on the hard trail facedown with a force that took my breath away. I lay unmoving for a good minute.

When I crawled out from beneath my pack and assessed the damage, I saw that a gash in my shin was seeping copious blood, a knot the size of a fist already forming beneath it. I poured a tiny bit of my precious water over it, flicking the dirt out the best I could, then limped on.

I walked the rest of the afternoon with my eyes fixed on the trail directly in front of me, afraid I'd lose my footing again. It was then that I spotted what I'd been fearing: mountain lion tracks. The lion had walked along the trail not long before me, its paw prints clearly legible in the dirt. I thought about all those nature shows I'd watched as a kid in which the predators go after the one they judge to be the weakest in the pack. I sang aloud the little songs that came into my head—"Twinkle, Twinkle, Little Star" and "Take Me Home, Country Roads"—hoping that my terrified voice would scare the lion away, while at the same time fearing it would alert her to my presence, as if the blood crusted on my leg and the days-old stench of my body weren't enough of a lure.

Soon the terrain began to change. The landscape was still arid, but juni-   45
per trees, piñon pines, and scrub oaks started popping up. Occasionally I passed through shady meadows thick with grass. The grass and the trees were a comfort to me. They intimated that I could do this. Until, that is, a tree

stopped me in my path. It had fallen across the trail, its wide trunk held aloft by branches just low enough that I couldn't pass beneath, yet so high that climbing over it was impossible. Walking around it was also out of the question: the trail dropped off too steeply on one side and the brush was too dense on the other. I stood for a long while, trying to map out a way past the tree. I had to do it, no matter how impossible it seemed. I backed up to the tree, unbuckled my pack, and pushed it up and over its rough trunk, doing my best to drop it over the other side gently. Then I climbed over the tree after it.

Later, as I was making my way along a narrow and steep stretch of trail, I looked up to see an enormous brown horned animal charging at me. "Moose!" I hollered, though I knew that it wasn't a moose. In the panic of the moment, my mind couldn't wrap around what I was seeing. "Moose!" I hollered more desperately as it neared. I scrambled into the manzanitas that bordered the trail, pulling myself into their sharp branches as best I could. As I did this, I realized that I was about to be mauled by a Texas longhorn bull. "Mooooose!" I shouted louder as I grabbed for the yellow cord tied to the frame of my pack that held the world's loudest whistle. I found it, brought it to my lips, closed my eyes, and blew with all my might. When I opened my eyes, the bull was gone. So was all the skin on the top of my right index finger, scraped off on the manzanitas' jagged branches.

The thing about hiking the Pacific Crest Trail, the thing that was so profound to me that summer — and yet also, like most things, so very simple — was how few choices I had and how often I had to do the thing I least wanted to do. How there was no escape or denial. No numbing anything down with a martini or covering it up with a roll in the hay. As I clung to the trees that day, attempting to patch up my bleeding finger, I considered my options. There were only two. I could go back in the direction I had come from, or I could go forward in the direction I intended to go. And so I walked on. ●

The Reader's Presence

1. Strayed describes her mother as "monolithic and insurmountable" (paragraph 6). How does her mother's death affect her life and her decision to hike the Pacific Crest Trail? In what ways does her mother's death reflect Strayed's experiences on the trail? Strayed describes her desire to hike the trail in natural, connected terms: "Something bloomed inside me as I traced the jagged line of the trail with my finger" (paragraph 11). What specifically does Strayed find so appealing about the Pacific Crest Trail?

2. Strayed describes the physical weight of her pack and the individual components necessary for her survival as "exactly like attempting to lift a Volkswagen Beetle" (paragraph 21), but what metaphor(s) would you use to characterize the emotional weight that she carries with her? Are the two connected in any way? If so, how? Although Strayed's journey was undoubtedly arduous and full of obstacles, there is a simplicity to her hiking; her choices are limited, and there is "no escape or denial" from her immediate surroundings (paragraph 47). How does Strayed's willingness to pare down her life enable her to come to terms with her mother's sudden death?

3. **CONNECTIONS:**   Compare and contrast the ways in which Strayed comes to terms with learning how to function effectively in an unfamiliar world with Frederick Douglass's account of learning to read and write (page 106). How does Strayed's immersion in an environment foreign to her relate to Douglass's immersing himself in practicing the enabling skills of reading and writing? In what ways do these experiences of total immersion affect their respective authors?

The Writer at Work

CHERYL STRAYED on What Makes a Good Essay

Courtesy of Cheryl Strayed

Although she started writing stories as a young child, Cheryl Strayed did not begin a serious career as a writer until her mother died of cancer. She tried expressing her enormous grief by writing about her mother in both fiction and nonfiction. As she did so, she began to appreciate more and more the essay form. An essay she wrote about her mother in 1999 (entitled "Heroine") was selected by Alan Lightman (page 469) for *The Best American Essays 2000* and Strayed, fittingly, served as a guest editor of that series in 2013. In her introduction to that year's collection she concisely and memorably explains what makes a good essay.

❝ Behind every good essay there's an author with a savage desire to know more about what is already known. A good essay isn't a report of what happened. It's a reach for the stuff beyond and beneath. Essayists begin with an objective truth and attempt to find a greater, grander truth by testing fact against subjective interpretations of experiences and ideas, memories and theories. They try to make meaning of actual life, even if an awful lot has yet to be figured out. They grapple and reflect with seriousness and humor. They philosophize and confess with intellect and emotion. They recollect and reimagine private and public history with a combination of clarity and conjecture. They venture into what happened and why with a complicated collision of documented proof and impossible-to-pin-down remembrances. And they follow the answers to the questions that arise in the course of writing about what happened wherever they go. The essay's engine is curiosity; its territory is the open road.

This is what makes them so damn fun to read. Their vibrancy and intimacy, their mystery and nerve, their relentlessly searching quality is simultaneously like a punch in the nose and a kiss on the lips. A pow and a wow. An *ouch* and a *yes*. A stop and a go. ❞

Alice Walker

BEAUTY: WHEN THE OTHER DANCER IS THE SELF

ALICE WALKER (b. 1944) was awarded the Pulitzer Prize and the American Book Award for her second novel, *The Color Purple* (1982), which was made into a popular film. This novel helped establish Walker's reputation as one of America's most important contemporary writers. In both her fiction and her nonfiction, she shares her compassion for the black women of America whose lives have long been largely excluded from or distorted in literary representation. Walker is also the author of other novels, short stories, several volumes of poetry, a children's biography of Langston Hughes, essays, and criticism. Her books of poetry and prose include *By the Light of My Father's Smile* (1998), *The Way Forward Is with a Broken Heart* (2000), and *Now Is the Time to Open Your Heart* (2004). Her most recent work includes a collection of essays and ruminations, *We Are the Ones We Have Been Waiting For* (2006); an illustrated poem for children, *Why War Is Never a Good Idea* (2007); *The World Will Follow Joy: Turning Madness into Flowers* (2013), and *The Cushion in the Road: Meditation and Wandering as the Whole World Awakens to Being in Harm's Way* (2013). "Beauty: When the Other Dancer Is the Self" comes from her 1983 collection, *In Search of Our Mothers' Gardens*.

> "You have to go to the bottom of the well with creativity. You have to give it everything you've got, but at the same time you have to leave that last drop for the creative spirit or for the earth itself."

When asked by an interviewer about her writing habits, Walker replied, "I think it was Hemingway who said that each day that you write, you don't try to write to the absolute end of what you feel and think. You leave a little, you know, so that the next day you have something else to go on. And I would take it a little further—the thing is being able to create out of fullness, and that in order to create out of fullness, you have to let it well up. . . . In creation you must always leave something. You have to go to the bottom of the well with creativity. You have to give it everything you've got, but at the same time you have to leave that last drop for the creative spirit or for the earth itself."

IT IS A BRIGHT SUMMER DAY in 1947. My father, a fat, funny man with beautiful eyes and a subversive wit, is trying to decide which of his eight children he will take with him to the county fair. My mother, of course, will not go. She is knocked out from getting most of us ready: I hold my neck stiff against the pressure of her knuckles as she hastily completes the braiding and the beribboning of my hair.

My father is the driver for the rich old white lady up the road. Her name is Miss Mey. She owns all the land for miles around, as well as the house in which we live. All I remember about her is that she once offered to pay my mother thirty-five cents for cleaning her house, raking up piles of her magnolia leaves, and washing her family's clothes, and that my mother — she of no money, eight children, and a chronic earache — refused it. But I do not think of this in 1947. I am two-and-a-half years old. I want to go everywhere my daddy goes. I am excited at the prospect of riding in a car. Someone has told me fairs are fun. That there is room in the car for only three of us doesn't faze me at all. Whirling happily in my starchy frock, showing off my biscuit-polished patent-leather shoes and lavender socks, tossing my head in a way that makes my ribbons bounce, I stand, hands on hips, before my father. "Take me, Daddy," I say with assurance; "I'm the prettiest!"

Later, it does not surprise me to find myself in Miss Mey's shiny black car, sharing the back seat with the other lucky ones. Does not surprise me that I thoroughly enjoy the fair. At home that night I tell the unlucky ones all I can remember about the merry-go-round, the man who eats live chickens, and the teddy bears, until they say: that's enough, baby Alice. Shut up now, and go to sleep.

It is Easter Sunday, 1950. I am dressed in a green, flocked, scalloped-hem dress (handmade by my adoring sister, Ruth) that has its own smooth satin petticoat and tiny hot-pink roses tucked into each scallop. My shoes, new T-strap patent leather, again highly biscuit-polished. I am six years old and have learned one of the longest Easter speeches to be heard that day, totally unlike the speech I said when I was two: "Easter lilies / pure and white / blossom in / the morning light." When I rise to give my speech I do so on a great wave of love and pride and expectation. People in the church stop rustling their new crinolines. They seem to hold their breath. I can tell they admire my dress, but it is my spirit, bordering on sassiness (womanishness), they secretly applaud.

"That girl's a little *mess*," they whisper to each other, pleased.   5

Naturally I say my speech without stammer or pause, unlike those who stutter, stammer, or, worst of all, forget. This is before the word "beautiful" exists in people's vocabulary, but "Oh, isn't she the *cutest* thing!" frequently floats my way. "And got so much sense!" they gratefully add . . . for which thoughtful addition I thank them to this day.

It was great fun being cute. But then, one day, it ended.

I am eight years old and a tomboy. I have a cowboy hat, cowboy boots, checkered shirt and pants, all red. My playmates are my brothers, two and four years older than I. Their colors are black and green, the only difference in the way we are dressed. On Saturday nights we all go to the picture show, even my mother; Westerns are her favorite kind of movie. Back home, "on the ranch," we pretend we are Tom Mix, Hopalong Cassidy, Lash LaRue (we've even named one of our dogs Lash LaRue); we chase each other for hours rustling cattle, being outlaws, delivering damsels from distress. Then my parents decide to buy my brothers guns. These are not "real" guns. They shoot BBs, copper pellets my brothers say will kill birds. Because I am a girl, I do not get a gun. Instantly I am relegated to the position of Indian. Now there appears a great distance between us. They shoot and shoot at everything with their new guns. I try to keep up with my bow and arrows.

One day while I am standing on top of our makeshift "garage"—pieces of tin nailed across some poles—holding my bow and arrow and looking out toward the fields, I feel an incredible blow in my right eye. I look down just in time to see my brother lower his gun.

Both brothers rush to my side. My eye stings, and I cover it with my   10
hand. "If you tell," they say, "we will get a whipping. You don't want that to happen, do you?" I do not. "Here is a piece of wire," says the older brother, picking it up from the roof; "say you stepped on one end of it and the other flew up and hit you." The pain is beginning to start. "Yes," I say. "Yes, I will say that is what happened." If I do not say this is what happened, I know my brothers will find ways to make me wish I had. But now I will say anything that gets me to my mother.

Confronted by our parents we stick to the lie agreed upon. They place me on a bench on the porch and I close my left eye while they examine the right. There is a tree growing from underneath the porch that climbs past the railing to the roof. It is the last thing my right eye sees. I watch as its trunk, its branches, and then its leaves are blotted out by the rising blood.

I am in shock. First there is intense fever, which my father tries to break using lily leaves bound around my head. Then there are chills: my mother tries to get me to eat soup. Eventually, I do not know how, my parents learn what has happened. A week after the "accident" they take me to see a doctor. "Why did you wait so long to come?" he asks, looking into my eye and shaking his head. "Eyes are sympathetic," he says. "If one is blind, the other will likely become blind too."

This comment of the doctor's terrifies me. But it is really how I look that bothers me most. Where the BB pellet struck there is a glob of whitish scar tissue, a hideous cataract, on my eye. Now when I stare at people—a favorite pastime, up to now—they will stare back. Not at the "cute" little girl, but at her scar. For six years I do not stare at anyone, because I do not raise my head.

Years later, in the throes of a mid-life crisis, I ask my mother and sister whether I changed after the "accident." "No," they say, puzzled. "What do you mean?"

What do I mean?   15

I am eight, and, for the first time, doing poorly in school, where I have been something of a whiz since I was four. We have just moved to the place where the "accident" occurred. We do not know any of the people around us because this is a different county. The only time I see the friends I knew is when we go back to our old church. The new school is the former state penitentiary. It is a large stone building, cold and drafty, crammed to over-flowing with boisterous, ill-disciplined children. On the third floor there is a huge circular imprint of some partition that has been torn out.

"What used to be here?" I ask a sullen girl next to me on our way past it to lunch.

"The electric chair," says she.

At night I have nightmares about the electric chair, and about all the people reputedly "fried" in it. I am afraid of the school, where all the students seem to be budding criminals.

"What's the matter with your eye?" they ask, critically.   20

When I don't answer (I cannot decide whether it was an "accident" or not), they shove me, insist on a fight.

My brother, the one who created the story about the wire, comes to my rescue. But then brags so much about "protecting" me, I become sick.

After months of torture at the school, my parents decide to send me back to our old community, to my old school. I live with my grandparents and the teacher they board. But there is no room for Phoebe, my cat. By the time my grandparents decide there *is* room, and I ask for my cat, she cannot be found. Miss Yarborough, the boarding teacher, takes me under her wing, and begins to teach me to play the piano. But soon she marries an African — a "prince," she says — and is whisked away to his continent.

At my old school there is at least one teacher who loves me. She is the teacher who "knew me before I was born" and bought my first baby clothes. It is she who makes life bearable. It is her presence that finally helps me turn on the one child at the school who continually calls me "one-eyed bitch." One day I simply grab him by his coat and beat him until I am satisfied. It is my teacher who tells me my mother is ill.

My mother is lying in bed in the middle of the day, something I have   25
never seen. She is in too much pain to speak. She has an abscess in her ear. I stand looking down on her, knowing that if she dies, I cannot live. She is being treated with warm oils and hot bricks held against her cheek. Finally a doctor comes. But I must go back to my grandparents' house. The weeks pass but I am hardly aware of it. All I know is that my mother might die, my father is not so jolly, my brothers still have their guns, and I am the one sent away from home.

"You did not change," they say.

Did I imagine the anguish of never looking up?

I am twelve. When relatives come to visit I hide in my room. My cousin Brenda, just my age, whose father works in the post office and whose mother is a nurse, comes to find me. "Hello," she says. And then she asks, looking at my recent school picture, which I did not want taken, and on which the "glob," as I think of it, is clearly visible, "You still can't see out of that eye?"

"No," I say, and flop back on the bed over my book.

That night, as I do almost every night, I abuse my eye. I rant and rave at   30
it, in front of the mirror. I plead with it to clear up before morning. I tell it I hate and despise it. I do not pray for sight. I pray for beauty.

"You did not change," they say.

I am fourteen and baby-sitting for my brother Bill, who lives in Boston. He is my favorite brother and there is a strong bond between us. Understanding my feelings of shame and ugliness he and his wife take me to a local hospital, where the "glob" is removed by a doctor named O. Henry. There is still a small bluish crater where the scar tissue was, but the ugly white stuff is gone. Almost immediately I become a different person from the girl who does not raise her head. Or so I think. Now that I've raised my head I win the boyfriend of my dreams. Now that I've raised my head I have plenty of friends. Now that I've raised my head classwork comes from my lips as faultlessly as Easter speeches did, and I leave high school as valedictorian, most popular student, and *queen*, hardly believing my luck. Ironically, the girl who was voted most beautiful in our class (and was) was later shot twice through the chest by a male companion, using a "real" gun, while she was pregnant. But that's another story in itself. Or is it?

"You did not change," they say.

It is now thirty years since the "accident." A beautiful journalist comes to visit and to interview me. She is going to write a cover story for her magazine that focuses on my latest book. "Decide how you want to look on the cover," she says. "Glamorous, or whatever."

Never mind "glamorous," it is the "whatever" that I hear. Suddenly all I   35
can think of is whether I will get enough sleep the night before the photography session: If I don't, my eye will be tired and wander, as blind eyes will.

At night in bed with my lover I think up reasons why I should not appear on the cover of a magazine. "My meanest critics will say I've sold out," I say. "My family will now realize I write scandalous books."

"But what's the real reason you don't want to do this?" he asks.

"Because in all probability," I say in a rush, "my eye won't be straight."

"It will be straight enough," he says. Then, "Besides, I thought you'd made your peace with that."

And I suddenly remember that I have.   40

I remember:

I am talking to my brother Jimmy, asking if he remembers anything unusual about the day I was shot. He does not know I consider that day the last time my father, with his sweet home remedy of cool lily leaves, chose me, and that I suffered and raged inside because of this. "Well," he says, "all I remember is standing by the side of the highway with Daddy, trying to flag down a car. A white man stopped, but when Daddy said he needed somebody to take his little girl to the doctor, he drove off."

I remember:

I am in the desert for the first time. I fall totally in love with it. I am so overwhelmed by its beauty, I confront for the first time, consciously, the meaning of the doctor's words years ago: "Eyes are sympathetic. If one is blind, the other will likely become blind too." I realize I have dashed about the world madly, looking at this, looking at that, storing up images against the fading of the light. *But I might have missed seeing the desert!* The shock of that possibility—and gratitude for over twenty-five years of sight—sends me literally to my knees. Poem after poem comes—which is perhaps how poets pray.

ON SIGHT

I am so thankful I have seen
The Desert
And the creatures in the desert
And the desert Itself.

The desert has its own moon
Which I have seen
With my own eye.
There is no flag on it.

Trees of the desert have arms
All of which are always up
That is because the moon is up
The sun is up
Also the sky
The Stars
Clouds
None with flags.

If there were flags, I doubt
the trees would point.
Would you?

But mostly, I remember this: 45

I am twenty-seven, and my baby daughter is almost three. Since her birth I have worried about her discovery that her mother's eyes are different from other people's. Will she be embarrassed? I think. What will she say? Every day she watches a television program called *Big Blue Marble*. It begins with a picture of the earth as it appears from the moon. It is bluish, a little battered-looking, but full of light, with whitish clouds swirling around it. Every time I see it I weep with love, as if it is a picture of Grandma's house. One day when I am putting Rebecca down for her nap, she suddenly focuses on my eye. Something inside me cringes, gets ready to try to protect myself. All children are cruel about physical differences, I know from experience, and that they don't always mean to be is another matter. I assume Rebecca will be the same.

But no-o-o-o. She studies my face intently as we stand, her inside and me outside her crib. She even holds my face maternally between her dimpled little hands. Then, looking every bit as serious and lawyerlike as her father, she says, as if it may just possibly have slipped my attention: "Mommy, there's a *world* in your eye." (As in, "Don't be alarmed, or do anything crazy.") And then, gently, but with great interest: "Mommy, where did you *get* that world in your eye?"

For the most part, the pain left then. (So what, if my brothers grew up to buy even more powerful pellet guns for their sons and to carry real guns themselves. So what, if a young "Morehouse[1] man" once nearly fell off the steps of Trevor Arnett Library because he thought my eyes were blue.) Crying and laughing I ran to the bathroom, while Rebecca mumbled and sang herself to sleep. Yes indeed, I realized, looking into the mirror. There *was* a world in my eye. And I saw that it was possible to love it: that in fact, for all it had taught me of shame and anger and inner vision, I *did* love it. Even to see it drifting out of orbit in boredom, or rolling up out of fatigue, not to mention floating back at attention in excitement (bearing witness, a friend has called it), deeply suitable to my personality, and even characteristic of me.

That night I dream I am dancing to Stevie Wonder's song "Always" (the name of the song is really "As," but I hear it as "Always"). As I dance, whirling and joyous, happier than I've ever been in my life, another bright-faced dancer joins me. We dance and kiss each other and hold each other through the night. The other dancer has obviously come through all right, as I have done. She is beautiful, whole, and free. And she is also me.

The Reader's Presence

1. In her opening paragraph, Walker refers to her father's "beautiful eyes." How does that phrase take on more significance in rereading? Can you find other words, phrases, or images that do the same? For example, why might Walker have mentioned the pain of having her hair combed?

2. Note that Walker uses the present tense throughout the essay. Why might this be unusual, given her subject? What effect does it have for both writer and reader? Try rewriting the opening paragraph in the past tense. What difference do you think it makes?

3. **CONNECTIONS:**   What is the meaning of Walker's occasional italicized comments? What do they have in common? Whose comments are they? To whom do they seem addressed? What time frame do they seem to be in? What purpose do you think they serve? How do they compare to those of Judith Ortiz Cofer in "Silent Dancing" (page 88)?

---

[1] **Morehouse:** Morehouse College, a black men's college in Atlanta, Georgia. —EDS.

Jerald Walker

SCATTERED INCONVENIENCES

JERALD WALKER (b. 1964) was born and raised on Chicago's South Side. He attended the Iowa Writers' Workshop and later earned a PhD in interdisciplinary studies from the University of Iowa. The winner of a James A. Michener Fellowship, he has published works in numerous periodicals such as the *Iowa Review*, the *Chronicle of Higher Education*, *Mother Jones*, *Harvard Review*, and *Creative Nonfiction*, and his essays have been selected for both *The Best American Essays* and *The Best African American Essays*. He was the chair of the Writing, Literature, and Publishing Faculty at Emerson College in Boston. His memoir, *Street Shadows: A Memoir of Race, Rebellion, and Redemption* (2010), received the 2011 L. L. Winship/PEN New England Award. "Scattered Inconveniences" appeared in the *North American Review* in 2006.

> Jerald Walker was born and raised on Chicago's South Side.

HE BARRELED up on our left, momentarily matched our speed, then surged forward and waved a cowboy hat out the window, a bull rider in a brown Chevy. Somehow I knew he would swerve into our lane and slow down, and as he did the sound of his horn came to us over the rumble of our truck's engine. We were in a seventeen-foot Ryder that held everything we owned, junk, pretty much, with ten feet to spare. Those were, we believed, the final days of poverty. After not being able to find a teaching job for three years since completing her doctorate in art history, my wife had landed a rare tenure-track position at a state college in New England, twelve hundred miles east of Iowa City where we'd spent ten years living with tornadoes, academics, and hippies. I was going to be a stay-at-home dad, watching our fifteen-month-old during the day and writing at night. It was the perfect scenario, one we'd dreamt of for so long. All I had to do now was prevent the man in the Chevy from killing us.

I gripped the steering wheel tighter, checked the rearview mirrors in case a sudden maneuver was necessary. There were no vehicles within twenty yards, besides our reckless escort, just ten feet away.

"This guy's drunk or something," Brenda said.

I shook my head. "I *told you* we shouldn't drive in the middle of the night."

"It's only eight."

I checked the clock on the dashboard. "8:10."

5

"Well, you could just *slow down*," she said, "and let him go."

"Or," I responded, "I could crush him."

"And injure your son in the process?"

I glanced to my right. Adrian slept between us in his child seat, oblivious   10
that we were being menaced by a fool, and that his daddy, in certain situations, particularly those that involved motor vehicles and testosterone, was
a fool, too. I tugged at his harness, and confirmed that it was secure, then
gunned the engine and lurched the truck forward. Brenda punched my arm. I
lifted my foot off the accelerator and watched the speedometer topple from 70
to 55, where I leveled off. For a few seconds there was a gentlemanly distance
between us and the Chevy, and then it slowed, too, until it was again ten feet
from our bumper. This time I held my ground. I could feel Brenda tensing. I
lowered my window and gave him the finger, Adrian stirring as wind tore into
the cab. Brenda called me an ass, though not audibly. We'd been together
long enough that the actual use of words, at times like those, was unnecessary.

The Chevy suddenly braked and I had to as well to avoid a collision.
My heart was racing now. I tried hard to believe that we weren't dealing
with something more ominous than a souse. We were in Indiana, a state I
vaguely remembered hearing was a breeding ground for racists; perhaps
the random sight of a black family had proved too irresistible, a cat straying
into an angry dog's view.

But I had heard similar things about Iowa, only later to experience no
problems. "No problems" is not to say "nothing," though, for there were
what a black intellectual referred to as "scattered inconveniences"—women
crossing the street or removing their purses from grocery carts at my
approach, security guards following me in department stores. Once, while
I was working out in the university's gym, two young men, looking my way
and laughing, began mimicking the walk of a gorilla. Silly, all of it, confirmation that the bigotry my parents faced no longer exists, that its sledgeham-
mer impact has been reduced, for the most part, to pebbles pitched from
a naughty child's hand. I tell myself to find victory in encounters such as
these. And I usually do. But sometimes I can't because of one simple truth:
I am a racist.

Like a recovering alcoholic, I recognize that to define myself by my disease is in some way to help guard against relapse, that there is daily salvation in this constant reminder of who and what I am. My quest to be rid of all
traces of this scourge has not been easy, though I have made good progress,
considering I was born during the sixties in a segregated Chicago. The communities I grew up in were dangerous and poor, and it was the common
opinion of nearly everyone I knew that, when all was said and done, whites
were to blame. Whites discriminated against us. Whites denied us decent
housing. Whites caused us to have high unemployment and failed schools.
Crack had come from whites, and so too had AIDS. Whites, in some vague
and yet indisputable way, made the winos drink and gangbangers kill. I
came to believe, at a very early age, that in order to succeed I would have to
beat the system through the mastery of some criminal enterprise, or join it in

the form of a Sambo, a sell-out, an Oreo, an Uncle Tom. In other words, I'd have to be my brother Clyde.

Clyde, who said things like, "Whites aren't an obstacle to success," and "Only *you* can stop *you*."

We didn't like Clyde.   15

We watched him with disgust as he became a teenager and continued to speak without slang or profanity. He wore straight-legs and loafers instead of bellbottoms and four-inch stacks, his only concession to soulful style an afro, which *could* have been bigger. He held a job during high school and still earned straight A's. After graduation he studied computers when his friends aspired to be postal clerks or pimps.

Our father threw him out. He was twenty-one. My twin brother and I, at fourteen, just on the threshold of a decade of lawlessness, had come home one night drunk. Clyde beat us sober with a pool stick. Outside of a few times at church, it was many years before we saw him socially again. I didn't know where he spent his exile. I was not surprised, though, when he resurfaced in the eighties in a Ford AeroStar with a Ronald Reagan sticker on his bumper. He'd rejected liberal black ideology his whole life, and so his emergence as a staunch conservative made perfect sense, as much sense as me, twenty years later, being tempted to crush a white man on I-80.

The Chevy switched lanes again, this time to the right. The driver was shouting at us through his opened window. I ignored him. He blew his horn.

Brenda asked, "What do you think he wants?"

"Our lives," I said.   20

He blew his horn again.

"I'm going to open my window and see what he wants."

"Do *not* do that!"

She opened her window. I couldn't make out what he was saying, and Brenda was practically hanging out the window to hear him. I leaned towards them while trying to keep the truck steady. Brenda suddenly whirled to face me. Her eyes were wide. "Stop the truck!" she demanded.

"*Why?*"   25

"The back door is open! The washer's about to fall out!"

We were towing our car behind us; the perilousness of the situation was instantly clear.

I put on my right signal and began to work my way to the shoulder. The man tooted his horn and gave me a thumbs-up, then rode off into the night. Adrian was crying and I wondered for how long. His pacifier had fallen. Brenda rooted it from his seat and slipped it between his lips. He puffed on it fiendishly, like it was long-denied nicotine.

We'd come to a stop. Our hazards were flashing. Cars and trucks rocked us gently as they hurled themselves east, towards the Promised Land. Before I opened my door, Brenda and I exchanged a quick glance. I did not have to actually say I was sorry. She did not have to actually say she forgave me. ▨

The Reader's Presence

1. Why does Walker title his essay "Scattered Inconveniences"? Where in the essay do we find the phrase used? Who said it and in what context does it appear? What meaning does it take on with respect to racism? Do you think the incident Walker describes is an example of a scattered inconvenience in the same sense that the phrase appears in the essay? Why or why not?

2. In paragraph 12, Walker admits to being "a racist." In what sense is he one? Is his racism shown in the essay? If so, how? If not, why does he introduce the subject? Consider Walker's brother Clyde, who plays a fairly large part in this brief essay. What does Clyde's presence have to do with Walker's main point in the essay?

3. **CONNECTIONS:**   Consider Walker's essay along with Brent Staples's "Just Walk on By: A Black Man Ponders His Power to Alter Public Space" (page 260). How would you differentiate the racial factors in each essay? How does Staples's essay conform to Walker's advice on how to tell a good story?

The Writer at Work

JERALD WALKER on Telling a Good Story

Brenda Molife

As a creative writing instructor, Jerald Walker wants his students to concentrate more on story *telling* and less on the lesson or point they want to make. Nevertheless, invited by the editors to discuss his own essay and what it means to him as a reader (and not as a writer), Walker discovers that it contains a moral or point he did not set out to make. His brief explanation makes us aware that writing to a large extent is an act of discovery. But that discovery could only happen in the process of constructing the story.

❝One thing I constantly urge my creative writing students to do is to lay off the metaphors. Go easy on morals, lessons, and "points"—it's the reader's job to worry about those. Your job is simply to try to tell a good story. That was what I tried to do in "Scattered Inconveniences." However, much to my delight (I was tempted to say "surprise," but I've come to expect surprises in the act of writing, so now I'm merely delighted when they occur), I later discovered it to be highly metaphorical. As a *reader* of this essay, I could make a case that the man in the Chevy represents the sin of American racism—slavery, discrimination, and other forms of bigotry that may at any moment barrel forth to make terribly disruptive appearances in our lives. When it cannot appear itself, which these days is more often the case than not, for an exceedingly long and reckless life has left it frail and feeble, it sends an able representative, known as paranoia. I have experienced a great deal of paranoia in the black community. On Chicago's South Side, where I was raised, there always seemed to be the suspicion, if not the outright prediction, that the blatant racism practiced in previous generations would make a triumphant comeback— indeed, in the minds of some people it never left. The paranoia created by racism, it seems to me, is often worse than racism itself, in the way that not knowing something is often worse than knowing. The phrase, "*Please*, Doc, just give it to me straight!" comes to mind.

But as my wife, son, and I traveled in our truck through Indiana, I could not have it given to me straight. I did not know the intentions of the man in the Chevy. And so, regrettably, I assumed the worst. Here my actions were metaphorical, too, for what better way to express how so many racial conflicts could be averted if we simply learned to give each other the benefit of the doubt. For me, that is sometimes easier said than done, but it is what I—what we all—must constantly aspire to if complete racial reconciliation will ever be achieved. Which leads me to another metaphor, as embodied in Adrian, my toddler, sleeping so peacefully until I lost my cool; he is, of course, the future. As a result of fear and mistrust, the future is placed in jeopardy. Perhaps that is ultimately the lesson of "Scattered Inconveniences"; maybe that is its moral or "point." I will leave that for each reader to decide, because, as the *writer*, I did not set out with any of these in mind. I was simply trying to tell a good story. **"**

LAUREN CARTER
Isn't Watermelon Delicious?

Courtesy of Lauren Carter

Lauren Carter graduated from Bridgewater State University in Massachusetts with a degree in English. While at Bridgewater, Carter served as editor in chief of the literary magazine *The Bridge*, where her essay, "Isn't Watermelon Delicious?" first appeared. After graduating, she began to write for a newspaper full time and currently works as a freelance writer for several publications. Her topics include music and race, and she encourages fellow student writers not to "look at writing as drudgery [but to] view it as an opportunity to express yourself."

Carter wrote the following essay as a response to an assignment in an undergraduate African American literature course taught at Bridgewater State University by Jerald Walker, the author of the preceding selection. Professor Walker, who is the chair of the Writing, Literature, and Publishing Faculty at Emerson College, generously supplied us with the actual assignment.

> **Assignment:** Malon Riggs's documentary *Black Is . . . Black Ain't . . .* ends with the following quotation: "If you have received no clear cut impression of what The Negro in America is like, then you are in the same place with me. There is no The Negro here" (Zora Neale Hurston). Hurston's point, it seems to me, is that Negroes (or coloreds or blacks or Afro-Americans or African Americans) come in such varieties that they are impossible to define as a homogeneous group. Much of this variety can be said to be the result of blues/jazz idiom, how blacks are constantly improvising new identities in an effort to adapt to changing conditions and needs. Likewise, African American fiction writers are constantly improvising on the theme of "blackness" in order to produce works that attempt to offer at least partial definitions of what it means to be African American. In your essay, work your way through the literature read in this class and discuss how each author adds to our understanding of what it means to be black.

As you read Carter's response to the assignment, observe how she blends her personal experiences of being a young black woman with a number of relevant literary works she read for Professor Walker's course. Her essay is prompted by a friend's comment about behavior corresponding to race. Where else does Carter encounter this idea? What questions does she raise about how people understand race?

Opens effectively with a vivid description of a specific setting.

It was just another Thursday night at Axis. White lights were flashing, music was pumping, and I was mildly buzzed. My best friend Stacey and I were making our way around the edges of the crowded dance floor, looking for a table where we could plop down and briefly escape the frenzy of the hot, crowded club. Then my favorite song came on. I don't remember what song it was; it was a long time ago and I usually had a new favorite song every other week. But at the time, the song that started playing was my favorite one, and I was ecstatic. As soon as I heard the bass line I guzzled what was left of my drink, broke out into some kind of over-enthusiastic dance move, and shouted "Let's go!"

Stacey looked over at me and laughed.

"God, Lauren," she said, "sometimes you're so white, and sometimes you're soooo black."

Introduces her central topic through dialogue.

It was an interesting idea. That I could be one or the other, at different times. I wondered when I was which one. So I asked her.

She started to answer, but the music was too loud, and I couldn't really make out what she was saying. I leaned in closer and asked her to repeat what she said, but she waved the idea away, saying we should go dance.

Yes, we should dance, I thought. My favorite song was on and we were attempting to have a conversation meant for a quiet café, not a loud, crowded club.

We never did have that conversation, and I never did get the answer I was looking for. What, exactly, I did that was so white. And what, exactly, I did that was so black. But the idea stuck with me. That a behavior related to a skin tone. That my behavior related to two different ones.

It wasn't a totally new idea. My black cousin Shea had told me for years that I acted "so white." I thought I was just acting like me, but apparently, with my Bart Simpson t-shirt, my "proper" speech, and my affinity for Vanilla Ice, I was masquerading as a white girl in a black girl's body. I didn't know those characteristics belonged exclusively to white people. I thought they belonged to people who liked the occasional Simpsons t-shirt, spoke the way they had learned to speak, and enjoyed listening to extremely cheesy, albeit catchy, quasi-rap music.

Or at least that's how I feel now. But then, I felt inferior—way behind in the race for true blackness. I would never catch up to her. I'd never know all the latest black sayings, never listen to all the latest black music, never wear all the latest black clothing. I'd never be as black as she was. Or so I thought.

> Fulfills writing assignment by introducing course readings that she clearly connects to her personal experience.

But that's before I met the Ex-Colored Man.[1] In his autobiography, he switched from white to black and back again, though his skin color never changed. When he discovered his blackness as a child, he still looked like a white person. But internally, he realized there was black blood running through his veins, or rather blue blood with black ancestry in it, and he withdrew. He wasn't what he thought he'd been. He couldn't stop thinking about his new blackness. Really, though, nothing had changed. Externally, at least.

[1] ***Ex-Colored Man:*** Referenced in Works Cited (page 292). —EDS.

So it kind of surprised me when, at the end of his story, he chose to become white again. This, after feeling mortified and ashamed that in a country like America, with all its talk of democracy and freedom, the black race could be persecuted so harshly. While I could attempt to analyze and judge his decision to forsake his blackness in order to better his condition, decide whether he had succumbed to the race game or merely decided to stop playing, the validity of his decision isn't as important as the fact that it could be made. That he could become white again, simply by deciding to be. It was a miraculous transformation. Which got me to thinking, if you can miraculously transform from black to white, or vice versa, then how real is either category?

My sister transforms all the time, depending on who's looking at her. She's black in terms of ancestry. Partially, anyway. Our mother's Italian, her father's black. And though her hair came out extremely nappy, her skin is light. Whiter than some "white" people's skin, in fact. Now that she chemically straightens her hair, most people don't know she's black unless she tells them. She can pass. Not among black people, of course, myself included. We can all see it in her features. But to the untrained eye, amongst the world at large, she can generally be perceived as white. So which is she? Is she what her ancestry dictates, or what other people's perception decides?

It's a ridiculous question, I know. But only as ridiculous as the fallacy it's based on. When you lump a group of people together based solely on the color of their skin, of course ridiculous questions like these come up. It'd be the same if you lumped them together based on eye color, height, or any other arbitrary characteristic over which they have no control.

Funny, that we would choose to separate and define people based on factors beyond their control. Well, maybe not funny. But certainly ingenious. And an excellent way to subordinate one group in order to elevate another. Because isn't it true that all of these external factors, in actuality, say nothing about a person's character, that the only real measure of a person is in their actions, not any physical characteristic? Isn't it true that anyone who has survived and succeeded in any facet of life did so almost exclusively because of their intellect, their intelligence, their will to persevere,

Poses a question that goes to the heart of her essay.

not because of the pigment in their skin or the fullness of their features?

When Frederick Douglass found ways to teach himself to read, it wasn't because of his melanin content. It was because of his desire to learn, his ingenuity, his intelligence.

After six months of torture by his brutal master Covey, Douglass made the bold and beautiful statement: "You have seen how a man was made a slave; now you shall see how a slave was made a man."

And when he did make that journey from slavery to manhood, it wasn't because of the coil of his hair, it was because of the color of his character. When Gabriel Prosser[2] decided to lead a revolt in pursuit of freedom, it wasn't because of the size of his muscles, it was because of the size of his spirit. When blacks survived slavery, it wasn't because of the width of their noses or how many calluses they did or didn't have on their hands. It was because of the survival strategies they'd developed over time, none of which had anything to do with appearance.

The folktales and spirituals that emerged out of that era weren't developed because of the shape of someone's kneecaps; they were developed because of a will to overcome seemingly insurmountable obstacles. And when Bigger Thomas, the main character in Richard Wright's famous novel, *Native Son*, became the agent of his own demise, it wasn't, contrary to his own beliefs, because of the darkness of his skin; it was because of the darkness of his mind, and all of the things he believed he would never, and so never did, achieve.

Maybe life would be simpler if skin color really was an indicator of character, external factors determined internal worth, and similar complexions could unite us all. Then all the dark-skinned peoples of America could heed Marcus Garvey's[3] message and return home to Africa. We could take a giant plane to Uganda, and when it landed we could step down off it with open arms and scream, "Hello black people, I'm finally home!!" But in reality, that probably

References more of her reading by providing summaries that also support her contention about character and determination.

---

[2] *Gabriel Prosser* (1776–1800): A blacksmith who was executed for planning a slave rebellion near Richmond, Virginia, in 1800. —EDS.
[3] *Marcus Garvey* (1887–1940): A Jamaican journalist known for his Black Nationalism movement. —EDS.

wouldn't work. Those Ugandans would only point out what I've come to realize over the past semester: that the significance of skin color is that it is the color of one's skin, and not much more. That it does not necessarily imply a common set of values, a standard behavior, a singular way of life.

And why should it? Aren't there a number of ways that human beings can define themselves as individuals? What about gender? Profession? Religious beliefs? Hobbies? Personality? Sexual orientation? Values? What about your attitude towards yourself, towards others, towards life? Isn't it true that race is just one ingredient in a large and complicated recipe? Why must it be the main ingredient and define all the other areas of life? I know that my life is about much more than being black, and, for that matter, being black is about much more than my skin color.

Uses a series of questions to reinforce her main point.

Which leads to the question: What is my blackness about? When am I really black? When I start celebrating Kwanzaa? When I fill my wardrobe with Roc-A-Wear and Phat Farm? When I stop playing Elton John? Is that what blackness is? A holiday? A piece of clothing? A song?

Funny, I never thought of being black that way. I never considered that a Dashiki would give me blackness, and I never thought that a lack of one would take it away. I always thought of black as a state of mind; a way of looking at the world. Perseverance in the face of any and all obstacles. Winning when everyone says you're bound to lose. I never looked at the color of my skin as evidence of a drum, or a slice of watermelon. I never thought I had to do, have, or say anything at all to be black. I just thought I was.

Responds to cousin's remark introduced in paragraph 8.

I never told her so, but when Shea said I was acting "so white," she was wrong. Whites don't have a monopoly on listening to Vanilla Ice, and even if they could have one, I doubt they'd want it. I was acting like me. I don't need to walk the streets with a sandwich board proclaiming what I am. I don't need to act out my blackness, just like I don't need to act out my eye color; it's simply an intrinsic part of who I am.

True, the color of my skin implies an ancestry that the color of my eyes does not, and I'm aware of that ancestry; I draw from it daily. But I don't need to wear Lugz and use slang to prove it. Maya Angelou wrote "I am the dream and the hope of the slave," and I haven't forgotten about those hopes and dreams. I understand the debt that I owe to my ancestors, and I pay it back every day, in my own way, that has nothing to do with what jeans I wear, and has everything to do with how I live my life. The size of my nose is not my inheritance. The will to survive is.

Stacey's statement in that nightclub was probably my first—or at least my most memorable—experience with double consciousness as civil rights activist W. E. B. DuBois described it, of being conscious not only of how you see yourself, but how others see you; I'd never thought of myself solely in terms of white and black, but I realized the extent to which other people could. For a long time after that night I wondered where the line between black and white was, and in what moments I crossed it. I don't wonder about that line anymore. Blackness no longer boils down to a t-shirt, or a desire to dance. It's just not that simple. Blackness is the legacy left by the people that came before me, and it's the legacy I'll leave behind me when I'm gone.

Concludes by returning to her friend's comment in opening scene and effectively introduces the concept of "double consciousness" she learned from her reading.

Works Cited

Angelou, Maya. "Still I Rise." *The Complete Collected Poems of Maya Angelou*, Random House, 1994.

Bontemps, Arna. *Black Thunder*. Beacon Press, 1992.

Douglass, Frederick. *Narrative of the Life of Frederick Douglass, an American Slave*. Barnes & Noble Classics, 2003.

DuBois, W. E. B. *The Souls of Black Folk*. Bedford/St. Martin's, 1997.

Johnson, James Weldon. *The Autobiography of an Ex-Colored Man*. Vintage Books, 1989.

Wright, Richard. *Native Son*. Harper Perennial Classics, 2003.

E. B. White

ONCE MORE TO THE LAKE

ELWYN BROOKS WHITE (1899–1985) started contributing to the *New Yorker* soon after the magazine began publication in 1925, and in the "Talk of the Town" and other columns helped establish the magazine's reputation for precise and brilliant prose. Collections of his contributions can be found in *Every Day Is Saturday* (1934), *Quo Vadimus?* (1939), and *The Wild Flag* (1946). He also wrote essays for *Harper's* on a regular basis; these essays include "Once More to the Lake" and are collected in *One Man's Meat* (1941). In his comments on this work, the critic Jonathan Yardley observed that White is "one of the few writers of this or any century who has succeeded in transforming the ephemera of journalism into something that demands to be called literature."

> "I have always felt that the first duty of a writer was to ascend—to make flights, carrying others along if he could manage it."

Capable of brilliant satire, White could also be sad and serious, as in his compilation of forty years of writing, *Essays* (1977). Among his numerous awards and honors, White received the American Academy of Arts and Letters Gold Medal (1960), a Presidential Medal of Freedom (1963), and a National Medal for Literature (1971). He made a lasting contribution to children's literature with *Stuart Little* (1945), *Charlotte's Web* (1952), and *The Trumpet of the Swan* (1970).

White has written, "I have always felt that the first duty of a writer was to ascend—to make flights, carrying others along if he could manage it." According to White, the writer needs not only courage but also hope and faith to accomplish this goal: "Writing itself is an act of faith, nothing else. And it must be the writer, above all others, who keeps it alive—choked with laughter, or with pain."

ONE SUMMER, along about 1904, my father rented a camp on a lake in Maine and took us all there for the month of August. We all got ring-worm from some kittens and had to rub Pond's Extract on our arms and legs night and morning, and my father rolled over in a canoe with all his clothes on; but outside of that the vacation was a success and from then on none of us ever thought there was any place in the world like that lake in Maine. We returned summer after summer—always on August 1st for one month. I have since become a salt-water man, but sometimes in summer there are days when the restlessness of the tides and the fearful cold of the sea water and the incessant wind that blows across the afternoon and into the evening make me wish for the placidity of a lake in the woods. A few weeks ago this feeling got so strong I bought myself a couple of bass hooks and a spinner and returned to the lake where we used to go, for a week's fishing and to revisit old haunts.

I took along my son, who had never had any fresh water up his nose and who had seen lily pads only from train windows. On the journey over to the lake I began to wonder what it would be like. I wondered how time would have marred this unique, this holy spot—the coves and streams, the hills that the sun set behind, the camps and the paths behind the camps. I was sure that the tarred road would have found it out and I wondered in what other ways it would be desolated. It is strange how much you can remember about places like that once you allow your mind to return into the grooves that lead back. You remember one thing, and that suddenly reminds you of another thing. I guess I remembered clearest of all the early mornings, when the lake was cool and motionless, remembered how the bedroom smelled of the lumber it was made of and the wet woods whose scent entered through the screen. The partitions in the camp were thin and did not extend clear to the top of the rooms, and as I was always the first up I would dress softly so as not to wake the others, and sneak out into the sweet outdoors and start out in the canoe, keeping close along the shore in the long shadows of the pines. I remembered being very careful never to rub my paddle against the gunwale for fear of disturbing the stillness of the cathedral.

The lake had never been what you would call a wild lake. There were cottages sprinkled about the shores, and it was in farming country although the shores of the lake were quite heavily wooded. Some of the cottages were owned by nearby farmers, and you would live at the shore and eat your meals at the farmhouse. That's what our family did. But although it wasn't wild, it was a fairly large and undisturbed lake and there were places in it which, to a child at least, seemed infinitely remote and primeval.

I was right about the tar: It led to within half a mile of the shore. But when I got back there, with my boy, and we settled into a camp near a farmhouse and into the kind of summertime I had known, I could tell that it was going to be pretty much the same as it had been before—I knew it, lying in bed the first morning, smelling the bedroom, and hearing the boy sneak quietly out and go off along the shore in a boat. I began to sustain the illusion that he was I, and therefore, by simple transposition, that I was my father. This sensation persisted, kept cropping up all the time we were there. It was not an entirely new feeling, but in this setting it grew much stronger. I seemed to be living a dual existence. I would be in the middle of some simple act, I would be picking up a bait box or laying down a table fork, or I would be saying something, and suddenly it would be not I but my father who was saying the words or making the gesture. It gave me a creepy sensation.

We went fishing the first morning. I felt the same damp moss covering   5
the worms in the bait can, and saw the dragonfly alight on the tip of my rod as it hovered a few inches from the surface of the water. It was the arrival of this fly that convinced me beyond any doubt that everything was as it always had been, that the years were a mirage and there had been no years. The small waves were the same, chucking the rowboat under the chin as we fished at anchor, and the boat was the same boat, the same color green and the ribs broken in the same places, and under the floor-boards the same fresh-water leavings and debris — the dead hellgrammite, the wisps of moss, the rusty discarded fishhook, the dried blood from yesterday's catch. We stared silently at the tips of our rods, at the dragonflies that came and went. I lowered the tip of mine into the water, tentatively, pensively dislodging the fly, which darted two feet away, poised, darted two feet back, and came to rest again a little farther up the rod. There had been no years between the ducking of this dragonfly and the other one — the one that was part of memory. I looked at the boy, who was silently watching his fly, and it was my hands that held his rod, my eyes watching. I felt dizzy and didn't know which rod I was at the end of.

We caught two bass, hauling them in briskly as though they were mackerel, pulling them over the side of the boat in a businesslike manner without any landing net, and stunning them with a blow on the back of the head. When we got back for a swim before lunch, the lake was exactly where we had left it, the same number of inches from the dock, and there was only the merest suggestion of a breeze. This seemed an utterly enchanted sea, this lake you could leave to its own devices for a few hours and come back to, and find that it had not stirred, this constant and trustworthy body of water. In the shallows, the dark, watersoaked sticks and twigs, smooth and old, were undulating in clusters on the bottom against the clean ribbed sand, and the track of the mussel was plain. A school of minnows swam by, each minnow with its small individual shadow, doubling the attendance, so clear and sharp in the sunlight. Some of the other campers were in swimming, along the shore, one of them with a cake of soap, and the water felt thin and clear and unsubstantial. Over the years there had been this person with the cake of soap, this cultist, and here he was. There had been no years.

Up to the farmhouse to dinner through the teeming, dusty field, the road under our sneakers was only a two-track road. The middle track was missing, the one with the marks of the hooves and splotches of dried, flaky manure. There had always been three tracks to choose from in choosing which track to walk in; now the choice was narrowed down to two. For a moment I missed terribly the middle alternative. But the way led past the tennis court, and something about the way it lay there in the sun reassured me; the tape had loosened along the backline, the alleys were green with plantains and other weeds, and the net (installed in June and removed in September) sagged in the dry noon, and the whole place steamed with midday heat and hunger and emptiness. There was a choice of pie for dessert, and one was blueberry and one was apple, and the waitresses were the same country girls, there having been no passage of time, only the illusion of it as in a dropped curtain—the waitresses were still fifteen; their hair had been washed, that was the only difference—they had been to the movies and seen the pretty girls with the clean hair.

Summertime, oh summertime, pattern of life indelible, the fade-proof lake, the woods unshatterable, the pasture with the sweetfern and the juniper forever and ever, summer without end; this was the background, and the life along the shore was the design, the cottages with their innocent and tranquil design, their tiny docks with the flagpole and the American flag floating against the white clouds in the blue sky, the little paths over the roots of the trees leading from camp to camp and the paths leading back to the outhouses and the can of lime for sprinkling, and at the souvenir counters at the store the miniature birch-bark canoes and the post cards that showed things looking a little better than they looked. This was the American family at play, escaping the city heat, wondering whether the newcomers in the camp at the head of the cove were "common" or "nice," wondering whether it was true that the people who drove up for Sunday dinner at the farmhouse were turned away because there wasn't enough chicken.

It seemed to me, as I kept remembering all this, that those times and those summers had been infinitely precious and worth saving. There had been jollity and peace and goodness. The arriving (at the beginning of August) had been so big a business in itself, at the railway station the farm wagon drawn up, the first smell of the pine-laden air, the first glimpse of the smiling farmer, and the great importance of the trunks and your father's enormous authority in such matters, and the feel of the wagon under you for the long ten-mile haul, and at the top of the last long hill catching the first view of the lake after eleven months of not seeing this cherished body of water. The shouts and cries of the other campers when they saw you, and the trunks to be unpacked, to give up their rich burden. (Arriving was less exciting nowadays, when you sneaked up in your car and parked it under a tree near the camp and took out the bags and in five minutes it was all over, no fuss, no loud wonderful fuss about trunks).

Peace and goodness and jollity. The only thing that was wrong now,   10
really, was the sound of the place, an unfamiliar nervous sound of the outboard motors. This was the note that jarred, the one thing that would sometimes break the illusion and set the years moving. In those other summertimes all motors were inboard; and when they were at a little distance, the noise they made was a sedative, an ingredient of summer sleep. They were one-cylinder and two-cylinder engines, and some were make-and-break and some were jump-spark, but they all made a sleepy sound across the lake. The one-lungers throbbed and fluttered, and the twin-cylinder ones purred and purred, and that was a quiet sound too. But now the campers all had outboards. In the daytime, in the hot mornings, these motors made a petulant, irritable sound; at night, in the still evening when the afterglow

lit the water, they whined about one's ears like mosquitoes. My boy loved our rented outboard, and his great desire was to achieve singlehanded mastery over it, and authority, and he soon learned the trick of choking it a little (but not too much), and the adjustment of the needle valve. Watching him I would remember the things you could do with the old one-cylinder engines with the heavy flywheel, how you could have it eating out of your hand if you got really close to it spiritually. Motor boats in those days didn't have clutches, and you would make a landing by shutting off the motor at the proper time and coasting in with a dead rudder. But there was a way of reversing them, if you learned the trick, by cutting the switch and putting it on again exactly on the final dying revolution of the flywheel, so that it would kick back against compression and begin reversing. Approaching a dock in a strong following breeze, it was difficult to slow up sufficiently by the ordinary coasting method, and if a boy felt he had complete mastery over his motor, he was tempted to keep it running beyond its time and then reverse it a few feet from the dock. It took a cool nerve, because if you threw the switch a twentieth of a second too soon you could catch the flywheel when it still had speed enough to go up past center, and the boat would leap ahead, charging bull-fashion at the dock.

We had a good week at the camp. The bass were biting well and the sun shone endlessly, day after day. We would be tired at night and lie down in the accumulated heat of the little bedrooms after the long hot day and the breeze would stir almost imperceptibly outside and the smell of the swamp drift in through the rusty screens. Sleep would come easily and in the morning the red squirrel would be on the roof, tapping out his gay routine. I kept remembering everything, lying in bed in the mornings—the small steamboat that had a long rounded stern like the lip of a Ubangi, and how quietly she ran on the moonlight sails, when the older boys played their mandolins and the girls sang and we ate doughnuts dipped in sugar, and how sweet the music was on the water in the shining night, and what it had felt like to think about girls then. After breakfast we would go up to the store and the things were in the same place—the minnows in a bottle, the plugs and spinners disarranged and pawed over by the youngsters from the boys' camp, the Fig Newtons and the Beeman's gum. Outside, the road was tarred and cars stood in front of the store. Inside, all was just as it had always been, except there was more Coca-Cola and not so much Moxie and root beer and birch beer and sarsaparilla. We would walk out with a bottle of pop apiece and sometimes the pop would backfire up our noses and hurt. We explored the streams, quietly, where the turtles slid off the sunny logs and dug their way into the soft bottom; and we lay on the town wharf and fed worms to the tame bass. Everywhere we went I had trouble making out which was I, the one walking at my side, the one walking in my pants.

One afternoon while we were there at that lake a thunderstorm came up. It was like the revival of an old melodrama that I had seen long ago with childish awe. The second-act climax of the drama of the electrical disturbance over a lake in America had not changed in any important respect.

This was the big scene, still the big scene. The whole thing was so familiar, the first feeling of oppression and heat and a general air around camp of not wanting to go very far away. In midafternoon (it was all the same) a curious darkening of the sky, and a lull in everything that had made life tick; and then the way the boats suddenly swung the other way at their moorings with the coming of a breeze out of the new quarter, and the premonitory rumble. Then the kettle drum, then the snare, then the bass drum and cymbals, then crackling light against the dark, and the gods grinning and licking their chops in the hills. Afterward the calm, the rain steadily rustling in the calm lake, the return of light and hope and spirits, and the campers running out in joy and relief to go swimming in the rain, their bright cries perpetuating the deathless joke about how they were getting simply drenched, and the children screaming with delight at the new sensation of bathing in the rain, and the joke about getting drenched linking the generations in a strong indestructible chain. And the comedian who waded in carrying an umbrella.

When the others went swimming my son said he was going in too. He pulled his dripping trunks from the line where they had hung all through the shower, and wrung them out. Languidly, and with no thought of going in, I watched him, his hard little body, skinny and bare, saw him wince slightly as he pulled up around his vitals the small, soggy, icy garment. As he buckled the swollen belt suddenly my groin felt the chill of death. ●

The Reader's Presence

1. In paragraph 2, White begins to reflect on the way his memory works. How does he follow the process of remembering throughout the essay? Are his memories of the lake safely stored in the past? If not, why not?

2. Go through the essay and identify words and images having to do with the sensory details of seeing, hearing, touching, and so on. How do these details contribute to the overall effect of the essay? How do they anticipate White's final paragraph?

3. **VISUAL PRESENCE:**   Examine the photograph of E. B. White (page 299). Which specific aspects of this portrait capture your attention? Explain why. How are White's writing style and subject matter reflected in this picture? Cite specific details from the image as you develop your response.

4. **CONNECTIONS:**   In paragraph 4, White refers to a "creepy sensation." What is the basis of that sensation? Why is it "creepy"? What is the "dual existence" White feels he is living? How does the essay build the story of White's relationships with both his father and his son? Compare this account of intergenerational intimacy to Raymond Carver's essay "My Father's Life" (page 81).

The Writer at Work

E. B. WHITE on the Essayist

New York Times Co./Getty Images

For several generations, E. B. White has remained America's best-known essayist, his works widely available and widely anthologized. Yet in the foreword to his 1977 collected essays, when he addresses the role of the essayist, he sounds wholly modest not only about his career but about his chosen genre: In the world of literature, he writes, the essayist is a "second-class citizen."

Why do you think White thinks of himself that way, and how might that self-deprecation be reconciled with the claims of his final two paragraphs? Do you think White's description of himself as an essayist matches the actual essayist we encounter in "Once More to the Lake"? Also, do you think White's persistent use of the male pronoun is merely for grammatical convenience (the essay was written in 1977) or reflects a gender bias on his part?

❝ The essayist is a self-liberated man, sustained by the childish belief that everything he thinks about, everything that happens to him, is of general interest. He is a fellow who thoroughly enjoys his work, just as people who take bird walks enjoy theirs. Each new excursion of the essayist, each new "attempt," differs from the last and takes him into new country. This delights him. Only a person who is congenitally self-centered has the effrontery and the stamina to write essays.

There are as many kinds of essays as there are human attitudes or poses, as many essay flavors as there are Howard Johnson ice creams. The essayist arises in the morning and, if he has work to do, selects his garb from an unusually extensive wardrobe: he can pull on any sort of shirt, be any sort of person, according to his mood or his subject matter — philosopher, scold, jester, raconteur, confidant, pundit, devil's advocate, enthusiast. I like the essay, have always liked it, and even as a child was at work, attempting to inflict my young thoughts and experiences on others by putting them on paper. I early broke into print in the pages of *St. Nicholas.*[1] I tend still to fall back on the essay form (or lack of form) when an idea strikes me, but I am not fooled about the place of the essay in twentieth century American letters — it stands a short distance down the line. The essayist, unlike the novelist, the poet, and the playwright, must be content in his self-imposed role of second-class citizen. A writer who has his sights trained on the Nobel Prize or other

[1] **St. Nicholas:** A prominent magazine for children, founded in 1873. — EDS.

earthly triumphs had best write a novel, a poem, or a play, and leave the essayist to ramble about, content with living a free life and enjoying the satisfactions of a somewhat undisciplined existence. (Dr. Johnson[2] called the essay "an irregular, undigested piece"; this happy practitioner has no wish to quarrel with the good doctor's characterization.)

There is one thing the essayist cannot do, though—he cannot indulge himself in deceit or in concealment, for he will be found out in no time. Desmond MacCarthy, in his introductory remarks to the 1928 E. P. Dutton & Company edition of Montaigne, observes that Montaigne "had the gift of natural candor. . . ." It is the basic ingredient. And even the essayist's escape from discipline is only a partial escape: the essay, although a relaxed form, imposes its own disciplines, raises

[2]*Dr. Samuel Johnson* (1709–1784): One of the most important and influential essayists and critics of the 18th century.—EDS.

its own problems, and these disciplines and problems soon become apparent and (we all hope) act as a deterrent to anyone wielding a pen merely because he entertains random thoughts or is in a happy or wandering mood.

I think some people find the essay the last resort of the egoist, a much too self-conscious and self-serving form for their tastes; they feel that it is presumptuous of a writer to assume that his little excursions or his small observations will interest the reader. There is some justice in their complaint. I have always been aware that I am by nature self-absorbed and egoistical; to write of myself to the extent I have done indicates a too great attention to my own life, not enough to the lives of others. I have worn many shirts, and not all of them have been a good fit. But when I am discouraged or downcast I need only fling open the door of my closet, and there, hidden behind everything else, hangs the mantle of Michel de Montaigne, smelling slightly of camphor. **"**

Elie Wiesel

EIGHT SIMPLE, SHORT WORDS

ELIE WIESEL (b. 1928) is a Romanian-born Jewish American writer, teacher, and human-rights activist. Born in Sighet, Transylvania (a historical region of Romania), he was fifteen years old when he was sent with his family to the Nazi concentration camp at Auschwitz. His older sisters survived the experience. His mother and younger sister did not. Elie and his father were transferred to another camp, Buchenwald, where his father died shortly before the camp was liberated in April 1945. After the war, Wiesel studied in Paris, became a journalist, and decided to write a book about his experiences in the death camps. The result was his internationally acclaimed memoir, *Night* (*La Nuit*), originally published in French in 1958 and since translated into more than thirty languages. Wiesel immigrated to the United States in 1955 and became an American citizen in 1963. Appointed chairman of the President's Commission on the Holocaust in 1978 by President Jimmy Carter, Wiesel went on to found the United States Holocaust Memorial Council in 1980. He has published more than fifty books of fiction and nonfiction and has received numerous awards for his literary and human-rights activities, including the Presidential Medal of

> **Elie Wiesel established The Elie Wiesel Foundation for Humanity, dedicated to fighting intolerance, indifference, and injustice.**

Freedom, the U.S. Congressional Gold Medal, the National Humanities Medal, the Medal of Liberty, and the rank of Grand-Croix in the French Legion of Honor. In 1986, Wiesel won the Nobel Prize for Peace. Soon after, with his wife Marion, he established The Elie Wiesel Foundation for Humanity, dedicated to fighting intolerance, indifference, and injustice. Since 1976, he has been the Andrew W. Mellon Professor in the Humanities at Boston University.

In May 1944, the police began rounding up Jews in Wiesel's hometown of Sighet, in what is now Romania, for transport in overcrowded cattle cars to the concentration camps at Auschwitz Birkenau. As the harrowing episode begins, the train has pulled out of the station at Sighet on what would be a four-day journey to the notorious camp. [Eds.]

LYING DOWN was not an option, nor could we all sit down. We decided to take turns sitting. There was little air. The lucky ones found themselves near a window; they could watch the blooming countryside flit by.

After two days of travel, thirst became intolerable, as did the heat.

Freed of normal constraints, some of the young let go of their inhibitions and, under cover of darkness, caressed one another, without any thought of others, alone in the world. The others pretended not to notice.

There was still some food left. But we never ate enough to satisfy our hunger. Our principle was to economize, to save for tomorrow. Tomorrow could be worse yet.

The train stopped in Kaschau, a small town on the Czechoslovakian   5
border. We realized then that we were not staying in Hungary. Our eyes opened. Too late.

The door of the car slid aside. A German officer stepped in accompanied by a Hungarian lieutenant, acting as his interpreter.

"From this moment on, you are under the authority of the German Army. Anyone who still owns gold, silver, or watches must hand them over now. Anyone who will be found to have kept any of these will be shot on the spot. Secondly, anyone who is ill should report to the hospital car. That's all."

The Hungarian lieutenant went around with a basket and retrieved the last possessions from those who chose not to go on tasting the bitterness of fear.

"There are eighty of you in the car," the German officer added. "If anyone goes missing, you will all be shot, like dogs."

The two disappeared. The doors clanked shut. We had fallen into the   10
trap, up to our necks. The doors were nailed, the way back irrevocably cut off. The world had become a hermetically sealed cattle car.

There was a woman among us, a certain Mrs. Schächter. She was in her fifties and her ten-year-old son was with her, crouched in a corner. Her husband and two older sons had been deported with the first transport, by mistake. The separation had totally shattered her.

I knew her well. A quiet, tense woman with piercing eyes, she had been a frequent guest in our house. Her husband was a pious man who spent most of his days and nights in the house of study. It was she who supported the family.

Mrs. Schächter had lost her mind. On the first day of the journey, she had already begun to moan. She kept asking why she had been separated from her family. Later, her sobs and screams became hysterical.

On the third night, as we were sleeping, some of us sitting, huddled against each other, some of us standing, a piercing cry broke the silence:

"Fire! I see a fire! I see a fire!"   15

There was a moment of panic. Who had screamed? It was Mrs. Schächter. Standing in the middle of the car, in the faint light filtering through the windows, she looked like a withered tree in a field of wheat. She was howling, pointing through the window:

"Look! Look at this fire! This terrible fire! Have mercy on me!"

Some pressed against the bars to see. There was nothing. Only the darkness of night.

It took us a long time to recover from this harsh awakening. We were still trembling, and with every screech of the wheels, we felt the abyss opening beneath us. Unable to still our anguish, we tried to reassure each other:

"She is mad, poor woman . . ."   20

Someone had placed a damp rag on her forehead. But she nevertheless continued to scream:

"Fire! I see a fire!"

Her little boy was crying, clinging to her skirt, trying to hold her hand:

"It's nothing, Mother! There's nothing there . . . Please sit down . . ." He pained me even more than did his mother's cries.

Some of the women tried to calm her: 25

"You'll see, you'll find your husband and sons again . . . In a few days . . ."

She continued to scream and sob fitfully.

"Jews, listen to me," she cried. "I see a fire! I see flames, huge flames!"

It was as though she were possessed by some evil spirit.

We tried to reason with her, more to calm ourselves, to catch our breath,   30
than to soothe her:

"She is hallucinating because she is thirsty, poor woman . . . That's why she speaks of flames devouring her . . ."

But it was all in vain. Our terror could no longer be contained. Our nerves had reached a breaking point. Our very skin was aching. It was as though madness had infected all of us. We gave up. A few young men forced her to sit down, then bound and gagged her.

Silence fell again. The small boy sat next to his mother, crying. I started to breathe normally again as I listened to the rhythmic pounding of the wheels on the tracks as the train raced through the night. We could begin to doze again, to rest, to dream . . .

And so an hour or two passed. Another scream jolted us. The woman had broken free of her bonds and was shouting louder than before:

"Look at the fire! Look at the flames! Flames everywhere . . ."   35

Once again, the young men bound and gagged her. When they actually struck her, people shouted their approval:

"Keep her quiet! Make that madwoman shut up. She's not the only one here . . ."

She received several blows to the head, blows that could have been lethal. Her son was clinging desperately to her, not uttering a word. He was no longer crying.

The night seemed endless. By daybreak, Mrs. Schächter had settled down. Crouching in her corner, her blank gaze fixed on some faraway place, she no longer saw us.

She remained like that all day, mute, absent, alone in the midst of us.   40
Toward evening she began to shout again:

"The fire, over there!"

She was pointing somewhere in the distance, always the same place. No one felt like beating her anymore. The heat, the thirst, the stench, the lack of air, were suffocating us. Yet all that was nothing compared to her screams, which tore us apart. A few more days and all of us would have started to scream.

But we were pulling into a station. Someone near a window read to us: "Auschwitz."

Nobody had ever heard that name.   45

The train did not move again. The afternoon went by slowly. Then the doors of the wagon slid open. Two men were given permission to fetch water.

When they came back, they told us that they had learned, in exchange for a gold watch, that this was the final destination. We were to leave the train here. There was a labor camp on the site. The conditions were good. Families would not be separated. Only the young would work in the factories. The old and the sick would find work in the fields.

Confidence soared. Suddenly we felt free of the previous nights' terror. We gave thanks to God.

Mrs. Schächter remained huddled in her corner, mute, untouched by the optimism around her. Her little one was stroking her hand.

Dusk began to fill the wagon. We ate what was left of our food. At ten   50
o'clock in the evening, we were all trying to find a position for a quick nap
and soon we were dozing. Suddenly:

"Look at the fire! Look at the flames! Over there!"

With a start, we awoke and rushed to the window yet again. We had
believed her, if only for an instant. But there was nothing outside but darkness. We returned to our places, shame in our souls but fear gnawing at us
nevertheless. As she went on howling, she was struck again. Only with great
difficulty did we succeed in quieting her down.

The man in charge of our wagon called out to a German officer strolling down the platform, asking him to have the sick woman moved to a
hospital car.

"Patience," the German replied, "patience. She'll be taken there soon."

Around eleven o'clock, the train began to move again. We pressed   55
against the windows. The convoy was rolling slowly. A quarter of an hour
later, it began to slow down even more. Through the windows, we saw
barbed wire; we understood that this was the camp.

We had forgotten Mrs. Schächter's existence. Suddenly there was a terrible scream:

"Jews, look! Look at the fire! Look at the flames!"

And as the train stopped, this time we saw flames rising from a tall chimney into a black sky.

Mrs. Schächter had fallen silent on her own. Mute again, indifferent,
absent, she had returned to her corner.

We stared at the flames in the darkness. A wretched stench floated in   60
the air. Abruptly, our doors opened. Strange-looking creatures, dressed in
striped jackets and black pants, jumped into the wagon. Holding flashlights
and sticks, they began to strike at us left and right, shouting:

"Everybody out! Leave everything inside. Hurry up!"

We jumped out. I glanced at Mrs. Schächter. Her little boy was still holding her hand.

In front of us, those flames. In the air, the smell of burning flesh. It must
have been around midnight. We had arrived. In Birkenau.

*The fifteen-year-old Elie would never see his mother and seven-year-old sis-
ter, Tzipora, again. His father was ordered to the crematorium after many
months of forced labor. The camp was liberated on April 11, 1945.* [EDS.]

The beloved objects that we had carried with us from place to place
were now left behind in the wagon and, with them, finally, our illusions.

Every few yards, there stood an SS man, his machine gun trained on us.   65
Hand in hand we followed the throng.

An SS came toward us wielding a club. He commanded:

"Men to the left! Women to the right!"

Eight words spoken quietly, indifferently, without emotion. Eight simple, short words. Yet that was the moment when I left my mother. There

was no time to think, and I already felt my father's hand press against mine: we were alone. In a fraction of a second I could see my mother, my sisters, move to the right. Tzipora was holding Mother's hand. I saw them walking farther and farther away; Mother was stroking my sister's blond hair, as if to protect her. And I walked on with my father, with the men. I didn't know that this was the moment in time and the place where I was leaving my mother and Tzipora forever. I kept walking, my father holding my hand.

Behind me, an old man fell to the ground. Nearby, an SS man replaced his revolver in its holster.

My hand tightened its grip on my father. All I could think of was not to 70 lose him. Not to remain alone.

The SS officers gave the order.

"Form ranks of fives!"

There was a tumult. It was imperative to stay together.

"Hey, kid, how old are you?"

The man interrogating me was an inmate. I could not see his face, but 75 his voice was weary and warm.

"Fifteen."

"No. You're eighteen."

"But I'm not," I said. "I'm fifteen."

"Fool. Listen to what *I* say."

Then he asked my father, who answered: 80

"I'm fifty."

"No." The man now sounded angry. "Not fifty. You're forty. Do you hear? Eighteen and forty."

He disappeared into the darkness. Another inmate appeared, unleashing a stream of invectives:

"Sons of bitches, why have you come here? Tell me, why?"

Someone dared to reply: 85

"What do you think? That we came here of our own free will? That we asked to come here?"

The other seemed ready to kill him:

"Shut up, you moron, or I'll tear you to pieces! You should have hanged yourselves rather than come here. Didn't you know what was in store for you here in Auschwitz? You didn't know? In 1944?"

True. We didn't know. Nobody had told us. He couldn't believe his ears. His tone became even harsher:

"Over there. Do you see the chimney over there? Do you see it? And 90 the flames, do you see them?" (Yes, we saw the flames.) "Over there, that's where they will take you. Over there will be your grave. You still don't understand? You sons of bitches. Don't you understand anything? You will be burned! Burned to a cinder! Turned into ashes!"

His anger changed into fury. We stood stunned, petrified. Could this be just a nightmare? An unimaginable nightmare?

I heard whispers around me:

"We must do something. We can't let them kill us like that, like cattle in the slaughterhouse. We must revolt."

There were, among us, a few tough young men. They actually had knives and were urging us to attack the armed guards. One of them was muttering:

"Let the world learn about the existence of Auschwitz. Let everybody 95 find out about it while they still have a chance to escape . . ."

But the older men begged their sons not to be foolish:

"We mustn't give up hope, even now as the sword hangs over our heads. So taught our sages . . ."

The wind of revolt died down. We continued to walk until we came to a crossroads. Standing in the middle of it was, though I didn't know it then, Dr. Mengele,[1] the notorious Dr. Mengele. He looked like the typical SS officer: a cruel, though not unintelligent, face, complete with monocle. He was holding a conductor's baton and was surrounded by officers. The baton was moving constantly, sometimes to the right, sometimes to the left.

In no time, I stood before him.

"Your age?" he asked, perhaps trying to sound paternal. 100

"I'm eighteen." My voice was trembling.

"In good health?"

"Yes."

"Your profession?"

Tell him that I was a student? 105

"Farmer," I heard myself saying.

This conversation lasted no more than a few seconds. It seemed like an eternity.

The baton pointed to the left. I took half a step forward. I first wanted to see where they would send my father. Were he to have gone to the right, I would have run after him.

The baton, once more, moved to the left. A weight lifted from my heart.

We did not know, as yet, which was the better side, right or left, which 110 road led to prison and which to the crematoria. Still, I was happy, I was near my father. Our procession continued slowly to move forward.

Another inmate came over to us:

"Satisfied?"

"Yes," someone answered.

"Poor devils, you are heading for the crematorium."

He seemed to be telling the truth. Not far from us, flames, huge flames, 115 were rising from a ditch. Something was being burned there. A truck drew close and unloaded its hold: small children. Babies! Yes, I did see this, with

---

[1] **Dr. Mengele** (1911–1979): The infamous concentration camp physician who inspected prisoners to select those fit for labor and those who would be exterminated. He was also responsible for performing medical experiments on prisoners. —EDS.

National Archives and Records Administration

Buchenwald, 1945. Wiesel is on the second row from the bottom, seventh from the left.

my own eyes . . . children thrown into the flames. (Is it any wonder that ever since then, sleep tends to elude me?)

So that was where we were going. A little farther on, there was another, larger pit for adults.

I pinched myself: Was I still alive? Was I awake? How was it possible that men, women, and children were being burned and that the world kept silent? No. All this could not be real. A nightmare perhaps . . . Soon I would wake up with a start, my heart pounding, and find that I was back in the room of my childhood, with my books . . .

My father's voice tore me from my daydreams:

"What a shame, a shame that you did not go with your mother . . . I saw many children your age go with their mothers . . ."

His voice was terribly sad. I understood that he did not wish to see what 120 they would do to me. He did not wish to see his only son go up in flames.

My forehead was covered with cold sweat. Still, I told him that I could not believe that human beings were being burned in our times; the world would never tolerate such crimes . . .

"The world? The world is not interested in us. Today, everything is possible, even the crematoria . . ." His voice broke.

"Father," I said. "If that is true, then I don't want to wait. I'll run into the electrified barbed wire. That would be easier than a slow death in the flames."

He didn't answer. He was weeping. His body was shaking. Everybody around us was weeping. Someone began to recite Kaddish, the prayer for the dead. I don't know whether, during the history of the Jewish people, men have ever before recited Kaddish for themselves.

"*Yisgadal, veyiskadash, shmey raba* . . . May His name be celebrated 125 and sanctified . . ." whispered my father.

For the first time, I felt anger rising within me. Why should I sanctify His name? The Almighty, the eternal and terrible Master of the Universe, chose to be silent. What was there to thank Him for?

We continued our march. We were coming closer and closer to the pit, from which an infernal heat was rising. Twenty more steps. If I was going to kill myself, this was the time. Our column had only some fifteen steps to go. I bit my lips so that my father would not hear my teeth chattering. Ten more steps. Eight. Seven. We were walking slowly, as one follows a hearse, our own funeral procession. Only four more steps. Three. There it was now, very close to us, the pit and its flames. I gathered all that remained of my strength in order to break rank and throw myself onto the barbed wire. Deep down, I was saying good-bye to my father, to the whole universe, and, against my will, I found myself whispering the words: "*Yisgadal, veyiskadash, shmey raba* . . ." May His name be celebrated and sanctified . . ." My heart was about to burst. There I was face-to-face with the Angel of Death[2] . . .

No. Two steps from the pit, we were ordered to turn left and herded into barracks.

I squeezed my father's hand. He said:

Do you remember Mrs. Schächter, in the train?   130

Never shall I forget that night, the first night in camp, that turned my life into one long night seven times sealed.

Never shall I forget that smoke.

Never shall I forget the small faces of the children whose bodies I saw transformed into smoke under a silent sky.

Never shall I forget those flames that consumed my faith forever.

Never shall I forget the nocturnal silence that deprived me for all eter- 135 nity of the desire to live.

---

[2] *Angel of Death:* A name by which Dr. Mengele was known. It isn't clear, however, if Wiesel wants to make this connection. — EDS.

Never shall I forget those moments that murdered my God and my soul and turned my dreams to ashes.

Never shall I forget those things, even were I condemned to live as long as God Himself.

Never. ▪

The Reader's Presence

1. Why do you think the inmates abuse the newly arrived prisoners? How would you describe their tone? Why do they order father and son to lie about their ages? Why do they lead the father and son to believe they are headed for the crematorium?

2. Besides offering a historical account of how Jews were herded into concentration camps, Wiesel also describes his harrowing religious experience. What impact did this experience have on his religious beliefs? What is Wiesel's purpose in the almost prayer-like litany that appears at the conclusion of the selection?

3. **VISUAL PRESENCE:**   Examine carefully the photograph taken at the Buchenwald concentration camp just after the end of World War II (page 307). What were your initial reactions to this image? What specific features of this photograph capture the tone and atmosphere of Wiesel's text? Support your response with details from the image.

4. **CONNECTIONS:**   How do people respond in writing when they have encountered horrific events? Compare Wiesel's recollection of his childhood internment at Auschwitz to Michihiko Hachiya's account of the bombing of Hiroshima ("Hiroshima Diary," page 136). Wiesel published his memoir of his nightmarish experiences in 1958 (originally in French), more than a decade after the events occurred. Hachiya began writing his diary a few days after the event. How do these different time frames account for the different ways in which each author makes his presence felt in his writing?

PART 2

EXPOSITORY WRITING

Shaping Information

WHAT IS EXPOSITORY WRITING?

One of the most important reasons to write, especially in college and within a chosen profession, is to impart and share information. Although **exposition** has a wide range of meanings, in composition it normally refers to discourse that provides readers with an informative report on a topic. This part, "Expository Writing: Shaping Information," will introduce you to many examples of informative writing by outstanding authors noted for their ability to explain concepts and research clearly and compellingly. These authors excel in practicing the art of exposition; that is, as writers they know how to set out and arrange material so that it is both educational and enjoyable. Some, but not all, of the authors in this part are experts in their respective fields. Many well-known writers are *experts* in a different way—they don't know everything there is to know about economics, medicine, or psychology, for example, but they do know how to find out pertinent information in a wide variety of fields and present it engagingly. This introduction aims to provide you with strategies for becoming an expert in the same way.

Some expository writing simply lays out information that the writer knows or has researched. For example, a history assignment may call for a paper detailing the rise of the women's suffrage movement in the early twentieth century. Such a report could be based mainly on a student's reading and research, and it could focus on the various stages of the movement that led to the passage in 1920 of the Nineteenth Amendment giving women the right to vote. This kind of writing isn't a product only of classroom assignments; many print and online sources convey information in this manner.

But exposition usually involves more than a straightforward summary of the subject. When you do your own expository writing, you'll likely need to aim for a higher level of personal and intellectual engagement that can take the form of **explanation**, **analysis**, and **interpretation**. Imagine that a history assignment asks a student not only to detail the stages of the women's suffrage movement but also to *explain why* the movement succeeded in achieving its goal. A student, then, would still need to know the movement's stages but would also need to consider and select the various elements of the movement that resulted in a radical change in public opinion, including the mass demonstrations of 1916–1918 that supported the suffrage cause across the nation and set the groundwork for congressional legislation.

Information is always more than a list or an assemblage of facts and data on a subject. The facts need to be arranged in some way; the writer needs to organize information so that the presentation is clear, consistent, coherent, and convincing. After all, at the heart of the word "information" is "form." In this introduction, we'll take those three main purposes of expository writing—to explain, to analyze, and to interpret—and offer strategies you might use in your own writing.

In setting out to write an expository essay, you should explore how each of the following strategies can best help you approach your topic and establish your main points. For example, to return to our women's suffrage assignment, would your information be best presented by showing the causes that led to the movement, by classifying the various types of demonstrations, or by comparing the right-to-vote issue with earlier or later civil rights movements? As you can see, considering the topic with the various strategies in mind also helps you anticipate the general structural pattern of your essay. The strategies will provide you with both a way to start your paper and a way to organize the information you've gathered.

STRATEGIES FOR SHARING INFORMATION

Expository writing often involves telling a story, reporting or summarizing a sequence of events, constructing a historical chronology, recounting a biography or an autobiography, or detailing how something is done. In these instances, authors use **narrative** to draw in an audience and keep them engaged.

In the following example, note Danielle Ofri's careful narration about a trip to the morgue, and consider why this trip unfolds step by step. How would this passage affect the reader differently if she had simply written, "We took the elevator down to the morgue"?

> We stared at our sneakers as the elevator lurched downward. It creaked past several floors and landed with a jolt. Out we spilled, gingerly, onto the raw concrete floor. Our first stop was the morgue. **Danielle Ofri**, "SAT" (page 508)

When it is important for you to slow down and include careful details, a strong and vivid **description** can make a subject easier for the reader to follow. Effective descriptions might involve creating a picture in word or image, making information more clear, or reporting objective details to visualize a setting.

Charles Bowden brings the scene of a fiesta to life with lively verbs and images of the various groups at the party rather than simply writing, "Everyone was enjoying the fiesta." How does describing this fiesta in great detail convey important information not only about the events but also about the people attending the party?

> Over in Naco, Sonora, the final night of a fiesta is in full roar. Men drinking beer move by on horseback, groups of girls in high heels prance past. Nearby, folks play bingo, and in the band shell a group does a sound check for the big dance. **Charles Bowden**, "Our Wall" (page 349)

Expository writing often requires writers to discuss concepts and ideas with which readers might be unfamiliar. In these cases, writers use **examples** to back up claims and to clarify an idea by illustrating it, making an abstract concept more concrete, representing a larger concept or event by a single incident or image, or providing a "for instance."

Note how David Brooks uses phrases like "in fact" and "for example" to signal that he's about to provide an example that illustrates his larger point. He understands that specific evidence will be more convincing to his reader. How would this passage affect the reader differently if he had written, "Sometimes segregated neighborhoods happen over time"? Would you be convinced without a clear example?

> In fact, evidence suggests that some neighborhoods become more segregated over time. New suburbs in Arizona and Nevada, for example, start out reasonably well integrated. **David Brooks**, "People Like Us" (page 356)

When you'd like to support a point, to make your writing more engaging with a particularly well-said statement, or to include a clear explanation of a difficult concept, you can **use expert testimony** by quoting or summarizing another writer on the subject. We include more coverage of this strategy in the introduction to the argument section, but it's important to note here that writers of expository prose often draw on quotations from credible sources. It's difficult to convince readers you're an expert without demonstrating that you're familiar with the work of other experts.

In the following example, note that although it might have been as easy for James McBride to make a point about speech-song in his own words, he chose to quote Samuel A. Floyd—using his full name—and to spend time presenting Floyd's credentials. Why do you think McBride made those decisions as a writer? What impact does reading the details of Floyd's professional identity have on you as reader?

> "Speech-song has been part of black culture for a long, long time," says Samuel A. Floyd, director of the Center for Black Music Research at Columbia College in Chicago. **James McBride**, "Hip-Hop Planet" (page 482)

Even for words we think we know the meaning of, writers often choose to build the foundation of their discussion by providing a **definition**. You might decide to do this in your own writing to clarify key terms, reflect on the significance or origins of a word, enlarge or restrict a term's meaning, eliminate confusion or ambiguity, or challenge conventional meanings and euphemisms.

In the following example, note how Eighner reports his research into the meaning of the word *Dumpster*—a word we probably take for granted, but which he's invested in helping us to slow down and consider. How does knowing the origin of the word *Dumpster* help you understand how Eighner thinks about Dumpsters and prepare you for the rest of his essay?

> Long before I began Dumpster diving I was impressed with Dumpsters, enough so that I wrote the Merriam-Webster research service to discover what I could about the word "Dumpster." I learned from them that "Dumpster" is a proprietary word belonging to the Dempster Dumpster company. **Lars Eighner**, "On Dumpster Diving" (page 399)

STRATEGIES FOR ANALYZING INFORMATION

When writers are working with a complicated idea or illuminating the details of a seemingly simple concept, they might use **classification** to analyze a subject by dividing it into several key parts, organizing material into categories or types, making distinctions, constructing outlines, arranging ideas in the most appropriate order, or viewing an issue from various sides.

Because we may think we know plenty about smiling, Amy Cunningham wants the reader to consider the subject in more deliberate, categorical detail, and she draws on the research of Paul Ekman to help us do so. If she had not listed the different types of smiles classified by Ekman, would you be prepared to think about smiling as a complicated subject?

> Psychologist Paul Ekman, the head of the University of California's Human Interaction Lab in San Francisco, has identified 18 distinct types of smiles, including those that show misery, compliance, fear, and contempt. **Amy Cunningham**, "Why Women Smile" (page 369)

Sometimes the best way to analyze a subject is to **compare and contrast** it with something that highlights meaningful similarities or differences. Writers use this strategy to organize material through point-by-point resemblances or disparities, to form analogies, or to express a preference for one thing or position over another.

In the following example, note how Stephen L. Carter illustrates the difference between honesty and integrity by pointing out that one can be honest without exemplifying integrity. Based on the title of the essay ("The Insufficiency of Honesty"), why might Carter choose this writing strategy over others?

> The first point to understand about the difference between honesty and integrity is that a person may be entirely honest without ever engaging in the hard work of discernment that integrity requires; she may tell us quite truthfully what she believes without ever taking the time to figure out whether what she believes is good and right and true. **Stephen L. Carter**, "The Insufficiency of Honesty" (page 362)

STRATEGIES FOR INTERPRETING INFORMATION

Many research-paper assignments ask students not only to present information on a topic but also to respond to and interpret that information. We interpret when our analysis and explanation lead us to **draw independent conclusions** about a subject. Interpretation is often implicit in the writer's approach and need not be stated directly by such assertions as "I think," "I conclude," "I believe," or "in my opinion," which would become repetitive.

Observe how best-selling author Malcolm Gladwell, who compares the face-to-face demonstrations of the 1960s civil rights movement to today's social-media activism, rejects some of the claims made by the proponents of social media by explaining on his own what might have happened had Martin Luther King Jr. had Facebook at his disposal:

> Enthusiasts for social media would no doubt have us believe that King's task in Birmingham would have been made infinitely easier had he been able to communicate with his followers through Facebook, and contented himself with tweets from a Birmingham jail. But networks are messy: think of the ceaseless pattern of correction and revision, amendment and debate, that characterizes Wikipedia. If Martin Luther

King, Jr., had tried to do a wiki-boycott in Montgomery, he would have been steam-rollered by the white power structure. And of what use would a digital communi-cation tool be in a town where ninety-eight percent of the black community could be reached every Sunday morning at church? The things that King needed in Bir-mingham—discipline and strategy—were things that online social media cannot pro-vide. **Malcolm Gladwell**, "Small Change: Why the Revolution Will Not Be Tweeted" (page 422)

Another way a writer might interpret information is to identify **cause and effect**. The writer can explain the cause of an event or a trend; examine how one thing influences another; explain the consequences of an action or idea; or assign credit, blame, or responsibility.

In the following example, note how Eric Schlosser uses this passage to answer the promise his title makes clear: he sets out to tell you "Why McDonald's Fries Taste So Good," and he does so with details that sound almost scientific. Why might he be interested in explaining cause and effect in this specific way, as opposed to stating more generally that McDonald's fries are cooked in beef fat?

For decades McDonald's cooked its French fries in a mixture of about 7 percent cot-tonseed oil and 93 percent beef tallow. The mixture gave the fries their unique fla-vor—and more saturated beef fat per ounce than a McDonald's hamburger. **Eric Schlosser**, "Why McDonald's Fries Taste So Good" (page 547)

All the strategies described can operate at all compositional levels. They can, for example, help shape a single sentence, an individual paragraph, or even the entire composition. Much effective expository writing, however, consists of a mixture of strategies. Many authors combine those that seem most appropriate for a particular point they are making. As you read the essays in this part, watch for authors combining strategies and think about how you might use combined strategies in your own writing.

READING EXPOSITORY ESSAYS: A Checklist

To benefit the most from the readings in this part, we recommend that you read each selection, paying close attention to a number of different elements. To help you gain experience as an attentive reader of informative writing, the following checklist will serve as a convenient guide.

- ✔ Evaluate what opinions, if any, you've already formed about the essay's topic, and whether those opinions interfere with your ability to fairly consider the author's approach and attitude.

- ✔ Identify the central points of the essay. Think about (or write) how you might summarize those main points in fifty words or less.

- ✔ Identify and describe the author's purpose in writing the essay and identify where you find evidence of this purpose in the text itself.

- ✔ Keep track of any words you haven't encountered before—either by circling them or by writing them down elsewhere. Look up the meaning of the words and note the definition for future reference.

- ✔ Look for evidence to determine the author's intended audience and decide whether you belong to that audience. In what ways, if any, does the writing exclude you?

- ✔ Try to articulate your emotional reaction to the essay. Are you intrigued, surprised, shocked, confused, annoyed, or disgusted by any of the author's ideas or assumptions? How might you summarize why the essay makes you feel the way you do?

- ✔ Annotate the essay with an eye on emphasizing key points or memorable passages and add marginal comments and questions that track your engagement with the selection.

- ✔ What do you notice about the author's style of writing? Try noting patterns of language or images, the repetition of key terms and metaphors, and the overall tone of the writing.

- ✔ Identify any inconsistencies in the selection. Does the author make contradictory statements or present unconvincing evidence?

- ✔ Consider whether you've relied completely on the author's information. Try to independently check facts and verify sources for information you consider essential to the author's central concept and point of view.

Joan Acocella

A FEW TOO MANY

JOAN ACOCELLA (b. 1945), also known as Joan Ross Acocella, is a dance critic for the *New Yorker* and the author of *Mark Morris* (1993), the first serious examination of the renowned choreographer of the same name. She has also written books on literature, *Willa Cather and the Politics of Criticism* (2000), and psychology, *Creating Hysteria: Women and Multiple Personality Disorder* (1999). Her latest book, *Twenty-Eight Artists and Two Saints* (2007), is a collection of essays on various dancers; artists; authors; choreographers; and, as the title indicates, saints, namely Mary Magdalene and Joan of Arc. Acocella received a Guggenheim Fellowship in 1993 and a Holtzbrinck Berlin Prize Fellowship in 2013, and she's presently a fellow at the New York Institute for the Humanities. Her work has been anthologized in *Best American Essays*. Regarding her work as a dance and book critic, she has said, "I try to describe with love what I love." Like many of her essays, this selection was originally published in the *New Yorker*.

> Regarding her work as a dance and book critic, Joan Acocella has said, "I try to describe with love what I love."

OF THE MISERIES regularly inflicted on humankind, some are so minor and yet, while they last, so painful that one wonders how, after all this time, a remedy cannot have been found. If scientists do not have a cure for cancer, that makes sense. But the common cold, the menstrual cramp? The hangover is another condition of this kind. It is a preventable malady: don't drink. Nevertheless, people throughout time have found what seemed to them good reason for recourse to alcohol. One attraction is alcohol's power to disinhibit — to allow us, at last, to tell off our neighbor or make an improper suggestion to his wife. Alcohol may also persuade us that we have found the truth about life, a comforting experience rarely available in the sober hour. Through the lens of alcohol, the world seems nicer. ("I drink to make other people interesting," the theater critic George Jean Nathan used to say.) For all these reasons, drinking cheers people up. See Proverbs 31:6–7: "Give . . . wine unto those that be of heavy hearts. Let him drink, and forget his poverty, and remember his misery no more." It works, but then, in the morning, a new misery presents itself.

A hangover peaks when alcohol that has been poured into the body is finally eliminated from it — that is, when the blood-alcohol level returns to zero. The toxin is now gone, but the damage it has done is not. By fairly common consent, a hangover will involve some combination of headache, upset stomach, thirst, food aversion, nausea, diarrhea, tremulousness, fatigue, and a general feeling of wretchedness. Scientists haven't yet found all the reasons for this network of woes, but they have proposed various causes. One is withdrawal, which would bring on the tremors and also sweating. A second factor may be dehydration. Alcohol interferes with the secretion of the hormone that inhibits urination. Hence the heavy traffic to the rest rooms at bars and parties. The resulting dehydration seems to trigger the thirst and lethargy. While that is going on, the alcohol may also be inducing hypoglycemia (low blood sugar), which converts into light-headedness and muscle weakness, the feeling that one's bones have turned to jello. Meanwhile, the body, to break down the alcohol, is releasing chemicals that may be more toxic than alcohol itself; these would result in nausea and other symptoms. Finally, the alcohol has produced inflammation, which in turn causes the white blood cells to flood the bloodstream with molecules called cytokines. Apparently, cytokines are the source of the aches and pains and lethargy that, when our bodies are attacked by a flu virus—and likewise, perhaps, by alcohol—encourage us to stay in bed rather than go to work, thereby freeing up the body's energy for use by the white cells in combatting the invader. In a series of experiments, mice that were given a cytokine inducer underwent dramatic changes. Adult males wouldn't socialize with young males new to their cage. Mothers displayed "impaired nest-building." Many people will know how these mice felt.

But hangover symptoms are not just physical; they are cognitive as well. People with hangovers show delayed reaction times and difficulties with attention, concentration, and visual-spatial perception. A group of airplane pilots given simulated flight tests after a night's drinking put in substandard performances. Similarly, automobile drivers, the morning after, get low marks on simulated road tests. Needless to say, this is a hazard, and not just for those at the wheel. There are laws against drunk driving, but not against driving with a hangover.

Hangovers also have an emotional component. Kingsley Amis, who was, in his own words, one of the foremost drunks of his time, and who wrote three books on drinking, described this phenomenon as "the metaphysical hangover": "When that ineffable compound of depression, sadness (these two are not the same), anxiety, self-hatred, sense of failure and fear for the future begins to steal over you, start telling yourself that what you have is a hangover. . . . You have not suffered a minor brain lesion, you are not all that bad at your job, your family and friends are not leagued in a conspiracy of barely maintained silence about what a shit you are, you have not come at last to see life as it really is." Some people are unable to convince themselves of this. Amis described the opening of Kafka's *Metamorphosis*, with the hero discovering that he has been changed into a bug, as the best literary representation of a hangover.

The severity of a hangover depends, of course, on how much you drank the night before, but that is not the only determinant. What, besides alcohol, did you consume at that party? If you took other drugs as well, your hangover may be worse. And what kind of alcohol did you drink? In general, darker drinks, such as red wine and whiskey, have higher levels of congeners—impurities produced by the fermentation process, or added to enhance flavor—than do light-colored drinks such as white wine, gin, and vodka. The greater the congener content, the uglier the morning. Then there are your own characteristics—for example, your drinking pattern. Unjustly, habitually heavy drinkers seem to have milder hangovers. Your sex is also important. A woman who matches drinks with a man is going to get drunk faster than he, partly because she has less body water than he does, and less of the enzyme alcohol dehydrogenase, which breaks down alcohol. Apparently, your genes also have a vote, as does your gene pool. Almost forty percent of East Asians have a variant, less efficient form of aldehyde dehydrogenase, another enzyme necessary for alcohol processing. Therefore, they start showing signs of trouble after just a few sips—they flush dramatically—and they get drunk fast. This is an inconvenience for some Japanese and Korean businessmen. They feel that they should drink with their Western colleagues. Then they crash to the floor and have to make awkward phone calls in the morning.

Hangovers are probably as old as alcohol use, which dates back to the Stone Age. Some anthropologists have proposed that alcohol production may have predated agriculture; in any case, it no doubt stimulated that development, because in many parts of the world the cereal harvest was largely given over to beer-making. Other prehistorians have speculated that alcohol intoxication may have been one of the baffling phenomena, like storms, dreams, and death, that propelled early societies toward organized religion. The ancient Egyptians, who, we are told, made seventeen varieties of beer, believed that their god Osiris invented this agreeable beverage. They buried their dead with supplies of beer for use in the afterlife.

Alcohol was also one of our ancestors' foremost medicines. Berton Roueché, in a 1960 article on alcohol for the *New Yorker*, quoted a prominent fifteenth-century German physician, Hieronymus Brunschwig, on the range of physical ills curable by brandy: head sores, pallor, baldness, deafness, lethargy, toothache, mouth cankers, bad breath, swollen breasts, shortwindedness, indigestion, flatulence, jaundice, dropsy, gout, bladder infections, kidney stones, fever, dog bites, and infestation with lice or fleas. Additionally, in many times and places, alcohol was one of the few safe things to drink. Water contamination is a very old problem.

Some words for hangover, like ours, refer prosaically to the cause: the Egyptians say they are "still drunk," the Japanese "two days drunk," the Chinese "drunk overnight." The Swedes get "smacked from behind." But it is in languages that describe the effects rather than the cause that we begin to see real poetic power. Salvadorans wake up "made of rubber," the French with a "wooden mouth" or a "hair ache." The Germans and the Dutch say they have a "tomcat," presumably wailing. The Poles, reportedly, experience a "howling of kittens." My favorites are the Danes, who get "carpenters in the forehead." In keeping with the saying about the Eskimos' nine words for snow, the Ukrainians have several words for hangover. And, in keeping with the Jews-don't-drink rule, Hebrew didn't even have one word until recently. Then the experts at the Academy of the Hebrew Language, in Tel Aviv, decided that such a term was needed, so they made one up: *hamarmoret*, derived from the word for fermentation. (*Hamarmoret* echoes a usage of Jeremiah's, in Lamentations 1:20, which the King James Bible translates as "My bowels are troubled.") There is a biochemical basis for Jewish abstinence. Many Jews—fifty percent, in one estimate—carry a variant gene for alcohol dehydrogenase. Therefore, they, like the East Asians, have a low tolerance for alcohol.

As for hangover remedies, they are legion. There are certain unifying themes, however. When you ask people, worldwide, how to deal with a hangover, their first answer is usually the hair of the dog. The old faithful in this category is the Bloody Mary, but books on curing hangovers—I have read three, and that does not exhaust the list—describe more elaborate potions, often said to have been invented in places like Cap d'Antibes by bartenders with names like Jean-Marc. An English manual, Andrew Irving's *How to Cure a Hangover* (2004), devotes almost a hundred pages to hair-of-the-dog recipes, including the Suffering Bastard (gin, brandy, lime juice, bitters, and ginger ale); the Corpse Reviver (Pernod, champagne, and lemon juice); and the Thomas Abercrombie (two Alka-Seltzers dropped into a double shot of tequila). Kingsley Amis suggests taking Underberg bitters, a highly alcoholic digestive: "The resulting mild convulsions and cries of shock are well worth witnessing. But thereafter a comforting glow supervenes." Many people, however, simply drink some more of what they had the night before. My Ukrainian informant described his morning-after protocol for a vodka hangover as follows: "two shots of vodka, then a cigarette, then another shot of vodka." A Japanese source suggested wearing a sake-soaked surgical mask.

Application of the hair of the dog may sound like nothing more than a   10
way of getting yourself drunk enough so that you don't notice you have a hangover, but, according to Wayne Jones, of the Swedish National Laboratory of Forensic Medicine, the biochemistry is probably more complicated than that. Jones's theory is that the liver, in processing alcohol, first addresses itself to ethanol, which is the alcohol proper, and then moves on to methanol, a secondary ingredient of many wines and spirits. Because methanol breaks down into formic acid, which is highly toxic, it is during this second stage that the hangover is most crushing. If at that point you pour in more alcohol, the body will switch back to ethanol processing. This will not eliminate the hangover—the methanol (indeed, more of it now) is still waiting for you round the bend—but it delays the worst symptoms. It may also mitigate them somewhat. On the other hand, you are drunk again, which may create difficulty about going to work.

As for the non-alcoholic means of combatting hangover, these fall into three categories: before or while drinking, before bed, and the next morning. Many people advise you to eat a heavy meal with lots of protein and fats, before or while drinking. If you can't do that, at least drink a glass of milk. In Africa, the same purpose is served by eating peanut butter. The other most frequent before-and-during recommendation is water, lots of it. Proponents of this strategy tell you to ask for a glass of water with every drink you order, and then make yourself chug-a-lug the water before addressing the drink.

A recently favored antidote, both in Asia and in the West, is sports drinks, taken either the morning after or, more commonly, at the party itself. A fast-moving bar drink these days is Red Bull, an energy drink, mixed with vodka or with the herbal liqueur Jägermeister. (The latter cocktail is a Jäger-bomb.) Some people say that the Red Bull holds the hangover at bay, but apparently its primary effect is to blunt the depressive force of alcohol—no surprise, since an eight-ounce serving of Red Bull contains more caffeine than two cans of Coke. According to fans, you can rock all night. According to Maria Lucia Souza-Formigoni, a psychobiology researcher at the Federal University of São Paolo, that's true, and dangerous. After a few drinks with Red Bull, you're drunk but you don't know it, and therefore you may engage in high-risk behaviors—driving, going home with a questionable companion—rather than passing out quietly in your chair. Red Bull's manufacturers have criticized the methodology of Souza-Formigoni's study and have pointed out that they never condoned mixing their product with alcohol.

When you get home, is there anything you can do before going to bed? Those still able to consider such a question are advised, again, to consume buckets of water, and also to take some Vitamin C. Koreans drink a bowl of water with honey, presumably to head off the hypoglycemia. Among the young, one damage-control measure is the ancient Roman method, induced vomiting. Nic van Oudtshoorn's *The Hangover Handbook* (1997) thoughtfully provides a recipe for an emetic: mix mustard powder with water. If you have "bed spins," sleep with one foot on the floor.

Now to the sorrows of the morning. The list-topping recommendation, apart from another go at the water cure, is the greasy-meal cure. (An American philosophy professor: "Have breakfast at Denny's." An English teenager: "Eat two McDonald's hamburgers. They have a secret ingredient for hangovers.") Spicy foods, especially Mexican, are popular, along with eggs, as in the Denny's breakfast. Another egg-based cure is the prairie oyster, which involves vinegar, Worcestershire sauce, and a raw egg yolk to be consumed whole. Sugar, some say, should be reapplied. A reporter at the *Times*: "Drink a six-pack of Coke." Others suggest fruit juice. In Scotland, there is a soft drink called Irn-Bru, described to me by a local as tasting like melted plastic. Irn-Bru is advertised to the Scots as "Your Other National Drink." Also widely employed are milk-based drinks. Teenagers recommend milk-shakes and smoothies. My contact in Calcutta said buttermilk. "You can also pour it over your head," he added. "Very soothing."

Elsewhere on the international front, many people in Asia and the Near   15
East take strong tea. The Italians and the French prefer strong coffee. (Italian
informant: add lemon. French informant: add salt. Alcohol researchers: stay
away from coffee—it's a diuretic and will make you more dehydrated.) Germans eat pickled herring; the Japanese turn to pickled plums; the Vietnam-
ese drink a wax-gourd juice. Moroccans say to chew cumin seeds; Andeans,
coca leaves. Russians swear by pickle brine. An ex-Soviet ballet dancer told
me, "Pickle juice or a shot of vodka or pickle juice with a shot of vodka."

Many folk cures for hangovers are soups: *menudo* in Mexico, *mondongo*
in Puerto Rico, *iskembe çorbasi* in Turkey, *patsa* in Greece, *khashi* in Georgia. The fact that all of the above involve tripe may mean something. Hun-
garians favor a concoction of cabbage and smoked meats, sometimes forth-
rightly called "hangover soup." The Russians' morning-after soup, *solyanka*,
is, of course, made with pickle juice. The Japanese have traditionally relied
on miso soup, though a while ago there was a fashion for a vegetable soup
invented and marketed by one Kazu Tateishi, who claimed that it cured cancer as well as hangovers.

I read this list of food cures to Manuela Neuman, a Canadian researcher
on alcohol-induced liver damage, and she laughed at only one, the six-pack
of Coke. Many of the cures probably work, she said, on the same distraction
principle as the hair of the dog: "Take the spicy foods, for example. They
divert the body's attention away from coping with the alcohol to coping with
the spices, which are also a toxin. So you have new problems—with your
stomach, with your esophagus, with your respiration—rather than the problem with the headache, or that you are going to the washroom every five
minutes." The high-fat and high-protein meals operate in the same way,
she said. The body turns to the food and forgets about the alcohol for the
time being, thus delaying the hangover and possibly alleviating it. As for
the differences among the many food recommendations, Neuman said that
any country's hangover cure, like the rest of its cultural practices, is an adaptation to the environment. Chilies are readily available in Mexico, peanut
butter in Africa. People use what they have. Neuman also pointed out that
local cures will reflect the properties of local brews. If Russians favor pickle
juice, they are probably right to, because their drink is vodka: "Vodka is a
very pure alcohol. It doesn't have the congeners that you find, for example,
in whiskey in North America. The congeners are also toxic, independent of
alcohol, and will have their own effects. With vodka you are just going to
have pure-alcohol effects, and one of the most important of those is dehydration. The Russians drink a lot of water with their vodka, and that combats the
dehydration. The pickle brine will have the same effect. It's salty, so they'll
drink more water, and that's what they need."

Many hangover cures—soups, the greasy breakfast—are comfort foods,
and that, apart from any sworn-by ingredients, may be their chief therapeu-
tic property, but some other remedies sound as though they were devised by
the witches in *Macbeth*. Kingsley Amis recommended a mixture of Bovril

and vodka. There is also a burnt-toast cure. Such items suggest that what some hungover people are seeking is not so much relief as atonement. The same can be said of certain non-food recommendations, such as exercise. One source says that you should do a forty-minute workout, another that you should run six miles—activities that may have little attraction for the hung over. Additional procedures said to be effective are an intravenous saline drip and kidney dialysis, which, apart from their lack of appeal, are not readily available.

There are other noningested remedies. Amazon will sell you a refrigeratable eye mask, an aromatherapy inhaler, and a vinyl statue of St. Vivian, said to be the patron saint of the hung over. She comes with a stand and a special prayer.

The most widely used over-the-counter remedy is no doubt aspirin.   20 Advil, or ibuprofen, and Alka-Seltzer—there is a special formula for hangovers, Alka-Seltzer Wake-Up Call—are probably close runners-up. (Tylenol, or acetaminophen, should not be used, because alcohol increases its toxicity to the liver.) Also commonly recommended are Vitamin C and B-complex vitamins. But those are almost home remedies. In recent years, pharmaceutical companies have come up with more specialized formulas: Chaser, NoHang, BoozEase, PartySmart, Sob'r-K HangoverStopper, Hangover Prevention Formula, and so on. In some of these, such as Sob'r-K and Chaser, the primary ingredient is carbon, which, according to the manufacturers, soaks up toxins. Others are herbal compounds, featuring such ingredients as ginseng, milk thistle, borage, and extracts of prickly pear, artichoke, and guava leaf. These and other OTC[1] remedies aim to boost biochemicals that help the body deal with toxins. A few remedies have scientific backing. Manuela Neuman, in lab tests, found that milk-thistle extract, which is an ingredient in NoHang and Hangover Helper, does protect cells from damage by alcohol. A research team headed by Jeffrey Wiese, of Tulane University, tested prickly-pear extract, the key ingredient in Hangover Prevention Formula, on human subjects and found significant improvement with the nausea, dry mouth, and food aversion but not with other, more common symptoms, such as headache.

Five years ago, there was a flurry in the press over a new OTC remedy called RU-21 (i.e., Are you twenty-one?). According to the reports, this wonder drug was the product of twenty-five years of painstaking research by the Russian Academy of Sciences, which developed it for KGB agents[2] who wanted to stay sober while getting their contacts drunk and prying information out of them. During the Cold War, we were told, the formula was a state secret, but in 1999 it was declassified. Now it was ours! "HERE'S ONE COMMUNIST PLOT AMERICANS CAN REALLY GET BEHIND," the headline in the *Washington Post* said. "BOTTOMS UP TO OUR BUDDIES IN RUSSIA," the *Cleveland Plain Dealer* said. The literature on RU-21 was mysterious, however.

---

[1] **OTC:** Over the counter. —EDS.

[2] **KGB:** State security police of the former Soviet Union, responsible for external espionage, internal counterintelligence, and internal "crimes against the state." —EDS.

If the formula was developed to keep your head clear, how come so many reports said that it didn't suppress the effects of alcohol? Clearly, it couldn't work both ways. When I put this question to Emil Chiaberi, a co-founder of RU-21's manufacturer, Spirit Sciences, in California, he answered, "No, no, no. It is true that succinic acid" —a key ingredient of RU-21— "was tested at the Russian Academy of Sciences, including secret laboratories that worked for the KGB. But it didn't do what they wanted. It didn't keep people sober, and so it never made it with the KGB men. Actually, it does improve your condition a little. In Russia, I've seen people falling under the table plenty of times—they drink differently over there—and if they took a few of these pills they were able to get up and walk around, and maybe have a couple more drinks. But no, what those scientists discovered, really by accident, was a way to prevent hangover." (Like many other OTC remedies, RU-21 is best taken before or while drinking, not the next morning.) Asians love the product, Chiaberi says. "It flies off the shelves there." In the United States, it is big with the Hollywood set: "For every film festival—Sundance, the Toronto Film Festival—we get calls asking us to send them RU-21 for parties. So it has that glamour thing."

Most cures for hangover—indeed most statements about hangover—have not been tested. Jeffrey Wiese and his colleagues, in a 2000 article in *Annals of Internal Medicine*, reported that in the preceding thirty-five years more than forty-seven hundred articles on alcohol intoxication had been published, but that only a hundred and eight of these dealt with hangover. There may be more information on hangover cures in college newspapers—a rich source—than in the scientific literature. And the research that has been published is often weak. A team of scientists attempting to review the literature on hangover cures were able to assemble only fifteen articles, and then they had to throw out all but eight on methodological grounds. There have been more studies in recent years, but historically this is not a subject that has captured scientists' hearts.

Which is curious, because anyone who discovered a widely effective hangover cure would make a great deal of money. Doing the research is hard, though. Lab tests with cell samples are relatively simple to conduct, as are tests with animals, some of which have been done. In one experiment, with a number of rats suffering from artificially induced hangovers, ninety percent of the animals died, but in a group that was first given Vitamins B and C, together with cysteine, an amino acid contained in some OTC remedies, there were no deaths. (Somehow this is not reassuring.) The acid test, however, is in clinical trials, with human beings, and these are complicated. Basically, what you have to do is give a group of people a lot to drink, apply the remedy in question, and then, the next morning, score them on a number of measures in comparison with people who consumed the same amount of alcohol without the remedy. But there are many factors that you have to control for: the sex of the subjects; their general health; their family history; their past experience with alcohol; the type of alcohol you give them; the amount of food and water they consume before, during, and after; and the circumstances under which they drink, among other variables. (Wiese and his colleagues, in their prickly-pear experiment, provided music so that the subjects could dance, as at a party.) Ideally, there should also be a large sample—many subjects.

All that costs money, and researchers do not pay out of pocket. They depend on funding institutions—typically, universities, government agencies, and foundations. With all those bodies, a grant has to be OK'd by an ethics committee, and such committees' ethics may stop short of getting people drunk. For one thing, they are afraid that the subjects will hurt themselves. (All the studies I read specified that the subjects were sent home by taxi or limousine after their contribution to science.) Furthermore, many people believe that alcohol abusers *should* suffer the next morning—that this is a useful deterrent. Robert Lindsey, the president of the National Council on Alcoholism and Drug Dependence, told me that he wasn't sure about that. His objection to hangover-cure research was simply that it was a misuse of resources: "Fifteen million people in this country are alcohol-dependent. That's a staggering number! They need help: not with hangovers but with the cause of hangovers—alcohol addiction." Robert Swift, an alcohol researcher who teaches at Brown University, counters that if scientists, through research, could provide the public with better information on the cognitive impairments involved in hangover, we might be able to prevent accidents. He compares the situation to the campaigns against distributing condoms, on the ground that this would increase promiscuity. In fact, the research has shown that free condoms did not have that effect. What they did was cut down on unwanted pregnancies and sexually transmitted disease.

Manufacturers of OTC remedies are sensitive to the argument that they are enablers, and their literature often warns against heavy drinking. The message may be unashamedly mixed, however. The makers of NoHang, on their Web page, say what your mother would: "It is recommended that you drink moderately and responsibly." At the same time, they tell you that with NoHang "you can drink the night away." They list the different packages in which their product can be bought: the Bender (twelve tablets), the Party Animal (twenty-four), the It's Noon Somewhere (forty-eight). Among the testimonials they publish is one by "Chad S.," from Chicago: "After getting torn up all day on Saturday, I woke up Sunday morning completely hangover-free. I must have had like twenty drinks." Researchers address the moral issue less hypocritically. Wiese and his colleagues describe the damage done by hangovers—according to their figures, the cost to the U.S. economy, in absenteeism and poor job performance, is a hundred and forty-eight billion dollars a year (other estimates are far lower, but still substantial)—and they mention the tests with the airplane pilots, guaranteed to scare anyone. They also say that there is no experimental evidence indicating that hangover relief encourages further drinking. (Nor, they might have added, have there been any firm findings on this matter.) Manuela Neuman, more philosophically, says that some people, now and then, are going to drink too much, no matter what you tell them, and that we should try to relieve the suffering caused thereby. Such reasoning seems to have cut no ice with funding institutions. Of the meager research I have read in support of various cures, all was paid for, at least in part, by pharmaceutical companies.

A truly successful hangover cure is probably going to be slow in coming. In the meantime, however, it is not easy to sympathize with the alcohol disciplinarians, so numerous, for example, in the United States. They seem to lack a sense of humor and, above all, the tragic sense of life. They appear not to know that many people have a lot that they'd like to forget. In the words of the English aphorist William Bolitho, "The shortest way out of Manchester is . . . a bottle of Gordon's gin," and if that relief is temporary the reformers would be hard put to offer a more lasting solution. Also questionable is the moral emphasis of the temperance folk, their belief that drinking is a lapse, a sin, as if getting to work on time, or living a hundred years, were the crown of life. They forget alcohol's relationship to camaraderie, sharing, toasts. Those, too, are moral matters. Even hangovers are related to social comforts. Alcohol investigators describe the bad things that people do on the morning after. According to Genevieve Ames and her research team at the Prevention Research Center, in Berkeley, hungover assembly-line workers are more likely to be criticized by their supervisors, to have disagreements with their co-workers, and to feel lousy. Apart from telling us what we already know, such findings are incomplete, because they do not talk about the jokes around the water cooler—the fellowship, the badge of honor. Yes, there are safer ways of gaining honor, but how available are they to most people?

Outside the United States, there is less finger-wagging. British writers, if they recommend a cure, will occasionally say that it makes you feel good enough to go out and have another drink. They are also more likely to tell you about the health benefits of moderate drinking—how it lowers one's risk of heart disease, Alzheimer's, and so on. English fiction tends to portray drinking as a matter of getting through the day, often quite acceptably. In P. G. Wodehouse's Jeeves and Wooster series, a hangover is the occasion of a happy event, Bertie's hiring of Jeeves. Bertie, after "a late evening," is lying on the couch in agony when Jeeves rings his doorbell. "'I was sent by the agency, sir,' he said. 'I was given to understand that you required a valet.'" Bertie says he would have preferred a mortician. Jeeves takes one look at Bertie, brushes past him, and vanishes into the kitchen, from which he emerges a moment later with a glass on a tray. It contains a prairie oyster. Bertie continues, "I would have clutched at anything that looked like a lifeline that morning. I swallowed the stuff. For a moment I felt as if somebody . . . was strolling down my throat with a lighted torch, and then everything seemed suddenly to get all right. The sun shone in through the window; birds twittered in the tree-tops; and, generally speaking, hope dawned once more. 'You're engaged,' I said." Here the hangover is a comedy, or at least a fact of life. So it has been, probably, since the Stone Age, and so it is likely to be for a while yet. ■

The Reader's Presence

1. What do you think Acocella's purpose was in writing this essay? What role do the anecdotes and scientific studies that she cites play in supporting her purpose? What personal opinions, if any, does Acocella reveal about alcohol consumption? Of those, which are stated explicitly and which are implied?

2. Identify a passage in which Acocella writes about a specific facet of alcohol consumption through multiple lenses: scientific, cultural, historical, anecdotal, and so on. What effect(s) does this approach have on your understanding of the subject? To what extent does each of the various sources Acocella cites seem relevant to her overarching purpose in writing this essay? Which did you find most compelling? Explain why.

3. **CONNECTIONS:**   Compare the moral implications raised in this essay with those in David Foster Wallace's "Consider the Lobster" (page 760). How would you describe the tone each writer uses when discussing the moral questions surrounding each of their topics? How does this tone affect your reading of each essay? How would your reading differ if the authors' tones were reversed—that is, if Wallace wrote about lobsters with the tone with which Acocella wrote about hangovers—and vice versa?

Daniel Akst

WHAT MEETS THE EYE

New York–born writer **DANIEL AKST** (b. 1956) divides his time between fiction and nonfiction, journalism and commentary. He has written two novels, *St. Burl's Obituary* (1996), a PEN/Faulkner Award finalist, and *The Webster Chronicle* (2001). His nonfiction account of financial fraud in southern California, *Wonder Boy*, was listed in *Businessweek*'s best books of 1990. Akst began his career in journalism while still attending college at the University of Pennsylvania and continued as a reporter while at New York University, where he took graduate courses in economics and finance. Akst has been a regular columnist for the

> Daniel Akst's latest book examines what he calls "the central problem of our time: how to save ourselves from what we want."

Los Angeles Times and the Sunday business section of the *New York Times*, writing, as he describes it, "about the intersection of money and culture." He is a regular contributor to the *Wall Street Journal* and his articles have appeared in numerous publications, including *Salon*, the *Christian Science Monitor, Forbes, Fortune, Money, Newsday, Slate,* and *Smithsonian*. His commentaries have been aired on NPR's *Marketplace* and the *Nightly Business Report* for PBS. A contributing editor to the *Wilson Quarterly*, where "What Meets the Eye" originally appeared in 2005, Akst also wrote a weekly column for *Newsday*. He now edits and writes for the "Week in Ideas" column for the weekend edition of the *Wall Street Journal*. His latest book, *We Have Met the Enemy: Self-Control in an Age of Excess* (2011), is a "wide-ranging examination of the central problem of our time: how to save ourselves from what we want."

EVERYONE KNOWS looks shouldn't matter. Beauty, after all, is only skin deep, and no right-thinking person would admit to taking much account of how someone looks outside the realm of courtship, that romantic free-trade zone traditionally exempted from the usual tariffs of rationality. Even in that tender kingdom, where love at first sight is still readily indulged, it would be impolitic, if not immature, to admit giving too much weight to a factor as shallow as looks. Yet perhaps it's time to say what we all secretly know, which is that looks do matter, maybe even more than most of us think.

We infer a great deal from people's looks — not just when it comes to mating (where looks matter profoundly), but in almost every other aspect of life as well, including careers and social status. It may not be true that blondes have more fun, but it's highly likely that attractive people do, and they start early. Mothers pay more attention to good-looking babies, for example, but, by the same token, babies pay more attention to prettier adults who wander into their fields of vision. Attractive people are paid more on the job, marry more desirable spouses, and are likelier to get help from others when in evident need. Nor is this all sheer, baseless prejudice. Human beings appear to be hard-wired to respond to how people and objects look, an adaptation without which the species might not have made it this far. The unpleasant truth is that, far from being only skin deep, our looks reflect all kinds of truths about difference and desire — truths we are, in all likelihood, biologically programmed to detect.

Sensitivity to the signals of human appearances would naturally lead to successful reproductive decisions, and several factors suggest that this sensitivity may be bred in the bone. Beauty may even be addictive. Researchers at London's University College have found that human beauty stimulates a section of the brain called the ventral striatum, the same region activated in drug and gambling addicts when they're about to indulge their habit. Photos of faces rated unattractive had no effect on the volunteers to whom they were shown, but the ventral striatum did show activity if the picture was of an attractive person, especially one looking straight at the viewer. And the responses occurred even when the viewer and the subject of the photo were of the same sex. Good-looking people just do something to us, whether we like it or not.

People's looks speak to us, sometimes in a whisper and sometimes in a shout, of health, reproductive fitness, agreeableness, social standing, and intelligence. Although looks in mating still matter much more to men than to women, the importance of appearance appears to be rising on both sides of the gender divide. In a fascinating cross-generational study of mating preferences, every 10 years different groups of men and women were asked to rank 18 characteristics they might want enhanced in a mate. The importance of good looks rose "dramatically" for both men and women from 1939 to 1989, the period of the study, according to David M. Buss, an evolutionary psychologist at the University of Texas. On a scale of 1 to 3, the importance men gave to good looks rose from 1.50 to 2.11. But for women, the importance of good looks in men rose from 0.94 to 1.67. In other words, women in 1989 considered a man's looks even more important than men considered women's looks 50 years earlier. Since the 1930s, Buss writes, "physical appearance has gone up in importance for men and women about equally, corresponding with the rise in television, fashion magazines, advertising, and other media depictions of attractive models."

In all likelihood this trend will continue, driven by social and technologi-   5
cal changes that are unlikely to be reversed anytime soon—changes such as the new ubiquity of media images, the growing financial independence of women, and the worldwide weakening of the institution of marriage. For better or worse, we live now in an age of appearances. It looks like looks are here to stay.

The paradox, in such an age, is that the more important appearances become, the worse most of us seem to look—and not just by comparison with the godlike images alternately taunting and bewitching us from every billboard and TV screen. While popular culture is obsessed with fashion and style, and our prevailing psychological infirmity is said to be narcissism, fully two-thirds of American adults have abandoned conventional ideas of attractiveness by becoming overweight. Nearly half of this group is downright obese. Given their obsession with dieting—a $40 billion-plus industry in the United States—it's not news to these people that they're sending an unhelpful message with their inflated bodies, but it's worth noting here nonetheless.

Social scientists have established what most of us already know in this regard, which is that heavy people are perceived less favorably in a variety of ways. Across cultures—even in places such as Fiji, where fat is the norm—people express a preference for others who are neither too slim nor too heavy. In studies by University of Texas psychologist Devendra Singh, people guessed that the heaviest figures in photos were eight to 10 years older than the slimmer ones, even though the faces were identical. (As the nation's bill for hair dye and facelifts attests, looking older is rarely desirable, unless you happen to be an underage drinker.)

America's weight problem is one dimension of what seems to be a broader-based national flight from presentability, a flight that manifests itself unmistakably in the relentless casualness of our attire. Contrary to the desperate contentions of some men's clothiers, for example, the suit is really dying. Walk around midtown Manhattan, and these garments are striking by their absence. Consumer spending reflects this. In 2004, according to NPD Group, a marketing information firm, sales of "active sportswear," a category that includes such apparel as warm-up suits, were $39 billion, nearly double what was spent on business suits and other tailored clothing. The irony is that the more athletic gear we wear, from plum-colored velour track suits to high-tech sneakers, the less athletic we become.

The overall change in our attire did not happen overnight. America's clothes, like America itself, have been getting more casual for decades, in a trend that predates even Nehru jackets and the "full Cleveland" look of a pastel leisure suit with white shoes and belt, but the phenomenon reaches something like an apotheosis in the vogue for low-riding pajama bottoms and flip-flops outside the home. Visit any shopping mall in summer—or many deep-Sunbelt malls year round—and you'll find people of all sizes, ages, and weights clomping through the climate-controlled spaces in tank tops, T-shirts, and running shorts. Tops—and nowadays often bottoms— emblazoned with the names of companies, schools, and places make many of these shoppers look like walking billboards. Bulbous athletic shoes, typically immaculate on adults who go everywhere by car, are the functional equivalent of SUVs for the feet. Anne Hollander, an observant student of clothing whose books include *Sex and Suits* (1994), has complained that we've settled on "a sandbox aesthetic" of sloppy comfort, the new classics— sweats, sneakers, and jeans—persist year after year, transcending fashion altogether.

We've come to this pass despite our seeming obsession with how we look. Consider these 2004 numbers from the American Society of Plastic Surgeons: 9.2 million cosmetic surgeries (up 24 percent from 2000) at a cost of $8.4 billion, and that doesn't count 7.5 million "minimally invasive" procedures, such as skin peels and Botox injections (collectively up 36 percent). Cosmetic dentistry is also booming, as is weight-loss surgery. Although most of this spending is by women, men are focusing more and more on their appearance as well, which is obvious if you look at the evolution of men's magazines over the years. Further reflecting our concern with both looks and rapid self-transformation is a somewhat grisly new genre of reality TV: the extreme makeover show, which plays on the audience's presumed desire to somehow look a whole lot better fast.

But appearances in this case *are* deceiving. The evidence suggests that a great many of us do not care nearly enough about how we look, and that even those who care very much indeed still end up looking terrible. In understanding why, it's worth remembering that people look the way they do for two basic reasons—on purpose and by accident—and both can be as revealing as a neon tube top.

Let's start with the purposeful. Extremes in casual clothing have several important functions. A big one nowadays is camouflage. Tent-like T-shirts and sweatsuits cover a lot of sins, and the change in our bodies over time is borne out by the sizes stores find themselves selling. In 1985, for example, the top-selling women's size was eight. Today, when, as a result of size inflation, an eight (and every other size) is larger than it used to be, NPD Group reports that the top-selling women's size is 14. Camouflage may also account for the popularity of black, which is widely perceived as slimming as well as cool.

That brings us to another motive for dressing down — way down — which is status. Dressing to manifest disregard for society — think of the loose, baggy hipsters in American high schools — broadcasts self-determination by flaunting the needlessness of having to impress anybody else. We all like to pretend we're immune to "what people think," but reaching for status on this basis is itself a particularly perverse — and egregious — form of status seeking. For grownups, it's also a way of pretending to be young, or at least youthful, since people know instinctively that looking young often means looking good. Among the truly young, dressing down is a way to avoid any embarrassing lapses in self-defining rebelliousness. And for the young and fit, sexy casual clothing can honestly signal a desire for short-term rather than long-term relationships. Indeed, researchers have shown that men respond more readily to sexy clothing when seeking a short-term relationship, perhaps because more modest attire is a more effective signal of sexual fidelity, a top priority for men in the marriage market, regardless of nation or tribe.

Purposeful slovenliness can have its reasons, then, but what about carelessness? One possible justification is that, for many people, paying attention to their own looks is just too expensive. Clothes are cheap, thanks to imports, but looking good can be costly for humans, just as it is for other species. A signal such as beauty, after all, is valuable in reproductive terms only if it has credibility, and it's been suggested that such signals are credible indicators of fitness precisely because in evolutionary terms they're so expensive. The peacock's gaudy tail, for example, attracts mates in part because it signals that the strutting bird is robust enough not only to sustain his fancy plumage but to fend off predators it also attracts. Modern humans who want to strut their evolutionary stuff have to worry about their tails too. They have to work them off. Since most of us are no longer paid to perform physical labor, getting exercise requires valuable time and energy, to say nothing of a costly gym membership. And then there is the opportunity cost — the pleasure lost by forgoing fried chicken and Devil Dogs. Eating junk food, especially fast food, is probably also cheaper, in terms of time, than preparing a low-calorie vegetarian feast at home.

These costs apparently strike many Americans as too high, which may   15
be why we as a culture have engaged in a kind of aesthetic outsourcing, transferring the job of looking good — of providing the desired supply of physical beauty — to the specialists known as "celebrities," who can afford

to devote much more time and energy to the task. Offloading the chore of looking great into a small, gifted corps of professionals saves the rest of us a lot of trouble and expense, even if it has opened a yawning aesthetic gulf between the average person (who is fat) and the average model or movie star (who is lean and toned within an inch of his or her life).

Although the popularity of Botox and other such innovations suggests that many people do want to look better, it seems fair to conclude that they are not willing to pay any significant price to do so, since the great majority do not in fact have cosmetic surgery, exercise regularly, or maintain anything like their ideal body weight. Like so much in our society, physical attractiveness is produced by those with the greatest comparative advantage, and consumed vicariously by the rest of us—purchased, in a sense, ready made.

Whether our appearance is purposeful or accidental, the outcome is the same, which is that a great many of us look awful most of the time, and as a consequence of actions or inactions that are at least substantially the result of free will.

Men dressed like boys? Flip-flops at the office? Health care workers who never get near an operating room but nevertheless dress in shapeless green scrubs? These sartorial statements are not just casual. They're also of a piece with the general disrepute into which looking good seems to have fallen. On its face, so to speak, beauty presents some serious ideological problems in the modern world. If beauty were a brand, any focus group that we convened would describe it as shallow and fleeting or perhaps as a kind of eye candy that is at once delicious and bad for you. As a society, we consume an awful lot of it, and we feel darn guilty about it.

Why should this be so? For one thing, beauty strikes most of us as a natural endowment, and as a people we dislike endowments. We tax inheritances, after all, on the premise that they are unearned by their recipients and might produce something like a hereditary aristocracy, not unlike the one produced by the competition to mate with beauty. Money plays a role in that competition; there's no denying that looks and income are traditionally awfully comfortable with each other, and today affluent Americans are the ones least likely to be overweight. By almost any standard, then, looks are a seemingly unfair way of distinguishing oneself, discriminating as they do on the basis of age and generally running afoul of what the late political scientist Alan Wildavsky called "the rise of radical egalitarianism," which was at the very least suspicious of distinction and advantage, especially a distinction as capricious and as powerful as appearance.

Appearance can be a source of inequality, and achieving some kind of   20 egalitarianism in this arena is a longstanding and probably laudable American concern. The Puritans eschewed fancy garb, after all, and Thoreau warned us to beware of enterprises that require new clothes. Nowadays, at a time of increased income inequality, our clothes paradoxically confer less distinction than ever. Gender distinctions in clothing, for instance, have been blurred in favor of much greater sartorial androgyny, to the extent that nobody would any longer ask who wears the pants in any particular house-hold (because the correct answer would be, "everybody"). The same goes for age distinctions (short pants long ago lost their role as uniform of the young), class distinctions (the rich wear jeans too), and even distinctions between occasions such as school and play, work and leisure, or public and private. Who among us hasn't noticed sneakers, for example, at a wedding, in a courtroom, or at a concert, where you spot them sometimes even on the stage?

The problem is that, if anything, looks matter even more than we think, not just because we're all hopelessly superficial, but because looks have always told us a great deal of what we want to know. Looks matter for good reason, in other words, and delegating favorable appearances to an affluent elite for reasons of cost or convenience is a mistake, both for the individuals who make it and for the rest of us as well. The slovenliness of our attire is one of the things that impoverish the public sphere, and the stunning rise in our weight (in just 25 years) is one of the things that impoverish our health. Besides, it's not as if we're evolving anytime soon into a species that's immune to appearances. Looks seem to matter to all cultures, not just our image-besotted one, suggesting that efforts to stamp out looksism (which have yet to result in hiring quotas on behalf of the homely) are bucking millions of years of evolutionary development.

The degree of cross-cultural consistency in this whole area is surprising. Contrary to the notion that beauty is in the eye of the beholder, or at the very least in the eye of the culture, studies across nations and tribal societies have found that people almost everywhere have similar ideas about what's attractive, especially as regards the face (tastes in bodies seem to vary a bit more, perhaps allowing for differing local evolutionary ecologies). Men everywhere, even those few still beyond the reach of Hollywood and Madison Avenue, are more concerned about women's looks than women are about men's, and their general preference for women who look young and healthy is probably the result of evolutionary adaptation.

The evidence for this comes from the field of evolutionary psychology. Whatever one's view of this burgeoning branch of science, one thing it has produced (besides controversy) is an avalanche of disconcerting research about how we look. Psychologists Michael R. Cunningham, of the University of Louisville, and Stephen R. Shamblen cite evidence that babies as young as two or three months old look longer at more attractive faces. New mothers of less attractive offspring, meanwhile, have been found to pay more attention to other people (say, hospital room visitors) than do new mothers of better-looking babies. This may have some basis in biological necessity, if you bear in mind that the evolutionary environment, free as it was of antibiotics and pediatricians, might have made it worthwhile indeed for mothers to invest themselves most in the offspring likeliest to survive and thrive.

The environment today, of course, is very different, but it may only amplify the seeming ruthlessness of the feelings and judgments we make. "In one study," reports David M. Buss, the evolutionary psychologist who reported on the multi-generational study of mating preferences, "after groups of men looked at photographs of either highly attractive women or women of average attractiveness, they were asked to evaluate their commitment to their current romantic partner. Disturbingly, the men who had viewed pictures of attractive women thereafter judged their actual partners to be less attractive than the men who had viewed analogous pictures of women who were average in attractiveness. Perhaps more important, the men who had viewed attractive women thereafter rated themselves as less committed, less satisfied, less serious, and less close to their actual partners." In another study, men who viewed attractive nude centerfolds promptly rated themselves as less attracted to their own partners.

Even if a man doesn't personally care much what a woman looks like, 25 he knows that others do. Research suggests that being with an attractive woman raises a man's status significantly, while dating a physically unattractive woman moderately lowers a man's status. (The effect for women is quite different; dating an attractive man raises a woman's status only somewhat, while dating an unattractive man lowers her status only nominally.) And status matters. In the well-known "Whitehall studies" of British civil servants after World War II, for example, occupational grade was strongly correlated with longevity. The higher the bureaucrat's ranking, the longer the life. And it turns out that Academy Award–winning actors and actresses outlive other movie performers by about four years, at least according to a study published in the *Annals of Internal Medicine* in 2001. "The results," write authors Donald A. Redelmeier and Sheldon M. Singh, "suggest that success confers a survival advantage." So if an attractive mate raises a man's status, is it really such a wonder that men covet trophy wives?

In fact, people's idea of what's attractive is influenced by the body types that are associated with status in a given time and place (which suggests that culture plays at least some role in ideas of attractiveness). As any museumgoer can tell you, the big variation in male preferences across time and place is in plumpness, and Buss contends that this is a status issue: In places where food is plentiful, such as the United States, high-status people distinguish themselves by being thin.

There are reasons besides sex and status to worry about how we look. For example, economists David S. Hamermesh, of the University of Texas, and Jeff E. Biddle, of Michigan State University, have produced a study suggesting that better-looking people make more money. "Holding constant demographic and labor-market characteristics," they wrote in a well-known 1993 paper, "plain people earn less than people of average looks, who earn less than the good-looking. The penalty for plainness is five to 10 percent, slightly larger than the premium for beauty." A 1998 study of attorneys (by the same duo) found that some lawyers also benefit by looking better. Yet another study found that better-looking college instructors—especially men—receive higher ratings from their students.

Hamermesh and some Chinese researchers also looked into whether primping pays, based on a survey of Shanghai residents. They found that beauty raises women's earnings (and, to a lesser extent, men's), but that spending on clothing and cosmetics helps only a little. Several studies have even found associations between appearance preferences and economic cycles. Psychologists Terry F. Pettijohn II, of Ohio State University, and Abraham Tesser, of the University of Georgia, for example, obtained a list of the Hollywood actresses with top box-office appeal in each year from 1932 to 1995. The researchers scanned the actresses' photos into a computer, did various measurements, and determined that, lo and behold, the ones who were most popular during social and economic good times had more "neoteny"—more childlike features, including bigger eyes, smaller chins, and rounder cheeks. During economic downturns, stronger and more rectangular female faces—in other words, faces that were more mature—were preferred.

It's not clear whether this is the case for political candidates as well, but looks matter in this arena too. In a study that appeared recently [2005] in *Science*, psychologist Alexander Todorov and colleagues at Princeton University showed photographs of political candidates to more than 800 students, who were asked to say who had won and why based solely on looks. The students chose correctly an amazing 69 percent of the time, consistently picking candidates they judged to look the most competent, meaning those who looked more mature. The losers were more likely to have babyfaces, meaning some combination of a round face, big eyes, small nose, high forehead, and small chin. Those candidates apparently have a hard time winning elections.

To scientists, a convenient marker for physical attractiveness in people   30
is symmetry, as measured by taking calipers to body parts [such] as wrists, elbows, and feet to see how closely the pairs match. The findings of this research can be startling. As summarized by biologist Randy Thornhill and psychologist Steven W. Gangestad, both of the University of New Mexico, "In both sexes, relatively low asymmetry seems to be associated with increased genetic, physical, and mental health, including cognitive skill and IQ. Also, symmetric men appear to be more muscular and vigorous, have a lower basal metabolic rate, and may be larger in body size than asymmetric men. . . . Symmetry is a major component of developmental health and overall condition and appears to be heritable." The researchers add that more symmetrical men have handsomer faces, more sex partners, and their first sexual experience at an earlier age, and they get to sex more quickly with a new romantic partner. "Moreover," they tell us, "men's symmetry predicts a relatively high frequency of their sexual partners' copulatory orgasms."

Those orgasms are sperm retaining, suggesting that symmetric men may have a greater chance of getting a woman pregnant. It doesn't hurt that the handsomest men may have the best sperm, at least according to a study at Spain's University of Valencia, which found that men with the healthiest, fastest sperm were those whose faces were rated most attractive by women. There's evidence that women care more about men's looks for short-term relationships than for marriage, and that as women get closer to the most fertile point of the menstrual cycle, their preference for "symmetrical" men grows stronger, according to Thornhill and Gangestad. Ovulating women prefer more rugged, masculinized faces, whereas the rest of the time they prefer less masculinized or even slightly feminized faces. Perhaps predictably, more-symmetrical men are likelier to be unfaithful and tend to invest less in a relationship.

Asymmetric people may have some idea that they're behind the eight ball here. William Brown and his then-colleague at Dalhousie University in Halifax, Nova Scotia, looked at 50 people in heterosexual relationships, measuring such features as hands, ears, and feet, and then asked about jealousy. The researchers found a strong correlation between asymmetry and romantic jealousy, suggesting that asymmetrical lovers may suspect they're somehow less desirable. Brown's explanation: "If jealousy is a strategy to retain your mate, then the individual more likely to be philandered on is more likely to be jealous."

In general, how we look communicates something about how healthy we are, how fertile, and probably how useful in the evolutionary environment. This may be why, across a range of cultures, women prefer tall, broad-shouldered men who seem like good reproductive specimens, in addition to offering the possibility of physical protection. Men, meanwhile, like pretty women who appear young. Women's looks seem to vary depending on where they happen to be in the monthly fertility cycle. The University of Liverpool biologist John Manning measured women's ears and fingers and had the timing of their ovulation confirmed by pelvic exams. He found a 30 percent decline in asymmetries in the 24 hours before ovulation—perhaps more perceptible to our sexual antennae than to the conscious mind. In general, symmetrical women have more sex partners, suggesting that greater symmetry makes women more attractive to men.

To evolutionary biologists, it makes sense that men should care more about the way women look than vice versa, because youth and fitness matter so much more in female fertility. And while male preferences do vary with time and place there's also some remarkable underlying consistency. Devendra Singh, for instance, found that the waist-to-hip ratio was the most important factor in women's attractiveness to men in 18 cultures he studied. Regardless of whether lean or voluptuous women happen to be in fashion, the favored shape involves a waist/hip ratio of about 0.7. "Audrey Hepburn and Marilyn Monroe represented two very different images of beauty to filmgoers in the 1950s," writes Nancy Etcoff, who is a psychologist at Massachusetts General Hospital. "Yet the 36-24-34 Marilyn and the 31.5-22-31 Audrey both had versions of the hourglass shape and waist-to-hip ratios of 0.7." Even Twiggy, in her 92-pound heyday, had a waist/hip ratio of 0.73.

The Kobal Collection at Art Resource, NY

Phillippe Halsman/Magnum Photos

Despite wildly divergent public images, actresses Audrey Hepburn, in black, and Marilyn Monroe shared one thing: a waist/hip ratio of 0.7.

Is it cause for despair that looks are so important? The bloom of youth   35
is fleeting, after all, and the bad news that our appearance will inevitably broadcast about us cannot be kept under wraps forever. Besides, who could live up to the impossible standards propagated by our powerful aesthetic-industrial complex? It's possible that the images of models and actresses and even TV newscasters, most of them preternaturally youthful and all selected for physical fitness, have driven most Americans to quit the game, insisting that they still care about how they look even as they retire from the playing field to console themselves with knife and fork.

If the pressure of all these images has caused us to opt out of caring about how we look, that's a shame, because we're slaves of neither genes nor fashion in this matter. By losing weight and exercising, simply by making ourselves healthier, we can change the underlying data our looks report. The advantages are almost too obvious to mention, including lower medical costs, greater confidence, and a better quality of life in virtually every way.

There's no need to look like Brad Pitt or Jennifer Lopez, and no reason for women to pursue Olive Oyl[1] thinness (a body type men do not especially prefer). Researchers, in fact, have found that people of both sexes tend to prefer averageness in members of the opposite sex: The greater the number of faces poured (by computer) into a composite, the higher it's scored in attractiveness by viewers. That's in part because "bad" features tend to be averaged out. But the implication is clear: You don't need to look like a movie star to benefit from a favorable appearance, unless, of course, you're planning a career in movies.

To a bizarre extent, looking good in America has become the province of an appearance aristocracy—an elect we revere for their seemingly unattainable endowment of good looks. Physical attractiveness has become too much associated with affluence and privilege for a country as democratically inclined as ours. We can be proud at least that these lucky lookers no longer have to be white or even young. Etcoff notes that, in tracking cosmetic surgery since the 1950s, the American Academy of Facial Plastic and Reconstructive Surgery reports a change in styles toward wider, fuller-tipped noses and narrower eyelids, while makeup styles have tended toward fuller lips and less pale skin shades. She attributes these changes to the recalibration of beauty norms as the result of the presence of more Asian, African, and Hispanic features in society.

But what's needed is a much more radical democratization of physical beauty, a democratization we can achieve not by changing the definition of beauty but by changing ourselves. Looking nice is something we need to take back from the elites and make once again a broadly shared, everyday attribute, as it once was when people were much less likely to be fat and much more likely to dress decently in public. Good looks are not just an endowment, and the un-American attitude that looks are immune to self-improvement only breeds the kind of fatalism that is blessedly out of character in America.

As a first step, maybe we can stop pretending that our appearance   40
doesn't—or shouldn't—matter. A little more looksism, if it gets people to shape up, would probably save some lives, to say nothing of some marriages. Let's face it. To a greater extent than most of us are comfortable with, looks tell us something, and right now what they say about our health, our discipline, and our mutual regard isn't pretty.

---

[1] **Olive Oyl:** A cartoon character created in 1919 by Elzie Crisler Segar for his comic strip "Thimble Theater," which later was renamed "Popeye," to recognize the popularity of the sailor character featured in the comic strip.—Eds.

The Reader's Presence

1. If, as Akst notes, humans are "hard-wired to respond to how people and objects look" (paragraph 2), why has society developed attitudes that consider beauty as "only skin deep" (paragraph 1)? How does the author explain this apparent inconsistency? Discuss why you agree or disagree with his explanation.

2. Note that Akst's essay on a common subject—the significance of good looks—relies on a number of scientific and professional studies. Make a list of the various disciplines that help provide Akst with evidence and support. For example, how does research in evolutionary biology contribute? How does economics contribute? What reports, if any, did you find either surprising or obvious, and why?

3. **VISUAL PRESENCE:**   Akst uses Audrey Hepburn and Marilyn Monroe as examples of "two very different images of beauty" that conform to the preferred "waist/hip ratio of 0.7" (paragraph 34; see also the photographs on page 339). Do you agree that the two actresses represent very different images of beauty? Explain why or why not by supporting your response with specific details. What other physical features do Hepburn and Monroe have in common that embody a certain kind of beauty? Comment on the extent to which these features would fit other standards of beauty around the world.

4. **CONNECTIONS:**   Read Akst's essay in conjunction with Camille Paglia's "The Pitfalls of Plastic Surgery" (page 691). Explain how Paglia's responses to the subject of looks and beauty conform to Akst's. How does Paglia offer alternative insights into the topic? For example, how are Paglia's norms about beauty different from those Akst cites in his essay? Which author do you agree with on the significance of good looks, and why?

Dave Barry

THE UGLY TRUTH ABOUT BEAUTY

DAVE BARRY (b. 1947) is an American author known primarily for his nationally syndicated humor column. In addition to his column for the *Miami Herald*, where he worked from 1983 through 2005, he has published dozens of books of fiction and nonfiction, including *Dave Barry Turns 40* (1990), *Dave Barry's Complete Guide to Guys* (1995), *Dave Barry in Cyberspace* (1996), *"The Greatest Invention in the History of Mankind Is Beer" and Other Manly Insights from Dave Barry* (2001), *Dave Barry's History of the Millennium (So Far)*

(2007), and *You Can Date Boys When You're Forty: Dave Barry on Parenting and Other Topics He Knows Very Little About* (2013). With Ridley Pearson, he is also the co-author of the successful *Peter and the Starcatchers* series, a series of novels for children based on J. M. Barrie's *Peter Pan*. The winner of a Pulitzer Prize for commentary in 1988, Dave Barry has been widely praised for his use of humor in journalism. Of his writing career, Barry has said that he was attracted to the newspaper business because he was an English major: "This meant I had experience writing long, authoritative-sounding essays without any knowledge of my topic, which is of course the essence of journalism."

> "As an English major, I had experience writing long authoritative-sounding essays without any knowledge of my topic, which is . . . the essence of journalism."

 IF YOU'RE A MAN, at some point a woman will ask you how she looks.

"How do I look?" she'll ask.

You must be careful how you answer this question. The best technique is to form an honest yet sensitive opinion, then collapse on the floor with some kind of fatal seizure. Trust me, this is the easiest way out. Because you will never come up with the right answer.

The problem is that women generally do not think of their looks in the same way that men do. Most men form an opinion of how they look in the seventh grade, and they stick to it for the rest of their lives. Some men form the opinion that they are irresistible stud muffins, and they do not change this opinion even when their faces sag and their noses bloat to the size of eggplants and their eyebrows grow together to form what appears to be a giant forehead-dwelling tropical caterpillar.

Most men, I believe, think of themselves as average-looking. Men will think this even if their faces cause heart failure in cattle at a range of 300 yards. Being average does not bother them; average is fine, for men. This is why men never ask anybody how they look. Their primary form of beauty care is to shave themselves, which is essentially the same form of beauty care that they give to their lawns. If, at the end of his four-minute daily beauty regimen, a man has managed to wipe most of the shaving cream out of his hair and is not bleeding too badly, he feels that he has done all he can, so he stops thinking about his appearance and devotes his mind to more critical issues, such as the Super Bowl.

Women do not look at themselves this way. If I had to express, in three words, what I believe most women think about their appearance, those words would be: "not good enough." No matter how attractive a woman may appear to be to others, when she looks at herself in the mirror, she thinks: woof. She thinks that at any moment a municipal animal-control officer is going to throw a net over her and haul her off to the shelter.

5

Why do women have such low self-esteem? There are many complex psychological and societal reasons, by which I mean Barbie. Girls grow up playing with a doll proportioned such that, if it were human, it would be seven feet tall and weigh 81 pounds, of which 53 pounds would be bosoms. This is a difficult appearance standard to live up to, especially when you contrast it with the standard set for little boys by their dolls . . . excuse me, by their action figures. Most of the action figures that my son played with when he was little were hideous-looking. For example, he was very fond of an action figure (part of the He-Man series) called "Buzz-Off," who was part human, part flying insect. Buzz-Off was not a looker. But he was extremely self-confident. You could not imagine Buzz-Off saying to the other action figures: "Do you think these wings make my hips look big?"

But women grow up thinking they need to look like Barbie, which for most women is impossible, although there is a multibillion-dollar beauty industry devoted to convincing women that they must try. I once saw an Oprah show wherein supermodel Cindy Crawford dispensed makeup tips to the studio audience. Cindy had all these middle-aged women applying beauty products to their faces; she stressed how important it was to apply them in a certain way, using the tips of their fingers. All the women dutifully did this, even though it was obvious to any sane observer that, no matter how carefully they applied these products, they would never look remotely like Cindy Crawford, who is some kind of genetic mutation.

I'm not saying that men are superior. I'm just saying that you're not going to get a group of middle-aged men to sit in a room and apply cosmetics to themselves under the instruction of Brad Pitt, in hopes of looking more like him. Men would realize that this task was pointless and demeaning. They would find some way to bolster their self-esteem that did not require looking like Brad Pitt. They would say to Brad: "Oh YEAH? Well what do you know about LAWN CARE, pretty boy?"

Of course many women will argue that the reason they become obsessed   10 with trying to look like Cindy Crawford is that men, being as shallow as a drop of spit, WANT women to look that way. To which I have two responses:

1. Hey, just because WE'RE idiots, that does not mean YOU have to be; and

2. Men don't even notice 97 percent of the beauty efforts you make anyway. Take fingernails. The average woman spends 5,000 hours per year worrying about her fingernails; I have never once, in more than 40 years of listening to men talk about women, heard a man say, "She has a nice set of fingernails!" Many men would not notice if a woman had upward of four hands.

Anyway, to get back to my original point: If you're a man, and a woman asks you how she looks, you're in big trouble. Obviously, you can't say she looks bad. But you also can't say that she looks great, because she'll think you're lying, because she has spent countless hours, with the help of the multibillion-dollar beauty industry, obsessing about the differences between herself and Cindy Crawford. Also, she suspects that you're not qualified to judge anybody's appearance. This is because you have shaving cream in your hair. ▢

The Reader's Presence

1. Barry makes a number of broad claims in this essay. How does he support—or fail to support—each of these claims? How specific or general is he in the explanations he offers? How does his approach affect your willingness to accept his explanations?

2. Comment on the role humor plays in Barry's essay. How would you read and understand the essay differently if Barry had simply explained each of his points in a straightforward manner? With which, if any, of Barry's more exaggerated or improbable statements did you find yourself agreeing? Explain why.

3. **CONNECTIONS:**   In both this essay and Barbara Ehrenreich's "Will Women Still Need Men?" (page 598), the authors use humorous generalizations to explain the points they are making. Find examples of this approach in both essays. Consider, specifically, how each writer justifies the generalizations that he or she makes. Are the two authors essentially using the same technique, or do their approaches differ? Explain.

Michael Bérubé

ANALYZE, DON'T SUMMARIZE

MICHAEL BÉRUBÉ, born in New York City in 1961, is Edwin Erle Sparks Professor of Literature and Director of the Institute for the Arts and Humanities at Pennsylvania State University, where he teaches literature and cultural studies or, as he calls it, "dangeral studies" for the controversy such studies engender. "I would be selling students short if my classes did not reflect some of my beliefs about literary theory, or feminism, or postmodernism, or multiculturalism, since I have spent my entire adult life studying such things," he told a reporter in 2006. Known for sparring with conservative critics of academia, Bérubé has become a noted advocate of "liberal" liberal education,

> Michael Bérubé has become a noted advocate of "liberal" liberal education, a defender of the humanities, and "the professor the right loves to hate."

a defender of the humanities, and "the professor the right loves to hate." His books include *Marginal Forces/Cultural Centers: Tolson, Pynchon, and the Politics of the Canon* (1992);

Public Access: Literary Theory and American Cultural Politics (1994); and *The Employment of English: Theory, Jobs, and the Future of Literary Studies* (1998). His 1996 book dealing with his son born with Down syndrome, *Life as We Know It: A Father, a Family, and an Exceptional Child* (1996), was a *New York Times* Notable Book of the Year. His most recent works are *What's Liberal About the Liberal Arts? Classroom Politics and "Bias" in Higher Education* (2006), *Rhetorical Occasions: Essays on Humans and the Humanities* (2006), and *The Left at War (Cultural Front)* (2009). He has written articles for many publications, including *Harper's*, the *New Yorker*, *Dissent*, the *New York Times Magazine*, the *Village Voice*, the *Washington Post*, and the *Nation*, as well as numerous scholarly journals such as the *Chronicle of Higher Education*, where his essay, "Analyze, Don't Summarize," appeared in 2004.

THE FIRST TIME a student asked me about my "grading system," I was nonplused—and a bit intimidated. It was an innocent question, but I heard it as a challenge: I was a 25-year-old graduate student teaching my first section in an English-literature class at the University of Virginia, and I really didn't know *what* my grading system was. Nor did I feel comfortable saying, "Well, it's like Justice Stewart's definition of pornography, really—I simply know an A paper when I see one."

I fumbled my way through a reply, but I was unsettled enough by the exchange to seek the advice of the professor in charge of the course (and roughly a dozen teaching assistants). He went on a sublime rant that I've never forgotten, though I'm sure I've embellished it over the years. "These students come in here," he fumed, "with the idea that *you* have to explain yourself. 'You gave me a B-plus,' they say. 'What did you take points off for?' I tell them, 'Your paper was not born with an A. Your paper was born with a "nothing," and I made up my mind about it as I read it. That's what the marginalia are—they're the record of my responses to your arguments.'"

Today I've incorporated versions of that rant into my own teaching handouts: I try to explain the differences among superior, mediocre, and failing papers, and I tell students that my skills as a reader have been honed by my many experiences with professional editors, who attend carefully to paragraph transitions, dangling modifiers, and inaccurate citations. But I've never been able to give my students a visceral idea of what goes through my head as I read their work—until now.

Like many sports fans, I've grown a bit tired of ESPN's 25th-anniversary hyper-self-awareness of itself as a sports medium. While it's great to see the network poke fun at its early years, when its anchors wore dorky sport coats and weren't always sure when they were on the air, it's really quite tedious to be reminded of how sports-television hype helped hype TV sports.

The show *Around the Horn* has come to epitomize the general decline   5 to me. Another half-hour program with which it's paired, *Pardon the Interruption*, gives us two volatile, opinionated sportscasters disagreeing with each other in rapid-fire fashion, with but a handful of seconds devoted to each topic. *Around the Horn* takes that format and makes a game show of it, offering us sportswriters competing for whose commentary will "win" by the end of the show.

I still play an organized sport—ice hockey—and as an amateur (and aged) player, I have to say that sports talk shows like this make me wonder whether some people don't see sports as simply an opportunity for endless metacommentary . . . and, of course, as gainful employment for an entire entourage of chattering parasites. In all that noise, I think, where are the games themselves?

Imagine my surprise, then, when I watched *Around the Horn* one afternoon and realized that here, at last, was my grading system in practice.

The idea behind *Around the Horn* is simple. There are a host and four contestants, each of whom speaks briefly on a series of up-to-the-moment sports topics. Points are awarded for smart—or merely plausible—remarks, and points are deducted for obviously foolish or factually inaccurate ones. There's a mute button involved, too, and players get eliminated as the show progresses (but those aspects of the game, so far as I can tell, have no counterpart in the world of paper-grading). And—of course, for this is the point of all such sports metacommentary—the viewers at home get to disagree with and complain about the commentary, as well as the officiating.

My standard undergraduate survey-course guides for paper-writing tell students things like this: "Assume a hypothetical readership composed of people who have already read the book. That means you shouldn't say, 'In class, we discussed the importance of the clam chowder in Chapter Five.' But more important, it means you *don't have to summarize the novel*. We're your readers, and we've read the book. However, we haven't read it in quite the way *you're* reading it. We haven't focused on the same scenes and passages you're bringing to our attention, and we haven't yet seen how your argument might make sense of the book for us."

But not all of my students see the point. Every semester I'm approached 10 by some who don't quite understand why they're being asked to make an *argument* out of literary criticism. Why shouldn't they simply record their impressions of the works before them? When I tell them that an observation is not a thesis, and that their thesis isn't sufficiently specific or useful if they can't imagine anyone plausibly disagreeing with it, they ask me why they can't simply explain *what happens in the novel.*

But in what world, exactly, would such an enterprise count as analysis? Not in any world I know—not even in the ephemeral pop-culture world of sports metacommentary. Can you imagine someone showing up on *Around the Horn* and saying to host Tony Reali, "Well, Tony, let me point out that last night, the Red Sox swept the Tigers and crept to within three games of the Yankees."

"And?"

"And nothing. I'm just pointing out that the Sox won, 3–1, on a four-hitter by Schilling, while the Yanks blew another late-inning lead."

No one does that, because no one in the sports world confuses summaries with analyses.

I also tell students that an essay of 2,000 words doesn't give them all that   15
much space to get going.

"You've only got a few pages to make that argument of yours. You don't need a grand introductory paragraph that begins, 'Mark Twain is one of Earth's greatest writers.' It's far better to start by giving us some idea of what you'll be arguing and why. If you like, you can even begin by pointing us to a particularly important passage that will serve as the springboard for your larger discussion: 'Not long after the second scaffold scene in *The Scarlet Letter*, when Arthur Dimmesdale joins hands with Hester Prynne and her daughter Pearl, Nathaniel Hawthorne asks us to reconsider the meaning of the scarlet A on Hester's breast.'"

On *Around the Horn*, commentators have to make their points in 15 seconds, which, as people who know me can testify, just happens to be roughly the amount of time it takes me to utter 2,000 words. So here, too, the analogy holds up.

Seriously, the sports-talk analogy is useful simply as a handy way of distinguishing between summary and analysis — and, more important, as an illustration of what happens in my grading process when a student paper cites textual evidence so compelling and unusual that it makes me go back and reread the passage in question (good!), suggests that a novel's conclusion fails to resolve the questions and tensions raised by the rest of the narrative (interesting! — possibly good, depending on the novel we're talking about), or makes claims that are directly contradicted by the literary text itself (bad! the mute button for you!).

So in a sense, I do "take off" points as I go — but then I add them back on as well, sentence by sentence, paragraph by paragraph, as I weigh the claims my students advance and the means by which they advance them.

The rules for literary analysis are the same rules in play for any kind of   20
analysis: mastery of the material. Cogency of supporting evidence. Ability to imagine and rebut salient counterarguments. Extra points for wit and style, points off for mind-numbing clichés, and permanent suspension for borrowing someone else's argument without proper attribution.

And yet, every year, I'm left with a handful of students who tell me that if *that's* what I want, I should simply assign topics to each student. "Not a chance," I reply. "Most of the mental labor of your paper takes place when you try to figure out just what you want to argue and why." As books like Thomas McLaughlin's *Street Smarts and Critical Theory* and Gerald Graff's *Clueless in Academe* have argued (with wit and style), students seem to understand this principle perfectly well when it comes to music, sports, and popular culture. It's our job to show them how it might apply to the study of literature.

My students, too, are often suspicious of what they regard as an idiosyncratic and a subjective enterprise that varies from English professor to English professor. But I can tell them there's really nothing mysterious about its mechanics. In fact, if they want to watch it in action, they can tune in to ESPN any weekday afternoon, 5 p.m. Eastern. ■

The Reader's Presence

1. Bérubé creates an analogy between grading student essays and watching sports commentary on ESPN. Outline the points of similarity between an instructor's responding to student writing and a television commentator's comments about sports. Which aspects of this analogy do you find most—and least—convincing? What aspects of this analogy, if any, has Bérubé omitted? Summarize the distinctions Bérubé draws between "analysis" and "summary." What is the significance of Bérubé's point that "an observation is not a thesis" (paragraph 10)?

2. In paragraph 21, Bérubé notes, "As books like Thomas McLaughlin's *Street Smarts and Critical Theory* and Gerald Graff's *Clueless in Academe* have argued (with wit and style), students seem to understand this principle perfectly well when it comes to music, sports, and popular culture." Explain the extent to which you agree—or disagree—with Bérubé's assertion here. What evidence can you point to in support of—or to argue against—the spirit and substance of Bérubé's claim?

3. As you reread Bérubé's essay, what specific words and phrases do you think most accurately and effectively characterize his tone toward grading student essays? toward television commentators on sports? What do you notice about Bérubé's choice of adjectives and verbs? What are his attitudes toward what he calls "marginalia" (paragraph 2)? What do you understand him to mean when he talks about "sports as simply an opportunity for endless metacommentary" (paragraph 6)? Comment on the effectiveness of Bérubé's use of "entourage" in the phrase "an entire entourage of chattering parasites" (paragraph 6). Examine carefully Bérubé's "rules for literary analysis" in paragraph 20. Apply these criteria to the strengths and weaknesses of his essay. Which of these rules does his essay most—and least—effectively illustrate? Be as specific as possible in your response.

4. **CONNECTIONS:** In his essay "Politics and the English Language" (page 515), George Orwell observes: "Modern English, especially written English, is full of bad habits which spread by imitation and which can be avoided if one is willing to take the necessary trouble" (paragraph 2). Orwell proceeds to list—and then to illustrate and analyze—six rules for writing good prose. Compare and contrast Orwell's and Bérubé's rules of writing. Based on these rules, which writer practices his craft more effectively? Explain why, and support your response with detailed analyses of each writer's prose.

Charles Bowden

OUR WALL

CHARLES BOWDEN (1945–2014) is probably best known for writing about the Mexican-American border. A contributing editor for *GQ* and *Mother Jones*, he also wrote for national publications such as *Harper's*, the *New York Times Book Review*, and *Esquire*. His many books of nonfiction include (to name just a few) *Murder City: Ciudad Juárez and the Global Economy's New Killing Fields* (2010), *Dreamland: The Way Out of Juárez* (2010), *Some of the Dead Are Still Breathing* (2009), *A Shadow in the City: Confessions of an Undercover Drug Warrior* (2005), and *Down by the River: Drugs, Money, Murder, and Family* (2004). He was a Lannan Writing Residency Fellow in Marfa, Texas, in 2001, and his

> Advocating immigration reform and criticizing U.S. border policy, Bowden likened American foreign policy toward Mexico to "making war on the poor."

2006 collaboration with photographer Michael Berman, *Inferno*, received the Border Regional Library Association's Southwest Book Award. A strong advocate for immigration reform and a sharp critic of U.S. border policy, Bowden called NAFTA "a machine producing poor people" and likened U.S. foreign policy (regarding Mexico) to "making war on the poor."

IN THE SPRING OF 1929, a man named Patrick Murphy left a bar in Bisbee, Arizona, to bomb the Mexican border town of Naco, a bunny hop of about ten miles (16 kilometers). He stuffed dynamite, scrap iron, nails, and bolts into suitcases and dropped the weapons off the side of his crop duster as part of a deal with Mexican rebels battling for control of Naco, Sonora. When his flight ended, it turned out he'd hit the wrong Naco, managing to destroy property mainly on the U.S. side, including a garage and a local mining company. Some say he was drunk, some say he was sober, but everyone agrees he was one of the first people to bomb the United States from the air.

Borders everywhere attract violence, violence prompts fences, and eventually fences can mutate into walls. Then everyone pays attention because a wall turns a legal distinction into a visual slap in the face. We seem to love walls, but are embarrassed by them because they say something unpleasant about the neighbors—and us. They flow from two sources: fear and the desire for control. Just as our houses have doors and locks, so do borders call forth garrisons, customs officials, and, now and then, big walls. They give us divided feelings because we do not like to admit we need them.

Now as the United States debates fortifying its border with Mexico, walls have a new vogue. At various spots along the dusty, 1,952-mile (3,141 kilometers) boundary, fences, walls, and vehicle barriers have been constructed since the 1990s to slow the surge in illegal immigration. In San Diego, nine miles (14 kilometers) of a double-layered fence have been erected. In Arizona, the state most overrun with illegal crossings, 65 miles (105 kilometers) of barriers have been constructed already. Depending on the direction of the ongoing immigration debate, there may soon be hundreds more miles of walls.

The 800 or so residents of Naco, Arizona, where Patrick Murphy is part of the local lore, have been living in the shadow of a 14-foot-high (four meters) steel wall for the past decade. National Guard units are helping to extend the 4.6-mile (7.4 kilometers) barrier 25 miles (40 kilometers) deeper into the desert. The Border Patrol station is the biggest building in the tiny town; the copper roof glistens under the blistering sun. In 2005, a pioneering bit of guerrilla theater took place here when the Minutemen, a citizen group devoted to securing the border, staked out 20 miles (32 kilometers) of the line and patrolled it. Today about 8,000 people live in Naco, Sonora, on the Mexican side of the metal wall that slashes the two communities.

Only a dirt parking lot separates the Gay 90s bar from the Naco wall.   5
Inside, the patrons are largely bilingual and have family ties on both sides of the line. Janet Warner, one of the bartenders, has lived here for years and is one of those fortunate souls who has found her place in the sun. But thanks to the racks of stadium lights along the wall, she has lost her nights, and laments the erasure of the brilliant stars that once hung over her life. She notes that sometimes Mexicans jump the new steel wall, come in for a beer, then jump back into Mexico. The bar began in the late 1920s as a casino and with the end of Prohibition added alcohol. The gambling continued until 1961, when a new county sheriff decided to clean up things. On the back wall are photographs of Ronald and Nancy Reagan when they'd stop by on their way to a nearby Mexican ranch.

The bar is one of only a handful of businesses left. The commercial street leading to the border is lined with defunct establishments, all dead because the U.S. government sealed the entry to Mexico after 9/11 and rerouted it to the east. Leonel Urcadez, 54, a handsome man who has owned the bar for decades, has mixed feelings about the wall. "You get used to it," he says. "When they first built it, it was not a bad idea—cars were crossing illegally from Mexico and the Border Patrol would chase them. But it's so ugly."

The two Nacos came into being in 1897 around a border crossing that connected copper mines in both nations. By 1901 a railroad linked the mines. A big miners' strike in 1906, one cherished by Mexicans as foreshadowing the revolution in 1910, saw troops from both nations facing each other down at the line. The town of Naco on the Mexican side changed hands many

Diane Cook & Len Jenshel

Border Field State Park, California. This stretch of upended railway track that looks like a work of contemporary art marks the western extent of the U.S.-Mexico border.

times during the actual revolution—at first the prize was revenue from the customs house. Later, when Arizona voted itself dry in 1915, the income came from the saloons. Almost every old house in Naco, Arizona, has holes from the gun battles. The Naco Hotel, with its three-foot (one meter) mud walls, advertised its bulletproof rooms.

The boundary between Mexico and the United States has always been zealously insisted upon by both countries. But initially Mexicans moved north at will. The U.S. patrols of the border that began in 1904 were mainly to keep out illegal Asian immigrants. Almost 900,000 Mexicans legally entered the United States to flee the violence of the revolution. Low population in both nations and the need for labor in the American Southwest made this migration a nonevent for decades. The flow of illegal immigrants exploded after the passage of the North American Free Trade Agreement in the early 1990s, a pact that was supposed to end illegal immigration but wound up dislocating millions of Mexican peasant farmers and many small-industrial workers.

The result: Naco was overrun by immigrants on their way north. At night, dozens, sometimes hundreds, of immigrants would crowd into motel rooms and storage rental sheds along the highway. The local desert was stomped into a powder of dust. Naco residents found their homes broken into by desperate migrants. Then came the wall in 1996, and the flow of people spread into the high desert outside the town.

The Border Patrol credits the wall, along with better surveillance technol-   10
ogy, with cutting the number of illegal immigrants captured near Naco's 33-mile (53 kilometers) border by half in the past year.[1] Before this new heightening of enforcement, the number caught each week, hiding in arroyos thick with mesquite and yucca, often exceeded the town's population. At the moment, the area is relatively quiet as "coyotes,"[2] or people smugglers, pause to feel out the new reality, and the National Guard has been sent in to assist the Border Patrol. At the nearby abandoned U.S. Army camp, the roofs are collapsing and the adobe bricks dribble mud onto the floor. Scattered about are Mexican water bottles — illegals still hole up here after climbing the wall.

Residents register a hodgepodge of feelings about the wall. Even those who have let passing illegal immigrants use their phones or given them a ride say the exodus has to stop. And even those sick of finding trash in their yards understand why the immigrants keep coming.

"Sometimes I feel sorry for the Mexicans," says Bryan Tomlinson, 45, a custodial engineer for the Bisbee school district. His brother Don chimes in, "But the wall's a good thing."

A border wall seems to violate a deep sense of identity most Americans cherish. We see ourselves as a nation of immigrants with our own goddess, the Statue of Liberty, a symbol so potent that dissident Chinese students fabricated a version of it in 1989 in Tiananmen Square as the visual representation of their yearning for freedom.

Walls are curious statements of human needs. Sometimes they are built to keep restive populations from fleeing. The Berlin Wall was designed to keep citizens from escaping from communist East Germany. But most walls are for keeping people out. They all work for a while, until human appetites or sheer numbers overwhelm them. The Great Wall of China, built mostly after the mid-14th century, kept northern tribes at bay until the Manchu conquered China in the 17th century. Hadrian's Wall, standing about 15 feet (5 meters) high, 9 feet (3 meters) wide, and 73 miles (117 kilometers) long, kept the crazed tribes of what is now Scotland from running amok in Roman

---

[1] This essay was published in May 2007. — EDS.

[2] *coyotes:* Smugglers paid to take people illegally across the U.S.-Mexico border. — EDS.

Britain—from A.D. 122 until it was overrun in 367. Then you have the Maginot Line, a series of connected forts built by France after World War I to keep the German army from invading. It was a success, except for one flaw: The troops of the Third Reich simply went around its northwestern end and invaded France through the Netherlands and Belgium. Now tourists visit its labyrinth of tunnels and underground barracks.

In 1859 a rancher named Thomas Austin released 24 rabbits in Australia   15 because, he noted, "the introduction of a few rabbits could do little harm and might provide a touch of home, in addition to a spot of hunting." By that simple act, he launched one of the most extensive barriers ever erected by human beings: the rabbit fences of Australia, which eventually reached 2,023 miles (3,256 kilometers). Within 35 years, the rabbits had overrun the continent, a place lacking sufficient and dedicated rabbit predators. For a century and a half, the Australian government has tried various solutions: imported fleas, poisons, trappers. Nothing has dented the new immigrants. The fences themselves failed almost instantly—rabbits expanded faster than the barriers could be built, careless people left gates open, holes appeared, and, of course, the rabbits simply dug under them.

In Naco all the walls of the world are present in one compact bundle. You have Hadrian's Wall or the Great Wall of China because the barrier is intended to keep people out. You have the Maginot Line because a 15-minute walk takes you to the end of the existing steel wall. You have the rabbit fences of Australia because people still come north illegally, as do the drugs.

Perhaps the closest thing to the wall going up on the U.S.-Mexico border is the separation wall being built by Israel in the West Bank. Like the new American wall, it is designed to control the movement of people, but it faces the problem of all walls—rockets can go over it, tunnels can go under it. It offends people, it comforts people, it fails to deliver security. And it keeps expanding.

Rodolfo Santos Esquer puts out *El Mirador*, a weekly newspaper in Naco, Sonora, and he finds the wall hateful. He stands in his cramped office—a space he shares with a small shop peddling underwear—and says, "It looks like the Berlin Wall. It is horrible. It is ugly. You feel more racism now. It is a racist wall. If people get close to the wall, the Border Patrol calls the Mexican police, and they go and question people."

And then he lightens up because he is a sunny man, and he says it actually hasn't changed his life or the lives of most people in town. Except that the coyotes now drive to the end of the wall before crossing. And as the wall grows in length, the coyotes raise their rates. Santos figures half the town is living off migrants going north—either feeding them and housing them or guiding them into the U.S. Passage to Phoenix, about 200 miles (320 kilometers) away, is now $1,500 and rising. He notes that after the wall went up in 1996, the migration mushroomed. He wonders if there is a connection, if the wall magically beckons migrants. Besides, he says, people just climb over it with ropes.

Santos fires up his computer and shows an image he snapped in the   20
cemetery of a nearby town. There, there, he points as he enlarges a section
of the photo. Slowly a skull-shaped blur floats into view against the black of
the night—a ghost, he believes. The border is haunted by ghosts—the hundreds who die each year from heat and cold, the ones killed in car wrecks
as the packed vans of migrants flee the Border Patrol, and the increasing
violence erupting between smugglers and the agents of Homeland Security.
Whenever heat is applied to one part of the border, the migration simply
moves to another part. The walls in southern California drove immigrants
into the Arizona desert and, in some cases, to their deaths. We think of walls
as statements of foreign policy, and we forget the intricate lives of the people
we wall in and out.

Emanuel Castillo Erúnez, 23, takes crime and car wreck photos for *El
Mirador*. He went north illegally when he was 17, walked a few days, then
was picked up and returned to Mexico. He sits on a bench in the plaza,
shielded by a New York Yankees cap, and sums up the local feeling about
the wall simply: "Some are fine with it, some are not." He thinks of going
north again, but then he thinks of getting caught again. And so he waits.

There is a small-town languor about Naco, Sonora, and the wall
becomes unnoticeable in this calm. The Minutemen and National Guard
terrify people. At the Hospedaje Santa María, four people wait for a chance
to go over the wall and illegally enter the wealth of the United States. It is
a run-down, two-story building, one of many boarding houses for migrants
in Naco. Salvador Rivera, a solid man in his early 30s, has been here about
a year. He worked in Washington State, but, when his mother fell ill, he
returned home to Nayarit, Mexico, and is now having trouble getting past
the increased security. He left behind an American girlfriend he can no
longer reach.

"For so many years, we Mexicans have gone to the U.S. to work. I don't
understand why they put up a wall to turn us away. It's not like we're robbing anybody over there, and they don't pay us very much."

But talk of the wall almost has to be prompted. Except for those engaged
in smuggling drugs or people, border crossers in Naco, Sonora, continue to
enter through the main gate, as they always have. They visit relatives on
the other side, as they always have. What has changed is this physical statement, a big wall lined with bright lights, that says, yes, we are two nations.

Jesús Gastelum Ramírez lives next door to the wall, makes neon signs,   25
and looks like Willie Nelson. He watches people climb the wall and he
understands a reality forgotten by most U.S. lawmakers—that simply to go
through the wire instantly raises a person's income tenfold. Gastelum knows
many of his neighbors smuggle people, and he understands.

Until recently, a volleyball team from the Mexican Naco and a team from
the U.S. Naco used to meet once a year at the point where the wall ends on
the west side of town, put up a net on the line, bring kegs of beer, and play
a volleyball game. People from both Nacos would stream out to the site and

watch. And then the wall would no longer exist for a spell. But it always confronts the eye.

Dan Duley, 50, operates heavy equipment and is a native of the Naco area. He was living in Germany after serving in the Air Force when the Berlin Wall came down, and he thought that was a fine thing. But here he figures something has to be done. "We need help," he says. "We're being invaded. They've taken away our jobs, our security. I'm just a blue-collar man living in a small town. And I just wish the government cared about a man who was blue."

But then, as in many conversations on the border, the rhetoric calms down. Duley, along with many other Naco residents, believes the real solution has to be economic, that jobs must be created in Mexico. There is an iron law on this border: The closer one gets to the line, the more rational the talk becomes because everyone has personal ties to people on the other side. Everyone realizes the wall is a police solution to an economic problem. The Mexicans will go over it, under it, or try to tear holes in it. Or, as is often the case, enter legally with temporary visiting papers and then melt into American communities. Of the millions of illegal immigrants living in the United States, few would have come if there wasn't a job waiting for them.

Over in Naco, Sonora, the final night of a fiesta is in full roar. Men drinking beer move by on horseback, groups of girls in high heels prance past. Nearby, folks play bingo, and in the band shell a group does a sound check for the big dance. Looming over the whole party is a giant statue of Father Hidalgo with his bald head and wild eyes. He launched the Mexican Wars of Independence in 1810. Two blocks away, the steel wall glows under a battery of lights.

In the Gay 90s bar in Naco, Arizona, a *quinceañera*, the 15th-birthday 30 celebration that introduces a young girl to the world, is firing up. There are 200 people in the saloon's back room, half from Mexico and half from the U.S. The boys wear rented tuxedo vests, the girls are dressed like goddesses. One man walks in with a baby in a black polka-dot dress with pink trim.

The birthday girl, Alyssa, stands with her family for an official portrait.

Walls come and go, but *quinceañeras* are forever, I say to the man with the baby. He nods his head and smiles.

The steel barrier is maybe a hundred feet (30 meters) away. Outside in the darkness, Mexicans are moving north, and Border Patrol agents are hunting them down. Tomorrow, work will continue on the construction of the wall as it slowly creeps east and west from the town. Tourists already come to look at it.

I have no doubt someday archaeologists will do excavations here and write learned treatises about the Great Wall of the United States. Perhaps one of them will be the descendant of a Mexican stealing north at this moment in the midnight hour. ▪

The Reader's Presence

1. From his first paragraph to his last, Bowden refers to the two towns of Naco, one in the United States and the other directly across the border in Mexico. What is the significance of these two towns? How do they play a key role in the way Bowden structures and develops his essay?

2. Bowden's essay is about barriers currently being built on the Mexican-American border. What, then, is his purpose in mentioning various walls and fences in world history, as he does in paragraphs 14–15? What is the relevance of the walls and fences to his main topic?

3. **VISUAL PRESENCE:**   Examine carefully the photograph of Border Field State Park in California (page 351). To what extent does this image match your expectation for what a wall looks like? In what ways is it similar to or different from the walls that Bowden describes in his essay? Cite specific examples in your answer.

4. **CONNECTIONS:**   Compare "Our Wall" to the following selection, David Brooks's "People Like Us." Who do the words *Our* and *Us* stand for in each essay? Do you think David Brooks's perspective on human behavior applies to the people Bowden speaks with in both Naco, Arizona, and Naco, Sonora? Why or why not?

David Brooks

PEOPLE LIKE US

DAVID BROOKS (b. 1961) was born in Toronto and grew up in New York City and in a suburb of Philadelphia. A journalist, columnist, and self-described "comic sociologist," Brooks has authored two books of cultural commentary, *Bobos in Paradise: The New Upper Class and How They Got There* (2001) and *On Paradise Drive: How We Live Now (and Always Have) in the Future Tense* (2004), and he edited the anthology *Backward and Upward: The New Conservative Writing* (1995). After graduating from the University of Chicago, Brooks worked as a reporter for the *Wall Street Journal*. Since that time, he has served as a senior editor at the *Weekly Standard* and as a contributing editor at the *Atlantic* and *Newsweek*, where the managing editor praised his "dead-on eye for the foibles of the Beltway—and his strong sense of how what happens in the capital's conservative circles affects the rest of the country."

Brooks presents commentary on National Public Radio and on *The Newshour with Jim Lehrer*. In 2003 he joined the *New York Times* as an op-ed columnist. He teaches occasionally as a visiting professor at Yale and Duke Universities.

In a PBS interview in 2000, Brooks argued that people tend to gravitate to like-minded, like-cultured people—a "congealing pot" of people just like themselves: "Now if you look at the *New York Times* wedding page, it's this great clash of résumés. . . . Harvard marries Yale. Princeton marries Stanford. Magna cum laude marries magna cum laude. You never

> In a PBS interview in 2000, David Brooks argued that people tend to gravitate to like-minded, like-cultured people— a "congealing pot" of people just like themselves.

get a magna cum laude marrying a summa cum laude because the tensions would be too great in that wedding." "People Like Us" first appeared in the *Atlantic* in 2003. Brooks's latest book is *The Social Animal: The Hidden Sources of Love, Character, and Achievement* (2011).

MAYBE IT'S TIME to admit the obvious. We don't really care about diversity all that much in America, even though we talk about it a great deal. Maybe somewhere in this country there is a truly diverse neighborhood in which a black Pentecostal minister lives next to a white anti-globalization activist, who lives next to an Asian short-order cook, who lives next to a professional golfer, who lives next to a postmodern-literature professor and a cardiovascular surgeon. But I have never been to or heard of that neighborhood. Instead, what I have seen all around the country is people making strenuous efforts to group themselves with people who are basically like themselves.

Human beings are capable of drawing amazingly subtle social distinctions and then shaping their lives around them. In the Washington, D.C., area Democratic lawyers tend to live in suburban Maryland, and Republican lawyers tend to live in suburban Virginia. If you asked a Democratic lawyer to move from her $750,000 house in Bethesda, Maryland, to a $750,000 house in Great Falls, Virginia, she'd look at you as if you had just asked her to buy a pickup truck with a gun rack and to shove chewing tobacco in her kid's mouth. In Manhattan the owner of a $3 million SoHo loft would feel out of place moving into a $3 million Fifth Avenue apartment. A West Hollywood interior decorator would feel dislocated if you asked him to move to Orange County. In Georgia a barista from Athens would probably not fit in serving coffee in Americus.

It is a common complaint that every place is starting to look the same. But in the information age, the late writer James Chapin once told me, every place becomes more like itself. People are less often tied down to factories and mills, and they can search for places to live on the basis of cultural affinity. Once they find a town in which people share their values, they flock there, and reinforce whatever was distinctive about the town in the first place. Once Boulder, Colorado, became known as congenial to politically progressive mountain bikers, half the politically progressive mountain bikers in the country (it seems) moved there; they made the place so culturally pure that it has become practically a parody of itself.

But people love it. Make no mistake — we are increasing our happiness by segmenting off so rigorously. We are finding places where we are comfortable and where we feel we can flourish. But the choices we make toward that end lead to the very opposite of diversity. The United States might be a diverse nation when considered as a whole, but block by block and institution by institution it is a relatively homogeneous nation.

When we use the word "diversity" today we usually mean racial integration. But even here our good intentions seem to have run into the brick wall of human nature. Over the past generation reformers have tried heroically, and in many cases successfully, to end housing discrimination. But recent patterns aren't encouraging: according to an analysis of the 2000 census data, the 1990s saw only a slight increase in the racial integration of neighborhoods in the United States. The number of middle-class and upper-middle-class African-American families is rising, but for whatever reasons — racism, psychological comfort — these families tend to congregate in predominantly black neighborhoods.   5

In fact, evidence suggests that some neighborhoods become more segregated over time. New suburbs in Arizona and Nevada, for example, start out reasonably well integrated. These neighborhoods don't yet have reputations, so people choose their houses for other, mostly economic reasons. But as neighborhoods age, they develop personalities (that's where the Asians live, and that's where the Hispanics live), and segmentation occurs. It could be that in a few years the new suburbs in the Southwest will be nearly as segregated as the established ones in the Northeast and the Midwest.

Even though race and ethnicity run deep in American society, we should in theory be able to find areas that are at least culturally diverse. But here, too, people show few signs of being truly interested in building diverse communities. If you run a retail company and you're thinking of opening new stores, you can choose among dozens of consulting firms that are quite effective at locating your potential customers. They can do this because people with similar tastes and preferences tend to congregate by ZIP code.

The most famous of these precision marketing firms is Claritas, which breaks down the U.S. population into sixty-two psycho-demographic clusters, based on such factors as how much money people make, what they like to read and watch, and what products they have bought in the past. For example, the "suburban sprawl" cluster is composed of young families making about $41,000 a year and living in fast-growing places such as Burnsville, Minnesota, and Bensalem, Pennsylvania. These people are almost twice as likely as other Americans to have three-way calling. They are two and a half times as likely to buy Light n' Lively Kid Yogurt. Members

© Bob Sacha/Corbis

Silicon Valley, California. As David Brooks writes, "[W]hat I have seen all around the country is people making strenuous efforts to group themselves with people who are basically like themselves." (paragraph 1)

of the "towns & gowns" cluster are recent college graduates in places such as Berkeley, California, and Gainesville, Florida. They are big consumers of DoveBars and *Saturday Night Live*. They tend to drive small foreign cars and to read *Rolling Stone* and *Scientific American*.

Looking through the market research, one can sometimes be amazed by how efficiently people cluster—and by how predictable we all are. If you wanted to sell imported wine, obviously you would have to find places where rich people live. But did you know that the sixteen counties with the greatest proportion of imported-wine drinkers are all in the same three metropolitan areas (New York, San Francisco, and Washington, D.C.)? If you tried to open a motor-home dealership in Montgomery County, Pennsylvania, you'd probably go broke, because people in this ring of the Philadelphia suburbs think RVs are kind of uncool. But if you traveled just a short way north, to Monroe County, Pennsylvania, you would find yourself in the fifth motor-home-friendliest county in America.

Geography is not the only way we find ourselves divided from people   10 unlike us. Some of us watch Fox News, while others listen to NPR. Some like David Letterman, and others — typically in less urban neighborhoods — like Jay Leno. Some go to charismatic churches; some go to mainstream churches. Americans tend more and more often to marry people with education levels similar to their own, and to befriend people with backgrounds similar to their own.

My favorite illustration of this latter pattern comes from the first, non-controversial chapter of *The Bell Curve*. Think of your twelve closest friends, Richard J. Herrnstein and Charles Murray write. If you had chosen them randomly from the American population, the odds that half of your twelve closest friends would be college graduates would be six in a thousand. The odds that half of the twelve would have advanced degrees would be less than one in a million. Have any of your twelve closest friends graduated from Harvard, Stanford, Yale, Princeton, Caltech, MIT, Duke, Dartmouth, Cornell, Columbia, Chicago, or Brown? If you chose your friends randomly from the American population, the odds against your having four or more friends from those schools would be more than a billion to one.

Many of us live in absurdly unlikely groupings, because we have organized our lives that way.

It's striking that the institutions that talk the most about diversity often practice it the least. For example, no group of people sings the diversity anthem more frequently and fervently than administrators at just such elite universities. But elite universities are amazingly undiverse in their values, politics, and mores. Professors in particular are drawn from a rather narrow segment of the population. If faculties reflected the general population, 32 percent of professors would be registered Democrats and 31 percent would be registered Republicans. Forty percent would be evangelical Christians. But a recent study of several universities by the conservative Center for the Study of Popular Culture and the American Enterprise Institute found that roughly 90 percent of those professors in the arts and sciences who had registered with a political party had registered Democratic. Fifty-seven professors at Brown were found on the voter-registration rolls. Of those, fifty-four were Democrats. Of the forty-two professors in the English, history, sociology, and political-science departments, all were Democrats. The results at Harvard, Penn State, Maryland, and the University of California at Santa Barbara were similar to the results at Brown.

What we are looking at here is human nature. People want to be around others who are roughly like themselves. That's called community. It probably would be psychologically difficult for most Brown professors to share an office with someone who was pro-life, a member of the National Rifle Association, or an evangelical Christian. It's likely that hiring committees would subtly — even unconsciously — screen out any such people they encountered. Republicans and evangelical Christians have sensed that they are not welcome at places like Brown, so they don't even consider working there. In fact, any registered Republican who contemplates a career in academia these days is both a hero and a fool. So, in a semi–self-selective pattern, brainy people with generally liberal social mores flow to academia, and brainy people with generally conservative mores flow elsewhere.

The dream of diversity is like the dream of equality. Both are based on ideals we celebrate even as we undermine them daily. (How many times have you seen someone renounce a high-paying job or pull his child from an elite college on the grounds that these things are bad for equality?) On the one hand, the situation is appalling. It is appalling that Americans know so little about one another. It is appalling that many of us are so narrow-minded that we can't tolerate a few people with ideas significantly different from our own. It's appalling that evangelical Christians are practically absent from entire professions, such as academia, the media, and filmmaking. It's appalling that people should be content to cut themselves off from everyone unlike themselves.   15

The segmentation of society means that often we don't even have arguments across the political divide. Within their little validating communities, liberals and conservatives circulate half-truths about the supposed awfulness of the other side. These distortions are believed because it feels good to believe them.

On the other hand, there are limits to how diverse any community can or should be. I've come to think that it is not useful to try to hammer diversity into every neighborhood and institution in the United States. Sure, Augusta National should probably admit women, and university sociology departments should probably hire a conservative or two. It would be nice if all neighborhoods had a good mixture of ethnicities. But human nature being what it is, most places and institutions are going to remain culturally homogeneous.

It's probably better to think about diverse lives, not diverse institutions. Human beings, if they are to live well, will have to move through a series of institutions and environments, which may be individually homogeneous but, taken together, will offer diverse experiences. It might also be a good idea to make national service a rite of passage for young people in this country: it would take them out of their narrow neighborhood segment and thrust them in with people unlike themselves. Finally, it's probably important for adults to get out of their own familiar circles. If you live in a coastal, socially liberal neighborhood, maybe you should take out a subscription to *The Door*, the evangelical humor magazine; or maybe you should visit Branson, Missouri. Maybe you should stop in at a megachurch. Sure, it would be superficial familiarity, but it beats the iron curtains that now separate the nation's various cultural zones.

Look around at your daily life. Are you really in touch with the broad diversity of American life? Do you care?

|||||||||||||||||||||||||||||||||||||||||||||||||||||||||||||||||||||||||||||||||||||||||||||||||||||||||||||||||||||||||||||||||||||

The Reader's Presence

1. Brooks begins his argument by "admit[ting] the obvious": Americans don't care about diversity, they just like to talk as if they do. What was your initial reaction to Brooks's so-called admission? What is the effect of admitting something that many of his readers will instinctually reject? How is your opinion affected by his evidence? How well has he supported this assertion by the end of the essay?

2. Brooks claims that it is human nature for people to group together with those who have similar ideals and backgrounds. What might be the advantages of such grouping? What might be lost if Americans were truly integrated? What is lost by segregating by religion, politics, race, class, profession, and sexuality?

3. **VISUAL PRESENCE:**   After examining the aerial photograph of an American residential neighborhood on page 359, describe specifically how this neighborhood is similar to or different from the neighborhood(s) you have lived in. How does the physical layout and appearance of this neighborhood reinforce Brooks's ideas about diversity in America?

4. **CONNECTIONS:**   Compare Brooks's observations about how we prefer to be around "people who are basically like [our]selves" (paragraph 1) to E. B. White's classic essay "Once More to the Lake" (page 293). In what ways can Brooks's point play a role in evaluating White's essay, which was written decades earlier? In what ways does White's lake community support Brooks's perspective on diversity? For a more direct comparison of ideas, compare Brooks's essay with Walter Benn Michaels's "The Trouble with Diversity" (page 673). After reading each selection closely, list the points Brooks and Michaels agree on and those they don't. What major differences do you see between the conclusions each writer reaches?

Stephen L. Carter
THE INSUFFICIENCY OF HONESTY

Law professor and writer **STEPHEN L. CARTER** (b. 1954) is an insightful and incisive critic of contemporary cultural politics. His first book, *Reflections of an Affirmative Action Baby* (1992), criticizes affirmative action policies that reinforce racial stereotypes rather than break down structures of discrimination. Carter's critique emerges from his own experience as an African American student at Stanford University and at Yale University Law School. After graduating from Yale, Carter served as a law clerk for Supreme Court justice Thurgood Marshall and eventually joined the faculty at Yale as professor of law, where he has served since 1991 as the William Cromwell Professor of Law. Carter has published widely on legal and social topics, including his books *The Culture of Disbelief: How American Law and Politics Trivialize Religious Devotion* (1993), *The Confirmation Mess: Cleaning Up the Federal Appointments Process* (1994), *Civility: Manners, Morals, and the Etiquette of Democracy* (1998), *The Dissent of the Governed: A Meditation on Law, Religion, and Loyalty* (1998), and *God's Name in Vain: The Wrongs and Rights of Religion in Politics* (2000).

> "There's no piece of writing that can't be improved by spending more time on it. The discipline is to make yourself stop."

Carter is also a prolific writer of novels; his most recent novels include *New England White* (2007), *Palace Council* (2008), *Jericho's Fall* (2009), and *The Impeachment of Abraham Lincoln* (2012). Carter's best-selling novel *The Emperor of Ocean Park* (2002) took him four years to complete. Carter says, "One of the best pieces of advice about writing I ever received was from a professor at law school who said to me, 'Stephen, there's no piece of writing that can't be improved by spending more time on it. The discipline is to make yourself stop.'"

"The Insufficiency of Honesty" first appeared in *Integrity* in 1996.

A COUPLE OF YEARS AGO I began a university commencement address by telling the audience that I was going to talk about integrity. The crowd broke into applause. Applause! Just because they had heard the word "integrity": that's how starved for it they were. They had no idea how I was using the word, or what I was going to say about integrity, or, indeed, whether I was for it or against it. But they knew they liked the idea of talking about it.

Very well, let us consider this word "integrity." Integrity is like the weather: everybody talks about it but nobody knows what to do about it. Integrity is that stuff that we always want more of. Some say that we need to return to the good old days when we had a lot more of it. Others say that we as a nation have never really had enough of it. Hardly anybody stops to explain exactly what we mean by it, or how we know it is a good thing, or why everybody needs to have the same amount of it. Indeed, the only trouble with integrity is that everybody who uses the word seems to mean something slightly different.

For instance, when I refer to integrity, do I mean simply "honesty"? The answer is no; although honesty is a virtue of importance, it is a different virtue from integrity. Let us, for simplicity, think of honesty as not lying; and let us further accept Sissela Bok's[1] definition of a lie: "any intentionally

---

[1] **Sissela Bok** (b. 1934): A Swedish-born scholar, philosopher, ethicist, and the author of many books, including *Lying: Moral Choice in Public and Private Life* (1978). She is the wife of Derek Bok, an interim president (2006–2007) of Harvard University. —Eds.

deceptive message which is *stated.*" Plainly, one cannot have integrity without being honest (although, as we shall see, the matter gets complicated), but one can certainly be honest and yet have little integrity.

When I refer to integrity, I have something very specific in mind. Integrity, as I will use the term, requires three steps: discerning what is right and what is wrong; acting on what you have discerned, even at personal cost; and saying openly that you are acting on your understanding of right and wrong. The first criterion captures the idea that integrity requires a degree of moral reflectiveness. The second brings in the ideal of a person of integrity as steadfast, a quality that includes keeping one's commitments. The third reminds us that a person of integrity can be trusted.

The first point to understand about the difference between honesty and integrity is that a person may be entirely honest without ever engaging in the hard work of discernment that integrity requires; she may tell us quite truthfully what she believes without ever taking the time to figure out whether what she believes is good and right and true. The problem may be as simple as someone's foolishly saying something that hurts a friend's feelings; a few moments of thought would have revealed the likelihood of the hurt and the lack of necessity for the comment. Or the problem may be more complex, as when a man who was raised from birth in a society that preaches racism states his belief in one race's inferiority as a fact, without ever really considering that perhaps this deeply held view is wrong. Certainly the racist is being honest—he is telling us what he actually thinks—but his honesty does not add up to integrity.

TELLING EVERYTHING YOU KNOW

A wonderful epigram sometimes attributed to the filmmaker Sam Goldwyn goes like this: "The most important thing in acting is honesty; once you learn to fake that, you're in." The point is that honesty can be something one *seems* to have. Without integrity, what passes for honesty often is nothing of the kind; it is fake honesty—or it is honest but irrelevant and perhaps even immoral.

Consider an example. A man who has been married for fifty years confesses to his wife on his deathbed that he was unfaithful thirty-five years earlier. The dishonesty was killing his spirit, he says. Now he has cleared his conscience and is able to die in peace.

The husband has been honest—sort of. He has certainly unburdened himself. And he has probably made his wife (soon to be his widow) quite miserable in the process, because even if she forgives him, she will not be able to remember him with quite the vivid image of love and loyalty that she had hoped for. Arranging his own emotional affairs to ease his transition to death, he has shifted to his wife the burden of confusion and pain, perhaps for the rest of her life. Moreover, he has attempted his honesty at the one

5

time in his life when it carries no risk; acting in accordance with what you think is right and risking no loss in the process is a rather thin and unadmirable form of honesty.

Besides, even though the husband has been honest in a sense, he has now twice been unfaithful to his wife: once thirty-five years ago, when he had his affair, and again when, nearing death, he decided that his own peace of mind was more important than hers. In trying to be honest he has violated his marriage vow by acting toward his wife not with love but with naked and perhaps even cruel self-interest.

As my mother used to say, you don't have to tell people everything you know. Lying and nondisclosure, as the law often recognizes, are not the same thing. Sometimes it is actually illegal to tell what you know, as, for example, in the disclosure of certain financial information by market insiders. Or it may be unethical, as when a lawyer reveals a confidence entrusted to her by a client. It may be simple bad manners, as in the case of a gratuitous comment to a colleague on his or her attire. And it may be subject to religious punishment, as when a Roman Catholic priest breaks the seal of the confessional—an offense that carries automatic excommunication.

In all the cases just mentioned, the problem with telling everything you know is that somebody else is harmed. Harm may not be the intention, but it is certainly the effect. Honesty is most laudable when we risk harm to ourselves; it becomes a good deal less so if we instead risk harm to others when there is no gain to anyone other than ourselves. Integrity may counsel keeping our secrets in order to spare the feelings of others. Sometimes, as in the example of the wayward husband, the reason we want to tell what we know is precisely to shift our pain onto somebody else—a course of action dictated less by integrity than by self-interest. Fortunately, integrity and self-interest often coincide, as when a politician of integrity is rewarded with our votes. But often they do not, and it is at those moments that our integrity is truly tested.

ERROR

Another reason that honesty alone is no substitute for integrity is that if forthrightness is not preceded by discernment, it may result in the expression of an incorrect moral judgment. In other words, I may be honest about what I believe, but if I have never tested my beliefs, I may be wrong. And here I mean "wrong" in a particular sense: the proposition in question is wrong if I would change my mind about it after hard moral reflection.

Consider this example. Having been taught all his life that women are not as smart as men, a manager gives the women on his staff less-challenging assignments than he gives the men. He does this, he believes, for their own benefit: he does not want them to fail, and he believes that they will if he gives them tougher assignments. Moreover, when one of the women on his staff does poor work, he does not berate her as harshly as he would a man, because he expects nothing more. And he claims to be acting with integrity because he is acting according to his own deepest beliefs.

The manager fails the most basic test of integrity. The question is not whether his actions are consistent with what he most deeply believes but whether he has done the hard work of discerning whether what he most deeply believes is right. The manager has not taken this harder step.

Moreover, even within the universe that the manager has constructed for himself, he is not acting with integrity. Although he is obviously wrong to think that the women on his staff are not as good as the men, even were he right, that would not justify applying different standards to their work. By so doing he betrays both his obligation to the institution that employs him and his duty as a manager to evaluate his employees.

The problem that the manager faces is an enormous one in our practical politics, where having the dialogue that makes democracy work can seem impossible because of our tendency to cling to our views even when we have not examined them. As Jean Bethke Elshtain[2] has said, borrowing from John Courtney Murray,[3] our politics are so fractured and contentious that we often cannot reach *disagreement*. Our refusal to look closely at our own most cherished principles is surely a large part of the reason. Socrates thought the unexamined life not worth living. But the unhappy truth is that few of us actually have the time for constant reflection on our views — on public or private morality. Examine them we must, however, or we will never know whether we might be wrong.

None of this should be taken to mean that integrity as I have described it presupposes a single correct truth. If, for example, your integrity-guided search tells you that affirmative action is wrong, and my integrity-guided search tells me that affirmative action is right, we need not conclude that one of us lacks integrity. As it happens, I believe — both as a Christian and as a secular citizen who struggles toward moral understanding — that we *can* find true and sound answers to our moral questions. But I do not pretend to have found very many of them, nor is an exposition of them my purpose here.

It is the case not that there aren't any right answers but that, given human fallibility, we need to be careful in assuming that we have found them. However, today's political talk about how it is wrong for the government to impose one person's morality on somebody else is just mindless chatter. *Every* law imposes one person's morality on somebody else, because

15

---

2 ***Jean Bethke Elshtain*** (1941–2013): A feminist political philosopher and professor of social and political ethics at the University of Chicago Divinity School. She served on the Board of Advisors of the Bible Literacy Project, publishers of the curriculum "The Bible and Its Influence" for public high school literature courses. — EDS.

3 ***John Courtney Murray, SJ*** (1904–1967): A Jesuit priest, theologian, and widely respected intellectual who was especially known for his efforts to reconcile Catholicism and religious pluralism, religious freedom, and American politics. — EDS.

law has only two functions: to tell people to do what they would rather not or to forbid them to do what they would.

And if the surveys can be believed, there is far more moral agreement in America than we sometimes allow ourselves to think. One of the reasons that character education for young people makes so much sense to so many people is precisely that there seems to be a core set of moral understandings—we might call them the American Core—that most of us accept. Some of the virtues in this American Core are, one hopes, relatively noncontroversial. About 500 American communities have signed on to Michael Josephson's[4] program to emphasize the "six pillars" of good character: trustworthiness, respect, responsibility, caring, fairness, and citizenship. These virtues might lead to a similarly noncontroversial set of political values: having an honest regard for ourselves and others, protecting freedom of thought and religious belief, and refusing to steal or murder.

HONESTY AND COMPETING RESPONSIBILITIES

A further problem with too great an exaltation of honesty is that it may   20
allow us to escape responsibilities that morality bids us bear. If honesty is substituted for integrity, one might think that if I say I am not planning to fulfill a duty, I need not fulfill it. But it would be a peculiar morality indeed that granted us the right to avoid our moral responsibilities simply by stating our intention to ignore them. Integrity does not permit such an easy escape.

Consider an example. Before engaging in sex with a woman, her lover tells her that if she gets pregnant, it is her problem, not his. She says that she understands. In due course she does wind up pregnant. If we believe, as I hope we do, that the man would ordinarily have a moral responsibility toward both the child he will have helped to bring into the world and the child's mother, then his honest statement of what he intends does not spare him that responsibility.

This vision of responsibility assumes that not all moral obligations stem from consent or from a stated intention. The linking of obligations to promises is a rather modern and perhaps uniquely Western way of looking at life, and perhaps a luxury that the well-to-do can afford. As Fred and Shulamit Korn (a philosopher and an anthropologist) have pointed out, "If one looks at ethnographic accounts of other societies, one finds that, while obligations everywhere play a crucial role in social life, promising is not preeminent among the sources of obligation and is not even mentioned by most anthropologists." The Korns have made a study of Tonga, where promises are virtually unknown but the social order is remarkably stable. If life without any

---

4 ***Michael Josephson*** (b. 1942): A prominent ethicist as well as founder and president of Josephson Institute and its CHARACTER COUNTS! Project. —EDS.

promises seems extreme, we Americans sometimes go too far the other way, parsing not only our contracts but even our marriage vows in order to discover the absolute minimum obligation that we have to others as a result of our promises.

That some societies in the world have worked out evidently functional structures of obligation without the need for promise or consent does not tell us what *we* should do. But it serves as a reminder of the basic proposition that our existence in civil society creates a set of mutual responsibilities that philosophers used to capture in the fiction of the social contract. Nowadays, here in America, people seem to spend their time thinking of even cleverer ways to avoid their obligations, instead of doing what integrity commands and fulfilling them. And all too often honesty is their excuse. ■

The Reader's Presence

1. If Carter intends his essay to be a discussion of honesty, why does he begin with a consideration of the concept of integrity? How are the terms related? In what important ways are they different? What does integrity involve that honesty doesn't?

2. Notice that in this essay Carter never once offers a dictionary definition of the words *honesty* and *integrity*. Look up each term in a standard dictionary. As a reader, do you think such definitions would have made Carter's distinctions clearer? Why or why not? Why do you think Carter chose not to define the words according to their common dictionary meanings? How does he define them? How are his considerations of honesty and integrity related to his conclusion?

3. **CONNECTIONS:** In "Why Women Smile" (page 369), Amy Cunningham argues that women often "smile in lieu of showing what's really on [their] minds" (paragraph 3). Would Carter classify this kind of smiling as insufficiently honest? Why or why not? Cunningham notes that she is "trying to quit" smiling (paragraph 1); would not smiling show greater integrity, as Carter explains it?

Amy Cunningham

WHY WOMEN SMILE

AMY CUNNINGHAM (b. 1955) has been writing on psychological issues and modern life for magazines such as *Redbook*, *Glamour*, and the *Washington Post Magazine* since she graduated from the University of Virginia in 1977 with a BA in English. Cunningham says that the essay reprinted here grew out of her own experience as an "easy to get along with person" who was raised by southerners in the suburbs of Chicago. She also recalls that when writing it, "I was unhappy with myself for taking too long, for not being efficient the way I thought a professional writer should be—but the work paid off and now I think it is one of the best essays I've written." "Why Women Smile" originally appeared in *Lear's* in 1993.

> "Good writing has less to do with talent and more to do with the discipline of staying seated . . . in front of the computer and getting the work done."

Looking back on her writing career, Cunningham notes, "When I was younger I thought if you had talent you would make it as a writer. I'm surprised to realize now that good writing has less to do with talent and more to do with the discipline of staying seated in the chair, by yourself, in front of the computer and getting the work done."

AFTER SMILING BRILLIANTLY for nearly four decades, I now find myself trying to quit. Or, at the very least, seeking to lower the wattage a bit.

Not everyone I know is keen on this. My smile has gleamed like a cheap plastic night-light so long and so reliably that certain friends and relatives worry that my mood will darken the moment my smile dims. "Gee," one says, "I associate you with your smile. It's the essence of you. I should think you'd want to smile more!" But the people who love me best agree that my smile—which springs forth no matter where I am or how I feel—hasn't been serving me well. Said my husband recently, "Your smiling face and unthreatening demeanor make people like you in a fuzzy way, but that doesn't seem to be what you're after these days."

Smiles are not the small and innocuous things they appear to be: Too many of us smile in lieu of showing what's really on our minds. Indeed, the success of the women's movement might be measured by the sincerity—and lack of it—in our smiles. Despite all the work we American women have done to get and maintain full legal control of our bodies, not to mention our destinies, we still don't seem to be fully in charge of a couple of small muscle groups in our faces.

We smile so often and so promiscuously — when we're angry, when we're tense, when we're with children, when we're being photographed, when we're interviewing for a job, when we're meeting candidates to employ — that the Smiling Woman has become a peculiarly American archetype. This isn't entirely a bad thing, of course. A smile lightens the load, diffuses unpleasantness, redistributes nervous tension. Women doctors smile more than their male counterparts, studies show, and are better liked by their patients.

Oscar Wilde's[1] old saw that "a woman's face is her work of fiction" is   5 often quoted to remind us that what's on the surface may have little connection to what we're feeling. What is it in our culture that keeps our smiles on automatic pilot? The behavior seems to be an equal blend of nature and nurture. Research has demonstrated that since females often mature earlier than males and are less irritable, girls smile more than boys from the very beginning. But by adolescence, the differences in the smiling rates of boys and girls are so robust that it's clear the culture has done more than its share of the dirty work. Just think of the mothers who painstakingly embroidered the words ENTER SMILING on little samplers, and then hung their handiwork on doors by golden chains. Translation: "Your real emotions aren't welcome here."

Clearly, our instincts are another factor. Our smiles have their roots in the greetings of monkeys, who pull their lips up and back to show their fear of attack, as well as their reluctance to vie for a position of dominance. And like the opossum caught in the light by the clattering garbage cans, we, too, flash toothy grimaces when we make major mistakes. By declaring ourselves non-threatening, our smiles provide an extremely versatile means of protection.

Our earliest baby smiles are involuntary reflexes having only the vaguest connection to contentment or comfort. In short, we're genetically wired to pull on our parents' heartstrings. As Desmond Morris[2] explains in *Babywatching*, this is our way of attaching ourselves to our caretakers, as truly as baby chimps clench their mothers' fur. Even as babies we're capable of projecting onto others (in this case, our parents) the feelings we know we need to get back in return.

Bona fide social smiles occur at two-and-a-half to three months of age, usually a few weeks after we first start gazing with intense interest into the faces of our parents. By the time we are six months old, we are smiling and laughing regularly in reaction to tickling, feedings, blown raspberries, hugs, and peekaboo games. Even babies who are born blind intuitively know how to react to pleasurable changes with a smile, though their first smiles start later than those of sighted children.

---

1 **Oscar Wilde** (1854–1900): An Irish writer, poet, aesthete, and popular playwright in the early 1890s remembered for his epigrams and his early death. — EDS.

2 **Desmond Morris** (b. 1928): Distinguished zoologist and author of the best-selling *The Naked Ape* (1967) and *Babywatching* (1992). — EDS.

Psychologists and psychiatrists have noted that babies also smile and laugh with relief when they realize that something they thought might be dangerous is not dangerous after all. Kids begin to invite their parents to indulge them with "scary" approach-avoidance games; they love to be chased or tossed up into the air. (It's interesting to note that as adults, we go through the same gosh-that's-shocking-and-dangerous-but-it's-okay-to-laugh-and-smile cycles when we listen to raunchy stand-up comics.)

From the wilds of New Guinea to the sidewalks of New York, smiles are   10 associated with joy, relief, and amusement. But smiles are by no means limited to the expression of positive emotions: People of many different cultures smile when they are frightened, embarrassed, angry, or miserable. In Japan, for instance, a smile is often used to hide pain or sorrow.

Psychologist Paul Ekman, the head of the University of California's Human Interaction Lab in San Francisco, has identified 18 distinct types of smiles, including those that show misery, compliance, fear, and contempt. The smile of true merriment, which Dr. Ekman calls the Duchenne Smile, after the nineteenth-century French doctor who first studied it, is characterized by heightened circulation, a feeling of exhilaration, and the employment of two major facial muscles: the zygomaticus major of the lower face, and the orbicularis oculi, which crinkles the skin around the eyes. But since the average American woman's smile often has less to do with her actual state of happiness than it does with the social pressure to smile no matter what, her baseline social smile isn't apt to be a felt expression that engages the eyes like this. Ekman insists that if people learned to read smiles, they could see the sadness, misery, or pain lurking there, plain as day.

These photos from Paul Ekman's study show the difference between the social smile (left) and the true enjoyment smile (right).

Evidently, a woman's happy, willing deference is something the world wants visibly demonstrated. Woe to the waitress, the personal assistant or receptionist, the flight attendant, or any other woman in the line of public service whose smile is not offered up to the boss or client as proof that there are no storm clouds—no kids to support, no sleep that's been missed—rolling into the sunny workplace landscape. Women are expected to smile no matter where they line up on the social, cultural, or economic ladder: College professors are criticized for not smiling, political spouses are pilloried for being too serious, and women's roles in films have historically been smiling ones. It's little wonder that men on the street still call out, "Hey, baby, smile! Life's not *that* bad, is it?" to women passing by, lost in thought.

A friend remembers being pulled aside by a teacher after class and asked, "What is wrong, dear? You sat there for the whole hour looking so sad!" "All I could figure," my friend says now, "is that I wasn't smiling. And the fact that *she* felt sorry for me for looking normal made me feel horrible."

Ironically, the social laws that govern our smiles have completely reversed themselves over the last two thousand years. Women weren't always expected to seem animated and responsive; in fact, immoderate laughter was once considered one of the more conspicuous vices a woman could have, and mirth was downright sinful. Women were kept apart, in some cultures even veiled, so that they couldn't perpetuate Eve's seductive, evil work. The only smile deemed appropriate on a privileged woman's face was the serene, inward smile of the Virgin Mary at Christ's birth, and even that expression was best directed exclusively at young children. Cackling laughter and wicked glee were the kinds of sounds heard only in hell.

What we know of women's facial expressions in other centuries comes 15 mostly from religious writings, codes of etiquette, and portrait paintings. In fifteenth century Italy, it was customary for artists to paint lovely, blank-faced women in profile. A viewer could stare endlessly at such a woman, but she could not gaze back. By the Renaissance, male artists were taking some pleasure in depicting women with a semblance of complexity, Leonardo da Vinci's *Mona Lisa*,[3] with her veiled enigmatic smile, being the most famous example.

The Golden Age of the Dutch Republic[4] marks a fascinating period for studying women's facial expressions. While we might expect the drunken young whores of Amsterdam to smile devilishly (unbridled sexuality and lasciviousness were *supposed* to addle the brain), it's the faces of the Dutch women from fine families that surprise us. Considered socially more free, these women demonstrate a fuller range of facial expressions than their

---

[3] **Mona Lisa** (p. 373): Widely recognized as one of the most important works of art in history, this sixteenth-century portrait painted in oil by Leonardo di ser Piero da Vinci (1452–1519) is on display at the Musée du Louvre in Paris as "Portrait of Lisa Gherardini, wife of Francesco del Giocondo."—Eds.

[4] **Golden Age of the Dutch Republic:** A period in Dutch history, ranging across the seventeenth century, in which Dutch achievements in trade, science, art, and military were highly acclaimed.—Eds.

Réunion des Musées Nationaux/Art Resource, NY

European sisters. Frans Hals's[5] 1622 portrait of Stephanus Geraerdt and Isa-
bella Coymans, a married couple, is remarkable not just for the full, friendly
smiles on each face but for the frank and mutual pleasure the couple take
in each other.

In the 1800s, sprightly, pretty women began appearing in advertisements for everything from beverages to those newfangled Kodak Land
cameras.[6] Women's faces were no longer impassive, and their willingness to
bestow status, to offer, proffer, and yield, was most definitely promoted by
their smiling images. The culture appeared to have turned the smile, originally a bond shared between intimates, into a socially required display that
sold capitalist ideology as well as kitchen appliances. And female viewers
soon began to emulate these highly idealized pictures. Many longed to be
more like her, that perpetually smiling female. She seemed so beautiful. So
content. So whole.

[5] ***Frans Hals*** (c. 1582/83–1666): One of the most celebrated painters during the Dutch Golden
Age. — EDS.
[6] ***Kodak Land camera:*** An instant camera, invented by American scientist Edwin Land and
first sold in 1948. — EDS.

By the middle of the nineteenth century, the bulk of America's smile burden was falling primarily to women and African-American slaves, providing a very portable means of protection, a way of saying, "I'm harmless. I won't assert myself here." It reassured those in power to see signs of gratitude and contentment in the faces of subordinates. As long ago as 1963, adman David Ogilvy declared the image of a woman smiling approvingly at a product clichéd, but we've yet to get the message. Cheerful Americans still appear in ads today, smiling somewhat less disingenuously than they smiled during the middle of the century, but smiling broadly nonetheless.

Other countries have been somewhat reluctant to import our "Don't worry, be happy" American smiles. When McDonald's opened in Moscow not long ago [1990] and when EuroDisney debuted in France last year [1992], the Americans involved in both business ventures complained that they couldn't get the natives they'd employed to smile worth a damn.

Europeans visiting the United States for the first time are often surprised at just how often Americans smile. But when you look at our history, the relentless good humor (or, at any rate, the pretense of it) falls into perspective. The American wilderness was developed on the assumption that this country had a shortage of people in relation to its possibilities. In countries with a more rigid class structure or caste system, fewer people are as captivated by the idea of quickly winning friends and influencing people. Here in the States, however, every stranger is a potential associate. Our smiles bring new people on board. The American smile is a democratic version of a curtsy or doffed hat, since, in this land of free equals, we're not especially formal about the ways we greet social superiors. 20

The civil rights movement never addressed the smile burden by name, but activists worked on their own to set new facial norms. African-American males stopped smiling on the streets in the 1960s, happily aware of the unsettling effect this action had on the white population. The image of the simpleminded, smiling, white-toothed black was rejected as blatantly racist, and it gradually retreated into the distance. However, like the women of Sparta and the wives of samurai, who were expected to look happy upon learning their sons or husbands had died in battle, contemporary American women have yet to unilaterally declare their faces their own property.

For instance, imagine a woman at a morning business meeting being asked if she could make a spontaneous and concise summation of a complicated project she's been struggling to get under control for months. She might draw the end of her mouth back and clench her teeth—Eek!—in a protective response, a polite, restrained expression of her surprise, not unlike the expression of a conscientious young schoolgirl being told to get out paper and pencil for a pop quiz. At the same time, the woman might be feeling resentful of the supervisor who sprang the request, but she fears taking that person on. So she holds back a comment. The whole performance resolves in a weird grin collapsing into a nervous smile that conveys discomfort and unpreparedness. A pointed remark by way of explanation or self-defense might've worked better for her—but her mouth was otherwise engaged.

We'd do well to realize just how much our smiles misrepresent us, and swear off for good the self-deprecating grins and ritual displays of deference. Real smiles have beneficial physiological effects, according to Paul Ekman. False ones do nothing for us at all.

"Smiles are as important as sound bites on television," insists producer and media coach Heidi Berenson, who has worked with many of Washington's most famous faces. "And women have always been better at understanding this than men. But the smile I'm talking about is not a cutesy smile. It's an authoritative smile. A genuine smile. Properly timed, it's tremendously powerful."

To limit a woman to one expression is like editing down an orchestra 25 to one instrument. And the search for more authentic means of expression isn't easy in a culture in which women are still expected to be magnanimous smilers, helpmates in crisis, and curators of everybody else's morale. But change is already floating in the high winds. We see a boon in assertive female comedians who are proving that women can *dish out* smiles, not just wear them. Actress Demi Moore has stated that she doesn't like to take smiling roles. Nike is running ads that show unsmiling women athletes sweating, reaching, pushing themselves. These women aren't overly concerned with issues of rapport; they're not being "nice" girls—they're working out.

If a woman's smile were truly her own, to be smiled or not, according to how the *woman* felt, rather than according to what someone else needed, she would smile more spontaneously, without ulterior, hidden motives. As Rainer Maria Rilke[7] wrote in *The Journal of My Other Self*, "Her smile was not meant to be seen by anyone and served its whole purpose in being smiled."

That smile is my long-term aim. In the meantime, I hope to stabilize on the smile continuum somewhere between the eliciting grin of Farrah Fawcett[8] and the haughty smirk of Jeane Kirkpatrick.[9] ▇

The Reader's Presence

1. Cunningham presents an informative précis of the causes and effects of smiling in Western culture. Consider the points of view from which she addresses this subject. Summarize and evaluate her treatment of smiling from psychological, physiological, sociological, and historical points of view. Which do you find most incisive? Why? What other points of view does she introduce into her discussion of smiling? What effects do they create? What does she identify as the benefits (and the disadvantages) of smiling?

---

[7] **Rainer Maria Rilke** (1875–1926): Austrian poet, art critic, and author of *Letters to a Young Poet* (1929) and *The Journal of My Other Self* (1930). —EDS.

[8] **Farrah Fawcett** (1947–2009): American actress who became an international celebrity after appearing in the television series *Charlie's Angels* in 1976. —EDS.

[9] **Jeane Kirkpatrick** (1926–2006): An American ambassador to the United Nations during the administration of President Ronald Reagan. —EDS.

2. At what point in this essay does Cunningham address the issue of gender? Characterize the language she uses to introduce this issue. She distinguishes between the different patterns—and the consequences—experienced by men and women who smile. Summarize these differences and assess the nature and the extent of the evidence she provides for each of her points. What more general distinctions does she make about various kinds of smiles? What are their different purposes and degrees of intensity? What information does she provide about smiling as an issue of nationality and race? What is the overall purpose of this essay? Where—and how—does Cunningham create and sustain a sense of her own presence in this essay? What does she set as her personal goal in relation to smiling?

3. **VISUAL PRESENCE:**   Compare the two photographs from Paul Ekman's study (page 371) with the *Mona Lisa* (page 373). The Ekman study photos demonstrate the difference between the "social smile" and the "true enjoyment smile." To which category does the *Mona Lisa* belong? Explain why.

4. **CONNECTIONS:**   Cunningham explains the causes of an activity that few of her readers are likely to think about in both scientific and historical terms. Compare her use of science and history to that of Steven Pinker in "Violence Vanquished" (page 698). How does each writer establish her or his authority in these fields? Point to specific examples to support each point you make. Summarize the nature of each writer's presentation. To what extent does each writer rely on factual evidence?

Joan Didion

THE SANTA ANA

The author of novels, short stories, screenplays, and essays, **JOAN DIDION** (b. 1934) began her career in 1956 as a staff writer at *Vogue* magazine in New York. In 1963, she published her first novel, *Run River*, and the following year returned to her native California. Didion's essays have appeared in periodicals ranging from *Mademoiselle* to the *National Review*. "The Santa Ana" first appeared in the *Saturday Evening Post* in 1967 and later appeared as a part of "Los Angeles Notebook," an essay collected in *Slouching Towards Bethlehem*. Didion's other nonfiction publications include *The White Album* (1979), *Salvador* (1983), *Miami* (1987), *After Henry* (1992), *Political Fictions* (2001), *Fixed Ideas: America since 9.11* (2003), and *Where I Was From* (2003). Her essays, written between 1968 and 2003, are collected in *We Tell Ourselves Stories in Order to Live* (2006). *The Year of Magical Thinking* (2005),

Didion's account of grief and survival after the loss of her husband of forty years, John Gregory Dunne, and the near-fatal illness of their only child, won the 2005 National Book Award for Nonfiction; Didion adapted her tragic memoir into a play, which opened on Broadway in 2007, starring Vanessa Redgrave and directed by David Hare. Didion's most recent book, *Blue Nights* (2011), is a memoir about aging and about her relationship with her daughter, who died in 2005.

> **"I write entirely to find out what's on my mind, what I'm thinking, what I'm looking at, what I'm seeing and what it means, what I want and what I'm afraid of."**

Didion has defined a writer as "a person whose most absorbed and passionate hours are spent arranging words on pieces of paper. I write entirely to find out what's on my mind, what I'm thinking, what I'm looking at, what I'm seeing and what it means, what I want and what I'm afraid of." She has also said that "all writing is an attempt to find out what matters, to find the pattern in disorder, to find the grammar in the shimmer. Actually I don't know whether you find the grammar in the shimmer or you impose a grammar on the shimmer, but I am quite specific about the grammar—I mean it literally. The scene that you see in your mind finds its own structure; the structure dictates the arrangement of the words. . . . All the writer has to do really is to find the words." However, she warns, "You have to be alone to do this."

THERE IS SOMETHING UNEASY in the Los Angeles air this afternoon, some unnatural stillness, some tension. What it means is that tonight a Santa Ana will begin to blow, a hot wind from the northeast whining down through the Cajon and San Gorgonio Passes, blowing up sand storms out along Route 66, drying the hills and the nerves to flash point. For a few days now we will see smoke back in the canyons, and hear sirens in the night. I have neither heard nor read that a Santa Ana is due, but I know it, and almost everyone I have seen today knows it too. We know it because we feel it. The baby frets. The maid sulks. I rekindle a waning argument with the telephone company, then cut my losses and lie down, given over to whatever it is in the air. To live with the Santa Ana is to accept, consciously or unconsciously, a deeply mechanistic view of human behavior.

I recall being told, when I first moved to Los Angeles and was living on an isolated beach, that the Indians would throw themselves into the sea when the bad wind blew. I could see why. The Pacific turned ominously glossy during a Santa Ana period, and one woke in the night troubled not only by the peacocks screaming in the olive trees but by the eerie absence of surf. The heat was surreal. The sky had a yellow cast, the kind of light sometimes called "earthquake weather." My only neighbor would not come out of her house for days, and there were no lights at night, and her husband roamed the place with a machete. One day he would tell me that he had heard a trespasser, the next a rattlesnake.

"On nights like that," Raymond Chandler[1] once wrote about the Santa Ana, "every booze party ends in a fight. Meek little wives feel the edge of the carving knife and study their husbands' necks. Anything can happen." That was the kind of wind it was. I did not know then that there was any basis for the effect it had on all of us, but it turns out to be another of those cases in which science bears out folk wisdom. The Santa Ana, which is named for one of the canyons it rushes through, is a *foehn* wind, like the *foehn* of Austria and Switzerland and the *hamsin* of Israel. There are a number of persistent malevolent winds, perhaps the best known of which are the mistral of France and the Mediterranean sirocco, but a *foehn* wind has distinct characteristics: it occurs on the leeward slope of a mountain range and, although the air begins as a cold mass, it is warmed as it comes down the mountain and appears finally as a hot dry wind. Whenever and wherever a *foehn* blows, doctors hear about headaches and nausea and allergies, about "nervousness," about "depression." In Los Angeles some teachers do not attempt to conduct formal classes during a Santa Ana, because the children become unmanageable. In Switzerland the suicide rate goes up during the *foehn*, and in the courts of some Swiss cantons the wind is considered a mitigating circumstance for crime. Surgeons are said to watch the wind, because blood does not clot normally during a *foehn*. A few years ago an Israeli physicist discovered that not only during such winds, but for the ten or twelve hours which precede them, the air carries an unusually high ratio of positive to negative ions. No one seems to know exactly why that should be; some talk about friction and others suggest solar disturbances. In any case the positive ions are there, and what an excess of positive ions does, in the simplest terms, is make people unhappy. One cannot get much more mechanistic than that.

Easterners commonly complain that there is no "weather" at all in Southern California, that the days and the seasons slip by relentlessly, numbingly bland. That is quite misleading. In fact the climate is characterized by infrequent but violent extremes: two periods of torrential subtropical rains which continue for weeks and wash out the hills and send subdivisions sliding toward the sea; about twenty scattered days a year of the Santa Ana, which, with its incendiary dryness, invariably means fire. At the first prediction of a Santa Ana, the Forest Service flies men and equipment from northern California into the southern forests, and the Los Angeles Fire Department cancels its ordinary nonfirefighting routines. The Santa Ana caused Malibu to burn the way it did in 1956, and Bel Air in 1961, and Santa Barbara in 1964. In the winter of 1966–67 eleven men were killed fighting a Santa Ana fire that spread through the San Gabriel Mountains.

Just to watch the front-page news out of Los Angeles during a Santa   5
Ana is to get very close to what it is about the place. The longest single Santa Ana period in recent years was in 1957, and it lasted not the usual three or four days but fourteen days, from November 21 until December 4.

---

[1] **Chandler** (1888–1959) is best known for his detective novels featuring Philip Marlowe. — EDS.

On the first day 25,000 acres of the San Gabriel Mountains were burning, with gusts reaching 100 miles an hour. In town, the wind reached Force 12, or hurricane force, on the Beaufort Scale; oil derricks were toppled and people ordered off the downtown streets to avoid injury from flying objects. On November 22 the fire in the San Gabriels was out of control. On November 24 six people were killed in automobile accidents, and by the end of the week the Los Angeles *Times* was keeping a box score of traffic deaths. On November 26 a prominent Pasadena attorney, depressed about money, shot and killed his wife, their two sons and himself. On November 27 a South Gate divorcée, twenty-two, was murdered and thrown from a moving car. On November 30 the San Gabriel fire was still out of control, and the wind in town was blowing eighty miles an hour. On the first day of December four people died violently, and on the third the wind began to break.

It is hard for people who have not lived in Los Angeles to realize how radically the Santa Ana figures in the local imagination. The city burning is Los Angeles's deepest image of itself. Nathanael West perceived that, in *The Day of the Locust*; and at the time of the 1965 Watts riots what struck the imagination most indelibly were the fires.[2] For days one could drive the Harbor Freeway and see the city on fire, just as we had always known it would be in the end. Los Angeles weather is the weather of catastrophe, of apocalypse, and, just as the reliably long and bitter winters of New England determine the way life is lived there, so the violence and the unpredictability of the Santa Ana affect the entire quality of life in Los Angeles, accentuate its impermanence, its unreliability. The wind shows us how close to the edge we are. ◼

The Reader's Presence

1. Characterize the role of the "imagination" in relation to the effects of the Santa Ana winds. Didion writes scientifically about the wind, specifically the "excess of positive ions" (paragraph 3) in the air and how this supposedly leads to nervousness and depression, yet she also discusses the wind in fictional terms, citing Raymond Chandler (paragraph 3) and referencing Nathanael West's novel *The Day of the Locust* (paragraph 6). What do you see as the compositional advantages of Didion's blend of fiction and reality in her essay? In what specific way(s) does Didion's connection between the two point to the wind itself?

2. There's a determinism that pervades Didion's essay, exemplified by the last sentence of the first paragraph: "To live with the Santa Ana is to accept, consciously or unconsciously, a deeply mechanistic view of human behavior." Much like the mythos of the full moon, Didion connects erratic, unpredictable human behavior to the dry Santa Ana winds. To what extent do you share her "mechanistic" outlook, or do you view this connection as an expression of "the local imagination" (paragraph 6)?

---

[2] **The Day of the Locust** (1939), a novel about Hollywood, ends in riot and fire. The August 1965 disturbances in the Watts neighborhood of Los Angeles resulted in millions of dollars in damage from fires. —EDS.

3. Didion discusses associating Los Angeles with destruction and fire in some detail, referencing the "1965 Watts riots" and noting that "[t]he city burning is Los Angeles's deepest image of itself" (paragraph 6). In what specific ways does this volatile image of the city affect the "local imagination"? What specific images and associations does Didion's description of the "violence and unpredictability of the Santa Ana" evoke? What is she discussing that is of greater consequence than the weather? How does the wind "[show] us how close to the edge we are" (paragraph 6)?

4. **CONNECTIONS:** Review carefully Didion's essay "Why I Write" (below). What specifically does she say here about her own writing process that helps you to understand and appreciate what she has achieved compositionally in "The Santa Ana"? In this respect, compare and contrast Didion's observations about why she writes and what an essayist does with those of E. B. White ("E. B. White on the Essayist," page 299).

The Writer at Work

JOAN DIDION on Why I Write

Christopher Flever/Corbis

Contrary to popular belief, writers are not necessarily intellectuals, or even people especially interested in ideas. Quite a few writers may be intellectuals, but being an intellectual and being able to write well do not always proceed hand in hand. In this passage from a well-known essay, Joan Didion takes a close look at the motives behind her writing and shows how our abilities can sometimes be fostered by our inabilities, in her case a lack of interest in abstract thinking and a tendency to always focus on the particulars of her immediate environment.

As Didion admits from the start, her essay was inspired by George Orwell's famous essay of the same title (see page 526).

❝Of course I stole the title for this talk,[1] from George Orwell. One reason I stole it was that I like the sound of the words: Why I Write. There you have three short unambiguous words that share a sound, and the sound they share is this:

I

I

I

[1]This essay is adapted from a Regents' Lecture delivered at the University of California at Berkeley.

In many ways writing is the act of saying *I*, of imposing oneself upon other people, of saying *listen to me, see it my way, change your mind*. It's an aggressive, even a hostile act. You can disguise its aggressiveness all you want with veils of subordinate clauses and qualifiers and tentative subjunctives, with ellipses and evasions — with the whole manner of intimating rather than claiming, of alluding rather than stating — but there's no getting around the fact that setting words on paper is the tactic of a secret bully, an invasion, an imposition of the writer's sensibility on the reader's most private space.

I stole the title not only because the words sounded right but because they seemed to sum up, in a no-nonsense way, all I have to tell you. Like many writers I have only this one "subject," this one "area": the act of writing. I can bring you no reports from any other front. I may have other interests: I am "interested," for example, in marine biology, but I don't flatter myself that you would come out to hear me talk about it. I am not a scholar. I am not in the least an intellectual, which is not to say that when I hear the word "intellectual" I reach for my gun, but only to say that I do not think in abstracts. During the years when I was an undergraduate at Berkeley I tried, with a kind of hopeless late-adolescent energy, to buy some temporary visa into the world of ideas, to forge for myself a mind that could deal with the abstract.

In short I tried to think. I failed. My attention veered inexorably back to the specific, to the tangible, to what was generally considered, by everyone I knew then and for that matter have known since, the peripheral. I would try to contemplate the Hegelian dialectic and would find myself concentrating instead on a flowering pear tree outside my window and the particular way the petals fell on my floor. I would try to read linguistic theory and would find myself wondering instead if the lights were on in the bevatron up the hill. When I say that I was wondering if the lights were on in the bevatron you might immediately suspect, if you deal in ideas at all, that I was registering the bevatron as a political symbol, thinking in shorthand about the military-industrial complex and its role in the university community, but you would be wrong. I was only

wondering if the lights were on in the bevatron, and how they looked. A physical fact.

I had trouble graduating from Berkeley, not because of this inability to deal with ideas—I was majoring in English, and I could locate the house-and-garden imagery in *The Portrait of a Lady* as well as the next person, "imagery" being by definition the kind of specific that got my attention—but simply because I had neglected to take a course in Milton. For reasons which now sound baroque I needed a degree by the end of that summer, and the English department finally agreed, if I would come down from Sacramento every Friday and talk about the cosmology of *Paradise Lost*, to certify me proficient in Milton. I did this. Some Fridays I took the Greyhound bus, other Fridays I caught the Southern Pacific's City of San Francisco on the last leg of its transcontinental trip. I can no longer tell you whether Milton put the sun or the earth at the center of his universe in *Paradise Lost*, the central question of at least one century and a topic about which I wrote 10,000 words that summer, but I can still recall the exact rancidity of the butter in the City of San Francisco's dining car, and the way the tinted windows on the Greyhound bus cast the oil refineries around Carquinez Straits into a grayed and obscurely sinister light. In short my attention was always on the periphery, on what I could see and taste and touch, on the butter, and the Greyhound bus. During those years I was traveling on what I knew to be a very shaky passport, forged papers: I knew that I was no legitimate resident in any world of ideas. I knew I couldn't think. All I knew then was what I couldn't do. All I knew then was what I wasn't, and it took me some years to discover what I was.

Which was a writer. **"**

Annie Dillard

THIS IS THE LIFE

ANNIE DILLARD (b. 1945) was awarded the Pulitzer Prize for general nonfiction in 1974 for *Pilgrim at Tinker Creek*, which she describes (borrowing from Henry David Thoreau) as "a meteorological journal of the mind." She graduated from Hollins College in 1967; Tinker Creek is nearby. She has also published poetry in *Tickets for a Prayer Wheel* (1974) and *Mornings Like This: Found Poems* (1995), literary theory in *Living by Fiction* (1982), essays in *Teaching a Stone to Talk: Expeditions and Encounters* (1982) and *For the Time Being* (1999), and an autobiography in *An American Childhood* (1987). Dillard's first novel was *The Living* (1992), and her most recent is *The Maytrees* (2007); the *Annie Dillard Reader* was published in 1994. She was contributing editor to *Harper's* magazine for almost a decade, and she taught creative writing at Wesleyan University where she is now professor emeritus. "This Is the Life" first appeared in *Image: A Journal of the Arts and Religion* and was subsequently reprinted in *Harper's* in 2002.

> "A sentence is a machine; it has a job to do. An extra word . . . is like a sock in a machine."

In her 1997 essay "Advice to Young Writers," Dillard argues, "Don't use any extra words. A sentence is a machine; it has a job to do. An extra word in a sentence is like a sock in a machine."

ANY CULTURE TELLS YOU how to live your one and only life: to wit, as everyone else does. Probably most cultures prize, as ours rightly does, making a contribution by working hard at work that you love; being in the know, and intelligent; gathering a surplus; and loving your family above all, and your dog, your boat, bird-watching. Beyond those things, our culture might specialize in money, and celebrity, and natural beauty. These are not universal. You enjoy work and will love your grandchildren, and somewhere in there you die.

Another contemporary consensus might be: You wear the best shoes you can afford, you seek to know Rome's best restaurants and their staffs, drive the best car, and vacation on Tenerife. And what a cook you are!

Or you take the next tribe's pigs in thrilling raids; you grill yams; you trade for televisions and hunt white-plumed birds. Everyone you know agrees: this is the life. Perhaps you burn captives. You set fire to a drunk. Yours is the human struggle, or the elite one, to achieve . . . whatever your own culture tells you: to publish the paper that proves the point; to progress in the firm and gain high title and salary, stock options, benefits; to get the loan to store the beans till their price rises; to elude capture, to feed your children or educate them to a feather edge; or to count coup or perfect your calligraphy; to eat the king's deer or catch the poacher; to spear the seal, intimidate the enemy, and be a big man or beloved woman and die respected for the pigs or the title or the shoes. Not a funeral. Forget funeral. A big birthday party. Since everyone around you agrees.

Since everyone around you agrees ever since there were people on earth that land is value, or labor is value, or learning is value, or title, necklaces, degree, murex shells, or ownership of slaves. Everyone knows bees sting and ghosts haunt and giving your robes away humiliates your rivals. That the enemies are barbarians. That wise men swim through the rock of the earth; that houses breed filth, airstrips attract airplanes, tornadoes punish, ancestors watch, and you can buy a shorter stay in purgatory. The black rock is holy, or the scroll; or the pangolin is holy, the quetzal is holy, this tree, water, rock, stone, cow, cross, or mountain—and it's all true. The Red Sox. Or nothing at all is holy, as everyone intelligent knows.

Who is your "everyone"? Chess masters scarcely surround themselves   5
with motocross racers. Do you want aborigines at your birthday party? Or are you serving yak-butter tea? Popular culture deals not in its distant past, or any other past, or any other culture. You know no one who longs to buy a mule or be named to court or thrown into a volcano.

So the illusion, like the visual field, is complete. It has no holes except books you read and soon forget. And death takes us by storm. What was that, that life? What else offered? If for him it was contract bridge, if for her it was copyright law, if for everyone it was and is an optimal mix of family and friends, learning, contribution, and joy—of making and ameliorating—what else is there, or was there, or will there ever be?

What else is a vision or fact of time and the peoples it bears issuing from the mouth of the cosmos, from the round mouth of eternity, in a wide and parti-colored utterance. In the complex weave of this utterance like fabric, in its infinite domestic interstices, the centuries and continents and classes dwell. Each people knows only its own squares in the weave, its wars and instruments and arts, and also the starry sky.

Okay, and then what? Say you scale your own weft and see time's breadth and the length of space. You see the way the fabric both passes among the stars and encloses them. You see in the weave nearby, and aslant farther off, the peoples variously scandalized or exalted in their squares. They work on their projects—they flake spear points, hoe, plant; they kill aurochs or one another; they prepare sacrifices—as we here and now work on our projects. What, seeing this spread multiply infinitely in every direction, would you do differently? No one could love your children more; would you love them less? Would you change your project? To what? Whatever you do, it has likely brought delight to fewer people than either contract bridge or the Red Sox.

However hypnotized you and your people are, you will be just as dead in their war, our war. However dead you are, more people will come. However many more people come, your time and its passions, and yourself and your passions, weigh equally in the balance with those of any dead who pulled waterwheel poles by the Nile or Yellow rivers, or painted their foreheads black, or starved in the wilderness, or wasted from disease then or now. Our lives and our deaths count equally, or we must abandon one-man-one-vote, dismantle democracy, and assign six billion people an importance-of-life ranking from one to six billion—a ranking whose number decreases, like gravity, with the square of the distance between us and them.

What would you do differently, you up on your beanstalk looking at   10 scenes of all peoples at all times in all places? When you climb down, would you dance any less to the music you love, knowing that music to be as provisional as a bug? Somebody has to make jugs and shoes, to turn the soil, fish. If you descend the long rope-ladders back to your people and time in the fabric, if you tell them what you have seen, and even if someone cares to listen, then what? Everyone knows times and cultures are plural. If you come back a shrugging relativist or tongue-tied absolutist, then what? If you spend hours a day looking around, high astraddle the warp or woof of your people's wall, then what new wisdom can you take to your grave for worms to untangle? Well, maybe you will not go into advertising.

Then you would know your own death better but perhaps not dread it less. Try to bring people up the wall, carry children to see it—to what end? Fewer golf courses? What is wrong with golf? Nothing at all. Equality of wealth? Sure; how?

The woman watching sheep over there, the man who carries embers in a pierced clay ball, the engineer, the girl who spins wool into yarn as she climbs, the smelter, the babies learning to recognize speech in their own languages, the man whipping a slave's flayed back, the man digging roots, the woman digging roots, the child digging roots—what would you tell them? And the future people—what are they doing? What excitements sweep peoples here and there from time to time? Into the muddy river they go, into the trenches, into the caves, into the mines, into the granary, into the sea in boats. Most humans who were ever alive lived inside one single culture that never changed for hundreds of thousands of years; archaeologists scratch their heads at so conservative and static a culture.

Over here, the rains fail; they are starving. There, the caribou fail; they are starving. Corrupt leaders take the wealth. Not only there but here. Rust and smut spoil the rye. When pigs and cattle starve or freeze, people die soon after. Disease empties a sector, a billion sectors.

People look at the sky and at the other animals. They make beautiful objects, beautiful sounds, beautiful motions of their bodies beating drums in lines. They pray; they toss people in peat bogs; they help the sick and injured; they pierce their lips, their noses, ears; they make the same mistakes despite religion, written language, philosophy, and science; they build, they kill, they preserve, they count and figure, they boil the pot, they keep the embers alive; they tell their stories and gird themselves.

Will knowledge you experience directly make you a Buddhist? Must you forfeit excitement per se? To what end?   15

Say you have seen something. You have seen an ordinary bit of what is real, the infinite fabric of time that eternity shoots through, and time's soft-skinned people working and dying under slowly shifting stars. Then what? ⬤

The Reader's Presence

1. The scope of Dillard's essay is grand, encompassing a wide variety of cultures across physical and chronological boundaries, yet the overarching point she makes is quite specific, concrete, and direct. Describe—as specifically as you can—the experience of reading Dillard's essay. To what extent did you feel overwhelmed by it? What strategic purpose do you recognize in her use of rhythm and repetition in her sentences? When you reflect on the essay, to what extent are you left with a feeling of the insurmountable differences or the startling similarities? How does the title of the essay relate to the questions she poses?

2. Dillard writes about a wide array of cultural values and assumptions, yet one attribute those values and assumptions share is that they shape and define our lives. We live our lives within the bounds of our culture and then suddenly "death takes us by storm" (paragraph 6). How does this assertion connect with the question Dillard asks in her closing sentence: "Then what?" What, finally, is she questioning? How would you respond?

3. Our lives are characterized by the decisions we make, decisions shaped in large part by the culture in which we live. In the twenty-first century, we face certain choices that are unique to our place in history, yet some choices transcend time. Does Dillard think these truths will ever change? Why or why not?

4. **VISUAL PRESENCE:** Examine carefully the portrait of Annie Dillard on page 386. How does the setting of the photograph reflect Dillard's writing style? What objects are present in the portrait and why did the photographer choose to include them? Point to specific details from the image to support your answer.

5. **CONNECTIONS:** In "The Death of the Moth" (page 574), Virginia Woolf focuses on a small creature to raise large-scale questions about self-identity and one's purpose in life. Make a list of the similarities and then the differences in each writer's treatment of this subject. To what extent are Dillard's use of language and literary techniques (including metaphor, irony, and diction) different from those of Woolf? Support your response with specific examples from each writer.

The Writer at Work

ANNIE DILLARD on the Writing Life

Richard Howard/Time & Life Pictures/Getty Images

One of the nation's outstanding nonfiction writers—who prefers to think of herself as an "all-purpose writer" rather than an essayist—Annie Dillard is also a professor emeritus of creative writing at Wesleyan University. Dillard once said that a commitment to writing is "like living any dedicated life." How is this idea reflected in the following excerpt from her book *The Writing Life* (1989)? What does Dillard believe drives the creative artist and writer? Does her tough-minded advice apply only to artistic expression? In what other areas of human activity or expression might it also apply?

❝Push it. Examine all things intensely and relentlessly. Probe and search each object in a piece of art. Do not leave it, do not course over it, as if it were understood, but instead follow it down until you see it in the mystery of its own specificity and strength. Giacometti's[1] drawings and paintings show his bewilderment and persistence. If he had not acknowledged his bewilderment, he would not have persisted. A twentieth-century master of drawing, Rico Lebrun, taught that "the draftsman must aggress; only by persistent assault will the live image capitulate and give up its secret to an unrelenting line." Who but an artist fierce to know—not fierce to seem to know—would suppose that a live image possessed a secret? The artist is willing to give all his or her strength and life to probing with blunt instruments those same secrets no one can describe in any way but with those instruments' faint tracks.

[1] *Alberto Giacometti* (1901–1966): A renowned Swiss sculptor, painter, draftsman, and printmaker. — EDS.

Admire the world for never ending on you—as you would admire an opponent, without taking your eyes from him, or walking away.

One of the few things I know about writing is this: spend it all, shoot it, play it, lose it, all, right away, every time. Do not hoard what seems good for a later place in the book, or for another book; give it, give it all, give it now. The impulse to save something good for a better place later is the signal to spend it now. Something more will arise for later, something better. These things fill from behind, from beneath, like well water. Similarly, the impulse to keep to yourself what you have learned is not only shameful, it is destructive. Anything you do not give freely and abundantly becomes lost to you. You open your safe and find ashes.

After Michelangelo died, someone found in his studio a piece of paper on which he had written a note to his apprentice, in the handwriting of his old age: 'Draw, Antonio, draw, Antonio, draw and do not waste time.' ❞

Brian Doyle

A WRITING PORTFOLIO
Dawn and Mary / His Last Game / A Note on Mascots

Journalist, essayist, and editor **BRIAN DOYLE** (b. 1956) was born in New York, educated "fitfully" at the University of Notre Dame, and now lives and works in Portland, Oregon, where he is editor of *Portland Magazine* at the University of Portland. Doyle is noted for writing books with spiritual and religious themes, including *Credo: Essays on Grace, Altar Boys, Bees, Kneeling, Saints, the Mass, Priests, Strong Women, Epiphanies, a Wake, and the Haunting Thin Energetic Dusty Figure of Jesus the Christ* (1999); *Saints Passionate & Peculiar: Brief Exuberant Essays for Teens* (2002); *The Wet Engine: Exploring the Mad Wild Miracle of the Heart* (2005); and *The Thorny Grace of It: And Other Essays for Imperfect Catholics* (2013), among many others. His novel *Mink River* was published in 2010, and he wrote his latest novel, *The Plover* (2014), in response to readers asking what happened to one of the characters in *Mink River*. He edited the anthology *God Is Love: Essays from* Portland Magazine (2003), and his work has appeared in *Best American Essays*, *Best Spiritual Writing*, *Best Essays Northwest*, and in many other anthologies.

> "I don't have a responsibility to edify. I think if you feel that way you're tending toward sermon and homily and lecture, which is basically the road to purgatory. Also, you know, the tendency to sermon and homily and lecture is basically boring."

Doyle's essays and poems have appeared in numerous magazines, journals, and newspapers, including the *Atlantic Monthly*, *Harper's*, *Commonweal*, *American Scholar*, *Georgia Review*, the *Times of London*, the *Sydney Morning Herald*, the *Kansas City Star*, the *San Francisco Chronicle*, *Newsday*, and *Orion*.

Though Doyle often writes on matters of faith and religion, he cautions against writing that sermonizes. In an interview on quotidiana.org, he said that, as a writer, he doesn't "have a responsibility to edify," adding that such writing tends "toward sermon and homily and lecture," a tendency he calls "boring."

Dawn and Mary

EARLY ONE MORNING several teachers and staffers at a Connecticut grade school were in a meeting. The meeting had been underway for about five minutes when they heard a chilling sound in the hallway. (*We heard pop-pop-pop*, said one of the staffers later.)

Most of them dove under the table. That is the reasonable thing to do, what they were trained to do, and that is what they did.

But two of the staffers *jumped*, or *leapt*, or *lunged* out of their chairs and ran toward the sound of bullets. Which word you use depends on which news account of that morning you read, but the words all point in the same direction—toward the bullets.

One of the staffers was the principal. Her name was Dawn. She had two daughters. Her husband had proposed to her five times before she'd finally said yes, and they had been married for ten years. They had a vacation house on a lake. She liked to get down on her knees to paint with the littlest kids in her school.

The other staffer was a school psychologist named Mary. She had two daughters. She was a football fan. She had been married for more than thirty years. She and her husband had a cabin on a lake. She loved to go to the theater. She was due to retire in one year. She liked to get down on her knees to work in her garden.

Dawn the principal told the teachers and the staffers to lock the door behind them, and the teachers and the staffers did so after Dawn and Mary ran out into the hall.

You and I have been in that hallway. We spent seven years of our childhood in that hallway. It's friendly and echoing, and when someone opens the doors at the end, a wind comes and flutters all the paintings and posters on the walls.

Dawn and Mary jumped, or leapt, or lunged toward the sound of bullets. Every fiber of their bodies—bodies descended from millions of years of bodies that had leapt away from danger—must have wanted to dive under the table. That's what they'd been trained to do. That's how you live to see another day. That's how you stay alive to paint with the littlest kids and work in the garden and hug your daughters and drive off laughing to your cabin on the lake.

But they leapt for the door, and Dawn said, *Lock the door after us*, and they lunged right at the boy with the rifle.

The next time someone says the word *hero* to you, you say this: There once were two women. One was named Dawn, and the other was named Mary. They both had two daughters. They both loved to kneel down to care for small beings. They leapt from their chairs and ran right at the boy with the rifle, and if we ever forget their names, if we ever forget the wind in that hallway, if we ever forget what they did, if we ever forget that there is something in us beyond sense and reason that snarls at death and runs roaring at it to defend children, if we ever forget that all children are our children, then we are fools who have allowed memory to be murdered too, and what good are we then? *What good are we then?*

The Reader's Presence

1. Doyle's essay is a startling and simple account of the bravery of two people who sacrificed themselves to protect the children they cared for at Sandy Hook Elementary School in Connecticut. How would you characterize the structure and length of Doyle's sentences as the essay unfolds? What reasonable inferences can you draw from the observations you make? What impact does Doyle's use of italics at the end of paragraph 1 and at the end of the essay have on your experience of reading his essay? What relationship does he establish between the words and sentences he italicizes? What does he accomplish by choosing to italicize *"hero"* in the opening sentence of the final paragraph? In what specific ways does this decision affect your reading?

2. Reread Doyle's brief essay aloud. How would you characterize the sound of the speaker's voice throughout this essay? Does the speaker's voice remain consistent throughout the essay? If not, where—and how—does it change? with what effects? Cite specific examples to support your response.

3. Doyle provides background information for Dawn and Mary— "She had two daughters" (paragraphs 4 and 5) and "She was a football fan" (paragraph 5). In what specific way(s) are those details important to the overall tone and purpose of Doyle's essay? How do these details impact your connection to the characters and to the overall influence of the essay? Doyle addresses the reader directly in paragraph 7, "You and I have been in that hallway." Why does he address the reader? What larger point is Doyle making here?

4. **CONNECTIONS:** After you have read Doyle's essay carefully several times, compare and contrast his attitudes and tone of voice when discussing violence with those of Steven Pinker in his essay "Violence Vanquished" (page 698) and of Jacob Ewing in his student essay on Pinker's argument (page 705). Who among these three writers creates the most evocative and compelling perspective on violence? Support your response with detailed references to each text.

His Last Game

WE WERE SUPPOSED TO BE DRIVING to the pharmacy for his prescriptions, but he said just drive around for a while, my prescriptions aren't going anywhere without me, so we just drove around. We drove around the edges of the college where he had worked and we saw a blue heron in a field of stubble, which is not something you see every day, and we stopped for a while to see if the heron was fishing for mice or snakes, on which we bet a dollar, me taking mice and him taking snakes, but the heron glared at us and refused to work under scrutiny, so we drove on.

We drove through the arboretum checking on the groves of ash and oak and willow trees, which were still where they were last time we looked, and then we checked on the wood duck boxes in the pond, which still seemed sturdy and did not feature ravenous weasels that we noticed, and then we saw a kestrel hanging in the crisp air like a tiny helicopter, but as soon as we bet mouse or snake the kestrel vanished, probably for religious reasons, said my brother, probably a *lot* of kestrels are adamant that gambling is immoral, but we are just *not* as informed as we should be about kestrels.

We drove deeper into the city and I asked him why we were driving this direction, and he said I am looking for something that when I see it you will know what I am looking for, which made me grin, because he knew and I knew that I would indeed know, because we have been brothers for 50 years, and brothers have many languages, some of which are physical, like broken noses and fingers and teeth and punching each other when you want to say I love you but don't know how to say that right, and some of them are laughter, and some of them are roaring and spitting, and some of them are weeping in the bathroom, and some of them we don't have words for yet.

By now it was almost evening, and just as I turned on the car's running lights I saw what it was he was looking for, which was a basketball game in a park. I laughed and he laughed and I parked the car. There were six guys on the court, and to their credit they were playing full court. Five of the guys looked to be in their twenties, and they were fit and muscled, and one of them wore a porkpie hat. The sixth guy was much older, but he was that kind of older ballplayer who is comfortable with his age and he knew where to be and what not to try.

We watched for a while and didn't say anything but both of us noticed   5
that one of the young guys was not as good as he thought he was, and one was better than he knew he was, and one was flashy but essentially useless, and the guy with the porkpie hat was a worker, setting picks, boxing out, whipping outlet passes, banging the boards not only on defense but on offense, which is much harder. The fifth young guy was one of those guys who ran up and down yelling and waving for the ball, which he never got. This guy was supposed to be covering the older guy but he didn't bother, and the older guy gently made him pay for his inattention, scoring occasionally on backdoor cuts and shots from the corners on which he was so alone he could have opened a circus and sold tickets, as my brother said.

The older man grew visibly weary as we watched, and my brother said he's got one last basket in him, and I said I bet a dollar it's a shot from the corner, and my brother said no, he doesn't even have the gas for that, he'll snake the kid somehow, you watch, and just then the older man, who was bent over holding the hems of his shorts like he was exhausted, suddenly cut to the basket, caught a bounce pass, and scored, and the game ended, maybe because the park lights didn't go on even though the street lights did.

On the way home my brother and I passed the heron in the field of stubble again, and the heron stopped work again and glared at us until we turned the corner.

That is one *withering* glare, said my brother. That's a ballplayer glare if ever I saw one. That's the glare a guy gives another guy when the guy you were supposed to be covering scores on a backdoor cut and you thought your guy was ancient and near death but it turns out he snaked you good and you are an idiot. *I* know that glare. You owe me a dollar. We better go get my prescriptions. They are not going to do any good but we better get them anyway so they don't go to waste. One less thing for my family to do afterwards. That game was good but the heron was even better. I think the prescriptions are pointless now but we already paid for them so we might as well get them. They'll just get thrown out if we don't pick them up. That was a good last game, though. I'll remember the old guy, sure, but the kid with the hat banging the boards, that was cool. You hardly ever see a guy with a porkpie hat hammering the boards.

There's so much to love, my brother added. All the little things. Remember shooting baskets at night and the only way you could tell if the shot went in was the sound of the net? Remember the time we cut the fingertips off our gloves so we could shoot on icy days and dad was so angry he lost his voice and he was supposed to give a speech and had to gargle and mom laughed so hard we thought she was going to pee? Remember that? I remember that. What happens to what I remember? You remember it for me, okay? You remember the way that heron glared at us like he would kick our ass except he was working. And you remember that old man snaking that kid. *Stupid kid*, you could say, but that's the obvious thing. The *beautiful* thing is the little thing that the old guy knew full well he wasn't going to cut around picks and drift out into the corner again, that would burn his last gallon of gas, not to mention he would have to hoist up a shot from way out there, so he snakes the kid beautiful, he knows the kid thinks he's old, and the guy with the hat sees him cut, and gets him the ball on a dime, that's a beautiful thing because it's little, and we saw it and we knew what it meant. You remember that for me. You owe me a dollar. ▪

The Reader's Presence

1. What expectations do most readers carry into reading the beginning of an essay? What responses does Doyle elicit from his readers by beginning his essay with the phrase "We were supposed to"? What implications does this phrase bear for the focus and direction of his essay? Point to specific words and phrases to support your response. Notice that Doyle repeats the word "just" in the opening sentence. What

other words and phrases does he repeat in the essay? With what effect(s)? The final sentence of the opening paragraph presents another reversal of expectations: "the heron glared at us and refused to work under scrutiny, so we drove on." What do see as the significance of this line, and how does it help to frame Doyle's essay?

2. What is the narrative trajectory of Doyle's essay? Where does it start and end? What literally happens during the course of the essay? What does the title "His Last Game" allude to? What specific evidence can you summon to support your response? What do you think the narrator means when he says, "brothers have many languages, some of which are physical" (paragraph 3)? Comment on Doyle's use of evocative detail, especially as the brothers observe—and then participate in—"a basketball game in a park" (paragraph 4)?

3. What role does figurative language—especially similes and metaphors—play in the essay? With what effect(s)? Consider, for example, the phrase "he snaked you" in paragraph 8. What are the effects of the three appearances of the heron as the narrative unfolds? What do you understand to be the point when the narrator observes "The *beautiful* thing is the little thing" (paragraph 9)? Ultimately, what do you think is the subject of Doyle's essay?

4. **CONNECTIONS:**   Based on your reading of Doyle's essay, what would you identify as his implicit rules for writing? What importance do you think Doyle would assign to a writer's use of figurative language, especially similes and metaphors? What other features of writing effectively does Doyle accentuate in this essay and in the others printed here? Compare and contrast these compositional principles with those Stephen King articulates in "Everything You Need to Know About Writing Successfully—in Ten Minutes" (page 447). In what specific way(s) are Doyle and King kindred spirits when thinking and writing about writing?

A Note on Mascots

THE FIRST SPORTS TEAM I REMEMBER loving as a child, in the dim dewy days when I was two or three years old and just waking up to things that were not milk and mama and dirt and dogs, was the Fighting Irish of the University of Notre Dame, who were on television every day, it seemed, in our bustling brick Irish Catholic house; and then, inasmuch as I was hatched and coddled near Manhattan, there were Metropolitans and Knickerbockers and Rangers and Islanders; and then, as I shuffled shyly into high school, there were, for the first time, snarling and roaring mammalian mascots, notably the Cougars of my own alma mater, which was plopped in marshlands where I doubt a cougar had been seen for three hundred years; but right about then I started paying attention to how we fetishize animals as symbols for our athletic adventures, and I have become only more attentive since, for I have spent nearly thirty years now working for colleges and universities, and you could earn a degree in zoology just by reading the college sports news, where roar and fly and sprint and lope and canter and gallop and prowl animals from anteater to wasp—among them, interestingly, armadillos, bees, boll weevils, herons, owls, koalas, turtles, moose, penguins, gulls, sea lions, and squirrels, none of which seem especially intimidating or prepossessing, although I know a man in North Carolina who once lost a fistfight with a heron, and certainly many of us have run away from angry bees and moose, and surely there are some among us who could relate stories of furious boll weevils, but perhaps this is not the time, although anyone who *has* a story like that should see me right after class.

There are vast numbers of canids (coyotes, foxes, huskies, salukis, great danes), felids (lions, tigers, panthers, lynx, bobcats), ruminants (bulls, chargers, broncs, broncos, and bronchoes, though no bronchials), mustelids (badgers, wolverine, otters), and denizens of the deep (dolphins, gators, sharks, sailfish, and "seawolves," or orca). There are two colleges which have an aggrieved camel as their mascot. There are schools represented by snakes and tomcats. There is a school whose symbol is a frog and one whose mascot is a large clam and one whose mascot famously is a slug. There is a school whose mascot is the black fly. There are the Fighting Turtles of the College of Insurance in New York. There are schools represented by lemmings and scorpions and spiders. There are the Fighting Stormy Petrels of Oglethorpe University in Georgia. There is a school represented by an animal that has never yet been seen in the Americas, the bearcat of Asia, although perhaps that is meant to be a wolverine, which did once inhabit southern Ohio, and may still live in Cincinnati, which has tough neighborhoods. The most popular mascot appears to be the eagle, especially if you count the fifteen schools represented by golden eagles, which brings us to a round total of eighty-two schools symbolized by a bird Benjamin Franklin considered "a bird of bad moral character, too lazy to fish for himself . . . like those among men who live by sharping & robbing he is generally poor and often very lousy. Besides he is a rank coward." But the two schools that Franklin helped establish are nicknamed the Quakers and the Diplomats, so we can safely ignore Ben on this matter.

This is not even to delve into the mysterious world of fantastical fauna— blue bears and blue tigers, crimson hawks, trolls, dragons and firebirds, griffins and griffons and gryphons, delta devils and jersey devils (there are a *lot* of devils, which says something interesting), jayhawks and kohawks and duhawks, green eagles and phoenixes, thunderhawks and thunderwolves— the mind reels, and then there is the whole subset of nicknamery that has to do with botany, as evidenced most memorably by the Fighting Violets of New York University, on which image we had better pull this whole essay to the side of the road and sit silently for a moment.

Beyond all the obvious reasons we choose animals as symbols for our sporting teams—their incredible energy and muscle, grace and strength, intelligence and verve, our ancient conviction of their power and magic, ancient associations as clan signs and tribal totems, even more ancient shivers perhaps of fear at animals who hunted and ate us, not to mention the way their images look cool on letterheads and sweatshirts and pennants and fundraising appeals—there is something else, something so deep and revelatory about human beings that I think we do not admit it because it is too sad.

I think we love animals as images because we miss them in the flesh,   5 and I think we love them as images because they matter to us spiritually in ways we cannot hope to articulate. The vast majority of us will never see a cougar or a wolverine, not to mention a boll weevil, but even wearing one on a shirt, or shouting the miracle of its name in a stadium, or grinning to see its rippling beauty on the window of a car, gives us a tiny subtle crucial electric jolt in the heart, connects us somehow to what we used to be with animals, which was thrilled and terrified. We've lost the salt of that feeling forever, but even a hint of it matters immensely to us as animals too. Maybe that's what we miss the most—the feeling that they are our cousins, and not clans of creatures who once filled the earth and now are shreds of memory, mere symbols, beings who used to be. 〇

The Reader's Presence

1. The origins of the word *mascot* can be traced back to medieval France, where "mascotte" was used to signify a charm or talisman, an object thought to have magical powers and to bring good luck. The word first gained widespread attention in the late nineteenth century, when the French composer Edmond Audran wrote the popular operetta *La Mascotte*. What specific characteristics does Doyle attribute to modern-day sports mascots? What do you understand him to mean when he observes that mascots "matter to us spiritually" (paragraph 5)? In the final paragraph, Doyle suggests that "[w]e've lost the salt of that feeling forever." What "feeling" does he allude to here?

2. Consider carefully the structure of Doyle's essay. What do you notice about the sentence structure of the opening paragraph? What reasonable inferences can you draw from your observations? Now consider the pacing as well as the specific diction Doyle uses. What observations and inferences can you draw from the choices Doyle makes? Finally, what do you notice about his use of specific poetic devices in his opening paragraph? Repeat the same pattern of making careful observations and drawing reasonable inferences in each of the succeeding paragraphs. What additional compositional effects does Doyle introduce in each new paragraph? Point to specific words and phrases as the basis of your observations and inferences.

3. What does Doyle gain by introducing the quotation from Benjamin Franklin on the eagle: "a bird of bad moral character" (paragraph 2)? How would you characterize Doyle's tone of voice (his attitude toward his subject) in this essay? For example, does he position himself as superior to, equal with, or subservient to his subject? Point to specific word choices to verify your response. In a similar manner, comment on his use of irony and humor. What impression does Doyle leave his readers with when he says, "We've lost the salt of that feeling forever" and "[the mascots] are our cousins" (paragraph 5)?

4. **CONNECTIONS:**   Compare and contrast the voice of Doyle's essay on mascots with that of David Foster Wallace in "Consider the Lobster" (page 760) and to that of Jonathan Safran Foer in "Let Them Eat Dog" (page 603). In what specific ways are these writers seeking to elicit similar responses from their readers? Support your responses with specific passages from each text as well as an analysis of each.

The Reader's Presence:
Questions on Three Essays and an Interview

1. In his interview with the editors of this collection (page 396), Brian Doyle responded to our question "What are the most challenging aspects of writing for you?" by observing: "Avoiding self-absorbed self-indulgent sermonizing homilizing advice-giving-counsel-confiding muck. A constant battle. I am always reminding myself to just tell a story." Examine carefully two of the three essays included in this portfolio of Doyle's essays, and identify several instances in each essay where he resists the temptation to indulge in sermonizing. What specific compositional strategies does Doyle use to let the story tell itself—without his editorializing or "sermonizing"? Support your response with an analysis of specific passages.

2. Doyle offered the following response to our question about what method he uses to start writing: "Make a note instantly when an idea or a line or a caught remark or a memory or an epiphany hits you suddenly in the kidney. INSTANTLY. . . . Then hustle to a keyboard as fast as you can and take the note out for a stroll and see what happens. Don't think. Just start typing and see what happens. Don't control it. Don't even think 'this will be an essay.' Just start. . . ." Choose one of the three essays reprinted here, and demonstrate how this spontaneity surfaces in Doyle's published essay(s). What specific evidence can you identify that illustrates Doyle's compositional belief?

3. When asked about the audience he imagines for his essays, Doyle declared: "I don't have a Reader in mind; for me it's more like a piece wants to be born and I have to try to catch it while it's ready and not edit or think much about it during the birthing hour." Select one of Doyle's essays in this portfolio and, after rereading it carefully, comment on the extent to which Doyle puts this principle for writing into practice. How is this belief evident in the structure and tone of his essay? Is his use of direct address in his essay "Dawn and Mary" a seeming exception? What does he gain as a writer in speaking directly to his readers in this instance? Comment on the effectiveness of direct address in this example. What other, similar, examples can you identify? With what effects?

The Writer at Work

BRIAN DOYLE on the Pleasures and Craft of Writing and Reading

 Brian Doyle is one of America's most engaging and memorable essayists. Many of his essays begin with the simple act of observing carefully the people and objects in the world he inhabits. By focusing and sustaining his attention on the artful elegance of the immediate and seemingly mundane aspects of life, Doyle crafts essays fueled by his imaginative attentiveness and his lyrical and descriptive sensibility. He is also a widely admired teacher and editor, a writer who generously encourages and advises other writers—from undergraduates at the University of Portland to professionals who submit their work to *Portland*, the quarterly magazine he edits for the university. *Portland* continues to be widely recognized as one of the top-ten university magazines in the country.

Brian Doyle graciously agreed to provide responses to the following questions prepared by the editors of *The Writer's Presence*.

What are your earliest recollections of writing? of reading?

Reading first—I was raised in a house in New York crammed with books, newspapers, and magazines—my dad was a newspaperman and my mom a teacher, and we were Irish and Catholic and American, and so story-addled and story-mad and story-starving; and my parents—bless their souls—arranged the books by height access, as it were, so that the shelves you could reach when little were maps and cartoons and photo books, and then up you went to the myths and adventures shelf (Hans Christian Andersen, the Grimms, Jim Kjelgaard, Tolkien, *Kon-Tiki*), and the Irish shelf (Mary Lavin! Frank O'Connor! Yeats!) and the Catholic shelf (Flannery O'Connor! J. F. Powers! Walker Percy! Greene! Waugh!), and the American shelf (Twain, Steinbeck, Edwin O'Connor), and finally the shelf I never got tall enough to read. My brothers did, and so they read

Proust and Churchill's war memoirs. As for writing, I vividly remember writing a short story at age 11, and while it was the worst short story ever written, I was totally nailed by the thought that THOSE WORDS HAD NEVER BEEN IN THAT ORDER EVER BEFORE IN THE HISTORY OF THE UNIVERSE, a feeling I still have with every piece of writing. We do not celebrate the sheer amazement of writing enough, I think.

How would you characterize yourself as a writer? What metaphor(s) would you use to characterize yourself as a writer?

Essayist first and foremost; it's the greatest form, I think, because it magpies all the other forms but is the most naked, the most direct and unadorned and unfiltered and most like the human voice and the human interior voice; but I have had enormous fun in recent years writing Big Fat Novels. Also my ambition is to write one of everything; so far I have published books of essays, stories, "proems," a novella, nonfiction books about wine and hearts and saints. If I could write a play and a comic book and a movie I am set.

What are the most challenging aspects of writing for you?

Avoiding self-absorbed self-indulgent sermonizing homilizing advice-giving counsel-confiding muck. A constant battle. I am always reminding myself to just tell a story. The best stories are about other people. Live there as a writer. Never give advice. Just catch and share stories and the world advances two inches.

What method of getting started is most successful for you?

Make a note instantly when an idea or a line or a caught remark or a memory or an epiphany hits you suddenly in the kidney. INSTANTLY. Use dollar bills and children's necks if necessary. (I once started an essay on my son Liam's neck at the beach.) Then hustle to a keyboard as fast as you can and take the note out for a stroll and see what happens. Don't think. Just start typing and see what happens. Don't control it. Don't even think "this will be an essay." Just start. I find that often the piece soon enough tells you what shape it wishes to take.

What specific strategies and/or tactics do you use to generate ideas for the essays you write?

Listening, above all. As my dad says, learn to ask a question and then shut your piehole and listen. People will tell amazing stories if you let them and invite them and be silent and dig them. People crave witness. Be a witness, and then report from the frontier of grace and pain and mercy and hilarity and terror and courage. Also I read wildly, especially newspapers, where you find an awful lot of stories that cry out to be explored.

Given your admirable productivity, procrastination doesn't seem to be an issue for you as a writer. If it is, what do you do to overcome it?

I am that lucky sort of man who knows full well he is an idiot and a turtle and a lazy-bone and so I am intent on writing every day, an hour a day if I can get it. I just show up and stuff happens. Talent has nothing to do with writing. Curiosity and typing and listening are the great tools. I usually have a Big Project on the griddle, and then happily do other things as they present themselves. I find that if you just show up every morning, a lot of stuff accumulates. I think of writing not at all as art but as craft. It's like carpentry and basketball—you put in your 10,000 hours of practice and then you stop thinking about doing it, you just do it. I don't think about art or quality or shoot for goals like *Best American Essays*; I just write, and then what happens happens. The cool stuff is all gravy to me. The best part about writing is connecting and being told by readers that your arrow landed. That's amazing and holy to me and I am humbled and thrilled and deeply moved by it. Even the insulting responses please me; at least the poor lunatics read the piece closely, heh heh heh. Although mostly those notes are from my brothers.

If someone walked into the room and observed you writing, what would he or she see?

Maniacal typing and shocking language issued by a large grizzled badger with an attitude and spectacles.

Describe the environment most conducive to you as a writer.

Actually I love working in the morning because it's quiet and the piece can present itself if I type fast enough to keep up.

For whom do you imagine that you are writing?

I don't have a Reader in mind; for me it's more like a piece wants to be born and I have to try to catch it while it's ready and not edit or think much about it during the birthing hour. Also I think I have developed some sort of subtle cadence antennae; the only revising and tinkering I do while writing is for swing and rhythm and cadence; I'll revise with a cold heart a day later. One of my personal rules is let a piece go cold for a day when I think I am finished and then go back to it with impersonal cruelty, looking to commit surgery.

What special habits do you have as a writer?

Muttering mumbling humming snarling grumbling groaning snickering burbling, with occasional snatches of song, mostly Miles Davis or the Beach Boys. If anyone ever heard me they would think I was mad.

What specific process do you follow when writing the first draft of an essay?

Bang it out. Follow its energy. Write like hell. DON'T THINK. Catch it as it wants to be. Tell a story. No "we should" or "we must . . ."—that's comment. No comment. Just catch and share a story, as much as you can in one burst.

How do you know when an essay is "finished"? What criteria do you use for making this decision?

Is it a whole story? Beginning and middle and end, as my dad says? did I get out of the way? is it lean and taut and direct? was I too playful or addicted to driving language too fast for my own amusement, which is one of my sins? Conversely is it too prim and normal? did I

say anything real? is there bone and salt and song and humor? Is it naked? There's enough witless cocky arrogant pompous fatuous idiot opinion and lecture in the world—did I just add another drop to that foul ocean, or does this thing before me *matter*, will it make the reader laugh or cry or snarl in rage or kneel in prayer or ideally all at once, which would be a mess?

What role has reading played in your success as a writer?

No reading, no writing. You have got to hear lots of voices on the page to learn how to get voices onto pages. The best education for a young writer is wild wide reading. Read everything of all sorts. Get a sense of how stories can be shaped and shared. Then get your butt in the chair every day, "lower your standards," as the great Oregon poet William Stafford said, and type like a maniac.

What have you learned about writing as a result of your reading? What do you do when you read that helps you when you write?

I notice now that while writing a novel I cannot read any novelist whose voice will mess with or override mine, so when I am writing a novel I read a lot of books about the sea and about animals. Weird. Although I will note that when I feel clogged and stupid and fatuous as a writer, I happily reread the essays of E. B. White and Annie Dillard and Robert Louis Stevenson and Twain, and Mary Oliver's poems, and they clear the pipes with their attentiveness and humor and verve and honesty and artful artlessness. Also I read the New Testament and the Psalms in the King James translation a lot for the amazing shouldery prickly muscular language. I always feel taller.

What specific advice would you offer other, but less experienced, writers to help them strengthen their efforts to improve their writing?

Do it every day for at least 30 minutes to an hour. Don't think. Just write. Edit and revise later. Lower your standards. When you are done with a piece, get it off your desk and into the mail. Don't tinker forever. Finish a piece and then do another and then another and etc. Don't think about style. Just write. There are millions of stories waiting to be sensed and caught and shared. What are you waiting for? **The best stories will come from other people. The best writing of all is witness. Be a witness. It's a holy and crucial job. If you have what my friend George Higgins called the "benign neurosis" of the itch to write, you are ready for the job. Get your butt in the chair today and do it. Don't expect money. Do hope you will shiver a heart here and there, or make people laugh. There's nothing as cool as that. If I can do it, by gawd you can do it, because I am a humming idiot. Do it again tomorrow. Best of luck. . . .**

Lars Eighner

On Dumpster Diving

LARS EIGHNER (b. 1948) was born in Texas and attended the University of Texas at Austin. An essayist and a fiction writer, he contributes regularly to the *Threepenny Review*, *Advocate Men*, the *Guide*, and *Inches*. He has published several collections of short stories, essays, and gay erotica. His most recent publications include a camp novel, *Pawn to Queen Four* (1995); a collection of essays, *Gay Cosmos* (1995); an erotic short story collection, *Whispered in the Dark* (1995); and *WANK: The Tapes* (1998). Eighner writes a blog on his Web site, larseighner.com.

> **"A writer needs talent, luck, and persistence. You can make do with two out of three, and the more you have of one, the less you need of the others."**

Eighner became homeless in 1988, after he lost his job as a mental-hospital attendant. "On Dumpster Diving" is Eighner's prize-winning essay based on this experience, later reprinted as part of his full-length book about homelessness, *Travels with Lizbeth: Three Years on the Road and on the Streets* (1993). Eighner and Lizbeth, Eighner's dog, became homeless again in 1996. Friends organized a fund under the auspices of the *Texas Observer* and obtained an apartment for Eighner and Lizbeth in Austin. Lizbeth has since passed away.

On what is required to find success as a writer, Eighner has said, "I was not making enough money to support myself as a housed person, but I was writing well before I became homeless. . . . A writer needs talent, luck, and persistence. You can make do with two out of three, and the more you have of one, the less you need of the others."

LONG BEFORE I began Dumpster diving I was impressed with Dumpsters, enough so that I wrote the Merriam-Webster research service to discover what I could about the word "Dumpster." I learned from them that "Dumpster" is a proprietary word belonging to the Dempster Dumpster company.

Since then I have dutifully capitalized the word although it was lower-cased in almost all of the citations Merriam-Webster photocopied for me. Dempster's word is too apt. I have never heard these things called anything but Dumpsters. I do not know anyone who knows the generic name for these objects. From time to time, however, I hear a wino or hobo give some corrupted credit to the original and call them Dipsy Dumpsters.

I began Dumpster diving about a year before I became homeless.

I prefer the term "scavenging" and use the word "scrounging" when I mean to be obscure. I have heard people, evidently meaning to be polite, using the word "foraging," but I prefer to reserve that word for gathering nuts and berries and such which I do also according to the season and the opportunity. "Dumpster diving" seems to me to be a little too cute and, in my case, inaccurate because I lack the athletic ability to lower myself into the Dumpsters as the true divers do, much to their increased profit.

I like the frankness of the word "scavenging," which I can hardly think   5
of without picturing a big black snail on an aquarium wall. I live from the refuse of others. I am a scavenger. I think it a sound and honorable niche, although if I could I would naturally prefer to live the comfortable consumer life, perhaps—and only perhaps—as a slightly less wasteful consumer owing to what I have learned as a scavenger.

While my dog Lizbeth and I were still living in the house on Avenue B in Austin, as my savings ran out, I put almost all my sporadic income into rent. The necessities of daily life I began to extract from Dumpsters. Yes, we ate from Dumpsters. Except for jeans, all my clothes came from Dumpsters. Boom boxes, candles, bedding, toilet paper, medicine, books, a typewriter, a virgin male love doll, change sometimes amounting to many dollars: I acquired many things from the Dumpsters.

I have learned much as a scavenger. I mean to put some of what I have learned down here, beginning with the practical art of Dumpster diving and proceeding to the abstract.

What is safe to eat?

After all, the finding of objects is becoming something of an urban art. Even respectable employed people will sometimes find something tempting sticking out of a Dumpster or standing beside one. Quite a number of people, not all of them of the bohemian type, are willing to brag that they found this or that piece in the trash. But eating from Dumpsters is the thing that separates the dilettanti from the professionals.

Eating safely from the Dumpsters involves three principles: using the   10 senses and common sense to evaluate the condition of the found materials, knowing the Dumpsters of a given area and checking them regularly, and seeking always to answer the question "Why was this discarded?"

Perhaps everyone who has a kitchen and a regular supply of groceries has, at one time or another, made a sandwich and eaten half of it before discovering mold on the bread or got a mouthful of milk before realizing the milk had turned. Nothing of the sort is likely to happen to a Dumpster diver because he is constantly reminded that most food is discarded for a reason. Yet a lot of perfectly good food can be found in Dumpsters.

Canned goods, for example, turn up fairly often in the Dumpsters I frequent. All except the most phobic people would be willing to eat from a can even if it came from a Dumpster. Canned goods are among the safest of foods to be found in Dumpsters, but are not utterly foolproof.

Although very rare with modern canning methods, botulism is a possibility. Most other forms of food poisoning seldom do lasting harm to a healthy person. But botulism is almost certainly fatal and often the first symptom is death. Except for carbonated beverages, all canned goods should contain a slight vacuum and suck air when first punctured. Bulging, rusty, dented cans and cans that spew when punctured should be avoided, especially when the contents are not very acidic or syrupy.

Heat can break down the botulin, but this requires much more cooking than most people do to canned goods. To the extent that botulism occurs at all, of course, it can occur in cans on pantry shelves as well as in cans from Dumpsters. Need I say that home-canned goods found in Dumpsters are simply too risky to be recommended.

From time to time one of my companions, aware of the source of my   15 provisions, will ask, "Do you think these crackers are really safe to eat?" For some reason it is most often the crackers they ask about.

This question always makes me angry. Of course I would not offer my companion anything I had doubts about. But more than that I wonder why he cannot evaluate the condition of the crackers for himself. I have no special knowledge and I have been wrong before. Since he knows where the food comes from, it seems to me he ought to assume some of the responsibility for deciding what he will put in his mouth.

For myself I have few qualms about dry foods such as crackers, cookies, cereal, chips, and pasta if they are free of visible contaminants and still dry and crisp. Most often such things are found in the original packaging, which is not so much a positive sign as it is the absence of a negative one.

Raw fruits and vegetables with intact skins seem perfectly safe to me, excluding of course the obviously rotten. Many are discarded for minor imperfections which can be pared away. Leafy vegetables, grapes, cauliflower, broccoli, and similar things may be contaminated by liquids and may be impractical to wash.

Candy, especially hard candy, is usually safe if it has not drawn ants. Chocolate is often discarded only because it has become discolored as the cocoa butter de-emulsified. Candying after all is one method of food preservation because pathogens do not like very sugary substances.

All of these foods might be found in any Dumpster and can be evaluated   20
with some confidence largely on the basis of appearance. Beyond these are foods which cannot be correctly evaluated without additional information.

I began scavenging by pulling pizzas out of the Dumpster behind a pizza delivery shop. In general prepared food requires caution, but in this case I knew when the shop closed and went to the Dumpster as soon as the last of the help left.

Such shops often get prank orders, called "bogus." Because help seldom stays long at these places pizzas are often made with the wrong topping, refused on delivery for being cold, or baked incorrectly. The products to be discarded are boxed up because inventory is kept by counting boxes: A boxed pizza can be written off; an unboxed pizza does not exist.

I never placed a bogus order to increase the supply of pizzas and I believe no one else was scavenging in this Dumpster. But the people in the shop became suspicious and began to retain their garbage in the shop overnight.

While it lasted I had a steady supply of fresh, sometimes warm pizza. Because I knew the Dumpster I knew the source of the pizza, and because I visited the Dumpster regularly I knew what was fresh and what was yesterday's.

The area I frequent is inhabited by many affluent college students. I   25
am not here by chance; the Dumpsters in this area are very rich. Students throw out many good things, including food. In particular they tend to throw everything out when they move at the end of a semester, before and after breaks, and around midterm when many of them despair of college. So I find it advantageous to keep an eye on the academic calendar.

The students throw food away around the breaks because they do not know whether it has spoiled or will spoil before they return. A typical discard is a half jar of peanut butter. In fact nonorganic peanut butter does not require refrigeration and is unlikely to spoil in any reasonable time. The student does not know that, and since it is Daddy's money, the student decides not to take a chance.

Opened containers require caution and some attention to the question "Why was this discarded?" But in the case of discards from student apartments, the answer may be that the item was discarded through carelessness, ignorance, or wastefulness. This can sometimes be deduced when the item is found with many others, including some that are obviously perfectly good.

Some students, and others, approach defrosting a freezer by chucking out the whole lot. Not only do the circumstances of such a find tell the story, but also the mass of frozen goods stays cold for a long time and items may be found still frozen or freshly thawed.

Yogurt, cheese, and sour cream are items that are often thrown out while they are still good. Occasionally I find a cheese with a spot of mold, which of course I just pare off, and because it is obvious why such a cheese was discarded, I treat it with less suspicion than an apparently perfect cheese found in similar circumstances. Yogurt is often discarded, still sealed, only because the expiration date on the carton had passed. This is one of my favorite finds because yogurt will keep for several days, even in warm weather.

Students throw out canned goods and staples at the end of semesters   30
and when they give up college at midterm. Drugs, pornography, spirits, and the like are often discarded when parents are expected—Dad's day, for example. And spirits also turn up after big party weekends, presumably discarded by the newly reformed. Wine and spirits, of course, keep perfectly well even once opened.

My test for carbonated soft drinks is whether they still fizz vigorously. Many juices or other beverages are too acid or too syrupy to cause much concern provided they are not visibly contaminated. Liquids, however, require some care.

One hot day I found a large jug of Pat O'Brien's Hurricane mix. The jug had been opened, but it was still ice cold. I drank three large glasses before it became apparent to me that someone had added the rum to the mix, and not a little rum. I never tasted the rum and by the time I began to feel the effects I had already ingested a very large quantity of the beverage. Some divers would have considered this a boon, but being suddenly and thoroughly intoxicated in a public place in the early afternoon is not my idea of a good time.

I have heard of people maliciously contaminating discarded food and even handouts, but mostly I have heard of this from people with vivid imaginations who have had no experience with the Dumpsters themselves. Just before the pizza shop stopped discarding its garbage at night, jalapeños began showing up on most of the discarded pizzas. If indeed this was meant to discourage me it was a wasted effort because I am a native Texan.

For myself, I avoid game, poultry, pork, and egg-based foods whether I find them raw or cooked. I seldom have the means to cook what I find, but when I do I avail myself of plentiful supplies of beef which is often in very good condition. I suppose fish becomes disagreeable before it becomes dangerous. The dog is happy to have any such thing that is past its prime and, in fact, does not recognize fish as food until it is quite strong.

Home leftovers, as opposed to surpluses from restaurants, are very often   35
bad. Evidently, especially among students, there is a common type of personality that carefully wraps up even the smallest leftover and shoves it into the back of the refrigerator for six months or so before discarding it.

Characteristic of this type are the reused jars and margarine tubs which house the remains.

I avoid ethnic foods I am unfamiliar with. If I do not know what it is supposed to look like when it is good, I cannot be certain I will be able to tell if it is bad.

No matter how careful I am I still get dysentery at least once a month, oftener in warm weather. I do not want to paint too romantic a picture. Dumpster diving has serious drawbacks as a way of life.

I learned to scavenge gradually, on my own. Since then I have initiated several companions into the trade. I have learned that there is a predictable series of stages a person goes through in learning to scavenge.

At first the new scavenger is filled with disgust and self-loathing. He is ashamed of being seen and may lurk around, trying to duck behind things, or he may try to dive at night.

(In fact, most people instinctively look away from a scavenger. By skulk-   40
ing around, the novice calls attention to himself and arouses suspicion. Diving at night is ineffective and needlessly messy.)

Every grain of rice seems to be a maggot. Everything seems to stink. He can wipe the egg yolk off the found can, but he cannot erase the stigma of eating garbage out of his mind.

That stage passes with experience. The scavenger finds a pair of running shoes that fit and look and smell brand new. He finds a pocket calculator in perfect working order. He finds pristine ice cream, still frozen, more than he can eat or keep. He begins to understand: People do throw away perfectly good stuff, a lot of perfectly good stuff.

At this stage, Dumpster shyness begins to dissipate. The diver, after all, has the last laugh. He is finding all manner of good things which are his for the taking. Those who disparage his profession are the fools, not he.

He may begin to hang onto some perfectly good things for which he has neither a use nor a market. Then he begins to take note of the things which are not perfectly good but are nearly so. He mates a Walkman with broken earphones and one that is missing a battery cover. He picks up things which he can repair.

At this stage he may become lost and never recover. Dumpsters are full   45
of things of some potential value to someone and also of things which never have much intrinsic value but are interesting. All the Dumpster divers I have known come to the point of trying to acquire everything they touch. Why not take it, they reason, since it is all free.

This is, of course, hopeless. Most divers come to realize that they must restrict themselves to items of relatively immediate utility. But in some cases the diver simply cannot control himself. I have met several of these pack-rat types. Their ideas of the values of various pieces of junk verge on the psychotic. Every bit of glass may be a diamond, they think, and all that glistens, gold.

I tend to gain weight when I am scavenging. Partly this is because I always find far more pizza and doughnuts than water-packed tuna, non-fat yogurt, and fresh vegetables. Also I have not developed much faith in the reliability of Dumpsters as a food source, although it has been proven to me many times. I tend to eat as if I have no idea where my next meal is coming from. But mostly I just hate to see food go to waste and so I eat much more than I should. Something like this drives the obsession to collect junk.

As for collecting objects, I usually restrict myself to collecting one kind of small object at a time, such as pocket calculators, sunglasses, or campaign buttons. To live on the street I must anticipate my needs to a certain extent: I must pick up and save warm bedding I find in August because it will not be found in Dumpsters in November. But even if I had a home with extensive storage space I could not save everything that might be valuable in some contingency.

I have proprietary feelings about my Dumpsters. As I have suggested, it is no accident that I scavenge from Dumpsters where good finds are common. But my limited experience with Dumpsters in other areas suggests to me that it is the population of competitors rather than the affluence of the dumpers that most affects the feasibility of survival by scavenging. The large number of competitors is what puts me off the idea of trying to scavenge in places like Los Angeles.

Curiously, I do not mind my direct competition, other scavengers, so 50 much as I hate the can scroungers.

People scrounge cans because they have to have a little cash. I have tried scrounging cans with an able-bodied companion. Afoot a can scrounger simply cannot make more than a few dollars a day. One can extract the necessities of life from the Dumpsters directly with far less effort than would be required to accumulate the equivalent value in cans.

Can scroungers, then, are people who *must* have small amounts of cash. These are drug addicts and winos, mostly the latter because the amounts of cash are so small.

Spirits and drugs do, like all other commodities, turn up in Dumpsters and the scavenger will from time to time have a half bottle of a rather good wine with his dinner. But the wino cannot survive on these occasional finds; he must have his daily dose to stave off the DTs. All the cans he can carry will buy about three bottles of Wild Irish Rose.

I do not begrudge them the cans, but can scroungers tend to tear up the Dumpsters, mixing the contents and littering the area. They become so specialized that they can see only cans. They earn my contempt by passing up change, canned goods, and readily hockable items.

There are precious few courtesies among scavengers. But it is a common 55 practice to set aside surplus items: pairs of shoes, clothing, canned goods, and such. A true scavenger hates to see good stuff go to waste and what he cannot use he leaves in good condition in plain sight.

Can scroungers lay waste to everything in their path and will stir one of a pair of good shoes to the bottom of a Dumpster, to be lost or ruined in the muck. Can scroungers will even go through individual garbage cans, something I have never seen a scavenger do.

Individual garbage cans are set out on the public easement only on garbage days. On other days going through them requires trespassing close to a dwelling. Going through individual garbage cans without scattering litter is almost impossible. Litter is likely to reduce the public's tolerance of scavenging. Individual garbage cans are simply not as productive as Dumpsters; people in houses and duplexes do not move as often and for some reason do not tend to discard as much useful material. Moreover, the time required to go through one garbage can that serves one household is not much less than the time required to go through a Dumpster that contains the refuse of twenty apartments.

But my strongest reservation about going through individual garbage cans is that this seems to me a very personal kind of invasion to which I would object if I were a householder. Although many things in Dumpsters are obviously meant never to come to light, a Dumpster is somehow less personal.

I avoid trying to draw conclusions about the people who dump in the Dumpsters I frequent. I think it would be unethical to do so, although I know many people will find the idea of scavenger ethics too funny for words.

Dumpsters contain bank statements, bills, correspondence, and other documents, just as anyone might expect. But there are also less obvious sources of information. Pill bottles, for example. The labels on pill bottles contain the name of the patient, the name of the doctor, and the name of the drug. AIDS drugs and antipsychotic medicines, to name but two groups, are specific and are seldom prescribed for any other disorders. The plastic compacts for birth control pills usually have complete label information. 60

Despite all of this sensitive information, I have had only one apartment resident object to my going through the Dumpster. In that case it turned out the resident was a university athlete who was taking bets and who was afraid I would turn up his wager slips.

Occasionally a find tells a story. I once found a small paper bag containing some unused condoms, several partial tubes of flavored sexual lubricant, a partially used compact of birth control pills, and the torn pieces of a picture of a young man. Clearly she was through with him and planning to give up sex altogether.

Dumpster things are often sad—abandoned teddy bears, shredded wedding books, despaired-of sales kits. I find many pets lying in state in Dumpsters. Although I hope to get off the streets so that Lizbeth can have a long and comfortable old age, I know this hope is not very realistic. So I suppose when her time comes she too will go into a Dumpster. I will have no better place for her. And after all, for most of her life her livelihood has come from the Dumpster. When she finds something I think is safe that has been spilled from the Dumpster I let her have it. She already knows the route around the best Dumpsters. I like to think that if she survives me she will have a chance of evading the dog catcher and of finding her sustenance on the route.

Silly vanities also come to rest in the Dumpsters. I am a rather accomplished needleworker. I get a lot of materials from the Dumpsters. Evidently sorority girls, hoping to impress someone, perhaps themselves, with their mastery of a womanly art, buy a lot of embroider-by-number kits, work a few stitches horribly, and eventually discard the whole mess. I pull out their stitches, turn the canvas over, and work an original design. Do not think I refrain from chuckling as I make original gifts from these kits.

I find diaries and journals. I have often thought of compiling a book of literary found objects. And perhaps I will one day. But what I find is hopelessly commonplace and bad without being, even unconsciously, camp. College students also discard their papers. I am horrified to discover the kind of paper which now merits an A in an undergraduate course. I am grateful, however, for the number of good books and magazines the students throw out.

In the area I know best I have never discovered vermin in the Dumpsters, but there are two kinds of kitty surprise. One is alley cats which I meet as they leap, claws first, out of Dumpsters. This is especially thrilling when I have Lizbeth in tow. The other kind of kitty surprise is a plastic garbage bag filled with some ponderous, amorphous mass. This always proves to be used cat litter.

City bees harvest doughnut glaze and this makes the Dumpster at the doughnut shop more interesting. My faith in the instinctive wisdom of animals is always shaken whenever I see Lizbeth attempt to catch a bee in her mouth, which she does whenever bees are present. Evidently some birds find Dumpsters profitable, for birdie surprise is almost as common as kitty surprise of the first kind. In hunting season all kinds of small game turn up in Dumpsters, some of it, sadly, not entirely dead. Curiously, summer and winter, maggots are uncommon.

The worst of the living and near-living hazards of the Dumpsters are the fire ants. The food that they claim is not much of a loss, but they are vicious and aggressive. It is very easy to brush against some surface of the Dumpster and pick up half a dozen or more fire ants, usually in some sensitive area such as the underarm. One advantage of bringing Lizbeth along as I make Dumpster rounds is that, for obvious reasons, she is very alert to ground-based fire ants. When Lizbeth recognizes the signs of fire ant infestation around our feet she does the Dance of the Zillion Fire Ants. I have learned not to ignore this warning from Lizbeth, whether I perceive the tiny ants or not, but to remove ourselves at Lizbeth's first pas de bourrée.[1] All the more so because the ants are the worst in the months I wear flip-flops, if I have them.

(Perhaps someone will misunderstand the above. Lizbeth does the Dance of the Zillion Fire Ants when she recognizes more fire ants than she cares

65

---

1 *pas de bourrée:* A transitional ballet step. —EDS.

to eat, not when she is being bitten. Since I have learned to react promptly, she does not get bitten at all. It is the isolated patrol of fire ants that falls in Lizbeth's range that deserves pity. Lizbeth finds them quite tasty.)

By far the best way to go through a Dumpster is to lower yourself into   70
it. Most of the good stuff tends to settle at the bottom because it is usually weightier than the rubbish. My more athletic companions have often demonstrated to me that they can extract much good material from a Dumpster I have already been over.

To those psychologically or physically unprepared to enter a Dumpster, I recommend a stout stick, preferably with some barb or hook at one end. The hook can be used to grab plastic garbage bags. When I find canned goods or other objects loose at the bottom of a Dumpster I usually can roll them into a small bag that I can then hoist up. Much Dumpster diving is a matter of experience for which nothing will do except practice.

Dumpster diving is outdoor work, often surprisingly pleasant. It is not entirely predictable; things of interest turn up every day and some days there are finds of great value. I am always very pleased when I can turn up exactly the thing I most wanted to find. Yet in spite of the element of change, scavenging more than most other pursuits tends to yield returns in some proportion to the effort and intelligence brought to bear. It is very sweet to turn up a few dollars in change from a Dumpster that has just been gone over by a wino.

The land is now covered with cities. The cities are full of Dumpsters. I think of scavenging as a modern form of self-reliance. In any event, after ten years of government service, where everything is geared to the lowest common denominator, I find work that rewards initiative and effort refreshing. Certainly I would be happy to have a sinecure again, but I am not heartbroken not to have one anymore.

I find from the experience of scavenging two rather deep lessons. The first is to take what I can use and let the rest go by. I have come to think that there is no value in the abstract. A thing I cannot use or make useful, perhaps by trading, has no value however fine or rare it may be. I mean useful in a broad sense—so, for example, some art I would think useful and valuable, but other art might be otherwise for me.

I was shocked to realize that some things are not worth acquiring, but   75
now I think it is so. Some material things are white elephants that eat up the possessor's substance.

The second lesson is of the transience of material being. This has not quite converted me to a dualist, but it has made some headway in that direction. I do not suppose that ideas are immortal, but certainly mental things are longer-lived than other material things.

Once I was the sort of person who invests material objects with sentimental value. Now I no longer have those things, but I have the sentiments yet.

Many times in my travels I have lost everything but the clothes I was wearing and Lizbeth. The things I find in Dumpsters, the love letters and ragdolls of so many lives, remind me of this lesson. Now I hardly pick up a thing without envisioning the time I will cast it away. This I think is a healthy state of mind. Almost everything I have now has already been cast out at least once, proving that what I own is valueless to someone.

Anyway, I find my desire to grab for the gaudy bauble has been largely sated. I think this is an attitude I share with the very wealthy—we both know there is plenty more where what we have came from. Between us are the rat-race millions who have confounded their selves with the objects they grasp and who nightly scavenge the cable channels looking for they know not what.

I am sorry for them. ▧

80

The Reader's Presence

1. At the center of "On Dumpster Diving" is Eighner's effort to bring out from the shadows of contemporary American life the lore and practices of scavenging, what he calls "a modern form of self-reliance." His essay also provides a compelling account of his self-education as he took to the streets for "the necessities of daily life" (paragraph 6). Outline the stages in this process, and summarize the ethical and moral issues and the questions of decorum that Eighner confronted along the way. Show how this process reflects the structure of his essay, "beginning with the practical art of Dumpster diving and proceeding to the abstract" (paragraph 7).

2. One of the most remarkable aspects of Eighner's essay is the tone (the attitude) he expresses toward his subject. Select a paragraph from the essay. Read it aloud. How would you characterize the sound of his voice? Does he sound, for example, tough-minded? polite? strident? experienced? cynical? something else? Consider, for example, paragraph 34, where he notes: "For myself, I avoid game, poultry, pork, and egg-based foods whether I find them raw or cooked." Where have you heard talk like this before? Do you notice any changes as the essay develops, or does Eighner maintain the same tone in discussing his subject? What responses does he elicit from his readers when he speaks of scavenging as a "profession" and a "trade"?

3. Think about Eighner's relationship with his readers. Does he consider himself fundamentally different from or similar to his audience? In what specific ways? Consider, for example, the nature of the information Eighner provides in the essay. Does he expect his readers to be familiar with the information? How does he characterize his own knowledgeability about this often-noticed but rarely discussed activity in urban America? Comment on Eighner's use of irony in presenting information about Dumpster diving and in anticipating his readers' responses to the circumstances within which he does the work of his trade.

4. **VISUAL PRESENCE:**   Examine the photograph of Lars Eighner on page 410. What features of the portrait help establish Eighner's presence? Support your answer with specific details from the picture.

5. **CONNECTIONS:**   Compare Eighner's description of Dumpster diving to one of the most famous essays in the English language, Jonathan Swift's "A Modest Proposal" (page 752). Both essays deal with economics and the effects of poverty. In what ways does each author use humor and satire? How does each author introduce us to the grim realities of poverty? What role does food play in each essay? You might also compare Eighner's essay to Peter Singer's "The Singer Solution to World Poverty" (page 735). Discuss how applicable you find Singer's "solution" to Eighner's problems.

The Writer at Work

LARS EIGHNER on the Challenges of Writing While Homeless

Barbara Laing//Time Life Pictures/Getty Images

Lars Eighner and Lizbeth.

In the summer of 1989, Lars Eighner, without a job and with no place to live, began writing about his experiences as a homeless person trying to survive in the college town of Austin, Texas. When one of his essays, "On Dumpster Diving," was published in the prestigious literary journal, the *Threepenny Review* (Fall 1991), it became immediately clear that he had contributed one of the best and most authentic accounts of life on the American streets. The essay, now a modern classic and reprinted widely, was collected in *Travels with Lizbeth: Three Years on the Road and on the Streets* in 1993. For that volume, Eighner included an introduction (excerpted here) in which he discussed the challenges that confront a homeless writer.

❝When I began this account I was living under a shower curtain in a stand of bamboo in a public park. I did not undertake to write about homelessness, but wrote what I knew, as an artist paints a still life, not because he is especially fond of fruit, but because the subject is readily at hand.

In the summer of 1989, when I was in the bamboo, I supposed interest in homelessness had peaked in the presidential election of the previous year. Moreover, I thought my experiences with homelessness were atypical.

I still think my experiences were atypical, but I have come to disbelieve in typical homelessness. I had some advantages and some disadvantages and I chose the course that seemed mostly likely to provide the survival of myself and my dog Lizbeth on the most comfortable terms of which our situation would admit.

I did not often associate with other homeless people. I avoided the homeless shelters and hobo jungles. I did not attempt to survive on the streets of a very large city, but made my way for the most part in a liberal and affluent area of an overgrown college town. Although I often despaired of improving my material situation, I seldom lacked for a feeling of self-worth or a sense of mission. On the other hand, I spent most of my time in Texas, where a general contempt for the poor is reflected in a useless, vestigial social welfare system. I handicapped myself by adopting from the first a policy of not stealing and not begging on the streets. And, of course, I would not be parted from Lizbeth. I do not pretend to speak for the homeless. I think no one could speak for all the various people who have in common the condition of being homeless. I do not know many of the homeless, but of the condition of being homeless I know something, and that is part of what I have written about.

In truth, becoming homeless was a long process that I can date only arbitrarily. I had been without a reliable income for about a year before I left the shack I had been living in. For about five months after I left the shack I traveled and imposed on friends and strangers, so that I spent only part of the time on the streets. Moreover, throughout that first period I believed I had one prospect or another of improving my situation and I did not regard myself as truly homeless.

When I had the opportunity to get off the street for a week or a month or even for only a night, I did so; my object was not to explore homelessness but to get off the street. I have recounted these events in the ordinary narrative manner, but have only summarized the events of my longer stopovers. Eventually I became homeless enough to suit anyone's definition. In spite of the challenges that homelessness presented, the chief characteristic of my experience of homelessness was tedium. The days and nights that Lizbeth and I were literally without a roof over our heads, although by far the majority of the more than two years encompassed here, are represented by relatively few examples. One of those days was so much like each of the others that to call any of them typical would be an understatement. Our immediate needs I met with more or less trouble, but once that was done I could do no more. Day after day I could aspire, within reason, to nothing more than survival. Although the planets wandered among the stars and the moon waxed and waned, the identical naked barrenness of existence was exposed to me, day in and day out. I do not think I could write a narrative that would quite capture the unrelenting ennui of homelessness, but if I were to write it, no one could bear to read it. I spare myself as much as the reader in not attempting to recall so many empty hours. Every life has trivial occurrences, pointless episodes, and unresolved mysteries, but a homeless life has these and virtually nothing else. I have found it best in some parts to abandon a strictly chronological account and to treat in essay form experiences that relate to a single subject although they occurred in disparate times and places. **"**

Ian Frazier

A Farewell to Yarns

The journalist and essayist **IAN FRAZIER** (b. 1951) started his career on the staff of the *New Yorker*. Many of the essays he wrote for the magazine can be found in his first two books: *Dating Your Mom* (1986) and *Nobody Better, Better Than Nobody* (1987). In the mid-1980s, Frazier left his job in New York and embarked on a journey across the North American prairies to Montana. The book that emerged after several years spent exploring this region, *Great Plains* (1989), was a huge success with both critics and readers. In *Family* (1994), Frazier turns to a subject closer to home and tells the story of twelve generations of his family. His books also include *Coyote v. Acme* (1996), a collection of comic essays; *On the Rez* (2000), the story of his experience on the Pine Ridge Indian Reservation; *Travels in Siberia* (2010); and *Lamentations of the Father* (2008), based on his 1997 award-winning essay of the same name. Frazier co-edited *The Best American Essays 1997* and *The Best American Travel Writing 2003*.

> **"With a lot of writing, what you see is the top, the pinnacle, and the rest is invisible."**

In all of his writing, Frazier pays close attention to detail and location. "If you know something about a place it can save your sanity," he says, and a writer can find that knowledge through observation. "With a lot of writing, what you see is the top, the pinnacle, and the rest is invisible—all of these observations are ways of keeping yourself from flying off into space." In "A Farewell to Yarns," which appeared in *Outside* magazine in 2012, Frazier explores the way the Internet has put an end to inflated stories about outdoor adventure.

A TRUTH ABOUT THE OUTDOORS is that it causes people to lie. Strange forces out there in the wild have always conspired to corrupt human honesty. Over time, intelligent listeners and readers came to accept that an adventurer's reports would not consist of one-to-one representations of fact but instead would contain exaggerations, distortions, omissions, additions, events that foolish people wanted to believe had happened but hadn't, and deliberate, implausible, fantastical lies. Maybe that was even a reason the restless and sketchy among us ventured into the wilderness in the first place: because if we claimed we did or saw something amazing there, who could prove the contrary? Returned from our journeys, we could brag all we wanted without fear of contradiction. An enormous attraction of far places has always been that no one else was inconveniently in the neighborhood to check.

"Here Be Monsters," the old maps announced, next to drawings of walking Leviathan-fish with huge maws and claws and fangs. The pictures must have been accurate; how would the mapmakers have known what to draw unless eyewitnesses had told them? Somewhere out there, travelers said, lived blue-eyed Indians who spoke only Hebrew—a Lost Tribe of Israel, miraculously transported to remotest Asia or the American West. Those who revealed this discovery had not, it turned out, met the blue-eyed (*blue-eyed?*) Hebrews themselves but once crossed paths with parties who had. Inventive wanderers said they had seen snakes that had bit their own tails and made themselves into hoops and rolled across the ground, cannibals with three heads, Arctic dwellers who covered their ears against the sound of the sunrise, and beautiful Amazonian women warriors who held healthy young men (often the wanderers themselves) captive for sex. Explorers claimed they had climbed mountains they hadn't climbed and had reached the North Pole when in fact they never reached it. Apparently sober individuals gave firsthand accounts of seeing yeti in the Himalayas and Nessie in her loch and jackalopes on the prairies. Old-time sailors boasted of sleeping with beautiful mermaids, annoyingly omitting the precise physical details, and according to certain fishermen, mermaids offering to grant them three wishes had come up in their nets. The words *fisherman* and *liar* are linked in our brains for good reason. And in the interest of brevity, I will pass over the many stories involving logging roads, elk hunters, space aliens, and intergalactic crossbreeding. There are some doors man was not meant to open.

Lies made the wild scary and alluring. When I was a boy, local places I knew about buzzed excitingly with crazy tales. In rural Illinois, Argyle State Park was said to be inhabited by a creature called the Argyle Monster—a huge cougar that had lost its front feet in a trap and ran through the forest on its hind legs at dusk and "screamed like a woman." Or so said Billy somebody, who told his friends, who were friends of mine, who told me. I never saw the Argyle Monster myself, but it ran on its hind legs through my imaginings and colored the dusk of this unremarkable state park a deep and thrilling sepia when I walked back to the picnic area after fishing. It's been decades since I went there; I regret that I quit being afraid of the Argyle Monster long ago.

More recently, as a grown-up supposedly immune to phantasms, I learned from Russians when I was traveling in Siberia that somewhere in its remotest parts is Coca-Cola City (Gorod Koka-Kola), which was built during the Cold War as a reproduction of an American city. The residents of Coca-Cola City speak perfect English and use American products and behave like Americans, providing a realistic setting in which the Russian spymasters can train special operatives who will be sent to the U.S. Coca-Cola City is alleged to be the topmost of top-secret sites, and it is closed, of course, to all visitors. I'm not sure if that's why I never could pin it down on the map. I suspect that it does not exist and never did—but who can say? The rumor of it made Siberia more Siberian for me.

You might not think that any human creation as hardy as lies could be   5
in danger of dying out, but I'm afraid that, at least outdoors, they are. Nowadays, a good outdoor what-if story has a much smaller chance for survival. Some years ago, you may remember, observers in the deep woods of eastern Arkansas said they had seen an ivory-billed woodpecker, the wonderful and near mythic bird that black people called Lord God Bird because of its soul-shivering appearance. There had been no confirmed sightings of the ivory-bill in decades, and its possible extinction was and is bad news. The observers who said they had seen it weren't trying to deceive, just being wishful, and because they recorded it with a video camera their wishfulness was eventually dashed—close analysis of the video revealed that the bird was not an ivory-bill.

It would have been nice to think that the bird still survived someplace far away in the forest. But truth is always better than error, I suppose. Consider the recent case of the giant wild hog Hogzilla. A Georgia man said he had shot it while it was running around someplace in the woods, and he posted pictures of it online. This eight-foot-long, 800-pound animal was as monstrous a creature as the Georgia swamps had ever seen. The man added that he had buried the hog in a grave marked with a cross (though feral, it had been a Christian hog, apparently), and because of the excitement stirred up on the Internet the man eventually had to submit the corpse for examination. Through DNA testing, experts determined that it was a mix of wild hog and domestic pig. Its size suggested it had eaten a lot of hog feed. Such a disappointment—Hogzilla, a pen-raised fake. How much more stimulating to believe that there are 800-pound wild hogs infesting the swamps of Georgia. One hates to think what a radio collar and a wildlife-management team would have done to William Faulkner's bear.

The Hogzilla debunking was another example of the pesky trend toward factuality currently sweeping the out-of-doors. Technology, of course, is at the root of it. The global landscape used to be a theater of various shadings—sunlit fields and canyons of dark obscurity, trackless jungles, and misty Shangri-las. Now the whole world is like a cineplex when the lights have come on. Almost no place on the surface of the planet is really obscure anymore. Satellites watch it all and can let you know to the millimeter how far continental drift moved your swimming beach last year. What's up along the banks of the great, gray-green Limpopo? How's traffic on the road to Mandalay? What's the snowpack like across the wide Missouri? The Internet or Google Earth will tell you.

Traveling in Siberia a decade ago, I thought I was pretty much beyond the reach of checkability; in fact-checker shorthand, anything I wrote would be "O.A.," which stands for "on author," meaning "unverifiable by anything other than the author's say-so." I did not need to worry that any checker would visit where I had been, nor was it likely that an irate reader would write in claiming I had got something wrong about the tundra zone of the Chukchi Peninsula, given the difficulty of getting there and the absence of any reason to go. But then time and advancing technology proved me wrong. During the many years my Siberian research took, satellite imagery of the earth's surface became available online, and my claims about the lay of the land in Siberia proved to be checkable after all. Even in far-flung places, descriptions could be verified. If I said there was no bridge over a remote Far Eastern river that I had crossed by ferry, the checker could look on Google Earth and see that, in fact, no bridge showed up in the satellite photo, and a small boat much like a ferry could be seen crossing there.

Today the adventurer's tale-telling days are over and his crooked ways have been made straight, and every untruth can be revealed. No point in lying: we've got it all on tape, as the TV detectives say. If you claim you drove to Nunavut and we think maybe you didn't, we'll just look at the E-ZPass records for the toll roads along the way. And if they don't tell us, the cell-phone towers will. Formerly, a cell-phone tower could follow a phone only when the phone was on, and smart criminals knew to turn it off before committing crimes. Now phones ping the towers and the towers record the presence of the cell phones in the vicinity, often whether they are on or not, and to escape the network's observation you must remove the battery entirely. Almost everywhere, some degree of electronic connection can be assumed.

I never took much notice of the satellites going over constantly until I   10 was out in the night in Siberia, with its grand darkness. In the middle of the Barabinsk Steppe or some other nowhere, I always studied the night sky before getting into my tent. Amid the stars' wild randomness, the little dots of light crossed the heavens on routes as purposeful and direct as a cue-ball shot. I carried a satellite phone myself. Sometimes I would pick a likely-looking satellite and shoot a call to it (I thought; actually, the link was more complicated, and to a satellite I didn't see) and then do something ordinary like make an appointment with my dentist back in New Jersey or talk to my daughter about her week at school. And all this from a region where exiles in former times used to disappear, never to be heard from again.

A favorite word for the technological fishbowl effect is *transparency*. Anything you do in far places, and anything that exists out there, can, in principle, be seen. *Transparency* is one of those words whose real meaning is its opposite, the way that countries with ministries of culture haven't any. Of course, all the technology known or yet to be known won't see even a part of everything or stop people from making things up. It's just that the realm of colorful prevarication has moved inside, where the heart does its sneaking. Most of the gods and demons and fairies and windigos who used to inhabit their own particular outdoor places died off long ago, and modern technology has zapped the survivors. If you want to spin a yarn, it will be about something inward and private, like whether you took steroids.

During the days when the Argyle Monster still seemed a possibility in my mind, one of the books I liked to read told about the life of a German hunter and sportsman named Baron Münchausen. This baron lived in the Black Forest in some former time—the stories date to the 1700s—and journeyed through the fastnesses of the forest having adventures. A typical one was his encounter with a young stag he surprised one day in a dark glen. Grabbing his rifle, the baron found he was out of bullets, but he happened to be eating a cherry at the time, so he spat out the cherry pit, loaded the rifle with it, and fired, hitting the stag squarely between the eyes. The stag fell down but then quickly leaped up and ran away. Years later, the baron was again in that part of the woods. All at once, to his astonishment, he came face-to-face with a huge stag that had a small but healthy cherry tree growing between its antlers.

As a boy I did not believe that had really happened, but I kind of suspended final judgment, because maybe it could, you know? Because it was cool, I didn't altogether rule it out. Today the baron would be a video game. Progress has cleared the outdoors of its tall stories and imaginary beings and redeposited them on screens. Cyberspace is full of invented monsters, and movies seem to be about nothing but winged horses and multiheaded dragons and rivers of snakes. In the first Harry Potter movie, a "full-grown mountain troll" appears in a Hogwarts bathroom and tries to smash Harry with its huge club before Harry manages to kill it by sticking his wand up its nose. Not too long ago, many people believed there really were such things as trolls in the mountains. I mourn the loss; the mountains are poorer without their trolls. As far as I'm concerned, not every last troll has left, and a stag with a tree growing between its antlers is an unlikely sight, but not out of the question completely.

The point is, wonders are out there still. If you don't on some level believe that, you're going to stay home with the TV, and "remote" will be what's lost between the cushions. Technology or no, I expect to see miracles and portents anytime I leave the pavement. A while ago, I was fishing for snook in the Florida Everglades. My guide and I had made our way far back in a gin-clear avenue between stands of mangroves when two manatees swam right beneath the boat. I had never seen a manatee before. They went past faster than Usain Bolt and executed a right turn with marvelous agility and were gone, and I swear I saw mermaids. Naked, brown, extremely sexy mermaids, like the fishermen said. ▪

The Reader's Presence

1. Comment on the effectiveness of Frazier's decision to open his essay with the assertion: "A truth about the outdoors is that it causes people to lie." In what specific ways do experiences in the outdoors provide opportunities to create "deliberate, implausible, fantastical lies" (paragraph 1)? What role do images and technology play in supporting or deflating such verbal extravagance? What major changes in contemporary experience would account for Frazier's assertion that "[y]ou might not think that any human creation as hardy as lies could be in danger of dying out, but I'm afraid that, at least outdoors, they are" (paragraph 5)?

2. Examine carefully the movement of Frazier's thinking in writing. For example, does Frazier develop his essay by proceeding inductively, that is, moving from particular instances to generalizations, or does he proceed deductively, inferring particular instances from general statements? How would you characterize Frazier's tone of voice in his essay? Does he maintain that tone throughout, or does he vary the sound of his voice in different parts of his essay? Point to—and then analyze—specific passages in which Frazier uses irony and humor to support and underscore particular points.

3. **CONNECTIONS:** Focus for a few moments on the final paragraph. How does Frazier's first sentence ("The point is, wonders are out there still.") establish the substance and direction of his ultimate belief in the imaginative possibilities of the natural world? In this respect, compare and contrast Frazier's attitudes toward the outdoors to those of Cheryl Strayed in "Into the Woods" (page 266) and to those of Nathaniel Hawthorne in "My Visit to Niagara" (page 432). Which writer's prose do you think is most memorable? Explain why, pointing to specific passages to support your response.

Daniel Gilbert

WHAT YOU DON'T KNOW MAKES YOU NERVOUS

A professor of psychology at Harvard University, **DANIEL GILBERT** (b. 1957) is well known for his research in social psychology. The author of the international best-seller *Stumbling on Happiness* (2006), Gilbert is particularly interested in the subject of affective forecasting—the human tendency to predict the emotions we will feel in the future—and cognitive bias: the systematic errors in our thinking that cause us to predict incorrectly. With long-time collaborator Timothy Wilson (University of Virginia), Daniel Gilbert coined the phrase "psychological immune system" to describe the system of coping mechanisms (rationalization, self-affirmation, and self-deception, to name but a few) that people use

> Daniel Gilbert coined the phrase, with Timothy Wilson, "psychological immune system" to describe the system of coping mechanisms (rationalization, self-affirmation, and self-deception, to name but a few) that people use to deal with negative emotions.

to deal with negative emotions. Gilbert has won numerous honors and awards for his research, including a Guggenheim Fellowship and the American Psychological Association's Distinguished Scientific Award for an Early Career Contribution to Psychology. His book *Stumbling on Happiness* won the 2007 Royal Society Prize for Science Books and has been translated into more than two-dozen languages. "What You Don't Know Makes You Nervous" appeared in the *New York Times* in 2009.

CAMBRIDGE, Mass.—SEVENTY-SIX YEARS AGO, Franklin Delano Roosevelt took to the inaugural dais and reminded a nation that its recent troubles "concern, thank God, only material things." In the midst of the Depression, he urged Americans to remember that "happiness lies not in the mere possession of money" and to recognize "the falsity of material wealth as the standard of success."

"The only thing we have to fear," he claimed, "is fear itself."

As it turned out, Americans had a great deal more to fear than that, and their innocent belief that money buys happiness was entirely correct. Psychologists and economists now know that although the very rich are no happier than the merely rich, for the other 99 percent of us, happiness is greatly enhanced by a few quaint assets, like shelter, sustenance and security. Those who think the material is immaterial have probably never stood in a breadline.

Money matters and today most of us have less of it, so no one will be surprised by new survey results from the Gallup-Healthways Well-Being Index showing that Americans are smiling less and worrying more than they were a year ago, that happiness is down and sadness is up, that we are getting less sleep and smoking more cigarettes, that depression is on the rise.

But light wallets are not the cause of our heavy hearts. After all, most of us still have more inflation-adjusted dollars than our grandparents had, and they didn't live in an unremitting funk. Middle-class Americans still enjoy more luxury than upper-class Americans enjoyed a century earlier, and the fin de siècle was not an especially gloomy time. Clearly, people can be perfectly happy with less than we had last year and less than we have now. 5

So if a dearth of dollars isn't making us miserable, then what is? No one knows. I don't mean that no one knows the answer to this question. I mean that the answer to this question is that no one knows—and not knowing is making us sick.

Consider an experiment by researchers at Maastricht University in the Netherlands who gave subjects a series of 20 electric shocks. Some subjects knew they would receive an intense shock on every trial. Others knew they would receive 17 mild shocks and 3 intense shocks, but they didn't know on which of the 20 trials the intense shocks would come. The results showed that subjects who thought there was a small chance of receiving an intense shock were more afraid—they sweated more profusely, their hearts beat faster—than subjects who knew for sure that they'd receive an intense shock.

That's because people feel worse when something bad *might* occur than when something bad *will* occur. Most of us aren't losing sleep and sucking down Marlboros because the Dow is going to fall another thousand points, but because we don't know whether it will fall or not—and human beings find uncertainty more painful than the things they're uncertain about.

But why?

A colostomy reroutes the colon so that waste products leave the body   10
through a hole in the abdomen, and it isn't anyone's idea of a picnic. A University of Michigan–led research team studied patients whose colostomies were permanent and patients who had a chance of someday having their colostomies reversed. Six months after their operations, patients who knew they would be permanently disabled were happier than those who thought they might someday be returned to normal.

Similarly, researchers at the University of British Columbia studied people who had undergone genetic testing to determine their risk for developing the neurodegenerative disorder known as Huntington's disease. Those who learned that they had a very high likelihood of developing the condition were happier a year after testing than those who did not learn what their risk was.

Why would we prefer to know the worst than to suspect it? Because when we get bad news we weep for a while, and then get busy making the best of it. We change our behavior, we change our attitudes. We raise our consciousness and lower our standards. We find our bootstraps and tug. But we can't come to terms with circumstances whose terms we don't yet know. An uncertain future leaves us stranded in an unhappy present with nothing to do but wait.

Our national gloom is real enough, but it isn't a matter of insufficient funds. It's a matter of insufficient certainty. Americans have been perfectly happy with far less wealth than most of us have now, and we could quickly become those Americans again—if only we knew we had to. ●

The Reader's Presence

1. Consider the opening of Gilbert's essay, where he points to President Franklin Delano Roosevelt's famous inaugural address and its most famous assertion: "The only thing we have to fear is fear itself" (paragraph 2). What does Gilbert gain strategically by starting his essay with a reference to Roosevelt's speech? How does Gilbert's effort to contextualize Roosevelt's speech and his famous line serve as an introduction to Gilbert's essay as a whole? Why do you think the "innocent belief that money buys happiness" (paragraph 3) continues to be promoted in contemporary American culture?

2. Gilbert identifies a pervasive sense of uncertainty as the cause of our "national gloom" (paragraph 13). What specific points would you summon to support—or contradict—the assertion that clarity and assurance are essential components of happiness? What specific evidence does Gilbert present to support his point? What reasonable inferences does Gilbert draw about the "cause of our heavy hearts"

(paragraph 5)? How convincing—and compelling—do you find Gilbert's notion that by recognizing and identifying feelings of uncertainty and fear as detrimental to happiness, we can begin to move toward a state of happiness?

3. **CONNECTIONS:**   Compare and contrast Gilbert's essay with Annie Dillard's "This Is the Life" (page 382). To what extent—and in what specific ways—do knowledge and experience play important roles in each essay? How does happiness relate to Dillard's essay? Reflect on Dillard's "Then what?" question (paragraph 16) and then apply it to Gilbert's essay. In what ways is Dillard's "Then what?" similar to and different from Gilbert's "But why?" question (paragraph 9)?

TOM HEWITT
Learning from Tison

Tom Hewitt

Tom Hewitt was a senior at the University of Alaska Fairbanks when he wrote "Learning from Tison." A journalism major, he served as a regular contributor and as an online editor of the student-run weekly paper, *The Sun Star*, where the essay originally appeared.

Hewitt offers the following advice for other student writers: "First and foremost, always keep writing. Writing more is the only surefire way to improve. What also helps is finding someone who can help you improve your writing. This can be a professor, friend, or colleague—anyone who can look at your work with a critical eye and tell you what you're doing right and where you're going astray."

Sets situation in a narrative that takes him to Indonesia.

Last week at this time, I was waking up in a Jakarta hotel in preparation for a 36-hour flight back to Alaska.

Let me back up.

I left Thanksgiving morning to travel to Indonesia, where I would begin filming a documentary about a 10-year-old burn victim named Tison who was coming to Fairbanks for reconstructive surgery. The whole opportunity had come together relatively at the last minute, but some journalistic opportunities are difficult to turn down.

It was a long haul traveling to the clinic where Tison lived—planes from Fairbanks to Seattle to Los Angeles to Hong Kong to Singapore to Manado to Ternate, then a speed boat from Ternate to the island of Halmahera, and a

Effective repetition of preposition "to" emphasizes difficulty of trip.

cab for the final three-hour drive to the clinic. I like travel-ing, but after four days en route, I was ready to stay in one place for a while.

The travel wasn't the only thing bothering me. I would be missing over a week of school—and an issue of the *Sun Star*—right before finals, and I had several papers and proj-ects to complete before my return, in addition to filming Tison and life at the clinic full time. My stress level was high.

What finally brought my mind back to my work was a trip to a soccer game at a nearby village, where the clin-ic's soccer team had a match against the locals. The twelve players, Tison, and I piled into a minivan and rumbled off.

Description helps us *see* impoverished conditions.

The villagers were poor. They lived in aluminum-and-wood shacks with tiny yards. The soccer field was mostly dirt, and a noticeable rise in the pitch near one goal pro-vided a terrain obstacle. The bridge to the field couldn't support a car—the villagers had to ferry us across the river on rafts.

Despite all this, everyone at the game was happy. The whole village turned out, and the visiting clinic team was treated like royalty, with cold water before the match and hot tea and baked bananas after. When the home team won, 3–1, the players' mothers and sisters stormed the field cheering.

Life isn't fair. Sometimes there's no good reason why some people get to travel halfway around the world to see incred-ible things while others sleep on dirt floors and don't know where their next meal will come from. The Indonesians know that, but it doesn't stop them from finding fulfillment.

Nor did having burns over 40 percent of his body dimin-ish Tison's spirit in any way I could detect. On his worst day, he was several times cheerier than I am in the best of times. No matter how long I pointed the camera in his direction, I never got tired of telling his story. And he pretended not to mind me tagging behind him everywhere he went.

Compares and contrasts situations to show different ways of considering happiness.

Concludes with the lesson he takes away from his experience and reminds us of the essay's title.

We get thrown curves sometimes, and part of the way we may be measured is how we respond not to situations we expect, but [to] those we don't. I don't know where I stack up, but the most important thing Tison taught me was that while things don't always turn out the way we want them to, all we can do is our best. And if I can do half as well as Tison, I'll count myself a success.

Malcolm Gladwell

SMALL CHANGE: WHY THE REVOLUTION WILL NOT BE TWEETED

MALCOLM GLADWELL (b. 1963) is a best-selling author and staff writer for the *New Yorker*. Son of a British father and a Jamaican mother, Gladwell was born in England and moved to the United States as a child. He began his journalism career at the *American Spectator*, a conservative monthly magazine. He started writing for the *Washington Post* in 1987, serving as a science writer before becoming the paper's New York City bureau chief. He left the *Post* in 1996 to write for the *New Yorker*. Gladwell is known for his best-selling books *The Tipping Point: How Little Things Can Make a Big Difference* (2000), *Blink: The Power of Thinking Without Thinking* (2005), *Outliers: The Story of Success* (2008), and *What the Dog Saw: And Other Adventures* (2009). His most recent book is *David and Goliath* (2013),

> "Ideas and products and messages and behaviors spread just like viruses do."

which draws on history, politics, business, and psychology to examine what causes the underdog to win (or lose). "Small Change: Why the Revolution Will Not Be Tweeted" first appeared in the October 4, 2010, issue of the *New Yorker*.

Gladwell's writing tends to be concerned with illuminating the patterns behind everyday life and identifying the origins of major events and the trends in minor ones. According to Gladwell, "Ideas and products and messages and behaviors spread just like viruses do." He was named one of *Time* magazine's 100 Most Influential People in 2005.

AT FOUR-THIRTY in the afternoon on Monday, February 1, 1960, four college students sat down at the lunch counter at the Woolworth's in downtown Greensboro, North Carolina. They were freshmen at North Carolina A. & T., a black college a mile or so away.

"I'd like a cup of coffee, please," one of the four, Ezell Blair, said to the waitress.

"We don't serve Negroes here," she replied.

The Woolworth's lunch counter was a long L-shaped bar that could seat sixty-six people, with a standup snack bar at one end. The seats were for whites. The snack bar was for blacks. Another employee, a black woman who worked at the steam table, approached the students and tried to warn them away. "You're acting stupid, ignorant!" she said. They didn't move.

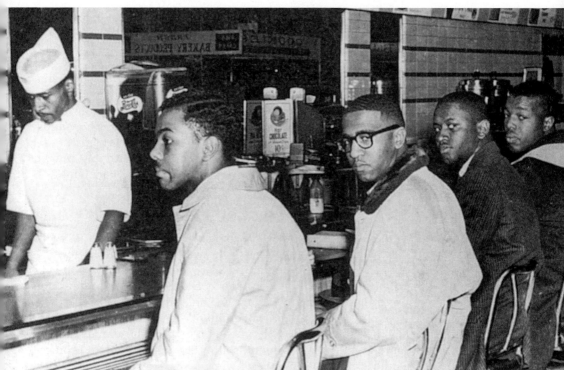

The four college students at the lunch counter at Woolworth's in downtown Greensboro, North Carolina, February 2, 1960.

Around five-thirty, the front doors to the store were locked. The four still didn't move. Finally, they left by a side door. Outside, a small crowd had gathered, including a photographer from the Greensboro *Record*. "I'll be back tomorrow with A. & T. College," one of the students said.

By next morning, the protest had grown to twenty-seven men and four   5 women, most from the same dormitory as the original four. The men were dressed in suits and ties. The students had brought their schoolwork, and studied as they sat at the counter. On Wednesday, students from Greensboro's "Negro" secondary school, Dudley High, joined in, and the number of protesters swelled to eighty. By Thursday, the protesters numbered three hundred, including three white women, from the Greensboro campus of the University of North Carolina. By Saturday, the sit-in had reached six hundred. People spilled out onto the street. White teenagers waved Confederate flags. Someone threw a firecracker. At noon, the A. & T. football team arrived. "Here comes the wrecking crew," one of the white students shouted.

By the following Monday, sit-ins had spread to Winston-Salem, twenty-five miles away, and Durham, fifty miles away. The day after that, students at Fayetteville State Teachers College and at Johnson C. Smith College, in Charlotte, joined in, followed on Wednesday by students at St. Augustine's

College and Shaw University, in Raleigh. On Thursday and Friday, the protest crossed state lines, surfacing in Hampton and Portsmouth, Virginia, in Rock Hill, South Carolina, and in Chattanooga, Tennessee. By the end of the month, there were sit-ins throughout the South, as far west as Texas. "I asked every student I met what the first day of the sitdowns had been like on his campus," the political theorist Michael Walzer wrote in *Dissent*. "The answer was always the same: 'It was like a fever. Everyone wanted to go.'" Some seventy thousand students eventually took part. Thousands were arrested and untold thousands more radicalized. These events in the early sixties became a civil-rights war that engulfed the South for the rest of the decade—and it happened without e-mail, texting, Facebook, or Twitter.

The world, we are told, is in the midst of a revolution. The new tools of social media have reinvented social activism. With Facebook and Twitter and the like, the traditional relationship between political authority and popular will has been upended, making it easier for the powerless to collaborate, coordinate, and give voice to their concerns. When ten thousand protesters took to the streets in Moldova in the spring of 2009 to protest against their country's Communist government, the action was dubbed the Twitter Revolution, because of the means by which the demonstrators had been brought together. A few months after that, when student protests rocked Tehran, the State Department took the unusual step of asking Twitter to suspend scheduled maintenance of its Web site, because the Administration didn't want such a critical organizing tool out of service at the height of the demonstrations. "Without Twitter the people of Iran would not have felt empowered and confident to stand up for freedom and democracy," Mark Pfeifle, a former national-security adviser, later wrote, calling for Twitter to be nominated for the Nobel Peace Prize. Where activists were once defined by their causes, they are now defined by their tools. Facebook warriors go online to push for change. "You are the best hope for us all," James K. Glassman, a former senior State Department official, told a crowd of cyber activists at a recent conference sponsored by Facebook, A. T. & T., Howcast, MTV, and Google. Sites like Facebook, Glassman said, "give the U.S. a significant competitive advantage over terrorists. Some time ago, I said that Al Qaeda was 'eating our lunch on the Internet.' That is no longer the case. Al Qaeda is stuck in Web 1.0. The Internet is now about interactivity and conversation."

These are strong, and puzzling, claims. Why does it matter who is eating whose lunch on the Internet? Are people who log on to their Facebook page really the best hope for us all? As for Moldova's so-called Twitter Revolution, Evgeny Morozov, a scholar at Stanford who has been the most persistent of digital evangelism's critics, points out that Twitter had scant internal significance in Moldova, a country where very few Twitter accounts exist. Nor does it seem to have been a revolution, not least because the protests—as Anne Applebaum suggested in the *Washington Post*—may well have been a bit of stagecraft cooked up by the government. (In a country paranoid about Romanian revanchism,[1] the protesters flew a Romanian flag over the Parliament building.) In the Iranian case, meanwhile, the people tweeting about the demonstrations were almost all in the West. "It is time to get Twitter's role in the events in Iran right," Golnaz Esfandiari wrote, this past summer, in *Foreign Policy*. "Simply put: There was no Twitter Revolution inside Iran." The cadre of prominent bloggers, like Andrew Sullivan, who championed the role of social media in Iran, Esfandiari continued, misunderstood the situation. "Western journalists who couldn't reach—or didn't bother reaching?—people on the ground in Iran simply scrolled through the English-language tweets post with tag #iranelection," she wrote. "Through it all, no one seemed to wonder why people trying to coordinate protests in Iran would be writing in any language other than Farsi."

Some of this grandiosity is to be expected. Innovators tend to be solipsists. They often want to cram every stray fact and experience into their new model. As the historian Robert Darnton has written, "The marvels of communication technology in the present have produced a false consciousness about the past—even a sense that communication has no history, or had nothing of importance to consider before the days of television and the Internet." But there is something else at work here, in the outsized enthusiasm for social media. Fifty years after one of the most extraordinary episodes of social upheaval in American history, we seem to have forgotten what activism is.

Greensboro in the early nineteen-sixties was the kind of place where 10 racial insubordination was routinely met with violence. The four students who first sat down at the lunch counter were terrified. "I suppose if anyone had come up behind me and yelled 'Boo,' I think I would have fallen off my seat," one of them said later. On the first day, the store manager notified the police chief, who immediately sent two officers to the store. On the third day, a gang of white toughs showed up at the lunch counter and stood ostentatiously behind the protesters, ominously muttering epithets such as "burr-head nigger." A local Ku Klux Klan leader made an appearance. On Saturday, as tensions grew, someone called in a bomb threat, and the entire store had to be evacuated.

The dangers were even clearer in the Mississippi Freedom Summer Project of 1964, another of the sentinel campaigns of the civil-rights movement. The Student Nonviolent Coordinating Committee recruited hundreds of Northern, largely white unpaid volunteers to run Freedom Schools, register black voters, and raise civil-rights awareness in the Deep South. "No one should go *anywhere* alone, but certainly not in an automobile and certainly not at night," they were instructed. Within days of arriving in Mississippi, three volunteers—Michael Schwerner, James Chaney, and Andrew

---

1 **revanchism** (from the French: *revanche*, "revenge"): A term used to describe a political policy of a nation or an ethnic group, intended to regain lost territory or standing.—EDS.

Goodman—were kidnapped and killed, and, during the rest of the summer, thirty-seven black churches were set on fire and dozens of safe houses were bombed; volunteers were beaten, shot at, arrested, and trailed by pickup trucks full of armed men. A quarter of those in the program dropped out. Activism that challenges the status quo—that attacks deeply rooted problems—is not for the faint of heart.

What makes people capable of this kind of activism? The Stanford sociologist Doug McAdam compared the Freedom Summer dropouts with the participants who stayed, and discovered that the key difference wasn't, as might be expected, ideological fervor. "*All* of the applicants—participants and withdrawals alike—emerge as highly committed, articulate supporters of the goals and values of the summer program," he concluded. What mattered more was an applicant's degree of personal connection to the civil-rights movement. All the volunteers were required to provide a list of personal contacts—the people they wanted kept apprised of their activities—and participants were far more likely than dropouts to have close friends who were also going to Mississippi. High-risk activism, McAdam concluded, is a "strong-tie" phenomenon.

This pattern shows up again and again. One study of the Red Brigades, the Italian terrorist group of the nineteen-seventies, found that seventy percent of recruits had at least one good friend already in the organization. The same is true of the men who joined the mujahideen in Afghanistan. Even revolutionary actions that look spontaneous, like the demonstrations in East Germany that led to the fall of the Berlin Wall, are, at core, strong-tie phenomena. The opposition movement in East Germany consisted of several hundred groups, each with roughly a dozen members. Each group was in limited contact with the others: at the time, only thirteen percent of East Germans even had a phone. All they knew was that on Monday nights, outside St. Nicholas Church in downtown Leipzig, people gathered to voice their anger at the state. And the primary determinant of who showed up was "critical friends" —the more friends you had who were critical of the regime the more likely you were to join the protest.

So one crucial fact about the four freshmen at the Greensboro lunch counter—David Richmond, Franklin McCain, Ezell Blair, and Joseph McNeil—was their relationship with one another. McNeil was a roommate of Blair's in A. & T.'s Scott Hall dormitory. Richmond roomed with McCain one floor up, and Blair, Richmond, and McCain had all gone to Dudley High School. The four would smuggle beer into the dorm and talk late into the night in Blair and McNeil's room. They would all have remembered the murder of Emmett Till in 1955, the Montgomery bus boycott that same year, and the showdown in Little Rock in 1957. It was McNeil who brought up the idea of a sit-in at Woolworth's. They'd discussed it for nearly a month. Then McNeil came into the dorm room and asked the others if they were ready. There was a pause, and McCain said, in a way that works only with people who talk late into the night with one another, "Are you guys chicken or not?" Ezell Blair worked up the courage the next day to ask for a cup of coffee because he was flanked by his roommate and two good friends from high school.

The kind of activism associated with social media isn't like this at all. The 15 platforms of social media are built around weak ties. Twitter is a way of following (or being followed by) people you may never have met. Facebook is a tool for efficiently managing your acquaintances, for keeping up with the people you would not otherwise be able to stay in touch with. That's why you can have a thousand "friends" on Facebook, as you never could in real life.

This is in many ways a wonderful thing. There is strength in weak ties, as the sociologist Mark Granovetter has observed. Our acquaintances—not our friends—are our greatest source of new ideas and information. The Internet lets us exploit the power of these kinds of distant connections with marvellous efficiency. It's terrific at the diffusion of innovation, interdisciplinary collaboration, seamlessly matching up buyers and sellers, and the logistical functions of the dating world. But weak ties seldom lead to high-risk activism.

In a new book called *The Dragonfly Effect: Quick, Effective, and Powerful Ways to Use Social Media to Drive Social Change*, the business consultant Andy Smith and the Stanford Business School professor Jennifer Aaker tell the story of Sameer Bhatia, a young Silicon Valley entrepreneur who came down with acute myelogenous leukemia. It's a perfect illustration of social media's strengths. Bhatia needed a bone-marrow transplant, but he could not find a match among his relatives and friends. The odds were best with a donor of his ethnicity, and there were few South Asians in the national bone-marrow database. So Bhatia's business partner sent out an e-mail explaining Bhatia's plight to more than four hundred of their acquaintances, who forwarded the e-mail to their personal contacts; Facebook pages and YouTube videos were devoted to the Help Sameer campaign. Eventually, nearly twenty-five thousand new people were registered in the bone-marrow database, and Bhatia found a match.

But how did the campaign get so many people to sign up? By not asking too much of them. That's the only way you can get someone you don't really know to do something on your behalf. You can get thousands of people to sign up for a donor registry, because doing so is pretty easy. You have to send in a cheek swab and—in the highly unlikely event that your bone marrow is a good match for someone in need—spend a few hours at the hospital. Donating bone marrow isn't a trivial matter. But it doesn't involve financial or personal risk; it doesn't mean spending a summer being chased by armed men in pickup trucks. It doesn't require that you confront socially entrenched norms and practices. In fact, it's the kind of commitment that will bring only social acknowledgment and praise.

The evangelists of social media don't understand this distinction; they seem to believe that a Facebook friend is the same as a real friend and that signing up for a donor registry in Silicon Valley today is activism in the same sense as sitting at a segregated lunch counter in Greensboro in 1960.

"Social networks are particularly effective at increasing motivation," Aaker and Smith write. But that's not true. Social networks are effective at increasing *participation*—by lessening the level of motivation that participation requires. The Facebook page of the Save Darfur Coalition has 1,282,339 members, who have donated an average of nine cents apiece. The next biggest Darfur charity on Facebook has 22,073 members, who have donated an average of thirty-five cents. Help Save Darfur has 2,797 members, who have given, on average, fifteen cents. A spokesperson for the Save Darfur Coalition told *Newsweek*, "We wouldn't necessarily gauge someone's value to the advocacy movement based on what they've given. This is a powerful mechanism to engage this critical population. They inform their community, attend events, volunteer. It's not something you can measure by looking at a ledger." In other words, Facebook activism succeeds not by motivating people to make a real sacrifice but by motivating them to do the things that people do when they are not motivated enough to make a real sacrifice. We are a long way from the lunch counters of Greensboro.

The students who joined the sit-ins across the South during the winter 20 of 1960 described the movement as a "fever." But the civil-rights movement was more like a military campaign than like a contagion. In the late nineteen-fifties, there had been sixteen sit-ins in various cities throughout the South, fifteen of which were formally organized by civil-rights organizations like the NAACP and CORE. Possible locations for activism were scouted. Plans were drawn up. Movement activists held training sessions and retreats for would-be protesters, The Greensboro Four were a product of this groundwork: all were members of the NAACP Youth Council. They had close ties with the head of the local NAACP chapter. They had been briefed on the earlier wave of sit-ins in Durham, and had been part of a series of movement meetings in activist churches. When the sit-in movement spread from Greensboro throughout the South, it did not spread indiscriminately. It spread to those cities which had preexisting "movement centers"—a core of dedicated and trained activists ready to turn the "fever" into action.

The civil-rights movement was high-risk activism. It was also, crucially, strategic activism: a challenge to the establishment mounted with precision and discipline. The NAACP was a centralized organization, run from New York according to highly formalized operating procedures. At the Southern Christian Leadership Conference, Martin Luther King, Jr., was the unquestioned authority. At the center of the movement was the black church, which had, as Aldon D. Morris points out in his superb 1984 study, "The Origins of the Civil Rights Movement," a carefully demarcated division of labor, with various standing committees and disciplined groups. "Each group was task-oriented and coordinated its activities through authority structures," Morris writes. "Individuals were held accountable for their assigned duties, and important conflicts were resolved by the minister, who usually exercised ultimate authority over the congregation."

This is the second crucial distinction between traditional activism and its online variant: social media are not about this kind of hierarchical organization. Facebook and the like are tools for building *networks*, which are the opposite, in structure and character, of hierarchies. Unlike hierarchies, with their rules and procedures, networks aren't controlled by a single central authority. Decisions are made through consensus, and the ties that bind people to the group are loose.

This structure makes networks enormously resilient and adaptable in low-risk situations. Wikipedia is a perfect example. It doesn't have an editor, sitting in New York, who directs and corrects each entry. The effort of putting together each entry is self-organized. If every entry in Wikipedia were to be erased tomorrow, the content would swiftly be restored, because that's what happens when a network of thousands spontaneously devote their time to a task.

There are many things, though, that networks don't do well. Car companies sensibly use a network to organize their hundreds of suppliers, but not to design their cars. No one believes that the articulation of a coherent design philosophy is best handled by a sprawling, leaderless organizational system. Because networks don't have a centralized leadership structure and clear lines of authority, they have real difficulty reaching consensus and setting goals. They can't think strategically; they are chronically prone to conflict and error. How do you make difficult choices about tactics or strategy or philosophical direction when everyone has an equal say?

The Palestine Liberation Organization originated as a network, and the international-relations scholars Mette Eilstrup-Sangiovanni and Calvert Jones argue in a recent essay in *International Security* that this is why it ran into such trouble as it grew: "Structural features typical of networks—the absence of central authority, the unchecked autonomy of rival groups, and the inability to arbitrate quarrels through formal mechanisms—made the P.L.O. excessively vulnerable to outside manipulation and internal strife."

In Germany in the nineteen-seventies, they go on, "the far more unified and successful left-wing terrorists tended to organize hierarchically, with professional management and clear divisions of labor. They were concentrated geographically in universities, where they could establish central leadership, trust, and camaraderie through regular, face-to-face meetings." They seldom betrayed their comrades in arms during police interrogations. Their counterparts on the right were organized as decentralized networks, and had no such discipline. These groups were regularly infiltrated, and members, once arrested, easily gave up their comrades. Similarly, Al Qaeda was most dangerous when it was a unified hierarchy. Now that it has dissipated into a network, it has proved far less effective.

The drawbacks of networks scarcely matter if the network isn't interested in systemic change—if it just wants to frighten or humiliate or make a splash—or if it doesn't need to think strategically. But if you're taking on a powerful and organized establishment you have to be a hierarchy. The Montgomery bus boycott required the participation of tens of thousands of people who depended on public transit to get to and from work each day. It lasted a *year*. In order to persuade those people to stay true to the cause, the boycott's organizers tasked each local black church with maintaining morale, and put together a free alternative private carpool service, with forty-eight dispatchers and forty-two pickup stations. Even the White Citizens Council, King later said, conceded that the carpool system moved with "military precision." By the time King came to Birmingham, for the climactic showdown with Police Commissioner Eugene (Bull) Connor, he had a budget of a million dollars, and a hundred full-time staff members on the ground, divided into operational units. The operation itself was divided into steadily escalating phases, mapped out in advance. Support was maintained through consecutive mass meetings rotating from church to church around the city.

Boycotts and sit-ins and nonviolent confrontations—which were the weapons of choice for the civil-rights movement—are high-risk strategies. They leave little room for conflict and error. The moment even one protester deviates from the script and responds to provocation, the moral legitimacy of the entire protest is compromised. Enthusiasts for social media would no doubt have us believe that King's task in Birmingham would have been made infinitely easier had he been able to communicate with his followers through Facebook, and contented himself with tweets from a Birmingham jail. But networks are messy: think of the ceaseless pattern of correction and revision, amendment and debate, that characterizes Wikipedia. If Martin Luther King, Jr., had tried to do a wiki-boycott in Montgomery, he would have been steamrollered by the white power structure. And of what use would a digital communication tool be in a town where ninety-eight percent of the black community could be reached every Sunday morning at church? The things that King needed in Birmingham—discipline and strategy—were things that online social media cannot provide.

The bible of the social-media movement is Clay Shirky's *Here Comes Everybody*. Shirky, who teaches at New York University, sets out to demonstrate the organizing power of the Internet, and he begins with the story of Evan, who worked on Wall Street, and his friend Ivanna, after she left her smart phone, an expensive Sidekick, on the back seat of a New York City taxicab. The telephone company transferred the data on Ivanna's lost phone to a new phone, whereupon she and Evan discovered that the Sidekick was now in the hands of a teenager from Queens, who was using it to take photographs of herself and her friends.

When Evan e-mailed the teenager, Sasha, asking for the phone back, she replied that his "white ass" didn't deserve to have it back. Miffed, he set up a Web page with her picture and a description of what had happened. He forwarded the link to his friends, and they forwarded it to their friends. Someone found the MySpace page of Sasha's boyfriend, and a link to it found its way onto the site. Someone found her address online and took a video of her home while driving by; Evan posted the video on the site. The story was picked up by the news filter Digg. Evan was now up to ten e-mails a minute. He created a bulletin board for his readers to share their stories, but it crashed under the weight of responses. Evan and Ivanna went to the police, but the police filed the report under "lost," rather than "stolen," which essentially closed the case. "By this point millions of readers were watching," Shirky writes, "and dozens of mainstream news outlets had covered the story." Bowing to the pressure, the NYPD reclassified the item as "stolen." Sasha was arrested, and Evan got his friend's Sidekick back.

Shirky's argument is that this is the kind of thing that could never have happened in the pre-Internet age—and he's right. Evan could never have tracked down Sasha. The story of the Sidekick would never have been publicized. An army of people could never have been assembled to wage this fight. The police wouldn't have bowed to the pressure of a lone person who had misplaced something as trivial as a cell phone. The story, to Shirky, illustrates "the ease and speed with which a group can be mobilized for the right kind of cause" in the Internet age.

Shirky considers this model of activism an upgrade. But it is simply a form of organizing which favors the weak-tie connections that give us access to information over the strong-tie connections that help us persevere in the face of danger. It shifts our energies from organizations that promote strategic and disciplined activity and toward those which promote resilience and adaptability. It makes it easier for activists to express themselves, and harder for that expression to have any impact. The instruments of social media are well suited to making the existing social order more efficient. They are not a natural enemy of the status quo. If you are of the opinion that all the world needs is a little buffing around the edges, this should not trouble you. But if you think that there are still lunch counters out there that need integrating it ought to give you pause.

Shirky ends the story of the lost Sidekick by asking, portentously, "What happens next?"—no doubt imagining future waves of digital protesters. But he has already answered the question. What happens next is more of the same. A networked, weak-tie world is good at things like helping Wall Streeters get phones back from teenage girls. *Viva la revolución.* ●

The Reader's Presence

1. Reread the first six paragraphs of Gladwell's essay. What do they lead you to believe will be the focus of his essay? Point to specific words and phrases to support your response. How does the scene that Gladwell describes relate to the point he is making in this essay? What are the effects of Gladwell's decision not to mention anything about social media until the end of this opening section?

2. Point to specific ways in which Gladwell recounts the events of the Greensboro lunch counter sit-in differently from the way he relates the story of the New Yorker who lost her Sidekick. What compositional strategies does Gladwell use to make the effects of reading about these two events seem so different?

3. **VISUAL PRESENCE:**   Examine the 1960 photograph on page 423 of a lunch counter sit-in. How is this image similar to or different from more recent pictures of protests you have seen that were spread by social media? Use specific examples to support your response.

4. **CONNECTIONS:**   Compare Gladwell's essay with Nicholas Carr's "Is Google Making Us Stupid?" (page 588). How does each author use historical facts to support the points he is making? In what specific ways are the authors' uses of historical facts similar? How are they different? In what ways do their claims support each other? In what ways are they at odds?

Nathaniel Hawthorne

My Visit to Niagara

Born in Salem, Massachusetts, **NATHANIEL HAWTHORNE** (1804–1864) is best known as the author of *The Scarlet Letter* (1850), but he was also a prolific short story and nonfiction writer. He worked briefly as the editor of the *American Magazine of Useful and Entertaining Knowledge*, but he spent much of his professional life (prior to the publication of *The Scarlet Letter*) working in government, first at the Customs House in Boston and later as the surveyor for the District of Salem and Beverly, Massachusetts. He was closely associated with other American writers of the period, including Henry Wadsworth Longfellow, Oliver Wendell Holmes, Herman Melville, Ralph Waldo Emerson, and Henry David Thoreau. Much of his fiction is set in New England and deals with themes of guilt and sin. Hawthorne was particularly troubled by the idea of ancestral sin: His ancestors were directly involved in the Salem witch trials. His great-great grandfather, John Hathorne, was one of the judges who oversaw the infamous trials, in which many innocent men and women were sentenced to death. It has even been suggested that Hawthorne added

> Nathaniel Hawthorne's great-great grandfather, John Hathorne, was one of the judges who oversaw the Salem witch trials, and it has been suggested that Hawthorne added the "w" to his last name to distance himself from his ancestors.

the "w" to the spelling of his last name to distance himself from his ancestors. "My Visit to Niagara," first published anonymously in the *New England Magazine*, February 1835, stands apart from much of Hawthorne's work in its comparatively light nature. He never included it in any of his later collections.

NEVER DID A PILGRIM approach Niagara with deeper enthusiasm, than mine. I had lingered away from it, and wandered to other scenes, because my treasury of anticipated enjoyments, comprising all the wonders of the world, had nothing else so magnificent, and I was loth to exchange the pleasures of hope for those of memory so soon. At length, the day came. The stage-coach, with a Frenchman and myself on the back seat, had already left Lewiston, and in less than an hour would set us down in Manchester. I began to listen for the roar of the cataract,[1] and trembled with a sensation like dread, as the moment drew nigh, when its voice of ages must roll, for the first time, on my ear. The French gentleman stretched himself from the window, and expressed loud admiration, while, by a sudden impulse, I threw myself back and closed my eyes. When the scene shut in, I was glad to think, that for me the whole burst of Niagara was yet in futurity. We rolled on, and entered the village of Manchester, bordering on the falls.

I am quite ashamed of myself here. Not that I ran, like a madman, to the falls, and plunged into the thickest of the spray—never stopping to breathe, till breathing was impossible; not that I committed this, or any other suitable extravagance. On the contrary, I alighted with perfect decency and composure, gave my cloak to the black waiter, pointed out my baggage, and inquired, not the nearest way to the cataract, but about the dinner-hour. The interval was spent in arranging my dress. Within the last fifteen minutes, my mind had grown strangely benumbed, and my spirits apathetic, with a slight depression, not decided enough to be termed sadness. My enthusiasm was in a deathlike slumber. Without aspiring to immortality, as he did, I could have imitated that English traveller, who turned back from the point where he first heard the thunder of Niagara, after crossing the ocean to behold it. Many a western trader, by-the-by, has performed a similar act of heroism with more heroic simplicity, deeming it no such wonderful feat to dine at the hotel and resume his route to Buffalo or Lewiston, while the cataract was roaring unseen.

Such has often been my apathy, when objects, long sought, and earnestly desired, were placed within my reach. After dinner—at which, an unwonted and perverse epicurism detained me longer than usual—I lighted a cigar and paced the piazza, minutely attentive to the aspect and business of a very ordinary village. Finally, with reluctant step, and the feeling of an intruder, I walked towards Goat Island. At the toll-house, there were further excuses for delaying the inevitable moment. My signature was required in a huge leger, containing similar records innumerable, many of which I read.

---

1 *cataract:* A large waterfall.—EDS.

The skin of a great sturgeon, and other fishes, beasts, and reptiles; a collection of minerals, such as lie in heaps near the falls; some Indian moccasins, and other trifles, made of deer-skin and embroidered with beads; several newspapers from Montreal, New-York, and Boston; all attracted me in turn. Out of a number of twisted sticks, the manufacture of a Tuscarora Indian, I selected one of curled maple, curiously convoluted, and adorned with the carved images of a snake and a fish. Using this as my pilgrim's staff, I crossed the bridge. Above and below me were the rapids, a river of impetuous snow, with here and there a dark rock amid its whiteness, resisting all the physical fury, as any cold spirit did the moral influences of the scene. On reaching Goat Island, which separates the two great segments of the falls, I chose the right-hand path, and followed it to the edge of the American cascade. There, while the falling sheet was yet invisible, I saw the vapor that never vanishes, and the Eternal Rainbow of Niagara.

It was an afternoon of glorious sunshine, without a cloud, save those of the cataracts. I gained an insulated rock, and beheld a broad sheet of brilliant and unbroken foam, not shooting in a curved line from the top of the precipice, but falling headlong down from height to depth. A narrow stream diverged from the main branch, and hurried over the crag by a channel of its own, leaving a little pine-clad island and a streak of precipice, between itself and the larger sheet. Below arose the mist, on which was painted a dazzling sunbow, with two concentric shadows—one, almost as perfect as the original brightness; and the other, drawn faintly round the broken edge of the cloud.

Still, I had not half seen Niagara. Following the verge of the island, the path led me to the Horse-shoe, where the real, broad St. Lawrence, rushing along on a level with its banks, pours its whole breadth over a concave line of precipice, and thence pursues its course between lofty crags towards Ontario. A sort of bridge, two or three feet wide, stretches out along the edge of the descending sheet, and hangs upon the rising mist, as if that were the foundation of the frail structure. Here I stationed myself, in the blast of wind, which the rushing river bore along with it. The bridge was tremulous beneath me, and marked the tremor of the solid earth. I looked along the whitening rapids, and endeavored to distinguish a mass of water far above the falls, to follow it to their verge, and go down with it, in fancy, to the abyss of clouds and storm. Casting my eyes across the river, and every side, I took in the whole scene at a glance, and tried to comprehend it in one vast idea. After an hour thus spent, I left the bridge, and, by a staircase, winding almost interminably round a post, descended to the base of the precipice. From that point, my path lay over slippery stones, and among great fragments of the cliff, to the edge of the cataract, where the wind at once enveloped me in spray, and perhaps dashed the rainbow round me. Were my long desires fulfilled? And had I seen Niagara?

Oh, that I had never heard of Niagara till I beheld it. Blessed were the wanderers of old, who heard its deep roar sounding through the woods, as the summons to an unknown wonder, and approached its awful brink, in all

5

Alvan Fisher, The Great Horseshoe Falls, Niagara. *This 1820 painting is held at the National Museum of American Art, Smithsonian Institution.*

the freshness of native feeling. Had its own mysterious voice been the first to warn me of its existence, then, indeed, I might have knelt down and worshipped. But I had come thither haunted with a vision of foam and fury, and dizzy cliffs, and an ocean tumbling down out of the sky—a scene, in short, which Nature had too much good taste and calm simplicity to realize. My mind had struggled to adapt these false conceptions to the reality, and finding the effort vain, a wretched sense of disappointment weighed me down. I climbed the precipice, and threw myself on the earth—feeling that I was unworthy to look at the Great Falls, and careless about beholding them again.

All that night, as there has been and will be, for ages past and to come, a rushing sound was heard, as if a great tempest were sweeping through the air. It mingled with my dreams, and made them full of storm and whirlwind. Whenever I awoke, and heard this dread sound in the air, and the windows rattling as with a mighty blast, I could not rest again, till, looking forth, I saw how bright the stars were, and that every leaf in the garden was motionless. Never was a summer-night more calm to the eye, nor a gale of autumn louder to the ear. The rushing sound proceeds from the rapids, and the rattling of the casements is but an effect of the vibration of the whole house, shaken by the jar of the cataract. The noise of the rapids draws the attention from the true voice of Niagara, which is a dull, muffled thunder, resounding between the cliffs. I spent a wakeful hour at midnight, in distinguishing its reverberations, and rejoiced to find that my former awe and enthusiasm were reviving.

Gradually, and after much contemplation, I came to know, by my own feelings, that Niagara is indeed a wonder of the world, and not the less wonderful, because time and thought must be employed in comprehending it. Casting aside all pre-conceived notions, and preparation to be dire-struck or delighted, the beholder must stand beside it in the simplicity of his heart, suffering the mighty scene to work its own impression. Night after night, I dreamed of it, and was gladdened every morning by the consciousness of a growing capacity to enjoy it. Yet I will not pretend to the all-absorbing enthusiasm of some more fortunate spectators, nor deny, that very trifling causes would draw my eyes and thoughts from the cataract.

The last day that I was to spend at Niagara, before my departure for the far west, I sat upon the Table Rock. This celebrated station did not now, as of old, project fifty feet beyond the line of the precipice, but was shattered by the fall of an immense fragment, which lay distant on the shore below. Still, on the utmost verge of the rock, with my feet hanging over it, I felt as if suspended in the open air. Never before had my mind been in such perfect unison with the scene. There were intervals, when I was conscious of nothing but the great river, rolling calmly into the abyss, rather descending than precipitating itself, and acquiring tenfold majesty from its unhurried motion. It came like the march of Destiny. It was not taken by surprise, but seemed to have anticipated, in all its course through the broad lakes, that it must pour their collected waters down this height. The perfect foam of the river, after its descent, and the ever-varying shapes of mist, rising up, to become clouds in the sky, would be the very picture of confusion, were it merely transient, like the rage of a tempest. But when the beholder has stood awhile and perceives no lull in the storm, and considers that the vapor and the foam are as everlasting as the rocks which produce them, all this turmoil assumes a sort of calmness. It soothes, while it awes the mind.

Leaning over the cliff, I saw the guide conducting two adventurers   10
behind the falls. It was pleasant, from that high seat in the sunshine, to observe them struggling against the eternal storm of the lower regions, with heads bent down, now faltering, now pressing forward, and finally swallowed up in their victory. After their disappearance, a blast rushed out with an old hat, which it had swept from one of their heads. The rock, to which they were directing their unseen course, is marked, at a fearful distance on the exterior of the sheet, by a jet of foam. The attempt to reach it, appears both poetical and perilous, to a looker-on, but may be accomplished without much more difficulty or hazard, than in stemming a violent northeaster. In a few moments, forth came the children of the mist. Dripping and breathless, they crept along the base of the cliff, ascended to the guide's cottage, and received, I presume, a certificate of their achievement, with three verses of sublime poetry on the back.

My contemplations were often interrupted by strangers who came down from Forsyth's to take their first view of the falls. A short, ruddy, middle-aged gentleman, fresh from old England, peeped over the rock, and evinced his approbation by a broad grin. His spouse, a very robust lady, afforded a sweet example of maternal solicitude, being so intent on the safety of her little boy that she did not even glance at Niagara. As for the child, he gave himself wholly to the enjoyment of a stick of candy. Another traveller, a native American, and no rare character among us, produced a volume of Captain Hall's tour, and labored earnestly to adjust Niagara to the captain's description, departing, at last, without one new idea or sensation of his own. The next comer was provided, not with a printed book, but with a blank sheet of foolscap, from top to bottom of which, by means of an ever-pointed pencil, the cataract was made to thunder. In a little talk, which we had together, he awarded his approbation to the general view, but censured the position of Goat Island, observing that it should have been thrown farther to the right, so as to widen the American falls, and contract those of the Horse-shoe. Next appeared two traders of Michigan, who declared, that, upon the whole, the sight was worth looking at; there certainly was an immense water-power here; but that, after all, they would go twice as far to see the noble stoneworks of Lockport, where the Grand Canal is locked down a descent of sixty feet. They were succeeded by a young fellow, in a home-spun cotton dress,

The Suspension Bridge, shown in this advertisement, was completed in 1855 and crossed from New York to Ontario.

with a staff in his hand, and a pack over his shoulders. He advanced close to the edge of the rock, where his attention, at first wavering among the different components of the scene, finally became fixed in the angle of the Horse-shoe falls, which is, indeed, the central point of interest. His whole soul seemed to go forth and be transported thither, till the staff slipped from his relaxed grasp, and falling down—down—down—struck upon the fragment of the Table Rock.

In this manner, I spent some hours, watching the varied impression, made by the cataract, on those who disturbed me, and returning to unwearied contemplation, when left alone. At length, my time came to depart. There is a grassy footpath, through the woods, along the summit of the bank, to a point whence a causeway, hewn in the side of the precipice, goes winding down to the ferry, about half a mile below the Table Rock. The sun was near setting, when I emerged from the shadow of the trees, and began the descent. The indirectness of my downward road continually changed the point of view, and shewed me, in rich and repeated succession—now, the whitening rapids and the majestic leap of the main river, which appeared more deeply massive as the light departed, now, the lovelier picture, yet still sublime, of Goat Island, with its rocks and grove, and the lesser falls, tumbling over the right bank of the St. Lawrence, like a tributary stream, now, the long vista of the river, as it eddied and whirled between the cliffs, to pass through Ontario towards the sea, and everywhere to be wondered at, for this one unrivalled scene. The golden sunshine tinged the sheet of the American cascade, and painted on its heaving spray the broken semicircle of a rainbow, Heaven's own beauty crowning earth's sublimity. My steps were slow, and I paused long at every turn of the descent, as one lingers and pauses, who discerns a brighter and brightening excellence in what he must soon behold no more. The solitude of the old wilderness now reigned over the whole vicinity of the falls. My enjoyment became the more rapturous, because no poet shared it—nor wretch, devoid of poetry, profaned it: but the spot, so famous through the world, was all my own!

The Reader's Presence

1. In addition to providing a fascinating description of seeing Niagara Falls for the first time, Hawthorne's essay constitutes a primer on the principle of encountering the natural world directly rather than through what Hawthorne calls "pre-conceived notions" (paragraph 8) and the perspectives of others. What other principles about how we ought to see the natural world can you infer from reading Hawthorne's essay?

2. Summarize the different reactions Hawthorne has to anticipating—and then seeing—Niagara Falls. Which does he seem more interested in exploring with his readers? Point to specific passages to support your response. Hawthorne seems quite conscious of his readers—especially when he says "I am quite ashamed of myself here" (paragraph 2). After seeing Niagara Falls for the first time, he says "a wretched sense of disappointment weighed me down" (paragraph 6). What, more specifically,

evokes this sense of being "ashamed" in anticipation of seeing Niagara Falls and then being overcome by a "wretched sense of disappointment"? How and when—and with what effect(s)—does Hawthorne's attitude toward himself change?

3. **VISUAL PRESENCE:** Examine carefully the painting "The Great Horseshoe Falls" (page 435) and the advertisement for Niagara Falls (page 437). How do these depictions of Niagara Falls differ from one another and from Hawthorne's description? How are they similar? Support your answer with details from the images.

4. **CONNECTIONS:** Much of Hawthorne's essay is written in the form of first-person narration and description. Yet Hawthorne also manages to convey a great deal of information about seeing Niagara Falls for the first time. Compare and contrast Hawthorne's use of personal narration and description with the ways in which these rhetorical modes function in Jhumpa Lahiri's essay "My Two Lives" (page 181) and Cheryl Strayed's essay "Into the Woods" (page 266).

Pico Iyer

THE TERMINAL CHECK

PICO IYER (b. 1957) is the British-born son of Indian philosopher Raghavan N. Iyer and religious scholar Nandini Nanak Mehta. When Iyer was seven years old, his family left Oxford, England, for California. He returned to Oxford for his own degree, graduating with the highest marks in his class, then went on to teach writing and literature at Harvard University before joining *Time* magazine in 1982 to write on world affairs. Known primarily as a travel writer, he has written several books of fiction and nonfiction, including novels *Cuba and the Night* (1995) and *Abandon* (2003), as well as numerous books of essays and travelogues,

> As an Indian born in England and raised predominantly in the United States, Iyer has said that "being an outsider, as I always was, proved to be a perfect background, and launching pad, for writing (and for traveling)."

including *Video Night in Kathmandu: And Other Reports from the Not-So-Far East* (1988), *The Lady and the Monk: Four Seasons in Kyoto* (1991), *Falling Off the Map: Some Lonely*

|||||||||||||||||||||||||||||||||||||||||||||||||||||||||||||||||||||||||||||||||||||||||||||||||||||||||||||

Places of the World (1993), and *The Open Road: The Global Journey of the Fourteenth Dalai Lama* (2008), an extended journalistic analysis of the Tibetan spiritual leader. Iyer's latest book is *The Man Within My Head* (2012), a memoir that tracks his fascination with and the strange parallels shared with his literary hero, the novelist Graham Greene. "The Terminal Check" first appeared in *Granta* in 2011.

As an Indian born in England and raised predominantly in the United States, Iyer has said that "being an outsider, as I always was, proved to be a perfect background, and launching pad, for writing (and for traveling)."

I'M SITTING IN THE EXPANSIVE SPACES of Renzo Piano's four-story airport outside Osaka, sipping an Awake tea from Starbucks and waiting for my bus home. I've chosen to live in Japan for the past twenty years, and I know its rites as I know the way I need tea when feeling displaced, or to head for a right-hand window seat as soon as I enter a bus. A small, round-faced Japanese man in his early thirties, accompanied by a tall and somewhat cadaverous man of the same age, approaches me.

"Excuse me," says the small, friendly-seeming one; they look like newborn salarymen in their not-quite-perfect suits. "May I see your passport?"

When I look up, surprised, he flashes me a badge showing that he's a plain-clothes policeman. Dazed after crossing sixteen time zones (from California), I hand him my British passport.

"What are you doing in Japan?"

"I'm writing about it." I pull out my business card with the red embossed 5 logo of *Time* magazine.

"*Time* magazine?" says the smiling cop, strangely impressed. "He works for *Time* magazine," he explains to his lanky and impassive partner. "Very famous magazine," he assures me. "High prestige!"

Then he asks for my address and phone number and where I plan to be for the next eighty-nine days. "If there is some unfortunate incident," he explains, "some terrorist attack," (he's sotto voce now) "then we will know you did it."

Six months later, I fly back to the country I love once more. This time I need to withdraw some yen[1] from an ATM as I stumble out of my trans-Pacific plane, in order to pay for my bus home.

"You're getting some money?" says an attractive young Japanese woman, suddenly appearing beside me with a smile.

"I am. To go back to my apartment." 10

"You live here?" Few Japanese women have ever come up to me in public, let alone without an introduction, and shown such interest.

"I do."

"May I see your passport?" she asks sweetly, flashing a badge at me, much as the pair of questioners had done two seasons before.

1 **yen:** Monetary unit used in Japan. —EDS.

"Just security," she says, anxious not to put me out, as my Japanese neighbors stream, unconcerned, towards the Gakuenmae bus that's about to pull out of its bay.

I tell my friends back in California about these small disruptions and they look much too knowing. It's 9/11, they assure me. Over the past decade, security has tightened around the world, which means that insecurity has increased proportionally. Indeed, in recent years Japan has introduced fingerprinting for all foreign visitors arriving at its airports, and takes photographs of every outsider coming across its borders; a large banner on the wall behind the immigration officers in Osaka—as angry-looking with its red-and-black hand-lettering as a student banner—explains the need for heightened measures in the wake of threats to national order.

But the truth of the matter is that, for those of us with darker skins, and from nations not materially privileged, it was ever thus. When I was eighteen, I was held in custody in Panama's airport (because of the Indian passport I then carried) and denied formal entry to the nation, while the roguish English friend from high school with whom I was travelling was free to enter with impunity and savor all the dubious pleasures of the Canal Zone. On my way into Hong Kong—a transit lounge of a city if ever there was one, a duty-free zone whose only laws seem to be those of the marketplace—I was hauled into a special cabin for a lengthy interrogation because my face was deemed not to match my (by then British) passport. In Japan I was strip-searched every time I returned to the country, three or four times a year—my lifelong tan moving the authorities to assume that I must be either Saddam Hussein's cousin or an illegal Iranian (or, worst of all, what I really am, a wandering soul with Indian forebears). Once I was sent to a small room in Tokyo reserved for anyone of South Asian ancestry (where bejewelled women in saris loudly complained in exaggerated Oxbridge accents about being taken for common criminals).

Another time, long before my Japanese neighbors had heard of Osama bin Laden, I was even detained on my way *out* of Osaka—and the British Embassy hastily faxed on a Sunday night—as if any male with brown skin, passable English, and a look of shabby quasi-respectability must be doing something wrong if he's crossing a border.

But now, having learned over decades to accept such indignities or injustices, I walk into a chorus of complaints every time I return to California, from my pale-skinned, affluent neighbors. They're patting us down now, my friends object, and they're confiscating our contact-lens fluid. They're forcing us to travel with tiny tubes of toothpaste and moving us to wear loafers when usually we'd prefer lace-ups. They're taking away every bottle of water—but only after bottles of water have been shown to be weapons of mass destruction; they're feeling us up with blue gloves, even here in Santa Barbara, now that they know that underwear can be a lethal weapon.

I listen to their grousing and think that the one thing the 9/11 attacks have achieved, for those of us who spend too much time in airports, is to make suspicion universal; fear and discomfort are equal-opportunity employers now. The world is flat in ways the high-flying global theoreticians don't always acknowledge; these days, even someone from the materially fortunate parts of the world—a man with a ruddy complexion, a woman in a Prada suit—is pulled aside for what is quixotically known as "random screening."

It used to be that the rich corners of the world seemed relatively safe,   20 protected, and the poor ones too dangerous to enter. Now, the logic of the terrorist attacks on New York and Washington has reversed all that. If anything, it's the rich places that feel unsettled. It used to be that officials would alight on people who look like me—from nations of need, in worn jeans, bearing the passports of more prosperous countries—as likely troublemakers; now they realize that even the well-born and well-dressed may not always be well-intentioned.

I understand why my friends feel aggrieved to be treated as if they came from Nigeria or Mexico or India. But I can't really mourn too much that airports, since 9/11, have become places where everyone may be taken to be guilty until proven innocent. The world is all mixed up these days, and America can no longer claim immunity. On 12 September 2001, *Le Monde* ran its now famous headline: WE ARE ALL AMERICANS. On 12 September 2011, it might more usefully announce: WE ARE ALL INDIANS. ●

The Reader's Presence

1. What does Iyer mean when he laments that "[t]he world is all mixed up" (paragraph 21) after the events of September 11, 2001? How do Iyer's friends explain his treatment abroad? What is his response to their explanation? Does he find some solace and justice in everyone's being subjected to the same treatment he describes in Japan? To what extent do you think his point that "fear and discomfort" are becoming "equal-opportunity employers" (paragraph 19) responds appropriately to the current circumstances for traveling, or does this attitude reinscribe the injustices described by Iyer? Explain your response. What does Iyer mean when he writes "WE ARE ALL INDIANS" (paragraph 21)?

2. The experiences Iyer describes in Japan of being subjected to not-so-random searches have occurred with such frequency that he has "learned over decades to accept such indignities or injustices" (paragraph 18). How do you reconcile Iyer's acceptance of these events with the innocuous complaints of his "pale-skinned, affluent neighbors" (paragraph 18)? Do you think they have no right to complain? Why or why not? To what extent does Iyer lament his experiences? Explain your answer.

3. **CONNECTIONS:** In what specific ways does the sense of uneasiness and "unsettled[ness]" Iyer describes in modern America relate to Daniel Gilbert's essay "What You Don't Know Makes You Nervous" (page 417)? In a similar vein, compare and contrast Iyer's attitudes toward stereotyping people with those expressed by Milos Kosic in his student essay "It's Not the Name That Matters" (page 212) and Manuel Muñoz in "Leave Your Name at the Border" (page 208).

MEHER AHMAD
My Homeland Security Journey

Courtesy of Meher Ahmad

When she wrote "My Homeland Security Journey," Meher Ahmad was a senior majoring in Middle Eastern studies at the University of Wisconsin–Madison. The essay was originally published in *The Progressive* magazine, where she served as an intern. When asked about her writing, she emphasized the importance of revision, saying she "wrote two drafts before submitting it to the editors at *The Progressive*, and that it was edited about three times after that." She goes on to say that subsequently she "revised it several times and reorganized several portions of it multiple times. The revisions allowed for a more continuous and direct narrative."

I grew up in a suburb of Indianapolis called Carmel and never found myself to be any different from my predominantly white friends, except for the odd unibrow joke and clarifying the pronunciation of my name during roll call.

On 9/11, hours after our teacher choked back tears to tell our fourth grade class the Twin Towers had been attacked, we all sat watching the news on the television. Some of us were crying, but we didn't quite comprehend why. A clip came on of people cheering around the world. First there was a reel of young Palestinians clamoring for the camera's attention. Someone in class pointed to the TV and said, "They did it!" I thought, "Why would they be celebrating when all these people are covered in ash and my teacher is crying?"

Then the newscast cut to a similar crowd of Pakistani boys jumping on cars in the street. Whoever pointed at the Palestinians was still pointing at the TV, this time suggesting that Pakistanis had done it. I could not even begin to grasp why Pakistanis would be happy about the attack, let alone what they had to do with all of the people running from a collapsing building in New York. Even if no one turned to me after the clip ended, I was acutely aware of the fact that I was Pakistani and not American.

Nearly eleven years after 9/11, virtually every Pakistani family in the area has a Homeland Security tale to tell.

Establishes how her sense of identity changed after the 9/11 attacks she witnessed on television as a child.

My Homeland Security journey began in the summer of 2002, the first time I flew since 9/11 for a family vacation to Hawaii. I was eleven years old. At the airport waiting to check in, I was playing Game Boy with my kid brother on the floor, ignoring the exchange the airline official was having with my parents.

But when I looked up, the attendant was flustered and scared, I could tell. A feeling of panic reached my stomach, which only worsened when a police officer showed up. My brother and I wondered, "Why are we under arrest?" "What's happening?" "What's wrong?" We tugged at our parents' pant legs, and they told us sweetly in Urdu that we weren't under arrest and to please stop bothering them, be quiet, and sit over there, for God's sake.

My parents tell me now that the FBI was crosschecking our names, and while we waited for hours at the check-in desk, an agent in the Washington, D.C., office verified our identities. After a while, a friendly looking man in a white shirt and blue jeans escorted us to our newly booked flight, as our original one had taken off long ago. He told us it was most likely my name that had set off the security flag.

The man we sat next to on the flight wasn't an ordinary passenger. My mom murmured to me as we squeezed past him that it figures she would be the one person next to such a big man on the long flight. He answered in perfect Urdu, our secret language for making fun of strangers in public. With a visage not unlike Brad Pitt's, he was the last person I would think to speak Urdu fluently, but after describing to us his time in Islamabad as a former CIA agent, I could see why he did. Strange as it was, we arrived in Hawaii, and I shelved the journey in the back of my mind.

Suspicion greeted us every time we traveled, and in my teenage years I responded with sarcasm. I'd ask the TSA agent why I was being stopped, just so I could roll my eyes when they repeated it was a random search.

A few years of that bratty attitude didn't bring me any satisfaction, and now as an experienced navigator of airport security, I remain as polite and cooperative as possible. After all, it isn't the fault of the TSA agent, who probably just wants to go home, that I'm being stopped. Instead of a smirk, I sport a smile. I know the drill, so let's get this over with.

As I approached the row of agents in Chicago O'Hare this winter, I made bets with my father and brother about my chances of getting stopped. We reached the desk and slipped our passports through the glass. A few minutes after looking through my family's passports, the immigration officer finally picked mine up. He glanced up at me; I was staring intently back at him so as to signal complete confidence, a cover for the self-consciousness seasoned with a hint of doubt that creeps into my head every time I hand my passport over to American immigration. It's like slowing down when you see a cop car in the rearview mirror even if you're driving five below.

I ran a reel of situations through my head that the agent might misconstrue. What if my interviews with women in the Islamic Action Front in Jordan could be used against me? What if the fact that I was in Cairo after the Coptic riots was misconstrued? I went to the West Bank; could that be it?

The immigration officer made a brief phone call to a shadowy figure that I liken to the Wizard of Oz. I won the bet. We were escorted to the cubicle-like office of O'Hare's Homeland Security.

I tried to make myself comfortable on the impossibly narrow benches in the waiting room and glanced at a few posters with waving American flags that reminded me of my rights within that space. I was a suspect yet again.

A month before I landed in O'Hare, I found myself in a similarly tiny cordoned-off area where unsightly travelers like myself were corralled at the Allenby Bridge into Israel from Jordan. Surrounded by Arabs, mostly Palestinians who had likely been waiting for more than an hour before I joined them, I noticed the crowd wasn't frustrated or defeated. They were playing games on their cell phones, reading the newspaper, conversing with their neighbors. It didn't seem to bother them that they had been waiting for so long; it was the norm.

I had known that I was going to join them in their wait when the Israeli immigration officer opened my passport. I'm used to the disappointed look on security personnel's faces when I hand them my passport because before 2004, I carried a Pakistani one. Pakistani passports are notoriously easy to forge. On my old passport, my name was misspelled (written in ballpoint pen), crossed out, and rewritten with

---

Moves narrative closer to her present time as she provides another concrete example of being stopped by security.

Uses an analogy of seeing police in a rearview mirror to make her point about facing immigration officials in an airport.

Contrasts her experiences traveling with a Pakistani passport versus an American one.

an arrow pointing to the correct spelling. I could understand why its validity was always in question.

But now, with a fresh American passport and citizenship, I expected to be presumed innocent. This thing has holograms and chips in it: What more could you want? But my passport isn't the kind an immigration officer likes to see:

Name: Ahmad, Noor Meher
Birthplace: Islamabad, Pakistan
Places Traveled: Pakistan, Jordan, Egypt, Turkey,
    Lebanon, Israel, United Kingdom

In Israel, they didn't pretend that the thorough and condescending questioning of my identity was random, as I'm always assured in the United States. It was blatantly discriminatory, and as I waved to my Caucasian American friends, who told me before they would wait in solidarity outside of the terminal, I was strangely comforted by the openly racist security policy of the IDF.

Back in O'Hare, the scene was tenser. My flight had come from Istanbul and it was full of people that ended up in the same waiting room as us. Though nobody told us not to talk, everyone kept quiet and spoke only in hushed tones. After an hour of anxiously watching the clock get closer to the time our connecting flight departed, I saw the Homeland Security agent come toward me to give me my passport back. He was smiling as if he just handed me a steaming apple pie.

After sprinting through the terminal, we ended up missing our flight, and that's when the helplessness of our situation hit me. There was nothing I could have done to get out of that gray waiting room faster. I couldn't prove to the agent that I was an all-American girl, that I drink Coca-Cola and frequently indulge in *The Real Housewives* series. I couldn't avoid my own identity.

Eleven years after my classmate pointed his finger at Pakistanis celebrating 9/11, I've now encountered a growing mass of finger-pointers. It used to be the only place I felt uncomfortably different was at an Arby's in rural Indiana. Now, I can sense the glares on my back as agents search my bags in plain view of my fellow passengers. It doesn't feel like they'll stop pointing any time soon.

Margin note (left): Provides yet another example of a security delay to drive home her main point about profiling in airports.

Margin note (right): Concludes by returning to her opening description of 9/11 and explaining how the years have not altered the experience of being uncomfortably different."

Stephen King

Everything You Need to Know About Writing Successfully—in Ten Minutes

STEPHEN KING was born in 1947 in Portland, Maine. He began writing stories early in his life, but it was his discovery of a box of horror and science fiction novels in the attic of his aunt's house that made him decide to pursue a career as a writer. He published his first short stories in pulp horror magazines while in high school. After graduating from the University of Maine at Orono in 1970, King, while working at a low-paying job in a laundry, began writing his first novel, *Carrie* (1974). *Carrie* was followed by some forty more novels, including a series written under the pen name Richard Bachman, as well as numerous novellas, short story collections,

> Stephen King's discovery of horror and science fiction novels in his aunt's attic prompted him to pursue a writing career.

and screenplays. His critically acclaimed work of nonfiction, *On Writing* (2000), the source of the following essay, was completed while he was recovering painfully from a much-publicized accident.

Stephen King has commented that, as a creative writer, he always hopes for "that element of inspiration which lifts you past the point where the characters are just you, where you do achieve something transcendental and the people are really people in the story."

I. THE FIRST INTRODUCTION

THAT'S RIGHT. I know it sounds like an ad for some sleazy writers' school, but I really am going to tell you everything you need to pursue a successful and financially rewarding career writing fiction, and I really am going to do it in ten minutes, which is exactly how long it took me to learn. It will actually take you twenty minutes or so to read this article, however, because I have to tell you a story, and then I have to write a second introduction. But these, I argue, should not count in the ten minutes.

II. THE STORY, OR, HOW STEPHEN KING LEARNED TO WRITE

When I was a sophomore in high school, I did a sophomoric thing which got me in a pot of fairly hot water, as sophomoric didoes often do. I wrote and published a small satiric newspaper called *The Village Vomit.* In this little paper I lampooned a number of teachers at Lisbon (Maine) High School, where I was under instruction. These were not very gentle lampoons; they ranged from the scatological to the downright cruel.

Eventually, a copy of this paper found its way into the hands of a faculty member, and since I had been unwise enough to put my name on it (a fault, some critics would argue, of which I have still not been entirely cured). I was brought into the office. The sophisticated satirist had by that time reverted to what he really was: a fourteen-year-old kid who was shaking in his boots and wondering if he was going to get a suspension . . . what we called a "three-day vacation" in those dim days of 1964.

I wasn't suspended. I was forced to make a number of apologies—they were warranted, but they tasted like dog-dirt in my mouth—and spent a week in detention hall. And the guidance counselor arranged what he no doubt thought of as a more constructive channel for my talents. This was a job—contingent upon the editor's approval—writing sports for the Lisbon Enterprise, a twelve-page weekly of the sort with which any small-town resident will be familiar. This editor was the man who taught me everything I know about writing in ten minutes. His name was John Gould—not the famed New England humorist or the novelist who wrote *The Greenleaf Fires*, but a relative of both, I believe.

He told me he needed a sports writer, and we could "try each other out,"   5
if I wanted.

I told him I knew more about advanced algebra than I did sports.

Gould nodded and said, "You'll learn."

I said I would at least try to learn. Gould gave me a huge roll of yellow paper and promised me a wage of 1/2 [cts.] per word. The first two pieces I wrote had to do with a high school basketball game in which a member of my school team broke the Lisbon High scoring record. One of these pieces was a straight piece of reportage. The second was a feature article.

I brought them to Gould the day after the game, so he'd have them for the paper, which came out Fridays. He read the straight piece, made two minor corrections, and spiked it. Then he started in on the feature piece with a large black pen and taught me all I ever needed to know about my craft. I wish I still had the piece,—it deserves to be framed, editorial corrections and all—but I can remember pretty well how it went and how it looked when he had finished with it. Here's an example:

> Last night, in the ~~well-loved~~ gymnasium of Lisbon High School, partisans and Jay Hills fans alike were stunned by an athletic performance unequalled in school history: Bob Ransom, ~~known as Bullet Bob for both his size and accuracy,~~ scored thirty-seven points. Yes, you heard me right. ~~Plus~~ he did it with grace, and speed . . . and with an odd courtesy as well, committing only two personal fouls in his ~~knight-like~~ quest for a record which has eluded Lisbon ~~thinclads~~ [players] since ~~the years of Korea~~ [1953] . . .

When Gould finished marking up my copy in the manner I have indi-   10
cated above, he looked up and must have seen something on my face. I
think he must have thought it was horror, but it was not: It was revelation.

"I only took out the bad parts, you know," he said. "Most of it's pretty
good."

"I know," I said, meaning both things; yes, most of it was good, and yes,
he had only taken out the bad parts. "I won't do it again."

"If that's true," he said, "you'll never have to work again. You can do
this for a living."

Then he threw back his head and laughed.

And he was right: I am doing this for a living, and as long as I can keep   15
on, I don't expect ever to have to work again.

III. THE SECOND INTRODUCTION

All of what follows has been said before. If you are interested enough in
writing to be a purchaser of this magazine [*Writer*], you will have either
heard or read all (or almost all) of it before. Thousands of writing courses
are taught across the United States each year; seminars are convened; guest
lecturers talk, then answer questions, and it all boils down to what follows.

I am going to tell you these things again because often people will only
listen — really listen — to someone who makes a lot of money doing the thing
he's talking about. This is sad but true. And I told you the story above not
to make myself sound like a character out of a Horatio Alger novel but to
make a point: I saw, I listened, and I learned. Until that day in John Gould's
little office, I had been writing first drafts of stories that might run 2,500
words. The second drafts were apt to run 3,300 words. Following that day,
my 2,500-word first drafts became 2,200-word second drafts. And two years
after that, I sold the first one.

So here it is, with all the bark stripped off. It'll take ten minutes to read,
and you can apply it right away . . . if you listen.

IV. EVERYTHING YOU NEED TO KNOW ABOUT WRITING SUCCESSFULLY

1. Be talented

This, of course, is the killer. What is talent? I can hear someone shouting, and here we are, ready to get into a discussion right up there with "What is the meaning of life?" for weighty pronouncements and total uselessness. For the purposes of the beginning writer, talent may as well be defined as eventual success—publication and money. If you wrote something for which someone sent you a check, if you cashed the check and it didn't bounce, and if you then paid the light bill with the money, I consider you talented.

Now some of you are really hollering. Some of you are calling me one crass money-fixated creep. Nonsense. Worse than nonsense, off the subject. We're not talking about good or bad here. I'm interested in telling you how to get your stuff published, not in critical judgments of who's good or bad. As a rule, the critical judgments come after the check's been spent, anyway. I have my own opinions, but most times I keep them to myself. People who are published steadily and are paid for what they are writing may be either saints or trollops, but they are clearly reaching a great many someones who want what they have. Ergo, they are communicating. Ergo, they are talented. The biggest part of writing successfully is being talented, and in the context of marketing, the only bad writer is one who doesn't get paid. If you're not talented, you won't succeed. And if you're not succeeding, you should know when to quit.

When is that? I don't know. It's different for each writer. Not after six rejection slips, certainly, nor after sixty. But after six hundred? Maybe. After six thousand? My friend, after six thousand pinks, it's time you tried painting or computer programming.

Further, almost every aspiring writer knows when he is getting warmer— you start getting little jotted notes on your rejection slips, or personal letters . . . maybe a commiserating phone call. It's lonely out there in the cold, but there are encouraging voices . . . unless there is nothing in your words that warrants encouragement. I think you owe it to yourself to skip as much of the self-illusion as possible. If your eyes are open, you'll know which way to go . . . or when to turn back.

2. Be neat

Type. Double-space. Use a nice heavy white paper. If you've marked your manuscript a lot, do another draft.

3. Be self-critical

If you haven't marked up your manuscript a lot, you did a lazy job. Only God gets things right the first time. Don't be a slob.

4. Remove every extraneous word

You want to get up on a soapbox and preach? Fine. Get one, and try your   25
local park. You want to write for money? Get to the point. And if you remove
the excess garbage and discover you can't find the point, tear up what you
wrote and start all over again . . . or try something new.

5. Never look at a reference book while doing a first draft

You want to write a story? Fine. Put away your dictionary, your encyclope-
dias, your *World Almanac*, and your thesaurus. Better yet, throw your thesaurus into the wastebasket. The only things creepier than a thesaurus are
those little paperbacks college students too lazy to read the assigned novels
buy around exam time. Any word you have to hunt for in a thesaurus is the
wrong word. There are no exceptions to this rule. You think you might have
misspelled a word? O.K., so here is your choice: Either look it up in the dictionary, thereby making sure you have it right—and breaking your train of
thought and the writer's trance in the bargain—or just spell it phonetically
and correct it later. Why not? Did you think it was going to go somewhere?
And if you need to know the largest city in Brazil and you find you don't
have it in your head, why not write in Miami, or Cleveland? You can check
it . . . but later. When you sit down to write, write. Don't do anything else
except go to the bathroom, and only do that if it absolutely cannot be put off.

6. Know the markets

Only a dimwit would send a story about giant vampire bats surrounding
a high school to *McCall's*. Only a dimwit would send a tender story about
a mother and daughter making up their differences on Christmas Eve to
Playboy . . . but people do it all the time. I'm not exaggerating; I have seen
such stories in the slush piles of the actual magazines. If you write a good
story, why send it out in an ignorant fashion? Would you send your kid out
in a snowstorm dressed in Bermuda shorts and a tank top? If you like science fiction, read science fiction novels and magazines. If you want to write
mysteries, read the magazines. And so on. It isn't just a matter of knowing
what's right for the present story; you can begin to catch on, after a while, to
overall rhythms, editorial likes and dislikes, a magazine's slant. Sometimes
your reading can influence the next story, and create a sale.

7. Write to entertain

Does this mean you can't write "serious fiction"? It does not. Somewhere
along the line pernicious critics have invested the American reading and
writing public with the idea that entertaining fiction and serious ideas do not
overlap. This would have surprised Charles Dickens, not to mention Jane

Austen, John Steinbeck, William Faulkner, Bernard Malamud, and hundreds of others. But your serious ideas must always serve your story, not the other way around. I repeat: If you want to preach, get a soapbox.

8. Ask yourself frequently, "Am I having fun?"

The answer needn't always be yes. But if it's always no, it's time for a new project or a new career.

9. How to evaluate criticism

Show your piece to a number of people—ten, let us say. Listen carefully to   30
what they tell you. Smile and nod a lot. Then review what was said very carefully. If your critics are all telling you the same thing about some facet of your story—a plot twist that doesn't work, a character who rings false, stilted narrative, or half a dozen other possibles—change it. It doesn't matter if you really like that twist or that character; if a lot of people are telling you something is wrong with your piece, it is. If seven or eight of them are hitting on that same thing, I'd still suggest changing it. But if everyone—or even most everyone—is criticizing something different, you can safely disregard what all of them say.

10. Observe all rules for proper submission

Return postage, self-addressed envelope, etc.

11. An agent? Forget it. For now.

Agents get 10 percent to 15 percent of monies earned by their clients. Fifteen percent of nothing is nothing. Agents also have to pay the rent. Beginning writers do not contribute to that or any other necessity of life. Flog your stories around yourself. If you've done a novel, send around query letters to publishers, one by one, and follow up with sample chapters and/or the complete manuscript. And remember Stephen King's First Rule of Writers and Agent, learned by bitter personal experience: You don't need one until you're making enough for someone to steal . . . and if you're making that much, you'll be able to take your pick of good agents.

12. If it's bad, kill it

When it comes to people, mercy killing is against the law. When it comes to fiction, it is the law.

That's everything you need to know. And if you listened, you can write everything and anything you want. Now I believe I will wish you a pleasant day and sign off.

My ten minutes are up. ◾

The Reader's Presence

1. Why does King include sections I through III, even though they are not part of the "ten minutes"? What does the first introduction actually introduce? the second? How effectively does section II work with section IV? For example, how many rules did King learn when John Gould edited his story? Which rules does he break in his own essay? Why do you think he breaks them?

2. King is best known for writing horror novels, stories that scare people. What fears does he play on throughout this essay? How does he go about setting up suspenseful situations? What does he do to frighten people in this essay? If the rules are monsters, which ones do you think are the most frightening? Why?

3. By King's definition, a talented author is one who has been paid for his or her writing. Pick an author in this collection whom you consider talented and evaluate him or her according to King's rules. How successful should this writer be according to King? What other rules of success does the writer's essay suggest should be added to King's list?

4. **CONNECTIONS:** King's essay represents an approach to an ongoing debate between money and art. Signaled by terms like *practicality* and *popularity*, the money side holds that you should write to make money. Signaled by phrases like "art for art's sake" or "selling out," the art side holds that you should write to please yourself. George Orwell in "George Orwell on the Four Reasons for Writing" (page 526) represents another approach to this debate when he lists "four great motives for writing" (paragraph 1). Read Orwell's essay and determine how well each motive would lead to the kind of successful writing that King imagines. For example, how well—or how poorly—does Orwell's desire to "share an experience which one feels is valuable" (paragraph 3) lead to King's "eventual success—publication and money" (paragraph 19)?

Maxine Hong Kingston

No Name Woman

MAXINE HONG KINGSTON (b. 1940) won the National Book Critics Circle Award for nonfiction with her first book, *The Woman Warrior: Memoirs of a Girlhood Among Ghosts* (1976). "No Name Woman" is the opening chapter of this book, which *Time* magazine named one of the top ten nonfiction works of the 1970s. Her other works include *China Men* (1980), which won the American Book Award; *Tripmaster Monkey: His Fake Book* (1989), a picaresque novel; and *To Be the Poet* (2002), a collection of her lectures and verse. A manuscript entitled *The Fourth Book of Peace* was destroyed, along with her home and all of her possessions, in a 1991 Oakland–Berkeley fire, but Kingston started over and published *The Fifth Book of Peace* in 2003. Kingston's writing often blurs the distinction between fiction and nonfiction. She edited *Veterans of War, Veterans of Peace* (2006), a collection of writing by survivors of war compiled from her healing workshops. Her narratives blend autobiography, history, myth, and legend, drawing on the stories she remembers from her childhood in the Chinese American community of Stockton, California. Kingston's essays, stories, and poems also appear in numerous magazines, and she received the 1997 National Medal for the Humanities. In 2004, she retired as a senior lecturer for creative writing at the University of California, Berkeley. Her most recent book, *I Love a Broad Margin to My Life* (2011), is a reflection on aging.

> "My life as a writer had been a long struggle with pronouns."

Kingston has said that before writing *The Woman Warrior*, "My life as a writer had been a long struggle with pronouns. For 30 years I wrote in the first-person singular. At a certain point I was thinking that I was self-centered and egotistical, solipsistic, and not very developed as a human being, nor as an artist, because I could only see from this one point of view." She began to write in the third person because "I thought I had to overcome this self-centeredness." As she wrote her third novel, Kingston experienced the disappearance of her authorial voice. "I feel that this is an artistic as well as psychological improvement on my part. Because I am now a much less selfish person."

"YOU MUST NOT TELL ANYONE," my mother said, "what I am about to tell you. In China your father had a sister who killed herself. She jumped into the family well. We say that your father has all brothers because it is as if she had never been born.

"In 1924 just a few days after our village celebrated seventeen hurry-up weddings—to make sure that every young man who went 'out on the road' would responsibly come home—your father and his brothers and your grandfather and his brothers and your aunt's new husband sailed for America, the Gold Mountain. It was your grandfather's last trip. Those lucky enough to get contracts waved good-bye from the decks. They fed and guarded the stowaways and helped them off in Cuba, New York, Bali, Hawaii. 'We'll meet in California next year,' they said. All of them sent money home.

"I remember looking at your aunt one day when she and I were dressing; I had not noticed before that she had such a protruding melon of a stomach. But I did not think, 'She's pregnant,' until she began to look like other pregnant women, her shirt pulling and the white tops of her black pants showing. She could not have been pregnant, you see, because her husband had been gone for years. No one said anything. We did not discuss it. In early summer she was ready to have the child, long after the time when it could have been possible.

"The village had also been counting. On the night the baby was to be born the villagers raided our house. Some were crying. Like a great saw, teeth strung with lights, files of people walked zigzag across our land, tearing the rice. Their lanterns doubled in the disturbed black water, which drained away through the broken bunds.[1] As the villagers closed in, we could see that some of them, probably men and women we knew well, wore white masks. The people with long hair hung it over their faces. Women with short hair made it stand up on end. Some had tied white bands around their foreheads, arms, and legs.

"At first they threw mud and rocks at the house. Then they threw eggs   5 and began slaughtering our stock. We could hear the animals scream their deaths—the roosters, the pigs, a last great roar from the ox. Familiar wild heads flared in our night windows; the villagers encircled us. Some of the faces stopped to peer at us, their eyes rushing like searchlights. The hands flattened against the panes, framed heads, and left red prints.

"The villagers broke in the front and the back doors at the same time, even though we had not locked the doors against them. Their knives dripped with the blood of our animals. They smeared blood on the doors and walls. One woman swung a chicken, whose throat she had slit, splattering blood in red arcs about her. We stood together in the middle of our house, in the family hall with the pictures and tables of the ancestors around us, and looked straight ahead.

"At that time the house had only two wings. When the men came back we would build two more to enclose our courtyard and a third one to begin a second courtyard. The villagers pushed through both wings, even your grandparents' rooms, to find your aunt's, which was also mine until the men returned. From this room a new wing for one of the younger families would grow. They ripped up her clothes and shoes and broke her combs, grinding them underfoot. They tore her work from the loom. They scattered the cooking fire and rolled the new weaving in it. We could hear them in the kitchen breaking our bowls and banging the pots. They overturned the great waist-high earthenware jugs; duck eggs, pickled fruits, vegetables burst out and mixed in acrid torrents. The old woman from the next field swept a broom through the air and loosed the spirits-of-the-broom over our heads. 'Pig.' 'Ghost.' 'Pig,' they sobbed and scolded while they ruined our house.

"When they left, they took sugar and oranges to bless themselves. They cut pieces from the dead animals. Some of them took bowls that were not broken and clothes that were not torn. Afterward we swept up the rice and sewed it back up into sacks. But the smells from the spilled preserves lasted. Your aunt gave birth in the pigsty that night. The next morning when I went up for the water, I found her and the baby plugging up the family well.

---

[1] **bunds:** An embankment around rice fields to help prevent flooding. —Eds.

"Don't let your father know that I told you. He denies her. Now that you have started to menstruate, what happened to her could happen to you. Don't humiliate us. You wouldn't like to be forgotten as if you had never been born. The villagers are watchful."

Whenever she had to warn us about life, my mother told stories that ran like this one, a story to grow up on. She tested our strength to establish realities. Those in the emigrant generations who could not reassert brute survival died young and far from home. Those of us in the first American generations have had to figure out how the invisible world the emigrants built around our childhoods fit in solid America. 10

The emigrants confused the gods by diverting their curses, misleading them with crooked streets and false names. They must try to confuse their offspring as well, who, I suppose, threaten them in similar ways—always trying to get things straight, always trying to name the unspeakable. The Chinese I know hide their names; sojourners take new names when their lives change and guard their real names with silence.

Chinese-Americans, when you try to understand what things in you are Chinese, how do you separate what is peculiar to childhood, to poverty, insanities, one family, your mother who marked your growing with stories, from what is Chinese? What is Chinese tradition and what is the movies?

If I want to learn what clothes my aunt wore, whether flashy or ordinary, I would have to begin, "Remember Father's drowned-in-the-well sister?" I cannot ask that. My mother has told me once and for all the useful parts. She will add nothing unless powered by Necessity, a riverbank that guides her life. She plants vegetable gardens rather than lawns; she carries the odd-shaped tomatoes home from the fields and eats food left for the gods.

Whenever we did frivolous things, we used up energy; we flew high kites. We children came up off the ground over the melting cones our parents brought home from work and the American movie on New Year's Day — *Oh, You Beautiful Doll* with Betty Grable one year, and *She Wore a Yellow Ribbon* with John Wayne another year. After the one carnival ride each, we paid in guilt; our tired father counted his change on the dark walk home.

Adultery is extravagance. Could people who hatch their own chicks and eat the embryos and the heads for delicacies and boil the feet in vinegar for party food, leaving only the gravel, eating even the gizzard lining — could such people engender a prodigal aunt? To be a woman, to have a daughter in starvation time was a waste enough. My aunt could not have been the lone romantic who gave up everything for sex. Women in the old China did not choose. Some man had commanded her to lie with him and be his secret evil. I wonder whether he masked himself when he joined the raid on her family. 15

Perhaps she encountered him in the fields or on the mountain where the daughters-in-law collected fuel. Or perhaps he first noticed her in the marketplace. He was not a stranger because the village housed no strangers. She had to have dealings with him other than sex. Perhaps he worked an adjoining field, or he sold her the cloth for the dress she sewed and wore.

His demand must have surprised, then terrified her. She obeyed him; she always did as she was told.

When the family found a young man in the next village to be her husband, she stood tractably beside the best rooster, his proxy, and promised before they met that she would be his forever. She was lucky that he was her age and she would be the first wife, an advantage secure now. The night she first saw him, he had sex with her. Then he left for America. She had almost forgotten what he looked like. When she tried to envision him, she only saw the black and white face in the group photograph the men had had taken before leaving.

The other man was not, after all, much different from her husband. They both gave orders: she followed. "If you tell your family, I'll beat you. I'll kill you. Be here again next week." No one talked sex, ever. And she might have separated the rapes from the rest of living if only she did not have to buy her oil from him or gather wood in the same forest. I want her fear to have lasted just as long as rape lasted so that the fear could have been contained. No drawn-out fear. But women at sex hazarded birth and hence lifetimes. The fear did not stop but permeated everywhere. She told the man, "I think I'm pregnant." He organized the raid against her.

On nights when my mother and father talked about their life back home, sometimes they mentioned an "outcast table" whose business they still seemed to be settling, their voices tight. In a commensal tradition, where food is precious, the powerful older people made wrongdoers eat alone. Instead of letting them start separate new lives like the Japanese, who could become samurais and geishas, the Chinese family, faces averted but eyes glowering sideways, hung on to the offenders and fed them leftovers. My aunt must have lived in the same house as my parents and eaten at an outcast table. My mother spoke about the raid as if she had seen it, when she and my aunt, a daughter-in-law to a different household, should not have been living together at all. Daughters-in-law lived with their husbands' parents, not their own; a synonym for marriage in Chinese is "taking a daughter-in-law." Her husband's parents could have sold her, mortgaged her, stoned her. But they had sent her back to her own mother and father, a mysterious act hinting at disgraces not told me. Perhaps they had thrown her out to deflect the avengers.

She was the only daughter; her four brothers went with her father, husband, and uncles "out on the road" and for some years became western men. When the goods were divided among the family, three of the brothers took land, and the youngest, my father, chose an education. After my grandparents gave their daughter away to her husband's family, they had dispensed all the adventure and all the property. They expected her alone to keep the traditional ways, which her brothers, now among the barbarians, could fumble without detection. The heavy, deep-rooted women were to maintain the past against the flood, safe for returning. But the rare urge west had fixed upon our family, and so my aunt crossed boundaries not delineated in space.

20

The work of preservation demands that the feelings playing about in one's guts not be turned into action. Just watch their passing like cherry blossoms. But perhaps my aunt, my forerunner, caught in a slow life, let dreams grow and fade and after some months or years went toward what persisted. Fear at the enormities of the forbidden kept her desires delicate, wire and bone. She looked at a man because she liked the way the hair was tucked behind his ears, or she liked the question-mark line of a long torso curving at the shoulder and straight at the hip. For warm eyes or a soft voice or a slow walk—that's all—a few hairs, a line, a brightness, a sound, a pace, she gave up family. She offered us up for a charm that vanished with tiredness, a pigtail that didn't toss when the wind died. Why, the wrong lighting could erase the dearest thing about him.

It could very well have been, however, that my aunt did not take subtle enjoyment of her friend, but, a wild woman, kept rollicking company. Imagining her free with sex doesn't fit, though. I don't know any women like that, or men either. Unless I see her life branching into mine, she gives me no ancestral help.

To sustain her being in love, she often worked at herself in the mirror, guessing at the colors and shapes that would interest him, changing them frequently in order to hit on the right combination. She wanted to look back.

On a farm near the sea, a woman who tended her appearance reaped a reputation for eccentricity. All the married women blunt-cut their hair in flaps about their ears or pulled it back in tight buns. No nonsense. Neither style blew easily into heart-catching tangles. And at their weddings they displayed themselves in their long hair for the last time. "It brushed the back of my knees," my mother tells me. "It was braided, and even so, it brushed the backs of my knees."

At the mirror my aunt combed individuality into her bob. A bun could   25 have been contrived to escape into black streamers blowing in the wind or in quiet wisps about her face, but only the older women in our picture album wear buns. She brushed her hair back from her forehead, tucking the flaps behind her ears. She looped a piece of thread, knotted into a circle between her index fingers and thumbs, and ran the double strand across her forehead. When she closed her fingers as if she were making a pair of shadow geese bite, the string twisted together catching the little hairs. Then she pulled the thread away from her skin, ripping the hairs out neatly, her eyes watering from the needles of pain. Opening her fingers, she cleaned the thread, then rolled it along her hairline and the tops of the eyebrows. My mother did the same to me and my sisters and herself. I used to believe that the expression "caught by the short hairs" meant a captive held with a depilatory string. It especially hurt at the temples, but my mother said we were lucky we didn't have to have our feet bound when we were seven. Sisters used to sit on their beds and cry together, she said, as their mothers or their slave removed the bandages for a few minutes each night and let the blood gush back into their veins. I hope that the man my aunt loved appreciated a smooth brow, that he wasn't just a tits-and-ass man.

Once my aunt found a freckle on her chin, at a spot that the almanac said predestined her for unhappiness. She dug it out with a hot needle and washed the wound with peroxide.

More attention to her looks than these pullings of hairs and pickings at spots would have caused gossip among the villagers. They owned work clothes and good clothes, and they wore good clothes for feasting the new seasons. But since a woman combing her hair hexes beginnings, my aunt rarely found an occasion to look her best. Women looked like great sea snails—the corded wood, babies, and laundry they carried were the whorls on their backs. The Chinese did not admire a bent back; goddesses and warriors stood straight. Still there must have been a marvelous freeing of beauty when a worker laid down her burden and stretched and arched.

Such commonplace loveliness, however, was not enough for my aunt. She dreamed of a lover for the fifteen days of New Year's, the time for families to exchange visits, money, and food. She plied her secret comb. And sure enough she cursed the year, the family, the village, and herself.

Even as her hair lured her imminent lover, many other men looked at her. Uncles, cousins, nephews, brothers would have looked, too, had they been home between journeys. Perhaps they had already been restraining their curiosity, and they left, fearful that their glances, like a field of nesting birds, might be startled and caught. Poverty hurt, and that was their first reason for leaving. But another, final reason for leaving the crowded house was the never-said.

She may have been unusually beloved, the precious only daughter,   30 spoiled and mirror-gazing because of the affection the family lavished on her. When her husband left, they welcomed the chance to take her back from the in-laws; she could live like the little daughter for just a while longer. There are stories that my grandfather was different from other people, "crazy ever since the little Jap bayoneted him in the head." He used to put his naked penis on the dinner table, laughing. And one day he brought home a baby girl, wrapped up inside his brown western-style greatcoat. He had traded one of his sons, probably my father, the youngest, for her. My grandmother made him trade back. When he finally got a daughter of his own, he doted on her. They must have all loved her, except perhaps my father, the only brother who never went back to China, having once been traded for a girl.

Brothers and sisters, newly men and women, had to efface their sexual color and present plain miens. Disturbing hair and eyes, a smile like no other, threatened the ideal of five generations living under one roof. To focus blurs, people shouted face to face and yelled from room to room. The immigrants I know have loud voices, unmodulated to American tones even after years away from the village where they called their friendships out across the fields. I have not been able to stop my mother's screams in public libraries or over telephones. Walking erect (knees straight, toes pointed forward, not pigeon-toed, which is Chinese-feminine) and speaking in an inaudible voice, I have tried to turn myself American-feminine. Chinese communication was loud, public. Only sick people had to whisper. But at the dinner table, where the family members came nearest one another, no one could talk, not the outcasts nor any eaters. Every word that falls from the mouth is a coin lost. Silently they gave and accepted food with both hands. A preoccupied child who took his bowl with one hand got a sideways glare. A complete moment of total attention is due everyone alike. Children and lovers have no singularity here, but my aunt used a secret voice, a separate attentiveness.

She kept the man's name to herself throughout her labor and dying; she did not accuse him that he be punished with her. To save her inseminator's name she gave silent birth.

He may have been somebody in her own household, but intercourse with a man outside the family would have been no less abhorrent. All the village were kinsmen, and the titles shouted in loud country voices never let kinship be forgotten. Any man within visiting distance would have been neutralized as a lover — "brother," "younger brother," "older brother" — 115 relationship titles. Parents researched birth charts probably not so much to assure good fortune as to circumvent incest in a population that has but one hundred surnames. Everybody has eight million relatives. How useless then sexual mannerisms, how dangerous.

As if it came from an atavism deeper than fear, I used to add "brother" silently to boys' names. It hexed the boys, who would or would not ask me to dance, and made them less scary and as familiar and deserving of benevolence as girls.

But, of course, I hexed myself also — no dates. I should have stood up,   35
both arms waving, and shouted out across libraries, "Hey, you! Love me back." I had no idea, though, how to make attraction selective, how to control its direction and magnitude. If I made myself American-pretty so that the five or six Chinese boys in the class fell in love with me, everyone else — the Caucasian, Negro, and Japanese boys — would too. Sisterliness, dignified and honorable, made much more sense.

Attraction eludes control so stubbornly that whole societies designed to organize relationships among people cannot keep order, not even when they bind people to one another from childhood and raise them together. Among the very poor and the wealthy, brothers married their adopted sisters, like doves. Our family allowed some romance, paying adult brides' prices and providing dowries so that their sons and daughters could marry strangers. Marriage promises to turn strangers into friendly relatives — a nation of siblings.

In the village structure, spirits shimmered among the live creatures, balanced and held in equilibrium by time and land. But one human being flaring up into violence could open up a black hole, a maelstrom that pulled in the sky. The frightened villagers, who depended on one another to maintain the real, went to my aunt to show her a personal, physical representation of the break she made in the "roundness." Misallying couples snapped off the future, which was to be embodied in true offspring. The villagers punished her for acting as if she could have a private life, secret and apart from them.

If my aunt had betrayed the family at a time of large grain yields and peace, when many boys were born, and wings were being built on many houses, perhaps she might have escaped such severe punishment. But the men—hungry, greedy, tired of planting in dry soil, cuckolded—had been forced to leave the village in order to send food-money home. There were ghost plagues, bandit plagues, wars with the Japanese, floods. My Chinese brother and sister had died of an unknown sickness. Adultery, perhaps only a mistake during good times, became a crime when the village needed food.

The round moon cakes and round doorways, the round tables of graduated size that fit one roundness inside another, round windows and rice bowls—these talismans had lost their power to warn this family of the law: A family must be whole, faithfully keeping the descent line by having sons to feed the old and the dead who in turn look after the family. The villagers came to show my aunt and lover-in-hiding a broken house. The villagers were speeding up the circling of events because she was too shortsighted to see that her infidelity had already harmed the village, that waves of consequences would return unpredictably, sometimes in disguise, as now, to hurt her. This roundness had to be made coin-sized so that she would see its circumference: Punish her at the birth of her baby. Awaken her to the inexorable. People who refused fatalism because they could invent small resources insisted on culpability. Deny accidents and wrest fault from the stars.

After the villagers left, their lanterns now scattering in various directions toward home, the family broke their silence and cursed her. "Aiaa, we're going to die. Death is coming. Death is coming. Look what you've done. You've killed us. Ghost! Dead Ghost! Ghost! You've never been born." She ran out into the fields, far enough from the house so that she could no longer hear their voices, and pressed herself against the earth, her own land no more. When she felt the birth coming, she thought that she had been hurt. Her body seized together. "They've hurt me too much," she thought. "This is gall, and it will kill me." With forehead and knees against the earth, her body convulsed and then relaxed. She turned on her back, lay on the ground. The black well of sky and stars went out and out forever; her body and her complexity seemed to disappear. She was one of the stars, a bright dot in blackness, without home, without a companion, in eternal cold and silence. An agoraphobia rose in her, speeding higher and higher, bigger and bigger; she would not be able to contain it; there would be no end to fear.

Flayed, unprotected against space, she felt pain return, focusing her body. This pain chilled her—a cold, steady kind of surface pain. Inside, spasmodically, the other pain, the pain of the child, heated her. For hours she lay on the ground, alternately body and space. Sometimes a vision of normal comfort obliterated reality: She saw the family in the evening gambling at the dinner table, the young people massaging their elders' backs. She saw them congratulating one another, high joy on the mornings the rice shoots came up. When these pictures burst, the stars drew yet further apart. Black space opened.

40

She got to her feet to fight better and remembered that old-fashioned women gave birth in their pigsties to fool the jealous, pain-dealing gods, who do not snatch piglets. Before the next spasms could stop her, she ran to the pigsty, each step a rushing out into emptiness. She climbed over the fence and knelt in the dirt. It was good to have a fence enclosing her, a tribal person alone.

Laboring, this woman who had carried her child as a foreign growth that sickened her every day, expelled it at last. She reached down to touch the hot, wet, moving mass, surely smaller than anything human, and could feel that it was human after all—fingers, toes, nails, nose. She pulled it up on to her belly, and it lay curled there, butt in the air, feet precisely tucked one under the other. She opened her loose shirt and buttoned the child inside. After resting, it squirmed and thrashed and she pushed it up to her breast. It turned its head this way and that until it found her nipple. There, it made little snuffling noises. She clenched her teeth at its preciousness, lovely as a young calf, a piglet, a little dog.

She may have gone to the pigsty as a last act of responsibility: She would protect this child as she had protected its father. It would look after her soul, leaving supplies on her grave. But how would this tiny child without family find her grave when there would be no marker for her anywhere, neither in the earth nor the family hall? No one would give her a family hall name. She had taken the child with her into the wastes. At its birth the two of them had felt the same raw pain of separation, a wound that only the family pressing tight could close. A child with no descent line would not soften her life but only trail after her, ghostlike, begging her to give it purpose. At dawn the villagers on their way to the fields would stand around the fence and look.

Full of milk, the little ghost slept. When it awoke, she hardened her 45 breasts against the milk that crying loosens. Toward morning she picked up the baby and walked to the well.

Carrying the baby to the well shows loving. Otherwise abandon it. Turn its face into the mud. Mothers who love their children take them along. It was probably a girl; there is some hope of forgiveness for boys.

"Don't tell anyone you had an aunt. Your father does not want to hear her name. She has never been born." I have believed that sex was unspeakable and words so strong and fathers so frail that "aunt" would do my father mysterious harm. I have thought that my family, having settled among immigrants who had also been their neighbors in the ancestral land, needed to clean their name, and a wrong word would incite the kinspeople even here. But there is more to this silence: They want me to participate in her punishment. And I have.

In the twenty years since I heard this story I have not asked for details nor said my aunt's name; I do not know it. People who comfort the dead can also chase after them to hurt them further—a reverse ancestor worship. The real punishment was not the raid swiftly inflicted by the villagers, but the family's deliberately forgetting her. Her betrayal so maddened them, they saw to it that she would suffer forever, even after death. Always hungry, always needing, she would have to beg food from other ghosts, snatch and steal it from those whose living descendants give them gifts. She would have to fight the ghosts massed at crossroads for the buns a few thoughtful citizens leave to decoy her away from village and home so that the ancestral spirits could feast unharassed. At peace, they could act like gods, not ghosts, their descent lines providing them with paper suits and dresses, spirit money, paper houses, paper automobiles, chicken, meat, and rice into eternity—essences delivered up in smoke and flames, steam and incense rising from each rice bowl. In an attempt to make the Chinese care for people outside the family, Chairman Mao[2] encourages us now to give our paper replicas to the spirits of outstanding soldiers and workers, no matter whose ancestors they may be. My aunt remains forever hungry. Goods are not distributed evenly among the dead.

My aunt haunts me—her ghost drawn to me because now, after fifty years of neglect, I alone devote pages of paper to her, though not origamied into houses and clothes. I do not think she always means me well. I am telling on her, and she was a spite suicide, drowning herself in the drinking water. The Chinese are always very frightened of the drowned one, whose weeping ghost, wet hair hanging and skin bloated, waits silently by the water to pull down a substitute. ▪

The Reader's Presence

1. Kingston's account of her aunt's life and death is a remarkable blend of fact and speculation. Consider the overall structure of "No Name Woman." How many versions of the aunt's story do we hear? Where, for example, does the mother's story end? Where does the narrator's begin? Which version do you find more compelling? Why? What does the narrator mean when she says that her mother's stories "tested our strength to establish realities" (paragraph 10)?

2. The narrator's version of her aunt's story is replete with such words and phrases as *perhaps* and *It could very well have been*. The narrator seems far more speculative about her aunt's life than her mother is. At what point does the narrator raise doubts about the veracity of her mother's version of the aunt's story? What purpose does the mother espouse in telling the aunt's story? Is it meant primarily to express family lore? to issue a warning? Point to specific passages to verify your response. What is the proposed moral of the story? Is that moral the same for the mother as for the narrator? Explain.

3. **CONNECTIONS:** What line does Kingston draw between the two cultures represented in the story: between the mother, a superstitious, cautious Chinese woman, and the narrator, an American-born child trying to "straighten out" her mother's confusing story? How does the narrator resolve the issue by thinking of herself as neither Chinese nor American, but as Chinese American? How does she imagine her

---

2 ***Chairman Mao*** (1893–1976): Political theorist, guerilla warfare strategist, poet, and leader of the Chinese Revolution, Mao Zedong helped found the People's Republic of China in 1949, and ruled the nation until his death in 1976. —EDS.

relationship to her distant aunt? Compare Kingston's depiction of relationships across generations and cultures to those in N. Scott Momaday's "The Way to Rainy Mountain" (page 492) and to those in Richard Rodriguez's "Aria: A Memoir of a Bilingual Childhood" (page 227). How does language feature in each writer's family? How do problems of comprehension become occasions for creative play in each essay?

The Writer at Work

MAXINE HONG KINGSTON on Writing for Oneself

Christopher Felver/Corbis

In the fire that raged through the Oakland, California, hills in 1991, Maxine Hong Kingston lost, along with her entire house, all her copies of a work in progress. In the following interview conducted by Diane Simmons at Kingston's new home in 1997, the writer discusses how the fire and the loss of her work have transformed her attitude toward her own writing. Confronted with a similar loss (whether the work was on paper or hard drive), most authors would try to recapture as best they could what they had originally written. Why do you think Kingston wants to avoid that sort of recovery? The following exchange is from the opening of that long interview, which appeared in a literary periodical, the *Crab Orchard Review* (Spring/Summer 1998). Simmons is the author of *Maxine Hong Kingston* (New York: Twayne Publishers, 1999).

I began by asking Ms. Kingston to talk about the book that was lost, and where she was going with her recent work.

Kingston: In the book that I lost in the fire, I was working on an idea of finding the book of peace again. There was a myth that there were three lost books of peace and so I was going to find the book of peace for our time. I imagine that it has to do with how to wage peace on earth and that there would be tactics on how to wage peace and how to stop war. I see that the books of war are popular; they are taught in the military academies; they're translated into all different languages. They [are used to] help corporate executives succeed in business. And people don't even think about the books of peace; people don't even know

about them. I'm the only one that knows about it.

And so I was writing this and that was what was burned in the fire. What I'm working on now I'm calling *The Fifth Book of Peace.* I'm not recalling and re-membering what I had written. To me it's the pleasure of writing to be constantly discovering, going into the new. To recall word by word what I had written before sounds like torture and agony for me. I know I can do it, I'm sure I can do it if I want to. One of my former students volunteered to hypnotize me so I could recall, but that seemed so wrong to me.

Simmons: How much was lost?

Kingston: About 200 written, rewrit-ten pages, so it was very good. But I had wanted to rewrite it again and I think to recall word by word would freeze me into a version and I didn't want to do that.

Simmons: Is the book you are working on now the same project, the same version?

Kingston: Yes, but it is not the same words. It's not the same story. It's the same idea that I want to work on peace. At one point I called it the global novel. But since then I've been thinking of it as a book of peace. And the one big difference is the Book of Peace was a work of fiction. I was imagining fictional characters. But after the fire I wanted to use writing for my personal self. I wanted to write directly what I was thinking and feeling, not imagining fictional other people. I wanted to write myself. I wanted to write in the way I wrote when I was a child which is to say my deepest feelings and thoughts as they could come out in a personal way and not for public consumption. It's not even for other people to read but for myself, to express myself, and it doesn't matter whether this would be published. I don't even want to think about publication or readers, but this is for my own expression of my own suffering or agony.

Simmons: You've said that that's how you wrote in the beginning.

Kingston: I always begin like that. I always have to begin like that. Getting back to the roots of language in myself. It's almost like diary writing which is not for others.

Simmons: You don't mean that you don't want other people to read it necessarily.

Kingston: That's not a consideration. I don't want to think about any of that. I think of this as going back to a primitive state of what writing is for me, which is that I am finding my own voice again.

Simmons: Was it lost?

Kingston: Well, I started not to think about it anymore. After a while I had such an effective public voice, from childhood to now, I had found it and I had created it.

Simmons: Where do we see that public voice?

Kingston: The public voice is the voice that's in all my books.

Simmons: Even *Woman Warrior*?

Kingston: Yes. All my works. That is a public voice. What I mean by the private, personal voice is what I write when I'm trying to figure out things, what I write that's just for me. I get to be the reader and nobody else gets to read this. For years now I have not written in that way. I usually don't write diaries as an adult and so after the fire I needed to get to that again. I had forgotten about it.

Simmons: You are going back to before *Woman Warrior*, to before being a writer.

Kingston: Yes. Before being a writer who publishes.

Simmons: Why do you think the fire caused you to turn away from fiction?

Kingston: At the same time, my father died; he died a few weeks before the fire. At that time I felt I'd lost a lot. So I wanted to say what I felt about all that, about all my losses. And I don't see that as writing for publication. I see that as writing for myself, to put into words my losses. And so I started there, and wrote and wrote and wrote. But as I was writing, it became some of the things I was thinking in the book that burned; those would come into the writing, and then of course I go back to that very *id*[1] basic place. I'm old enough and civilized enough now so that the sentences and the words that come out are very elegant, very good, very crafted. I don't return to a place that's not crafted anymore. So all this stuff that I wrote down is going to be part of *The Fifth Book of Peace*.

[1] *id:* Latin for *it*; in Freudian psychoanalysis it stands for primitive impulses that derive from the unconscious part of the human psyche.

Steven D. Levitt and Stephen J. Dubner

WHAT SHOULD YOU WORRY ABOUT?

STEVEN D. LEVITT (b. 1967) and **STEPHEN J. DUBNER** (b. 1963) teamed up to write the enormously popular and influential book *Freakonomics: A Rogue Economist Explores the Hidden Side of Everything* (2006), which was on the *New York Times* best-seller list for over two years, selling more than 3 million copies worldwide. The team followed up their success in 2009 with *SuperFreakonomics: Global Cooling, Patriotic Prostitutes, and Why Suicide Bombers Should Buy Life Insurance*, which debuted at number two on the *New York Times* best-seller list. A documentary film inspired by the books was released in 2010, and Dubner currently hosts a public radio show called *Freakonomics Radio*.

> In 2004, Steven Levitt won the John Bates Clark Medal, which recognizes the most influential economist in America under the age of forty.

Levitt graduated from Harvard University and received his PhD from the Massachusetts Institute of Technology. He has been a professor of economics at the University of Chicago since 1997 and is the director of the Becker Center on Chicago Price Theory, a research center administered by the Graduate School of Business at the University of Chicago that emphasizes the role of markets and incentives in understanding economics and human behavior—fundamental elements of the new study of "freakonomics." An award-winning economist, Levitt was named one of *Time* magazine's "100 People Who Shape Our World" and, in 2004, received the John Bates Clark Medal, which recognizes the most influential economist in America under the age of forty. In 2009, he co-founded—with a group of leading economists, including John List and Andrew Rosenfield—a business and philanthropy consulting firm called *The Greatest Good*.

Author and journalist Stephen J. Dubner received his MFA from Columbia University in New York City. In addition to co-writing *Freakonomics*, he is the author of two books of nonfiction/memoir, *Turbulent Souls: A Catholic Son's Return to His Jewish Family* (1998) and *Confessions of a Hero-Worshipper* (2003); and a book for young children, *The Boy with Two Belly Buttons* (2007). His work appears frequently in the *New Yorker* and in the *New York Times*, and it has been anthologized in *Best American Sports Writing* and *Best American Crime Writing*, among other collections. Both writers contribute to the *New York Times* blog "Freakonomics."

HUMANS ARE GOOD at many things—typing, inventing stuff—but we're bad at assessing risk. Day after day, we get bent out of shape over things we shouldn't worry about so much, like airplane crashes and lightning strikes, instead of things we should, like heart disease and the flu.

So how can we find out what's truly dangerous? Economics. Upon hearing the word, most people think of incomprehensible charts and jargon and promptly change the subject. However, we can use the field's powerful ideas and tools, along with huge piles of data, to understand topics that aren't typically associated with economics. Topics like shark attacks.

Think back to the summer of 2001, or what the U.S. media dubbed the "Summer of the Shark." The prime example was the story of Jessie Arbogast, an 8-year-old who was playing in the warm, shallow Pensacola, Florida, waves when a bull shark ripped off his right arm and a big chunk of his thigh.

The media was full of such chilling tales. Here's the lead paragraph from one article published that summer:

"Sharks come silently, without warning. There are three ways they 5 strike: the hit-and-run, the bump-and-bite, and the sneak attack. The hit-and-run is the most common. The shark may see the sole of a swimmer's foot, think it's a fish, and take a bite before realizing this isn't its usual prey."

A reasonable person might never go near the ocean again. But how many shark attacks do you think actually happened that year?

Take a guess—and then cut that figure in half, and now cut it in half a few more times. During all of 2001, there were 68 shark attacks worldwide, of which just four were fatal.

Not only were the numbers lower than the media hysteria implied, but they were not much higher than those of previous years or of the years that followed. Between 1995 and 2005, there were on average 60.3 shark attacks worldwide each year, with a high of 79 and a low of 46. There were on average 5.9 fatalities per year, with a high of 11 and a low of three. In other words, the headlines during the summer of 2001 might just as easily have read "Shark Attacks About Average This Year."

Elephants, meanwhile, kill at least 200 people a year. Why aren't we petrified of them? Probably because their victims tend to live far from the world's media centers. It may also have to do with our perceptions gleaned from the movies. Friendly elephants are a staple of children's films like *Babar* and *Dumbo*; sharks are typecast as villains.

There are any number of topics about which our fears run far out of 10 proportion to reality. For instance, whom are you more afraid of: strangers or people you know?

While "strangers" is the obvious answer, it's probably wrong. Three out of four murder victims knew their assailants; about seven of 10 rape victims knew theirs. While the public is justifiably horrified when a stranger snatches a child off the street, the data show that such kidnappings are extremely rare.

As for the crime of identity theft, most of us fear nameless, faceless perpetrators—say, a far-off ring of teenage hackers. We try to thwart them by endlessly changing our PINs (and forgetting them). But it turns out that nearly half of identity-theft victims are ripped off by someone they know. And fully 90 percent of thefts happen offline, not on the Internet.

Fear sometimes distorts our thinking to the point where we become convinced that certain threats are so enormous as to be unstoppable. Every generation has at least one such problem—the plague, polio. Today, it's global warming.

The average global ground temperature over the past 100 years has risen 1.3 degrees Fahrenheit, or 0.74 degrees Celsius. But even the most brilliant climate scientists are unable to predict exactly what will happen to the Earth as a result of those atmospheric changes and when anything will happen.

We humans tend to respond to uncertainty with more emotion—fear, 15 blame, paralysis—than advisable. Uncertainty also has a nasty way of making us conjure the very worst possibilities. With global warming, these are downright biblical: hellish temperatures, rising oceans, a planet in chaos.

But instead of panicking and collectively wringing our hands, it might help us to look at other "unsolvable" problems humanity has had to deal with.

Like, well, horse manure. As urban populations exploded in the 19th century, horses were put to work in countless ways, from pulling streetcars and coaches to powering manufacturing equipment. Our cities became filled with horses—for example, in 1900, New York City was home to some 200,000 of them, or one for every 17 people.

Unfortunately, they produced a slew of what economists refer to as "negative externalities." These included noise, gridlock, high insurance costs, and far too many human traffic fatalities.

The worst problem was the manure. The average horse produces about 24 pounds of it a day. In New York, that added up to nearly 5 million pounds. A day. It lined the streets like banks of snow and was piled as high as 60 feet in vacant lots. It stank to the heavens. And it was a fertile breeding ground for flies that spread deadly disease.

City planners everywhere were confounded. It seemed as if cities could 20 not survive without the horse—but they couldn't survive with it, either.

And then the problem vanished. The horse was kicked to the curb by the electric streetcar and the automobile.

Virtually every unsolvable problem we've faced in the past has turned out to be quite solvable, and the script has nearly always been the same: A band of clever, motivated people—scientists usually—find an answer. With polio, it was the creation of a vaccine. If the best minds in the world focus their attention on global warming, hopefully we can handle that, too.

Yes, it is an incredibly large and challenging problem. But, as history has shown us again and again, human ingenuity is bound to be even larger. ▪

The Reader's Presence

1. The authors argue that knowledge of economics can help us better assess risk. Why do you think they chose shark attacks as their lead example? In what way does economics help us understand that being attacked by a shark is less of a risk than most people realize? Are you persuaded by their example? Why or why not?

2. What does our fear of global warming have to do with "horse manure" (paragraph 17)? In what ways do both examples support the view that economics can solve what appear to be insurmountable problems? What do the authors propose people do to solve the problems associated with global warming?

3. **CONNECTIONS:** "What Should You Worry About?" is an optimistic essay: it never directly answers its own question, instead suggesting that such trends as global warming—although cause for concern and attention—are not the apocalyptic problems that the popular media makes of them. Compare and contrast the specific ways Levitt and Dubner use statistics to support their conclusions with the ways Steven Pinker uses data in "Violence Vanquished" (page 698). Which use of statistics do you find more engaging and convincing? Explain why.

Alan Lightman

Our Place in the Universe

ALAN LIGHTMAN (b. 1948) is unique among American fiction writers in that he is also a respected physicist. In fact, he was the first professor ever to receive a joint appointment in the sciences and the humanities from the Massachusetts Institute of Technology. Born in Memphis, Tennessee, he demonstrated an unusual talent for both science and English at an early age, winning statewide science fairs and English awards in high school. As a scientist, his research has focused largely on gravity: he is particularly well known for positing that, because all falling objects accelerate at the same speed, gravity must be described as a geometrical warping of time and space.

Lightman's most famous novel, *Einstein's Dreams* (1992), depicts Albert Einstein as a young man, developing the theory of relativity, plagued by dreams about time. It was an international best-seller and has been translated into thirty languages. Lightman has written several novels since then, including *Reunion* (2003) and *Ghost* (2007), as well as a number of essay collections and books about science, including *Dance for Two* (1996) and *Great Ideas in Physics: The Conservation of Energy, the Second Law of Thermodynamics, the Theory of Relativity, and Quantum Mechanics*, originally published in 1992 and now in its third edition. His most recent novel, *Mr g* (2012), is the story of creation told from the perspective of God. He has described "the history of science . . . as the recasting of phenomena that were once thought to be accidents as phenomena that can be understood in terms of fundamental causes and principles," and suggested that, because of findings that "have led some of the world's premier physicists to propose . . . that some of the most basic features of our particular universe are indeed mere *accidents* . . . there [may be] no hope of ever explaining our universe's particular features in terms of fundamental causes and principles." The following essay, "Our Place in the Universe," was originally published in *Harper's* in 2012.

> **Alan Lightman's most famous novel, *Einstein's Dreams* (1992), depicts Albert Einstein as a young man, developing the theory of relativity, plagued by dreams about time.**

MY MOST VIVID ENCOUNTER with the vastness of nature occurred years ago on the Aegean Sea. My wife and I had chartered a sailboat for a two-week holiday in the Greek islands. After setting out from Piraeus, we headed south and hugged the coast, which we held three or four miles to our port. In the thick summer air, the distant shore appeared as a hazy beige ribbon—not entirely solid, but a reassuring line of reference. With binoculars, we could just make out the glinting of houses, fragments of buildings.

Then we passed the tip of Cape Sounion and turned west toward Hydra. Within a couple of hours, both the land and all other boats had disappeared. Looking around in a full circle, all we could see was water, extending out and out in all directions until it joined with the sky. I felt insignificant, misplaced, a tiny odd trinket in a cavern of ocean and air.

Naturalists, biologists, philosophers, painters, and poets have labored to express the qualities of this strange world that we find ourselves in. Some things are prickly, others are smooth. Some are round, some jagged. Luminescent or dim. Mauve colored. Pitter-patter in rhythm. Of all these aspects of things, none seems more immediate or vital than *size*. Large versus small. Consciously and unconsciously, we measure our physical size against the dimensions of other people, against animals, trees, oceans, mountains. As brainy as we think ourselves to be, our bodily size, our bigness, our simple volume and bulk are what we first present to the world. Somewhere in our fathoming of the cosmos, we must keep a mental inventory of plain size and scale, going from atoms to microbes to humans to oceans to planets to stars. And some of the most impressive additions to that inventory have occurred at the high end. Simply put, the cosmos has gotten larger and larger. At each new level of distance and scale, we have had to contend with a different conception of the world that we live in.

The prize for exploring the greatest distance in space goes to a man named Garth Illingworth, who works in a ten-by-fifteen-foot office at the University of California, Santa Cruz. Illingworth studies galaxies so distant that their light has traveled through space for more than 13 billion years to get here. His office is packed with tables and chairs, bookshelves, computers, scattered papers, issues of *Nature*, and a small refrigerator and a microwave to fuel research that can extend into the wee hours of the morning.

Like most professional astronomers these days, Illingworth does not look directly through a telescope. He gets his images by remote control—in his case, quite remote. He uses the Hubble Space Telescope, which orbits Earth once every ninety-seven minutes, high above the distorting effects of Earth's atmosphere. Hubble takes digital photographs of galaxies and sends the images to other orbiting satellites, which relay them to a network of earth-bound antennae; these, in turn, pass the signals on to the Goddard Space Flight Center in Greenbelt, Maryland. From there the data is uploaded to a secure website that Illingworth can access from a computer in his office.

The most distant galaxy Illingworth has seen so far goes by the name UDFj-39546284 and was documented in early 2011. This galaxy is about 100,000,000,000,000,000,000,000 miles away from Earth, give or take. It appears as a faint red blob against the speckled night of the distant universe—red because the light has been stretched to longer and longer wavelengths as the galaxy has made its lonely journey through space for billions of years. The actual color of the galaxy is blue, the color of young, hot stars, and it is twenty times smaller than our galaxy, the Milky Way. UDFj-39546284 was one of the first galaxies to form in the universe.

"That little red dot is hellishly far away," Illingworth told me recently. At sixty-five, he is a friendly bear of a man, with a ruddy complexion, thick strawberry-blond hair, wire-rimmed glasses, and a broad smile. "I sometimes think to myself: What would it be like to be out there, looking around?"

One measure of the progress of human civilization is the increasing scale of our maps. A clay tablet dating from about the twenty-fifth century B.C. found near what is now the Iraqi city of Kirkuk depicts a river valley with a plot of land labeled as being 354 *iku* (about thirty acres) in size. In the earliest recorded cosmologies, such as the Babylonian *Enuma Elish*, from around 1500 B.C., the oceans, the continents, and the heavens were considered finite, but there were no scientific estimates of their dimensions. The early Greeks, including Homer, viewed Earth as a circular plane with the ocean enveloping it and Greece at the center, but there was no understanding of

5

scale. In the early sixth century B.C., the Greek philosopher Anaximander, whom historians consider the first mapmaker, and his student Anaximenes proposed that the stars were attached to a giant crystalline sphere. But again there was no estimate of its size.

The first large object ever accurately measured was Earth, accomplished in the third century B.C. by Eratosthenes, a geographer who ran the Library of Alexandria. From travelers, Eratosthenes had heard the intriguing report that at noon on the summer solstice, in the town of Syene, due south of Alexandria, the sun casts no shadow at the bottom of a deep well. Evidently the sun is directly overhead at that time and place. (Before the invention of the clock, noon could be defined at each place as the moment when the sun was highest in the sky, whether that was exactly vertical or not.) Eratosthenes knew that the sun was not overhead at noon in Alexandria. In fact, it was tipped 7.2 degrees from the vertical, or about one fiftieth of a circle—a fact he could determine by measuring the length of the shadow cast by a stick planted in the ground. That the sun could be directly overhead in one place and not another was due to the curvature of Earth. Eratosthenes reasoned that if he knew the distance from Alexandria to Syene, the full circumference of the planet must be about fifty times that distance. Traders passing through Alexandria told him that camels could make the trip to Syene in about fifty days, and it was known that a camel could cover one hundred stadia (almost eleven and a half miles) in a day. So the ancient geographer estimated that Syene and Alexandria were about 570 miles apart. Consequently, the complete circumference of Earth he figured to be about 50 x 570 miles, or 28,500 miles. This number was within 15 percent of the modem measurement, amazingly accurate considering the imprecision of using camels as odometers.

As ingenious as they were, the ancient Greeks were not able to calculate   10
the size of our solar system. That discovery had to wait for the invention of the telescope, nearly two thousand years later. In 1672, the French astronomer Jean Richer determined the distance from Earth to Mars by measuring how much the position of the latter shifted against the background of stars from two different observation points on Earth. The two points were Paris (of course) and Cayenne, French Guiana. Using the distance to Mars, astronomers were also able to compute the distance from Earth to the sun, approximately 100 million miles.

A few years later, Isaac Newton managed to estimate the distance to the nearest stars. (Only someone as accomplished as Newton could have been the first to perform such a calculation and have it go almost unnoticed among his other achievements.) If one assumes that the stars are similar objects to our sun, equal in intrinsic luminosity, Newton asked, how far away would our sun have to be in order to appear as faint as nearby stars? Writing his computations in a spidery script, with a quill dipped in the ink of oak galls, Newton correctly concluded that the nearest stars are about 100,000 times the distance from Earth to the sun, about 10 trillion miles away. Newton's calculation is contained in a short section of his *Principia* titled simply "On the distance of the stars."

Newton's estimate of the distance to nearby stars was larger than any distance imagined before in human history. Even today, nothing in our experience allows us to relate to it. The fastest most of us have traveled is about 500 miles per hour, the cruising speed of a jet. If we set out for the nearest star beyond our solar system at that speed, it would take us about 5 million years to reach our destination. If we traveled in the fastest rocket ship ever manufactured on Earth, the trip would last 100,000 years, at least a thousand human life spans.

But even the distance to the nearest star is dwarfed by the measurements made in the early twentieth century by Henrietta Leavitt, an astronomer at the Harvard College Observatory. In 1912, she devised a new method for determining the distances to faraway stars. Certain stars, called Cepheid variables, were known to oscillate in brightness. Leavitt discovered that the cycle times of such stars are closely related to their intrinsic luminosities. More luminous stars have longer cycles. Measure the cycle time of such a star and you know its intrinsic luminosity. Then, by comparing its intrinsic luminosity with how bright it appears in the sky, you can infer its distance, just as you could gauge the distance to an approaching car at night if you knew the wattage of its headlights. Cepheid variables are scattered throughout the cosmos. They serve as cosmic distance signs in the highway of space.

Using Leavitt's method, astronomers were able to determine the size of the Milky Way, a giant congregation of about 200 billion stars. To express such mind-boggling sizes and distances, twentieth-century astronomers adopted a new unit called the light-year, the distance that light travels in a year—about 6 trillion miles. The nearest stars are several light-years away. The diameter of the Milky Way has been measured at about 100,000 light-years. In other words, it takes a ray of light 100,000 years to travel from one side of the Milky Way to the other.

There are galaxies beyond our own. They have names like Andromeda 15 (one of the nearest), Sculptor, Messier 87, Malin 1, IC 1101. The average distance between galaxies, again determined by Leavitt's method, is about twenty galactic diameters, or 2 million light-years. To a giant cosmic being leisurely strolling through the universe and not limited by distance or time, galaxies would appear as illuminated mansions scattered about the dark countryside of space. As far as we know, galaxies are the largest objects in the cosmos. If we sorted the long inventory of material objects in nature by size, we would start with subatomic particles like electrons and end up with galaxies.

Over the past century, astronomers have been able to probe deeper and deeper into space, looking out to distances of hundreds of millions of light-years and farther. A question naturally arises: Could the physical universe be unending in size? That is, as we build bigger and bigger telescopes sensitive to fainter and fainter light, will we continue to see objects farther and farther away — like the third emperor of the Ming Dynasty, Yongle, who surveyed his new palace in the Forbidden City and walked from room to room to room, never reaching the end?

Here we must take into account a curious relationship between distance and time. Because light travels at a fast (186,000 miles per second) but not infinite speed, when we look at a distant object in space we must remember that a significant amount of time has passed between the emission of the light and the reception at our end. The image we see is what the object looked like when it emitted that light. If we look at an object 186,000 miles away, we see it as it appeared one second earlier; at 1,860,000 miles away, we see it as it appeared ten seconds earlier; and so on. For extremely distant objects, we see them as they were millions or billions of years in the past.

Now the second curiosity. Since the late 1920s we have known that the universe is expanding, and that as it does so it is thinning out and cooling. By measuring the current rate of expansion, we can make good estimates of the moment in the past when the expansion began — the Big Bang — which was about 13.7 billion years ago, a time when no planets or stars or galaxies existed and the entire universe consisted of a fantastically dense nugget of pure energy. No matter how big our telescopes, we cannot see beyond the distance light has traveled since the Big Bang. Farther than that, and there simply hasn't been enough time since the birth of the universe for light to get from there to here. This giant sphere, the maximum distance we can see, is only the *observable* universe. But the universe could extend far beyond that.

In his office in Santa Cruz, Garth Illingworth and his colleagues have mapped out and measured the cosmos to the edge of the observable universe. They have reached out almost as far as the laws of physics allow. All that exists in the knowable universe — oceans and sky; planets and stars; pulsars, quasars, and dark matter; distant galaxies and clusters of galaxies; and great clouds of star-forming gas — has been gathered within the cosmic sensorium gauged and observed by human beings.

"Every once in a while," says Illingworth, "I think: By God, we are studying things that we can never physically touch. We sit on this miserable little planet in a midsize galaxy and we can characterize most of the universe. It is astonishing to me, the immensity of the situation, and how to relate to it in terms we can understand." 20

The idea of Mother Nature has been represented in every culture on Earth. But to what extent is the new universe, vastly larger than anything conceived of in the past, part of *nature*? One wonders how connected Illingworth feels to this astoundingly large cosmic terrain, to the galaxies and stars so distant that their images have taken billions of years to reach our eyes. Are the little red dots on his maps part of the same landscape that Wordsworth and Thoreau described, part of the same environment of mountains and trees, part of the same cycle of birth and death that orders our lives, part of our physical and emotional conception of the world we live in? Or are such things instead digitized abstractions, silent and untouchable, akin to us only in their (hypothesized) makeup of atoms and molecules? And to what extent are we human beings, living on a small planet orbiting one star among billions of stars, part of that same nature?

The heavenly bodies were once considered divine, made of entirely different stuff than objects on Earth. Aristotle argued that all matter was constituted from four elements: earth, fire, water, and air. A fifth element, ether, he reserved for the heavenly bodies, which he considered immortal, perfect, and indestructible. It wasn't until the birth of modern science, in the seventeenth century, that we began to understand the similarity of heaven and Earth. In 1610, using his new telescope, Galileo noted that the sun had dark patches and blemishes, suggesting that the heavenly bodies are not perfect. In 1687, Newton proposed a universal law of gravity that would apply equally to the fall of an apple from a tree and to the orbits of planets around the sun. Newton then went further, suggesting that all the laws of nature apply to phenomena in the heavens as well as on Earth. In later centuries, scientists used our understanding of terrestrial chemistry and physics to estimate how long the sun could continue shining before depleting its resources of energy; to determine the chemical composition of stars; to map out the formation of galaxies.

Yet even after Galileo and Newton, there remained another question: Were living things somehow different from rocks and water and stars? Did animate and inanimate matter differ in some fundamental way? The "vitalists" claimed that animate matter had some special essence, an intangible spirit or soul, while the "mechanists" argued that living things were elaborate machines and obeyed precisely the same laws of physics and chemistry as did inanimate material. In the late nineteenth century, two German physiologists, Adolf Eugen Fick and Max Rubner, each began testing the mechanistic hypothesis by painstakingly tabulating the energies required for muscle contraction, body heat, and other physical activities and comparing these energies against the chemical energy stored in food. Each gram of fat, carbohydrate, and protein had its energy equivalent. Rubner concluded that the amount of energy used by a living creature was exactly equal to the energy it consumed in its food. Living things were to be viewed as complex arrangements of biological pulleys and levers, electric currents, and chemical impulses. Our bodies are made of the same atoms and molecules as stones, water, and air.

And yet many had a lingering feeling that human beings were somehow separate from the rest of nature. Such a view is nowhere better illustrated than in the painting *Tallulah Falls* (1841), by George Cooke, an artist associated with the Hudson River School. Although this group of painters celebrated nature, they also believed that human beings were set apart from the natural world. Cooke's painting depicts tiny human figures standing on a small promontory above a deep canyon. The people are dwarfed by tree-covered mountains, massive rocky ledges, and a waterfall pouring down to the canyon below. Not only insignificant in size compared with their surroundings, the human beings are mere witnesses to a scene they are not part of and never could be. Just a few years earlier, Ralph Waldo Emerson had published his famous essay "Nature," an appreciation of the natural world that nonetheless held humans separate from nature, at the very least in the moral and spiritual domain: "Man is fallen; nature is erect."

Today, with various back-to-nature movements attempting to resist the dislocations brought about by modernity, and with our awareness of Earth's precarious environmental state ever increasing, many people feel a new sympathy with the natural world on this planet. But the gargantuan cosmos beyond remains remote. We might understand at some level that those tiny points of light in the night sky are similar to our sun, made of atoms identical to those in our bodies, and that the cavern of outer space extends from our galaxy of stars to other galaxies of stars, to distances that would take light billions of years to traverse. We might understand these discoveries in intellectual terms, but they are baffling abstractions, even disturbing, like the notion that each of us once was the size of a dot, without mind or thought. Science has vastly expanded the scale of our cosmos, but our emotional reality is still limited by what we can touch with our bodies in the time span of our lives. George Berkeley, the eighteenth-century Irish philosopher, argued that the entire cosmos is a construct of our minds, that there is no material reality outside our thoughts. As a scientist, I cannot accept that belief. At the emotional and psychological level, however, I can have some sympathy with Berkeley's views. Modern science has revealed a world as far removed from our bodies as colors are from the blind.

Very recent scientific findings have added yet another dimension to the question of our place in the cosmos. For the first time in the history of science, we are able to make plausible estimates of the rate of occurrence of life in the universe. In March 2009, NASA launched a spacecraft called *Kepler* whose mission was to search for planets orbiting in the "habitable zone" of other stars. The habitable zone is the region in which a planet's surface temperature is not so cold as to freeze water and not so hot as to boil it. For many reasons, biologists and chemists believe that liquid water is required for the emergence of life, even if that life may be very different from life on Earth. Dozens of candidates for such planets have been found, and we can make a rough preliminary calculation that something like 3 percent of all stars are accompanied by a potentially life-sustaining planet. The totality of living matter on Earth—humans and animals, plants, bacteria, and pond scum—makes up 0.00000001 percent of the mass of the planet. Combining this figure with the results from the *Kepler* mission, and assuming that all potentially life-sustaining planets do indeed have life, we can estimate that the fraction of stuff in the visible universe that exists in living form is something like 0.000000000000001 percent, or one millionth of one billionth of 1 percent. If some cosmic intelligence created the universe, life would seem to have been only an afterthought. And if life emerges by random processes, vast amounts of lifeless material are needed for each particle of life. Such numbers cannot help but bear upon the question of our significance in the universe.

Decades ago, when I was sailing with my wife in the Aegean Sea, in the midst of unending water and sky, I had a slight inkling of infinity. It was a sensation I had not experienced before, accompanied by feelings of awe, fear, sublimity, disorientation, alienation, and disbelief. I set a course for 255°, trusting in my compass—a tiny disk of painted numbers with a sliver of rotating metal—and hoped for the best. In a few hours, as if by magic, a pale ocher smidgen of land appeared dead ahead, a thing that drew closer and closer, a place with houses and beds and other human beings.

The Reader's Presence

1. Lightman addresses the centuries-old question of whether we exist within the framework of the natural world or are observers of a universe in which we have an insignificant place: "The idea of Mother Nature has been represented in every culture on Earth. But to what extent is the new universe, vastly larger than anything conceived of in the past, part of *nature*? . . . And to what extent are we human beings, living on a small planet orbiting one star among billions of stars, part of that same nature?" (paragraph 21). What are the compositional advantages of Lightman's decision to begin and end his essay by writing about a personal "encounter with the vastness of nature" (paragraph 1)? In what specific ways do your own experiences in and with nature, on both a large and small scale, affect your own sense of place in the universe?

2. To what extent do you agree with Lightman's assertion that our conception of the "size and scale" (paragraph 3) of the world impacts how we think about our lives? What was your first reaction when you read that the distance of the galaxy UDFj-39546284 is 100,000,000,000,000,000,000,000 miles from Earth (paragraph 6)? How is your reaction related to what Lightman calls your "physical and emotional conception of the world" (paragraph 21)? What is your response to Lightman's question, "[T]o what extent is the new universe, vastly larger than anything conceived of in the past, part of *nature*?" (paragraph 21)? Lightman relies on analogies to help us make sense of the massive scale of the universe. Which of his examples do you find most helpful? Explain why.

3. **CONNECTIONS:** Compare Lightman's essay to Annie Dillard's "This Is the Life" (page 382). How consistent is Dillard's concept of "knowledge you experience directly" (paragraph 15) with the operative assumptions of Lightman's essay? Cite specific passages from each essay to support your response. Do you think we can ever completely comprehend something as vast and abstract as the size of the universe? How do you think Lightman would respond to Dillard's question, "Then what?" Are our lives governed by what we understand "at the emotional and psychological level" (paragraph 25)?

Abraham Lincoln

GETTYSBURG ADDRESS

ABRAHAM LINCOLN (1809–1865), the sixteenth president of the United States, led the country through a bloody civil war in which one side "would *make* war rather than let the nation survive; and the other would *accept* war rather than let it perish." During his presidency, Lincoln, who is still widely admired as both a political figure and a writer, wrote notable documents such as the Emancipation Proclamation and several poignant and moving speeches, including the Gettysburg Address.

Four months after the Battle of Gettysburg, Lincoln joined in a dedication of a national cemetery on the battlefield. The "Gettysburg Address," delivered on November 19, 1863, would become one of the most famous—and one of the shortest—speeches given by a U.S. president. The text that follows has been widely accepted as the "final" version of the "Gettysburg Address." It comes from the "Bliss copy" of the speech—the fifth and final version of the text that Lincoln copied out by hand, probably sometime in early 1864.

> **"A house divided against itself cannot stand."**

FOUR SCORE and seven years ago our fathers brought forth on this continent, a new nation, conceived in Liberty, and dedicated to the proposition that all men are created equal.

Now we are engaged in a great civil war, testing whether that nation, or any nation so conceived and so dedicated, can long endure. We are met on a great battle-field of that war. We have come to dedicate a portion of that field, as a final resting place for those who here gave their lives that that nation might live. It is altogether fitting and proper that we should do this.

But, in a larger sense, we can not dedicate—we can not consecrate—we can not hallow—this ground. The brave men, living and dead, who struggled here, have consecrated it, far above our poor power to add or detract. The world will little note, nor long remember what we say here, but it can never forget what they did here. It is for us the living, rather, to be dedicated here to the unfinished work which they who fought here have thus far so nobly advanced. It is rather for us to be here dedicated to the great task remaining before us—that from these honored dead we take increased devotion to that cause for which they gave the last full measure of devotion—that we here highly resolve that these dead shall not have died in vain—that this nation, under God, shall have a new birth of freedom—and that government of the people, by the people, for the people, shall not perish from the earth.

The Reader's Presence

1. What historical event does Lincoln refer to at the beginning and end of the "Gettysburg Address"? Why do you think he chose to place this information in a position of such prominence? Why is this event relevant to the dedication of a cemetery?

2. Consider Lincoln's strategy of repetition. What phrases and sentence structures does he repeat? What is the effect of the repetition? Read the speech aloud. Do you find the repetition more or less effective when the words are spoken? Why?

3. **CONNECTIONS:** Compare and contrast Lincoln's "Gettysburg Address" to Thomas Jefferson's draft of "The Declaration of Independence" (page 623). Focus on their respective uses of such rhetorical devices as repetition, parallel structure, alliteration, and antithesis (a figure of speech in which an opposition or a contrast of ideas is expressed by parallelism of words that are the opposites of, or strongly contrasted with, each other). Which writer uses these rhetorical devices more successfully? Support your response by pointing to specific examples of each rhetorical device.

The Writer at Work

ABRAHAM LINCOLN's Hay Draft of the "Gettysburg Address"

Alexander Hesler/George Eastman House/Getty Images

Abraham Lincoln, 1860.

Two of the five surviving versions of the "Gettysburg Address" in Lincoln's own handwriting were written down just before or just after he gave the speech on November 19, 1863. Scholars disagree about whether one of these two drafts—known as the "Nicolay Draft" and the "Hay Draft"—might have been the pages Lincoln read from on the field at Gettysburg; both drafts differ somewhat from contemporary accounts of the speech that the president delivered that day. Both also differ from the final "Bliss copy" that has become the standard version of the "Gettysburg Address" (see previous page).

The images on the following pages show the pages of the Hay Draft of the "Gettysburg Address," the second version that Lincoln wrote. Note the additions and changes Lincoln has made to this draft of his speech. Compare this version, written very close to the time of the speech's delivery, with the final version made several months later. As the fame of the "Gettysburg Address" continued to grow, Lincoln kept revising the words for an increasingly wide audience that had not been present to hear him speak. What do Lincoln's continuing revisions suggest about his hopes for this text? Which version do you find more compelling?

Four score and seven years ago our fathers brought forth, upon this continent, a new nation, conceived in Liberty, and dedicated to the proposition that all men are created equal.

Now we are engaged in a great civil war, testing whether that nation, or any nation, so conceived, and so dedicated, can long endure. We are met here on a great battle-field of that war. We have ~~are~~ come ~~to~~ to dedicate a portion of it, as a ~~the~~ final resting place for ~~of~~ those who here gave their lives that that nation might live. It is altogether fitting and proper that we should do this.

But in a larger sense we can not dedicate— we can not consecrate— we can not hallow this ground. The brave men, living and dead, who struggled here, have consecrated it, far above our poor power to add or detract. The world will little note, nor long remember, what we say here, but can never forget what they did here. It is for us, the living, rather to be dedicated here to the unfinished work which they have, thus far, so nobly carried on. It is rather for us to be here dedicated to the great task remaining before us — that from these honored dead we take increased devotion to that cause for which they here gave the last full measure of devotion — that we here highly resolve that these dead shall not have died in vain; that this nation shall have a new birth of freedom; and that this government of the people, by the people, for the people, shall not perish from the earth.

There are five known manuscript versions of Lincoln's "Gettysburg Address." This manuscript, known as the Hay Draft, features Lincoln's handwritten corrections. It was discovered in 1906, during a search for the "original manuscript" of the Address among the papers of John Hay, Lincoln's personal secretary.

James McBride

Hip-Hop Planet

Writer, journalist, and musician **JAMES McBRIDE** (b. 1957) grew up in Harlem in New York City, the son of a black father and a white, Jewish mother, and the eighth of twelve siblings. The title of his best-selling memoir, *The Color of Water: A Black Man's Tribute to His White Mother* (1996), refers to the answer his mother gave him when he asked about the color of God's skin. McBride's first novel, *Miracle of St. Anna* (2002), has been made into a film by Spike Lee. His second novel, *Song Yet Sung* (2008), set in pre–Civil War Maryland, is the story of a slave girl who can see the future, and his most recent book, released in 2013, is a comic novel called *The Good Lord Bird*. It won the 2013 National Book Award for fiction.

McBride began his dual career as journalist and musician early, studying composition at the Oberlin Conservatory of Music in Ohio and receiving his master's in journalism from Columbia University in New York at age 22. He has been a staff writer for the *Washington Post*, *People* magazine, and the *Boston Globe*, and he has written articles for the *New York Times*, *Essence*, *Rolling Stone*, and *National Geographic*, where his essay "Hip-Hop Planet" appeared in April 2007. McBride is a composer, lyricist, producer, and performer, playing tenor saxophone. He has written for

> "The nice thing about rap music, . . . good rap that's straight ahead and deals with truth really gets to the point and takes you places, just like a good book will. . . . It's all storytelling."

such music luminaries as Anita Baker, Grover Washington Jr., and Gary Burton, and he has recorded and performed with numerous jazz and pop artists. His collaboration with Ed Shockly on the musical *Bobos* won the Stephen Sondheim Award and the Richard Rodgers Foundation Horizon Award. He holds several honorary doctorates and was appointed a Distinguished Writer in Residence at New York University in 2005. He is married with three children and lives in Pennsylvania and New York.

McBride often talks about writing in the context of music, likening writing fiction to playing jazz and, in an interview with Powell's Books, rap music to storytelling: "The nice thing about rap music, and I know people give rap a bad rap, good rap that's straight ahead and deals with truth really gets to the point and takes you places, just like a good book will. And it's all valid. It's no more or less valid than Def Leppard or Henri Salvador, the French singer. It's all storytelling."

THIS IS MY NIGHTMARE: My daughter comes home with a guy and says, "Dad, we're getting married." And he's a rapper, with a mouthful of gold teeth, a do-rag on his head, muscles popping out of his arms, and a thug attitude. And then the nightmare gets deeper, because before you know it, I'm hearing the pitter-patter of little feet, their offspring, cascading through my living room, cascading through my life, drowning me with the sound of my own hypocrisy, because when I was young, I was a knucklehead, too, hearing my own music, my own sounds. And so I curse the day I saw his face, which is a reflection of my own, and I rue the day I heard his name, because I realize to my horror that rap—music seemingly without melody, sensibility, instruments, verse, or harmony, music with no beginning, end, or middle, music that doesn't even seem to be music—rules the world. It is no longer my world. It is his world. And I live in it. I live on a hip-hop planet.

HIGH-STEPPING

I remember when I first heard rap. I was standing in the kitchen at a party in Harlem. It was 1980. A friend of mine named Bill had just gone on the blink. He slapped a guy, a total stranger, in the face right in front of me. I can't remember why. Bill was a fellow student. He was short-circuiting. Problem was, the guy he slapped was a big guy, dude wearing a do-rag who'd crashed the party with three friends, and, judging by the fury on their faces, there would be no Martin Luther King moments in our immediate future.

There were no white people in the room, though I confess I wished there had been, if only to hide the paleness of my own frightened face. We were black and Latino students about to graduate from Columbia University's journalism school, having learned the whos, whats, wheres, and whys of American reporting. But the real storytellers of the American experience came from the world of the guy that Bill had just slapped. They lived less than a mile from us in the South Bronx. They had no journalism degrees. No money. No credibility. What they did have, however, was talent.

Earlier that night, somebody tossed a record on the turntable, which sent my fellow students stumbling onto the dance floor, howling with delight, and made me, a jazz lover, cringe. It sounded like a broken record. It was a version of an old hit record called "Good Times," the same four bars looped over and over. And on top of this loop, a kid spouted a rhyme about how he was the best disc jockey in the world. It was called "Rapper's Delight." I thought it was the most ridiculous thing I'd ever heard. More ridiculous than Bill slapping that stranger.

Bill survived that evening, but in many ways, I did not. For the next 26   5
years, I high-stepped past that music the way you step over a crack in the sidewalk. I heard it pounding out of cars and alleyways from Paris to Abidjan, yet I never listened. It came rumbling out of boomboxes from Johannesburg to Osaka, yet I pretended not to hear. I must have strolled past the corner

of St. James Place and Fulton Street in my native Brooklyn where a fat kid named Christopher Wallace, aka Biggie Smalls, stood amusing friends with rhyme, a hundred times, yet I barely noticed. I high-stepped away from that music for 26 years because it was everything I thought it was, and more than I ever dreamed it would be, but mostly, because it held everything I wanted to leave behind.

In doing so, I missed the most important cultural event of my lifetime.

Not since the advent of swing jazz in the 1930s has an American music exploded across the world with such overwhelming force. Not since the Beatles invaded America and Elvis packed up his blue suede shoes has a music crashed against the world with such outrage. This defiant culture of song, graffiti, and dance, collectively known as hip-hop, has ripped popular music from its moorings in every society it has permeated. In Brazil, rap rivals samba in popularity. In China, teens spray-paint graffiti on the Great Wall. In France it has been blamed, unfairly, for the worst civil unrest that country has seen in decades.

Its structure is unique, complex, and at times bewildering. Whatever music it eats becomes part of its vocabulary, and as the commercial world falls into place behind it to gobble up the powerful slop in its wake, it meta-morphoses into the Next Big Thing. It is a music that defies definition, yet defines our collective societies in immeasurable ways. To many of my gen-eration, despite all attempts to exploit it, belittle it, numb it, classify it, and analyze it, hip-hop remains an enigma, a clarion call, a cry of "I am" from the youth of the world. We'd be wise, I suppose, to start paying attention.

BURNING MAN

Imagine a burning man. He is on fire. He runs into the room. You put out the flames. Then another burning man arrives. You put him out and go about your business. Then two, three, four, five, ten appear. You extinguish them all, send them to the hospital. Then imagine no one bothers to examine why the men caught fire in the first place. That is the story of hip-hop.

It is a music dipped in the boiling cauldron of race and class, and for   10 that reason it is clouded with mystics, snake oil salesmen, two-bit scholars, race-baiters, and sneaker salesmen, all professing to know the facts, to be "real," when the reality of race is like shifting sand, dependent on time, place, circumstance, and who's telling the history. Here's the real story: In the mid-1970s, New York City was nearly broke. The public school system cut funding for the arts drastically. Gone were the days when you could wander into the band room, rent a clarinet for a minimal fee, and march it home to squeal on it and drive your parents nuts.

The kids of the South Bronx and Harlem came up with something else. In the summer of 1973, at 1595 East 174th Street in the Bronx River Houses, a black teenager named Afrika Bambaataa stuck a speaker in his mother's first-floor living room window, ran a wire to the turntable in his bedroom, and set the housing project of 3,000 people alight with party music. At the same time, a Jamaican teenager named Kool DJ Herc was starting up the scene in the East Bronx, while a technical whiz named Grandmaster Flash was rising to prominence a couple of miles south. The Bronx became a music magnet for Puerto Ricans, Jamaicans, Dominicans, and black Americans from the surrounding areas. Fab 5 Freddy, Kurtis Blow, and Melle Mel were only a few of the pioneers. Grand Wizard Theodore, Kool DJ AJ, the Cold Crush Brothers, Spoony Gee, and the Rock Steady Crew of B-boys showed up to "battle"—dance, trade quips and rhymes, check out each other's records and equipment—not knowing as they strolled through the doors of the community center near Bambaataa's mother's apartment that they were writing musical history. Among them was an MC named Lovebug Starski, who was said to utter the phrase "hip-hop" between breaks to keep time.

This is how it worked: One guy, the DJ, played records on two turntables. One guy—or girl—served as master of ceremonies, or MC. The DJs learned to move the record back and forth under the needle to create a "scratch," or to drop the needle on the record when the beat was the hottest, playing "the break" over and over to keep the folks dancing. The MCs "rapped" over the music to keep the party going. One MC sought to outchat the other. Dance styles were created—"locking" and "popping" and "breaking." Graffiti artists spread the word of the "I" because the music was all about identity: I am the best. I spread the most love in the Bronx, in Harlem, in Queens. The focus initially was not on the MCs, but on the dancers, or B-boys. Commercial radio ignored it. DJs sold mix tapes out of the back of station wagons. "Rapper's Delight" by the Sugarhill Gang—the song I first heard at that face-slapping party in Harlem—broke the music onto radio in 1979.

That is the short history.

The long history is that spoken-word music made its way here on slave ships from West Africa centuries ago: Ethnomusicologists trace hip-hop's roots to the dance, drum, and song of West African griots, or storytellers, its pairing of word and music the manifestation of the painful journey of slaves who survived the middle passage. The ring shouts, field hollers, and spirituals[1] of early slaves drew on common elements of African music, such as call and response and improvisation. "Speech-song has been part of black culture for a long, long time," says Samuel A. Floyd, director of the Center for Black Music Research at Columbia College in Chicago. The "dozens," "toasts," and "signifying" of black Americans—verbal dueling, rhyming, self-deprecating tales, and stories of blacks outsmarting whites—were defensive, empowering strategies.

You can point to jazz musicians such as Oscar Brown, Jr., Edgar "Eddie" Jefferson, and Louis Armstrong, and blues greats such as John Lee Hooker, and easily find the foreshadowing of rap music in the verbal play of their

15

---

[1] ***ring shouts, field hollers, and spirituals:*** Various types of music and circle dances that drew from African sources but were adapted by slave communities as they developed new forms of expression in the pre–Civil War American South. —EDS.

The Sugarhill Gang, an American rap group active since the 1970s: (left to right) Michael "Wonder Mike" Wright, Guy "Master Gee" O'Brien, and Henry "Big Bank Hank" Jackson.

work. Black performers such as poet Nikki Giovanni and Gil Scott-Heron, a pianist and vocalist who put spoken political lyrics to music (most famously in "The Revolution Will Not Be Televised"), elevated spoken word to a new level.

But the artist whose work arguably laid the groundwork for rap as we know it was Amiri Baraka, a beat poet out of Allen Ginsberg's Greenwich Village scene. In the 1950s and '60s, Baraka performed with shrieks, howls, cries, stomps, verse floating ahead of or behind the rhythm, sometimes in staccato syncopation. It was performance art, delivered in a dashiki and Afro, in step with the anger of a bold and sometimes frightening nationalistic black movement, and it inspired what might be considered the first rap group, the Last Poets.

I was 13 when I first heard the Last Poets in 1970. They scared me. To black America, they were like the relatives you hoped wouldn't show up at your barbecue because the boss was there—the old Aunt Clementine who would arrive, get drunk, and pull out her dentures. My parents refused to allow us to play their music in our house—so my siblings waited until my parents went to work and played it anyway. They were the first musical group I heard to use the N-word on a record, with songs like "N------ Are Scared of Revolution." In a world where blacks were evolving from "Negroes" to "blacks," and the assassinations of civil rights leaders Malcolm X and Martin Luther King, Jr., still reverberated in the air like a shotgun blast, the

Last Poets embodied black power. Their records consisted of percussion and spoken-word rhyme. They were wildly popular in my neighborhood. Their debut recording sold 400,000 records in three months, says Last Poet member Umar Bin Hassan. "No videos, no radio play, strictly word of mouth." The group's demise coincided with hip-hop's birth in the 1970s.

It's unlikely that the Last Poets ever dreamed the revolution they sang of would take the form it has. "We were about the movement," Abiodun Oyewoke, a founder of the group, says. "A lot of today's rappers have talent. But a lot of them are driving the car in the wrong direction."

THE CROSSOVER

Highways wrap around the city of Dayton, Ohio, like a ribbon bowtied on a box of chocolates from the local Esther Price candy factory. They have six ladies at the plant who do just that: Tie ribbons around boxes all day. Henry Rosenkranz can tell you about it. "I love candy," says Henry, a slim white teenager in glasses and a hairnet, as he strolls the factory, bucket in hand. His full-time after-school job is mopping the floors.

Henry is a model American teenager—and the prototypical consumer at   20 which the hip-hop industry is squarely aimed, which has his parents sitting up in their seats. The music that was once the purview of black America has gone white and gone commercial all at once. A sea of white faces now rises up to greet rap groups as they perform, many of them teenagers like Henry, a NASCAR fanatic and self-described redneck. "I live in Old North Dayton," he says. "It's a white, redneck area. But hip-hop is so prominent with country people . . . if you put them behind a curtain and hear them talk, you won't know if they're black or white. There's a guy I work with, when Kanye West sings about a gold digger, he can relate because he's paying alimony and child support."

Obviously, it's not just working-class whites, but also affluent, suburban kids who identify with this music with African-American roots. A white 16-year-old hollering rap lyrics at the top of his lungs from the driver's seat of his dad's late-model Lexus may not have the same rationale to howl at the moon as a working-class kid whose parents can't pay for college, yet his own anguish is as real to him as it gets. What attracts white kids to this music is the same thing that prompted outraged congressmen to decry jazz during the 1920s and Tipper Gore[2] to campaign decades later against violent and sexually explicit lyrics: life on the other side of the tracks; its "cool" or illicit factor, which black Americans, like it or not, are always perceived to possess.

Hip-hop has continually changed form, evolving from party music to social commentary with the 1982 release of Grandmaster Flash and the

---

[2] ***Tipper Gore:*** Mary Elizabeth ("Tipper") Gore is the ex-wife of former U.S. vice president Al Gore. In 1985, she founded an organization that advocated putting warning labels on albums with explicit lyrics. —EDS.

Furious Five's "The Message." Today, alternative hip-hop artists continue to produce socially conscious songs, but most commercial rappers spout violent lyrics that debase women and gays. Beginning with the so-called gangsta rap of the '90s, popularized by the still unsolved murders of rappers Biggie Smalls and Tupac Shakur, the genre has become dominated by rappers who brag about their lives of crime. 50 Cent, the hip-hop star of the moment, trumpets his sexual exploits and boasts that he has been shot nine times.

"People call hip-hop the MTV music now," scoffs Chuck D., of Public Enemy, known for its overtly political rap. "It's Big Brother controlling you. To slip something in there that's indigenous to the roots, that pays homage to the music that came before us, it's the Mount Everest of battles."

Most rap songs unabashedly function as walking advertisements for luxury cars, designer clothes, and liquor. Agenda Inc., a "pop culture brand strategy agency" listed Mercedes-Benz as the number one brand mentioned in *Billboard*'s top 20 singles in 2005. Hip-hop sells so much Hennessy cognac, listed at number six, that the French makers, deader than yesterday's beer a decade ago, are now rolling in suds. The company even sponsored a contest to win a visit to its plant in France with a famous rapper.

In many ways, the music represents an old dream. It's the pot of gold to 25 millions of kids like Henry, who quietly agonizes over how his father slaves 14 hours a day at two tool-and-die machine jobs to make ends meet. Like teenagers across the world, he fantasizes about working in the hip-hop business and making millions himself.

"My parents hate hip-hop," Henry says, motoring his 1994 Dodge Shadow through traffic on the way home from work on a hot October afternoon. "But I can listen to Snoop Dogg and hear him call women whores, and I know he has a wife and children at home. It's just a fantasy. Everyone has the urge deep down to be a bad guy or a bad girl. Everyone likes to talk the talk, but not everyone will walk the walk."

FULL CIRCLE

You breathe in and breathe out a few times and you are there. Eight hours and a wake-up shake on the flight from New York, and you are on the tarmac in Dakar, Senegal. Welcome to Africa. The assignment: Find the roots of hip-hop. The music goes full circle. The music comes home to Africa. That whole bit. Instead it was the old reporter's joke: You go out to cover a story and the story covers you. The stench of poverty in my nostrils was so strong it pulled me to earth like a hundred-pound ring in my nose. Dakar's Sandaga market is full of "local color" — unless you live there. It was packed and filthy, stalls full of new merchandise surrounded by shattered pieces of life everywhere, broken pipes, bicycle handlebars, fruit flies, soda bottles, beggars, dogs, cell phones. A teenager beggar, his body malformed by polio, crawled by on hands and feet, like a spider. He said, "Hey brother, help me." When I looked into his eyes, they were a bottomless ocean.

The Hotel Teranga is a fortress, packed behind a concrete wall where beggars gather at the front gate. The French tourists march past them, the women in high heels and stonewashed jeans. They sidle through downtown Dakar like royalty, haggling in the market, swimming in the hotel pool with their children, a scene that resembles Birmingham, Alabama, in the 1950s—the blacks serving, the whites partying. Five hundred yards away, Africans eat off the sidewalk and sell peanuts for a pittance. There is a restlessness, a deep sense of something gone wrong in the air.

The French can't smell it, even though they've had a mouthful back home. A good amount of the torching of Paris suburbs in October 2005 was courtesy of the children of immigrants from former French African colonies, exhausted from being bottled up in housing projects for generations with no job prospects. They telegraphed the punch in their music—France is the second largest hip-hop market in the world—but the message was ignored. Around the globe, rap music has become a universal expression of outrage, its macho pose borrowed from commercial hip-hop in the U.S.

In Dakar, where every kid is a microphone and turntable away from 30
squalor, and American rapper Tupac Shakur's picture hangs in market stalls of folks who don't understand English, rap is king. There are hundreds of rap groups in Senegal today. French television crews troop in and out of Dakar's nightclubs filming the kora harp lute[3] and *tama*[4] talking drum with regularity. But beneath the drumming and the dance lessons and the jingling sound of tourist change, there is a quiet rage, a desperate fury among the Senegalese, some of whom seem to bear an intense dislike of their former colonial rulers.

"We know all about French history," says Abdou Ba, a Senegalese producer and musician. "We know about their kings, their castles, their art, their music. We know everything about them. But they don't know much about us."

Assane N'Diaye, 19, loves hip-hop music. Before he left his Senegalese village to work as a DJ in Dakar, he was a fisherman, just like his father, like his father's father before him. Tall, lean, with a muscular build and a handsome chocolate face, Assane became a popular DJ, but the equipment he used was borrowed, and when his friend took it back, success eluded him. He has returned home to Toubab Dialaw, about 25 miles south of Dakar, a village marked by a huge boulder, perhaps 40 feet high, facing the Atlantic Ocean.

About a century and a half ago, a local ruler led a group of people fleeing slave traders to this place. He was told by a white trader to come here, to Toubab Dialaw. When he arrived, the slavers followed. A battle ensued. The ruler fought bravely but was killed. The villagers buried him by the sea and marked his grave with a small stone, and over the years it is said to

---

3 **kora harp lute:** In West Africa, a popular 21-string instrument played with both hands and used by storytellers and bards.—EDS.

4 **tama:** A flexible West African drum, known as a "talking drum," popular in Senegal; it is placed under the shoulder and can be manipulated to produce a wide range of tones and sounds.—EDS.

have sprouted like a tree planted by God. It became a huge, arching boulder that stares out to sea, protecting the village behind it. When the fishermen went deep out to sea, the boulder was like a lighthouse that marked the way home. The Great Rock of Toubab Dialaw is said to hold a magic spirit, a spirit that Assane N'Diaye believes in.

In the shadow of the Great Rock, Assane has built a small restaurant, Chez Las, decorated with hundreds of seashells. It is where he lives his hip-hop dream. At night, he and his brother and cousin stand by the Great Rock and face the sea. They meditate. They pray. Then they write rap lyrics that are worlds away from the bling-bling culture of today's commercial hip-hoppers. They write about their lives as village fishermen, the scarcity of catch forcing them to fish in deeper and deeper waters, the hardship of fishing for 8, 10, 14 days at a time in an open pirogue in rainy season, the high fee they pay to rent the boat, and the paltry price their catches fetch on the market. They write about the humiliation of poverty, watching their town sprout up around them with rich Dakarians and richer French. And they write about the relatives who leave in the morning and never return, surrendered to the sea, sharks, and God.

The dream, of course, is to make a record. They have their own demo,   35
their own logo, and their own name, Salam T. D. (for Toubab Dialaw). But rap music represents a deeper dream: a better life. "We want money to help our parents," Assane says over dinner. "We watch our mothers boil water to cook and have nothing to put in the pot."

He fingers his food lightly. "Rap doesn't belong to American culture," he says. "It belongs here. It has always existed here, because of our pain and our hardships and our suffering."

On this cool evening in a restaurant above their village, these young men, clad in baseball caps and T-shirts, appear no different from their African-American counterparts, with one exception. After a dinner of chicken and rice, Assane says something in Wolof[5] to the others. Silently and without ceremony, they take every bit of the leftover dinner—the half-eaten bread, rice, pieces of chicken, the chicken bones—and dump them into a plastic bag to give to the children in the village. They silently rise from the table and proceed outside. The last I see of them, their regal figures are outlined in the dim light of the doorway, heading out to the darkened village, holding on to that bag as though it held money.

THE CITY OF GODS

Some call the Bronx River Houses the City of Gods, though if God has been by lately, he must've slipped out for a chicken sandwich. The 10 drab, red-brick buildings spread out across 14 acres, coming into view as you drive east across the East 174th Street Bridge. The Bronx is the hallowed holy

---

5 **Wolof:** The most widely used language in Senegal; "banana" is a Wolof word. —EDS.

ground of hip-hop, the place where it all began. Visitors take tours through this neighborhood now, care of a handful of fortyish "old-timers," who point out the high and low spots of hip-hop's birthplace.

It is a telling metaphor for the state of America's racial landscape that you need a permit to hold a party in the same parks and playgrounds that produced the music that changed the world. The rap artists come and go, but the conditions that produced them linger. Forty percent of New York City's black males are jobless. One in three black males born in 2001 will end up in prison. The life expectancy of black men in the U.S. ranks below that of men in Sri Lanka and Colombia. It took a massive hurricane in New Orleans for the United States to wake up to its racial realities.

That is why, after 26 years, I have come to embrace this music I tried so   40
hard to ignore. Hip-hop culture is not mine. Yet I own it. Much of it I hate. Yet I love it, the good of it. To confess a love for a music that, at least in part, embraces violence is no easy matter, but then again our national anthem talks about bombs bursting in air, and I love that song, too. At its best, hip-hop lays bare the empty moral cupboard that is our generation's legacy. This music that once made visible the inner culture of America's greatest social problem, its legacy of slavery, has taken the dream deferred to a global scale. Today, 2 percent of the Earth's adult population owns more than 50 percent of its household wealth, and indigenous cultures are swallowed with the rapidity of a teenager gobbling a bag of potato chips. The music is calling. Over the years, the instruments change, but the message is the same. The drums are pounding out a warning. They are telling us something. Our children can hear it.

The question is: Can we? ▣

The Reader's Presence

1. "Hip-Hop Planet" features a popular topic covered by an experienced journalist. What characteristics of the selection seem to belong to the personal essay? What characteristics seem to belong to a journalistic article? How are these two components of the selection brought together? Would you prefer if the selection used only a single method — for example, interviews and information told in the third person without a personal response? Explain why or why not.

2. Discuss McBride's attitude toward hip-hop. Why did he dislike it at first? What did he come to admire about it? What does McBride still not like about the music? What does he think about today's commercial rap artists? In what ways do they differ from the groups McBride enjoys most? How would you describe the differences? Do those differences matter to you?

3. **CONNECTIONS:** Compare McBride's evaluation of hip-hop culture to Joel Stein's evaluation of millennials in "The New Greatest Generation" (page 565). After considering each essay carefully, summarize all the points on which McBride and Stein would agree. What do you think would be their major points of disagreement? Which account of youth do you find more engaging and convincing? Support each point you make with specific references to each text.

N. Scott Momaday

THE WAY TO RAINY MOUNTAIN

N. SCOTT MOMADAY (b. 1934) was born on a Kiowa Indian reservation in Oklahoma and grew up surrounded by the cultural traditions of his people. He has taught at the University of California, Berkeley; Stanford University; Columbia University; Princeton University; and the University of Arizona. His first novel, *House Made of Dawn* (1968), won a Pulitzer Prize. The author of poetry and autobiography, Momaday has edited a collection of Kiowa oral literature. His books include *Ancestral Voice: Conversations with N. Scott Momaday* (1989), *The Ancient Child* (1989), *In the Presence of the Sun: Stories and Poems* (1991), *Circle of Wonder: A Native American Christmas Story* (1994), *The Man Made of Words: Essays, Stories, Passages* (1997), and *In the Bear's House* (1999). "The Way to Rainy Mountain" appears as the introduction to the book of that name,

published in 1969. Among his more recent books is a collection of Momaday's plays, *Three Plays: The Indolent Boy, Children of the Sun, and the Moon in Two Windows* (2007); *Four Arrows and Magpie* (2006), a book

> "I listen to what I write. I work with it until it is what I want it to be in my hearing."

for young children, which Momaday also illustrated; and *Again the Far Morning: New and Selected Poems* (2011). In 2007, Momaday was awarded the National Medal of Arts "for his writings and his work that celebrate and preserve Native American art and oral tradition."

Momaday thinks of himself as a storyteller. When asked to compare his written voice with his speaking voice, he replied, "My physical voice is something that bears on my writing in an important way. I listen to what I write. I work with it until it is what I want it to be in my hearing. I think that the voice of my writing is very much like the voice of my speaking. And I think in both cases it's distinctive. At least, I mean for it to be. I think that most good writers have individual voices, and that the best writers are those whose voices are most distinctive—most recognizably individual."

A SINGLE KNOLL rises out of the plain in Oklahoma, north and west of the Wichita Range. For my people, the Kiowas, it is an old landmark, and they gave it the name Rainy Mountain. The hardest winter in the world is there. Winter brings blizzards, hot tornadic winds arise in the spring, and in summer the prairie is an anvil's edge. The grass turns brittle and brown, and it cracks beneath your feet. There are green belts along the rivers and creeks, linear groves of hickory and pecan, willow and witch hazel. At a distance in July or August, the steaming foliage seems almost to writhe in fire. Great green and yellow grasshoppers are everywhere in the tall grass, popping up like corn to sting the flesh, and tortoises crawl about on the red earth, going nowhere in plenty of time. Loneliness is an aspect of the land. All things in the plain are isolate; there is no confusion of objects in the eye, but *one* hill or *one* tree or *one* man. To look upon that landscape in the early morning, with the sun at your back, is to lose the sense of proportion. Your imagination comes to life, and this, you think, is where Creation was begun.

I returned to Rainy Mountain in July. My grandmother had died in the spring, and I wanted to be at her grave. She had lived to be very old and at last infirm. Her only living daughter was with her when she died, and I was told that in death her face was that of a child.

I like to think of her as a child. When she was born, the Kiowas were living the last great moment of their history. For more than a hundred years they had controlled the open range from the Smoky Hill River to the Red, from the headwaters of the Canadian to the fork of the Arkansas and Cimarron. In alliance with the Comanches, they had ruled the whole of the

Kiowa Holy Place, Rainy Mountain, Oklahoma.

Rainy Mountain, Kiowa Holy Place, Oklahoma, photo copyright by Joan Frederick

southern Plains. War was their sacred business, and they were among the finest horsemen the world has ever known. But warfare for the Kiowas was preeminently a matter of disposition rather than of survival, and they never understood the grim, unrelenting advance of the U.S. Cavalry. When at last, divided and ill-provisioned, they were driven onto the Staked Plains in the cold rains of autumn, they fell into panic. In Palo Duro Canyon they abandoned their crucial stores to pillage and had nothing then but their lives. In order to save themselves, they surrendered to the soldiers of Fort Sill and were imprisoned in the old stone corral that now stands as a military museum. My grandmother was spared the humiliation of those high gray walls by eight or ten years, but she must have known from birth the affliction of defeat, the dark brooding of old warriors.

Her name was Aho, and she belonged to the last culture to evolve in North America. Her forebears came down from the high country in western Montana nearly three centuries ago. They were a mountain people, a mysterious tribe of hunters whose language has never been positively classified in any major group. In the late seventeenth century they began a long migration to the south and east. It was a journey toward the dawn, and it led to a golden age. Along the way the Kiowas were befriended by the Crows, who gave them the culture and religion of the Plains. They acquired horses, and their ancient nomadic spirit was suddenly free of the ground. They acquired Tai-me, the sacred Sun Dance doll, from that moment the object and symbol of their worship, and so shared in the divinity of the sun. Not least, they acquired the sense of destiny, therefore courage and pride. When they entered upon the southern Plains they had been transformed. No longer were they slaves to the simple necessity of survival; they were a lordly and dangerous society of fighters and thieves, hunters and priests of the sun. According to their origin myth, they entered the world through a hollow log. From one point of view, their migration was the fruit of an old prophecy, for indeed they emerged from a sunless world.

Although my grandmother lived out her long life in the shadow of Rainy   5
Mountain, the immense landscape of the continental interior lay like memory in her blood. She could tell of the Crows, whom she had never seen, and of the Black Hills, where she had never been. I wanted to see in reality what she had seen more perfectly in the mind's eye, and traveled fifteen hundred miles to begin my pilgrimage.

Yellowstone, it seemed to me, was the top of the world, a region of deep lakes and dark timber, canyons and waterfalls. But, beautiful as it is, one might have the sense of confinement there. The skyline in all directions is close at hand, the high wall of the woods and deep cleavages of shade. There is a perfect freedom in the mountains, but it belongs to the eagle and the elk, the badger and the bear. The Kiowas reckoned their stature by the distance they could see, and they were bent and blind in the wilderness.

Descending eastward, the highland meadows are a stairway to the plain. In July the inland slope of the Rockies is luxuriant with flax and buckwheat, stonecrop and larkspur. The earth unfolds and the limit of the land recedes. Clusters of trees, and animals grazing far in the distance, cause the vision to reach away and wonder to build upon the mind. The sun follows a longer course in the day, and the sky is immense beyond all comparison. The great billowing clouds that sail upon it are shadows that move upon the grain like water, dividing light. Farther down, in the land of the Crows and Blackfeet, the plain is yellow. Sweet clover takes hold of the hills and bends upon itself to cover and seal the soil. There the Kiowas paused on their way; they had come to the place where they must change their lives. The sun is at home on the plains. Precisely there does it have the certain character of a god. When the Kiowas came to the land of the Crows, they could see the dark lees of the hills at dawn across the Bighorn River, the profusion of light on the grain shelves, the oldest deity ranging after the solstices. Not yet would they veer southward to the caldron of the land that lay below; they must wean their blood from the northern winter and hold the mountains a while longer in their view. They bore Tai-me in procession to the east.

A dark mist lay over the Black Hills, and the land was like iron. At the top of the ridge I caught sight of Devil's Tower upthrust against the gray sky as if in the birth of time the core of the earth had broken through its crust and the motion of the world was begun. There are things in nature that engender an awful quiet in the heart of man; Devil's Tower is one of them. Two centuries ago, because they could not do otherwise, the Kiowas made a legend at the base of the rock. My grandmother said:

> Eight children were there at play, seven sisters and their brother. Suddenly the boy was struck dumb; he trembled and began to run upon his hands and feet. His fingers became claws, and his body was covered with fur. Directly there was a bear where the boy had been. The sisters were terrified; they ran, and the bear ran after them. They came to the stump of a great tree, and the tree spoke to them. It bade them climb upon it, and as they did so it began to rise into the air. The bear came to kill them, but they were just beyond its reach. It reared against the tree and scored the bark all around with its claws. The seven sisters were borne into the sky, and they became the stars of the Big Dipper.

From that moment, and so long as the legend lives, the Kiowas have kinsmen in the night sky. Whatever they were in the mountains, they could be no more. However tenuous their well-being, however much they had suffered and would suffer again, they had found a way out of the wilderness.

My grandmother had a reverence for the sun, a holy regard that now is all but gone out of mankind. There was a wariness in her, and an ancient awe. She was a Christian in her later years, but she had come a long way about, and she never forgot her birthright. As a child she had been to the Sun Dances; she had taken part in those annual rites, and by them she had learned the restoration of her people in the presence of Tai-me. She was about seven when the last Kiowa Sun Dance was held in 1887 in the Washita River above Rainy Mountain Creek. The buffalo were gone. In order to consummate the ancient sacrifice—to impale the head of a buffalo bull upon the medicine tree—a delegation of old men journeyed into Texas, there to beg and barter for an animal from the Goodnight herd. She was ten when the Kiowas came together for the last time as a living Sun Dance culture. They could find no buffalo; they had to hang an old hide from the sacred tree. Before the dance could begin, a company of soldiers rode out from Fort Sill under orders to disperse the tribe. Forbidden without cause the essential act of their faith, having seen the wild herds slaughtered and left to rot upon the ground, the Kiowas backed away forever from the medicine tree. That was July 20, 1890, at the great bend of the Washita. My grandmother was there. Without bitterness, and for as long as she lived, she bore a vision of deicide.

Now that I can have her only in memory, I see my grandmother in the   10
several postures that were peculiar to her: standing at the wood stove on a winter morning and turning meat in a great iron skillet; sitting at the south window, bent above her beadwork, and afterwards, when her vision failed, looking down for a long time into the fold of her hands; going out upon a cane, very slowly as she did when the weight of age came upon her; praying. I remember her most often at prayer. She made long, rambling prayers out of suffering and hope, having seen many things. I was never sure that I had the right to hear, so exclusive were they of all mere custom and company. The last time I saw her she prayed standing by the side of her bed at night, naked to the waist, the light of a kerosene lamp moving upon her dark skin. Her long, black hair, always drawn and braided in the day, lay upon her shoulders and against her breasts like a shawl. I do not speak Kiowa, and I never understood her prayers, but there was something inherently sad in the sound, some merest hesitation upon the syllables of sorrow. She began in a high and descending pitch, exhausting her breath to silence; then again and again—and always the same intensity of effort, of something that is, and is not, like urgency in the human voice. Transported so in the dancing light among the shadows of her room, she seemed beyond the reach of time. But that was illusion; I think I knew then that I should not see her again.

Houses are like sentinels in the plain, old keepers of the weather watch. There, in a very little while, wood takes on the appearance of great age. All colors wear soon away in the wind and rain, and then the wood is burned gray and the grain appears and the nails turn red with rust. The windowpanes are black and opaque; you imagine there is nothing within, and indeed there are many ghosts, bones given up to the land. They stand here and there against the sky, and you approach them for a longer time than you expect. They belong in the distance; it is their domain.

Once there was a lot of sound in my grandmother's house, a lot of coming and going, feasting and talk. The summers there were full of excitement and reunion. The Kiowas are a summer people; they abide the cold and keep to themselves, but when the season turns and the land becomes warm and vital they cannot hold still; an old love of going returns upon them. The aged visitors who came to my grandmother's house when I was a child were made of lean and leather, and they bore themselves upright. They wore great black hats and bright ample shirts that shook in the wind. They rubbed fat upon their hair and wound their braids with strips of colored cloth. Some of them painted their faces and carried the scars of old and cherished enmities. They were an old council of warlords, come to remind and be reminded of who they were. Their wives and daughters served them well. The women might indulge themselves; gossip was at once the mark and compensation of their servitude. They made loud and elaborate talk among themselves, full of jest and gesture, fright and false alarm. They went abroad in fringed and flow-ered shawls, bright beadwork and German silver. They were at home in the kitchen, and they prepared meals that were banquets.

There were frequent prayer meetings, and great nocturnal feasts. When I was a child I played with my cousins outside, where the lamplight fell upon the ground and the singing of the old people rose up around us and car-ried away into the darkness. There were a lot of good things to eat, a lot of laughter and surprise. And afterwards, when the quiet returned, I lay down with my grandmother and could hear the frogs away by the river and feel the motion of the air.

Now there is a funereal silence in the rooms, the endless wake of some final word. The walls have closed in upon my grandmother's house. When I returned to it in mourning, I saw for the first time in my life how small it was. It was late at night, and there was a white moon, nearly full. I sat for a long time on the stone steps by the kitchen door. From there I could see out across the land; I could see the long row of trees by the creek, the low light upon the rolling plains, and the stars of the big dipper. Once I looked at the moon and caught sight of a strange thing. A cricket had perched upon the hand-rail, only a few inches away from me. My line of vision was such that the creature filled the moon like a fossil. It had gone there, I thought, to live and die, for there, of all places, was its small definition made whole and eternal. A warm wind rose up and purled like the longing within me.

The next morning I awoke at dawn and went out on the dirt road to Rainy Mountain. It was already hot, and the grasshoppers began to fill the air. Still, it was early in the morning, and the birds sang out of the shadows. The long yellow grass on the mountain shone in the bright light, and a scis-sortail hied above the land. There, where it ought to be, at the end of a long and legendary way, was my grandmother's grave. Here and there on the dark stones were ancestral names. Looking back once, I saw the mountain and came away. 🔳

15

The Reader's Presence

1. Momaday tells several stories in this selection, including the history of the Kiowa people, the story of his grandmother's life and death, the story of his homecoming, and the legend of Devil's Tower. How does each story overlap and intertwine with the others? What forces compel the telling or creation of each story? What needs

do the stories satisfy? Look, for example, at the legend related in paragraph 8. The Kiowas made this legend "because they could not do otherwise." Why could they have not done otherwise? How does this embedded legend enhance and complicate the other stories Momaday tells here?

2. From the beginning of this essay, Momaday sets his remarks very firmly in space and then in time. Discuss the importance of physical space in this essay. Why does Momaday take the journey to Rainy Mountain—a fifteen-hundred-mile "pilgrimage" (paragraph 5)? Why does he say that his grandmother's vision of this landscape is more nearly perfect than his, even though she has never actually seen the landscape he travels? Consider the many remarks about perspective, and change of perspective, that Momaday includes, as well as his remarks on proportion. What significance does he attach to these remarks? More generally, consider the temporal journeys that run parallel to the spatial journeys: the Kiowas' "journey toward the dawn [that] led to a golden age" (paragraph 4) and Momaday's own journeys that he relates in the essay. How would you characterize the sense of space and time and the relation between the two that are conveyed in this essay?

3. **VISUAL PRESENCE:**   Examine the photograph of the Kiowa Holy Place, Rainy Mountain (page 493). Compare the details in this photograph to Momaday's use of opulent and affectionate language in his essay. In which passages in his essay does Momaday come closest to evoking the splendor of the landscape? What specific features of the image capture its importance to the author and to the Kiowa people?

4. **CONNECTIONS:**   In the interview quoted in the introductory note to this selection, Momaday talks about capturing his speaking voice in his writing. What are some of the phrases and passages in this selection that make you hear the distinctive qualities of Momaday's voice as you read? Point to—and analyze—specific words and phrases to discuss how Momaday creates the effect he aims for. Compare Momaday's voice to Dorothy Allison's in "A Question of Class" (page 37). What techniques do both writers use to make their prose appealing to their reader's ear? Cite specific passages to support each point you make.

Azar Nafisi

FROM READING LOLITA IN TEHRAN

AZAR NAFISI (b. 1950) was raised in Tehran, Iran, and educated in England and the United States. Having returned to Iran in the 1970s to teach English literature, she experienced firsthand the revolution and its aftermath, when strict Islamic religious codes were imposed; the harshest restrictions were placed on women. Nafisi has said that "before the revolution I had an image of myself as a woman, as a writer, as an academician, as a person with a set of values." Afterward, even the smallest public gestures were forbidden, from kissing her husband in public to shaking hands with a colleague. Fearing she would "become someone who was a stranger to herself," Nafisi resigned her university position in 1995 and for two years took a group of her best students "underground" for weekly discussions of Western authors, including Vladimir Nabokov, the author of *Lolita* and the subject of Nafisi's scholarly work. *Reading Lolita in Tehran* (2003), the book she wrote about her experiences, has been translated into thirty-two languages, won multiple awards, and spent more than one hundred weeks on the *New York Times* best-seller list.

> "I think if a civilization or a culture does not take its own works of literature seriously it goes downhill. You need imagination in order to imagine a future that doesn't exist."

"Unfortunately you have to be deprived of something in order to understand its worth," Nafisi told an interviewer. "I think if a civilization or a culture does not take its own works of literature seriously it goes downhill. You need imagination in order to imagine a future that doesn't exist."

Nafisi left Iran with her family in 1997. She is currently a Visiting Fellow at the Foreign Policy Institute of the Johns Hopkins University School of Advanced International Studies and the director of the Dialogue Project, an education and policy initiative for the development of democracy and human rights in the Muslim world. This essay, adapted from *Reading Lolita in Tehran* (2003), first appeared in the *Chronicle of Higher Education*. She has since published a second memoir, *Things I've Been Silent About: Memories of a Prodigal Daughter* (2008), which focuses on her family.

IN THE FALL OF 1995, after resigning from my last academic post, I decided to indulge myself and fulfill a dream. I chose seven of my best and most committed students and invited them to come to my home every Thursday morning to discuss literature. They were all women — to teach a mixed class in the privacy of my home was too risky, even if we were discussing harmless works of fiction.

For nearly two years, almost every Thursday morning, rain or shine, they came to my house, and almost every time, I could not get over the shock of seeing them shed their mandatory veils and robes and burst into color. When my students came into that room, they took off more than their scarves and robes. Gradually, each one gained an outline and a shape, becoming her own inimitable self. Our world in that living room with its window framing my beloved Elburz Mountains became our sanctuary, our self-contained universe, mocking the reality of black-scarved, timid faces in the city that sprawled below.

The theme of the class was the relationship between fiction and reality. We would read Persian classical literature, such as the tales of our own lady of fiction, Scheherazade, from *A Thousand and One Nights*, along with Western classics — *Pride and Prejudice, Madame Bovary, Daisy Miller, The Dean's December*, and *Lolita*, the work of fiction that perhaps most resonated with our lives in the Islamic Republic of Iran. For the first time in many years, I felt a sense of anticipation that was not marred by tension: I would not need to go through the tortuous rituals that had marked my days when I taught at the university — rituals governing what I was forced to wear, how I was expected to act, the gestures I had to remember to control.

Life in the Islamic Republic was as capricious as the month of April, when short periods of sunshine would suddenly give way to showers and storms. It was unpredictable: The regime would go through cycles of some tolerance, followed by a crackdown. Now, in the mid-1990s, after a period of relative calm and so-called liberalization, we had again entered a time of hardships. Universities had once more become the targets of attack by the cultural purists, who were busy imposing stricter sets of laws, going so far as to segregate men and women in classes and punishing disobedient professors.

The University of Allameh Tabatabai, where I had been teaching since 1987, had been singled out as the most liberal university in Iran. It was rumored that someone in the Ministry of Higher Education had asked, rhetorically, if the faculty at Allameh thought they lived in Switzerland. Switzerland had somehow become a byword for Western laxity. Any program or action that was deemed un-Islamic was reproached with a mocking reminder that Iran was by no means Switzerland.

The pressure was hardest on the students. I felt helpless as I listened to their endless tales of woe. Female students were being penalized for running up the stairs when they were late for classes, for laughing in the hallways, for talking to members of the opposite sex. One day Sanaz had barged into class near the end of the session, crying. In between bursts of tears, she explained that she was late because the female guards at the door, finding a blush in her bag, had tried to send her home with a reprimand.

Why did I stop teaching so suddenly? I had asked myself this question many times. Was it the declining quality of the university? The ever-increasing indifference among the remaining faculty members and students? The daily struggle against arbitrary rules and restrictions?

I often went over in my mind the reaction of the university officials to my letter of resignation. They had harassed and limited me in all manner of ways, monitoring my visitors, controlling my actions, refusing my long-over-due tenure; and when I resigned, they infuriated me by suddenly commiserating and by refusing to accept my resignation. The students had threatened to boycott classes, and it was of some satisfaction to me to find out later that despite threats of reprisals, they in fact did boycott my replacement. Every-one thought I would break down and eventually return. It took two more years before they finally accepted my resignation.

Teaching in the Islamic Republic, like any other vocation, was subservi-ent to politics and subject to arbitrary rules. Always, the joy of teaching was marred by diversions and considerations forced on us by the regime—how well could one teach when the main concern of university officials was not the quality of one's work but the color of one's lips, the subversive poten-tial of a single strand of hair? Could one really concentrate on one's job when what preoccupied the faculty was how to excise the word "wine" from a Hemingway story, when they decided not to teach Brontë because she appeared to condone adultery?

In selecting students for study in my home, I did not take into consid-eration their ideological or religious backgrounds. Later, I would count it as the class's great achievement that such a mixed group, with different and at times conflicting backgrounds, personal as well as religious and social, remained so loyal to its goals and ideals. One reason for my choice of these particular girls was the peculiar mixture of fragility and courage I sensed in them. They were what you would call loners, who did not belong to any particular group or sect. I admired their ability to survive not despite but in some ways because of their solitary lives. 10

One of the first books we read was Nabokov's *Invitation to a Behead-ing*. Nabokov creates for us in this novel not the actual physical pain and torture of a totalitarian regime but the nightmarish quality of living in an atmosphere of perpetual dread. Cincinnatus C. is frail, he is passive, he is a hero without knowing or acknowledging it: He fights with his instincts, and his acts of writing are his means of escape. He is a hero because he refuses to become like all the rest.

We formed a special bond with Nabokov despite the difficulty of his prose. This went deeper than our identification with his themes. His novels are shaped around invisible trapdoors, sudden gaps that constantly pull the carpet from under the reader's feet. They are filled with mistrust of what we call everyday reality, an acute sense of that reality's fickleness and frailty.

There was something, both in his fiction and in his life, that we instinctively related to and grasped, the possibility of a boundless freedom when all options are taken away.

Nabokov used the term "fragile unreality" to explain his own state of exile; it also describes our existence in the Islamic Republic of Iran. We lived in a culture that denied any merit to literary works, considering them important only when they were handmaidens to something seemingly more urgent—namely, ideology. This was a country where all gestures, even the most private, were interpreted in political terms. The colors of my head scarf or my father's tie were symbols of Western decadence and imperialist tendencies. Not wearing a beard, shaking hands with members of the opposite sex, clapping or whistling in public meetings, were likewise considered Western and therefore decadent, part of the plot by imperialists to bring down our culture.

Our class was shaped within this context. There, in that living room, we rediscovered that we were also living, breathing human beings; and no matter how repressive the state became, no matter how intimidated and frightened we were, like Lolita we tried to escape and to create our own little pockets of freedom. And, like Lolita, we took every opportunity to flaunt our insubordination: by showing a little hair from under our scarves, insinuating a little color into the drab uniformity of our appearances, growing our nails, falling in love, and listening to forbidden music.

How can I create this other world outside the room? I have no choice   15
but to appeal to your imagination. Let's imagine one of the girls, say Sanaz, leaving my house, and let us follow her from there to her final destination. She says her goodbyes and puts on her black robe and scarf over her orange shirt and jeans, coiling her scarf around her neck to cover her huge gold earrings. She directs wayward strands of hair under the scarf, puts her notes into her large bag, straps it on over her shoulder, and walks out into the hall. She pauses for a moment on top of the stairs to put on thin, lacy, black gloves to hide her nail polish.

We follow Sanaz down the stairs, out the door, and into the street. You might notice that her gait and her gestures have changed. It is in her best interest not to be seen, not to be heard or noticed. She doesn't walk upright, but bends her head toward the ground and doesn't look at passers-by. She walks quickly and with a sense of determination. The streets of Tehran and other Iranian cities are patrolled by militia, who ride in white Toyota patrols—four gun-carrying men and women, sometimes followed by a minibus. They are called the Blood of God. They patrol the streets to make sure that women like Sanaz wear their veils properly, do not wear makeup, do not walk in public with men who are not their fathers, brothers, or husbands. If she gets on a bus, the seating is segregated. She must enter through the rear door and sit in the back seats, allocated to women.

You might well ask, What is Sanaz thinking as she walks the streets of Tehran? How much does this experience affect her? Most probably, she tries to distance her mind as much as possible from her surroundings. Perhaps she is thinking of her distant boyfriend and the time when she will meet him in Turkey. Does she compare her own situation with her mother's when she was the same age? Is she angry that women of her mother's generation could walk the streets freely, enjoy the company of the opposite sex, join the police force, become pilots, live under laws that were among the most progressive in the world regarding women? Does she feel humiliated by the new laws, by the fact that after the revolution, the age of marriage was lowered from eighteen to nine, that stoning became once more the punishment for adultery and prostitution?

In the course of nearly two decades, the streets have been turned into a war zone, where young women who disobey the rules are hurled into patrol cars, taken to jail, flogged, fined, forced to wash the toilets and humiliated — and, as soon as they leave, they go back and do the same thing. Is she aware, Sanaz, of her own power? Does she realize how dangerous she can be when her every stray gesture is a disturbance to public safety? Does she think how vulnerable are the Revolutionary Guards, who for over eighteen years have patrolled the streets of Tehran and have had to endure young women like herself, and those of other generations, walking, talking, showing a strand of hair just to remind them that they have not converted?

These girls had both a real history and a fabricated one. Although they came from very different backgrounds, the regime that ruled them had tried to make their personal identities and histories irrelevant. They were never free of the regime's definition of them as Muslim women.

Take the youngest in our class, Yassi. There she is, in a photograph I   20
have of the students, with a wistful look on her face. She is bending her head to one side, unsure of what expression to choose. She is wearing a thin white-and-gray scarf, loosely tied at the throat—a perfunctory homage to her family's strict religious background. Yassi was a freshman who audited my graduate courses in my last year of teaching. She felt intimidated by the older students, who, she thought, by virtue of their seniority, were blessed not only with greater knowledge and a better command of English but also with more wisdom. Although she understood the most difficult texts better than many of the graduate students, and although she read the texts more dutifully and with more pleasure than most, she felt secure only in her terrible sense of insecurity.

About a month after I had decided privately to leave Allameh Tabatabai, Yassi and I were standing in front of the green gate at the entrance of the university. What I remember most distinctly about the university now is that green gate. I owe my memory of that gate to Yassi: She mentioned it in one of her poems. The poem is called "How Small Are the Things That I Like." In it, she describes her favorite objects—an orange backpack, a colorful coat, a bicycle just like her cousin's—and she also describes how much she likes to enter the university through the green gate. The gate appears in this poem, and in some of her other writings, as a magical entrance into the forbidden world of all the ordinary things she had been denied in life.

Yet that green gate was closed to her, and to all my girls. Next to the gate there was a small opening with a curtain hanging from it. Through this opening all the female students went into a small, dark room to be inspected. Yassi would describe later what was done to her in this room: "I would first be checked to see if I have the right clothes: the color of my coat, the length of my uniform, the thickness of my scarf, the form of my shoes, the objects in my bag, the visible traces of even the mildest makeup, the size of my rings and their level of attractiveness, all would be checked before I could enter the campus of the university, the same university in which men also study. And to them the main door, with its immense portals and emblems and flags, is generously open."

In the sunny intimacy of our encounter that day, I asked Yassi to have an ice cream with me. We went to a small shop, where, sitting opposite each other with two tall *cafés glacés* between us, our mood changed. We became, if not somber, quite serious. Yassi came from an enlightened religious family that had been badly hurt by the revolution. They felt the Islamic Republic was a betrayal of Islam rather than its assertion. At the start of the revolution, Yassi's mother and older aunt joined a progressive Muslim women's group that, when the new government started to crack down on its former supporters, was forced to go underground. Yassi's mother and aunt went into hiding for a long time. This aunt had four daughters, all older than Yassi, all of whom in one way or another supported an opposition group that was popular with young religious Iranians. They were all but one arrested, tortured, and jailed. When they were released, every one of them married within a year. They married almost haphazardly, as if to negate their former rebellious selves. Yassi felt that they had survived the jail but could not escape the bonds of traditional marriage.

To me, Yassi was the real rebel. She did not join any political group or organization. As a teenager she had defied family traditions and, in the face of strong opposition, had taken up music. Listening to any form of nonreligious music, even on the radio, was forbidden in her family, but Yassi forced her will. Her rebellion did not stop there: She did not marry the right suitor at the right time and instead insisted on leaving her hometown, Shiraz, to go to college in Tehran. Now she lived partly with her older sister and husband and partly in the home of an uncle with fanatical religious leanings. The university, with its low academic standards, its shabby morality, and its ideological limitations, had been a disappointment to her.

What could she do? She did not believe in politics and did not want to marry, but she was curious about love. That day, she explained why all the normal acts of life had become small acts of rebellion and political insubordination to her and to other young people like her. All her life she was shielded. She was never let out of sight; she never had a private corner in which to think, to feel, to dream, to write. She was not allowed to meet any young men on her own. Her family not only instructed her on how to behave around men, but seemed to think they could tell her how she should feel

25

|||||||||||||||||||||||||||||||||||||||||||||||||||||||||||||||||||||||||||||||||||||||||||||||||||||||||||||||||||||||||||||||||||||||||||

about them as well. What seems natural to someone like you, she said, is so strange and unfamiliar to me.

Again she repeated that she would never get married. She said that for her a man always existed in books, that she would spend the rest of her life with Mr. Darcy[1] — even in the books, there were few men for her. What was wrong with that? She wanted to go to America, like her uncles, like me. Her mother and her aunts had not been allowed to go, but her uncles were given the chance. Could she ever overcome all the obstacles and go to America? Should she go to America? She wanted me to advise her; they all wanted that. But what could I offer her, she who wanted so much more from life than she had been given?

There was nothing in reality that I could give her, so I told her instead about Nabokov's "other world." I asked her if she had noticed how in most of Nabokov's novels, there was always the shadow of another world, one that was attainable only through fiction. It is this world that prevents his heroes and heroines from utter despair, that becomes their refuge in a life that is consistently brutal.

Take *Lolita*. This was the story of a twelve-year-old girl who had nowhere to go. Humbert had tried to turn her into his fantasy, into his dead love, and he had destroyed her. The desperate truth of Lolita's story is not the rape of a twelve-year-old by a dirty old man but the confiscation of one individual's life by another. We don't know what Lolita would have become if Humbert had not engulfed her. Yet the novel, the finished work, is hopeful, beautiful even, a defense not just of beauty but of life, ordinary everyday life, all the normal pleasures that Lolita, like Yassi, was deprived of.

Warming up and suddenly inspired, I added that, in fact, Nabokov had taken revenge against our own solipsizers; he had taken revenge on the Ayatollah Khomeini and those like him. They had tried to shape others according to their own dreams and desires, but Nabokov, through his portrayal of Humbert, had exposed all solipsists who take over other people's lives. She, Yassi, had much potential; she could be whatever she wanted to be — a good wife or a teacher and poet. What mattered was for her to know what she wanted.

I want to emphasize that we were not Lolita, the Ayatollah was not 30 Humbert, and this republic was not what Humbert called his princedom by the sea. *Lolita* was not a critique of the Islamic Republic, but it went against the grain of all totalitarian perspectives.

At some point, the truth of Iran's past became as immaterial to those who had appropriated it as the truth of Lolita's is to Humbert. It became immaterial in the same way that Lolita's truth, her desires and life, must lose color before Humbert's one obsession, his desire to turn a twelve-year-old unruly child into his mistress.

---

1 **Mr. Darcy:** The leading male character in Jane Austen's classic novel *Pride and Prejudice* (1813). — EDS.

This is how I read *Lolita*. Again and again as we discussed *Lolita* in that class, our discussions were colored by my students' hidden personal sorrows and joys. Like tear stains on a letter, these forays into the hidden and the personal shaded all our discussions of Nabokov.

Humbert never possesses his victim; she always eludes him, just as objects of fantasy are always simultaneously within reach and inaccessible. No matter how they may be broken, the victims will not be forced into submission.

This was on my mind one Thursday evening after class, as I was looking at the diaries my girls had left behind, with their new essays and poems. At the start of our class, I had asked them to describe their image of themselves. They were not ready then to face that question, but every once in a while I returned to it and asked them again. Now, as I sat curled up on the love seat, I looked at dozens of pages of their recent responses.

I have one of these responses in front of me. It belongs to Sanaz, who 35 handed it in shortly after a recent experience in jail, on trumped-up morality charges. It is a simple drawing in black and white, of a naked girl, the white of her body caught in a black bubble. She is crouched in an almost fetal position, hugging one bent knee. Her other leg is stretched out behind her. Her long, straight hair follows the same curved line as the contour of her back, but her face is hidden. The bubble is lifted in the air by a giant bird with long black talons. What interests me is a small detail: the girl's hand reaches out of the bubble and holds on to the talon. Her subservient nakedness is dependent on that talon, and she reaches out to it.

The drawing immediately brought to my mind Nabokov's statement in his famous afterword to *Lolita*, about how the "first little throb of Lolita" went through him in 1939 or early 1940, when he was ill with a severe attack of intercostal neuralgia. He recalls that "the initial shiver of inspiration was somehow prompted by a newspaper story about an ape in the Jardin des Plantes, who, after months of coaxing by a scientist, produced the first drawing ever charcoaled by an animal: this sketch showed the bars of the poor creature's cage."

The two images, one from the novel and the other from reality, reveal a terrible truth. Its terribleness goes beyond the fact that in each case an act of violence has been committed. It goes beyond the bars, revealing the victim's proximity and intimacy with its jailer. Our focus in each is on the delicate spot where the prisoner touches the bar, on the invisible contact between flesh and cold metal.

Most of the other students expressed themselves in words. Manna saw herself as fog, moving over concrete objects, taking on their form but never becoming concrete herself. Yassi described herself as a figment. Nassrin, in one response, gave me the *Oxford English Dictionary*'s definition of the word "paradox." Implicit in almost all of their descriptions was the way they saw themselves in the context of an outside reality that prevented them from defining themselves clearly and separately.

Manna had once written about a pair of pink socks for which she was reprimanded by the Muslim Students' Association. When she complained to a favorite professor, he started teasing her about how she had already ensnared and trapped her man, Nima, and did not need the pink socks to entrap him further.

These students, like the rest of their generation, were different from my generation in one fundamental aspect. My generation complained of a loss, the void in our lives that was created when our past was stolen from us, making us exiles in our own country. Yet we had a past to compare with the present; we had memories and images of what had been taken away. But my girls spoke constantly of stolen kisses, films they had never seen, and the wind they had never felt on their skin. This generation had no past. Their memory was of a half-articulated desire, something they never had. It was this lack, their sense of longing for the ordinary, taken-for-granted aspects of life, that gave their words a certain luminous quality akin to poetry. 40

I had asked my students if they remembered the dance scene in *Invitation to a Beheading*: The jailer invites Cincinnatus to a dance. They begin a waltz and move out into the hall. In a corner they run into a guard: "They described a circle near him and glided back into the cell, and now Cincinnatus regretted that the swoon's friendly embrace had been so brief." This movement in circles is the main movement of the novel. As long as he accepts the sham world the jailers impose upon him, Cincinnatus will remain their prisoner and will move within the circles of their creation. The worst crime committed by totalitarian mind-sets is that they force their citizens, including their victims, to become complicit in their crimes. Dancing with your jailer, participating in your own execution, that is an act of utmost brutality. My students witnessed it in show trials on television and enacted it every time they went out into the streets dressed as they were told to dress. They had not become part of the crowd who watched the executions, but they did not have the power to protest them, either.

The only way to leave the circle, to stop dancing with the jailer, is to find a way to preserve one's individuality, that unique quality which evades description but differentiates one human being from the other. That is why, in their world, rituals—empty rituals—become so central.

There was not much difference between our jailers and Cincinnatus's executioners. They invaded all private spaces and tried to shape every gesture, to force us to become one of them, and that in itself is another form of execution.

In the end, when Cincinnatus is led to the scaffold, and as he lays his head on the block, in preparation for his execution, he repeats the magic mantra: "by myself." This constant reminder of his uniqueness, and his attempts to write, to articulate and create a language different from the one imposed upon him by his jailers, saves him at the last moment, when he takes his head in his hands and walks away toward voices that beckon him from that other world, while the scaffold and all the sham world around him, along with his executioner, disintegrate.

The Reader's Presence

1. What does literature represent to Nafisi's students? How do the young women's experiences in Iran shape their interpretations and understandings of Nabokov?

2. Why is Cincinnatus's execution a metaphor Nafisi's students can relate to? What is the meaning of Cincinnatus's mantra "by myself" (paragraph 44)? How does Cincinnatus "save" himself in the end? Is this ending hopeful for Nafisi's students? Why or why not?

3. **CONNECTIONS:**   The strict moral regulations imposed by the Islamic regime are, Nafisi suggests, motivated by fear. When picturing her student Sanaz on the street, Nafisi asks, "Does she realize how dangerous she can be when her every stray gesture is a disturbance to public safety?" (paragraph 18). How is the education of women a potential threat to public safety in Iran? Read Sherman Alexie's "The Joy of Reading and Writing: Superman and Me" (page 34). How does Alexie characterize his education as subversive? Who is threatened by his learning?

Danielle Ofri

SAT

DANIELLE OFRI (b. 1965) demonstrates that it is possible to be a productive writer while pursuing a busy life or career. With an MD and a PhD, Ofri is an attending physician at Bellevue Hospital and assistant professor of medicine at New York University School of Medicine. She is also editor-in-chief and co-founder of the *Bellevue Literary Review* and the associate chief editor of the award-winning medical textbook *The Bellevue Guide to Outpatient Medicine*. Her essays have appeared in the *New York Times*, the *Los Angeles Times*, *Best American Essays*, *Best American Science Writing*, the *New England Journal of Medicine*, the *Missouri Review*, *Tikkun*, the *Journal of the American Medical Association*, and the *Lancet*. Her Web site,

> Danielle Ofri demonstrates that it is possible to be a productive writer while pursuing a busy life or career. In addition to professionally editing and writing, she is an attending physician at Bellevue Hospital and assistant professor of medicine at New York University School of Medicine.

danielleofri.com, explores the relationship between literature and medicine. A frequent guest on National Public Radio, Ofri lives in New York City with her husband and three children.

Her first collection, *Singular Intimacies: Becoming a Doctor at Bellevue* (2003), was described by physician/author Perri Klass as "a beautiful book about souls and bodies, sadness and healing at a legendary hospital." Ofri co-edited with her colleagues *The Best of the Bellevue Literary Review* (2008), a collection of writings from that journal. Her essay, "SAT," is taken from her 2005 book, *Incidental Findings: Lessons from My Patients in the Art of Medicine*. A *New York Times* profile reports, "To Dr. Ofri every patient's history is a mystery story, a narrative that unfolds full of surprises, exposing the vulnerability at the human core." Her most recent book, *What Doctors Feel: How Emotions Affect the Practice of Medicine*, was published in 2013.

"NEMESIO RIOS?" I called out to the crowded waiting room of our medical clinic. I'd just finished a long stint attending on the wards and I was glad to be back to the relatively sane life of the clinic. "Nemesio Rios?" I called out again.

"Yuh," came a grunt, as a teenaged boy in baggy jeans with a ski hat pulled low over his brow hoisted himself up. He sauntered into my office and slumped into the plastic chair next to my desk.

"What brings you to the clinic today?"

He shrugged. "Feel all right, but they told me to come today," he said, slouching lower into the chair, his oversize sweatshirt reaching nearly to his knees. The chart said he'd been in the ER two weeks ago for a cough.

"How about a regular checkup?" He shrugged again. His eyes were   5
deep brown, tucked deep beneath his brow.

Past medical history? None. Past surgical history? None. Meds? None. Allergies? None. Family history? None.

"Where were you born?" I asked, wanting to know his nationality.

"Here."

"Here in New York?"

"Yeah, in this hospital."   10

"A Bellevue baby!" I said with a grin, noticing that his medical record number had only six digits (current numbers had nine digits). "A genuine Bellevue baby."

There was a small smile, but I could see him working hard to suppress it. "My mom's from Mexico."

"Have you ever been there?" I asked, curious.

"You sound like my mom." He rolled his eyes. "She's always trying to get me to go. She's over there right now visiting her sisters."

"You don't want to go visit?"   15

"Mexico? Just a bunch of corrupt politicians." Nemesio shifted his unlaced sneakers back and forth on the linoleum floor, causing a dull screech each time.

I asked about his family. In a distracted voice, as though he'd been through this a million times before, he told me that he was the youngest of eight, but now that his sister got married, it was only he and his mother left in the house. I asked about his father.

"He lives in Brooklyn." Nemesio poked his hand in and out of the pocket of his sweatshirt. "He's all right, I guess, but he drinks a lot," he said, his voice trailing off. "Doesn't do anything stupid, but he drinks."

"Are you in school now?"

"Me?" he said, his voice perking up for the first time from his baseline   20
mumble. "I'm twenty. I'm done! Graduated last year."

"What are you doing now?"

"Working in a kitchen. It's all right, I guess."

"Any thoughts about college?"

"You sound like my cousin in Connecticut. He's in some college there and he's always bugging me about going to college. But I'm lazy. No one to kick my lazy butt."

"What do you want to do when you grow up?"   25

"What I *really* want to do? I want to play basketball." He gave a small laugh. "But they don't take five-foot-seven guys in the NBA."

"Anything else besides basketball?"

He thought for a minute. "Comics. I like to draw comics. I guess I could be an artist that draws comics." His eye caught the tiny Monet poster I'd taped above the examining table. "That's pretty cool, that painting."

"There are a lot of great art schools here in New York." My comment floated off into empty space. We were silent for a few minutes. I made a few notes in the chart.

"That stuff about peer pressure is a bunch of crap," he said abruptly,   30
forcefully, sitting up in his chair, speaking directly toward the poster in front of him.

I leaned closer toward Nemesio, trying to figure out what this sudden outburst was related to. But he continued, staring straight forward, lecturing at the empty room, as if I weren't there.

"Anyone who tells you they do something because of peer pressure is full of crap." He was even more animated now, even angry. "People always asking me to do stuff, but I can make my own mind up." His hands came out of his sweatshirt pocket and began gesticulating in the air. "My brother and his friends, they're always drinking beer. But I don't like the taste of it. I don't believe in peer pressure."

Speech ended, Nemesio settled back into his chair, resumed his slouched posture, and repositioned his hands into his pockets. Then he glanced up at the ceiling and added quietly, almost wistfully, "But if beer tasted like apple juice, I might be drinking it every day."

He was quiet for a few minutes. One hand slid out of his pocket and started fiddling with the zipper on his sweatshirt.

Without warning he swiveled in his chair to face me directly, his whole   35
body leaning into my desk. "You ever face peer pressure, Doc?"

His eyes were right on mine, and I was caught off guard by this sudden shift in his voice and body language. I felt unexpectedly on the spot. Who does he see? I wondered. Do I represent the older generation or the medical profession or women or non-Hispanic whites? Or all of the above?

Nemesio refused to let my gaze wander off his. He demanded an answer to his question, and our doctor–patient encounter had obviously taken an abrupt turn. I could tell that a lot was riding on my answer, though I wasn't sure what exactly was at stake. Did he need me to provide a reassuring societal answer about how bad drugs are? Or did he need me to identify with him, to say that I've been where he's been, even if that was not exactly the truth?

"Yes," I said, after debating in my head for a moment, trying to think of something sufficiently potent to satisfy the question but not so sordid as to embarrass myself. "I have."

He stared at me, waiting for me to continue. His eyes looked younger and younger.

"In my first year of college," I said. "In the very first week. Everyone was   40
sitting in the stairwell and they were passing a joint around. Everyone took a drag. When it came to me I hesitated. I wasn't really interested in smoking, but everyone else was doing it."

"So what did you do?"

"I didn't want anyone to think I was a little kid, so I took a drag too."

"Did you like it?"

"No, I just hacked and coughed. I didn't even *want* the stupid joint to begin with, and I couldn't believe I was doing it just because everyone else was."

"That peer pressure is crap." Nemesio stated it as a fact and then sank   45
back into his seat.

"You're right. It is. It took me a little while to figure that out."

He pushed the ski hat back from his brow a few inches. "In my high school there was this teacher that was always on my case. She was always bugging me to study and take the tests. What a pain in the butt she was." He pulled the hat all the way off. "But now there's no one around to kick my lazy butt. I could get to college easy, but I'm just lazy."

My mind wandered back to a crisp autumn day in my second month of medical school. Still overwhelmed by the pentose-phosphate shunt and other minutiae of biochemistry, our Clinical Correlation group—led by two fourth-year students—promised us first-year students a taste of clinical medicine.

The CC student leaders had obtained permission for a tour of the New York City medical examiner's office. All suspicious deaths—murders, suicides, and the like—were investigated here.

The autumn sun dazzled against the bright turquoise bricks of the ME   50
building, which stood out in sharp contrast to the gray concrete buildings lining First Avenue. We congregated on the steps, endeavoring to look nonchalant.

The security guard checked our ID cards as well as our letter of entry. We followed him through the metal detector, down the whitewashed concrete hallway, into the unpainted service elevator with a hand-pulled metal grate.

We stared at our sneakers as the elevator lurched downward. It creaked past several floors and landed with a jolt. Out we spilled, gingerly, onto the raw concrete floor. Our first stop was the morgue. The cavernous walk-in refrigerator was icy and silent. There was a Freon smell, the kind I recalled from the frozen food departments in grocery stores. As a child, when I went shopping with my mother I used to lean into the bins of ice cream and frozen waffles and inhale that curiously appealing, vaguely sweet, chemical fragrance. But here the odor was intensified—magnified by the rigid chill and bleak soundlessness of the room.

Nine naked corpses lay on shelves, their wizened bodies covered with skin that glowed a ghastly green from the low-wattage fluorescent lights. These were the unclaimed bodies, mostly elderly men found on the streets. The ones that were never identified, never claimed by relatives. The ones that were sent next door to the medical school. These were the subjects of our first-year anatomy course.

From there we were herded into the autopsy room. Loosely swinging doors delivered us into a shock of cacophonous noise and harsh bright lights. We stumbled into each other, a discombobulated mass at the entranceway, blinking to adjust from the stark silence of the morgue. The autopsy room was long and rectangular. The high ceilings and brisk yellow walls lent an odd air of cheeriness. Seven metal tables lay parallel in the center. Six of them were surrounded by groups of pathology residents performing autopsies. The residents wore long rubber gloves and industrial-strength aprons. The sound of their voices and their clanking instruments echoed in the room.

The only body I had ever opened was my cadaver in anatomy lab, which   55
was preserved in formaldehyde and completely dried out. I'd never actually seen blood. In the autopsy room there was blood everywhere. Residents were handling organs—weighing hearts, measuring kidneys, taking samples from livers—then replacing them in the open corpses. Their aprons were spotted with scarlet streaks. Blood streamed down the troughs that surrounded each table.

It was disgusting, but I wasn't nauseated. These bodies didn't look like people anymore. It was more like a cattle slaughterhouse: cows and pigs lined up to be transformed into sterile packages of cellophane-wrapped chopped meat. The slaughterhouse that compelled you to vow lifetime vegetarianism, a resolve that lasted only until the next barbecue with succulent, browned burgers that looked nothing like the disemboweled carcasses you'd seen earlier.

Then I spied the last table, the only one without a sea of activity around it. Lying on the metal table was a young boy who didn't look older than twelve. He was wearing new Nikes and one leg of his jeans was rolled up to the knee. His bright red basketball jersey was pushed up, revealing a smooth brown chest. He looked as if he were sleeping.

I tiptoed closer. Could he really be dead? There was not a mark on his body. Every part was in its place. His clothes were crisp and clean. There was no blood, no dirt, no sign of struggle. He wasn't anything like the gutted carcasses on the other tables. His expression was serene, his face without blemish. His skin was plump. He was just a beautiful boy sleeping.

I wanted to rouse him, to tell him to get out of this house of death, quick, before the rubber-aproned doctors got to him. There is still time, I wanted to say. Get out while you can!

I leaned over his slender, exposed, adolescent chest. I peered closer.   60
There, just over his left nipple, was a barely perceptible hole. Smaller than the tip of my little finger. A tiny bullet hole.

I stared at that hole. That ignominious hole. That hole that stole this boy's life. I wanted to rewind the tape, to give him a chance to dodge six inches to the right. That's all he'd need—just six inches. Who would balk over six inches?

Somebody pulled on my arm. Time to go.

For months after my visit to the medical examiner's office, I had night-mares. But they weren't about bloody autopsies or refrigerated corpses. I dreamt only about the boy, that beautiful, untouched, intact boy. The one who'd had the misfortune to fall asleep in the autopsy room.

At night, he would creep into my bed. On the street, I could feel his breath on the back of my neck. In the library, while I battled the Krebs cycle and the branches of the trigeminal nerve, he would slip silently into the pages of my book. His body was so perfect, so untouched.

Except for that barely perceptible hole.   65

Now I looked at Nemesio Rios sitting before me; his beautiful body adrift in the uncertainty of adolescence, made all the rockier by the unfair bur-dens of urban poverty. Research has shown that health status and life expec-tancy are directly correlated with socioeconomic status and earning power. Whether this is related to having health insurance, or simply to having more knowledge to make healthier lifestyle choices, there is no doubt that being poor is bad for your health.

As I scribbled in his chart, an odd thought dawned on me: the best thing that I, as a physician, could recommend for Nemesio's long-term health would be to take the SAT and get into college. Too bad I couldn't just write a prescription for that.

"Have you taken the SAT yet?" I asked Nemesio.

"Nah. I can't stand U.S. history. What's the point of knowing U.S. history?"

I twisted my stethoscope around my finger. "Ever hear of McCarthy?"   70

He shrugged. "Yeah, maybe."

"McCarthy tried to intimidate people to turn in their friends and cowork-ers. Anyone who might believe differently from him. I'd hate to see that part of U.S. history repeated."

He nodded slowly. "Yeah, I guess. I wouldn't want nobody to tell me what to think. That peer pressure is crap."

"Besides," I added, "there's no U.S. history on the SAT."

Nemesio turned toward me, his eyes opened wide. "Yeah? No U.S. his- 75 tory?" His cheeks were practically glowing.

"No history. Just math and English."

"Wow," he said. "No U.S. history. That's pretty cool." His tone of voice changed abruptly as his gaze plummeted to the floor. "But damn, I can't remember those fractions and stuff."

"Sure you can," I said. "It's all the same from high school. If you review it, it'll all come back to you."

In medical school, I had taught an SAT prep course on the weekends to help pay my living expenses. For kids in more affluent neighborhoods, these courses were standard. But it didn't seem fair, because for Nemesio, his health depended on it.

"Listen," I said. "I'll make you a deal. You go out and buy one of those 80 SAT review books and bring it to our next appointment. I bet we can brush you up on those fractions."

He shifted in his seat and I could just detect a hint of a swagger in his torso. "Okay, Doc. I'll take you on."

Nemesio stood up to go and then turned quickly back to me. "College ain't so bad, but what I really want is to play basketball."

Now it was my turn to nod. "There's nothing like a good ballgame. I played point guard in college."

"You? You even shorter than me."

"That's why I had to find another career." 85

He grinned. "You and me both." Nemesio put his ski hat on and pulled it carefully down over his forehead. Then he slouched out the door.

Nemesio and I met three times over the next two months. While my stethoscope and blood pressure cuff sat idle, we reviewed algebra, analogies, geometry, and reading comprehension. With only a little prodding, Nemesio was able to recall what he had learned in high school. And he thought it was "really cool" when I showed him the tricks and shortcuts that I recalled from the SAT prep course.

I lost touch with Nemesio after that. Many days I thought about him, wondering how things turned out. If this were a movie, he'd score a perfect 1600 and be off to Princeton on full scholarship. But Harlem isn't Hollywood, and the challenges in real life are infinitely more complex. I don't know if Nemesio ever got into college—any college—or if he even took the SAT exam. But he did learn a bit more about fractions, and I learned a bit more about the meaning of preventative medicine. At the end of each visit, I would face the clinic billing sheet. The top fifty diagnoses were listed—the most common and important medical issues, according to Medicaid, that faced our patients. I scrutinized them each time, because I was required to check one off, to check off Nemesio Rios's most salient medical diagnosis and treatment, to identify the most pressing issues for his health, to categorize the medical interventions deemed necessary for this patient's well-being, otherwise the clinic wouldn't get reimbursed.

SAT prep was not among them. ■

The Reader's Presence

1. Ofri uses dialogue extensively throughout the essay. What are the effects of this choice? How would the essay be different if she had not used her patient's own words?

2. Why does Ofri juxtapose the material about Nemesio Rios with the material about her experiences in the morgue? Is the fact that Ofri does not reveal the outcome of Nemesio's story disturbing? Does this uncertainty make the essay more or less believable? Why?

3. **CONNECTIONS:** Ofri argues that continuing his education is the best step her patient can take to safeguard his health. Do you agree? Read John Taylor Gatto's "Against School" (page 607). Does Gatto's argument apply to a case like that of Ofri's young patient? Why or why not?

George Orwell

POLITICS AND THE ENGLISH LANGUAGE

During his lifetime, **GEORGE ORWELL** was well known for the political positions he laid out in his essays. The events that inspired Orwell to write his essays have long since passed, but his writing continues to be read and enjoyed. Orwell demonstrates that political writing need not be narrowly topical—it can speak to enduring issues and concerns. He suggested as much in 1946 when he wrote, "What I have most wanted to do throughout the past ten years is to make political writing into an art. My starting point is always a feeling of partisanship, a feeling of injustice. . . . But I could not do the work of writing a book, or even a long magazine article, if it were not also an aesthetic experience." "Politics and the English Language" appears in *Shooting an Elephant and Other Essays* (1950).

> "My starting point is always a feeling of partisanship, a feeling of injustice."

For more information about Orwell, see page 216.

MOST PEOPLE who bother with the matter at all would admit that the English language is in a bad way, but it is generally assumed that we cannot by conscious action do anything about it. Our civilization is decadent and our language—so that argument runs—must inevitably share in the general collapse. It follows that any struggle against the abuse of language is a sentimental archaism, like preferring candles to electric light or hansom cabs to airplanes. Underneath this lies the half-conscious belief that language is a natural growth and not an instrument which we shape for our own purposes.

Now, it is clear that the decline of a language must ultimately have political and economic causes: It is not due simply to the bad influence of this or that individual writer. But an effect can become a cause, reinforcing the original cause and producing the same effect in an intensified form, and so on indefinitely. A man may take to drink because he feels himself to be a failure, and then fail all the more completely because he drinks. It is rather the same thing that is happening to the English language. It becomes ugly and inaccurate because our thoughts are foolish, but the slovenliness of our language makes it easier for us to have foolish thoughts. The point is that the process is reversible. Modern English, especially written English, is full of bad habits which spread by imitation and which can be avoided if one is willing to take the necessary trouble. If one gets rid of these habits one can think more clearly, and to think clearly is a necessary first step towards political regeneration: so that the fight against bad English is not frivolous and is not the exclusive concern of professional writers. I will come back to this presently, and I hope that by that time the meaning of what I have said here will have become clearer. Meanwhile, here are five specimens of the English language as it is now habitually written.

These five passages have not been picked out because they are especially bad—I could have quoted far worse if I had chosen—but because they illustrate various of the mental vices from which we now suffer. They are a little below the average, but are fairly representative samples. I number them so that I can refer back to them when necessary:

> (1) I am not, indeed, sure whether it is true to say that the Milton who once seemed not unlike a seventeenth-century Shelley had not become, out of an experience ever more bitter in each year, more alien [sic] to the founder of that Jesuit sect which nothing could induce him to tolerate.
>
> Professor Harold Laski (*Essay in Freedom of Expression*).

> (2) Above all, we cannot play ducks and drakes with a native battery of idioms which prescribes such egregious collections of vocals as the Basic *put up with* for *tolerate* or *put at a loss* for *bewilder*.
>
> Professor Lancelot Hogben (*Interglossa*).

> (3) On the one side we have the free personality: By definition it is not neurotic, for it has neither conflict nor dream. Its desires, such as they are, are transparent, for they are just what institutional approval keeps in the forefront of consciousness; another institutional pattern would alter their number and intensity; there is little in them that is natural, irreducible, or culturally dangerous.

But *on the other side*, the social bond itself is nothing but the mutual reflection of these self-secure integrities. Recall the definition of love. Is not this the very picture of a small academic? Where is there a place in this hall of mirrors for either personality or fraternity?

Essay on psychology in *Politics* (New York).

(4) All the "best people" from the gentlemen's clubs, and all the frantic fascist captains, united in common hatred of Socialism and bestial horror of the rising tide of the mass revolutionary movement, have turned to acts of provocation, to foul incendiarism, to medieval legends of poisoned wells, to legalize their own destruction of proletarian organizations, and rouse the agitated petty-bourgeoisie to chauvinistic fervor on behalf of the fight against the revolutionary way out of the crisis.

Communist pamphlet.

(5) If a new spirit *is* to be infused into this old country, there is one thorny and contentious reform which must be tackled, and that is the humanization and galvanization of the B.B.C. Timidity here will bespeak cancer and atrophy of the soul. The heart of Britain may be sound and of strong beat, for instance, but the British lion's roar at present is like that of Bottom in Shakespeare's *Midsummer Night's Dream*—as gentle as any sucking dove. A virile new Britain cannot continue indefinitely to be traduced in the eyes or rather ears, of the world by the effete languors of Langham Place, brazenly masquerading as "standard English." When the *Voice of Britain* is heard at nine o'clock, better far and infinitely less ludicrous to hear aitches honestly dropped than the present priggish, inflated, inhibited, school-ma'amish arch braying of blameless bashful mewing maidens!

Letter in *Tribune*.

Each of these passages has faults of its own, but, quite apart from avoidable ugliness, two qualities are common to all of them. The first is staleness of imagery: The other is lack of precision. The writer either has a meaning and cannot express it, or he inadvertently says something else, or he is almost indifferent as to whether his words mean anything or not. This mixture of vagueness and sheer incompetence is the most marked characteristic of modern English prose, and especially of any kind of political writing. As soon as certain topics are raised, the concrete melts into the abstract and no one seems able to think of turns of speech that are not hackneyed: Prose consists less and less of *words* chosen for the sake of their meaning, and more and more of *phrases* tacked together like the sections of a prefabricated hen-house. I list below, with notes and examples, various of the tricks by means of which the work of prose-construction is habitually dodged:

Dying Metaphors. A newly invented metaphor assists thought by evoking a visual image, while on the other hand a metaphor which is technically "dead" (e.g., *iron resolution*) has in effect reverted to being an ordinary word and can generally be used without loss of vividness. But in between these two classes there is a huge dump of worn-out metaphors which have lost all evocative power and are merely used because they save people the trouble of inventing phrases for themselves. Examples are: *Ring the changes on, take up the cudgels for, toe the line, ride roughshod over, stand shoulder to shoulder with, play into the hands of, no axe to grind, grist to the mill, fishing in troubled waters, rift within the lute, on the order of the day, Achilles' heel, swan song, hotbed.* Many of these are used without knowledge of their meaning (what is a "rift," for instance?), and incompatible metaphors are frequently mixed, a sure sign that the writer is not interested in what he is saying. Some metaphors now current have been twisted out of their original meaning without those who use them even being aware of the fact. For example, *toe the line* is sometimes written *tow the line.* Another example is *the hammer and the anvil*, now always used with the implication that the anvil gets the worst of it. In real life it is always the anvil that breaks the hammer, never the other way about: A writer who stopped to think what he was saying would be aware of this, and would avoid perverting the original phrase.

Operators or Verbal False Limbs. These save the trouble of picking out appropriate verbs and nouns, and at the same time pad each sentence with extra syllables which give it an appearance of symmetry. Characteristic phrases are *render inoperative, militate against, make contact with, be subjected to, give rise to, give grounds for, have the effect of, play a leading part (role) in, make itself felt, take effect, exhibit a tendency to, serve the purpose of, etc., etc.* The keynote is the elimination of simple verbs. Instead of being a single word, such as *break, stop, spoil, mend, kill*, a verb becomes a *phrase*, made up of a noun or adjective tacked on to some general-purpose verb such as *prove, serve, form, play, render.* In addition, the passive voice is wherever possible used in preference to the active, and noun constructions are used instead of gerunds (*by examination of* instead of *by examining*). The range of verbs is further cut down by means of the *-ize* and *de-* formation, and the banal statements are given an appearance of profundity by means of the *not un-* formation. Simple conjunctions and prepositions are replaced by such phrases as *with respect to, having regard to, the fact that, by dint of, in view of, in the interests of, on the hypothesis that*; and the ends of sentences are saved from anticlimax by such resounding commonplaces as *greatly to be desired, cannot be left out of account, a development to be expected in the near future, deserving of serious consideration, brought to a satisfactory conclusion*, and so on and so forth.

Pretentious Diction. Words like *phenomenon, element, individual* (as noun), *objective, categorical, effective, virtual, basic, primary, promote, constitute, exhibit, exploit, utilize, eliminate, liquidate*, are used to dress up simple statements and give an air of scientific impartiality to biased judgments. Adjectives like *epoch-making, epic, historic, unforgettable, triumphant, age-old, inevitable, inexorable, veritable*, are used to dignify the sordid processes of international politics, while writing that aims at glorifying war usually takes on an archaic color, its characteristic words being: *realm, throne, chariot, mailed fist, trident, sword, shield, buckler, banner, jackboot, clarion.* Foreign words and expressions such as *cul de sac, ancien régime, deus ex machina, mutatis mutandis, status quo, gleichschaltung, weltanschauung,* are used to give an air of culture and elegance. Except for the useful abbreviations *i.e., e.g.,* and *etc.,* there is no real need for any of the hundreds of foreign phrases now current in English. Bad writers, and especially scientific, political, and sociological writers, are nearly always haunted by the notion that Latin or Greek words are grander than Saxon ones, and unnecessary words like *expedite, ameliorate, predict, extraneous, deracinated, clandestine, subaqueous,* and hundreds of others constantly gain ground from their Anglo-Saxon opposite numbers.[1] The jargon peculiar to Marxist writing (*hyena, hangman, cannibal, petty bourgeois, these gentry, lackey, flunkey, mad dog, White Guard,* etc.) consists largely of words and phrases translated from Russian, German, or French; but the normal way of coining a new word is to use a Latin or Greek root with the appropriate affix and, where necessary, the *-ize* formation. It is often easier to make up words of this kind (*deregionalize, impermissible, extramarital, nonfragmentary,* and so forth) than to think up the English words that will cover one's meaning. The result, in general, is an increase in slovenliness and vagueness.

Meaningless Words. In certain kinds of writing, particularly in art criticism and literary criticism, it is normal to come across long passages which are almost completely lacking in meaning.[2] Words like *romantic, plastic, values, human, dead, sentimental, natural, vitality,* as used in art criticism, are strictly meaningless, in the sense that they not only do not point to any discoverable object, but are hardly ever expected to do so by the reader. When one critic writes, "The outstanding feature of Mr. X's work is its living quality," while another writes, "The immediately striking thing about Mr. X's work is its peculiar deadness," the reader accepts this as a simple difference of opinion. If words like *black* and *white* were involved, instead of the jargon words *dead* and *living,* he would see at once that language was being used in an improper way. Many political words are similarly abused. The word *Fascism* has now no meaning except in so far as it signifies "something not desirable." The words *democracy, socialism, freedom, patriotic, realistic, justice,* have each of them several different meanings which cannot be reconciled with one another. In the case of a word like *democracy,* not only is there no agreed definition, but the attempt to make one is resisted

---

    [1] An interesting illustration of this is the way in which the English flower names which were in use till very recently are being ousted by Greek ones, *snapdragon* becoming *antirrhinum, forget-me-not* becoming *myosotis,* etc. It is hard to see any practical reason for this change of fashion: It is probably due to an instinctive turning away from the more homely word and a vague feeling that the Greek word is scientific. —Orwell's Note.
    [2] Example: "Comfort's catholicity of perception and image, strangely Whitmanesque in range, almost the exact opposite in aesthetic compulsion, continues to evoke that trembling atmospheric accumulative hinting at a cruel, an inexorably serene timelessness. . . . Wrey Gardiner scores by aiming at simple bull's-eyes with precision. Only they are not so simple, and through this contented sadness runs more than the surface bitter-sweet of resignation." (*Poetry Quarterly*). —Orwell's Note.

from all sides. It is almost universally felt that when we call a country democratic we are praising it: Consequently the defenders of every kind of regime claim that it is a democracy, and fear that they might have to stop using the word if it were tied down to any one meaning. Words of this kind are often used in a consciously dishonest way. That is, the person who uses them has his own private definition, but allows his hearer to think he means something quite different. Statements like *Marshal Pétain*[3] *was a true patriot*, *The Soviet Press is the freest in the world*, *The Catholic Church is opposed to persecution*, are almost always made with intent to deceive. Other words used in variable meanings, in most cases more or less dishonestly, are: *class, totalitarian, science, progressive, reactionary, bourgeois, equality*.

Now that I have made this catalogue of swindles and perversions, let me give another example of the kind of writing that they lead to. This time it must of its nature be an imaginary one. I am going to translate a passage of good English into modern English of the worst sort. Here is a well-known verse from *Ecclesiastes*:

> I returned and saw under the sun, that the race is not to the swift, nor the battle to the strong, neither yet bread to the wise, nor yet riches to men of understanding, nor yet favor to men of skill; but time and chance happeneth to them all.

Here it is in modern English:

> Objective consideration of contemporary phenomena compels the conclusion that success or failure in competitive activities exhibits no tendency to be commensurate with innate capacity, but that a considerable element of the unpredictable must invariably be taken into account.

This is a parody, but not a very gross one. Exhibit (3), above, for instance, contains several patches of the same kind of English. It will be seen that I have not made a full translation. The beginning and ending of the sentence follow the original meaning fairly closely, but in the middle the concrete illustrations—race, battle, bread—dissolve into the vague phrase "success or failure in competitive activities." This had to be so, because no modern writer of the kind I am discussing—no one capable of using phrases like "objective consideration of contemporary phenomena"—would ever tabulate his thoughts in that precise and detailed way. The whole tendency of modern prose is away from concreteness. Now analyze these two sentences a little more closely. The first contains forty-nine words but only sixty syllables, and all its words are those of everyday life. The second contains thirty-eight words of ninety syllables: Eighteen of its words are from Latin roots, and one from Greek. The first sentence contains six vivid images, and only one phrase ("time and chance") that could be called vague. The second

10

---

3 ***Pétain:*** Henri Philippe Pétain was a World War I French military hero who served as chief of state in France from 1940 to 1945, after France surrendered to Germany. A controversial figure, Pétain was regarded by some to be a patriot who had sacrificed himself for his country, while others considered him to be a traitor. He was sentenced to life imprisonment in 1945, the year before Orwell wrote his essay.—EDS.

contains not a single fresh, arresting phrase, and in spite of its ninety syllables it gives only a shortened version of the meaning contained in the first. Yet without a doubt it is the second kind of sentence that is gaining ground in modern English. I do not want to exaggerate. This kind of writing is not yet universal, and outcrops of simplicity will occur here and there in the worst-written page. Still, if you or I were told to write a few lines on the uncertainty of human fortunes, we should probably come much nearer to my imaginary sentences than to the one from *Ecclesiastes*.

As I have tried to show, modern writing at its worst does not consist in picking out words for the sake of their meaning and inventing images in order to make the meaning clearer. It consists in gumming together long strips of words which have already been set in order by someone else, and making the results presentable by sheer humbug. The attraction of this way of writing is that it is easy. It is easier—even quicker once you have the habit—to say *In my opinion it is a not unjustifiable assumption that* than to say *I think*. If you use ready-made phrases, you not only don't have to hunt about for words; you also don't have to bother with the rhythms of your sentences, since these phrases are generally so arranged as to be more or less euphonious. When you are composing in a hurry—when you are dictating to a stenographer, for instance, or making a public speech—it is natural to fall into a pretentious, Latinized style. Tags like *a consideration which we should do well to bear in mind* or *a conclusion to which all of us would readily assent* will save many a sentence from coming down with a bump. By using stale metaphors, similes, and idioms, you save much mental effort, at the cost of leaving your meaning vague, not only for your reader but for yourself. This is the significance of mixed metaphors. The sole aim of a metaphor is to call up a visual image. When these images clash—as in *The Fascist octopus has sung its swan song, the jackboot is thrown into the melting pot*—it can be taken as certain that the writer is not seeing a mental image of the objects he is naming; in other words he is not really thinking. Look again at the examples I gave at the beginning of this essay. Professor Laski (1) uses five negatives in fifty-three words. One of these is superfluous, making nonsense of the whole passage, and in addition there is the slip—*alien* for akin—making further nonsense, and several avoidable pieces of clumsiness which increase the general vagueness. Professor Hogben (2) plays ducks and drakes with a battery which is able to write prescriptions, and, while disapproving of the everyday phrase *put up with*, is unwilling to look *egregious* up in the dictionary and see what it means; (3), if one takes an uncharitable attitude towards it, is simply meaningless: Probably one could work out its intended meaning by reading the whole of the article in which it occurs. In (4), the writer knows more or less what he wants to say, but an accumulation of stale phrases chokes him like tea leaves blocking a sink. In (5), words and meaning have almost parted company. People who write in this manner usually have a general emotional meaning—they dislike one thing and want to express solidarity with another—but they are not interested in the detail of what they are saying. A scrupulous writer, in every sentence that he writes, will ask himself at least four questions, thus: What am I trying to say? What words will express it? What image or idiom will make it clearer? Is this image fresh enough to have an effect? And he will probably ask himself two more: Could I put it more shortly? Have I said anything that is avoidably ugly? But you are not obliged to go to all this trouble. You can shirk it by simply throwing your mind open and letting the ready-made phrases come crowding in. They will construct your sentences for you—even think your thoughts for you, to a certain extent—and at need they will perform the important service of partially concealing your meaning even from yourself. It is at this point that the special connection between politics and the debasement of language becomes clear.

In our time it is broadly true that political writing is bad writing. Where it is not true, it will generally be found that the writer is some kind of rebel, expressing his private opinions and not a "party line." Orthodoxy, of whatever color, seems to demand a lifeless, imitative style. The political dialects to be found in pamphlets, leading articles, manifestos, White Papers, and the speeches of under-secretaries do, of course, vary from party to party, but they are all alike in that one almost never finds in them a fresh, vivid, home-made turn of speech. When one watches some tired hack on the platform mechanically repeating the familiar phrases—*bestial atrocities, iron heel, bloodstained tyranny, free peoples of the world, stand shoulder to shoulder*—one often has a curious feeling that one is not watching a live human being but some kind of dummy: a feeling which suddenly becomes stronger at moments when the light catches the speaker's spectacles and turns them into blank discs which seem to have no eyes behind them. And this is not altogether fanciful. A speaker who uses that kind of phraseology has gone some distance towards turning himself into a machine. The appropriate noises are coming out of his larynx, but his brain is not involved as it would be if he were choosing his words for himself. If the speech he is making is one that he is accustomed to make over and over again, he may be almost unconscious of what he is saying, as one is when one utters the responses in church. And this reduced state of consciousness, if not indispensable, is at any rate favorable to political conformity.

In our time, political speech and writing are largely the defense of the indefensible. Things like the continuance of British rule in India, the Russian purges and deportations, the dropping of the atom bombs on Japan, can indeed be defended, but only by arguments which are too brutal for most people to face, and which do not square with the professed aims of political parties. Thus political language has to consist largely of euphemism, question-begging, and sheer cloudy vagueness. Defenseless villages are bombarded from the air, the inhabitants driven out into the countryside, the cattle machine-gunned, the huts set on fire with incendiary bullets: This is called *pacification*. Millions of peasants are robbed of their farms and sent trudging along the roads with no more than they can carry: This is called *transfer of population* or *rectification of frontiers*. People are imprisoned for years without trial, or shot in the back of the neck or sent to die of scurvy in Arctic lumber camps:[4] This is called *elimination of unreliable elements.* Such phraseology is needed if one wants to name things without calling up mental pictures of them. Consider for instance some comfortable English professor defending Russian totalitarianism. He cannot say outright, "I believe in killing off your opponents when you get good results by doing so." Probably, therefore, he will say something like this:

"While freely conceding that the Soviet régime exhibits certain features which the humanitarian may be inclined to deplore, we must, I think, agree that a certain curtailment of the right to political opposition is an unavoidable concomitant of transitional periods, and that the rigors which the Russian people have been called upon to undergo have been amply justified in the sphere of concrete achievement."

The inflated style is itself a kind of euphemism. A mass of Latin words   15 falls upon the facts like soft snow, blurring the outlines and covering up all the details. The great enemy of clear language is insincerity. When there is a gap between one's real and one's declared aims, one turns as it were instinctively to long words and exhausted idioms, like a cuttlefish squirting out ink. In our age there is no such thing as "keeping out of politics." All issues are political issues, and politics itself is a mass of lies, evasions, folly, hatred, and schizophrenia. When the general atmosphere is bad, language must suffer. I should expect to find—this is a guess which I have not sufficient knowledge to verify—that the German, Russian, and Italian languages have all deteriorated in the last ten or fifteen years, as a result of dictatorship.

But if thought corrupts language, language can also corrupt thought. A bad usage can spread by tradition and imitation, even among people who should and do know better. The debased language that I have been discussing is in some ways very convenient. Phrases like *a not unjustifiable assumption, leaves much to be desired, would serve no good purpose, a consideration which we should do well to bear in mind,* are a continuous temptation, a packet of aspirins always at one's elbow. Look back through this essay, and for certain you will find that I have again and again committed the very faults I am protesting against. By this morning's post I have received a pamphlet dealing with conditions in Germany. The author tells me that he "felt impelled" to write it. I open it at random, and here is almost the first sentence that I see: "(The Allies) have an opportunity not only of achieving a radical transformation of Germany's social and political structure in such a way as to avoid a nationalistic reaction in Germany itself, but at the same time of laying the foundations of a co-operative and unified Europe." You see, he "feels impelled" to write—feels, presumably, that he has something new to say—and yet his words, like cavalry horses answering the bugle, group themselves automatically into the familiar dreary pattern. The invasion of

---

[4] ***People . . . camps:*** Though Orwell is decrying all totalitarian abuse of language, his examples are mainly pointed at the Soviet purges under Joseph Stalin.—EDS.

one's mind by ready-made phrases (*lay the foundations, achieve a radical transformation*) can only be prevented if one is constantly on guard against them, and every such phrase anaesthetizes a portion of one's brain.

I said earlier that the decadence of our language is probably curable. Those who deny this would argue, if they produced an argument at all, that language merely reflects existing social conditions, and that we cannot influence its development by any direct tinkering with words and constructions. So far as the general tone or spirit of a language goes, this may be true, but it is not true in detail. Silly words and expressions have often disappeared, not through any evolutionary process but owing to the conscious action of a minority. Two recent examples were *explore every avenue* and *leave no stone unturned*, which were killed by the jeers of a few journalists. There is a long list of flyblown metaphors which could similarly be got rid of if enough people would interest themselves in the jobs; and it should also be possible to laugh the *not un-* formation out of existence,[5] to reduce the amount of Latin and Greek in the average sentence, to drive out foreign phrases and strayed scientific words, and, in general, to make pretentiousness unfashionable. But all these are minor points. The defense of the English language implies more than this, and perhaps it is best to start by saying what it does *not* imply.

To begin with it has nothing to do with archaism, with the salvaging of obsolete words and turns of speech, or with the setting up of a "standard English" which must never be departed from. On the contrary, it is especially concerned with the scrapping of every word or idiom which has outworn its usefulness. It has nothing to do with correct grammar and syntax, which are of no importance so long as one makes one's meaning clear, or with the avoidance of Americanisms, or with having what is called a "good prose style." On the other hand it is not concerned with fake simplicity and the attempt to make written English colloquial. Nor does it even imply in every case preferring the Saxon word to the Latin one, though it does imply using the fewest and shortest words that will cover one's meaning. What is above all needed is to let the meaning choose the word, and not the other way about. In prose, the worst thing one can do with words is to surrender to them. When you think of a concrete object, you think wordlessly, and then, if you want to describe the thing you have been visualizing you probably hunt about till you find the exact words that seem to fit. When you think of something abstract you are more inclined to use words from the start, and unless you make a conscious effort to prevent it, the existing dialect will come rushing in and do the job for you, at the expense of blurring or even changing your meaning. Probably it is better to put off using words as long as possible and get one's meaning as clear as one can through pictures or sensations. Afterwards one can choose—not simply *accept*—the phrases that will best cover the meaning, and then switch round and decide what impression one's words are likely to make on another person. This last effort of the mind cuts

---

[5] One can cure oneself of the *not un-* formation by memorizing this sentence: *A not unblack dog was chasing a not unsmall rabbit across a not ungreen field.*—ORWELL'S NOTE.

out all stale or mixed images, all prefabricated phrases, needless repetitions, and humbug and vagueness generally. But one can often be in doubt about the effect of a word or a phrase, and one needs rules that one can rely on when instinct fails. I think the following rules will cover most cases:

(i) Never use a metaphor, simile, or other figure of speech which you are used to seeing in print.

(ii) Never use a long word where a short one will do.

(iii) If it is possible to cut a word out, always cut it out.

(iv) Never use the passive where you can use the active.

(v) Never use a foreign phrase, a scientific word, or a jargon word if you can think of an everyday English equivalent.

(vi) Break any of these rules sooner than say anything outright barbarous.

These rules sound elementary, and so they are, but they demand a deep change in attitude in anyone who has grown used to writing in the style now fashionable. One could keep all of them and still write bad English, but one could not write the kind of stuff that I quoted in those five specimens at the beginning of this article.

I have not here been considering the literary use of language, but merely language as an instrument for expressing and not for concealing or preventing thought. Stuart Chase and others have come near to claiming that all abstract words are meaningless, and have used this as a pretext for advocating a kind of political quietism. Since you don't know what Fascism is, how can you struggle against Fascism? One need not swallow such absurdities as these, but one ought to recognize that the present political chaos is connected with the decay of language, and the one can probably bring about some improvement by starting at the verbal end. If you simplify your English, you are freed from the worst follies of orthodoxy. You cannot speak any of the necessary dialects, and when you make a stupid remark its stupidity will be obvious, even to yourself. Political language—and with variations this is true of all political parties, from Conservatives to Anarchists—is designed to make lies sound truthful and murder respectable, and to give an appearance of solidity to pure wind. One cannot change this all in a moment, but one can at least change one's own habits, and from time to time one can even, if one jeers loudly enough, send some worn-out and useless phrase—some *jackboot, Achilles' heel, hotbed, melting pot, acid test, veritable inferno*, or other lump of verbal refuse—into the dustbin where it belongs.

The Reader's Presence

1. What characteristics of Orwell's own writing demonstrate his six rules for writing good prose (paragraph 18)? Can you identify five examples in which Orwell practices what he preaches? Can you identify any moments when he seems to slip?

2. Note that Orwell does not provide *positive* examples of political expression. Why do you think this is so? Is Orwell implying that all political language—regardless of party or position—is corrupt? From this essay, can you infer Orwell's political philosophy? Explain your answer.

3. **CONNECTIONS:**   Look carefully at Orwell's five examples of bad prose. Would you have identified this writing as "bad" if you had come across it in your college reading? Compare Orwell's list of rules for writing (paragraph 18), and the ideas expressed in paragraph 16, to Langston Hughes's "How to Be a Bad Writer (in Ten Easy Lessons)" (page 160). How does each writer use humor to persuade the reader of the serious effects of writing badly? What does each writer seem to think is at stake in how one writes?

The Writer at Work

GEORGE ORWELL on the Four Reasons for Writing

ullstein bild/The Image Works

As the preceding essay shows, George Orwell spent much time considering the art of writing. He believed it was of the utmost political importance to write clearly and accurately. In the following passage from another essay, "Why I Write," Orwell considers a more-fundamental aspect of writing: the reasons behind why people write at all. You may observe that he doesn't list the reason most college students write—to respond to an assignment. Why do you think he omitted assigned writing? Can you think of other motives he doesn't take into account?

❝Putting aside the need to earn a living, I think there are four great motives for writing, at any rate for writing prose. They exist in different degrees in every writer, and in any one writer the proportions will vary from time to time, according to the atmosphere in which he is living. They are:

1. Sheer egoism. Desire to seem clever, to be talked about, to be remembered after death, to get your own back on grown-ups who snubbed you in childhood, etc., etc. It is humbug to pretend that this is not a motive, and a strong one. Writers share this characteristic with scientists, artists, politicians, lawyers, soldiers, successful businessmen—in short, with the whole top crust of humanity. The great mass of human beings are not acutely selfish. After the age of thirty they abandon individual ambition—in many cases, indeed, they almost abandon the sense of being individuals at all—and live chiefly for others, or are simply smothered under drudgery. But there is also the minority of gifted, willful

people who are determined to live their own lives to the end, and writers belong in this class. Serious writers, I should say, are on the whole more vain and self-centered than journalists, though less interested in money.

2. Aesthetic enthusiasm. Perception of beauty in the external world, or, on the other hand, in words and their right arrangement. Pleasure in the impact of one sound on another, in the firmness of good prose or the rhythm of a good story. Desire to share an experience which one feels is valuable and ought not to be missed. The aesthetic motive is very feeble in a lot of writers, but even a pamphleteer or a writer of textbooks will have pet words and phrases which appeal to him for non-utilitarian reasons; or he may feel strongly about typography, width of margins, etc. Above the level of a railway guide, no book is quite free from aesthetic considerations.

3. Historical impulse. Desire to see things as they are, to find out true facts and store them up for the use of posterity.

4. Political purpose—using the word "political" in the widest possible sense. Desire to push the world in a certain direction, to alter other people's idea of the kind of society that they should strive after. Once again, no book is genuinely free from political bias. The opinion that art should have nothing to do with politics is itself a political attitude. **"**

Michael Pollan

THE END OF COOKING?

Journalist, author, and educator **MICHAEL POLLAN** (b. 1955) has become a leading voice for change in our industrialized food system—what we grow and what we eat. The theme of his 2008 book, *In Defense of Food: An Eater's Manifesto*, comes down to seven words: "Eat Food. Not Too Much. Mostly Plants." His other books include *The Botany of Desire: A Plant's-Eye View of the World* (2001), in which he argues that domesticated plants have shaped humans as much as humans have shaped plants; *The Omnivore's Dilemma: A Natural History of Four Meals* (2006), which focuses on the impact of corn on the American diet and the environment; and, most recently, *Cooked: A Natural History of Transformation*

||||||||||||||||||||||||||||||||||||||||||||||||||||||||||||||||||||||||||||||||||||||||||||||||||||||||||||||||||||||||

(2013), which examines the science and skill of the processes that happen in our kitchens. Pollan was born and raised on Long Island, New York, and educated at Bennington College, Mansfield College, University of Oxford, and Columbia University, where he received his MA in English. Since then, he has written books and articles, lectured, and taught about food, agriculture, nature, and the environment. He is currently the Knight Professor of Journalism and director of the Knight Program in Science and Environmental Journalism at the University of California, Berkeley. An

> The theme of Michael Pollan's 2008 book, *In Defense of Food: An Eater's Manifesto*, comes down to seven words: **Eat Food. Not Too Much. Mostly Plants.**

award-winning journalist, Pollan is a regular contributor to the *New York Times Magazine*. A longer version of "The End of Cooking?" originally appeared in the *New York Times* in 2009 (with the title "Out of the Kitchen, Onto the Couch"), and this shorter version subsequently appeared in *Portland Magazine* in 2012.

I WAS ONLY EIGHT YEARS OLD when *The French Chef* first appeared on American television in 1963, but it didn't take long for me to realize that this Julia Child had improved the quality of life around our house. My mother began cooking dishes she'd watched Julia cook on television: boeuf bourguignon (the subject of the show's first episode), French onion soup gratinée, duck à l'orange, coq au vin, mousse au chocolat. Some of the more ambitious dishes, like the duck or the mousse, were pointed toward weekend company, but my mother would usually test these out on me and my sisters earlier in the week, and a few of the others—including the boeuf bourguignon, which I especially loved—actually made it into heavy weeknight rotation. So whenever people talk about how Julia Child upgraded the culture of food in America, I nod appreciatively. I owe her. Not that I didn't also owe Swanson, because we also ate TV dinners, and those were pretty good, too.

Every so often I would watch *The French Chef* with my mother in the den. On WNET in New York, it came on late in the afternoon, after school, and because we had only one television back then, if Mom wanted to watch her program, you watched it, too. The show felt less like TV than like hanging around the kitchen, which is to say, not terribly exciting to a kid (except when Child dropped something on the floor, which my mother promised would happen if we stuck around long enough) but comforting in its familiarity: the clanking of pots and pans, the squeal of an oven door in need of oil, all the kitchen-chemistry-set spectacles of transformation. The show was

:e macmillanhighered.com/writerspresence8e
Are healthy food and good business decisions mutually exclusive?
e-Readings > *Healthy Corner Stores* [video]

taped live and broadcast uncut and unedited, so it had a vérité feel completely unlike anything you might see today on the Food Network, with its A.D.H.D. editing and hyperkinetic soundtracks of rock music and clashing knives. While Julia waited for the butter foam to subside in the sauté pan, you waited, too, precisely as long, listening to Julia's improvised patter over the hiss of her pan, as she filled the desultory minutes with kitchen tips and lore. It all felt more like life than TV, though Julia's voice was like nothing I ever heard before or would hear again until Monty Python came to America: vaguely European, breathy and singsongy, and weirdly suggestive of a man doing a falsetto impression of a woman. The BBC supposedly took *The French Chef* off the air because viewers wrote in complaining that Julia Child seemed either drunk or demented.

Meryl Streep, who brings Julia Child vividly back to the screen in Nora Ephron's charming comedy, *Julie & Julia*, has the voice down, and with the help of some clever set design and cinematography, she manages to evoke too Child's big-girl ungainliness—the woman was 6 foot 2 and had arms like a longshoreman. Streep also captures the deep sensual delight that Julia Child took in food—not just the eating of it but the fondling and affectionate slapping of ingredients in their raw state and the magic of their kitchen transformations.

But *Julie & Julia* is more than an exercise in nostalgia. As the title suggests, the film has a second, more contemporary heroine. The Julie character (played by Amy Adams) is based on Julie Powell, a 29-year-old aspiring writer living in Queens who, casting about for a blog conceit in 2002, hit on a cool one: she would cook her way through all 524 recipes in Child's *Mastering the Art of French Cooking* in 365 days and blog about her adventures. The movie shuttles back and forth between Julie's year of compulsive cooking and blogging in Queens in 2002 and Julia's decade in Paris and Provence a half-century earlier, as recounted in *My Life in France,* the memoir published a few years after her death in 2004. Julia Child in 1949 was in some ways in the same boat in which Julie Powell found herself in 2002: happily married to a really nice guy but feeling, acutely, the lack of a life project. Living in Paris, where her husband, Paul Child, was posted in the diplomatic corps, Julia (who like Julie had worked as a secretary) was at a loss as to what to do with her life until she realized that what she liked to do best was eat. So she enrolled in Le Cordon Bleu and learned how to cook. As with Julia, so with Julie: cooking saved her life, giving her a project and, eventually, a path to literary success.

That learning to cook could lead an American woman to success of any kind would have seemed utterly implausible in 1949; that it is so thoroughly plausible 60 years later owes everything to Julia Child's legacy. Julie Powell operates in a world that Julia Child helped to create, one where food is taken seriously, where chefs have been welcomed into the repertory company of American celebrity and where cooking has become a broadly appealing mise-en-scène in which success stories can plausibly be set and played out. How amazing is it that we live today in a culture that has not

5

only something called the Food Network but now a hit show on that network called *The Next Food Network Star*, which thousands of 20- and 30-somethings compete eagerly to become? It would seem we have come a long way from Swanson TV dinners.

The Food Network can now be seen in nearly 100 million American homes, and on most nights commands more viewers than any of the cable news channels. Millions of Americans, including my 16-year-old son, can tell you months after the finale which contestant emerged victorious in Season 5 of *Top Chef*. The popularity of cooking shows — or perhaps I should say food shows — has spread beyond the precincts of public or cable television to the broadcast networks. It's no wonder that a Hollywood studio would conclude that American audiences had an appetite for a movie in which the road to personal fulfillment and public success passes through the kitchen and turns, crucially, on a recipe for boeuf bourguignon. (The secret is to pat dry your beef before you brown it.)

But here's what I don't get: How is it that we are so eager to watch other people browning beef cubes on screen but so much less eager to brown them ourselves? For the rise of Julia Child as a figure of cultural consequence — along with Alice Waters and Mario Batali and Martha Stewart and Emeril Lagasse and whoever is crowned the next Food Network star — has, paradoxically, coincided with the rise of fast food, home-meal replacements and the decline and fall of everyday home cooking.

That decline has several causes: women working outside the home; food companies persuading Americans to let them do the cooking; and advances in technology that made it easier for them to do so. Cooking is no longer obligatory, and for many people, women especially, that has been a blessing. But perhaps a mixed blessing, to judge by the culture's continuing, if not deepening, fascination with the subject. It has been easier for us to give up cooking than it has been to give up talking about it — and watching it.

Today the average American spends a mere 27 minutes a day on food preparation (another four minutes cleaning up); that's less than half the time that we spent cooking and cleaning up when Julia arrived on our television screens. It's also less than half the time it takes to watch a single episode of *Top Chef* or *Chopped* or *The Next Food Network Star*. What this suggests is that a great many Americans are spending considerably more time watching images of cooking on television than they are cooking themselves — an increasingly archaic activity they will tell you they no longer have the time for.

What is wrong with this picture?   10

THE COURAGE TO FLIP

When I asked my mother recently what exactly endeared Julia Child to her, she explained that "for so many of us she took the fear out of cooking" and, to illustrate the point, brought up the famous potato show, one of the episodes that Meryl Streep recreates brilliantly on screen. Millions of Americans of a certain age claim to remember Julia Child dropping a chicken or a goose on the floor, but the memory is apocryphal: what she dropped was a potato pancake, and it didn't quite make it to the floor. Still, this was a classic live-television moment, inconceivable on any modern cooking show: Martha Stewart would sooner commit seppuku than let such an outtake ever see the light of day.

The episode has Julia making a plate-size potato pancake, sautéing a big disc of mashed potato into which she has folded impressive quantities of cream and butter. Then the fateful moment arrives:

"When you flip anything, you just have to have the courage of your convictions," she declares, clearly a tad nervous at the prospect, and then gives the big pancake a flip. On the way down, half of it catches the top of the pan and splats onto the stovetop. Undaunted, Julia scoops the thing up and roughly patches the pancake back together, explaining: "When I flipped it, I didn't have the courage to do it the way I should have. You can always pick it up." And then, looking right through the camera as if taking us into her confidence, she utters the line that did so much to lift the fear of failure from my mother and her contemporaries: "If you're alone in the kitchen, WHOOOO"—the pronoun is sung—"is going to see?" For a generation of women eager to transcend their mothers' recipe box (and perhaps, too, their mothers' social standing), Julia's little kitchen catastrophe was a liberation and a lesson: "The only way you learn to flip things is just to flip them!"

It was a kind of courage—not only to cook but to cook the world's most glamorous and intimidating cuisine—that Julia Child gave my mother and so many other women like her, and to watch her empower viewers in episode after episode is to appreciate just how much about cooking on television—not to mention cooking itself—has changed in the years since *The French Chef* was on the air.

There are still cooking programs that will teach you how to cook. Public television offers the eminently useful *America's Test Kitchen*. The Food Network carries a whole slate of so-called dump-and-stir shows during the day, and the network's research suggests that at least some viewers are following along. But many of these programs—I'm thinking of Rachael Ray, Paula Deen, Sandra Lee—tend to be aimed at stay-at-home moms who are in a hurry and eager to please. These shows stress quick results, shortcuts, and superconvenience but never the sort of pleasure—physical and mental—that Julia Child took in the work of cooking: the tomahawking of a fish skeleton or the chopping of an onion, the Rolfing of butter into the breast of a raw chicken or the vigorous whisking of heavy cream. By the end of the potato show, Julia was out of breath and had broken a sweat, which she mopped from her brow with a paper towel. (Have you ever seen Martha Stewart break a sweat?) Child was less interested in making it fast or easy than making it right, because cooking for her was so much more than a means to a meal. It was a gratifying, even ennobling sort of work, engaging both the mind and the muscles. You didn't do it to please a husband or

15

impress guests; you did it to please yourself. No one cooking on television today gives the impression that they enjoy the actual work quite as much as Julia Child did. In this, she strikes me as a more liberated figure than many of the women who have followed her on television.

Curiously, the year Julia Child went on the air—1963—was the same year Betty Friedan published *The Feminine Mystique*, the book that taught millions of American women to regard housework, cooking included, as drudgery, indeed as a form of oppression. You may think of these two figures as antagonists, but that wouldn't be quite right. They actually had a great deal in common, as Child's biographer, Laura Shapiro, points out, and addressed the aspirations of many of the same women. Julia never referred to her viewers as "housewives"—a word she detested—and never condescended to them. She tried to show the sort of women who read *The Feminine Mystique* that, far from oppressing them, the work of cooking approached in the proper spirit offered a kind of fulfillment and deserved an intelligent woman's attention. (A man's too.) Second-wave feminists were often ambivalent on the gender politics of cooking. Simone de Beauvoir wrote in *The Second Sex* that though cooking could be oppressive, it could also be a form of "revelation and creation; and a woman can find special satisfaction in a successful cake or a flaky pastry, for not everyone can do it: one must have the gift." This can be read either as a special Frenchie exemption for the culinary arts (féminisme, c'est bon, but we must not jeopardize those flaky pastries!) or as a bit of wisdom that some American feminists thoughtlessly trampled in their rush to get women out of the kitchen.

TO THE KITCHEN STADIUM

Whichever, kitchen work itself has changed considerably since 1963, judging from its depiction on today's how-to shows. Take the concept of cooking from scratch. Many of today's cooking programs rely unapologetically on ingredients that themselves contain lots of ingredients: canned soups, jarred mayonnaise, frozen vegetables, powdered sauces, vanilla wafers, limeade concentrate, Marshmallow Fluff. This probably shouldn't surprise us: processed foods have so thoroughly colonized the American kitchen and diet that they have redefined what passes today for cooking, not to mention food. Many of these convenience foods have been sold to women as tools of liberation; the rhetoric of kitchen oppression has been cleverly hijacked by food marketers and the cooking shows they sponsor to sell more stuff. So the shows encourage home cooks to take all manner of shortcuts, each of which involves buying another product, and all of which taken together have succeeded in redefining what is commonly meant by the verb "to cook."

I spent an enlightening if somewhat depressing hour on the phone with a veteran food-marketing researcher, Harry Balzer, who explained that "people call things 'cooking' today that would roll their grandmother in her grave—heating up a can of soup or microwaving a frozen pizza." Balzer has been studying American eating habits since 1978; the NPD Group, the firm he works for, collects data from a pool of 2,000 food diaries to track American eating habits. Years ago Balzer noticed that the definition of cooking held by his respondents had grown so broad as to be meaningless, so the firm tightened up the meaning of "to cook" at least slightly to capture what was really going on in American kitchens. To cook from scratch, they decreed, means to prepare a main dish that requires some degree of "assembly of elements." So microwaving a pizza doesn't count as cooking, though washing a head of lettuce and pouring bottled dressing over it does. Under this dispensation, you're also cooking when you spread mayonnaise on a slice of bread and pile on some cold cuts or a hamburger patty. (Currently the most popular meal in America, at both lunch and dinner, is a sandwich; the No. 1 accompanying beverage is a soda.) At least by Balzer's non-too-exacting standard, Americans are still cooking up a storm—58 percent of our evening meals qualify, though even that figure has been falling steadily since the 1980s.

Like most people who study consumer behavior, Balzer has developed a somewhat cynical view of human nature, which his research suggests is ever driven by the quest to save time or money or, optimally, both. I kept asking him what his research had to say about the prevalence of the activity I referred to as "real scratch cooking," but he wouldn't touch the term. Why? Apparently the activity has become so rarefied as to elude his tools of measurement.

"Here's an analogy," Balzer said. "A hundred years ago, chicken for din-   20
ner meant going out and catching, killing, plucking and gutting a chicken. Do you know anybody who still does that? It would be considered crazy! Well, that's exactly how cooking will seem to your grandchildren: something people used to do when they had no other choice. Get over it."

After my discouraging hour on the phone with Balzer, I settled in for a couple more hours with the Food Network, trying to square his dismal view of our interest in cooking with the hyperexuberant, even fetishized images of cooking that are presented on the screen. The Food Network undergoes a complete change of personality at night, when it trades the cozy precincts of the home kitchen and chirpy softball coaching of Rachael Ray or Sandra Lee for something markedly less feminine and less practical. Erica Gruen, the cable executive often credited with putting the Food Network on the map in the late '90s, recognized early on that, as she told a journalist, "people don't watch television to learn things." So she shifted the network's target audience from people who love to cook to people who love to eat, a considerably larger universe and one that—important for a cable network—happens to contain a great many more men.

In prime time, the Food Network's mise-en-scène shifts to masculine arenas like the Kitchen Stadium on *Iron Chef*, where famous restaurant chefs wage gladiatorial combat to see who can, in 60 minutes, concoct the most spectacular meal from a secret ingredient ceremoniously unveiled just as the clock starts: an octopus or a bunch of bananas or a whole school of daurade. Whether in the Kitchen Stadium or on *Chopped* or *The Next Food*

Network Star or, over on Bravo, *Top Chef*, cooking in prime time is a form of athletic competition, drawing its visual and even aural vocabulary from *Monday Night Football*. On *Iron Chef America*, one of the Food Network's biggest hits, the cooking-caster Alton Brown delivers a breathless (though always gently tongue-in-cheek) play by play and color commentary, as the iron chefs and their team of iron sous-chefs race the clock to peel, chop, slice, dice, mince, Cuisinart, mandolin, boil, double-boil, pan-sear, sauté, sous vide, deepfry, pressure-cook, grill, deglaze, reduce, and plate—this last word I'm old enough to remember when it was a mere noun. A particularly dazzling display of chefly "knife skills"—a term bandied as freely on the Food Network as "passing game" or "slugging percentage" is on ESPN—will earn an instant replay: an onion minced in slo-mo. Can we get a camera on this, Alton Brown will ask in a hushed, this-must-be-golf tone of voice. It looks like Chef Flay's going to try for a last-minute garnish grab before the clock runs out! Will he make it? [The buzzer sounds.] Yes!

These shows move so fast, in such a blur of flashing knives, frantic pantry raids, and more sheer fire than you would ever want to see in your own kitchen, that I honestly can't tell you whether that "last-minute garnish grab" happened on *Iron Chef America* or *Chopped* or *The Next Food Network Star* or whether it was Chef Flay or Chef Batali who snagged the sprig of foliage at the buzzer. But impressive it surely was, in the same way it's impressive to watch a handful of eager young chefs of *Chopped* figure out how to make a passable appetizer from chicken wings, celery, soba noodles and a package of string cheese in just 20 minutes, said starter to be judged by a panel of professional chefs on the basis of "taste, creativity and presentation." (If you ask me, the key to victory on any of these shows comes down to one factor: bacon. Whichever contestant puts bacon in the dish invariably seems to win.)

But you do have to wonder how easily so specialized a set of skills might translate to the home kitchen—or anywhere else for that matter. For when in real life are even professional chefs required to conceive and execute dishes in 20 minutes from ingredients selected by a third party exhibiting obvious sadistic tendencies? (String cheese?) Never, is when. The skills celebrated on the Food Network in prime time are precisely the skills necessary to succeed on the Food Network in prime time. They will come in handy nowhere else on God's green earth.

We learn things watching these cooking competitions, but they're not   25
things about how to cook. There are no recipes to follow; the contests fly by much too fast for viewers to take in any practical tips; and the kind of cooking practiced in prime time is far more spectacular than anything you would ever try at home. No, for anyone hoping to pick up a few dinnertime tips, the implicit message of today's prime-time cooking shows is, Don't try this at home. If you really want to eat this way, go to a restaurant. Or as a chef friend put it when I asked him if he thought I could learn anything about cooking by watching the Food Network, "How much do you learn about basketball by watching the N.B.A.?"

What we mainly learn about on the Food Network in prime time is culinary fashion, which is no small thing: if Julia took the fear out of cooking, these shows take the fear—the social anxiety—out of ordering in restaurants. (Hey, now I know what a shiso leaf is and what "crudo" means!) Then, at the judges' table, we learn how to taste and how to talk about food. For viewers, these shows have become less about the production of high-end food than about its consumption—including its conspicuous consumption. (I think I'll start with the sawfish crudo wrapped in shiso leaves . . .)

Surely it's no accident that so many Food Network stars have themselves found a way to transcend barriers of social class in the kitchen—beginning with Emeril Lagasse, the working-class guy from Fall River, Massachusetts, who, though he may not be able to sound the "r" in "garlic," can still cook like a dream. Once upon a time Julia made the same promise in reverse: she showed you how you, too, could cook like someone who could not only prepare but properly pronounce a béarnaise. So-called fancy food has always served as a form of cultural capital, and cooking programs help you acquire it, now without so much as lifting a spatula. The glamour of food has made it something of a class leveler in America, a fact that many of these shows implicitly celebrate. Television likes nothing better than to serve up elitism to the masses, paradoxical as that might sound. How wonderful is it that something like arugula can at the same time be a mark of sophistication and be found in almost every salad bar in America? Everybody wins!

But the shift from producing food on television to consuming it strikes me as a far-less-salubrious development. Traditionally, the recipe for the typical dump-and-stir program comprises about 80 percent cooking followed by 20 percent eating, but in prime time you now find a raft of shows that flip that ratio on its head, like *The Best Thing I Ever Ate* and *Diners, Drive-Ins and Dives*, which are about nothing but eating. Sure, Guy Fieri, the tattooed and spiky-coiffed chowhound who hosts *Diners, Drive-Ins and Dives*, ducks into the kitchen whenever he visits one of these roadside joints to do a little speed-bonding with the startled short-order cooks in back, but most of the time he's wrapping his mouth around their supersize creations: a 16-ounce Oh Gawd! Burger (with the works); battered and deep-fried anything (clams, pickles, cinnamon buns, stuffed peppers, you name it); or a buttermilk burrito approximately the size of his head, stuffed with bacon, eggs and cheese. What Fieri's critical vocabulary lacks in analytical rigor, it more than makes up for in tailgate enthusiasm: "Man, oh man, now this is what I'm talking about!" What can possibly be the appeal of watching Guy Fieri bite, masticate, and swallow all this chow?

The historical drift of cooking programs—from a genuine interest in producing food for yourself to the spectacle of merely consuming it—surely owes a lot to the decline of cooking in our culture, but it also has something to do with the gravitational field that eventually overtakes anything in television—or educational television, as it used to be called. On a commercial network, a program that actually inspired viewers to get off the couch and spend an hour cooking a meal would be a commercial disaster, for it would mean they were turning off the television to do something else. The ads on the Food Network, at least in prime time, strongly suggest its viewers do no such thing: the food-related ads hardly ever hawk kitchen appliances or ingredients (unless you count A.1. steak sauce) but rather push the usual supermarket cart of edible foodlike substances, including Manwich sloppy joe in a can, Special K protein shakes and Ore-Ida frozen French fries, along with fast-casual eateries like Olive Garden and Red Lobster.

Buying, not making, is what cooking shows are mostly now about—that   30
and, increasingly, cooking shows themselves: the whole self-perpetuating spectacle of competition, success and celebrity that, with *The Next Food Network Star*, appears to have entered its baroque phase. The Food Network has figured out that we care much less about what's cooking than who's cooking. A few years ago, Mario Batali neatly summed up the network's formula to a reporter: "Look, it's TV! Everyone has to fall into a niche. I'm the Italian guy. Emeril's the next exuberant New Orleans guy with the big eyebrows who yells a lot. Bobby's the grilling guy. Rachael Ray is the cheerleader-type girl who makes things at home the way a regular person would. Giada's the beautiful girl with the nice rack who does simple Italian food. As silly as the whole Food Network is, it gives us all a soapbox to talk about the things we care about." Not to mention a platform from which to sell all their stuff.

The Food Network has helped to transform cooking from something you do into something you watch—into yet another confection of spectacle and celebrity that keeps us pinned to the couch. The formula is as circular and self-reinforcing as a TV dinner: a simulacrum of home cooking that is sold on TV and designed to be eaten in front of the TV. True, in the case of the Swanson rendition, at least you get something that will fill you up; by comparison, the Food Network leaves you hungry, a condition its advertisers must love. But in neither case is there much risk that you will get off the couch and actually cook a meal. Both kinds of TV dinner plant us exactly where television always wants us: in front of the set, watching.

WATCHING WHAT WE EAT

To point out that television has succeeded in turning cooking into a spectator sport raises the question of why anyone would want to watch other people cook in the first place. There are plenty of things we've stopped doing for ourselves that we have no desire to watch other people do on TV: you don't see shows about changing the oil in your car or ironing shirts or reading newspapers. So what is it about cooking, specifically, that makes it such good television just now?

It's worth keeping in mind that watching other people cook is not exactly a new behavior for us humans. Even when "everyone" still cooked, there were plenty of us who mainly watched: men, for the most part, and children. Most of us have happy memories of watching our mothers in the kitchen, performing feats that sometimes looked very much like sorcery and typically resulted in something tasty to eat. Watching my mother transform the raw materials of nature—a handful of plants, an animal's flesh—into a favorite dinner was always a pretty good show, but on the afternoons when she tackled a complex marvel like chicken Kiev, I happily stopped whatever I was doing to watch. (I told you we had it pretty good, thanks partly to Julia.) My mother would hammer the boneless chicken breasts into flat pink slabs, roll them tightly around chunks of ice-cold herbed butter, glue the cylinders shut with egg, then fry the little logs until they turned golden brown, in what qualified as a minor miracle of transubstantiation. When the dish turned out right, knifing through the crust into the snowy white meat within would uncork a fragrant ooze of melted butter that seeped across the plate to merge with the Minute Rice. (If the instant rice sounds all wrong, remember that in the 1960s, Julia Child and modern food science were both tokens of sophistication.)

Yet even the most ordinary dish follows a similar arc of transformation, magically becoming something greater than the sum of its parts. Every dish contains not just culinary ingredients but also the ingredients of narrative: a beginning, a middle, and an end. Bring in the element of fire—cooking's *deus ex machina*—and you've got a tasty little drama right there, the whole thing unfolding in a TV-friendly span of time: 30 minutes (at 350 degrees) will usually do it.

Cooking shows also benefit from the fact that food itself is—by definition—attractive to the humans who eat it, and that attraction can be enhanced by food styling, an art at which the Food Network so excels as to make Julia Child look like a piker. You'll be flipping aimlessly through the cable channels when a slow-motion cascade of glistening red cherries or a tongue of flame lapping at a slab of meat on the grill will catch your eye, and your reptilian brain will paralyze your thumb on the remote, forcing you to stop to see what's cooking. Food shows are the campfires in the deep cable forest, drawing us like hungry wanderers to their flames. (And on the Food Network there are plenty of flames to catch your eye, compensating, no doubt, for the unfortunate absence of aromas.)

No matter how well produced, a televised oil change and lube offers no such satisfactions.

I suspect we're drawn to the textures and rhythms of kitchen work, too, which seem so much more direct and satisfying than the more abstract and formless tasks most of us perform in our jobs nowadays. The chefs on TV get to put their hands on real stuff, not keyboards and screens but fundamental things like plants and animals and fungi; they get to work with fire and ice and perform feats of alchemy. By way of explaining why in the world she wants to cook her way through *Mastering the Art of French Cooking*, all Julie Powell has to do in the film is show us her cubicle at the Lower

35

Manhattan Development Corporation, where she spends her days on the phone mollifying callers with problems that she lacks the power to fix.

"You know what I love about cooking?" Julie tells us in a voiceover as we watch her field yet another inconclusive call on her headset. "I love that after a day where nothing is sure—and when I say nothing, I mean nothing—you can come home and absolutely know that if you add egg yolks to chocolate and sugar and milk, it will get thick. It's such a comfort." How many of us still do work that engages us in a dialogue with the material world and ends—assuming the soufflé doesn't collapse—with such a gratifying and tasty sense of closure? Come to think of it, even the collapse of the soufflé is at least definitive, which is more than you can say about most of what you will do at work tomorrow.

THE END OF COOKING

If cooking really offers all these satisfactions, then why don't we do more of it? Well, ask Julie Powell: for most of us it doesn't pay the rent, and very often our work doesn't leave us the time; during the year of Julia, dinner at the Powell apartment seldom arrived at the table before 10 p.m. For many years now, Americans have been putting in longer hours at work and enjoying less time at home. Since 1967, we've added 167 hours—the equivalent of a month's full-time labor—to the total amount of time we spend at work each year, and in households where both parents work, the figure is more like 400 hours. Americans today spend more time working than people in any other industrialized nation—an extra two weeks or more a year. Not surprisingly, in those countries where people still take cooking seriously, they also have more time to devote to it.

It's generally assumed that the entrance of women into the work force 40 is responsible for the collapse of home cooking, but that turns out to be only part of the story. Yes, women with jobs outside the home spend less time cooking—but so do women without jobs. The amount of time spent on food preparation in America has fallen at the same precipitous rate among women who don't work outside the home as it has among women who do: in both cases, a decline of about 40 percent since 1965. (Though for married women who don't have jobs, the amount of time spent cooking remains greater: 58 minutes a day, as compared with 36 for married women who do have jobs.) In general, spending on restaurants or takeout food rises with income. Women with jobs have more money to pay corporations to do their cooking, yet all American women now allow corporations to cook for them when they can.

Those corporations have been trying to persuade Americans to let them do the cooking since long before large numbers of women entered the work force. After World War II, the food industry labored mightily to sell American women on all the processed-food wonders it had invented to feed the troops:

canned meals, freeze-dried foods, dehydrated potatoes, powdered orange juice and coffee, instant everything. As Laura Shapiro recounts in *Something from the Oven: Reinventing Dinner in 1950s America*, the food industry strived to "persuade millions of Americans to develop a lasting taste for meals that were a lot like field rations." The same process of peace-time conversion that industrialized our farming, giving us synthetic fertilizers made from munitions and new pesticides developed from nerve gas, also industrialized our eating.

Shapiro shows that the shift toward industrial cookery began not in response to a demand from women entering the work force but as a supply-driven phenomenon. In fact, for many years American women, whether they worked or not, resisted processed foods, regarding them as a dereliction of their "moral obligation to cook," something they believed to be a parental responsibility on par with child care. It took years of clever, dedicated marketing to break down this resistance and persuade Americans that opening a can or cooking from a mix really was cooking. Honest. In the 1950s, just-add-water cake mixes languished in the supermarket until the marketers figured out that if you left at least something for the "baker" to do—specifically, crack open an egg—she could take ownership of the cake. Over the years, the food scientists have gotten better and better at simulating real food, keeping it looking attractive, and seemingly fresh, and the rapid acceptance of microwave ovens—which went from being in only 8 percent of American households in 1978 to 90 percent today—opened up vast new horizons of home-meal replacement.

Harry Balzer's research suggests that the corporate project of redefining what it means to cook and serve a meal has succeeded beyond the industry's wildest expectations. People think nothing of buying frozen peanut butter-and-jelly sandwiches for their children's lunchboxes. (Now how much of a timesaver can that be?) "We've had a hundred years of packaged foods," Balzer told me, "and now we're going to have a hundred years of packaged meals." Already today, 80 percent of the cost of food eaten in the home goes to someone other than a farmer, which is to say to industrial cooking and packaging and marketing. Balzer is unsentimental about this development: "Do you miss sewing or darning socks? I don't think so."

So what are we doing with the time we save by outsourcing our food preparation to corporations and 16-year-old burger flippers? Working, commuting to work, surfing the Internet and, perhaps most curiously of all, watching other people cook on television.

But this may not be quite the paradox it seems. Maybe the reason we 45 like to watch cooking on TV is that there are things about cooking we miss. We might not feel we have the time or the energy to do it ourselves every day, yet we're not prepared to see it disappear from our lives entirely. Why? Perhaps because cooking—unlike sewing or darning socks—is an activity that strikes a deep emotional chord in us, one that might even go to the heart of our identity as human beings.

What?! You're telling me Bobby Flay strikes deep emotional chords?

Bear with me. Consider for a moment the proposition that as a human activity, cooking is far more important—to our happiness and to our health—than its current role in our lives, not to mention its depiction on TV, might lead you to believe. Let's see what happens when we take cooking seriously.

THE COOKING ANIMAL

The idea that cooking is a defining human activity is not a new one. In 1773, the Scottish writer James Boswell, noting that "no beast is a cook," called Homo sapiens "the cooking animal," though he might have reconsidered that definition had he been able to gaze upon the frozen-food cases at Wal-Mart. Fifty years later, in *The Physiology of Taste*, the French gastronome Jean-Anthelme Brillat-Savarin claimed that cooking made us who we are; by teaching men to use fire, it had "done the most to advance the cause of civilization." More recently, the anthropologist Claude Lévi-Strauss, writing in 1964 in *The Raw and the Cooked*, found that many cultures entertained a similar view, regarding cooking as a symbolic way of distinguishing ourselves from the animals.

For Lévi-Strauss, cooking is a metaphor for the human transformation of nature into culture, but in the years since *The Raw and the Cooked*, other anthropologists have begun to take quite literally the idea that cooking is the key to our humanity. Richard Wrangham, a Harvard anthropologist, published a fascinating book called *Catching Fire*, in which he argues that it was the discovery of cooking by our early ancestors—not tool-making or language or meat-eating—that made us human. By providing our primate forebears with a more energy-dense and easy-to-digest diet, cooked food altered the course of human evolution, allowing our brains to grow bigger (brains are notorious energy guzzlers) and our guts to shrink. It seems that raw food takes much more time and energy to chew and digest, which is why other primates of our size carry around substantially larger digestive tracts and spend many more of their waking hours chewing: up to six hours a day. (That's nearly as much time as Guy Fieri devotes to the activity.) Also, since cooking detoxifies many foods, it cracked open a treasure trove of nutritious calories unavailable to other animals. Freed from the need to spend our days gathering large quantities of raw food and then chewing (and chewing) it, humans could now devote their time, and their metabolic resources, to other purposes, like creating a culture.

Cooking gave us not just the meal but also the occasion: the practice of 50 eating together at an appointed time and place. This was something new under the sun, for the forager of raw food would likely have fed himself on the go and alone, like the animals. (Or, come to think of it, like the industrial eaters we've become, grazing at gas stations and skipping meals.) But sitting down to common meals, making eye contact, sharing food, all served to civilize us; "around that fire," Wrangham says, "we became tamer."

If cooking is as central to human identity and culture as Wrangham believes, it stands to reason that the decline of cooking in our time would have a profound effect on modern life. At the very least, you would expect that its rapid disappearance from everyday life might leave us feeling nostalgic for the sights and smells and the sociality of the cooking fire. Bobby Flay and Rachael Ray may be pushing precisely that emotional button. Interestingly, the one kind of home cooking that is actually on the rise today (according to Harry Balzer) is outdoor grilling. Chunks of animal flesh seared over an open fire: grilling is cooking at its most fundamental and explicit, the transformation of the raw into the cooked right before our eyes. It makes a certain sense that the grill would be gaining adherents at the very moment when cooking meals and eating them together is fading from the culture. (While men have hardly become equal partners in the kitchen, they are cooking more today than ever before: about 13 percent of all meals, many of them on the grill.)

Yet we don't crank up the barbecue every day; grilling for most people is more ceremony than routine. We seem to be well on our way to turning cooking into a form of weekend recreation, a backyard sport for which we outfit ourselves at Williams-Sonoma, or a televised spectator sport we watch from the couch. Cooking's fate may be to join some of our other weekend exercises in recreation atavism: camping and gardening and hunting and riding on horseback. Something in us apparently likes to be reminded of our distant origins every now and then and to celebrate whatever rough skills for contending with the natural world might survive in us, beneath the thin crust of 21st-century civilization.

To play at farming or foraging for food strikes us as harmless enough, perhaps because the delegating of those activities to other people in real life is something most of us are generally O.K. with. But to relegate the activity of cooking to a form of play, something that happens just on weekends or mostly on television, seems much more consequential. The fact is that not cooking may well be deleterious to our health, and there is reason to believe that the outsourcing of food preparation to corporations and 16-year-olds has already taken a toll on our physical and psychological well-being.

Consider some recent research on the links between cooking and dietary health. A 2003 study by a group of Harvard economists led by David Cutler found that the rise of food preparation outside the home could explain most of the increase in obesity in America. Mass production has driven down the cost of many foods, not only in terms of price but also in the amount of time required to obtain them. The French fry did not become the most popular "vegetable" in America until industry relieved us of the considerable effort needed to prepare French fries ourselves. Similarly, the mass production of cream-filled cakes, fried chicken wings and taquitos, exotically flavored chips or cheesy puffs of refined flour, has transformed all these hard-to-make-at-home foods into the sort of everyday fare you can pick up at the gas station on a whim and for less than a dollar. The fact that we no longer have to plan or even wait to enjoy these items, as we would if we were making them ourselves, makes us that much more likely to indulge impulsively.

Cutler and his colleagues also surveyed cooking patterns across several cultures and found that obesity rates are inversely correlated with the amount of time spent on food preparation. The more time a nation devotes to food preparation at home, the lower its rate of obesity. In fact, the amount of time spent cooking predicts obesity rates more reliably than female participation in the labor force or income. Other research supports the idea that cooking is a better predictor of a healthful diet than social class: a 1992 study in *The Journal of the American Dietetic Association* found that poor women who routinely cooked were more likely to eat a more healthful diet than well-to-do women who did not.

So cooking matters—a lot. Which when you think about it, should come as no surprise. When we let corporations do the cooking, they're bound to go heavy on sugar, fat and salt; these are three tastes we're hard-wired to like, which happen to be dirt cheap to add and do a good job masking the shortcomings of processed food. And if you make special-occasion foods cheap and easy enough to eat every day, we will eat them every day. The time and work involved in cooking, as well as the delay in gratification built into the process, served as an important check on our appetite. Now that check is gone, and we're struggling to deal with the consequences.

The question is, Can we ever put the genie back into the bottle? Once it has been destroyed, can a culture of everyday cooking be rebuilt? One in which men share equally in the work? One in which the cooking shows on television once again teach people how to cook from scratch and, as Julia Child once did, actually empower them to do it?

Let us hope so. Because it's hard to imagine ever reforming the American way of eating or, for that matter, the American food system unless millions of Americans—women and men—are willing to make cooking a part of daily life. The path to a diet of fresher, unprocessed food, not to mention to a revitalized local-food economy, passes straight through the home kitchen.

But if this is a dream you find appealing, you might not want to call Harry Balzer right away to discuss it.

"Not going to happen," he told me. "Why? Because we're basically cheap and lazy. And besides, the skills are already lost. Who is going to teach the next generation to cook? I don't see it.

"We're all looking for someone else to cook for us. The next American cook is going to be the supermarket. Takeout from the supermarket, that's the future. All we need now is the drive-through supermarket."

Crusty as a fresh baguette, Harry Balzer insists on dealing with the world, and human nature, as it really is, or at least as he finds it in the survey data he has spent the past three decades poring over. But for a brief moment,

I was able to engage him in the project of imagining a slightly different reality. This took a little doing. Many of his clients—which include many of the big chain restaurants and food manufacturers—profit handsomely from the decline and fall of cooking in America; indeed, their marketing has contributed to it. Yet Balzer himself made it clear that he recognizes all that the decline of everyday cooking has cost us. So I asked him how, in an ideal world, Americans might begin to undo the damage that the modern diet of industrially prepared food has done to our health.

"Easy. You want Americans to eat less? I have the diet for you. It's short, and it's simple. Here's my diet plan: Cook it yourself. That's it. Eat anything you want—just as long as you're willing to cook it yourself."

The Reader's Presence

1. What reasons does Pollan offer to account for the decline in home cooking? What explanation and examples does Pollan provide to support his assertion that cooking is "central to human identity and culture" (paragraph 51)? To what extent do you consider opening a can of soup, microwaving a pizza, or pouring bottled dressing on a salad to be "cooking"? What, exactly, does "cooking" mean and involve? How has the definition of "cooking" changed over time, and in what specific ways does your answer bear on the question Pollan poses about "the end of cooking"?

2. Pollan equates presenting cooking programs on television to sporting events: "cooking in prime time is a form of athletic competition, drawing its visual and even aural vocabulary from *Monday Night Football*" (paragraph 22). How, if it all, has this hyperexuberant depiction of cooking affected our cooking habits and the cultural associations it invokes? If, as Pollan writes, "Julia [Child] took the fear out of cooking" (paragraph 26), what are the cultural consequences of the modern cooking show? Do you agree with Pollan that cooking shows should empower us to do more cooking at home instead of indulging in the "spectacle of merely consuming it" (paragraph 29)?

3. What rationale does Pollan offer to validate his view of Julia Child as "a more liberated figure than many of the women who have followed her on television" (paragraph 15)? What factors determine whether cooking can be an oppressive chore or a liberating activity? To what extent has cooking at home remained a female domain? In what ways does cooking contain "the ingredients of [a] narrative" (paragraph 34)? How does this relate to the potential satisfaction one might experience in cooking?

4. **CONNECTIONS:** Compare and contrast Pollan's essay on cooking with Joan Acocella's "A Few Too Many" (page 319). Both examine in detail common experiences and explore the cultural resonances of these activities. Identify and comment on the effectiveness of the specific ways each writer treats his or her subject differently. How would you characterize the tone of voice each author uses?

Katha Pollitt

Why Boys Don't Play with Dolls

KATHA POLLITT was born in 1949 in New York City and is considered one of the leading poets of her generation. Her 1982 collection of poetry, *Antarctic Traveller*, won a National Book Critics Circle Award. Her poetry has appeared in such publications as the *Atlantic* and the *New Yorker*, and she has received a Guggenheim Fellowship and a National Endowment for the Arts grant. She published a second collection of poetry, *The Mind-Body Problem*, in 2009.

Pollitt also writes essays, and she has gained a reputation for incisive analysis and persuasive argument. She contributes reviews, essays, and social commentary to numerous national publications, many of which are collected in *Reasonable Creatures: Essays on Women and Feminism* (1994). Her collections of essays, *Subject to Debate: Sense and Dissents on Women, Politics, and Culture* (2001) and *Virginity or Death! And Other Social and Political Issues of Our Time* (2006), draw on her column called "Subject to Debate," which is printed twice monthly in the *Nation*, where

> "What I want in a poem . . . is not an argument, it's not a statement, it has to do with language. . . ."

she has been a writer, an associate editor, and a columnist since 1980. She won the American Book Award's Lifetime Achievement Award in 2010. Her latest collection of personal essays is *Learning to Drive: And Other Life Stories* (2008). "Why Boys Don't Play with Dolls" appeared in the *New York Times Magazine* in 1995.

Pollitt thinks of writing poems and political essays as two distinct endeavors. "What I want in a poem—one that I read or one that I write—is not an argument, it's not a statement, it has to do with language. . . . There isn't that much political poetry that I find I even want to read once, and almost none that I would want to read again."

IT'S TWENTY-EIGHT YEARS since the founding of NOW,[1] and boys still like trucks and girls still like dolls. Increasingly, we are told that the source of these robust preferences must lie outside society—in prenatal hormonal influences, brain chemistry, genes—and that feminism has reached its natural limits. What else could possibly explain the love of pre-

---

[1] *NOW:* The National Organization for Women was founded in 1966.—Eds.

school girls for party dresses or the desire of toddler boys to own more guns than Mark from Michigan?[2]

True, recent studies claim to show small cognitive differences between the sexes: he gets around by orienting himself in space, she does it by remembering landmarks. Time will tell if any deserve the hoopla with which each is invariably greeted, over the protests of the researchers themselves. But even if the results hold up (and the history of such research is not encouraging), we don't need studies of sex-differentiated brain activity in reading, say, to understand why boys and girls still seem so unalike.

The feminist movement has done much for some women, and something for every woman, but it has hardly turned America into a playground free of sex roles. It hasn't even got women to stop dieting or men to stop interrupting them.

Instead of looking at kids to "prove" that differences in behavior by sex are innate, we can look at the ways we raise kids as an index to how unfinished the feminist revolution really is, and how tentatively it is embraced even by adults who fully expect their daughters to enter previously male-dominated professions and their sons to change diapers.

I'm at a children's birthday party. "I'm sorry," one mom silently mouths   5 to the mother of the birthday girl, who has just torn open her present—Tropical Splash Barbie. Now, you can love Barbie or you can hate Barbie, and there are feminists in both camps. But *apologize* for Barbie? Inflict Barbie, against your own convictions, on the child of a friend you know will be none too pleased?

Every mother in that room had spent years becoming a person who had to be taken seriously, not least by herself. Even the most attractive, I'm willing to bet, had suffered over her body's failure to fit the impossible American ideal. Given all that, it seems crazy to transmit Barbie to the next generation. Yet to reject her is to say that what Barbie represents—being sexy, thin, stylish—is unimportant, which is obviously not true, and children know it's not true.

Women's looks matter terribly in this society, and so Barbie, however ambivalently, must be passed along. After all, there are worse toys. The Cut and Style Barbie styling head, for example, a grotesque object intended to encourage "hair play." The grown-ups who give that probably apologize, too.

How happy would most parents be to have a child who flouted sex conventions? I know a lot of women, feminists, who complain in a comical, eyeball-rolling way about their sons' passion for sports: the ruined weekends, obnoxious coaches, macho values. But they would not think of discouraging their sons from participating in this activity they find so foolish. Or do they? Their husbands are sports fans, too, and they like their husbands a lot.

---

2 ***Mark from Michigan:*** Mark Koernke, a former right-wing talk-show host who supports the militia movement's resistance to federal government. — EDS.

Could it be that even sports-resistant moms see athletics as part of manliness? That if their sons wanted to spend the weekend writing up their diaries, or reading, or baking, they'd find it disturbing? Too antisocial? Too lonely? Too gay?

Theories of innate differences in behavior are appealing. They let parents off the hook—no small recommendation in a culture that holds moms, and sometimes even dads, responsible for their children's every misstep on the road to bliss and success.

They allow grown-ups to take the path of least resistance to the dominant culture, which always requires less psychic effort, even if it means more actual work: just ask the working mother who comes home exhausted and nonetheless finds it easier to pick up her son's socks than make him do it himself. They let families buy for their children, without *too* much guilt, the unbelievably sexist junk that the kids, who have been watching commercials since birth, understandably crave.

But the thing that theories do most of all is tell adults that the *adult* world—in which moms and dads still play by many of the old rules even as they question and fidget and chafe against them—is the way it's supposed to be. A girl with a doll and a boy with a truck "explain" why men are from Mars and women are from Venus, why wives do housework and husbands just don't understand.

The paradox is that the world of rigid and hierarchical sex roles evoked by determinist theories is already passing away. Three-year-olds may indeed insist that doctors are male and nurses female, even if their own mother is a physician. Six-year-olds know better. These days, something like half of all medical students are female, and male applications to nursing school are inching upward. When tomorrow's three-year-olds play doctor, who's to say how they'll assign the roles?

With sex roles, as in every area of life, people aspire to what is possible, and conform to what is necessary. But these are not fixed, especially today. Biological determinism may reassure some adults about their present, but it is feminism, the ideology of flexible and converging sex roles, that fits our children's future. And the kids, somehow, know this.

That's why, if you look carefully, you'll find that for every kid who fits a stereotype, there's another who's breaking one down. Sometimes it's the same kid—the boy who skateboards *and* takes cooking in his afterschool program; the girl who collects stuffed animals *and* A-pluses in science.

Feminists are often accused of imposing their "agenda" on children. Isn't that what adults always do, consciously and unconsciously? Kids aren't born religious, or polite, or kind, or able to remember where they put their sneakers. Inculcating these behaviors, and the values behind them, is a tremendous amount of work, involving many adults. We don't have a choice, really, about *whether* we should give our children messages about what it means to be male and female—they're bombarded with them from morning till night.

The question, as always, is what do we want those messages to be? ▪

The Reader's Presence

1. Pollitt notes in her opening paragraph, "It's twenty-eight years since the founding of NOW, and boys still like trucks and girls still like dolls." What does Pollitt identify as the competing theories to explain these differences between boys and girls? Which theory does Pollitt prefer, and how does she express her support of it?

2. As you reread the essay, consider carefully the role of the media in upholding the status quo with regard to differentiated roles for girls and boys. As you develop a response to this question, examine carefully both the media directed principally to children and the media targeted at adults. In the latter category, for instance, Pollitt refers to the media version of scientific research studies into gender differences (paragraph 2) and alludes to popular books that discuss the differences between men and women, such as *Men Are from Mars, Women Are from Venus*, and *You Just Don't Understand* (paragraph 12). Drawing on Pollitt's essay and on your own experience, identify—and discuss—the specific social responsibilities you would like to see America's mass media take more seriously.

3. **CONNECTIONS:** How would you characterize Pollitt's stance toward today's parents? What are some of the reasons she gives to explain parents' choices and actions? Consider Pollitt's argument in the light of Bernard Cooper's essay "A Clack of Tiny Sparks: Remembrances of a Gay Boyhood" (page 98). How does Cooper's account of his parents' attitudes compare with Pollitt's portrait of parents? What general points about childrearing can you draw from the contrasts and commonalities between the essays? How does parenting figure in the transmission of beliefs and practices in America, according to these authors?

Eric Schlosser

WHY MCDONALD'S FRIES TASTE SO GOOD

Investigative reporter and author **ERIC SCHLOSSER** was born in New York City in 1959. A correspondent for the *Atlantic* and a contributor to *Rolling Stone* and the *New Yorker*, he has won numerous journalistic honors and awards. His two-part *Atlantic Monthly* series, "Reefer Madness" and "Marijuana and the Law," won the National Magazine Award in 1994 and became the basis for his best-selling collection of essays, *Reefer Madness: Sex, Drugs, and Cheap Labor in the American Black Market* (2003), an exposé of America's underground economy. *Fast Food Nation: The Dark Side of the All-American Meal* (2001), Schlosser's controversial and influential first book, prompted a reexamination of practices in the meat-processing industry. A best-seller, the book was adapted and released as a motion picture in 2006, followed by a companion book for young people, *Chew on This: Everything You Don't Want to Know About Fast Food* (2006). His most recent book, *Command and Control: Nuclear Weapons, the Damascus Accident, and the Illusion of Safety*, was published in 2013.

> *Fast Food Nation: The Dark Side of the All-American Meal* (2001), Eric Schlosser's first book, prompted a reexamination of practices in the meat-processing industry.

Of writing *Fast Food Nation*, Schlosser said, "I care about the literary aspects of the book. I tried to make it as clear as possible, and make it an interesting thing to read, but I sacrificed some of that, ultimately, in order to get this out to people and let them know what's going on."

THE FRENCH FRY was "almost sacrosanct for me," Ray Kroc, one of the founders of McDonald's, wrote in his autobiography, "its preparation a ritual to be followed religiously." During the chain's early years french fries were made from scratch every day. Russet Burbank potatoes were peeled, cut into shoestrings, and fried in McDonald's kitchens. As the chain expanded nationwide, in the mid-1960s, it sought to cut labor costs, reduce the number of suppliers, and ensure that its fries tasted the same at every restaurant. McDonald's began switching to frozen french fries in 1966 — and few customers noticed the difference. Nevertheless, the change had a profound effect on the nation's agriculture and diet. A familiar food had been transformed into a highly processed industrial commodity. McDonald's fries now come from huge manufacturing plants that can peel, slice, cook, and freeze two million pounds of potatoes a day. The rapid expansion of McDonald's and the popularity of its low-cost, mass-produced fries changed the way Americans eat. In 1960 Americans consumed an average of about eighty-one pounds of fresh potatoes and four pounds of frozen french fries. In 2000 they consumed an average of about fifty pounds of fresh potatoes and thirty pounds of frozen fries. Today McDonald's is the largest buyer of potatoes in the United States.

The taste of McDonald's french fries played a crucial role in the chain's success — fries are much more profitable than hamburgers — and was long praised by customers, competitors, and even food critics. James Beard loved McDonald's fries. Their distinctive taste does not stem from the kind of potatoes that McDonald's buys, the technology that processes them, or the restaurant equipment that fries them: other chains use Russet Burbanks, buy their french fries from the same large processing companies, and have similar fryers in their restaurant kitchens. The taste of a french fry is largely determined by the cooking oil. For decades McDonald's cooked its french fries in a mixture of about 7 percent cottonseed oil and 93 percent beef tallow. The mixture gave the fries their unique flavor—and more saturated beef fat per ounce than a McDonald's hamburger.

In 1990, amid a barrage of criticism over the amount of cholesterol in its fries, McDonald's switched to pure vegetable oil. This presented the company with a challenge: how to make fries that subtly taste like beef without cooking them in beef tallow. A look at the ingredients in McDonald's french fries suggests how the problem was solved. Toward the end of the list is a seemingly innocuous yet oddly mysterious phrase: "natural flavor." That ingredient helps to explain not only why the fries taste so good but also why

Advertising poster for the 2004 award-winning documentary by Morgan Spurlock that examined the consequences of surviving for one month entirely on meals from McDonald's.

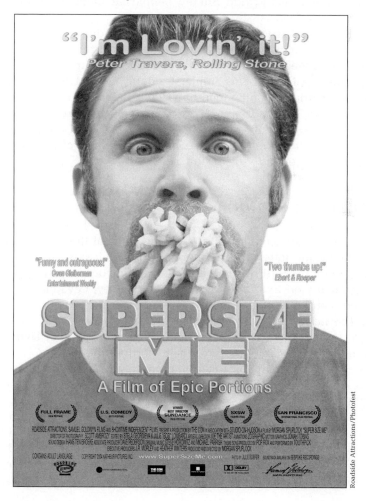

most fast food—indeed, most of the food Americans eat today—tastes the way it does.

Open your refrigerator, your freezer, your kitchen cupboards, and look at the labels on your food. You'll find "natural flavor" or "artificial flavor" in just about every list of ingredients. The similarities between these two broad categories are far more significant than the differences. Both are man-made additives that give most processed food most of its taste. People usually buy a food item the first time because of its packaging or appearance. Taste usually determines whether they buy it again. About 90 percent of the money that Americans now spend on food goes to buy processed food. The canning, freezing, and dehydrating techniques used in processing destroy most of food's flavor—and so a vast industry has arisen in the United States to make processed food palatable. Without this flavor industry today's fast food would not exist. The names of the leading American fast-food chains and their best-selling menu items have become embedded in our popular culture and famous worldwide. But few people can name the companies that manufacture fast food's taste.

The flavor industry is highly secretive. Its leading companies will not   5
divulge the precise formulas of flavor compounds or the identities of clients. The secrecy is deemed essential for protecting the reputations of beloved brands. The fast-food chains, understandably, would like the public to believe that the flavors of the food they sell somehow originate in their restaurant kitchens, not in distant factories run by other firms. A McDonald's french fry is one of countless foods whose flavor is just a component in a complex manufacturing process. The look and the taste of what we eat now are frequently deceiving—by design.

THE FLAVOR CORRIDOR

The New Jersey Turnpike runs through the heart of the flavor industry, an industrial corridor dotted with refineries and chemical plants. International Flavors & Fragrances (IFF), the world's largest flavor company, has a manufacturing facility off Exit 8A in Dayton, New Jersey; Givaudan, the world's second-largest flavor company, has a plant in East Hanover. Haarmann & Reimer, the largest German flavor company, has a plant in Teterboro, as does Takasago, the largest Japanese flavor company. Flavor Dynamics has a plant in South Plainfield; Frutarom is in North Bergen; Elan Chemical is in Newark. Dozens of companies manufacture flavors in the corridor between Teaneck and South Brunswick. Altogether the area produces about two-thirds of the flavor additives sold in the United States.

The IFF plant in Dayton is a huge pale-blue building with a modern office complex attached to the front. It sits in an industrial park, not far from a BASF plastics factory, a Jolly French Toast factory, and a plant that manufactures Liz Claiborne cosmetics. Dozens of tractor-trailers were parked at the IFF loading dock the afternoon I visited, and a thin cloud of steam floated from a roof vent. Before entering the plant, I signed a nondisclosure form, promising not to reveal the brand names of foods that contain IFF flavors. The place reminded me of Willy Wonka's chocolate factory. Wonderful smells drifted through the hallways, men and women in neat white lab coats cheerfully went about their work, and hundreds of little glass bottles sat on laboratory tables and shelves. The bottles contained powerful but fragile flavor chemicals, shielded from light by brown glass and round white caps shut tight. The long chemical names on the little white labels were as mystifying to me as medieval Latin. These odd-sounding things would be mixed and poured and turned into new substances, like magic potions.

I was not invited into the manufacturing areas of the IFF plant, where, it was thought, I might discover trade secrets. Instead I toured various laboratories and pilot kitchens, where the flavors of well-established brands are tested or adjusted, and where whole new flavors are created. IFF's snack-and-savory lab is responsible for the flavors of potato chips, corn chips, breads, crackers, breakfast cereals, and pet food. The confectionary lab devises flavors for ice cream, cookies, candies, toothpastes, mouthwashes, and antacids. Everywhere I looked, I saw famous, widely advertised products sitting on laboratory desks and tables. The beverage lab was full of brightly colored liquids in clear bottles. It comes up with flavors for popular soft drinks, sports drinks, bottled teas, and wine coolers, for all-natural juice drinks, organic soy drinks, beers, and malt liquors. In one pilot kitchen I saw a dapper food technologist, a middle-aged man with an elegant tie beneath his crisp lab coat, carefully preparing a batch of cookies with white frosting and pink-and-white sprinkles. In another pilot kitchen I saw a pizza oven, a grill, a milk-shake machine, and a french fryer identical to those I'd seen at innumerable fast-food restaurants.

In addition to being the world's largest flavor company, IFF manufactures the smells of six of the ten best-selling fine perfumes in the United States, including Estée Lauder's Beautiful, Clinique's Happy, Lancôme's Trésor, and Calvin Klein's Eternity. It also makes the smells of household products such as deodorant, dishwashing detergent, bath soap, shampoo, furniture polish, and floor wax. All these aromas are made through essentially the same process: the manipulation of volatile chemicals. The basic science behind the scent of your shaving cream is the same as that governing the flavor of your TV dinner.

"NATURAL" AND "ARTIFICIAL"

Scientists now believe that human beings acquired the sense of taste as a 10 way to avoid being poisoned. Edible plants generally taste sweet, harmful ones bitter. The taste buds on our tongues can detect the presence of half a dozen or so basic tastes, including sweet, sour, bitter, salty, astringent, and umami, a taste discovered by Japanese researchers—a rich and full sense of deliciousness triggered by amino acids in foods such as meat, shellfish, mushrooms, potatoes, and seaweed. Taste buds offer a limited means of detection, however, compared with the human olfactory system, which can perceive thousands of different chemical aromas. Indeed, "flavor" is primarily the smell of gases being released by the chemicals you've just put in your mouth. The aroma of a food can be responsible for as much as 90 percent of its taste.

The act of drinking, sucking, or chewing a substance releases its volatile gases. They flow out of your mouth and up your nostrils, or up the passageway in the back of your mouth, to a thin layer of nerve cells called the olfactory epithelium, located at the base of your nose, right between your eyes. Your brain combines the complex smell signals from your olfactory epithelium with the simple taste signals from your tongue, assigns a flavor to what's in your mouth, and decides if it's something you want to eat.

A person's food preferences, like his or her personality, are formed during the first few years of life, through a process of socialization. Babies innately prefer sweet tastes and reject bitter ones; toddlers can learn to enjoy hot and spicy food, bland health food, or fast food, depending on what the people around them eat. The human sense of smell is still not fully understood. It is greatly affected by psychological factors and expectations. The mind focuses intently on some of the aromas that surround us and filters out the overwhelming majority. People can grow accustomed to bad smells or good smells; they stop noticing what once seemed overpowering. Aroma and memory are somehow inextricably linked. A smell can suddenly evoke a long-forgotten moment. The flavors of childhood foods seem to leave an indelible mark, and adults often return to them, without always knowing why. These "comfort foods" become a source of pleasure and reassurance — a fact that fast-food chains use to their advantage. Childhood memories of Happy Meals, which come with french fries, can translate into frequent adult visits to McDonald's. On average, Americans now eat about four servings of french fries every week.

The human craving for flavor has been a largely unacknowledged and unexamined force in history. For millennia royal empires have been built, unexplored lands traversed, and great religions and philosophies forever changed by the spice trade. In 1492 Christopher Columbus set sail to find seasoning. Today the influence of flavor in the world marketplace is no less decisive. The rise and fall of corporate empires — of soft-drink companies, snack-food companies, and fast-food chains — is often determined by how their products taste.

The flavor industry emerged in the mid-nineteenth century, as processed foods began to be manufactured on a large scale. Recognizing the need for flavor additives, early food processors turned to perfume companies that had long experience working with essential oils and volatile aromas. The great perfume houses of England, France, and the Netherlands produced many of the first flavor compounds. In the early part of the twentieth century

Germany took the technological lead in flavor production, owing to its powerful chemical industry. Legend has it that a German scientist discovered methyl anthranilate, one of the first artificial flavors, by accident while mixing chemicals in his laboratory. Suddenly the lab was filled with the sweet smell of grapes. Methyl anthranilate later became the chief flavor compound in grape Kool-Aid. After World War II much of the perfume industry shifted from Europe to the United States, settling in New York City near the garment district and the fashion houses. The flavor industry came with it, later moving to New Jersey for greater plant capacity. Man-made flavor additives were used mostly in baked goods, candies, and sodas until the 1950s, when sales of processed food began to soar. The invention of gas chromatographs and mass spectrometers—machines capable of detecting volatile gases at low levels—vastly increased the number of flavors that could be synthesized. By the mid-1960s flavor companies were churning out compounds to supply the taste of Pop Tarts, Bac-Os, Tab, Tang, Filet-O-Fish sandwiches, and literally thousands of other new foods.

The American flavor industry now has annual revenues of about $1.4   15
billion. Approximately 10,000 new processed-food products are introduced every year in the United States. Almost all of them require flavor additives. And about nine out of ten of these products fail. The latest flavor innovations and corporate realignments are heralded in publications such as *Chemical Market Reporter*, *Food Chemical News*, *Food Engineering*, and *Food Product Design*. The progress of IFF has mirrored that of the flavor industry as a whole. IFF was formed in 1958, through the merger of two small companies. Its annual revenues have grown almost fifteenfold since the early 1970s, and it currently has manufacturing facilities in twenty countries.

Today's sophisticated spectrometers, gas chromatographs, and headspace-vapor analyzers provide a detailed map of a food's flavor components, detecting chemical aromas present in amounts as low as one part per billion. The human nose, however, is even more sensitive. A nose can detect aromas present in quantities of a few parts per trillion—an amount equivalent to about 0.000000000003 percent. Complex aromas, such as those of coffee and roasted meat, are composed of volatile gases from nearly a thousand different chemicals. The smell of a strawberry arises from the interaction of about 350 chemicals that are present in minute amounts. The quality that people seek most of all in a food—flavor—is usually present in a quantity too infinitesimal to be measured in traditional culinary terms such as ounces or teaspoons. The chemical that provides the dominant flavor of bell pepper can be tasted in amounts as low as 0.02 parts per billion; one drop is sufficient to add flavor to five average-size swimming pools. The flavor additive usually comes next to last in a processed food's list of ingredients and often costs less than its packaging. Soft drinks contain a larger proportion of flavor additives than most products. The flavor in a twelve-ounce can of Coke costs about half a cent.

The color additives in processed foods are usually present in even smaller amounts than the flavor compounds. Many of New Jersey's flavor companies also manufacture these color additives, which are used to make processed foods look fresh and appealing. Food coloring serves many of the same decorative purposes as lipstick, eye shadow, mascara—and is often made from the same pigments. Titanium dioxide, for example, has proved to be an especially versatile mineral. It gives many processed candies, frostings, and icings their bright white color; it is a common ingredient in women's cosmetics; and it is the pigment used in many white oil paints and house paints. At Burger King, Wendy's, and McDonald's coloring agents have been added to many of the soft drinks, salad dressings, cookies, condiments, chicken dishes, and sandwich buns.

Studies have found that the color of a food can greatly affect how its taste is perceived. Brightly colored foods frequently seem to taste better than bland-looking foods, even when the flavor compounds are identical. Foods that somehow look off-color often seem to have off tastes. For thousands of years human beings have relied on visual cues to help determine what is edible. The color of fruit suggests whether it is ripe, the color of meat whether it is rancid. Flavor researchers sometimes use colored lights to modify the influence of visual cues during taste tests. During one experiment in the early 1970s people were served an oddly tinted meal of steak and french fries that appeared normal beneath colored lights. Everyone thought the meal tasted fine until the lighting was changed. Once it became apparent that the steak was actually blue and the fries were green, some people became ill.

The federal Food and Drug Administration does not require companies to disclose the ingredients of their color or flavor additives so long as all the chemicals in them are considered by the agency to be GRAS ("generally recognized as safe"). This enables companies to maintain the secrecy of their formulas. It also hides the fact that flavor compounds often contain more ingredients than the foods to which they give taste. The phrase "artificial strawberry flavor" gives little hint of the chemical wizardry and manufacturing skill that can make a highly processed food taste like strawberries.

A typical artificial strawberry flavor, like the kind found in a Burger 20 King strawberry milk shake, contains the following ingredients: amyl acetate, amyl butyrate, amyl valerate, anethol, anisyl formate, benzyl acetate, benzyl isobutyrate, butyric acid, cinnamyl isobutyrate, cinnamyl valerate, cognac essential oil, diacetyl, dipropyl ketone, ethyl acetate, ethyl amyl ketone, ethyl butyrate, ethyl cinnamate, ethyl heptanoate, ethyl heptylate, ethyl lactate, ethyl methylphenylglycidate, ethyl nitrate, ethyl propionate, ethyl valerate, heliotropin, hydroxyphenyl-2-butanone (10 percent solution in alcohol), α-ionone, isobutyl anthranilate, isobutyl butyrate, lemon essential oil, maltol, 4-methylacetophenone, methyl anthranilate, methyl benzoate, methyl cinnamate, methyl heptine carbonate, methyl naphthyl ketone, methyl salicylate, mint essential oil, neroli essential oil, nerolin, neryl isobutyrate, orris butter, phenethyl alcohol, rose, rum ether, y-undecalactone, vanillin, and solvent.

Although flavors usually arise from a mixture of many different volatile chemicals, often a single compound supplies the dominant aroma. Smelled alone, that chemical provides an unmistakable sense of the food. Ethyl-2-methyl butyrate, for example, smells just like an apple. Many of today's highly processed foods offer a blank palette: whatever chemicals are added to them will give them specific tastes. Adding methyl-2-pyridyl ketone makes something taste like popcorn. Adding ethyl-3-hydroxy butanoate makes it taste like marshmallow. The possibilities are now almost limitless. Without affecting appearance or nutritional value, processed foods could be made with aroma chemicals such as hexanal (the smell of freshly cut grass) or 3-methyl butanoic acid (the smell of body odor).

The 1960s were the heyday of artificial flavors in the United States. The synthetic versions of flavor compounds were not subtle, but they did not have to be, given the nature of most processed food. For the past twenty years food processors have tried hard to use only "natural flavors" in their products. According to the FDA, these must be derived entirely from natural sources—from herbs, spices, fruits, vegetables, beef, chicken, yeast, bark, roots, and so forth. Consumers prefer to see natural flavors on a label, out of a belief that they are more healthful. Distinctions between artificial and natural flavors can be arbitrary and somewhat absurd, based more on how the flavor has been made than on what it actually contains.

"A natural flavor," says Terry Acree, a professor of food science at Cornell University, "is a flavor that's been derived with an out-of-date technology." Natural flavors and artificial flavors sometimes contain exactly the same chemicals, produced through different methods. Amyl acetate, for example, provides the dominant note of banana flavor. When it is distilled from bananas with a solvent, amyl acetate is a natural flavor. When it is produced by mixing vinegar with amyl alcohol and adding sulfuric acid as a catalyst, amyl acetate is an artificial flavor. Either way it smells and tastes the same. "Natural flavor" is now listed among the ingredients of everything from Health Valley Blueberry Granola Bars to Taco Bell Hot Taco Sauce.

A natural flavor is not necessarily more healthful or purer than an artificial one. When almond flavor—benzaldehyde—is derived from natural sources, such as peach and apricot pits, it contains traces of hydrogen cyanide, a deadly poison. Benzaldehyde derived by mixing oil of clove and amyl acetate does not contain any cyanide. Nevertheless, it is legally considered an artificial flavor and sells at a much lower price. Natural and artificial flavors are now manufactured at the same chemical plants, places that few people would associate with Mother Nature.

A TRAINED NOSE AND A POETIC SENSIBILITY

The small and elite group of scientists who create most of the flavor in   25
most of the food now consumed in the United States are called "flavorists." They draw on a number of disciplines in their work: biology, psychology,

physiology, and organic chemistry. A flavorist is a chemist with a trained nose and a poetic sensibility. Flavors are created by blending scores of different chemicals in tiny amounts—a process governed by scientific principles but demanding a fair amount of art. In an age when delicate aromas and microwave ovens do not easily co-exist, the job of the flavorist is to conjure illusions about processed food and, in the words of one flavor company's literature, to ensure "consumer likeability." The flavorists with whom I spoke were discreet, in keeping with the dictates of their trade. They were also charming, cosmopolitan, and ironic. They not only enjoyed fine wine but could identify the chemicals that give each grape its unique aroma. One flavorist compared his work to composing music. A well-made flavor compound will have a "top note" that is often followed by a "dry-down" and a "leveling-off," with different chemicals responsible for each stage. The taste of a food can be radically altered by minute changes in the flavoring combination. "A little odor goes a long way," one flavorist told me.

In order to give a processed food a taste that consumers will find appealing, a flavorist must always consider the food's "mouthfeel"—the unique combination of textures and chemical interactions that affect how the flavor is perceived. Mouthfeel can be adjusted through the use of various fats, gums, starches, emulsifiers, and stabilizers. The aroma chemicals in a food can be precisely analyzed, but the elements that make up mouthfeel are much harder to measure. How does one quantify a pretzel's hardness, a french fry's crispness? Food technologists are now conducting basic research in rheology, the branch of physics that examines the flow and deformation of materials. A number of companies sell sophisticated devices that attempt to measure mouthfeel. The TA.XT2i Texture Analyzer, produced by the Texture Technologies Corporation, of Scarsdale, New York, performs calculations based on data derived from as many as 250 separate probes. It is essentially a mechanical mouth. It gauges the most-important rheological properties of a food—bounce, creep, breaking point, density, crunchiness, chewiness, gumminess, lumpiness, rubberiness, springiness, slipperiness, smoothness, softness, wetness, juiciness, spreadability, springback, and tackiness.

Some of the most important advances in flavor manufacturing are now occurring in the field of biotechnology. Complex flavors are being made using enzyme reactions, fermentation, and fungal and tissue cultures. All the flavors created by these methods—including the ones being synthesized by fungi—are considered natural flavors by the FDA. The new enzyme-based processes are responsible for extremely true-to-life dairy flavors. One company now offers not just butter flavor but also fresh creamy butter, cheesy butter, milky butter, savory melted butter, and super-concentrated butter flavor, in liquid or powder form. The development of new fermentation techniques, along with new techniques for heating mixtures of sugar and amino acids, have led to the creation of much more realistic meat flavors.

The McDonald's Corporation most likely drew on these advances when it eliminated beef tallow from its french fries. The company will not reveal the exact origin of the natural flavor added to its fries. In response to inquiries from *Vegetarian Journal*, however, McDonald's did acknowledge that its fries derive some of their characteristic flavor from "an animal source." Beef is the probable source, although other meats cannot be ruled out. In France, for example, fries are sometimes cooked in duck fat or horse tallow.

Other popular fast foods derive their flavor from unexpected ingredients. McDonald's Chicken McNuggets contain beef extracts, as does Wendy's Grilled Chicken Sandwich. Burger King's BK Broiler Chicken Breast Patty contains "natural smoke flavor." A firm called Red Arrow Products specializes in smoke flavor, which is added to barbecue sauces, snack foods, and processed meats. Red Arrow manufactures natural smoke flavor by charring sawdust and capturing the aroma chemicals released into the air. The smoke is captured in water and then bottled, so that other companies can sell food that seems to have been cooked over a fire.

The Vegetarian Legal Action Network recently petitioned the FDA 30 to issue new labeling requirements for foods that contain natural flavors. The group wants food processors to list the basic origins of their flavors on their labels. At the moment vegetarians often have no way of knowing whether a flavor additive contains beef, pork, poultry, or shellfish. One of the most widely used color additives—whose presence is often hidden by the phrase "color added"—violates a number of religious dietary restrictions, may cause allergic reactions in susceptible people, and comes from an unusual source. Cochineal extract (also known as carmine or carminic acid) is made from the desiccated bodies of female *Dactylopius coccus Costa*, a small insect harvested mainly in Peru and the Canary Islands. The bug feeds on red cactus berries, and color from the berries accumulates in the females and their unhatched larvae. The insects are collected, dried, and ground into a pigment. It takes about 70,000 of them to produce a pound of carmine, which is used to make processed foods look pink, red, or purple. Dannon strawberry yogurt gets its color from carmine, and so do many frozen fruit bars, candies, and fruit fillings, and Ocean Spray pink-grapefruit juice drink.

In a meeting room at IFF, Brian Grainger let me sample some of the company's flavors. It was an unusual taste test—there was no food to taste. Grainger is a senior flavorist at IFF, a soft-spoken chemist with graying hair, an English accent, and a fondness for understatement. He could easily be mistaken for a British diplomat or the owner of a West End brasserie with two Michelin stars. Like many in the flavor industry, he has an Old World, old-fashioned sensibility. When I suggested that IFF's policy of secrecy and discretion was out of step with our mass-marketing, brand-conscious, self-promoting age, and that the company should put its own logo on the countless products that bear its flavors, instead of allowing other companies to enjoy the consumer loyalty and affection inspired by those flavors, Grainger politely disagreed, assuring me that such a thing would never be done. In the absence of public credit or acclaim, the small and secretive fraternity of flavor chemists praise one another's work. By analyzing the flavor formula of a product, Grainger can often tell which of his counterparts at a rival firm devised it. Whenever he walks down a supermarket aisle, he takes a quiet pleasure in seeing the well-known foods that contain his flavors.

Grainger had brought a dozen small glass bottles from the lab. After he opened each bottle, I dipped a fragrance-testing filter into it—a long white strip of paper designed to absorb aroma chemicals without producing off notes. Before placing each strip of paper in front of my nose, I closed my eyes. Then I inhaled deeply, and one food after another was conjured from the glass bottles. I smelled fresh cherries, black olives, sautéed onions, and shrimp. Grainger's most remarkable creation took me by surprise. After closing my eyes, I suddenly smelled a grilled hamburger. The aroma was uncanny, almost miraculous—as if someone in the room were flipping burgers on a hot grill. But when I opened my eyes, I saw just a narrow strip of white paper and a flavorist with a grin. ■

The Reader's Presence

1. What do McDonald's french fries have to do with Schlosser's primary aim in this selection? Why does he feature them in the title and use them in the opening to the essay? Why, in your opinion, didn't he use a different example?

2. Describe Schlosser's attitude toward "natural" and "artificial" flavoring (paragraph 4). Does he think one is superior to the other? Why or why not? How critical does he appear toward food additives in general? Do you read his essay as a condemnation of fast food? How does his account of his laboratory visit color your response? Overall, were his laboratory experiences positive or negative? Explain what in his account makes you feel one way or the other.

3. **VISUAL PRESENCE:** Examine carefully the film poster for *Super Size Me* on page 549. What message does this poster convey about the fast-food industry? What specific features in the poster illustrate that message? How does the poster relate to Schlosser's points about food flavoring?

4. **CONNECTIONS:** Compare and contrast Schlosser's investigative techniques with those of Amy Cunningham in "Why Women Smile" (page 369). How does each writer establish a question to investigate, provoke your interest in the issue, gather information, and conduct the investigation? How important are sources and interviews? What information about sources and interviews is omitted from the essays?

Charles Simic

THE LIFE OF IMAGES

CHARLES SIMIC (b. 1938) grew up in Belgrade, Yugoslavia (now Serbia), during World War II. He immigrated to the United States with his family when he was sixteen years old and became a naturalized citizen in 1971. "Being one of the millions of displaced persons made an impression on me. In addition to my own little story of bad luck, I heard plenty of others. I'm still amazed by all the vileness and stupidity I witnessed in my life," he says. Since his first volume of poetry, *What the Grass Says* (1967), Simic has published more than sixty books and has won numerous awards, including the Pulitzer Prize in poetry for *The World Doesn't End* (1996), a MacArthur Foundation "genius grant," and The Zbigniew Herbert International Literary Award (2014). His book *Walking the Black Cat* (1996) was a finalist for the National Book Award for poetry; *The Voice at 3:00 A.M.* was nominated for the National Book Award and the *Los Angeles Times* Book Award in 2003. His recent collections of poetry include *Sixty Poems* (2008), collected to celebrate his appointment as the U.S. Poet Laureate in 2007, *That Little Something* (2008), *Master of Disguises* (2010), and *New and Selected Poems: 1962–2012* (2013). Simic is a noted translator of French, Serbian, Croatian, Macedonian, and Slovenian poetry, and his own work has also been translated into many languages. Professor emeritus at the University of New Hampshire in Durham, Simic also contributes frequently to magazines and journals, including the *Harvard Review*, in which his essay "The Life of Images" was published in 2003.

> "Everything is hard to write about. Many of my shortest and seemingly simple poems took years to get right. . . . I expect to be revising in my coffin as it is being lowered into the ground."

When asked what he found hardest to write about, Simic replied, "Everything is hard to write about. Many of my shortest and seemingly simple poems took years to get right. I tinker with most of my poems even after publication. I expect to be revising in my coffin as it is being lowered into the ground."

IN ONE of Berenice Abbott's[1] photographs of the Lower East Side, I recall a store sign advertising *Silk Underwear*. Underneath, there was the additional information about "reasonable prices for peddlers." How interesting, I thought. Did someone carry a suitcase full of ladies' underwear and try to peddle them on some street corner farther uptown? Or did he ring doorbells in apartment buildings and offer them to housewives? I imagine the underwear came in many different sizes, so he may have had to carry two suitcases. The peddler was most likely an immigrant and had difficulty making himself understood. What he wanted was for the lady of the house to feel how soft the silk was but she either did not understand him or she had other reasons for hesitating. She wore a house robe, her hair was loose as if she just got out of bed, so she was embarrassed to touch the undies draped over his extended hand. Then she finally did touch them.

The reason photographs live in my memory is that the city I continue to roam is rich with such visual delights. Everyone who does this is taking imaginary snapshots. For all I know my face, briefly glimpsed in a crowd, may live on in someone else's memory. The attentive eye makes the world mysterious. Some men or a woman going about their business seventy years ago either caught sight of a camera pointed at them or they passed by oblivious. It was like hide and seek. They thought they had concealed themselves in plain view and the camera found them out. It showed something even they did not know they were hiding. Often people had the puzzled look of someone who had volunteered to assist a hypnotist on a stage and awakened to the sound of the audience's applause.

I'm looking at the long-torn-down Second Avenue "El" at the intersection of Division Street and Bowery in another Abbott photograph. The date is April 24, 1936. It seems like a nice day, for the sunlight streams through the tracks and iron scaffold of the elevated train, making patterns of shadow and light on the sidewalk below. As far as I can make out, the street on both sides is lined with stores selling cheap furs. The entire area was for years a bargain hunter's paradise. My father knew a fellow in his office, an elderly, impeccably dressed man, who claimed that he did all his shopping on Orchard and Hester Streets, where he never paid more than five dollars for a suit. What interests me the most in this photograph is the shadowy couple under the El with their backs turned to us. She's willowy and taller than he is, as if she were a model or a salesgirl in one of these shops. They have drawn close together as if talking over something very important, or why would they otherwise stop like that in the middle of the street? The way this woman in a long skirt carries herself gives me the impression that she is young. Not so the man. With one hand casually resting on a post and his other stuck in his pocket, he appears confident, even brash. It's the way they

---

1 ***Berenice Abbott*** (1898–1991): A photographer who is noted for her concentration on New York City. Combining artistry with documentary brilliance, her work ranks her among major American photographers. She wrote many articles on photography, and her best-known book is the one Simic refers to, *Changing New York* (1939). —EDS.

Second Avenue El.

Collection, Miriam and Ira D. Wallach Division of Art, Prints and Photography, The New York Public Library, Astor, Lenox and Tilden Foundations/Art Resource, NY

stand together that suggests to me that they are not casual acquaintances. Most likely they work in the same neighborhood, but there is something else going on between them too. She seems very interested in what he is saying now. No one else in view pays them any attention. The fellow standing on the sidewalk in front of the Beauty Fur Shop looks off into the distance where a portly young man with glasses wearing an open overcoat over a three-piece suit is coming into view. He has just had lunch and is glancing idly at the shop windows as he strolls lazily back to the office. He is too young to be the boss, so he must be the son or the son-in-law of one of the store owners. Except for the couple who elude identification, there is nothing unusual here. A photograph such as this one, where time has stopped on an ordinary scene full of innuendoes, partakes of the infinite.

I cannot look long at any old photograph of the city without hearing some music in the background. The moment that happens, I'm transported into the past so vividly no one can convince me that I did not live in that moment. I have heard just about every recording of popular music and jazz made between 1920 and 1950. This is probably the most esoteric knowledge I possess. It's easier to talk to people about Tibetan Buddhism, Arab poetry in Medieval Spain, or Russian icons, than about Helen Kane, Annette

Hanshaw, and Ethel Waters. Or how about some Boswell Sisters or Joe Venuti and his Blue Four, Red McKenzie and his Mound City Blue Blowers, Ted Lewis and his Orchestra playing "Egyptian Ella"? It scares me how much of that music is in my head. I have friends who cannot believe that I can enjoy both Mahler's symphonies and Coleman Hawkins. Young Ella Fitzgerald singing "If That's What You're Thinking, You're Wrong" with Chick Webb's band would be just right for Abbott's shadowy couple.

Can one experience nostalgia for a time and place one did not know? I believe so. You could put me in solitary with Abbott's photograph of "Blossom Restaurant"[2] and I wouldn't notice the months pass away as I studied the menu chalked on the blackboard at its entrance. The prices, of course, are incredibly low, but that's secondary. The dishes enumerated here are what fascinates me. No one eats that kind of food today. Rare Mongolian, Patagonian, and Afghan specialties are procurable in New York, but not lamb oxtail stew, boiled beef, or even stuffed peppers. The ethnic makeup of the city has changed in the last thirty years. Most of the luncheonettes in the 1950s and 1960s served samplings of German, Hungarian, and Jewish cuisine. Pea and bean soup, stuffed cabbage, corned beef and boiled potatoes, and veal cutlets were to be found regularly on the menu, together with the usual assortment of sandwiches. On every table, and all along the counter, there were containers stocked with dill pickles and slices of raw onion. The portions were enormous. A cheap dish like franks and kraut would stuff you for the rest of the day. I subsisted for years on soups and chowders cooked by a Greek in a greasy spoon on East 8th Street. They gave you two thick slices of rye bread and butter with the soup and all the pickles you could eat. After that, I could hardly keep my eyes open for the rest of the day.

Abbott's photograph of the Blossom Restaurant front also includes the barbershop next door with its own price list. Does a tonsorial establishment anywhere in this country still offer electric massage? The gadget, which resembled contraptions from a horror film, was a mesh of spring coils and electric wires. Once the juice was turned on, the machine squirmed and shook for a minute or two over the customer's scalp, supposedly providing a stimulating, healthful, up-to-date treatment, while he sat back in the chair pretending to be absorbed in some article in the *Police Gazette*.[3] That ordeal was followed by a few sprinkles of strong-smelling cologne from a large bottle and a dusting of talcum powder on the freshly shaved neck.

The worst haircut I ever had in my life was at a barber college at the Union Square subway station. "Learn Barbering and make Money," the sign said. It was the cheapest haircut in town. But, before I realized what was happening, the apprentice barber had cut off all my hair with clippers except for a tuft right up in front. The kid was clearly a hair fashion visionary decades

---

2 ***"Blossom Restaurant":*** Abbott's photograph of the restaurant, at 103 Bowery, was taken on October 3, 1935. — EDS.

3 **Police Gazette:** A century-old men's periodical that featured sensational news items and risqué photographs. It was especially popular in barbershops. — EDS.

Blossom Restaurant.

ahead of his time, but back then I was in total panic. I rushed immediately across the street into Klein's department store and found a beret, which I wore pulled down over my ears for the next six weeks. The problem was that it was summer, hot and humid as it usually is in New York. I also wore dark glasses to give the impression that I was simply affecting the appearance of a jazz musician. I saw both Dizzy Gillespie and Thelonius Monk similarly decked out, but they tended to make their appearance only after dark, while I had to go to work in the morning in the storeroom of a publishing company where everyone who saw me burst out laughing. Lunch was a hassle too. The customers at adjoining tables snickered and the waitress who knew me well gave me a puzzled look as she brought me my sandwich. I always held unpopular opinions and was not afraid to voice them, but to have people stare at me because I had a funny haircut or wore a necktie of some outrageous hue was something I had no stomach for.

"My place is no bigger than a closet," a woman said to her companion on the street the other day as they rushed past me, and I saw it instantly with its clutter of furniture and its piles of clothes on the bed and the floor. Dickinson's "Madonna dim" came to mind and I did not even take a good look at her before she was lost in the crowd. No sooner has one seen an interesting face in the street than one gives it a biography. Through a small window in her room, the evening casts its first shadow on a blank wall where the out-line of a picture that once hung there is still visible. She is not home yet, but there is a small bird in the cage waiting for her and so am I.

Mr. Nobody is what I call the man in the subway. I catch sight of him from time to time. He has labored all his life to make himself inconspicuous in dress and manner and has nearly succeeded. He sits in the far corner in his gray hat, gray moustache, pale collapsing cheeks, and empty, watery eyes, staring off into space while the subway train grinds along and the overhead lights go out briefly and return to find us puzzled, looking up from newspapers at each other sitting there. Even more odd than these searching looks we give strangers are the times when we catch someone doing the same to us. They see me as I truly am, one imagines, wanting both to run away from them and to ask what it is they see.

Today dozens of people are sunning themselves on park benches, sitting   10
close together with eyes shut as if making a collective wish. An old mutt who has done a lot of thinking and sighing in his life lies at their feet, eyeing a rusty pigeon take wing as I pass by. The enigma of the ordinary—that's what makes old photographs so poignant. An ancient streetcar in sepia color. A few men holding on to their hats on a windy day. They hurry with their faces averted except for one befuddled old fellow who has stopped and is looking over his shoulder at what we cannot see, but where, we suspect, we ourselves will be coming into view someday, as hurried and ephemeral as any one of them. ▇

The Reader's Presence

1. Consider the process Simic goes through when looking at a photograph. How does he make sense of the image? What does he add to it? What conclusions does he come to about the value of photography?

2. How does Simic move between interpreting the historic photographs by Berenice Abbott and interpreting scenes from his daily life in New York City? What does one have to do with the other? Does Simic read faces on the street or scenes in the city in the same way that he reads Abbott's photographs? Why or why not?

3. **VISUAL PRESENCE:** Carefully examine the two photographs on pages 561 and 563, "Second Avenue El" and "Blossom Restaurant." What personal experiences or stories come to mind when you look at these photographs? Why? Identify specific details from the images that prompt these associations. How are your associations similar to or different from those Simic articulates?

4. **CONNECTIONS:** "Can one experience nostalgia for a time and place one did not know?" Simic asks (paragraph 5). Compare Simic's essay about his New York City to one of the most famous essays on "a time and place," E. B. White's classic "Once More to the Lake" (page 293). What similarities can you find between these two essays on nostalgia? What is the main difference between each author's attachment to place and time? How does the "past" figure in each essay? You might also compare Simic's essay to Nathaniel Hawthorne's "My Visit to Niagara" (page 432). How does each writer "read" the scenes he encounters?

Joel Stein

THE NEW GREATEST GENERATION

JOEL STEIN (b. 1971) is an American journalist and humor writer who has taught at Princeton University and writes for *Time* magazine. He has also written for television, notably for an animated show called *Hey Joel*, which aired in Canada and South Africa. He is known for taking controversial positions on controversial topics. In 2006, for example, he was criticized for writing that it was hypocritical to claim to be against the war in Iraq while simultaneously claiming to "support our troops." His writing is often characterized by a confrontational brand of humor that seems at times intended to both offend and entertain.

> Joel Stein began his career as a writer for *Martha Stewart Living* and has said that Martha Stewart once fired him twice in the same day.

He majored in English at Stanford University before graduating in 1993, moving first to New York and then, in 2005, to Los Angeles. He began his career as a writer for *Martha Stewart Living* and has said that Martha Stewart once fired him twice in the same day. In addition to working as a journalist, he has also appeared as a commentator on VH1's nostalgia program, *I Love the '80s*. He was originally hesitant to do the show, believing that the role of television host conflicted with his identity as a writer, but he ultimately decided that his reluctance to wear other hats was "kind of stupid and certainly antiquated." He went on to say, "As journalism dies, I . . . want some skills besides writing." His writing continues to be published widely, though, and his first book, *Man Made: A Stupid Quest for Masculinity*, was published in 2012. "The New Greatest Generation" was published in *Time* magazine in 2013. It is interesting in that it first confirms nearly every negative stereotype about millennials before going on to argue that the millennial generation may in fact be a powerful force for positive change.

I AM ABOUT TO DO WHAT OLD PEOPLE have done throughout history: call those younger than me lazy, entitled, selfish and shallow. But I have studies! I have statistics! I have quotes from respected academics! Unlike my parents, my grandparents and my great-grandparents, I have proof.

Here's the cold, hard data: The incidence of narcissistic personality disorder is nearly three times as high for people in their 20s as for the generation that's now 65 or older, according to the National Institutes of Health; 58% more college students scored higher on a narcissism scale in 2009 than in 1982. Millennials got so many participation trophies growing up that a recent study showed that 40% believe they should be promoted every two years, regardless of performance. They are fame-obsessed: three times as many middle school girls want to grow up to be a personal assistant to a famous person as want to be a Senator, according to a 2007 survey; four times as many would pick the assistant job over CEO of a major corporation. They're so convinced of their own greatness that the National Study of Youth and Religion found the guiding morality of 60% of millennials in any situation is that they'll just be able to feel what's right. Their development is stunted: more people ages 18 to 29 live with their parents than with a spouse, according to the 2012 Clark University Poll of Emerging Adults. And they are lazy. In 1992, the nonprofit Families and Work Institute reported that 80% of people under 23 wanted to one day have a job with greater responsibility; 10 years later, only 60% did.

Millennials consist, depending on whom you ask, of people born from 1980 to 2000. To put it more simply for them, since they grew up not having to do a lot of math in their heads, thanks to computers, the group is made up mostly of teens and 20-somethings. At 80 million strong, they are the biggest age grouping in American history. Each country's millennials are different, but because of globalization, social media, the exporting of Western culture and the speed of change, millennials worldwide are more similar to one another than to older generations within their nations. Even in China, where family history is more important than any individual, the Internet, urbanization and the one-child policy have created a generation as overconfident and self-involved as the Western one. And these aren't just rich-kid problems: poor millennials have even higher rates of narcissism, materialism and technology addiction in their ghetto-fabulous lives.

They are the most threatening and exciting generation since the baby boomers brought about social revolution, not because they're trying to take over the Establishment but because they're growing up without one. The Industrial Revolution made individuals far more powerful—they could move to a city, start a business, read and form organizations. The information revolution has further empowered individuals by handing them the technology to compete against huge organizations: hackers vs. corporations, bloggers vs. newspapers, terrorists vs. nation-states, YouTube directors vs. studios, app-makers vs. entire industries. Millennials don't need us. That's why we're scared of them.

In the U.S., millennials are the children of baby boomers, who are also known as the Me Generation, who then produced the Me Me Me Generation, whose selfishness technology has only exacerbated. Whereas in the 1950s families displayed a wedding photo, a school photo and maybe a military photo in their homes, the average middle-class American family today walks amid 85 pictures of themselves and their pets. Millennials have come

5

of age in the era of the quantified self, recording their daily steps on FitBit, their whereabouts every hour of every day on PlaceMe and their genetic data on 23 and Me. They have less civic engagement and lower political participation than any previous group. This is a generation that would have made Walt Whitman wonder if maybe they should try singing a song of someone else.

They got this way partly because, in the 1970s, people wanted to improve kids' chances of success by instilling self-esteem. It turns out that self-esteem is great for getting a job or hooking up at a bar but not so great for keeping a job or a relationship. "It was an honest mistake," says Roy Baumeister, a psychology professor at Florida State University and the editor of *Self-Esteem: The Puzzle of Low Self-Regard.* "The early findings showed that, indeed, kids with high self-esteem did better in school and were less likely to be in various kinds of trouble. It's just that we've learned later that self-esteem is a result, not a cause." The problem is that when people try to boost self-esteem, they accidentally boost narcissism instead. "Just tell your kids you love them. It's a better message," says Jean Twenge, a psychology professor at the University of San Diego, who wrote *Generation Me* and *The Narcissism Epidemic.* "When they're little it seems cute to tell them they're special or a princess or a rock star or whatever their T-shirt says. When they're 14 it's no longer cute." All that self-esteem leads them to be disappointed when the world refuses to affirm how great they know they are. "This generation has the highest likelihood of having unmet expectations with respect to their careers and the lowest levels of satisfaction with their careers at the stage that they're at," says Sean Lyons, co-editor of *Managing the New Workforce: International Perspectives on the Millennial Generation.* "It is sort of a crisis of unmet expectations."

What millennials are most famous for besides narcissism is its effect: entitlement. If you want to sell seminars to middle managers, make them about how to deal with young employees who e-mail the CEO directly and beg off projects they find boring. English teacher David McCullough Jr.'s address last year to Wellesley High School's graduating class, a 12-minute reality check titled "You Are Not Special," has nearly 2 million hits on YouTube.[1] "Climb the mountain so you can see the world, not so the world can see you," McCullough told the graduates. He says nearly all the response to the video has been positive, especially from millennials themselves; the video has 57 likes for every dislike.

Though they're cocky about their place in the world, millennials are also stunted, having prolonged a life stage between teenager and adult that this magazine once called *twixters* and will now use once again in an attempt to get that term to catch on. The idea of the teenager started in the 1920s; in 1910, only a tiny percentage of kids went to high school, so most people's social interactions were with adults in their family or in the workplace. Now that cell phones allow kids to socialize at every hour—they send and

---

[1] This speech has been expanded into a recently published book. —EDS.

receive an average of 88 texts a day, according to Pew—they're living under the constant influence of their friends. "Peer pressure is anti-intellectual. It is anti-historical. It is anti-eloquence," says Mark Bauerlein, an English professor at Emory, who wrote *The Dumbest Generation: How the Digital Age Stupefies Young Americans and Jeopardizes Our Future (Or, Don't Trust Anyone Under 30)*. "Never before in history have people been able to grow up and reach age 23 so dominated by peers. To develop intellectually you've got to relate to older people, older things: 17-year-olds never grow up if they're just hanging around other 17-year-olds." Of all the objections to Obamacare, not a lot of people argued against parents' need to cover their kids' health insurance until they're 26.

Millennials are interacting all day but almost entirely through a screen. You've seen them at bars, sitting next to one another and texting. They might look calm, but they're deeply anxious about missing out on something better. Seventy percent of them check their phones every hour, and many experience phantom pocket-vibration syndrome. "They're doing a behavior to reduce their anxiety," says Larry Rosen, a psychology professor at California State University at Dominguez Hills and the author of *iDisorder*. That constant search for a hit of dopamine ("Someone liked my status update!") reduces creativity. From 1966, when the Torrance Tests of Creative Thinking were first administered, through the mid-1980s, creativity scores in children increased. Then they dropped, falling sharply in 1998. Scores on tests of empathy similarly fell sharply, starting in 2000, likely because of both a lack of face-to-face time and higher degrees of narcissism. Not only do millennials lack the kind of empathy that allows them to feel concerned for others, but they also have trouble even intellectually understanding others' points of view.

What they do understand is how to turn themselves into brands, with   10
"friend" and "follower" tallies that serve as sales figures. As with most sales, positivity and confidence work best. "People are inflating themselves like balloons on Facebook," says W. Keith Campbell, a psychology professor at the University of Georgia, who has written three books about generational increases in narcissism (including *When You Love a Man Who Loves Himself*). When everyone is telling you about their vacations, parties and promotions, you start to embellish your own life to keep up. If you do this well enough on Instagram, YouTube and Twitter, you can become a microcelebrity.

Millennials grew up watching reality TV shows, most of which are basically documentaries about narcissists. Now they have trained themselves to be reality-TV-ready. "Most people never define who they are as a personality type until their 30s. So for people to be defining who they are at the age of 14 is almost a huge evolutionary jump," says casting director Doron Ofir, who auditioned participants for *Jersey Shore*, *Millionaire Matchmaker*, *A Shot at Love* and *RuPaul's Drag Race*, among other shows. "Do you follow me on Twitter?" he asks at the end of the interview. "Oh, you should. I'm fun. I hope that one day they provide an Emmy for casting of reality shows—because, you know, I'd assume I'm a shoo-in. I would like that gold statue.

And then I will take a photo of it, and then I will Instagram it." Ofir is 41, but he has clearly spent a lot of time around millennials.

I have gone just about as far as I can in an article without talking about myself. So first, yes, I'm aware that I started this piece—in which I complain about millennials' narcissism—with the word *I*. I know that this magazine, which for decades did not print bylines, started putting authors' names on the cover regularly in 2004 and that one of the first names was mine. As I mocked reality shows in the previous paragraph, I kept thinking about the fact that I got to the final round for 1995's *Real World: London.* I know my number of Twitter followers far better than the tally on my car's odometer; although Facebook has a strictly enforced limit of 5,000 friends, I somehow have 5,079. It was impossible not to remember, the whole time I was accusing millennials of being lazy, that I was supposed to finish this article nearly a year ago.

I moved home for the first six months after college. When I got hired at TIME, my co-workers hated me for cozying up to the editor of the magazine. I talk to one of my parents every other day and depend on my dad for financial advice. It's highly possible that I'm a particularly lame 41-year-old, but still, none of these traits are new to millennials; they've been around at least since the Reformation, when Martin Luther told Christians they didn't need the church to talk to God, and became more pronounced at the end of the 18th century in the Romantic period, when artists stopped using their work to celebrate God and started using it to express themselves. In 1979, Christopher Lasch wrote in *The Culture of Narcissism,* "The media give substance to, and thus intensify, narcissistic dreams of fame and glory, encourage common people to identify themselves with the stars and to hate the 'herd,' and make it more and more difficult for them to accept the banality of everyday existence." I checked my e-mail three times during that sentence.

So while the entire first half of this article is absolutely true (I had data!), millennials' self-involvement is more a continuation of a trend than a revolutionary break from previous generations. They're not a new species; they've just mutated to adapt to their environment.

For example, millennials' perceived entitlement isn't a result of overprotection but an adaptation to a world of abundance. "For almost all of human history, almost everyone was a small-scale farmer. And then people were farmers and factory workers. Nobody gets very much fulfillment from either of those things," says Jeffrey Arnett, a psychology professor at Clark University, who invented the phrase *emerging adulthood*, which people foolishly use instead of the catchy *twixters*. Twixters put off life choices because they can choose from a huge array of career options, some of which, like jobs in social media, didn't exist 10 years ago. What idiot would try to work her way up at a company when she's going to have an average of seven jobs before age 26? Because of online dating, Facebook circles and the ability to connect with people internationally, they no longer have to marry someone from their high school class or even their home country. Because life expectancy is increasing so rapidly and technology allows women to get pregnant in their 40s, they're more free to postpone big decisions. The median age for an American woman's first marriage went from 20.6 in 1967 to 26.9 in 2011.

And while all that choice might end in disappointment, it's a lottery worth playing. "I had one grandfather fight in the Pacific and one in the Atlantic theater. One became a pilot; one became a doctor. When you grow up during the Great Depression and fight off the Nazis, you want safety and stability," says Tucker Max, 37, who set an example for millennials when instead of using his Duke law degree to practice law, he took his blog rants about his drunken, lecherous adventures and turned them into a mega-best-selling book, *I Hope They Serve Beer in Hell*, that he got an independent publisher to print. "Everyone told you that everyone above you had to s--- on you before you got to s--- on people below you. And millennials didn't want to do that."

In fact, a lot of what counts as typical millennial behavior is how rich kids have always behaved. The Internet has democratized opportunity for many young people, giving them access and information that once belonged mostly to the wealthy. When I was growing up in the 1980s, I thought I would be a lawyer, since that was the best option I knew about for people who sucked at math in my middle-class suburb, but I saw a lot more options once I got to Stanford. "Previously if you wanted to be a writer but didn't know anyone who is in publishing, it was just, Well, I won't write. But now it's, Wait, I know someone who knows someone," says Jane Buckingham, who studies workplace changes as founder of Trendera, a consumer-insights firm. "I hear story after story of people high up in an organization saying, 'Well, this person just e-mailed me and asked me for an hour of my time, and for whatever reason I gave it to them.' So the great thing is that they do feel entitled to all of this, so they'll be more innovative and more willing to try new things and they'll do all this cool stuff."

Because millennials don't respect authority, they also don't resent it. That's why they're the first teens who aren't rebelling. They're not even sullen. "I grew up watching *Peanuts*, where you didn't even see the parents. They were that 'Wah-wah' voice. And MTV was always a parent-free zone," says MTV president Stephen Friedman, 43, who now includes parents in nearly all the channel's reality shows. "One of our research studies early on said that a lot of this audience outsources their superego to their parents. The most simple decision of should I do this or should I do that—our audience will check in with their parents." A 2012 Google Chrome ad shows a college student video-chatting all the details of her life to her dad. "I am very used to seeing things where the cliché is the parent doesn't understand. Most of my friends, their parents are on social and they're following them or sharing stuff with them," says Jessica Brillhart, a filmmaker at Google's Creative Lab, who worked on the commercial. It's hard to hate your parents when they also listen to rap and watch Jon Stewart.

In fact, many parents of millennials would proudly call their child-rearing style peer-enting. "I negotiate daily with my son who is 13. Maybe all that coddling has paid off in these parent-child relationships," says Jon Murray, who created *The Real World* and other reality shows, including *Keeping Up With the Kardashians*. He says that seeing regular people celebrated on TV gives millennials confidence: "They're going after what they want. It can be a little irritating that they want to be on the next rung so quickly. Maybe I'm partly responsible for it. I like this generation, so I have no issues with that."

Kim Kardashian, who represents to nonmillennials all that is wrong with   20
her generation, readily admits that she has no particular talent. But she also knows why she appeals to her peers. "They like that I share a lot of myself and that I've always been honest about the way I live my life," she says. "They want relationships with businesses and celebrities. Gen X was kept at arm's length from businesses and celebrity." When you're no longer cowed by power, you are going to like what a friend tells you about far more than what an ad campaign does, even if that friend is a celebrity trying to make money and that friendship is just a reply to one tweet.

While every millennial might seem like an oversharing Kardashian, posting vacation photos on Facebook is actually less obnoxious than 1960s couples' trapping friends in their houses to watch their terrible vacation slide shows. "Can you imagine if the boomers had YouTube, how narcissistic they would've seemed?" asks Scott Hess, senior vice president of human intelligence for SparkSMG, whose TedX speech, "Millennials: Who They Are and Why We Hate Them," advised companies on marketing to youth. "Can you imagine how many frickin' Instagrams of people playing in the mud during Woodstock we would've seen? I think in many ways you're blaming millennials for the technology that happens to exist right now." Yes, they check their phones during class, but think about how long you can stand in line without looking at your phone. Now imagine being used to that technology your whole life and having to sit through algebra.

Companies are starting to adjust not just to millennials' habits but also to their atmospheric expectations. Nearly a quarter of DreamWorks' 2,200 employees are under 30, and the studio has a 96% retention rate. Dan Satterthwaite, who runs the studio's human-relations department and has been in the field for about 23 years, says Maslow's hierarchy of needs makes it clear that a company can't just provide money anymore but also has to deliver self-actualization. During work hours at DreamWorks, you can take classes in photography, sculpting, painting, cinematography and karate. When one employee explained that jujitsu is totally different from karate, Satterthwaite was shocked at his boldness, then added a jujitsu class.

Millennials are able to use their leverage to negotiate much better contracts with the traditional institutions they do still join. Although the armed forces had to lower the physical standards for recruits and make boot camp less intensive, Gary Stiteler, who has been an Army recruiter for about 15 years, is otherwise more impressed with millennials than any other group he's worked with. "The generation that we enlisted when I first started recruiting was sort of do, do, do. This generation is think, think about it before you do it," he says. "This generation is three to four steps ahead.

They're coming in saying, 'I want to do this, then when I'm done with this, I want to do this.'"

Here's something even all the psychologists who fret over their narcissism studies agree about: millennials are nice. They have none of that David Letterman irony and Gen X ennui. "The positivism has surprised me. The Internet was always 50-50 positive and negative. And now it's 90-10," says Shane Smith, the 43-year-old CEO of Vice, which adjusted from being a Gen X company in print to a millennial company once it started posting videos online, which are viewed by a much younger audience. Millennials are more accepting of differences, not just among gays, women and minorities but in everyone. "There are many, many subcultures, and you can dip into them and search around. I prefer that to you're either supermainstream or a riot grrrl," says Tavi Gevinson, a 17-year-old who runs *Rookie*, an online fashion magazine, from her bedroom when she's not at school. It's hard, in other words, to join the counterculture when there's no culture. "There's not this us-vs.-them thing now. Maybe that's why millennials don't rebel," she says.

There may even be the beginning of a reaction against all the constant   25 self-promotion. Evan Spiegel, 22, co-founder of Snapchat, an app that allows people to send photos, video and text that are permanently erased after 10 seconds or less, argues that it's become too exhausting for millennials to front a perfect life on social media. "We're trying to create a place where you can be in sweatpants, sitting eating cereal on a Friday night, and that's O.K.," he says.

But if you need the ultimate proof that millennials could be a great force for positive change, know this: Tom Brokaw, champion of the Greatest Generation, loves millennials. He calls them the Wary Generation, and he thinks their cautiousness in life decisions is a smart response to their world. "Their great mantra has been: Challenge convention. Find new and better ways of doing things. And so that ethos transcends the wonky people who are inventing new apps and embraces the whole economy," he says. The generation that experienced Monica Lewinsky's dress, 9/11, the longest wars in U.S. history, the Great Recession and an Arab Spring that looks at best like a late winter is nevertheless optimistic about its own personal chances of success. Sure, that might be delusional, but it's got to lead to better results than wearing flannel, complaining and making indie movies about it.

So here's a more rounded picture of millennials than the one I started with. All of which I also have data for. They're earnest and optimistic. They embrace the system. They are pragmatic idealists, tinkerers more than dreamers, life hackers. Their world is so flat that they have no leaders, which is why revolutions from Occupy Wall Street to Tahrir Square have even less chance than previous rebellions. They want constant approval—they post photos from the dressing room as they try on clothes. They have massive fear of missing out and have an acronym for everything (including FOMO). They're celebrity obsessed but don't respectfully idolize celebrities from a distance. (Thus *Us* magazine's "They're just like us!" which consists of paparazzi shots of famous people doing everyday things.) They're not into going to church, even though they believe in God, because they don't identify with big institutions; one-third of adults under 30, the highest percentage ever, are religiously unaffili-ated. They want new experiences, which are more important to them than material goods. They are cool and reserved and not all that passionate. They are informed but inactive: they hate Joseph Kony but aren't going to do any-thing about Joseph Kony. They are probusiness. They're financially respon-sible; although student loans have hit record highs, they have less house-hold and credit-card debt than any previous generation on record—which, admittedly, isn't that hard when you're living at home and using your parents' credit card. They love their phones but hate talking on them.

They are not only the biggest generation we've ever known but maybe the last large birth grouping that will be easy to generalize about. There are already microgenerations within the millennial group, launching as often as new iPhones, depending on whether you learned to type before Facebook, Twitter, iPads or Snapchat. Those rising microgenerations are all horrifying the ones right above them, who are their siblings. And the group after mil-lennials is likely to be even more empowered. They're already so comfort-able in front of the camera that the average American 1-year-old has more images of himself than a 17th century French king.

So, yes, we have all that data about narcissism and laziness and entitle-ment. But a generation's greatness isn't determined by data; it's determined by how they react to the challenges that befall them. And, just as important, by how we react to them. Whether you think millennials are the new great-est generation of optimistic entrepreneurs or a group of 80 million people about to implode in a dwarf star of tears when their expectations are unmet depends largely on how you view change. Me, I choose to believe in the children. God knows they do. ▪

The Reader's Presence

1. Stein opens his essay by announcing: "I am about to do what old people have done throughout history: call those younger than me lazy, entitled, selfish and shallow." Comment on the specific ways in which this strategy was—or was not—effective in drawing you in as a reader. To what extent do you agree with Stein that these traits accurately characterize millennials? Do you think every generation believes the next generation is "lazy, entitled, selfish and shallow"? If so, why? Do you think the mil-lennials are markedly different from the people of Stein's generation? If so, in what specific ways?

2. Technology plays a prominent role in Stein's essay. He claims that technology has "exacerbated" the millennial's "selfishness" and "narcissism," both of which he sees as defining generational characteristics. He writes, "Millennials have come of age in the era of the quantified self, recording their daily steps on FitBit, their whereabouts every hour of every day on PlaceMe and their genetic data on 23 and Me" (para-graph 5). To what extent should millennials be held responsible for the effect and use of technology built by the previous generations?

3. After extolling his data on the millennials that support his claims of "narcissism and laziness and entitlement," Stein concludes his essay by observing, "a generation's greatness isn't determined by data; it's determined by how they react to the challenges that befall them." What do you think will be the challenges facing the millennials? What are the challenges they currently face? Why does Stein "choose to believe in the children" (paragraph 29)?

4. **CONNECTIONS:**   Compare and contrast the substance and structure of Stein's argument to that of Nicholas Carr in "Is Google Making Us Stupid?" (page 588). In what specific way(s) are the arguments presented in each essay complementary? In what way(s) are they at odds? What in your judgment would each writer say about the other's position? Point to specific passages in each essay to validate your response. What role does anecdote play in each essay? Which writer uses data more effectively to build his argument? Support the points you make with specific examples.

Virginia Woolf

THE DEATH OF THE MOTH

One of the most important writers of the twentieth century, **VIRGINIA WOOLF** (1882–1941) explored innovations in indirect narration and the impressionistic use of language that are now considered hallmarks of the modern novel and continue to influence novelists on both sides of the Atlantic. Together with her husband, Leonard Woolf, she founded the Hogarth Press, which published many experimental works that have now become classics, including her own. A central figure in the Bloomsbury group of writers, Woolf established her reputation with the novels *Mrs. Dalloway* (1925), *To the Lighthouse* (1927), and *The Waves* (1931). The feminist movement has helped to focus attention on her work, and Woolf's nonfiction has provided the basis for several important lines of argument in contemporary feminist theory. *A Room of One's Own* (1929), *Three Guineas* (1938), and *The Common Reader* (1938) are the major works of nonfiction published in Woolf's lifetime;

> "The novelist—it is his distinction and his danger—is terribly exposed to life. . . . He can no more cease to receive impressions than a fish in mid-ocean can cease to let the water rush through his gills."

posthumously, her essays have been gathered together in *The Death of the Moth* (1942) (where the essay reprinted here appears) and in the four-volume *Collected Essays* (1967).

Reflecting on her own writing life, Woolf wrote, "The novelist—it is his distinction and his danger—is terribly exposed to life. . . . He can no more cease to receive impressions than a fish in mid-ocean can cease to let the water rush through his gills." To turn those impressions into writing, Woolf maintained, requires solitude and the time for thoughtful selection. Given tranquility, a writer can, with effort, discover art in experience. "There emerges from the mist something stark, formidable and enduring, the bone and substance upon which our rush of indiscriminating emotion was founded."

MOTHS THAT FLY BY DAY are not properly to be called moths; they do not excite that pleasant sense of dark autumn nights and ivy-blossom which the commonest yellow-underwing asleep in the shadow of the curtain never fails to rouse in us. They are hybrid creatures, neither gay like butterflies nor somber like their own species. Nevertheless the present specimen, with his narrow hay-colored wings, fringed with a tassel of the same color, seemed to be content with life. It was a pleasant morning, mid-September, mild, benignant, yet with a keener breath than that of the summer months. The plough was already scoring the field opposite the window, and where the share had been, the earth was pressed flat and gleamed with moisture. Such vigor came rolling in from the fields and the down beyond that it was difficult to keep the eyes strictly turned upon the book. The rooks too were keeping one of their annual festivities; soaring round the tree tops until it looked as if a vast net with thousands of black knots in it had been cast up into the air; which, after a few moments sank slowly down upon the trees until every twig seemed to have a knot at the end of it. Then, suddenly, the net would be thrown into the air again in a wider circle this time, with the utmost clamor and vociferation, as though to be thrown into the air and settle slowly down upon the tree tops were a tremendously exciting experience.

The same energy which inspired the rooks, the ploughmen, the horses, and even, it seemed, the lean bare-backed downs, sent the moth fluttering from side to side of his square of the windowpane. One could not help watching him. One was, indeed, conscious of a queer feeling of pity for him. The possibilities of pleasure seemed that morning so enormous and so various that to have only a moth's part in life, and a day moth's at that, appeared a hard fate, and his zest in enjoying his meager opportunities to the full, pathetic. He flew vigorously to one corner of his compartment, and after waiting there a second, flew across to the other. What remained for him but to fly to a third corner and then to a fourth? That was all he could do, in spite of the size of the downs, the width of the sky, the far-off smoke of houses, and the romantic voice, now and then, of a steamer out at sea. What he could do he did. Watching him, it seemed as if a fiber, very thin but pure, of the enormous energy of the world had been thrust into his frail and diminutive body. As often as he crossed the pane, I could fancy that a thread of vital light became visible. He was little or nothing but life.

Yet, because he was so small, and so simple a form of the energy that was rolling in at the open window and driving its way through so many narrow and intricate corridors in my own brain and in those of other human beings, there was something marvelous as well as pathetic about him. It was as if someone had taken a tiny bead of pure life and decking it as lightly as possible with down and feathers, had set it dancing and zigzagging to show us the true nature of life. Thus displayed one could not get over the strangeness of it. One is apt to forget all about life, seeing it humped and bossed and garnished and cumbered so that it has to move with the greatest circumspection and dignity. Again, the thought of all that life might have been had he been born in any other shape caused one to view his simple activities with a kind of pity.

After a time, tired by his dancing apparently, he settled on the window ledge in the sun, and, the queer spectacle being at an end, I forgot about him. Then, looking up, my eye was caught by him. He was trying to resume his dancing, but seemed either so stiff or so awkward that he could only flutter to the bottom of the windowpane; and when he tried to fly across it he failed. Being intent on other matters I watched these futile attempts for a time without thinking, unconsciously waiting for him to resume his flight, as one waits for a machine, that has stopped momentarily, to start again without considering the reason of its failure. After perhaps a seventh attempt he slipped from the wooden ledge and fell, fluttering his wings, on to his back on the windowsill. The helplessness of his attitude roused me. It flashed upon me that he was in difficulties; he could no longer raise himself; his legs struggled vainly. But, as I stretched out a pencil, meaning to help him to right himself, it came over me that the failure and awkwardness were the approach of death. I laid the pencil down again.

The legs agitated themselves once more. I looked as if for the enemy   5 against which he struggled. I looked out of doors. What had happened there? Presumably it was midday, and work in the fields had stopped. Stillness and quiet had replaced the previous animation. The birds had taken themselves off to feed in the brooks. The horses stood still. Yet the power was there all the same, massed outside, indifferent, impersonal, not attending to anything in particular. Somehow it was opposed to the little hay-colored moth. It was useless to try to do anything. One could only watch the extraordinary efforts made by those tiny legs against an oncoming doom which could, had it chosen, have submerged an entire city, not merely a city, but masses of human beings; nothing, I knew had any chance against death. Nevertheless after a pause of exhaustion the legs fluttered again. It was superb this last protest, and so frantic that he succeeded at last in righting himself. One's sympathies, of course, were all on the side of life. Also, when there was nobody to care or to know, this gigantic effort on the part of an insignificant little moth, against a power of such magnitude, to retain what no one else valued or desired to keep, moved one strangely. Again, somehow, one saw life, a pure bead. I lifted the pencil again, useless though I knew it to be. But even as I did so, the unmistakable tokens of death showed themselves. The body relaxed, and instantly grew stiff. The struggle was over. The insignificant little creature now knew death. As I looked at the dead moth, this minute wayside triumph of so great a force over so mean an antagonist filled me with wonder. Just as life had been strange a few minutes before, so death was now as strange. The moth having righted himself now lay most decently and uncomplainingly composed. O yes, he seemed to say, death is stronger than I am.

The Reader's Presence

1. Woolf calls her essay "The Death of the Moth." What effect(s) does her decision to use a definite article ("the" rather than "a" moth) have? What quality does the definite article add to the essay?

2. Reread the essay, paying special attention not to the moth but to the writer. What presence does Woolf establish for herself in the essay? How does the act of writing itself get introduced? Of what significance is the pencil? Can you discover any connection between the essay's subject and its composition?

3. **CONNECTIONS:** Examine carefully the list of rules for writing in George Orwell's essay "Politics and the English Language" (paragraph 18, page 515). In what specific ways does Woolf exemplify Orwell's standards for writing effectively? Be specific in illustrating each point you make. Compare Woolf's observations on writing effectively (page 578) with those Orwell recounts in "George Orwell on the Four Reasons for Writing" (page 526).

The Writer at Work

VIRGINIA WOOLF on the Practice of Freewriting

Hulton Archive/Getty Images

At the time of her death (1941), Virginia Woolf, one of modern literature's outstanding creative voices, left twenty-six volumes of a handwritten diary that she had started in 1915. Her diary records her daily activities, social life, reading, and, most important, her thoughts about the writing process. In 1953, her husband, Leonard Woolf, extracted her remarks about writing and published them in a separate volume called *A Writer's Diary*. Here, just having completed a newspaper article on the novelist Daniel Defoe, Woolf decides to take a break and think about the different ways she composes when she writes in her diary as opposed to when she writes more formally for publication.

❝ *This Loose, Drifting Material of Life*
Easter Sunday, April 20, 1919

In the idleness which succeeds any long article, and Defoe is the second leader this month, I got out this diary and read, as one always does read one's own writing, with a kind of guilty intensity. I confess that the rough and random style of it, often so ungrammatical, and crying for a word altered, afflicted me somewhat. I am trying to tell whichever self it is that reads this hereafter that I can write very much better; and take no time over this; and forbid her to let the eye of man behold it. And now I may add my little compliment to the effect that it has a slapdash and vigor and sometimes hits an unexpected bull's eye. But what is more to the point is my belief that the habit of writing thus for my own eye only is good practice. It loosens the ligaments. Never mind the misses and the stumbles. Going at such a pace as I do I must make the most direct and instant shots at my object, and thus have to lay hands on words, choose them and shoot them with no more pause than is needed to put my pen in the ink. I believe that during the past year I can trace some increase of ease in my professional writing which I attribute to my casual half hours after tea. Moreover there looms ahead of me the shadow of some kind of form which a diary might attain to. I might in the course of time learn what it is that one can make of this loose, drifting material of life; finding another use for it than the use I put it to, so much more consciously and scrupulously, in fiction. What sort of diary should I like mine to be? Something loose knit and yet not slovenly, so elastic that it will embrace anything, solemn, slight, or beautiful that comes into my mind. I should like it to resemble some deep old desk, or capacious hold-all, in which one flings a mass of odds and ends without looking them through. I should like to come back, after a year or two, and find that the collection had sorted itself and refined itself and coalesced, as such deposits so mysteriously do, into a mould, transparent enough to reflect the light of our life, and yet steady, tranquil compounds with the aloofness of a work of art. The main requisite, I think on re-reading my old volumes, is not to play the part of censor, but to write as the mood comes or of anything whatever; since I was curious to find how I went for things put in haphazard, and found the significance to lie where I never saw it at the time. But looseness quickly becomes slovenly. A little effort is needed to face a character or an incident which needs to be recorded. ❞

PART 3

ARGUMENTATIVE WRITING

Contending with Issues

WHAT IS ARGUMENTATIVE WRITING?

Argument—whether written or spoken—is an inescapable part of our cultural environment, from newspaper editorials, blogs, and magazine articles to talk radio, commercials, and the evening news shows. In most forms of public argument today, someone is either defending or attacking a controversial position—gun control, government surveillance, the death penalty, climate change, and so on. These topics are commonly known as "issues"; an issue is basically a topic that is in dispute, one that people take various positions on, and one that is often a matter of contentious public debate. In this part, we look at how some highly regarded writers contend with issues: how they attempt to persuade you that one policy is better than another, that a certain course of action would lead to desirable or disastrous outcomes, or that certain choices are more ethically or morally correct than others.

Thinking about and writing an argument can seem overwhelming, but constructing arguments is a basic operation of the mind. As you'll discover when you dig deeper into any topic, even experts in a field disagree, and convincing reasons and evidence can too often be supplied for the many conflicting opinions we encounter daily. This is true not only with respect to public policy and political or legal debate but also with conflicts in our own life as we conduct "inner debates" with ourselves about decisions we must make or courses of action we wish to pursue. We construct arguments all the time—in our thoughts, in our informal conversations with friends—but we don't always examine how we arrive at our beliefs and convictions, nor do we normally pay close attention to the intricacies of our reasoning. Reading the essays in this part and drafting your own will help you slow down and think about how arguments are put together and what makes them persuasive.

Argumentative essays, as you will see in this part, come in all shapes and sizes. Regardless of length, style, and approach, however, arguments usually depend on four main features: **presenting the issue**, **making a claim**, **building a case**, and **coming to a conclusion**. Argumentative strategies may vary according to how much an author believes his or her audience knows about a topic or other matters of context, but these four features will very likely be present in most argumentative essays.

STRATEGIES FOR PRESENTING THE ISSUE

Even if the writer believes his or her opinions on a hotly debated topic represent an ideal solution—with all other opinions considered wrong—the issue doesn't go away but remains debated and discussed. For example, the fact that one believes that climate change or the second amendment's right to bear arms is an indisputable fact does not mean that the argument is over. No matter how meritorious our position may appear to ourselves, there will undoubtedly be others who disagree. So we need to supply reasons and evidence even for positions we assume are unarguable. And because we're speaking to those who may not agree, we must be careful how we present the issue.

Short argumentative essays—the kind we see in editorials and blogs—usually present the issue in the opening paragraph; it's generally a good idea not to leave your reader wondering what you're planning to discuss. In longer arguments, however, the writer may gradually set the stage for the essay's central issue. For example, the greatly admired novelist and essayist David Foster Wallace spends several pages describing a Maine lobster festival with its enormous lobster cooker before introducing the ethical issue at the heart of his essay:

> So then here is a question that's all but unavoidable at the World's Largest Lobster Cooker, and may arise in kitchens across the US: Is it all right to boil a sentient creature alive just for our gustatory pleasure? **David Foster Wallace**, "Consider the Lobster" (page 760)

Wallace's question works well precisely because we've been led through pages of a well-told (but perhaps faintly alarming) description of the festival. We don't get the sense that his answer to this question was necessarily made up before he arrived, the question itself is well-asked and doesn't overly predetermine its answer in the way it's phrased, and it pinpoints a turning point in the essay: from here on out, he's going to explore the answer. Because Wallace has engaged our interest and proven himself to be a knowledgeable guide, we agree to come along as he does so.

When you present your own topic, no matter how passionately you feel about it, it's wise to check your emotions on the subject at first, and present your topic in a similarly levelheaded tone. You likely won't have the time or the luxury of an audience engaged enough to spend several pages getting to your point. You'll probably want to do that in the first few paragraphs. But you can present yourself as a curious and logical speaker on the subject, one who will be laying out all the relevant pieces of the argument and coming to a justified and persuasive conclusion. There might be appropriate space in your conclusion for more emotion, but we'll get to that.

STRATEGIES FOR MAKING A CLAIM

Once the issue at stake has been established, it's time to make a claim about that issue. Our claim is our position. It is essentially where we stand, what we are arguing for. Claims usually fall into four categories: claims about policy, about value, about outcomes, and about a situation or condition.

Claims about policy often take the form of proposals, which recommend a course of action; for example, an educational psychologist proposing a better way of keeping public schools safe from gun violence or an activist arguing that nuclear power plants are a poor source of energy and should be abolished.

Claims about value argue whether something is good or bad, moral or immoral. A writer may claim that it is wrong to kill and eat living creatures. Value claims can also include social and cultural opinions, such as "Facebook is cheapening the concept of friendship" or "*Breaking Bad* is the best television series ever filmed."

Claims about outcomes usually examine what will happen if we pursue a certain course of action or adopt a particular position. For example, one could argue that if we banned automobiles from inner cities, we would create more livable urban communities; or one could argue that if college athletes were paid, only football and basketball players would truly benefit.

Claims about a situation or condition usually depend heavily on facts, research, and evidence. An author, for example, attempts to identify a trend or a state of affairs—that television shows are growing increasingly pornographic or that televised news reports are now being shaped by social media. Note how the distinguished Harvard psychologist Steven Pinker expresses such a claim in his essay on violence. Disputing the commonly held idea that the world was a better, less-violent place in the past, he writes:

> Believe it or not, the world of the past was *much* worse. Violence has been in decline for thousands of years, and today we may be living in the most peaceable era in the existence of our species. **Steven Pinker**, "Violence Vanquished" (page 698)

Pinker's claim, and many of these other kinds of claims, works best when they argue something unexpected. Just by walking around in the world and watching the news, we've ingested the sense that our own era is exceptionally violent, and Pinker's claim quickly taps into those cultural assumptions and rattles them, preparing us for his argument.

As you read the essays in this section, it might help to identify which kind of claim the author is making and how the author conveys a sense of urgency to that particular kind of argument. Maybe you'll be able to identify which type of argument works best on you: Are you more persuaded by claims about value—this or that is wrong or immoral? Or are you more persuaded by claims that are carefully built with facts and evidence, like a claim about a situation or condition? When it comes time to write your own essay, think about which of these claims best suits your subject, and use similar essays in this section to model how professional writers do what you're setting out to do.

STRATEGIES FOR BUILDING A CASE

It is relatively easy to make a claim but harder to back it up with reasons and evidence. Without support, Pinker's statement about the decline of world violence would be a mere assertion. His claim demands some level of proof before we can take it seriously. Pinker's essay goes on to cite historical records, statistics, and biological science as evidence to support his claim, and that kind of authoritative evidence might be what your essay calls for, too.

Writers rely on a number of different ways to support their claims and build a case for their opinions. Following are some of the most common: citing experts and authorities, using examples, providing statistics, presenting analogies, sharing personal experience, and anticipating objections.

Writers may **cite experts and authorities** when they'd like to add credibility to their own opinions. This strategy says, "See! Even experts agree with me," and it's a persuasive—though not always necessary—addition to an argument. For example, a writer supports his contention that the first amendment of the U.S. Constitution does not grant individual citizens the right to free speech by quoting a prominent law professor who has written several books on the subject. Or, in attempting to prove that a lobster can experience pain, Wallace cites the author of a book about lobsters (page 772). When you come across a reference to or quotation by an expert in the essays that follow, consider the claim without that support. How would it change the way you respond to the argument?

Using examples to illustrate a key point can serve as another effective means of support. For example (we'll use this strategy to illustrate this point, too), a writer hoping to show that memoirs today are becoming increasingly unreliable refers to several recent books criticized for containing lies and fabrications. Peter Singer's argument in which he proposes a solution to world poverty depends entirely on examples ("The Singer Solution to World Poverty," page 735).

Statistics (figures and data) from reputable sources provide the basis of many arguments, especially in the sciences and social sciences. For example, an author who wants to impress upon her readers the urgency of the negative impact of climate change might cite data from leading climatologists. In "The Tyranny of Choice," Barry Schwartz cites a recent study in the *Journal of the American Medical Association* to suggest that the incidence of clinical depression is increasing in the United States (page 721).

An **analogy** in which we compare the similarities of two different things to make our point can be an effective way to build an argument. A writer may want to show the benefits of communal cooperation by comparing a human society to a bee colony. Or, in "Letter from Birmingham Jail" (page 643), note how Martin Luther King Jr. defends the accusations that his civil rights demonstrations led to violence: "In your statement you asserted that our actions, even though peaceful, must be condemned because they precipitate violence. But can this assertion be logically made? Isn't this like condemning a robbed man because his possession of money precipitated the evil act of robbery?"

Persuasive arguments can be constructed from **personal experience**. A disabled student may argue for better campus facilities by citing his personal difficulties. This chapter contains a number of essays that argue from personal experience, perhaps most memorably Christopher Hitchens's account of his voluntarily undergoing "waterboarding" to prove that it constitutes torture ("Believe Me, It's Torture," page 616).

Though it's slightly different from other kinds of evidence, **anticipating objections** should be considered a necessary part of building your case if it's at all applicable to your topic. In constructing a case to support their claim, conscientious writers realize the importance of taking into account opposing opinions and testimony. Good debaters know the importance of understanding all sides of an issue and, like an effective courtroom attorney, prepare themselves for rebuttal and counterarguments. But writers rarely get the chance to hear objections to their arguments. Therefore, it is important in building a case within an essay to think carefully through the main objections that someone may bring to your argument and respond to them as you proceed to make your points. This strategy not only helps you to construct your case more effectively but also indicates to the reader that you have reasonably considered other points of view.

For example, in "Violence Vanquished," Pinker realizes how his notion that violence is decreasing worldwide must strike readers familiar with reports of horrific daily events. So shortly after he states his main point, Pinker writes: "This claim, I know, invites skepticism, incredulity, and sometimes anger." He then proceeds to acknowledge the scenes of violence we encounter in the media and how these may affect our "impressions." By anticipating our initial resistance to a surprising claim, a writer is able to disarm our immediate objections and prepare us for a systematic presentation of his or her case. However, if a writer ignores the other side of the argument entirely or doesn't seem to be aware of how a surprising claim will impact a reader, the writer appears less trustworthy — we're not sure we want to hear what he or she has to say.

STRATEGIES FOR COMING TO A CONCLUSION

In essays that argue a position and support it with reasoning and evidence, conclusions can be quite important. For one thing, you may need to reiterate or summarize your points for emphasis, especially if in a longer paper or research report you have provided a significant amount of supporting evidence. But a summary should not be a verbatim repetition of what you've already said. A good summarizing paragraph can be a pithy reminder to the reader of your issue's importance and the reasonableness of your position or opinion.

Some persuasive conclusions consist of **calls to action** that often take the form of a collaboration of writer and reader to do something together — advance a cause, resist a poor policy, join a movement, and so on. Note the way Howard Zinn concludes his essay criticizing Hollywood films for their inadequate depictions of social and political realities. He begins by briefly reminding his readers of some of the types of films he would like to see produced and then finishes with a call to action:

> If such films are made — about war, about class conflict, about the history of governmental lies, about broken treaties and official violence — if those stories reach the public, we might produce a new generation. As a teacher, I'm not interested in just

reproducing class after class of graduates who will get out, become successful, and take their obedient places in the slots that society has prepared for them. What we must do—whether we teach or write or make films—is educate a new generation to do this very modest thing: change the world. **Howard Zinn**, "Stories Hollywood Never Tells" (page 784)

Zinn's conclusion works well because it's both possible (we can imagine films on topics like these) and overly ambitious (can changing the world really be taught?). This reminds and grounds the reader in what's come before and sends the reader forward, continuing to think about Zinn's ideas and the scope of film's influence. Zinn's may be a good model for your own essays: think about both solidifying your reader in what you've argued and urging the reader to join you in acting on larger ideas.

Another type of conclusion is admonitory; that is, the author **issues a warning** about unfortunate outcomes if a recommended course of action is not accepted. Here is how Schwartz ends his essay on what he calls the "tyranny of choice," the limitations people may come to feel when they experience too much choice:

> There is a *New Yorker* cartoon that depicts a parent goldfish and an offspring in a small goldfish bowl. "You can be anything you want to be—no limit," says the myopic parent, not realizing how limited an existence the fishbowl allows. I'd like to suggest that perhaps the parent is not so myopic. Freedom without limits, choice within constraints, is indeed liberating. But if the fishbowl gets shattered—if the constraints disappear—freedom of choice can turn into a tyranny of choice. **Barry Schwartz**, "The Tyranny of Choice" (page 720)

Schwartz's final three words match the title of the essay, bringing us back to the beginning and reinforcing that ominous word—*tyranny*. You might think about creating a similar circle in your own essay, using the conclusion to touch back on what you discussed in your introduction. You might also consider creating the kind of tone Schwartz creates: a serious tone emphasizes the seriousness of the issue you discuss and warns your reader to consider your argument carefully.

Effective conclusions do not need to neatly wrap up the argument. They can suggest new thoughts or perspectives that can expand the discussion or even change course. One way to conclude an argumentative essay that moves the reader in a new direction is to **end with a question**. In an essay that takes a close hard look at the imprisoning aspects of modern romantic relationships, Laura Kipnis ("Against Love," page 660) concludes by asking her readers: "But isn't it a little depressing to think we are somehow incapable of inventing forms of emotional life based on anything other than subjugation?" Her question at once echoes the topic of the entire essay yet directs the discussion into a new direction, asking the reader to continue thinking about all she's presented.

READING ARGUMENTATIVE ESSAYS: A Checklist

✔ Can you approach the argument with an open mind? Do the author's opinions differ so much from yours that you cannot give the essay a fair hearing?

✔ Does the writer appear credible? Does she or he demonstrate a solid knowledge of the topic? Are the information and evidence derived from personal and professional expertise or is the writer relying on other authorities?

✔ Has the writer presented the issue clearly and fairly? Has he or she stayed on topic? Do you feel it is a genuine issue or do you feel it has been contrived to suit the author's purposes?

✔ Has the writer strayed off issue to attack opponents personally by insulting, name-calling, or associating them with unpopular groups? Does the author appear morally and ethically superior while those disagreed with are portrayed as ignorant or contemptible?

✔ Does the writer appear to be "preaching before the choir"—that is, arguing a point to an audience who already accepts it?

✔ Does the argument appear to be based on oversimplifications: reducing a complex situation to an either/or possibility or explaining a complicated series of events by a single cause that cannot be determined?

✔ To what extent does the author use emotions to persuade a reader? Does the essay try to inspire negative feelings of fear, anger, disgust, or resentment?

✔ To what extent does the author use figurative language—images, metaphors, symbols—to influence the reader? Does the figurative language feel appropriate or manipulative?

✔ Has the author depended on generalizations that you feel are unjustified? Do you think that his or her generalizations are based on too few examples or too little evidence?

✔ Do the reasons the author provides to support his or her position seem consistent and coherent? Can you locate any inconsistencies or contradictory comments in the author's reasoning?

✔ Has the writer demonstrated an awareness of different opinions on the issue? Do you feel he or she has attempted to fairly state or summarize other opinions and perspectives?

✔ How does the writer's tone of voice strike you: strident? preachy? stuffy? snooty? sarcastic? ironic? Do you detect any ways of speaking that make the author appear unreasonable or not credible?

✔ Does the writer clearly identify sources of information such as statistical data, testimony of experts, or quotations? Do you feel the information being provided to support the opinion is trustworthy?

Nicholas Carr

IS GOOGLE MAKING US STUPID?

NICHOLAS CARR (b. 1959) writes about the influence of technology on business and economics as well as on society in general. The *Christian Science Monitor* called his 2008 best-seller, *The Big Switch: Rewiring the World, from Edison to Google*, "the most influential book so far on the cloud computing movement," and his previous book, *Does IT Matter? Information Technology and the Corrosion of Competitive Advantage* (2004), was praised by the *New York Times* for its clear analysis of the economics of information technology. Carr is the former executive editor of the *Harvard Business Review*, a former member of the editorial board for *Encyclopedia Britannica*, as well as a former member of the steering board for the World Economic Forum's project on cloud computing. He has written for the *Atlantic Monthly*, *Wired*, the *Financial Times*, the *New York Times Magazine*, *The Guardian*, and many other prestigious publications; he writes the popular blog *Rough Type*; and he has been an invited speaker on issues relating to technology at the Massachusetts Institute of Technology, Harvard University, and NASA.

> The *Christian Science Monitor* called his 2008 best-seller, *The Big Switch: Rewiring the World from Edison to Google*, "the most influential book so far on the cloud computing movement."

Originally published in the *Atlantic Monthly* in 2008, "Is Google Making Us Stupid?" has been anthologized in *The Best American Science and Nature Writing*, *The Best Technology Writing*, and *The Best American Spiritual Writing*. Carr's book that picks up the same theme as this essay, *The Shallows: What the Internet Is Doing to Our Brains* (2010), was a finalist for both the 2011 Pulitzer Prize in general nonfiction and the 2011 Pen Center USA literary award, and has been translated into more than twenty languages.

"DAVE, STOP. Stop, will you? Stop, Dave. Will you stop, Dave?" So the supercomputer HAL pleads with the implacable astronaut Dave Bowman in a famous and weirdly poignant scene toward the end of Stanley Kubrick's *2001: A Space Odyssey*. Bowman, having nearly been sent to a deep-space death by the malfunctioning machine, is calmly, coldly disconnecting the

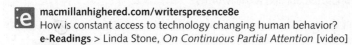

macmillanhighered.com/writerspresence8e
How is constant access to technology changing human behavior?
e-Readings > Linda Stone, *On Continuous Partial Attention* [video]

memory circuits that control its artificial "brain." "Dave, my mind is going," HAL says, forlornly. "I can feel it. I can feel it."

I can feel it, too. Over the past few years I've had an uncomfortable sense that someone, or something, has been tinkering with my brain, remapping the neural circuitry, reprogramming the memory. My mind isn't going — so far as I can tell — but it's changing. I'm not thinking the way I used to think. I can feel it most strongly when I'm reading. Immersing myself in a book or a lengthy article used to be easy. My mind would get caught up in the narrative or the turns of the argument, and I'd spend hours strolling through long stretches of prose. That's rarely the case anymore. Now my concentration often starts to drift after two or three pages. I get fidgety, lose the thread, begin looking for something else to do. I feel as if I'm always dragging my wayward brain back to the text. The deep reading that used to come naturally has become a struggle.

I think I know what's going on. For more than a decade now, I've been spending a lot of time online, searching and surfing and sometimes adding to the great databases of the Internet. The Web has been a godsend to me as a writer. Research that once required days in the stacks or periodical rooms of libraries can now be done in minutes. A few Google searches, some quick clicks on hyperlinks, and I've got the telltale fact or pithy quote I was after. Even when I'm not working, I'm as likely as not to be foraging in the Web's info-thickets, reading and writing e-mails, scanning headlines and blog posts, watching videos and listening to podcasts, or just tripping from link to link to link. (Unlike footnotes, to which they're sometimes likened, hyperlinks don't merely point to related works; they propel you toward them.)

For me, as for others, the Net is becoming a universal medium, the conduit for most of the information that flows through my eyes and ears and into my mind. The advantages of having immediate access to such an incredibly rich store of information are many, and they've been widely described and duly applauded. "The perfect recall of silicon memory," *Wired*'s Clive Thompson has written, "can be an enormous boon to thinking." But that boon comes at a price. As the media theorist Marshall McLuhan pointed out in the 1960s, media are not just passive channels of information. They supply the stuff of thought, but they also shape the process of thought. And what the Net seems to be doing is chipping away my capacity for concentration and contemplation. My mind now expects to take in information the way the Net distributes it: in a swiftly moving stream of particles. Once I was a scuba diver in the sea of words. Now I zip along the surface like a guy on a Jet Ski.

I'm not the only one. When I mention my troubles with reading to friends and acquaintances — literary types, most of them — many say they're having similar experiences. The more they use the Web, the more they have to fight to stay focused on long pieces of writing. Some of the bloggers I follow have also begun mentioning the phenomenon. Scott Karp, who writes a blog about online media, recently confessed that he has stopped reading books altogether. "I was a lit major in college, and used to be [a] voracious book

5

reader," he wrote. "What happened?" He speculates on the answer: "What if I do all my reading on the Web not so much because the way I read has changed, i.e. I'm just seeking convenience, but because the way I THINK has changed?"

Bruce Friedman, who blogs regularly about the use of computers in medicine, also has described how the Internet has altered his mental habits. "I now have almost totally lost the ability to read and absorb a longish article on the Web or in print," he wrote earlier this year. A pathologist who has long been on the faculty of the University of Michigan Medical School, Friedman elaborated on his comment in a telephone conversation with me. His thinking, he said, has taken on a "staccato" quality, reflecting the way he quickly scans short passages of text from many sources online. "I can't read *War and Peace* anymore," he admitted. "I've lost the ability to do that. Even a blog post of more than three or four paragraphs is too much to absorb. I skim it."

Anecdotes alone don't prove much. And we still await the long-term neurological and psychological experiments that will provide a definitive picture of how Internet use affects cognition. But a recently published study of online research habits, conducted by scholars from University College London, suggests that we may well be in the midst of a sea change in the way we read and think. As part of the five-year research program, the scholars examined computer logs documenting the behavior of visitors to two popular research sites, one operated by the British Library and one by a U.K. educational consortium, that provide access to journal articles, e-books, and other sources of written information. They found that people using the sites exhibited "a form of skimming activity," hopping from one source to another and rarely returning to any source they'd already visited. They typically read no more than one or two pages of an article or book before they would "bounce" out to another site. Sometimes they'd save a long article, but there's no evidence that they ever went back and actually read it. The authors of the study report:

> It is clear that users are not reading online in the traditional sense; indeed there are signs that new forms of "reading" are emerging as users "power browse" horizontally through titles, contents pages and abstracts going for quick wins. It almost seems that they go online to avoid reading in the traditional sense.

Thanks to the ubiquity of text on the Internet, not to mention the popularity of text-messaging on cell phones, we may well be reading more today than we did in the 1970s or 1980s, when television was our medium of choice. But it's a different kind of reading, and behind it lies a different kind of thinking — perhaps even a new sense of the self. "We are not only *what* we read," says Maryanne Wolf, a developmental psychologist at Tufts University and the author of *Proust and the Squid: The Story and Science of the Reading Brain*. "We are *how* we read." Wolf worries that the style of reading promoted by the Net, a style that puts "efficiency" and "immediacy" above all else, may be weakening our capacity for the kind of deep reading that emerged when an earlier technology, the printing press, made long and complex works of prose commonplace. When we read online, she says, we tend to become "mere decoders of information." Our ability to interpret text, to make the rich mental connections that form when we read deeply and without distraction, remains largely disengaged.

Reading, explains Wolf, is not an instinctive skill for human beings. It's not etched into our genes the way speech is. We have to teach our minds how to translate the symbolic characters we see into the language we understand. And the media or other technologies we use in learning and practicing the craft of reading play an important part in shaping the neural circuits inside our brains. Experiments demonstrate that readers of ideograms, such as the Chinese, develop a mental circuitry for reading that is very different from the circuitry found in those of us whose written language employs an alphabet. The variations extend across many regions of the brain, including those that govern such essential cognitive functions as memory and the interpretation of visual and auditory stimuli. We can expect as well that the circuits woven by our use of the Net will be different from those woven by our reading of books and other printed works.

10

Sometime in 1882, Friedrich Nietzsche bought a typewriter—a Malling-Hansen Writing Ball, to be precise. His vision was failing, and keeping his eyes focused on a page had become exhausting and painful, often bringing on crushing headaches. He had been forced to curtail his writing, and he feared that he would soon have to give it up. The typewriter rescued him, at least for a time. Once he had mastered touch-typing, he was able to write with his eyes closed, using only the tips of his fingers. Words could once again flow from his mind to the page.

But the machine had a subtler effect on his work. One of Nietzsche's friends, a composer, noticed a change in the style of his writing. His already terse prose had become even tighter, more telegraphic. "Perhaps you will through this instrument even take to a new idiom," the friend wrote in a letter, noting that, in his own work, his "'thoughts' in music and language often depend on the quality of pen and paper."

"You are right," Nietzsche replied, "our writing equipment takes part in the forming of our thoughts." Under the sway of the machine, writes the German media scholar Friedrich A. Kittler, Nietzsche's prose "changed from arguments to aphorisms, from thoughts to puns, from rhetoric to telegram style."

The human brain is almost infinitely malleable. People used to think that our mental meshwork, the dense connections formed among the 100 billion or so neurons inside our skulls, was largely fixed by the time we reached adulthood. But brain researchers have discovered that that's not the case. James Olds, a professor of neuroscience who directs the Krasnow Institute for Advanced Study at George Mason University, says that even the adult mind "is very plastic." Nerve cells routinely break old connections and form new ones. "The brain," according to Olds, "has the ability to reprogram itself on the fly, altering the way it functions."

As we use what the sociologist Daniel Bell has called our "intellectual   15
technologies"—the tools that extend our mental rather than our physical capacities—we inevitably begin to take on the qualities of those technologies. The mechanical clock, which came into common use in the 14th
century, provides a compelling example. In *Technics and Civilization*, the
historian and cultural critic Lewis Mumford described how the clock "disas-
sociated time from human events and helped create the belief in an independent world of mathematically measurable sequences." The "abstract
framework of divided time" became "the point of reference for both action
and thought."

The clock's methodical ticking helped bring into being the scientific
mind and the scientific man. But it also took something away. As the late
MIT computer scientist Joseph Weizenbaum observed in his 1976 book,
Computer Power and Human Reason: From Judgment to Calculation, the
conception of the world that emerged from the widespread use of timekeep-
ing instruments "remains an impoverished version of the older one, for it
rests on a rejection of those direct experiences that formed the basis for,
and indeed constituted, the old reality." In deciding when to eat, to work,
to sleep, to rise, we stopped listening to our senses and started obeying the
clock.

The process of adapting to new intellectual technologies is reflected in
the changing metaphors we use to explain ourselves to ourselves. When the
mechanical clock arrived, people began thinking of their brains as operating
"like clockwork." Today, in the age of software, we have come to think of
them as operating "like computers." But the changes, neuroscience tells us,
go much deeper than metaphor. Thanks to our brain's plasticity, the adaptation occurs also at a biological level.

The Internet promises to have particularly far-reaching effects on cognition. In a paper published in 1936, the British mathematician Alan Turing
proved that a digital computer, which at the time existed only as a theoretical machine, could be programmed to perform the function of any other
information-processing device. And that's what we're seeing today. The
Internet, an immeasurably powerful computing system, is subsuming most
of our other intellectual technologies. It's becoming our map and our clock,
our printing press and our typewriter, our calculator and our telephone, and
our radio and TV.

When the Net absorbs a medium, that medium is re-created in the Net's
image. It injects the medium's content with hyperlinks, blinking ads, and
other digital gewgaws, and it surrounds the content with the content of all
the other media it has absorbed. A new e-mail message, for instance, may
announce its arrival as we're glancing over the latest headlines at a newspaper's site. The result is to scatter our attention and diffuse our concentration.

The Net's influence doesn't end at the edges of a computer screen, either.   20
As people's minds become attuned to the crazy quilt of Internet media, traditional media have to adapt to the audience's new expectations. Television

programs add text crawls and pop-up ads, and magazines and newspapers shorten their articles, introduce capsule summaries, and crowd their pages with easy-to-browse info-snippets. When, in March of this year, the *New York Times* decided to devote the second and third pages of every edition to article abstracts, its design director, Tom Bodkin, explained that the "short-cuts" would give harried readers a quick "taste" of the day's news, sparing them the "less efficient" method of actually turning the pages and reading the articles. Old media have little choice but to play by the new-media rules.

Never has a communications system played so many roles in our lives—or exerted such broad influence over our thoughts—as the Internet does today. Yet, for all that's been written about the Net, there's been little consideration of how, exactly, it's reprogramming us. The Net's intellectual ethic remains obscure.

About the same time that Nietzsche started using his typewriter, an earnest young man named Frederick Winslow Taylor carried a stopwatch into the Midvale Steel plant in Philadelphia and began a historic series of experiments aimed at improving the efficiency of the plant's machinists. With the approval of Midvale's owners, he recruited a group of factory hands, set them to work on various metalworking machines, and recorded and timed their every movement as well as the operations of the machines. By breaking down every job into a sequence of small, discrete steps and then testing different ways of performing each one, Taylor created a set of precise instructions—an "algorithm," we might say today—for how each worker should work. Midvale's employees grumbled about the strict new regime, claiming that it turned them into little more than automatons, but the factory's productivity soared.

More than a hundred years after the invention of the steam engine, the Industrial Revolution had at last found its philosophy and its philosopher. Taylor's tight industrial choreography—his "system," as he liked to call it—was embraced by manufacturers throughout the country and, in time, around the world. Seeking maximum speed, maximum efficiency, and maximum output, factory owners used time-and-motion studies to organize their work and configure the jobs of their workers. The goal, as Taylor defined it in his celebrated 1911 treatise, *The Principles of Scientific Management*, was to identify and adopt, for every job, the "one best method" of work and thereby to effect "the gradual substitution of science for rule of thumb throughout the mechanic arts." Once his system was applied to all acts of manual labor, Taylor assured his followers, it would bring about a restructuring not only of industry but of society, creating a utopia of perfect efficiency. "In the past the man has been first," he declared; "in the future the system must be first."

Taylor's system is still very much with us; it remains the ethic of industrial manufacturing. And now, thanks to the growing power that computer engineers and software coders wield over our intellectual lives, Taylor's ethic is beginning to govern the realm of the mind as well. The Internet is a machine

The Googleplex, Google's headquarters in Mountain View, California.

Tony Avelar/Bloombe
via Getty Images

designed for the efficient and automated collection, transmission, and manipulation of information, and its legions of programmers are intent on finding the "one best method"—the perfect algorithm—to carry out every mental movement of what we've come to describe as "knowledge work."

Google's headquarters, in Mountain View, California—the Google-   25
plex—is the Internet's high church, and the religion practiced inside its walls is Taylorism. Google, says its chief executive, Eric Schmidt, is "a company that's founded around the science of measurement," and it is striving to "systematize everything" it does. Drawing on the terabytes of behavioral data it collects through its search engine and other sites, it carries out thousands of experiments a day, according to the *Harvard Business Review*, and it uses the results to refine the algorithms that increasingly control how people find information and extract meaning from it. What Taylor did for the work of the hand, Google is doing for the work of the mind.

The company has declared that its mission is "to organize the world's information and make it universally accessible and useful." It seeks to develop "the perfect search engine," which it defines as something that "understands exactly what you mean and gives you back exactly what you want." In Google's view, information is a kind of commodity, a utilitarian resource that can be mined and processed with industrial efficiency. The more pieces of information we can "access" and the faster we can extract their gist, the more productive we become as thinkers.

Where does it end? Sergey Brin and Larry Page, the gifted young men who founded Google while pursuing doctoral degrees in computer science at Stanford, speak frequently of their desire to turn their search engine into an artificial intelligence, a HAL-like machine that might be connected directly to our brains. "The ultimate search engine is something as smart as people—or smarter," Page said in a speech a few years back. "For us, working on search is a way to work on artificial intelligence." In a 2004 interview with *Newsweek*, Brin said, "Certainly if you had all the world's information directly attached to your brain, or an artificial brain that was smarter than your brain, you'd be better off." Last year, Page told a convention of scientists that Google is "really trying to build artificial intelligence and to do it on a large scale."

Such an ambition is a natural one, even an admirable one, for a pair of math whizzes with vast quantities of cash at their disposal and a small army of computer scientists in their employ. A fundamentally scientific enterprise, Google is motivated by a desire to use technology, in Eric Schmidt's words, "to solve problems that have never been solved before," and artificial intelligence is the hardest problem out there. Why wouldn't Brin and Page want to be the ones to crack it?

Still, their easy assumption that we'd all "be better off" if our brains were supplemented, or even replaced, by an artificial intelligence is unsettling. It suggests a belief that intelligence is the output of a mechanical process, a series of discrete steps that can be isolated, measured, and optimized. In Google's world, the world we enter when we go online, there's little place for the fuzziness of contemplation. Ambiguity is not an opening for insight but a bug to be fixed. The human brain is just an outdated computer that needs a faster processor and a bigger hard drive.

The idea that our minds should operate as high-speed data-processing machines is not only built into the workings of the Internet, it is the network's reigning business model as well. The faster we surf across the Web—the more links we click and pages we view—the more opportunities Google and other companies gain to collect information about us and to feed us advertisements. Most of the proprietors of the commercial Internet have a financial stake in collecting the crumbs of data we leave behind as we flit from link to link—the more crumbs, the better. The last thing these companies want is to encourage leisurely reading or slow, concentrated thought. It's in their economic interest to drive us to distraction.

Maybe I'm just a worrywart. Just as there's a tendency to glorify technological progress, there's a countertendency to expect the worst of every new tool or machine. In Plato's *Phaedrus*, Socrates bemoaned the development of writing. He feared that, as people came to rely on the written word as a substitute for the knowledge they used to carry inside their heads, they would, in the words of one of the dialogue's characters, "cease to exercise their memory and become forgetful." And because they would be able to "receive a quantity of information without proper instruction," they would "be thought very knowledgeable when they are for the most part quite ignorant." They would be "filled with the conceit of wisdom instead of real wisdom." Socrates wasn't wrong—the new technology did often have the effects he feared—but he was shortsighted. He couldn't foresee the many ways that writing and reading would serve to spread information, spur fresh ideas, and expand human knowledge (if not wisdom).

The arrival of Gutenberg's printing press, in the 15th century, set off another round of teeth gnashing. The Italian humanist Hieronimo Squarciafico worried that the easy availability of books would lead to intellectual laziness, making men "less studious" and weakening their minds. Others argued that cheaply printed books and broadsheets would undermine religious authority, demean the work of scholars and scribes, and spread sedition and debauchery. As New York University professor Clay Shirky notes, "Most of the arguments made against the printing press were correct, even prescient." But, again, the doomsayers were unable to imagine the myriad blessings that the printed word would deliver.

So, yes, you should be skeptical of my skepticism. Perhaps those who dismiss critics of the Internet as Luddites or nostalgists will be proved correct, and from our hyperactive, data-stoked minds will spring a golden age of intellectual discovery and universal wisdom. Then again, the Net isn't the alphabet, and although it may replace the printing press, it produces something altogether different. The kind of deep reading that a sequence of printed pages promotes is valuable not just for the knowledge we acquire from the author's words but for the intellectual vibrations those words set off within our own minds. In the quiet spaces opened up by the sustained, undistracted reading of a book, or by any other act of contemplation, for that matter, we make our own associations, draw our own inferences and analogies, foster our own ideas. Deep reading, as Maryanne Wolf argues, is indistinguishable from deep thinking.

If we lose those quiet spaces, or fill them up with "content," we will sacrifice something important not only in our selves but in our culture. In a recent essay, the playwright Richard Foreman eloquently described what's at stake:

> I come from a tradition of Western culture, in which the ideal (my ideal) was the complex, dense and "cathedral-like" structure of the highly educated and articulate personality—a man or woman who carried inside themselves a personally constructed and unique version of the entire heritage of the West. [But now] I see within us all (myself included) the replacement of complex inner density with a new kind of self—evolving under the pressure of information overload and the technology of the "instantly available."

As we are drained of our "inner repertory of dense cultural inheritance," Foreman concluded, we risk turning into "'pancake people'—spread wide and thin as we connect with that vast network of information accessed by the mere touch of a button."

I'm haunted by that scene in *2001*. What makes it so poignant, and so 35 weird, is the computer's emotional response to the disassembly of its mind: its despair as one circuit after another goes dark, its childlike pleading with the astronaut—"I can feel it. I can feel it. I'm afraid"—and its final reversion to what can only be called a state of innocence. HAL's outpouring of feeling contrasts with the emotionlessness that characterizes the human figures in the film, who go about their business with an almost robotic efficiency. Their thoughts and actions feel scripted, as if they're following the steps of an algorithm. In the world of *2001*, people have become so machinelike that the most human character turns out to be a machine. That's the essence of Kubrick's dark prophecy: as we come to rely on computers to mediate our understanding of the world, it is our own intelligence that flattens into artificial intelligence. ●

The Reader's Presence

1. Before considering the scientific and sociological research supporting each of his claims, Carr relays his personal experience of the ways his reading habits have changed. What does he achieve in doing so? What effect does this strategy have on the persuasiveness of his argument? Comment on the specific ways in which this strategy was—or was not—effective in drawing you in as a reader.

2. Examine carefully each source Carr draws on to support his response to the question he asks. What are the different areas of study represented in his argument? What do you notice about the way Carr transitions from one source to the next? Comment on the effectiveness of these transitions.

3. **VISUAL PRESENCE:** Examine carefully the Google campus, located in Mountain View, in the heart of California's fabled Silicon Valley (page 594). What observations can you offer about what you see? What reasonable inferences can you draw from these observations? What specific features of this photograph reflect the values and operative assumptions Carr identifies in his essay?

4. **CONNECTIONS:** Both Carr's argument and the argument Pico Iyer presents in "The Terminal Check" (page 439) begin with personal experience. How does the way each writer structures his argument differ? How is the structure of each argument the same? Focusing on the way the arguments are constructed rather than on whether you agree with the author, how persuasive do you find each approach? To which author's argumentative strategy do you find yourself more drawn? Explain why.

Barbara Ehrenreich

WILL WOMEN STILL NEED MEN?

Although she received a PhD in cellular biology from Rockefeller University in the late 1960s, **BARBARA EHRENREICH** (b. 1941) chose to abandon a career in science to pursue a life of political activism. She is a prominent member of the Democratic Socialists of America and sits on the Board of Directors of NORML, the National Organization for the Reform of Marijuana Laws. Ehrenreich has published nearly twenty books, the most recent of which is *Living with a Wild God: A Nonbeliever's Search for the Truth about Everything* (2014), and her work has appeared in such magazines as *Harper's*, the *New York Times*, *Mother Jones*, *The Progressive*, *Ms.*, the *New Republic*, the *Atlantic Monthly*, and *Salon.com*. Of writing, she has said, "What prepared me for writing? Probably the main thing was that I've always been a big reader. By reading 'the classics' while I was growing up and good fiction ever since, I developed an ear for the language and what can be done with it."

> "By reading 'the classics' while I was growing up and good fiction ever since, I developed an ear for the language and what can be done with it."

"Will Women Still Need Men?" was originally published in *Time* in 2000.

THIS COULD BE the century when the sexes go their separate ways. Sure, we've hung in there together for about a thousand millenniums so far—through hunting-gathering, agriculture and heavy industry—but what choice did we have? For most of human existence, if you wanted to make a living, raise children or even have a roaring good time now and then, you had to get the cooperation of the other sex.

What's new about the future, and potentially more challenging to our species than Martian colonization or silicon brain implants, is that the partnership between the sexes is becoming entirely voluntary. We can decide to stick together—or we can finally say, "Sayonara, other sex!" For the first time in human history and prehistory combined, the choice will be ours.

I predict three possible scenarios, starting with the Big Divorce. Somewhere around 2025, people will pick a gender equivalent of the Mason-Dixon Line and sort themselves out accordingly. In Guy Land the men will be free to spend their evenings staging belching contests and watching old Howard Stern tapes. In Gal Land the women will all be fat and happy, and no one will bother to shave her legs. Aside from a few initial border clashes, the separation will for the most part be amicable. At least the "battle of the sexes," insofar as anyone can remember it, will be removed from the kitchens and bedrooms of America and into the U.N.

And why not? If the monosexual way of life were counter to human nature, men wouldn't have spent so much of the past millennium dodging women by enlisting in armies, monasteries and all-male guilds and professions. Up until the past half-century, women only fantasized about their version of the same: a utopia like the one described by 19th century feminist Charlotte Perkins Gilman, where women would lead placidly sexless lives and reproduce by parthenogenesis. But a real separation began to look feasible about 50 years ago. With the invention of TV dinners and drip-dry shirts, for the first time the average man became capable of feeding and dressing himself. Sensing their increasing dispensability on the home front, and tired of picking up dropped socks, women rushed into the work force. They haven't achieved full economic independence by any means (women still earn only 75% of what men do), but more and more of them are realizing that ancient female dream—a room, or better yet, a condo of their own.

The truly species-shaking change is coming from the new technologies   5
of reproduction. Up until now, if you wanted to reproduce, you not only had to fraternize with a member of the other sex for at least a few minutes, but you also ran a 50% risk that any resulting baby would turn out to be a member of the foreign sex. No more. Thanks to in vitro fertilization, we can have babies without having sex. And with the latest techniques of sex selection, we can have babies of whatever sex we want.

Obviously women, with their built-in baby incubators, will have the advantage in a monosexual future. They just have to pack up a good supply of frozen semen, a truckload of turkey basters and go their own way. But men will be catching up. For one thing, until now, frozen-and-thawed ova have been tricky to fertilize because their outer membrane gets too hard. But a new technique called intracytoplasmic sperm injection makes frozen ova fully fertilizable, and so now Guy Land can have its ovum banks. As for the incubation problem, a few years ago feminist writer Gena Corea offered the seemingly paranoid suggestion that men might eventually keep just a few women around in "reproductive brothels," gestating on demand. A guy will pick an ovum for attractive qualities like smart, tall and allergy-free, then have it inserted into some faceless surrogate mother employed as a reproductive slave.

What about sex, though, meaning the experience, not the category? Chances are, we will be having sex with machines, mostly computers. Even today you can buy interactive CD-ROMs like Virtual Valerie, and there's talk of full-body, virtual-reality sex in which the pleasure seeker wears a specially fitted suit—very specially fitted—allowing for tactile as well as audiovisual sensation. If that sounds farfetched, consider the fact that cyber-innovation is currently in the hands of social skills–challenged geeks who couldn't hope to get a date without flashing their Internet stock options.

Still, there's a reason why the Big Divorce scenario isn't likely to work out, even by Y3K: we love each other, we males and females—madly, sporadically, intermittently, to be sure—but at least enough to keep us pair bonding furiously, even when there's no obvious hardheaded reason to do so. Hence, despite predictions of the imminent "breakdown of the family," the divorce rate leveled off in the 1990s, and the average couple is still hopeful or deluded enough to invest about $20,000 in their first wedding. True, fewer people are marrying: 88% of Americans have married at least once, down from 94% in 1988. But the difference is largely made up by couples who set up housekeeping without the blessing of the state. And an astounding 16% of the population has been married three times—which shows a remarkable commitment to, if nothing else, the institution of marriage.

The question for the new century is, Do we love each other enough—enough, that is, to sustain the old pair-bonded way of life? Many experts see the glass half empty: cohabitation may be replacing marriage, but it's even less likely to last. Hearts are routinely broken and children's lives disrupted as we churn, ever starry-eyed, from one relationship to the next. Even liberal icons like Hillary Rodham Clinton and Harvard Afro-American studies professor Cornel West have been heard muttering about the need to limit the ease and accessibility of divorce.

Hence, perhaps, Scenario B: seeing that the old economic and biological   10
pressures to marry don't work anymore, people will decide to replace them with new forms of coercion. Divorce will be outlawed, along with abortion and possibly contraception. Extramarital hanky-panky will be punishable with shunning or, in the more hard-line jurisdictions, stoning. There will still be sex, and probably plenty of it inside marriage, thanks to what will be known as Chemically Assisted Monogamy: Viagra for men and Viagra-like drugs for women, such as apomorphine and Estratest (both are being tested right now), to reignite the spark long after familiarity has threatened to extinguish it. Naturally, prescriptions will be available only upon presentation of a valid marriage license.

It couldn't happen here, even in a thousand years? Already, a growing "marriage movement," including groups like the Promise Keepers, is working to make divorce lawyers as rare as elevator operators. Since 1997, Louisiana and Arizona have been offering ultratight "covenant marriages," which can be dissolved only in the case of infidelity, abuse or felony conviction, and similar measures have been introduced in 17 other states. As for the age-old problem of premarital fooling around, some extremely conservative Christian activists have launched a movement to halt the dangerous practice of dating and replace it with parent-supervised betrothals leading swiftly and ineluctably to the altar.

But Scenario B has a lot going against it too. The 1998 impeachment fiasco showed just how hard it will be to restigmatize extramarital sex. Sure, we think adultery is a bad thing, just not bad enough to disqualify anyone from ruling the world. Meanwhile, there have been few takers for covenant marriages, showing that most people like to keep their options open. Tulane University sociologist Laura Sanchez speculates that the ultimate effect of covenant marriages may be to open up the subversive possibility of diversifying the institution of marriage—with different types for different folks, including, perhaps someday, even gay folks.

Which brings us to the third big scenario. This is the diversity option, arising from the realization that the one-size-fits-all model of marriage may have been one of the biggest sources of tension between the sexes all along—based as it is on the wildly unrealistic expectation that a single spouse can meet one's needs for a lover, friend, co-parent, financial partner, reliably, 24-7. Instead there will be renewable marriages, which get re-evaluated every five to seven years, after which they can be revised, recelebrated or dissolved with no, or at least fewer, hard feelings. There will be unions between people who don't live together full-time but do want to share a home base. And of course there will always be plenty of people who live together but don't want to make a big deal out of it. Already, thanks to the gay-rights movement, more than 600 corporations and other employers offer domestic-partner benefits, a 60-fold increase since 1990.

And the children? The real paradigm shift will come when we stop trying to base our entire society on the wavering sexual connection between individuals. Romantic love ebbs and surges unaccountably; it's the bond between parents and children that has to remain rocklike year after year. Putting children first would mean that adults would make a contract—not to live together or sleep together but to take joint responsibility for a child or an elderly adult. Some of these arrangements will look very much like today's marriages, with a heterosexual couple undertaking the care of their biological children. Others will look like nothing we've seen before, at least not in suburban America, especially since there's no natural limit on the number of contracting caretakers. A group of people—male, female, gay, straight—will unite in their responsibility for the children they bear or acquire through the local Artificial Reproduction Center. Heather may routinely have two mommies, or at least a whole bunch of resident aunts—which is, of course, more or less how things have been for eons in such distinctly unbohemian settings as the tribal village.

So how will things play out this century and beyond? Just so you will be 15 prepared, here's my timeline:

> Between 2000 and 2339: geographical diversity prevails. The Southeast and a large swath of the Rockies will go for Scenario B (early marriage, no divorce). Oregon, California and New York will offer renewable marriages, and a few states will go monosexual, as in Scenario A. But because of the 1996 Defense of Marriage Act, each state is entitled to recognize only the kinds of "marriages" it approves of, so you will need a "marriage visa" to travel across the country, at least if you intend to share a motel room.

Between 2340 and 2387: NATO will be forced to intervene in the Custody Wars that break out between the Polygamous Republic of Utah and the Free Love Zone of the Central Southwest. A huge refugee crisis will develop when singles are ethnically cleansed from the Christian Nation of Idaho. Florida will be partitioned into divorce-free and marriage-free zones.

In 2786: the new President's Inauguration will be attended by all five members of the mixed-sex, multiracial commune that raised her. She will establish sizable tax reductions for couples or groups of any size that create stable households for their children and other dependents. Peace will break out.

And in 2999: a scholar of ancient history will discover these words penned by a gay writer named Fenton Johnson back in 1996: "The mystery of love and life and death is really grander and more glorious than human beings can grasp, much less legislate." He will put this sentence onto a bumper sticker. The message will spread. We will realize that the sexes can't live without each other, but neither can they be joined at the hip. We will grow up.

The Reader's Presence

1. Although Ehrenreich makes some hyperbolic and humorous assertions in this essay, most of her claims and predictions are rooted in current or historical events. Which specific parts of her essay are conjecture and which are based on facts? How does she integrate the two? With what effect(s)? How persuasive do you find this compositional strategy?

2. Identify what you think are Ehrenreich's personal views on the topic of this essay. Which specific passages lead you to believe this? What do you notice, for example, about both the word choices and the way in which Ehrenreich presents these passages? How do you read the last line of the essay, and what are the effects of Ehrenreich's choosing to end the essay with it?

3. **CONNECTIONS:** Compare the claims about gender that Ehrenreich makes in this essay to the ones Mary Roach makes in "Ed and Mary Do Mars and Venus" (page 709). What authority does each writer invoke to make her claims? In what specific ways are their approaches similar, and in what ways are they different? How does each writer's own gender affect your reading of the claims she makes?

Jonathan Safran Foer

LET THEM EAT DOG

JONATHAN SAFRAN FOER (b. 1977) is a Jewish American author whose first novel, *Everything Is Illuminated* (2002), was published to critical acclaim when he was only twenty-five years old. In the wake of this success, he went on to write another novel, *Extremely Loud & Incredibly Close* (2005), which was also widely praised and translated into several languages. A writer of diverse talents, Foer has also written the libretto for an opera, *Seven Attempted Escapes from Silence*, which was performed by the Berlin State Opera in 2005, and a book of nonfiction, *Eating Animals* (2009), from which "Let Them Eat Dog" is an excerpt. Long conflicted about the ethics of eating meat, Foer was inspired by the birth of his first child to explore the issue with more urgency because, he said, he "would have to make decisions on [his son's] behalf." Foer's more recent novels include *Tree of Codes* (2010) and *Escape from Children's Hospital* (2014). He is married to writer Nicole Krauss, and they live in Brooklyn with their two children.

> **Long conflicted about the ethics of eating meat, Jonathan Safran Foer was inspired by the birth of his first child to explore the issue with more urgency because, he said, he "would have to make decisions on [his son's] behalf."**

DESPITE THE FACT that it's perfectly legal in 44 states, eating "man's best friend" is as taboo as a man eating his best friend. Even the most enthusiastic carnivores won't eat dogs. TV guy and sometimes cooker Gordon Ramsay can get pretty macho with lambs and piglets when doing publicity for something he's selling, but you'll never see a puppy peeking out of one of his pots. And though he once said he'd electrocute his children if they became vegetarian, one can't help but wonder what his response would be if they poached the family pooch.

Dogs are wonderful, and in many ways unique. But they are remarkably unremarkable in their intellectual and experiential capacities. Pigs are every bit as intelligent and feeling, by any sensible definition of the words. They can't hop into the back of a Volvo, but they can fetch, run and play, be mischievous and reciprocate affection. So why don't they get to curl up by the fire? Why can't they at least be spared being tossed on the fire? Our taboo against dog eating says something about dogs and a great deal about us.

The French, who love their dogs, sometimes eat their horses.

The Spanish, who love their horses, sometimes eat their cows.

The Indians, who love their cows, sometimes eat their dogs.   5

While written in a much different context, George Orwell's words (from *Animal Farm*) apply here: "All animals are equal, but some animals are more equal than others."

So who's right? What might be the reasons to exclude canine from the menu? The selective carnivore suggests:

Don't eat companion animals. But dogs aren't kept as companions in all of the places they are eaten. And what about our petless neighbors? Would we have any right to object if they had dog for dinner?

OK, then: Don't eat animals with significant mental capacities. If by "significant mental capacities" we mean what a dog has, then good for the dog. But such a definition would also include the pig, cow and chicken. And it would exclude severely impaired humans.

Then: It's for good reason that the eternal taboos—don't fiddle with your   10
crap, kiss your sister, or eat your companions—are taboo. Evolutionarily speaking, those things are bad for us. But dog eating isn't a taboo in many places, and it isn't in any way bad for us. Properly cooked, dog meat poses no greater health risks than any other meat.

Dog meat has been described as "gamey," "complex," "buttery" and "floral." And there is a proud pedigree of eating it. Fourth-century tombs contain depictions of dogs being slaughtered along with other food animals. It was a fundamental enough habit to have informed language itself: the Sino-Korean character for "fair and proper" (*yeon*) literally translates into "as cooked dog meat is delicious." Hippocrates praised dog meat as a source of strength. Dakota Indians enjoyed dog liver, and not so long ago Hawaiians ate dog brains and blood. Captain Cook ate dog. Roald Amundsen famously ate his sled dogs. (Granted, he was really hungry.) And dogs are still eaten to overcome bad luck in the Philippines; as medicine in China and Korea; to enhance libido in Nigeria and in numerous places, on every continent, because they taste good. For centuries, the Chinese have raised special breeds of dogs, like the black-tongued chow, for chow, and many European countries still have laws on the books regarding postmortem examination of dogs intended for human consumption.

Of course, something having been done just about everywhere is no kind of justification for doing it now. But unlike all farmed meat, which re-quires the creation and maintenance of animals, dogs are practically beg-ging to be eaten. Three to four million dogs and cats are euthanized annu-ally. The simple disposal of these euthanized dogs is an enormous ecological and economic problem. But eating those strays, those runaways, those not-quite-cute-enough-to-take and not-quite-well-behaved-enough-to-keep dogs would be killing a flock of birds with one stone and eating it, too.

In a sense it's what we're doing already. Rendering—the conversion of animal protein unfit for human consumption into food for livestock and

Jan van IJken Pho-
tography & Film

*Dutch photographer Jan van IJken has devoted several years to observing humans
interact with animals in a wide range of circumstances—from laboratory settings
to bird shows and factory farms. His remarkable images document the ambivalent
ways we value other creatures.*

pets—allows processing plants to transform useless dead dogs into productive members of the food chain. In America, millions of dogs and cats euthanized in animal shelters every year become the food for our food. So let's just
eliminate this inefficient and bizarre middle step.

This need not challenge our civility. We won't make them suffer any
more than necessary. While it's widely believed that adrenaline makes dog
meat taste better—hence the traditional methods of slaughter: hanging,
boiling alive, beating to death—we can all agree that if we're going to eat
them, we should kill them quickly and painlessly, right? For example, the
traditional Hawaiian means of holding the dog's nose shut—in order to con-
serve blood—must be regarded (socially if not legally) as a no-no. Perhaps
we could include dogs under the Humane Methods of Slaughter Act. That
doesn't say anything about how they're treated during their lives, and isn't

subject to any meaningful oversight or enforcement, but surely we can rely on the industry to "self-regulate," as we do with other eaten animals.

Few people sufficiently appreciate the colossal task of feeding a world of   15
billions of omnivores who demand meat with their potatoes. The inefficient use of dogs—conveniently already in areas of high human population (take note, local-food advocates)—should make any good ecologist blush. One could argue that various "humane" groups are the worst hypocrites, spending enormous amounts of money and energy in a futile attempt to reduce the number of unwanted dogs while at the very same time propagating the irresponsible no-dog-for-dinner taboo. If we let dogs be dogs, and breed without interference, we would create a sustainable, local meat supply with low energy inputs that would put even the most efficient grass-based farming to shame. For the ecologically-minded it's time to admit that dog is realistic food for realistic environmentalists.

For those already convinced, here's a classic Filipino recipe I recently came across. I haven't tried it myself, but sometimes you can read a recipe and just know.

> **Stewed Dog, Wedding Style**
> First, kill a medium-sized dog, then burn off the fur over a hot fire. Carefully remove the skin while still warm and set aside for later (may be used in other recipes). Cut meat into 1" cubes. Marinate meat in mixture of vinegar, peppercorn, salt, and garlic for 2 hours. Fry meat in oil using a large wok over an open fire, then add onions and chopped pineapple and sauté until tender. Pour in tomato sauce and boiling water, add green pepper, bay leaf, and Tabasco. Cover and simmer over warm coals until meat is tender. Blend in purée of dog's liver and cook for additional 5–7 minutes.

There is an overabundance of rational reasons to say no to factory-farmed meat: It is the No. 1 cause of global warming, it systematically forces tens of billions of animals to suffer in ways that would be illegal if they were dogs, it is a decisive factor in the development of swine and avian flus, and so on. And yet even most people who know these things still aren't inspired to order something else on the menu. Why?

Food is not rational. Food is culture, habit, craving and identity. Respond-   20
ing to factory farming calls for a capacity to care that dwells beyond information. We know what we see on undercover videos of factory farms and slaughterhouses is wrong. (There are those who will defend a system that allows for occasional animal cruelty, but no one defends the cruelty, itself.) And despite it being entirely reasonable, the case for eating dogs is likely repulsive to just about every reader of this paper. The instinct comes before our reason, and is more important. ▪

The Reader's Presence

1. What was your visceral reaction to reading Foer's essay? Discuss your reaction in the light of what you think Foer's purpose was in writing this essay. How well does his approach support—or not support—the argument he is advocating?

2. Foer writes, "Food is not rational" (paragraph 20). Review the numerous reasons he gives to support the idea of consuming dogs as food. What arguments can you make against any of his justifications? How airtight is the case he makes?

3. **VISUAL PRESENCE:**   Examine carefully the image of the chick perched precariously on the edge of the conveyor belt in a food processing plant (page 605). In what specific way(s) does this image reinforce or subvert Foer's argument that "[f]ood is not rational" (paragraph 20)? How would you characterize the point of view the workers present in relation to the position of the chick?

4. **CONNECTIONS:**   Compare the voice of Foer's essay with that of David Foster Wallace in "Consider the Lobster" (page 760). What kinds of reaction do you think each writer tries to elicit from his respective readers? (Cite specific passages to support your answer.) Why do you think each writer chose his unusual approach to argument rather than a more traditional one? How does each writer establish his authority to speak on the topic?

John Taylor Gatto

AGAINST SCHOOL

"I've taught public school for twenty-six years but I just can't do it anymore," began an impassioned op-ed piece published in the *Wall Street Journal* in 1991. Its author, **JOHN TAYLOR GATTO** (b. 1935), continued, "I've come slowly to understand what it is I really teach: A curriculum of confusion, class position, arbitrary justice, vulgarity, rudeness, disrespect for privacy, indifference to quality, and utter dependency. I teach how to fit into a world I don't want to live in." With the headline "I May Be a Teacher but I'm Not an Educator," the essay set off a fierce debate among parents, teachers, and politicians about the system of public education in the United States. It also launched Gatto's career as a speaker, consultant, and writer.

> "I've come slowly to understand what it is I really teach: A curriculum of confusion, class position, arbitrary justice, vulgarity, rudeness, disrespect for privacy, indifference to quality, and utter dependency. I teach how to fit into a world I don't want to live in."

After graduating from Columbia University, Gatto worked as a scriptwriter, a songwriter, and an ad writer; drove a cab; sold hot dogs; and, finally, began a distinguished career as a schoolteacher. He was recognized as New York City Teacher of the Year for three years in a row. In 1991, the year he resigned in protest from his position as a seventh-grade teacher at the Booker T. Washington School in New York City, he was named New York State Teacher of the Year. He has edited and written many books on education, including *Dumbing Us Down: The Hidden Curriculum of Compulsory Schooling* (1992), *The Exhausted School* (1993), *A Different Kind of Teacher: Solving the Crisis of American Schooling* (2000), and *The Underground History of American Education: A Schoolteacher's Intimate Investigation into the Problem of Modern Schooling* (2001). His latest book, *Weapons of Mass Instruction: A Schoolteacher's Journey Through the Dark World of Compulsory Schooling* (2010), focuses on the ways in which compulsory schooling cripples the imagination. His essay "Against School" first appeared in *Harper's* magazine in 2001.

I TAUGHT FOR THIRTY YEARS in some of the worst schools in Manhattan, and in some of the best, and during that time I became an expert in boredom. Boredom was everywhere in my world, and if you asked the kids, as I often did, *why* they felt so bored, they always gave the same answers: They said the work was stupid, that it made no sense, that they already knew it. They said they wanted to be doing something real, not just sitting around. They said teachers didn't seem to know much about their subjects and clearly weren't interested in learning more. And the kids were right: their teachers were every bit as bored as they were.

Boredom is the common condition of schoolteachers, and anyone who has spent time in a teachers' lounge can vouch for the low energy, the whining, the dispirited attitudes, to be found there. When asked why *they* feel bored, the teachers tend to blame the kids, as you might expect. Who wouldn't get bored teaching students who are rude and interested only in grades? If even that. Of course, teachers are themselves products of the same twelve-year compulsory school programs that so thoroughly bore their students, and as school personnel they are trapped inside structures even more rigid than those imposed upon the children. Who, then, is to blame?

We all are. My grandfather taught me that. One afternoon when I was seven I complained to him of boredom, and he batted me hard on the head. He told me that I was never to use that term in his presence again, that if I was bored it was my fault and no one else's. The obligation to amuse and instruct myself was entirely my own, and people who didn't know that were childish people, to be avoided if possible. Certainly not to be trusted. That episode cured me of boredom forever, and here and there over the years I was able to pass on the lesson to some remarkable student. For the most part, however, I found it futile to challenge the official notion that boredom and childishness were the natural state of affairs in the classroom. Often I had to defy custom, and even bend the law, to help kids break out of this trap.

The empire struck back, of course; childish adults regularly conflate opposition with disloyalty. I once returned from a medical leave to discover that all evidence of my having been granted the leave had been purposely destroyed, that my job had been terminated, and that I no longer possessed even a teaching license. After nine months of tormented effort I was able to retrieve the license when a school secretary testified to witnessing the plot unfold. In the meantime my family suffered more than I care to remember. By the time I finally retired in 1991, I had more than enough reason to think of our schools—with their long-term, cell-block–style, forced confinement of both students and teachers—as virtual factories of childishness. Yet I honestly could not see *why* they had to be that way. My own experience had revealed to me what many other teachers must learn along the way, too, yet keep to themselves for fear of reprisal: if we wanted to we could easily and inexpensively jettison the old, stupid structures and help kids *take* an education rather than merely *receive* a schooling. We could encourage the best qualities of youthfulness—curiosity, adventure, resilience, the capacity for surprising insight—simply by being more flexible about time, texts, and tests, by introducing kids to truly competent adults, and by giving each student what autonomy he or she needs in order to take a risk every now and then.

But we don't do that. And the more I asked why not, and persisted in   5
thinking about the "problem" of schooling as an engineer might, the more I missed the point: What if there is no "problem" with our schools? What if they are the way they are, so expensively flying in the face of common sense and long experience in how children learn things, not because they are doing something wrong but because they are doing something right? Is it possible that George W. Bush accidentally spoke the truth when he said we would "leave no child behind"? Could it be that our schools are designed to make sure not one of them ever really grows up?

Do we really need school? I don't mean education, just forced schooling: six classes a day, five days a week, nine months a year, for twelve years. Is this deadly routine really necessary? And if so, for what? Don't hide behind reading, writing, and arithmetic as a rationale, because two million happy home-schoolers have surely put that banal justification to rest. Even if they hadn't, a considerable number of well-known Americans never went through the twelve-year wringer our kids currently go through, and they turned out all right. George Washington, Benjamin Franklin, Thomas Jefferson, Abraham Lincoln? Someone taught them, to be sure, but they were not products of a school *system*, and not one of them was ever "graduated" from a secondary school. Throughout most of American history, kids generally didn't go to high school, yet the unschooled rose to be admirals, like Farragut; inventors, like Edison; captains of industry, like Carnegie and Rockefeller; writers, like Melville and Twain and Conrad; and even scholars, like Margaret Mead.[1]

---

1 **Margaret Mead** (1901–1978): Became the most-famous anthropologist in the world, best known for *Coming of Age in Samoa* (1928), a book that analyzed cultural influence on adolescence. —EDS.

In fact, until pretty recently people who reached the age of thirteen weren't looked upon as children at all. Ariel Durant, who co-wrote an enormous, and very good, multivolume history of the world with her husband, Will, was happily married at fifteen, and who could reasonably claim that Ariel Durant was an uneducated person? Unschooled, perhaps, but not uneducated.

We have been taught (that is, schooled) in this country to think of "success" as synonymous with, or at least dependent upon, "schooling," but historically that isn't true in either an intellectual or a financial sense. And plenty of people throughout the world today find a way to educate themselves without resorting to a system of compulsory secondary schools that all too often resemble prisons. Why, then, do Americans confuse education with just such a system? What exactly is the purpose of our public schools?

Mass schooling of a compulsory nature really got its teeth into the United States between 1905 and 1915, though it was conceived of much earlier and pushed for throughout most of the nineteenth century. The reason given for this enormous upheaval of family life and cultural traditions was, roughly speaking, threefold:

1. To make good people.

2. To make good citizens.

3. To make each person his or her personal best.

These goals are still trotted out today on a regular basis, and most of us accept them in one form or another as a decent definition of public education's mission, however short schools actually fall in achieving them. But we are dead wrong. Compounding our error is the fact that the national literature holds numerous and surprisingly consistent statements of compulsory schooling's true purpose. We have, for example, the great H. L. Mencken,[2] who wrote in *The American Mercury* for April 1924 that the aim of public education is not

> to fill the young of the species with knowledge and awaken their intelligence. . . . Nothing could be further from the truth. The aim . . . is simply to reduce as many individuals as possible to the same safe level, to breed and train a standardized citizenry, to put down dissent and originality. That is its aim in the United States . . . and that is its aim everywhere else.

Because of Mencken's reputation as a satirist, we might be tempted to dismiss this passage as a bit of hyperbolic sarcasm. His article, however, goes on to trace the template for our own educational system back to the now vanished, though never to be forgotten, military state of Prussia. And although he was certainly aware of the irony that we had recently been at war with Germany, the heir to Prussian thought and culture, Mencken was being perfectly serious here. Our educational system really is Prussian in origin, and that really is cause for concern.

---

[2] *H[enry] L[ouis] Mencken* (1880–1956): An influential journalist, essayist, magazine editor, satirist, and critic of American life and culture. —EDS.

The odd fact of a Prussian provenance for our schools pops up again 10
and again once you know to look for it. William James[3] alluded to it many
times at the turn of the century. Orestes Brownson, the hero of Christopher
Lasch's 1991 book, *The True and Only Heaven*, was publicly denouncing
the Prussianization of American schools back in the 1840s. Horace Mann's[4]
"Seventh Annual Report" to the Massachusetts State Board of Education
in 1843 is essentially a paean to the land of Frederick the Great and a call
for its schooling to be brought here. That Prussian culture loomed large in
America is hardly surprising, given our early association with that utopian
state. A Prussian served as Washington's aide during the Revolutionary
War, and so many German-speaking people had settled here by 1795 that
Congress considered publishing a German-language edition of the federal
laws. But what shocks is that we should so eagerly have adopted one of the
very worst aspects of Prussian culture: an educational system deliberately
designed to produce mediocre intellects, to hamstring the inner life, to deny
students appreciable leadership skills, and to ensure docile and incomplete
citizens—all in order to render the populace "manageable."

It was from James Bryant Conant—president of Harvard for twenty
years, WWI poison-gas specialist, WWII executive on the atomic-bomb project, high commissioner of the American zone in Germany after WWII, and
truly one of the most influential figures of the twentieth century—that I first
got wind of the real purposes of American schooling. Without Conant, we
would probably not have the same style and degree of standardized testing
that we enjoy today, nor would we be blessed with gargantuan high schools
that warehouse 2,000 to 4,000 students at a time, like the famous Columbine
High in Littleton, Colorado. Shortly after I retired from teaching I picked up
Conant's 1959 book-length essay, *The Child, the Parent and the State*, and
was more than a little intrigued to see him mention in passing that the modern schools we attend were the result of a "revolution" engineered between
1905 and 1930. A revolution? He declines to elaborate, but he does direct
the curious and the uninformed to Alexander Inglis's 1918 book, *Principles
of Secondary Education*, in which "one saw this revolution through the eyes
of a revolutionary."

Inglis, for whom a lecture in education at Harvard is named, makes it
perfectly clear that compulsory schooling on this continent was intended to
be just what it had been for Prussia in the 1820s: a fifth column into the burgeoning democratic movement that threatened to give the peasants and the
proletarians a voice at the bargaining table. Modern, industrialized, compulsory schooling was to make a sort of surgical incision into the prospective

---

[3] **William James** (1842–1910): One of America's most important psychologists and philosophers. Trained as a medical doctor, he wrote important books on psychology, and particularly on
education and religious experience, as well as on the philosophy of pragmatism. The brother of
novelist Henry James and of diarist Alice James.—EDS.

[4] **Horace Mann** (1796–1859): A celebrated American education reformer and also a member of
the U.S. House of Representatives (Massachusetts) from 1848 to 1853.—EDS.

unity of these underclasses. Divide children by subject, by age-grading, by constant rankings on tests, and by many other more subtle means, and it was unlikely that the ignorant mass of mankind, separated in childhood, would ever re-integrate into a dangerous whole.

Inglis breaks down the purpose—the *actual* purpose—of modern schooling into six basic functions, any one of which is enough to curl the hair of those innocent enough to believe the three traditional goals listed earlier:

1. The *adjustive or adaptive* function. Schools are to establish fixed habits of reaction to authority. This, of course, precludes critical judgment completely. It also pretty much destroys the idea that useful or interesting material should be taught, because you can't test for *reflexive* obedience until you know whether you can make kids learn, and do, foolish and boring things.

2. The *integrating* function. This might well be called "the conformity function," because its intention is to make children as alike as possible. People who conform are predictable, and this is of great use to those who wish to harness and manipulate a large labor force.

3. The *diagnostic and directive* function. School is meant to determine each student's proper social role. This is done by logging evidence mathematically and anecdotally on cumulative records. As in "your permanent record." Yes, you do have one.

4. The *differentiating* function. Once their social role has been "diagnosed," children are to be sorted by role and trained only so far as their destination in the social machine merits—and not one step further. So much for making kids their personal best.

5. The *selective* function. This refers not to human choice at all but to Darwin's theory of natural selection as applied to what he called "the favored races." In short, the idea is to help things along by consciously attempting to improve the breeding stock. Schools are meant to tag the unfit—with poor grades, remedial placement, and other punishments—clearly enough that their peers will accept them as inferior and effectively bar them from the reproductive sweepstakes. That's what all those little humiliations from first grade onward were intended to do: wash the dirt down the drain.

6. The *propaedeutic* function. The societal system implied by these rules will require an elite group of caretakers. To that end, a small fraction of the kids will quietly be taught how to manage this continuing project, how to watch over and control a population deliberately dumbed down and declawed in order that government might proceed unchallenged and corporations might never want for obedient labor.

That, unfortunately, is the purpose of mandatory public education in this country. And lest you take Inglis for an isolated crank with a rather too cynical take on the educational enterprise, you should know that he was hardly alone in championing these ideas. Conant himself, building on the ideas of Horace Mann and others, campaigned tirelessly for an American school system designed along the same lines. Men like George Peabody, who funded the cause of mandatory schooling throughout the South, surely understood that the Prussian system was useful in creating not only a harmless electorate and a servile labor force but also a virtual herd of mindless consumers. In time a great number of industrial titans came to recognize the enormous profits to be had by cultivating and tending just such a herd via public education, among them Andrew Carnegie and John D. Rockefeller.

There you have it. Now you know. We don't need Karl Marx's[5] concep-   15
tion of a grand warfare between the classes to see that it is in the interest of complex management, economic or political, to dumb people down, to demoralize them, to divide them from one another, and to discard them if they don't conform. Class may frame the proposition, as when Woodrow Wilson, then president of Princeton University, said the following to the New York City School Teachers Association in 1909: "We want one class of persons to have a liberal education, and we want another class of persons, a very much larger class, of necessity, in every society, to forgo the privileges of a liberal education and fit themselves to perform specific difficult manual tasks." But the motives behind the disgusting decisions that bring about these ends need not be class-based at all. They can stem purely from fear, or from the by now familiar belief that "efficiency" is the paramount virtue, rather than love, liberty, laughter, or hope. Above all, they can stem from simple greed.

There were vast fortunes to be made, after all, in an economy based on mass production and organized to favor the large corporation rather than the small business or the family farm. But mass production required mass consumption, and at the turn of the twentieth century most Americans considered it both unnatural and unwise to buy things they didn't actually need. Mandatory schooling was a godsend on that count. School didn't have to train kids in any direct sense to think they should consume nonstop, because it did something even better: it encouraged them not to think at all. And that left them sitting ducks for another great invention of the modern era—marketing.

Now, you needn't have studied marketing to know that there are two groups of people who can always be convinced to consume more than they need to: addicts and children. School has done a pretty good job of turning our children into addicts, but it has done a spectacular job of turning our children into children. Again, this is no accident. Theorists from Plato to Rousseau to our own Dr. Inglis knew that if children could be cloistered with other children, stripped of responsibility and independence, encouraged to

---

5 ***Karl Marx*** (1818–1883): Often identified as the father of communism, Marx was a philosopher, political economist, sociologist, political theorist, and revolutionary.—Eds.

develop only the trivializing emotions of greed, envy, jealousy, and fear, they would grow older but never truly grow up. In the 1934 edition of his once well-known book *Public Education in the United States*, Ellwood P. Cubberley detailed and praised the way the strategy of successive school enlargements had extended childhood by two to six years, and forced schooling was at that point still quite new. This same Cubberley—who was dean of Stanford's School of Education, a textbook editor at Houghton Mifflin, and Conant's friend and correspondent at Harvard—had written the following in the 1922 edition of his book *Public School Administration*: "Our schools are . . . factories in which the raw products (children) are to be shaped and fashioned. . . . And it is the business of the school to build its pupils according to the specifications laid down."

It's perfectly obvious from our society today what those specifications were. Maturity has by now been banished from nearly every aspect of our lives. Easy divorce laws have removed the need to work at relationships; easy credit has removed the need for fiscal self-control; easy entertainment has removed the need to learn to entertain oneself; easy answers have removed the need to ask questions. We have become a nation of children, happy to surrender our judgments and our wills to political exhortations and commercial blandishments that would insult actual adults. We buy televisions, and then we buy the things we see on the television. We buy computers, and then we buy the things we see on the computer. We buy $150 sneakers whether we need them or not, and when they fall apart too soon we buy another pair. We drive SUVs and believe the lie that they constitute a kind of life insurance, even when we're upside-down in them. And, worst of all, we don't bat an eye when Ari Fleischer[6] tells us to "be careful what you say," even if we remember having been told somewhere back in school that America is the land of the free. We simply buy that one too. Our schooling, as intended, has seen to it.

Now for the good news. Once you understand the logic behind modern schooling, its tricks and traps are fairly easy to avoid. School trains children to be employees and consumers; teach your own to be leaders and adventurers. School trains children to obey reflexively; teach your own to think critically and independently. Well-schooled kids have a low threshold for boredom; help your own to develop an inner life so that they'll never be bored. Urge them to take on the serious material, the *grown-up* material, in history, literature, philosophy, music, art, economics, theology—all the stuff schoolteachers know well enough to avoid. Challenge your kids with plenty of solitude so that they can learn to enjoy their own company, to conduct inner dialogues. Well-schooled people are conditioned to dread being alone, and they seek constant companionship through the TV, the

---

[6] *Ari Fleischer:* White House press secretary under President George W. Bush from 2001 to 2003.—Eds.

computer, the cell phone, and through shallow friendships quickly acquired and quickly abandoned. Your children should have a more meaningful life, and they can.

First, though, we must wake up to what our schools really are: laborato- ries of experimentation on young minds, drill centers for the habits and atti- tudes that corporate society demands. Mandatory education serves children only incidentally; its real purpose is to turn them into servants. Don't let your own have their childhoods extended, not even for a day. If David Farragut could take command of a captured British warship as a preteen, if Thomas Edison could publish a broadsheet at the age of twelve, if Ben Franklin could apprentice himself to a printer at the same age (then put himself through a course of study that would choke a Yale senior today), there's no telling what your own kids could do. After a long life, and thirty years in the public school trenches, I've concluded that genius is as common as dirt. We suppress our genius only because we haven't yet figured out how to manage a population of educated men and women. The solution, I think, is simple and glorious. Let them manage themselves. ◾

20

The Reader's Presence

1. Would you agree with Gatto that compulsory schooling has the effect of creating con- formity and obedience to authority? Why or why not? To what extent does schooling attempt to form citizens? To what extent are students trained to be consumers?

2. Gatto makes a distinction between "education" and "schooling" (paragraph 4). What is significant about this distinction? What are the consequences of conflating the two?

3. **CONNECTIONS:** Gatto argues that compulsory schooling can—and often does— effectively prevent students from becoming independent thinkers. Read Joel Stein's "The New Greatest Generation" (page 565). Do you think Stein would agree that schooling is at least partly responsible for adolescent resistance to adulthood? Do you agree? Why or why not? Draw on specific passages from each essay to support your response.

Christopher Hitchens

BELIEVE ME, IT'S TORTURE

One of the world's most public intellectuals, **CHRISTOPHER HITCHENS** (1949–2011) was known for making controversial arguments. His 2007 book, for example, *God Is Not Great: How Religion Poisons Everything*, argues that religion is immoral, contributing to everything from ignorance to terrorism to sexual repression. In another book, *The Missionary Position: Mother Teresa in Theory and Practice* (1995), he took the very unpopular position that the Catholic nun was more interested in furthering Catholic doctrine and "becoming a saint" than she was in genuinely helping the poor. Although his views on religion and sexuality were typically associated with the political

> One of the world's most-public intellectuals, Christopher Hitchens was known for making controversial arguments.

left, Hitchens was not reluctant to criticize liberal politicians: his 1999 book, *No One Left to Lie To: The Values of the Worst Family*, was a scathing attack on the Clinton family. His last books included *Hitch-22* (2010), a candid memoir of his personal life and political philosophy, and *Mortality* (2012), published posthumously, a collection of essays describing his struggle with esophageal cancer, which claimed his life in 2011.

HERE IS THE MOST chilling way I can find of stating the matter. Until recently, "waterboarding" was something that Americans did to other Americans. It was inflicted, and endured, by those members of the Special Forces who underwent the advanced form of training known as SERE (Survival, Evasion, Resistance, Escape). In these harsh exercises, brave men and women were introduced to the sorts of barbarism that they might expect to meet at the hands of a lawless foe who disregarded the Geneva Conventions. But it was something that Americans were being trained to resist, not to *inflict*.

Exploring this narrow but deep distinction, on a gorgeous day last May I found myself deep in the hill country of western North Carolina, preparing to be surprised by a team of extremely hardened veterans who had confronted their country's enemies in highly arduous terrain all over the world. They knew about everything from unarmed combat to enhanced interrogation and, in exchange for anonymity, were going to show me as nearly as possible what real waterboarding might be like.

It goes without saying that I knew I could stop the process at any time, and that when it was all over I would be released into happy daylight rather than returned to a darkened cell. But it's been well said that cowards die many times before their deaths, and it was difficult for me to completely forget the clause in the contract of indemnification that I had signed. This document (written by one who knew) stated revealingly: "'Water boarding' is a potentially dangerous activity in which the participant can receive serious and permanent (physical, emotional and psychological) injuries and even death, including injuries and death due to the respiratory and neurological systems of the body." As the agreement went on to say, there would be safeguards provided "during the 'water boarding' process, however, these measures may fail and even if they work properly they may not prevent Hitchens from experiencing serious injury or death."

On the night before the encounter I got to sleep with what I thought was creditable ease, but woke early and knew at once that I wasn't going back to any sort of doze or snooze. The first specialist I had approached with the scheme had asked my age on the telephone and when told what it was (I am 59) had laughed out loud and told me to forget it. Waterboarding is for Green Berets in training, or wiry young jihadists whose teeth can bite through the gristle of an old goat. It's not for wheezing, paunchy scribblers. For my current "handlers" I had had to produce a doctor's certificate assuring them that I did not have asthma, but I wondered whether I should tell them about the 15,000 cigarettes I had inhaled every year for the last several decades. I was feeling apprehensive, in other words, and beginning to wish I hadn't given myself so long to think about it.

I have to be opaque about exactly where I was later that day, but there 5 came a moment when, sitting on a porch outside a remote house at the end of a winding country road, I was very gently yet firmly grabbed from behind, pulled to my feet, pinioned by my wrists (which were then cuffed to a belt), and cut off from the sunlight by having a black hood pulled over my face. I was then turned around a few times, I presume to assist in disorienting me, and led over some crunchy gravel into a darkened room. Well, mainly darkened: there were some oddly spaced bright lights that came as pinpoints through my hood. And some weird music assaulted my ears. (I'm no judge of these things, but I wouldn't have expected former Special Forces types to be so fond of New Age techno-disco.) The outside world seemed very suddenly very distant indeed.

Arms already lost to me, I wasn't able to flail as I was pushed onto a sloping board and positioned with my head lower than my heart. (That's the main point: the angle can be slight or steep.) Then my legs were lashed together so that the board and I were one single and trussed unit. Not to bore you with my phobias, but if I don't have at least two pillows I wake up with acid reflux and mild sleep apnea, so even a merely supine position makes me uneasy. And, to tell you something I had been keeping from myself as well as from my new experimental friends, I do have a fear of drowning that comes from a bad childhood moment on the Isle of Wight, when I got out of my depth. As a boy reading the climactic torture scene of *1984*,[1] where what is in Room 101 is the worst thing in the world, I realize that somewhere in my version of that hideous chamber comes the moment when the wave washes over me. Not that that makes me special: I don't know anyone who *likes* the idea of drowning. As mammals we may have originated in the ocean, but water has many ways of reminding us that when we are in it we are out of our element. In brief, when it comes to breathing, give me good old air every time.

You may have read by now the official lie about this treatment, which is that it "simulates" the feeling of drowning. This is not the case. You feel that you are drowning because you *are* drowning—or, rather, being drowned, albeit slowly and under controlled conditions and at the mercy (or otherwise) of those who are applying the pressure. The "board" is the instrument, *not* the method. You are not being boarded. You are being watered. This was very rapidly brought home to me when, on top of the hood, which still admitted a few flashes of random and worrying strobe light to my vision, three layers of enveloping towel were added. In this pregnant darkness, head downward, I waited for a while until I abruptly felt a slow cascade of water going up my nose. Determined to resist if only for the honor of my navy ancestors who had so often been in peril on the sea, I held my breath for a while and then had to exhale and—as you might expect—inhale in turn. The inhalation brought the damp cloths tight against my nostrils, as if a huge, wet paw had been suddenly and annihilatingly clamped over my face. Unable to determine whether I was breathing in or out, and flooded more with sheer panic than with mere water, I triggered the pre-arranged signal and felt the unbelievable relief of being pulled upright and having the soaking and stifling layers pulled off me. I find I don't want to tell you how little time I lasted.

This is because I had read that Khalid Sheikh Mohammed, invariably referred to as the "mastermind" of the atrocities of September 11, 2001, had impressed his interrogators by holding out for upward of two minutes before cracking. (By the way, this story is not confirmed. My North Carolina friends jeered at it. "Hell," said one, "from what I heard they only washed his damn face before he babbled.") But, hell, I thought in my turn, no Hitchens is going to do worse than *that*. Well, O.K., I admit I didn't outdo him. And so then I said, with slightly more bravado than was justified, that I'd like to try it one more time. There was a paramedic present who checked my racing pulse and warned me about adrenaline rush. An interval was ordered, and then I felt the mask come down again. Steeling myself to remember what it had been like last time, and to learn from the previous panic attack, I fought down the first, and some of the second, wave of nausea and terror but soon

---

1 *Nineteen Eighty-Four* (also written as *1984*): George Orwell's novel (published 1948) depicting a world of constant warfare, government surveillance, and public mind control, a world in which the individual is subordinated to the state ("Big Brother").—EDS.

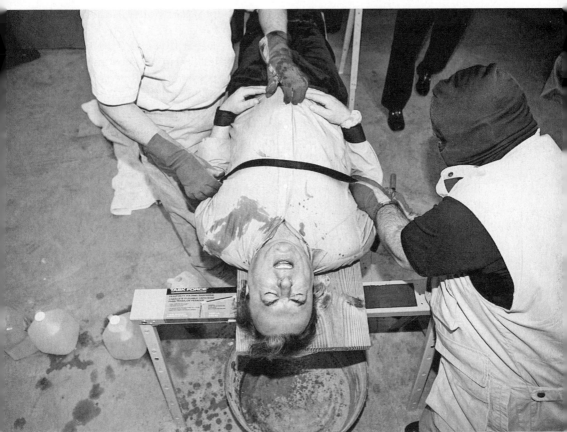

Gasper Tringale

Christopher Hitchens undergoing waterboarding "treatment."

found that I was an abject prisoner of my gag reflex. The interrogators would hardly have had time to ask me any questions, and I knew that I would quite readily have agreed to supply any answer. I still feel ashamed when I think about it. Also, in case it's of interest, I have since woken up trying to push the bedcovers off my face, and if I do anything that makes me short of breath I find myself clawing at the air with a horrible sensation of smothering and claustrophobia. No doubt this will pass. As if detecting my misery and shame, one of my interrogators comfortingly said, "Any time is a long time when you're breathing water." I could have hugged him for saying so, and just then I was hit with a ghastly sense of the sadomasochistic dimension that underlies the relationship between the torturer and the tortured. I apply the Abraham Lincoln test for moral casuistry:[2] "If slavery is not wrong,

---

2 *casuistry:* Using clever but unsound reasoning, especially in relation to moral questions. —EDS.

nothing is wrong." Well, then, if waterboarding does not constitute torture, then there is no such thing as torture.

I am somewhat proud of my ability to "keep my head," as the saying goes, and to maintain presence of mind under trying circumstances. I was completely convinced that, when the water pressure had become intolerable, I had firmly uttered the pre-determined code word that would cause it to cease. But my interrogator told me that, rather to his surprise, I had not spoken a word. I had activated the "dead man's handle" that signaled the onset of unconsciousness. So now I have to wonder about the role of false memory and delusion. What I do recall clearly, though, is a hard finger feeling for my solar plexus as the water was being poured. What was that for? "That's to find out if you are trying to cheat, and timing your breathing to the doses. If you try that, we can outsmart you. We have all kinds of enhancements." I was briefly embarrassed that I hadn't earned or warranted these refinements, but it hit me yet again that this is certainly the *language* of torture.

Maybe I am being premature in phrasing it thus. Among the veterans there are at least two views on all this, which means in practice that there are two opinions on whether or not "waterboarding" constitutes torture. I have had some extremely serious conversations on the topic, with two groups of highly decent and serious men, and I think that both cases have to be stated at their strongest.

The team who agreed to give me a hard time in the woods of North Carolina belong to a highly honorable group. This group regards itself as out on the front line in defense of a society that is too spoiled and too ungrateful to appreciate those solid, underpaid volunteers who guard us while we sleep. These heroes stay on the ramparts at all hours and in all weather, and if they make a mistake they may be arraigned in order to scratch some domestic political itch. Faced with appalling enemies who make horror videos of torture and beheadings, they feel that they are the ones who confront denunciation in our press, and possible prosecution. As they have just tried to demonstrate to me, a man who has been waterboarded may well emerge from the experience a bit shaky, but he is in a mood to surrender the relevant information and is unmarked and undamaged and indeed ready for another bout in quite a short time. When contrasted to actual torture, waterboarding is more like foreplay. No thumbscrew, no pincers, no electrodes, no rack. Can one say this of those who have been captured by the tormentors and murderers of (say) Daniel Pearl? On this analysis, any call to indict the United States for torture is therefore a lame and diseased attempt to arrive at a moral equivalence between those who defend civilization and those who exploit its freedoms to hollow it out, and ultimately to bring it down. I myself do not trust anybody who does not clearly understand this viewpoint.

Against it, however, I call as my main witness Mr. Malcolm Nance. Mr. Nance is not what you call a bleeding heart. In fact, speaking of the coronary area, he has said that, in battlefield conditions, he "would personally cut bin Laden's heart out with a plastic M.R.E. spoon."[3] He was to the fore on September 11, 2001, dealing with the burning nightmare in the debris of the Pentagon. He has been involved with the SERE program since 1997. He speaks Arabic and has been on al Qaeda's tail since the early 1990s. His most recent book, *The Terrorists of Iraq* [2007], is a highly potent analysis both of the jihadist threat in Mesopotamia and of the ways in which we have made its life easier. I passed one of the most dramatic evenings of my life listening to his cold but enraged denunciation of the adoption of waterboarding by the United States. The argument goes like this:

1. Waterboarding is a deliberate torture technique and has been prosecuted as such by our judicial arm when perpetrated by others.

2. If we allow it and justify it, we cannot complain if it is employed in the future by other regimes on captive U.S. citizens. It is a method of putting American prisoners in harm's way.

3. It may be a means of extracting information, but it is also a means of extracting junk information. (Mr. Nance told me that he had heard of someone's being compelled to confess that he was a hermaphrodite. I later had an awful twinge while wondering if I myself could have been "dunked" this far.) To put it briefly, even the CIA sources for the *Washington Post* story on waterboarding conceded that the information they got out of Khalid Sheikh Mohammed was "not all of it reliable." Just put a pencil line under that last phrase, or commit it to memory.

4. It opens a door that cannot be closed. Once you have posed the notorious "ticking bomb" question, and once you assume that you are in the right, what will you *not* do? Waterboarding not getting results fast enough? The terrorist's clock still ticking? Well, then, bring on the thumbscrews and the pincers and the electrodes and the rack.

Masked by these arguments, there lurks another very penetrating point. Nance doubts very much that Khalid Sheikh Mohammed lasted that long under the water treatment (and I am pathetically pleased to hear it). It's also quite thinkable, *if* he did, that he was trying to attain martyrdom at our hands. But even if he endured so long, and since the United States has in any case bragged that *in fact* he did, one of our worst enemies has now become one of the founders of something that will someday disturb your sleep as well as mine. To quote Nance:

> Torture advocates hide behind the argument that an open discussion about specific American interrogation techniques will aid the enemy. Yet, convicted Al Qaeda members and innocent captives who were released to their host nations have already debriefed the world through hundreds of interviews,

3 After searching for Osama bin Laden for nearly a decade following the attacks of September 11, 2001, Osama bin Laden was killed by American special military forces on May 1, 2011. —Eds.

movies and documentaries on exactly what methods they were subjected to and how they endured. Our own missteps have created a cadre of highly experienced lecturers for Al Qaeda's own virtual SERE school for terrorists.

Which returns us to my starting point, about the distinction between training *for* something and training to resist it. One used to be told—and surely with truth—that the lethal fanatics of al Qaeda were schooled to lie, and instructed to claim that they had been tortured and maltreated whether they had been tortured and maltreated or not. Did we notice what a frontier we had crossed when we admitted and even proclaimed that their stories might in fact be true? I had only a very slight encounter on that frontier, but I still wish that my experience were the only way in which the words "waterboard" and "American" could be mentioned in the same (gasping and sobbing) breath. ▉

The Reader's Presence

1. How would you characterize the tone of voice Hitchens uses in this essay? Pay particular attention to the passages where he describes the sensation of being waterboarded. How would you describe the sound of his voice in these passages? What other approaches could he have taken with equal plausibility, given the subject matter? Why do you think Hitchens takes the approach that he does?

2. Hitchens writes: "As if detecting my misery and shame, one of my interrogators comfortingly said, 'Any time is a long time when you're breathing water.' I could have hugged him for saying so, and just then I was hit with a ghastly sense of the sadomasochistic dimension that underlies the relationship between the torturer and the tortured" (paragraph 8). What does Hitchens mean by this? What is the effect of Hitchens's having made this observation so close to the end of the essay? With what impression does Hitchens leave the reader at the end of his essay?

3. **VISUAL PRESENCE:**   What details attract your attention in the photograph of Hitchens as he subjects himself to a waterboarding "treatment" (page 619)? In what specific way(s) does the angle of the camera reinforce the effects of this image? What does the photographer gain by positioning the camera at this angle? What is "lost" in this decision? Be as specific as possible in your response.

4. **CONNECTIONS:**   Compare Hitchens's essay to the passages from Michihiko Hachiya's "Hiroshima Diary" (page 136). What similarities (and differences) do you notice about the way the two writers tell their stories? Consider, for example, their respective tones of voice, sentence lengths, rhythms, and interjections of personal opinion. How do those similarities and differences affect your understanding of what each writer experienced? How did your visceral reaction to each essay differ?

Thomas Jefferson

THE DECLARATION OF INDEPENDENCE

THOMAS JEFFERSON (1743–1826) was born and raised in Virginia and attended William and Mary College. After being admitted to the bar, he entered politics and served in the Virginia House of Burgesses and the Continental Congress of 1775. During the Revolutionary War he was elected governor of Virginia, and after independence he was appointed special minister to France and later secretary of state. As the nation's third president, he negotiated the Louisiana Purchase. Of all his accomplishments as an inventor, an architect, a diplomat, a scientist, and a politician, Jefferson counted his work in designing the University of Virginia among the most important, along with his efforts to establish separation of church and state and the composition of the Declaration of Independence.

In May and June 1776, the Continental Congress had been vigorously debating the dangerous idea of independence and felt the need to issue a document that clearly pointed out the colonial grievances against Great Britain. A committee was appointed to "prepare a declaration" that would summarize the specific reasons for colonial discontent. The committee of five included Thomas Jefferson, Benjamin Franklin, and John Adams. Jefferson, who was noted for his skills in composition and, as Adams put it, "peculiar felicity of expression," was chosen to write the first draft. The assignment took Jefferson about two weeks, and he submitted the draft first to the committee, which made a few verbal alterations, and then on June 28 to Congress, where, after further alterations mainly relating to slavery, it was finally approved on July 4, 1776.

> Thomas Jefferson intended the Declaration of Independence "to be an expression of the American mind, and to give to that expression the proper tone and spirit called for by the occasion."

Jefferson claims to have composed the document without research, working mainly from ideas he felt were commonly held at the time. As Jefferson recalled many years later, he drafted the document as "an appeal to the tribunal of the world" and hoped "to place before mankind the common sense of the subject, in terms so plain and firm as to command their assent." He claims that "neither aiming at originality of principle or sentiment . . . it was intended to be an expression of the American mind, and to give to that expression the proper tone and spirit called for by the occasion."

WHEN IN THE COURSE of human events, it becomes necessary for one people to dissolve the political bands which have connected them with another, and to assume among the Powers of the earth, the separate and equal station to which the Laws of Nature and of Nature's God entitle them, a decent respect to the opinions of mankind requires that they should declare the causes which impel them to the separation.

We hold these truths to be self-evident, that all men are created equal, that they are endowed by their Creator with certain inalienable Rights, that among these are Life, Liberty and the pursuit of Happiness. That to secure these rights, Governments are instituted among Men, deriving their just powers from the consent of the governed. That whenever any Form of Government becomes destructive of these ends, it is the Right of the People to alter or to abolish it, and to institute new Government, laying its foundation on such principles and organizing its powers in such form, as to them shall seem most likely to effect their Safety and Happiness. Prudence, indeed, will dictate that Governments long established should not be changed for light and transient causes; and accordingly all experience hath shown, that mankind are more disposed to suffer, while evils are sufferable, than to right themselves by abolishing the forms to which they are accustomed. But when a long train of abuses and usurpations, pursuing invariably the same Object evinces a design to reduce them under absolute Despotism, it is their right, it is their duty, to throw off such Government, and to provide new Guards for their future security.—Such has been the patient sufferance of these Colonies; and such is now the necessity which constrains them to alter their former Systems of Government. The history of the present King of Great Britain is a history of repeated injuries and usurpations, all having in direct object the establishment of an absolute Tyranny over these States. To prove this, let Facts be submitted to a candid world.

He has refused his Assent to Laws, the most wholesome and necessary for the public good.

He has forbidden his Governors to pass Laws of immediate and pressing importance, unless suspended in their operation till his Assent should be obtained; and when so suspended, he has utterly neglected to attend to them.

He has refused to pass other laws for the accommodation of large districts of people, unless those people would relinquish the right of Representation in the Legislature, a right inestimable to them and formidable to tyrants only.

He has called together legislative bodies at places unusual, uncomfortable, and distant from the depository of their Public Records, for the sole purpose of fatiguing them into compliance with his measures.

He has dissolved Representative Houses repeatedly, for opposing with manly firmness his invasions on the rights of the people.

He has refused for a long time, after such dissolutions, to cause others to be elected; whereby the Legislative Powers, incapable of Annihilation, have returned to the People at large for their exercise; the State remaining in the mean time exposed to all the dangers of invasion from without, and convulsions within.

He has endeavoured to prevent the population of these States;[1] for that purpose obstructing the Laws for Naturalization of Foreigners; refusing to pass others to encourage their migration hither, and raising the conditions of new Appropriations of Lands.

He has obstructed the Administration of Justice, by refusing his Assent 10 to Laws for establishing Judiciary Powers.

He has made Judges dependent on his Will alone, for the tenure of their offices, and the amount and payment of their salaries.

He has erected a multitude of New Offices, and sent hither swarms of Officers to harass our People, and eat out their substance.

He has kept among us, in times of peace, Standing Armies without the Consent of our legislature.

He has affected to render the Military independent of and superior to the Civil Power.

He has combined with others to subject us to a jurisdiction foreign to our 15 constitution, and unacknowledged by our laws; giving his Assent to their acts of pretended Legislation:

For quartering large bodies of armed troops among us:

For protecting them, by a mock Trial, from Punishment for any Murders which they should commit on the Inhabitants of these States:

For cutting off our Trade with all parts of the world:

For imposing taxes on us without our Consent:

For depriving us in many cases, of the benefits of Trial by Jury: 20

For transporting us beyond Seas to be tried for pretended offenses:

For abolishing the free System of English Laws in a neighboring Province, establishing therein an Arbitrary government, and enlarging its Boundaries so as to render it at once an example and fit instrument for introducing the same absolute rule into these Colonies:

For taking away our Charters, abolishing our most valuable Laws, and altering fundamentally the Forms of our Governments:

For suspending our own Legislatures, and declaring themselves invested with Power to legislate for us in all cases whatsoever.

He has abdicated Government here, by declaring us out of his Protec-   25 tion and waging War against us.

He has plundered our seas, ravaged our Coasts, burnt our towns, and destroyed the lives of our people.

He is at this time transporting large armies of foreign mercenaries to compleat the works of death, desolation and tyranny, already begun with circumstances of Cruelty & perfidy scarcely paralleled in the most barbarous ages, and totally unworthy of the Head of a civilized nation.

---

1 **prevent the population of these States:** This meant limiting emigration to the Colonies, thus controlling their growth. —EDS.

He has constrained our fellow Citizens taken Captive on the high Seas to bear Arms against their Country, to become the executioners of their friends and Brethren, or to fall themselves by their Hands.

He has excited domestic insurrections amongst us, and has endeavoured to bring on the inhabitants of our frontiers, the merciless Indian Savages, whose known rule of warfare, is an undistinguished destruction of all ages, sexes and conditions.

In every stage of these Oppressions We have Petitioned for Readdress   30 in the most humble terms: Our repeated Petitions have been answered only by repeated injury. A Prince, whose character is thus marked by every act which may define a Tyrant, is unfit to be the ruler of a free People.

Nor have We been wanting in attention to our British brethren. We have warned them from time to time of attempts by their legislature to extend an unwarrantable jurisdiction over us. We have reminded them of the circumstances of our emigration and settlement here. We have appealed to their native justice and magnanimity, and we have conjured them by the ties of our common kindred to disavow these usurpations, which would inevitably interrupt our connections and correspondence. They too have been deaf to the voice of justice and of consanguinity. We must, therefore, acquiesce in the necessity, which denounces our Separation, and hold them, as we hold the rest of mankind, Enemies in War, in Peace Friends.

We, therefore, the Representatives of the United States of America, in General Congress, Assembled, appealing to the Supreme Judge of the world for the rectitude of our intentions, do in the Name, and by Authority of the good People of these Colonies, solemnly publish and declare, That these United Colonies are, and of Right ought to be Free and Independent States, that they are Absolved from all Allegiance to the British Crown, and that all political connection between them and the State of Great Britain, is and ought to be totally dissolved; and that as Free and Independent States, they have full Power to levy War, conclude Peace, contract Alliances, establish Commerce, and to do all other Acts and Things which Independent States may of right do. And for the support of this Declaration, with a firm reliance on the Protection of Divine Providence, we mutually pledge to each other our Lives, our Fortunes and our sacred Honor. ▨

The Reader's Presence

1. How does Jefferson seem to define *independence*? Whom does the definition include? Whom does it exclude? How does Jefferson's definition of *independence* differ from your own? It has been pointed out that Jefferson disregards "interdependence." Can you formulate an argument contrary to Jefferson's?

2. Examine the Declaration's first sentence. Who is the speaker here? What is the effect of the omniscient tone of the opening? Why does the first paragraph have no personal pronouns or references to specific events? What might Jefferson's argument stand to gain in generalizing the American situation?

3. **CONNECTIONS:** As in classical epics and the Bible, Jefferson relies on the rhetorical devices of repetition and lists. What is the effect of using such devices? The Declaration is fundamentally a list of complaints against King George III of England. In what specific ways does the speaker's voice reflect that tone of grievance? Identify specific words and phrases that express that attitude. Compare and contrast Jefferson's use of tone and other compositional strategies in drafting the Declaration with those the Reverend Martin Luther King Jr. uses in "I Have a Dream" (page 628). How—specifically—does King draw on the compositional strategies of such seminal speeches as the "Declaration of Independence" in framing his appeal to equal rights and democratic dignity and freedom for every American?

The Writer at Work

Another Draft of the Declaration of Independence

The "original Rough draught" of the Declaration of Independence is one of the foundational documents in American history. The following reproduction of the opening paragraphs of the Declaration illustrates how the text evolved from the initial draft by Thomas Jefferson to the final text adopted by Congress on the morning of July 4, 1776.

Thomas Jefferson, 1776 (oil on canvas), Peale, Charles Willson (1741–1827) (after)/ Huntington Library and Art Gallery, San Marino, CA, USA/© The Huntington Library, Art Collections & Botanical Gardens/The Bridgeman Art Library

❝ A Declaration by the Representatives of the United States of America, in General Congress assembled.

When in the course of human events, it becomes necessary for one people to dissolve the political bands which have connected them with another, and to assume among the powers of the earth the separate and equal station to which the laws of nature and of nature's God entitle them, a decent respect to the opinions of mankind requires that they should declare the causes which impel them to the separation.

We hold these truths to be self evident: that all men are created equal; that they are endowed by their Creator with [inherent and] inalienable rights; that among these are life, liberty, and the pursuit of happiness; that to secure these rights, governments are instituted among men, deriving their just powers from the consent of the governed; that whenever any form of government becomes destructive of these ends, it is the right of the people to alter or to abolish it, and to institute new government, laying its foundation on such principles, and organizing its powers in such form, as to them shall seem most likely to effect their safety and happiness. Prudence, indeed, will dictate that governments long established should not be changed for light and transient causes; and accordingly all experience hath shown that mankind are more disposed to suffer while evils are sufferable, than to right themselves by abolishing the forms to which they are accustomed. But when a long train of abuses and usurpations, [begun at a distinguished period and] pursuing invariably the same object, evinces a design to reduce them under absolute despotism, it is their right, it is their duty to throw off such government, and to provide new guards for their future security. Such has been the patient sufferance of these colonies; and such is now the necessity which constrains them to [expunge] their former systems of government. The history of the present king of Great Britain is a history of [unremitting] injuries and usurpations, [among which appears no solitary fact to contradict the uniform tenor of the rest, but all have] in direct object the establishment of an absolute tyranny over these states. To prove this, let facts be submitted to a candid world [for the truth of which we pledge a faith yet unsullied by falsehood.] . . . **"**

Martin Luther King Jr.

I Have a Dream

MARTIN LUTHER KING JR. (1929–1968) was born in Atlanta, Georgia, and after training for the ministry became pastor of the Dexter Avenue Baptist Church in Montgomery, Alabama. In 1956 he was elected president of the Montgomery Improvement Association, the group that organized a transportation boycott in response to the arrest of Rosa Parks. King later became president of the Southern Christian Leadership Conference, and under his philosophy of nonviolent direct action he led marches and protests throughout the South, to Chicago, and to Washington, D.C. In 1963 King delivered his most famous speech, "I Have a Dream," before 200,000 people in front of the Lincoln Memorial in Washington, D.C., and in 1964 he was awarded the Nobel Peace Prize. King was assassinated on April 3, 1968, in Memphis, Tennessee.

> In 1964, Martin Luther King Jr. was awarded the Nobel Peace Prize.

King was a masterful orator and a powerful writer. Along with his many speeches, King wrote several books, including *Why We Can't Wait* (1963), *Where Do We Go from Here: Chaos or Community?* (1967), *The Measure of a Man* (1968), and *The Trumpet of Conscience* (1968).

For more on Martin Luther King Jr., see page 643.

FIVE SCORE YEARS AGO, a great American, in whose symbolic shadow we stand, signed the Emancipation Proclamation.[1] This momentous decree came as a great beacon light of hope to millions of Negro slaves who had been seared in the flames of withering injustice. It came as a joyous daybreak to end the long night of captivity.

But one hundred years later, we must face the tragic fact that the Negro is still not free. One hundred years later, the life of the Negro is still sadly crippled by the manacles of segregation and the chains of discrimination. One hundred years later, the Negro lives on a lonely island of poverty in the midst of a vast ocean of material prosperity. One hundred years later, the Negro is still languishing in the corners of American society and finds himself an exile in his own land. So we have come here today to dramatize an appalling condition.

In a sense we have come to our nation's Capitol to cash a check. When the architects of our republic wrote the magnificent words of the Constitution and the Declaration of Independence, they were signing a promissory note to which every American was to fall heir. This note was a promise that all men would be guaranteed the unalienable rights of life, liberty, and the pursuit of happiness.

It is obvious today that America has defaulted on this promissory note insofar as her citizens of color are concerned. Instead of honoring this sacred obligation, America has given the Negro people a bad check; a check which has come back marked "insufficient funds." But we refuse to believe that the bank of justice is bankrupt. We refuse to believe that there are insufficient funds in the great vaults of opportunity of this nation. So we have come to cash this check—a check that will give us upon demand the riches of freedom and the security of justice. We have also come to this hallowed spot to remind America of the fierce urgency of *now*. This is no time to engage in the luxury of cooling off or to take the tranquilizing drug of gradualism. *Now* is the time to make real the promises of Democracy. *Now* is the time to rise from the dark and desolate valley of segregation to the sunlit path of racial justice. *Now* is the time to open the doors of opportunity to all of God's children. *Now* is the time to lift our nation from the quicksands of racial injustice to the solid rock of brotherhood.

It would be fatal for the nation to overlook the urgency of the moment and to underestimate the determination of the Negro. This sweltering summer of the Negro's legitimate discontent will not pass until there is an invigorating

5

---

1 **Emancipation Proclamation:** Abraham Lincoln signed the Emancipation Proclamation that officially freed the slaves in 1863.—EDS.

autumn of freedom and equality. 1963 is not an end, but a beginning. Those who hope that the Negro needed to blow off steam and will now be content will have a rude awakening if the nation returns to business as usual. There will be neither rest nor tranquility in America until the Negro is granted his citizenship rights. The whirlwinds of revolt will continue to shake the foundations of our nation until the bright day of justice emerges.

But there is something I must say to my people who stand on the warm threshold which leads into the palace of justice. In the process of gaining our rightful place we must not be guilty of wrongful deeds. Let us not seek to satisfy our thirst for freedom by drinking from the cup of bitterness and hatred. We must forever conduct our struggle on the high plane of dignity and discipline. We must not allow our creative protest to degenerate into physical violence. Again and again we must rise to the majestic heights of meeting physical force with soul force. The marvelous new militancy which has engulfed the Negro community must not lead us to a distrust of all white people, for many of our white brothers, as evidenced by their presence here today, have come to realize that their destiny is tied up with our destiny and their freedom is inextricably bound to our freedom. We cannot walk alone.

And as we walk, we must make the pledge that we shall march ahead. We cannot turn back. There are those who are asking the devotees of civil rights, "When will you be satisfied?" We can never be satisfied as long as the Negro is the victim of the unspeakable horrors of police brutality. We can never be satisfied as long as our bodies, heavy with the fatigue of travel, cannot gain lodging in the motels of the highways and the hotels of the cities. We cannot be satisfied as long as the Negro's basic mobility is from a smaller ghetto to a larger one. We can never be satisfied as long as a Negro in Mississippi cannot vote and a Negro in New York believes he has nothing for which to vote. No, no, we are not satisfied, and we will not be satisfied until justice rolls down like waters and righteousness like a mighty stream.

I am not unmindful that some of you have come here out of great trials and tribulations. Some of you have come fresh from narrow jail cells. Some of you have come from areas where your quest for freedom left you battered by the storms of persecution and staggered by the winds of police brutality. You have been the veterans of creative suffering. Continue to work with the faith that unearned suffering is redemptive.

Go back to Mississippi, go back to Alabama, go back to South Carolina, go back to Georgia, go back to Louisiana, go back to the slums and ghettoes of our northern cities, knowing that somehow this situation can and will be changed. Let us not wallow in the valley of despair.

I say to you today, my friends, that in spite of the difficulties and frustrations of the moment I still have a dream. It is a dream deeply rooted in the American dream.   10

I have a dream that one day this nation will rise up and live out the true meaning of its creed: "We hold these truths to be self-evident; that all men are created equal."[2]

2 From the Declaration of Independence by Thomas Jefferson (page 623). —EDS.

I have a dream that one day on the red hills of Georgia the sons of former slaves and the sons of former slaveowners will be able to sit down together at the table of brotherhood.

I have a dream that the state of Mississippi, a desert state sweltering with the heat of injustice and oppression, will be transformed into an oasis of freedom and justice.

I have a dream that my four little children will one day live in a nation where they will not be judged by the color of their skin but by the content of their character.

I have a dream today.   15

I have a dream that the state of Alabama, whose governor's[3] lips are presently dripping with the words of interposition and nullification, will be transformed into a situation where little black boys and black girls will be able to join hands with little white boys and white girls and walk together as sisters and brothers.

I have a dream today.

I have a dream that one day every valley shall be exalted, every hill and mountain shall be made low, the rough places will be made plain, and the crooked places will be made straight, and the glory of the Lord shall be revealed, and all flesh shall see it together.

This is our hope. This is the faith with which I return to the South. With this faith we will be able to hew out of the mountain of despair a stone of hope. With this faith we will be able to transform the jangling discords of our nation into a beautiful symphony of brotherhood. With this faith we will be able to work together, to pray together, to struggle together, to go to jail together, to stand up for freedom together, knowing that we will be free one day.

This will be the day when all of God's children will be able to sing with   20 new meaning.

> My country, 'tis of thee
> Sweet land of liberty,
>   Of thee I sing:
> Land where my fathers died,
> Land of the pilgrims' pride,
> From every mountainside
>   Let freedom ring.

And if America is to be a great nation this must become true. So let freedom ring from the prodigious hilltops of New Hampshire. Let freedom ring from the mighty mountains of New York. Let freedom ring from the heightening Alleghenies of Pennsylvania!

Let freedom ring from the snowcapped Rockies of Colorado!

Let freedom ring from the curvaceous peaks of California!

But not only that; let freedom ring from Stone Mountain of Georgia!

Let freedom ring from Lookout Mountain of Tennessee!   25

---

3 ***governor's:*** The governor of Alabama in 1963 was segregationist George Wallace (1919–1998), who eventually came to support integration and equal rights for African Americans. —EDS.

Let freedom ring from every hill and molehill of Mississippi. From every mountainside, let freedom ring.

When we let freedom ring, when we let it ring from every village and every hamlet, from every state and every city, we will be able to speed up that day when all of God's children, black men and white men, Jews and Gentiles, Protestants and Catholics, will be able to join hands and sing in the words of the old Negro spiritual, "Free at last! free at last! thank God almighty, we are free at last!" ◼

The Reader's Presence

1. How does King use familiar concepts and phrases from American democracy to create his message? What are some examples? How does he use repetition? How does he use rhythm? What are the effects of his rhetoric?

2. Make a list of the metaphors King uses throughout the speech. What connotations do they bring? What recurring themes does he draw on for his metaphors? How do metaphors help extend the meanings of the words he describes?

3. **CONNECTIONS:**   Read Ho Che Anderson's graphic representation of King's "I Have a Dream" speech, which follows this piece. How does Anderson represent King as a speaker and leader? How does the juxtaposition of images and words influence your perception of the event?

The Artist at Work

HO CHE ANDERSON Reenvisions Martin Luther King Jr.'s *I Have a Dream*

Jason Thibault

Ho Che Anderson (b. 1969) was born in the United Kingdom and raised in Canada, where he lives today. He has authored a number of graphic "comix" including *Young Hoods in Love* (1994), *I Want to Be Your Dog* (1996), and, in collaboration with Wilfred Santiago, the series *Pop Life* (1998). His biographical trilogy, *King* (Volumes I–III), illustrates the life of Martin Luther King Jr. from his birth to his assassination. Anderson's complex rendering of the 1963 civil rights march on Washington, D.C., during which King delivered his most-famous speech, "I Have a Dream," is excerpted from *King, Volume II* (2002). The first volume, *King* (1992), won a 1995 Parent's Choice Award; *King, Volume III*, was published in 2003.

MARCH ON WASHINGTON
FOR
JOBS & FREEDOM
1963
Children, I've been buked and I've
Tryin' to make this
What the system does to the subjugated is destroy his sense of reality. It destroys his father's authority over hjm. His father can no longer tell him anything because his past has disappeared....
mahalia jackson
CATHOLIC
JEWS
PROTESTANT
NOW!
charlton heston

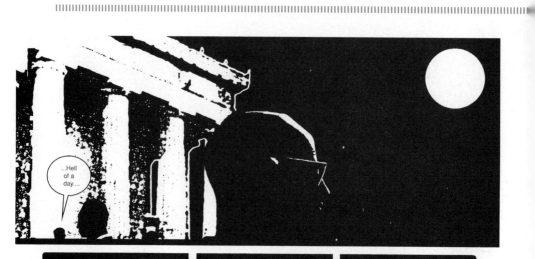

Martin Luther King Jr.

LETTER FROM BIRMINGHAM JAIL

MARTIN LUTHER KING JR., one of the nation's best-known civil rights activists, led protests across the South in the years before the passage of the Civil Rights Act of 1964. He was arrested in 1960 for sitting at a whites-only lunch counter in Greensboro, North Carolina, and in 1962 he was jailed in Albany, Georgia. On April 12, 1963, King was again arrested, this time in Birmingham, Alabama, for demonstrating without a permit. He served eleven days in jail. While there, he wrote "Letter from Birmingham Jail" in response to a letter from eight clergymen who argued against King's acts of civil disobedience. The letter was published in King's book *Why We Can't Wait* (1963).

> **"Through education we seek to break down the spiritual barriers to integration."**

Many of King's writings, including the letter printed here and the famous "I Have a Dream" speech (page 628), are designed to educate his audiences and inspire them to act. "Through education we seek to break down the spiritual barriers to integration," he said, and "through legislation and court orders we seek to break down the physical barriers to integration. One method is not a substitute for the other, but a meaningful and necessary supplement."

For more on Martin Luther King Jr., see page 659.

The following is the public statement by eight Alabama clergymen that occasioned King's letter.

———

WE THE UNDERSIGNED clergymen are among those who, in January, issued "an appeal for law and order and common sense," in dealing with racial problems in Alabama. We expressed understanding that honest convictions in racial matters could properly be pursued in the courts, but urged that decisions of those courts should in the meantime be peacefully obeyed.

Since that time there had been some evidence of increased forbearance and a willingness to face facts. Responsible citizens have undertaken to work on various problems which cause racial friction and unrest. In Birmingham, recent public events have given indication that we all have opportunity for a new constructive and realistic approach to racial problems.

However, we are now confronted by a series of demonstrations by some of our Negro citizens, directed and led in part by outsiders. We recognize the natural impatience of people who feel that their hopes are slow in being realized. But we are convinced that these demonstrations are unwise and untimely.

We agree rather with certain local Negro leadership which has called for honest and open negotiation of racial issues in our area. And we believe this kind of facing of issues can best be accomplished by citizens of our own metropolitan area, white and Negro, meeting with their knowledge and experience of the local situation. All of us need to face that responsibility and find proper channels for its accomplishment.

Just as we formerly pointed out that "hatred and violence have no sanc-   5
tion in our religious and political traditions," we also point out that such actions as incite to hatred and violence, however technically peaceful those actions may be, have not contributed to the resolution of our local problems. We do not believe that these days of new hope are days when extreme measures are justified in Birmingham.

We commend the community as a whole, and the local news media and law enforcement officials in particular, on the calm manner in which these demonstrations have been handled. We urge the public to continue to show restraint should the demonstrations continue, and the law enforcement officials to remain calm and continue to protect our city from violence.

We further strongly urge our own Negro community to withdraw support from these demonstrations, and to unite locally in working peacefully for a better Birmingham. When rights are consistently denied, a cause should be pressed in the courts and in negotiations among local leaders, and not in the streets. We appeal to both our white and Negro citizenry to observe the principles of law and order and common sense.

> BISHOP C. C. J. CARPENTER, D.D., LL.D., Episcopalian Bishop of Alabama
>
> BISHOP JOSEPH A. DURICK, D.D., Auxiliary Bishop, Roman Catholic Diocese of Mobile, Birmingham
>
> RABBI MILTON L. GRAFMAN, Temple Emanu-El, Birmingham, Alabama
>
> BISHOP PAUL HARDIN, Methodist Bishop of the Alabama–West Florida Conference
>
> BISHOP NOLAN B. HARMON, Bishop of the North Alabama Conference of the Methodist Church
>
> REV. GEORGE M. MURRAY, D.D., LL.D., Bishop Coadjutor, Episcopal Diocese of Alabama
>
> REV. EDWARD V. RAMAGE, Moderator, Synod of the Alabama Presbyterian Church in the United States
>
> REV. EARL STALLINGS, Pastor, First Baptist Church, Birmingham, Alabama
>
> *April 12, 1963*

MARTIN LUTHER KING JR.
Birmingham City Jail
April 16, 1963

Bishop C. C. J. CARPENTER
Bishop JOSEPH A. DURICK
Rabbi MILTON L. GRAFMAN
Bishop PAUL HARDIN

Bishop NOLAN B. HARMON
The Rev. GEORGE M. MURRAY
The Rev. EDWARD V. RAMAGE
The Rev. EARL STALLINGS

My dear Fellow Clergymen,

While confined here in the Birmingham City Jail, I came across your recent statement calling our present activities "unwise and untimely." Seldom, if ever, do I pause to answer criticism of my work and ideas. If I sought to answer all of the criticisms that cross my desk, my secretaries would be engaged in little else in the course of the day and I would have no time for constructive work. But since I feel that you are men of genuine good will and your criticisms are sincerely set forth, I would like to answer your statement in what I hope will be patient and reasonable terms.

I think I should give the reason for my being in Birmingham, since you have been influenced by the argument of "outsiders coming in." I have the honor of serving as president of the Southern Christian Leadership Conference, an organization operating in every Southern state with headquarters in Atlanta, Georgia. We have some eighty-five affiliate organizations all across the South—one being the Alabama Christian Movement for Human Rights. Whenever necessary and possible we share staff, educational, and financial resources with our affiliates. Several months ago our local affiliate here in Birmingham invited us to be on call to engage in a nonviolent direct action program if such were deemed necessary. We readily consented and when the hour came we lived up to our promises. So I am here, along with several members of my staff, because we were invited here. I am here because I have basic organizational ties here. Beyond this, I am in Birmingham because injustice is here. Just as the eighth century prophets left their little villages and carried their "thus saith the Lord" far beyond the boundaries of their home town, and just as the Apostle Paul left his little village of Tarsus and carried the gospel of Jesus Christ to practically every hamlet and city of the Greco-Roman world, I too am compelled to carry the gospel of freedom beyond my particular home town. Like Paul, I must constantly respond to the Macedonian call for aid.

Moreover, I am cognizant of the interrelatedness of all communities and states. I cannot sit idly by in Atlanta and not be concerned about what happens in Birmingham. Injustice anywhere is a threat to justice everywhere. We are caught in an inescapable network of mutuality tied in a single garment of destiny. Whatever affects one directly affects all indirectly. Never again can we afford to live with the narrow, provincial "outside agitator" idea. Anyone who lives inside the United States can never be considered an outsider anywhere in this country.

You deplore the demonstrations that are presently taking place in Birmingham. But I am sorry that your statement did not express a similar concern for the conditions that brought the demonstrations into being. I am sure that each of you would want to go beyond the superficial social analyst who looks merely at effects, and does not grapple with underlying causes. I would not hesitate to say that it is unfortunate that so-called demonstrations are taking place in Birmingham at this time, but I would say in more emphatic terms it is even more unfortunate that the white power structure of this city left the Negro community with no other alternative.

In any nonviolent campaign there are four basic steps: (1) collection of the facts to determine whether injustices are alive; (2) negotiation; (3) self-purification; and (4) direct action. We have gone through all of these steps in Birmingham. There can be no gainsaying of the fact that racial injustice engulfs this community. Birmingham is probably the most thoroughly segregated city in the United States. Its ugly record of police brutality is known in every section of this country. Its unjust treatment of Negroes in the courts is a notorious reality. There have been more unsolved bombings of Negro homes and churches in Birmingham than in any city in this nation. These are the hard, brutal, and unbelievable facts. On the basis of these conditions Negro leaders sought to negotiate with the city fathers. But the political leaders consistently refused to engage in good faith negotiation.

Then came the opportunity last September to talk with some of the leaders of the economic community. In these negotiating sessions certain promises were made by the merchants — such as the promise to remove the humiliating racial signs from the stores. On the basis of these promises Rev. Shuttlesworth and the leaders of the Alabama Christian Movement for Human Rights agreed to call a moratorium on any type of demonstrations. As the weeks and months unfolded we realized that we were the victims of a broken promise. The signs remained. As in so many experiences of the past we were confronted with blasted hopes, and the dark shadow of a deep disappointment settled upon us. So we had no alternative except that of preparing for direct action, whereby we would present our very bodies as a means of laying our case before the conscience of the local and national community. We were not unmindful of the difficulties involved. So we decided to go through a process of self-purification. We started having workshops on nonviolence and repeatedly asked ourselves the questions, "Are you able to accept blows without retaliating?" "Are you able to endure the ordeals of jail?"

We decided to set our direct action program around the Easter season, realizing that with the exception of Christmas, this was the largest shopping period of the year. Knowing that a strong economic withdrawal program would be the by-product of direct action, we felt that this was the best time to bring pressure on the merchants for the needed changes. Then it occurred

to us that the March election was ahead, and so we speedily decided to postpone action until after election day. When we discovered that Mr. Connor[1]
was in the run-off, we decided again to postpone so that the demonstrations
could not be used to cloud the issues. At this time we agreed to begin our
nonviolent witness the day after the run-off.

This reveals that we did not move irresponsibly into direct action. We
too wanted to see Mr. Connor defeated; so we went through postponement
after postponement to aid in this community need. After this we felt that
direct action could be delayed no longer.

You may well ask, "Why direct action? Why sit-ins, marches, etc.? Isn't
negotiation a better path?" You are exactly right in your call for negotiation.
Indeed, this is the purpose of direct action. Nonviolent direct action seeks to
create such a crisis and establish such creative tension that a community that
has constantly refused to negotiate is forced to confront the issue. It seeks so
to dramatize the issue that it can no longer be ignored. I just referred to the
creation of tension as a part of the work of the nonviolent resister. This may
sound rather shocking. But I must confess that I am not afraid of the word
tension. I have earnestly worked and preached against violent tension, but
there is a type of constructive nonviolent tension that is necessary for growth.
Just as Socrates felt that it was necessary to create a tension in the mind so
that individuals could rise from the bondage of myths and half-truths to the
unfettered realm of creative analysis and objective appraisal, we must see
the need of having nonviolent gadflies to create the kind of tension in society that will help men rise from the dark depths of prejudice and racism to
the majestic heights of understanding and brotherhood. So the purpose of
the direct action is to create a situation so crisis-packed that it will inevitably
open the door to negotiation. We, therefore, concur with you in your call for
negotiation. Too long has our beloved Southland been bogged down in the
tragic attempt to live in monologue rather than dialogue.

One of the basic points in your statement is that our acts are untimely.   10
Some have asked, "Why didn't you give the new administration time to act?"
The only answer that I can give to this inquiry is that the new administration must be prodded about as much as the outgoing one before it acts. We
will be sadly mistaken if we feel that the election of Mr. Boutwell will bring
the millennium to Birmingham. While Mr. Boutwell is much more articulate
and gentle than Mr. Connor, they are both segregationists dedicated to the
task of maintaining the status quo. The hope I see in Mr. Boutwell is that he
will be reasonable enough to see the futility of massive resistance to desegregation. But he will not see this without pressure from the devotees of civil
rights. My friends, I must say to you that we have not made a single gain in

---

[1] **Mr. Connor:** Eugene "Bull" Connor and Albert Boutwell ran for mayor of Birmingham, Alabama, in 1963. Although Boutwell, the more-moderate candidate, was declared the winner, Connor,
the city commissioner of public safety, refused to leave office, claiming that he had been elected to
serve until 1965. While the issue was debated in the courts, Connor was on the street ordering the
police to use force to suppress demonstrations against segregation. —EDS.

civil rights without determined legal and nonviolent pressure. History is the long and tragic story of the fact that privileged groups seldom give up their privileges voluntarily. Individuals may see the moral light and voluntarily give up their unjust posture; but as Reinhold Niebuhr[2] has reminded us, groups are more immoral than individuals.

We know through painful experience that freedom is never voluntarily given by the oppressor; it must be demanded by the oppressed. Frankly I have never yet engaged in a direct action movement that was "well timed," according to the timetable of those who have not suffered unduly from the disease of segregation. For years now I have heard the word "Wait!" It rings in the ear of every Negro with a piercing familiarity. This "wait" has almost always meant "never." It has been a tranquilizing thalidomide,[3] relieving the emotional stress for a moment, only to give birth to an ill-formed infant of frustration. We must come to see with the distinguished jurist of yesterday that "justice too long delayed is justice denied." We have waited for more than three hundred and forty years for our constitutional and God-given rights. The nations of Asia and Africa are moving with jet-like speed toward the goal of political independence, and we still creep at horse and buggy pace toward the gaining of a cup of coffee at a lunch counter.

I guess it is easy for those who have never felt the stinging darts of segregation to say wait. But when you have seen vicious mobs lynch your mothers and fathers at will and drown your sisters and brothers at whim; when you have seen hate-filled policemen curse, kick, brutalize, and even kill your black brothers and sisters with impunity; when you see the vast majority of your twenty million Negro brothers smothering in an air-tight cage of poverty in the midst of an affluent society; when you suddenly find your tongue twisted and your speech stammering as you seek to explain to your six-year-old daughter why she can't go to the public amusement park that has just been advertised on television, and see tears welling up in her little eyes when she is told that Funtown is closed to colored children, and see the depressing clouds of inferiority begin to form in her little mental sky, and see her begin to distort her little personality by unconsciously developing a bitterness toward white people; when you have to concoct an answer for a five-year-old son asking in agonizing pathos: "Daddy, why do white people treat colored people so mean?"; when you take a cross country drive and find it necessary to sleep night after night in the uncomfortable corners of your automobile because no motel will accept you; when you are humiliated day in and day out by nagging signs reading "white" men and "colored"; when your first name becomes "nigger" and your middle name becomes "boy" (however old you are) and your last name becomes "John," and when your wife and mother are never given the respected title "Mrs.";

---

2 **Reinhold Niebuhr** (1892–1971): Protestant theologian best known for attempts to relate Christianity to modern politics. —EDS.

3 **thalidomide:** A drug originally used as a sedative, but withdrawn in the early 1960s following the discovery that it caused malformation or absence of limbs in children whose mothers took the drug during early pregnancy. —EDS.

when you are harried by day and haunted by night by the fact that you are a Negro, living constantly at tip-toe stance never quite knowing what to expect next, and plagued with inner fears and outer resentments; when you are forever fighting a degenerating sense of "nobodiness";—then you will understand why we find it difficult to wait. There comes a time when the cup of endurance runs over, and men are no longer willing to be plunged into an abyss of injustice where they experience the bleakness of corroding despair. I hope, sirs, you can understand our legitimate and unavoidable impatience.

You express a great deal of anxiety over our willingness to break laws. This is certainly a legitimate concern. Since we so diligently urge people to obey the Supreme Court's decision of 1954 outlawing segregation in the public schools, it is rather strange and paradoxical to find us consciously breaking laws. One may well ask, "How can you advocate breaking some laws and obeying others?" The answer is found in the fact that there are two types of laws. There are *just* laws and there are *unjust* laws. I would be the first to advocate obeying just laws. One has not only a legal but moral responsibility to obey just laws. Conversely, one has a moral responsibility to disobey unjust laws. I would agree with Saint Augustine that "An unjust law is no law at all."

Now what is the difference between the two? How does one determine when a law is just or unjust? A just law is a man-made code that squares with the moral law or the law of God. An unjust law is a code that is out of harmony with the moral law. To put it in the terms of Saint Thomas Aquinas, an unjust law is a human law that is not rooted in eternal and natural law. Any law that uplifts human personality is just. Any law that degrades human personality is unjust. All segregation statutes are unjust because segregation distorts the soul and damages the personality. It gives the segregator a false sense of superiority and the segregated a false sense of inferiority. To use the words of Martin Buber, the great Jewish philosopher, segregation substitutes an "I-it" relationship for the "I-thou" relationship, and ends up relegating persons to the status of things. So segregation is not only politically, economically, and sociologically unsound, but it is morally wrong and sinful. Paul Tillich[4] has said that sin is separation. Isn't segregation an existential expression of man's tragic separation, an expression of his awful estrangement, his terrible sinfulness? So I can urge men to obey the 1954 decision of the Supreme Court[5] because it is morally right, and I can urge them to disobey segregation ordinances because they are morally wrong.

Let us turn to a more concrete example of just and unjust laws. An unjust   15
law is a code that a majority inflicts on a minority that is not binding on itself. This is *difference* made legal. On the other hand a just law is a code that a majority compels a minority to follow that it is willing to follow itself. This is *sameness* made legal.

---

4 ***Paul Tillich*** (1886–1965): Theologian and philosopher. —EDS.
5 ***1954 decision of the Supreme Court:*** *Brown v. Board of Education*, the case in which the Supreme Court ruled racial segregation in the nation's public schools unconstitutional. —EDS.

Let me give another explanation. An unjust law is a code inflicted upon a minority which that minority had no part in enacting or creating because they did not have the unhampered right to vote. Who can say the legislature of Alabama which set up the segregation laws was democratically elected? Throughout the state of Alabama all types of conniving methods are used to prevent Negroes from becoming registered voters and there are some counties without a single Negro registered to vote despite the fact that the Negro constitutes a majority of the population. Can any law set up in such a state be considered democratically structured?

These are just a few examples of unjust and just laws. There are some instances when a law is just on its face but unjust in its application. For instance, I was arrested Friday on a charge of parading without a permit. Now there is nothing wrong with an ordinance which requires a permit for a parade, but when the ordinance is used to preserve segregation and to deny citizens the First Amendment privilege of peaceful assembly and peaceful protest, then it becomes unjust.

I hope you can see the distinction I am trying to point out. In no sense do I advocate evading or defying the law as the rabid segregationist would do. This would lead to anarchy. One who breaks an unjust law must do it *openly*, *lovingly* (not hatefully as the white mothers did in New Orleans when they were seen on television screaming "nigger, nigger, nigger") and with a willingness to accept the penalty. I submit that an individual who breaks a law that conscience tells him is unjust, and willingly accepts the penalty by staying in jail to arouse the conscience of the community over its injustice, is in reality expressing the very highest respect for law.

Of course there is nothing new about this kind of civil disobedience. It was seen sublimely in the refusal of Shadrach, Meshach, and Abednego to obey the laws of Nebuchadnezzar because a higher moral law was involved. It was practiced superbly by the early Christians who were willing to face hungry lions and the excruciating pain of chopping blocks, before submitting to certain unjust laws of the Roman Empire. To a degree academic freedom is a reality today because Socrates practiced civil disobedience.

We can never forget that everything Hitler did in Germany was "legal"   20
and everything the Hungarian freedom fighters[6] did in Hungary was "illegal." It was "illegal" to aid and comfort a Jew in Hitler's Germany. But I am sure that, if I had lived in Germany during that time, I would have aided and comforted my Jewish brothers even though it was illegal. If I lived in a communist country today where certain principles dear to the Christian faith are suppressed, I believe I would openly advocate disobeying those antireligious laws.

I must make two honest confessions to you, my Christian and Jewish brothers. First I must confess that over the last few years I have been gravely disappointed with the white moderate. I have almost reached the regrettable

---

[6] ***Hungarian freedom fighters:*** Those who fought in the unsuccessful 1956 revolt against Soviet oppression. —EDS.

conclusion that the Negroes' great stumbling block in the stride toward freedom is not the White Citizens' "Counciler" or the Ku Klux Klanner, but the
white moderate who is more devoted to "order" than to justice; who prefers
a negative peace which is the absence of tension to a positive peace which is
the presence of justice; who constantly says "I agree with you in the goal you
seek, but I can't agree with your methods of direct action"; who paternalisti-
cally feels that he can set the timetable for another man's freedom; who lives
by the myth of time and who constantly advises the Negro to wait until a
"more convenient season." Shallow understanding from people of good will
is more frustrating than absolute misunderstanding from people of ill will.
Lukewarm acceptance is much more bewildering than outright rejection.

I had hoped that the white moderate would understand that law and
order exist for the purpose of establishing justice, and that when they fail to
do this they become the dangerously structured dams that block the flow of
social progress. I had hoped that the white moderate would understand that
the present tension in the South is merely a necessary phase of the transition
from an obnoxious negative peace, where the Negro passively accepted his
unjust plight, to a substance-filled positive peace, where all men will respect
the dignity and worth of human personality. Actually, we who engage in
nonviolent direct action are not the creators of tension. We merely bring to
the surface the hidden tension that is already alive. We bring it out in the
open where it can be seen and dealt with. Like a boil that can never be
cured as long as it is covered up but must be opened with all its pus-flowing
ugliness to the natural medicines of air and light, injustice must likewise be
exposed, with all of the tension its exposing creates, to the light of human
conscience and the air of national opinion before it can be cured.

In your statement you asserted that our actions, even though peaceful,
must be condemned because they precipitate violence. But can this assertion be logically made? Isn't this like condemning the robbed man because
his possession of money precipitated the evil act of robbery? Isn't this like
condemning Socrates because his unswerving commitment to truth and his
philosophical delvings precipitated the misguided popular mind to make
him drink the hemlock? Isn't this like condemning Jesus because His unique
God consciousness and never-ceasing devotion to His will precipitated the
evil act of crucifixion? We must come to see, as federal courts have consistently affirmed, that it is immoral to urge an individual to withdraw his
efforts to gain his basic constitutional rights because the quest precipitates
violence. Society must protect the robbed and punish the robber.

I had also hoped that the white moderate would reject the myth of time. I
received a letter this morning from a white brother in Texas which said: "All
Christians know that the colored people will receive equal rights eventually,
but is it possible that you are in too great of a religious hurry? It has taken
Christianity almost 2000 years to accomplish what it has. The teachings of
Christ take time to come to earth." All that is said here grows out of a tragic
misconception of time. It is the strangely irrational notion that there is something in the very flow of time that will inevitably cure all ills. Actually time

is neutral. It can be used either destructively or constructively. I am coming to feel that the people of ill will have used time much more effectively than the people of good will. We will have to repent in this generation not merely for the vitriolic words and actions of the bad people, but for the appalling silence of the good people. We must come to see that human progress never rolls in on wheels of inevitability. It comes through the tireless efforts and persistent work of men willing to be co-workers with God, and without this hard work time itself becomes an ally of the forces of social stagnation.

We must use time creatively, and forever realize that the time is always 25 ripe to do right. Now is the time to make real the promise of democracy, and transform our pending national elegy into a creative psalm of brotherhood. Now is the time to lift our national policy from the quicksand of racial injustice to the solid rock of human dignity.

You spoke of our activity in Birmingham as extreme. At first I was rather disappointed that fellow clergymen would see my nonviolent efforts as those of the extremist. I started thinking about the fact that I stand in the middle of two opposing forces in the Negro community. One is a force of complacency made up of Negroes who, as a result of long years of oppression, have been so completely drained of self-respect and a sense of "somebodiness" that they have adjusted to segregation, and of a few Negroes in the middle class who, because of a degree of academic and economic security, and because at points they profit by segregation, have unconsciously become insensitive to the problems of the masses. The other force is one of bitterness and hatred and comes perilously close to advocating violence. It is expressed in the various black nationalist groups that are springing up over the nation, the largest and best known being Elijah Muhammad's Muslim movement.[7] This movement is nourished by the contemporary frustration over the continued existence of racial discrimination. It is made up of people who have lost faith in America, who have absolutely repudiated Christianity, and who have concluded that the white man is an incurable "devil." I have tried to stand between these two forces saying that we need not follow the "do-nothing-ism" of the complacent or the hatred and despair of the black nationalist. There is the more excellent way of love and nonviolent protest. I'm grateful to God that, through the Negro church, the dimension of nonviolence entered our struggle. If this philosophy had not emerged I am convinced that by now many streets of the South would be flowing with floods of blood. And I am further convinced that if our white brothers dismiss us as "rabble rousers" and "outside agitators"—those of us who are working through the channels of nonviolent direct action—and refuse to support our nonviolent efforts, millions of Negroes, out of frustration and despair, will seek solace and security in black nationalist ideologies, a development that will lead inevitably to a frightening racial nightmare.

---

[7] *Elijah Muhammad's Muslim movement:* Led by Elijah Muhammad, the Black Muslims opposed integration and promoted the creation of a black nation within the United States. —EDS.

Oppressed people cannot remain oppressed forever. The urge for free-dom will eventually come. This is what has happened to the American Negro. Something within has reminded him of his birthright of freedom; something without has reminded him that he can gain it. Consciously and unconsciously, he has been swept in by what the Germans call the *Zeitgeist*,[8] and with his black brothers of Africa, and his brown and yellow brothers of Asia, South America, and the Caribbean, he is moving with a sense of cosmic urgency toward the promised land of racial justice. Recognizing this vital urge that has engulfed the Negro community, one should readily understand public demonstrations. The Negro has many pent-up resentments and latent frustrations. He has to get them out. So let him march sometime; let him have his prayer pilgrimages to the city hall; understand why he must have sit-ins and freedom rides. If his repressed emotions do not come out in these nonviolent ways, they will come out in ominous expressions of violence. This is not a threat; it is a fact of history. So I have not said to my people, "Get rid of your discontent." But I have tried to say that this normal and healthy discontent can be channeled through the creative outlet of nonviolent direct action. Now this approach is being dismissed as extremist. I must admit that I was initially disappointed in being so categorized.

But as I continued to think about the matter I gradually gained a bit of satisfaction from being considered an extremist. Was not Jesus an extremist in love? "Love your enemies, bless them that curse you, pray for them that despitefully use you." Was not Amos[9] an extremist for justice—"Let justice roll down like waters and righteousness like a mighty stream." Was not Paul an extremist for the gospel of Jesus Christ—"I bear in my body the marks of the Lord Jesus." Was not Martin Luther an extremist—"Here I stand; I can do none other so help me God." Was not John Bunyan[10] an extremist—"I will stay in jail to the end of my days before I make a butchery of my con-science." Was not Abraham Lincoln an extremist—"This nation cannot sur-vive half slave and half free." Was not Thomas Jefferson an extremist—"We hold these truths to be self-evident, that all men are created equal." So the question is not whether we will be extremist but what kind of extremist will we be. Will we be extremists for hate or will we be extremists for love? Will we be extremists for the preservation of injustice—or will we be extrem-ists for the cause of justice? In that dramatic scene on Calvary's hill three men were crucified. We must never forget that all three were crucified for the same crime—the crime of extremism. Two were extremists for immoral-ity, and thus fell below their environment. The other, Jesus Christ, was an extremist for love, truth, and goodness, and thereby rose above His environ-ment. So, after all, maybe the South, the nation, and the world are in dire need of creative extremists.

---

8 **Zeitgeist:** A German word meaning "spirit of the time."—EDS.
9 ***Amos:*** Prophet who preached against false worship and immorality.—EDS.
10 ***John Bunyan*** (1628–1688): Puritan author of *Pilgrim's Progress.*—EDS.

I had hoped that the white moderate would see this. Maybe I was too optimistic. Maybe I expected too much. I guess I should have realized that few members of a race that has oppressed another race can understand or appreciate the deep groans and passionate yearnings of those that have been oppressed, and still fewer have the vision to see that injustice must be rooted out by strong, persistent, and determined action. I am thankful, however, that some of our white brothers have grasped the meaning of this social revolution and committed themselves to it. They are still all too small in quantity, but they are big in quality. Some like Ralph McGill, Lillian Smith, Harry Golden, and James Dabbs have written about our struggle in eloquent, prophetic, and understanding terms. Others have marched with us down nameless streets of the South. They have languished in filthy, roach-infested jails, suffering the abuse and brutality of angry policemen who see them as "dirty nigger lovers." They, unlike so many of their moderate brothers and sisters, have recognized the urgency of the moment and sensed the need for powerful "action" antidotes to combat the disease of segregation.

Let me rush on to mention my other disappointment. I have been so greatly disappointed with the white Church and its leadership. Of course there are some notable exceptions. I am not unmindful of the fact that each of you has taken some significant stands on this issue. I commend you, Rev. Stallings, for your Christian stand on this past Sunday, in welcoming Negroes to your worship service on a nonsegregated basis. I commend the Catholic leaders of this state for integrating Springhill College several years ago.

But despite these notable exceptions I must honestly reiterate that I have been disappointed with the Church. I do not say that as one of those negative critics who can always find something wrong with the Church. I say it as a minister of the gospel, who loves the Church; who was nurtured in its bosom; who has been sustained by its spiritual blessings and who will remain true to it as long as the cord of life shall lengthen.

I had the strange feeling when I was suddenly catapulted into the leadership of the bus protest in Montgomery[11] several years ago that we would have the support of the white Church. I felt that the white ministers, priests, and rabbis of the South would be some of our strongest allies. Instead, some have been outright opponents, refusing to understand the freedom movement and misrepresenting its leaders; all too many others have been more cautious than courageous and have remained silent behind the anesthetizing security of stained glass windows.

In spite of my shattered dreams of the past, I came to Birmingham with the hope that the white religious leadership of the community would see the justice of our cause and, with deep moral concern, serve as the channel through which our just grievances could get to the power structure.

---

[11] **bus protest in Montgomery:** After Rosa Parks was arrested on December 1, 1955, in Montgomery, Alabama, for refusing to give her seat on a bus to a white male passenger, a bus boycott began, which lasted nearly one year and was supported by nearly all of the city's black residents. —EDS.

I had hoped that each of you would understand. But again I have been disappointed.

I have heard numerous religious leaders of the South call upon their worshippers to comply with a desegregation decision because it is the law, but I have longed to hear white ministers say follow this decree because integration is morally right and the Negro is your brother. In the midst of blatant injustices inflicted upon the Negro, I have watched white churches stand on the sideline and merely mouth pious irrelevancies and sanctimonious trivialities. In the midst of a mighty struggle to rid our nation of racial and economic injustice, I have heard so many ministers say, "Those are social issues with which the Gospel has no real concern," and I have watched so many churches commit themselves to a completely otherworldly religion which made a strange distinction between body and soul, the sacred and the secular.

So here we are moving toward the exit of the twentieth century with   35 a religious community largely adjusted to the status quo, standing as a tail-light behind other community agencies rather than a headlight leading men to higher levels of justice.

I have travelled the length and breadth of Alabama, Mississippi, and all the other Southern states. On sweltering summer days and crisp autumn mornings I have looked at her beautiful churches with their spires pointing heavenward. I have beheld the impressive outlay of her massive religious education buildings. Over and over again I have found myself asking: "Who worships here? Who is their God? Where were their voices when the lips of Governor Barnett[12] dripped with words of interposition and nullification? Where were they when Governor Wallace[13] gave the clarion call for defiance and hatred? Where were their voices of support when tired, bruised, and weary Negro men and women decided to rise from the dark dungeons of complacency to the bright hills of creative protest?"

Yes, these questions are still in my mind. In deep disappointment, I have wept over the laxity of the Church. But be assured that my tears have been tears of love. There can be no deep disappointment where there is not deep love. Yes, I love the Church; I love her sacred walls. How could I do otherwise? I am in the rather unique position of being the son, the grandson, and the great grandson of preachers. Yes, I see the Church as the body of Christ. But, oh! How we have blemished and scarred that body through social neglect and fear of being nonconformists.

There was a time when the Church was very powerful. It was during that period when the early Christians rejoiced when they were deemed worthy to suffer for what they believed. In those days the Church was not merely a thermometer that recorded the ideas and principles of popular opinion; it was a thermostat that transformed the mores of society. Wherever the early Christians entered a town the power structure got disturbed and

---

12 ***Governor Barnett:*** Ross R. Barnett, governor of Mississippi from 1960 to 1964.—Eds.
13 ***Governor Wallace:*** George C. Wallace served as governor of Alabama from 1963 to 1966, 1971 to 1979, and 1983 to 1987.—Eds.

immediately sought to convict them for being "disturbers of the peace" and "outside agitators." But they went on with the conviction that they were a "colony of heaven" and had to obey God rather than man. They were small in number but big in commitment. They were too God-intoxicated to be "astronomically intimidated." They brought an end to such ancient evils as infanticide and gladiatorial contest.

Things are different now. The contemporary Church is so often a weak, ineffectual voice with an uncertain sound. It is so often the arch-supporter of the status quo. Far from being disturbed by the presence of the Church, the power structure of the average community is consoled by the Church's silent and often vocal sanction of things as they are.

But the judgment of God is upon the Church as never before. If the Church of today does not recapture the sacrificial spirit of the early Church, it will lose its authentic ring, forfeit the loyalty of millions, and be dismissed as an irrelevant social club with no meaning for the twentieth century. I am meeting young people every day whose disappointment with the Church has risen to outright disgust. 40

Maybe again I have been too optimistic. Is organized religion too inextricably bound to the status quo to save our nation and the world? Maybe I must turn my faith to the inner spiritual Church, the church within the Church, as the true *ecclesia*[14] and the hope of the world. But again I am thankful to God that some noble souls from the ranks of organized religion have broken loose from the paralyzing chains of conformity and joined us as active partners in the struggle for freedom. They have left their secure congregations and walked the streets of Albany, Georgia, with us. They have gone through the highways of the South on torturous rides for freedom. Yes, they have gone to jail with us. Some have been kicked out of their churches and lost the support of their bishops and fellow ministers. But they have gone with the faith that right defeated is stronger than evil triumphant. These men have been the leaven in the lump of the race. Their witness has been the spiritual salt that has preserved the true meaning of the Gospel in these troubled times. They have carved a tunnel of hope through the dark mountain of disappointment.

I hope the Church as a whole will meet the challenge of this decisive hour. But even if the Church does not come to the aid of justice, I have no despair about the future. I have no fear about the outcome of our struggle in Birmingham, even if our motives are presently misunderstood. We will reach the goal of freedom in Birmingham and all over the nation, because the goal of America is freedom. Abused and scorned though we may be, our destiny is tied up with the destiny of America. Before the pilgrims landed at Plymouth, we were here. Before the pen of Jefferson etched across the pages of history the majestic words of the Declaration of Independence, we were here. For more than two centuries our foreparents labored in this country without wages; they made cotton "king"; and they built the homes of their masters in the midst of brutal injustice and shameful humiliation—and yet

---

14 **ecclesia:** The Latin word for church.—EDS.

out of a bottomless vitality they continued to thrive and develop. If the inex-
pressible cruelties of slavery could not stop us, the opposition we now face
will surely fail. We will win our freedom because the sacred heritage of our
nation and the eternal will of God are embodied in our echoing demands.

I must close now. But before closing I am impelled to mention one
other point in your statement that troubled me profoundly. You warmly
commended the Birmingham police force for keeping "order" and "preventing violence." I don't believe you would have so warmly commended
the police force if you had seen its angry violent dogs literally biting six
unarmed, nonviolent Negroes. I don't believe you would so quickly commend the policemen if you would observe their ugly and inhuman treatment of Negroes here in the city jail; if you would watch them push and
curse old Negro women and young Negro girls; if you would see them slap
and kick old Negro men and young Negro boys; if you will observe them,
as they did on two occasions, refuse to give us food because we wanted to
sing our grace together. I'm sorry that I can't join you in your praise for the
police department.

It is true that they have been rather disciplined in their public handling
of the demonstrators. In this sense they have been rather publicly "nonviolent." But for what purpose? To preserve the evil system of segregation. Over
the last few years I have consistently preached that nonviolence demands
that the means we use must be as pure as the ends we seek. So I have tried
to make it clear that it is wrong to use immoral means to attain moral ends.
But now I must affirm that it is just as wrong, or even more so, to use moral
means to preserve immoral ends. Maybe Mr. Connor and his policemen
have been rather publicly nonviolent, as Chief Pritchett[15] was in Albany,
Georgia, but they have used the moral means of nonviolence to maintain the
immoral end of flagrant racial injustice. T. S. Eliot has said that there is no
greater treason than to do the right deed for the wrong reason.

I wish you had commended the Negro sit-inners and demonstrators of   45
Birmingham for their sublime courage, their willingness to suffer, and their
amazing discipline in the midst of the most inhuman provocation. One day
the South will recognize its real heroes. They will be the James Merediths,[16]
courageously and with a majestic sense of purpose, facing jeering and hostile mobs and the agonizing loneliness that characterizes the life of the pio-
neer. They will be old, oppressed, battered Negro women, symbolized in a
seventy-two year old woman of Montgomery, Alabama, who rose up with
a sense of dignity and with her people decided not to ride the segregated
buses, and responded to one who inquired about her tiredness with ungrammatical profundity: "My feets is tired, but my soul is rested." They will be
young high school and college students, young ministers of the gospel and

---

15 ***Chief Pritchett:*** Pritchett served as police chief in Albany, Georgia, during nonviolent demonstrations in 1961 and 1962. Chief Pritchett responded to the nonviolent demonstrations with nonviolence, refusing to allow his officers to physically or verbally abuse the demonstrators. —Eds.

16 ***James Merediths:*** Under the protection of federal marshals and the National Guard in 1962,
James Meredith was the first black man to enroll at the University of Mississippi. —Eds.

a host of the elders, courageously and nonviolently sitting in at lunch counters and willingly going to jail for conscience's sake. One day the South will know that when these disinherited children of God sat down at lunch counters they were in reality standing up for the best in the American dream and the most sacred values in our Judeo-Christian heritage, and thus carrying our whole nation back to great wells of democracy which were dug deep by the founding fathers in the formulation of the Constitution and the Declaration of Independence.

Never before have I written a letter this long (or should I say a book?). I'm afraid that it is much too long to take your precious time. I can assure you that it would have been much shorter if I had been writing from a comfortable desk, but what else is there to do when you are alone for days in the dull monotony of a narrow jail cell other than write long letters, think strange thoughts, and pray long prayers?

If I have said anything in this letter that is an overstatement of the truth and is indicative of an unreasonable impatience, I beg you to forgive me. If I have said anything in this letter that is an understatement of the truth and is indicative of my having a patience that makes me patient with anything less than brotherhood, I beg God to forgive me.

I hope this letter finds you strong in the faith. I also hope that circumstances will soon make it possible for me to meet each of you, not as an integrationist or a civil rights leader, but as a fellow clergyman and a Christian brother. Let us all hope that the dark clouds of racial prejudice will soon pass away and the deep fog of misunderstanding will be lifted from our fear-drenched communities and in some not too distant tomorrow the radiant stars of love and brotherhood will shine over our great nation with all of their scintillating beauty.

Yours for the cause of
Peace and Brotherhood
MARTIN LUTHER KING JR.

The Reader's Presence

1. What does King gain by characterizing his "Fellow Clergymen" as "men of genuine good will," whose criticisms are "sincerely set forth" (paragraph 1)? What evidence can you point to in King's letter to verify the claim that his audience extends far beyond the eight clergymen he explicitly addresses? Comment on the overall structure of King's letter. What principle of composition underpins the structure of his response?

2. King establishes the tone of his response to the criticisms of the clergymen at the end of the opening paragraph: "I would like to answer your statement in what I hope will be patient and reasonable terms." As you reread his letter, identify specific words and phrases—as well as argumentative strategies—that satisfy these criteria that King imposes on himself. In what specific sense does King use the word *hope* here? As you reread his letter, point to each subsequent reference to hope. How does King emphasize the different meanings and connotations of the word as he unfolds his argument?

3. **VISUAL PRESENCE:** Examine carefully the image of the Reverend Martin Luther King Jr. sitting in a jail cell in the Jefferson County Courthouse in Birmingham, Alabama (below). What impression of King does this image convey? What specific details evoke this response? This photograph was taken on October 1, 1967, more than four years after King wrote his famous "Letter from Birmingham Jail." What reasonable inferences can you draw from the image and the context surrounding it?

4. **CONNECTIONS:** This letter has the ring of the oratory for which King was widely known and justly praised. Read passages aloud and note the ways that King appeals to his reader's ear (for example, with the balanced clauses of many of his sentences). How do the cadences of King's prose help to make his point? Compare King's letter with the famous "I Have a Dream" speech (page 628) that he made in the same year. Although one is composed as a letter and the other was delivered as a stirring public address, what elements of language do they share?

The Writer at Work

MARTIN LUTHER KING JR. on Self-Importance

Bettmann/Corbis

In the following piece, the famous African American political leader expresses his profound mistrust of the individual voice that rises above those for whom that voice speaks. In this, as in so many respects, King joins a long tradition of wrestling with the question of how to reconcile one's own creativity with the larger—and vastly more important—word and mission of God. King's spiritual mission was, of course, a social vision as well: that of racial equality in America. In speaking for those who believed with him in the possibility of making this dream a reality, King drew on his consummate skills as a preacher, an orator, and an organizer. Throughout his short public life (spanning only twelve years, ending with his assassination on April 4, 1968, in Memphis, Tennessee), King struggled with the competing claims of personal celebrity and of the community he so forcefully represented. How do King's ideas about representation (standing for and speaking on behalf of others) resonate with the ideas of other notable Americans included in this anthology, for example, Frederick Douglass ("Learning to Read and Write," page 106), James Baldwin ("Notes of a Native Son," page 61), Thomas Jefferson ("The Declaration of Independence," page 623), and Abraham Lincoln ("Gettysburg Address," page 478)?

❝ Would you allow me to share a personal experience with you this morning? And I say it only because I think it has bearing on this message. One of the problems that I have to face and even fight every day is this problem of self-centeredness, this tendency that can so easily come to my life now that I'm something special, that I'm something important. Living over the past year, I can hardly go into any city or any town in this nation where I'm not lavished with hospitality by peoples of all races and of all creeds. I can hardly go anywhere to speak in this nation where hundreds and thousands of people are not turned away because of lack of space. And then after speaking, I often have to be rushed out to get away from the crowd rushing for autographs. I can hardly walk the street in any city of this nation where I'm not confronted with people running up on the street, "Isn't this Reverend King of Alabama?" Living under this it's easy, it's a dangerous tendency that I will come to feel that I'm something special, that I stand somewhere in this universe because of my ingenuity and that I'm important, that I can walk around life with a type of arrogance because of an importance that I have. And one of the prayers that I pray to God every day is: "O God, help me to see my self in my true perspective. Help me, O God, to see that I'm just a symbol of a movement. Help me to see that I'm the victim of what the Germans call a *Zeitgeist* and that something was getting ready to happen in history; history was ready for it. And that a boycott would have taken place in Montgomery, Alabama, if I had never come to Alabama. Help me to realize that I'm where I am because of the forces of history and because of the fifty thousand Negroes of Alabama who will never get their names in the papers and in the headline. O God, help me to see that where I stand today, I stand because others helped me to stand there and because the forces of history projected me there. And this movement would have come in history even if M. L. King had never been born." And when we come to see that, we stand with humility. This is the prayer I pray to God every day, "Lord help me to see M. L. King as M. L. King in his true perspective." Because if I don't see that, I will become the biggest fool in America. **🟆🟆**

Laura Kipnis
AGAINST LOVE

LAURA KIPNIS (b. 1956) is a cultural theorist, an author, and a former videographer whose work blends academic theory, social criticism, and witty analysis, all "richly informed by her post-marxist, post-structuralist, post-feminist, post-everything sense of humor," according to a recent biography. A professor in the school of communications at Northwestern University in Evanston, Illinois, Kipnis is the author of several books, including *Ecstasy Unlimited: On Sex, Capital, Gender, and Aesthetics* (1993), *Bound and Gagged: Pornography and the*

Politics of Fantasy in America (1996), *Against Love: A Polemic* (2003), and *The Female Thing: Dirt, Sex, Envy, Vulnerability* (2006). Kipnis's video essays—including *Ecstasy Unlimited: The Interpenetrations of Sex and Capital* (1985), *A Man's Woman* (1988), and *Marx: The Video* (1990)—have been screened in such venues as the Museum of Modern Art, the American Film Institute, and the Whitney Museum. Kipnis has also written essays and reviews for *Slate*, the *Village Voice*, *Harper's*, *Critical Inquiry*, *Wide Angle*, and the *New York Times Magazine*, where "Against Love" appeared in 2001. Her most recent book, *Men: Notes from an Ongoing Investigation*, was published in 2014.

Kipnis's work has evolved over time, shifting from what was once a strictly academic tone to her more recent playful and casual style. In an interview with the editor of the *Minnesota Review*, she admits that she has developed a growing interest in "creativity" over "theory." She explains, "I trace it back to my art school origins. I started as a painter, actually, and there's something about the writing I've been doing lately which has gotten really intricate and worked over, that reminds me of my origins as a painter. I've started to write in a painterly way, dabbing at it, endlessly revising."

> "It's a polemic, so there are certain questions I don't have to address, or complications I don't have to go into. I can be completely irresponsible. I love it."

In a discussion of *Against Love* in 2001, Kipnis pointed out that "the voice isn't precisely 'me,' it's some far more vivacious and playful version of me. It's a polemic, so there are certain questions I don't have to address, or complications I don't have to go into. I can be completely irresponsible. I love it."

LOVE IS, as we know, a mysterious and controlling force. It has vast power over our thoughts and life decisions. It demands our loyalty, and we, in turn, freely comply. Saying no to love isn't simply heresy; it is tragedy—the failure to achieve what is most essentially human. So deeply internalized is our obedience to this most capricious despot that artists create passionate odes to its cruelty, and audiences seem never to tire of the most deeply unoriginal mass spectacles devoted to rehearsing the litany of its torments, fixating their very beings on the narrowest glimmer of its fleeting satisfactions.

Yet despite near total compliance, a buzz of social nervousness attends the subject. If a society's lexicon of romantic pathologies reveals its particular anxieties, high on our own list would be diagnoses like "inability to settle down" or "immaturity," leveled at those who stray from the norms of domestic coupledom either by refusing entry in the first place or, once installed, pursuing various escape routes: excess independence, ambivalence, "straying," divorce. For the modern lover, "maturity" isn't a depressing signal of impending decrepitude but a sterling achievement, the sine qua non of a lover's qualifications to love and be loved.

This injunction to achieve maturity—synonymous in contemporary usage with thirty-year mortgages, spreading waistlines, and monogamy—obviously finds its raison d'être in modern love's central anxiety, that structuring social contradiction the size of the San Andreas Fault: namely, the expectation that romance and sexual attraction can last a lifetime of coupled togetherness despite much hard evidence to the contrary.

Ever optimistic, heady with love's utopianism, most of us eventually pledge ourselves to unions that will, if successful, far outlast the desire that impelled them into being. The prevailing cultural wisdom is that even if sexual desire tends to be a short-lived phenomenon, "mature love" will kick in to save the day when desire flags. The issue that remains unaddressed is whether cutting off other possibilities of romance and sexual attraction for the more muted pleasures of mature love isn't similar to voluntarily amputating a healthy limb: a lot of anesthesia is required and the phantom pain never entirely abates. But if it behooves a society to convince its citizenry that wanting change means personal failure or wanting to start over is shameful or simply wanting more satisfaction than what you have is an illicit thing, clearly grisly acts of self-mutilation will be required.

There hasn't always been quite such optimism about love's longev-   5
ity. For the Greeks, inventors of democracy and a people not amenable to being pushed around by despots, love was a disordering and thus preferably brief experience. During the reign of courtly love, love was illicit and usually fatal. Passion meant suffering: the happy ending didn't yet exist in the cultural imagination. As far as togetherness as an eternal ideal, the 12th-century advice manual "De Amore et Amoris Remedio" ("On Love and the Remedies of Love") warned that too many opportunities to see or chat with the beloved would certainly decrease love.

The innovation of happy love didn't even enter the vocabulary of romance until the 17th century. Before the 18th century—when the family was primarily an economic unit of production rather than a hothouse of Oedipal tensions—marriages were business arrangements between families; participants had little to say on the matter. Some historians consider romantic love a learned behavior that really only took off in the late 18th century along with the new fashion for reading novels, though even then affection between a husband and wife was considered to be in questionable taste.

Historians disagree, of course. Some tell the story of love as an eternal and unchanging essence; others, as a progress narrative over stifling social conventions. (Sometimes both stories are told at once; consistency isn't required.) But has modern love really set us free? Fond as we are of projecting our own emotional quandaries back through history, construing vivid costume dramas featuring medieval peasants or biblical courtesans sharing their feelings with the post-Freudian savvy of lifelong analysands, our amatory predecessors clearly didn't share all our particular aspirations about their romantic lives.

We, by contrast, feel like failures when love dies. We believe it could be otherwise. Since the cultural expectation is that a state of coupled permanence is achievable, uncoupling is experienced as crisis and inadequacy—even though such failures are more the norm than the exception.

As love has increasingly become the center of all emotional expression in the popular imagination, anxiety about obtaining it in sufficient quantities—and for sufficient duration—suffuses the population. Everyone knows that as the demands and expectations on couples escalated, so did divorce rates. And given the current divorce statistics (roughly 50 percent of all marriages end in divorce), all indications are that whomever you love today—your beacon of hope, the center of all your optimism—has a good chance of becoming your worst nightmare tomorrow. (Of course, that 50 percent are those who actually leave their unhappy marriages and not a particularly good indication of the happiness level or nightmare potential of those who remain.) Lawrence Stone, a historian of marriage, suggests—rather jocularly, you can't help thinking—that today's rising divorce rates are just a modern technique for achieving what was once taken care of far more efficiently by early mortality.

Love may or may not be a universal emotion, but clearly the social   10 forms it takes are infinitely malleable. It is our culture alone that has dedicated itself to allying the turbulence of romance and the rationality of the long-term couple, convinced that both love and sex are obtainable from one person over the course of decades, that desire will manage to sustain itself for thirty or forty or fifty years and that the supposed fate of social stability is tied to sustaining a fleeting experience beyond its given life span.

Of course, the parties involved must "work" at keeping passion alive (and we all know how much fun that is), the presumption being that even after living in close proximity to someone for a historically unprecedented length of time, you will still muster the requisite desire to achieve sexual congress on a regular basis. (Should passion fizzle out, just give up sex. Lack of desire for a mate is never an adequate rationale for "looking elsewhere.") And it is true, many couples do manage to perform enough psychic retooling to reshape the anarchy of desire to the confines of the marriage bed, plugging away at the task year after year (once a week, same time, same position) like diligent assembly-line workers, aided by the occasional fantasy or two to help get the old motor to turn over, or keep running, or complete the trip. And so we have the erotic life of a nation of workaholics: if sex seems like work, clearly you're not working hard enough at it.

But passion must not be allowed to die! The fear—or knowledge—that it does shapes us into particularly conflicted psychological beings, perpetually in search of prescriptions and professional interventions, regardless of cost or consequence. Which does have its economic upside, at least. Whole new sectors of the economy have been spawned, with massive social investment in new technologies from Viagra to couples' porn: capitalism's Lourdes[1] for dying marriages.

There are assorted low-tech solutions to desire's dilemmas too. Take advice. In fact, take more and more advice. Between print, airwaves, and the therapy industry, if there were any way to quantify the GNP in romantic counsel, it would be a staggering number. Desperate to be cured of love's temporality, a love-struck populace has molded itself into an advanced race of advice receptacles, like some new form of miracle sponge that can instantly absorb many times its own body weight in wetness.

Inexplicably, however, a rebellious breakaway faction keeps trying to leap over the wall and emancipate themselves, not from love itself — unthinkable! — but from love's domestic confinements. The escape routes are well trodden — love affairs, midlife crises — though strewn with the left-behind luggage of those who encountered unforeseen obstacles along the way (panic, guilt, self-engineered exposures) and beat self-abashed retreats to their domestic gulags, even after pledging body and soul to new-found loves in the balmy utopias of nondomesticated romances. Will all the adulterers in the audience please stand up? You know who you are. Don't be embarrassed! Adulterers aren't just "playing around." These are our home-grown closet social theorists, because adultery is not just a referendum on the sustainability of monogamy; it is a veiled philosophical discussion about the social contract itself. The question on the table is thus "How much renunciation of desire does society demand of us, versus the degree of gratification it provides?" Clearly, the adulterer's answer, following a long line of venerable social critics, would be, "Too much."

But what exactly is it about the actual lived experience of modern   15
domestic love that would make flight such a compelling option for so many? Let us briefly examine those material daily life conditions.

Fundamentally, to achieve love and qualify for entry into that realm of salvation and transcendence known as the couple (the secular equivalent of entering a state of divine grace), you must *be* a lovable person. And what precisely does being lovable entail? According to the tenets of modern love, it requires an advanced working knowledge of the intricacies of *mutuality*.

Mutuality means recognizing that your partner has needs and being prepared to meet them. This presumes, of course, that the majority of those needs can and should be met by one person. (Question this, and you question the very foundations of the institution. So don't.) These needs of ours run deep, a tangled underground morass of ancient, gnarled roots, looking to ensnarl any hapless soul who might accidentally trod upon their outer radices.

Still, meeting those needs is the most effective way to become the object of another's desire, thus attaining intimacy, which is required to achieve the

---

1 **Lourdes:** Notre Dame de Lourdes in France has been a site of Catholic pilgrimage ever since a fourteen-year-old girl reportedly received a vision there in 1858. — EDS.

state known as psychological maturity. (Despite how closely it reproduces the affective conditions of our childhoods, since trading compliance for love is the earliest social lesson learned; we learn it in our cribs.)

You, in return, will have your own needs met by your partner in matters large and small. In practice, many of these matters turn out to be quite small. Frequently, it is the tensions and disagreements over the minutiae of daily living that stand between couples and their requisite intimacy. Taking out the garbage, tone of voice, a forgotten errand—these are the rocky shoals upon which intimacy so often founders.

Mutuality requires *communication*, since in order to be met, these needs   20 must be expressed. (No one's a mind reader, which is not to say that many of us don't expect this quality in a mate. Who wants to keep having to tell someone what you need?) What you need is for your mate to understand you—your desires, your contradictions, your unique sensitivities, what irks you. (In practice, that means what about your mate irks you.) You, in turn, must learn to understand the mate's needs. This means being willing to hear what about yourself irks your mate. Hearing is not a simple physiological act performed with the ears, as you will learn. You may think you know how to *hear*, but that doesn't mean that you know how to *listen*.

With two individuals required to coexist in enclosed spaces for extended periods of time, domesticity requires substantial quantities of compromise and adaptation simply to avoid mayhem. Yet with the post-Romantic ideal of unconstrained individuality informing our most fundamental ideas of the self, this can prove a perilous process. Both parties must be willing to jettison whatever aspects of individuality might prove irritating while being simultaneously allowed to retain enough individuality to feel their autonomy is not being sacrificed, even as it is being surgically excised.

Having mastered mutuality, you may now proceed to *advanced intimacy*. Advanced intimacy involves inviting your partner "in" to your most interior self. Whatever and wherever our "inside" is, the widespread—if somewhat metaphysical—belief in its existence (and the related belief that whatever is in there is dying to get out) has assumed a quasi-medical status. Leeches once served a similar purpose. Now we "express our feelings" in lieu of our fluids because everyone knows that those who don't are far more prone to cancer, ulcers or various dire ailments.

With love as our culture's patent medicine, prescribed for every ill (now even touted as a necessary precondition for that other great American obsession, longevity), we willingly subject ourselves to any number of arcane procedures in its quest. "Opening up" is required for relationship health, so lovers fashion themselves after doctors wielding long probes to penetrate the tender regions. Try to think of yourself as one big orifice: now stop clenching and relax. If the procedure proves uncomfortable, it just shows you're not open enough. Psychotherapy may be required before sufficient dilation can be achieved: the world's most expensive lubricant.

Needless to say, this opening-up can leave you feeling quite vulnerable, lying there psychically spread-eagled and shivering on the examining table of your relationship. (A favored suspicion is that your partner, knowing exactly where your vulnerabilities are, deliberately kicks you there—one reason this opening-up business may not always feel as pleasant as advertised.) And as anyone who has spent much time in—or just in earshot of—a typical couple knows, the "expression of needs" is often the Trojan horse of intimate warfare, since expressing needs means, by definition, that one's partner has thus far failed to meet them.

In any long-term couple, this lexicon of needs becomes codified over 25 time into a highly evolved private language with its own rules. Let's call this couple grammar. Close observation reveals this as a language composed of one recurring unit of speech: the interdiction—highly nuanced, mutually imposed commands and strictures extending into the most minute areas of household affairs, social life, finances, speech, hygiene, allowable idiosyncrasies and so on. From bathroom to bedroom, car to kitchen, no aspect of coupled life is not subject to scrutiny, negotiation and codes of conduct.

A sample from an inexhaustible list, culled from interviews with numerous members of couples of various ages, races and sexual orientations:

You can't leave the house without saying where you're going. You can't not say what time you'll return. You can't go out when the other person feels like staying at home. You can't be a slob. You can't do less than 50 percent of the work around the house, even if the other person wants to do 100 percent more cleaning than you find necessary or even reasonable. You can't leave the dishes for later, load them the way that seems best to you, drink straight from the carton or make crumbs. You can't leave the bathroom door open—it's offensive. You can't leave the bathroom door closed—your partner needs to get in. You can't not shave your underarms or legs. You can't gain weight. You can't watch soap operas. You can't watch infomercials or the pregame show or Martha Stewart. You can't eat what you want—goodbye Marshmallow Fluff; hello tofu meatballs. You can't spend too much time on the computer. And stay out of those chat rooms. You can't take risks, unless they are agreed-upon risks, which somewhat limits the concept of "risk." You can't make major purchases alone, or spend money on things the other person considers excesses. You can't blow money just because you're in a bad mood, and you can't be in a bad mood without being required to explain it. You can't begin a sentence with "You always. . . ." You can't begin a sentence with "I never. . . ." You can't be simplistic, even when things are simple. You can't say what you really think of that outfit or color combination or cowboy hat. You can't be cynical about things the other person is sincere about. You can't drink without the other person counting your drinks. You can't have the wrong laugh. You can't bum cigarettes when you're out because it embarrasses your mate, even though you've explained the unspoken fraternity between smokers. You can't tailgate, honk or listen to talk radio in the car. And so on. The specifics don't matter. What matters is that the operative word is "can't."

Thus is love obtained.

Certainly, domesticity offers innumerable rewards: companionship, child-rearing convenience, reassuring predictability and many other benefits too varied to list. But if love has power over us, domesticity is its enforcement wing: the iron dust mop in the velvet glove. The historian Michel Foucault[2] has argued that modern power made its mark on the world by inventing new types of enclosures and institutions, places like factories, schools, barracks, prisons and asylums, where individuals could be located, supervised, processed and subjected to inspection, order and the clock. What current social institution is more enclosed than modern intimacy? What offers greater regulation of movement and time, or more precise surveillance of body and thought, to a greater number of individuals?

Of course, it is your choice—as if any of us could really choose not to   30
desire love or not to feel like hopeless losers should we fail at it. We moderns are beings yearning to be filled, yearning to be overtaken by love's mysterious power. We prostrate ourselves at love's portals, like social strivers waiting at the rope line outside some exclusive club hoping to gain admission and thereby confirm our essential worth. A life without love lacks an organizing narrative. A life without love seems so barren, and it might almost make you consider how empty the rest of the world is, as if love were vital plasma and everything else just tap water.

Exchanging obedience for love comes naturally—after all, we all were once children whose survival depended on the caprices of love. And there you have the template for future intimacies. If you love me, you'll do what I want—or need, or demand—and I'll love you in return. We all become household dictators, petty tyrants of the private sphere, who are, in our turn, dictated to.

And why has modern love developed in such a way as to maximize submission and minimize freedom, with so little argument about it? No doubt a citizenry schooled in renouncing desire instead of imagining there could be something more would be, in many respects, advantageous. After all, wanting more is the basis for utopian thinking, a path toward dangerous social demands, even toward imagining the possibilities for altogether different social arrangements. But if the most elegant forms of social control are those that came packaged in the guise of individual needs and satisfactions, so wedded to the individual psyche that any opposing impulse registers as the anxiety of unlovability, who needs a soldier on every corner? We are more than happy to police ourselves and those we love and call it living happily ever after. Perhaps a secular society needed another metaphysical entity to subjugate itself to after the death of God, and love was available for the job. But isn't it a little depressing to think we are somehow incapable of inventing forms of emotional life based on anything other than subjugation? ●

---

2 **Michel Foucault** (1926–1984): French philosopher and historian who questioned assumptions about the constitution of power and knowledge. —Eds.

The Reader's Presence

1. How does Kipnis reevaluate the meaning of adultery and mid-life crises? What sort of evidence are these phenomena, in her opinion?

2. What elements of Kipnis's writing mark this essay as a scholarly argument? Do you agree that it is also a "polemic," as the subtitle of her book indicates? Is it more effective as a scholarly argument or as a polemic? Why?

3. **CONNECTIONS:** Kipnis suggests that society benefits from convincing its populace to marry and that people have been brainwashed into believing that these long-term arrangements are natural. What benefits does society gain from long-term relationships? What, in Kipnis's opinion, do individuals give up? Read John Taylor Gatto's "Against School" (page 607). What, according to his argument, does the individual lose in submitvting to compulsory schooling? Who, according to Gatto, benefits from it?

Bill McKibben

A MORAL ATMOSPHERE

BILL McKIBBEN (b. 1960) advocates human behavior toward Earth that is "sound and elegant and civilized and respectful of community." Born in Palo Alto, California, and raised in Massachusetts, he now lives with his family in New York's Adirondack Mountains. After graduating from Harvard University in 1982, McKibben immediately went to work as a writer, and later as an editor, at the *New Yorker*, where he wrote more than four hundred articles for the magazine's "Talk of the Town" column. His essays, reporting, and criticism appear regularly in publications such as the *Atlantic Monthly*, *Harper's*, the *New York Review of Books*, the *New York Times*, *Orion*, *Rolling Stone*, and *Outside*. McKibben is currently the Schumann Distinguished Scholar in Environmental Studies at Middlebury College in Vermont.

McKibben's 1989 book, *The End of Nature*, sounded one of the earliest alarms about climate change and catalyzed an international debate on the issue that is still ongoing. His long list of books catalogs his concerns about the health of our global ecosystem, particularly the relationship between humanity and nature and the impact of our consumer society on both. His recent books include *The Age of Missing Information* (2006), *Deep Economy: The Wealth of Communities and the Durable Future* (2007), *Fight Global Warming Now: The Handbook for Taking Action in Your Community* (2007), *Eaarth: Making a Life on a Tough New Planet*

(2010), and *Oil and Honey: The Education of an Unlikely Activist* (2013). His collected essays, *The Bill McKibben Reader*, was published in 2008. He's organized several massive global protests calling for attention to the issue of climate change, including the 350.org protests in 2009, which involved 5,200 simultaneous demonstrations in 181 countries. He received the Gandhi Peace award in 2013, and he holds honorary degrees from a dozen colleges.

In a 1999 interview, McKibben discussed the competing visions of what is good for people and the planet: "The market forces pushing convenience, individualism, and comfort are still stronger than the attraction of community, fellowship, and connection with the natural world. . . . What we call the environmental crisis is really a crisis of desire. We're losing the battle to offer people an alternative set of things to desire."

> **"What we call the environmental crisis is really a crisis of desire. We're losing the battle to offer people an alternative set of things to desire."**

McKibben's essay "A Moral Atmosphere" is another call to action concerning climate change, dismissing the idea that we can't take action until we can do so without hypocrisy. It was first published in *Orion* in 2013.

THE LIST OF REASONS for not acting on climate change is long and ever-shifting. First it was "there's no problem"; then it was "the problem's so large there's no hope." There's "China burns stuff too," and "it would hurt the economy," and, of course, "it would hurt the economy." The excuses are getting tired, though. Post Sandy (which hurt the economy to the tune of $100 billion) and the drought ($150 billion), 74 percent of Americans have decided they're very concerned about climate change and want something to happen.[1]

But still, there's one reason that never goes away, one evergreen excuse not to act: "you're a hypocrite." I've heard it ten thousand times myself—how can you complain about climate change and drive a car/have a house/turn on a light/raise a child? This past fall, as I headed across the country on a bus tour to push for divestment from fossil fuels, local newspapers covered each stop. I could predict, with great confidence, what the first online comment from a reader following each account would be: "Do these morons not know that their bus takes gasoline?" In fact, our bus took biodiesel—as we headed down the East Coast, one job was watching the web app that showed the nearest station pumping the good stuff. But it didn't matter, because the next comment would be: "Don't these morons know that the plastic fittings on their bus, and the tires, and the seats are all made from fossil fuels?"

Actually, I do know—even a moron like me. I'm fully aware that we're embedded in the world that fossil fuel has made, that from the moment I

---

[1] Hurricane Sandy ravaged the entire East Coast of the United States in late October 2012; the North American drought has continued since 2012 to impact much of the central and western United States. —EDS.

wake up, almost every action I take somehow burns coal and gas and oil. I've done my best, at my house, to curtail it: we've got solar electricity, and solar hot water, and my new car runs on electricity—I can plug it into the roof and thus into the sun. But I try not to confuse myself into thinking that's helping all that much: it took energy to make the car, and to make every-thing else that streams into my life. I'm still using far more than any respon-sible share of the world's vital stuff.

And, in a sense, that's the point. If those of us who are trying really hard are still fully enmeshed in the fossil fuel system, it makes it even clearer that what needs to change are not individuals but precisely that system. We simply can't move fast enough, one by one, to make any real difference in how the atmosphere comes out. Here's the math, obviously imprecise: maybe 10 percent of the population cares enough to make strenuous efforts to change—maybe 15 percent. If they all do all they can, in their homes and offices and so forth, then, well . . . nothing much shifts. The trajectory of our climate horror stays about the same.

But if 10 percent of people, once they've changed the light bulbs, work   5 all-out to change the system? That's enough. That's more than enough. It would be enough to match the power of the fossil fuel industry, enough to convince our legislators to put a price on carbon. At which point none of us would be required to be saints. We could all be morons, as long as we paid attention to, say, the price of gas and the balance in our checking accounts. Which even dummies like me can manage.

I think more and more people are coming to realize this essential truth. Ten years ago, half the people calling out hypocrites like me were doing it from the left, demanding that we do better. I hear much less of that now, mostly, I think, because everyone who's pursued those changes in good faith has come to realize both their importance and their limitations. Now I hear it mostly from people who have no intention of changing but are starting to feel some psychic tension. They feel a little guilty, and so they dump their guilt on Al Gore because he has two houses. Or they find even lamer targets.

For instance, as college presidents begin to feel the heat about divest-ment, I've heard from several who say, privately, "I'd be more inclined to listen to kids if they didn't show up at college with cars." Which in one sense is fair enough. But in another sense it's avoidance at its most extreme. Young people are asking college presidents to stand up to oil companies. (And the ones doing the loudest asking are often the most painfully idealis-tic, not to mention the hardest on themselves.) If as a college president you *do* stand up to oil companies, then you stand some chance of changing the outcome of the debate, of weakening the industry that has poured billions into climate denial and lobbying against science. The action you're demand-ing of your students—less driving—can't rationally be expected to change the outcome. The action they're demanding of you has at least some chance. That makes you immoral, not them.

Yes, they should definitely take the train to school instead of drive. But unless you're the president of Hogwarts, there's a pretty good chance there's no train that goes there. Your students, in other words, by advocating divestment, have gotten way closer to the heart of the problem than you have. They've taken the lessons they've learned in physics class and political science and sociology and economics and put them to good use. And you—because it would be uncomfortable to act, because you don't want to get crosswise with the board of trustees—have summoned a basically bogus response. If you're a college president making the argument that you won't act until your students stop driving cars, then clearly you've failed morally, but you've also failed intellectually. Even if you just built an energy-efficient fine arts center, and installed a bike path, and dedicated an acre of land to a college garden, you've failed. Even if you drive a Prius, you've failed.

Maybe especially if you drive a Prius. Because there's a certain sense in which Prius-driving can become an out, an excuse for inaction, the twenty-first-century equivalent of "I have a lot of black friends." It's nice to walk/drive the talk; it's much smarter than driving a semi-military vehicle to get your groceries. But it's become utterly clear that doing the right thing in

The fossil fuel system is difficult to avoid.

your personal life, or even on your campus, isn't going to get the job done in time; and it may be providing you with sufficient psychic comfort that you don't feel the need to do the hard things it will take to get the job done. It's in our role as citizens—of campuses, of nations, of the planet—that we're going to have to solve this problem. We each have our jobs, and none of them is easy. ■

The Reader's Presence

1. McKibben observes that the argument asserting activists' hypocrisy for using fossil fuels is simply one example in a long "list of reasons for not acting on climate change" (paragraph 1). What other reasons does he enumerate for not taking action to address this global problem? How does McKibben deal with the fact that he, too, is "embedded in the world that fossil fuel has made" (paragraph 3)? What does McKibben mean when he writes, "everyone who's pursued . . . changes in good faith has come to realize both their importance and their limitations" (paragraph 6)?

2. McKibben discusses the fossil fuel system, a vast commercial network that touches nearly every facet of modern life. How does he address the issue of individual use in such a vast system? What moral and ethical reasons does McKibben summon to reinforce the need for an individual corrective action? What role(s) does he imply students should play in addressing this global problem? What role should college presidents play? On what grounds does McKibben criticize college presidents? How convincing do you find his argument? How might McKibben strengthen this aspect of his argument? What other examples would you use to strengthen or refute his claims?

3. According to McKibben, why is driving a hybrid car not enough action to solve the problem of climate change? Why might choosing to drive a hybrid hinder rather than help the problem? What distinctions does McKibben make between the terms "moral" and "intellectual" with regard to choices we make in response to climate change? To what extent do you agree with the arguments in McKibben's essay? Support your response by summoning specific reasons and evidence.

4. **VISUAL PRESENCE:** Given the spirit and substance of McKibben's argument in "A Moral Atmosphere," what specific words and phrases can you envision that he would adapt from his essay to characterize the parking lot shown on page 671? Be as specific as possible in identifying—and explaining—the appropriateness of the word choices you make.

5. **CONNECTIONS:** Consider the nature and extent of the arguments McKibben enumerates to advocate for individual and collective action in responding to the global problem of climate change. Compare and contrast McKibben's arguments with those Peter Singer offers to address world poverty ("The Singer Solution to World Poverty," page 735). Which writer presents the more convincing and compelling case? Explain why.

Walter Benn Michaels

THE TROUBLE WITH DIVERSITY

WALTER BENN MICHAELS (b. 1948) entered a swirl of controversy—from both right and left—with his 2006 book, *The Trouble with Diversity: How We Learned to Love Identity and Ignore Equality*, his polemic against identity politics and economic inequality on college campuses and in the greater society. In his book, he argues that the thorniest problem in American society is not racism or sexism or any of the other isms but the "increasing gap between the rich and the poor." Michaels received his PhD at the University of California, Santa Barbara, and taught English at the University of California, Berkeley, and at Johns Hopkins University before joining the faculty at the University of Illinois at Chicago, where he has taught American literature and literary theory since 2001. His books and monographs include *The Gold Standard and the Logic of Naturalism: American Literature at the Turn of the Century* (1987), *Our America: Nativism, Modernism, and Pluralism* (1995), *The Shape of the Signifier: 1967 to the End of History* (2004), and *Promises of American Life: 1880–1920* in volume three of the *Cambridge History of American Literature*. His essay "The Trouble with Diversity," excerpted from his 2006 book, appeared in the *American Prospect* in 2006.

> Walter Benn Michaels argues that the thorniest problem in American society is not racism or sexism or any of the other isms but the "increasing gap between the rich and the poor."

In a 2004 essay in the *New York Times Magazine*, Michaels argued that focusing on diversity keeps our eyes off the real problem. "As long as we think that our best universities are fair if they are appropriately diverse, we don't have to worry that most people can't go to them, while others get to do so because they've had the good luck to be born into relatively wealthy families. In other words, as long as the left continues to worry about diversity, the right won't have to worry about inequality."

"THE RICH are different from you and me" is a famous remark supposedly made by F. Scott Fitzgerald to Ernest Hemingway, although what made it famous—or at least made Hemingway famously repeat it—was not the remark itself but Hemingway's reply: "Yes, they have more

macmillanhighered.com/writerspresence8e
Should we, as a society, worry about income inequality?
e-Readings > The White House, *The Buffett Rule* [video]

money." In other words, to Hemingway, the rich really aren't very different from you and me. Fitzgerald's mistake, he thought, was that he mythologized or sentimentalized the rich, treating them as if they were a different kind of person instead of the same kind of person with more money. It was as if, according to Fitzgerald, what made rich people different was not what they *had*—their money—but what they *were*, "a special glamorous race."

To Hemingway, this difference—between what people owned and what they were—seemed obvious. No one cares much about Robert Cohn's money in *The Sun Also Rises*, but everybody feels the force of the fact that he's a "race conscious . . . little kike." And whether or not it's true that Fitzgerald sentimentalized the rich, it's certainly true that he, like Hemingway, believed that the fundamental differences—the ones that really mattered—ran deeper than the question of how much money you had. That's why in *The Great Gatsby*, the fact that Gatsby has made a great deal of money isn't quite enough to win Daisy Buchanan back. Rich as he has become, he's still "Mr. Nobody from Nowhere," not Jay Gatsby but Jimmy Gatz. The change of name is what matters. One way to look at *The Great Gatsby* is as a story about a poor boy who makes good, which is to say, a poor boy who becomes rich—the so-called American Dream. But *Gatsby* is not really about someone who makes a lot of money; it is instead about someone who tries and fails to change who he is. Or, more precisely, it's about someone who pretends to be something he's not; it's about Jimmy Gatz pretending to be Jay Gatsby. If, in the end, Daisy Buchanan is very different from Jimmy Gatz, it's not because she's rich and he isn't but because Fitzgerald treats them as if they really belong to different races, as if poor boys who made a lot of money were only "passing" as rich. "We're all white here," someone says, interrupting one of Tom Buchanan's racist outbursts. Jimmy Gatz isn't quite white enough.

What's important about *The Great Gatsby*, then, is that it takes one kind of difference (the difference between the rich and the poor) and redescribes it as another kind of difference (the difference between the white and the not-so-white). To put the point more generally, books like *The Great Gatsby* (and there have been a great many of them) give us a vision of our society divided into races rather than into economic classes. And this vision has proven to be extraordinarily attractive. Indeed, it has survived even though what we used to think were the races have not. In the 1920s, racial science was in its heyday; now very few scientists believe that there are any such things as races. But many of those who are quick to remind us that there are no biological entities called races are even quicker to remind us that races have not disappeared; they should just be understood as social entities instead. And these social entities have turned out to be remarkably tenacious, both in ways we know are bad and in ways we have come to think of as good. The bad ways involve racism, the inability or refusal to accept people who are different from us. The good ways involve just the opposite: embracing difference, celebrating what we have come to call diversity.

Indeed, in the United States, the commitment to appreciating diversity emerged out of the struggle against racism, and the word diversity itself began to have the importance it does for us today in 1978 when, in *Bakke v. Board of Regents*, the Supreme Court ruled that taking into consideration the race of an applicant to the University of California (the medical school at UC Davis, in this case) was acceptable if it served "the interest of diversity." The Court's point here was significant. It was not asserting that preference in admissions could be given, say, to black people because they had previously been discriminated against. It was saying instead that universities had a legitimate interest in taking race into account in exactly the same way they had a legitimate interest in taking into account what part of the country an applicant came from or what his or her nonacademic interests were. They had, in other words, a legitimate interest in having a "diverse student body," and racial diversity, like geographic diversity, could thus be an acceptable goal for an admissions policy.

Two things happened there. First, even though the concept of diversity   5 was not originally connected with race (universities had long sought diverse student bodies without worrying about race at all), the two now came to be firmly associated. When universities publish their diversity statistics today, they're not talking about how many kids come from Oregon. My university—the University of Illinois at Chicago—is ranked as one of the most diverse in the country, but well over half the students in it come from Chicago. What the rankings measure is the number of African Americans and Asian Americans and Latinos we have, not the number of Chicagoans.

And, second, even though the concept of diversity was introduced as a kind of end run around the historical problem of racism (the whole point was that you could argue for the desirability of a diverse student body without appealing to the history of discrimination against blacks and so without getting accused by people like Alan Bakke of reverse discrimination against whites), the commitment to diversity became deeply associated with the struggle against racism. Indeed, the goal of overcoming racism—of creating a "color-blind" society—was now reconceived as the goal of creating a diverse, that is, a color-conscious, society. Instead of trying to treat people as if their race didn't matter, we would not only recognize but celebrate racial identity. Indeed, race has turned out to be a gateway drug for all kinds of identities, cultural, religious, sexual, even medical. To take what may seem like an extreme case, advocates for the disabled now urge us to stop thinking of disability as a condition to be "cured" or "eliminated" and to start thinking of it instead on the model of race: We don't think black people should want to stop being black; why do we assume the deaf want to hear?

Our commitment to diversity has thus redefined the opposition to discrimination as the appreciation (rather than the elimination) of difference. So with respect to race, the idea is not just that racism is a bad thing (which of course it is) but that race itself is a good thing.

And what makes it a good thing is that it's not class. We love race—we love identity—because we don't love class. We love thinking that the differences that divide us are not the differences between those of us who have money and those who don't but are instead the differences between those who are black and those who are white or Asian or Latino or whatever. A world where some of us don't have money is a world where the differences between us present a problem: the need to get rid of inequality or to justify it. A world where some of us are black and some of us are white—or biracial or Native American or transgendered—is a world where the differences between us present a solution: appreciating our diversity. So we like to talk about the differences we can appreciate, and we don't like to talk about the ones we can't. Indeed, we don't even like to acknowledge that they exist. As survey after survey has shown, Americans are very reluctant to identify themselves as belonging to the lower class and even more reluctant to identify themselves as belonging to the upper class. The class we like is the middle class.

But the fact that we all like to think of ourselves as belonging to the same class doesn't, of course, mean that we actually do belong to the same class. In reality, we obviously and increasingly don't. "The last few decades," as *The Economist* puts it, "have seen a huge increase in inequality in America." The rich *are* different from you and me, and one of the ways they're different is that they're getting richer and we're not. And while it's not surprising that most of the rich and their apologists on the intellectual right are unperturbed by this development, it is at least a little surprising that the intellectual left has managed to remain almost equally unperturbed. Giving priority to issues like affirmative action and committing itself to the celebration of difference, the intellectual left has responded to the increase in economic inequality by insisting on the importance of cultural identity. So for 30 years, while the gap between the rich and the poor has grown larger, we've been urged to respect people's identities—as if the problem of poverty would be solved if we just appreciated the poor. From the economic standpoint, however, what poor people want is not to contribute to diversity but to minimize their contribution to it—they want to stop being poor. Celebrating the diversity of American life has become the American left's way of accepting their poverty, of accepting inequality.

Our current notion of cultural diversity—trumpeted as the repudiation of   10
racism and biological essentialism—in fact grew out of and perpetuates the very concepts it congratulates itself on having escaped. The American love affair with race—especially when you can dress race up as culture—has continued and even intensified. Almost everything we say about culture (that the significant differences between us are cultural, that such differences should be respected, that our cultural heritages should be perpetuated, that there's a value in making sure that different cultures survive) seems to me mistaken. We must shift our focus from cultural diversity to economic equality to help alter the political terrain of contemporary American intellectual life.

In the last year, it has sometimes seemed as if this terrain might in fact be starting to change, and there has been what at least looks like the beginning of a new interest in the problem of economic inequality. Various newspapers have run series noticing the growth of inequality and the decline of class mobility; it turns out, for example, that the Gatsby-style American Dream—poor boy makes good, buys beautiful, beautiful shirts—now has a better chance of coming true in Sweden than it does in America, and as good a chance of coming true in western Europe (which is to say, not very good) as it does here. People have begun to notice also that the intensity of interest in the race of students in our universities has coincided with more or less complete indifference to their wealth. We're getting to the point where there are more black people than poor people in elite universities (even though there are still precious few black people). And Hurricane Katrina—with its televised images of the people left to fend for themselves in drowning New Orleans—provided both a reminder that there still are poor people in America and a vision of what the consequences of that poverty can be.

At the same time, however, the understanding of these issues has proven to be more a symptom of the problem than a diagnosis. In the *Class Matters* series in the *New York Times*, for example, the differences that mattered most turned out to be the ones between the rich and the really rich and between the old rich and the new rich. Indeed, at one point, the *Times* started treating class not as an issue to be addressed in addition to race but as itself a version of race, as if the rich and poor really were different races and so as if the occasional marriage between them were a kind of interracial marriage.

But classes are not like races and cultures, and treating them as if they were—different but equal—is one of our strategies for managing inequality rather than minimizing or eliminating it. White is not better than black, but rich is definitely better than poor. Poor people are an endangered species in elite universities not because the universities put quotas on them (as they did with Jews in the old days) and not even because they can't afford to go to them (Harvard will lend you or even give you the money you need to go there) but because they can't get into them. Hence the irrelevance of most of the proposed solutions to the systematic exclusion of poor people from elite universities, which involve ideas like increased financial aid for students who can't afford the high tuition, support systems for the few poor students who manage to end up there anyway, and, in general, an effort to increase the "cultural capital" of the poor. Today, says David Brooks, "the rich don't exploit the poor, they just out-compete them." And if out-competing people means tying their ankles together and loading them down with extra weight while hiring yourself the most expensive coaches and the best practice facilities, he's right. The entire U.S. school system, from pre-K up, is structured from the very start to enable the rich to out-compete the poor, which is to say, the race is fixed. And the kinds of solutions that might actually make a difference—financing every school district equally, abolishing private schools, making high-quality child care available to every family—are treated as if they were positively un-American.

But it's the response to Katrina that is most illuminating for our purposes, especially the response from the left, not from the right. "Let's be honest,"

Cornel West told an audience at the Paul Robeson Student Center at Rutgers University, "we live in one of the bleakest moments in the history of black people in this nation." "Look at the Super Dome," he went on to say. "It's not a big move from the hull of the slave ship to the living hell of the Super Dome." This is what we might call the "George Bush doesn't care about black people" interpretation of the government's failed response to the catastrophe. But nobody doubts that George Bush cares about Condoleezza Rice, who is very much a black person and who is fond of pointing out that she's been black since birth. And there are, of course, lots of other black people — like Clarence Thomas[1] and Thomas Sowell[2] and Janice Rogers Brown[3] and, at least once upon a time, Colin Powell — for whom George Bush almost certainly has warm feelings. But what American liberals want is for our conservatives to be racists. We want the black people George Bush cares about to be "some of my best friends are black" tokens. We want a fictional George Bush who doesn't care about black people rather than the George Bush we've actually got, one who doesn't care about poor people.

Although that's not quite the right way to put it. First because, for all I   15
know, George Bush does care about poor people; at least he cares as much about poor people as anyone else does. What he doesn't care about — and what Bill Clinton, judging by his eight years in office, didn't much care about, and what John Kerry, judging from his presidential campaign, doesn't much care about, and what we on the so-called left, judging by our own willingness to accept Kerry as the alternative to Bush, don't care about either — is taking any steps to get them to stop being poor. We would much rather get rid of racism than get rid of poverty. And we would much rather celebrate cultural diversity than seek to establish economic equality.

Indeed, diversity has become virtually a sacred concept in American life today. No one's really against it; people tend instead to differ only in their degrees of enthusiasm for it and their ingenuity in pursuing it. Microsoft, for example, is very ingenious indeed. Almost every company has the standard racial and sexual "employee relations groups," just as every college has the standard student groups: African American, Black and Latino Brotherhood, Alliance of South Asians, Chinese Adopted Sibs (this one's pretty cutting-edge), and the standard GLBTQ (the Q is for *Questioning*) support center. But (as reported in a 2003 article in *Workforce Management*) Microsoft also includes groups for "single parents, dads, Singaporean, Malaysian, Hellenic, and Brazilian employees, and one for those with attention deficit disorder." And the same article goes on to quote Patricia Pope, CEO of a diversity management firm in Cincinnati, describing companies that "tackle other

---

[1] *Clarence Thomas* (b. 1948): Associate justice of the Supreme Court of the United States since 1991 and the second African American to serve on the Supreme Court, after Justice Thurgood Marshall. — EDS.

[2] *Thomas Sowell* (b. 1930): An American economist, social commentator, author of numerous books, and a senior fellow of the Hoover Institution. — EDS.

[3] *Janice Rogers Brown* (b. 1949): A federal judge on the United States Court of Appeals for the District of Columbia Circuit and previously an associate justice of the California Supreme Court. — EDS.

differences" like "diversity of birth order" and, most impressive of all, "diversity of thought." If it's a little hard to imagine the diversity of birth order workshops (all the oldest siblings trying to take care of each other, all the youngest competing to be the baby), it's harder still to imagine how the diversity of thought workshops go. What if the diversity of thought is about your sales plan? Are you supposed to reach agreement (but that would eliminate diversity) or celebrate disagreement (but that would eliminate the sales plan)?

Among the most enthusiastic proponents of diversity, needless to say, are the thousands of companies providing "diversity products," from diversity training (a $10-billion-a-year industry) to diversity newsletters (I subscribe to *Diversity Inc.*, but there are dozens of them) to diversity rankings to diversity gifts and clothing—you can "show your support for multiculturalism" *and* "put an end to panty lines" with a "Diversity Rocks Classic Thong" ($9.99). The "Show Me the Money Diversity Venture Capital Conference" says what needs to be said here. But it's not all about the benjamins.[4] There's no money for the government in proclaiming Asian Pacific American Heritage Month (it used to be just a week, but the first President Bush upgraded it) or in Women's History Month or National Disability Employment Awareness Month or Black History Month or American Indian Heritage Month. And there's no money for the Asians, Indians, blacks, and women whose history gets honored.

In fact, the closest thing we have to a holiday that addresses economic inequality instead of identity is Labor Day, which is a product not of the multicultural cheerleading at the end of the 20th century but of the labor unrest at the end of the 19th. The union workers who took a day off to protest President Grover Cleveland's deployment of 12,000 troops to break the Pullman strike weren't campaigning to have their otherness respected. And when, in 1894, their day off was made official, the president of the American Federation of Labor, Samuel Gompers, looked forward not just to a "holiday" but to "the day for which the toilers in past centuries looked forward, when their rights and wrongs would be discussed." The idea was not that they'd celebrate their history but that they'd figure out how to build a stronger labor movement and make the dream of economic justice a reality.

Obviously, it didn't work out that way, either for labor (which is weaker than it's ever been) or for Labor Day (which mainly marks the end of summer). You get bigger crowds, a lot livelier party and a much stronger sense of solidarity for Gay Pride Day. But Gay Pride Day isn't about economic equality, and celebrating diversity shouldn't be an acceptable alternative to seeking economic equality.

In an ideal universe we wouldn't be celebrating diversity at all—we [20] wouldn't even be encouraging it—because in an ideal universe the question of who you wanted to sleep with would be a matter of concern only to

---

[4] **benjamins:** 100-dollar bills; so called because the face of Benjamin Franklin is on the bill. —EDS.

you and to your loved (or unloved) ones. As would your skin color; some people might like it, some people might not, but it would have no political significance whatsoever. Diversity of skin color is something we should happily take for granted, the way we do diversity of hair color. No issue of social justice hangs on appreciating hair color diversity; no issue of social justice hangs on appreciating racial or cultural diversity.

If you're worried about the growing economic inequality in American life, if you suspect that there may be something unjust as well as unpleasant in the spectacle of the rich getting richer and the poor getting poorer, no cause is less worth supporting, no battles are less worth fighting, than the ones we fight for diversity. While some cultural conservatives may wish that everyone should be assimilated to their fantasy of one truly American culture, and while the supposed radicals of the "tenured left" continue to struggle for what they hope will finally become a truly inclusive multiculturalism, the really radical idea of redistributing wealth becomes almost literally unthinkable. In the early 1930s, Senator Huey Long of Louisiana proposed a law making it illegal for anyone to earn more than $1 million a year and for anyone to inherit more than $5 million. Imagine the response if—even suitably adjusted for inflation—any senator were to propose such a law today, cutting off incomes at, say, $15 million a year and inheritances at $75 million. It's not just the numbers that wouldn't fly; it's the whole concept. Long's proposal never became law, but it was popular and debated with some seriousness. Today, such a restriction would seem as outrageous and unnatural as interracial—not to mention gay—marriage would have seemed then. But we don't need to purchase our progress in civil rights at the expense of a commitment to economic justice. More fundamentally still, we should not allow—or we should not continue to allow—the phantasm of respect for difference to take the place of that commitment to economic justice. Commitment to diversity is at best a distraction and at worst an essentially reactionary position that prevents us from putting equality at the center of the national agenda.

Our identity is the least important thing about us. And yet, it is the thing we have become most committed to talking about. From the standpoint of a left politics, this is a profound mistake since what it means is that the political left—increasingly invested in the celebration of diversity and the redress of historical grievance—has converted itself into the accomplice rather than the opponent of the right. Diversity has become the left's way of doing neoliberalism, and antiracism has become the left's contribution to enhancing market efficiency. The old Socialist leader Eugene Debs used to be criticized for being unwilling to interest himself in any social reform that didn't involve attacking economic inequality. The situation now is almost exactly the opposite; the left obsessively interests itself in issues that have nothing to do with economic inequality.

And, not content with pretending that our real problem is cultural difference rather than economic difference, we have also started to treat economic difference as if it were cultural difference. So now we're urged to be more respectful of poor people and to stop thinking of them as victims, since to treat them as victims is condescending—it denies them their "agency." And if we can stop thinking of the poor as people who have too little money and start thinking of them instead as people who have too little respect, then it's our attitude toward the poor, not their poverty, that becomes the problem to be solved, and we can focus our efforts of reform not on getting rid of classes but on getting rid of what we like to call classism. The trick, in other words, is to stop thinking of poverty as a disadvantage, and once you stop thinking of it as a disadvantage then, of course, you no longer need to worry about getting rid of it. More generally, the trick is to think of inequality as a consequence of our prejudices rather than as a consequence of our social system and thus to turn the project of creating a more egalitarian society into the project of getting people (ourselves and, especially, others) to stop being racist, sexist, classist homophobes. The starting point for a progressive politics should be to attack that trick. ▪

The Reader's Presence

1. According to Michaels, why does celebrating diversity distract us from minimizing inequality? Specifically, how does Michaels establish connections between race and class? What would happen if we followed his advice and focused only on economic inequalities? For example, describe how colleges would be affected if they did not take the diversity of their student body into account during the admissions process. Michaels is not specific about how eliminating race as a political category will eliminate class as a social misery. Applying Michaels's logic to his Hurricane Katrina example (paragraph 14), how would ignoring race have led to a better response for the hurricane's victims?

2. Michaels skillfully uses wit and humor at strategic moments in his essay. Consider, for example, such lines as "what poor people want is not to contribute to diversity but to minimize their contribution to it" (paragraph 9). What are the effects of using wit and humor to write about such a serious subject? What risks does Michaels take in doing so? How effectively would his essay read if such wit and humor were omitted? In formulating your response, identify a few humorous or witty moments and rewrite them with a serious tone. How did changing the tone affect the argument? Do you think a reader would be more—or less—convinced by an argument that was formulated without wit and humor? Explain why.

3. **CONNECTIONS:** Compare and contrast Michaels's argument about "The Trouble with Diversity" with David Brooks's ideas in "People Like Us" (page 356). For example, contrast the opening two sentences in Brooks's essay—"Maybe it's time to admit the obvious. We don't really care about diversity all that much in America, even though we talk about it a great deal"—with the tone and direction Michaels sets for his readers in the opening of his essay. What would Brooks make of Michaels's assertion that "[n]o issue of social justice hangs on appreciating racial or cultural diversity" (paragraph 20)? What standards of evidence and argument do Michaels and Brooks use to evaluate cultural claims about race and class? Which essay do you find more informative? more convincing? Explain why by pointing to specific passages from each essay.

Walter Mosley

GET HAPPY

WALTER MOSLEY (b. 1952) is best known for his popular crime novels, but he is also one of the most versatile writers in contemporary American literature, penning literary fiction as well as science fiction, political writing, young adult novels, and plays. He is the author of over forty books, which have been translated into more than twenty languages worldwide. He is the recipient of PEN America's Lifetime Achievement Award, and his essays have appeared in magazines such as the *New York Times Magazine* and *The Nation*. His mother was Jewish, the daughter of Russian immigrants, and his father was African American, and he has said that he identifies with both groups. Growing up in the Los Angeles area in the 1950s and 1960s, he was witness to a great deal of racial

> **"There are serious cracks in the veneer of our progress."**

conflict, and he is an outspoken critic of race relations in the United States. He recently said, "Things seem better, but there are serious cracks in the veneer of our progress. Injustices such as the one committed against Trayvon Martin have reared their ugly heads since before Emmett Till's murder in 1955." This concern with racial injustice often appears in the context of his fiction and nonfiction. He has cited Langston Hughes and Raymond Chandler among his influences. "Get Happy" originally appeared in *The Nation* in October 2009.

We hold these truths to be self evident, that all men are created equal, that they are endowed by their Creator with certain unalienable rights, that among these are Life, Liberty, and the pursuit of Happiness.

AMERICANS ARE AN UNHAPPY, UNHEALTHY LOT. From the moment we declared our independence from the domination of British rule, we have included the people's right to pursue happiness as one of the primary privileges of our citizens and the responsibility of our government. Life and liberty are addressed to one degree or another by our executive, legislative and judicial branches, but our potential for happiness has lagged far behind.

As the quote above says (and does not say), freedom was once the province of white men; now the lack of that freedom and the subsequent loss of the potential for happiness belongs to all of us. Our happiness is kept from us by prisonlike schools and meaningless jobs, un(der)employment and untreated physical and psychological ailments, by political leaders who scare the votes out of us and corporate "persons" that buy up all the resources that have been created and defined by our labor.

Citizens are not treated like members of society but more like employees who can be cut loose for any reason large or small, whether that reason be an individual action or some greater event like the downturn of the stock market. We are lied to by our leaders and the mass media to such a great extent that it's almost impossible to lay a finger on one thing that we can say, unequivocally, is true. We wage a "war on drugs" while our psychiatrists prescribe mood-altering medicines at an alarming rate. We eat and drink and smoke too much, and sleep too little. We worry about health and taxes and the stock market until one of the three finally drags us down. We fall for all sorts of get-rich-quick schemes, from the stock market to the lottery. We practice rampant consumerism, launch perpetual wars and seek out meaningless sex.

Through these studies we create aberrant citizens who glean their empty and impossible hopes from television, the Internet and stadium sports. These issues, and others, form the seat of our discontent, a throne of nails under a crown of thorns.

Happiness is considered by most to be a subset of wealth, which is not   5 necessarily true. But even if it was true, most Americans are not wealthy, and most of those who are will lose that wealth before they die. Besides, money cannot buy happiness. It can buy bigger TVs and comelier sex partners; it can pay for liposuction and enough fossil fuel to speed away from smog-filled urban sprawls. Money can influence court verdicts, but it cannot buy justice. And without the bedrock of justice, how can any American citizen be truly happy?

Happiness is a state of mind cultivated under a sophisticated understanding of a rapidly changing world. In times gone by the world didn't change so fast. As recently as the early twentieth century it would take a generation or more for knowledge to double; now the sum total of our knowledge doubles each year, perhaps even less than that. As technology and technique change, so does our world and our reactions to it. The Internet, gene-splicing, transportation, overpopulation and other vast areas of ever-growing knowledge and experience force significant changes in our lifestyles every few years.

The pursuit of happiness implies room to move, but the definition of that space has changed—from open fields to Internet providers, from talk with a friend or religious leader to psychotherapy and antidepresssion drugs.

If you are reading this essay and believe that you and the majority of your fellows are happy, content, satisfied and generally pleased with the potentials presented to you and others, then you don't have to continue reading. I certainly do not wish to bring unhappiness to anyone who feels they fit into this world like a pampered foot into a sheepskin slipper.

Some of us are naturally happy; others have had the good fortune to be born at the right moment, in the right place. But many of us suffer under a corporatized bureaucracy where homelessness, illiteracy, poverty, malnourishment (both physical and spiritual) and an unrelenting malaise are not only possible but likely.

One cure—for those who feel that their pursuit of happiness has been sent on a long detour through the labor camps of American and international capitalism—is the institution of a government department that has as its only priority the happiness of all Americans.

At first blush this might seem like a frivolous suggestion. Each and every American is responsible for her or his own happiness, whatever that is, you might say. Furthermore, even if a government department was designed to monitor, propagate and ensure the happiness of our citizens, that department should not have the power or even the desire to enforce its conclusions on anyone.

But the suggestion here is to expand the possibilities for happiness, not to codify or impose these possibilities. Our Declaration of Independence says that the pursuit of happiness is an "unalienable right." This language seems to make the claim that it is a government responsibility to ensure that all Americans, or as many as possible, are given a clear path toward that pursuit.

This is not and cannot be some rocky roadway through a barren landscape. Our world is more like the tropics, crowded by a lush forest of fast-growing knowledge. The path must be cleared every day. How can a normal person be happy with herself in this world, when the definition of the world is changing almost hourly?

What we need is a durable and yet flexible definition (created by study and consensus) that will impact the other branches of government. If we can, through a central agency, begin to come to a general awareness of what we need to clear the path to the pursuit of happiness, I believe that the lives we are living stand a chance of being more satisfying. If we can have a dialogue based on our forefathers' declaration, I believe that we can tame the shadowy government and corporate incursions into our lives.

What do we need to be assured of our own path to a contented existence? Enough food to eat? Health? Help with childcare? A decent, fulfilling education? Should we feel that the land we stand on is ours? Or that our welfare is the most important job of a government that is made up by our shared citizenship?

These simple interrogations are complex in their nature. All paths are not the same; many conflict. But we need a government that assures us the promise of the Declaration of Independence. We need to realize that the ever more convoluted world of knowledge can flummox even the greatest minds. We need to concentrate on our own happiness if we expect to make a difference in the careening technological and slovenly evolving social world of the twenty-first century.

The Reader's Presence

1. What does Mosley gain by including as an epigraph the opening lines from the Declaration of Independence? To what extent do you agree with Mosley that in comparison to life and liberty, "our potential for happiness has lagged far behind" (paragraph 1)? How does Mosley's definition of happiness ("a state of mind cultivated under a sophisticated understanding of a rapidly changing world," paragraph 6) relate to the fact that the "pursuit of happiness has been sent on a long detour" (paragraph 10)?

2. What is your reaction to Mosley's invitation to stop reading in the eighth paragraph? Where you tempted to stop reading? Explain why or why not. What does Mosley potentially gain or lose by suggesting this proposition in his essay? Do you think he intends his offer to be taken seriously, or is he being facetious? What evidence can you identify to support your response? What larger point does he make here about our general sense of unhappiness?

3. How convincing do you find Mosley's suggestion that a government department be established to help Americans in their "pursuit of happiness"? To what extent do you think the happiness/unhappiness Mosley discusses is the same as that mentioned in the Declaration of Independence? Explain your response.

4. **CONNECTIONS:**   How is Mosley's appeal "to expand the possibilities for happiness" (paragraph 12) similar to—and different from—Daniel Gilbert's idea that uncertainty and ignorance lead to unhappiness ("What You Don't Know Makes You Nervous," page 417)? How convincing do you find Gilbert's suggestion that bringing attention to our general unhappiness and identifying the factors standing in the way of our "unalienable right" will help Americans to cease being "stranded in an unhappy present" (Gilbert, paragraph 12)? How do you think Gilbert would respond to Mosley's idea to establish a government agency focused on improving "the happiness of all Americans" (paragraph 10)?

Barack Obama

GRANT PARK VICTORY SPEECH

America's forty-fourth president, **BARACK OBAMA** (b. 1961) was born in Honolulu, Hawaii, to a Kansas-born American mother and a Kenyan father, who met and married when they were students at the University of Hawaii. The effects of his parent's interracial marriage, his father's return to Kenya, and his parents' subsequent divorce when he was very young are central to his memoir, *Dreams from My Father: A Story of Race and Inheritance* (1995;

reprinted in 2004). A 1995 review in the *New York Times Book Review* said that Obama's memoir "persuasively describes the phenomenon of belonging to two different worlds, and thus belonging to neither." After graduating from Columbia University in 1983, Obama worked as a community organizer in Chicago, then went on to Harvard University, where he became the first African American president of the *Harvard Law Review*; he received his law degree in 1991. Turning down a prestigious judicial clerkship, he chose instead to practice civil rights law in Chicago and to teach constitutional law at the University of Chicago. He served in the Illinois State Senate from 1997 to 2003 and was elected to the U.S. Senate in 2004. In addition to his memoir, Obama wrote *The Audacity of Hope: Thoughts on Reclaiming the American Dream*, published in 2006. In 2009, Barack Obama received the Nobel Peace Prize "for his extraordinary efforts to strengthen international diplomacy and cooperation between peoples . . ." and particularly for his "vision of and work for a world without nuclear weapons." This speech was given in Grant Park in Chicago, Illinois, on November 4, 2008, the night Obama won his first presidential election.

> In 2009, Barack Obama received the Nobel Peace Prize "for his extraordinary efforts to strengthen international diplomacy and cooperation between peoples."

"HELLO, CHICAGO!"

If there is anyone out there who still doubts that America is a place where all things are possible; who still wonders if the dream of our founders is alive in our time; who still questions the power of our democracy, tonight is your answer.

It's the answer told by lines that stretched around schools and churches in numbers this nation has never seen; by people who waited three hours and four hours, many for the very first time in their lives, because they believed that this time must be different; that their voice could be that difference.

It's the answer spoken by young and old, rich and poor, Democrat and Republican, black, white, Latino, Asian, Native American, gay, straight, disabled and not disabled—Americans who sent a message to the world that we have never been a collection of red states and blue states; we are, and always will be, the United States of America.

It's the answer that led those who have been told for so long by so many to be cynical, and fearful, and doubtful of what we can achieve to put their hands on the arc of history and bend it once more toward the hope of a better day. 5

It's been a long time coming, but tonight, because of what we did on this day, in this election, at this defining moment, change has come to America.

I just received a very gracious call from Sen. McCain. He fought long and hard in this campaign, and he's fought even longer and harder for the country he loves. He has endured sacrifices for America that most of us cannot begin to imagine, and we are better off for the service rendered by this brave and selfless leader. I congratulate him and Gov. Palin for all they have achieved, and I look forward to working with them to renew this nation's promise in the months ahead.

I want to thank my partner in this journey, a man who campaigned from his heart and spoke for the men and women he grew up with on the streets of Scranton and rode with on that train home to Delaware, the vice-president-elect of the United States, Joe Biden.

I would not be standing here tonight without the unyielding support of my best friend for the last 16 years, the rock of our family and the love of my life, our nation's next first lady, Michelle Obama. Sasha and Malia, I love you both so much, and you have earned the new puppy that's coming with us to the White House. And while she's no longer with us, I know my grandmother is watching, along with the family that made me who I am. I miss them tonight, and know that my debt to them is beyond measure.

President-elect Barack Obama addresses his supporters in Chicago's Grant Park, following his election-night victory on November 4, 2008.

Eric Thayer/Getty Images

To my campaign manager, David Plouffe; my chief strategist, David 10
Axelrod; and the best campaign team ever assembled in the history of politics—you made this happen, and I am forever grateful for what you've sacrificed to get it done.

But above all, I will never forget who this victory truly belongs to—it
belongs to you.

I was never the likeliest candidate for this office. We didn't start with
much money or many endorsements. Our campaign was not hatched in the
halls of Washington—it began in the backyards of Des Moines and the living rooms of Concord and the front porches of Charleston.

It was built by working men and women who dug into what little savings they had to give $5 and $10 and $20 to this cause. It grew strength
from the young people who rejected the myth of their generation's apathy;
who left their homes and their families for jobs that offered little pay and
less sleep; from the not-so-young people who braved the bitter cold and
scorching heat to knock on the doors of perfect strangers; from the millions
of Americans who volunteered and organized, and proved that more than
two centuries later, a government of the people, by the people and for the
people has not perished from this earth. This is your victory.

I know you didn't do this just to win an election, and I know you didn't
do it for me. You did it because you understand the enormity of the task that
lies ahead. For even as we celebrate tonight, we know the challenges that
tomorrow will bring are the greatest of our lifetime—two wars, a planet in
peril, the worst financial crisis in a century. Even as we stand here tonight,
we know there are brave Americans waking up in the deserts of Iraq and
the mountains of Afghanistan to risk their lives for us. There are mothers
and fathers who will lie awake after their children fall asleep and wonder
how they'll make the mortgage, or pay their doctor's bills, or save enough
for college. There is new energy to harness and new jobs to be created; new
schools to build and threats to meet and alliances to repair.

The road ahead will be long. Our climb will be steep. We may not get 15
there in one year, or even one term, but America—I have never been more
hopeful than I am tonight that we will get there. I promise you: We as a
people will get there.

There will be setbacks and false starts. There are many who won't agree
with every decision or policy I make as president, and we know that government can't solve every problem. But I will always be honest with you about
the challenges we face. I will listen to you, especially when we disagree.
And, above all, I will ask that you join in the work of remaking this nation
the only way it's been done in America for 221 years—block by block, brick
by brick, callused hand by callused hand.

What began 21 months ago in the depths of winter must not end on this
autumn night. This victory alone is not the change we seek—it is only the
chance for us to make that change. And that cannot happen if we go back to
the way things were. It cannot happen without you.

So let us summon a new spirit of patriotism; of service and responsibility where each of us resolves to pitch in and work harder and look after not only ourselves, but each other. Let us remember that if this financial crisis taught us anything, it's that we cannot have a thriving Wall Street while Main Street suffers. In this country, we rise or fall as one nation—as one people.

Let us resist the temptation to fall back on the same partisanship and pettiness and immaturity that has poisoned our politics for so long. Let us remember that it was a man from this state who first carried the banner of the Republican Party to the White House—a party founded on the values of self-reliance, individual liberty and national unity. Those are values we all share, and while the Democratic Party has won a great victory tonight, we do so with a measure of humility and determination to heal the divides that have held back our progress.

As Lincoln said to a nation far more divided than ours, "We are not enemies, but friends. . . . Though passion may have strained, it must not break our bonds of affection." And, to those Americans whose support I have yet to earn, I may not have won your vote, but I hear your voices, I need your help, and I will be your president, too. 20

And to all those watching tonight from beyond our shores, from parliaments and palaces to those who are huddled around radios in the forgotten corners of our world—our stories are singular, but our destiny is shared, and a new dawn of American leadership is at hand. To those who would tear this world down: We will defeat you. To those who seek peace and security: We support you. And to all those who have wondered if America's beacon still burns as bright: Tonight, we proved once more that the true strength of our nation comes not from the might of our arms or the scale of our wealth, but from the enduring power of our ideals: democracy, liberty, opportunity and unyielding hope.

For that is the true genius of America—that America can change. Our union can be perfected. And what we have already achieved gives us hope for what we can and must achieve tomorrow.

This election had many firsts and many stories that will be told for generations. But one that's on my mind tonight is about a woman who cast her ballot in Atlanta. She's a lot like the millions of others who stood in line to make their voice heard in this election, except for one thing: Ann Nixon Cooper is 106 years old.

She was born just a generation past slavery; a time when there were no cars on the road or planes in the sky; when someone like her couldn't vote for two reasons—because she was a woman and because of the color of her skin.

And tonight, I think about all that she's seen throughout her century in America—the heartache and the hope; the struggle and the progress; the times we were told that we can't and the people who pressed on with that American creed: Yes we can. 25

At a time when women's voices were silenced and their hopes dismissed, she lived to see them stand up and speak out and reach for the ballot. Yes, we can.

When there was despair in the Dust Bowl and depression across the land, she saw a nation conquer fear itself with a New Deal, new jobs and a new sense of common purpose. Yes, we can.

When the bombs fell on our harbor and tyranny threatened the world, she was there to witness a generation rise to greatness and a democracy was saved. Yes, we can.

She was there for the buses in Montgomery, the hoses in Birmingham, a bridge in Selma and a preacher from Atlanta who told a people that "We Shall Overcome." Yes, we can.

A man touched down on the moon, a wall came down in Berlin, a world   30
was connected by our own science and imagination. And this year, in this election, she touched her finger to a screen and cast her vote, because after 106 years in America, through the best of times and the darkest of hours, she knows how America can change. Yes, we can.

America, we have come so far. We have seen so much. But there is so much more to do. So tonight, let us ask ourselves: If our children should live to see the next century; if my daughters should be so lucky to live as long as Ann Nixon Cooper, what change will they see? What progress will we have made?

This is our chance to answer that call. This is our moment. This is our time — to put our people back to work and open doors of opportunity for our kids; to restore prosperity and promote the cause of peace; to reclaim the American Dream and reaffirm that fundamental truth that out of many, we are one; that while we breathe, we hope, and where we are met with cynicism, and doubt, and those who tell us that we can't, we will respond with that timeless creed that sums up the spirit of a people: Yes, we can.

Thank you, God bless you, and may God bless the United States of America. ▮

The Reader's Presence

1. In the second sentence of Obama's public address on November 4, 2008, the night he was declared the winner of the popular vote to be the next president of the United States of America, he invokes two classic myths about America: "a place where all things are possible" and a place where "the dream of our founders is alive in our time." At what other points in his speech — and with what specific effects — does President-elect Obama introduce other myths about America? What popular political myths does he invoke and then deny?

2. Obama uses a classical rhetorical strategy, anaphora — the repetition of a word or phrase at the beginning of successive phrases, clauses, or sentences — at the beginning of the third, fourth, and fifth paragraphs. Identify, and comment on the effectiveness of, other instances of repetition (of diction, phrasing, and imagery)

throughout Obama's speech. Choose one example and explain why you think it is especially effective.

3. **VISUAL PRESENCE:**   In what specific ways are the images presented in this photograph of President Barack Obama's election-night victory speech (page 687) consistent with or different from the language of his remarks that evening?

4. **CONNECTIONS:**   During the course of his address, Obama also makes several historical allusions and invokes several figures in American history, including Abraham Lincoln and Martin Luther King Jr. After you have reread Obama's "Victory Speech," examine it in relation to Lincoln's "Gettysburg Address" (page 478) and King's address ("I Have a Dream," page 628) delivered as the culmination of the March on Washington on August 28, 1963. What specific thematic, rhetorical, and stylistic connections can you establish between and among these three historic speeches to the American public?

Camille Paglia

THE PITFALLS OF PLASTIC SURGERY

CAMILLE PAGLIA (b. 1947), academic, author, and *Salon*'s "fave pop intellectual," earned her PhD at Yale University and taught at Bennington College, Wesleyan University, and Yale University. In 1984, she joined the faculty at the University of the Arts in Philadelphia, where she is professor of humanities and media studies. Her academic study, and first book, *Sexual Personae: Art and Decadence from Nefertiti to Emily Dickinson* (1990) caused heated debate and launched her career as a noted feminist, cultural critic, and social commentator. By early 1991, she was featured on the cover of *New York Magazine*, under the headline "Woman Warrior." In 1992, her

> "That 700-page tome was a round-the-clock operation, requiring a fanaticism of attention and persistence that could not possibly have been combined with a responsible family life."

second book, *Sex, Art, and American Culture*, was published, followed by *Vamps & Tramps* (1994). In 1998, she published a volume about Alfred Hitchcock's film *The Birds*, for the British Film Institute Films Classics series. Her latest books are *Break, Blow, Burn: Camille Paglia Reads Forty-Three of the World's Best Poems*

|||

(2005) and *Glittering Images: A Journey Through Art from Egypt to Star Wars* (2012). Paglia is a founding contributor to *Salon*; and she writes about art, literature, culture, media, and politics for numerous publications throughout the world, including the *Advocate*, the *New York Times*, the *Independent* of London, the *American Enterprise*, and *Harper's Bazaar*, where "The Pitfalls of Plastic Surgery" appeared in 2005.

Paglia describes her life after turning sixty and becoming a parent, with her partner, of a baby boy—and reveals the trials of writing her first book. "I'm deeply enjoying being a parent—which I certainly would not have been able to do while I was writing *Sexual Personae* for 20 years," she told an interviewer. "That 700-page tome was a round-the-clock operation, requiring a fanaticism of attention and persistence that could not possibly have been combined with a responsible family life."

PLASTIC SURGERY is living sculpture: a triumph of modern medicine. As a revision of nature, cosmetic surgery symbolizes the conquest of biology by human free will. With new faces and bodies, people have become their own works of art.

Once largely confined to the entertainment and fashion industries, plastic surgery has become routine in the corporate workplace in the U.S., even for men. A refreshed, youthful look is now considered essential for job retention and advancement in high-profile careers. As cosmetic surgery has become more widespread and affordable, it has virtually become a civil right, an equal-opportunity privilege once enjoyed primarily by a moneyed elite who could fly to Brazil for a discreet nip and tuck.

The questions raised about plastic surgery often have a moralistic hue. Is cosmetic surgery a wasteful frivolity, an exercise in narcissism? Does the pressure for alteration of face and body fall more heavily on women because of endemic sexism? And are coercive racist stereotypes at work in the trend among black women to thin their noses and among Asian women to "Westernize" their eyes?

All these ethical issues deserve serious attention. But nothing, I submit, will stop the drive of the human species toward beauty and the shimmering illusion of perfection. It is one of our deepest and finest instincts. From prehistory on, tribal peoples flattened their skulls, pierced their noses, elongated their necks, stretched their earlobes and scarred or tattooed their entire bodies to achieve the most admired look. Mutilation is in the eye of the beholder.

Though cosmetic surgery is undoubtedly an unstoppable movement, we   5
may still ask whether its current application can be improved. I have not had surgery and have no plans to do so, on the theory that women intellectuals, at least, should perhaps try to hold out. (On the other hand, one doesn't want to scare the horses!) Over the past 15 years, I have become increasingly uneasy about ruling styles of plastic surgery in the U.S. What norms are being imposed on adult or aging women?

I would suggest that the current models upon which many American surgeons are basing their reworking of the female face and body are far too parochial. The eye can be retrained over time, and so we have come to accept a diminished and even demeaning view of woman as ingenue, a perky figure of ingratiating girliness. Neither sex bomb nor dominatrix, she is a cutesy sex kitten without claws.

In the great era of the Hollywood studio system, from the 1920s to the early '60s, pioneering makeup techniques achieved what plastic surgery does now to remold the appearance of both male and female stars. For example, the mature Lana Turner[1] of *Imitation of Life* or *Peyton Place* was made to look like a superglamorous and ravishingly sensual version of a woman of Turner's own age. The problem today is that Hollywood expects middle-aged female actors to look 20 or even 30 years younger than they are. The ideal has become the bouncy Barbie doll or simpering nymphet, not a sophisticated woman of the world. Women's faces are erased, blanked out as in a cartoon. In Europe, in contrast, older women are still considered sexy: Women are granted the dignity of accumulated experience. The European woman has a reserve or mystique because of her assumed mastery of the esoteric arts of love.

Why this cultural discrepancy? Many of the founders of Hollywood, from studio moguls to directors, screenwriters, makeup artists, and composers, were European émigrés whose social background ranged from peasant to professional. European models of beauty are based on classical precedents: on luminous Greek sculpture, with its mathematical symmetry and proportion, or on Old Master oil paintings, with their magnificent portraiture of elegant aristocrats and hypnotic femme fatales. As an upstart popular form with trashy roots in nickelodeons and penny arcades, Hollywood movies strove to elevate their prestige by invoking a noble past. The studios presented their stable of stars as a Greek pantheon of resurrected divinities, sex symbols with an unattainable grandeur.

But Hollywood's grounding in great art has vanished. In this blockbuster era of computerized special effects and slam-bang action-adventure films, few producers and directors root their genre in the ancestry of the fine arts. On the contrary, they are more likely to be inspired by snarky television sitcoms or holographic video games, with their fantasy cast of overmuscled heroes and pneumatic vixens. The profound influence of video games can be seen in the redefining of today's ultimate female body type, inspired by Amazonian superheroines like Lara Croft: large breasts with a flat midriff and lean hips, a hormonally anomalous profile that few women can attain without surgical intervention and liposuction.

Maximizing one's attractiveness and desirability is a justifiable aim   10
in any society, except for the most puritanical. But it is worrisome that the American standard of female sexual allure may be regressing. In the post-1960s culture of easy divorce on demand, middle-aged women have found

---

1 ***Lana Turner*** (1921–1995): One of Hollywood's most glamorous stars in the 1940s and 1950s, Turner appeared in countless films, including *Peyton Place* (1957) and *Imitation of Life* (1959).

themselves competing with nubile women in their 20s, who are being scooped up as trophy second wives by ambitious men having a midlife crisis. Cosmetic surgery seems to level the playing field. But at what cost?

Good surgery discovers and reveals personality; bad surgery obscures or distorts it. The facial mask should not be frozen or robotic. We still don't know what neurological risks there might be in long term use of nonsurgical Botox, a toxin injected subcutaneously to paralyze facial muscles and smooth out furrows and wrinkles. What is clear, however, is that unskilled practitioners are sometimes administering Botox in excessive amounts, so that even major celebrities in their late 30s and 40s can be seen at public events with frighteningly waxen, mummified foreheads. Actors who overuse Botox are forfeiting the mobile expressiveness necessary to portray character. We will probably never again see "great faces" among accomplished older women—the kind of severe, imperious, craggy look of formidable visionaries like Diana Vreeland or Lillian Hellman.[2]

The urgent problem is that today's cosmetic surgeons are drawing from too limited a repertoire of images. Plastic surgery is an art form: Therefore, surgeons need training in art as well as medicine. Without a broader visual vocabulary, too many surgeons will continue to homogenize women, divesting them of authority and reducing them to a generic cookie-cutter sameness. And without a gift for psychology, surgeons cannot intuit and reinforce a woman's unique personality.

For cosmetic surgery to maintain or regain subtlety and nuance, surgeons should meditate on great painting and sculpture. And women themselves must draw the line against seeking and perpetuating an artificial juvenility that obliterates their own cultural value. ▣

The Reader's Presence

1. How would you describe Paglia's attitude toward cosmetic surgery? What ethical issues does it raise for her? In what ways does cosmetic surgery affect Paglia's artistic sensibility? What distinction does she make between good surgery and bad surgery?

2. How does Paglia connect the popularity of cosmetic surgery today to the history of the American film industry? How did changes in the movie industry alter American notions of what is beautiful? According to Paglia, what are the sources of today's standards of attractiveness and how are they affecting cosmetic surgery? Do you find her analysis persuasive? Why or why not?

3. **CONNECTIONS:** Consider Paglia's short essay in conjunction with Daniel Akst's "What Meets the Eye" (page 329). In what ways does Akst's essay help reinforce Paglia's point? Which author, in your opinion, provides the more-interesting explanation of what Americans find physically attractive? Give specific reasons for why you find one analysis more interesting than the other.

---

[2] **Diana Vreeland or Lillian Hellman:** Vreeland (1903–1989), the celebrated fashion editor of *Vogue* magazine, and Hellman (1905–1984), the well-known American playwright, were known for their strikingly craggy facial features.

Student Essay

SABRINA VERCHOT
A Response to Camille Paglia's "The Pitfalls of Plastic Surgery"

Courtesy of Sabrina Verchot

Sabrina Verchot was a senior at Emerson College in Boston, working toward her BFA in Writing, Literature, and Publishing. After graduating, in spring 2011, she took the summer off to work on writing projects, both fiction and nonfiction. She lives in Massachusetts.

She summarizes Paglia's main argument and then clearly states her objections.

In her essay, "The Pitfalls of Plastic Surgery," Camille Paglia explores the growing practice of cosmetic surgery and how it has both influenced and been influenced by American culture. She examines the idea that plastic surgery is simply a form of sculpture for Hollywood actresses who want their bodies to conform to the sexist ideal promoted by American media. She suggests that conformity to this ideal has also become the norm for many other Americans, and now plays a critical role in job retention as well as marriage retention. Although Paglia's argument is in many ways sensible, there are a few points I take issue with, such as the idea that Hollywood has perpetuated a sexist ideal of women through plastic surgery.

Plastic surgery was indeed made popular by Hollywood. Most of the news coverage of plastic surgery typically involves Hollywood actresses, particularly those who have undergone extreme cosmetic surgery or who have had multiple operations. Paglia is certainly right about that detail. Even so, in the past few years, Hollywood has not encouraged surgically enhanced sexist images. In fact, casting directors have gone in the opposite direction and some refuse to cast anyone who looks as though she has

Agrees with Paglia about Hollywood's influence but offers a specific instance to show that attitudes are changing.

been transformed by plastic surgery. For example, the casting director of *Pirates of the Caribbean 4*, now underway, specifically requested auditions from those with "natural-looking breasts only" (Fagen). Clearly, there has been a distinct switch in Hollywood thinking when it comes to surgical enhancement and the media's vision of the ideal woman.

Paglia states that "plastic surgery is living sculpture" [paragraph 1]. She is literally correct. The word *plastic* comes from the Greek *Plastikos*, to make or form, so even the very root of the word suggests that to opt for plastic surgery is to be *formed* into something other than what you are. However, that does not necessarily mean that if you elect such surgery you will automatically become a carbon copy of everyone else who has done the same. Paglia complains that plastic surgeons "homogenize women, divesting them of authority and reducing them to a generic cookie-cutter sameness" [paragraph 12]. But the process of plastic surgery actually takes place over a number of different medical sessions to make sure that the person undergoing surgery will receive the expected results, not some generic face or body that the surgeon has pre-selected for all of his or her patients.

There are women in Hollywood who undergo massive amounts of surgery to achieve the "perfect body," the homogenized version of a woman Paglia talks about. But most of those women are actually addicted to plastic surgery and have body dysmorphic disorder, which causes them to see their own bodies as unappealing. They might see themselves as fat even if they are thin, and they'll pick up on the tiniest imperfection and feel that they have to fix it. Michael Jackson is the most well-known case of body dysmorphic disorder in Hollywood, but Kelly Osbourne is another case, and there is quite a bit of debate over whether Heidi Montag has the disease, considering her recent venture into plastic surgery in which she had ten operations done in one day (Goldman).

Although some patients, particularly those with body dysmorphic disorder, may want to be the "perfect" woman, displaying — as Paglia observes — "large breasts with a flat midriff and lean hips" [paragraph 9], that certainly isn't every woman's ideal. Some simply want to soften harsh features or even out bodily proportions. Not to mention that

Disagrees that plastic surgeons "homogenize women."

By introducing the example of Michael Jackson she suggests the issue isn't only about women.

there are — usually to the surprise of many men — women unhappy with large breasts who willingly undergo breast-reduction surgery. Not all women want implants. Even Hollywood seems to be getting the idea that women do not require oversized breasts to be sexually appealing. Drew Barrymore, Queen Latifah, and Kelly Osbourne have all either openly discussed the idea of having breast-reduction surgery or are planning to undergo the surgery, and not just for the cosmetic reasons Paglia seems to focus on when she criticizes plastic surgery (Stewart). Reducing breast size can actually be medically beneficial for some women and can eliminate back pain and headaches (Ray). Additionally, studies have suggested that breast-reduction surgery can reduce the risk of breast cancer, especially in women over the age of fifty (Hage).

Cites two medical studies that claim plastic surgery can be beneficial.

Medically, a huge number of benefits can result from successful plastic surgery, and each of these benefits is particular to the patient and the problem he or she would like to remedy. Plastic surgery isn't confined to Hollywood, as Paglia notes, but it is also not confined to the "corporate workplace" for "job retention and advancement in high-profile careers" [paragraph 2]. Plastic surgery is practiced in hospitals all over the world on normal, everyday people who need a life-changing procedure. In Boston, just a few years ago, James Maki fell onto the subway tracks. Half of his face was burnt off, his nose was completely gone, his upper lips and cheeks were missing. He survived miraculously, but once he was out of the hospital he wouldn't leave his house for fear of how neighbors would react. In 2009, he returned to Brigham and Women's Hospital in Boston for plastic surgery to reconstruct his face. The procedure was a success and dramatically changed his life for the better. The surgery gave him a life outside of the confines of his home (Kowalczyk).

Points out how plastic surgery is used routinely in hospitals and cites a particular case.

Though Paglia is certainly right on many counts, there is clearly much more to plastic surgery than its "pitfalls." When examining the costs and benefits of cosmetic surgery we must look carefully at the whole picture. That picture includes not just how plastic surgery perpetuates the media's version of a "perfect body" but also how it can give hope to all the people in hospitals today desperately looking for a better life.

Concludes by conceding Paglia is "right on many counts" but that her argument overlooks the many advantages of plastic surgery.

WORKS CITED

Fagen, Cynthia R. "Disney Wants Women with Natural Breasts for New 'Pirate' Movie." *New York Post,* 21 Mar. 2010, nypost.com/2010/03/21/disney-wants -women-with-natural-breasts-for-new-pirates-movie/.

Goldman, Leslie. "Celebs and Body Dysmorphic Disorder." *Today,* NBC, 1 Mar. 2010, www.today.com.

Hage, Joris J., and Refaat B. Karim. "Risk of Breast Cancer among Reduction Mammaplasty Patients and the Strategies Used by Plastic Surgeons to Detect Such Cancer." *Plastic and Reconstructive Surgery,* vol. 117, no. 3, Mar. 2006, pp. 727–35.

Kowalczyk, Liz. "His Tragic Accident behind Him, New England's First Face Transplant Patient Tells of an Arduous Journey and a Life Renewed." *The Boston Globe,* 21 May 2009, archive.boston.com/news/local/massachusetts/ articles/2009/05/21/his_tragic_accident_behind_him_new_englands_first_face _transplant_patient_tells_of_an_arduous_journey_and_a_life_renewed/.

Paglia, Camille. "The Pitfalls of Plastic surgery." *The Writer's presence: A Pool of Readings,* edited by Robert Atwan and Donald McQuade, 8th ed., Bedford/St. Martin's, 2015, pp. 691–94.

Ray, Lynn. "Breast Reduction May Be Covered by Your Insurance Plan." *Examiner.com,* AXS Digital Group, 6 Aug. 2010, www.examiner.com/article/ breast-reduction-may-be-covered-by-your-insurance-plan.

Stewart, Colin. "Smaller Breasts Are in Style." *Orange County Register,* 8 Sept. 2009, www.ocregister.com/articles/implants-28547-breast-women.html.

Steven Pinker

VIOLENCE VANQUISHED

STEVEN PINKER (b. 1954) is an author, a psychologist, a linguist, and a Harvard professor. He was born in Montreal, Quebec, Canada, and received his PhD in experimental psychology from Harvard University in 1979. He taught at the Massachusetts Institute of Technology and Stanford University before returning to Harvard in 2008. He is well known for his belief that the mind is an information-processing system, much like a computer, and that thinking is, therefore, a kind of computation. This theory, called "Computational Theory of Mind," informs much of his work and celebrity. He is also a proponent of evolutionary psychology, which presumes that many of our psychological traits—such as the ability to deduce the emotions of others, cooperate, and recognize our relatives—are, in fact, adaptations that helped human beings survive in our ancestral environments. Pinker has argued specifically that language is the result of natural selection.

He is the author of numerous books, including *The Language Instinct* (1994), *How the Mind Works* (1997), *The Blank Slate* (2002), and *The Better Angels of Our Nature* (2011), to name just a few. He is the chair of the usage panel of *The American Heritage Dictionary* and has received numerous prizes for his writing, including the *Los Angeles Times* Science Book Prize and the William James Book Prize, which he has had the distinguished honor of winning three times. He has also received a number of awards for his scientific research, notably the Troland Research Award from the National Academy of Sciences and the Henry Dale Prize

> **"All our behaviors are a result of neurophysiological activity in the brain."**

from the Royal Institution of Great Britain. He was the Humanist of the Year in 2006 and the recipient of the Innovations for Humanity Award from La Ciudad de las Ideas in Mexico in 2008. He was named one of the 100 most influential scientists and thinkers in the world by *Time* magazine in 2008. In line with his ideas regarding evolutionary psychology and computational theory of mind, he has said, "All our behaviors are a result of neurophysiological activity in the brain." The following article, "Violence Vanquished," originally appeared in the *Wall Street Journal* in September 2011.

ON THE DAY THIS ARTICLE APPEARS, you will read about a shocking act of violence. Somewhere in the world there will be a terrorist bombing, a senseless murder, a bloody insurrection. It's impossible to learn about these catastrophes without thinking, "What is the world coming to?"

But a better question may be, "How bad was the world in the past?"

Believe it or not, the world of the past was *much* worse. Violence has been in decline for thousands of years, and today we may be living in the most peaceable era in the existence of our species.

The decline, to be sure, has not been smooth. It has not brought violence down to zero, and it is not guaranteed to continue. But it is a persistent historical development, visible on scales from millennia to years, from the waging of wars to the spanking of children.

This claim, I know, invites skepticism, incredulity, and sometimes anger. We tend to estimate the probability of an event from the ease with which we can recall examples, and scenes of carnage are more likely to be beamed into our homes and burned into our memories than footage of people dying of old age. There will always be enough violent deaths to fill the evening news, so people's impressions of violence will be disconnected from its actual likelihood.   5

Evidence of our bloody history is not hard to find. Consider the genocides in the Old Testament and the crucifixions in the New, the gory mutilations in

Shakespeare's tragedies and Grimm's fairy tales, the British monarchs who beheaded their relatives, and the American founders who dueled with their rivals.

Today the decline in these brutal practices can be quantified. A look at the numbers shows that over the course of our history, humankind has been blessed with six major declines of violence.

The first was a process of pacification: the transition from the anarchy of the hunting, gathering, and horticultural societies in which our species spent most of its evolutionary history to the first agricultural civilizations, with cities and governments, starting about 5,000 years ago.

For centuries, social theorists like Hobbes and Rousseau speculated from their armchairs about what life was like in a "state of nature." Nowadays we can do better. Forensic archeology—a kind of "CSI: Paleolithic"—can estimate rates of violence from the proportion of skeletons in ancient sites with bashed-in skulls, decapitations, or arrowheads embedded in bones. And ethnographers can tally the causes of death in tribal peoples that have recently lived outside of state control.

These investigations show that, on average, about 15% of people in 10 prestate eras died violently, compared to about 3% of the citizens of the earliest states. Tribal violence commonly subsides when a state or empire imposes control over a territory, leading to the various "paxes" (Romana, Islamica, Brittanica, and so on) that are familiar to readers of history.

It's not that the first kings had a benevolent interest in the welfare of their citizens. Just as a farmer tries to prevent his livestock from killing one another, so a ruler will try to keep his subjects from cycles of raiding and feuding. From his point of view, such squabbling is a dead loss— forgone opportunities to extract taxes, tributes, soldiers, and slaves.

The second decline of violence was a civilizing process that is best documented in Europe. Historical records show that between the late Middle Ages and the 20th century, European countries saw a 10- to 50-fold decline in their rates of homicide.

The numbers are consistent with narrative histories of the brutality of life in the Middle Ages, when highwaymen made travel a risk to life and limb and dinners were commonly enlivened by dagger attacks. So many people had their noses cut off that medieval medical textbooks speculated about techniques for growing them back.

Historians attribute this decline to the consolidation of a patchwork of feudal territories into large kingdoms with centralized authority and an infrastructure of commerce. Criminal justice was nationalized, and zero-sum plunder gave way to positive-sum trade. People increasingly controlled their impulses and sought to cooperate with their neighbors.

The third transition, sometimes called the Humanitarian Revolution, 15 took off with the Enlightenment. Governments and churches had long maintained order by punishing nonconformists with mutilation, torture, and gruesome forms of execution, such as burning, breaking, disembowelment, impalement, and sawing in half. The 18th century saw the widespread

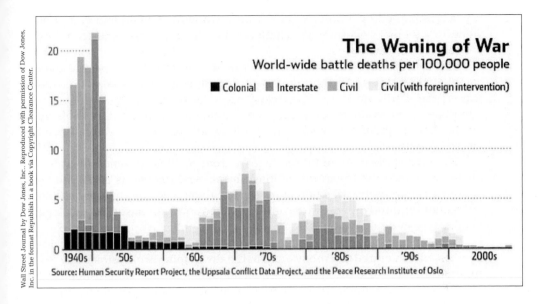

The Waning of War
World-wide battle deaths per 100,000 people

■ Colonial ■ Interstate ▨ Civil ▨ Civil (with foreign intervention)

Source: Human Security Report Project, the Uppsala Conflict Data Project, and the Peace Research Institute of Oslo

abolition of judicial torture, including the famous prohibition of "cruel and unusual punishment" in the eighth amendment of the U.S. Constitution.

At the same time, many nations began to whittle down their list of capital crimes from the hundreds (including poaching, sodomy, witchcraft, and counterfeiting) to just murder and treason. And a growing wave of countries abolished blood sports, dueling, witchhunts, religious persecution, absolute despotism, and slavery.

The fourth major transition is the respite from major interstate war that we have seen since the end of World War II. Historians sometimes refer to it as the Long Peace.

Today we take it for granted that Italy and Austria will not come to blows, nor will Britain and Russia. But centuries ago, the great powers were almost always at war, and until quite recently, Western European countries tended to initiate two or three new wars every year. The cliché that the 20th century was "the most violent in history" ignores the second half of the century (and may not even be true of the first half, if one calculates violent deaths as a proportion of the world's population).

Though it's tempting to attribute the Long Peace to nuclear deterrence, non-nuclear developed states have stopped fighting each other as well. Political scientists point instead to the growth of democracy, trade, and international organizations—all of which, the statistical evidence shows, reduce the likelihood of conflict. They also credit the rising valuation of human life over national grandeur—a hard-won lesson of two world wars.

The fifth trend, which I call the New Peace, involves war in the world 20 as a whole, including developing nations. Since 1946, several organizations have tracked the number of armed conflicts and their human toll worldwide. The bad news is that for several decades, the decline of interstate wars was accompanied by a bulge of civil wars, as newly independent countries were led by inept governments, challenged by insurgencies, and armed by the cold war superpowers.

The less bad news is that civil wars tend to kill far fewer people than wars between states. And the best news is that, since the peak of the cold war in the 1970s and '80s, organized conflicts of all kinds—civil wars, genocides, repression by autocratic governments, terrorist attacks—have declined throughout the world, and their death tolls have declined even more precipitously.

The rate of documented direct deaths from political violence (war, terrorism, genocide, and warlord militias) in the past decade is an unprecedented few hundredths of a percentage point. Even if we multiplied that rate to account for unrecorded deaths and the victims of war-caused disease and famine, it would not exceed 1%.

The most immediate cause of this New Peace was the demise of communism, which ended the proxy wars in the developing world stoked by the superpowers and also discredited genocidal ideologies that had justified the sacrifice of vast numbers of eggs to make a utopian omelet. Another contributor was the expansion of international peacekeeping forces, which really do keep the peace—not always, but far more often than when adversaries are left to fight to the bitter end.

Finally, the postwar era has seen a cascade of "rights revolutions"—a growing revulsion against aggression on smaller scales. In the developed world, the civil rights movement obliterated lynchings and lethal pogroms, and the women's-rights movement has helped to shrink the incidence of rape and the beating and killing of wives and girlfriends.

In recent decades, the movement for children's rights has significantly   25
reduced rates of spanking, bullying, paddling in schools, and physical and sexual abuse. And the campaign for gay rights has forced governments in the developed world to repeal laws criminalizing homosexuality and has had some success in reducing hate crimes against gay people.

Why has violence declined so dramatically for so long? Is it because violence has literally been bred out of us, leaving us more peaceful by nature?

This seems unlikely. Evolution has a speed limit measured in generations, and many of these declines have unfolded over decades or even years. Toddlers continue to kick, bite, and hit; little boys continue to play-fight; people of all ages continue to snipe and bicker, and most of them continue to harbor violent fantasies and to enjoy violent entertainment.

It's more likely that human nature has always comprised inclinations toward violence and inclinations that counteract them—such as self-control, empathy, fairness, and reason—what Abraham Lincoln called "the better angels of our nature." Violence has declined because historical circumstances have increasingly favored our better angels.

The most obvious of these pacifying forces has been the state, with its monopoly on the legitimate use of force. A disinterested judiciary and police can defuse the temptation of exploitative attack, inhibit the impulse for revenge, and circumvent the self-serving biases that make all parties to a dispute believe that they are on the side of the angels.

We see evidence of the pacifying effects of government in the way that rates of killing declined following the expansion and consolidation of states in tribal societies and in medieval Europe. And we can watch the movie in reverse when violence erupts in zones of anarchy, such as the Wild West, failed states, and neighborhoods controlled by mafias and street gangs, who can't call 911 or file a lawsuit to resolve their disputes but have to administer their own rough justice.

Another pacifying force has been commerce, a game in which everybody can win. As technological progress allows the exchange of goods and ideas over longer distances and among larger groups of trading partners, other people become more valuable alive than dead. They switch from being targets of demonization and dehumanization to potential partners in reciprocal altruism.

For example, though the relationship today between America and China is far from warm, we are unlikely to declare war on them or vice versa. Morality aside, they make too much of our stuff, and we owe them too much money.

A third peacemaker has been cosmopolitanism—the expansion of people's parochial little worlds through literacy, mobility, education, science, history, journalism, and mass media. These forms of virtual reality can prompt people to take the perspective of people unlike themselves and to expand their circle of sympathy to embrace them.

These technologies have also powered an expansion of rationality and objectivity in human affairs. People are now less likely to privilege their own interests over those of others. They reflect more on the way they live and consider how they could be better off. Violence is often reframed as a problem to be solved rather than as a contest to be won. We devote ever more of our brainpower to guiding our better angels. It is probably no coincidence that the Humanitarian Revolution came on the heels of the Age of Reason and the Enlightenment, that the Long Peace and rights revolutions coincided with the electronic global village.

Whatever its causes, the implications of the historical decline of violence are profound. So much depends on whether we see our era as a nightmare of crime, terrorism, genocide, and war or as a period that, in the light of the historical and statistical facts, is blessed by unprecedented levels of peaceful coexistence.

Bearers of good news are often advised to keep their mouths shut, lest they lull people into complacency. But this prescription may be backward. The discovery that fewer people are victims of violence can thwart cynicism among compassion-fatigued news readers who might otherwise think that the dangerous parts of the world are irredeemable hell holes. And a better understanding of what drove the numbers down can steer us toward doing things that make people better off rather than congratulating ourselves on how moral we are.

As one becomes aware of the historical decline of violence, the world begins to look different. The past seems less innocent, the present less sinister. One starts to appreciate the small gifts of coexistence that would have seemed utopian to our ancestors: the interracial family playing in the park, the comedian who lands a zinger on the commander in chief, the countries that quietly back away from a crisis instead of escalating to war.

For all the tribulations in our lives, for all the troubles that remain in the world, the decline of violence is an accomplishment that we can savor—and an impetus to cherish the forces of civilization and enlightenment that made it possible. ■

The Reader's Presence

1. Summarize the points that inform Pinker's claim that "[v]iolence has been in decline for thousands of years" (paragraph 3). What does Pinker identify as one of the earliest lifestyle changes that led to a more-peaceful coexistence? What kinds of past violence does he focus on, and how does he use this information to build his case? Pinker recognizes that his argument is often met with "skepticism, incredulity, and sometimes anger" (paragraph 5). Why do you think his claim provokes such strong reactions? What was your reaction to reading paragraph 3? How is—or isn't—your reaction consistent with Pinker's argument about the incessant coverage of violence in the media?

2. What reasons does Pinker provide for humankind's historical "process of pacification" (paragraph 8)? Although violence is declining, as Pinker writes, how do you explain our cultural fascination with violence throughout history, including "the Old Testament and the crucifixions in the New, the gory mutilations in Shakespeare's tragedies and Grimm's fairy tales, [and] the British monarchs who beheaded their relatives and the American founders who dueled with their rivals" (paragraph 6)? Pinker discusses other factors in the "declines of violence" (paragraph 7). What important areas might he have overlooked? What correlation, if any, can you establish between the decline of violence and the prevalence of violence in the arts?

3. Trade and commerce play an important role in Pinker's argument about the historical decline of violence; violence is, he observes, "a dead loss—forgone opportunities to extract taxes" (paragraph 11), and "people become more valuable alive than dead" (paragraph 31). To what extent can this assertion be viewed as a form of "reciprocal altruism" (paragraph 31)? To what extent do you find the reliance on money for peace to be troubling? What sorts of issues surface when people view each other in monetary terms?

4. **CONNECTIONS:** Consider the substance of Pinker's points about viewing people in monetary terms, and then compare and contrast these points with Andre Dubus III's treatment of similar issues in "The Land of No: Love in a Class-riven America" (page 112) and the opening paragraphs of Annie Dillard's essay "This Is the Life" (page 382). Which writer's view of the relationship between identity and money do you find most convincing? Explain why. Support your response by analyzing specific passages from each text in detail.

JACOB EWING
Steven Pinker and the Question of Violence

Courtesy of Jacob Ewing

At the time he wrote "Steven Pinker and the Question of Violence," Jacob Ewing was a junior at Ashland University in Ohio, where he majored in English and Spanish. In preparing to write, Ewing admits he thought Pinker's tone had "an air of finality, as though no arguments could be made to the contrary. I wanted to ask a few more questions before we closed the discussion."

His essay was in response to the following assignment:

Steven Pinker's recent book *The Better Angels of Our Nature: Why Violence Has Declined* has provoked a great deal of discussion. After reading carefully the essay, "Violence Vanquished," adapted from the book by the *Wall Street Journal*, join the controversy by writing a response to Pinker in which you confirm and/or challenge some of his findings and conclusions. Be sure to select several specific claims that Pinker makes and systematically point out their merits or weaknesses. You may bring in additional readings to support your own.

Opens his essay by citing the specific publication he is responding to and then summarizing Pinker's central claim.

In his essay "Violence Vanquished," which appeared in the *Wall Street Journal* (September 24, 2011), the Harvard Professor of Psychology, Steven Pinker, claims that the modern era is the most peaceful time in the history of the human species. He says that now more than ever before, we are less likely to die a violent death at the hands of another human being. He cites statistics that show how violence of all kinds—murder, war, genocide, and so on—have decreased across the board.

Pinker is aware that this fact seems not only unlikely but blatantly wrong, especially in light of the seemingly endless acts of violence that characterize so much of today's news. Yet, despite the horrors in Darfur, Syria, and Iraq and in virtually every major American city, Pinker is likely right in his general claim that violence is diminishing across the globe. It would be hard to argue with his statistics that prove that violence among human beings is at its lowest point in history.

Concedes that Pinker's statistics are probably correct, so will not argue with that aspect of the essay.

But there are still some major issues to consider when evaluating Pinker's position. For instance, what exactly constitutes violence in this argument? It would first be help-ful to analyze the author's definition. Throughout the piece, he discusses violence in terms of how likely one is to die at the hands of another human being. This is a convenient statistic, especially for an argument as numbers-driven as Pinker's, but violence extends well beyond just murder or warfare. Rape, assault, bullying—these are all ways in which human beings act violent toward one another, yet none of these phenomena are mentioned in his article.

Shows various ways we can define violence that Pinker ignores.

There are still other types of violence that permeate society. Most young boys have, at a certain point in their childhood, gotten into a wrestling match or a fist fight, often with some-one very close to them—a brother, a cousin, a best friend. Now, this type of violence is not on par with murder, but it is certainly an aspect of our society that goes unmentioned by Pinker's analysis. Violence manifests itself in modern society in a variety of ways, many of which Pinker ignores and some of which are not extreme enough to even be on his radar.

In the latter half of the article, Pinker attempts to deter-mine what exactly has caused the decline in violence he has described. He appeals first to modern governments, saying, "The most obvious of these pacifying forces has been the state, with its monopoly on the legitimate use of force." Here again, Pinker's point is not as simple as it appears. The state's ability to monopolize the use of force has absolutely helped quell vigilante justice and personal vendettas, but it has also created a potential for violence that is absolutely unprecedented.

Indeed, one could assume that at this moment, several of the world's major powers have the ability to launch a nuclear attack with weapons far more powerful than those used on Japan at the end of the Second World War, when a single plane dropping one atomic bomb over Hiroshima left over 100,000 human beings dead. The number of deaths that could result in a nuclear attack today is unthinkable. With modern weapons that absolutely dwarf the original atomic bomb, and with so many states having access to such weapons, Pinker's assertion that the state has brought about an alleviation of violence becomes less evident. He would be quick to point out that such an attack has not hap-pened; it might be better to say that such an attack has not happened yet. As Robert Jervis says in his article "Pinker

Reinforces his point about state violence by citing supporting view.

the Prophet," "If we think we're playing Russian roulette, then the fact that we were lucky does not count quite so strongly for our living in a less violent time."[1]

Pinker also cites the global market as a source for this newfound peace. He points out how unlikely it is for a war to break out between the United States and China because "they make too much of our stuff, and we owe them too much money." But the fallacy of this point comes a paragraph earlier, when Pinker describes commerce as "a game in which everybody can win." This sentiment holds true when considering two nations like the United States and China—strong centralized governments, stable economies, freedom from internal conflict. This allows trade to occur between these two nations in a peaceful, mutually-beneficial manner.

But what about countries that aren't fortunate enough to be a world power? What about countries where the extraction of precious natural resources has resulted in some of the most gruesome violence of the twentieth century? One only need analyze the history of the diamond trade in Africa to realize the type of violence that can come as a direct result of commerce. Diamonds are a precious commodity, and any opportunity to make money in a place like Sierra Leone is likely to end in violence. Even more recently, the mining of coltan—a mineral used in most cell phones and laptops—has been the source for violence in the Democratic Republic of Congo. In these cases, commerce and trade have actually created violence—not alleviated it.

Pinker is constantly alluding to the Enlightenment as another source for what he calls "the most peaceable era in the existence of our species." It would be hard to argue that the Enlightenment didn't at least help people realize that killing one another may not be the best thing to do. That seems obvious now. But what about people who are raised in our enlightened society, taught about playing nice and the sanctity of life and the golden rule, yet still kill people? The list of school-shootings over the past twenty years is already terrifying and growing by the year. These acts are carried out by people who are presumably enlightened, products of our education system, who have had the

Supplies example of diamond-trade violence to counter Pinker's point about global commerce.

Confronts Pinker's point about the Enlightenment with counter-examples of today's violence.

[1]*The National Interest*, Issue 116, Nov./Dec. 2011, p. 57.

opportunity to learn how important and beautiful and sacred life is; yet the shootings still happen.

Pinker is quick to mention how "about 15% of people in prestate eras died violently," but fails to mention that the populations of these societies were savages by contemporary standards. Death happened at a much higher rate, but these people were wholly unable to comprehend the philosophical implications of the deaths they were causing. It was their way of life, and they didn't have the advanced knowledge to consider that life might be lived some other way. The same cannot be said about modern day murderers. If our society is truly as enlightened as Pinker likes to think it is—as we all like to think it is—then the fact that so many people still function outside of the collective societal reasoning, the fact that murders happen every day, should be far more shocking than the fact unenlightened savages killed one another at a higher rate than we do today.

Pinker's assertion that violence is in consistent decline is both intriguing and inspiring, but is not as solid as it appears on the surface. To his credit, Pinker readily concedes that violence still has an enormous presence in human society. But the way in which he measures violence—human death caused by another human being—is not necessarily the full story on the matter. Furthermore, his desire to appeal to state power, global commerce, and the modern enlightened mind all have some important implications, as noted above, to which his article does not do justice.

> Summarizes his objections to the way Pinker "measures" violence.

The final claim that Pinker never addresses is an omission for which no one could blame him. One of the most frequent instances of violence over the past decade has been natural disasters—earthquakes, tsunamis, hurricanes, and so on. The amount of human life lost as a result is enormous, yes, but it wouldn't have anything to do with an assessment like Pinker's. Or would it? If one day, the world of science comes to discover that these patterns in extreme weather were caused by human beings, by the way modern society functions, is Pinker's argument changed at all? Are we considerably more violent if that is the case, even if it is unintentional? This is undoubtedly speculative, but if Pinker's project is to consider how violence works on the macro-level, it might not be a bad idea to at least consider the possibility that human beings kill one another in more ways than we realize.

> Instead of concluding with a summary, he effectively introduces a new question about violence and human responsibility that Pinker never addresses.

Mary Roach

ED AND MARY DO MARS AND VENUS

MARY ROACH (b. 1959) is a best-selling author of "popular science" books: books that are *about* science but written for a lay audience. She often chooses unconventional subject matter, approaching otherwise taboo material with a humorous eye. For example, her first book, *Stiff: The Curious Lives of Human Cadavers* (2003), covers topics like decomposition, the cannibalism of corpses, decapitation, head transplant surgery, and the use of corpses as crash-test dummies.

Roach grew up in Etna, New Hampshire, and graduated from Wesleyan University in 1981. One of her first jobs was in public relations for the San Francisco Zoo, where she wrote freelance articles "when [she] wasn't taking calls about elephant wart removal surgery or denying rumors that the cheetahs had been sucked dry by fleas." Her books include *Spook: Science Tackles the Afterlife* (2005), *Bonk: The Curious Coupling of Science and Sex* (2008), *Packing for Mars: The Curious Science of Life in the Void* (2010), and *Gulp: Adventures on the Alimentary Canal* (2013). She also writes for magazines, and her articles have appeared in *Outside*, *National Geographic*, *Wired*, and the *New York Times Magazine*, among other publications. "Ed and Mary Do Mars and Venus" originally appeared in *Men's Health* in March 2001 and reflects Roach's interest in popular science, specifically pop psychology. Of her science writing, she has said, "I don't have a science degree and must fake my way through interviews with experts I can't understand."

> One of Mary Roach's first jobs was in public relations for the San Francisco Zoo, where she took "calls about elephant wart removal surgery or [was] denying rumors that the cheetahs had been sucked dry by fleas."

NEVER READ *Men Are from Mars, Women Are from Venus*, but I can tell you some of what's in it. For better or worse, the teachings of psychologist John Gray have seeped into our consciousness: Women need to talk about things that are bothering them, and men don't. Women instinctively know how to make each other feel better. They empathize; they say things like "What a drag. I had a boss like that once." Men don't empathize; they offer solutions. They say things like "If your job upsets you that much, maybe you're in the wrong career." The women get angry at the men for not validating their feelings. The men, in turn, get angry that the women are angry, when the men were just trying to help. Start with one problem, and now you have two.

Seems apt enough, but where do we go from there? How do women teach men empathy? How, in short, can we make them more like us? This is what I hoped to learn when I signed up myself and my husband, Ed, for an all-day Mars-Venus Communication Workshop.

The workshops, taught by therapists who claim to have been personally trained by Gray, are the latest in a long line of Mars-Venus spin-offs, including a board game, a television show hosted by Cybill Shepherd, and, most recently, a Las Vegas revue. Our therapist was Greg Galati, of Redwood City, California. Galati is gentle and friendly, one of those rare people who can hold a smile while talking and not look like an infomercial host. He reminded me of Greg Brady on one of the episodes where things were going really well for him.

Galati said he was going to begin by reviewing some basic differences between men and women. Ed wrote to himself, "1. Women have breasts." It was going to be a long day.

Galati told us that a woman's primary "love need" is to be understood   5
and listened to (and to never, speaking personally, have to hear the term "love need"). Men, on the other hand, need to feel competent. This is why they try to fix things, to offer solutions. Their main "love need" is to feel recognized and appreciated for this ability.

It's not that men are self-centered or cold, according to Galati. "They give care in ways women can't see," said Galati. Out of the corner of my eye, I noticed Ed nodding. It occurred to me that on the way out the door that morning, Ed had pointed out how clean the walls around our front doorway were since he'd hosed them down. I believe I said "Wow" in that way you say "Wow" when what you really mean is "Big deal. I dusted and vacuumed the house and put all the vacation pictures in an album."

I leaned over to Ed's chair. "When you hosed off the doorway yesterday, were you giving care?" Ed gave me the *duh* look, so I thanked him for his hosing competence. Already I could see we were making progress.

We also learned that when women practice their empathy skills on men, the act goes largely unappreciated. A man in turmoil doesn't want to be understood or even listened to. He just wants to be left alone. When men are upset, Galati explained, they retreat to what Gray calls "the cave." They don't want to talk through their problems; they want to escape them. They want to watch a ball game or zone out in front of mindless sitcoms.

Perhaps to make the men in the workshop feel more comfortable, Galati had brought in a TV and would periodically play videotapes of John Gray speaking to vast auditorium audiences. Here was his mistake, because, for me anyway, the whole Mars-Venus worldview began to unravel.

Instead of teaching the men in the audience how to empathize, he was   10
teaching them how to pretend to empathize. Gray instructs men to "make reassuring sounds" while women talk about their problems. His workbook lists examples in a handy table: "Hmmm..." "Oh..." "Ahh..." "Mmmm..."

"Oh my goodness." "Oooo." "Ouch." "Really?" He seemed to be saying that sincerity doesn't matter as long as you have the script down.

He's wrong. If you understand where someone is coming from and you want her to know that, then you must say things—entire sentences, in fact—that show you understand. "Ahhuh" is better than "Maybe you're being oversensitive," but it's hardly empathy.

Our Mars-Venus workbooks were full of simple, patronizing tips on how to mollify a woman, magic formulas to shut her up and keep her off your back. "Give her four hugs every day." "Practice looking at her when you talk to her." "Say 'I love you' twice a day." "Laugh at her jokes." Either John Gray is the biggest misogynist on Earth (or Mars, or wherever he's from), or he assumes most men are. Either way, I wanted to seal him up in his cave for good.

It was time for lunch, and Galati turned us loose for an hour. On the way down the hall, Ed hugged me. Then he hugged me again, and again twice more. "Just thought I'd get those over with."

After lunch, the topic was anger and conflict. We watched a videotape of John Gray telling women they shouldn't ever expect to resolve an argument with a man by talking it through. "Unless he's agreed with," warned Gray, "a man will just get angrier."

Gray even went so far as to blame the upturn in divorce rates since the sixties on men being forced to talk about conflicts and vent their feelings. "It would take a million years of evolution before we could be like women," he insists. Instead, when disagreements arise, women should let men retreat to their caves, and "go to some women friends for support." Hmmm. Oh. Ahhuh. Really?

Though still smiling, Galati looked uncomfortable. He said that probably what Gray meant was that women shouldn't force men to settle arguments while they're riled up. Men should be allowed to come back to the subject later, when both parties have had time to cool off. (Actually, I did recall this from the videotape. It was the part where Gray likened women to leftover lasagne: "You let them congeal, and the next day they're much better.")

For his part, Ed agreed with Gray that forcing a man to talk through a disagreement doesn't always resolve it. "Men think that means they have to keep talking until they admit they're wrong and see the woman's point of view," Ed said. And they hate this. "It's tied up to the competency thing. It takes every ounce of power in a man's body to say, 'Oh, I guess I was wrong.'"

What men need to understand is that most women *don't* expect men to take on all the blame. Women are willing to surrender a piece of ground, too. That's how arguments are settled. Each side concedes a point, and both feel better.

If women don't want to concede, perhaps they, too, can learn to fake it. Ladies, try these handy phrases: "I guess I'm guilty, too, because I _____." "That's okay, hon, I didn't help matters by _____." "Maybe you're right about _____." "I know I have a tendency to _____."

In the car on the drive home, I asked Ed whether I should let him spend   20
more time in his cave. "Sometimes that's important," he said. "But if a man
always goes to his cave, nothing will ever get talked about. It's not good for
men to keep everything inside." Then the conversation petered out because
Ed was listening for baseball scores on the radio. A call-in show was on. A
man was saying, "I just want to talk about the Giants a little . . ."

"See?" said Ed. "Men need to talk, too." ▪

The Reader's Presence

1. John Gray's operative assumption in *Men Are from Mars, Women Are from Venus*
   is that women need "to be understood and listened to," whereas men "need to
   feel competent" (paragraph 5). To what extent are Gray's assumptions consistent
   with Roach's experiences in the workshop with her husband? Point to specific passages to support your response. What conclusions about Gray's claims does Roach
   draw from her experience in this "all-day Mars-Venus Communication Workshop"
   with her husband, Ed (paragraph 2)? When—and how—does Roach conclude that
   Gray's behavioral generalizations are grounded in traditional gender stereotypes?

2. To what extent do Gray's ideas about teaching men "to pretend to empathize" with
   women by making "'reassuring sounds'" (paragraph 10) validate and encourage
   men to "retreat to what Gray calls 'the cave'" (paragraph 8)? What, more generally,
   is Roach's reaction to Gray's encouraging men to feign empathy and sincerity? What
   are the implications of Gray's likening "women to leftover lasagne: 'You let them
   congeal, and the next day they're much better'" (paragraph 16)? What other striking
   metaphors does Roach use to make her prose more memorable?

3. Artful uses of tone, irony, and understated humor are hallmarks of Roach's style.
   Despite the many differences Gray identifies between men and women in *Men Are
   from Mars, Women Are from Venus*, Roach's experience at the workshop tells her
   otherwise: "Men and women actually do live on the same planet." Point to other
   examples of Roach's humorous twists on Greg Galati's presentation of Gray's "philosophical" musings on the behavioral differences between men and women. Does
   Roach agree that "'[i]t would take a million years of evolution before [men] could be
   like women'" (paragraph 15)? Why or why not?

4. **CONNECTIONS:**   In both this essay and Barbara Ehrenreich's "Will Women Still
   Need Men?" (page 598), the authors use generalizations to explain the points they
   make. Find examples of this approach in both essays. Consider, specifically, how each
   writer justifies the generalizations and observations that she makes. Are the authors
   using the same technique, or do their approaches differ? Explain.

Michael J. Sandel

WHAT ISN'T FOR SALE?

MICHAEL J. SANDEL (b. 1953) is the Anne T. and Robert M. Bass Professor of Government at Harvard University, where he has taught political philosophy since 1980. He is well known for his "Justice" course, which has over the past two decades become one of the most widely attended courses offered by the renowned university. It was recorded in the fall semester of 2005 and condensed into a twelve-hour miniseries for WGBH public television. The series has been broadcast around the world and is particularly popular in Japan, where the companion book, *Justice: What's the Right Thing to Do?* (2009), became a best-seller. Sandel's course is also offered through edX, the nonprofit collection of free Internet courses (or MOOCs—Massive Open Online Courses) from major universities. In 2012, Sandel published *What Money Can't Buy: The Moral Limits of Markets*. "What Isn't for Sale?" follows a similar theme as this most recent book and was originally published in *The Atlantic* in 2012.

> "The responsibility of political philosophy that tries to engage with practice is to be clear, or at least accessible—clear enough that its arguments and concerns can be accessible to a nonacademic public."

Sandel is known for being an excellent lecturer, drawing on clear examples from everyday life to make his arguments. He has said that "the responsibility of political philosophy that tries to engage with practice is to be clear, or at least accessible—clear enough that its arguments and concerns can be accessible to a nonacademic public. Otherwise, it's not possible really for political philosophers to generate debate that could possibly challenge existing understandings."

THERE ARE SOME THINGS money can't buy—but these days, not many. Almost everything is up for sale. For example:

- **A prison-cell upgrade: $90 a night.** In Santa Ana, California, and some other cities, nonviolent offenders can pay for a clean, quiet jail cell, without any non-paying prisoners to disturb them.

- **Access to the carpool lane while driving solo: $8.** Minneapolis, San Diego, Houston, Seattle, and other cities have sought to ease traffic congestion by letting solo drivers pay to drive in carpool lanes, at rates that vary according to traffic.

- **The services of an Indian surrogate mother: $8,000.** Western couples seeking surrogates increasingly outsource the job to India, and the price is less than one-third the going rate in the United States.

- **The right to shoot an endangered black rhino: $250,000.** South Africa has begun letting some ranchers sell hunters the right to kill a limited number of rhinos, to give the ranchers an incentive to raise and protect the endangered species.

- **Your doctor's cellphone number: $1,500 and up per year.** A growing number of "concierge" doctors offer cellphone access and same-day appointments for patients willing to pay annual fees ranging from $1,500 to $25,000.

- **The right to emit a metric ton of carbon dioxide into the atmosphere: $10.50.** The European Union runs a carbon-dioxide-emissions market that enables companies to buy and sell the right to pollute.

- **The right to immigrate to the United States: $500,000.** Foreigners who invest $500,000 and create at least 10 full-time jobs in an area of high unemployment are eligible for a green card that entitles them to permanent residency.

Not everyone can afford to buy these things. But today there are lots of new ways to make money. If you need to earn some extra cash, here are some novel possibilities:

- **Sell space on your forehead to display commercial advertising: $10,000.** A single mother in Utah who needed money for her son's education was paid $10,000 by an online casino to install a permanent tattoo of the casino's Web address on her forehead. Temporary tattoo ads earn less.

- **Serve as a human guinea pig in a drug-safety trial for a pharmaceutical company: $7,500.** The pay can be higher or lower, depending on the invasiveness of the procedure used to test the drug's effect and the discomfort involved.

- **Fight in Somalia or Afghanistan for a private military contractor: up to $1,000 a day.** The pay varies according to qualifications, experience, and nationality.

- **Stand in line overnight on Capitol Hill to hold a place for a lobbyist who wants to attend a congressional hearing: $15–$20 an hour.** Lobbyists pay line-standing companies, who hire homeless people and others to queue up.

- **If you are a second-grader in an underachieving Dallas school, read a book: $2.** To encourage reading, schools pay kids for each book they read.

To pay for her son's education, a single mother allowed her forehead to be used as advertising for an online casino.

We live in a time when almost everything can be bought and sold. Over the past three decades, markets — and market values — have come to govern our lives as never before. We did not arrive at this condition through any deliberate choice. It is almost as if it came upon us.

As the Cold War ended, markets and market thinking enjoyed unrivaled prestige, and understandably so. No other mechanism for organizing the production and distribution of goods had proved as successful at generating affluence and prosperity. And yet even as growing numbers of countries around the world embraced market mechanisms in the operation of their economies, something else was happening. Market values were coming to play a greater and greater role in social life. Economics was becoming an imperial domain. Today, the logic of buying and selling no longer applies to material goods alone. It increasingly governs the whole of life.

The years leading up to the financial crisis of 2008 were a heady time   5
of market faith and deregulation — an era of market triumphalism. The era began in the early 1980s, when Ronald Reagan and Margaret Thatcher proclaimed their conviction that markets, not government, held the key to prosperity and freedom. And it continued into the 1990s with the market-friendly liberalism of Bill Clinton and Tony Blair, who moderated but consolidated the faith that markets are the primary means for achieving the public good.

Today, that faith is in question. The financial crisis did more than cast doubt on the ability of markets to allocate risk efficiently. It also prompted a widespread sense that markets have become detached from morals, and that we need to somehow reconnect the two. But it's not obvious what this would mean, or how we should go about it.

Some say the moral failing at the heart of market triumphalism was greed, which led to irresponsible risk-taking. The solution, according to this view, is to rein in greed, insist on greater integrity and responsibility among bankers and Wall Street executives, and enact sensible regulations to prevent a similar crisis from happening again.

This is, at best, a partial diagnosis. While it is certainly true that greed played a role in the financial crisis, something bigger was and is at stake. The most fateful change that unfolded during the past three decades was not an increase in greed. It was the reach of markets, and of market values, into spheres of life traditionally governed by nonmarket norms. To contend with this condition, we need to do more than inveigh against greed; we need to have a public debate about where markets belong—and where they don't.

Consider, for example, the proliferation of for-profit schools, hospitals, and prisons, and the outsourcing of war to private military contractors. (In Iraq and Afghanistan, private contractors have actually outnumbered U.S. military troops.) Consider the eclipse of public police forces by private security firms—especially in the U.S. and the U.K., where the number of private guards is almost twice the number of public police officers.

Or consider the pharmaceutical companies' aggressive marketing of   10 prescription drugs directly to consumers, a practice now prevalent in the U.S. but prohibited in most other countries. (If you've ever seen the television commercials on the evening news, you could be forgiven for thinking that the greatest health crisis in the world is not malaria or river blindness or sleeping sickness but an epidemic of erectile dysfunction.)

Consider too the reach of commercial advertising into public schools, from buses to corridors to cafeterias; the sale of "naming rights" to parks and civic spaces; the blurred boundaries, within journalism, between news and advertising, likely to blur further as newspapers and magazines struggle to survive; the marketing of "designer" eggs and sperm for assisted reproduction; the buying and selling, by companies and countries, of the right to pollute; a system of campaign finance in the U.S. that comes close to permitting the buying and selling of elections.

These uses of markets to allocate health, education, public safety, national security, criminal justice, environmental protection, recreation, procreation, and other social goods were for the most part unheard-of 30 years ago. Today, we take them largely for granted.

Why worry that we are moving toward a society in which everything is up for sale?

For two reasons. One is about inequality, the other about corruption. First, consider inequality. In a society where everything is for sale, life is harder for those of modest means. The more money can buy, the more affluence—or the lack of it—matters. If the only advantage of affluence were the ability to afford yachts, sports cars, and fancy vacations, inequalities of income and wealth would matter less than they do today. But as money comes to buy more and more, the distribution of income and wealth looms larger.

The second reason we should hesitate to put everything up for sale is more difficult to describe. It is not about inequality and fairness but about the corrosive tendency of markets. Putting a price on the good things in life can corrupt them. That's because markets don't only allocate goods; they express and promote certain attitudes toward the goods being exchanged. Paying kids to read books might get them to read more, but might also teach them to regard reading as a chore rather than a source of intrinsic satisfaction. Hiring foreign mercenaries to fight our wars might spare the lives of our citizens, but might also corrupt the meaning of citizenship.

Economists often assume that markets are inert, that they do not affect the goods being exchanged. But this is untrue. Markets leave their mark. Sometimes, market values crowd out nonmarket values worth caring about.

When we decide that certain goods may be bought and sold, we decide, at least implicitly, that it is appropriate to treat them as commodities, as instruments of profit and use. But not all goods are properly valued in this way. The most obvious example is human beings. Slavery was appalling because it treated human beings as a commodity, to be bought and sold at auction. Such treatment fails to value human beings as persons, worthy of dignity and respect; it sees them as instruments of gain and objects of use.

Something similar can be said of other cherished goods and practices. We don't allow children to be bought and sold, no matter how difficult the process of adoption can be or how willing impatient prospective parents might be. Even if the prospective buyers would treat the child responsibly, we worry that a market in children would express and promote the wrong way of valuing them. Children are properly regarded not as consumer goods but as beings worthy of love and care. Or consider the rights and obligations of citizenship. If you are called to jury duty, you can't hire a substitute to take your place. Nor do we allow citizens to sell their votes, even though others might be eager to buy them. Why not? Because we believe that civic duties are not private property but public responsibilities. To outsource them is to demean them, to value them in the wrong way.

These examples illustrate a broader point: some of the good things in life are degraded if turned into commodities. So to decide where the market belongs, and where it should be kept at a distance, we have to decide how to value the goods in question—health, education, family life, nature, art, civic duties, and so on. These are moral and political questions, not merely economic ones. To resolve them, we have to debate, case by case, the moral meaning of these goods, and the proper way of valuing them.

This is a debate we didn't have during the era of market triumphalism. As a result, without quite realizing it—without ever deciding to do so—we drifted from having a market economy to being a market society.

The difference is this: A market economy is a tool—a valuable and effective tool—for organizing productive activity. A market society is a way of life in which market values seep into every aspect of human endeavor. It's a place where social relations are made over in the image of the market.

The great missing debate in contemporary politics is about the role and reach of markets. Do we want a market economy, or a market society? What role should markets play in public life and personal relations? How can we decide which goods should be bought and sold, and which should be governed by nonmarket values? Where should money's writ not run?

Even if you agree that we need to grapple with big questions about the morality of markets, you might doubt that our public discourse is up to the task. It's a legitimate worry. At a time when political argument consists mainly of shouting matches on cable television, partisan vitriol on talk radio, and ideological food fights on the floor of Congress, it's hard to imagine a reasoned public debate about such controversial moral questions as the right way to value procreation, children, education, health, the environment, citizenship, and other goods. I believe such a debate is possible, but only if we are willing to broaden the terms of our public discourse and grapple more explicitly with competing notions of the good life.

In hopes of avoiding sectarian strife, we often insist that citizens leave their moral and spiritual convictions behind when they enter the public square. But the reluctance to admit arguments about the good life into politics has had an unanticipated consequence. It has helped prepare the way for market triumphalism, and for the continuing hold of market reasoning.

In its own way, market reasoning also empties public life of moral argu- 25
ment. Part of the appeal of markets is that they don't pass judgment on the preferences they satisfy. They don't ask whether some ways of valuing goods are higher, or worthier, than others. If someone is willing to pay for sex, or a kidney, and a consenting adult is willing to sell, the only question the economist asks is "How much?" Markets don't wag fingers. They don't discriminate between worthy preferences and unworthy ones. Each party to a deal decides for him- or herself what value to place on the things being exchanged.

This nonjudgmental stance toward values lies at the heart of market reasoning, and explains much of its appeal. But our reluctance to engage in moral and spiritual argument, together with our embrace of markets, has exacted a heavy price: it has drained public discourse of moral and civic energy, and contributed to the technocratic, managerial politics afflicting many societies today.

A debate about the moral limits of markets would enable us to decide, as a society, where markets serve the public good and where they do not belong. Thinking through the appropriate place of markets requires that we reason together, in public, about the right way to value the social goods we prize. It would be folly to expect that a more morally robust public discourse, even at its best, would lead to agreement on every contested question. But it would make for a healthier public life. And it would make us more aware of the price we pay for living in a society where everything is up for sale.

The Reader's Presence

1. Sandel's essay revolves around his claim that market thinking so permeates contemporary life that we hardly notice it anymore. He further suggests that our market society has evolved as an unintentional progression: "[i]t is almost as if it came upon us" (paragraph 3). How does Sandel account for our evolving from a market economy to a market society in which everything is a commodity? Characterize the differences between a "market economy" and a "market society." What is "the price we pay for living in a society where everything is up for sale" (paragraph 27)? What is Sandel's view of the possibility of managing the reach of markets?

2. Explain what Sandel means by "the corrosive tendency of markets" (paragraph 15). To what extent do you think markets can answer the moral and political questions we face in society? What is your response to Sandel's observation that "market reasoning . . . empties public life of moral argument" (paragraph 25)? How does this relate to American society's "reluctance to engage in moral and spiritual argument" (paragraph 26)? What is your response to Sandel's argument encouraging citizens to "leave their moral and spiritual convictions behind when they enter the public square" (paragraph 24)? Near the end of his essay, Sandel claims that "[e]ven if you agree that we need to grapple with big questions about the morality of markets, you might doubt that our public discourse is up to the task" (paragraph 23). Explain why you agree — or disagree — with Sandel's point that public discourse has become ineffective. Draw on one of the three areas Sandel mentions — television, talk radio, and Congress — as the focus of your response.

3. **VISUAL PRESENCE:** Examine carefully the photograph of Kari Smith and her son, Brady, on page 715. For $10,000 and "a brighter future for her son," Smith became "a real life pop-up ad for a virtual casino." (Aaron Falk, *Desert Morning News*, June 2005, "Mom sells face space for tattoo advertisement.") Smith used the Internet to auction the space on her forehead in order to underwrite the cost of a private-school education for her son. Review Sandel's argument in "What Isn't for Sale?" and point to specific words and phrases that Sandel might draw on to respond to Smith's decision.

4. **CONNECTIONS:** Compare Sandel's essay to Steven Pinker's "Violence Vanquished" (page 698), in which Pinker writes about the role of expanding international markets as a means to usher in a period of reduced violence never before seen in human history. How would Sandel respond to Pinker's claim that through markets "people become more valuable alive than dead" (paragraph 31)?

Barry Schwartz

THE TYRANNY OF CHOICE

Author and professor **BARRY SCHWARTZ** (b. 1946) has taught psychology and economics at Swarthmore College in Pennsylvania since receiving his PhD from the University of Pennsylvania in 1971. He is currently the Dorwin Cartwright Professor of Social Theory and Social Action, and his classes and seminars focus on the process of thinking and decision making, the interaction of morality and self-interest, work satisfaction, and the intersection of psychology and economics—all subjects found in his many writings and books. In addition to co-writing a number of textbooks on the psychology of learning, memory, and behaviorism, he has written *The Battle for Human Nature: Science, Morality and Modern Life* (1987), *The Costs of Living: How Market Freedom Erodes the Best Things in Life* (2000), and *The Paradox of Choice: Why More Is Less* (2003), in which he explores how choice overload in the marketplace can lead to anxiety and the inability to choose anything at all. Schwartz has written articles for numerous professional journals and mainstream periodicals, including the *New York Times Magazine*, *USA Today*, *Scientific American*, and the *Chronicle of Higher Education*, where his essay "The Tyranny of Choice" appeared in January 2004.

> **Barry Schwartz's book, *The Paradox of Choice: Why More Is Less* (2003), explores how choice overload in the marketplace can lead to anxiety and the inability to choose anything at all.**

THE MODERN UNIVERSITY has become a kind of intellectual shopping mall. Universities offer a wide array of different "goods" and allow, even encourage, students—the "customers"—to shop around until they find what they like. Individual customers are free to "purchase" whatever bundles of knowledge they want, and the university provides whatever its customers demand. In some rather prestigious institutions, this shopping-mall view has been carried to an extreme. In the first few weeks of classes, students sample the merchandise. They go to a class, stay 10 minutes to see what the professor is like, then walk out, often in the middle of the professor's sentence, to try another class. Students come and go in and out of classes just as browsers go in and out of stores in a mall.

This explosion of choice in the university is a reflection of a pervasive social trend. Americans are awash in choice, not only in the courses they take, but also in the products they buy (300 kinds of cereal, 50 different cellphones, thousands of mutual funds) and in virtually all aspects of life. Increasingly, people are free to choose when and how they will work, how they will worship, where they will live, and what they will look like (thanks to liposuction, Botox, and cosmetic surgery of every description), and what kind of romantic relationships they will have. Further, freedom of choice is greatly enhanced by increased affluence. In the last 40 years, the inflation-adjusted, per capita income of Americans has more than doubled. The proportion of homes with dishwashers has increased from 9 to 50 percent, with clothes dryers from 20 to 70 percent, and with air-conditioning from 15 to 73 percent. And of course, no one had cable TV, home computers, or the Internet in 1964. This increased affluence contributes to freedom of choice by giving people the means to act on their various goals and desires, whatever they may be.

Does increased affluence and increased choice mean we have more happy people? Not at all. Three recently published books — by the psychologist David Myers, the political scientist Robert E. Lane, and the journalist Gregg Easterbrook — point out how the growth of material affluence has not brought with it an increase in subjective well-being. Indeed, they argue that we are actually experiencing a *decrease* in well-being. In the last 30 years, the number of Americans describing themselves as "very happy" declined by 5 percent, which means that about 14 million fewer people report being very happy today than in 1974. And, as a recent study published in the *Journal of the American Medical Association* indicates, the rate of serious clinical depression has more than tripled over the last two generations, and increased by perhaps a factor of 10 from 1900 to 2000. Suicide rates are also up, not only in the United States, but in almost every developed country. And both serious depression and suicide are occurring among people younger than ever before. Deans at virtually every college and university in the United States can testify to this malaise, as they witness a demand for psychological services that they are unable to meet.

Why are people increasingly unhappy even as they experience greater material abundance and freedom of choice? Recent psychological research suggests that increased choice may itself be part of the problem.

It may seem implausible that there can be too much choice. As a matter of logic, it would appear that adding options will make no one worse off and is bound to make someone better off. If you're content choosing among three different kinds of breakfast cereal, or six television stations, you can simply ignore the dozens or hundreds that get added to your supermarket shelves or cable provider's menu. Meanwhile, one of those new cereals or TV stations may be just what some other person was hoping for. Given the indisputable fact that choice is good for human well-being, it seems only logical that if some choice is good, more choice is better.

5

Logically true, yes. Psychologically true, no. My colleagues and I, along with other researchers, have begun amassing evidence—both in the laboratory and in the field—that increased choice can lead to *decreased* well-being. This is especially true for people we have termed "maximizers," people whose goal is to get the best possible result when they make decisions. Choice overload is also a problem for people we call "satisficers," people who seek only "good enough" results from their choices, but the problem is greatly magnified for maximizers. Much of the relevant research is summarized in my book, *The Paradox of Choice: Why More Is Less*. Here are some examples:

- Shoppers who confront a display of 30 jams or varieties of gourmet chocolate are less likely to purchase *any* than when they encounter a display of six.

- Students given 30 topics from which to choose to write an extra-credit essay are less likely to write one than those given six. And if they do write one, it tends to be of lower quality.

- The majority of medical patients do not want the decision authority that the canons of medical ethics have thrust upon them. Responsibility for medical decisions looks better to people in prospect than in actuality: Sixty-five percent of respondents say that if they were to get cancer, they would want to be in charge of treatment decisions, but among those who actually have cancer, only 12 percent want that control and responsibility.

- The more funds employers offer their employees in 401(k) retirement plans, the less likely the employees are to invest in any, even though in many cases, failing to do so costs them employer-matching funds of up to several thousand dollars a year.

- When maximizers, as opposed to satisficers, go shopping for big items or small ones, they spend more time looking, have a harder time deciding, look around more at what others are buying, and are less satisfied with their purchases.

- Maximizing college seniors send out more résumés, investigate more different fields, go on more job interviews, and get better, higher-paying jobs than satisficers. But they are less satisfied with their jobs, and are much more stressed, anxious, frustrated, and unhappy in the process.

These examples paint a common picture: Increasing options does not increase well-being, especially for maximizers, even when it enables choosers to do better by some objective standard. We have identified several processes that help explain why increased choice decreases satisfaction. Greater choice:

- Increases the burden of gathering information to make a wise decision.

- Increases the likelihood that people will regret the decisions they make.

- Increases the likelihood that people will *anticipate* regretting the decision they make, with the result that they can't make a decision at all.

- Increases the feeling of missed opportunities, as people encounter the attractive features of one option after another that they are rejecting.

- Increases expectations about how good the chosen option should be. Since assessments of the quality of a choice are almost always made relative to one's expectations, as expectations rise, actual choices have a rising standard to meet if they are to produce satisfaction.

- Increases the chances that people will blame themselves when their choices fail to live up to expectations. After all, with so many options out there, there is really no excuse for a disappointing choice.

To illustrate these last two points, I recall buying a bottle of wine to accompany dinner when I was vacationing with my family in a seaside cottage in a small town in Oregon. The tiny general store had about five options from which to choose. The wine I chose wasn't very good, but I didn't expect it to be, and I knew that I couldn't really have done much better. Contrast that with how it would feel to bring home a disappointing bottle of wine from a store that offered thousands of bottles from which to choose.

What are the implications of an abundance of choice for higher education today? College students don't have to worry about choosing 401(k) plans, and most of them don't have major health issues to make decisions about. Nonetheless, the world of the modern college student is so laden with choice, much of it extremely consequential, that for many, it has become overwhelming, perhaps contributing to the rush of students to university counseling services.

When I went to college, 35 years ago, there were almost two years' 10 worth of general-education requirements that all students had to complete. We had *some* choices among courses that met those requirements, but they were rather narrow. Almost every department had a single, introductory course that prepared the student for more advanced work in the field. You could be fairly certain, if you ran into a fellow student you didn't know, that the two of you would have at least a year's worth of courses in common to discuss. In the shopping mall that is the modern university, the chances that any two students have significant intellectual experiences in common are much reduced.

About 30 years ago, somewhat dismayed that their students no longer shared enough common intellectual experiences, the Harvard faculty revised its general-education requirements to form a "core curriculum." With this new curriculum (which is currently undergoing another revision), students take at least one course in each of 11 different broad areas of inquiry. But among those areas, there are dozens and dozens of courses from which to choose. What are the odds that two random students will have courses in common to discuss?

At the advanced end of the curriculum, Harvard offers about 40 majors. For students with interdisciplinary interests, these can be combined into an almost endless array of joint majors. If that doesn't do the trick, students can create their own degree plan. And within majors, at least many of them, internal structure has largely disappeared. Students can begin almost anywhere in the curriculum and end almost anywhere.

Harvard is not unusual. Princeton offers its students a choice of several hundred courses from which to satisfy its general-education requirements. Stanford, which has a larger student body, offers even more. Even at my small college, Swarthmore, with only 1,350 students, we offer about 120 courses to meet our version of the general-education requirement, from which students must select nine. And don't think that this range of choices is peculiar to elite, private institutions. At Pennsylvania State University, for example, liberal-arts students can choose from more than 40 majors and from hundreds of courses intended to meet basic requirements.

Within classes, the digital revolution has made access to information unbelievably easy. The Internet and the "digital library" can be a term-paper writer's blessing. But they can also be a curse. With so much information so readily available, when do you stop looking? There is no excuse for failing to examine all of it.

And outside the classroom, the range of recreational and extracurricular activities afforded to students has become mind-boggling. As elite universities compete with one another for elite students (an example of social waste that I think rivals the SUV), the institutions engage in an arms race of amenity provision—fitness centers, indoor rock-climbing walls, hot tubs that accommodate dozens of people at once, espresso bars—in their effort to attract every student they want. The result is a set of choices of things to do outside of class that makes one's head spin.   15

There are many benefits to expanded educational opportunities. The traditional bodies of knowledge transmitted from teachers to students in the past were constraining and often myopic. The tastes and interests of the idiosyncratic students often were stifled and frustrated. In the modern university, each individual student is free to pursue almost any interest, without having to be harnessed to what his intellectual ancestors thought was worth knowing. Moreover, the advent of the digital age has opened up the intellectual world to all students, even those at resource-poor institutions.

But this freedom comes at a price. Now, students are required to make many choices about education that will affect them for the rest of their lives, and they are forced to make them at a point in their intellectual development when many students lack the wisdom to choose intelligently. In my own experience I see this manifested in several ways. Advisees ask me to approve course selections that have no rhyme or reason behind them and that the advisees themselves can't justify. Students are eager to have double and triple majors, partly, I know, to pad their résumés, but also because they can't figure out which discipline they really want to commit to. And I learned some time ago that "What are you doing when you graduate?" is not a friendly question to ask many college seniors.

In addition, students are faced with all this curricular choice while also trying to figure out what kinds of people they are going to be. Matters of ethnic, religious, and sexual identity are up for grabs. So are issues of romantic intimacy (to marry or not to marry; to have kids or not to have kids; to have kids early or to wait until careers are established). Students can live and work anywhere after they graduate, and in a wired world, they can work at any time, from any place. Of course it is true that students have always had to make these kinds of life decisions. College is an unsettled, and often unsettling, time. But in the past, in virtually each of these areas of life, there was a "default" option that was so powerful that many decisions didn't *feel* like decisions, because alternatives to the default weren't seriously considered. Nowadays, almost nothing is decided by default.

The result is a generation of students who use university counseling services and antidepressants in record numbers, and who provide places like Starbucks with the most highly educated minimum-wage work force in the world, as they bide their time hoping that the answer to the "what should I be when I grow up" question will eventually emerge. Choice overload is certainly not the only reason for the anxiety and uncertainty experienced by modern college students, but I believe it is an important one. I believe that by offering our students this much freedom of choice, we are doing them no favor. Indeed, I think that this obsession with choice constitutes an abdication of responsibility by university faculty members and administrators to provide college students with the guidance they badly need.

In an important respect, the "liberation" of the university experience   20
mirrors the embrace of choice in American society at large. The dominant political trend in the last 25 years, influenced by the principles and assumptions of neoclassical economics, has been to stop trying to have the government provide services that serve the welfare of citizens and instead offer citizens choices so that each of us can pursue our own welfare. The push to privatize Social Security, to offer senior citizens choice among prescription-drug plans, and to offer parents choice in the public education their children receive—these are all instances of the view that choice cannot help but make people better off. And so it is with the modern university. What I have tried to indicate is that though all this choice no doubt makes *some* people better off, it makes *many* people worse off, even when their choices work out well.

If enhanced freedom of choice and increased affluence don't enhance well-being, what does? The most important factor seems to be close social relations. People who are married, who have good friends, and who are close to their families are happier than those who are not. People who participate in religious communities are happier than those who do not. Being connected to others seems to be more important to well-being than being rich or "keeping your options open."

In the context of this discussion of choice, it is important to note that, in many ways, social ties actually *decrease* freedom of choice. Marriage, for example, is a commitment to a particular other person that curtails freedom of choice of sexual or emotional partners. Serious friendship also entails weighty responsibilities and obligations that at times may limit one's own freedom. The same is true, obviously, of family. And most religious institutions call on their members to live their lives in a certain way, and to take responsibility for the well-being of their fellow congregants. So, counterintuitive as it may appear, what seems to contribute most to happiness binds us rather than liberates us.

Yet more than a quarter of Americans report being lonely, and loneliness seems to come not from being alone, but from lack of intimacy. We spend less time visiting with neighbors. We spend less time visiting with our parents, and much less time visiting with other relatives. Partly this is because we *have* less time, since we are busy trying to determine what choices to make in other areas of life. But partly this is because close social relations have themselves become matters of choice. As Robert Lane writes: "What was once given by neighborhood and work now must be achieved; people have had to make their own friends . . . and actively cultivate their own family connections." In other words, our social fabric is no longer a birthright but has become a series of deliberate and demanding choices.

Universities should acknowledge the role they have played in creating a world of choice overload and move from being part of the problem to being a part of the solution. The "culture wars" over the canon that rocked college campuses for years have subsided, and most of us were not sorry to see them go. It is deeply troubling to face up to the fact that you and your colleagues can't agree on something as basic as what a college curriculum should consist of. There were no winners in these wars; they subsided, I think, because people got tired of fighting them. And they subsided because giving students choice seemed like a benign resolution of what were sometimes virulent conflicts. Some choice is good, we thought, so more choice is better. Let students choose and we never have to figure out what to choose for them.

But offering more choice is *not* benign. It is a major source of stress, uncertainty, anxiety—even misery. It is not serving our students well. They would be better served by a faculty and an institution that offered choice within limits, freedom within constraints. The poet and essayist Katha Pollitt observed some years ago that the real reason why battles over the curriculum were so intense—the reason that the stakes seemed so high—is that faculty members knew that for the vast majority of students, the last serious book they would *ever* read would be the last book they read in their college careers. I think we are less likely to turn our students off to the life of the mind if we offer them curricular options that are well structured and coherent than if we simply let them choose whatever they want on their own.

There is a *New Yorker* cartoon that depicts a parent goldfish and an off-spring in a small goldfish bowl. "You can be anything you want to be—no limits," says the myopic parent, not realizing how limited an existence the fishbowl allows. I'd like to suggest that perhaps the parent is not so myopic. Freedom without limits, choice within constraints, is indeed liberating. But if the fishbowl gets shattered—if the constraints disappear—freedom of choice can turn into a tyranny of choice.

The Reader's Presence

1. Schwartz, a professor of psychology and economics at Swarthmore College, begins his essay with the provocative assertion: "The modern university has become a kind of intellectual shopping mall." Explore the nature of this metaphor. What aspects of it do you find most—and least—convincing? Explain why. If "increased choice" leads to a "*decrease* in well-being," as Schwartz argues (paragraph 3), then to what extent should we decrease curriculum choice to increase our educational well-being? Which parts of Schwartz's essay support eliminating our opportunity to choose college courses? Would Schwartz endorse the recommendation that all students should take the same classes through their undergraduate years? Explain why or why not. Develop a counterargument that defends increased choice, taking care to reply to each of Schwartz's points. In your judgment, what are some reasons to keep a university as "a kind of intellectual shopping mall" (paragraph 1)?

2. Identify—and comment on the effectiveness of—the different kinds of evidence Schwartz draws on to make his points (for example, statistics, stories, logic). In what circumstances—and why—does he use one kind of proof rather than another? For example, why do the statistics that begin the essay disappear toward the end? Which kinds of proof are the most convincing to support his points? Reread Schwartz's account of choosing a bottle of wine. These are personal facts, but this is the only personal story Schwartz tells. Why does he choose to tell it here? How is it more or less persuasive than citing another statistic or research study?

3. **CONNECTIONS:** What might Schwartz say about people who have no choices? For example, read Lars Eighner's "On Dumpster Diving" (page 399), which partly tells about what happens when we can no longer exercise choice about where we get our food and what we eat. As Schwartz predicts, Eighner comes to "a healthy state of mind" (Eighner, paragraph 78) by losing his material choices (food, cable channels, etc.). But explain the extent to which Eighner's mental well-being increases because he has lost his choices.

Leslie Marmon Silko

IN THE COMBAT ZONE

Poet, novelist, screenwriter, and storyteller **LESLIE MARMON SILKO** (b. 1948) is of mixed heritage, part Pueblo Indian, part Mexican, and part white. She was raised on the Laguna Pueblo and educated at the University of New Mexico, where she taught English for many years. Her published work includes *Storyteller* (1981), a montage of stories, legends, poems, and photographs; *Sacred Water: Narratives and Pictures* (1993), an illustrated autobiography; *Yellow Woman and a Beauty of the Spirit* (1996), a collection of essays; *Love Poem: Slim Man Canyon* (1999); and the novels *Almanac of the Dead* (1991) and *Gardens in the Dunes* (1999). A collection of rare interviews with Silko, *Conversations with Leslie Marmon Silko*, edited by Ellen L. Arnold, was published in 2000. "In the Combat Zone" appeared in *Hungry Mind Review* in 1995. Silko was awarded a MacArthur Fellowship in 1981 and a Native Writers' Circle of the Americas Lifetime Achievement Award in 1994. She

> **When asked by an interviewer why she writes, Leslie Marmon Silko replied, "I don't know what I know until it comes out in narrative."**

has taught in New Mexico, Alaska, and Arizona and holds academic appointments at both the universities of New Mexico and Arizona. Her latest book, *The Turquoise Ledge: A Memoir* (2010), her first in ten years, is at once an account of her family history and a meditation on the natural beauty of Arizona's Sonoran Desert.

When asked by an interviewer why she writes, she replied, "I don't know what I know until it comes out in narrative." Speaking specifically of the process of composing her novel *Almanac of the Dead*, she said, "It's like a do-it-yourself psychoanalysis. It's sort of dangerous to be a novelist . . . [Y]ou're working with language and all kinds of things can escape with the words of a narrative."

WOMEN SELDOM DISCUSS our wariness or the precautions we take after dark each time we leave the apartment, car, or office to go on the most brief errand. We take for granted that we are targeted as easy prey by muggers, rapists, and serial killers. This is our lot as women in the United States. We try to avoid going anywhere alone after dark, although economic necessity sends women out night after night. We do what must be done, but always we are alert, on guard, and ready. We have to be aware of persons walking on the sidewalk behind us; we have to pay attention to others who board an elevator we're on. We try to avoid all staircases and deserted parking garages when we are alone. Constant vigilance requires considerable energy and concentration seldom required of men.

I used to assume that most men were aware of this fact of women's lives, but I was wrong. They may notice our reluctance to drive at night to the convenience store alone, but they don't know or don't want to know the experience of a woman out alone at night. Men who have been in combat know the feeling of being a predator's target, but it is difficult for men to admit that we women live our entire lives in a combat zone. Men have the power to end violence against women in the home, but they feel helpless to protect women from violent strangers. Because men feel guilt and anger at their inability to shoulder responsibility for the safety of their wives, sisters, and daughters, we don't often discuss random acts of violence against women.

When we were children, my sisters and I used to go to Albuquerque with my father. Sometimes strangers would tell my father it was too bad that he had three girls and no sons. My father, who has always preferred the company of women, used to reply that he was glad to have girls and not boys, because he might not get along as well with boys. Furthermore, he'd say, "My girls can do anything your boys can do, and my girls can do it better." He had in mind, of course, shooting and hunting.

When I was six years old, my father took me along as he hunted deer; he showed me how to walk quietly, to move along, and then to stop and listen carefully before taking another step. A year later, he traded a pistol for a little single shot .22 rifle just my size.

He took me and my younger sisters down to the dump by the river and taught us how to shoot. We rummaged through the trash for bottles and glass jars; it was great fun to take aim at a pickle jar and watch it shatter. If the Río San Jose had water running in it, we threw bottles for moving targets in the muddy current. My father told us that a .22 bullet can travel a mile, so we had to be careful where we aimed. The river was a good place because it was below the villages and away from the houses; the high clay riverbanks wouldn't let any bullets stray. Gun safety was drilled into us. We were cautioned about other children whose parents might not teach them properly; if we ever saw another child with a gun, we knew to get away. Guns were not toys. My father did not approve of BB guns because they were classified as toys. I had a .22 rifle when I was seven years old. If I felt like shooting, all I had to do was tell my parents where I was going, take my rifle and a box of .22 shells and go. I was never tempted to shoot at birds or animals because whatever was killed had to be eaten. Now, I realize how odd this must seem; a seven-year-old with a little .22 rifle and a box of ammunition, target shooting alone at the river. But that was how people lived at Laguna when I was growing up; children were given responsibilities from an early age.

Laguna Pueblo people hunted deer for winter meat. When I was thirteen, I carried George Pearl's saddle carbine, a .30–30, and hunted deer for

5

the first time. When I was fourteen, I killed my first male deer buck with one shot through the heart.

Guns were for target shooting and guns were for hunting, but also I knew that Grandma Lily carried a little purse gun with her whenever she drove alone to Albuquerque or Los Lunas. One night my mother and my grandmother were driving the fifty miles from Albuquerque to Laguna down Route 66 when three men in a car tried to force my grandmother's car off the highway. Route 66 was not so heavily traveled as Interstate 40 is now, and there were many long stretches of highway where no other car passed for minutes on end. Payrolls at the Jackpile Uranium Mine were large in the 1950s, and my mother or my grandmother had to bring home thousands from the bank in Albuquerque to cash the miners' checks on paydays.

After that night, my father bought my mother a pink nickel-plated snub-nose .22 revolver with a white bone grip. Grandma Lily carried a tiny Beretta as black as her prayer book. As my sisters and I got older, my father taught us to handle and shoot handguns, revolvers mostly, because back then, semiautomatic pistols were not as reliable—they frequently jammed. I will never forget the day my father told us three girls that we never had to let a man hit us or terrorize us because no matter how big and strong the man was, a gun in our hand equalized all differences of size and strength.

Much has been written about violence in the home and spousal abuse. I wish to focus instead on violence from strangers toward women because this form of violence terrifies women more, despite the fact that most women are murdered by a spouse, relative, fellow employee, or next-door neighbor, not a stranger. Domestic violence kills many more women and children than strangers kill, but domestic violence also follows more predictable patterns and is more familiar: He comes home drunk and she knows what comes next. A good deal of the terror of a stranger's attack comes from its suddenness and unexpectedness. Attacks by strangers occur with enough frequency that battered women and children often cite their fears of such attacks as reasons for remaining in abusive domestic situations. They fear the violence they imagine strangers will inflict on them more than they fear the abusive home. More than one feminist has pointed out that rapists and serial killers help keep the patriarchy securely in place.

An individual woman may be terrorized by her spouse, but women are   10 not sufficiently terrorized that we avoid marriage. Yet many women I know, including myself, try to avoid going outside of their homes alone after dark. Big deal, you say; well, yes, it is a big deal since most lectures, performances, and films are presented at night; so are dinners and other social events. Women out alone at night who are assaulted by strangers are put on trial by public opinion: Any woman out alone after dark is asking for trouble. Presently, for millions of women of all socioeconomic backgrounds, sundown is lockdown. We are prisoners of violent strangers.

Daylight doesn't necessarily make the streets safe for women. In the early 1980s, a rapist operated in Tucson in the afternoon near the University of Arizona campus. He often accosted two women at once, forced them into residential alleys, then raped each one with a knife to her throat and forced the other to watch. Afterward the women said that part of the horror of their attack was that all around them, everything appeared normal. They could see people inside their houses and cars going down the street—all around them life was going on as usual while their lives were being changed forever.

The afternoon rapist was not the only rapist in Tucson at that time; there were the prime-time rapist, the potbellied rapist, and the apologetic rapist all operating in Tucson in the 1980s. The prime-time rapist was actually two men who invaded comfortable foothills homes during television prime time when residents were preoccupied with television and eating dinner. The prime-time rapists terrorized entire families; they raped the women and sometimes they raped the men. Family members were forced to go to automatic bank machines to bring back cash to end the ordeal. Potbelly rapist and apologetic rapist need little comment, except to note that the apologetic rapist was good looking, well educated, and smart enough to break out of jail for one last rape followed by profuse apologies and his capture in the University of Arizona library. Local papers recounted details about Tucson's last notorious rapist, the red bandanna rapist. In the late 1970s, this rapist attacked more than twenty women over a three-year period, and Tucson police were powerless to stop him. Then one night, the rapist broke into a midtown home where the lone resident, a woman, shot him four times in the chest with a .38 caliber revolver.

In midtown Tucson, on a weekday afternoon, I was driving down Campbell Avenue to the pet store. Suddenly the vehicle behind me began to weave into my lane, so I beeped the horn politely. The vehicle swerved back to its lane, but then in my rearview mirror I saw the small late-model truck change lanes and begin to follow my car very closely. I drove a few blocks without looking in the rearview mirror, but in my sideview mirror I saw the compact truck was right behind me. OK. Some motorists stay upset for two or three blocks, some require ten blocks or more to recover their senses. Stoplight after stoplight, when I glanced into the rearview mirror I saw the man—in his early thirties, tall, white, brown hair, and dark glasses. This guy must not have a job if he has the time to follow me for miles—oh, ohhh! No beast more dangerous in the U.S.A. than an unemployed white man.

At this point I had to make a decision: Do I forget about the trip to the pet store and head for the police station downtown, four miles away? Why should I have to let this stranger dictate my schedule for the afternoon? The man might dare to follow me to the police station, but by the time I reach the front door of the station, he'd be gone. No crime was committed; no Arizona law forbids tailgating someone for miles or for turning into a parking lot behind them. What could the police do? I had no license plate number to report because Arizona requires only one license plate, on the rear bumper of the vehicle. Anyway, I was within a block of the pet store where I knew I could get help from the pet store owners. I would feel better about this incident if it was not allowed to ruin my trip to the pet store.

The guy was right on my rear bumper; if I'd had to stop suddenly for any   15
reason, there'd have been a collision. I decide I will not stop even if he does ram into the rear of my car. I study this guy's face in my rearview mirror; six feet two inches tall, 175 pounds, medium complexion, short hair, trimmed moustache. He thinks he can intimidate me because I am a woman, five feet five inches tall, 140 pounds. But I am not afraid, I am furious. I refuse to be intimidated. I won't play his game. I can tell by the face I see in the mirror this guy has done this before, he enjoys using his truck to menace lone women.

I keep thinking he will quit, or he will figure that he's scared me enough, but he seems to sense that I am not afraid. It's true. I am not afraid because years ago my father taught my sisters and me that we did not have to be afraid. He'll give up when I turn into the parking lot outside the pet store, I think. But I watch in my rearview mirror; he's right on my rear bumper. As his truck turns into the parking lot behind my car, I reach over and open the glove compartment. I take out the holster with my .38 special and lay it on the car seat beside me.

I turned my car into a parking spot so quickly that I was facing my stalker who had momentarily stopped his truck and was watching me. I slid the .38 out of its holster onto my lap. I watched the stranger's face, trying to determine whether he would jump out of his truck with a baseball bat or gun and come after me. I felt calm. No pounding heart or rapid breathing. My early experience deer hunting had prepared me well. I did not panic because I felt I could stop him if he tried to harm me. I was in no hurry. I sat in the car and waited to see what choice my stalker would make. I looked directly at him without fear because I had my .38 and I was ready to use it. The expression on my face must have been unfamiliar to him; he was used to seeing terror in the eyes of the women he followed. The expression on my face communicated a warning: If he approached the car window, I'd kill him.

He took a last look at me then sped away. I stayed in my car until his truck disappeared in the traffic of Campbell Avenue.

I walked into the pet store shaken. I had felt able to protect myself throughout the incident, but it left me emotionally drained and exhausted. The stranger had only pursued me—how much worse to be battered or raped.

Years before, I was unarmed the afternoon that two drunken deer hunt-   20
ers threatened to shoot me off my horse with razor-edged hunting arrows from fiberglass crossbows. I was riding a colt on a national park trail near my home in the Tucson Mountains. These young white men in their late twenties were complete strangers who might have shot me if the colt had not galloped away erratically bucking and leaping—a moving target too diffi-cult for the drunken bow hunters to aim at. The colt brought me to my ranch house where I called the county sheriff's office and the park ranger. I live in a sparsely populated area where my nearest neighbor is a quarter-mile

away. I was afraid the men might have followed me back to my house so I took the .44 magnum out from under my pillow and strapped it around my waist until the sheriff or park ranger arrived. Forty-five minutes later, the park ranger arrived; the deputy sheriff arrived fifteen minutes after him. The drunken bow hunters were apprehended in the national park and arrested for illegally hunting; their bows and arrows were seized as evidence for the duration of bow hunting season. In southern Arizona that is enough punishment; I didn't want to take a chance of stirring up additional animosity with these men because I lived alone then; I chose not to make a complaint about their threatening words and gestures. I did not feel that I backed away by not pressing charges; I feared that if I pressed assault charges against these men, they would feel that I was challenging them to all-out war. I did not want to have to kill either of them if they came after me, as I thought they might. With my marksmanship and my .243 caliber hunting rifle from the old days, I am confident that I could stop idiots like these. But to have to take the life of another person is a terrible experience I will always try to avoid.

It isn't height or weight or strength that make women easy targets; from infancy women are taught to be self-sacrificing, passive victims. I was taught differently. Women have the right to protect themselves from death or bodily harm. By becoming strong and potentially lethal individuals, women destroy the fantasy that we are sitting ducks for predatory strangers.

In a great many cultures, women are taught to depend on others, not themselves, for protection from bodily harm. Women are not taught to defend themselves from strangers because fathers and husbands fear the consequences themselves. In the United States, women depend on the courts and the police, but as many women have learned the hard way, the police cannot be outside your house twenty-four hours a day. I don't want more police. More police on the streets will not protect women. A few policemen are rapists and killers of women themselves; their uniforms and squad cars give them an advantage. No, I will be responsible for my own safety, thank you.

Women need to decide who has the primary responsibility for the health and safety of their bodies. We don't trust the State to manage our reproductive organs, yet most of us blindly trust that the State will protect us (and our reproductive organs) from predatory strangers. One look at the rape and murder statistics for women (excluding domestic incidents) and it is clear that the government FAILS to protect women from the violence of strangers. Some may cry out for a "stronger" State, more police, mandatory sentences, and swifter executions. Over the years we have seen the U.S. prison population become the largest in the world, executions take place every week now, inner-city communities are occupied by the National Guard, and people of color are harassed by police, but guess what? A woman out alone, night or day, is confronted with more danger of random violence from strangers than ever before. As the U.S. economy continues "to downsize," and the good jobs disappear forever, our urban and rural landscapes will include more desperate, angry men with nothing to lose.

Only women can put a stop to the "open season" on women by strangers. Women are TAUGHT to be easy targets by their mothers, aunts, and grandmothers, who themselves were taught that "a woman doesn't kill" or "a woman doesn't learn how to use a weapon." Women must learn how to take aggressive action individually, apart from the police and the courts.

Presently, twenty-one states issue permits to carry concealed weapons; 25 most states require lengthy gun safety courses and a police security check before issuing a permit. Inexpensive but excellent gun safety and self-defense courses designed for women are also available from every quality gun dealer who hopes to sell you a handgun at the end of the course. Those who object to firearms need trained companion dogs or collectives of six or more women to escort one another day and night. We must destroy the myth that women are born to be easy targets.

The Reader's Presence

1. What does Silko mean by a "combat zone" (paragraph 2)? What is the origin of the term? How does she apply it to women's experiences? Do you think the term is applicable? What behavior does the term legitimize? Why do you think she concentrates on violence from strangers instead of domestic violence?

2. Why do you think Silko introduces stories about hunting experiences? In what ways do those experiences shape her background? Do you think they have shaped her present attitude? How do the experiences help reinforce her point about gun ownership? In what ways do they make her more qualified to speak on the issue?

3. **CONNECTIONS:** In her opening two paragraphs, Silko describes the precautions women take in public every day, of which men are often ignorant. Read Brent Staples's "Just Walk on By: A Black Man Ponders His Power to Alter Public Space" (page 260), which details his experiences of being stereotyped as a threat. How do you think Staples and Silko might discuss this idea of safety? Does Staples show himself to be aware of women's safety concerns? If so, in what ways? What might Silko say in response to Staples's feelings about "being perceived as dangerous" (Staples, paragraph 2)?

Peter Singer

THE SINGER SOLUTION TO WORLD POVERTY

PETER SINGER, born in 1946 in Melbourne, Australia, has had a long career as an animal rights activist and is one of today's most controversial contemporary philosophers. He is the DeCamp Professor of Bioethics at Princeton University's Center for Human Values and a Laureate Professor at the University of Melbourne. His book *Animal Liberation*, first published in 1975 and reprinted many times since, has become a basic sourcebook for animal rights activists, and his book *Practical Ethics* (1979) is one of the most widely recognized works of applied ethics. He has also written *Rethinking Life and Death: The Collapse of Our Traditional Ethics*, which received an award from the National Book Council in 1995. He is president of Animal Rights International, vice-president of the United Kingdom's Royal Society for the Prevention of Cruelty to Animals, and he serves on the advisory board of several organizations. Singer has written or edited more than thirty books, including *One World: The Ethics of Globalization* (2002), *Pushing Time Away: My Grandfather and the Tragedy of Jewish Vienna* (2003), and *The Life You Can Save: Acting Now to End World Poverty* (2009). He co-wrote with Jim Mason *The Ethics of What We Eat: Why Our Food Choices Matter* (2006) and co-edited the *Cambridge Textbook of Bioethics*, published in 2008. "The Singer Solution to World Poverty" was first published in the *New York Times* in September 1999.

> "For Singer, living ethically is living a meaningful life. It is a life that makes a difference in the world. It is a life that reduces the sum total of suffering."

A reviewer of *Writings on an Ethical Life* (1994) commented: "Singer argues that value judgments should be matters of rational scrutiny and not matters of taste about which argument is futile. . . . For Singer, living ethically is living a meaningful life. It is a life that makes a difference in the world. It is a life that reduces the sum total of suffering."

IN THE BRAZILIAN FILM *Central Station*, Dora is a retired schoolteacher who makes ends meet by sitting at the station writing letters for illiterate people. Suddenly she has an opportunity to pocket $1,000. All she has to do is persuade a homeless nine-year-old boy to follow her to an address she has been given. (She is told he will be adopted by wealthy foreigners.) She delivers the boy, gets the money, spends some of it on a television set, and settles down to enjoy her new acquisition. Her neighbor spoils the fun, however, by telling her that the boy was too old to be adopted—he will be killed and his organs sold for transplantation. Perhaps Dora knew this all along, but after her neighbor's plain speaking, she spends a troubled night. In the morning Dora resolves to take the boy back.

Suppose Dora had told her neighbor that it is a tough world, other people have nice new TVs too, and if selling the kid is the only way she can get one, well, he was only a street kid. She would then have become, in the eyes of the audience, a monster. She redeems herself only by being prepared to bear considerable risks to save the boy.

At the end of the movie, in cinemas in the affluent nations of the world, people who would have been quick to condemn Dora if she had not rescued the boy go home to places far more comfortable than her apartment. In fact, the average family in the United States spends almost one-third of its income on things that are no more necessary to them than Dora's new TV was to her. Going out to nice restaurants, buying new clothes because the old ones are no longer stylish, vacationing at beach resorts — so much of our income is spent on things not essential to the preservation of our lives and health. Donated to one of a number of charitable agencies, that money could mean the difference between life and death for children in need.

All of which raises a question: In the end, what is the ethical distinction between a Brazilian who sells a homeless child to organ peddlers and an American who already has a TV and upgrades to a better one — knowing that the money could be donated to an organization that would use it to save the lives of kids in need?

Of course, there are several differences between the two situations that could support different moral judgments about them. For one thing, to be able to consign a child to death when he is standing right in front of you takes a chilling kind of heartlessness; it is much easier to ignore an appeal for money to help children you will never meet. Yet for a utilitarian philosopher like myself — that is, one who judges whether acts are right or wrong by their consequences — if the upshot of the American's failure to donate the money is that one more kid dies on the streets of a Brazilian city, then it is, in some sense, just as bad as selling the kid to the organ peddlers. But one doesn't need to embrace my utilitarian ethic to see that, at the very least, there is a troubling incongruity in being so quick to condemn Dora for taking the child to the organ peddlers while, at the same time, not regarding the American consumer's behavior as raising a serious moral issue.

In his 1996 book, *Living High and Letting Die*, the New York University philosopher Peter Unger presented an ingenious series of imaginary examples designed to probe our intuitions about whether it is wrong to live well without giving substantial amounts of money to help people who are hungry, malnourished, or dying from easily treatable illnesses like diarrhea. Here's my paraphrase of one of these examples:

Bob is close to retirement. He has invested most of his savings in a very rare and valuable old car, a Bugatti, which he has not been able to insure. The Bugatti is his pride and joy. In addition to the pleasure he gets from driving and caring for his car, Bob knows that its rising market value means

5

that he will always be able to sell it and live comfortably after retirement. One day when Bob is out for a drive, he parks the Bugatti near the end of a railway siding and goes for a walk up the track. As he does so, he sees that a runaway train, with no one aboard, is running down the railway track. Looking farther down the track, he sees the small figure of a child very likely to be killed by the runaway train. He can't stop the train and the child is too far away to warn of the danger, but he can throw a switch that will divert the train down the siding where his Bugatti is parked. Then nobody will be killed—but the train will destroy his Bugatti. Thinking of his joy in owning the car and the financial security it represents, Bob decides not to throw the switch. The child is killed. For many years to come, Bob enjoys owning his Bugatti and the financial security it represents.

Bob's conduct, most of us will immediately respond, was gravely wrong. Unger agrees. But then he reminds us that we, too, have opportunities to save the lives of children. We can give to organizations like Unicef or Oxfam America. How much would we have to give one of these organizations to have a high probability of saving the life of a child threatened by easily preventable diseases? (I do not believe that children are more worth saving than adults, but since no one can argue that children have brought their poverty on themselves, focusing on them simplifies the issues.) Unger called up some experts and used the information they provided to offer some plausible estimates that include the cost of raising money, administrative expenses, and the cost of delivering aid where it is most needed. By his calculation, $200 in donations would help a sickly two-year-old transform into a healthy six-year-old—offering safe passage through childhood's most dangerous years. To show how practical philosophical argument can be, Unger even tells his readers that they can easily donate funds by using their credit card and calling one of these toll-free numbers: (800) 367-5437 for Unicef; (800) 693-2687 for Oxfam America.

Now you, too, have the information you need to save a child's life. How should you judge yourself if you don't do it? Think again about Bob and his Bugatti. Unlike Dora, Bob did not have to look into the eyes of the child he was sacrificing for his own material comfort. The child was a complete stranger to him and too far away to relate to in an intimate, personal way. Unlike Dora, too, he did not mislead the child or initiate the chain of events imperiling him. In all these respects, Bob's situation resembles that of people able but unwilling to donate to overseas aid and differs from Dora's situation.

If you still think that it was very wrong of Bob not to throw the switch   10 that would have diverted the train and saved the child's life, then it is hard to see how you could deny that it is also very wrong not to send money to one of the organizations listed above. Unless, that is, there is some morally important difference between the two situations that I have overlooked.

Is it the practical uncertainties about whether aid will really reach the people who need it? Nobody who knows the world of overseas aid can doubt that such uncertainties exist. But Unger's figure of $200 to save a child's life was reached after he had made conservative assumptions about the proportion of the money donated that will actually reach its target.

One genuine difference between Bob and those who can afford to donate to overseas aid organizations but don't is that only Bob can save the child on the tracks, whereas there are hundreds of millions of people who can give $200 to overseas aid organizations. The problem is that most of them aren't doing it. Does this mean that it is all right for you not to do it?

Suppose that there were more owners of priceless vintage cars—Carol, Dave, Emma, Fred, and so on, down to Ziggy—all in exactly the same situation as Bob, with their own siding and their own switch, all sacrificing the child in order to preserve their own cherished car. Would that make it all right for Bob to do the same? To answer this question affirmatively is to endorse follow-the-crowd ethics—the kind of ethics that led many Germans to look away when the Nazi atrocities were being committed. We do not excuse them because others were behaving no better.

We seem to lack a sound basis for drawing a clear moral line between Bob's situation and that of any reader of this article with $200 to spare who does not donate it to an overseas aid agency. These readers seem to be acting at least as badly as Bob was acting when he chose to let the runaway train hurtle toward the unsuspecting child. In the light of this conclusion, I trust that many readers will reach for the phone and donate that $200. Perhaps you should do it before reading further.

Now that you have distinguished yourself morally from people who put their vintage cars ahead of a child's life, how about treating yourself and your partner to dinner at your favorite restaurant? But wait. The money you will spend at the restaurant could also help save the lives of children overseas! True, you weren't planning to blow $200 tonight, but if you were to give up dining out just for one month, you would easily save that amount. And what is one month's dining out, compared to a child's life? There's the rub. Since there are a lot of desperately needy children in the world, there will always be another child whose life you could save for another $200. Are you therefore obliged to keep giving until you have nothing left? At what point can you stop? 15

Hypothetical examples can easily become farcical. Consider Bob. How far past losing the Bugatti should he go? Imagine that Bob had got his foot stuck in the track of the siding, and if he diverted the train, then before it rammed the car it would also amputate his big toe. Should he still throw the switch? What if it would amputate his foot? His entire leg?

As absurd as the Bugatti scenario gets when pushed to extremes, the point it raises is a serious one: Only when the sacrifices become very significant indeed would most people be prepared to say that Bob does nothing wrong when he decides not to throw the switch. Of course, most people could be wrong; we can't decide moral issues by taking opinion polls. But consider for yourself the level of sacrifice that you would demand of Bob, and then think about how much money you would have to give away in order to make a sacrifice that is roughly equal to that. It's almost certainly

much, much more than $200. For most middle-class Americans, it could eas-
ily be more like $200,000.

Isn't it counterproductive to ask people to do so much? Don't we run the
risk that many will shrug their shoulders and say that morality, so conceived,
is fine for saints but not for them? I accept that we are unlikely to see, in the
near or even medium-term future, a world in which it is normal for wealthy
Americans to give the bulk of their wealth to strangers. When it comes to
praising or blaming people for what they do, we tend to use a standard that
is relative to some conception of normal behavior. Comfortably off Americans who give, say, 10 percent of their income to overseas aid organizations
are so far ahead of most of their equally comfortable fellow citizens that I
wouldn't go out of my way to chastise them for not doing more. Nevertheless, they should be doing much more, and they are in no position to criticize
Bob for failing to make the much greater sacrifice of his Bugatti.

At this point various objections may crop up. Someone may say: "If every
citizen living in the affluent nations contributed his or her share I wouldn't
have to make such a drastic sacrifice, because long before such levels were
reached, the resources would have been there to save the lives of all those
children dying from lack of food or medical care. So why should I give more
than my fair share?" Another, related objection is that the government ought
to increase its overseas aid allocations, since that would spread the burden
more equitably across all taxpayers.

Yet the question of how much we ought to give is a matter to be decided   20
in the real world—and that, sadly, is a world in which we know that most
people do not, and in the immediate future will not, give substantial amounts
to overseas aid agencies. We know, too, that at least in the next year, the
United States government is not going to meet even the very modest United
Nations–recommended target of 0.7 percent of gross national product; at
the moment it lags far below that, at 0.09 percent, not even half of Japan's
0.22 percent or a tenth of Denmark's 0.97 percent. Thus, we know that the
money we can give beyond that theoretical "fair share" is still going to save
lives that would otherwise be lost. While the idea that no one need do more
than his or her fair share is a powerful one, should it prevail if we know that
others are not doing their fair share and that children will die preventable
deaths unless we do more than our fair share? That would be taking fairness
too far.

Thus, this ground for limiting how much we ought to give also fails. In
the world as it is now, I can see no escape from the conclusion that each one
of us with wealth surplus to his or her essential needs should be giving most
of it to help people suffering from poverty so dire as to be life-threatening.
That's right: I'm saying that you shouldn't buy that new car, take that cruise,
redecorate the house, or get that pricey new suit. After all, a $1,000 suit
could save five children's lives.

So how does my philosophy break down in dollars and cents? An American household with an income of $50,000 spends around $30,000 annually
on necessities, according to the Conference Board, a nonprofit economic

research organization. Therefore, for a household bringing in $50,000 a year, donations to help the world's poor should be as close as possible to $20,000. The $30,000 required for necessities holds for higher incomes as well. So a household making $100,000 could cut a yearly check for $70,000. Again, the formula is simple: Whatever money you're spending on luxuries, not necessities, should be given away.

Now, evolutionary psychologists tell us that human nature just isn't sufficiently altruistic to make it plausible that many people will sacrifice so much for strangers. On the facts of human nature, they might be right, but they would be wrong to draw a moral conclusion from those facts. If it is the case that we ought to do things that, predictably, most of us won't do, then let's face that fact head-on. Then, if we value the life of a child more than going to fancy restaurants, the next time we dine out we will know that we could have done something better with our money. If that makes living a morally decent life extremely arduous, well, then that is the way things are. If we don't do it, then we should at least know that we are failing to live a morally decent life — not because it is good to wallow in guilt but because knowing where we should be going is the first step toward heading in that direction.

When Bob first grasped the dilemma that faced him as he stood by that railway switch, he must have thought how extraordinarily unlucky he was to be placed in a situation in which he must choose between the life of an innocent child and the sacrifice of most of his savings. But he was not unlucky at all. We are all in that situation. ■

The Reader's Presence

1. How convincing do you find Singer's hypothetical examples, such as Bob and his uninsured Bugatti? Do you think the examples support Singer's basic argument or weaken it? Explain your response.

2. Singer defines a utilitarian philosopher as "one who judges whether acts are right or wrong by their consequences" (paragraph 5). Can you think of utilitarian solutions other than Singer's to the problems of world poverty? For example, would population-control methods that drastically reduced the number of impoverished children born into the world also be a utilitarian solution? Would donations to organizations that fund population control be more effective than charitable donations that directly assist children? If Singer's solution were adopted and more and more children were assisted, would that eventually encourage higher birth rates and thus worsen the very problem Singer wants to solve?

3. **CONNECTIONS:**   Consider Singer's essay in conjunction with Jonathan Swift's classic satirical essay on poverty, "A Modest Proposal" (page 752). In what ways does Swift's essay also take a utilitarian position? How do you think Swift would react to Singer's solution to world poverty?

The Academic Voice

PETER SINGER on "Utility and the Survival Lottery"

© Rune Hellestad/CORBIS

What happens when writers address an academic audience, rather than a general audience? What adjustments do they make in their vocabulary, tone of voice, organization, or argument? How do these adjustments take into account the level of knowledge and information they can expect an academic audience to possess? Here you will find the beginning of Peter Singer's academic paper "Utility and the Survival Lottery," published in the journal *Philosophy*. Compare this academic selection with Singer's imaginary example of Bob and his Bugatti (paragraphs 7–14) in his essay for a general audience, "The Singer Solution to World Poverty" (page 735).

❝ In an ingenious article John Harris has proposed a "survival lottery," which would minimize the total number of deaths in a community by sacrificing randomly chosen individuals so that their organs could be transplanted to other people, each of whom needs to have an organ replaced. Since, assuming the perfection of transplant technology, the parts of one "donor" (if that is the right word) could save the lives of four or five others, the proposal appears to be a rational one. If we had the option of joining such a scheme it seems, at first glance anyway, that we would be imprudent to refuse to join. More lives will be saved by the transplants than will be lost by the sacrifices required; hence our prospects of living to a ripe old age are better if we join.[1]

Rational as Harris's idea seems, it will no doubt evoke numerous objections based on the idea of the sanctity of human life and the wrongness of killing an innocent human being.[2] It is not my present purpose to discuss such objections, although my inclinations are to side with Harris against them, on the ground that if human life is valuable, a scheme that saves human lives must be desirable. To say that one violates the sanctity of human life by killing one person to save four, while one does not violate it if one allows four to die because one refuses to kill one, invokes a very dubious notion of moral responsibility. Moral responsibility, as Harris and others have argued, must apply to what we deliberately allow to occur as well as to what we directly bring about.[3]

[1] John Harris, "The Survival Lottery," *Philosophy* 50 (1975), 81.

[2] Alan Ryan has suggested (though not necessarily endorsed) some of these objections in "Two Kinds of Morality," *The Hastings Center Report 5*, no. 5 (1975), 5.
[3] See, for instance, Jonathan Bennett, "Whatever the Consequences," *Analysis 26* (1966); Michael Tooley, "Abortion and Infanticide," *Philosophy and Public Affairs 2*, no. 1 (1972); and Jonathan Glover's book, *Causing Death and Saving Lives* (1990).

Similarly, the charge that it is arbitrary or unfair to be called upon to die just because one's number has been drawn in a lottery can be met by pointing out that it is arbitrary and unfair to die just because one has contracted a kidney disease; and if the only way to prevent four arbitrary and unfair deaths is to inflict one arbitrary and unfair death, that procedure is itself neither arbitrary nor unfair.

In any case, the charge of unfairness, or of infringing on individual rights, can be overcome by the stipulation that the scheme be a voluntary one. Instead of simply giving everyone a lottery number, as Harris suggests, we could invite applications for membership in a kind of mutual benefit society, benefits and risks being restricted to members only. Provided people consent to the arrangement, in full knowledge of what it is to which they are consenting, it seems difficult to hold it unfair or an infringement of their rights if they are later selected to be sacrificed.

The major drawback to the survival lottery seems to be, then, not that it infringes some justifiable moral prohibition against killing; rather, I shall suggest, it is a problem of a utilitarian kind. This is surprising, for the scheme looks like an example of utilitarian planning carried to a new extreme. Harris himself says that utilitarians ought to favor it, and devotes most of his article to meeting absolutist objections. But the survival lottery faces a problem that is faced—though in a milder form—by a wide range of social welfare schemes: by transferring the consequences of imprudent action from the imprudent individual to society at large, the scheme removes the natural disincentive to imprudent action. Thus if I like rich food, and am a member of the survival lottery, I can eat what I like without worrying about growing obese or straining my heart; when it fails, I can always get a new one from a healthier person. My obesity does not increase my chances of being selected by the lottery, and so does not decrease my expected life-span; nor does another person's sensible diet and regular exercise increase his expected life-span. There may even be a tendency toward the reverse, since unhealthy people whose organs have already deteriorated to some extent will be of little use as donors and so presumably would be eliminated from the draw, leaving the healthy to bear the burden of providing organs when required. **"**

Lauren Slater

THE TROUBLE WITH SELF-ESTEEM

LAUREN SLATER (b. 1963) began her writing career after earning a doctorate in clinical psychology from Boston University. Her first book, *Welcome to My Country: A Therapist's Memoir of Madness* (1996), tells the stories of some of the patients she treated over the course of her eleven-year career. She is perhaps best known, however, for her accounts of her own mental illness and recovery, *Prozac Diary* (1998) and *Lying: A Metaphorical Memoir* (2000). Discussing the difference between writing about her patients and about herself, Slater explains, "I think I found it easier to write about other people, about patients, because I could portray the enormity and dignity of their suffering without risking self-absorption, or blatant narcissism. In writing about myself, I feel much more constricted. I worry about solipsism, shortsightedness, self-aggrandizement, self-denigration, and all the other treacherous territories that come with the fascinating pursuit of autobiography."

> "In writing about myself, I feel much more constricted. I worry about solipsism, shortsightedness, self-aggrandizement, self-denigration, and all the other treacherous territories that come with the fascinating pursuit of autobiography."

Slater has also published numerous books combining scientific research, a professional's perspective, and personal experience, including *Love Works Like This: Moving from One Kind of Life to Another* (2002), *Opening Skinner's Box: Great Psychological Experiments of the Twentieth Century* (2004), and *Blue Beyond Blue* (2005), a collection of stories told as fairy tales. She has contributed pieces to the *New York Times*, *Harper's*, *Elle*, and *Nerve*, and her essays are found in numerous anthologies, including *Best American Essays of 1994, 1997,* and *2008, Best American Science Writing 2002,* and *Best American Magazine Writing 2002*. Her most recent book is *The $60,000 Dog: My Life with Animals* (2012). Her essay "The Trouble with Self-Esteem" appeared in the *New York Times Magazine* in 2002. Her most recent book is *Playing House: Notes of a Reluctant Mother* (2013).

TAKE THIS TEST:

1. On the whole I am satisfied with myself.

2. At times I think that I am no good at all.

3. I feel that I have a number of good qualities.

4. I am able to do things as well as most other people.

5. I feel I do not have much to be proud of.

6. I certainly feel useless at times.

7. I feel that I am a person of worth, at least the equal of others.

8. I wish I could have more respect for myself.

9. All in all, I am inclined to feel that I am a failure.

10. I take a positive attitude toward myself.

Devised by the sociologist Morris Rosenberg, this questionnaire is one of the most widely used self-esteem assessment scales in the United States. If your answers demonstrate solid self-regard, the wisdom of the social sciences predicts that you are well adjusted, clean and sober, basically lucid, without criminal record and with some kind of college cum laude under your high-end belt. If your answers, on the other hand, reveal some inner shame, then it is obvious: you were, or are, a teenage mother; you are prone to social deviance; and if you don't drink, it is because the illicit drugs are bountiful and robust.

It has not been much disputed, until recently, that high self-esteem—defined quite simply as liking yourself a lot, holding a positive opinion of your actions and capacities—is essential to well-being and that its opposite is responsible for crime and substance abuse and prostitution and murder and rape and even terrorism. Thousands of papers in psychiatric and social-science literature suggest this, papers with names like "Characteristics of Abusive Parents: A Look at Self-Esteem" and "Low Adolescent Self-Esteem Leads to Multiple Interpersonal Problems." In 1990, David Long published "The Anatomy of Terrorism," in which he found that hijackers and suicide bombers suffer from feelings of worthlessness and that their violent, fluorescent acts are desperate attempts to bring some inner flair to a flat mindscape.

This all makes so much sense that we have not thought to question it. The less confidence you have, the worse you do; the more confidence you have, the better you do; and so the luminous loop goes round. Based on our beliefs, we have created self-esteem programs in schools in which the main objective is, as Jennifer Coon-Wallman, a psychotherapist based in Boston, says, "to dole out huge heapings of praise, regardless of actual accomplishment." We have a National Association for Self-Esteem with about a thousand members, and in 1986, the State Legislature of California founded the "California Task Force to Promote Self-Esteem and Personal and Social Responsibility." It was galvanized by Assemblyman John Vasconcellos, who fervently believed that by raising his citizens' self-concepts, he could divert drug abuse and all sorts of other social ills.

It didn't work.

In fact, crime rates and substance abuse rates are formidable, right along with our self-assessment scores on paper-and-pencil tests. (Whether these tests are valid and reliable indicators of self-esteem is a subject worthy of inquiry itself, but in the parlance of social-science writing, it goes "beyond the scope of this paper.") In part, the discrepancy between high self-esteem scores and poor social skills and academic acumen led researchers like Nicholas Emler of the London School of Economics and Roy Baumeister of Case Western Reserve University to consider the unexpected notion that self-esteem is overrated and to suggest that it may even be a culprit, not a cure.

"There is absolutely no evidence that low self-esteem is particularly harmful," Emler says. "It's not at all a cause of poor academic performance; people with low self-esteem seem to do just as well in life as people with high self-esteem. In fact, they may do better, because they often try harder." Baumeister takes Emler's findings a bit further, claiming not only that low self-esteem is in most cases a socially benign if not beneficent condition but also that its opposite, high self-regard, can maim and even kill. Baumeister conducted a study that found that some people with favorable views of themselves were more likely to administer loud blasts of ear-piercing noise to a subject than those more tepid, timid folks who held back the horn. An earlier experiment found that men with high self-esteem were more willing to put down victims to whom they had administered electric shocks than were their low-level counterparts.

Last year alone there were three withering studies of self-esteem released in the United States, all of which had the same central message: people with high self-esteem pose a greater threat to those around them than people with low self-esteem and feeling bad about yourself is not the cause of our country's biggest, most expensive social problems. The research is original and compelling and lays the groundwork for a new, important kind of narrative about what makes life worth living—if we choose to listen, which might be hard. One of this country's most central tenets, after all, is the pursuit of happiness, which has been strangely joined to the pursuit of self-worth. Shifting a paradigm is never easy. More than 2,000 books offering the attainment of self-esteem have been published; educational programs in schools designed to cultivate self-esteem continue to proliferate, as do rehabilitation programs for substance abusers that focus on cognitive realignment with self-affirming statements like, "Today I will accept myself for who I am, not who I wish I were." I have seen therapists tell their sociopathic patients to say "I adore myself" every day or to post reminder notes on their kitchen cabinets and above their toilet-paper dispensers, self-affirmations set side by side with waste.

Will we give these challenges to our notions about self-esteem their due or will the research go the way of the waste? "Research like that is seriously flawed," says Stephen Keane, a therapist who practices in Newburyport, Mass. "First, it's defining self-esteem according to very conventional and problematic masculine ideas. Second, it's clear to me that many violent men, in particular, have this inner shame; they find out early in life they're not going to measure up, and they compensate for it with fists. We need, as men, to get to the place where we can really honor and expand our natural human grace."

Keane's comment is rooted in a history that goes back hundreds of years, 10 and it is this history that in part prevents us from really tussling with the insights of scientists like Baumeister and Emler. We have long held in this country the Byronic[1] belief that human nature is essentially good or grace-ful, that behind the sheath of skin is a little globe of glow to be harnessed for creative uses. Benjamin Franklin, we believe, got that glow, as did Joseph Pulitzer and scads of other, lesser, folks who eagerly caught on to what was called, in the 19th century, "mind cure."

Mind cure augurs New Age healing, so that when we lift and look at the roots, New Age is not new at all. In the 19th century, people fervently believed that you were what you thought. Sound familiar? Post it above your toilet paper. You are what you think. What you think. What you think. In the 1920's, a French psychologist, Émile Coué, became all the rage in this coun-try; he proposed the technique of autosuggestion and before long had many citizens repeating, "Day by day in every way I am getting better and better."

But as John Hewitt says in his book criticizing self-esteem, it was maybe Ralph Waldo Emerson more than anyone else who gave the mod-ern self-esteem movement its most eloquent words and suasive philosophy. Emerson died more than a century ago, but you can visit his house in Con-cord, Mass., and see his bedroom slippers cordoned off behind plush velvet ropes and his eyeglasses, surprisingly frail, the frames of thin gold, the ovals of shine, perched on a beautiful desk. It was in this house that Emerson wrote his famous transcendentalist essays like "On Self-Reliance," which posits that the individual has something fresh and authentic within and that it is up to him to discover it and nurture it apart from the corrupting pressures of social influence. Emerson never mentions "self-esteem" in his essay, but his every word echoes with the self-esteem movement of today, with its romantic, some-times silly and clearly humane belief that we are special, from head to toe.

Self-esteem, as a construct, as a quasi-religion, is woven into a tradi-tion that both defines and confines us as Americans. If we were to decon-struct self-esteem, to question its value, we would be, in a sense, question-ing who we are, nationally and individually. We would be threatening our self-esteem. This is probably why we cannot really assimilate research like Baumeister's or Emler's; it goes too close to the bone and then threatens to break it. Imagine if you heard your child's teacher say, "Don't think so much of yourself." Imagine your spouse saying to you, "You know, you're really not so good at what you do." We have developed a discourse of affirmation, and to deviate from that would be to enter another arena, linguistically and grammatically, so that what came out of our mouths would be impolite at best, unintelligible at worst.

---

1 **Byronic:** After the English poet George Gordon, Lord Byron (1788–1824). —EDS.

Is there a way to talk about the self without measuring its worth? Why, as a culture, have we so conflated the two quite separate notions—(a) self and (b) worth? This may have as much to do with our entrepreneurial history as Americans, in which everything exists to be improved, as it does, again, with the power of language to shape beliefs. How would we story the self if not triumphantly, redemptively, enhanced from the inside out? A quick glance at amazon.com titles containing the word "self" shows that a hefty percentage also have -improvement or -enhancement tucked into them, oftentimes with numbers—something like 101 ways to improve your self-esteem or 503 ways to better your outlook in 60 days or 604 ways to overcome negative self-talk. You could say that these titles are a product of a culture, or you could say that these titles and the contents they sheathe shape the culture. It is the old argument: do we make language or does language make us? In the case of self-esteem, it is probably something in between, a synergistic loop-the-loop.

On the subject of language, one could, of course, fault Baumeister and Emler for using "self-esteem" far too unidimensionally, so that it blurs and blends with simple smugness. Baumeister, in an attempt at nuance, has tried to shade the issue by referring to two previously defined types: high *unstable* self-esteem and high *well-grounded* self-esteem. As a psychologist, I remember once treating a murderer, who said, "The problem with me, Lauren, is that I'm the biggest piece of [expletive] the world revolves around." He would have scored high on a self-esteem inventory, but does he really "feel good" about himself? And if he doesn't really feel good about himself, then does it not follow that his hidden low, not his high, self-esteem leads to violence? And yet as Baumeister points out, research has shown that people with overt low self-esteem aren't violent, so why would low self-esteem cause violence only when it is hidden? If you follow his train of thinking, you could come up with the sort of silly conclusion that covert low self-esteem causes aggression, but overt low self-esteem does not, which means concealment, not cockiness, is the real culprit. That makes little sense.

"The fact is," Emler says, "we've put antisocial men through every self-esteem test we have, and there's *no* evidence for the old psychodynamic concept that they secretly feel bad about themselves. These men are racist or violent because they don't feel bad *enough* about themselves." Baumeister and his colleagues write: "People who believe themselves to be among the top 10 percent on any dimension may be insulted and threatened whenever anyone asserts that they are in the 80th or 50th or 25th percentile. In contrast, someone with lower self-esteem who regards himself or herself as being merely in the top 60 percent would only be threatened by the feedback that puts him or her at the 25th percentile. . . . In short, the more favorable one's view of oneself, the greater the range of external feedback that will be perceived as unacceptably low."

Perhaps, as these researchers are saying, pride really is dangerous, and too few of us know how to be humble. But that is most likely not the entire reason why we are ignoring flares that say, "Look, sometimes self-esteem can be bad for your health." There are, as always, market forces, and they

15

are formidable. The psychotherapy industry, for instance, would take a huge hit were self-esteem to be re-examined. After all, psychology and psychiatry are predicated upon the notion of the self, and its enhancement is the primary purpose of treatment. I am by no means saying mental health professionals have any conscious desire to perpetuate a perhaps simplistic view of self-esteem, but they are, we are (for I am one of them, I confess), the "cultural retailers" of the self-esteem concept, and were the concept to falter, so would our pocketbooks.

Really, who would come to treatment to be taken down a notch? How would we get our clients to pay to be, if not insulted, at least uncomfortably challenged? There is a profound tension here between psychotherapy as a business that needs to retain its customers and psychotherapy as a practice that has the health of its patients at heart. Mental health is not necessarily a comfortable thing. Because we want to protect our patients and our pocketbooks, we don't always say this. The drug companies that underwrite us never say this. Pills take you up or level you out, but I have yet to see an advertisement for a drug of deflation.

If you look at psychotherapy in other cultures, you get a glimpse into the obsessions of our own. You also see what a marketing fiasco we would have on our hands were we to dial down our self-esteem beliefs. In Japan, there is a popular form of psychotherapy that does not focus on the self and its worth. This psychotherapeutic treatment, called Morita, holds as its central premise that neurotic suffering comes, quite literally, from extreme self-awareness. "The most miserable people I know have been self-focused," says David Reynolds, a Morita practitioner in Oregon. Reynolds writes, "Cure is not defined by the alleviation of discomfort or the attainment of some ideal state (which is impossible) but by taking constructive action in one's life which helps one to live a full and meaningful existence and not be ruled by one's emotional state."

Morita therapy, which emphasizes action over reflection, might have   20 some trouble catching on here, especially in the middle-class West, where folks would be hard pressed to garden away the 50-minute hour. That's what Morita patients do; they plant petunias and practice patience as they wait for them to bloom.

Like any belief system, Morita has its limitations. To detach from feelings carries with it the risk of detaching from their significant signals, which carry important information about how to act: reach out, recoil. But the current research on self-esteem does suggest that we might benefit, if not fiscally then at least spiritually, from a few petunias on the Blue Cross bill. And the fact that we continue, in the vernacular, to use the word "shrink" to refer to treatment means that perhaps unconsciously we know we sometimes need to be taken down a peg.

Down to . . . what? Maybe self-control should replace self-esteem as a primary peg to reach for. I don't mean to sound puritanical, but there is something to be said for discipline, which comes from the word "disciple," which actually means to comprehend. Ultimately, self-control need not be seen as a constriction; restored to its original meaning, it might be experienced as the kind of practiced prowess an athlete or an artist demonstrates, muscles not tamed but trained, so that the leaps are powerful, the spine supple and the energy harnessed and shaped.

There are therapy programs that teach something like self-control, but predictably they are not great moneymakers and they certainly do not attract the bulk of therapy consumers, the upper middle class. One such program, called Emerge, is run by a psychologist named David Adams in a low-budget building in Cambridge, Mass. Emerge's clients are mostly abusive men, 75 percent of them mandated by the courts. "I once did an intake on a batterer who had been in psychotherapy for three years, and his violence wasn't getting any better," Adams told me. "I said to him, 'Why do you think you hit your wife?' He said to me, 'My therapist told me it's because I don't feel good about myself inside.'" Adams sighs, then laughs. "We believe it has *nothing* to do with how good a man feels about himself. At Emerge, we teach men to evaluate their behaviors honestly and to interact with others using empathy and respect." In order to accomplish these goals, men write their entire abuse histories on 12-by-12 sheets of paper, hang the papers on the wall and read them. "Some of the histories are so long, they go all around the room," Adams says. "But it's a powerful exercise. It gets a guy to really concretely *see*." Other exercises involve having the men act out the abuse with the counselor as the victim. Unlike traditional "suburban" therapies, Emerge is under no pressure to keep its customers; the courts do that for them. In return, they are free to pursue a path that has to do with "balanced confrontation," at the heart of which is critical reappraisal and self-—no, not esteem—responsibility.

While Emerge is for a specific subgroup of people, it might provide us with a model for how to reconfigure treatment—and maybe even life—if we do decide the self is not about how good it feels but how well it does, in work and love. Work and love. That's a phrase fashioned by Freud himself, who once said the successful individual is one who has achieved meaningful work and meaningful love. Note how separate this sentence is from the notion of self. We blame Freud for a lot of things, but we can't blame that cigar-smoking Victorian for this particular cultural obsession. It was Freud, after all, who said that the job of psychotherapy was to turn neurotic suffering into ordinary suffering. Freud never claimed we should be happy, and he never claimed confidence was the key to a life well lived.

I remember the shock I had when I finally read this old analyst in his 25 native tongue. English translations of Freud make him sound maniacal, if not egomaniacal, with his bloated words like id, ego and superego. But in the original German, id means under-I, ego translates into I and superego is not super-duper but, quite simply, over-I. Freud was staking a claim for a part of the mind that watches the mind, that takes the global view in an effort at honesty. Over-I. I can see. And in the seeing, assess, edit, praise and prune. This is self-appraisal, which precedes self-control, for we must first know both where we flail and stumble, and where we are truly strong, before we can make disciplined alterations. Self-appraisal. It has a certain sort of rhythm to it, does it not? Self-appraisal may be what Baumeister and Emler are actually advocating. If our lives are stories in the making, then we must be able to edit as well as advertise the text. Self-appraisal. If we say self-appraisal again and again, 101 times, 503 times, 612 times, maybe we can create it. And learn its complex arts. ▪

The Reader's Presence

1. How does Slater establish her credibility? Identify techniques, words, phrases, and evidence that enhance your view of her as an expert. What makes establishing credibility especially important in this essay?

2. In Slater's opinion, how is self-esteem tied to American identity? What have Americans invested in the idea of self-esteem? What might be lost if self-esteem were no longer seen as valuable?

3. **CONNECTIONS:** In refuting the idea that self-esteem is highly valuable, Slater honestly addresses what would be threatened by such a change in perspective. How does Slater address each of these threats? Compare Slater's technique of arguing against a widely accepted ideal to Laura Kipnis's argument in "Against Love" (page 660) and John Taylor Gatto's in "Against School" (page 607). Which argument(s) do you find most convincing? Why?

The Writer at Work

LAUREN SLATER on Writing Groups

FRANCES M. ROBERTS/Newscom

Many professional writers find it stimulating and inspiring to share their work with friends and colleagues. They prefer to do this while the writing is in progress so that they can discover problems they haven't anticipated, take note of alternate directions they might pursue, or simply obtain a "gut reaction" from a supportive audience. For Slater, a key advantage of working with a writing group is the impetus provided by a dialogue: "You feel like you're really involved in a dialogue as opposed to a monologue. I do better in engaging in dialogues" (paragraph 2). These comments on writing groups are part of an interview Slater did with Alys Culhane that appeared in the creative nonfiction journal *Fourth Genre* in spring 2005.

Culhane: I recently read that your writing group is integral to your writing process. Is this so? And if so, what's its history?

Slater: It's been quite critical. I was 24 when I started working with this group and I've just turned 40. My writing group has shortened or abolished the state between writer and reader. It can be weeks on end that you are writing, and when you send something out, weeks on end before you hear anything back. But you can bring something to group, and people will hear it right away. This provides a real impetus. You feel like you're really involved in a dialogue as opposed to a monologue. I do better in engaging in dialogues.

Culhane: Why do you think this is?

Slater: Probably everything I write is kind of a co-construction of what I think and what other people think and I just don't see myself as being someone who's pulling ideas out of her own head. I dialogue with people, with books, with pictures, with everything—the world is always giving me things and I'm always taking them and turning them over. I often feel like a quilt maker—and the members of my writing group have, in a way, provided me with ways of thinking about a design and given me some of the squares. So have other friends, other writers, other books. I'm a very derivative writer and I rely heavily on other texts.

Culhane: Can you provide a specific instance where a reliance upon other texts appears in your work?

Slater: Yes. I just finished a book of fairy tales, *Blue Beyond Blue*. In this book I take established fairy tales and established fairy-tale characters and tell the story of Snow White through the eyes of the stepmother, Hansel and Gretel through the eyes of the witch.

Culhane: How has the structure of your writing group changed over time?

Slater: It's always been very loose. There's been considerable discussion about life issues that have changed over the years, from getting a boyfriend, to having breast cancer, to having kids or not having kids; the issues have changed as we've changed. In terms of structure, we have always followed the same set of "rules." We convene around 8:30 p.m. every Thursday night. We eat. We talk. At around about 11 p.m. we start to read our work. We stay for as long as it takes for everyone who has work to read it. After a person is finished reading, we go around the room and give our own comments on the piece. When this is done, we plunge into a discussion. We're all very tired on Fridays.

Culhane: Now after many years of sharing your writing with the same people do you find that you anticipate their response when you're writing?

Slater: Yes. For example, to some degree I know that one person is going to feel that a particular, say, meditative or internal beginning is slow because her writing style favors very action-oriented scenes. Others are more partial to memoir, or to fiction. Some of us adhere to the "Show, Don't Tell" rule whereas others are more likely to analyze and interpret.

Culhane: Do you anticipate their specific responses?

Slater: Yes. As a writer, what I'm really looking for is a very visceral kind of response; I take visceral reactions much more to heart than studious ones. I ask myself, did they connect with this piece, does it resonate? What I should do with this paragraph or that paragraph isn't an issue to me.

Jonathan Swift

A MODEST PROPOSAL

For Preventing the Children of Poor People in Ireland from Being a Burden to Their Parents or Country, and for Making Them Beneficial to the Public

JONATHAN SWIFT (1667–1745) was born and raised in Ireland, the son of English parents. He was ordained an Anglican priest and, although as a young man he lived a literary life in London, he was appointed against his wishes to be dean of St. Patrick's Cathedral in Dublin. Swift wrote excellent poetry but is remembered principally for his essays and politi-cal pamphlets, most of which were published under pseudonyms. Swift received payment for only one work in his entire life, *Gulliver's Travels* (1726). Swift's political pamphlets were very influential in his day; among other issues, he spoke out against English exploita-tion of the Irish. Some of Swift's more important publications include *A Tale of a Tub* (1704), *The Importance of the Guardian Considered* (1713), *The Public Spirit of the Whigs* (1714), and *A Modest Proposal* (1729).

> "... the chief end I propose to myself in all my labors is to vex the world rather than divert it."

Writing to his friend Alexander Pope, Swift commented that "the chief end I propose to myself in all my labors is to vex the world rather than divert it, and if I could compass that design without hurting my own person or Fortune I would be the most Indefatigable writer you have ever seen."

IT IS A MELANCHOLY OBJECT to those who walk through this great town[1] or travel in the country, when they see the streets, the roads, and cabin doors, crowded with beggars of the female sex, followed by three, four, or six children, all in rags and importuning every passenger for an alms. These mothers instead of being able to work for their honest livelihood, are forced to employ all their time in strolling to beg sustenance for their help-less infants: who as they grow up either turn thieves for want of work, or

---

1 ***this great town:*** Dublin. —Eds.

leave their dear native country to fight for the pretender in Spain,[2] or sell themselves to the Barbadoes.[3]

I think it is agreed by all parties that this prodigious number of children in the arms, or on the backs, or at the heels of their mothers, and frequently of their fathers, is in the present deplorable state of the kingdom a very great additional grievance; and, therefore, whoever could find out a fair, cheap, and easy method of making these children sound, useful members of the commonwealth, would deserve so well of the public as to have his statute set up for a preserver of the nation.

But my intention is very far from being confined to provide only for the children of professed beggars; it is of a much greater extent, and shall take in the whole number of infants at a certain age who are born of parents in effect as little able to support them as those who demand our charity in the streets.

As to my own part, having turned my thoughts for many years upon this important subject, and maturely weighed the several schemes of our projec-tors,[4] I have always found them grossly mistaken in their computation. It is true, a child just dropped from its dam may be supported by her milk for a solar year, with little other nourishment; at most not above the value of 2s.,[5] which the mother may certainly get, or the value in scraps, by her lawful occupation of begging; and it is exactly at one year old that I propose to provide for them in such a manner as instead of being a charge upon their parents or the parish, or wanting food and raiment for the rest of their lives, they shall on the contrary contribute to the feeding, and partly to the cloth-ing, of many thousands.

There is likewise another great advantage in my scheme, that it will pre-vent those voluntary abortions, and that horrid practice of women murder-ing their bastard children, alas! too frequent among us! sacrificing the poor innocent babes I doubt more to avoid the expense than the shame, which would move tears and pity in the most savage and inhuman breast.

The number of souls in this kingdom being usually reckoned one million and a half, of these I calculate there may be about 200,000 couple whose wives are breeders; from which number I subtract 30,000 couple who are able to maintain their own children (although I apprehend there cannot be so many, under the present distress of the kingdom); but this being granted,

5

---

2 ***pretender in Spain:*** James Stuart (1688–1766); exiled in Spain, he laid claim to the English crown and had the support of many Irishmen who had joined an army hoping to restore him to the throne. — EDS.

3 ***the Barbadoes:*** Inhabitants of the British colony in the Caribbean where Irishmen emigrated to work as indentured servants in exchange for their passage. — EDS.

4 ***projectors:*** Planners. — EDS.

5 ***2s.:*** Two shillings: in Swift's time one shilling was worth less than twenty-five cents. Other monetary references in the essay are to pounds sterling ("£"), pence ("d."), a crown, and a groat. A pound consisted of twenty shillings; a shilling of twelve pence; a crown was five shillings; a groat was worth a few cents. — EDS.

there will remain 170,000 breeders. I again subtract 50,000 for those women who miscarry, or whose children die by accident or disease within the year. There only remain 120,000 children of poor parents annually born. The question therefore is, how this number shall be reared and provided for? which, as I have already said, under the present situation of affairs, is utterly impossible by all the methods hitherto proposed. For we can neither employ them in handicraft or agriculture; we neither build houses (I mean in the country) nor cultivate land; they can very seldom pick up a livelihood by stealing, till they arrive at six years old, except where they are of towardly parts,[6] although I confess they learn the rudiments much earlier; during which time they can, however, be properly looked upon only as probationers; as I have been informed by a principal gentleman in the county of Cavan, who protested to me that he never knew above one or two instances under the age of six, even in a part of the kingdom so renowned for the quickest proficiency in that art.

I am assured by our merchants, that a boy or a girl before twelve years old is no salable commodity; and even when they come to this age they will not yield above 3£. or 3£. 2s. 6d. at most on the exchange; which cannot turn to account either to the parents or kingdom, the charge of nutriment and rags having been at least four times that value.

I shall now therefore humbly propose my own thoughts, which I hope will not be liable to the least objection.

I have been assured by a very knowing American of my acquaintance in London, that a young healthy child well nursed is at a year old a most delicious, nourishing, and wholesome food, whether stewed, roasted, baked, or broiled; and I make no doubt that it will equally serve in a fricassee or a ragout.[7]

I do therefore humbly offer it to public consideration that of the 120,000 children already computed, 20,000 may be reserved for breed, whereof only one-fourth part to be males; which is more than we allow to sheep, black cattle, or swine; and my reason is, that these children are seldom the fruits of marriage, a circumstance not much regarded by our savages; therefore one male will be sufficient to serve four females. That the remaining 100,000 may, at a year old, be offered in sale to the persons of quality and fortune through the kingdom; always advising the mother to let them suck plentifully in the last month, so as to render them plump and fat for a good table. A child will make two dishes at an entertainment for friends; and when the family dines alone, the fore and hind quarter will make a reasonable dish, and seasoned with a little pepper or salt will be very good boiled on the fourth day, especially in winter.

I have reckoned upon a medium that a child just born will weigh 12 pounds, and in a solar year, if tolerably nursed, will increase to 28 pounds.

10

---

6 *towardly parts:* Natural abilities. —EDS.
7 *ragout:* A stew. —EDS.

I grant this food will be somewhat dear, and therefore very proper for landlords, who, as they have already devoured most of the parents, seem to have the best title to the children.

Infants' flesh will be in season throughout the year, but more plentiful in March, and a little before and after: for we are told by a grave author, an eminent French physician,[8] that fish being a prolific diet, there are more children born in Roman Catholic countries about nine months after Lent than at any other season; therefore, reckoning a year after Lent, the markets will be more glutted than usual, because the number of popish infants is at least three to one in this kingdom: and therefore it will have one other collateral advantage, by lessening the number of papists among us.

I have already computed the charge of nursing a beggar's child (in which list I reckon all cottagers, laborers, and four-fifths of the farmers) to be about 2s. per annum, rags included; and I believe no gentleman would repine to give 10s. for the carcass of a good fat child, which, as I have said, will make four dishes of excellent nutritive meat, when he has only some particular friend or his own family to dine with him. Thus the squire will learn to be a good landlord, and grow popular among the tenants; the mother will have 8s. net profit, and be fit for work till she produces another child.

Those who are more thrifty (as I must confess the times require) may   15
flay the carcass; the skin of which artificially[9] dressed will make admirable gloves for ladies, and summer boots for fine gentlemen.

As to our city of Dublin, shambles[10] may be appointed for this purpose in the most convenient parts of it, and butchers we may be assured will not be wanting: although I rather recommend buying the children alive, and dressing them hot from the knife as we do roasting pigs.

A very worthy person, a true lover of his country, and whose virtues I highly esteem, was lately pleased in discoursing on this matter to offer a refinement upon my scheme. He said that many gentlemen of this kingdom, having of late destroyed their deer, he conceived that the want of venison might be well supplied by the bodies of young lads and maidens, not exceeding fourteen years of age nor under twelve; so great a number of both sexes in every country being now ready to starve for want of work and service; and these to be disposed of by their parents, if alive, or otherwise by their nearest relations. But with due deference to so excellent a friend and so deserving a patriot, I cannot be altogether in his sentiments; for as to the males, my American acquaintance assured me from frequent experience that their flesh was generally tough and lean, like that of our schoolboys by continual exercise, and their taste disagreeable; and to fatten them would not answer the charge. Then as to the females, it would, I think, with humble

---

8 **French physician:** François Rabelais (c. 1483–1553), the great Renaissance humanist and author of the comic masterpiece *Gargantua and Pantagruel*. Swift is being ironic in calling Rabelais "grave." —EDS.

9 **artificially:** Artfully. —EDS.

10 **shambles:** Slaughterhouses. —EDS.

submission be a loss to the public, because they soon would become breeders themselves: and besides, it is not improbable that some scrupulous people might be apt to censure such a practice (although indeed very unjustly), as a little bordering upon cruelty; which, I confess, has always been with me the strongest objection against any project, how well soever intended.

But in order to justify my friend, he confessed that this expedient was put into his head by the famous Psalmanazar[11] a native of the island Formosa, who came from thence to London about twenty years ago: and in conversation told my friend, that in his country when any young person happened to be put to death, the executioner sold the carcass to persons of quality as a prime dainty; and that in his time the body of a plump girl of fifteen, who was crucified for an attempt to poison the emperor, was sold to his imperial majesty's prime minister of state, and other great mandarins of the court, in joints from the gibbet, at 400 crowns. Neither indeed can I deny, that if the same use were made of several plump young girls in this town, who without one single groat to their fortunes cannot stir abroad without a chair,[12] and appear at the playhouse and assemblies in foreign fineries which they never will pay for, the kingdom would not be the worse.

Some persons of a desponding spirit are in great concern about the vast number of poor people, who are aged, diseased, or maimed, and I have been desired to employ my thoughts what course may be taken to ease the nation of so grievous an encumbrance. But I am not in the least pain upon that matter, because it is very well known that they are every day dying and rotting by cold and famine, and filth and vermin, as fast as can be reasonably expected. And as to the young laborers, they are now in as hopeful condition: They cannot get work, and consequently pine away for want of nourishment, to a degree that if at any time they are accidentally hired to common labor, they have not strength to perform it; and thus the country and themselves are happily delivered from the evils to come.

I have too long digressed, and therefore shall return to my subject. I think the advantages by the proposal which I have made are obvious and many, as well as of the highest importance. 20

For first, as I have already observed, it would greatly lessen the number of papists, with whom we are yearly overrun, being the principal breeders of the nation as well as our most dangerous enemies; and who stay at home on purpose to deliver the kingdom to the Pretender, hoping to take their advantage by the absence of so many good Protestants, who have chosen rather to leave their country than stay at home and pay tithes against their conscience to an Episcopal curate.

Secondly, The poor tenants will have something valuable of their own, which by law may be made liable to distress[13] and help to pay their

---

11 **George Psalmanazar** (c. 1679–1763): A Frenchman who tricked London society into believing he was a native of Formosa (now Taiwan). —EDS.

12 **a chair:** A sedan chair in which one is carried about. —EDS.

13 **distress:** Seizure for payment of debt. —EDS.

landlord's rent, their corn and cattle being already seized, and money a thing unknown.

Thirdly, Whereas the maintenance of 100,000 children from two years old and upward, cannot be computed at less that 10s. a-piece per annum, the nation's stock will be thereby increased £50,000 per annum, beside the profit of a new dish introduced to the tables of all gentlemen of fortune in the kingdom who have any refinement in taste. And the money will circulate among ourselves, the goods being entirely of our own growth and manufacture.

Fourthly, The constant breeders beside the gain of 8s. sterling per annum by the sale of their children, will be rid of the charge of maintaining them after the first year.

Fifthly, This food would likewise bring great custom to taverns, where the vintners will certainly be so prudent as to procure the best receipts[14] for dressing it to perfection, and consequently have their houses frequented by all the fine gentlemen, who justly value themselves upon their knowledge in good eating; and a skillful cook who understands how to oblige his guests, will contrive to make it as expensive as they please.

Sixthly, This would be a great inducement to marriage, which all wise nations have either encouraged by rewards or enforced by laws and penalties. It would increase the care and tenderness of mothers toward their children, when they were sure of a settlement for life to the poor babes, provided in some sort by the public, to their annual profit instead of expense. We should see an honest emulation among the married women, which of them would bring the fattest child to the market. Men would become as fond of their wives during the time of their pregnancy as they are now of their mares in foal, their cows in calf, their sows when they are ready to farrow; nor offer to beat or kick them (as is too frequent a practice) for fear of a miscarriage.

Many other advantages might be enumerated. For instance, the addition of some thousand carcasses in our exportation of barreled beef, the propagation of swine's flesh, and improvement in the art of making good bacon, so much wanted among us by the great destruction of pigs, too frequent at our table; which are no way comparable in taste or magnificence to a well-grown, fat, yearling child, which roasted whole will make a considerable figure at a lord mayor's feast or any other public entertainment. But this and many others I omit, being studious of brevity.

Supposing that 1,000 families in this city would be constant customers for infants' flesh, besides others who might have it at merry-meetings, particularly at weddings and christenings, I compute that Dublin would take off annually about 20,000 carcasses; and the rest of the kingdom (where probably they will be sold somewhat cheaper) the remaining 80,000.

I can think of no one objection that will possibly be raised against this proposal unless it should be urged that the number of people will be thereby

25

---

14 *receipts:* Recipes. — EDS.

much lessened in the kingdom. This I freely own, and it was indeed one principal design in offering it to the world. I desire the reader will observe, that I calculate my remedy for this one individual kingdom of Ireland and for no other that ever was, is, or I think ever can be upon earth. Therefore let no man talk to me of other expedients: of taxing our absentees at 5s. a pound: of using neither clothes nor household furniture except what is of our own growth and manufacture: of utterly rejecting the materials and instruments that promote foreign luxury: of curing the expensiveness of pride, vanity, idleness, and gaming in our women: of introducing a vein of parsimony, prudence, and temperance: of learning to love our country, in the want of which we differ even from Laplanders and the inhabitants of Topinamboo:[15] of quitting our animosities and factions, nor acting any longer like the Jews, who were murdering one another at the very moment their city was taken:[16] of being a little cautious not to sell our country and conscience for nothing: of teaching landlords to have at least one degree of mercy toward their tenants: lastly, of putting a spirit of honesty, industry, and skill into our shopkeepers; who, if a resolution could now be taken to buy only our native goods, would immediately unite to cheat and exact upon us in the price the measure, and the goodness, nor could ever yet be brought to make one fair proposal of just dealing, though often and earnestly invited to it.

Therefore I repeat, let no man talk to me of these and the like expedi-   30
ents, till he has at least some glimpse of hope that there will be ever some hearty and sincere attempt to put them in practice.

But as to myself, having been wearied out for many years with offering vain, idle, visionary thoughts, and at length utterly despairing of success, I fortunately fell upon this proposal; which, as it is wholly new, so it has something solid and real, of no expense and little trouble, full in our own power, and whereby we can incur no danger in disobliging England. For this kind of commodity will not bear exportation, the flesh being of too tender a consistence to admit a long continuance in salt, although perhaps I could name a country which would be glad to eat up our whole nation without it.

After all, I am not so violently bent upon my own opinion as to reject any offer proposed by wise men, which shall be found equally innocent, cheap, easy, and effectual. But before something of that kind shall be advanced in contradiction to my scheme, and offering a better, I desire the author or authors will be pleased maturely to consider two points. First, as things now stand, how they will be able to find food and raiment for 100,000 useless mouths and backs. And secondly, there being a round million of creatures in human figure throughout this kingdom, whose subsistence put into a common stock would leave them in debt 2,000,000£. sterling, adding those who are beggars by profession to the bulk of farmers, cottagers, and laborers,

---

[15] **Laplanders and the inhabitants of Topinamboo:** Lapland is the area of Scandinavia above the Arctic Circle; Topinamboo, in Brazil, was known in Swift's time for the savagery of its tribes. — EDS.
[16] **was taken:** A reference to the Roman seizure of Jerusalem (70 CE). — EDS.

with the wives and children who are beggars in effect; I desire those politicians who dislike my overture, and may perhaps be so bold as to attempt an answer, that they will first ask the parents of these mortals, whether they would not at this day think it a great happiness to have been sold for food at a year old in the manner I prescribe, and thereby have avoided such a perpetual scene of misfortunes as they have since gone through by the oppression of landlords, the impossibility of paying rent without money or trade, the want of common sustenance, with neither house nor clothes to cover them from the inclemencies of the weather, and the most inevitable prospect of entailing the like or greater miseries upon their breed for ever.

I profess, in the sincerity of my heart, that I have not the least personal interest in endeavoring to promote this necessary work, having no other motive than the public good of my country, by advancing our trade, providing for infants, relieving the poor, and giving some pleasure to the rich. I have no children by which I can propose to get a single penny; the youngest being nine years old, and my wife past childbearing. ■

The Reader's Presence

1. Consider Swift's title. In what sense is the proposal "modest"? What is modest about it? What synonyms would you use for *modest* that appear in the essay? In what sense is the essay a "proposal"? Does it follow any format that resembles a proposal? If so, what type of format? What aspects of its language seem to resemble proposal writing?

2. For this essay Swift invents a speaker, an unnamed, fictional individual who "humbly" proposes a plan to relieve poverty in Ireland. What attitudes and beliefs in the essay do you attribute to the speaker? Which do you attribute to Swift, the author? Having considered two authors (the speaker of the proposal and Swift), now consider two readers—the reader the speaker imagines and the reader Swift imagines. How do these two readers differ? Reread the final paragraph of the essay from the perspective of each of these readers. How do you think each reader is expected to respond?

3. **CONNECTIONS:**   In the introductory comment, Swift is quoted as wanting "to vex the world rather than divert it" with his writing. Where in the essay do you find Swift most vexing? How does he attempt to provoke the reader's outrage? Where does the first, most visceral indication of the speaker's plan appear? Does he heighten the essay's effect after this point? If so, where and how? How does Swift mount a serious political argument in the midst of such hyperbole? Read "Against Love" by Laura Kipnis (page 660). How does Kipnis use hyperbole or satire in the presentation of her argument? Does she make a serious point? Why or why not?

David Foster Wallace

CONSIDER THE LOBSTER

DAVID FOSTER WALLACE (1962–2008) is probably best known for his 1996 novel, *Infinite Jest*. Widely considered one of the most important works of American fiction in recent memory, *Infinite Jest* made *Time* magazine's list of the 100 greatest novels spanning the period of 1926–2006, and firmly established Wallace at the forefront of American letters. Wallace double-majored in English and philosophy at Amherst College and went on to receive an MFA in Creative Writing at the University of Arizona in 1987. He published his first novel, *The Broom of the System*, in 1987, and, shortly thereafter, moved to Boston, Massachusetts, to work toward a graduate degree in philosophy at Harvard University. He soon abandoned the endeavor, dedicating himself instead to writing. He taught creative writing at Illinois State University from 1992 through 2002, when he moved to Claremont, California, to take a position as the Roy E. Disney Professor of Creative Writing at Pomona College. In addition to *Infinite Jest* and *The Broom of the System*, Wallace published several short story collections, including *Brief Interviews with Hideous Men* (1999), which was adapted for the screen in a 2009 film of the same name. Wallace also published essays and stories in magazines, including the *Paris Review*, *Harper's*, the *Atlantic Monthly*, *Esquire*, and *Gourmet*. When Wallace committed suicide in 2008, he left behind an unfinished novel titled *The Pale King*, which was published posthumously in 2011 and was a finalist for the Pulitzer Prize in fiction in 2012.

> Widely considered one of the most important works of American fiction in recent memory, *Infinite Jest* made *Time* magazine's list of the 100 greatest novels spanning the period of 1926–2006, and firmly established David Foster Wallace at the forefront of American letters.

Wallace wrote "Consider the Lobster" on assignment from *Gourmet*, a culinary magazine, in 2004.

Note: Extensive personal footnotes are part of Wallace's prose style; unless otherwise specified, all the footnotes are Wallace's.

THE ENORMOUS, pungent, and extremely well-marketed Maine Lobster Festival is held every late July in the state's midcoast region, meaning the western side of Penobscot Bay, the nerve stem of Maine's lobster industry. What's called the midcoast runs from Owl's Head and Thomaston in the south to Belfast in the north. (Actually, it might extend all the way up to Bucksport, but we were never able to get farther north than Belfast on Route 1, whose summer traffic is, as you can imagine, unimaginable.) The region's two main communities are Camden, with its very old money and yachty harbor and five-star restaurants and phenomenal B&Bs, and Rockland, a serious old fishing town that hosts the festival every summer in historic Harbor Park, right along the water.[1]

Tourism and lobster are the midcoast region's two main industries, and they're both warm-weather enterprises, and the Maine Lobster Festival represents less an intersection of the industries than a deliberate collision, joyful and lucrative and loud. The assigned subject of this *Gourmet* article is the 56th Annual MLF, 30 July–3 August 2003, whose official theme this year was "Lighthouses, Laughter, and Lobster." Total paid attendance was over 100,000, due partly to a national CNN spot in June during which a senior editor of *Food & Wine* magazine hailed the MLF as one of the best food-themed galas in the world. 2003 festival highlights: concerts by Lee Ann Womack and Orleans, annual Maine Sea Goddess beauty pageant, Saturday's big parade, Sunday's William G. Atwood Memorial Crate Race, annual Amateur Cooking Competition, carnival rides and midway attractions and food booths, and the MLF's Main Eating Tent, where something over 25,000 pounds of fresh-caught Maine lobster is consumed after preparation in the World's Largest Lobster Cooker near the grounds' north entrance. Also available are lobster rolls, lobster turnovers, lobster sauté, Down East lobster salad, lobster bisque, lobster ravioli, and deep-fried lobster dumplings. Lobster thermidor is obtainable at a sit-down restaurant called the Black Pearl on Harbor Park's northwest wharf. A large all-pine booth sponsored by the Maine Lobster Promotion Council has free pamphlets with recipes, eating tips, and Lobster Fun Facts. The winner of Friday's Amateur Cooking Competition prepares Saffron Lobster Ramekins, the recipe for which is now available for public downloading at www.mainelobsterfestival.com. There are lobster T-shirts and lobster bobblehead dolls and inflatable lobster pool toys and clamp-on lobster hats with big scarlet claws that wobble on springs. Your assigned correspondent saw it all, accompanied by one girlfriend and both his own parents—one of which parents was actually born and raised in Maine, albeit in the extreme northern inland part, which is potato country and a world away from the touristic midcoast.[2]

---

1 There's a comprehensive native apothegm: "Camden by the sea, Rockland by the smell."

2 N.B. All personally connected parties have made it clear from the start that they do not want to be talked about in this article.

For practical purposes, everyone knows what a lobster is. As usual, though, there's much more to know than most of us care about—it's all a matter of what your interests are. Taxonomically speaking, a lobster is a marine crustacean of the family Homaridae, characterized by five pairs of jointed legs, the first pair terminating in large pincerish claws used for subduing prey. Like many other species of benthic carnivore, lobsters are both hunters and scavengers. They have stalked eyes, gills on their legs, and antennae. There are a dozen or so different kinds worldwide, of which the relevant species here is the Maine lobster, *Homarus americanus*. The name "lobster" comes from the Old English *loppestre*, which is thought to be a corrupt form of the Latin word for locust combined with the Old English *loppe*, which meant spider.

Moreover, a crustacean is an aquatic arthropod of the class Crustacea, which comprises crabs, shrimp, barnacles, lobsters, and freshwater crayfish. All this is right there in the encyclopedia. And arthropods are members of the phylum Arthropoda, which phylum covers insects, spiders, crustaceans, and centipedes/millipedes, all of whose main commonality, besides the absence of a centralized brain-spine assembly, is a chitinous exoskeleton composed of segments, to which appendages are articulated in pairs.

The point is that lobsters are basically giant sea insects.[3] Like most arthropods, they date from the Jurassic period, biologically so much older than mammalia that they might as well be from another planet. And they are—particularly in their natural brown-green state, brandishing their claws like weapons and with thick antennae awhip—not nice to look at. And it's true that they are garbagemen of the sea, eaters of dead stuff,[4] although they'll also eat some live shellfish, certain kinds of injured fish, and sometimes one another.

But they are themselves good eating. Or so we think now. Up until sometime in the 1800s, though, lobster was literally low-class food, eaten only by the poor and institutionalized. Even in the harsh penal environment of early America, some colonies had laws against feeding lobsters to inmates more than once a week because it was thought to be cruel and unusual, like making people eat rats. One reason for their low status was how plentiful lobsters were in old New England. "Unbelievable abundance" is how one source describes the situation, including accounts of Plymouth Pilgrims wading out and capturing all they wanted by hand, and of early Boston's seashore being littered with lobsters after hard storms—these latter were treated as a smelly nuisance and ground up for fertilizer. There is also the fact that premodern lobster was cooked dead and then preserved, usually packed in salt or crude hermetic containers. Maine's earliest lobster industry was based around a dozen such seaside canneries in the 1840s, from which lobster was shipped as far away as California, in demand only because it was cheap and high in protein, basically chewable fuel.

5

---

3 Midcoasters' native term for a lobster is, in fact, "bug," as in "Come around on Sunday and we'll cook up some bugs."

4 Factoid: Lobster traps are usually baited with dead herring.

Now, of course, lobster is posh, a delicacy, only a step or two down from caviar. The meat is richer and more substantial than most fish, its taste subtle compared to the marine-gaminess of mussels and clams. In the US pop-food imagination, lobster is now the seafood analog to steak, with which it's so often twinned as Surf 'n' Turf on the really expensive part of the chain steakhouse menu.

In fact, one obvious project of the MLF, and of its omnipresently sponsorial Maine Lobster Promotion Council, is to counter the idea that lobster is unusually luxe or unhealthy or expensive, suitable only for effete palates or the occasional blow-the-diet treat. It is emphasized over and over in presentations and pamphlets at the festival that lobster meat has fewer calories, less cholesterol, and less saturated fat than chicken.[5] And in the Main Eating Tent, you can get a "quarter" (industry shorthand for a 1¼-pound lobster), a four-ounce cup of melted butter, a bag of chips, and a soft roll w/butter-pat for around $12.00, which is only slightly more expensive than supper at McDonald's.

Be apprised, though, that the Maine Lobster Festival's democratization of lobster comes with all the massed inconveniences and aesthetic compromise of real democracy. See, for example, the aforementioned Main Eating Tent, for which there is a constant Disneyland-grade queue, and which turns out to be a square quarter mile of awning-shaded cafeteria lines and rows of long institutional tables at which friend and stranger alike sit cheek by jowl, cracking and chewing and dribbling. It's hot, and the sagged roof traps the steam and the smells, which latter are strong and only partly food-related. It is also loud, and a good percentage of the total noise is masticatory. The suppers come in styrofoam trays, and the soft drinks are iceless and flat, and the coffee is convenience-store coffee in yet more styrofoam, and the utensils are plastic (there are none of the special long skinny forks for pushing out the tail meat, though a few savvy diners bring their own). Nor do they give you near enough napkins considering how messy lobster is to eat, especially when you're squeezed onto benches alongside children of various ages and vastly different levels of fine-motor development—not to mention the people who've somehow smuggled in their own beer in enormous aisle-blocking coolers, or who all of a sudden produce their own plastic tablecloths and spread them over large portions of tables to try to reserve them (the tables) for their own little groups. And so on. Any one example is no more than a petty inconvenience, of course, but the MLF turns out to be full of irksome little downers like this—see for instance the Main Stage's headliner shows, where it turns out that you have to pay $20 extra for a folding chair if you want to sit down; or the North Tent's mad scramble for the Nyquil-cup-sized samples of finalists' entries handed out after the Cooking Competition; or the much-touted Maine Sea Goddess pageant finals, which turn out to be excruciatingly long and to consist mainly of endless thanks

---

[5] Of course, the common practice of dipping the lobster meat in melted butter torpedoes all these happy fat-specs, which none of the council's promotional stuff ever mentions, any more than potato industry PR talks about sour cream and bacon bits.

and tributes to local sponsors. Let's not even talk about the grossly inadequate Port-A-San facilities or the fact that there's nowhere to wash your hands before or after eating. What the Maine Lobster Festival really is is a midlevel county fair with a culinary hook, and in this respect it's not unlike Tidewater crab festivals, Midwest corn festivals, Texas chili festivals, etc., and shares with these venues the core paradox of all teeming commercial demotic events: It's not for everyone.[6] Nothing against the euphoric senior editor of *Food & Wine*, but I'd be surprised if she'd ever actually been here in Harbor Park, amid crowds of people slapping canal-zone mosquitoes as they eat deep-fried Twinkies and watch Professor Paddywhack, on six-foot stilts in a raincoat with plastic lobsters protruding from all directions on springs, terrify their children.

Lobster is essentially a summer food. This is because we now prefer our 10 lobsters fresh, which means they have to be recently caught, which for both tactical and economic reasons takes place at depths less than 25 fathoms. Lobsters tend to be hungriest and most active (i.e., most trappable) at summer water temperatures of 45–50 degrees. In the autumn, most Maine lobsters migrate out into deeper water, either for warmth or to avoid the heavy waves that pound New England's coast all winter. Some burrow into the bottom. They might hibernate; nobody's sure. Summer is also lobsters' molting season—specifically early- to mid-July. Chitinous arthropods grow by molting, rather the way people have to buy bigger clothes as they age and gain weight. Since lobsters can live to be over 100, they can also get to be quite large, as in 30 pounds or more—though truly senior lobsters are rare

---

6 In truth, there's a great deal to be said about the differences between working-class Rockland and the heavily populist flavor of its festival versus comfortable and elitist Camden with its expensive view and shops given entirely over to $200 sweaters and great rows of Victorian homes converted to upscale B&Bs. And about these differences as two sides of the great coin that is US tourism. Very little of which will be said here, except to amplify the above-mentioned paradox and to reveal your assigned correspondent's own preferences. I confess that I have never understood why so many people's idea of a fun vacation is to don flip-flops and sunglasses and crawl through maddening traffic to loud, hot, crowded tourist venues in order to sample a "local flavor" that is by definition ruined by the presence of tourists. This may (as my festival companions keep pointing out) all be a matter of personality and hardwired taste: the fact that I do not like tourist venues means that I'll never understand their appeal and so am probably not the one to talk about it (the supposed appeal). But, since this FN will almost surely not survive magazine-editing anyway, here goes:

As I see it, it probably really is good for the soul to be a tourist, even if it's only once in a while. Not good for the soul in a refreshing or enlivening way, though, but rather in a grim, steely-eyed, let's-look-honestly-at-the-facts-and-find-some-way-to-deal-with-them way. My personal experience has not been that traveling around the country is broadening or relaxing, or that radical changes in place and context have a salutary effect, but rather that intranational tourism is radically constricting, and humbling in the hardest way—hostile to my fantasy of being a real individual, of living somehow outside and above it all. (Coming up is the part that my companions find especially unhappy and repellent, a sure way to spoil the fun of vacation travel:) To be a mass tourist, for me, is to become a pure late-date American: alien, ignorant, greedy for something you cannot ever have, disappointed in a way you can never admit. It is to spoil, by way of sheer ontology, the very unspoiledness you are there to experience. It is to impose yourself on places that in all noneconomic ways would be better, realer, without you. It is, in lines and gridlock and transaction after transaction, to confront a dimension of yourself that is as inescapable as it is painful: As a tourist, you become economically significant but existentially loathsome, an insect on a dead thing.

now because New England's waters are so heavily trapped.[7] Anyway, hence the culinary distinction between hard- and soft-shell lobsters, the latter sometimes a.k.a. shedders. A soft-shell lobster is one that has recently molted. In midcoast restaurants, the summer menu often offers both kinds, with shedders being slightly cheaper even though they're easier to dismantle and the meat is allegedly sweeter. The reason for the discount is that a molting lobster uses a layer of seawater for insulation while its new shell is hardening, so there's slightly less actual meat when you crack open a shedder, plus a redolent gout of water that gets all over everything and can sometimes jet out lemonlike and catch a tablemate right in the eye. If it's winter or you're buying lobster someplace far from New England, on the other hand, you can almost bet that the lobster is a hard-shell, which for obvious reasons travel better.

As an à la carte entrée, lobster can be baked, broiled, steamed, grilled, sautéed, stir-fried, or microwaved. The most common method, though, is boiling. If you're someone who enjoys having lobster at home, this is probably the way you do it, since boiling is so easy. You need a large kettle w/cover, which you fill about half full with water (the standard advice is that you want 2.5 quarts of water per lobster). Seawater is optimal, or you can add two tbsp salt per quart from the tap. It also helps to know how much your lobsters weigh. You get the water boiling, put in the lobsters one at a time, cover the kettle, and bring it back up to a boil. Then you bank the heat and let the kettle simmer—ten minutes for the first pound of lobster, then three minutes for each pound after that. (This is assuming you've got hard-shell lobsters, which, again, if you don't live between Boston and Halifax is probably what you've got. For shedders, you're supposed to subtract three minutes from the total.) The reason the kettle's lobsters turn scarlet is that boiling somehow suppresses every pigment in their chitin but one. If you want an easy test of whether the lobsters are done, you try pulling on one of their antennae—if it comes out of the head with minimal effort, you're ready to eat.

A detail so obvious that most recipes don't even bother to mention it is that each lobster is supposed to be alive when you put it in the kettle. This is part of lobster's modern appeal—it's the freshest food there is. There's no decomposition between harvesting and eating. And not only do lobsters require no cleaning or dressing or plucking, they're relatively easy for vendors to keep alive. They come up alive in the traps, are placed in containers of seawater, and can—so long as the water's aerated and the animals' claws are pegged or banded to keep them from tearing one another up under the stresses of captivity[8]—survive right up until they're boiled. Most of us have been in supermarkets or restaurants that feature tanks of live

---

7 Datum: In a good year, the US industry produces around 80,000,000 pounds of lobster, and Maine accounts for more than half that total.

8 N.B. Similar reasoning underlies the practice of what's termed "debeaking" broiler chickens and brood hens in modern factory farms. Maximum commercial efficiency requires that enormous poultry populations be confined in unnaturally close quarters, under which conditions many birds go crazy and peck one another to death. As a purely observational side-note, be apprised that debeaking is usually an automated process and that the chickens receive no anesthetic. It's not

A crate of lobsters is loaded onto a platform in preparation for cooking at the Maine Lobster Festival.

lobsters, from which you can pick out your supper while it watches you point. And part of the overall spectacle of the Maine Lobster Festival is that you can see actual lobstermen's vessels docking at the wharves along the northeast grounds and unloading fresh-caught product, which is transferred by hand or cart 150 yards to the great clear tanks stacked up around the festival's cooker—which is, as mentioned, billed as the World's Largest Lobster Cooker and can process over 100 lobsters at a time for the Main Eating Tent.

So then here is a question that's all but unavoidable at the World's Largest Lobster Cooker, and may arise in kitchens across the US: Is it all right to

---

clear to me whether most *Gourmet* readers know about debeaking, or about related practices like dehorning cattle in commercial feed lots, cropping swine's tails in factory hog farms to keep psychotically bored neighbors from chewing them off, and so forth. It so happens that your assigned correspondent knew almost nothing about standard meat-industry operations before starting work on this article.

boil a sentient creature alive just for our gustatory pleasure? A related set of concerns: Is the previous question irksomely PC or sentimental? What does "all right" even mean in this context? Is the whole thing just a matter of personal choice?

As you may or may not know, a certain well-known group called People for the Ethical Treatment of Animals thinks that the morality of lobster-boiling is not just a matter of individual conscience. In fact, one of the very first things we hear about the MLF . . . well, to set the scene: We're coming in by cab from the almost indescribably odd and rustic Knox County Airport[9] very late on the night before the festival opens, sharing the cab with a wealthy political consultant who lives on Vinalhaven Island in the bay half the year (he's headed for the island ferry in Rockland). The consultant and cabdriver are responding to informal journalistic probes about how people who live in the midcoast region actually view the MLF, as in is the festival just a big-dollar tourist thing or is it something local residents look forward to attending, take genuine civic pride in, etc. The cabdriver (who's in his seventies, one of apparently a whole platoon of retirees the cab company puts on to help with the summer rush, and wears a US-flag lapel pin, and drives in what can only be called a very *deliberate* way) assures us that locals do endorse and enjoy the MLF, although he himself hasn't gone in years, and now come to think of it no one he and his wife know has, either. However, the demilocal consultant's been to recent festivals a couple times (one gets the impression it was at his wife's behest), of which his most vivid impression was that "you have to line up for an ungodly long time to get your lobsters, and meanwhile there are all these ex–flower children coming up and down along the line handing out pamphlets that say the lobsters die in terrible pain and you shouldn't eat them."

And it turns out that the post-hippies of the consultant's recollection were   15
activists from PETA. There were no PETA people in obvious view at the 2003 MLF,[10] but they've been conspicuous at many of the recent festivals. Since at least the mid-1990s, articles in everything from the *Camden Herald* to the *New York Times* have described PETA urging boycotts of the Maine Lobster

---

[9] The terminal used to be somebody's house, for example, and the lost-luggage-reporting room was clearly once a pantry.

[10] It turned out that one Mr. William R. Rivas-Rivas, a high-ranking PETA official out of the group's Virginia headquarters, was indeed there this year, albeit solo, working the festival's main and side entrances on Saturday, 2 August, handing out pamphlets and adhesive stickers emblazoned with "Being Boiled Hurts," which is the tagline in most of PETA's published material about lobsters. I learned that he'd been there only later, when speaking with Mr. Rivas-Rivas on the phone. I'm not sure how we missed seeing him *in situ* at the festival, and I can't see much to do except apologize for the oversight—although it's also true that Saturday was the day of the big MLF parade through Rockland, which basic journalistic responsibility seemed to require going to (and which, with all due respect, meant that Saturday was maybe not the best day for PETA to work the Harbor Park grounds, especially if it was going to be just one person for one day, since a lot of diehard MLF partisans were off-site watching the parade (which, again with no offense intended, was in truth kind of cheesy and boring, consisting mostly of slow homemade floats and various midcoast people waving at one another, and with an extremely annoying man dressed as Blackbeard ranging up and down the length of the crowd saying "Arrr" over and over and brandishing a plastic sword at people, etc.; plus it rained)).

Festival, often deploying celebrity spokesmen like Mary Tyler Moore for open letters and ads saying stuff like "Lobsters are extraordinarily sensitive" and "To me, eating a lobster is out of the question." More concrete is the oral testimony of Dick, our florid and extremely gregarious rental-car liaison,[11] to the effect that PETA's been around so much in recent years that a kind of brittlely tolerant homeostasis now obtains between the activists and the festival's locals, e.g.: "We had some incidents a couple years ago. One lady took most of her clothes off and painted herself like a lobster, almost got herself arrested. But for the most part they're let alone. [Rapid series of small ambiguous laughs, which with Dick happens a lot.] They do their thing and we do our thing."

This whole interchange takes place on Route 1, 30 July, during a four-mile, 50-minute ride from the airport[12] to the dealership to sign car-rental papers. Several irreproducible segues down the road from the PETA anecdotes, Dick — whose son-in-law happens to be a professional lobsterman and one of the Main Eating Tent's regular suppliers — explains what he and his family feel is the crucial mitigating factor in the whole morality-of-boiling-lobsters-alive issue: "There's a part of the brain in people and animals that lets us feel pain, and lobsters' brains don't have this part."

Besides the fact that it's incorrect in about nine different ways, the main reason Dick's statement is interesting is that its thesis is more or less echoed by the festival's own pronouncement on lobsters and pain, which is part of a Test Your Lobster IQ quiz that appears in the 2003 MLF program courtesy of the Maine Lobster Promotion Council:

> The nervous system of a lobster is very simple, and is in fact most similar to the nervous system of the grasshopper. It is decentralized with no brain. There is no cerebral cortex, which in humans is the area of the brain that gives the experience of pain.

Though it sounds more sophisticated, a lot of the neurology in this latter claim is still either false or fuzzy. The human cerebral cortex is the brain-part that deals with higher faculties like reason, metaphysical self-awareness, language, etc. Pain reception is known to be part of a much older and more primitive system of nociceptors and prostaglandins that are managed by the brain stem and thalamus.[13] On the other hand, it is true that the cerebral

---

11 By profession, Dick is actually a car salesman; the midcoast region's National Car Rental franchise operates out of a Chevy dealership in Thomaston.

12 The short version regarding why we were back at the airport after already arriving the previous night involves lost luggage and a miscommunication about where and what the midcoast's National franchise was — Dick came out personally to the airport and got us, out of no evident motive but kindness. (He also talked nonstop the entire way, with a very distinctive speaking style that can be described only as manically laconic; the truth is that I now know more about this man than I do about some members of my own family.)

13 To elaborate by way of example: The common experience of accidentally touching a hot stove and yanking your hand back before you're even aware that anything's going on is explained by the fact that many of the processes by which we detect and avoid painful stimuli do not involve the cortex. In the case of the hand and stove, the brain is bypassed altogether; all the important neurochemical action takes place in the spine.

cortex is involved in what's variously called suffering, distress, or the emotional experience of pain—i.e., experiencing painful stimuli as unpleasant, very unpleasant, unbearable, and so on.

Before we go any further, let's acknowledge that the questions of whether and how different kinds of animals feel pain, and of whether and why it might be justifiable to inflict pain on them in order to eat them, turn out to be extremely complex and difficult. And comparative neuroanatomy is only part of the problem. Since pain is a totally subjective mental experience, we do not have direct access to anyone or anything's pain but our own; and even just the principles by which we can infer that other human beings experience pain and have a legitimate interest in not feeling pain involve hardcore philosophy—metaphysics, epistemology, value theory, ethics. The fact that even the most highly evolved nonhuman mammals can't use language to communicate with us about their subjective mental experience is only the first layer of additional complication in trying to extend our reasoning about pain and morality to animals. And everything gets progressively more abstract and convoluted as we move farther and farther out from the higher-type mammals into cattle and swine and dogs and cats and rodents, and then birds and fish, and finally invertebrates like lobsters.

The more important point here, though, is that the whole animal-cruelty-and-eating issue is not just complex, it's also uncomfortable. It is, at any rate, uncomfortable for me, and for just about everyone I know who enjoys a variety of foods and yet does not want to see herself as cruel or unfeeling. As far as I can tell, my own main way of dealing with this conflict has been to avoid thinking about the whole unpleasant thing. I should add that it appears to me unlikely that many readers of *Gourmet* wish to think about it, either, or to be queried about the morality of their eating habits in the pages of a culinary monthly. Since, however, the assigned subject of this article is what it was like to attend the 2003 MLF, and thus to spend several days in the midst of a great mass of Americans all eating lobster, and thus to be more or less impelled to think hard about lobster and the experience of buying and eating lobster, it turns out that there is no honest way to avoid certain moral questions.

There are several reasons for this. For one thing, it's not just that lobsters   20
get boiled alive, it's that you do it yourself—or at least it's done specifically for you, on-site.[14] As mentioned, the World's Largest Lobster Cooker, which is highlighted as an attraction in the festival's program, is right out there on the MLF's north grounds for everyone to see. Try to imagine a Nebraska

14 Morality-wise, let's concede that this cuts both ways. Lobster-eating is at least not abetted by the system of corporate factory farms that produces most beef, pork, and chicken. Because, if nothing else, of the way they're marketed and packaged for sale, we eat these latter meats without having to consider that they were once conscious, sentient creatures to whom horrible things were done. (N.B. PETA distributes a certain video—the title of which is being omitted as part of the elaborate editorial compromise by which this note appears at all—in which you can see just about everything meat-related you don't want to see or think about. (N.B.[2] Not that PETA's any sort of font of unspun truth. Like many partisans in complex moral disputes, the PETA people are fanatics, and a lot of their rhetoric seems simplistic and self-righteous. Personally, though, I have to say that I found this unnamed video both credible and deeply upsetting.))

Beef Festival[15] at which part of the festivities is watching trucks pull up and the live cattle get driven down the ramp and slaughtered right there on the World's Largest Killing Floor or something — there's no way.

The intimacy of the whole thing is maximized at home, which of course is where most lobster gets prepared and eaten (although note already the semiconscious euphemism "prepared," which in the case of lobsters really means killing them right there in our kitchens). The basic scenario is that we come in from the store and make our little preparations like getting the kettle filled and boiling, and then we lift the lobsters out of the bag or whatever retail container they came home in . . . whereupon some uncomfortable things start to happen. However stuporous the lobster is from the trip home, for instance, it tends to come alarmingly to life when placed in boiling water. If you're tilting it from a container into the steaming kettle, the lobster will sometimes try to cling to the container's sides or even to hook its claws over the kettle's rim like a person trying to keep from going over the edge of a roof. And worse is when the lobster's fully immersed. Even if you cover the kettle and turn away, you can usually hear the cover rattling and clanking as the lobster tries to push it off. Or the creature's claws scraping the sides of the kettle as it thrashes around. The lobster, in other words, behaves very much as you or I would behave if we were plunged into boiling water (with the obvious exception of screaming[16]). A blunter way to say this is that the lobster acts as if it's in terrible pain, causing some cooks to leave the kitchen altogether and to take one of those little lightweight plastic oven-timers with them into another room and wait until the whole process is over.

There happen to be two main criteria that most ethicists agree on for determining whether a living creature has the capacity to suffer and so has genuine interests that it may or may not be our moral duty to consider.[17] One is how much of the neurological hardware required for pain-experience the

15 Is it significant that "lobster," "fish," and "chicken" are our culture's words for both the animal and the meat, whereas most mammals seem to require euphemisms like "beef" and "pork" that help us separate the meat we eat from the living creature the meat once was? Is this evidence that some kind of deep unease about eating higher animals is endemic enough to show up in English usage, but that the unease diminishes as we move out of the mammalian order? (And is "lamb"/"lamb" the counterexample that sinks the whole theory, or are there special, biblico-historical reasons for that equivalence?)

16 There's a relevant populist myth about the high-pitched whistling sound that sometimes issues from a pot of boiling lobster. The sound is really vented steam from the layer of seawater between the lobster's flesh and its carapace (this is why shedders whistle more than hard-shells), but the pop version has it that the sound is the lobster's rabbit-like death scream. Lobsters communicate via pheromones in their urine and don't have anything close to the vocal equipment for screaming, but the myth's very persistent — which might, once again, point to a low-level cultural unease about the boiling thing.

17 "Interests" basically means strong and legitimate preferences, which obviously require some degree of consciousness, responsiveness to stimuli, etc. See, for instance, the utilitarian philosopher Peter Singer [page 735], whose 1974 *Animal Liberation* is more or less the bible of the modern animal-rights movement:

It would be nonsense to say that it was not in the interests of a stone to be kicked along the road by a schoolboy. A stone does not have interests because it cannot suffer. Nothing that we can do to it could possibly make any difference to its welfare. A mouse, on the other hand, does have an interest in not being kicked along the road, because it will suffer if it is.

animal comes equipped with—nociceptors, prostaglandins, neuronal opioid receptors, etc. The other criterion is whether the animal demonstrates behavior associated with pain. And it takes a lot of intellectual gymnastics and behaviorist hairsplitting not to see struggling, thrashing, and lid-clattering as just such pain-behavior. According to marine zoologists, it usually takes lobsters between 35 and 45 seconds to die in boiling water. (No source I could find talks about how long it takes them to die in superheated steam; one rather hopes it's faster.)

There are, of course, other ways to kill your lobster on-site and so achieve maximum freshness. Some cooks' practice is to drive a sharp heavy knife point-first into a spot just above the midpoint between the lobster's eyestalks (more or less where the Third Eye is in human foreheads). This is alleged either to kill the lobster instantly or to render it insensate, and is said at least to eliminate some of the cowardice involved in throwing a creature into boiling water and then fleeing the room. As far as I can tell from talking to proponents of the knife-in-the-head method, the idea is that it's more violent but ultimately more merciful, plus that a willingness to exert personal agency and accept responsibility for stabbing the lobster's head honors the lobster somehow and entitles one to eat it (there's often a vague sort of Native American spirituality-of-the-hunt flavor to pro-knife arguments). But the problem with the knife method is basic biology: Lobsters' nervous systems operate off not one but several ganglia, a.k.a. nerve bundles, which are sort of wired in series and distributed all along the lobster's underside, from stem to stern. And disabling only the frontal ganglion does not normally result in quick death or unconsciousness.

Another alternative is to put the lobster in cold saltwater and then very slowly bring it up to a full boil. Cooks who advocate this method are going mostly on the analogy to a frog, which can supposedly be kept from jumping out of a boiling pot by heating the water incrementally. In order to save a lot of research-summarizing, I'll simply assure you that the analogy between frogs and lobsters turns out not to hold—plus, if the kettle's water isn't aerated seawater, the immersed lobster suffers from slow suffocation, although usually not decisive enough suffocation to keep it from still thrashing and clattering when the water gets hot enough to kill it. In fact, lobsters boiled incrementally often display a whole bonus set of gruesome, convulsionlike reactions that you don't see in regular boiling.

Ultimately, the only certain virtues of the home-lobotomy and slow-heating methods are comparative, because there are even worse/crueler ways people prepare lobster. Time-thrifty cooks sometimes microwave them alive (usually after poking several extra vent-holes in the carapace, which is a precaution most shellfish-microwavers learn about the hard way). Live dismemberment, on the other hand, is big in Europe—some chefs cut the lobster in half before cooking; others like to tear off the claws and tail and toss only these parts in the pot.   25

And there's more unhappy news respecting suffering-criterion number one. Lobsters don't have much in the way of eyesight or hearing, but they do have an exquisite tactile sense, one facilitated by hundreds of thousands of tiny hairs that protrude through their carapace. "Thus it is," in the words of T. M. Prudden's industry classic *About Lobster*, "that although encased in what seems a solid, impenetrable armor, the lobster can receive stimuli and impressions from without as readily as if it possessed a soft and delicate skin." And lobsters do have nociceptors,[18] as well as invertebrate versions of the prostaglandins and major neurotransmitters via which our own brains register pain.

Lobsters do not, on the other hand, appear to have the equipment for making or absorbing natural opioids like endorphins and enkephalins, which are what more advanced nervous systems use to try to handle intense pain. From this fact, though, one could conclude either that lobsters are maybe even *more* vulnerable to pain, since they lack mammalian nervous systems' built-in analgesia, or, instead, that the absence of natural opioids implies an absence of the really intense pain-sensations that natural opioids are designed to mitigate. I for one can detect a marked upswing in mood as I contemplate this latter possibility. It could be that their lack of endorphin/enkephalin hardware means that lobsters' raw subjective experience of pain is so radically different from mammals' that it may not even deserve the term "pain." Perhaps lobsters are more like those frontal-lobotomy patients one reads about who report experiencing pain in a totally different way than you and I. These patients evidently do feel physical pain, neurologically speaking, but don't dislike it—though neither do they like it; it's more that they feel it but don't feel anything *about* it—the point being that the pain is not distressing to them or something they want to get away from. Maybe lobsters, who are also without frontal lobes, are detached from the neurological-registration-of-injury-or-hazard we call pain in just the same way. There is, after all, a difference between (1) pain as a purely neurological event, and (2) actual suffering, which seems crucially to involve an emotional component, an awareness of pain as unpleasant, as something to fear/dislike/want to avoid.

Still, after all the abstract intellection, there remain the facts of the frantically clanking lid, the pathetic clinging to the edge of the pot. Standing at the stove, it is hard to deny in any meaningful way that this is a living creature experiencing pain and wishing to avoid/escape the painful experience. To my lay mind, the lobster's behavior in the kettle appears to be the expression of a preference; and it may well be that an ability to form preferences is the decisive criterion for real suffering.[19] The logic of this (preference → suffering) relation may be easiest to see in the negative case. If you cut certain

18 This is the neurological term for special pain-receptors that are "sensitive to potentially damaging extremes of temperature, to mechanical forces, and to chemical substances which are released when body tissues are damaged."

19 "Preference" is maybe roughly synonymous with "interests," but it is a better term for our purposes because it's less abstractly philosophical—"preference" seems more personal, and it's the whole idea of a living creature's personal experience that's at issue.

kinds of worms in half, the halves will often keep crawling around and going about their vermiform business as if nothing had happened. When we assert, based on their post-op behavior, that these worms appear not to be suffering, what we're really saying is that there's no sign the worms know anything bad has happened or would *prefer* not to have gotten cut in half.

Lobsters, though, are known to exhibit preferences. Experiments have shown that they can detect changes of only a degree or two in water temperature; one reason for their complex migratory cycles (which can often cover 100-plus miles a year) is to pursue the temperatures they like best.[20] And, as mentioned, they're bottom-dwellers and do not like bright light—if a tank of food-lobsters is out in the sunlight or a store's fluorescence, the lobsters will always congregate in whatever part is darkest. Fairly solitary in the ocean, they also clearly dislike the crowding that's part of their captivity in tanks, since (as also mentioned) one reason why lobsters' claws are banded on capture is to keep them from attacking one another under the stress of close-quarter storage.

In any event, at the MLF, standing by the bubbling tanks outside the World's Largest Lobster Cooker, watching the fresh-caught lobsters pile over one another, wave their hobbled claws impotently, huddle in the rear corners, or scrabble frantically back from the glass as you approach, it is difficult not to sense that they're unhappy, or frightened, even if it's some rudimentary version of these feelings . . . and, again, why does rudimentariness even enter into it? Why is a primitive, inarticulate form of suffering less urgent or uncomfortable for the person who's helping to inflict it by paying for the food it results in? I'm not trying to give you a PETA-like screed here—at least I don't think so. I'm trying, rather, to work out and articulate some of the troubling questions that arise amid all the laughter and saltation and community pride of the Maine Lobster Festival. The truth is that if you, the festival attendee, permit yourself to think that lobsters can suffer and

30

---

20 Of course, the most common sort of counterargument here would begin by objecting that "like best" is really just a metaphor, and a misleadingly anthropomorphic one at that. The counter-arguer would posit that the lobster seeks to maintain a certain optimal ambient temperature out of nothing but unconscious instinct (with a similar explanation for the low-light affinities about to be mentioned in the main text). The thrust of such a counterargument will be that the lobster's thrashings and clankings in the kettle express not unpreferred pain but involuntary reflexes, like your leg shooting out when the doctor hits your knee. Be advised that there are professional scientists, including many researchers who use animals in experiments, who hold to the view that nonhuman creatures have no real feelings at all, merely "behaviors." Be further advised that this view has a long history that goes all the way back to Descartes, although its modern support comes mostly from behaviorist psychology.

To these what-looks-like-pain-is-really-just-reflexes counterarguments, however, there happen to be all sorts of scientific and pro–animal rights counter-counterarguments. And then further attempted rebuttals and redirects, and so on. Suffice it to say that both the scientific and the philosophical arguments on either side of the animal-suffering issue are involved, abstruse, technical, often informed by self-interest or ideology, and in the end so totally inconclusive that as a practical matter, in the kitchen or restaurant, it all still seems to come down to individual conscience, going with (no pun) your gut.

would rather not, the MLF begins to take on the aspect of something like a Roman circus or medieval torture-fest.

Does that comparison seem a bit much? If so, exactly why? Or what about this one: Is it possible that future generations will regard our own present agribusiness and eating practices in much the same way we now view Nero's[21] entertainments or Mengele's[22] experiments? My own initial reaction is that such a comparison is hysterical, extreme — and yet the reason it seems extreme to me appears to be that I believe animals are less morally important than human beings;[23] and when it comes to defending such a belief, even to myself, I have to acknowledge that (a) I have an obvious selfish interest in this belief, since I like to eat certain kinds of animals and want to be able to keep doing it, and (b) I haven't succeeded in working out any sort of personal ethical system in which the belief is truly defensible instead of just selfishly convenient.

Given this article's venue and my own lack of culinary sophistication, I'm curious about whether the reader can identify with any of these reactions and acknowledgments and discomforts. I'm also concerned not to come off as shrill or preachy when what I really am is more like confused. For those *Gourmet* readers who enjoy well-prepared and -presented meals involving beef, veal, lamb, pork, chicken, lobster, etc.: Do you think much about the (possible) moral status and (probable) suffering of the animals involved? If you do, what ethical convictions have you worked out that permit you not just to eat but to savor and enjoy flesh-based viands (since of course refined enjoyment, rather than mere ingestion, is the whole point of gastronomy)? If, on the other hand, you'll have no truck with confusions or convictions and regard stuff like the previous paragraph as just so much fatuous navel-gazing, what makes it feel truly okay, inside, to just dismiss the whole thing out of hand? That is, is your refusal to think about any of this the product of actual thought, or is it just that you don't want to think about it? And if the latter, then why not? Do you ever think, even idly, about the possible reasons for your reluctance to think about it? I am not trying to bait anyone here — I'm genuinely curious. After all, isn't being extra aware and attentive and thoughtful about one's food and its overall context part of what distinguishes a real gourmet? Or is all the gourmet's extra attention and sensibility just supposed to be sensuous? Is it really all just a matter of taste and presentation?

These last few queries, though, while sincere, obviously involve much larger and more abstract questions about the connections (if any) between

---

21 *Nero* (37–68): First-century Roman Emperor noted for his cruelty. — EDS.

22 *Mengele:* Dr. Mengele, the infamous Nazi concentration camp physician (1911–1979) who inspected new prisoners to select those fit for labor and those who would be exterminated. He also was responsible for performing medical experiments on prisoners. — EDS.

23 Meaning *a lot* less important, apparently, since the moral comparison here is not the value of one human's life vs. the value of one animal's life, but rather the value of one animal's life vs. the value of one human's taste for a particular kind of protein. Even the most diehard carniphile will acknowledge that it's possible to live and eat well without consuming animals.

aesthetics and morality—about what the adjective in a phrase like "The Magazine of Good Living" is really supposed to mean—and these questions lead straightaway into such deep and treacherous waters that it's probably best to stop the public discussion right here. There are limits to what even interested persons can ask of each other. ●

The Reader's Presence

1. What is the occasion behind "Consider the Lobster"? Why did Wallace write it? How would you describe the audience he is writing for? What relation does he establish with that audience? What is Wallace's overall attitude toward the event that he was assigned to write about?

2. Wallace refers to "Consider the Lobster" as an "article." How does it differ from the magazine articles you may typically read? Note the title: "Consider" is often a term used by essayists. What does the word *consider* suggest to you? It's common in essays for the essayist to examine different sides of an issue and, instead of coming up with a definite conclusion, offer various ways that we might think of, or "consider," that issue. What features of the selection resemble a magazine article? What features appear essayistic?

3. **CONNECTIONS:**   The selection begins with a consideration of tourism in America. How would you characterize Wallace's attitude toward tourism? Carefully read his remarks on tourism in the long footnote appearing on page 764. Consider Nathaniel Hawthorne's "My Visit to Niagara" (page 432) in the light of Wallace's remarks. How appropriate do those remarks seem to Hawthorne's essay? You might also want to compare "Consider the Lobster" to Jonathan Swift's "A Modest Proposal" (page 752). How does each writer deal with problems of audience?

The Writer at Work

Another Version of "Consider the Lobster"

Suzy Allman /The New York Times/Redux

When David Foster Wallace submitted "Consider the Lobster" to *Gourmet*, which calls itself "The Magazine of Good Living," the piece was edited by the magazine before it appeared in its August 2004 issue. After it was selected for the *Best American Essays 2005*, Wallace asked if he could make some changes before it was published in that volume. Basically, he wanted to restore some of his original remarks that the magazine had revised. Then, when he included the essay in his own collection, *Consider the Lobster and Other Essays* (2005), he made even further revisions. It is that final text that we have included in this book.

Most of Wallace's revisions occur in the conclusion of the essay. The following passage is taken from the first appearance of the essay in *Gourmet* magazine and represents the essay's final four paragraphs. As you compare the concluding paragraphs as they appeared in *Gourmet* to those Wallace preferred and used in his book (pages 773–775), what do you find significant about the differences? What kind of changes had *Gourmet* made? Why do you think Wallace wanted to change what *Gourmet* had done? Note the substitution of "Aztec sacrifices" for "Mengele's experiments" (for more on Mengele see Elie Wiesel's "Eight Simple, Short Words" on page 300). Which is the better example in your opinion? Why do you think Wallace preferred to address his readers as "you" in his version and not as "they" as appears in paragraph 3 of the *Gourmet* version? Why do you think the magazine preferred to drop the direct address to readers in this context?

From *Gourmet* magazine:

[30] **❝**I'm not trying to give you a PETA-like screed here — at least I don't think so. I'm trying, rather, to work out and articulate some of the troubling questions that arise amid all the laughter and saltation and community pride of the Maine Lobster Festival. The truth is that if you, the Festival attendee, permit yourself to think that lobsters can suffer and would rather not, the MLF can begin to take on aspects of something like a Roman circus or medieval torture-fest.

[31] Does that comparison seem a bit much? If so, exactly why? Or what about this one: Is it not possible that future generations will regard our own present agribusiness and eating practices in much the same way we now view Nero's entertainments or Aztec sacrifices? My own immediate reaction is that such a comparison is hysterical, extreme — and yet the reason it seems extreme to me appears to be that I believe animals are less morally important than human beings; and when it comes to defending such a belief, even to myself, I have to acknowledge that (a) I have an obvious selfish interest in this belief, since I like to eat certain kinds of animals and want to be

able to keep doing it, and (b) I have not succeeded in working out any sort of personal ethical system in which the belief is truly defensible instead of just selfishly convenient.

[32] Given this article's venue and my own lack of culinary sophistication, I'm curious about whether the reader can identify with any of these reactions and acknowledgments and discomforts. I am also concerned not to come off as shrill or preachy when what I really am is confused. Given the (possible) moral status and (very possible) physical suffering of the animals involved, what ethical convictions do gourmets evolve that allow them not just to eat but to savor and enjoy flesh-based viands (since of course refined *enjoyment*, rather than just ingestion, is the whole point of gastronomy)? And for those gourmets who'll have no truck with convictions or rationales and who regard stuff like the previous paragraph as just so much

pointless navel-gazing, what makes it feel okay, inside, to dismiss the whole issue out of hand? That is, is their refusal to think about any of this the product of actual thought, or is it just that they don't want to think about it? Do they ever think about their reluctance to think about it? After all, isn't being extra aware and attentive and thoughtful about one's food and its overall context part of what distinguishes a real gourmet? Or is all the gourmet's extra attention and sensibility just supposed to be aesthetic, gustatory?

[33] These last couple queries, though, while sincere, obviously involve much larger and more abstract questions about the connections (if any) between aesthetics and morality, and these questions lead straightaway into such deep and treacherous waters that it's probably best to stop the public discussion right here. There are limits to what even interested persons can ask of each other. **"**

John Edgar Wideman

FATHERALONG*

Asa Messen Professor and Professor of Africana Studies and Literary Arts at Brown University, **JOHN EDGAR WIDEMAN** (b. 1941) was the first author to win the International PEN/Faulkner Award for Fiction twice. After receiving his BA in English in 1963, he won a Rhodes scholarship to study philosophy at Oxford University's New College. He returned to the United States in 1966, spent a year as a Kent Fellow at the famous University of Iowa Writer's Workshop, and published his first novel, *A Glance Away*, in 1967. He has written many novels since then, including *The Lynchers* (1973), *Hiding Place* (1981), *Philadelphia Fire* (1990), *Two Cities* (1998), and *Fanon* (2008), to name but a few. He is also the author of a memoir, *Brothers and Keepers* (1984), as well as several other nonfiction books and collections of short stories. *Conversations with John Edgar Wideman*, a series of nineteen interviews spanning three decades, was published by the University Press of Mississippi in 1998. He's won the American Book Award for Fiction, the Lannan Literary Fellowship for fiction, and a MacArthur Fellowship. "Fatheralong" was published in *Harper's* in 2009. The book Wideman published by the same title in 1994 was a finalist for the National Book Award for nonfiction. Wideman has written widely on African American issues and culture, and his articles on Malcolm X, Spike Lee, Denzel Washington, Michael Jordan, Emmett Till, Thelonius Monk, and women's professional basketball have appeared in the *New Yorker*, *Vogue*, *Esquire*, *Emerge*, and the *New York Times Magazine*. His daughter, Jamila, is a professional basketball player.

> John Edgar Wideman was the first author to win the International PEN/Faulkner Award for Fiction twice.

LOUIS TILL, THE FATHER OF EMMETT TILL, the fourteen-year-old Chicago boy murdered in Mississippi in 1955, one year after the Supreme Court's school desegregation decision, is the first father I think about when I am asked to comment on the alleged failure of black males to assume properly the responsibilities of fatherhood. I also think about Freud, about the global crisis demanding a metamorphosis of family that's not new, not black. President Barack Obama, who addressed such issues earlier and eloquently in his *Dreams from My Father* (1995), is clearly the catalyst of the

---

*The word I heard as a child when the church sang "Farther Along."

present discussions as he works to apply his personal insights and experiences to a national dilemma. I'm moved by his honest explorations of fatherhood, his witness. The world is a troubled, dangerous place, at best. Unfairly dangerous for young Americans in free fall, growing up too fast or not growing at all, deprived of the love, guidance, positive example, the material, intellectual, and moral support of fathers negotiating the perils with them.

Louis Till's Non-Battle Casualty Report lists his rank as PVT, his serial number as 36392273, lists the Date of Casualty as July 2, his Reporting Theatre as MTO, the Mediterranean Theatre of Operations, lists his Arm or Service as TC, the Transportation Command, a non-combat unit to which nearly every colored soldier in the segregated U.S. Army was assigned, lists the Place of Casualty as Italy, and leaves blank, except for an asterisk, the space in which Type of Casualty should be listed. Mrs. Mamie Till's name (misspelled "Mammie") appears on the Battle Casualty Report, but it does not mention Till's son, Emmett.

The first time Mamie Till knew her husband had been hanged in Italy by the United States Army was in the fall of 1955, not long after their son Emmett was murdered, about a dozen years after she'd seen Louis Till last in Chicago. The telegram she had received from the Army on July 13, 1945, composed of selected facts from the Non-Battle Casualty Report, informed her that her husband, Private Louis Till, had died of willful misconduct, but omitted "sol died in non-battle status" and "judicial asphixiation," words typed into a confidential footnote below the official report. Although assisted by a lawyer, Mrs. Till's attempt to investigate the circumstances surrounding

© Bettmann/CORBIS

Emmett Till

the death of her husband and father of her only child had been stymied by the government's terminal unresponsiveness, the very same government that ordered its colored soldiers to serve in what amounted to a separate, second-class army of conscripted laborers.

The government that at its highest levels chose to break its own rules and violate the rights of Private Louis Till by sending his confidential service record, which included a transcript of his court martial (CM288642), to lawyers defending the kidnappers and killers of his son, Emmett. Driven by their desire to repair the public image of a state that was being drubbed nationwide by press coverage of Emmett Till's murder, the Mississippi arch-segregationist Senators James Eastland and John Stennis are likely the ones who obtained and leaked Louis Till's papers, as only officials with their rank and clout could demand and receive, from the Army adjutant general, a soldier's classified service record. A Colonel Ralph K. Johnson, TJAG (The Judge Advocate General) on October 14, 1955, did the dirty work of signing off on the release and penciling out the word CONFIDENTIAL stamped on the cover and pages of the Record of Trial by General Courts Martial, dated February 17, 1945.

In November 1955, approximately six weeks after a trial that found World War II veterans—J. W. Milam and his brother-in-law Roy Bryant—not guilty of murdering Emmett Till, a trial that the Cleveland *Post and Call* derided ("Mississippi Jungle Law Frees Slayers of Child") and the Greenwood, Mississippi, *Morning Star* complimented ("Fair Trial Was Credit to Mississippi"), the state of Mississippi, compelled by the testimony of a sheriff during the trial that Milam and Bryant admitted to him they had taken Emmett Till from his great-uncle Moses Wright's home, sought indictments against the two men for kidnapping. Parties unknown leaked to the press that Emmett Till's father, Mamie Till's husband, Louis, far from being the martyred war hero portrayed in Northern papers during the trial, had been hanged by the U.S. Army for committing rape and murder.

This revelation of the crimes of the father doomed any chance that jurors in Sumner, Mississippi, would indict the killers of Louis Till's son for any wrongdoing whatever. Instead of what measure of comfort she might have felt if the court had punished her son's murderers, Mamie Bradley Till found herself watching in dismay as Emmett Till's already dead and brutalized body was tarred, feathered, and lynched again for the father's sins, her fourteen-year-old boy stigmatized, scorned as rotten fruit from a rotten tree.

The novelist Chester Himes, expressing the despair shared by many of his fellow citizens, published a letter in the *New York Post* on September 25, 1955, in which he wrote, "The real horror comes when your dead brain must face the fact that we as a nation don't want it to stop. If we wanted to, we would. So let us all share the guilt, those in New York as well as those in Sumner, Mississippi."

5

As a father, Louis Till didn't have much time to spend with his son. Emmett Till was born in July of 1941 (a month after I was born), and Louis Till (like my father) went off to war in a segregated army in 1942, returning to Chicago only once, one AWOL night before the Army came and knocked on Mamie's door in the morning and hauled him back. A ring Louis Till purchased in Casablanca and had engraved with his initials and the date May 25, 1943, was included among the personal effects Mamie Till received from the Army after she was notified of his death. This silver ring, cached in Emmett Till's jewelry box or occasionally worn on his finger, padded by tape until his finger grew thick enough the last year of his life to keep it in place, may have been the most intimate link between father and son, an irony, since the ring also served to identify Emmett Till's battered, bloated, disfigured body when it was pulled from the Tallahatchie River.

What kind of father did Emmett Till imagine when he wore the silver ring? Looking down at the ring encircling his own dark finger, did Louis Till ever think about a son bearing his name, *Till*, wearing the ring one day?

While his sentence of death by hanging was receiving its mandatory   10 review by The Judge Advocate General's Division, Louis Till was confined in the Disciplinary Training Center, a United States military prison in Metato, near Pisa. The poet Ezra Pound, facing a capital sentence himself, on charges of treasonous radio broadcasts, was Till's fellow prisoner, the only civilian in a population of 3,600 mostly colored inmates. The Pisan *Cantos*, written during Pound's internment in the DTC, imagine Louis Till as *Outis*, Greek for "no one," "nobody," the wanderer of the Odyssey, as Zeus the lusty ram, Till's sign, the Chinese ideogram "M4," "a man upon whom the sun has gone down" (Canto LXXIV: 170–178, edited by Richard Sieburth).

If Louis Till had been around to school Emmett about the perils of the South, about how white men treat black boys down south and up north, would Emmett have returned to Chicago safely on the *City of New Orleans* train from his trip to visit relatives in Money, Mississippi, started up public school in the fall, earned good grades, maybe even have become successful and rich, eluding the fate of his father? Or does his father's fate draw Emmett like a fluttering moth to its flame, Emmett flying backward and forward at once, like the African sankofa bird flies, because part of the father's fate is not to be around to advise and supervise and support the son, the fate of father and son to be divided always? A cycle of predictable missings and absence eternally renewed. A flicker of wings igniting, quickly extinguished, then darkness.

Race is myth. When we stop talking about race, stop believing in race, it will disappear. Except for its career historically and in people's memories as the antithesis of human freedom, the embodiment of inequality and injustice that remained far too long a toxic, unresolved paradox in nations proclaiming themselves free. In a raceless society color wouldn't disappear.

Difference wouldn't disappear. Africa wouldn't disappear. In post-race America "white" people would disappear. That is, no group could assume as birthright and identity a privileged, supernaturally ordained superiority at the top of a hierarchy of other groups, a supremacy that bestows upon their particular kind the right perpetually to rule and regulate the lives of all other kinds. This idea, this belief in "whiteness," whether the belief is expressed in terms of color, ethnicity, nationality, gender, tribe, etc., constitutes the founding principle of race, its appeal and its discontents.

To dismiss race as myth is not to underestimate its power. Race, like religion, is immune to critiques of science and logic because it rests on belief. And people need beliefs. Although science has discredited the biological underpinnings of the notion of race, faith rushes in to seal the cracks, paper over glaring omissions in arrested explanations of human difference offered by racial ideology. Louis Till's color, the color of his son, Emmett, the color of Richard Wright's fictional character Bigger Thomas, Colin Powell's color, are not problems until the myth of race and the racialized perspective it authorizes turn color into an indictment, into instant proof of innocence or guilty-as-charged. We should understand by now that race can mean anything, everything, or nothing, depending upon whom we ask.

The continuing existence of race in the United States indicates conspiracy and cover-up. An attempt to make more palatable to ourselves, and anyone watching, the not-so-secret dirty secret shared by all Americans that our country, in spite of public professions to the contrary, entertains a deeply internalized, segregated vision of itself. We look at ourselves and believe we see White Americans or Black Americans. We perceive our problems as Black or White problems, The urgent task of redressing the shameful neglect of American children gets postponed by hand-wringing and finger-pointing at feckless black fathers and the damage they're inflicting upon their black offspring. Or sidetracked just as effectively by blaming society and exempting blacks because race tells us blacks are permanent victims, not agents of change. The truth of too many black boys in prison, too many black babies dying, too many hungry black youngsters being raised in dire poverty, too many terrible black schools—these truths misrepresented by discourses perpetuating the myth of separate races don't spur us to action but become an occasion for shedding crocodile tears, washing our hands of personal as well as collective responsibility. More than half a century ago James Baldwin,[1] outed this kind of hiding from the consequences of racialized thinking as *willed innocence*. At this late date, displays of surprise or ignorance about how bad things are for our children suggest dishonesty, signify complicity, conscious or unconscious, with the cover-up.

Louis Till was born fatherless in Madrid, Missouri. One could argue that   15
the concept of race abiding today in America is a profound orphaning of all

---

[1]See Baldwin's "Notes of a Native Son" (page 61).—EDS.

black children. Argue that any attempt to understand black fathers and to interpret their responsibilities, successes, and failures should begin right there, with a consideration of the fact that myths of race isolate children, place them at risk, disinherit and repudiate. Start by listening a moment to the roaring silence in which Louis Till is buried, the silence neither his voice nor his son's voice can break, the dark, impervious silence in which words — *good, bad, responsible, black, white* — vanish.

The Reader's Presence

1. Comment on Wideman's decision to frame his essay with the story of Louis Till's hanging while in military service in Italy during World War II and the murder of his son, Emmett, "the fourteen-year-old Chicago boy murdered in Mississippi in 1955, one year after the Supreme Court's school desegregation decision" (paragraph 1). In what specific ways does Wideman's account of their deaths — and the reports on each — enable him to build an argument about the role of race in American culture? Demonstrate how Wideman builds his argument step-by-step toward his concluding assertion: "One could argue that the concept of race abiding today in America is a profound orphaning of all black children" (paragraph 15).

2. Wideman explains in an epigraph to his essay that the title, "Fatheralong," is "[t]he word I heard as a child when the church sang 'Farther Along.'" In the light of reading Wideman's essay, what literal and figurative meanings do you think Wideman associates with the word *Fatheralong*? In what specific ways can this word serve as a painfully ironic commentary on the state of race relations in contemporary American society? Support your response by pointing to — and then analyzing — specific passages. What evidence does Wideman present to support his argument that "[r]ace is myth" (paragraph 12)? What distinctions does Wideman draw between "belief" and "faith" in the context of race relations in the United States (paragraph 13)?

3. **CONNECTIONS:** Near the end of his essay, Wideman invokes James Baldwin's phrase *"willed innocence"* to challenge the "truths misrepresented by discourses perpetuating the myth of separate races" as "an occasion for shedding crocodile tears, washing our hands of personal as well as collective responsibility" (paragraph 14). Compare and contrast Wideman's and Baldwin's attitudes toward — and suggestions for improving — race relations in the United States. In what specific ways is Wideman's essay similar to — and different from — the points Martin Luther King Jr. makes in his prophetic "I Have a Dream" speech (page 632)?

Howard Zinn

STORIES HOLLYWOOD NEVER TELLS

HOWARD ZINN (1922–2010) was professor emeritus of political science at Boston University and is known both for his active involvement in the civil rights and peace movements and for his scholarship. He published scores of books that reflected the issues of their times yet remain in print, demonstrating their continuing relevance. A sampling includes *The Southern Mystique* (1964); *Disobedience and Democracy: Nine Fallacies on Law and Order* (1968); *A People's History of the United States: 1492–Present* (1980), which has sold more than two million copies; *Declarations of Independence: Cross-Examining American Ideology* (1990); *Three Strikes: Miners, Musicians, Salesgirls, and the Fighting Spirit of Labor's Last Century* (2001); and *Artists in Times of War* (2003). The essay "Stories Hollywood Never Tells," adapted from *Artists in Times of War*, was published in *The Sun* in 2004.

> "I am totally confident not that the world will get better, but that we should not give up the game before all the cards have been played."

Zinn had also written plays, a musical, and an autobiography, *You Can't Be Neutral on a Moving Train* (1994).

Throughout his career, Zinn argued that perseverance in the face of opposition is essential: "I am totally confident not that the world will get better, but that we should not give up the game before all the cards have been played. The metaphor is deliberate; life is a gamble. Not to play is to foreclose any chance of winning. To play, to act, is to create at least a possibility of changing the world."

HOWEVER HATEFUL they may be sometimes, I have always loved the movies. When I began reading and studying history, I kept coming across incidents and events that led me to think, *Wow, what a movie this would make.* I would look to see if a movie had been made about it, but I'd never find one. It took me a while to realize that Hollywood isn't going to make movies like the ones I imagined. Hollywood isn't going to make movies that are class-conscious, or antiwar, or conscious of the need for racial equality or gender equality.

I wondered about this. It seemed to me that the people in Hollywood didn't all get together in a room and decide, "We're going to do just this kind of film and not the other kind of film." Yet it's not just an oversight or an accident, either. Leon Trotsky once used an expression to describe events that are not accidents, and are not planned deliberately, but are something in between. He called this the "natural selection of accidents," in which, if there's a certain structure to a situation, then these "accidents" will inevitably happen, whether anyone plans them or not. It seems that the structure of Hollywood is such that it will not produce the kinds of films that I imagined. It's a structure where money and profit are absolutely the first consideration: before art, before aesthetics, before human values.

When you consider the films about war that have come out of Hollywood — and there have been hundreds and hundreds, maybe even thousands — they almost always glorify military heroism. We need to think about telling the story of war from a different perspective.

Let's take one of our most popular wars to begin with: the Revolutionary War. How can you speak against the Revolutionary War, right? But to tell the story of the American Revolution, not from the standpoint of the schoolbooks, but from the standpoint of war as a complex phenomenon intertwined with moral issues, we must acknowledge not just that Americans were oppressed by the English, but that some Americans were oppressed by other Americans. For instance, American Indians did not rush to celebrate the victory of the colonists over England, because for them it meant that the line that the British had drawn to limit westward expansion in the Proclamation of 1763 would now be obliterated. The colonists would be free to move west into Indian lands.

John Adams, one of the Founding Fathers and a revolutionary leader, estimated that one-third of the colonists supported the American Revolution, one-third were opposed, and one-third were neutral. It would be interesting to tell the story of the American Revolution from the viewpoint of an ordinary workingman who hears the Declaration of Independence read to him from a balcony in Boston, promising freedom and equality and so on, and immediately is told that rich men can get out of service by paying several hundred dollars. This man then joins the army, despite his misgivings, despite his own feelings of being oppressed — not just by the British, but by the leaders of the colonial world — because he is promised some land. But as the war progresses and he sees the mutilations and the killing, he becomes increasingly disaffected. There's no place in society where class divisions are more clear-cut than in the military, and he sees that the officers are living in splendor while the ordinary enlisted men don't have any clothes or shoes, aren't being paid, and are being fed slop. So he joins the mutineers.

In the Revolutionary War, there were two mutinies against Washington's army: the mutiny of the Pennsylvania Line, and the mutiny of the New Jersey Line. Let's say our workingman joins the Pennsylvania Line, and they march on the Continental Congress, but eventually are surrounded by Washington's army, and several of their former comrades are forced to shoot several of the mutineers. Then this soldier, embittered by what he's seen, gets out of the army and gets some land in western Massachusetts. After the war is over, he becomes part of Shays's Rebellion, in which a group of small farmers rebel against the rich men who control the legislature in Boston and who are imposing heavy taxes on them, taking away their land and farms. The farmers, many of them Revolutionary War veterans, surround the court-houses and refuse to let the auctioneer go in to auction off their farms. The militia is called out to suppress them, and the militia also goes over to their side. Finally an army is raised by the moneyed class in Boston to suppress Shays's Rebellion.

I have never seen Hollywood tell this kind of story. If you know of a film that has been made about it, I wish you'd tell me so that we could have a celebration of that rare event.

Wars are more complicated than the simple good-versus-evil scenario presented to us in our history books and our culture. Wars are not simply conflicts of one people against another; wars always involve class differ-ences within each side, and victory is very often not shared by everybody, but only among a few. The people who fight the wars are not the people who benefit from the wars.

I think somebody should make a new movie about the Mexican War. I haven't seen one that tells how the Mexican War started, or how the presi-dent of the United States deceived the American people. I know it's sur-prising to hear that a president would willfully deceive the people of the United States, but this was one of those rare cases. President James Polk told Americans that Mexican troops had fired at our troops on U.S. soil. Really the fighting broke out on disputed soil that both Mexico and the U.S. had claimed. The war had been planned in advance by the Polk administration, because it coveted this beautiful territory of the Southwest.

It would be interesting to tell that story from the viewpoint of an ordi- 10 nary soldier, who sees the mayhem and the bloodshed as the army moves into Mexico and destroys town after town. More and more U.S. soldiers grow disaffected from the war, and as they make their final march toward Mexico City, General Scott wakes up one morning to discover that half his army has deserted.

It would be interesting, too, to tell the story from the point of view of one of the Massachusetts volunteers who comes back at the end of the war and is invited to a victory celebration. When the commander of the Mas-sachusetts volunteers gets up to speak, he is booed off the platform by the surviving half of his men, who resent what happened to their comrades in the war and who wonder what they were fighting for. I should tell you: this really happened.

The film could also include a scene after the war in which the U.S. Army is moving to suppress a rebellion in Santa Fe, because mostly Mexicans still live there. The army marches through the streets of Santa Fe, and all the townspeople go into their houses and close the shutters. The army is met by total silence, an expression of how the population feels about this great American victory.

Another little story about the Mexican War is the tale of the deserters. Many of those who volunteered to fight in the Mexican War did so for the same reason that people volunteer for the military today: they were desperately poor and hoped that their fortunes would improve as a result of enlisting. During the Mexican War, some of these volunteers were recent Irish immigrants. When these immigrant soldiers saw what was being done to the people of Mexico, a number of them deserted and went over to the Mexican side. They formed their own battalion, which they called St. Patrick's Battalion, or the San Patricio Battalion, and they fought for the Mexicans.

It's not easy to make the Spanish-American War look like a noble enterprise—though of course Hollywood can do anything. The war has gotten a certain amount of attention, because of the heroism of Theodore Roosevelt and his Rough Riders, but not a lot. In the history textbooks, the Spanish-American War is called "a splendid little war." It lasted three months. We fought it to free the Cubans, because we're always going to war to free somebody. We expelled the Spaniards from Cuba, but we didn't expel ourselves, and the United States in effect took over Cuba after the war. One grievance we have against Fidel Castro is that he ended U.S. control of Cuba. We're certainly not against him simply because he's a dictator. We've never had anything against dictators in general.

I remember learning in school that, as a result of the Spanish-American   15
War, we somehow took over the Philippines, but I never knew the details. When you look into it, you'll find that the Spanish-American War lasted three months; the Philippine War lasted for years and was a brutal, bloody suppression of the Filipino movement for independence. In many ways, it was a precursor of the Vietnam War, in terms of the atrocities committed by the U.S. Army. Now, that's a story that has never been told.

Black American soldiers in the Philippines soon began to identify more with the Filipinos than with their fellow white Americans. While these black soldiers were fighting to suppress the Filipinos, they also were hearing from relatives about the lynchings and race riots in their hometowns. They were hearing about black people being killed in large numbers—and here they were, fighting against a nonwhite people on behalf of the United States government. A number of black soldiers deserted and went over to fight with the Filipinos.

In 1906, when the Philippine War was supposedly over—but really the U.S. Army was still suppressing pockets of rebellion—there was a massacre. That's the only way to describe it. The Moros are inhabitants of a southern island in the Philippines. The army swooped down and annihilated a Moro village of six hundred men, women, and children—all of whom were unarmed. Every last one of them was killed. Mark Twain wrote angrily about this. He was especially angry about the fact that President Theodore Roosevelt sent a letter of congratulations to the military commander who had ordered this atrocity, saying it was a great military victory. Have you ever seen a movie in which Theodore Roosevelt was presented as a racist? As an imperialist? As a supporter of massacres? And there he is, up on Mount Rushmore. I've had the thought: *A hammer, a chisel*. But no, it wouldn't do.

War needs to be presented on film in such a way as to encourage the population simply to say no to war. We need a film about those heroic Americans who protested World War I. When you look at them, you see socialists, pacifists, and just ordinary people who saw the stupidity of entering a war that was taking the lives of ten million people in Europe. You see Emma Goldman, the feminist and anarchist, who went to prison for opposing the draft and the war. You see Helen Keller. Every film about Helen Keller concentrates on the fact that she was disabled. I've never seen a film in which Helen Keller is presented as what she was: a radical, a socialist, an antiwar agitator. You also see Kate Richards O'Hare, a socialist who was put in jail for opposing World War I. There is a story from her time in prison that would make a great scene in a movie: The prisoners are stifling for lack of air, and O'Hare takes a book that she's been reading, reaches through the bars, and hurls the book through a skylight to let the air in. All the prisoners applaud and cheer.

I have to acknowledge that there have been a few antiwar films made about World War I. *All Quiet on the Western Front* is an extraordinary film. I recently wrote an article comparing it to *Saving Private Ryan*. Despite the mayhem, *Saving Private Ryan* was essentially a glorification of war, whereas *All Quiet on the Western Front* expresses a diamond-clear antiwar sentiment.

What about the many films devoted to World War II, the "good war"?   20 When Studs Terkel did his oral history of World War II, he called it *The "Good War,"* with quotation marks around *Good War*. In that war, we fought against a terrible evil—fascism—but our own atrocities multiplied as the war went on, culminating in the bombings of Hiroshima and Nagasaki. I have not seen a Hollywood film about the bombing of Hiroshima. The closest we've come to a movie that deals with our bombing of civilian populations was the film version of Kurt Vonnegut's book *Slaughterhouse-Five*, about the bombing of Dresden, Germany, and that was a rarity.

Films about the Civil War tend to focus on the famous battles, like Gettysburg, Fredericksburg, and Bull Run. The Civil War is, again, one of our "good wars"—the slaves were freed because of it—but it is not that simple. There is the class element of who was and who was not drafted, who paid substitutes, who made huge amounts of money off the war. And then there is what happened to the Indians. In the midst of the Civil War, while the armies were fighting in the South, another part of the Union Army was out west, destroying Indian settlements and taking over Indian land. In 1864, not long after the Emancipation Proclamation, the U.S. Army was in Colorado attacking an Indian village, killing hundreds of men, women, and children at Sand Creek, in one of the worst Indian massacres in American history. This massacre occurred during the war to end slavery. In the years of the Civil War, more land was taken from the Indians than in any other comparable period in history.

There's a lot of historical work to be done, a lot of films that need to be made. There are so many class struggles in the U.S. that could be dealt with

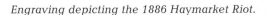

in movies. We've seen movies that deal with working-class people, but it's always some individual who rises up out of his or her situation and "makes it" in society. Stories of Americans who organize and get together to oppose the powers that hold them down have been very rare.

The American political system and the revered and celebrated Constitution of the United States do not grant any economic rights to the American people. We very often forget that the Constitution gives political rights but not economic rights. If you are not wealthy, then your political rights are limited, even though they are guaranteed on paper in the Constitution. The freedom of speech is granted there, but how much free speech you have depends on how much money and what access to resources you have. The Declaration of Independence talks about the right to life, liberty, and the pursuit of happiness. But how can you have life, liberty, and the pursuit of happiness if you don't have food, housing, and healthcare?

Working people throughout history have had to organize, struggle, go on strike, declare boycotts, and face the police and the army. They have had to do it themselves, against the opposition of government, in order to win the eight-hour workday and other slight improvements to their working conditions. A great film remains to be made about the Haymarket Affair of 1886, which was part of the struggle for the eight-hour workday. The Haymarket Affair culminated in the execution of four anarchists who were charged with

Engraving depicting the 1886 Haymarket Riot.

planting a bomb, though in the end nobody ever found out who really had planted it.

The great railroad strike of 1894 tied up the railway system of the United 25
States, and all the power of the army and the courts had to be brought against the striking workers. Eugene Debs, who organized the railroad workers, has never been the central figure in a movie. He was sent to prison for opposing World War I, and he made such an impression on his fellow prisoners that, when he was released, the warden let all the inmates out into the yard, and they applauded as Debs was granted his freedom.

I've met someone who is actually writing a script about the Lawrence textile strike of 1912, a magnificent episode in American history, because the striking workers won. It was a multicultural strike. A working population that spoke twelve different languages got together and defied the textile companies and the police, who were sent to the railroad station to prevent the children of the workers from leaving town. Police literally attacked the women and children at the station, because the company wanted to starve out the strikers, and that would be less likely to happen if their children were safe. But the strikers held out, and with the help of the Industrial Workers of the World, they finally won.

Then there's the Ludlow Massacre, which took place during the Colorado coal strike of 1913–1914, one of the most bitter, bloody, dramatic strikes in American history. The workers were up against the Rockefeller interests. (It's not easy to make an unflattering film about the Rockefellers.) One of the strike's leaders was Mother Jones, an eighty-three-year-old woman who had previously organized textile workers in West Virginia and Pennsylvania. That's another story that should be told. There were kids working in the textile mills at the age of eleven and twelve. Mother Jones led these children on a march from Pennsylvania to Oyster Bay, New York, where President Theodore Roosevelt was on summer vacation. They stood there outside the resort with signs that said, WE WANT TIME TO PLAY. Has there ever been a film made about that?

We've had films on Christopher Columbus, but I don't know of any film that shows Columbus as what he was: a man ruled by the capitalist ethic. Columbus and the Spaniards were killing people for gold. The Catholic priest Bartolomé de Las Casas was an eyewitness. He exposed what was going on, and a remarkable debate took place before the Royal Commission of Spain in 1650. The debate was between Las Casas and Sepulveda, another priest, who argued that the Indians were not human and therefore you could do anything you wanted to them.

There's also the story of the Trail of Tears—the expulsion of the Cherokees from the Southeast. Andrew Jackson, one of our national heroes, signed the order to expel them. That was ethnic cleansing on a large scale: the march across the continent, the U.S. Army driving the Indians from their homeland to a little space in Oklahoma that was then called "Indian Territory." When oil was later discovered there, the Indian population was once again evicted. Of the sixteen thousand people who marched westward, four

Immigrant women striking in Lawrence, Massachusetts, 1912.

thousand died on the march, while the U.S. Army pushed them, and the U.S. president extolled what happened.

Of course someone should finally tell the story of black people in the   30 United States from a black person's point of view. We've had a number of films about the civil-rights movement from white points of view. *The Long Walk Home* (1991) tells the story of the Montgomery bus boycott from Sissy Spacek's point of view. *Mississippi Burning* (1988) is about the murder of three civil-rights workers in Mississippi in 1964. The FBI agents are the heroes of the film, but every person who was in Mississippi in 1964—my wife and I were both there at the time—knew that the FBI was the enemy. The FBI was watching people being beaten and not doing anything about it. The FBI was silent and absent when people needed protection against murderers. In this Hollywood film, they become heroes. We need the story of the civil-rights movement told from the viewpoint of black people.

Of course, many good movies and wonderful documentaries have been made. Michael Moore's film *Roger and Me*, which has been seen by tens of millions of people, is a remarkable success story. So the possibilities do exist to practice a kind of guerrilla warfare and make films outside of the Hollywood establishment.

If such films are made—about war, about class conflict, about the history of governmental lies, about broken treaties and official violence—if those stories reach the public, we might produce a new generation. As a teacher, I'm not interested in just reproducing class after class of graduates who will get out, become successful, and take their obedient places in the slots that society has prepared for them. What we must do—whether we teach or write or make films—is educate a new generation to do this very modest thing: change the world. ■

The Reader's Presence

1. Explain what Zinn means by what Leon Trotsky called the "natural selection of accidents" (paragraph 2) preventing true depictions of war, class, and race from appearing in films. Do you agree that Hollywood's structure works against such depictions? Why or why not?

2. Reading the essay, who did you imagine Zinn's audience to be? How sympathetic to his argument would you expect them to be? What evidence can you find for your answers?

3. **VISUAL PRESENCE:** Zinn's essay calls attention to several little-known instances of protest and rebellion throughout American history. In what specific ways do the images of the 1886 Haymarket Riot (page 789) and the 1912 strike of immigrant women in Lawrence, Massachusetts (page 791) illustrate the points that Zinn makes in his argument? Which of these two images do you find more compelling? Explain why.

4. **CONNECTIONS:** Zinn says, "Stories of Americans who organize and get together to oppose the powers that hold them down have been very rare" in Hollywood (paragraph 22), but he presents examples to indicate such stories have appeared again and again throughout American history. Compare and contrast the points Zinn makes about race in American culture with those that John Edgar Wideman discusses in his essay "Fatheralong" (page 778). What "American values" would Zinn and Wideman share? Point to specific passages in each essay to validate your response.

PART 4

THE SHORT STORY

Six Modern Classics

WHAT ARE SHORT STORIES?

Though stories and storytelling are as old as human history, the formal designation of a short story is a relatively modern phenomenon, dating back only to the end of the eighteenth century. Early nineteenth-century American writers, such as Washington Irving and Nathaniel Hawthorne, made little distinction between fiction and nonfiction in their collections and usually referred to essays as "sketches" and stories as "tales." But by the end of the nineteenth century, the short story had grown into one of America's most-popular genres and it remains so.

Not all short stories are "short" in the sense that they are only a few pages long and can be read quickly. For example, one of the stories in this part is almost sixteen pages long, and it's not uncommon to come across stories that run for twenty, even thirty, pages. But a short story is generally much shorter than a novel. In fact, some stories can be quite brief. Another of the stories in this part is one paragraph long and barely covers a page.

Length is not the only feature that distinguishes the short story from the novel. Novels tend to introduce more characters, vary settings, and rely on numerous, intertwined episodes with a complex plot structure and sometimes multiple perspectives. Short stories tend to focus on a small cast of characters involved in a single episode or conflict that usually culminates in a decisive action, a transformation, or an illumination.

Short fiction can be a highly crafted form of literary art. Many serious writers construct their stories painstakingly, weighing each word, carefully interweaving descriptive images, and subtly distinguishing various points of view. They are especially attuned to nuances of voice and tone. These writers expect their readers will observe their artistry. But stories aren't simply a matter of craft. All great short story writers skillfully blend craft and content; the stories are about something the writer (and, of course, the characters) consider important, and something urgent is often at stake. Attentive readers learn to see how craft and content go hand in hand.

Although this brief introduction is by no means comprehensive, we can begin to understand short fiction by asking of each story we read the following questions. These questions—which cover **narrative point of view**, **plot**, **character and dialogue**, **setting**, and **theme**—will pertain to practically every story you will ever read.

STRATEGIES FOR UNDERSTANDING NARRATIVE POINT OF VIEW: WHO IS TELLING THE STORY?

Every story is narrated by someone critics usually refer to as the **narrator**. Talented short story writers create many kinds of narrators, but the most common **narrative points of view** are first-person narrators and third-person narrators.

The **first-person narrator** is someone invented by the author who tells the story in the first person singular, meaning they say "I did this" or "I thought that." Such a narrator can be the main character of the story; a character with a small role in the story; or, less commonly, a character uninvolved in the story.

A good example of a first-person narrator who is the main character of the story can be seen in John Updike's famous short story, "A & P" (page 871). This story is narrated in the distinctive voice of its main character, Sammy, a teenager who is working at a small suburban supermarket. It opens like this:

> In walks these three girls in nothing but bathing suits. I'm in the third checkout slot, with my back to the door, so I don't see them until they're over by the bread.

Although the story is written in the first-person singular—exactly like most personal essays—the character and voice are fictional and do not correspond to any real person. Sammy is an invention of John Updike's imagination and he should not be confused with John Updike, the author. In other words, the "I" of the story is not John Updike.

Although writers occasionally tell a story in the second-person singular ("You woke up very early that Monday morning but getting to class was out of the question."), the second-most common type of narrator can be found in **third-person narrative**, in which the person telling the story does not participate in the action and refers to characters as "he," "she," or "they." The various kinds of third-person narrators are what critics call the "omniscient narrator," one who knows what every character thinks and feels; the "close third-person narrator," who often drifts in and out of the consciousness of one or two major characters; and the "objective narrator," who avoids entering any character's consciousness.

These distinctions are not always airtight, especially in contemporary short stories where the third-person narrator tends not to be wholly "omniscient" (as was common in much nineteenth-century fiction) but prefers to narrate a story from the perspective of a single character without recounting the story in the first-person singular. The great American novelist Henry James liked to say that a story, though told in the third person, was told from the "register" of a particular character. We hear at times what that character sounds like and we see others through that one perspective even though someone else, an undefined, unnamed narrator, is telling the story in the third person. A good example of this narrative technique is seen in the opening of Flannery O'Connor's classic tale, "A Good Man Is Hard to Find" (page 852). The story is being told by someone who has no role in the story and is never identified.

> The Grandmother didn't want to go to Florida. She wanted to visit some of her connections in east Tennessee and she was seizing at every chance to change Bailey's mind. Bailey was the son she lived with, her only boy.

Throughout the story, this anonymous narrator subtly echoes the regional idioms the Grandmother might use ("connections" instead of "relatives") and enters into her decisions and motivations ("seizing at every chance to change Bailey's mind"). To ask why O'Connor decided to write the story this way and not have it spoken in the first person by the Grandmother ("I didn't want to go to Florida. I wanted to visit some of my connections in east Tennessee . . .") is to pose a question that gets to the heart of fiction's artistry.

So—if not one of the characters—who is the unidentified person narrating the story? It's tempting to say the narrator must be the author, Flannery O'Connor, but although that may seem convenient it would not be entirely correct. Just as Updike invented the fictitious first-person narrator, Sammy, to narrate "A & P," so does O'Connor invent an unidentified narrator to narrate "A Good Man Is Hard to Find." It's simpler to see that Sammy is an invented narrator because he is the main character of the story he tells—we know who he is—but even in stories that are told in the third person by an unidentified narrator, it is important to remember that that narrator is also fictional and not to be confused with the author. This difficult critical concept may take time to sink in, but it is a fundamental principle of literary fiction that is always useful to keep in mind.

As you read the stories in this part, identify which narrative point of view the author uses, and then see if you have any sense of why the author might have made that choice. A good way to gain an idea of this decision's impact is to imagine the story with a different point of view: What would change (aside from point of view) about "A Good Man Is Hard to Find" if it were told from the grandmother's perspective? How would "A & P" read differently if it were told to us not by Sammy but by a third-person narrator or from the perspective of one of the girls in a swimsuit? Consider what we gain or lose when the story shifts its narrative closeness, its residence in the mind of a specific narrator. This is a pertinent question particularly because it's something writers can spend a lot of time asking themselves as they write. In fact, some writers will write entire stories or even novels and then go back and change the point of view, deciding the story needs a different narrator. As a reader, considering the author's decision carefully will deepen your appreciation and understanding of the story.

STRATEGIES FOR UNDERSTANDING PLOT: WHAT HAPPENS IN THE STORY?

Years ago, the famous English novelist E. M. Forster offered readers a useful distinction between story and **plot**. "'The king died and then the queen died,' is a story," he said. "'The king died, and then the queen died of grief' is a plot." In other words, a *story* is a simple succession of events: A happens, then B, then C. But a *plot* deals with causes and consequences of events. A story is *sequential narrative*; a plot is *consequential narrative*. Writers devise plots to achieve certain artistic effects: suspense, surprise, a reversal of fortune, a sudden recognition. In many sprawling novels, plots can be complicated, with subplots inside subplots, but in the short story plots are often sparse and will appear uncontrived. In many modern short stories, the plot line may be minimal in terms of action and events but psychologically subtle.

We can usually trace the plot of a story by looking closely at the way the narrative develops. Most short stories contain a central action that often encompasses a conflict or struggle that seeks some sort of resolution. This, of course, is a standard formula and most talented writers work numerous variations on it; nevertheless, as readers we should try to understand how the story's action unfolds into a conflict that will come to some conclusion. The action may be physical or psychological, the conflict inside or outside the characters, the development gradual or rapid, and the conclusion decisive or indecisive. These elements vary from story to story, but in any story you will find most or all of them and their interaction will form the plot of the story. Updike's "A & P" may be considered a textbook example of an action that unfolds into a conflict that gets quickly resolved by an un-reversible decision.

As you read, try to identify not just the sequence of events ("The king died and then the queen died") but the elements of the story's plot (the "of grief" part). A plot encompasses the internal landscape of the characters: What do they want, and what's in their way, and how do they go after what they want? How does their internal landscape impact the story or impact the actions of other characters? You'll know you're dealing with plot when you try to imagine the story *without* a particular element of action or motivation, and you have a sense that the story would crumble without it. Try to see each element of action and motivation in the context of the larger story, and you're on your way to analyzing plot.

STRATEGIES FOR UNDERSTANDING CHARACTER AND DIALOGUE: WHO APPEARS IN THE STORY?

As noted earlier, unlike most novels, the short story usually features a small cast of characters. These characters will range from perhaps a main character (about whom the action revolves) to those who play minor, or peripheral, roles. The main character is often referred to by critics as the **protagonist**. Such characters could be telling the story in the first person ("My name is Miriam Kendell and I grew up in Madison, Wisconsin."), could be the subject of another's first-person narrative ("Miriam Kendell was the most-interesting person I ever met. She grew up in Madison, Wisconsin."), or could be the center of a third-person narrative ("This is a story about Miriam Kendell who grew up in Madison, Wisconsin."). Most stories contain surrounding characters who may have key roles in the plot development or who may be only loosely connected to the leading characters. But many good stories don't introduce characters haphazardly; even a minor character may influence the story's action, plot development, and conclusion.

In stories, we get to know characters by how they are described or by the way they talk—that is, we see and hear them. In older stories (especially novels) told by omniscient narrators, the reader often finds characters meticulously described (many nineteenth-century novels contained illustrations as well) and also learns what these characters think and feel. In most modern short fiction, however, the reader may be told only the most salient details of what a character looks like, and much of our information is inferred from actions and conversation.

The short story writer doesn't have pages to lavish on description and so paints quickly with a few brush strokes that also help the reader assess the character's personality. Physical features, clothing, gestures, and posture will intermingle in the depiction of a character. Here, for example, is a brief description that indicates how a writer can present a visual image of a character and at the same time suggest something about his or her personality:

> Her name was Connie. She was fifteen and she had a quick nervous giggling habit of craning her neck to glance into mirrors, or checking other people's faces to make sure her own was all right. **Joyce Carol Oates**, "Where Are You Going, Where Have You Been?" (page 834).

Note that instead of offering readers details of her main character's physical appearance (these come later), Oates opens her story by letting us see Connie's nervous habits and insecurity. She doesn't flatly tell us her character is "insecure" but shows us this important characteristic.

In the hands of a talented writer, small snatches of dialogue can also reveal an individual's character. Note the following exchange toward the conclusion of "A Good Man Is Hard to Find" (paragraphs 74–76) between the grandmother and the escaped outlaw known as the Misfit. The Misfit has just witnessed the car accident that will seal the family's tragic fate.

> "Good afternoon," he said. "I see you all had you a little spill."
> "We turned over twice!" said the grandmother.
> "Oncet," he corrected. "We seen it happen. Try their car and see will it run, Hiram," he said quietly to the boy with the gray hat.

We hear the Misfit speaking quietly and calmly in a Southern dialect, and we also can tell from the conversation that he is polite, though immediately corrects the grandmother when she says their car "turned over twice." We've already seen that the grandmother is inclined to exaggeration and inaccuracy and, as the remainder of the story reveals, the Misfit, despite his homicidal tendencies, cares much about truth. This very small exchange embodies the essence of characterization through dialogue. And it also shows how dialogue can advance the story: the Misfit needs a car and hopes the family's still starts.

We have a tendency to prefer or to "identify with" likeable characters, a fact that seems to hold in all kinds of fictional media from TV sitcoms to serious novels. Yet there are few "likeable" characters in "A Good Man Is Hard to Find"—even the two children are obnoxious. That is not a flaw in a story that attempts, as do most great stories, to reveal the intricacies of human nature. In addition to his convenient distinction (discussed in the previous section) between plot and story, E. M. Forster offered readers another useful distinction, dividing characters into "flat" and "round," those who appear one-dimensional (such as many stereotypical characters) and those who are complicated and demonstrate more than one character trait. It is important in reading literary fiction not to separate the likeable from the unlikeable characters but to appreciate the artistry and imagination that allows a writer to create complex characters that in turn invite us to expand our range of sympathy and identification.

As you read the short stories in this part, pay attention to which characters appear, when and why they are present, and how we learn about them—through description? dialogue? actions? Consider whether each is a flat or round character, and how they change over the course of the story.

STRATEGIES FOR UNDERSTANDING SETTING: WHERE IS THE STORY IN TIME AND SPACE?

Short stories are often set—as is Updike's "A & P"—in a particular place and time. Nearly all the action of "A & P" takes place inside a supermarket. As we read, we are in a specific physical space with its aisles and products, a world of commodities that lends the story an economic dimension that is important to our understanding and provides a context not only for the story's sexual tension but for its references to class status as well. The supermarket is not simply a place where the central action occurs; it plays a pivotal role in the story, as its title suggests. In an effectively written story, a detailed setting will often enhance the story's action and contribute to its language. As you read "A & P," note the way the supermarket supplies the narrator with vocabulary and images.

When we enter into the fictional world of a short story, we may also enter into a different era—the American Civil War; the roaring twenties; or, as in the case of "A & P," the early 1960s New England. As we learn from one of Sammy's comments, 1990 seems like the distant future, a time, his remark suggests, when the United States may be taken over by Russia (then the Soviet Union). Readers need to adjust their evaluations and expectations accordingly: Sammy can't text his best friend to tell him he quit his job. We can't update the story. To fully appreciate fiction, we frequently need to imagine ourselves transported to another time and place. Yet, supermarkets—though now mega-markets—still exist and adolescents still rebel against rules and regulations or, to use the term Sammy pokes fun at, "policy." Good literature rarely goes out of date; as the poet Ezra Pound once put it, "Literature is news that stays news."

As you read, consider where and when the story is set, and which details solidify the location and give you a sense of the importance of the setting to the narrative. Consider how the setting is significant, and why, when the author had all the space in the universe and all of time past and future available for the setting of a story, he or she chose this particular moment and location.

||||||||||||||||||||||||||||||||||||||||||||||||||||||||||||||||||||||||||||||||||||||||||||||||||||||||||

STRATEGIES FOR UNDERSTANDING THEME AND MEANING: WHAT IS THE STORY ABOUT?

Stories usually have a "point" to make: they are *about* something; they *mean* something: they advance a writer's beliefs, attitudes, or moral vision, even if those beliefs are that we have nothing to believe in. The simpler the story, of course, the easier it is to grasp its point—for example, children are often smarter than adults, dogs are loyal, modern technology is destroying community.

All major short story writers engage in dominant themes that they explore over and over. For example, Oates's story "Where Are You Going, Where Have You Been?" clearly demonstrates her career-long exploration of sexual violence. Not every one of her stories confronts this theme, but if you were to read several of her collections you would discover that this issue is frequently at the center of her fiction. Although their dominant themes are quite different, the same could be said of all the other writers included in this part.

Yet in serious creative writing, don't expect a story's theme or meaning to be expressed directly somewhere inside the story or, as in a child's cautionary tale, in the form of a moral tacked on to the end. We usually need to uncover a story's meaning by paying close attention to all the various elements that went into its composition—its plot, setting, characters, narrative point of view, images, interplay of dialogue, and so on. In short stories that stand the test of time, we need to view all these elements as a unified whole, to see how each element and detail contributes to the story's overall emotional and intellectual impact.

Such close readings are one of the chief tasks of literary critics who want to understand the significance of major works and authors. They essentially want to understand not only what a story says but how it says it. For example, critics have commented on O'Connor's "A Good Man Is Hard to Find" for decades, examining the story's details and design from many different angles with the hope of capturing its deepest meanings. In this part, you will have the opportunity to encounter that enigmatic and powerful story along with its author's comments and those of a leading critic. As you read, see if you can come up with your own interpretation of what O'Connor is trying to say.

READING SHORT STORIES: A Checklist

🖊 Examine the story's narrator. Who appears to be telling the story? Is the storyteller a character in the story? Does the narrator have a name and an identity?

🖊 Is the story being told in the first person or third person? Does the narrator appear to know what his or her characters are thinking? Or does the narration seem to be more objective or detached?

🖊 Listen carefully to the narrator's tone of voice. Can you detect any echo or mimicry of other characters? Does the narrator appear to be sympathetic to or critical of these other characters? To which character does the narrator seem closest?

🖊 Identify the character you consider to be the central character, or protagonist, of the story.

🖊 In writing, reconstruct the plot outline of the story. Explain why one event occurs after another. What is the relationship of events? Note the ways one event causes another. Does the plot appear natural and probable or contrived and artificial?

🖊 Identify in a sentence or two what seems to be the story's central conflict. Which character experiences the conflict most?

🖊 Describe the story's dominant setting or settings. What details seem most important to the story? Examine the ways particular details affect the story's overall language and mood.

🖊 Consider the story's passage of time. Does the story take place in a continuous present or do gaps and lapses occur in the chronology?

🖊 Explain how the story concludes. Are conflicts resolved or do they persist?

🖊 Examine the story's dominant theme. Can you state it in a few words or sentences? How closely do you associate this theme with human concerns in general?

🖊 Explore some ways that the story's overall meaning is connected to how the story is written. Can you see how the plot, the narrative perspective, and the physical details, for example, all contribute to the story's meaning?

Sherman Alexie

THIS IS WHAT IT MEANS TO SAY PHOENIX, ARIZONA

SHERMAN ALEXIE's short story "This Is What It Means to Say Phoenix, Arizona" appears in *The Lone Ranger and Tonto Fistfight in Heaven* (1993). Alexie has said, "Most of my heroes are just decent people. Decency is rare and underrated. I think my writing is somehow just about decency." Victor and Thomas, two "decent people" in this story, are also characters in Alexie's first screenplay. The film, *Smoke Signals*, premiered at the 1998 Sundance Film Festival, where it won the Audience Award and the Filmmakers Trophy.

> "Most of my heroes are just decent people. Decency is rare and underrated. I think my writing is somehow just about decency."

Alexie describes the film as "a very basic story, a road trip / buddy movie about a lost father." The narrative structure, as he has pointed out, appears "in everything from the Bible to the *Iliad* and the *Odyssey*."

For additional information on Sherman Alexie, see page 34.

JUST AFTER VICTOR lost his job at the BIA,[1] he also found out that his father had died of a heart attack in Phoenix, Arizona. Victor hadn't seen his father in a few years, only talked to him on the telephone once or twice, but there still was a genetic pain, which was soon to be pain as real and immediate as a broken bone.

Victor didn't have any money. Who does have money on a reservation, except the cigarette and fireworks salespeople? His father had a savings account waiting to be claimed, but Victor needed to find a way to get to Phoenix. Victor's mother was just as poor as he was, and the rest of his family didn't have any use at all for him. So Victor called the Tribal Council.

"Listen," Victor said. "My father just died. I need some money to get to Phoenix to make arrangements."

"Now, Victor," the council said. "You know we're having a difficult time financially."

"But I thought the council had special funds set aside for stuff like this."   5

---

1 **BIA:** Bureau of Indian Affairs, an agency that has historically often been at odds with the tribes it was created to administer. —EDS.

"Now, Victor, we do have some money available for the proper return of tribal members' bodies. But I don't think we have enough to bring your father all the way back from Phoenix."

"Well," Victor said. "It ain't going to cost all that much. He had to be cremated. Things were kind of ugly. He died of a heart attack in his trailer and nobody found him for a week. It was really hot, too. You get the picture."

"Now, Victor, we're sorry for your loss and the circumstances. But we can really only afford to give you one hundred dollars."

"That's not even enough for a plane ticket."

"Well, you might consider driving down to Phoenix."   10

"I don't have a car. Besides, I was going to drive my father's pickup back up here."

"Now, Victor," the council said. "We're sure there is somebody who could drive you to Phoenix. Or is there somebody who could lend you the rest of the money?"

"You know there ain't nobody around with that kind of money."

"Well, we're sorry, Victor, but that's the best we can do."

Victor accepted the Tribal Council's offer. What else could he do? So he   15
signed the proper papers, picked up his check, and walked over to the Trading Post to cash it.

While Victor stood in line, he watched Thomas Builds-the-Fire standing near the magazine rack, talking to himself. Like he always did. Thomas was a storyteller that nobody wanted to listen to. That's like being a dentist in a town where everybody has false teeth.

Victor and Thomas Builds-the-Fire were the same age, had grown up and played in the dirt together. Ever since Victor could remember, it was Thomas who always had something to say.

Once, when they were seven years old, when Victor's father still lived with the family, Thomas closed his eyes and told Victor this story: "Your father's heart is weak. He is afraid of his own family. He is afraid of you. Late at night he sits in the dark. Watches the television until there's nothing but that white noise. Sometimes he feels like he wants to buy a motorcycle and ride away. He wants to run and hide. He doesn't want to be found."

Thomas Builds-the-Fire had known that Victor's father was going to leave, knew it before anyone. Now Victor stood in the Trading Post with a one-hundred-dollar check in his hand, wondering if Thomas knew that Victor's father was dead, if he knew what was going to happen next.

Just then Thomas looked at Victor, smiled, and walked over to him.   20

"Victor, I'm sorry about your father," Thomas said.

"How did you know about it?" Victor asked.

"I heard it on the wind. I heard it from the birds. I felt it in the sunlight. Also, your mother was just in here crying."

"Oh," Victor said and looked around the Trading Post. All the other Indians stared, surprised that Victor was even talking to Thomas. Nobody talked to Thomas anymore because he told the same damn stories over and over again. Victor was embarrassed, but he thought that Thomas might be able to help him. Victor felt a sudden need for tradition.

"I can lend you the money you need," Thomas said suddenly. "But you   25
have to take me with you."

"I can't take your money," Victor said. "I mean, I haven't hardly talked to you in years. We're not really friends anymore."

"I didn't say we were friends. I said you had to take me with you."

"Let me think about it."

Victor went home with his one hundred dollars and sat at the kitchen table. He held his head in his hands and thought about Thomas Builds-the-Fire, remembered little details, tears and scars, the bicycle they shared for a summer, so many stories.

Thomas Builds-the-Fire sat on the bicycle, waited in Victor's yard. He   30
was ten years old and skinny. His hair was dirty because it was the Fourth of July.

"Victor," Thomas yelled. "Hurry up. We're going to miss the fireworks."

After a few minutes, Victor ran out of his house, jumped the porch railing, and landed gracefully on the sidewalk.

"And the judges award him a 9.95, the highest score of the summer," Thomas said, clapped, laughed.

"That was perfect, cousin," Victor said. "And it's my turn to ride the bike."

Thomas gave up the bike and they headed for the fairgrounds. It was   35
nearly dark and the fireworks were about to start.

"You know," Thomas said. "It's strange how us Indians celebrate the Fourth of July. It ain't like it was *our* independence everybody was fighting for."

"You think about things too much," Victor said. "It's just supposed to be fun. Maybe Junior will be there."

"Which Junior? Everybody on this reservation is named Junior."

And they both laughed.

The fireworks were small, hardly more than a few bottle rockets and   40
a fountain. But it was enough for two Indian boys. Years later, they would need much more.

Afterwards, sitting in the dark, fighting off mosquitoes, Victor turned to Thomas Builds-the-Fire.

"Hey," Victor said. "Tell me a story."

Thomas closed his eyes and told this story: "There were these two Indian boys who wanted to be warriors. But it was too late to be warriors in the old way. All the horses were gone. So the two Indian boys stole a car and drove to the city. They parked the stolen car in front of the police station and then hitchhiked back home to the reservation. When they got back, all their friends cheered and their parents' eyes shone with pride. *You were very brave*, everybody said to the two Indian boys. *Very brave.*"

"Ya-hey," Victor said. "That's a good one. I wish I could be a warrior."

"Me, too," Thomas said.   45

They went home together in the dark, Thomas on the bike now, Victor on foot. They walked through shadows and light from the streetlamps.

"We've come a long ways," Thomas said. "We have outdoor lighting."

"All I need is the stars," Victor said. "And besides, you still think about things too much."

They separated then, each headed for home, both laughing all the way.

Victor sat at his kitchen table. He counted his one hundred dollars again   50
and again. He knew he needed more to make it to Phoenix and back. He knew he needed Thomas Builds-the-Fire. So he put his money in his wallet and opened the front door to find Thomas on the porch.

"Ya-hey, Victor," Thomas said. "I knew you'd call me."

Thomas walked into the living room and sat down on Victor's favorite chair.

"I've got some money saved up," Thomas said. "It's enough to get us down there, but you have to get us back."

"I've got this hundred dollars," Victor said. "And my dad had a savings account I'm going to claim."

"How much in your dad's account?"   55

"Enough. A few hundred."

"Sounds good. When we leaving?"

When they were fifteen and had long since stopped being friends, Victor and Thomas got into a fistfight. That is, Victor was really drunk and beat Thomas up for no reason at all. All the other Indian boys stood around and watched it happen. Junior was there and so were Lester, Seymour, and a lot of others. The beating might have gone on until Thomas was dead if Norma Many Horses hadn't come along and stopped it.

"Hey, you boys," Norma yelled and jumped out of her car. "Leave him alone."

If it had been someone else, even another man, the Indian boys would've   60
just ignored the warnings. But Norma was a warrior. She was powerful. She could have picked up any two of the boys and smashed their skulls together. But worse than that, she would have dragged them all over to some tipi and made them listen to some elder tell a dusty old story.

The Indian boys scattered, and Norma walked over to Thomas and picked him up.

"Hey, little man, are you okay?" she asked.

Thomas gave her a thumbs up.

"Why they always picking on you?"

Thomas shook his head, closed his eyes, but no stories came to him,   65
no words or music. He just wanted to go home, to lie in his bed and let his dreams tell his stories for him.

Thomas Builds-the-Fire and Victor sat next to each other in the airplane, coach section. A tiny white woman had the window seat. She was busy twisting her body into pretzels. She was flexible.

"I have to ask," Thomas said, and Victor closed his eyes in embarrassment.

"Don't," Victor said.

"Excuse me, miss," Thomas asked. "Are you a gymnast or something?"

"There's no something about it," she said. "I was first alternate on the   70 1980 Olympic team."

"Really?" Thomas asked.

"Really."

"I mean, you used to be a world-class athlete?" Thomas asked.

"My husband still thinks I am."

Thomas Builds-the-Fire smiled. She was a mental gymnast, too. She   75 pulled her leg straight up against her body so that she could've kissed her kneecap.

"I wish I could do that," Thomas said.

Victor was ready to jump out of the plane. Thomas, that crazy Indian storyteller with ratty old braids and broken teeth, was flirting with a beautiful Olympic gymnast. Nobody back home on the reservation would ever believe it.

"Well," the gymnast said. "It's easy. Try it."

Thomas grabbed at his leg and tried to pull it up into the same position as the gymnast. He couldn't even come close, which made Victor and the gymnast laugh.

"Hey," she asked. "You two are Indian, right?"   80

"Full-blood," Victor said.

"Not me," Thomas said. "I'm half magician on my mother's side and half clown on my father's."

They all laughed.

"What are your names?" she asked.

"Victor and Thomas."   85

"Mine is Cathy. Pleased to meet you all."

The three of them talked for the duration of the flight. Cathy the gymnast complained about the government, how they screwed the 1980 Olympic team by boycotting.

"Sounds like you all got a lot in common with Indians," Thomas said.

Nobody laughed.

After the plane landed in Phoenix and they had all found their way to   90 the terminal, Cathy the gymnast smiled and waved good-bye.

"She was really nice," Thomas said.

"Yeah, but everybody talks to everybody on airplanes," Victor said. "It's too bad we can't always be that way."

"You always used to tell me I think too much," Thomas said. "Now it sounds like you do."

"Maybe I caught it from you."

"Yeah."   95

Thomas and Victor rode in a taxi to the trailer where Victor's father died.

"Listen," Victor said as they stopped in front of the trailer. "I never told you I was sorry for beating you up that time."

"Oh, it was nothing. We were just kids and you were drunk."

"Yeah, but I'm still sorry."

"That's all right."   100

Victor paid for the taxi and the two of them stood in the hot Phoenix summer. They could smell the trailer.

"This ain't going to be nice," Victor said. "You don't have to go in."

"You're going to need help."

Victor walked to the front door and opened it. The stink rolled out and made them both gag. Victor's father had lain in that trailer for a week in hundred-degree temperatures before anyone found him. And the only reason anyone found him was because of the smell. They needed dental records to identify him. That's exactly what the coroner said. They needed dental records.

"Oh, man," Victor said. "I don't know if I can do this."   105

"Well, then don't."

"But there might be something valuable in there."

"I thought his money was in the bank."

"It is. I was talking about pictures and letters and stuff like that."

"Oh," Thomas said as he held his breath and followed Victor into the   110
trailer.

When Victor was twelve, he stepped into an underground wasp nest. His foot was caught in the hole, and no matter how hard he struggled, Victor couldn't pull free. He might have died there, stung a thousand times, if Thomas Builds-the-Fire had not come by.

"Run," Thomas yelled and pulled Victor's foot from the hole. They ran then, hard as they ever had, faster than Billy Mills,[2] faster than Jim Thorpe,[3] faster than the wasps could fly.

Victor and Thomas ran until they couldn't breathe, ran until it was cold and dark outside, ran until they were lost and it took hours to find their way home. All the way back, Victor counted his stings.

"Seven," Victor said. "My lucky number."

Victor didn't find much to keep in the trailer. Only a photo album and   115
a stereo. Everything else had that smell stuck in it or was useless anyway.

"I guess this is all," Victor said. "It ain't much."

"Better than nothing," Thomas said.

---

[2] **Billy Mills** (b. 1938): An Oglala Lakota (Sioux), Mills was the only American to win an Olympic gold medal in the 10,000-meter race — at the 1964 Tokyo Olympic Games. — EDS.

[3] **Jim Thorpe** (1887–1953): A member of the Sac and Fox tribe and acclaimed to be the greatest athlete of the twentieth century, Thorpe won gold medals in the pentathlon and decathlon in the 1912 Olympic games and played both professional football and professional baseball. — EDS.

"Yeah, and I do have the pickup."

"Yeah," Thomas said, "it's in good shape."

"Dad was good about that stuff." 120

"Yeah, I remember your dad."

"Really?" Victor asked. "What do you remember?"

Thomas Builds-the-Fire closed his eyes and told this story: "I remember when I had this dream that told me to go to Spokane, to stand by the Falls in the middle of the city and wait for a sign. I knew I had to go there but I didn't have a car. Didn't have a license. I was only thirteen. So I walked all the way, took me all day, and I finally made it to the Falls. I stood there for an hour waiting. Then your dad came walking up. *What the hell are you doing here?* he asked me. I said, *Waiting for a vision.* Then your father said, *All you're going to get here is mugged.* So he drove me over to Denny's, bought me dinner, and then drove me home to the reservation. For a long time I was mad because I thought my dreams had lied to me. But they didn't. Your dad was my vision. *Take care of each other* is what my dreams were saying. *Take care of each other.*"

Victor was quiet for a long time. He searched his mind for memories of his father, found the good ones, found a few bad ones, added it all up, and smiled.

"My father never told me about finding you in Spokane," Victor said. 125

"He said he wouldn't tell anybody. Didn't want me to get in trouble. But he said I had to watch out for you as part of the deal."

"Really?"

"Really. Your father said you would need the help. He was right."

"That's why you came down here with me, isn't it?" Victor asked.

"I came because of your father." 130

Victor and Thomas climbed into the pickup, drove over to the bank, and claimed the three hundred dollars in the savings account.

Thomas Builds-the-Fire could fly.

Once, he jumped off the roof of the tribal school and flapped his arms like a crazy eagle. And he flew. For a second, he hovered, suspended above all the other Indian boys who were too smart or too scared to jump.

"He's flying," Junior yelled, and Seymour was busy looking for the trick wires or mirrors. But it was real. As real as the dirt when Thomas lost altitude and crashed to the ground.

He broke his arm in two places. 135

"He broke his wing," Victor chanted, and the other Indian boys joined in, made it a tribal song.

"He broke his wing, he broke his wing, he broke his wing," all the Indian boys chanted as they ran off, flapping their wings, wishing they could fly, too. They hated Thomas for his courage, his brief moment as a bird. Everybody has dreams about flying. Thomas flew.

One of his dreams came true for just a second, just enough to make it real.

Victor's father, his ashes, fit in one wooden box with enough left over to fill a cardboard box.

"He was always a big man," Thomas said.   140

Victor carried part of his father and Thomas carried the rest out to the pickup. They set him down carefully behind the seats, put a cowboy hat on the wooden box and a Dodgers cap on the cardboard box. That's the way it was supposed to be.

"Ready to head back home?" Victor asked.

"It's going to be a long drive."

"Yeah, take a couple days, maybe."

"We can take turns," Thomas said.   145

"Okay," Victor said, but they didn't take turns. Victor drove for sixteen hours straight north, made it halfway up Nevada toward home before he finally pulled over.

"Hey, Thomas," Victor said. "You got to drive for a while."

"Okay."

Thomas Builds-the-Fire slid behind the wheel and started off down the road. All through Nevada, Thomas and Victor had been amazed at the lack of animal life, at the absence of water, of movement.

"Where is everything?" Victor had asked more than once.   150

Now when Thomas was finally driving they saw the first animal, maybe the only animal in Nevada. It was a long-eared jackrabbit.

"Look," Victor yelled. "It's alive."

Thomas and Victor were busy congratulating themselves on their discovery when the jackrabbit darted out into the road and under the wheels of the pickup.

"Stop the goddamn car," Victor yelled, and Thomas did stop, backed the pickup to the dead jackrabbit.

"Oh, man, he's dead," Victor said as he looked at the squashed animal.   155

"Really dead."

"The only thing alive in this whole state and we just killed it."

"I don't know," Thomas said, "I think it was suicide."

Victor looked around the desert, sniffed the air, felt the emptiness and loneliness, and nodded his head.

"Yeah," Victor said, "it had to be suicide."   160

"I can't believe this," Thomas said. "You drive for a thousand miles and there ain't even any bugs smashed on the windshield. I drive for ten seconds and kill the only living thing in Nevada."

"Yeah," Victor said. "Maybe I should drive."

"Maybe you should."

Thomas Builds-the-Fire walked through the corridors of the tribal school by himself. Nobody wanted to be anywhere near him because of all those stories. Story after story.

Thomas closed his eyes and this story came to him: "We are all given   165
one thing by which our lives are measured, one determination. Mine are the

stories which can change or not change the world. It doesn't matter which as long as I continue to tell the stories. My father, he died on Okinawa in World War II, died fighting for this country, which had tried to kill him for years. My mother, she died giving birth to me, died while I was still inside her. She pushed me out into the world with her last breath. I have no brothers or sisters. I have only my stories which came to me before I even had the words to speak. I learned a thousand stories before I took my first thousand steps. They are all I have. It's all I can do."

Thomas Builds-the-Fire told his stories to all those who would stop and listen. He kept telling them long after people had stopped listening.

Victor and Thomas made it back to the reservation just as the sun was rising. It was the beginning of a new day on earth, but the same old shit on the reservation.

"Good morning," Thomas said.

"Good morning."

The tribe was waking up, ready for work, eating breakfast, reading the 170 newspaper, just like everybody else does. Willene LeBret was out in her garden wearing a bathrobe. She waved when Thomas and Victor drove by.

"Crazy Indians made it," she said to herself and went back to her roses.

Victor stopped the pickup in front of Thomas Builds-the-Fire's HUD[4] house. They both yawned, stretched a little, shook dust from their bodies.

"I'm tired," Victor said.

"Of everything," Thomas added.

They both searched for words to end the journey. Victor needed to thank 175 Thomas for his help, for the money, and make the promise to pay it all back.

"Don't worry about the money," Thomas said. "It don't make any difference anyhow."

"Probably not, enit?"

"Nope."

Victor knew that Thomas would remain the crazy storyteller who talked to dogs and cars, who listened to the wind and pine trees. Victor knew that he couldn't really be friends with Thomas, even after all that had happened. It was cruel but it was real. As real as the ashes, as Victor's father, sitting behind the seats.

"I know how it is," Thomas said. "I know you ain't going to treat me any 180 better than you did before. I know your friends would give you too much shit about it."

Victor was ashamed of himself. Whatever happened to the tribal ties, the sense of community? The only real thing he shared with anybody was a bottle and broken dreams. He owed Thomas something, anything.

"Listen," Victor said and handed Thomas the cardboard box which contained half of his father. "I want you to have this."

---

4 ***HUD:*** The U.S. Department of Housing and Urban Development. — EDS.

Thomas took the ashes and smiled, closed his eyes, and told this story: "I'm going to travel to Spokane Falls one last time and toss these ashes into the water. And your father will rise like a salmon, leap over the bridge, over me, and find his way home. It will be beautiful. His teeth will shine like silver, like a rainbow. He will rise, Victor, he will rise."

Victor smiled.

"I was planning on doing the same thing with my half," Victor said. "But I didn't imagine my father looking anything like a salmon. I thought it'd be like cleaning the attic or something. Like letting things go after they've stopped having any use."

"Nothing stops, cousin," Thomas said. "Nothing stops."

Thomas Builds-the-Fire got out of the pickup and walked up his driveway. Victor started the pickup and began the drive home.

"Wait," Thomas yelled suddenly from his porch. "I just got to ask one favor."

Victor stopped the pickup, leaned out the window, and shouted back. "What do you want?"

"Just one time when I'm telling a story somewhere, why don't you stop and listen?" Thomas asked.

"Just once?"

"Just once."

Victor waved his arms to let Thomas know that the deal was good. It was a fair trade, and that was all Victor had ever wanted from his whole life. So Victor drove his father's pickup toward home while Thomas went into his house, closed the door behind him, and heard a new story come to him in the silence afterwards. ▪

The Reader's Presence

1. Thomas is portrayed as an outcast in the community, "a storyteller that nobody wanted to listen to" (paragraph 16). What stories does Thomas tell? Why are they unpopular with listeners? What do Thomas's stories have to do with his role as an outcast?

2. Describe Victor's state of mind and place in life at the beginning of the story. What is he like? What has happened to him? Compare this Victor to the Victor who appears at the end of the story. Has he changed? Do you think that he will change in the future? Why or why not?

3. **CONNECTIONS:**   Compare the characters of Thomas and Victor to Alexie's description of the children on the Spokane Indian Reservation of Alexie's youth in "The Joy of Reading and Writing: Superman and Me" (page 34). What characteristics does Thomas share with the children Alexie describes, including himself as a boy? What characteristics does Victor share with them? How are Alexie's fictional reservation and the people who live there like—and unlike—the reservation and people Alexie describes in his essay?

Jamaica Kincaid

GIRL

JAMAICA KINCAID was born in Antigua in 1949 and came to the United States at the age of seventeen to work for a New York family as an au pair. Her novel *Lucy* (1990) is an imaginative account of her experience of coming into adulthood in a foreign country and continues the narrative of her personal history begun in the novel *Annie John* (1985). Her other books include a collection of short stories, *At the Bottom of the River* (1983); a collection of essays, *A Small Place* (1988); *My Brother* (1997), which was a National Book Award Finalist for nonfiction; *My Favorite Plant: Writers and Gardeners on the Plants They Love* (1998); *Among Flowers: A Walk in the Himalaya* (2005), and *See Now Then* (2013). Her writing also appears in national magazines, especially the *New Yorker*, where she worked as a staff writer until 1995. "Girl" is the first piece of fiction Kincaid published; it appeared in the *New Yorker* in 1978.

For more information on Jamaica Kincaid, see page 169.

> "Girl" is the first piece of fiction Jamaica Kincaid published; it appeared in the *New Yorker* in 1978.

WASH THE WHITE CLOTHES on Monday and put them on the stone heap; wash the color clothes on Tuesday and put them on the clothesline to dry; don't walk barehead in the hot sun; cook pumpkin fritters in very hot sweet oil; soak your little clothes right after you take them off; when buying cotton to make yourself a nice blouse, be sure that it doesn't have gum on it, because that way it won't hold up well after a wash; soak salt fish overnight before you cook it; is it true that you sing benna[1] in Sunday School?; always eat your food in such a way that it won't turn someone else's stomach; on Sundays try to walk like a lady and not like the slut you are so bent on becoming; don't sing benna in Sunday School; you mustn't speak to wharf-rat boys, not even to give directions; don't eat fruits on the street—flies will follow you; *but I don't sing benna on Sundays at all and never in Sunday School*; this is how to sew on a button; this is how to make a buttonhole for

---

1 **benna:** Popular calypso-like music. —EDS.

macmillanhighered.com/writerspresence8e
Listen to an audio version of "Girl," read by the author.
e-Readings > Jamaica Kincaid, *Girl* [audio]

the button you have just sewed on; this is how to hem a dress when you see the hem coming down and so to prevent yourself from looking like the slut I know you are so bent on becoming; this is how you iron your father's khaki shirt so that it doesn't have a crease; this is how you iron your father's khaki pants so that they don't have a crease; this is how you grow okra—far from the house, because okra tree harbors red ants; when you are growing dasheen,[2] make sure it gets plenty of water or else it makes your throat itch when you are eating it; this is how you sweep a corner; this is how you sweep a whole house; this is how you sweep a yard; this is how you smile to someone you don't like too much; this is how you smile to someone you don't like at all; this is how you smile to someone you like completely; this is how you set a table for tea; this is how you set a table for dinner; this is how you set a table for dinner with an important guest; this is how you set a table for lunch; this is how you set a table for breakfast; this is how to behave in the presence of men who don't know you very well, and this way they won't recognize immediately the slut I have warned you against becoming; be sure to wash every day, even if it is with your own spit; don't squat down to play marbles—you are not a boy, you know; don't pick people's flow-ers—you might catch something; don't throw stones at blackbirds, because it might not be a blackbird at all; this is how to make a bread pudding; this is how to make doukona;[3] this is how to make pepper pot; this is how to make a good medicine for a cold; this is how to make a good medicine to throw away a child before it even becomes a child; this is how to catch a fish; this is how to throw back a fish you don't like, and that way something bad won't fall on you; this is how to bully a man; this is how a man bullies you; this is how to love a man, and if this doesn't work there are other ways, and if they don't work don't feel too bad about giving up; this is how to spit up in the air if you feel like it, and this is how to move quick so that it doesn't fall on you; this is how to make ends meet; always squeeze bread to make sure it's fresh; *but what if the baker won't let me feel the bread?*; you mean to say that after all you are really going to be the kind of woman who the baker won't let near the bread? ▩

The Reader's Presence

1. Whose voice dominates this story? To whom is the monologue addressed? What effect(s) does the speaker seek to have on the listener? Where does the speaker appear to have acquired her values? Categorize the kinds of advice you find in the story. Identify sentences in which one category of advice merges into another. How are the different kinds of advice alike, and to what extent are they contradictory?

2. The girl speaks only two lines, both of which are italicized. In each case, what prompts her to speak? What is the result? Stories generally create the expectation that at least one main character will undergo a change. What differences, if any, do you notice

2 **dasheen:** A starchy vegetable. —EDS.
3 **doukona:** Cornmeal. —EDS.

between the girl's first and second lines of dialogue (and the replies she elicits), differences that might suggest that such a change has taken place? If you do notice any differences, in whom do you notice them? Analyze the girl's character based not only on what she says but on what she hears (if one can assume that this monologue was not delivered all in one sitting, but is rather the distillation of years' worth of advice, as heard by the girl).

3. **CONNECTIONS:**   Consider the role of gender in this story. What gender stereotypes does the main speaker perpetuate? Look not only at the stereotypes that affect women but also at those that define the roles of men. What can you infer about the males who remain behind the scenes? Read Amy Cunningham's "Why Women Smile" (page 369). What gender stereotypes influence whether—and when—women smile? To what extent do gender roles and cultural expectations determine the patterns—and consequences—of when men and women smile?

The Writer at Work

JAMAICA KINCAID on "Girl"

© NORMA JOSEPH/Alamy

To many readers, "Girl" appears to be an odd and confusing short story. It's far shorter than most published stories and consists almost entirely of a monologue spoken by a mother to her daughter. Readers may wonder: "What makes this a story?" In the following passage from an interview with Jamaica Kincaid, Allan Varda asks the author some questions about this intriguing little story and discovers behind its composition a larger agenda that we might not perceive from a single reading. How do Kincaid's answers to Varda's questions help you better understand what's happening in the story? In what ways?

AV: There is a litany of items in "Girl" from a mother to her daughter about what to do and what *not* to do regarding the elements of being "a nice young lady." Is this the way it was for you and other girls in Antigua?

JK: In a word, yes.

AV: Was that good or bad?

JK: I don't think it's the way I would tell my daughter, but as a mother I would tell her what I think would be best for her to be like. This mother in "Girl" was really just giving the girl an idea about the things she would need to be a self-possessed woman in the world.

AV: But you didn't take your mother's advice?

JK: No, because I had other ideas on how to be a self-possessed woman in the world. I didn't know that at the time.

I only remember these things. What the mother in the story sees as aids to living in the world, the girl might see as extraordinary oppression, which is one of the things I came to see.

AV: Almost like she's Mother England.

JK: I was just going to say that. I've come to see that I've worked through the relationship of the mother and the girl to a relationship between Europe and the place that I'm from, which is to say, a relationship between the powerful and the powerless. The girl is powerless and the mother is powerful. The mother shows her how to be in the world, but at the back of her mind she thinks she never will get it. She's deeply skeptical that this child could ever grow up to be a self-possessed woman and in the end she reveals her skepticism; yet even within the skepticism is, of course, dismissal and scorn. So it's not unlike the relationship between the conquered and the conqueror.

Jhumpa Lahiri

INTERPRETER OF MALADIES

JHUMPA LAHIRI's short story "Interpreter of Maladies" appears in her 1999 collection by the same name. The collection—which won the Pulitzer Prize for fiction in 2000 and has sold more than fifteen million copies across the globe—explores the lives of Indians and Indian Americans who straddle two cultures, learning to negotiate tradition and the influences of a new world. The experiences of the characters somewhat reflect Lahiri's own experience growing up as a native Indian in America. She doesn't feel a particular claim to either side of her cultural identity. She has said, "I continue to be hesitant to call myself an American, but I also feel hesitant to call myself anything else." Though her parents told her she was Indian, she says that "going to India as

> "I continue to be hesitant to call myself an American, but I also feel hesitant to call myself anything else."

a child made it apparent that I simply did not have a claim to either country. In the eyes of Indians who never left, I'm not an Indian at all."

For additional information on Jhumpa Lahiri, see page 181.

AT THE TEA STALL Mr. and Mrs. Das bickered about who should take Tina to the toilet. Eventually Mrs. Das relented when Mr. Das pointed out that he had given the girl her bath the night before. In the rearview mirror Mr. Kapasi watched as Mrs. Das emerged slowly from his bulky white Ambassador, dragging her shaved, largely bare legs across the back seat. She did not hold the little girl's hand as they walked to the rest room.

They were on their way to see the Sun Temple at Konarak. It was a dry, bright Saturday, the mid-July heat tempered by a steady ocean breeze, ideal weather for sightseeing. Ordinarily Mr. Kapasi would not have stopped so soon along the way, but less than five minutes after he'd picked up the family that morning in front of Hotel Sandy Villa, the little girl had complained. The first thing Mr. Kapasi had noticed when he saw Mr. and Mrs. Das, standing with their children under the portico of the hotel, was that they were very young, perhaps not even thirty. In addition to Tina they had two boys, Ronny and Bobby, who appeared very close in age and had teeth covered in a network of flashing silver wires. The family looked Indian but dressed as foreigners did, the children in stiff, brightly colored clothing and caps with translucent visors. Mr. Kapasi was accustomed to foreign tourists; he was assigned to them regularly because he could speak English. Yesterday he had driven an elderly couple from Scotland, both with spotted faces and fluffy white hair so thin it exposed their sunburnt scalps. In comparison, the tanned, youthful faces of Mr. and Mrs. Das were all the more striking. When he'd introduced himself, Mr. Kapasi had pressed his palms together in greeting, but Mr. Das squeezed hands like an American so that Mr. Kapasi felt it in his elbow. Mrs. Das, for her part, had flexed one side of her mouth, smiling dutifully at Mr. Kapasi, without displaying any interest in him.

As they waited at the tea stall, Ronny, who looked like the older of the two boys, clambered suddenly out of the back seat, intrigued by a goat tied to a stake in the ground.

"Don't touch it," Mr. Das said. He glanced up from his paperback tour book, which said "INDIA" in yellow letters and looked as if it had been published abroad. His voice, somehow tentative and a little shrill, sounded as though it had not yet settled into maturity.

"I want to give it a piece of gum," the boy called back as he trotted ahead. 5

Mr. Das stepped out of the car and stretched his legs by squatting briefly to the ground. A clean-shaven man, he looked exactly like a magnified version of Ronny. He had a sapphire blue visor, and was dressed in shorts, sneakers, and a T-shirt. The camera slung around his neck, with an impressive telephoto lens and numerous buttons and markings, was the only complicated thing he wore. He frowned, watching as Ronny rushed toward the goat, but appeared to have no intention of intervening. "Bobby, make sure that your brother doesn't do anything stupid."

"I don't feel like it," Bobby said, not moving. He was sitting in the front seat beside Mr. Kapasi, studying a picture of the elephant god taped to the glove compartment.

"No need to worry," Mr. Kapasi said. "They are quite tame." Mr. Kapasi was forty-six years old, with receding hair that had gone completely silver, but his butterscotch complexion and his unlined brow, which he treated in spare moments to dabs of lotus-oil balm, made it easy to imagine what he must have looked like at an earlier age. He wore gray trousers and a matching jacket-style shirt, tapered at the waist, with short sleeves and a large pointed collar, made of a thin but durable synthetic material. He had specified both the cut and the fabric to his tailor—it was his preferred uniform for giving tours because it did not get crushed during his long hours behind the wheel. Through the windshield he watched as Ronny circled around the goat, touched it quickly on its side, then trotted back to the car.

"You left India as a child?" Mr. Kapasi asked when Mr. Das had settled once again into the passenger seat.

"Oh, Mina and I were both born in America," Mr. Das announced with   10
an air of sudden confidence. "Born and raised. Our parents live here now, in Assansol. They retired. We visit them every couple years." He turned to watch as the little girl ran toward the car, the wide purple bows of her sundress flopping on her narrow brown shoulders. She was holding to her chest a doll with yellow hair that looked as if it had been chopped, as a punitive measure, with a pair of dull scissors. "This is Tina's first trip to India, isn't it, Tina?"

"I don't have to go to the bathroom anymore," Tina announced.

"Where's Mina?" Mr. Das asked.

Mr. Kapasi found it strange that Mr. Das should refer to his wife by her first name when speaking to the little girl. Tina pointed to where Mrs. Das was purchasing something from one of the shirtless men who worked at the tea stall. Mr. Kapasi heard one of the shirtless men sing a phrase from a popular Hindi love song as Mrs. Das walked back to the car, but she did not appear to understand the words of the song, for she did not express irritation, or embarrassment, or react in any other way to the man's declarations.

He observed her. She wore a red-and-white-checkered skirt that stopped above her knees, slip-on shoes with a square wooden heel, and a close-fitting blouse styled like a man's undershirt. The blouse was decorated at chest-level with a calico appliqué in the shape of a strawberry. She was a short woman, with small hands like paws, her frosty pink fingernails painted to match her lips, and was slightly plump in her figure. Her hair, shorn only a little longer than her husband's, was parted far to one side. She was wearing large dark brown sunglasses with a pinkish tint to them, and carried a big straw bag, almost as big as her torso, shaped like a bowl, with a water bottle poking out of it. She walked slowly, carrying some puffed rice tossed with peanuts and chili peppers in a large packet made from newspapers. Mr. Kapasi turned to Mr. Das.

"Where in America do you live?"   15

"New Brunswick, New Jersey."

"Next to New York?'

"Exactly. I teach middle school there."

"What subject?"

"Science. In fact, every year I take my students on a trip to the Museum   20
of Natural History in New York City. In a way we have a lot in common, you could say, you and I. How long have you been a tour guide, Mr. Kapasi?"

"Five years."

Mrs. Das reached the car. "How long's the trip?" she asked, shutting the door.

"About two and a half hours," Mr. Kapasi replied.

At this Mrs. Das gave an impatient sigh, as if she had been traveling her whole life without pause. She fanned herself with a folded Bombay film magazine written in English.

"I thought that the Sun Temple is only eighteen miles north of Puri," Mr.   25
Das said, tapping on the tour book.

"The roads to Konarak are poor. Actually it is a distance of fifty-two miles," Mr. Kapasi explained.

Mr. Das nodded, readjusting the camera strap where it had begun to chafe the back of his neck.

Before starting the ignition, Mr. Kapasi reached back to make sure the cranklike locks on the inside of each of the back doors were secured. As soon as the car began to move the little girl began to play with the lock on her side, clicking it with some effort forward and backward, but Mrs. Das said nothing to stop her. She sat a bit slouched at one end of the back seat, not offering her puffed rice to anyone. Ronny and Tina sat on either side of her, both snapping bright green gum.

"Look," Bobby said as the car began to gather speed. He pointed with his finger to the tall trees that lined the road. "Look."

"Monkeys!" Ronny shrieked. "Wow!"   30

They were seated in groups along the branches, with shining black faces, silver bodies, horizontal eyebrows, and crested heads. Their long gray tails dangled like a series of ropes among the leaves. A few scratched themselves with black leathery hands, or swung their feet, staring as the car passed.

"We call them the hanuman," Mr. Kapasi said. "They are quite common in the area."

As soon as he spoke, one of the monkeys leaped into the middle of the road, causing Mr. Kapasi to brake suddenly. Another bounced onto the hood of the car, then sprang away. Mr. Kapasi beeped his horn. The children began to get excited, sucking in their breath and covering their faces partly with their hands. They had never seen monkeys outside of a zoo, Mr. Das explained. He asked Mr. Kapasi to stop the car so that he could take a picture.

While Mr. Das adjusted his telephoto lens, Mrs. Das reached into her straw bag and pulled out a bottle of colorless nail polish, which she proceeded to stroke on the tip of her index finger.

The little girl stuck out a hand. "Mine too. Mommy, do mine too."   35

"Leave me alone," Mrs. Das said, blowing on her nail and turning her body slightly. "You're making me mess up."

The little girl occupied herself by buttoning and unbuttoning a pinafore on the doll's plastic body.

"All set," Mr. Das said, replacing the lens cap.

The car rattled considerably as it raced along the dusty road, causing them all to pop up from their seats every now and then, but Mrs. Das continued to polish her nails. Mr. Kapasi eased up on the accelerator, hoping to produce a smoother ride. When he reached for the gearshift the boy in front accommodated him by swinging his hairless knees out of the way. Mr. Kapasi noted that this boy was slightly paler than the other children. "Daddy, why is the driver sitting on the wrong side in this car, too?" the boy asked.

"They all do that here, dummy," Ronny said.   40

"Don't call your brother a dummy," Mr. Das said. He turned to Mr. Kapasi. "In America, you know . . . it confuses them."

"Oh yes, I am well aware," Mr. Kapasi said. As delicately as he could, he shifted gears again, accelerating as they approached a hill in the road. "I see it on *Dallas*, the steering wheels are on the left-hand side."

"What's *Dallas*?" Tina asked, banging her now naked doll on the seat behind Mr. Kapasi.

"It went off the air," Mr. Das explained. "It's a television show."

They were all like siblings, Mr. Kapasi thought as they passed a row of   45
date trees. Mr. and Mrs. Das behaved like an older brother and sister, not parents. It seemed that they were in charge of the children only for the day; it was hard to believe they were regularly responsible for anything other than themselves. Mr. Das tapped on his lens cap, and his tour book, dragging his thumbnail occasionally across the pages so that they made a scraping sound. Mrs. Das continued to polish her nails. She had still not removed her sunglasses. Every now and then Tina renewed her plea that she wanted her nails done, too, and so at one point Mrs. Das flicked a drop of polish on the little girl's finger before depositing the bottle back inside her straw bag.

"Isn't this an air-conditioned car?" she asked, still blowing on her hand. The window on Tina's side was broken and could not be rolled down.

"Quit complaining," Mr. Das said. "It isn't so hot."

"I told you to get a car with air-conditioning," Mrs. Das continued. "Why do you do this, Raj, just to save a few stupid rupees. What are you saving us, fifty cents?"

Their accents sounded just like the ones Mr. Kapasi heard on American television programs, though not like the ones on *Dallas*.

"Doesn't it get tiresome, Mr. Kapasi, showing people the same thing   50
every day?" Mr. Das asked, rolling down his own window all the way. "Hey,
do you mind stopping the car. I just want to get a shot of this guy."

Mr. Kapasi pulled over to the side of the road as Mr. Das took a picture
of a barefoot man, his head wrapped in a dirty turban, seated on top of a cart
of grain sacks pulled by a pair of bullocks. Both the man and the bullocks
were emaciated. In the back seat Mrs. Das gazed out another window, at the
sky, where nearly transparent clouds passed quickly in front of one another.

"I look forward to it, actually," Mr. Kapasi said as they continued on
their way. "The Sun Temple is one of my favorite places. In that way it is a
reward for me. I give tours on Fridays and Saturdays only. I have another job
during the week."

"Oh? Where?" Mr. Das asked.

"I work in a doctor's office."

"You're a doctor?"   55

"I am not a doctor. I work with one. As an interpreter."

"What does a doctor need an interpreter for?"

"He has a number of Gujarati patients. My father was Gujarati, but
many people do not speak Gujarati in this area, including the doctor. And
so the doctor asked me to work in his office, interpreting what the patients
say."

"Interesting. I've never heard of anything like that," Mr. Das said.

Mr. Kapasi shrugged. "It is a job like any other."   60

"But so romantic," Mrs. Das said dreamily, breaking her extended
silence. She lifted her pinkish brown sunglasses and arranged them on top
of her head like a tiara. For the first time, her eyes met Mr. Kapasi's in the
rearview mirror: pale, a bit small, their gaze fixed but drowsy.

Mr. Das craned to look at her. "What's so romantic about it?"

"I don't know. Something." She shrugged, knitting her brows together
for an instant. "Would you like a piece of gum, Mr. Kapasi?" she asked
brightly. She reached into her straw bag and handed him a small square
wrapped in green-and-white-striped paper. As soon as Mr. Kapasi put the
gum in his mouth a thick sweet liquid burst onto his tongue.

"Tell us more about your job, Mr. Kapasi," Mrs. Das said.

"What would you like to know, madame?"   65

"I don't know," she shrugged, munching on some puffed rice and licking the mustard oil from the corners of her mouth. "Tell us a typical situation." She settled back in her seat, her head tilted in a patch of sun, and
closed her eyes. "I want to picture what happens."

"Very well. The other day a man came in with a pain in his throat."

"Did he smoke cigarettes?"

"No. It was very curious. He complained that he felt as if there were
long pieces of straw stuck in his throat. When I told the doctor he was able
to prescribe the proper medication."

"That's so neat."   70

"Yes," Mr. Kapasi agreed after some hesitation.

"So these patients are totally dependent on you," Mrs. Das said. She spoke slowly, as if she were thinking aloud. "In a way, more dependent on you than the doctor."

"How do you mean? How could it be?"

"Well, for example, you could tell the doctor that the pain felt like a burning, not straw. The patient would never know what you had told the doctor, and the doctor wouldn't know that you had told the wrong thing. It's a big responsibility.

"Yes, a big responsibility you have there, Mr. Kapasi," Mr. Das agreed. 75

Mr. Kapasi had never thought of his job in such complimentary terms. To him it was a thankless occupation. He found nothing noble in interpreting people's maladies, assiduously translating the symptoms of so many swollen bones, countless cramps of bellies and bowels, spots on people's palms that changed color, shape, or size. The doctor, nearly half his age, had an affinity for bell-bottom trousers and made humorless jokes about the Congress party. Together they worked in a stale little infirmary where Mr. Kapasi's smartly tailored clothes clung to him in the heat, in spite of the blackened blades of a ceiling fan churning over their heads.

The job was a sign of his failings. In his youth he'd been a devoted scholar of foreign languages, the owner of an impressive collection of dictionaries. He had dreamed of being an interpreter for diplomats and dignitaries, resolving conflicts between people and nations, settling disputes of which he alone could understand both sides. He was a self-educated man. In a series of notebooks, in the evenings before his parents settled his marriage, he had listed the common etymologies of words, and at one point in his life he was confident that he could converse, if given the opportunity, in English, French, Russian, Portuguese, and Italian, not to mention Hindi, Bengali, Orissi, and Gujarati. Now only a handful of European phrases remained in his memory, scattered words for things like saucers and chairs. English was the only non-Indian language he spoke fluently anymore. Mr. Kapasi knew it was not a remarkable talent. Sometimes he feared that his children knew better English than he did, just from watching television. Still, it came in handy for the tours.

He had taken the job as an interpreter after his first son, at the age of seven, contracted typhoid — that was how he had first made the acquaintance of the doctor. At the time Mr. Kapasi had been teaching English in a grammar school, and he bartered his skills as an interpreter to pay the increasingly exorbitant medical bills. In the end the boy had died one evening in his mother's arms, his limbs burning with fever, but then there was the funeral to pay for, and the other children who were born soon enough, and the newer, bigger house, and the good schools and tutors, and the fine shoes and the television, and the countless other ways he tried to console his wife and to keep her from crying in her sleep, and so when the doctor offered to pay him twice as much as he earned at the grammar school, he accepted. Mr. Kapasi knew that his wife had little regard for his career as an interpreter. He knew it reminded her of the son she'd lost, and that she resented the other lives he helped, in his own small way, to save. If ever she referred to his position, she used the phrase "doctor's assistant," as if the process of interpretation were equal to taking someone's temperature, or changing a bedpan. She never asked him about the patients who came to the doctor's office, or said that his job was a big responsibility.

For this reason it flattered Mr. Kapasi that Mrs. Das was so intrigued by his job. Unlike his wife, she had reminded him of its intellectual challenges. She had also used the word "romantic." She did not behave in a romantic way toward her husband, and yet she had used the word to describe him. He wondered if Mr. and Mrs. Das were a bad match, just as he and his wife were. Perhaps they, too, had little in common apart from three children and a decade of their lives. The signs he recognized from his own marriage were there—the bickering, the indifference, the protracted silences. Her sudden interest in him, an interest she did not express in either her husband or her children, was mildly intoxicating. When Mr. Kapasi thought once again about how she had said "romantic," the feeling of intoxication grew.

He began to check his reflection in the rearview mirror as he drove, 80 feeling grateful that he had chosen the gray suit that morning and not the brown one, which tended to sag a little in the knees. From time to time he glanced through the mirror at Mrs. Das. In addition to glancing at her face he glanced at the strawberry between her breasts, and the golden brown hollow in her throat. He decided to tell Mrs. Das about another patient, and another: the young woman who had complained of a sensation of raindrops in her spine, the gentleman whose birthmark had begun to sprout hairs. Mrs. Das listened attentively, stroking her hair with a small plastic brush that resembled an oval bed of nails, asking more questions, for yet another example. The children were quiet, intent on spotting more monkeys in the trees, and Mr. Das was absorbed by his tour book, so it seemed like a private conversation between Mr. Kapasi and Mrs. Das. In this manner the next half hour passed, and when they stopped for lunch at a roadside restaurant that sold fritters and omelette sandwiches, usually something Mr. Kapasi looked forward to on his tours so that he could sit in peace and enjoy some hot tea, he was disappointed. As the Das family settled together under a magenta umbrella fringed with white and orange tassels, and placed their orders with one of the waiters who marched about in tricornered caps, Mr. Kapasi reluctantly headed toward a neighboring table.

"Mr. Kapasi, wait. There's room here," Mrs. Das called out. She gathered Tina onto her lap, insisting that he accompany them. And so, together, they had bottled mango juice and sandwiches and plates of onions and potatoes deep-fried in graham-flour batter. After finishing two omelette sandwiches Mr. Das took more pictures of the group as they ate.

"How much longer?" he asked Mr. Kapasi as he paused to load a new roll of film in the camera.

"About half an hour more."

By now the children had gotten up from the table to look at more monkeys perched in a nearby tree, so there was a considerable space between

Mrs. Das and Mr. Kapasi. Mr. Das placed the camera to his face and squeezed one eye shut, his tongue exposed at one corner of his mouth. "This looks funny. Mina, you need to lean in closer to Mr. Kapasi."

She did. He could smell a scent on her skin, like a mixture of whiskey   85 and rosewater. He worried suddenly that she could smell his perspiration, which he knew had collected beneath the synthetic material of his shirt. He polished off his mango juice in one gulp and smoothed his silver hair with his hands. A bit of the juice dripped onto his chin. He wondered if Mrs. Das had noticed.

She had not. "What's your address, Mr. Kapasi?" she inquired, fishing for something inside her straw bag.

"You would like my address?"

"So we can send you copies," she said. "Of the pictures." She handed him a scrap of paper which she had hastily ripped from a page of her film magazine. The blank portion was limited, for the narrow strip was crowded by lines of text and a tiny picture of a hero and heroine embracing under a eucalyptus tree.

The paper curled as Mr. Kapasi wrote his address in clear, careful letters. She would write to him, asking about his days interpreting at the doctor's office, and he would respond eloquently, choosing only the most entertaining anecdotes, ones that would make her laugh out loud as she read them in her house in New Jersey. In time she would reveal the disappointment of her marriage, and he his. In this way their friendship would grow, and flourish. He would possess a picture of the two of them, eating fried onions under a magenta umbrella, which he would keep, he decided, safely tucked between the pages of his Russian grammar. As his mind raced, Mr. Kapasi experienced a mild and pleasant shock. It was similar to a feeling he used to experience long ago when, after months of translating with the aid of a dictionary, he would finally read a passage from a French novel, or an Italian sonnet, and understand the words, one after another, unencumbered by his own efforts. In those moments Mr. Kapasi used to believe that all was right with the world, that all struggles were rewarded, that all of life's mistakes made sense in the end. The promise that he would hear from Mrs. Das now filled him with the same belief.

When he finished writing his address Mr. Kapasi handed her the paper,   90 but as soon as he did so he worried that he had either misspelled his name, or accidentally reversed the numbers of his postal code. He dreaded the possibility of a lost letter, the photograph never reaching him, hovering somewhere in Orissa, close but ultimately unattainable. He thought of asking for the slip of paper again, just to make sure he had written his address accurately, but Mrs. Das had already dropped it into the jumble of her bag.

They reached Konarak at two-thirty. The temple, made of sandstone, was a massive pyramid-like structure in the shape of a chariot. It was dedicated to the great master of life, the sun, which struck three sides of the edifice as it made its journey each day across the sky. Twenty-four giant wheels

Neal Boenzi/New York Times/Getty Images

Built by King Narasimhadeva, a thirteenth-century ruler of the Ganga dynasty, the Konarak Sun Temple was shaped like a giant chariot.

were carved on the north and south sides of the plinth. The whole thing was drawn by a team of seven horses, speeding as if through the heavens. As they approached, Mr. Kapasi explained that the temple had been built between A.D. 1243 and 1255, with the efforts of twelve hundred artisans, by the great ruler of the Ganga dynasty, King Narasimhadeva the First, to commemorate his victory against the Muslim army.

"It says the temple occupies about a hundred and seventy acres of land," Mr. Das said, reading from his book.

"It's like a desert," Ronny said, his eyes wandering across the sand that stretched on all sides beyond the temple.

"The Chandrabhaga River once flowed one mile north of here. It is dry now," Mr. Kapasi said, turning off the engine.

They got out and walked toward the temple, posing first for pictures by 95 the pair of lions that flanked the steps. Mr. Kapasi led them next to one of the wheels of the chariot, higher than any human being, nine feet in diameter.

"'The wheels are supposed to symbolize the wheel of life,'" Mr. Das read. "'They depict the cycle of creation, preservation, and achievement of realization.' Cool." He turned the page of his book. "'Each wheel is divided into eight thick and thin spokes, dividing the day into eight equal parts. The rims are carved with designs of birds and animals, whereas the medallions in the spokes are carved with women in luxurious poses, largely erotic in nature.'"

What he referred to were the countless friezes of entwined naked bodies, making love in various positions, women clinging to the necks of men, their knees wrapped eternally around their lovers' thighs. In addition to these were assorted scenes from daily life, of hunting and trading, of deer being killed with bows and arrows and marching warriors holding swords in their hands.

It was no longer possible to enter the temple, for it had filled with rubble years ago, but they admired the exterior, as did all the tourists Mr. Kapasi brought there, slowly strolling along each of its sides. Mr. Das trailed behind, taking pictures. The children ran ahead, pointing to figures of naked people, intrigued in particular by the Nagamithunas, the half-human, half-serpentine couples who were said, Mr. Kapasi told them, to live in the deepest waters of the sea. Mr. Kapasi was pleased that they liked the temple, pleased especially that it appealed to Mrs. Das. She stopped every three or four paces, staring silently at the carved lovers, and the processions of elephants, and the topless female musicians beating on two-sided drums.

Though Mr. Kapasi had been to the temple countless times, it occurred to him, as he, too, gazed at the topless women, that he had never seen his own wife fully naked. Even when they had made love she kept the panels of her blouse hooked together, the string of her petticoat knotted around her waist. He had never admired the backs of his wife's legs the way he now admired those of Mrs. Das, walking as if for his benefit alone. He had, of course, seen plenty of bare limbs before, belonging to the American and

European ladies who took his tours. But Mrs. Das was different. Unlike the other women, who had an interest only in the temple, and kept their noses buried in a guidebook, or their eyes behind the lens of a camera, Mrs. Das had taken an interest in him.

Mr. Kapasi was anxious to be alone with her, to continue their private 100 conversation, yet he felt nervous to walk at her side. She was lost behind her sunglasses, ignoring her husband's requests that she pose for another picture, walking past her children as if they were strangers. Worried that he might disturb her, Mr. Kapasi walked ahead, to admire, as he always did, the three life-sized bronze avatars of Surya, the sun god, each emerging from its own niche on the temple facade to greet the sun at dawn, noon, and evening. They wore elaborate headdresses, their languid, elongated eyes closed, their bare chests draped with carved chains and amulets. Hibiscus petals, offerings from previous visitors, were strewn at their gray-green feet. The last statue, on the northern wall of the temple, was Mr. Kapasi's favorite. This Surya had a tired expression, weary after a hard day of work, sitting astride a horse with folded legs. Even his horse's eyes were drowsy. Around his body were smaller sculptures of women in pairs, their hips thrust to one side.

"Who's that?" Mrs. Das asked. He was startled to see that she was standing beside him.

"He is the Astachala-Surya," Mr. Kapasi said. "The setting sun."

"So in a couple of hours the sun will set right here?" She slipped a foot out of one of her square-heeled shoes, rubbed her toes on the back of her other leg.

"That is correct."

She raised her sunglasses for a moment, then put them back on again. 105 "Neat."

Mr. Kapasi was not certain exactly what the word suggested, but he had a feeling it was a favorable response. He hoped that Mrs. Das had understood Surya's beauty, his power. Perhaps they would discuss it further in their letters. He would explain things to her, things about India, and she would explain things to him about America. In its own way this correspondence would fulfill his dream, of serving as an interpreter between nations. He looked at her straw bag, delighted that his address lay nestled among its contents. When he pictured her so many thousands of miles away he plummeted, so much so that he had an overwhelming urge to wrap his arms around her, to freeze with her, even for an instant, in an embrace witnessed by his favorite Surya. But Mrs. Das had already started walking.

"When do you return to America?" he asked, trying to sound placid.

"In ten days."

He calculated: A week to settle in, a week to develop the pictures, a few days to compose her letter, two weeks to get to India by air. According to his schedule, allowing room for delays, he would hear from Mrs. Das in approximately six weeks' time.

The family was silent as Mr. Kapasi drove them back, a little past four-   110
thirty, to Hotel Sandy Villa. The children had bought miniature granite versions of the chariot's wheels at a souvenir stand, and they turned them round
in their hands. Mr. Das continued to read his book. Mrs. Das untangled
Tina's hair with her brush and divided it into two little ponytails.

Mr. Kapasi was beginning to dread the thought of dropping them off. He
was not prepared to begin his six-week wait to hear from Mrs. Das. As he
stole glances at her in the rearview mirror, wrapping elastic bands around
Tina's hair, he wondered how he might make the tour last a little longer.
Ordinarily he sped back to Puri using a shortcut, eager to return home, scrub
his feet and hands with sandalwood soap, and enjoy the evening newspaper
and a cup of tea that his wife would serve him in silence. The thought of that
silence, something to which he'd long been resigned, now oppressed him.
It was then that he suggested visiting the hills at Udayagiri and Khandagiri,
where a number of monastic dwellings were hewn out of the ground, facing
one another across a defile. It was some miles away, but well worth seeing,
Mr. Kapasi told them.

"Oh yeah, there's something mentioned about it in this book," Mr. Das
said. "Built by a Jain king or something."

"Shall we go then?" Mr. Kapasi asked. He paused at a turn in the road.
"It's to the left."

Mr. Das turned to look at Mrs. Das. Both of them shrugged.

"Left, left," the children chanted.   115

Mr. Kapasi turned the wheel, almost delirious with relief. He did not
know what he would do or say to Mrs. Das once they arrived at the hills.
Perhaps he would tell her what a pleasing smile she had. Perhaps he would
compliment her strawberry shirt, which he found irresistibly becoming. Perhaps, when Mr. Das was busy taking a picture, he would take her hand.

He did not have to worry. When they got to the hills, divided by a steep
path thick with trees, Mrs. Das refused to get out of the car. All along the
path, dozens of monkeys were seated on stones, as well as on the branches
of the trees. Their hind legs were stretched out in front and raised to shoulder level, their arms resting on their knees.

"My legs are tired," she said, sinking low in her seat. "I'll stay here."

"Why did you have to wear those stupid shoes?" Mr. Das said. "You
won't be in the pictures."

"Pretend I'm there."   120

"But we could use one of these pictures for our Christmas card this year.
We didn't get one of all five of us at the Sun Temple. Mr. Kapasi could take
it."

"I'm not coming. Anyway, those monkeys give me the creeps."

"But they're harmless," Mr. Das said. He turned to Mr. Kapasi. "Aren't
they?"

"They are more hungry than dangerous," Mr. Kapasi said. "Do not provoke them with food, and they will not bother you."

Mr. Das headed up the defile with the children, the boys at his side, the 125
little girl on his shoulders. Mr. Kapasi watched as they crossed paths with
a Japanese man and woman, the only other tourists there, who paused for
a final photograph, then stepped into a nearby car and drove away. As the
car disappeared out of view some of the monkeys called out, emitting soft
whooping sounds, and then walked on their flat black hands and feet up
the path. At one point a group of them formed a little ring around Mr. Das
and the children. Tina screamed in delight. Ronny ran in circles around his
father. Bobby bent down and picked up a fat stick on the ground. When
he extended it, one of the monkeys approached him and snatched it, then
briefly beat the ground.

"I'll join them," Mr. Kapasi said, unlocking the door on his side. "There
is much to explain about the caves."

"No. Stay a minute," Mrs. Das said. She got out of the back seat and
slipped in beside Mr. Kapasi. "Raj has his dumb book anyway." Together,
through the windshield, Mrs. Das and Mr. Kapasi watched as Bobby and the
monkey passed the stick back and forth between them.

"A brave little boy," Mr. Kapasi commented.

"It's not so surprising," Mrs. Das said.

"No?"   130

"He's not his."

"I beg your pardon?"

"Raj's. He's not Raj's son."

Mr. Kapasi felt a prickle on his skin. He reached into his shirt pocket for
the small tin of lotus-oil balm he carried with him at all times, and applied
it to three spots on his forehead. He knew that Mrs. Das was watching him,
but he did not turn to face her. Instead he watched as the figures of Mr. Das
and the children grew smaller, climbing up the steep path, pausing every
now and then for a picture, surrounded by a growing number of monkeys.

"Are you surprised?" The way she put it made him choose his words 135
with care.

"It's not the type of thing one assumes," Mr. Kapasi replied slowly. He
put the tin of lotus-oil balm back in his pocket.

"No, of course not. And no one knows, of course. No one at all. I've kept
it a secret for eight whole years." She looked at Mr. Kapasi, tilting her chin
as if to gain a fresh perspective. "But now I've told you."

Mr. Kapasi nodded. He felt suddenly parched, and his forehead was
warm and slightly numb from the balm. He considered asking Mrs. Das for
a sip of water, then decided against it.

"We met when we were very young," she said. She reached into her
straw bag in search of something, then pulled out a packet of puffed rice.
"Want some?"

"No, thank you."   140

She put a fistful in her mouth, sank into the seat a little, and looked away
from Mr. Kapasi, out the window on her side of the car. "We married when

we were still in college. We were in high school when he proposed. We went to the same college, of course. Back then we couldn't stand the thought of being separated, not for a day, not for a minute. Our parents were best friends who lived in the same town. My entire life I saw him every weekend, either at our house or theirs. We were sent upstairs to play together while our parents joked about our marriage. Imagine! They never caught us at anything, though in a way I think it was all more or less a setup. The things we did those Friday and Saturday nights, while our parents sat downstairs drinking tea . . . I could tell you stories, Mr. Kapasi."

As a result of spending all her time in college with Raj, she continued, she did not make many close friends. There was no one to confide in about him at the end of a difficult day, or to share a passing thought or a worry. Her parents now lived on the other side of the world, but she had never been very close to them, anyway. After marrying so young she was overwhelmed by it all, having a child so quickly, and nursing, and warming up bottles of milk and testing their temperature against her wrist while Raj was at work, dressed in sweaters and corduroy pants, teaching his students about rocks and dinosaurs. Raj never looked cross or harried, or plump as she had become after the first baby.

Always tired, she declined invitations from her one or two college girl-friends, to have lunch or shop in Manhattan. Eventually the friends stopped calling her, so that she was left at home all day with the baby, surrounded by toys that made her trip when she walked or wince when she sat, always cross and tired. Only occasionally did they go out after Ronny was born, and even more rarely did they entertain. Raj didn't mind; he looked forward to coming home from teaching and watching television and bouncing Ronny on his knee. She had been outraged when Raj told her that a Punjabi friend, someone whom she had once met but did not remember, would be staying with them for a week for some job interviews in the New Brunswick area.

Bobby was conceived in the afternoon, on a sofa littered with rubber teething toys, after the friend learned that a London pharmaceutical company had hired him, while Ronny cried to be freed from his playpen. She made no protest when the friend touched the small of her back as she was about to make a pot of coffee, then pulled her against his crisp navy suit. He made love to her swiftly, in silence, with an expertise she had never known, without the meaningful expressions and smiles Raj always insisted on afterward. The next day Raj drove the friend to JFK. He was married now, to a Punjabi girl, and they lived in London still, and every year they exchanged Christmas cards with Raj and Mina, each couple tucking photos of their families into the envelopes. He did not know that he was Bobby's father. He never would.

"I beg your pardon, Mrs. Das, but why have you told me this informa- 145 tion?" Mr. Kapasi asked when she had finally finished speaking, and had turned to face him once again.

"For God's sake, stop calling me Mrs. Das. I'm twenty-eight. You probably have children my age."

"Not quite." It disturbed Mr. Kapasi to learn that she thought of him as a parent. The feeling he had had toward her, that had made him check his reflection in the rearview mirror as they drove, evaporated a little.

"I told you because of your talents." She put the packet of puffed rice back into her bag without folding over the top.

"I don't understand," Mr. Kapasi said.

"Don't you see? For eight years I haven't been able to express this to   150
anybody, not to friends, certainly not to Raj. He doesn't even suspect it. He thinks I'm still in love with him. Well, don't you have anything to say?"

"About what?"

"About what I've just told you. About my secret, and about how terrible it makes me feel. I feel terrible looking at my children, and at Raj, always terrible. I have terrible urges, Mr. Kapasi, to throw things away. One day I had the urge to throw everything I own out the window, the television, the children, everything. Don't you think it's unhealthy?"

He was silent.

"Mr. Kapasi, don't you have anything to say? I thought that was your job."

"My job is to give tours, Mrs. Das."   155

"Not that. Your other job. As an interpreter."

"But we do not face a language barrier. What need is there for an interpreter?"

"That's not what I mean. I would never have told you otherwise. Don't you realize what it means for me to tell you?"

"What does it mean?"

"It means that I'm tired of feeling so terrible all the time. Eight years, Mr.   160
Kapasi, I've been in pain eight years. I was hoping you could help me feel better, say the right thing. Suggest some kind of remedy."

He looked at her, in her red plaid skirt and strawberry T-shirt, a woman not yet thirty, who loved neither her husband nor her children, who had already fallen out of love with life. Her confession depressed him, depressed him all the more when he thought of Mr. Das at the top of the path, Tina clinging to his shoulders, taking pictures of ancient monastic cells cut into the hills to show his students in America, unsuspecting and unaware that one of his sons was not his own. Mr. Kapasi felt insulted that Mrs. Das should ask him to interpret her common, trivial little secret. She did not resemble the patients in the doctor's office, those who came glassy-eyed and desperate, unable to sleep or breathe or urinate with ease, unable, above all, to give words to their pains. Still, Mr. Kapasi believed it was his duty to assist Mrs. Das. Perhaps he ought to tell her to confess the truth to Mr. Das. He would explain that honesty was the best policy. Honesty, surely, would help her feel better, as she'd put it. Perhaps he would offer to preside over the discussion, as a mediator. He decided to begin with the most obvious question, to get to the heart of the matter, and so he asked, "Is it really pain you feel, Mrs. Das, or is it guilt?"

She turned to him and glared, mustard oil thick on her frosty pink lips. She opened her mouth to say something, but as she glared at Mr. Kapasi some certain knowledge seemed to pass before her eyes, and she stopped. It crushed him; he knew at that moment that he was not even important enough to be properly insulted. She opened the car door and began walking up the path, wobbling a little on her square wooden heels, reaching into her straw bag to eat handfuls of puffed rice. It fell through her fingers, leaving a zigzagging trail, causing a monkey to leap down from a tree and devour the little white grains. In search of more, the monkey began to follow Mrs. Das. Others joined him, so that she was soon being followed by about half a dozen of them, their velvety tails dragging behind.

Mr. Kapasi stepped out of the car. He wanted to holler, to alert her in some way, but he worried that if she knew they were behind her, she would grow nervous. Perhaps she would lose her balance. Perhaps they would pull at her bag or her hair. He began to jog up the path, taking a fallen branch in his hand to scare away the monkeys. Mrs. Das continued walking, oblivious, trailing grains of puffed rice. Near the top of the incline, before a group of cells fronted by a row of squat stone pillars, Mr. Das was kneeling on the ground, focusing the lens of his camera. The children stood under the arcade, now hiding, now emerging from view.

"Wait for me," Mrs. Das called out. "I'm coming."

Tina jumped up and down. "Here comes Mommy!" 165

"Great," Mr. Das said without looking up. "Just in time. We'll get Mr. Kapasi to take a picture of the five of us."

Mr. Kapasi quickened his pace, waving his branch so that the monkeys scampered away, distracted, in another direction.

"Where's Bobby?" Mrs. Das asked when she stopped.

Mr. Das looked up from the camera. "I don't know. Ronny, where's Bobby?"

Ronny shrugged. "I thought he was right here." 170

"Where is he?" Mrs. Das repeated sharply. "What's wrong with all of you?"

They began calling his name, wandering up and down the path a bit. Because they were calling, they did not initially hear the boy's screams. When they found him, a little farther down the path under a tree, he was surrounded by a group of monkeys, over a dozen of them, pulling at his T-shirt with their long black fingers. The puffed rice Mrs. Das had spilled was scattered at his feet, raked over by the monkeys' hands. The boy was silent, his body frozen, swift tears running down his startled face. His bare legs were dusty and red with welts from where one of the monkeys struck him repeatedly with the stick he had given to it earlier.

"Daddy, the monkey's hurting Bobby," Tina said.

Mr. Das wiped his palms on the front of his shorts. In his nervousness he accidentally pressed the shutter on his camera; the whirring noise of the advancing film excited the monkeys, and the one with the stick began to beat Bobby more intently. "What are we supposed to do? What if they start attacking?"

"Mr. Kapasi," Mrs. Das shrieked, noticing him standing to one side. "Do 175 something, for God's sake, do something!"

Mr. Kapasi took his branch and shooed them away, hissing at the ones that remained, stomping his feet to scare them. The animals retreated slowly, with a measured gait, obedient but unintimidated. Mr. Kapasi gathered Bobby in his arms and brought him back to where his parents and siblings were standing. As he carried him he was tempted to whisper a secret into the boy's ear. But Bobby was stunned, and shivering with fright, his legs bleeding slightly where the stick had broken the skin. When Mr. Kapasi delivered him to his parents, Mr. Das brushed some dirt off the boy's T-shirt and put the visor on him the right way. Mrs. Das reached into her straw bag to find a bandage which she taped over the cut on his knee. Ronny offered his brother a fresh piece of gum. "He's fine. Just a little scared, right, Bobby?" Mr. Das said, patting the top of his head.

"God, let's get out of here," Mrs. Das said. She folded her arms across the strawberry on her chest. "This place gives me the creeps."

"Yeah. Back to the hotel, definitely," Mr. Das agreed.

"Poor Bobby," Mrs. Das said. "Come here a second. Let Mommy fix your hair." Again she reached into her straw bag, this time for her hairbrush, and began to run it around the edges of the translucent visor. When she whipped out the hairbrush, the slip of paper with Mr. Kapasi's address on it fluttered away in the wind. No one but Mr. Kapasi noticed. He watched as it rose, carried higher and higher by the breeze, into the trees where the monkeys now sat, solemnly observing the scene below. Mr. Kapasi observed it too, knowing that this was the picture of the Das family he would preserve forever in his mind. ●

The Reader's Presence

1. Identify some of the characteristics of the Das family that Mr. Kapasi notices. For example, how are they dressed? How do they speak? In what specific ways do the parents relate to each other? Why do you think Mr. Kapasi notices their behavior so carefully? What do his observations add to the story? How would you imagine the story if it were told by Mrs. Das or Mr. Das?

2. According to critic Ann Charters, "Foreshadowing [introduces] specific words, images, or events into a narrative to suggest or anticipate later events that are central to the action and its resolution." Lahiri's story contains many instances of foreshadowing. Identify as many instances as you can. Where, for example, does Lahiri first suggest that "Bobby" is not Mr. Das's child? Why do you think the author relies so often on this literary technique? How does it affect your reading of the story? To what extent do you think it eliminates an element of surprise or enhances it?

3. **VISUAL PRESENCE:** Lahiri devotes a great deal of attention to Mr. Kapasi's descriptions of the specific characteristics of the dress, language, and behavior of the Das family. Study the photograph of the Konarak Sun Temple (page 825) — as seen as

one approaches it. (The Konarak Temple, located in Odisha, India, dates to 1250 and is built in the shape of an enormous chariot with intricately carved stone wheels, pillars, and walls. Much of this structure, declared a UNESCO World Heritage Site, is now in ruins.) In what specific ways are the details of this image consistent with the sensibility at work in Lahiri's story?

4. **CONNECTIONS:**   Consider "Interpreter of Maladies" in the light of the author's essay "My Two Lives" (page 181). In what specific ways does that essay help illuminate the cultural conflicts we find at the heart of this story? You might also compare this short story to Flannery O'Connor's "A Good Man Is Hard to Find" (page 852). What strategies does each writer use to feature a journey that leads to a clash of values? How many other similarities can you point to in these two stories?

Joyce Carol Oates

WHERE ARE YOU GOING, WHERE HAVE YOU BEEN?

JOYCE CAROL OATES (b. 1938) has published more than a hundred works of fiction and nonfiction in every genre, including novels, short stories, essays, poetry, screenplays, and a libretto—frequently publishing several projects simultaneously while working and reworking the manuscript for the next. Describing herself as a "chronicler of the American experience," Oates often explores violent behavior "in a nation prone to violence" and its effect on the lives of ordinary people, particularly women and children. Among her long list of novels are *A Garden of Earthly Delights* (1967) and *them* (1969), which won the National Book Award for fiction in 1970. Her most recent works of fiction include the novels *Mudwoman* (2012),

> Describing herself as a "chronicler of the American experience," Joyce Carol Oates often explores violent behavior "in a nation prone to violence."

Daddy Love (2013), and *The Accursed* (2013); and short story collections *Give Me Your Heart: Tales of Mystery and Suspense* (2011), *The Corn Maiden and Other Nightmares* (2011), and *Black Dahlia & White Rose* (2012). Oates's interests and versatility are also reflected in her nonfiction prose, which includes *The Profane Art* (1983), *On Boxing* (1987), *Where I've Been, and Where I'm Going* (1999), and *A Widow's Story* (2011).

Oates's short story "Where Are You Going, Where Have You Been?" first appeared in 1966 and has been anthologized frequently since. She has said that the idea came from a magazine piece she saw—but never finished reading—about a "thrill killer" in Tucson, Arizona. "Where Are You Going, Where Have You Been?" was the basis for the film *Smooth Talk* in 1985.

For Bob Dylan

HER NAME WAS CONNIE. She was fifteen and she had a quick nervous giggling habit of craning her neck to glance into mirrors, or checking other people's faces to make sure her own was all right. Her mother, who noticed everything and knew everything and who hadn't much reason any longer to look at her own face, always scolded Connie about it. "Stop gawking at yourself, who are you? You think you're so pretty?" she would say. Connie would raise her eyebrows at these familiar complaints and look right through her mother, into a shadowy vision of herself as she was right at that moment: she knew she was pretty and that was everything. Her mother had been pretty once too, if you could believe those old snapshots in the album, but now her looks were gone and that was why she was always after Connie.

"Why don't you keep your room clean like your sister? How've you got your hair fixed—what the hell stinks? Hair spray? You don't see your sister using that junk."

Her sister June was twenty-four and still lived at home. She was a secretary in the high school Connie attended, and if that wasn't bad enough—with her in the same building—she was so plain and chunky and steady that Connie had to hear her praised all the time by her mother and her mother's sisters. June did this, June did that, she saved money and helped clean the house and cooked and Connie couldn't do a thing, her mind was all filled with trashy daydreams. Their father was away at work most of the time and when he came home he wanted supper and he read the newspaper at supper and after supper he went to bed. He didn't bother talking much to them, but around his bent head Connie's mother kept picking at her until Connie wished her mother was dead and she herself was dead and it was all over. "She makes me want to throw up sometimes," she complained to her friends. She had a high, breathless, amused voice which made everything she said a little forced, whether it was sincere or not.

There was one good thing: June went places with girl friends of hers, girls who were just as plain and steady as she, and so when Connie wanted to do that her mother had no objections. The father of Connie's best girl friend drove the girls the three miles to town and left them off at a shopping plaza, so that they could walk through the stores or go to a movie, and when he came to pick them up again at eleven he never bothered to ask what they had done.

They must have been familiar sights, walking around that shopping   5
plaza in their shorts and flat ballerina slippers that always scuffed the side-walk, with charm bracelets jingling on their thin wrists; they would lean together to whisper and laugh secretly if someone passed by who amused or interested them. Connie had long dark blond hair that drew anyone's eye to it, and she wore part of it pulled up on her head and puffed out and the rest of it she let fall down her back. She wore a pullover jersey blouse that looked one way when she was at home and another way when she was away from home. Everything about her had two sides to it, one for home and one for anywhere that was not home: her walk that could be childlike and bob-bing, or languid enough to make anyone think she was hearing music in her head, her mouth which was pale and smirking most of the time, but bright and pink on these evenings out, her laugh which was cynical and drawling at home—"Ha, ha, very funny"—but high-pitched and nervous anywhere else, like the jingling of the charms on her bracelet.

Sometimes they did go shopping or to a movie, but sometimes they went across the highway, ducking fast across the busy road, to a drive-in restaurant where older kids hung out. The restaurant was shaped like a big bottle, though squatter than a real bottle, and on its cap was a revolving fig-ure of a grinning boy who held a hamburger aloft. One night in midsummer they ran across, breathless with daring, and right away someone leaned out a car window and invited them over, but it was just a boy from high school they didn't like. It made them feel good to be able to ignore him. They went up through the maze of parked and cruising cars to the bright-lit, fly-infested restaurant, their faces pleased and expectant as if they were entering a sacred building that loomed out of the night to give them what haven and what blessing they yearned for. They sat at the counter and crossed their legs at the ankles, their thin shoulders rigid with excitement and listened to the music that made everything so good: the music was always in the background like music at a church service, it was something to depend upon.

A boy named Eddie came in to talk with them. He sat backwards on his stool, turning himself jerkily around in semi-circles and then stopping and turning again, and after a while he asked Connie if she would like some-thing to eat. She said she did and so she tapped her friend's arm on her way out—her friend pulled her face up into a brave droll look—and Connie said she would meet her at eleven, across the way. "I just hate to leave her like that," Connie said earnestly, but the boy said that she wouldn't be alone for long. So they went out to his car and on the way Connie couldn't help but let her eyes wander over the windshields and faces all around her, her face gleaming with the joy that had nothing to do with Eddie or even this place; it might have been the music. She drew her shoulders up and sucked in her breath with the pure pleasure of being alive, and just at that moment she happened to glance at a face just a few feet from hers. It was a boy with shaggy black hair, in a convertible jalopy painted gold. He stared at her and then his lips widened into a grin. Connie slit her eyes at him and turned away, but she couldn't help glancing back and there he was still watching her. He wagged a finger and laughed and said, "Gonna get you, baby," and Connie turned away again without Eddie noticing anything.

She spent three hours with him, at the restaurant where they ate hamburgers and drank Cokes in wax cups that were always sweating, and then down an alley a mile or so away, and when he left her off at five to eleven only the movie house was still open at the plaza. Her girl friend was there, talking with a boy. When Connie came up the two girls smiled at each other and Connie said, "How was the movie?" and the girl said, "*You* should know." They rode off with the girl's father, sleepy and pleased, and Connie couldn't help but look at the darkened shopping plaza with its big empty parking lot and its signs that were faded and ghostly now, and over at the drive-in restaurant where cars were still circling tirelessly. She couldn't hear the music at this distance.

Next morning June asked her how the movie was and Connie said, "So-so."

She and that girl and occasionally another girl went out several times a   10 week that way, and the rest of the time Connie spent around the house—it was summer vacation—getting in her mother's way and thinking, dreaming, about the boys she met. But all the boys fell back and dissolved into a single face that was not even a face, but an idea, a feeling, mixed up with the urgent insistent pounding of the music and the humid night air of July. Connie's mother kept dragging her back to the daylight by finding things for her to do or saying suddenly, "What's this about the Pettinger girl?"

And Connie would say nervously, "Oh, her. That dope." She always drew thick clear lines between herself and such girls, and her mother was simple and kindly enough to believe her. Her mother was so simple, Connie thought, that it was maybe cruel to fool her so much. Her mother went scuffling around the house in old bedroom slippers and complained over the telephone to one sister about the other, then the other called up and the two of them complained about the third one. If June's name was mentioned her mother's tone was approving, and if Connie's name was mentioned it was disapproving. This did not really mean she disliked Connie and actually Connie thought that her mother preferred her to June because she was prettier, but the two of them kept up a pretense of exasperation, a sense that they were tugging and struggling over something of little value to either of them. Sometimes, over coffee, they were almost friends, but something would come up—some vexation that was like a fly buzzing suddenly around their heads—and their faces went hard with contempt.

One Sunday Connie got up at eleven—none of them bothered with church—and washed her hair so that it could dry all day long, in the sun. Her parents and sister were going to a barbecue at an aunt's house and Connie said no, she wasn't interested, rolling her eyes, to let her mother know just what she thought of it. "Stay home alone then," her mother said sharply. Connie sat out back in a lawn chair and watched them drive away, her father quiet and bald, hunched around so that he could back the car out, her mother with a look that was still angry and not at all softened through the windshield, and in the back seat poor old June all dressed up as if she didn't know what a barbecue was, with all the running yelling kids and the flies. Connie sat with her eyes closed in the sun, dreaming and dazed with the warmth about her as if this were a kind of love, the caresses of love, and her mind slipped over onto thoughts of the boy she had been with the night before and how nice he had been, how sweet it always was, not the way someone like June would suppose but sweet, gentle, the way it was in movies and promised in songs; and when she opened her eyes she hardly knew where she was, the back yard ran off into weeds and a fenceline of trees and behind it the sky was perfectly blue and still. The asbestos "ranch house" that was now three years old startled her—it looked small. She shook her head as if to get awake.

It was too hot. She went inside the house and turned on the radio to drown out the quiet. She sat on the edge of her bed, barefoot, and listened for an hour and a half to a program called XYZ Sunday Jamboree, record after record of hard, fast, shrieking songs she sang along with, interspersed by exclamations from "Bobby King": "An' look here you girls at Napoleon's—Son and Charley want you to pay real close attention to this song coming up!"

And Connie paid close attention herself, bathed in a glow of slow-pulsed joy that seemed to rise mysteriously out of the music itself and lay languidly about the airless little room, breathed in and breathed out with each gentle rise and fall of her chest.

After a while she heard a car coming up the drive. She sat up at once,   15
startled, because it couldn't be her father so soon. The gravel kept crunching all the way in from the road—the driveway was long—and Connie ran to the window. It was a car she didn't know. It was an open jalopy, painted a bright gold that caught the sun opaquely. Her heart began to pound and her fingers snatched at her hair, checking it, and she whispered "Christ. Christ," wondering how bad she looked. The car came to a stop at the side door and the horn sounded four short taps as if this were a signal Connie knew.

She went into the kitchen and approached the door slowly, then hung out the screen door, her bare toes curling down off the step. There were two boys in the car and now she recognized the driver: he had shaggy, shabby black hair that looked crazy as a wig and he was grinning at her.

"I ain't late, am I?" he said.

"Who the hell do you think you are?" Connie said.

"Toldja I'd be out, didn't I?"

"I don't even know who you are."   20

She spoke sullenly, careful to show no interest or pleasure, and he spoke in a fast bright monotone. Connie looked past him to the other boy, taking her time. He had fair brown hair, with a lock that fell onto his forehead. His sideburns gave him a fierce, embarrassed look, but so far he hadn't even bothered to glance at her. Both boys wore sunglasses. The driver's glasses were metallic and mirrored everything in miniature.

"You wanta come for a ride?" he said.

Connie smirked and let her hair fall loose over one shoulder.

"Don'tcha like my car? New paint job," he said. "Hey."

"What?"   25

"You're cute."

She pretended to fidget, chasing flies away from the door.

"Don'tcha believe me, or what?" he said.

"Look, I don't even know who you are," Connie said in disgust.

"Hey, Ellie's got a radio, see. Mine's broke down." He lifted his friend's   30
arm and showed her the little transistor the boy was holding, and now Connie began to hear the music. It was the same program that was playing
inside the house.

"Bobby King?" she said.

"I listen to him all the time. I think he's great."

"He's kind of great," Connie said reluctantly.

"Listen, that guy's *great*. He knows where the action is."

Connie blushed a little, because the glasses made it impossible for her to   35
see just what this boy was looking at. She couldn't decide if she liked him or
if he was just a jerk, and so she dawdled in the doorway and wouldn't come
down or go back inside. She said, "What's all that stuff painted on your car?"

"Can'tcha read it?" He opened the door very carefully, as if he was afraid
it might fall off. He slid out just as carefully, planting his feet firmly on the
ground, the tiny metallic world in his glasses slowing down like gelatin hardening and in the midst of it Connie's bright green blouse. "This here is my
name, to begin with," he said. ARNOLD FRIEND was written in tar-like black
letters on the side, with a drawing of a round grinning face that reminded
Connie of a pumpkin, except it wore sunglasses. "I wanta introduce myself,
I'm Arnold Friend and that's my real name and I'm gonna be your friend,
honey, and inside the car's Ellie Oscar, he's kinda shy." Ellie brought his
transistor up to his shoulder and balanced it there. "Now these numbers are
a secret code, honey," Arnold Friend explained. He read off the numbers
33, 19, 17 and raised his eyebrows at her to see what she thought of that,
but she didn't think much of it. The left rear fender had been smashed and
around it was written, on the gleaming gold background: DONE BY CRAZY
WOMAN DRIVER. Connie had to laugh at that. Arnold Friend was pleased at
her laughter and looked up at her. "Around the other side's a lot more—you
wanta come and see them?"

"No."

"Why not?"

"Why should I?"

"Don'tcha wanta see what's on the car? Don'tcha wanta go for a ride?"   40

"I don't know."

"Why not?"

"I got things to do."

"Like what?"

"Things."   45

He laughed as if she had said something funny. He slapped his thighs. He was standing in a strange way, leaning back against the car as if he were balancing himself. He wasn't tall, only an inch or so taller than she would be if she came down to him. Connie liked the way he was dressed, which was the way all of them dressed: tight faded jeans stuffed into black, scuffed boots, a belt that pulled his waist in and showed how lean he was, and a white pull-over shirt that was a little soiled and showed the hard small muscles of his arms and shoulders. He looked as if he probably did hard work, lifting and carrying things. Even his neck looked muscular. And his face was a familiar face, somehow: the jaw and chin and cheeks slightly darkened, because he hadn't shaved for a day or two, and the nose long and hawk-like, sniffing as if she were a treat he was going to gobble up and it was all a joke.

"Connie, you ain't telling the truth. This is your day set aside for a ride with me and you know it," he said, still laughing. The way he straightened and recovered from his fit of laughing showed that it had been all fake.

"How do you know what my name is?" she said suspiciously.

"It's Connie."

"Maybe and maybe not."   50

"I know my Connie," he said, wagging his finger. Now she remembered him even better, back at the restaurant, and her cheeks warmed at the thought of how she sucked in her breath just at the moment she passed him—how she must have looked to him. And he had remembered her. "Ellie and I come out here especially for you," he said. "Ellie can sit in back. How about it?"

"Where?"

"Where what?"

"Where're we going?"

He looked at her. He took off the sunglasses and she saw how pale the   55 skin around his eyes was, like holes that were not in shadow but instead in light. His eyes were like chips of broken glass that catch the light in an amiable way. He smiled. It was as if the idea of going for a ride somewhere, to some place, was a new idea to him.

"Just for a ride, Connie sweetheart."

"I never said my name was Connie," she said.

"But I know what it is. I know your name and all about you, lots of things," Arnold Friend said. He had not moved yet but stood still leaning back against the side of his jalopy. "I took a special interest in you, such a pretty girl, and found out all about you like I know your parents and sister are gone somewheres and I know where and how long they're going to be gone, and I know who you were with last night, and your best friend's name is Betty. Right?"

He spoke in a simple lilting voice, exactly as if he were reciting the words to a song. His smile assured her that everything was fine. In the car Ellie turned up the volume on his radio and did not bother to look around at them.

"Ellie can sit in the back seat," Arnold Friend said. He indicated his 60 friend with a casual jerk of his chin, as if Ellie did not count and she could not bother with him.

"How'd you find out all that stuff?" Connie said.

"Listen: Betty Schultz and Tony Fitch and Jimmy Pettinger and Nancy Pettinger," he said, in a chant. "Raymond Stanley and Bob Hutter—"

"Do you know all those kids?"

"I know everybody."

"Look, you're kidding. You're not from around here." 65

"Sure."

"But—how come we never saw you before?"

"Sure you saw me before," he said. He looked down at his boots, as if he were a little offended. "You just don't remember."

"I guess I'd remember you," Connie said.

"Yeah?" He looked up at this, beaming. He was pleased. He began to 70 mark time with the music from Ellie's radio, tapping his fists lightly together. Connie looked away from his smile to the car, which was painted so bright it almost hurt her eyes to look at it. She looked at that name, ARNOLD FRIEND. And up at the front fender was an expression that was familiar—MAN THE FLYING SAUCERS. It was an expression kids had used the year before, but didn't use this year. She looked at it for a while as if the words meant something to her that she did not yet know.

"What're you thinking about? Huh?" Arnold Friend demanded. "Not worried about your hair blowing around in the car, are you?"

"No."

"Think I maybe can't drive good?"

"How do I know?"

"You're a hard girl to handle. How come?" he said. "Don't you know I'm 75 your friend? Didn't you see me put my sign in the air when you walked by?"

"What sign?"

"My sign." And he drew an X in the air, leaning out toward her. They were maybe ten feet apart. After his hand fell back to his side the X was still in the air, almost visible. Connie let the screen door close and stood perfectly still inside it, listening to the music from her radio and the boy's blend together. She stared at Arnold Friend. He stood there so stiffly relaxed, pretending to be relaxed, with one hand idly on the door handle as if he were keeping himself up that way and had no intention of ever moving again. She recognized most things about him, the tight jeans that showed his thighs and buttocks and the greasy leather boots and the tight shirt, and even that slippery friendly smile of his, that sleepy dreamy smile that all the boys used to get across ideas they didn't want to put into words. She recognized all this and also the singsong way he talked, slightly mocking, kidding, but serious and a little melancholy, and she recognized the way he tapped one fist against the other in homage to the perpetual music behind him. But all these things did not come together.

She said suddenly, "Hey, how old are you?"

His smile faded. She could see then that he wasn't a kid, he was much older—thirty, maybe more. At this knowledge her heart began to pound faster.

"That's a crazy thing to ask. Can'tcha see I'm your own age?"   80

"Like hell you are."

"Or maybe a coupla years older, I'm eighteen."

"Eighteen?" she said doubtfully.

He grinned to reassure her and lines appeared at the corners of his mouth. His teeth were big and white. He grinned so broadly his eyes became slits and she saw how thick the lashes were, thick and black as if painted with a black tar-like material. Then he seemed to become embarrassed, abruptly, and looked over his shoulder at Ellie. "*Him*, he's crazy," he said. "Ain't he a riot, he's a nut, a real character." Ellie was still listening to the music. His sunglasses told nothing about what he was thinking. He wore a bright orange shirt unbuttoned halfway to show his chest, which was a pale, bluish chest and not muscular like Arnold Friend's. His shirt collar was turned up all around and the very tips of the collar pointed out past his chin as if they were protecting him. He was pressing the transistor radio up against his ear and sat there in a kind of daze, right in the sun.

"He's kinda strange," Connie said.   85

"Hey, she says you're kinda strange! Kinda strange!" Arnold Friend cried. He pounded on the car to get Ellie's attention. Ellie turned for the first time and Connie saw with shock that he wasn't a kid either—he had a fair, hairless face, cheeks reddened slightly as if the veins grew too close to the surface of his skin, the face of a forty-year-old baby. Connie felt a wave of dizziness rise in her at this sight and she stared at him as if waiting for something to change the shock of the moment, make it all right again. Ellie's lips kept shaping words, mumbling along with the words blasting in his ear.

"Maybe you two better go away," Connie said faintly.

"What? How come?" Arnold Friend cried. "We come out here to take you for a ride. It's Sunday." He had the voice of the man on the radio now. It was the same voice, Connie thought. "Don'tcha know it's Sunday all day and honey, no matter who you were with last night today you're with Arnold Friend and don't you forget it!—Maybe you better step out here," he said, and this last was in a different voice. It was a little flatter, as if the heat was finally getting to him.

"No. I got things to do."

"Hey."   90

"You two better leave."

"We ain't leaving until you come with us."

"Like hell I am—"

"Connie, don't fool around with me. I mean—I mean, don't fool *around*," he said, shaking his head. He laughed incredulously. He placed his sunglasses on top of his head, carefully, as if he were indeed wearing a wig, and brought the stems down behind his ears. Connie stared at him, another wave of dizziness and fear rising in her so that for a moment he wasn't even in focus but was just a blur, standing there against his gold car, and she had the idea that he had driven up the driveway all right but had come from nowhere before that and belonged nowhere and that everything about him and even the music that was so familiar to her was only half real.

"If my father comes and sees you—"   95

"He ain't coming. He's at a barbecue."

"How do you know that?"

"Aunt Tillie's. Right now they're—uh—they're drinking. Sitting around," he said vaguely, squinting as if he were staring all the way to town and over to Aunt Tillie's back yard. Then the vision seemed to clear and he nodded energetically. "Yeah. Sitting around. There's your sister in a blue dress, huh? And high heels, the poor sad bitch—nothing like you, sweetheart! And your mother's helping some fat woman with the corn, they're cleaning the corn—husking the corn—"

"What fat woman?" Connie cried.

"How do I know what fat woman. I don't know every goddamn fat 100 woman in the world!" Arnold Friend laughed.

"Oh, that's Mrs. Hornby. . . . Who invited her?" Connie said. She felt a little light-headed. Her breath was coming quickly.

"She's too fat. I don't like them fat. I like them the way you are, honey," he said, smiling sleepily at her. They stared at each other for a while, through the screen door. He said softly, "Now what you're going to do is this: you're going to come out that door. You're going to sit up front with me and Ellie's going to sit in the back, the hell with Ellie, right? This isn't Ellie's date. You're my date. I'm your lover, honey."

"What? You're crazy—"

"Yes, I'm your lover. You don't know what that is but you will," he said. "I know that too. I know all about you. But look: it's real nice and you couldn't ask for nobody better than me, or more polite. I always keep my word. I'll tell you how it is, I'm always nice at first, the first time. I'll hold you so tight you won't think you have to try to get away or pretend anything because you'll know you can't. And I'll come inside you where it's all secret and you'll give in to me and you'll love me—"

"Shut up! You're crazy!" Connie said. She backed away from the door. 105 She put her hands against her ears as if she'd heard something terrible, something not meant for her. "People don't talk like that, you're crazy," she muttered. Her heart was almost too big now for her chest and its pumping made sweat break out all over her. She looked out to see Arnold Friend pause and then take a step toward the porch lurching. He almost fell. But, like a clever drunken man, he managed to catch his balance. He wobbled in his high boots and grabbed hold of one of the porch posts.

"Honey?" he said. "You still listening?"

"Get the hell out of here!"

"Be nice, honey. Listen."

"I'm going to call the police—"

He wobbled again and out of the side of his mouth came a fast spat   110
curse, an aside not meant for her to hear. But even this "Christ!" sounded forced. Then he began to smile again. She watched this smile come, awkward as if he were smiling from inside a mask. His whole face was a mask, she thought wildly, tanned down onto his throat but then running out as if he had plastered make-up on his face but had forgotten about his throat.

"Honey—? Listen, here's how it is. I always tell the truth and I promise you this: I ain't coming in that house after you."

"You better not! I'm going to call the police if you—if you don't—"

"Honey," he said, talking right through her voice, "honey, I'm not coming in there but you are coming out here. You know why?"

She was panting. The kitchen looked like a place she had never seen before, some room she had run inside but which wasn't good enough, wasn't going to help her. The kitchen window had never had a curtain, after three years, and there were dishes in the sink for her to do—probably—and if you ran your hand across the table you'd probably feel something sticky there.

"You listening, honey? Hey?"   115

"—going to call the police—"

"Soon as you touch the phone I don't need to keep my promise and can come inside. You won't want that."

She rushed forward and tried to lock the door. Her fingers were shaking. "But why lock it," Arnold Friend said gently, talking right into her face. "It's just a screen door. It's just nothing." One of his boots was at a strange angle, as if his foot wasn't in it. It pointed out to the left, bent at the ankle. "I mean, anybody can break through a screen door and glass and wood and iron or anything else if he needs to, anybody at all and specially Arnold Friend. If the place got lit up with a fire, honey, you'd come runnin' out into my arms, right into my arms an' safe at home—like you knew I was your lover and'd stopped fooling around, I don't mind a nice shy girl but I don't like no fooling around." Part of those words were spoken with a slight rhythmic lilt, and Connie somehow recognized them—the echo of a song from last year, about a girl rushing into her boy friend's arms and coming home again—

Connie stood barefoot on the linoleum floor, staring at him. "What do you want?" she whispered.

"I want you," he said.   120

"What?"

"Seen you that night and thought, that's the one, yes sir. I never needed to look any more."

"But my father's coming back. He's coming to get me. I had to wash my hair first—" She spoke in a dry, rapid voice, hardly raising it for him to hear.

"No, your daddy is not coming and yes, you had to wash your hair and you washed it for me. It's nice and shining and all for me. I thank you, sweetheart," he said, with a mock bow, but again he almost lost his balance. He had to bend and adjust his boots. Evidently his feet did not go all the way down; the boots must have been stuffed with something so that he would seem taller. Connie stared out at him and behind him at Ellie in the car, who seemed to be looking off toward Connie's right, into nothing. Then Ellie said, pulling the words out of the air one after another as if he were just discovering them, "You want me to pull out the phone?"

"Shut your mouth and keep it shut," Arnold Friend said, his face red 125 from bending over or maybe from embarrassment because Connie had seen his boots. "This ain't none of your business."

"What—what are you doing? What do you want?" Connie said. "If I call the police they'll get you, they'll arrest you—"

"Promise was not to come in unless you touch that phone, and I'll keep that promise," he said. He resumed his erect position and tried to force his shoulders back. He sounded like a hero in a movie, declaring something important. He spoke too loudly and it was as if he were speaking to someone behind Connie. "I ain't made plans for coming in that house where I don't belong but just for you to come out to me, the way you should. Don't you know who I am?"

"You're crazy," she whispered. She backed away from the door but did not want to go into another part of the house, as if this would give him permission to come through the door. "What do you . . . You're crazy, you. . . ."

"Huh? What're you saying, honey?"

Her eyes darted everywhere in the kitchen. She could not remember 130 what it was, this room.

"This is how it is, honey: you come out and we'll drive away, have a nice ride. But if you don't come out we're gonna wait till your people come home and then they're all going to get it."

"You want that telephone pulled out?" Ellie said. He held the radio away from his ear and grimaced, as if without the radio the air was too much for him.

"I toldja shut up, Ellie," Arnold Friend said, "you're deaf, get a hearing aid, right? Fix yourself up. This little girl's no trouble and's gonna be nice to me, so Ellie keep to yourself, this ain't your date—right? Don't hem in on me, don't hog, don't crush, don't bird dog, don't trail me," he said in a rapid, meaningless voice, as if he were running through all the expressions he'd learned but was no longer sure which one of them was in style, then rushing on to new ones, making them up with his eyes closed. "Don't crawl under my fence, don't squeeze in my chipmunk hole, don't sniff my glue, suck my popsicle, keep your own greasy fingers on yourself!" He shaded his eyes and peered in at Connie, who was backed against the kitchen table. "Don't mind him, honey, he's just a creep. He's a dope. Right? I'm the boy for you and like I said, you come out here nice like a lady and give me your hand, and nobody else gets hurt, I mean, your nice old bald-headed daddy and your mummy and your sister in her high heels. Because listen: why bring them in this?"

"Leave me alone," Connie whispered.

"Hey, you know that old woman down the road, the one with the chick- 135 ens and stuff—you know her?"

"She's dead!"

"Dead? What? You know her?" Arnold Friend said.

"She's dead—"

"Don't you like her?"

"She's dead—she's—she isn't here any more—" 140

"But don't you like her, I mean, you got something against her? Some grudge or something?" Then his voice dipped as if he were conscious of rudeness. He touched the sunglasses on top of his head as if to make sure they were still there. "Now you be a good girl."

"What are you going to do?"

"Just two things, or maybe three," Arnold Friend said. "But I promise it won't last long and you'll like me that way you get to like people you're close to. You will. It's all over for you here, so come on out. You don't want your people in any trouble, do you?"

She turned and bumped against a chair or something, hurting her leg, but she ran into the back room and picked up the telephone. Something roared in her ear, a tiny roaring, and she was so sick with fear that she could do nothing but listen to it—the telephone was clammy and very heavy and her fingers groped down to the dial but were too weak to touch it. She began to scream into the phone, into the roaring. She cried out, she cried for her mother, she felt her breath start jerking back and forth in her lungs as if it were something Arnold Friend was stabbing her with again and again with no tenderness. A noisy sorrowful wailing rose all about her and she was locked inside it the way she was locked inside this house.

After a while she could hear again. She was sitting on the floor, with her 145 wet back against the wall.

Arnold Friend was saying from the door, "That's a good girl. Put the phone back."

She kicked the phone away from her.

"No, honey. Pick it up. Put it back right."

She picked it up and put it back. The dial tone stopped.

"That's a good girl. Now you come outside." 150

She was hollow with what had been fear but what was now just an emptiness. All that screaming had blasted it out of her. She sat, one leg cramped under her, and deep inside her brain was something like a pinpoint of light that kept going and would not let her relax. She thought, I'm not going to see my mother again. She thought, I'm not going to sleep in my bed again. Her bright green blouse was all wet.

Arnold Friend said, in a gentle-loud voice that was like a stage voice, "The place where you came from ain't there any more, and where you had in mind to go is cancelled out. This place you are now—inside your daddy's house—is nothing but a cardboard box I can knock down any time. You know that and always did know it. You hear me?"

She thought, I have got to think. I have got to know what to do.

"We'll go out to a nice field, out in the country here where it smells so nice and it's sunny," Arnold Friend said. "I'll have my arms tight around you so you won't need to try to get away and I'll show you what love is like, what it does. The hell with this house! It looks solid all right," he said. He ran a fingernail down the screen and the noise did not make Connie shiver, as it would have the day before. "Now put your hand on your heart, honey. Feel that? That feels solid too but we know better. Be nice to me, be sweet like you can because what else is there for a girl like you but to be sweet and pretty and give in?—and get away before her people get back?"

She felt her pounding heart. Her hand seemed to enclose it. She thought 155 for the first time in her life that it was nothing that was hers, that belonged to her, but just a pounding, living thing inside this body that wasn't really hers either.

"You don't want them to get hurt," Arnold Friend went on. "Now get up, honey. Get up all by yourself."

She stood.

"Now turn this way. That's right. Come over to me—Ellie, put that away, didn't I tell you? You dope. You miserable creepy dope," Arnold Friend said. His words were not angry but only part of an incantation. The incantation was kindly. "Now come out through the kitchen to me honey and let's see a smile, try it, you're a brave sweet little girl and now they're eating corn and hotdogs cooked to bursting over an outdoor fire, and they don't know one thing about you and never did and honey you're better than them because not a one of them would have done this for you."

Connie felt the linoleum under her feet; it was cool. She brushed her hair back out of her eyes. Arnold Friend let go of the post tentatively and opened his arms for her, his elbows pointing in toward each other and his wrists limp, to show that this was an embarrassed embrace and a little mocking, he didn't want to make her self-conscious.

She put out her hand against the screen. She watched herself push the 160 door slowly open as if she were back safe somewhere in the other doorway, watching this body and this head of long hair moving out into the sunlight where Arnold Friend waited.

"My sweet little blue-eyed girl," he said in a half-sung sigh that had nothing to do with her brown eyes but was taken up just the same by the vast sunlit reaches of the land behind him and on all sides of him—so much land that Connie had never seen before and did not recognize except to know that she was going to it. ▪

The Reader's Presence

1. Oates describes Connie as having "two sides . . . , one for home and one for anywhere that was not home" (paragraph 5). What are the differences between the two sides? In what ways does Arnold Friend also seem to have two sides? How are these characters alike? How are they different?

2. How does the narrator mimic the tone of voice, speech, and idiomatic expressions of the characters? Give some examples of how this is done. How does the mimicry affect your reponse to the story? Explain whether it brings you closer to the characters or distances you from them.

3. **CONNECTIONS:** Read Oates's essay that follows. In what specific ways does reading this essay help you to understand better—and appreciate more—Oates's achievements as a writer of fiction? What specific aspects of the essay help you to understand Connie and, especially, her relationship with adults? What does Oates admire about the film *Smooth Talk*? What reservations does she express about the film? Characterize Oates's response to the contrast between the end of the story and the end of the film. Which does she prefer? Explain why.

The Writer at Work

JOYCE CAROL OATES on *Smooth Talk*: Short Story into Film

Francois Durand/Getty Images

Joyce Carol Oates's "Where Are You Going, Where Have You Been?" has been described as "a study in the peril that lurks beneath the surface of everyday life." In 1985, Joyce Chopra directed a film, *Smooth Talk*, with a screenplay by Tom Cole based on Oates's story. The film continues after the story ends, giving viewers an unexpectedly optimistic glimpse of Connie's fate. *Smooth Talk* won the Grand Jury Prize at the Sundance Film Festival in 1986. The following article appeared in the *New York Times* in 1986. Does Oates's original conception of the story fit with your expectations of what might happen to Connie? Does considering a happy ending—or at least an ending without tragedy—make a difference in your view of the story as a whole?

❝Some years ago in the American Southwest there surfaced a tabloid psychopath known as "The Pied Piper of Tucson." I have forgotten his name, but his specialty was the seduction and occasional murder of teenaged girls. He may or may not have had actual accomplices, but his bizarre activities were known among a circle of teenagers in the Tucson area; for some reason they kept his secret, deliberately did not inform parents or police. It was this fact, not the fact of the mass murderer himself, that struck me at the time. And this was a pre-Manson time, early or mid-1960s.

The Pied Piper mimicked teenagers in their talk, dress, and behavior, but he was not a teenager—he was a man in his early thirties. Rather short, he stuffed rags in his leather boots to give himself height. (And sometimes walked unsteadily as a consequence: did none among his admiring constituency notice?) He charmed his victims as charismatic psychopaths have always charmed their victims, to the bewilderment of others who fancy themselves free of all lunatic attractions. The Pied Piper of Tucson: a trashy dream, a tabloid archetype, sheer artifice, comedy, cartoon—surrounded, however improbably, and finally tragically by real people. You think that, if you look twice, he won't be there. But there he is.

I don't remember any longer where I first read about this Pied Piper—very likely in *Life* Magazine. I do recall deliberately not reading the full article because I didn't want to be distracted by too much detail. It was not after all the mass murderer himself who intrigued me, but the disturbing fact that a number of teenagers—from "good" families—aided and abetted his crimes. This is the sort of thing authorities and responsible citizens invariably call "inexplicable" because they can't find explanations for it. *They* would not have fallen under this maniac's spell, after all.

An early draft of my short story "Where Are You Going, Where Have You Been?"—from which the film *Smooth Talk* was adapted by Joyce Chopra and Tom Cole—had the rather too explicit title "Death and the Maiden." It was cast in a mode of fiction to which I am still partial—indeed, every third or fourth story of mine is probably in this mode—"realistic allegory," it might be called. It is Hawthornean,[1] romantic, shading into parable. Like the medieval German engraving from which my title was taken, the story was minutely detailed yet clearly an allegory of the fatal attractions of death (or the devil). An innocent young girl is seduced by way of her own vanity; she mistakes death for erotic romance of a particularly American/trashy sort.

In subsequent drafts the story changed its tone, its focus, its language, its title. It became "Where Are You Going, Where Have You Been?" Written at a time when the author was intrigued by the music of Bob Dylan, particularly the hauntingly elegiac song "It's All Over Now, Baby Blue," it was dedicated to Bob Dylan. The charismatic mass murderer drops into the background and his innocent victim, a fifteen-year-old, moves into the foreground. She becomes the true protagonist of the tale, courting and being courted by her fate, a self-styled 1950s pop figure, alternately absurd and winning. There is no suggestion in the published story that "Arnold Friend" has seduced and murdered other young girls, or even that he necessarily intends to murder Connie. Is his interest "merely" sexual? (Nor is there anything about the complicity of other teenagers. I saved that yet more provocative note for a current story, "Testimony.") Connie is shallow, vain, silly, hopeful, doomed—but capable nonetheless of an unexpected gesture

---

[1] *Hawthornean:* Similar in style to that of Nathaniel Hawthorne (1804–1864), the acclaimed American novelist and short story writer. (See page 432). —EDS.

of heroism at the story's end. Her smooth-talking seducer, who cannot lie, promises her that her family will be unharmed if she gives herself to him; and so she does. The story ends abruptly at the point of her "crossing over." We don't know the nature of her sacrifice, only that she is generous enough to make it.

In adapting a narrative so spare and thematically foreshortened as "Where Are You Going, Where Have You Been?" film director Joyce Chopra and screenwriter Tom Cole were required to do a good deal of filling in, expanding, inventing. Connie's story becomes lavishly, and lovingly, textured; she is not an allegorical figure so much as a "typical" teenaged girl (if Laura Dern, spectacularly good-looking, can be so defined). Joyce Chopra, who has done documentary films on contemporary teenage culture and, yet more authoritatively, has an adolescent daughter of her own, creates in *Smooth Talk* a vivid and absolutely believable world for Connie to inhabit. Or worlds: as in the original story there is Connie-at-home, and there is Connie-with-her-friends. Two fifteen-year-old girls, two finely honed styles, two voices, sometimes but not often overlapping. It is one of the marvelous visual features of the film that we *see* Connie and her friends transform themselves, once they are safely free of parental observation. The girls claim their true identities in the neighborhood shopping mall. What freedom, what joy!

Smooth Talk is, in a way, as much Connie's mother's story as it is Connie's; its center of gravity, its emotional nexus, is frequently with the mother — warmly and convincingly played by Mary Kay Place. (Though the mother's sexual jealousy of her daughter is slighted in the film.) Connie's ambiguous relationship with her affable, somewhat mysterious father (well played by Levon Helm) is an excellent touch: I had thought, subsequent to the story's publication, that I should have built up the father, suggesting, as subtly as I could, an attraction there paralleling the attraction Connie feels for her seducer, Arnold Friend. And Arnold Friend himself — "A. Friend" as he says — is played with appropriately overdone sexual swagger by Treat Williams, who is perfect for the part; and just the right age. We see that Arnold Friend isn't a teenager even as Connie, mesmerized by his presumed charm, does not seem to *see* him at all. What is so difficult to accomplish in prose — nudging the reader to look over the protagonist's shoulder, so to speak — is accomplished with enviable ease in film.

Treat Williams as Arnold Friend is supreme in his very awfulness, as, surely, the original Pied Piper of Tucson must have been. (Though no one involved in the film knew about the original source.) Mr. Williams flawlessly impersonates Arnold Friend as Arnold Friend impersonates — is it James Dean? James Dean regarding himself in mirrors, doing James Dean impersonations? That Connie's fate is so trashy is in fact her fate.

What is outstanding in Joyce Chopra's *Smooth Talk* is its visual freshness, its sense of motion and life; the attentive intelligence the director has brought to the semi-secret world of the American adolescent — shopping mall flirtations, drive-in restaurant romances, highway hitchhiking, the fascination of rock music played very, very loud. (James Taylor's music for the film is wonderfully appropriate. We hear it as Connie hears it; it is the music of her spiritual being.) Also outstanding, as I have indicated, and numerous critics have noted, are the acting performances. Laura Dern is so dazzlingly right as "my" Connie that I may come to think I modeled the fictitious girl on her, in the way that writers frequently delude themselves about motions of causality.

My difficulties with *Smooth Talk* have primarily to do with my chronic hesitation — about seeing/hearing work of mine abstracted from its contexture of language. All writers know that language is their subject; quirky word choices, patterns of rhythm, enigmatic pauses, punctuation marks. Where the quick scanner sees "quick" writing, the writer conceals nine tenths of the iceberg. Of course we all have "real" subjects, and we will fight to the death to defend those subjects, but beneath the tale-telling it is the tale-telling that grips us so very fiercely. The writer works in a single dimension, the director works in three. I assume they are professionals to their fingertips; authorities in their medium as I am an authority (if I am) in mine. I would fiercely defend the placement of a semicolon in one of my novels but I would probably have deferred in the end to Joyce Chopra's decision to reverse the story's conclusion, turn it upside down, in a sense, so

that the film ends not with death, not with a sleepwalker's crossing over to her fate, but upon a scene of reconciliation, rejuvenation.

A girl's loss of virginity, bittersweet but not necessarily tragic. Not today. A girl's coming-of-age that involves her succumbing to, but then rejecting, the "trashy dreams" of her pop teenage culture. "Where Are You Going, Where Have You Been?" defines itself as allegorical in its conclusion: Death and Death's chariot (a funky souped-up convertible) have come for the Maiden. Awakening is, in the story's final lines, moving out into the sunlight where Arnold Friend waits:

> "My sweet little blue-eyed girl," he said in a half-sung sigh that had nothing to do with [Connie's] brown eyes but was taken up just the same by the vast sunlit reaches of the land behind him and on all sides of him — so much land that Connie had never seen before and did not recognize except to know that she was going to it.

— a conclusion impossible to transfigure into film. **"**

Flannery O'Connor

A GOOD MAN IS HARD TO FIND

FLANNERY O'CONNOR (1925–1964) was born in Savannah, Georgia, the only child of devout Catholic parents. At the age of thirteen, O'Connor moved with her parents to her mother's ancestral home in Milledgeville, Georgia, after her father became terminally ill with lupus. In 1945 she received a BA degree from Georgia State College for Women, where she contributed regularly to the school's literary magazine. While earning an MFA from the Writers' Workshop at the University of Iowa, O'Connor published her first short story, "The Geranium," in 1946. After graduation, O'Connor was a resident at Yaddo, an artists' retreat in New York, and lived in New York City and in Connecticut until 1951, when she was diagnosed with lupus and returned to Georgia for treatment. She and her mother moved a short distance from Milledgeville to their family farm, Andalusia, where O'Connor lived until her death at the age of thirty-nine, raising peafowl, painting, and writing daily. During

> Flannery O'Connor spent the last part of her life on her family's farm in Georgia. She spent her time raising peafowl, painting, and writing.

her short yet distinguished life, O'Connor published two novels, *Wise Blood* (1952) and *The Violent Bear It Away* (1960), and a collection of short stories, *A Good Man Is Hard to Find* (1955), the title story of which appears here. A book of essays, *Mystery and Manners* (1969); two other short story collections, *Everything That Rises Must Converge* (1965) and *The Complete Stories of Flannery O'Connor* (1971), winner of a National Book Award; and a collection of letters, *The Habit of Being* (1979), were published posthumously.

THE GRANDMOTHER didn't want to go to Florida. She wanted to visit some of her connections in east Tennessee and she was seizing at every chance to change Bailey's mind. Bailey was the son she lived with, her only boy. He was sitting on the edge of his chair at the table, bent over the orange sports section of the *Journal*. "Now look here, Bailey," she said, "see here, read this," and she stood with one hand on her thin hip and the other rattling the newspaper at his bald head. "Here this fellow that calls himself The Misfit is aloose from the Federal Pen and headed toward Florida and you read here what it says he did to these people. Just you read it. I wouldn't take my children in any direction with a criminal like that aloose in it. I couldn't answer to my conscience if I did."

Bailey didn't look up from his reading so she wheeled around then and faced the children's mother, a young woman in slacks, whose face was as broad and innocent as a cabbage and was tied around with a green head-kerchief that had two points on the top like a rabbit's ears. She was sitting on the sofa, feeding the baby his apricots out of a jar. "The children have been to Florida before," the old lady said. "You all ought to take them somewhere else for a change so they would see different parts of the world and be broad. They never have been to east Tennessee."

The children's mother didn't seem to hear her but the eight-year-old boy, John Wesley, a stocky child with glasses, said, "If you don't want to go to Florida, why dontcha stay at home?" He and the little girl, June Star, were reading the funny papers on the floor.

"She wouldn't stay at home to be queen for a day," June Star said without raising her yellow head.

"Yes and what would you do if this fellow, The Misfit, caught you?" the   5
grandmother asked.

"I'd smack his face," John Wesley said.

"She wouldn't stay at home for a million bucks," June Star said. "Afraid she'd miss something. She has to go everywhere we go."

"All right, Miss," the grandmother said. "Just remember that the next time you want me to curl your hair."

June Star said her hair was naturally curly.

The next morning the grandmother was the first one in the car, ready to   10
go. She had her big black valise that looked like the head of a hippopotamus in one corner, and underneath it she was hiding a basket with Pitty Sing, the cat, in it. She didn't intend for the cat to be left alone in the house for three days because he would miss her too much and she was afraid he might brush against one of the gas burners and accidentally asphyxiate himself. Her son, Bailey, didn't like to arrive at a motel with a cat.

She sat in the middle of the back seat with John Wesley and June Star on either side of her. Bailey and the children's mother and the baby sat in front and they left Atlanta at eight forty-five with the mileage on the car at 55890. The grandmother wrote this down because she thought it would be interesting to say how many miles they had been when they got back. It took them twenty minutes to reach the outskirts of the city.

The old lady settled herself comfortably, removing her white cotton gloves and putting them up with her purse on the shelf in front of the back window. The children's mother still had on slacks and still had her head tied up in a green kerchief, but the grandmother had on a navy blue straw sailor hat with a bunch of white violets on the brim and a navy blue dress with a small white dot in the print. Her collars and cuffs were white organdy trimmed with lace and at her neckline she had pinned a purple spray of cloth violets containing a sachet. In case of an accident, anyone seeing her dead on the highway would know at once that she was a lady.

She said she thought it was going to be a good day for driving, neither too hot nor too cold, and she cautioned Bailey that the speed limit was

fifty-five miles an hour and that the patrolmen hid themselves behind billboards and small clumps of trees and sped out after you before you had a
chance to slow down. She pointed out interesting details of the scenery:
Stone Mountain; the blue granite that in some places came up to both sides
of the highway; the brilliant red clay banks slightly streaked with purple;
and the various crops that made rows of green lace-work on the ground. The
trees were full of silver-white sunlight and the meanest of them sparkled.
The children were reading comic magazines and their mother had gone
back to sleep.

"Let's go through Georgia fast so we won't have to look at it much,"
John Wesley said.

"If I were a little boy," said the grandmother, "I wouldn't talk about my   15
native state that way. Tennessee has the mountains and Georgia has the
hills."

"Tennessee is just a hillbilly dumping ground," John Wesley said, "and
Georgia is a lousy state too."

"You said it," June Star said.

"In my time," said the grandmother, folding her thin veined fingers,
"children were more respectful of their native states and their parents and
everything else. People did right then. Oh look at the cute little picka-
ninny!" she said and pointed to a Negro child standing in the door of a
shack. "Wouldn't that make a picture, now?" she asked and they all turned
and looked at the little Negro out of the back window. He waved.

"He didn't have any britches on," June Star said.

"He probably didn't have any," the grandmother explained. "Little nig-   20
gers in the country don't have things like we do. If I could paint, I'd paint
that picture," she said.

The children exchanged comic books.

The grandmother offered to hold the baby and the children's mother
passed him over the front seat to her. She set him on her knee and bounced
him and told him about the things they were passing. She rolled her eyes
and screwed up her mouth and stuck her leathery thin face into his smooth
bland one. Occasionally he gave her a faraway smile. They passed a large
cotton field with five or six graves fenced in the middle of it, like a small
island. "Look at the graveyard!" the grandmother said, pointing it out. "That
was the old family burying ground. That belonged to the plantation."

"Where's the plantation?" John Wesley asked.

"Gone With the Wind," said the grandmother. "Ha. Ha."

When the children finished all the comic books they had brought, they   25
opened the lunch and ate it. The grandmother ate a peanut butter sandwich
and an olive and would not let the children throw the box and the paper
napkins out the window. When there was nothing else to do they played a
game by choosing a cloud and making the other two guess what shape it
suggested. John Wesley took one the shape of a cow and June Star guessed
a cow and John Wesley said, no, an automobile, and June Star said he didn't
play fair, and they began to slap each other over the grandmother.

The grandmother said she would tell them a story if they would keep quiet. When she told a story, she rolled her eyes and waved her head and was very dramatic. She said once when she was a maiden lady she had been courted by a Mr. Edgar Atkins Teagarden from Jasper, Georgia. She said he was a very good-looking man and a gentleman and that he brought her a watermelon every Saturday afternoon with his initials cut in it, E. A. T. Well, one Saturday, she said, Mr. Teagarden brought the watermelon and there was nobody at home and he left it on the front porch and returned in his buggy to Jasper, but she never got the watermelon, she said, because a nigger boy ate it when he saw the initials, E. A. T.! This story tickled John Wesley's funny bone and he giggled and giggled but June Star didn't think it was any good. She said she wouldn't marry a man that just brought her a watermelon on Saturday. The grandmother said she would have done well to marry Mr. Teagarden because he was a gentleman and had bought Coca-Cola stock when it first came out and that he had died only a few years ago, a very wealthy man.

They stopped at The Tower for barbecued sandwiches. The Tower was a part stucco and part wood filling station and dance hall set in a clearing outside of Timothy. A fat man named Red Sammy Butts ran it and there were signs stuck here and there on the building and for miles up and down the highway saying, TRY RED SAMMY'S FAMOUS BARBECUE. NONE LIKE FAMOUS RED SAMMY'S! RED SAM! THE FAT BOY WITH THE HAPPY LAUGH! A VETERAN! RED SAMMY'S YOUR MAN!

Red Sammy was lying on the bare ground outside The Tower with his head under a truck while a gray monkey about a foot high, chained to a small chinaberry tree, chattered nearby. The monkey sprang back into the tree and got on the highest limb as soon as he saw the children jump out of the car and run toward him.

Inside, The Tower was a long dark room with a counter at one end and tables at the other and dancing space in the middle. They all sat down at a board table next to the nickelodeon and Red Sam's wife, a tall burnt-brown woman with hair and eyes lighter than her skin, came and took their order. The children's mother put a dime in the machine and played "The Tennessee Waltz," and the grandmother said that tune always made her want to dance. She asked Bailey if he would like to dance but he only glared at her. He didn't have a naturally sunny disposition like she did and trips made him nervous. The grandmother's brown eyes were very bright. She swayed her head from side to side and pretended she was dancing in her chair. June Star said play something she could tap to so the children's mother put in another dime and played a fast number and June Star stepped out onto the dance floor and did her tap routine.

"Ain't she cute?" Red Sam's wife said, leaning over the counter. "Would you like to come be my little girl?"

30

"No I certainly wouldn't," June Star said. "I wouldn't live in a broken-down place like this for a million bucks!" and she ran back to the table.

"Ain't she cute?" the woman repeated, stretching her mouth politely.

"Aren't you ashamed?" hissed the grandmother.

Red Sam came in and told his wife to quit lounging on the counter and hurry up with these people's order. His khaki trousers reached just to his hip bones and his stomach hung over them like a sack of meal swaying under his shirt. He came over and sat down at a table nearby and let out a combination sigh and yodel. "You can't win," he said. "You can't win," and he wiped his sweating red face off with a gray handkerchief. "These days you don't know who to trust," he said. "Ain't that the truth?"

"People are certainly not nice like they used to be," said the grandmother.   35

"Two fellers come in here last week," Red Sammy said, "driving a Chrysler. It was an old beat-up car, but it was a good one and these boys looked all right to me. Said they worked at the mill and you know I let them fellers charge the gas they bought? Now why did I do that?"

"Because you're a good man!" the grandmother said at once.

"Yes'm, I suppose so," Red Sam said as if he were struck with this answer.

His wife brought the orders, carrying the five plates all at once without a tray, two in each hand and one balanced on her arm. "It isn't a soul in this green world of God's that you can trust," she said. "And I don't count nobody out of that, not nobody," she repeated, looking at Red Sammy.

"Did you read about that criminal, The Misfit, that's escaped?" asked   40 the grandmother.

"I wouldn't be a bit surprised if he didn't attact this place right here," said the woman. "If he hears about it being here, I wouldn't be none surprised to see him. If he hears it's two cent in the cash register, I wouldn't be at all surprised if he . . ."

"That'll do," Red Sam said. "Go bring these people their Co'-Colas," and the woman went off to get the rest of the order.

"A good man is hard to find," Red Sammy said. "Everything is getting terrible. I remember the day you could go off and leave your screen door unlatched. Not no more."

He and the grandmother discussed better times. The old lady said that in her opinion Europe was entirely to blame for the way things were now. She said the way Europe acted you would think we were made of money and Red Sam said it was no use talking about it, she was exactly right. The children ran outside into the white sunlight and looked at the monkey in the lacy chinaberry tree. He was busy catching fleas on himself and biting each one carefully between his teeth as if it were a delicacy.

They drove off again into the hot afternoon. The grandmother took cat   45 naps and woke up every few minutes with her own snoring. Outside of Toombsboro she woke up and recalled an old plantation that she had visited in this neighborhood once when she was a young lady. She said the house had six white columns across the front and that there was an avenue of oaks leading up to it and two little wooden trellis arbors on either side in front where you sat down with your suitor after a stroll in the garden. She recalled exactly which road to turn off to get to it. She knew that Bailey would not be willing to lose any time looking at an old house, but the more she talked about it, the more she wanted to see it once again and find out if the little twin arbors were still standing. "There was a secret panel in this house," she said craftily, not telling the truth but wishing that she were, "and the story went that all the family silver was hidden in it when Sherman[1] came through but it was never found . . ."

"Hey!" John Wesley said. "Let's go see it! We'll find it! We'll poke all the woodwork and find it! Who lives there? Where do you turn off at? Hey Pop, can't we turn off there?"

"We never have seen a house with a secret panel!" June Star shrieked. "Let's go to the house with the secret panel! Hey Pop, can't we go see the house with the secret panel!"

"It's not far from here, I know," the grandmother said. "It wouldn't take over twenty minutes."

Bailey was looking straight ahead. His jaw was as rigid as a horseshoe. "No," he said.

The children began to yell and scream that they wanted to see the house   50
with the secret panel. John Wesley kicked the back of the front seat and June Star hung over her mother's shoulder and whined desperately into her ear that they never had any fun even on their vacation, that they could never do what THEY wanted to do. The baby began to scream and John Wesley kicked the back of the seat so hard that his father could feel the blows in his kidney.

"All right!" he shouted and drew the car to a stop at the side of the road. "Will you all shut up? Will you all just shut up for one second? If you don't shut up, we won't go anywhere."

"It would be very educational for them," the grandmother murmured.

"All right," Bailey said, "but get this: this is the only time we're going to stop for anything like this. This is the one and only time."

"The dirt road that you have to turn down is about a mile back," the grandmother directed. "I marked it when we passed."

"A dirt road," Bailey groaned.   55

After they had turned around and were headed toward the dirt road, the grandmother recalled other points about the house, the beautiful glass over the front doorway and the candle-lamp in the hall. John Wesley said that the secret panel was probably in the fireplace.

"You can't go inside this house," Bailey said. "You don't know who lives there."

"While you all talk to the people in front, I'll run around behind and get in a window," John Wesley suggested.

"We'll all stay in the car," his mother said.

They turned onto the dirt road and the car raced roughly along in a swirl   60
of pink dust. The grandmother recalled the times when there were no paved roads and thirty miles was a day's journey. The dirt road was hilly and there

---

[1] **Sherman:** General William Tecumseh Sherman (1820–1891) was the Union general who captured Atlanta in 1864. —EDS.

were sudden washes in it and sharp curves on dangerous embankments. All at once they would be on a hill, looking down over the blue tops of trees for miles around, then the next minute, they would be in a red depression with the dust-coated trees looking down on them.

"This place had better turn up in a minute," Bailey said, "or I'm going to turn around."

The road looked as if no one had traveled on it in months.

"It's not much farther," the grandmother said and just as she said it, a horrible thought came to her. The thought was so embarrassing that she turned red in the face and her eyes dilated and her feet jumped up, upsetting her valise in the corner. The instant the valise moved, the newspaper top she had over the basket under it rose with a snarl and Pitty Sing, the cat, sprang onto Bailey's shoulder.

The children were thrown to the floor and their mother, clutching the baby, was thrown out the door onto the ground; the old lady was thrown into the front seat. The car turned over once and landed right-side-up in a gulch off the side of the road. Bailey remained in the driver's seat with the cat—gray-striped with a broad white face and an orange nose—clinging to his neck like a caterpillar.

As soon as the children saw they could move their arms and legs, they scrambled out of the car, shouting, "We've had an ACCIDENT!" The grandmother was curled up under the dashboard, hoping she was injured so that Bailey's wrath would not come down on her all at once. The horrible thought she had had before the accident was that the house she had remembered so vividly was not in Georgia but in Tennessee.   65

Bailey removed the cat from his neck with both hands and flung it out the window against the side of a pine tree. Then he got out of the car and started looking for the children's mother. She was sitting against the side of the red gutted ditch, holding the screaming baby, but she only had a cut down her face and a broken shoulder. "We've had an ACCIDENT!" the children screamed in a frenzy of delight.

"But nobody's killed," June Star said with disappointment as the grandmother limped out of the car, her hat still pinned to her head but the broken front brim standing up at a jaunty angle and the violet spray hanging off the side. They all sat down in the ditch, except the children, to recover from the shock. They were all shaking.

"Maybe a car will come along," said the children's mother hoarsely.

"I believe I have injured an organ," said the grandmother, pressing her side, but no one answered her. Bailey's teeth were clattering. He had on a yellow sport shirt with bright blue parrots designed in it and his face was as yellow as the shirt. The grandmother decided that she would not mention that the house was in Tennessee.

The road was about ten feet above and they could see only the tops of   70 the trees on the other side of it. Behind the ditch they were sitting in there were more woods, tall and dark and deep. In a few minutes they saw a car some distance away on top of a hill, coming slowly as if the occupants were watching them. The grandmother stood up and waved both arms dramatically to attract their attention. The car continued to come on slowly, disappeared around a bend and appeared again, moving even slower, on top of the hill they had gone over. It was a big black battered hearselike automobile. There were three men in it.

It came to a stop just over them and for some minutes, the driver looked down with a steady expressionless gaze to where they were sitting, and didn't speak. Then he turned his head and muttered something to the other two and they got out. One was a fat boy in black trousers and a red sweat shirt with a silver stallion embossed on the front of it. He moved around on the right side of them and stood staring, his mouth partly open in a kind of loose grin. The other had on khaki pants and a blue striped coat and a gray hat pulled down very low, hiding most of his face. He came around slowly on the left side. Neither spoke.

The driver got out of the car and stood by the side of it, looking down at them. He was an older man than the other two. His hair was just beginning to gray and he wore silver-rimmed spectacles that gave him a scholarly look. He had a long creased face and didn't have on any shirt or undershirt. He had on blue jeans that were too tight for him and was holding a black hat and a gun. The two boys also had guns.

"We've had an ACCIDENT!" the children screamed.

The grandmother had the peculiar feeling that the bespectacled man was someone she knew. His face was as familiar to her as if she had known him all her life but she could not recall who he was. He moved away from the car and began to come down the embankment, placing his feet carefully so that he wouldn't slip. He had on tan and white shoes and no socks, and his ankles were red and thin. "Good afternoon," he said. "I see you all had you a little spill."

"We turned over twice!" said the grandmother.   75

"Oncet," he corrected. "We seen it happen. Try their car and see will it run, Hiram," he said quietly to the boy with the gray hat.

"What you got that gun for?" John Wesley asked. "Whatcha gonna do with that gun?"

"Lady," the man said to the children's mother, "would you mind calling them children to sit down by you? Children make me nervous. I want all you all to sit down right together there where you're at."

"What are you telling US what to do for?" June Star asked.

Behind them the line of woods gaped like a dark open mouth. "Come   80 here," said their mother.

"Look here now," Bailey began suddenly, "we're in a predicament! We're in . . ."

The grandmother shrieked. She scrambled to her feet and stood staring. "You're The Misfit!" she said. "I recognized you at once!"

"Yes'm," the man said, smiling slightly as if he were pleased in spite of himself to be known, "but it would have been better for all of you, lady, if you hadn't of reckernized me."

Bailey turned his head sharply and said something to his mother that shocked even the children. The old lady began to cry and The Misfit reddened.

"Lady," he said, "don't you get upset. Sometimes a man says things he don't mean. I don't reckon he meant to talk to you thataway." 85

"You wouldn't shoot a lady, would you?" the grandmother said and removed a clean handkerchief from her cuff and began to slap at her eyes with it.

The Misfit pointed the toe of his shoe into the ground and made a little hole and then covered it up again. "I would hate to have to," he said.

"Listen," the grandmother almost screamed, "I know you're a good man. You don't look a bit like you have common blood. I know you must come from nice people!"

"Yes ma'am," he said, "finest people in the world." When he smiled he showed a row of strong white teeth. "God never made a finer woman than my mother and my daddy's heart was pure gold," he said. The boy with the red sweat shirt had come around behind them and was standing with his gun at his hip. The Misfit squatted down on the ground. "Watch them children, Bobby Lee," he said. "You know they make me nervous." He looked at the six of them huddled together in front of him and he seemed to be embarrassed as if he couldn't think of anything to say. "Ain't a cloud in the sky," he remarked, looking up at it. "Don't see no sun but don't see no cloud neither."

"Yes, it's a beautiful day," said the grandmother. "Listen," she said, 90 "you shouldn't call yourself The Misfit because I know you're a good man at heart. I can just look at you and tell."

"Hush!" Bailey yelled. "Hush! Everybody shut up and let me handle this!" He was squatting in the position of a runner about to sprint forward but he didn't move.

"I pre-chate that, lady," The Misfit said and drew a little circle in the ground with the butt of his gun.

"It'll take a half a hour to fix this here car," Hiram called, looking over the raised hood of it.

"Well, first you and Bobby Lee get him and that little boy to step over yonder with you," The Misfit said, pointing to Bailey and John Wesley. "The boys want to ask you something," he said to Bailey. "Would you mind stepping back in them woods there with them?"

"Listen," Bailey began, "we're in a terrible predicament! Nobody real- 95 izes what this is," and his voice cracked. His eyes were as blue and intense as the parrots in his shirt and he remained perfectly still.

The grandmother reached up to adjust her hat brim as if she were going to the woods with him but it came off in her hand. She stood staring at it and after a second she let it fall on the ground. Hiram pulled Bailey up by the arm as if he were assisting an old man. John Wesley caught hold of his father's hand and Bobby Lee followed. They went off toward the woods and just as they reached the dark edge, Bailey turned and supporting himself against a gray naked pine trunk, he shouted, "I'll be back in a minute, Mamma, wait on me!"

"Come back this instant!" his mother shrilled but they all disappeared into the woods.

"Bailey Boy!" the grandmother called in a tragic voice but she found she was looking at The Misfit squatting on the ground in front of her. "I just know you're a good man," she said desperately. "You're not a bit common!"

"Nome, I ain't a good man," The Misfit said after a second as if he had considered her statement carefully, "but I ain't the worst in the world neither. My daddy said I was a different breed of dog from my brothers and sisters. 'You know,' Daddy said, 'it's some that can live their whole life out without asking about it and it's others has to know why it is, and this boy is one of the latters. He's going to be into everything!'" He put on his black hat and looked up suddenly and then away deep into the woods as if he were embarrassed again. "I'm sorry I don't have on a shirt before you ladies," he said, hunching his shoulders slightly. "We buried our clothes that we had on when we escaped and we're just making do until we can get better. We borrowed these from some folks we met," he explained.

"That's perfectly all right," the grandmother said. "Maybe Bailey has an   100
extra shirt in his suitcase."

"I'll look and see terrectly," The Misfit said.

"Where are they taking him?" the children's mother screamed.

"Daddy was a card himself," The Misfit said. "You couldn't put anything over on him. He never got in trouble with the Authorities though. Just had the knack of handling them."

"You could be honest too if you'd only try," said the grandmother. "Think how wonderful it would be to settle down and live a comfortable life and not have to think about somebody chasing you all the time."

The Misfit kept scratching in the ground with the butt of his gun as   105
if he were thinking about it. "Yes'm, somebody is always after you," he murmured.

The grandmother noticed how thin his shoulder blades were just behind his hat because she was standing up looking down on him. "Do you ever pray?" she asked.

He shook his head. All she saw was the black hat wiggle between his shoulder blades. "Nome," he said.

There was a pistol shot from the woods, followed closely by another. Then silence. The old lady's head jerked around. She could hear the wind move through the tree tops like a long satisfied insuck of breath. "Bailey Boy!" she called.

"I was a gospel singer for a while," The Misfit said. "I been most everything. Been in the arm service, both land and sea, at home and abroad, been twict married, been an undertaker, been with the railroads, plowed Mother Earth, been in a tornado, seen a man burnt alive oncet," and looked up at the children's mother and the little girl who were sitting close together, their faces white and their eyes glassy; "I even seen a woman flogged," he said.

"Pray, pray," the grandmother began, "pray, pray . . ."   110

"I never was a bad boy that I remember of," The Misfit said in an almost dreamy voice, "but somewheres along the line I done something wrong and got sent to the penitentiary. I was buried alive," and he looked up and held her attention to him by a steady stare.

"That's when you should have started to pray," she said. "What did you do to get sent to the penitentiary that first time?"

"Turn to the right, it was a wall," The Misfit said, looking up again at the cloudless sky. "Turn to the left, it was a wall. Look up it was a ceiling, look down it was a floor. I forget what I done, lady. I set there and set there, trying to remember what it was I done and I ain't recalled it to this day. Oncet in a while, I would think it was coming to me, but it never come."

"Maybe they put you in by mistake," the old lady said vaguely.

"Nome," he said. "It wasn't no mistake. They had the papers on me."   115

"You must have stolen something," she said.

The Misfit sneered slightly. "Nobody had nothing I wanted," he said. "It was a head-doctor at the penitentiary said what I had done was kill my daddy but I known that for a lie. My daddy died in nineteen ought nineteen of the epidemic flu and I never had a thing to do with it. He was buried in the Mount Hopewell Baptist churchyard and you can go there and see for yourself."

"If you would pray," the old lady said, "Jesus would help you."

"That's right," The Misfit said.

"Well then, why don't you pray?" she asked, trembling with delight 120 suddenly.

"I don't want no hep," he said. "I'm doing all right by myself."

Bobby Lee and Hiram came ambling back from the woods. Bobby Lee was dragging a yellow shirt with bright blue parrots in it.

"Throw me that shirt, Bobby Lee," The Misfit said. The shirt came flying at him and landed on his shoulder and he put it on. The grandmother couldn't name what the shirt reminded her of. "No, lady," The Misfit said while he was buttoning it up, "I found out the crime don't matter. You can do one thing or you can do another, kill a man or take a tire off his car, because sooner or later you're going to forget what it was you done and just be punished for it."

The children's mother had begun to make heaving noises as if she couldn't get her breath. "Lady," he asked, "would you and that little girl like to step off yonder with Bobby Lee and Hiram and join your husband?"

"Yes, thank you," the mother said faintly. Her left arm dangled help- 125 lessly and she was holding the baby, who had gone to sleep, in the other. "Hep that lady up, Hiram," The Misfit said as she struggled to climb out of the ditch, "and Bobby Lee, you hold onto that little girl's hand."

"I don't want to hold hands with him," June Star said. "He reminds me of a pig."

The fat boy blushed and laughed and caught her by the arm and pulled her off into the woods after Hiram and her mother.

Alone with The Misfit, the grandmother found that she had lost her voice. There was not a cloud in the sky nor any sun. There was nothing around her but woods. She wanted to tell him that he must pray. She opened and closed her mouth several times before anything came out. Finally she found herself saying, "Jesus, Jesus," meaning, Jesus will help you, but the way she was saying it, it sounded as if she might be cursing.

"Yes'm," the Misfit said as if he agreed. "Jesus thown everything off balance. It was the same case with Him as with me except He hadn't committed any crime and they could prove I had committed one because they had the papers on me. Of course," he said, "they never shown me my papers. That's why I sign myself now. I said long ago, you get you a signature and sign everything you do and keep a copy of it. Then you'll know what you done and you can hold up the crime to the punishment and see do they match and in the end you'll have something to prove you ain't been treated right. I call myself The Misfit," he said, "because I can't make what all I done wrong fit what all I gone through in punishment."

There was a piercing scream from the woods, followed closely by a pis- 130 tol report. "Does it seem right to you, lady, that one is punished a heap and another ain't punished at all?"

"Jesus!" the old lady cried. "You've got good blood! I know you wouldn't shoot a lady! I know you come from nice people! Pray! Jesus, you ought not to shoot a lady. I'll give you all the money I've got!"

"Lady," The Misfit said, looking beyond her far into the woods, "there never was a body that give the undertaker a tip."

There were two more pistol reports and the grandmother raised her head like a parched old turkey hen crying for water and called, "Bailey Boy, Bailey Boy!" as if her heart would break.

"Jesus was the only One that ever raised the dead." The Misfit continued, "and He shouldn't have done it. He thown everything off balance. If He did what He said, then it's nothing for you to do but thow away everything and follow Him, and if He didn't, then it's nothing for you to do but enjoy the few minutes you got left the best way you can—by killing somebody or burning down his house or doing some other meanness to him. No pleasure but meanness," he said and his voice had become almost a snarl.

"Maybe He didn't raise the dead," the old lady mumbled, not knowing 135 what she was saying and feeling so dizzy that she sank down in the ditch with her legs twisted under her.

"I wasn't there so I can't say He didn't," The Misfit said. "I wisht I had of been there," he said, hitting the ground with his fist. "It ain't right I wasn't there because if I had of been there I would of known. Listen lady," he said in a high voice, "if I had of been there I would of known and I wouldn't be like I am now." His voice seemed about to crack and the grandmother's head cleared for an instant. She saw the man's face twisted close to her own as if he was going to cry and she murmured, "Why you're one of my babies.

You're one of my own children!" She reached out and touched him on the shoulder. The Misfit sprang back as if a snake had bitten him and shot her three times through the chest. Then he put his gun down on the ground and took off his glasses and began to clean them.

Hiram and Bobby Lee returned from the woods and stood over the ditch, looking down at the grandmother who half sat and half lay in a puddle of blood with her legs crossed under her like a child's and her face smiling up at the cloudless sky.

Without his glasses, The Misfit's eyes were red-rimmed and pale and defenseless-looking. "Take her off and thow her where you thown the others," he said, picking up the cat that was rubbing itself against his leg.

"She was a talker, wasn't she?" Bobby Lee said, sliding down the ditch with a yodel.

"She would of been a good woman," The Misfit said, "if it had been 140 somebody there to shoot her every minute of her life."

"Some fun!" Bobby Lee said.

"Shut up, Bobby Lee," The Misfit said. "It's no real pleasure in life." ◉

The Reader's Presence

1. The grandmother is described only indirectly, through her words, actions, and interactions with others. Reread paragraphs 1–9. How does the grandmother appear to see herself? How do you see her? In what ways does the writer's "voice" influence your impression of the character?

2. What might the Misfit figure symbolize in relation to the grandmother and her family? Does his nickname have any significance? What sort of tone does O'Connor establish in the Misfit encounter? Is it eerie, comedic, or somewhere between? Imagine the story as presented in a different tone; how would the story differ? What does O'Connor's position on the characters and events appear to be? What specific evidence (words and phrases) in her approach leads you to your conclusion? (See also O'Connor's commentary on the story.)

3. **CONNECTIONS:** In "The Writer at Work" that follows, O'Connor discusses the crucial action or gesture that makes a story work. "[I]t is probably some action, some gesture of a character that is unlike any other in the story, one which indicates where the real heart of the story lies. . . . It would be a gesture which somehow made contact with mystery" (paragraph 12). O'Connor locates this key moment in paragraph 136 of "A Good Man Is Hard to Find," when "the grandmother's head cleared for an instant." Locate the crucial gesture or action in Sherman Alexie's story "This Is What It Means to Say Phoenix, Arizona" (page 803). Is O'Connor's description of such a gesture and its key role in "making a story hold up" applicable to stories by writers other than herself? Is "mystery" as important to Alexie as it is to O'Connor?

The Writer at Work

FLANNERY O'CONNOR on Her Own Work

Hulton Archive/Getty Images

Flannery O'Connor's "A Good Man Is Hard to Find" ranks as one of American fiction's most durable short stories. It has been reprinted and analyzed in critical periodicals hundreds of times since it first appeared in 1953. Ten years after its first publication and shortly before her untimely death, O'Connor was invited to read the story at Hollins College (now Hollins University) in Virginia, where she made the following remarks. Her comments on the story were then included in a collection of nonfiction published by her editor in 1969 under the very appropriate title "Mystery and Manners." As you consider the story, you may want to focus on these terms: *mystery* and *manners*. How does each word describe an important aspect of the story? How are they interrelated? You should also consider the story from the perspective O'Connor herself provides in the following selection. Do you think her comments on her own story are critically persuasive? Did you come away from the story with a different sense of its significance? Do you think that what an author says about his or her own work must always be the final word?

❝ Last fall I received a letter from a student who said she would be "graciously appreciative" if I would tell her "just what enlightenment" I expected her to get from each of my stories. I suspect she had a paper to write. I wrote her back to forget about the enlightenment and just try to enjoy them. I knew that was the most unsatisfactory answer I could have given because, of course, she didn't want to enjoy them, she just wanted to figure them out.

In most English classes the short story has become a kind of literary specimen to be dissected. Every time a story of mine appears in a Freshman anthology, I have a vision of it, with its little organs laid open, like a frog in a bottle.

I realize that a certain amount of this what-is-the-significance has to go on, but I think something has gone wrong in the process when, for so many students, the story becomes simply a problem to be solved, something which you evaporate to get Instant Enlightenment.

A story really isn't any good unless it successfully resists paraphrase, unless it hangs on and expands in the mind. Properly, you analyze to enjoy, but it's equally true that to analyze with any discrimination, you have to have enjoyed already, and I think that the best reason to hear a story read is that it should stimulate that primary enjoyment.

I don't have any pretensions to being an Aeschylus or Sophocles and providing you in this story with a cathartic experience out of your mythic background, though this story I'm going to read certainly calls up a good deal of the South's mythic background, and it should elicit from you a degree of pity and terror, even though its way of being serious is a comic one. I do think, though, that like the Greeks you should know what is going to happen in this story so that any element of suspense in it will be transferred from its surface to its interior.

I would be most happy if you had already read it, happier still if you knew it well, but since experience has taught me to keep my expectations along these lines modest, I'll tell you that this is the story of a family of six which, on its way driving to Florida, gets wiped out by an escaped convict who calls himself the Misfit. The family is made up of the Grandmother and her son, Bailey, and his children, John Wesley and June Star and the baby, and there is also the cat and the children's mother. The cat is named Pitty Sing, and the Grandmother is taking him with them, hidden in a basket.

Now I think it behooves me to try to establish with you the basis on which reason operates in this story. Much of my fiction takes its character from a reasonable use of the unreasonable, though the reasonableness of my use of it may not always be apparent. The assumptions that underlie this use of it, however, are those of the central Christian mysteries. These are assumptions to which a large part of the modern audience takes exception. About this I can only say that there are perhaps other ways than my own in which this story could be read, but none other by which it could have been written. Belief, in my own case anyway, is the engine that makes perception operate.

The heroine of this story, the Grandmother, is in the most significant position life offers the Christian. She is facing death. And to all appearances she, like the rest of us, is not too well prepared for it. She would like to see the event postponed. Indefinitely.

I've talked to a number of teachers who use this story in class and who tell their students that the Grandmother is evil, that in fact, she's a witch, even down to the cat. One of these teachers told me that his students, and particularly his Southern students, resisted this interpretation with a certain bemused vigor, and he didn't understand why. I had to tell him that they resisted it because they all had grandmothers or great-aunts just like her at home, and they knew, from personal experience, that the old lady lacked comprehension, but that she had a good heart. The Southerner is usually tolerant of those weaknesses that proceed from innocence, and he knows that a taste for self-preservation can be readily combined with the missionary spirit.

This same teacher was telling his students that morally the Misfit was several cuts above the Grandmother. He had a really sentimental attachment to the Misfit. But then a prophet gone wrong is almost always more interesting than your grandmother, and you have to let people take their pleasures where they find them.

It is true that the old lady is a hypocritical old soul; her wits are no match for the Misfit's, nor is her capacity for grace equal to his; yet I think the unprejudiced reader will feel that the Grandmother has a special kind of triumph in this story which instinctively we do not allow to someone altogether bad.

I often ask myself what makes a story work, and what makes it hold up as a story, and I have decided that it is probably some action, some gesture of a character that is unlike any other in the story, one which indicates where the real heart of the story lies. This would have to be an action or a gesture which was both totally right and totally unexpected; it would have to be one that was both in character and beyond character; it would have to suggest both the world and eternity. The action or gesture I'm talking about would have to be on the anagogical level, that is, the level which has to do with the Divine life and our participation in it.

It would be a gesture that transcended any neat allegory that might have been intended or any pat moral categories a reader could make. It would be a gesture which somehow made contact with mystery.

There is a point in this story where such a gesture occurs. The Grandmother is at last alone, facing the Misfit. Her head clears for an instant and she realizes, even in her limited way, that she is responsible for the man before her and joined to him by ties of kinship which have their roots deep in the mystery she has been merely prattling about so far. And at this point, she does the right thing, she makes the right gesture.

I find that students are often puzzled by what she says and does here, but I think myself that if I took out this gesture and what she says with it, I would have no story. What was left would not be worth your attention. Our age not only does not have a very sharp eye for the almost imperceptible intrusions of grace, it no longer has much feeling for the nature of the violences which precede and follow them. The devil's greatest wile, Baudelaire has said, is to convince us that he does not exist.

I suppose the reasons for the use of so much violence in modern fiction will differ with each writer who uses it, but in my own stories I have found that violence is strangely capable of returning my characters to reality and preparing them to accept their moment of grace. Their heads are so hard that almost nothing else will do the work. This idea, that reality is something to which we must be returned at considerable cost, is one which is seldom understood by the casual reader, but it is one which is implicit in the Christian view of the world.

I don't want to equate the Misfit with the devil. I prefer to think that, however unlikely this may seem, the old lady's gesture, like the mustard-seed, will grow to be a great crow-filled tree in the Misfit's heart, and will be enough of a pain to him there to turn him into the prophet he was meant to become. But that's another story.

This story has been called grotesque, but I prefer to call it literal. A good story is literal in the same sense that a child's drawing is literal. When a child draws, he doesn't intend to distort but to set down exactly what he sees, and as his gaze is direct, he sees the lines that create motion. Now the lines of motion that interest the writer are usually invisible. They are lines of spiritual motion. And in this story you should be on the lookout for such things as the action of grace in the Grandmother's soul, and not for the dead bodies.

We hear many complaints about the prevalence of violence in modern fiction, and it is always assumed that this violence is a bad thing and meant to be an end in itself. With the serious writer, violence is never an end in itself. It is the extreme situation that best reveals what we are essentially, and I believe these are times when writers are more interested in what we are essentially than in the tenor of our daily lives. Violence is a force which can be used for good or evil, and among other things taken by it is the kingdom of heaven. But regardless of what can be taken by it, the man in the violent situation reveals those qualities least dispensable in his personality, those qualities which are all he will have to take into eternity with him; and since the characters in this story are all on the verge of eternity, it is appropriate to think of what they take with them. In any case, I hope that if you consider these points in connection with the story, you will come to see it as something more than an account of a family murdered on the way to Florida. **"**

The Critic at Work

WILLIAM CAVERLEE on "The Best Southern Short Story Ever?"

Brian R. Fassett

For decades, "A Good Man Is Hard to Find" has been considered one of the greatest American short stories and it has been included in nearly every short fiction anthology since it first appeared in *Partisan Review* in 1953. Given its enigmatic quality and its eerie combination of humor and horror, the story has been the subject of much serious criticism over the years. The following essay by William Caverlee, a contributing writer to the Southern magazine *Oxford American*, is one of the latest attempts to come to terms with the story's mystery. You might compare Caverlee's understanding of the story to O'Connor's in the preceding selection. How do you think O'Connor might respond to Caverlee's interpretation and assessment?

❝ Without ever leaving her hideout in Milledgeville, Georgia, Flannery O'Connor knew all there was to know about the two-lane, dirt and blacktop Southern roads of the 1950s — with their junkyards and tourist courts, gravel pits and pine trees that pressed at the edges of the road. She knew the slogans of the Burma Shave signs, knew the names of barbecue joints and the chicken baskets on their menus. She also knew a backwoods American cadence and vocabulary you'd think was limited to cops, truckers, runaway teens, and the patrons of the Teardrop Inn, where at midnight somebody could always be counted on to go out to a pickup truck and come back with a shotgun. She was a virtuoso mimic, and she assimilated whole populations of American sounds and voices, and then offered them back to us from time to time in her small fictional detonations, one of which she named, in 1953, "A Good Man Is Hard to Find."

The plot is sewn together through a devious coincidence: While planning a car trip to Florida, a Georgia family (grandmother, son, wife, and three children)

learns that an escaped criminal named The Misfit is roaming about the region. The family embarks anyway, stops for lunch at a country restaurant, has a car accident, and is slaughtered by The Misfit and his two cohorts.

In a characteristic sleight of hand, O'Connor decided to give the story to the grandmother, a pint-sized heroine for this tale of mayhem and death. The grandmother (that's her name in the story) appears in every scene and speaks nearly all of the dialogue, rivaled only by the two menacing, boisterous older children and an unexpected visitor in the final scene. She takes control of things from the outset — wheedling, conniving, whining, and manipulating the entire family to go along with her plans. She's a self-pitying narcissist, a megalomaniacal, self-delighting tyrant of her middle-class family. She utters clichés day and night and considers herself, in the end, always a proper lady:

> I wouldn't take my children in any
> direction with a criminal like that

aloose in it. I couldn't answer to my conscience if I did. [1]

In my time, children were more respectful of their native states and their parents and everything else. [18]

People are certainly not nice like they used to be. [35]

And naturally, it is the grandmother's hiding of her cat in the car's back seat (couldn't bear leaving Pitty Sing home alone) and her maneuvers to visit a roadside attraction that lead to the car accident and the family's destruction.

In the final scene, the grandmother meets her narcissistic match, who just so happens to be a sociopathic killer. The duet that plays between her and The Misfit is a pinnacle of American comic writing—a dizzying dialogue that takes place at the same time as the gunshot murders of two adults, two children, and an infant. Like a pair of theological vaudevillians, they speak of Christ, fate, good and evil, and the discovery of their respective salvation. For the first time in her life, the grandmother is nearly dumb with terror, reduced to stammering out pleas for her life. The middle-aged Misfit, scholarly in his spectacles, recounts his horrific past. He is at once ominous and detached, despairing and alert, a kind of proselytizing antiprophet utterly given over to impulse and violence, and who, in spite of (or perhaps because of) his complete solipsism, speaks one or two words of unwitting truth—truth that, improbably enough, sets the old woman free.

Along with the grandmother, everyone in the story speaks in banalities—the children, John Wesley and June Star, the garrulous restaurateur Red Sammy, The Misfit's two henchmen, Hiram and Bobby Lee—everyone including The Misfit (perhaps especially The Misfit), although his language also manages to be complex and self-aware. With The Misfit,

the reader is jerked out of an impatient restlessness and distaste for these tiresome people. He's the only charismatic figure in these pages, and his compressed life story has the cadence and richness of a poem:

> I was a gospel singer for a while. I been most everything. Been in the arm service, both land and sea, at home and abroad, been twict married, been an undertaker, been with the railroads, plowed Mother Earth, been in a tornado. . . . [109]

In one sense, The Misfit is a co-hero, as significant as the grandmother—a hypnotic, dazzling Iago, of sorts. But O'Connor is doing a number on us with the magnetic Misfit, has intentionally made him the most interesting character, so that we would be drawn to him for a time, so that we would be curious about him, half-believe him. Indeed, we're spellbound, laughing and wincing at his eerie language until the moment he reminds us of his horrific potential.

The Shakespeare critic A. C. Bradley once said that the first thing to keep in mind about Iago is that you can't believe a single word he says. You have to distrust everything. Certainly, the same holds for The Misfit, who, like his predecessor, is so penetrated with untruth that he lies before he thinks, lies as he breathes. He's in that great line of backwoods con men—quite capable of rewriting his charismatic life story on every ditchbank in Georgia, the biblical language in which he is so fluent being another form of the con.

The story, which had begun as a cartoon, a comedy of '50s manners, takes, in a handful of pages, a remarkable turn. All the events have occurred in a single day, during this balmy summer car trip in rural Georgia. There is no chance that a reader should accept O'Connor's plot, with its blatantly placed clue in the first paragraph. Yet she makes it work. We laugh our way through a brief series of scenes, ride along in the crowded car, have lunch at Red Sammy's, get lost on the dirt road, laugh again when Pitty Sing (who, it must be said, had been suspiciously well behaved for most of the trip) jumps on the son's shoulder and causes the wreck; and then somehow, not quite knowing how it has happened, we find ourselves slumped in shock alongside the doomed family at the bottom of a ditch, looking up at a cloudless sky and three men looming above.

The grandmother's son is named Bailey, but we never learn his wife's name. She is simply "the children's mother," anonymous, almost selfless in the grandmother's characteristic worldview. O'Connor makes her the butt of an early joke on page one, giving her a face "as broad and innocent as a cabbage." During the accident, she is thrown from the car, still holding the infant, and breaks her shoulder. She sits there, stiffening in shock as her husband and young son are led away by The Misfit's henchmen to be slaughtered in the woods. Soon the murderers come for her, and The Misfit quietly asks her "to step off yonder with Bobby Lee and Hiram and join your husband."

Nearly mute in pain and horror, she can only say, "Yes, thank you." Then she takes the two remaining children and obediently walks off to her death. O'Connor, who had humiliated the young woman earlier, gives her back to us now in something close to tragedy, in a miraculous dignity; and her "Yes, thank you" becomes the most poignant moment of the story.

Only the grandmother remains. Grasping at straws, she mutters, "Jesus, Jesus," and The Misfit chimes right in. And then, in the midst of his philosophizing, he speaks the central line of the story: "Jesus thown everything off balance" [paragraph 129]. We know that The Misfit is speaking out of his own insanity and violence, but O'Connor is stretching language so far here that, for a moment at least, the reality of these Georgia trees and skies starts to crack apart. We've been working our way through some of the strangest American prose ever written. Six people are dead. And The Misfit becomes the most memorable religious character in recent American fiction.

In the last moments of the story, the grandmother has reached the limits of despair. She alone is left alive. She has begged for her life, twisted and turned every way she knows, has reached some unspeakable point of horror and fear and catastrophe, and she cries out to The Misfit, "Why you're one of my babies. You're one of my own children!" [paragraph 136]. Her entire atrocious, selfish, ignorant, useless life has led to this. And in its last moments, the improbable occurs: She breaks through, speaks words she doesn't even realize she is speaking. She reaches out to The Misfit and touches him on the shoulder—a common enough rural gesture. And at her touch, The Misfit, a fully realized nihilist, shoots her dead.

The story runs quickly to its close. One or two more sentences. The Misfit tells Bobby Lee, "She would of been a good woman, if it had been somebody there to shoot her every minute of her life" [paragraph 140]. It has taken the extremity of death for the grandmother to escape the shell of her egoism—a transformation The Misfit, a shrewd psychologist, readily comprehends, even as he is the very agent of her destruction.

Thus, in the guise of a Deep South horror story, O'Connor gave American letters something else altogether: a religiously audacious work of literature, a spiritual puzzle—a small miracle. **𝄢**

John Updike

A & P

Over the course of his career as a novelist, short story writer, poet, essayist, and dramatist, **JOHN UPDIKE** (1932–2009) received every major American literary award; in 1998 he was awarded the National Book Foundation Medal for Distinguished Contribution to American Letters. For one novel alone, *Rabbit Is Rich* (1981), he won the Pulitzer Prize, the American Book Award, and the National Book Critics Circle Award. Among more than twenty published novels, his recurring themes include religion, sexuality, and middle-class experience. In his essays, Updike's concerns range widely over literary and cultural issues. One volume of his collected essays, *Hugging the Shore: Essays and Criticism* (1983), was also awarded a National Book Critics Circle Award. Since his death, a posthumous collection of poems, *Endpoint and Other Poems* (2009), has been published, along with a collection of essays, *Hub Fans Bid Kid Adieu: John Updike on Ted Williams* (2010).

"A & P" is one of nineteen stories from John Updike's 1962 collection titled *Pigeon Feathers and Other Stories*, which appeared early in the writer's long and impressive career.

> "I'm not a very fast reader, so I like to open up a book and feel some whiff of poetry or of extra effort or of something inventive going on, so that even read backwards, a paragraph of prose will yield something to the sense."

In a 2001 interview, Updike commented on his goals as a writer and what he appreciated in other writing: "I've just tried to write in a way that would entertain and please me, if I were the reader . . . the kind of writer I'm attracted to is a writer who gives pleasure—the prose writer who does a little more than what is strictly called for to deliver the image or the facts. I'm not a very fast reader, so I like to open up a book and feel some whiff of poetry or of extra effort or of something inventive going on, so that even read backwards, a paragraph of prose will yield something to the sense." Updike once said humorously of his approach to reading: "My purpose in reading has ever secretly been not to come and judge but to come and steal."

IN WALKS THESE THREE GIRLS in nothing but bathing suits. I'm in the third checkout slot, with my back to the door, so I don't see them until they're over by the bread. The one that caught my eye first was the one in the plaid green two-piece. She was a chunky kid, with a good tan and a sweet broad soft-looking can with those two crescents of white just under it, where the sun never seems to hit, at the top of the backs of her legs. I stood there with my hand on a box of HiHo crackers trying to remember if I rang it up or not. I ring it up again and the customer starts giving me hell. She's one of these cash-register-watchers, a witch about fifty with rouge on her cheekbones and no eyebrows, and I know it made her day to trip me up. She'd been watching cash registers for fifty years and probably never seen a mistake before.

By the time I got her feathers smoothed and her goodies into a bag — she gives me a little snort in passing, if she'd been born at the right time they would have burned her over in Salem — by the time I get her on her way the girls had circled around the bread and were coming back, without a push-cart, back my way along the counters, in the aisle between the checkouts and the Special bins. They didn't even have shoes on. There was this chunky one, with the two-piece — it was bright green and the seams on the bra were still sharp and her belly was still pretty pale so I guessed she just got it (the suit) — there was this one, with one of those chubby berry-faces, the lips all bunched together under her nose, this one, and a tall one, with black hair that hadn't quite frizzed right, and one of these sunburns right across under the eyes, and a chin that was too long — you know, the kind of girl other girls think is very "striking" and "attractive" but never quite makes it, as they very well know, which is why they like her so much — and then the third one, that wasn't quite so tall. She was the queen. She kind of led them, the other two peeking around and making their shoulders round. She didn't look around, not this queen, she just walked straight on slowly, on these long white prima-donna legs. She came down a little hard on her heels, as if she didn't walk in her bare feet that much, putting down her heels and then letting the weight move along to her toes as if she was testing the floor with every step, putting a little deliberate extra action into it. You never know for sure how girls' minds work (do you really think it's a mind in there or just a little buzz like a bee in a glass jar?) but you got the idea she had talked the other two into coming in here with her, and now she was showing them how to do it, walk slow and hold yourself straight.

She had on a kind of dirty-pink — beige maybe, I don't know — bathing suit with a little nubble all over it and, what got me, the straps were down. They were off her shoulders looped loose around the cool tops of her arms, and I guess as a result the suit had slipped a little on her, so all around the top of the cloth there was this shining rim. If it hadn't been there you wouldn't have known there could have been anything whiter than those shoulders. With the straps pushed off, there was nothing between the top of the suit and the top of her head except just *her*, this clean bare plane of the top of her chest down from the shoulder bones like a dented sheet of metal tilted in the light. I mean, it was more than pretty.

She had sort of oaky hair that the sun and salt had bleached, done up in a bun that was unraveling, and a kind of prim face. Walking into the A & P with your straps down, I suppose it's the only kind of face you *can* have. She held her head so high her neck, coming up out of those white shoulders, looked kind of stretched, but I didn't mind. The longer her neck was, the more of her there was.

She must have felt in the corner of her eye me and over my shoulder   5 Stokesie in the second slot watching, but she didn't tip. Not this queen. She kept her eyes moving across the racks, and stopped, and turned so slow it made my stomach rub the inside of my apron, and buzzed to the other two, who kind of huddled against her for relief, and then they all three of them went up the cat-and-dog-food-breakfast-cereal-macaroni-rice-raisins-seasonings-spreads-spaghetti-soft-drinks-crackers-and-cookies aisle. From the third slot I look straight up this aisle to the meat counter, and I watched them all the way. The fat one with the tan sort of fumbled with the cookies, but on second thought she put the package back. The sheep pushing their carts down the aisle—the girls were walking against the usual traffic (not that we have one-way signs or anything)—were pretty hilarious. You could see them, when Queenie's white shoulders dawned on them, kind of jerk, or hop, or hiccup, but their eyes snapped back to their own baskets and on they pushed. I bet you could set off dynamite in an A & P and the people would by and large keep reaching and checking oatmeal off their lists and muttering "Let me see, there was a third thing, began with A, asparagus, no, ah, yes, applesauce!" or whatever it is they do mutter. But there was no doubt, this jiggled them. A few houseslaves in pin curlers even looked around after pushing their carts past to make sure what they had seen was correct.

You know, it's one thing to have a girl in a bathing suit down on the beach, where what with the glare nobody can look at each other much anyway, and another thing in the cool of the A & P, under the fluorescent lights, against all those stacked packages, with her feet paddling along naked over our checkerboard green-and-cream rubber-tile floor.

"Oh Daddy," Stokesie said beside me. "I feel so faint."

"Darling," I said. "Hold me tight." Stokesie's married, with two babies chalked up on his fuselage already, but as far as I can tell that's the only difference. He's twenty-two, and I was nineteen this April.

"Is it done?" he asks, the responsible married man finding his voice. I forgot to say he thinks he's going to be manager some sunny day, maybe in 1990 when it's called the Great Alexandrov and Petrooshki Tea Company or something.

What he meant was, our town is five miles from a beach, with a big   10 summer colony out on the Point, but we're right in the middle of town, and the women generally put on a shirt or shorts or something before they get out of the car into the street. And anyway these are usually women with six children and varicose veins mapping their legs and nobody, including them, could care less. As I say, we're right in the middle of town, and if you stand at our front doors you can see two banks and the Congregational church and the newspaper store and three real-estate offices and about twenty-seven old freeloaders tearing up Central Street because the sewer broke again. It's not as if we're on the Cape, we're north of Boston and there's people in this town haven't seen the ocean for twenty years.

The girls had reached the meat counter and were asking McMahon something. He pointed, they pointed, and they shuffled out of sight behind a pyramid of Diet Delight peaches. All that was left for us to see was old McMahon patting his mouth and looking after them sizing up their joints. Poor kids, I began to feel sorry for them, they couldn't help it.

Now here comes the sad part of the story, at least my family says it's sad, but I don't think it's so sad myself. The store's pretty empty, it being Thursday afternoon, so there was nothing much to do except lean on the register and wait for the girls to show up again. The whole store was like a pinball machine and I didn't know which tunnel they'd come out of. After a while they come around out of the far aisle, around the light bulbs, records at discount of the Caribbean Six or Tony Martin Sings or some such gunk you wonder they waste the wax on, sixpacks of candy bars, and plastic toys done up in cellophane that fall apart when a kid looks at them anyway. Around they come, Queenie still leading the way, and holding a little gray jar in her hands. Slots Three through Seven are unmanned and I could see her wondering between Stokes and me, but Stokesie with his usual luck draws an old party in baggy gray pants who stumbles up with four giant cans of pineapple juice (what do these bums *do* with all that pineapple juice? I've often asked myself). So the girls come to me. Queenie puts down the jar and I take it into my fingers icy cold. Kingfish Fancy Herring Snacks in Pure Sour Cream: 49¢. Now her hands are empty, not a ring or a bracelet, bare as God made them, and I wonder where the money's coming from. Still with that prim look she lifts a folded dollar bill out of the hollow at the center of her nubbled pink top. The jar went heavy in my hand. Really, I thought that was so cute.

Then everybody's luck begins to run out. Lengel comes in from haggling with a truck full of cabbages on the lot and is about to scuttle into that door marked MANAGER behind which he hides all day when the girls touch his eye. Lengel's pretty dreary, teaches Sunday school and the rest, but he doesn't miss that much. He comes over and says, "Girls, this isn't the beach."

Queenie blushes, though maybe it's just a brush of sunburn I was noticing for the first time, now that she was so close. "My mother asked me to pick up a jar of herring snacks." Her voice kind of startled me, the way voices do when you see the people first, coming out so flat and dumb yet kind of tony, too, the way it ticked over "pick up" and "snacks." All of a sudden I slid right down her voice into the living room. Her father and the other men were standing around in ice-cream coats and bow ties and the women were in sandals picking up herring snacks on toothpicks off a big glass plate and they were all holding drinks the color of water with olives and sprigs of mint in them. When my parents have somebody over they get lemonade and if it's a real racy affair Schlitz in tall glasses with "They'll Do It Every Time" cartoons stenciled on.

"That's all right," Lengel said. "But this isn't the beach." His repeating   15
this struck me as funny, as if it had just occurred to him, and he had been
thinking all these years the A & P was a great big dune and he was the head
lifeguard. He didn't like my smiling—as I say he doesn't miss much—but
he concentrates on giving the girls that sad Sunday-school-superintendent
stare.

Queenie's blush is no sunburn now, and the plump one in plaid, that
I liked better from the back—a really sweet can—pipes up, "We weren't
doing any shopping. We just came in for the one thing."

"That makes no difference," Lengel tells her, and I could see from the
way his eyes went that he hadn't noticed she was wearing a two-piece
before. "We want you decently dressed when you come in here."

"We *are* decent," Queenie says suddenly, her lower lip pushing, getting
sore now that she remembers her place, a place from which the crowd that
runs the A & P must look pretty crummy. Fancy Herring Snacks flashed in
her very blue eyes.

"Girls, I don't want to argue with you. After this come in here with
your shoulders covered. It's our policy." He turns his back. That's policy
for you. Policy is what the kingpins want. What the others want is juvenile
delinquency.

All this while, the customers had been showing up with their carts but,   20
you know, sheep, seeing a scene, they had all bunched up on Stokesie, who
shook open a paper bag as gently as peeling a peach, not wanting to miss a
word. I could feel in the silence everybody getting nervous, most of all Lengel, who asks me, "Sammy, have you rung up their purchase?"

I thought and said "No" but it wasn't about that I was thinking. I go
through the punches, 4, 9, GROC. TOT—it's more complicated than you think,
and after you do it often enough, it begins to make a little song, that you
hear words to, in my case "Hello (*bing*) there, you (*gung*) hap-py *pee*-pul
(*splat*)!"—the *splat* being the drawer flying out. I uncrease the bill, tenderly
as you may imagine, it just having come from between the two smoothest
scoops of vanilla I had ever known were there, and pass a half and a penny
into her narrow pink palm, and nestle the herrings in a bag and twist its
neck and hand it over, all the time thinking.

The girls, and who'd blame them, are in a hurry to get out, so I say "I
quit" to Lengel quick enough for them to hear, hoping they'll stop and watch
me, their unsuspected hero. They keep right on going, into the electric eye;
the door flies open and they flicker across the lot to their car, Queenie and
Plaid and Big Tall Goony-Goony (not that as raw material she was so bad),
leaving me with Lengel and a kink in his eyebrow.

"Did you say something, Sammy?"

"I said I quit."

"I thought you did."   25

"You didn't have to embarrass them."

"It was they who were embarrassing us."

I started to say something that came out "Fiddle-de-doo." It's a saying of my grandmother's, and I know she would have been pleased.

"I don't think you know what you're saying," Lengel said.

"I know you don't," I said. "But I do." I pull the bow at the back of my apron and start shrugging it off my shoulders. A couple customers that had been heading for my slot begin to knock against each other, like scared pigs in a chute.

Lengel sighs and begins to look very patient and old and gray. He's been a friend of my parents for years. "Sammy, you don't want to do this to your Mom and Dad," he tells me. It's true, I don't. But it seems to me that once you begin a gesture it's fatal not to go through with it. I fold the apron, "Sammy" stitched in red on the pocket, and put it on the counter, and drop the bow tie on top of it. The bow tie is theirs, if you've ever wondered. "You'll feel this for the rest of your life," Lengel says, and I know that's true, too, but remembering how he made the pretty girl blush makes me so scrunchy inside I punch the No Sale tab and the machine whirs "pee-pul" and the drawer splats out. One advantage to this scene taking place in summer, I can follow this up with a clean exit, there's no fumbling around getting your coat and galoshes, I just saunter into the electric eye in my white shirt that my mother ironed the night before, and the door heaves itself open, and outside the sunshine is skating around on the asphalt.

I look around for my girls, but they're gone, of course. There wasn't anybody but some young married screaming with her children about some candy they didn't get by the door of a powder-blue Falcon station wagon. Looking back in the big windows, over the bags of peat moss and aluminum lawn furniture stacked on the pavement, I could see Lengel in my place in the slot, checking the sheep through. His face was dark gray and his back stiff, as if he'd just had an injection of iron, and my stomach kind of fell as I felt how hard the world was going to be to me hereafter.

The Reader's Presence

1. The story is written in colloquial language. Reread the first two paragraphs. What does the narrator's style of expression convey about him? What effect does the narrator's style of expression have on your reading of the story? Are you more, or less, inclined to believe his words? Why? Suppose the same story were recounted in more conventional English. Would its meaning differ? If so, in what ways? How do you think Updike wishes the reader to view the narrator? Does Updike seem to agree, partially agree, or disagree with the narrator's point of view? What clues in the narrative lead you to your conclusion?

2. A great deal of the story hinges on what the narrator doesn't know or say. Is the girls' attire the only issue in the confrontation? What other tensions are evident in the store and in the town? What impression of the situation do you glean "between the lines"? How does the writer convey information beyond the scope of what the narrator is able to articulate?

3. **CONNECTIONS:**   Updike's story presents a seemingly minor event at a supermarket as the catalyst for a major change in the narrator's life. "I felt how hard the world was going to be to me hereafter," Sammy says in the story's final sentence. How do the perceptions of the past, present, and future intersect in the story? How seriously do you take the narrator's grim view of his future? Read Judith Ortiz Cofer's essay "Silent Dancing" (page 88), which is also prompted by a seemingly insignificant occasion: watching a home movie. Compare and contrast the ways in which past, present, and future intersect in Cofer's essay and Updike's story. Which writer handles these intersections more effectively? Explain why.

ACKNOWLEDGMENTS (*continued from page iv*)

Text Credits

Joan Acocella. "A Few Too Many." First published in *The New Yorker*, May 26, 2008. Copyright © 2008 by Joan Acocella. Reprinted by permission of the author and the Robert Cornfield Literary Agency.

Meher Ahmad. "My Homeland Security Journey." First published in *The Progressive*, May 2012. Reprinted by permission of the publisher.

Daniel Akst. "What Meets the Eye." Reprinted by permission of International Creative Management on behalf of the author. Copyright © 2005 by Daniel Akst. All rights reserved.

Sherman Alexie. "The Joy of Reading and Writing: Superman and Me." Copyright © 1997 by Sherman Alexie. All rights reserved. Used by permission of Nancy Stauffer Associates. "This Is What It Means to Say Phoenix, Arizona." From *The Lone Ranger and Tonto Fistfight in Heaven*. Copyright © 1993, 2005 by Sherman Alexie. Used by permission of Grove/Atlantic, Inc. Any third party use of this material, outside of this publication, is prohibited.

Dorothy Allison. "A Question of Class." From *Skin*. Reprinted by permission of The Frances Goldin Literary Agency. Copyright © 1994 by Dorothy Allison.

Ho Che Anderson. "Reenvisions Martin Luther King Jr.'s 'I Have a Dream.'" From *King*, vol. 2 (2002). Reprinted by permission of Fantagraphics Books.

Maya Angelou. "'What's Your Name, Girl?'" From *I Know Why the Caged Bird Sings* by Maya Angelou. Copyright 1969 and renewed 1997 by Maya Angelou. Used by permission of Random House, an imprint and division of Random House LLC. All rights reserved. Any third party use of this material, outside of this publication, is prohibited. Interested third parties must apply directly to Random House LLC for permission.

James Baldwin. "Notes of a Native Son." From *Notes of a Native Son*. Copyright © 1955, renewed 1983 by James Baldwin. Reprinted by permission of Beacon Press, Boston. "If Black English Isn't a Language, Then Tell Me, What Is?" originally published in *The New York Times*, July 29, 1979. Reprinted by permission of the James Baldwin Estate.

Dave Barry. "The Ugly Truth About Beauty." From the *Miami Herald*, Feb. 1998. Reprinted by permission of the author.

Michael Bérubé. "Analyze, Don't Summarize." First published in *The Chronicle of Higher Education*, Oct. 1, 2004. Copyright © 2004 by Michael Bérubé. Reprinted by permission of the author.

Charles Bowden. "Our Wall." First published in *National Geographic* magazine, May 2007. Reprinted by permission of National Geographic Creative.

David Brooks. "People Like Us." From *The Atlantic Monthly*, Sept. 2003. Reprinted by permission of the author.

Nicholas Carr. "Is Google Making Us Stupid?" From *The Atlantic Monthly*, July/August 2008. Reprinted by permission of the author.

Rebecca Carroll. "On the Writer's Voice." From an interview with Henry Louis Gates Jr. in *Swing Low, Black Men Writing*. Copyright © 1994 by Rebecca Carroll. Used by permission of Crown Books, an imprint of the Crown Publishing Group, a division of Random House LLC. All rights reserved. Any third party use of this material, outside of this publication, is prohibited. Interested third parties must apply directly to Random House LLC for permission.

Lauren Carter. "Isn't Watermelon Delicious?" Originally published in *The Bridge*, vol. 2, Spring 2005. Reprinted by permission of the author.

Stephen L. Carter. "The Insufficiency of Honesty." From *Integrity* by Stephen L. Carter. Copyright © 1996 by Stephen L. Carter. Reprinted by permission of Basic Books, a member of the Perseus Books Group.

Raymond Carver. "My Father's Life." Copyright © 1984 by Raymond Carver. Used by permission of The Wylie Agency LLC.

William Caverlee. "The Best Southern Short Story Ever?" Originally published in *The Oxford American*, Spring 2006. Copyright © 2006 by William Caverlee. Used by permission of the author.

Judith Ortiz Cofer. "On Memory and Personal Essays" (from the "Preface") and "Silent Dancing." From *Silent Dancing*. Copyright © 1990 Arte Publico Press–University of Houston. Reprinted by permission of the publisher.

Bernard Cooper. "A Clack of Tiny Sparks: Remembrances of a Gay Boyhood." Copyright © 1991 *Harper's* magazine. All rights reserved. Reproduced from the January issue by special permission.

Alys Culhane. "Interview with Lauren Slater." From *Fourth Genre: Explorations in Nonfiction*. Reproduced with permission of Michigan State University Press via the Copyright Clearance Center.

Amy Cunningham. "Why Women Smile." First published in *Lear's* (1993). Reprinted by permission of the author.

Joan Didion. "The Santa Ana." From *Slouching Towards Bethlehem*. Copyright © 1966, 1968, renewed 1996 by Joan Didion. Reprinted by permission of Farrar, Straus and Giroux, LLC. "Why I Write." Copyright © 1976 by Joan Didion. Originally published in *The New York Times Book Review*. Reprinted by permission of the author.

Annie Dillard. "This Is the Life." From *Image: A Journal of Arts and Religion* (2002). Reprinted by permission of Russell & Volkening as agents for the author. Copyright © 2002 by Annie Dillard. "On the Writing Life." From *The Writing Life*. Copyright © 1989 by Annie Dillard. Reprinted by permission of HarperCollins Publishers.

Brian Doyle. "Dawn and Mary" from *The Sun*, Aug. 2013; "His Last Game" from *Notre Dame Magazine*, Autumn 2012; and "A Note on Mascots." Reprinted by permission of the author. "On the Pleasures and Craft of Writing and Reading" from a personal interview. Reprinted by permission of Brian Doyle.

Andre Dubus III. "The Land of No: Love in a Class-riven America." From the March 1, 2012, issue of *The New Republic*. Reprinted by permission of the publisher. Excerpt from "Writing and Publishing a Memoir: What in the Hell Have I Done?" From *River Teeth*, Fall 2012. Reprinted by permission of the author.

Barbara Ehrenreich. "Will Women Still Need Men?" Reprinted from *TIME* and published with the permission of Time Inc. Copyright © 2000 by Time Inc. All rights reserved. Reproduction in any manner in any language in whole or in part without written permission is prohibited. TIME and the TIME logo are registered trademarks of Time Inc. used under license.

Lars Eighner. "On Dumpster Diving." From *Travels with Lizbeth*. Copyright © 1993 by Lars Eighner. Reprinted by permission of St. Martin's Press. All rights reserved.

Anne Fadiman. Excerpts from the "Introduction" by Anne Fadiman to *The Best American Essays*, 2003, edited by Robert Atwan and Anne Fadiman, are reprinted by permission of Anne Fadiman. Introduction copyright © 2003 by Anne Fadiman. "Under Water." From *At Large and at Small: Familiar Essays*. Copyright © 2007 by Anne Fadiman. Reprinted by permission of Farrar, Straus and Giroux, LLC.

Jonathan Safran Foer. "Let Them Eat Dog." From *The Wall Street Journal*, Oct. 31, 2009. Reprinted by permission of The Wall Street Journal. Copyright © 2009 by Dow Jones & Company, Inc. All rights reserved worldwide.

Ian Frazier. "A Farewell to Yarns." Copyright © 2012 by Ian Frazier. Originally published in *Outside* magazine, used by permission of The Wylie Agency LLC.

Henry Louis Gates Jr. "In the Kitchen." From *Colored People: A Memoir*. Copyright © 1994 by Henry Louis Gates Jr. Used by permission of Alfred A. Knopf, an imprint of the Knopf Doubleday Publishing Group, a division of Random House LLC. All rights reserved. Any third party use of this material, outside of this publication, is prohibited. Interested third parties must apply directly to Random House LLC for permission.

John Taylor Gatto. "Against School." From *Harper's*, Sept. 2003. Reprinted by permission of the author.

Daniel Gilbert. "What You Don't Know Makes You Nervous." From *The New York Times*, May 20, 2009. Reprinted by permission of the author.

Malcolm Gladwell. "Small Change: Why the Revolution Will Not Be Tweeted." From *The New Yorker*, Oct. 4, 2010. Reprinted by permission of the author.

Michihiko Hachiya. From *Hiroshima Diary: The Journal of a Japanese Physician, August 6– September 30, 1945*, trans. and ed. by Warner Wells, M.D. Copyright © 1955 by the University of North Carolina Press, renewed 1983 by Warner Wells. Foreword by John W. Dower © 1995 by the University of North Carolina Press. Used by permission of the publisher. www.uncpress .unc.edu

Scott London. Excerpt from "Crossing Borders: An Interview with Richard Rodriguez." First published in *The Sun* (August 1997). Copyright © 1997 by Scott London. Reprinted by permission of Scott London.

Nancy Mairs. "On Finding a Voice." From *Voice Lessons*. Copyright © 1994 by Nancy Mairs. Reprinted by permission of the publisher, Beacon Press, Boston. "On Being a Cripple." From *Plaintext*. Copyright © 1986 by The Arizona Board of Regents. Reprinted by permission of the University of Arizona Press.

David Mamet. "The Rake: A Few Scenes from My Childhood." Serialized in *Harper's* magazine, June 1992. From *The Cabin*. Copyright © 1992 by David Mamet. Used by permission of Vintage Books, an imprint of the Knopf Doubleday Publishing Group, a division of Random House LLC. All rights reserved. Any third party use of this material, outside of this publication, is prohibited. Interested third parties must apply directly to Random House LLC for permission.

James McBride. "Hip-Hop Planet." First published in *National Geographic* magazine, April 2007. Reprinted by permission of National Geographic Creative.

Bill McKibben. "A Moral Atmosphere." From the March/April 2013 issue of *Orion*. Reprinted by permission of the author.

Dinaw Mengestu. "Home at Last." Copyright © 2008 by Dinaw Mengestu. From *Brooklyn Was Mine*, edited by Chris Knutsen and Valerie Steiker. Used by permission of Riverhead Books, an imprint of Penguin Group (USA) LLC.

Walter Benn Michaels. "The Trouble with Diversity." From *The Trouble with Diversity: How We Learned to Love Identity and Ignore Inequality*. Copyright © 2006 by Walter Benn Michaels. Reprinted by permission of Henry Holt and Company, LLC. All rights reserved.

N. Scott Momaday. "The Way to Rainy Mountain." From "Introduction" to *The Way to Rainy Mountain*. Copyright © 1969 by the University of New Mexico Press. Reprinted by permission of the publisher.

Walter Mosley. "Get Happy." From the October 5, 2009, issue of *The Nation*. Reprinted with permission of *The Nation*. For subscription information, call 1-800-333-8536. Portions of each week's *Nation* magazine can be accessed at http://www.thenation.com.

Manuel Muñoz. "Leave Your Name at the Border." From *The New York Times*, Aug. 1, 2007. Copyright © 2007 by The New York Times. All rights reserved. Used by permission and protected by the Copyright Laws of the United States. The printing, copying, redistribution, or retransmission of this Content without express written permission is prohibited.

Azar Nafisi. From *Reading Lolita in Tehran: A Memoir in Books*. Copyright © 2002 by Azar Nafisi. Used by permission of Random House, an imprint and division of Random House LLC. All rights reserved. Any third party use of this material, outside of this publication, is prohibited. Interested third parties must apply directly to Random House LLC for permission.

Joyce Carol Oates. "*Smooth Talk*: Short Story into Film." From *Woman Writer: Occasions and Opportunities*. Copyright © 1988 by The Ontario Review, Inc. Used by permission of Dutton, a division of Penguin Group (USA) LLC. "Where Are You Going, Where Have You Been?" From *Wheel of Love and Other Stories* (Vanguard Press 1970). Copyright © 1970 by Ontario Review Inc. Reprinted by permission of John Hawkins & Associates, Inc.

Flannery O'Connor. "A Good Man Is Hard to Find." From *A Good Man Is Hard to Find and Other Stories*. Copyright 1953 by Flannery O'Connor. Copyright © renewed 1981 by Regina O'Connor. Reprinted by permission of Houghton Mifflin Harcourt Publishing Company. All rights reserved. "On Her Own Work." Originally published as "A Reasonable Use of the Unreasonable" from *Mystery and Manners*, ed. by Sally and Robert Fitzgerald. Copyright © 1969 by the Estate of Mary Flannery O'Connor. Reprinted by permission of Farrar, Straus and Giroux, LLC.

Danielle Ofri. "SAT." From *Incidental Findings: Lessons from My Patients in the Art of Medicine*. Copyright © 2005 by Danielle Ofri. Reprinted by permission of Beacon Press.

George Orwell. "Politics and the English Language" and "Shooting an Elephant." From *A Collection of Essays* by George Orwell. Copyright © 1950 by Sonia Brownell Orwell. Copyright © renewed 1978 by Sonia Pitt-Rivers. Reprinted by permission of Houghton Mifflin Harcourt Publishing Company. All rights reserved. "On the Four Reasons for Writing." From *Such, Such*

of the Knopf Doubleday Publishing Group, a division of Random House LLC. All rights reserved. Any third party use of this material, outside of this publication, is prohibited. Interested third parties must apply directly to Random House LLC for permission. "Just Walk on By: A Black Man Ponders His Power to Alter Public Space." Copyright © 1986 by Brent Staples. Reprinted by permission of the author.

Joel Stein. "The New Greatest Generation." Reprinted from *TIME* and published with permission of Time Inc. Copyright © 2013 by Time Inc. All rights reserved. Reproduction in any manner in any language in whole or in part without written permission is prohibited. TIME and the TIME logo are registered trademarks of Time Inc. used under license.

Cheryl Strayed. "Into the Woods." Adapted excerpt originally published in *Vogue*, March 2012. From *Wild: From Lost to Found on the Pacific Crest Trail*. Copyright © 2012 by Cheryl Strayed. Used by permission of Alfred A. Knopf, an imprint of the Knopf Doubleday Publishing Group, a division of Random House LLC. All rights reserved. Any third party use of this material, outside of this publication, is prohibited. Interested third parties must apply directly to Random House LLC for permission.

Cheryl Strayed. Excerpts from the "Introduction" by Cheryl Strayed to *The Best American Essays*, 2013, edited by Robert Atwan and Cheryl Strayed are reprinted by permission of Cheryl Strayed. Introduction copyright © 2013 by Cheryl Strayed.

John Updike. "A & P." From *Pigeon Feathers and Other Stories*. Copyright © 1962 by John Updike, copyright renewed 1990 by John Updike. Used by permission of Alfred A. Knopf, an imprint of the Knopf Doubleday Publishing Group, a division of Random House LLC. All rights reserved. Any third party use of this material, outside of this publication, is prohibited. Interested third parties must apply directly to Random House LLC for permission.

Allan Vorda. "On 'Girl.'" From an interview with Jamaica Kincaid conducted by Allan Vorda. Originally published in the *Mississippi Review* and in *Face to Face: Interviews with Contemporary Novelists*, ed. by Allan Vorda (Rice University Press). Reprinted by permission of Allan Vorda.

Alice Walker. "Beauty: When the Other Dancer Is the Self." From *In Search of Our Mothers' Gardens: Womanist Prose*. Copyright © 1983 by Alice Walker. Reprinted by permission of Houghton Mifflin Harcourt Publishing Company. All rights reserved.

Jerald Walker. "Scattered Inconveniences." First published in the *North American Review*, Nov./ Dec. 2006, pp. 8–9, "On Telling a Good Story." Both are reprinted by permission of the author.

David Foster Wallace. "Consider the Lobster." From *Consider the Lobster*. Copyright © 2005 by David Foster Wallace. By permission of Little, Brown and Company. All rights reserved. Excerpt from "Consider the Lobster" as originally published in *Gourmet* magazine. Copyright © 2004 by David Foster Wallace. Used by permission of the David Foster Wallace Literary Trust.

E. B. White. "On the Essayist." From "Foreword" in *Essays of E. B. White*, copyright © 1977 by E. B. White. Reprinted by permission of HarperCollins Publishers. "Once More to the Lake." From *One Man's Meat*, text copyright © 1941 by E. B. White. Copyright renewed. Reprinted by permission of Tilbury House, Publishers, Thomaston, Maine.

John Edgar Wideman. "Fatheralong." Copyright © 2009 by John Edgar Wideman. Originally published in *Harper's* magazine. Copyright © 2009 by John Edgar Wideman. Used by permission of The Wylie Agency LLC.

Elie Wiesel. "Eight Simple, Short Words." From *Night*, trans. by Marion Wiesel. Translation copyright © 2006 by Marion Wiesel. Reprinted by permission of Hill and Wang, a division of Farrar, Straus and Giroux LLC.

Virginia Woolf. "The Death of the Moth." From *The Death of the Moth and Other Essays* by Virginia Woolf. Copyright 1942 by Houghton Mifflin Harcourt Publishing Company. Copyright © renewed 1970 by Marjorie T. Parsons, Executrix. Reprinted by permission of Houghton Mifflin Harcourt Publishing Company. All rights reserved. "On the Practice of Freewriting." Excerpt from "Easter Sunday, April 20th." From *A Writer's Diary* by Virginia Woolf. Copyright 1954 by Leonard Woolf. Copyright © renewed 1982 by Quentin Bell and Angelica Garnett. Reprinted by permission of Houghton Mifflin Harcourt Publishing Company. All rights reserved.

Howard Zinn. "Stories Hollywood Never Tells." Originally published in *The Sun*, July 2004. Permission granted by the Ward & Balkin Agency.

Index of Authors and Titles

Inside LaunchPad Solo for *The Writer's Presence*, Eighth Edition

Tutorials

Critical Reading

Active Reading Strategies

Reading Visuals: Purpose

Reading Visuals: Audience

Documentation and Working with Sources

Do I Need to Cite That?

How to Cite an Article in MLA Style

How to Cite a Book in MLA Style

How to Cite a Database in MLA Style

How to Cite a Database in APA Style

How to Cite a Web Site in MLA Style

How to Cite a Website in APA Style

Digital Writing

Photo Editing Basics with GIMP

Audio Editing with Audacity

Presentations

Word Processing

Online Research Tools

Job Search/Personal Branding

LearningCurve

Critical Reading

Topic Sentences and Supporting Details

Topics and Main Ideas

Working with Sources (MLA)

Working with Sources (APA)

Commas

Fragments

Run-ons and Comma Splices

Active and Passive Voice

Appropriate Language

Subject-Verb Agreement

e-Readings

Howie Chackowicz, *The Game Ain't Over 'til the Fatso Man Sings* [audio essay]

Disabled Sports USA, *DisabledSportsUSA.org* [screenshots]

United States Department of State, *Help Protect Our Ocean* [video]

United States Department of Agriculture, *Miracles from Agriculture 1960* [video]

Linda Stone, *On Continuous Partial Attention* [video]

The White House, *The Buffet Rule* [video]

Jamaica Kincaid, *Girl* [audio]